FORAGES / *The Science of Grassland Agriculture*

The Science of Grassland

"Take not too much of a land, weare not out all the fatnesse, but leave it in some heart."

—By Pliny the Elder, A.D. 23–79, from his *Historiae Naturalis*, in 37 volumes

FORAGES

Agriculture Third Edition

Under Editorial Authorship of

MAURICE E. HEATH
PURDUE UNIVERSITY

DARREL S. METCALFE
UNIVERSITY OF ARIZONA

ROBERT F. BARNES
AGRICULTURAL RESEARCH SERVICE, USDA

&

WITH 93 ADDITIONAL CONTRIBUTING AUTHORS
SELECTED FOR THEIR RECOGNIZED LEADERSHIP
IN THE FIELD OF GRASSLAND AGRICULTURE

&

The Iowa State University Press / Ames, Iowa, U.S.A.

&

© 1951, 1962, 1973 The Iowa State University Press
Ames, Iowa 50010. All rights reserved

Composed and printed by
The Iowa State University Press

First edition, 1951
Second printing, 1952
Revised printing, 1953

Second edition, 1962
Second printing, 1963
Revised printing, 1966
Fourth printing, 1967

Fifth printing, 1969
Sixth printing, 1972
Third edition, 1973

Second printing, 1974
Third printing, 1975
Fourth printing, 1976
Revised printing, 1978

Library of Congress Cataloging in Publication Data

Heath, Maurice E   1910–
    Forages; the science of grassland agriculture.
    Previous editions are entered under H. D. Hughes.
    1. Forage plants—United States.   I. Metcalfe, Darrel S.,
1913–   joint author. II. Barnes, Robert F., 1933–
joint author. III. Hughes, Harold De Mott, 1882–1969.
Forages. IV. Title.
SB193.H4 1973   633′.2   73–13561
ISBN 0–8138–0680–1

THIS VOLUME IS RESPECTFULLY DEDICATED ❧

To the Memory of Those gone on before, who, envisioning the needs of the future and the possibility of better things, lived purposefully, giving of themselves.

In Recognition of Those of our own day, who, endowed with leadership ability in research and education, continue to stimulate us to more productive effort.

For the Inspiration of Those who today follow on, but who tomorrow, building upon established foundations, will be charged with the responsibility of solving the new problems with which those of their day will be confronted.

GRASS – HAY – PASTURE

FROM GENESIS TO REVELATION

Genesis 1–12:
And the earth brought forth GRASS . . . whose seed was in itself, after its kind: and God saw that it was good.

Genesis 47–4:
They said moreover unto Pharaoh, for to sojourn in the land are we come; for thy servants have no PASTURE for their flocks; for the famine is sore in the land of Canaan. . . .

Deuteronomy 11–15:
And I will seed GRASS in thy fields for the cattle, that thou mayest eat and be full.

1 Kings 4–23:
Ten fat oxen and twenty oxen out of the PASTURES, and an hundred sheep, beside harts, and roebucks, and fallow deer, and fatted fowl. . . .

1 Kings 18–5:
And Ahab said to Obadiah, Go into the land, unto all fountains of water, and unto all brooks; peradventure we may find GRASS to save the horses and the mules alive, that we lose not all the beasts.

Psalms 65–13:
The PASTURES are clothed with flocks; the valleys also are covered over with corn; they shout for joy, they also sing.

Psalms 104–14:
He causeth the GRASS to grow for the cattle, and herb for the service of man; that he may bring forth food out of the earth.

Proverbs 19–12:
The king's wrath is as the roaring of a lion; but his favor is as dew upon the GRASS.

Isaiah 15–6:
For the waters of Nimrim shall be desolate: for the HAY is withered away, the GRASS faileth, there is no green thing.

Isaiah 40–8:
The GRASS withereth, the flower fadeth; but the word of the Lord shall stand forever.

Joel 1–18:
How do the beasts groan, the herds of cattle are perplexed, because they have no PASTURE; yea the flocks of sheep are made desolate.

Joel 1–20:
The beasts of the field cry unto thee; for the rivers of waters are dried up and the fire hath devoured the PASTURES of the wilderness.

Matthew 14–19:
And he commanded the multitude to sit down on the GRASS, and he took the five loaves and the two fishes, and looking up to heaven, he blessed and brake, and gave the loaves to his disciples, and the disciples to the multitude.

Revelation 9–4:
And it was commanded that they should not hurt the GRASS of the earth, neither any green thing. . . .

—After E. W. HAMILTON
Milwaukee, Wisconsin

CONTENTS

&

vii

PART III / *Forage Production Practice*

PART IV / *Forage Utilization*

THE LAST OF THE VIRGIN SOD

We broke today on the homestead
   The last of the virgin sod,
And a haunting feeling oppressed me
   That we'd marred a work of God.

A fragrance rose from the furrow,
   A fragrance both fresh and old;
It was fresh with the dew of morning,
   Yet aged with time untold.

The creak of leather and clevis,
   The rip of the coulter blade,
And we wreck what God with the labor
   Of a million years had made.

I thought, while laying the last land,
   Of the tropical sun and rains,
Of the jungles, glaciers and oceans
   Which had helped to make these plains.

Of monsters, horrid and fearful,
   Which reigned in the land we plow,
And it seemed to me so presumptuous
   Of man to claim it now.

So when, today on the homestead,
   We finished the virgin sod,
Is it strange I almost regretted
   To have marred that work of God.

RUDOLPH RUSTE

PREFACE

※

Authorship *※*

A most important aspect of this book is its authorship. Sixty-six new authors and co-authors have been added to the thirty carried forward from the second edition. The chapters are written by individuals recognized as specialists in forage production and utilization, and they have drawn from broad and varied experience to present the subject matter covered.

Basic Fundamental Principles *※*

Most chapters have been entirely reorganized and rewritten, bringing them thoroughly up to date. A few have been combined, several dropped, and eight new chapters have been added. Recognition is given in this revision to the trend toward more fundamental and basic principles and their application.

Profuse Citations *※*

Authors have been generous in providing references to pertinent and significant research—the who, what, where, and when of some 2600 citations. The ready availability of these adds greatly to the value of *Forages* for the researcher and teacher.

Uniformity—Avoidance of Repetition *※*

It has been the responsibility of the editors to organize and unify the entire text in both expression and level of presentation, at the same time preserving the individuality of the chapter authors insofar as possible.

The editors have also attempted to avoid repetition, conflict, and overlapping in subject matter, while recognizing the desirability of making each chapter complete within itself.

Wide Selection and Application *※*

In the sixty-five chapters much more is presented than can be covered adequately in any one course; for example, some chapters apply to specific geographic areas. This makes wide selection possible according to the area and subject matter to be emphasized.

Equal care has been given to selecting material of interest and value to those in the Northeast, the deep South, the Southwest, the West including Alaska and Hawaii, and the Corn Belt and the eastern Great Plains of the United States. Much of the material has universal application.

Think Metric ❧

With the urging of scientific societies and the federal government, the metric system has been used throughout the text. For easy transition a set of conversions from the metric to the English system is provided immediately following the Preface.

Forages Abroad ❧

Through the years *Forages* has received much recognition and use abroad. It has been translated into Spanish and is widely used by the Spanish-speaking countries, especially those in Central and South America.

In Memoriam—PROFESSOR H(AROLD) D(EMOTT) HUGHES, 1882–1969 ❧

Professor Hughes, Iowa State University, coordinated all efforts on the first and second editions of *Forages* as chairman of the editorial committee. He also authored several chapters. He will long be remembered for his enthusiastic forage leadership and his many contributions to forage management.

MAURICE E. HEATH
DARREL S. METCALFE
ROBERT F. BARNES

THE METRIC SYSTEM

*

The International System of Units* (SI) is based on seven base units as follows:

Measure	Base unit	Symbol
length	meter	m
mass	kilogram	kg
time	second	s
electric current	ampere	A
thermodynamic temperature	kelvin	K
amount of substance	mole	mol
luminous intensity	candela	cd

Following are prefixes and their meanings, suggested for use with units of the metric system:

Multiples and submultiples	Prefix	Meaning	Symbol
$1,000,000 = 10^6$	mega	one million times	M
$1,000 = 10^3$	kilo	one thousand times	k
$100 = 10^2$	hecto	one hundred times	h
$10 = 10^1$	deka	ten times	dk
The unit $= 1$			
$0.1 = 10^{-1}$	deci	one tenth of	d
$0.01 = 10^{-2}$	centi	one hundredth of	c
$0.001 = 10^{-3}$	milli	one thousandth of	m
$0.000,001 = 10^{-6}$	micro	one millionth of	μ
$0.000,000,001 = 10^{-9}$	nano	one billionth of	n
$0.000,000,000,001 = 10^{-12}$	pico	one trillionth of	p

CONVERSION FROM A METRIC UNIT TO THE ENGLISH EQUIVALENT

Metric Unit	English Unit Equivalent
Length	
kilometer (km)	0.621 mile (mi)
meter (m) —— to —→	1.094 yard (yd)
meter (m) —— to —→	3.281 foot (ft)
centimeter (cm)	0.394 inch (in.)
millimeter (mm)	0.039 inch (in.)
Area	
kilometer² (km²)	0.386 mile² (mi²)
kilometer² (km²)	247.1 acre
hectare (ha) —— to —→	2.471 acre (A)

* Additional information may be found in the 1972 Standard Metric Practice Guide: A Guide to the Use of SI—The International System of Units. *In:* Annual Book of ASTM Standards, pt. 30, general test methods, designation E 380-72, pp. 1184–1217. Amer. Soc. for Testing and Materials (ASTM), Philadelphia.

Metric Unit	*English Unit Equivalent*

Volume

meter³ (m³)	1.308 yard³ (yd³)
meter³ (m³)	35.316 foot³ (ft³)
hectoliter (hl)	3.532 foot³ (ft³)
hectoliter (hl)	2.838 bushel (U.S.) (bu)
liter (l)	1.057 quart (U.S. liq.) (qt)

Mass

ton (t)	1.102 ton
• quintal (q) ——— to ———→	220.5 pound (lb) *= 100 kg = 1 q*
• kilogram (kg) ——— to ——→	2.205 pound (lb)
gram (g)	0.00221 pound (lb)

• 1000 kg = 1 metric ton

Yield or Rate

ha = 2.47 A

ton/hectare (t/ha)	0.446 ton/acre
hectoliter/hectare (hl/ha)	7.013 bushel/acre
kilogram/hectare (kg/ha)	0.892 pound/acre
quintal/hectare (q/ha)	89.24 pound /acre
quintal/hectare (q/ha)	0.892 hundredweight/acre

Pressure

bar (10⁶ dynes/cm²)	14.5 pound/inch² (psi)
bar (bar)	0.9869 atmosphere (atm)
atmosphere (atm or atmos)	14.7 pound/inch² (psi)
(an "atmosphere" may be	
specified in metric	
or English units)	

bar (10^6 dynes/cm²) — 14.5 pound/inch² (psi)

Temperature

Celsius (C) $1.80C + 32 =$ Fahrenheit (F)
kelvin (K) $= C + 273.15$

Light

lux (lx)	0.0929 foot-candle (ft-c)
candela (cd) $= 1$ lumen (lm)	
lux (lx) $= 1$ lm/m²	
lambert (L) $= 1$ lm/cm²	295.7 candle/foot²

Time

second (s)   second (s)

Work and Energy

calorie (cal) 3.97×10^{-3} British thermal unit (Btu)
kilocalorie (kcal) $= 1000$ cal
megacalorie (Mcal) $= 1000$ kcal
erg (erg) $= 2.39 \times 10^{-8}$ cal
joule (J) $= 1 \times 10^7$ ergs

PART I

❧

FORAGES AND A PRODUCTIVE AGRICULTURE

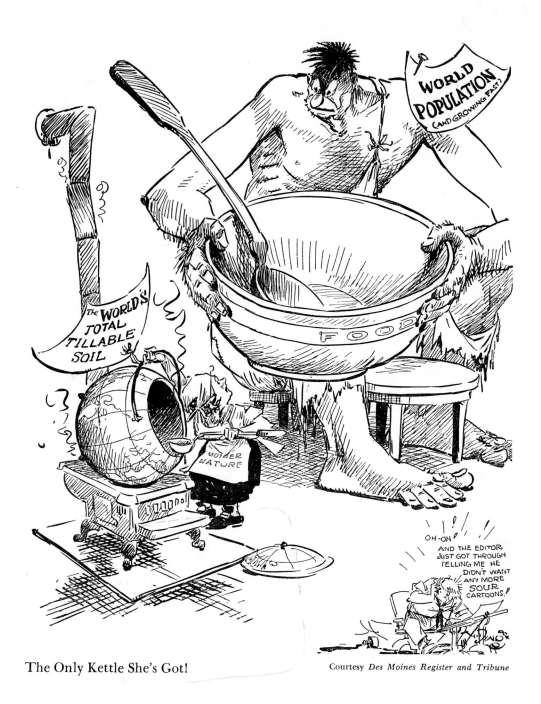

The Only Kettle She's Got!

Courtesy *Des Moines Register and Tribune*

MAURICE E. HEATH / *Purdue University*

1

FORAGES IN A CHANGING WORLD

❧

Eᴀʀʟʏ ʀᴇᴄᴏɢɴɪᴛɪᴏɴ of the high value of grass is indicated by a writer in the Book of Psalms thousands of years ago, "He causeth the grass to grow for the cattle." Moses promised the Children of Israel, as their reward if they accepted the commandments of God, that they would have "Grass in their fields for their cattle." Again, "In the habitation of dragons shall be grass," and again, "The Lord shall give to everyone grass in the fields." The want of grass was recognized as the symbol of desolation, "The hay is withered away, the grass faileth." The theme of grazing runs all through the Books of Genesis and Exodus.

❧ THE IMPORTANT ROLE OF GRASS

About 12,000 years ago the grassy tundra of Alaska's interior formed a natural haven for 31 species of land mammals (Fig. 1.1). Eighteen species were grazers; 11 of the 31 species are now extinct but 9 of the living species may still be found in Alaska, the remainder on other continents.[1]

❧ MAURICE E. HEATH is Associate Professor of Agronomy at Purdue University. Trained in agronomy at Iowa State University, he worked many years with the Soil Conservation Service on grassland problems of the central Corn Belt and the 12 northeastern states. He is concerned with the improvement of forage-animal-land use efficiencies on fragipan hill land soils.

Grazing lands were vital to primitive man long before cattle were domesticated. Man's first attempts to control his fate, to provide for future need instead of remaining the victim of droughts or other untoward circumstances, must have been on grasslands where the young calves, lambs, and kids he caught and tamed could find forage. It was also on grasslands, after he had reached the food-producing as distinguished from the food-gathering stage, that primitive man developed more rapidly.[2]

The culture of grass as we now know it is mainly a product of European and American civilization. In Great Britain, haymaking and the scythe date from 750 B.C. The amount of livestock kept through the winter depended on the success or failure of the hay harvest.[3] Columella (Roman) about A.D. 50 described in great detail the growing of hay crops and the significance of proper curing.[4]

Making hay from harvested forage undoubtedly is a very ancient agricultural practice. But the conversion of green forage into cured hay capable of being stored

In previous editions this chapter was written by H. D. Hughes, deceased.

1. Gutherie, Russell D. 1972. Recreating a vanished world. *Nat. Geographic* 141:294–301.
2. Smithsonian Institution. 1931. Old and new plant lore. Scientific Ser. 11.
3. Franklin, T. Bedford. 1953. British Grasslands. Faber and Faber, London.
4. Pendergrass, Webster. 1954. Research, education and related activities in grassland agriculture. Ph.D. thesis, Harvard Univ.

FIG. 1.1. *Alaska's interior . . . 12,000 years ago . . . haven for 31 species of mammals . . . 18 species were grazers.* The density of the region's population is exaggerated; probably not all these species appeared in any single summer, but discoveries elsewhere in central Alaska prove that they existed at the same time. (Gutherie, 1972.[1])

and used through a considerable period is believed to have had a more important part in a changing world than most realize. It is associated with a stabilized agriculture.

The Anglo-Saxons produced the first enclosed meadows in the Midlands of Britain about A.D. 800. The value of a change of pasture to the health of cattle and sheep was well known to the Monks of Kelso as early as 1165. About 1400 the Monks of Couper were alternating two years of wheat and five years of grass, later called ley farming (crop rotation).[3]

Red clover was cultivated in Italy as early as 1550, somewhat later in western Europe, in England by 1645, and in Massachusetts in 1747. Its influence on civilization and European Agriculture is said to have been greater than the potato and much more than any other forage plant. Red clover not only increased the abundance of animal feed and manure but also added nitrogen to the soil.[5]

❧ WORLD POPULATIONS, FOOD, AND FORAGES

In 1650 the world population was 545 million, about 14% of that today. At the beginning of the twentieth century it stood at approximately 1.6 billion. It is anticipated that world population may increase by the end of this century to more than 7 billion. To what extent and how long can the earth continue to produce the food necessary for this rapidly increasing population? There has been no such increase in the world food supply. It seems certain that the next 40 or 50 years will produce a series of crises the dimensions of which cannot yet be measured. (See Fig. 1.2.)[6-9]

It is recognized that this is in marked

5. Piper, Charles V. 1924. Forage Plants and Their Culture, rev. ed., p. 143. Macmillan, New York.

6. Osborn, Fairchild. 1957. Renewable resources and human populations. *In* America's Natural Resources. Roland Press, New York.
7. Bear, Firman E. 1960. How many people can we feed? *In* Food for America's Future. McGraw-Hill, New York.
8. Borgstrom, Georg. 1972. The Hungry Planet. Collier Books, New York.
9. Ware, Thomas M. 1967. Agriculture in American foreign policy. *In* Maximizing Agricultural Productivity, pp. 1–13. Proc. 16th Ann. Meet. Agr. Res. Inst., Natl. Acad. Sci.

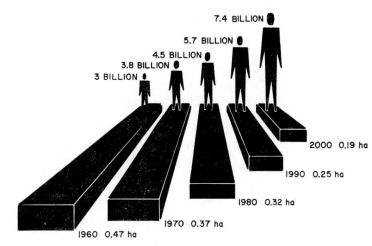

FIG. 1.2. Growth of world population in relation to the decrease in arable or tillable land per capita. (Ware, 1967.[9])

7.4 BILLION
5.7 BILLION
4.5 BILLION
3.8 BILLION
3 BILLION

2000 0.19 ha
1990 0.25 ha
1980 0.32 ha
1970 0.37 ha
1960 0.47 ha

contrast to the U.S. and to certain other limited areas where, as a result of greatly improved methods, reserves and surpluses of such crops as wheat and corn have accumulated. But our local present abundance should not blind us to world conditions. On a world basis we are not keeping pace.

From the earliest centuries through modern times, famine has repeatedly depopulated great areas. Millions have died from starvation. A famine in 1125 is reported to have cut the German population by half. In China, 9.5 million are said to have died of starvation in 1877–78. In 1846–47 the failure of the Irish potato crop resulted in 2–3 million deaths from starvation.

In the Volga Valley and Ukraine area of Russia some 20 million faced death from starvation in 1921–23, before the American Relief Administration under the direction of Herbert Hoover came to the rescue with $80 million worth of food and medicines, contributed largely by American religious and charitable organizations.[10] As late as 1943 the Bengal (India) area lost 1.5 million people before emergency relief arrived.[11]

Famines have most often resulted from climatic causes, but whole civilizations have declined from grandeur to penury

and woe because of failure to protect once fertile and productive soils. Increasing populations demanded cereal foods, with no thought to the conservation of the soil. There was no appreciation of the value of sod crops and their ability to hold the soil against destructive erosion.

In a relatively few years much of the land in those parts of the U.S. longest under the plow became so gullied and eroded that it was worthless for cropping. It was allowed to revert to weeds and brush, and parts of it returned to forest cover. Some 20 million ha of our once good cropland has been ruined for further cultivation, while another hectarage of equal proportions has been badly damaged. This land equals the hectarage of the three great Corn Belt states of Ohio, Illinois, and Iowa.[12]

❧ FORAGES IN COLONIAL TIMES

The efforts of the first English colonists in the seventeenth century to produce food could hardly be called agricultural production. In general, they resembled primitive tribes in the hunting and gathering stage of development. It was only by adopting the plants, cultivation, and harvesting methods of the natives that starvation was

10. Hoover, Herbert. 1961. An American Epic, vol. 3. Regnery, Chicago.

11. Encyclopaedia Britannica. 1956. Famine.

12. Bennett, H. H. 1940. Our soil can be saved. *In* Farmers in a Changing World, pp. 429–40. USDA Yearbook Agr.

escaped. It is estimated that, measured in farm values, 57% of our present agricultural production is of plants domesticated by the American Indian–corn, peanuts, potatoes, sweet potatoes, tobacco, pumpkins, squash, beans, and others.[13]

Since the Indian of the Atlantic Coast area had no herbivorous domestic animals, he had no need for forage plants. Such forage as there was consisted mostly of coarse and unpalatable swamp grasses, low in feeding value. For some time the need for forages was not pressing. There were few domestic animals in the early colonies, and these had been imported with considerable difficulty. The long ocean voyage in tiny ships was difficult, and many animals did not survive.[14] Gradually, however, livestock numbers increased and such grasses and clovers as had been used in England began to make their appearance in the settlements.

As early as the beginning of the eighteenth century the hectarage of grasses in woods and enclosed meadows did not keep pace with the increase in livestock. Lands worn out by overtillage and then abandoned to weed fallow made poor pasture. Perhaps half the average farm was a vast "pasture," mostly overrun with sourgrass, briars, and bushes. Farmers continued to cut hay chiefly from natural meadows and marshy areas.[15]

English settlers on the Atlantic Coast brought their name *meadow* for native grassland suitable for mowing. The French in Canada and adjoining the mid-U.S. used *prairie* for similar grassland, and the Spanish in Florida used the word *savanna*. All have been included in American English.[16,17]

Between 1780 and 1820 many trials with grassland plants were made in England, the most famous was at Woburn Abbey. Various grasses and legumes were grown in small plots, and yields were determined and analyzed for nutritive value. Results were published as a book sold at home and abroad. Although the work would be considered very crude by the modern researcher, the results were referred to in the U.S. for about 50 years.[18]

Late in the 1700s agricultural societies began to be formed in the U.S. similar to those of England and Germany; by 1860 there were over 900.[19] Among the earlier ones was the Philadelphia Society for the Promotion of Agriculture. The questions raised by members are indicative of the interest in forages at that time. The following recorded communication of April 1778 is typical.

Next, we should enquire what kinds of grasses we have in this and ye Neighboring Provinces and what kinds of them are best for Bankd, watered or bottom meadows; and when they may be sowd to ye best advantage, and what quantity is to be allowed to an acre; —likewise what grasses ye are best for pasture; whether white or Red clover or blue grass; when and in what quantities to ye acre, they should be sowd . . . how long white, or Red clover, will grow with vigor, before it must be renewed by Plowing: and how our meadows may be best kept rich, while fresh; or how they may be best renewd when worn and decayed. . . .[20]

During the first 100 years following the Revolution agricultural technology improved more than in the previous 2000 years. Farmers were quick to accept new mechanical labor-saving equipment, but were much slower to adopt scientific methods, which for a long time were referred to by many as "book farming."[19] It was not until many years later that findings of

13. Edwards, Everett E. 1940. American agriculture—The first 300 years. *In* Farmers in a Changing World, pp. 171–276. USDA Yearbook Agr.
14. Carrier, Lyman. 1923. The Beginnings of Agriculture in America. McGraw-Hill, New York.
15. Edwards, Everett E. 1948. The settlement of the grasslands. *In* Grass, pp. 16–25. USDA Yearbook Agr.
16. Bidwell, P. W., and J. I. Falconer. 1941. History of Agriculture in the Northern United States, 1620–1860, pp. 20, 108. Reprint. Peter Smith, New York.
17. Gray, L. C. 1958. History of Agriculture in the Southern United States to 1860, vol. 1, pp. 56, 57, 107, 148–50, 324. Reprint. Peter Smith, New York.

18. Sinclair, George. About 1820. Hortus Gramineus Woburnensis, 4th ed. London.
19. Johnstone, Paul. 1940. Old ideals versus new ideas in farm life. *In* Farmers in a Changing World, pp. 111–70. USDA Yearbook Agr.
20. Philadelphia Society for Promoting Agriculture. 1939. Memoirs, vol. 6.

research agencies were accepted readily and applied generally as they became available. As a result, whereas the average U.S. farm worker was producing only enough food and fiber for approximately four others in 1850 and for seven in 1900, by 1950 he was producing enough for 16 and by 1970 for approximately 47 others. In spite of the continued rapid increase in the U.S. population the increase in food production has been even more rapid.

❧ THE GREAT AMERICAN PRAIRIES

From primitive times to the present, man's history has been largely influenced by grasslands. Civilization began on the grasslands and civilizations have vanished with their destruction.[21]

Although a heavy forest growth originally covered nearly all the eastern U.S., about 40% of our 770 million ha were grasslands. There were thousands of indigenous species of grass, thriving under a variety of soil and climatic conditions. Some were palatable and nutritious the year through, when lush or when cured in place. Others were palatable for only a few weeks in the early spring.

As the pioneer farmers pushed westward across the Alleghenies during and following the Revolution, they were confronted by the necessity of clearing heavy forest growths before crops could be grown, just as had been necessary for all farmers during the two centuries of the Colonial period. The idea had become pretty well fixed that land that grew only grass was inferior. As settlers entered western areas where there was a choice between forest and prairie, forest-covered soils were favored. Forests seemingly loomed large in the thinking of pioneer farmers. The forest growth had sheltered the game that once constituted the chief source of meat, and it supplied logs for cabins, stock shelters, fuel, and fences. Fencing materials were important. The problem of fences on the prairies remained essentially un-

Fig. 1.3. . . . growth and decay of . . . native grasses through thousands of years resulted in deep, rich black soil. Iowa State Univ. photo.

solved until the invention of barbed wire in 1874.[13,15,22]

The pioneers hesitated on the edge of the large prairies with their seemingly endless growth of big grass. There was a sense of vastness about them that seemed overwhelming and the impression of a greatness that could not be subdued. Indeed, some contended that they would not be brought under cultivation for centuries.[15]

Originally, there were about 283 million ha of grass-covered native prairie stretching from Ohio westward. In Iowa 85% was tall-grass prairie. In general, the most fertile deep soils were formed under the vegetative growth of the prairies. The growth and decay of these heavy-sodding native grasses through the thousands of years resulted in deep, rich black soil. (See Fig. 1.3.)

The main grasslands of the central and Great Lake states were dominated by grasses so tall with stands so dense that the early settlers' cattle could be found only by the tinkling of cowbells and the waving of the grasses. (See Fig. 1.4.) So tough and thick were the sods of these

21. Costello, David F. 1957. Grasslands: America's Natural Resources. Roland Press, New York.

22. Hayter, Earl W. 1939. Barbed wire fencing—A prairie invention. Agr. Hist. 13:189–207.

Fig. 1.4. . . . *large prairie areas were covered with . . . native grasses.* Pictured is big bluestem grown for seed increase at Ames, Iowa. *SCS photo.*

prairie grasses that some farmers preferred not to break sod until after the stand had been weakened by heavy grazing and repeated mowing. From three to seven yoke of oxen were required to break new fields.[10] Further west, the short-grass prairie extended from Texas northward into Canada and eastward from the mountains to mid-Kansas, Nebraska, and the Dakotas. The six Great Plains states included a grassland area of about 98 million ha, or about 30% of the western grazing land. Here the native short grasses such as grama grasses and buffalograss were in greatest abundance, though some of the tall grasses predominated toward the eastern margin of the area. The only extensive tall-grass native grazing area remaining is in the flint hills area of eastern Kansas.[19]

The impression of early explorers was that the growth of grass on these vast prairie areas was such that they would endlessly support countless herds and flocks. How wrong they were! By 1880 continued overstocking had reduced the carrying capacity of most of the western range to only a fraction of its original capacity. Great areas became almost worthless.

Centers of origin for large cattle herds

occurred on the frontier from Pennsylvania to Florida for a short time and continued westward across the country. Other centers of origin were the Spanish missions in southern Texas and California. From these areas the name *ranch* has been widely accepted for a large animal-producing organization. The area available for grazing native vegetation was known as *range*. No such distinctive names were used in the East, probably due to the short-time existence of ranching there. Ranches with large herds increased in numbers most rapidly after 1870 from central Texas northward and westward.[23,24]

Some appreciation of the natural grazing wealth originally provided can be gained from the numbers of herbage-consuming wildlife that roamed the great prairies in early days: 60 million buffalo, 40 million whitetail deer, 40 million antelope, and 10 million elk. To this array must be added the hundreds of millions of prairie dogs, jackrabbits, and cottontails, all forage consumers.[25]

FORAGES AND CONTINUED PRODUCTIVITY

Anywhere in the world the face of the land faithfully reflects the culture of the people who live upon it. Where the land is poor and worn, so are the people who strive to maintain themselves on its inhospitable surface. And where the land is rich and bountiful, the people who inhabit it have an opportunity to live a rich and bountiful life.[26]

An increasing number of people have become convinced that we must have "a more secure agriculture," "a balanced agriculture," and "greater permanence in farming." This means the year-to-year and generation-to-generation assurance that we can continue to use land efficiently in pro-

23. Chapline, W. R., and C. K. Cooperrider. 1941. Climate and grazing. *In* Climate and Man, pp. 459–76. USDA Yearbook Agr.
24. Edwards, Everett E. 1948. The settlement of grasslands. *In* Grass, pp. 16–25. USDA Yearbook Agr.
25. Seton, Ernest Thompson. 1929. Lives of Game Animals, vol. 3. Doubleday, Garden City.
26. Van Dersal, William R. 1943. The American Land. Oxford, New York.

ducing crops and at the same time maintain its fertility. Permanence in agriculture is a goal always to be sought everywhere.[27]

Adapted grasses and legumes are now generally recognized as the chief tools in soil improvement and conservation. The direct benefit from sod crops in rotation has been recognized and evaluated over many years under a great variety of environmental conditions. Much evidence has been accumulated on the extent to which they increase the permeability and water-holding capacity of a given soil. Much has been learned about the effect of grass roots on the granulation of soil particles and the relation of this characteristic to the resistance of soil to destructive erosion.

INTERNATIONAL GRASSLAND CONGRESS

Recognition of the worldwide need to make better use of grasslands resulted in the International Grassland Congress, the first of which met in Germany in 1927. In Australia in 1970 the eleventh Congress attracted 750 members from 51 countries. The sixth, in the U.S. in 1952, had more than 1200 delegates and members present. Over 300 were from countries other than the U.S. The foreword to the sixth Congress proceedings emphasizes the world's food problems and explains the role of the Congress in helping to solve them:

The specter of hunger stalks the world. . . . Increasing population is exerting steadily mounting pressure on food production capacities. Exploitive systems of farming are taking heavy toll of soil productivity. . . . We must find new resources for production. We must reverse the downward trend in soil productivity. And for the attainment of both of these necessary objectives, grassland farming is the most effective weapon in agriculture's arsenal. . . . More than half the total land surface of the earth is in grazing lands. Most of these enormous acreages are unimproved. Improvement practices, based on research findings, can result in vast increases in production and in

the utilization of livestock feed from these grasslands. And the grasslands provide the major raw material for the production of meat, milk, and other animal products. . . . Soil is the basic resource of all agriculture. . . . Sound soil management practices must be built around grasses and legumes. . . . The doctrines and teachings of science transcend national borders. . . . The . . . Congress provides the opportunity for scientists and technicians from various parts of the world to exchange information concerning the production, improvement, management, and use of grasslands.[28] [See Fig. 1.5.]

GRASSLAND ORGANIZATIONS

Through the influence of the International Grassland Congresses more grassland organizations and activities have developed within and among many countries. For example, in 1944 steps were taken in England to organize the British Grassland Society which held its first meeting in 1945. Its main purpose is to focus greater scientific attention on all aspects of grasslands. In 1955 the first county grassland society was organized in Surrey. This movement has grown into 47 local county grassland societies.[29]

Grassland organizations are very active in New Zealand and Australia. The European Grassland Federation was formed in 1963 by grassland organizations from 13 countries. Their objective is a closer working relationship and a greater interchange of scientific and applied information.[30]

In the western U.S. the Range Management Society was established in 1948 and is very active in fostering the science and art of range management.[31] In 1944 the Joint Committee on Grassland Farming was formed and is now the American Forage and Grassland Council. It attempts

27. Cardon, P. V. 1948. Our aim: An introduction. *In* Grass, pp. 1–5. USDA Yearbook Agr.

28. Editors. 1952. Foreword, Proc. 6th Int. Grassl. Congr., pp. v–vi (State College, Pa.).
29. Jones, Martin. 1970. The history and development of the British Grassland Society. *J. Brit. Grassl. Soc.* 25:-195–97.
30. European Grassland Federation. 1963. Business session minutes (9–27–63) and EGF constitution. *In* The Agronomic Evaluation of Grassland. Proc. 1st Symp. Grassland Res. Inst. (Hurley, England).
31. Pachanec, Joseph F. 1948. Our range society. *J. Range Manage.* 1:1–2.

to bring together public service and industry (including farm) leadership to strengthen the educational and research aspects of forages and grasslands in American agriculture.[32]

❧ CHANGING CONDITIONS

Changes in market demands, tariff barriers, governmental regulations, farm power, and other farm equipment and production factors and methods result in significant changes and variations in land use and types of farming.

The humid South, from Arkansas and Louisiana eastward, once produced all the cotton grown in the country. Between 1940 and 1970 the cotton hectarage fell from 5 million to 1.9 million, while beef cow numbers increased six times to more than 6 million head.[33,34] This somewhat reflects the change in land use and the increased emphasis on forage production and utilization.

The decline in the number of draft animals on farms has been a much greater factor in accounting for the increase in farm products for sale than is generally realized. About 32 million ha of cropland were used immediately following the first World War to grow grain and hay to feed horses and mules. This was more than 20% of the total crop hectarage harvested at that time. As the number of horses and mules decreased, millions of ha of pasture land and large amounts of labor and other production resources as well as feed grain and hay ha were shifted to the production of food and fiber crops. Since the mid-1930s the number of horses and mules on farms has decreased from 16.5 million to less than 2.5 million. If there had been no diversion of land use from growing feed for work animals, assuming that yield levels and other factors had remained the same, the U.S. would have been faced with crop shortages rather than surpluses in recent years.[35]

Vegetative cover is recognized as particularly important from the standpoint of rainfall conservation. It slows down the movement of rainwater from the time it hits the soil surface to its entry through river channels into the sea. The availability and control of water is fast becoming one of our most serious national problems. Approximately 25% of the U.S. population are in serious trouble because of an inadequate water supply or water of unsatisfactory quality. Today our total per capita use of water is more than 545 liters/day. Our total national use has increased approximately four times in 50 years. Many have no appreciation of the vast quantities of water necessary for our industrial processes or the relation of forage cover to the conservation of soil and water.[6]

It is recognized that only about 10% of the caloric value of the feeds consumed by livestock become available to man in animal products such as milk or meat. One-third of the land area of the world is classified as range or grassland on which livestock are grazed.

In general, such lands are not suited to cultivation. Food can be obtained from them only through the consumption of native forage by livestock. Whole populations are almost entirely dependent upon livestock products from the forage of these vast areas. Cultural and agricultural types and practices vary greatly from one area and part of the world to another. This may be illustrated by the fact that on a world basis more people consume milk and milk products from goats than from cows. Cows' milk is nearly unavailable and unknown in many parts of the world.

Forages play a vital role in U.S. milk production. The average annual fat production per cow increased from 75 kg in 1925 to 142 kg in 1970. But the consuming public is rapidly losing interest in

32. Amer. Forage Grassl. Council. 1966. New council name. *Grassl. Progr.* 7:(summer)4.
33. USDA. Agricultural statistics. 1941, 1971.
34. USDC. 1940, 1970. U.S. Agr. Census.

35. Higbee, Edward. 1958. American Agriculture. Wiley, New York.

Fig. 1.5. . . . *grasslands provide the major raw material . . . meat, milk, and other animal products.* These replacement dairy heifers are utilizing cropland pasture. *Ill. SCS photo.*

milk fat. The annual per capita consumption of butter has dropped from 8 to 2 kg. People are now using milk instead of cream on fruit and cereals. Skim milk, once considered fairly worthless, is now bottled and sold for human consumption at a price only a few cents less than that of whole milk. Such is the relation between consumption demands and production.[36]

FORAGE PROGRAMS AND SYSTEMS

Many of our agricultural enterprises are so interrelated that to consider one phase without at the same time considering several others is likely to lead to false conclusions.

Forage programs and systems relate directly to the research of the soil physicist, the soil chemist, and the plant scientist; to the investigations in soil management and soil fertility; to the results obtained by those who deal with the problems of soil conservation through erosion control; and also to the cash grain farmer, and to the livestock producer with his summer grazing procedures and winter feeding systems.

They go even farther, in fact, and must be given high priority in the thinking of the agricultural economist. They influence to a significant degree not only short-time procedures but also the longtime na-

tional economy. It is believed that the material in the following chapters will lead the way to more efficient and profitable forage opportunities.

TIME REQUIRED FOR CHANGES

Some years ago when writing about the time required for the introduction of new ideas, William Newton Clarke said:

First the idea must be seen in enthusiastic vision by someone, and enunciated for the world to hear. It must get abroad among men, and be somewhat widely considered. It must come to be deemed important. Then it must be ignored, recognized, restated, ridiculed, refuted, denied, doubted, admitted, discussed, affirmed, believed, accepted, taught to adults, taught to children, wrought into literature, put into practice, tested by its fruits, allowed to modify other ideas, embodied in institutions; and in the course of some generations it will sink in among the certainties that are assured and acted upon without question and without thought. For this process two hundred years is but a short period.[37]

But that statement was made before the day of high-pressure sales programs; before the airwaves were crowded with commercially sponsored news and informational and educational programs; before we had agricultural agents in practically every county; before state colleges had

36. Herrington, B. L. 1959. Research in composition of milk. N.Y. Agr. Exp. Sta. Farm Research, vol. 25, no. 3, p. 10.

37. Clarke, William N. 1909. Sixty Years with the Bible. Scribners, New York.

their agricultural extension divisions with their corps of specialists and their well-organized information bureaus with radio stations at their command. That was before profusely illustrated information booklets were generally available; before the day of television in every home; before the day of the Farmer's Home Administration, the Soil Conservation Service, and other similar action agencies; before the organization of watershed areas, with funds, equipment, and trained personnel available to demonstrate the value of proved conservation practices; and finally, before the day of Soil Conservation Districts, organized in nearly every county in large parts of many states, with soil conservationists available to work with every individual farmer willing to cooperate.

We are not willing today to accept the idea that two hundred years is a short period in which to expect new ideas to sink in among the certainties that are assured, to be acted upon without question and without thought.[37]

Progress toward a grassland agriculture has been made; this progress will be more apparent and rapid in the years ahead.[38]

38. Voisen, André. 1960. Grass Productivity. Philosophical Library, New York.

❧ QUESTIONS

1. Discuss some of the early forage practices in Europe and Great Britain that were later used by the colonists in America.
2. How important are forages in relation to the expanding world population? Why?
3. What is the origin and meaning of the words *meadow, prairie,* and *savanna?*
4. What was the importance of the great American prairie to the American Indian? How has the prairie contributed to present-day agricultural production?
5. Name several organizations which give emphasis to forage and grassland research and education.
6. List four specific examples of large agricultural changes in the U.S. during this century that involved forages and grasslands.

MAURICE E. HEATH / *Purdue University*

2

GRASSLAND AGRICULTURE

❧

GRASSLAND AGRICULTURE is a farming system which emphasizes the importance of grasses and legumes in livestock and land management.[1,2] Farmers who plan row crop and livestock production around their grassland acres are grassland farmers. The main feature of grassland agriculture is its dependence on grasses, legumes, and other forage for proper land use and increased animal profitability. High-quality forages are emphasized in livestock production. Grains complement the available forage in feeding practices. (See Fig. 2.1.)

Grassland farming, simply defined, is the proper use of grass in agriculture. . . . Its integration into a farming program accomplishes many things: It covers the land to protect it from the weather; . . . as pasture and meadow it provides inexpensive, high-quality livestock feed in the form of pasture, hay, and silage; and in all its forms it is easily cared for and harvested mechanically. . . . This integration has become the science of grassland farming. . . . Grasslanding embodies many fields of endeavor. All the soil, crop, and livestock sciences are ingredients in this basic system of farming.[3]

In the latter part of the nineteenth century western Europe began to develop a scientific grassland agriculture based on the

results of research.[4] During the nationwide soil conservation movement in the 1930s and early 1940s, much emphasis was placed on the expanded use of grasses and legumes for soil protection. World War II generated heavy grain production which started the trend in the 1950s of higher grain patterns for dairy and beef feeding.[5] However, scientific grassland agriculture was first given national recognition by the USDA and state agencies in 1950, when a joint voluntary program was announced to assist farmers and ranchers in intensifying grassland farming practices, based whenever possible upon research findings.[6]

❧ WHY GRASSLAND AGRICULTURE?

When grassland agriculture is practiced intensively, organic matter is renewed, soil erosion prevented, gully formation arrested, and soil tilth improved; therefore, soil conservation becomes an opportunity instead of a problem. Grass, when properly used,

1. Harlan, Jack R. 1956. Theory and Dynamics of Grassland Agriculture. Van Nostrand, Princeton.
2. Ahlgren, G. H. 1956. Forage Crops, 2nd ed. McGraw-Hill, New York.
3. American Grassland Council. 1959. American Grassland Council, Its History, Plans, and Objectives. State College, Pa.
4. Pendergrass, Webster. 1954. Research, education, and related activities in grassland farming. Ph.D. thesis, Harvard Univ.
5. McCloud, Darrell E. 1965. Grassland agriculture for the future. Proc. Amer. Forage and Grassl. Counc. 2nd Natl. Grassl. Field Day and Conf., pp. 49–54.
6. Cardon, P. V. 1952. Our concept of grassland agriculture. Proc. 6th Int. Grassl. Congr., State College, Pa.

❧ MAURICE E. HEATH. *See Chapter 1.*

FIG. 2.1. *Grasslanding embodies many fields of endeavor . . . soil, crop, and livestock sciences are ingredients in this basic system of farming.* A Lancaster County, Pa., view of contour strip-cropping, showing a partially completed soil conservation farm plan. *SCS photo.*

counters the devastating influence of erosion.

The USDA classified 579 million ha of farmland and other privately owned land in the U.S. as to longtime use capabilities (Fig. 2.2).[7] Results show that 56% of the land (Classes I–IV) can be used with limited to intensive tillage practices (see Terminology for definition of land classes). Crop options may include forages, grains, and other crops; however, the remaining 44% of the land (Classes V–VII) is limited to permanent vegetation for grazing, forestry, or wildlife. Range and pasture crops become the only alternative for much of this land.[7]

A fallacious concept in the U.S. regarding forages has been pointed out:

. . . that the spigot of agricultural abundance is turned off by planting land down to grass, and that it is turned on by ploughing the grasslands for the production of row crops. This is a concept based on our having been, for generations, row and cash crop farmers. . . . I am convinced that grasslands are productive, and that grassland improvement has an essential role to play in increased agricultural production. . . . We are a meat-eating and milk-drinking nation . . . grasslands provide the major raw materials for the production of beef, mutton, and dairy products.[8]

Due to the exploding world population, humans are competing with livestock for feed grains. The pressure of people on the world's food supply is a powerful force. Here in the U.S. a growing population and greater consumption of red meat have in-

7. USDA. 1971. National inventory of soil and water conservation needs, 1967. Stat. Bull. 461.

8. Myers, W. M. 1952. Our greatest grassland potential. *Crops and Soils.* 4:9–12.

creased demand for beef and other animal products. This in turn will require greater production from the forage and grassland ha.[5]

In grassland agriculture the emphasis is on getting the greatest overall benefit from the forage ha. This does not mean putting the entire farm in forages. Some farms could be reorganized to operate more profitably in the long run by increasing the number of ha in forages. Others might adjust to fewer ha with greater attention to getting the most from each. (See Fig. 2.3.)

❦ A GRASSLAND PHILOSOPHY

A sound national grassland philosophy must be developed before a grassland agriculture will be practiced generally on individual farms. Soil and climate, together with factors governing production and utilization of grasses and legumes, determine the intensity of grassland agriculture in different parts of the country. The forage plants common in range country will be quite different from those of humid areas, but the principles to be followed are similar, regardless of location. These principles concern productivity as measured by response to management when forages are made central to the farm and ranch operations. It has been emphasized that grassland agriculture is a *longtime program* directed toward increased production from improved grasslands and more efficient use of high-quality forage, rich in protein, minerals, and protective vitamins.[9]

9. Wisconsin College of Agriculture Grassland Committee. 1948. Turn to grassland farming now. Wis. Agr. Exp. Sta. Stencil Bull. 4.

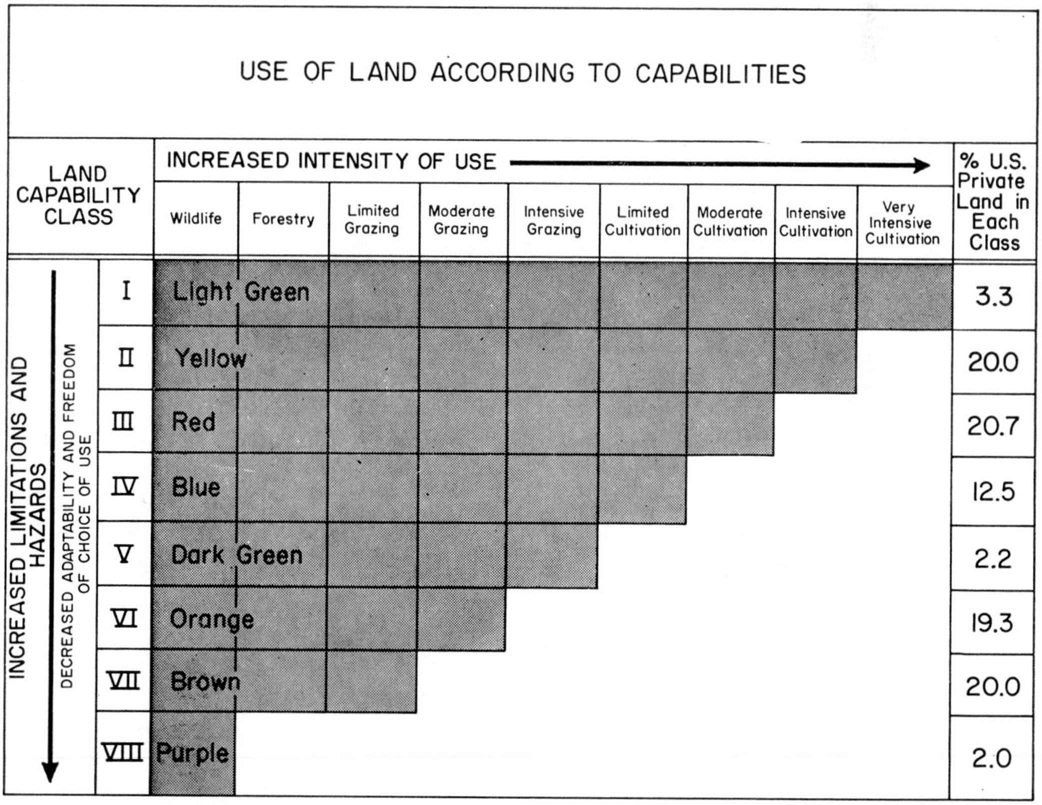

USE OF LAND ACCORDING TO CAPABILITIES

LAND CAPABILITY CLASS		INCREASED INTENSITY OF USE ⟶									% U.S. Private Land in Each Class
		Wildlife	Forestry	Limited Grazing	Moderate Grazing	Intensive Grazing	Limited Cultivation	Moderate Cultivation	Intensive Cultivation	Very Intensive Cultivation	
I		Light Green									3.3
II		Yellow									20.0
III		Red									20.7
IV		Blue									12.5
V		Dark Green									2.2
VI		Orange									19.3
VII		Brown									20.0
VIII		Purple									2.0

INCREASED LIMITATIONS AND HAZARDS

DECREASED ADAPTABILITY AND FREEDOM OF CHOICE OF USE

FIG. 2.2. Percent of U.S. farm and other privately owned lands by land capability classes as related to permanent land limitations and safe land use. All land in Classes I through VII (98%) is suitable for forage-animal production. However, Classes I through IV (56.5%) may also be used for intensive to limited cultivated crop production. *SCS chart.*

Fɪɢ. 2.3. This uplifted hectare of corn stimulates the imagination to visualize all that contributes to low costs per unit of production. *Pioneer Hi-Bred, Inc., photo.*

Shifts from a cash crop system to one emphasizing forage production and utilization with livestock require additional skills and a much higher type of management by the farm operator. One of the greatest regional shifts in forage emphasis has been in the southern and southeastern states. Since 1925 there has been a vast shift from corn and cotton to grasslands. Presently, 45% of the national beef cow herd is located within this area and is increasing.[10] (See Fig. 2.4.)

New Zealand is a country with a strong national grassland philosophy. Until the 1920s the grassland farmer was not viewed as a real farmer because he did not grow grain crops. The concept that grassland production *is* crop production immediately made him the most important crop farmer in New Zealand rather than a mere grazier.

An overall coherent land-forage-animal agriculture is nationally promoted. New Zealand, with much rugged terrain, is twice the size of North Carolina. In 1969 it had a population of 60 million sheep and 8.6 million cattle.[11-13]

Successful grassland agriculture requires sound farm management that will result in the greatest return possible over many years. It involves balancing the physical factors of production at a high level and at the same time providing the American people with an adequate diet.

FORAGES AND MAN

It has been shown that 30% of our families do not have as much calcium in their diets as is recommended, while nearly

10. Pope, L. S. 1972. Forages and cattle—Challenges for the south. Proc. Amer. Forage and Grassl. Counc., 5th Res.-Ind. Conf., pp. 20–24.

11. Levy, Sir E. Bruce. 1970. Grasslands of New Zealand, 3rd ed. A. R. Shearer, Govt. Printer, Wellington.
12. Dept. of Statistics. 1970. New Zealand pocket digest of statistics. A. R. Shearer, Govt. Printer, Wellington.
13. Smallfield, P. W. 1970. The Grassland Revolution in New Zealand. Hodder and Stoughton, Auckland.

TABLE 2.1 ⚘ Percentage of essential food nutrients consumed by U.S. population, furnished by milk and dairy products

Nutrient	Percent	Nutrient	Percent
Food energy	11.7	Iron	2.2
Protein	22.5	Vitamin A	11.5
Fat	17.0	Thiamin	9.9
Carbohydrate	7.2	Riboflavin	43.0
Calcium	76.2	Niacin	1.7
Phosphorus	36.7	Ascorbic acid	4.7

Source: Hanson, 1972.[15]

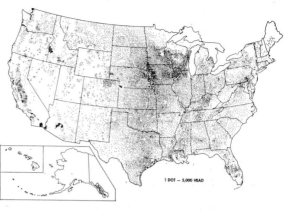

FIG. 2.4. Distribution of all cattle and calves throughout the U.S.

10% were substandard in their protein allowances.[14] Seventy-six percent of our food Ca and 36% of our P are from dairy products, largely derived from forages rich in Ca and P. Other essential food elements for good nutrition are furnished by milk and dairy products (Table 2.1).[15]

Animal products are currently furnishing 72% of the protein contained in our food supply.[16] Americans have become better fed; the protein source from animal products has increased more than 26% since 1910.[17] Domestic beef production doubled in the period 1948–68. Most estimates call for another doubling of beef demand by the year 2000.[18] (See Fig. 2.5.[19]) The intensification of grassland agriculture through applied technology provides one of the greatest expandable food resources for our ever-growing population.[20]

⚘ FORAGES AND LIVESTOCK IN THE NATIONAL ECONOMY

In grassland agriculture a high direct value of forages as livestock feed exists as well as many complementary benefits.

FEED FOR LIVESTOCK

Forages furnished 54.4% of all feed units consumed by the U.S. livestock industry in 1970 (Fig. 2.6).[21] Beef cattle were the largest market, consuming 66.8% of all forage; dairy cattle consumed 21.3%. Beef and dairy cattle together account for 88.1% of the U.S. forage market (Fig. 2.7).[21]

The feed from forages utilized by the U.S. livestock industry in 1970 amounted to 208 million t of feed units. A feed unit is a kilogram or ton of corn or its equivalent in other feed. At $44/t this

21. Allen, George C., Earl F. Hodges, and Margaret Devers. 1972. National and state livestock-feed relationships. Suppl. ERS-USDA Res. Serv. Stat. Bull. 446.

14. LeBovit, Corinne, and Faith Clark. 1959. Are we well fed? *In* Food, pp. 620–28. USDA Yearbook Agr.
15. Hanson, A. A. 1972. Importance of forages to agriculture. Amer. Soc. Agron. Forage Fert. Symp. In Press.
16. FAO. 1972. Production Yearbook 1971, vol. 25. Rome.
17. Byerly, T. C. 1966. The relation of animal agriculture to world food shortages, pp. 31–44. Proc. Agr. Res. Inst.
18. Hodgson, H. J., and R. E. Hodgson. 1970. Changing patterns in beef cattle production. *Agr. Sci. Rev.* 8:16–24.
19. Van Arsdall, Roy N., and Melvin D. Skold. 1973. Cattle raising in the U.S. ERS-USDA Agr. Econ. Rept. 235.
20. Myers, W. M. 1952. Your greatest opportunity is grass. *Country Gentleman* 122:20–21, 42–43.

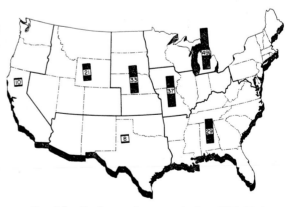

FIG. 2.5. Beef cow increase during 1970–80 is the estimated percent growth in numbers of beef cows by regions.

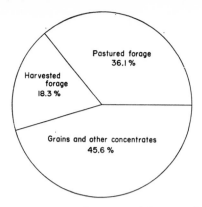

FIG. 2.6. Source and percent of forage and concentrate feeds consumed by the U.S. livestock industry in 1970. Harvested and pastured forage furnished 54.4% of the total feed units.

amounted to $9.15 billion, equal to 44% of the cash sales of all U.S. crops marketed in 1970 and 2.8 times the cash sales of all corn.[21-23]

Forage legumes not only provide feed for livestock but furnish large quantities of essential N for the growth of companion grasses. However, the commercial developments of N in the 1950s and 1960s now afford the grassland farmer an alternative source of N for use on his grass crops.[24]

Even idle grass has value in soil protection and organic matter renewal, but it is the value of forages as livestock feed that will largely determine their use and hectarage on farms throughout the country. With an increasing number of new forage species and improved cultivars, all-year grazing is becoming a reality in an ever-increasing area in the South. In the North the grazing period is being lengthened.[25]

An adequate reserve of forage at all times in the form of unused pasturage, grass silage, or hay is required in an intensive grassland agriculture. This is one of the keys to successful grassland-livestock management. A forage reserve such as hay or silage is needed to bridge such emergencies as a severe winter, a late spring, a summer drought, or a partial crop failure. In the more humid areas, rainy weather makes it difficult to capture the full nutrient value of the forage crops in the form of hay. Here the grassland farmer finds he can conserve these valuable nutrients as silage. Grassland farmers are finding that high-quality grass silage is the nearest they can come to good pasturage during winter cold and summer drought.

The economy of pasture is due chiefly to the saving in labor, equipment use, and power. The animals gather their own feed, spreading manure as they graze. However, the U.S. census does not provide animal production information (yield/ha) for range and pasture lands as it does for grain and other crops. Also, there is very little comparative economic data on land-forage-animal systems.[26]

❧ COMPLEMENTARY BENEFITS FROM FORAGE

In a grassland agriculture many direct complementary benefits are derived from forages. These are considered in some detail in other chapters. A few of the most evident and important are mentioned here.

ADAPTABILITY TO MANY SOIL SITUATIONS

A broad range of soil-climate environments exists throughout the U.S. Nearly half the land in farms is unsuitable for tilled crops; however, there are nearly 100 grass species of major forage importance in the U.S. and a third that number of legumes. This diversity of adaptation in forage species makes possible a more complete and intensive use of our total land resources.[27]

IMPROVEMENT OF SOIL DRAINAGE

In a grassland agriculture, grasses are teamed with legumes wherever possible since they supplement each other. Not only do legumes penetrate the subsoil and im-

22. USDA. 1971. Agricultural statistics.
23. Hodgson, H. J. 1968. Importance of forages in livestock production in the U.S., pp. 11–24. Amer. Soc. Agron. Spec. Publ. 13.
24. Scarseth, George D. 1969. The magic element for agricultural abundance—Nitrogen. In Man and His Earth, pp. 117–37. Iowa State Univ. Press, Ames.
25. Van Keuren, R. W., and E. W. Klosterman. 1967. Winter pasture system for Ohio beef cows. Ohio Rept. Res. Dev. 52 (5): 67–69.

26. Hanson, A. A. 1969. Future of forages in animal production. Proc. Natl. Conf. Forage Qual. and Util., pp. VI–V10. Nebr. Center Continuing Education, Lincoln.
27. McCloud, D. E. 1970. Innovations resulting from forage research, pp. 64–67. Proc. Amer. Forage and Grassl. Counc., 3rd Res.-Ind. Conf.

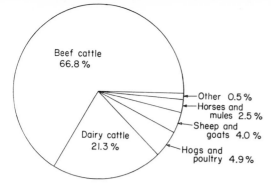

Beef cattle
66.8%

Dairy cattle
21.3%

Other 0.5%
Horses and
mules 2.5%
Sheep and
goats 4.0%
Hogs and
poultry 4.9%

Fig. 2.7. Percent of the total forage feed units in the U.S. consumed by each livestock category in 1970.

prove drainage but the fibrous grass roots permeate the plow layer, the quantity gradually diminishing with depth. The roots of some of the taller growing grasses may go down 2 m or more. A comparison of dry-weight grass root yields from different areas shows a range of from less than 2.2 t to more than 22 t/ha, depending on the species, location, and soil depth.[28] A high-quality grass-legume sod increases water percolation. Tile lines made useless by soil compaction from excessive row-cropping have functioned again when the optimum ratio of sod crops to row crops was used.

PROTECTION OF SOILS

On nonforested ha, adapted grass-legume combinations furnish excellent protection to soils on erodible, sloping lands. Forages, when compared to clean cultivated row crops or fallow, have been shown to be from 200 to 2000 times more effective in preventing soil loss. Effectiveness varies with soil type, forage management, and amount and intensity of precipitation.[29]

Close-growing forages protect the soil surface from the beating action of rain. It has been shown that the energy from rain beating on the soil surface may exceed 269 t-meters/ha/25 mm of rain.[30] The energy in 25 mm of rain falling within a half-hour is enough to raise an 18-cm layer of

soil 30 cm. Such energy will largely be dissipated by a grass-legume hay or pasture canopy capable of producing 7 t/ha or more of dry matter. Grass roots, when plowed for row crop production, furnish protection to the soil surface by holding and binding soil particles together and increasing percolation.

⚘ SOIL-FORAGE-ANIMAL SYSTEMS

In developing a soil-forage-animal system the grassland farmer begins planning his operations with the forage seeding. Choice of forage species and cultivars is all-important. Companion grasses are selected which associate well with legumes. Or a grass species may be used alone with fertilizer N. Factors such as lime, seedbed, fertilizer needs, weed control, and ultimate forage utilization are considered. When a companion cereal crop is used with the forage seeding, the management should ensure the forage stand.

Intensive grassland practices in the more humid or irrigated areas show that some of the highest forage yields are grown on land capability classes I, II, and III. It is here that alfalfa or alfalfa-grass mixtures may combine well with the grain crops for animal production. Corn and sorghum also are becoming more popular for high-energy silages in dairy and beef cattle enterprises. Classes IV–VII lands usually are in continuous grass-legumes, except for such periodic reestablishment of legumes as may be necessary. Depending on the soil, this may be accomplished by partially subduing the grass sod by tillage or chemicals. The use of sod-planted corn or sorghum for silage or grain has been used in certain situations.

GRASSLAND PROBLEMS AND RESEARCH

Many of the problems confronting the grassland farmer today are so broad as to be beyond the scope of any one specialist. State and federal research teams have been organized in a number of locations by assigning a number of scientists to work to-

28. Troughton, Arthur. 1957. The underground organs of herbage grasses. Commonwealth Bur. of Pastures and Field Crops, Bull. 44. Hurley, Berkshire, England.
29. Heath, Maurice E. 1961. Forage dynamics in soil conservation. *J. Soil Water Conserv.* 16:105–10.
30. Wischmeier, Walter H., and Dwight D. Smith. 1958. Rainfall energy and its relationship to soil loss. Trans. Amer. Geophys. Union 39:285–91.

gether in studying and analyzing grassland problems. One such problem being studied is how to best utilize the greater quantities of forages needed for proper land use. Soil, crop, animal, farm management, and soil conservation specialists are teamed to pool their resources and to study interacting factors and their effects on each other.[31,32]

Research on grassland problems is a trinity study: the forage itself, the animal which grazes or consumes it, and the soil it anchors and nourishes. Investigators must constantly remind themselves that their function is to provide new ideas and new approaches to grassland problems. The more their work becomes an accepted part of farm practice, the more successful they can count themselves as researchers. It is the scientist's responsibility, not the farmer's, to show how forage can best be disciplined. Funds devoted to grasslands research are investments repaid many times in new knowledge for increased efficiency in grassland agriculture. This results in greater abundance of animal products and in human health.[33,34]

As yet, we do not observe big forage science centers developing in the U.S. as in other countries with a strong national grassland philosophy. Several mission-oriented national laboratories to study land-forage-animal systems would help give coherence and national direction to the forage and grassland phases of American agriculture.[35]

GRASSLAND EDUCATION

Intensive grassland agriculture requires that grassland research results be presented by specialist teams. Each specialist needs to correlate his subject matter responsibility to the whole grassland farming operation of the individual farm and ranch as well as to the opportunities of larger areas.[36,37] A number of states have organized state forage and grassland councils so the many diverse forage interests in public service and industry can work together more effectively.

Many counties have pooled their leadership, information, and other resources to work with grassland agriculture. Some local county grassland committees or councils have analyzed the potentials of a grassland agriculture for their particular area and planned a course of action. Such committees or councils usually include various agricultural workers, farm leaders, farm credit representatives, farm equipment dealers, farm editors, representatives of local industry, and others.[38] Such local teamwork helps speed the trend toward grassland agriculture while maintaining a well-balanced overall approach.

36. Burcalow, F. V., and George M. Werner. 1957. Extension methods of evaluating pasture in Wisconsin, p. 80. Amer. Soc. Agron. Abstr.
37. Morgan, N. D. 1972. Selling a forage educational program, pp. 168–70. Clemson Univ. Southern Pasture and Forage Crop Improvement Conf. Rept.
38. Thompson, Warren C. 1970. Organizing and using a county forage council, pp. 99–100. Univ. Georgia Southern Pasture and Forage Conf. Rept.

❧ QUESTIONS

1. What is grassland agriculture? A grassland farmer?
2. Why is a national grassland philosophy important in implementing a grassland agriculture on farms and ranches?
3. What percent of the total feed units consumed by livestock in the U.S. is furnished by forages? What portion of protein of the U.S. human diet is of animal source?
4. Why is grassland agriculture so closely linked with livestock production?
5. What are some of the more important complementary benefits derived from the use of forages in grassland agriculture?
6. What are the advantages of teamwork in research and education in rendering assistance to the grassland farmer?
7. What is meant by research on grassland problems being a trinity study?
8. Develop a countywide grassland agriculture program that ultimately would result in a highly productive and profitable agriculture for your home area.

31. Weiss, Martin G. 1959. Integration of programs in genetics, pathology, and entomology. In Grasslands. AAAS Publ. 53.
32. Davies, William. 1954. The Grass Crop, Its Development, Use, and Maintenance. E. and F. N. Spon, Ltd., London.
33. Duckham, A. N. 1958. Grassland research and the future. J. Brit. Grassl. Soc. 13:165–69.
34. Myers, W. M. 1951. Research needs of the grasslands program. Proc. Assoc. Land Grant Coll. and Univ., Houston, Texas.
35. Weinberg, Alvin M. 1967. Reflections on Big Science. M.I.T. Press, Cambridge, Mass.

VICTOR E. JACOBS / *University of Missouri*

3

FORAGE PRODUCTION ECONOMICS

⚘

T HE IMPORTANCE of forages has been well established. In 1971 the U.S. hay crop alone was valued in excess of $3 billion. The January inventory of cattle, primary consumers of forage, was appraised in excess of $20 billion in 1970.[1,2] Despite the importance of forages, it is generally recognized that technology has been more sparingly used on forage crops than on major grain, fiber, and horticultural crops. Yield improvement potentials are large for forage crops, especially in the humid areas, but actual attainment depends on their profitability.

This discussion is concerned with economic evaluation of alternative forage production and utilization practices. No attempt is made to determine profitabilities of specific practices for particular areas. Nor is any comprehensive review of production economics attempted. Selected economic concepts and methods of analysis with particular relevance to forage evaluation and decision making are presented.

⚘ FORAGE PRODUCTION AND LOCATION

A brief summation of the reasons for forage production, along with some economic

⚘ VICTOR E. JACOBS is Professor of Agricultural Economics and Extension Economist at the University of Missouri. He holds the M.S. degree from the University of Illinois and the Ph.D. from Kansas State Univerity. His primary interest is the economics of beef-forage production systems.

concepts of forage location, may be useful for building an economic perspective.

Livestock feed requirements often require production of forages, especially for ruminants. While all-concentrate rations have been sparingly used to finish cattle, the breeding herds, dairy herds, and backgrounding enterprises commonly require forage.

By-product utilization often requires forage crops to fill the calendar gaps. Grain crop residues are often available as a nearly free feed that is usable by ruminants. But pasture and hay or silage must also be produced to feed the animals when grain crop residues are not available.

Soil and water conservation is a particularly important objective served by solid-seeded perennial forage crops as opposed to annual grain, fiber, and horticultural crops requiring annual tillage and periods without adequate soil cover.

Benefits to other crops commonly motivate production of forage crops. Provision of legume-fixed nitrogen and the breaking of insect, weed, or disease life cycles often result in a benefit not reflected in forage yield but in the yields of other crops produced in rotation with forages.

These reasons all imply complementary effects between forage and other crops. Conservation of soil fertility is reflected in reduced costs or improved returns from future

1. ERS, USDA. 1971. Feed situation, p. 21. Nov.
2. ERS, USDA. 1971. Livestock and meat statistics. Suppl. 1970 Stat. Bull. 333, Table 3, p. 1. June.

crops. Facilitating a livestock enterprise may result in more productive use of family labor, management potentials, and other resources. Yield increases of crops produced in rotation with forages result in economic benefits in excess of the market value of the forage itself. Where such external benefits accrue, they should be accounted as income from the forage crop and added to the market value of the forage itself.

In many situations, forages are competitive with other crops. When competitive, the comparative advantage of forage crop production is determined by an interaction between cost structure and land-climate productivity. Perennial forages as well as reseeding annuals and biennials tend to have relatively low direct production costs because they do not require annual seedbed preparation, seed, or clean cultivation. Conversely, the bulky nature of a forage crop results in higher harvesting, handling,

FIG. 3.1. . . . *pasture and hay . . . produced where low production costs are an advantage.* Pictured is a dallisgrass-bermudagrass-carpetgrass-clover mixed lowland pasture in Georgia. *USDA photo.*

storage, and transportation costs per unit of product value relative to grain crops.

Even pasture has high harvest or utilization costs whenever the ownership costs of the animals are considered as yield-associated or harvest costs. When it is profitable to produce both types of crops in a particular area, they will tend to be segregated by soil and climate productivity. The perennial forage crop will, because of lower fixed production costs, tend to occupy the less productive land. As land quality and grain yield potential increase, the grain crop with its lower per unit harvesting costs tends to catch up and finally become economically superior as land productivity increases. A smaller percentage of the additional grain yield is absorbed by additional harvesting costs.

Thus it is not surprising to find pasture and hay produced on the nongrain land where low production costs are an advantage. (See Fig. 3.1.) Grains are produced on the highest quality land, where lower yield-associated costs of harvest, handling, transportation, and storage are relatively more important.

❧ FORAGE AS AN ECONOMIC COMMODITY

The bulky nature of forage affects more than its location relative to grain crops. In fact, this attribute is very central to problems of valuation and utilization and to determining the kind of market that forages face.

When corn is worth $44/t, hay may be worth only $27, silage $9–$13, and the standing forage worth only $3–$4/t of green weight. With these lower values per ton of material, harvesting, handling, storage, and transportation costs bulk much larger as a percentage of crop value. Reductions in yield or carrying capacity of up to 50% are commonly accepted for grazing as pasture to avoid costs of mechanical harvesting. Production of 1 t of 85% dry matter (DM) hay requires the removal of 3.25 t of water from a standing crop of forage containing 80% moisture. In humid areas where natural curing is difficult, much of this additional water is harvested, handled, transported, and stored as silage at considerable cost.

Any handling and transportation function that costs $7/t adds only 16% to the cost of $44/t of grain, 26% to $27/t of hay, and 64% to the cost of $11/t silage.

Several important economic implications of these higher harvest, handling, storage, and transportation costs are noted below.

A smaller percentage of eventual forage value remains to pay for any yield-increasing practice. Additional hay may be worth $27/t at feeding time, but only $10 may remain to pay for its production if $17/t is required to harvest, transport, and store the added ton.

Dependence on livestock to harvest pasture limits efficiency when livestock numbers must be set or fixed in advance. While the combine may harvest whatever grain is produced, the harvest capability of livestock is limited by the number available. To avoid the poor-year risks of distress sale (at low prices), reduced performance, or the cost of purchased feed, conservative stocking rates are often accepted at the cost of underutilization in years of superior yield.

Markets for forage tend to be more local, imperfect, poorly organized, and less dependable. The greater cost of transporting hay, the often prohibitive costs of transporting silage, and the impossibility of transporting pasture usually mean a more local market with fewer buyers and sellers. Local variations in weather are more important, and dependability of both supply and demand is reduced. Therefore, most forage is used by the same operator who produced it, with his own livestock serving as the market.

Seasonal production is important. In much of the U.S., 60% or more of the forage is produced in only 25% or less of the calendar year. Since livestock (especially breeding livestock) require feed on a year-round basis, much forage must be harvested to match supply to year-round demands. When harvest, transport, handling, and storage costs are high relative to crop value (as with forage) this seasonality of production carries a larger cost. As will be seen later, production practices or species that level out seasonal production are worth more. Practices that add only to yield in already surplus periods are worth substantially less.

❧ FORAGE VALUATION AND THE YIELDS AND VALUES DILEMMA

Economic profitability of any crop (or yield-increasing practice) ultimately comes down to a comparison of crop value (or added value) with crop cost (or added cost). A necessary preliminary to this comparison, however, is the determination of crop value. This is where difficulties and inconsistencies unique to forage are most commonly encountered. One of the difficulties is found in the choice of a generally acceptable yield unit. Pasture yields, for instance, are variously reported in tons of hay equivalent or DM, animal unit months (AUM's) of carrying capacity, beef or milk produced per ha, or as nutritional components such as total digestible nutrients (TDN) and protein. Even seemingly simple measures such as tons of forage are complicated by differing DM percentages, shrink, and harvest losses.

A Pasture Example

It will be assumed that a cool-season pasture is being evaluated at a midwestern experiment station. On this pasture 225-kg "tester" steers are grazed to measure animal performance or pasture quality. These steers are stocked continuously during the periods the pasture is used. Additional steers (called "put-and-take" animals) are added and removed as needed to standardize the supply of forage available to the testers. This permits a more controlled comparison of animal performance between experimental pastures. Total steer-days are recorded for both the testers and the more variably stocked put-and-take steers. The performance of the put-and-take steers is ignored because of weighing errors over short periods. The results are as follows:

The tester steers gain 0.7 kg/day. The steer-days accumulated per ha include 300 from the testers and 200 from the put-and-take steers for a total of 500 steer-days/ha. These 500 steer-days multiplied by the tester's daily performance of 0.7 kg of gain gives an estimated production of 350 kg beef/ha.

When steers are sold at the end of the pasture period for 66¢/kg, the apparent gross value of the final product (beef) is 350 kg at 66¢ or $231/ha. A contrasting approach would be to value the more direct product or carrying capacity. Since a 225-kg steer consumes approximately 0.6 as much as a 454-kg animal, the 500 steer-days convert to 500 × 0.6 or 300 animal-unit days or 10 AUM's/ha. When pasture rents for $4/AUM, a gross direct crop value of only $40/ha results rather than $231. The simplest approach is the latter, the measurement and valuation of the direct product. It can be contended that the final salable product is the only economic reason for producing the pasture and that carrying capacity is also ambiguous and dependent on stocking intensity, failing to take into account differences in quality of pasture.

INTERPRETATION OF FINAL PRODUCT YIELDS

The question is whether final product yields (beef, milk) are reasonably unambiguous stable constants of a specific pasture or whether they are only relative to very particular circumstances of production. In fact, the latter will be found to be true. Animal age, class, condition, and system of utilization sometimes are more important determinants of final product yield than the pasture or treatment ostensibly being measured.

YOUNG ANIMALS ARE MORE EFFICIENT. According to the National Research Council requirements a full-fed 200-kg calf requires 3.7 kg TDN to gain 1.0 kg/day. A full-fed 400-kg two-year-old requires 8.0 kg TDN to gain 1.4 kg/day. Even though the two-year-old gains 40% faster, the final product yield of the calf is still 54% larger from the same amount of feed or area.[3]

THIN ANIMALS ARE MORE EFFICIENT. In a Beltsville nutritional experiment, very thin 230-kg heifers and very fleshy 547-kg herdmates were both switched to an ad libitum ration of grass hay.[4] The very thin heifers (from a low-energy level prior to the ration change) actually consumed slightly more total feed per day than the 547-kg heifers and gained nearly 5 times as much over the first 84 days. While these differences in previous energy level (and thus differences in initial fleshing) were somewhat extreme, the results strongly indicate the effect of fleshing or condition. The thin animals actually produced over 4.5 times as much gain from the same amount of feed.

COMPENSATION SHRINKS EARLY ADVANTAGES. The tendency of animals to compensate in later performance for differences in nutrition and performance in earlier periods complicates economic evaluation where performance differences occur. A particular pasture may appear to be superior (or inferior) because of a substantial performance advantage (or disadvantage). When animals are sold at the end of the period in question, such differences are reflected directly in differing sale weights. When the pasture (or ration) is used early, with other feeds used in an intervening period prior to sale, performance differences are gradually eroded with compensating higher or lower performances in future periods. Thus a gain superiority of 20 kg/head in period A may directly cause a 10-kg smaller gain in period B. The only salable result of the 20-kg difference in gain in period A is the 10-kg difference still remaining when the animal is eventually sold. The only relevant performance difference in an economic sense is that remaining at sale time.

BEEF COWS PRODUCE LESS. The primary reason beef cows are used in place of young steers or heifers in the utiliza-

3. National Research Council. 1970. Nutrient Requirements of Beef Cattle, 4th ed., rev., pp. 22–3. Natl. Acad. Sci., Washington, D.C.

4. Wiltbank, J. N. et al. 1965. Influence of total feed and protein intake on reproductive performance in the beef female through second calving. USDA Tech. Bull. 1314, p. 42.

tion of pasture and other forage is that more dollars are realized per kilogram of animal production. In much of the U.S., steers and heifers will produce 50% or more additional beef per ha than a beef breeding herd.

FINAL PRODUCT DEPENDS ON WHEN THE PASTURE IS USED. Utilization systems commonly employed on experimental pastures tend to produce a "best of all worlds" level of final product yield. When put-and-take animals are used to vary stocking rate and maintain a more constant forage supply, a more immature forage also results. It is generally known that a perennial forage may decline in dry matter digestibility from 70% or above to below 50% as it advances in maturity. Grazing managements that maintain a more immature plant produce more gain per ha and per animal. Where a steer may gain 0.7 kg/day or more during rapid growth periods on an immature forage, the same steer may gain little or nothing (even lose weight) when pastured on the same forage when it is stockpiled at a more advanced stage of maturity.

OPTIMAL MANAGEMENT IS NOT NECESSARILY ECONOMICALLY OPTIMAL. Animals and grazing managements may be selected that appear optimal from the standpoint of total final product. It cannot, however, be assumed that these systems are economically optimal and should therefore be employed by farmers or that the yields so produced are necessarily good indicators of even relative pasture value for farmers.

For example, paying the extra price for very young thin animals cannot be automatically assumed profitable, even though it results in maximum gains per ha. Neither is it necessarily profitable to own larger numbers for shorter periods to maximize performance of cool-season grasses. Warm-season species may cost more, yield less, or require better land for annual seedings. Thus it may be economically optimal to allow cool-season surpluses to accumulate (in mature less digestible form) for use during the summer, despite the lower gains per ha and per animal. It cannot be automatically assumed that a forage or forage system that was superior for steers or dairy cows is also superior for a beef breeding herd. Higher forage palatability or digestibility may result in more steer gain or milk per ha even though fewer tons of DM or AUM's of carrying capacity are produced. With the beef cow, an unsalable addition of 80–90 kg of cow weight may be the primary result of this superior forage quality.

Thus whether a pasture (or other feed) produces 100 or 500 kilograms of animal product per ha may have very little to do with the basic agronomic characteristics of the forage itself. Such differences can result entirely from differences in animals and utilization systems, none of which can automatically be assumed superior just because they produce more final product per ha. Neither are the relative rankings of alternative forages necessarily stable. The nutritionally superior pasture or other forage that excels for steers or dairy cows may well rank behind a lower quality forage of greater carrying capacity when used for beef breeding cows.

Certain specific attributes should ideally be measured and valued separately and independently. Carrying capacity, nutritive quality, and seasonal distribution of growth are three such attributes; all have independent effects on the economic value of a pasture. The relative economic importance of each will depend on the system in which the forage is employed. If an economic evaluation is made on the basis of gross final product yields alone, the foregoing limitations should be remembered; but more important, the final product yield must be valued and costs debited in a manner consistent with the actual system of utilization employed. It is to this problem we now turn.

ECONOMICS OF FORAGE VALUES AND FINAL PRODUCT YIELDS

Forage valuation or pricing commonly is required in two classes of decision problems: (1) To compare alternative uses of the same land resources, it is usually necessary to determine the residual economic return remaining to pay for the use of land and overhead; and (2) when yield-increasing inputs or technologies are being considered, it is necessary to determine the residual economic return (net of other yield-associated costs) remaining to pay for the yield-increasing input or technology. In either case, we are interested in the net value of product remaining after deducting all other yield-associated or utilization costs. That portion of gross product value resulting from harvesting, transportation, storage, or animal ownership costs incurred to get the product to the point, form, or time at which value is assessed is not a result of, nor creditable to, the yield-increasing input.

CONSISTENCY BETWEEN ALL ELEMENTS OF THE ANALYSIS IS IMPERATIVE. Forage may be priced or valued standing unharvested in the field; behind the baler; after it is hauled to storage; after a six-month storage period; or after transformation into milk, meat, or wool. Each successive stage through which it progresses toward a final consumable product results in a higher value because other costs or inputs have been incorporated. A standing hay crop may be worth only $11/t (90% DM basis), as opposed to $20 behind the baler, $26 in storage, and $30 at feeding time. Gross values should rise further after transformation into beef or milk since many more costs have by then been incorporated into the final product produced.

In the hay example used above, only the $11/t standing forage value may be credited directly to the fertilizer that produced it, not its $30/t value after the expenditure of perhaps $9 for mowing, raking, and baling; $6 for hauling to storage; and $4 for storage and shrinkage up to feeding time. In short, the price selected, the additional costs deducted, and the yield itself (or shrinkage of yield) all need to be consistent with one another and with some defined place, form, and time with respect to the product being valued. While hay bales

may weigh 25–30 kg at harvest, they may weigh only 20–25 kg at the point fed. Care must be exercised not to apply a feeding-time price to a harvest-time yield or the reverse.

FINAL PRODUCT VALUATION REQUIRES USE OF RESIDUAL IMPUTATION. Because of the less than perfect market pricing of forages such as pasture and the difficulty in assigning values to differing qualities, many prefer to start with the final product. Thus pastures are commonly characterized in popular articles as having produced 400 kg of beef, or 5000 kg of milk, or other animal or final product yields per ha. This is analogous to characterizing some quantity of iron ore as having an output of 5000 automobiles. All the additional milk or beef produced from fertilization is not creditable to the fertilizer. In fact, the pasture and other forage used to produce milk represent only a minor share of the total inputs used. Feed represents about 50% of the cost of producing milk, with forage commonly amounting to only 50% of the feed.

Residual imputation is a means of valuing backward from final product values. Described simply, this amounts to taking final product value as income, deducting all other expenses or costs required to transform the standing forage into the final product, and imputing the remaining value or residual back to the forage or other input being priced. Such a backward valuation requires that the production function be homogeneous and linear and that all other inputs are priced at their marginal-value product.[5] Any pure profit (or loss) of the total enterprise is imputed back (or credited) to the single input being residually valued. Such residually estimated values are extremely sensitive to variations in management, product price, or other costs. Their sensitivity increases as the input being valued decreases as a percentage share of total costs.

5. Heady, Earl O. 1952. Economics of Agricultural Production and Resource Use, pp. 407–8. Prentice-Hall, New York.

In Table 3.1 we can see some reasons for the caution of economists. If the operator were a superior dairyman and received 10% more milk from the same inputs, an additional $60 profit would result, all of which is credited to the pasture, even though it represented only 8% of the total inputs used. Similarly, with poorer management and 10% less production the entire $60 loss is imputed back to the pasture, resulting in a residual value of minus $10 for the six-month pasture. Similar effects may be estimated for above (or below) average product price. Each 10% change in final product quantity or price results in a 120% change in the residually estimated pasture value. When a more direct valuation approach can be consistently and appropriately used, it is preferable. More direct yield measures such as AUM's offer fewer pitfalls and allow yield to be priced in accordance with differences in forage quality.

Price margins on purchased replacements are a particular concern in forage valuation for cattle grazing enterprises. While one occasionally reads about a 300-kg gain per ha at a 66¢/kg selling price, this seldom reflects reality. Because less beef is normally produced per ha with a beef breeding herd than with grazing of young cattle, a price structure has developed that tends to equalize returns between alternative uses of the same forage. When a 320-kg steer sells for 70¢ per kg, his 180-kg replacement may cost 84¢/kg, resulting in a price loss or negative price margin on the purchased weight of 14¢/kg. When the 320-kg feeder brings only 57¢ per kg, his 180-kg replacement may cost 64¢ with a 7¢ negative price

margin. Normally, the higher the price level, the larger the negative price margin. In this manner the price signals for more or less beef are relayed back to the original source, the calf producer.

Also, a compensatory price structure tends to develop to equalize returns between seasons. Since pasture gains commonly are believed cheap to produce, the price of younger, thinner animals is competitively forced up at the beginning of the pasture season with a reverse movement at the end. Combining both effects, the 1966–70 Kansas City price of all 272-kg feeder steers averaged 65.34¢/kg in May, while 340-kg steers averaged only 58.47¢/kg in September. The 6.87¢ negative price margin on the initial 272 kg represents an $18.69 ownership cost per steer. The 68-kg gain produced actually sold for only 31¢/kg (net of negative price margins on initial weight) even though the total steer sold for over 58¢/kg. The only economic gain is the increase in value per head. Thus the 340-kg feeder at 58.47¢/kg brought $198.50 in September. Deducting 272 kg at 65.34¢/kg ($177.72/head) leaves a gross gain per head of $21.08, or 31¢/kg of gain. Other animal ownership costs such as interest, death loss, and labor must be deducted to arrive at the residual return remaining for pasture. Neglect of price margins, whether positive or negative, is indeed serious.

❦ FORAGE VALUE MORE THAN GROSS YIELD

Simple physical yields such as tons, beef, or milk per ha are commonly used as indicators of net economic worth. Economic value, however, depends on much more than gross physical yield, and these other aspects should be considered in evaluating alternative forages and treatments.

Seasonal production patterns affect pasture values. Where cool-season species predominate, 70% or more of production often occurs in a calendar period representing only 20–25% of the livestock year; thus, 45–50% of annual production (the 70% produced minus the 20–25% used during the

TABLE 3.1 ❦ A hypothetical example of residual pricing of forage from a dairy enterprise

Pricing	Normal	10% More	10% Less
Gross income per cow	$600	$660	$540
Minus: all nonfeed costs	300	300	300
Minus: hay, grain, silage	250	250	250
Remaining for six-month pasture	$ 50	$110	−$ 10

period) must be used in a later period, or animal demands must be modified to match the seasonal production pattern. The latter alternative is not possible with a breeding herd (a 12-month business). Seasonal price movements often make it a very marginal possibility even for the grazer of young cattle. Larger negative price margins and other animal costs absorbed for short gain periods represent a substantial cost of varying animal numbers to match seasonal pasture growth.

Surplus spring growth is also mechanically harvested and stored for later use, but at a significant addition to cost. Some of the surplus is commonly accumulated or stockpiled for use during the summer. Reduced animal performance then becomes the cost incurred as forage quality deteriorates with advancing maturity.

Thus additional forage produced in an already surplus period inevitably incurs one or more of these additional costs. Additional pasture produced outside the primary surplus period is worth substantially more than additional forage produced in a surplus period. This premium for nonsurplus production is either equal to (1) the differing net value received for the gain (net of price margins and other ownership costs), (2) the added harvesting cost required to conserve surplus forage into the deficit period, or (3) the superiority of animal performance on the more immature growth of the pasture produced in the deficit period over that on stockpiled surplus with its lower digestibility. Thus a treatment, system, or species that provides additional production in nonsurplus periods has a substantially higher value than one that provides additional product in an already surplus period.

An improved beef per ha criterion can be developed. Gross beef yield per ha is commonly reported, but it is often not a satisfactory indicator of even the relative economic value of a forage. Animal ownership or harvesting costs must be paid before anything remains for the pasture. When negative price margins on initial weight claim $20/head and other animal ownership, sale, and transport costs total an ad-

ditional $15/head, we have a total per head fixed cost of $35. When the steer sells for 70¢/kg, the first 50 kg of gain per steer is required to pay these per head costs with nothing remaining for the pasture. A pasture that carries 10 steers/ha gaining only 50 kg/head may leave nothing for pasture even though 500 kg of gain are produced per ha. Conversely, a pasture that carries only 2.5 steers/ha but produces gains of 100 kg/head leaves a surplus gain of 50 kg/head and 2.5 × 50 or 125 kg/ha of surplus gain. At a selling price of 70¢/kg, this 125 kg/ha of surplus gain allows an $87.50 rental for pasture usage even though only 50% as much gain is produced per ha as in the earlier case with a residual pasture return of zero. The economic importance of season-long pasture quality is obvious. Since quality is strongly related to stage of maturity, seasonal balance in growth patterns assumes a marked economic importance where young cattle are being grazed. Only the gain in excess of ownership costs per head remains for pasture.

The physical yield criterion or model implied above is relatively simple:

$$\begin{array}{ccc} \text{Effective} & & \text{Surplus gain} & & \text{Animals} \\ \text{pasture} & = & \text{per head} & \times & \text{per unit} \\ \text{value} & & & & \text{area} \end{array}$$

where surplus gain is defined as the excess gain per head above that (valued at sale price) required to pay all per head costs including price loss on initial weight.

❧ A TOTAL SYSTEMS APPROACH

Forage is but one variable or input among many used in livestock production. Whether the decision at hand is the choice of forage species or the choice of fertilizer or other treatments, the relevant economic question is, What is the total economic impact of that choice within the system in which it is used? (See Fig. 3.2.) Accurate economic assessment can be approached only if we strive for this ideal in our economic analysis.

Differing seasonal distributions of production of alternative species and treatments can be evaluated in a total systems approach. A penalty of additional harvest-

FIG. 3.2. *Forage . . . one input . . . livestock production.* This herd of 500 beef cows in southwest Indiana is carried on improved well-managed permanent pasture during the growing season. The cows utilize grain crop residues, including ear drop and cornstalks, during the winter months. *Purdue Univ. photo.*

ing cost can be assessed against additional yield in a surplus period, but not against additional production in a nonsurplus period. Differences in season-long forage quality can be assessed with the allegedly improved beef per ha model presented above. Quality can be assessed differently for a cow herd than for young steers and heifers. When most of the gain from added quality is received only as unsalable additions to weight and condition of the mother cow, less economic value should be placed on quality and relatively more on carrying capacity than with steers. When several months intervene between an early feeding period and eventual sale, compensation will narrow initial performance differences of alternative forages. The higher quality forage should then be credited only with the performance advantage expected to remain at sale time rather than that observed at the end of the early phase itself.

Maximum generality in forage evaluation depends on concepts and coefficients that permit accurate forecasting of performance of varied animals under varied utilization systems. Much forage research (especially of pasture) is conducted with particular animals employed in a specific system of utilization. Application at the farm level, however, usually requires forecasting the performance of different animals employed in a different system of utilization than that employed at the research station. Cooperation between the plant and animal scientist and the economist is required for continued development of concepts and coefficients to achieve this desired transferability of research and for the tailoring of experimental results to the forecasting needs of farm decision makers. Scales and record systems at the farm level are also necessary if performances are to be known and alternatives accurately assessed.

Finally, forages must be consistently measured, priced, and costed on a time, place, and form-specific basis. Because of their bulk, yield-associated or utilization costs are important and must be taken into account. Simple gross-yield measures are inadequate for reflecting total systems impact since performance and other costs are affected by seasonal distribution, quality, and other attributes. A total systems perspective is required.

❧ QUESTIONS

1. Identify the two major differences in cost structure between perennial forages and annual grain crops and describe how they affect the location of these crops relative to climate and land quality.
2. Name three reasons why forages may complement other crop production or produce benefits in excess of the market value of the direct forage product.
3. Why is it necessary that yields, prices, and costs all be determined on a time, place, and form-specific basis?
4. When forage values are to be estimated from final product yields (beef or milk), why is residual imputation necessary and what are the major pitfalls to be observed?
5. When 200-kg steers are purchased for 75¢/kg to utilize pasture, gain 100 kg, and sell for 60¢/kg at the end of the pasture season, what is the gross increase (in dollar terms) per kilogram of gain produced?
6. Why is the seasonal production pattern of an alternative forage or treatment often important in determining its net value per unit of product?
7. Identify and discuss several factors that must be taken into account in generalizing from the systems-specific results of a particular grazing experiment to an equally systems-specific forecast of performance with different animals in an alternative system of utilization of the same forage.

GEORGE M. BROWNING / *Iowa State University*
and Association of North Central Agricultural Experiment Stations

4

FORAGES AND SOIL CONSERVATION

⋇

W HEN the white man came to this continent, he found the land covered with native grasses, legumes, and timber. In most parts there were relatively few animals to consume the forages, and the Indians made little use of the timber. As a result, the above-ground growth was returned to the surface to decompose and become incorporated with the soil. The root systems of plants also contributed to the accumulation of organic matter in the soil, and the stems and leaves protected the soil surface from the beating action of rain. The loose spongy condition of the soil was ideal for maximum absorption of water; therefore, soil erosion was not a problem. To the early settler the supply of land and timber appeared to be unlimited. Thus there was little incentive to protect and conserve these resources. But as the population increased, man needed more food for himself and feed for his livestock; timber was needed for fuel and shelter. Subsequently, he plowed the virgin prairie and cleared the timber; and erosion took its toll from intertilled crops such as corn, tobacco, and cotton grown without supporting conservation

measures. Modern farming practices made possible the development of a great agricultural and industrial nation but destroyed nature's blanket of protective vegetation. In general, our system has been exploitative. With the use of conservation methods of farming the same development, or more, could have been achieved. But only since the 1950s have the farmer and the general public been awakened to the real consequences of misusing farmland and other resources.

As the nation's population increases, our per capita land resources dwindle, and the demand on land and water resources presses ever harder against the limits of the natural environment.

⋇ USE OF OUR LAND

The distribution of the 0.93 billion ha of land in the 50 states is shown in Table 4.1.[1] As one of 213 million Americans, your pro rata share of land is 4.2 ha. In 1940 the land base to support each man, woman, and child was 7 ha. Based on the estimated population, it will be only 2.6 ha in 2000.

Not all your 4.2-ha share is available to do with as you please. Some of the land is already taken up by cities, towns, airports, and highways. About 0.8 ha are

⋇ GEORGE M. BROWNING is Regional Director of the North Central Agricultural Experiment Stations. He received the M.S. and Ph.D. degrees from the University of West Virginia. He served with the SCS and as associate director of the Iowa station.

1. USDA. 1967. National inventory of soil and water conservation needs. Stat. Bull. 461.

TABLE 4.1 🍂 Distribution of total land area, 50 states

Land type	Hectares (000)	Percent
Locally Controlled Land		
Privately owned land	536,892	58.5
Nonfederal public land	24,811	2.7
Indian land	20,397	2.2
Small water areas	2,873	0.3
Urban and built-up areas	24,684	2.7
Federal	307,369	33.6
Total land area, 50 states	917,026	100.0

producing food and fiber, and some of the land is barren mountaintop, desert, or frozen tundra. We need to use our remaining land resources more efficiently to meet our food and fiber needs and preserve a livable and pleasant environment.

About 66% of our land (0.58 billion ha) is owned in individual parcels by private citizens; by business and industry; by states, counties, and cities; and by other units of local government. About 308 million ha or 33% of our land is public, administered by the federal government in the general interest.

The welfare of the public and the nation depends more on how the nonpublic land is used and managed, for it is this land that furnishes most of our food, fiber, lumber, and other products that either are essential or add to our pleasure and comfort. Private land (locally controlled land) is the space on which we build our houses, erect our towns and cities, run railroads, and construct highways and airports. For all its importance, the use and care of this land is nonetheless dependent on the millions of day-to-day decisions made by private users.

The uses made of the nation's locally controlled rural land are shown in Figure 4.1.[2] Land use is divided among three major productive purposes: cropland, 30%; pasture and range, 34%; and forest, 32%. About half the arable land is used for cultivated crops; but if an increase in food production is needed, cropland

2. USDA. 1971. Two-thirds of our land: A national inventory. SCS Program Aid 984.

acreage could be expanded without encroaching on other land use. By concentrating tillage farming on the land best suited for it and planning other uses in harmony with the natural features and capability of the land, we can have sufficient land for all our needs.

Although we have abundant soil resources for the foreseeable future, 60% of locally controlled land is not cared for adequately. Sediment and other pollutants from improperly treated land foul streams and lakes and destroy recreation and aesthetic values. Data from the national land-use inventory show that 64% of the 177 million ha of cropland needs additional conservation treatment.[2] Similarly, 67% of the 195 million ha of pasture and rangeland, 62% of the 187 million ha of forest land, and 28% of the 23 million ha of other land is inadequately treated.

When row crops are grown, there are times when no cover exists to protect the soil against erosion and leaching. An estimated 89 million ha of U.S. crop and grazing land have been seriously damaged. An additional 314 million ha of crop, grazing, and forest land have been eroded to some degree. Of the 186 million ha

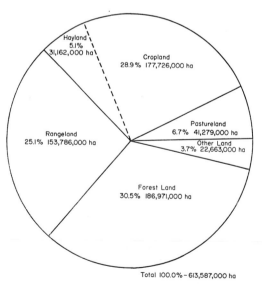

FIG. 4.1. Predominant use of nonfederal rural land in 1967.

FIG. 4.2. *Wind erosion is estimated to be active . . . 181,000,000 ha . . . in the Great Plains area.* This view is not somewhere in the semiarid West but is a roadside in the central Corn Belt after a spring blow. *Iowa SCS photo.*

now comprising the farms and ranches of the U.S., all but about 40 million ha are subject to erosion unless protected.[3]

An estimated 2.7 billion t of solid materials are lost from fields and pastures each year through water erosion. This soil contains 83 million t of the five principal elements of plant food (N, P, K, Ca, Mg).[4] Wind erosion is prevalent over more than 181 million ha of farmland and grazing land in the Great Plains area from Texas to North Dakota and in other parts of the West (Fig. 4.2).

❧ WATERSHED MANAGEMENT

Vegetation is probably the most influential variable in the hydrologic cycle and also the most manipulated by man. Infiltration of water is largely dependent on vegetation. Plants with dense canopies such as forages protect the soil surface and increase infiltration as opposed to a bare soil where direct rainfall puddles the soil surface (Fig. 4.3). Soil mosture content

3. USDA. 1953. Our productive land. Inf. Bull. 106.
4. Bennett, H. H., and W. R. Chapline. 1928. Soil erosion, a national menace. USDA Circ. 33.

FIG. 4.3. *Plants . . . such as forages protect . . . where . . . rainfall puddles the soil surface.* The camera lens catches a raindrop (top) as it is about to reach the surface of a saturated soil. As the drop strikes, it disperses surface materials much as a small explosion does. *USDA photos.*

has a significant effect on infiltration and percolation, but it is a function of infiltration and evapotranspiration which are both dependent on vegetation.

A bare soil surface will soon dry, reducing the amount of water returning to the atmosphere, whereas the plant root system extends to a large volume of soil and continues to withdraw water as long as the atmosphere is demanding water from the plant and water is available in the root zone. Grasses use water from early spring to late fall compared with corn which has lush growth for only two to three months. Since grasses have shallower roots but use more water than other crops, the soil beneath grass often is drier, causing higher infiltration rates.

Stream flow and erosion are the result of complex processes. The relative effect of factors such as rainfall, soil erodibility, length of slope, slope gradient, cropping and management, and erosion control practices varies among locations.

Increased emphasis is being placed on multipurpose watershed management of soil and water resources in view of growing populations and affluence coupled with reduced resources. Thus it is imperative to relate all available information to the development of effective con-

servation programs for a wide variety of conditions.

In one study, runoff and erosion were found to be less from a field-size watershed in grass than from a comparable watershed in continuous corn (Fig. 4.4).[5] Other workers demonstrated that soils of a watershed developed on a deep loess mantle were moderately permeable.[6] Slopes ranged from 2–4% on ridges and valleys and from 12–18% on the sides. For the 6-year period 1964–69, sheet erosion from corn was 67.3 t/ha or 100 times the 0.67 t/ha loss from a well-managed smooth bromegrass pasture. Data for 1967 compared with 1964–67 (Fig. 4.4) illustrate the effectiveness of a sod crop in controlling sheet erosion in a year when amount and intensity of rainfall was above average. In 1967 during a 30-day period 508 mm of rain fell, 100–200 mm more than expected for a 100-year return period. In addition the maximum 30-minute storm intensity was three times the average annual value for this location. Soil loss from

5. Saxton, K. E., R. G. Spomer, and L. A. Kramer. 1971. Hydrology and erosion of loessial watersheds. Proc. Amer. Soc. Civil Eng., Hydraulic Div. 97 (HY 11): 1835–51.
6. Oschwald, W. R., F. F. Riecken, R. I. Dideriksen, W. H. Scholtes, and F. W. Schaller. 1965. Principal soils of Iowa. Spec. Rept. 42, Dept. Agron., Iowa State Univ., Ames.

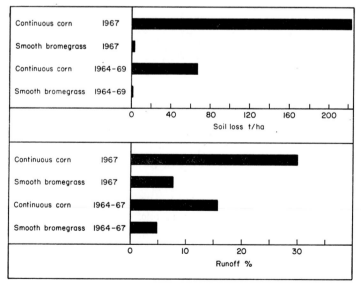

Fig. 4.4. Soil loss and runoff of Treynor, Iowa, watersheds.

contoured corn was 222.2 t/ha in 1967 or 3.3 times greater than the 5-year average, whereas the soil loss from smooth brome-grass pasture was only 1.35 t/ha (a slight increase over the 5-year average loss of 0.67 t/ha), an acceptable level of control. Data from the Treynor, Iowa, watersheds are in general agreement with results obtained from small plots on the same type of soil at the western Iowa experimental farm near Castana, where soil loss from contoured corn was 100 times that from a smooth bromegrass–alfalfa sod.

Research workers have found that the 1964–69 average annual water yield from base flow from a watershed in well-managed smooth bromegrass pasture was 17% more than from a comparable watershed in contoured corn.[5] In 1967, a year when the amount and intensity of rainfall was higher than normal, the base flow was 45% higher from smooth bromegrass than from corn. The higher water yield as base flow reflects the higher infiltration rate under grass since total stream flow, which is made up of base flow and surface runoff, was less from grass than from corn.

PEAK RATES OF STREAM FLOW

Peak rates of stream flow are primarily the result of amount of surface runoff, its time distribution, and the channel system through which it must flow. The amount and time distribution of runoff is a result of the rainfall rates minus infiltration rates. The flow system on upland areas varies from overland flow in thin sheets, to small rills or channels, to well-defined channels and waterways. Dense vegetation, conservation practices, and good farm management will reduce the runoff volumes, causing a similar reduction in peak rates. For 82 comparable storms on the Treynor, Iowa, watershed, peak runoff rates from the grass were found to be less than 10% of those from the contoured corn watersheds.[7]

✤ CONTROL OF RUNOFF AND EROSION

CANOPY INTERCEPTION

Anyone who has walked through a field of grass, hay, or corn after a rain realizes that a considerable portion of the precipitation clings to the leaves and later must either pass down the stalks of the plant to the soil or be lost by evaporation.[8] One study finds that 35.8% of the 274 mm of rain that fell between April 27 and September 15 was intercepted by alfalfa.[9] Similar studies with corn for the period May 27 to September 15 show that 15.5% of the 180 mm of rain that fell in 27 storms was intercepted by corn. Oats intercepted 6.9% of the 173 mm of rain that fell in 35 storms from April 15 to June 30. General conclusions indicate that interception of rainfall increases directly with the increase of vegetative cover. Forages with their dense covering of leaves and stems afford maximum canopy interception of rainfall.[9]

Although forages intercept an appreciable amount of rainfall, their greatest benefit is in controlling erosion by protecting the surface of the soil from the beating action of the raindrops.[10]

TYPE AND AMOUNT OF VEGETATIVE COVER

Numerous studies are available showing the effect of protecting the soil surface with vegetation or mulch to reduce runoff and erosion. The formation of a compact surface layer which greatly reduced the infiltration rate has been described and photographed, and the effect of mulch in preventing the formation of such a layer has been demonstrated.[11]

The effect of forages on runoff and ero-

7. Saxton, K. E., and R. G. Spomer. 1968. Effects of conservation on the hydrology of loessal watersheds. Trans. Amer. Soc. Agr. Engineers 11:848–49, 853.

8. Horton, R. E. 1919. Rainfall interception. *Monthly Weather Rev.* 47:603–23.
9. Haynes, J. L. 1940. Ground rainfall under vegetative canopy of crops. *J. Amer. Soc. Agron.* 32:176–84.
10. Hendrickson, B. H. 1934. The choking of pore space in the soil and its relation to runoff and erosion. Proc. 15th Amer. Geophys. Union, Pt. 2, pp. 500–505.
11. Duley, F. L., and L. L. Kelley. 1939. Effect of soil types, slope and surface condition on intake of water. Nebr. Agr. Exp. Sta. Res. Bull. 112.

sion has been shown to be directly related to the type and amount of growth. A rate of runoff of 3.3 cm/hour from a heavily grazed poor pasture sod has been found.[12] On a heavily grazed good sod, the rate of runoff was about 1.3 cm/hour. On heavily manured excellent sod, lightly grazed but clipped, less than 2.5 mm/hour of rainfall was lost as runoff.

Many studies have shown that the type and amount of vegetative cover has a major effect on sheet and rill erosion. Data have been summarized on the effects of cover, management, and conservation practices on several soils from 10,000 plot-years of runoff and soil loss from 47 research stations in 24 states.[13] Data show that soil loss from fourth-year corn at a high fertility level with conventional tillage was 125 times that from highly productive grass-legume sod (Table 4.2).[14] Grassland permanently in sod had an effect similar to that of a heavy mulch in allowing a high rate of water intake.[11] When the grass and debris were removed from the surface, the rate of intake decreased rapidly.

Pasture management practices, including the intensity of grazing and lime and fertilizer use, stimulate the amount and density of growing cover and greatly influence the amount of runoff and erosion.

A four-year Dixon Springs, Ill., station study showed a soil loss of 3973 kg/ha from a treated and severely grazed pasture. This is in contrast to 380 kg from a fertilized and moderately grazed pasture. The total percentage of rainfall loss as runoff was 17.3% for the severely grazed and 3.4% for the moderately grazed pastures. The additional moisture available to the moderately grazed areas also was effective in stimulating greater forage growth.[15]

TABLE 4.2 ❧ Effect of cover on soil loss

Cover and management	Soil loss, percentage of that from fallow
Fourth-year corn, low quality, conventional tillage	65
Fourth-year corn, high fertility, conventional tillage	50
Moderately productive grass-legumes	0.6
Highly productive grass-legumes	0.4

It has been shown that a vigorous thick cover growth cushions the beating action of raindrops and slows down the movement of surface runoff. Roots of such cover help hold the soil in place and improve soil tilth, thus making the soil more porous and better able to absorb rainfall. Rapid-growing, vigorous cover growth is possible only on soils of high natural fertility or with adequate fertilization. High fertility is a prerequisite of successful erosion control (Table 4.2).

SOIL TEMPERATURE. Some of the highest rates of runoff occur in early spring when the ground is frozen; erosion can be serious at this time unless the land is protected with vegetation. In addition to protecting the surface from erosion, a good cover of forages may keep the soil from freezing and thus allow greater percolation of water.[16]

A four-year study indicates that, in exceptionally cold weather, soil protected by vegetation and a layer of snow may have 14 C higher temperature than bare soil at a 7.6 cm depth and that the soil temperature fluctuates less under sod than where the soil is bare.[17]

Snow depth and frost penetration studies were made during the winter of

12. Alderfer, R. B., and R. I. Robinson. 1947. Runoff from pastures in relation to grazing intensity and soil erosion. *J. Amer. Soc. Agron.* 39:948–58.
13. Wischmeier, W. H., and D. D. Smith. 1965. Predicting rainfall-erosion losses from cropland east of the Rocky Mountains. USDA Agr. Handbook 282.
14. Johnson, H. P., K. E. Saxton, and D. W. DeBoer. 1969. The effect of man on water yield, peak runoff and sedimentation. Proc. Iowa Acad. Sci. 76:153–66.

15. Gard, L. E., R. F. Fuelleman, C. A. Van Doren, and W. G. Kammlade. 1934. Runoff from pasture land as affected by the soil treatment and grazing management. *J. Amer. Soc. Agron.* 35:332–47.
16. USDA. 1940. Influences of vegetation and watershed treatment on runoff, erosion, and stream flow. Misc. Publ. 397.
17. Bouyoucos, George J. 1916. Soil temperature. Mich. Agr. Exp. Sta. Tech. Bull. 26.

1935–36 on the Big Creek watershed in north central Missouri.[16] Average frost penetration was 63.5 cm on bare land, 30.5 cm with vegetative cover not over 12.7 cm tall, and 12.7 cm where the vegetative cover was taller. Average snow accumulation was in reverse order. On bare land the average snow depth ranged from 0–10 cm, whereas snow accumulated to 25–61 cm where the vegetative cover was over 12.7 cm tall.

WATER PENETRATION. The rate of water penetration in undisturbed orchard sods was found to be approximately five times that in adjacent areas which had been cultivated with little vegetation present and was subjected to disturbance and some compaction by spray rigs and farm machinery. The high infiltration rate of about 12.7 cm/hour found on the sodded areas may be explained by the loose and friable condition that developed over a period of years from the accumulation of vegetation that was allowed to grow undisturbed.[18] Worm holes, insect burrows, and channels left by decayed roots also were factors in the development of the unusually high infiltration rate.

Channels left by decayed roots perform an important function in water infiltration, storage of water, and soil and water conservation. These roots spread out through the soil in an amazingly complicated network, the denseness of the roots depending on the type and amount of the vegetation. This network is particularly dense close to the surface; below 60 cm it is somewhat less so. The growing tips of living roots force their way into minute cracks in the soil granules, expand and enlarge the opening, or break the granules into still finer particles. When the roots die, which happens annually with one-third or more, they soon decay and leave channels through which water may penetrate the soil. The beneficial effects from roots of grass and plants like alfalfa and sweetclover are much greater than from those of most intertilled crops because of

the extent of their root systems and the size of the channels resulting from root decay.

ROLE OF FORAGES

The USDA, in cooperation with various state stations, has reported the results of studies on factors affecting erosion and methods of control for important soil and climatic areas throughout the U.S.[19-26] A summary emphasizing the role of forages in reducing runoff and erosion is shown in Table 4.3. These factors vary widely for different soils and with the degree of slope. The most outstanding differences are between the runoff and erosion from row crops versus sod crops. For example, Muskingum silt loam in Ohio had a soil loss of 222.6 t/ha from continuous corn and 0.045 t/ha from a Kentucky bluegrass sod. From row crops, 40.3% of the total rainfall was lost as runoff, whereas only 4.8% was lost from the bluegrass sod. Approximately 7500 years would be required to erode 2.5 cm of soil under Kentucky bluegrass. In contrast, the loss under con-

18. Browning, G. M., and R. H. Sudds. 1942. Some physical and chemical properties of the principal orchard soils in the eastern panhandle of West Virginia. W. Va. Agr. Exp. Sta. Bull. 303.
19. Daniel, H. A., H. M. Elwell, and M. B. Cox. 1943. Investigations in erosion control and reclamation of eroded land at the Red Plains conservation experiment station, Guthrie, Oklahoma, 1930–40. USDA Tech. Bull. 837.
20. Hill, H. O., W. J. Peevy, A. G. McCall, and F. G. Bell. 1944. Investigations in erosion control and reclamation of eroded land at the Blackland conservation experiment station, Temple, Texas, 1931–41. USDA Tech. Bull. 859.
21. Horner, G. M., A. G. McCall, and F. G. Bell. 1944. Investigations in erosion control and the reclamation of eroded land at the Palouse conservation experiment station, Pullman, Wash., 1931–42. USDA Tech. Bull. 860.
22. Copley, T. L., L. A. Forrest, A. G. McCall, and F. G. Bell. 1944. Investigations in erosion control and reclamation of eroded land at the central Piedmont conservation experiment station, Statesville, North Carolina, 1930–40. USDA Tech. Bull. 873.
23. Smith, D. D., D. M. Whitt, A. W. Zingg, A. G. McCall, and F. G. Bell. 1945. Investigations in erosion control and reclamation of eroded Shelby and related soils at the conservation experiment station, Bethany, Missouri, 1930–42. USDA Tech. Bull. 883.
24. Borst, H. L., A. G. McCall, and F. G. Bell. 1945. Investigations in erosion control and the reclamation of eroded land at the northwest Appalachian conservation experiment station, Zanesville, Ohio, 1934–42. USDA Tech. Bull. 888.
25. Browning, G. M., R. A. Norton, A. G. McCall, and F. G. Bell. 1948. Investigations in erosion control and the reclamation of eroded land at the Missouri Valley loess conservation experiment station, Clarinda, Iowa, 1931–42. USDA Tech. Bull. 959.
26. Hooton, D. R., H. V. Jordan, D. D. Porter, P. M. Jenkins, and J. E. Adams. 1949. Influence of fertilizers on growth rates, fruiting habits, and fiber characters of cotton. USDA Tech. Bull. 979.

TABLE 4.3 ❧ Effect of row and sod crops on runoff and erosion on different soils

Soil type	Location	Slope (%)	Soil loss (t/ha)		Runoff (%)	
			Row crop*	Sod	Row crop*	Sod
Marshall silt loam	Iowa	9.0	85.6	.067	18.7	1.3
Shelby loam	Mo.	8.0	114.1	.359	27.1	8.1
Muskingum silt loam	Ohio	12.0	222.6	.045	40.3	4.8
Stephenville fine sandy loam	Okla.	7.7	42.4	.045	12.5	1.0
Cecil clay loam	N.C.	10.0	70.0	.695	12.4	1.9
Kervin fine sandy loam	Texas	8.7	53.8	.179	19.9	1.0
Kervin fine sandy loam	Texas	16.5	137.0	.011	14.4	0.3
Nacogdoches sandy loam	Texas	10.0	14.6	.011	13.9	0.3
Austin clay	Texas	4.0	46.2	.045	13.6	0.05
Austin black clay	Texas	2.0	17.5	.179	10.5	1.2
Fayette silt loam	Wis.	16.0	250.4	.224	29.2	0.55

* Row crop was continuous corn on Marshall, Shelby, Muskingum, Fayette, and Austin soils. Cotton was grown on the Stephenville, Cecil, Kervin, and Nacogdoches soils. The sod crop was either Kentucky bluegrass or bermudagrass.

tinuous corn would require 1.5 years to remove 2.5 cm of soil by erosion.

The data in Table 4.3 are average annual losses that include all types of rainfall. The greatest value of perennial close-growing forages in controlling erosion is during rains of high intensity, most of which occur during May, June, and July, the season when intertilled crops leave the land vulnerable to erosion. Sods give year-round protection. Soil and water losses from corn and from sod for a single hard, driving rain on two soils are shown in Table 4.4. The erosion and runoff from corn was of the same magnitude on the two soils; the same is true for erosion under the sod. Percentage runoff under sod varies widely between the soils; for Marshall it is 2.3% and for Shelby 39.0%. Differences in rate and amount of rainfall and in soil permeability also influence runoff. When the rate of rainfall exceeds its infiltration into the soil, runoff is a problem even with a good vegetative cover.

Forages are also effective as surface mulches to reduce runoff and erosion (Fig. 4.5). The formation of an impervious layer at the soil surface, often only a few mm thick, can be largely prevented with a cover of residue or by a growing forage crop.

The average infiltration rate for six widely different soils has been found to be 0.6 cm/hour on a bare cultivated area.[11] In contrast, adjacent areas covered with mulch had an infiltration rate of 1.9 cm/hour. It has been concluded that the beneficial effect of surface mulch was in the elimination of the raindrop impact rather than the reduction of overland flow velocity.[27]

GRASS WATERWAYS

A mat of grass and grass roots is unequaled in holding soil. Severe erosion and gullies develop where natural drainage ways are not maintained in sod to permit the safe disposal of excess rainfall. Grass waterways may be considered

27. Borst, H. L., and Russell Woodburn. 1942. The effect of mulching and methods of cultivation on runoff and erosion from Muskingum silt loam. *Agr. Eng.* 23:19–22.

TABLE 4.4 ❧ Runoff and erosion from corn and sod during a single intense rain on Marshall and Shelby soils

Soil type	Location	Rainfall (mm)	Soil loss (t/ha)		Runoff (%)	
			Corn	Sod	Corn	Sod
Shelby loam	Mo.		103.1	.112	68.0	39.0
Marshall silt loam	Iowa	95.5	83.0		70.0	2.3

FIG. 4.5. *Forages . . . effectively used as surface mulches . . . reduce runoff and erosion.* Shown is an erosive slope seeded without a mulch (left) and with a mulch (right). *Iowa SCS photo.*

the basis of such successful erosion control practices as effective rotation, strip cropping, contour farming, terracing, gully control, and intelligent farming in general.

Plant cover protects the waterway channel surface from the erosive action of flowing water and reduces the movement of soil particles from the channel bed. This protective action varies with the kind of vgetation and uniformity of cover. Type and amount of vegetation in the waterway have a marked effect on the capacity and stability of these channels. Graphs have been developed for determining the maximum conditions under which different types of vegetation are effective in resisting the erosive action of runoff water in grass waterways.[28]

Steps in the preparation and seeding of a grass waterway have been outlined.[29-31] Important considerations are the size of the area to be drained, the width of the waterway, preparation of the seedbed, manure and fertilizer treatments, grass mixtures, seeding rates, and maintenance.

FARM MANAGEMENT PRACTICES

STRIP-CROPPING. Strip-cropping is the arrangement in alternate strips of erosive intertilled crops and small-grain crops with conserving grasses and legumes at right angles to the natural slope of the land. This has been shown to be effective in reducing runoff and erosion. Close-

growing forage crops are the key to successful strip-cropping. The strip of meadow serves as a buffer to slow down and disperse the rate of runoff from the intertilled area. Velocity of the silt-laden water is reduced as it enters the sod strip, causing the deposition of much of the silt. The strip also prevents concentration of water in low areas which would in time develop gullies if it were allowed to flow uncontrolled from the field. Studies at soil erosion experiment stations have shown that, on the average, fields that are strip cropped lose only about 25% as much soil as comparable fields that are not.[32] Factors to consider in developing a strip-cropping plan and assessing its effect on general farm operations have been discussed by a number of workers.[33-35] (See Fig. 4.6.)

CONTOUR FARMING. Planting crops on the contour not only reduces the cost of production per hectare, with a de-

28. Ree, W. O., and B. J. Palmer. 1949. Flow of water in channels protected by vegetative linings. USDA Tech. Bull. 967.
29. Tascher, W. R., and Marion W. Clark. 1942. Conserving soil with natural grass waterways. Mo. Agr. Ext. Serv. Circ. 438.
30. Leffler, Allan T. 1945. Contouring and grass waterways made easy. Iowa Agr. Ext. Serv. Bull. 63 (rev.).
31. Zeasman, O. R. 1941. Grass waterways control and prevent gullies. Wis. Ext. Serv. Circ. 320.
32. Browning, G. M., C. L. Parish, and John Glass. 1947. A method for determining the use and limitations of rotation and conservation practices in the control of soil erosion in Iowa. *J. Amer. Soc. Agron.* 39:65–73.
33. Tower, Harold E., and Harry H. Gardner. 1943. Strip cropping for war production. USDA Farmers' Bull. 1919.
34. Peterson, J. B., and L. E. Clapp. 1943. Following the contour. Iowa Agr. Exp. Sta. Ext. Serv. Bull. 53.
35. Thorfinson, M. A. 1942. Contour strip cropping. Minn. Agr. Ext. Serv. Folder 108.

FIG. 4.6. *Strip-cropping . . . shown to be effective in reducing runoff and erosion.* A cropping pattern for rolling terrain near Decorah, Iowa, is illustrated by the area surrounding the Washington Prairie Church, one of the "Great American Churches" featured in 1950 in *Christian Century* and *Life* magazines.

TABLE 4.5 ❧ Annual soil loss in tons per hectare and water loss in percent of rainfall at six locations when farmed on the contour and uphill and downhill

Location	Slope percent	Crop	Soil loss (t/ha)		Water loss (% rainfall)	
			Con- toured	Up and down hill	Con- toured	Up and down hill
Temple, Tex., 1931–40	4	Corn-oats-cotton	9.6	24.9	5.0	8.3
Zanesville, Ohio, 1939–40	12	Corn	34.5	128.5	4.1	6.8
Guthrie, Okla., 1932–35	6.8	Cotton (with winter wheat cover)	55.2	123.8	9.9	11.1
Hays, Kans., 1934–38	4.5	Wheat	3.4	4.7	9.8	13.0
		Kafir	1.6	30.5	2.6	20.4
Temple, Tex., 1932–41	3.5	Cotton	13.2	35.2	4.6	13.6
Clarinda, Iowa, 1933–37	8	Corn	16.4	62.1	1.8	10.2
Castana, Iowa, 1948–58	12	Corn-oats (sweetclover)	12.3	59.2	5.0	11.1

crease in the power required and the machinery operation costs, but also aids in saving soil and water, with resulting increases in yields per hectare. The effectiveness of contour farming in reducing soil loss and runoff is shown in Table 4.5 and Figure 4.7. Average annual soil loss for the six locations, with 34 cropping seasons considered, was 5.8 t/ha for contour farming compared to 18 t/ha for uphill and downhill farming. Water loss in percentage of rainfall for the two methods was 5.5 and 12%, respectively.[36]

COVER CROPS. Planting of cover crops is an important part of a good cropping system. Such crops are planted in or following erosive intertilled crops to help prevent erosion and the leaching of plant nutrients. This is particularly true in those sections where mild winters leave farmland unprotected from the ravages of erosion during frequently occurring high-intensity rains. In North Carolina a cropping system without a cover crop lost 72.2 t/ha of soil and 11% of the total rainfall. In a system with cover crops, 40.8 t/ha of soil and 7.2% of the rainfall were lost.[37] On a Dunmore silt loam soil in Virginia, on fallow land, 22.9% of the rainfall was

lost as percolate. When a rye and vetch cover crop was used, only 16.2% of the rainfall was lost, indicating a reduction of 29% as the result of the cover crop.[38]

CROP ROTATION. Food and fiber requirements for the U.S. population necessitate the production of intertilled crops. The productivity of the land can be maintained if the proper balance of depleting row crops and conserving forages is combined with supporting practices such as contouring, strip-cropping, and terraces which are adapted to the capabilities of the land.[39-41]

The main value of crop rotation from the standpoint of erosion control lies in the sod crop and the reduction in soil cultivation or soil tillage. Sod crops and grass in particular produce an excellent physical soil condition which is essential in erosion control.[42] Crop rotation alone will not control erosion, but it is fundamental to erosion control and a perma-

36. Tower, Harold E. 1946. Strip cropping for conservation and production. USDA Farmers' Bull. 1981.
37. Copley, T. L., L. A. Forrest, A. G. McCall, and F. G. Bell. 1944. Investigations in erosion control and reclamation of eroded land at the central Piedmont conservation experiment station, Statesville, North Carolina, 1930–40. USDA Tech. Bull. 873.

38. Hill, H. H. 1943. The effects of rye, lespedeza, and cowpeas when used as cover crops. Va. Agr. Exp. Sta. Tech. Bull. 83.
39. Hays, Orville, and Noble Clark. 1941. Cropping systems that help control erosion. Wis. Agr. Exp. Sta. Bull. 452.
40. Smith, D. D., D. M. Whitt, and M. F. Miller, 1948. Cropping systems for soil conservation. Mo. Agr. Exp. Sta. Bull. 518.
41. Browning, G. M., R. A. Norton, A. G. McCall, and F. G. Bell. 1948. Investigations in erosion control and the reclamation of eroded land. USDA Tech. Bull. 959.
42. Bradfield, Richard. 1937. Soil conservation from the standpoint of soil physics. J. Amer. Soc. Agron. 29:85–92.

FIG. 4.7. *Forages . . . effective as surface mulches.* Effects of crops and degrees and lengths of slope on soil loss and runoff have been determined. Runoff water and soil from these experimental plots are caught and accurate determinations of losses are made. *Iowa SCS photo.*

nent agriculture. It has been seriously neglected in the past but must be recognized and practiced. The introduction of crop rotations adequate for erosion control when supplemented by supporting practices, fertilizer and manure use, and good farm management will aid materially in stabilizing crop production and in developing a sound and permanent agriculture.

Crop rotations with adequate sod crops are the key to good soil tilth. Soils that contain a high percentage of large, stable granules, as a result of sod crops in the rotation, are more resistant to the erosive action of raindrops than soils depleted of organic matter through intensive growth of intertilled crops. Studies at erosion experiment stations show that, on the average, erosion from corn following a sod crop is only about half that from corn following a clean-tilled crop in the rotation.

The effect on soil aggregation of crops grown on Marshall silt loam for an 11-year period showed that clover turned down before corn in the corn-oats-clover rotation increased the aggregates 27% as compared with continuous corn.[41] In all cases sod crops have almost doubled the amount of stable aggregates present in contrast to the situation under continuous corn. The increased aggregation that results from close-cropping vegetation emphasizes the importance of including sod crops regularly in the rotation. This maintains a stable structure that resists the action of tillage implements and the beating

action of raindrops during the period when the land is in intertilled crops.

Crops differ materially in the type and amount of residue they leave in the soil.[43,44] Chemical composition and amount of residue also influence the amount and stability of the aggregates.[45] Materials which decompose rapidly, such as legumes, bring about aggregation in a relatively short period, two or three weeks under field conditions, but lose their effectiveness within two or three months. On the other hand, more carbonaceous materials such as the grasses require a longer period to affect aggregation, but they have a more lasting effect on soil structure.

❧ SEDIMENTATION

Silt accumulating in natural and artificial reservoirs is rapidly decreasing their storage capacity and leaves the water unsuited for recreational purposes. The seriousness of the reservoir-silting problem, particularly from an economic and engineering standpoint, deserves special consideration. There were more than 8400 dams and reservoirs in the U.S. in 1940.[16] A conservative estimate would place the initial investment at more than $2 billion. The usefulness of at least 20% of the

43. Woodruff, C. M. 1939. Variations in the state and stability of aggregation as a result of different methods of cropping. *Soil Sci. Soc. Amer.* 4:13–18.
44. Shively, S. E., and J. E. Weaver. 1939. Amount of underground plant material in different grassland climates. Nebr. Conserv. Bull. 21.
45. Browning, G. M., and F. M. Milan. 1944. Effect of different types of organic material and lime on soil aggregation. *Soil Sci.* 57:91–106.

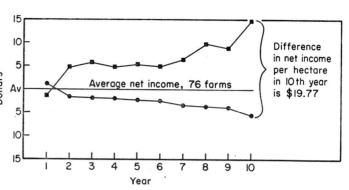

FIG. 4.8. The average annual net earnings per ha of 20 "high-conservation" and 20 "low-conservation" farms compared with the average of 76 comparable farms in the same Illinois county. *John Deere and Co. data.*

reservoirs, representing an estimated 75% of the total investment, is in water storage alone. When storage is unavailable as a result of silting, their value will largely have disappeared. Of 56 reservoirs examined by the Soil Conservation Service in the southern Piedmont region in 1934, 13 major reservoirs with dams averaging 9.1 m in height were found to have been completely filled by eroded material within an average period of 29.4 years.

Numerous examples could be cited showing the damage by siltation to reservoirs where the watershed was not adequately protected by forages and other conservation measures. The story of Lake Decatur is typical.[46] The citizens of Decatur, Ill., built a 1134-ha lake at a cost of $2 million to provide a water supply and recreational facilities for the community. In 25 years this lake lost more than 25% of its capacity by silting of precious topsoil from the fertile prairie in the watershed. Damage to the reservoir as well as to the farmland of the area would not have occurred if wise land use and conservation measures had been adopted on the entire watershed.

Studies have shown that reservoir sedimentation, largely man-induced, is a serious problem in Iowa.[14] About 6% of the upper-level conservation pool of the Coralville reservoir was occupied by sediment five years after construction. At the present rate of sedimentation, the reservoir will be seriously impaired in 75 years. A

46. Walker, E. D. 1949. The story of a lake. Ill. Ext. Circ. 644.

permanent pool of a small reservoir in Mills County, Iowa, heavily row cropped and with inadequate conservation measures, was filled in 12 years. Surveys of similar reservoirs in Lucas County, Iowa, where better conservation practices were used, showed annual storage losses of from less than 1 to 2½% of the permanent pool.[47]

❧ RESULTS OF CONSERVATION PRACTICES

Soil and water conserving practices when properly applied result in an increase in net return per hectare, with greater increases as the years pass. In an Illinois study "high-conservation" farms in each of three county groups averaged $11.79, $16.95, and $15.84 more annual net earnings per hectare than comparable "low-conservation" farms. The annual average net earnings per hectare through a ten-year period are shown in Figure 4.8. Capitalizing the increases shown at 5%, the earning value of the "high-conservation" farms was $195, $139, and $128 more than for the comparable "low-conservation" farms.[48]

47. ERS-SCS, USDA. 1965. Watershed program evaluation, Honey Creek, Iowa. Bull. ERS-204.
48. Sauer, E. L., and H. C. M. Case. 1954. Soil conservation pays off. Ill. Agr. Exp. Sta. Bull. 575.

❧ QUESTIONS

1. Discuss the extent of land damage by erosion in the U.S.
2. What is canopy interception? How is it related to soil conservation?

3. What is the relative effectiveness of clean-tilled row crops and forages in controlling runoff and erosion?
4. What forages, if any, are used for cover crops? How do they influence soil conservation?
5. Under what conditions is strip-cropping recommended? How effective is it as a conservation measure? What determines its effectiveness?
6. Under what conditions would forages be used as surface mulches? What effect do mulches have on runoff and erosion?
7. Define soil tilth. What relation do crop rotations have to it?
8. Discuss crop rotations in relation to soil conservation.
9. How does the type and amount of vegetative cover affect soil conservation?
10. What effect does vegetative cover have on soil temperature? How does this relate to soil conservation?

T. H. TAYLOR AND W. C. TEMPLETON, JR.
University of Kentucky

5

GRASSLAND ECOSYSTEM CONCEPTS

❧

Many interacting factors are involved in the growing and utilization of grassland crops. The more important of these are the physical environment, plants, domestic livestock, and decomposer organisms. A working knowledge of the effects and interrelationships of each factor is essential for efficient use of our grassland resources on a sustained basis. The aim of this chapter is to introduce and discuss some of the more important concepts relative to grassland ecosystems.

Living organisms with their nonliving environment taken as a whole constitute an ecosystem, a term introduced by Tansley in 1935.[1] An ecosystem has been defined as an open system comprising plants, animals, organic residues, atmospheric gases, water, and minerals that are involved together in the flow of energy and the circulation of matter.[2] An ecosystem results from the integration of all living and nonliving factors of the environment for a defined segment of space and time.[3]

Natural grassland ecosystems have built-in homeostatic mechanisms (i.e., checks and balances) or forces and counterforces, which tend to maintain them in a more or less stable condition. However, these buffer limits can easily be exceeded by man. The plowing of vast areas of subhumid and semiarid grasslands in the U.S. and other areas of the world to grow more grain crops has greatly disturbed natural ecosystems. Where moisture is limited, overgrazing reduces desirable grasses, forbs, and shrubs, which are replaced by mesquite, cacti, weedy grasses, and other less desirable plants.[4] However, man can wisely manipulate forces within the ecosystem, which may lead to practical increases in productivity.

❧ MAIN COMPONENTS OF A GRASSLAND ECOSYSTEM

For the purpose of description and analysis, use is made of the four main elements

❧ TIMOTHY H. TAYLOR is Professor of Agronomy at the University of Kentucky. He received the M.S. degree from the University of Kentucky and the Ph.D. from Pennsylvania State University. His specialty is the ecology of humid temperate grasslands, and he has worked in grassland management research.

❧ WILLIAM C. TEMPLETON, JR., is Professor of Agronomy at the University of Kentucky. He received the M.S. degree from the University of Illinois and the Ph.D. from Purdue University. Pasture utilization and management is his primary interest, and he has served as a consultant on pastures in the U.S., Mexico, and Venezuela.

1. Tansley, A. G. 1935. The use and abuse of vegetational concepts and terms. *Ecology* 16:284–307.
2. Spedding, C. R. W. 1971. Grassland Ecology, pp. 4–5, 109. Oxford Univ. Press, London.
3. Van Dyne, George M. 1969. Some mathematical models of grassland ecosystems. *In* The Grassland Ecosystem, p. 4. Colo. State Univ. Sci. Ser. 2.
4. Love, R. Merton. 1961. The range—Natural plant communities or modified ecosystems. *J. Brit. Grassl. Soc.* 16:89–99.

of an ecosystem as described by Odum.[5]

Abiotic substances are nonliving components of the environment such as water; sunlight; oxygen; carbon dioxide; organic compounds; soil; such plant nutrients as N, P, K, Ca, and Mg; and such minor nutrients as Cu, Co, I, and Fe.

The climate of the region, a physical phenomenon, exerts profound effects on the living components of an ecosystem.

Producer organisms in a grassland ecosystem are green herbaceous plants, often members of the grass or legume family. Other green plants such as broadleaf weeds and shrubs may occupy a prominent place among the producer organisms in some grassland communities. Through photosynthesis these plants synthesize food utilized in their own life processes. Plants or plant parts in turn are used as food by consumer organisms of the ecosystem.

Consumer organisms (animals) which feed directly on the plants are designated primary consumers, while animals which feed on these are called secondary consumers. The former are also called herbivores and the latter carnivores. Our main concern in grassland studies is with the herbivores, or herbage-consuming animals. These may be either domesticated or wild game animals. Examples of ruminating, cud-chewing herbivores are cattle, sheep, goats, and deer; nonruminating animals that may live entirely on herbaceous plants include horses and asses, rabbits, and meadow voles. Primary consumer organisms also may include many species of slugs, insects, nematodes, birds, rodents, and other animals. Secondary consumers are represented by spiders, toads, lizards, snakes, dogs, housecats, and coyotes. Odum mentions that no one as yet has made a complete census of the consumer organisms in a pond or meadow ecosystem.[5]

Decomposer organisms are of two main groups, microflora and fauna. Decomposition by invading organisms begins before death of the plant parts themselves, with some bacterial and fungal decomposition preceding utilization by soil invertebrate organisms.[6] Earthworms and dung beetles are among the important decomposers in grasslands. Upon decay of all the organisms that remain a part of the ecosystem (i.e., plants, consumers, and decomposers), the chemicals contained in them are released and may then be reused in the system. The importance of decomposers in a grassland ecosystem often is not appreciated, but these organisms occur in great abundance in well-managed grasslands and are of great significance.

❧ MODIFICATION OF ECOSYSTEM COMPONENTS

Grassland management involves manipulation and use by man of the abiotic substances, producers, consumers, and decomposers of grassland ecosystems. Depending on the nature of the management, productivity may be increased, maintained, or decreased. Productivity as used here refers to animals and animal products useful to man. In the real world of the farmer or rancher, economic consideration must be applied to all aspects of inputs to and outputs from grasslands. A grassland ecosystem is an excellent example of a renewable resource, and if properly managed the system may be productive over a very long time (Fig. 5.1).

PHYSICAL ENVIRONMENT

Grassland management consists to a great degree of willful actions taken by the operator, farmer, or rancher to modify the environment of plants. Assume a particular grassland habitat has soils that are acid, low in available P, and poorly drained. Each of these conditions may limit productivity, but all are readily amenable to change. The low pH may be raised to a favorable level by adding ground limestone; P fertilizer may be applied (Chapter

5. Odum, E. P. 1971. Fundamentals of Ecology, 3rd ed., pp. 8–39, 83. W. B. Saunders, Philadelphia.

6. Clark, F. E., and E. A. Paul. 1970. The microflora of grassland. *Advan. Agron.* 22:375–435.

FIG. 5.1. *Grassland ecosystem . . . renewable resource . . . properly managed . . . may be productive over a very long time.* An environment in which the climax vegetation is deciduous hardwood trees is illustrated in this man-managed grassland ecosystem. J. D. Gay, Jr., Brookview Farm, Pine Grove, Ky., photo.

38) and an appropriate drainage system developed. In some dry areas irrigation of grasslands tremendously alters the botanical composition and productivity of the ecosystem and may be economically feasible.

GRASSLAND PLANTS

Through selection, hybridization, and irradiation man can change the genetic composition of plants; listed in this book are many examples that have been changed by plant breeders so they may serve man's needs better. In addition, the botanical composition of grassland communities may be deliberately altered. Examples are the introduction of legumes into grassy swards through renovation techniques;[7] replacement of weedy, low-yielding species with plants having higher yield potential;[8] imposition of grazing management schemes that alter botanical composition and sward yield;[9] and decrease in legume content caused by liberal use of fertilizer N.[10] Moreover, man can change the leaf area index

(LAI) of a grassland community by altering the stocking rate per unit of land or by mechanically harvesting the herbage. The concept of LAI was introduced in 1947 to denote the leaf area per unit of land area.[11] This indicates the relative area available for photosynthesis, although stems, petioles, leaf sheaths, and inflorescences also intercept light and contribute in varying degrees to this process.

DOMESTIC ANIMALS

The selection and breeding of livestock for special purposes has been in progress since man domesticated animals for his use. Examples of selection of animals for high milk production are the Holstein dairy cow and the Toggenberg dairy goat. Many of the sheep breeds have been selected for wool quality as well as adaptability to special environmental conditions. Some beef cattle have been selected from work stock of an earlier period. The work horse as contrasted with the Thoroughbred illustrates man's influence on this species.[12] Through animal domestication followed by a very long period of selection, man has many highly specialized animals to serve his needs.

In addition to animal breeding and

7. Taylor, T. H., E. M. Smith, and W. C. Templeton, Jr. 1969. Use of minimum tillage and herbicide for establishing legumes in Kentucky bluegrass, *Poa pratensis* L., swards. *Agron. J.* 61:761–66.

8. Rogler, G. A., and R. J. Lorenz. 1970. Beef production from Russian wildrye, *Elymus junceus* Fisch., in the United States. Proc. 11th Int. Grassl. Congr., pp. 835–38 (Surfers Paradise, Queensland, Aust.).

9. Brougham, R. W. 1960. The effects of frequent hard grazing at different times of the year on the productivity and species yields of a grass-clover pasture. *N.Z. J. Agr. Res.* 3:125–36.

10. Templeton, W. C., Jr., and T. H. Taylor. 1966. Some effects of nitrogen, phosphorus and potassium fertilization on botanical composition of a tall fescue–white clover sward. *Agron. J.* 58:569–72.

11. Watson, D. J. 1947. Comparative studies on the growth of field crops. I. Variation in net assimilation rate and leaf area between species and varieties and within and between years. *Am. Bot.* (London) 11:41–76.

12. Briggs, H. M., and D. M. Briggs. 1969. Modern Breeds of Livestock, 3rd ed., pp. 517–23. Macmillan, London.

selection man has developed other useful skills in animal production, e.g., immunizing animals against diseases, castrating males, controlling internal parasites, and using feed additives. Time of giving birth has been controlled in some species to harmonize feed production and nutrient needs of the animals.

OTHER BIOTIC FACTORS

In addition to living herbage plants and domestic livestock deliberately brought together in a man-managed grassland ecosystem, there may be other biota within the system that exert powerful influences on the efficiency of animal production. For example, legumes in the plant community will be much higher producing if inoculated with the correct rhizobia. Plants that are too highly competitive toward each other should not be grown in association.[13] Level of soil acidity or alkalinity and N availability may affect the microfloral population and its activity and in turn alter the rate of decomposition of organic matter.

Estimate places the biomass of bacteria and fungi in grassland soils at approximately 200 g/sq m to a depth of 30 cm, or approximately 2.18 t/ha.[9] Disappearance of dung droppings in a pasture may be directly related to the number and activity of dung beetles. A strong positive correlation between weight of earthworms and pasture production has been noted.[14] Better pastures had over 3.4 million earthworms/ha, with a total liveweight of approximately 2129 kg/ha.

A multitude of pests may lower the productive capacity, nutritive value, and length of life of grassland plants; among them are viruses, bacteria, fungi, nematodes, insects, rodents, and rabbits. Significant progress has been made by plant breeders in the development of plants pos-

TABLE 5.1 ❧ Estimated forage consumption by several small-animal species on the Santa Rita experimental range, near Tucson, Ariz., 1937

Species	Forage consumed per animal per year (kg)	Forage consumed per ha per year (kg)
Allen jackrabbit	79.5	39.2
California jackrabbit	54.7	1.1
Arizona cottontail	24.9	4.5
Round-tailed ground squirrel	3.7	5.6
Bannertail kangaroo rat	2.5	10.1
Merriam kangaroo rat	1.1	2.2
Total		62.7*

Source: Reynolds and Martin, 1968.[15]
* Total consumption by rodents and rabbits was estimated to be approximately 40% of the forage produced.

sessing tolerance, resistance, or immunity to certain plant pathogens. In the establishment of tame or cultivated pastures, consideration should be given to the use of improved cultivars and strains (Chapters 11, 13–32). In the case of natural grasslands, however, it is sometimes not practical or even possible to lessen losses from some pests.

Control of insects and other undesirable animals frequently must be considered in both cultivated and natural grasslands. Rodents and rabbits are often very destructive in ranges and other extensive areas of natural grasslands, consuming appreciable amounts of forage. They may be especially troublesome during periods of range improvement when plants on newly seeded areas are becoming established. Losses that may occur on ranges from small animals have been determined (Table 5.1).[15] Considering that production of forage under dry-range conditions may only be from less than 100 kg to a few hundred kilograms per ha, the importance of such losses is better appreciated. Not all small animals found in grasslands are harmful. Before any control program is initiated, competent advice should be sought from specialists.

13. Blaser, R. E., W. H. Skrdla, and T. H. Taylor. 1952. Ecological and physiological factors in compounding forage seed mixtures. *Advan. Agron.* 4:179–219.
14. Sears, P. D., and L. T. Evans. 1953. Pasture growth and soil fertility. III. The influence of red and white clovers, superphosphate, lime, and dung and urine on soil composition and on earthworm and grass-grub populations. *N.Z. J. Sci. Tech.* 35:42–52.

15. Reynolds, Hudson G., and S. Clark Martin. 1968. Managing grass-shrub cattle ranges in the Southwest. *U.S. Forest Serv. Agr. Handbook 162, rev.*

TABLE 5.2 ❧ Average daily liveweight gains and parasite burdens of control and parasitized steers grazing irrigated and nonirrigated pastures in Canada

Pasture treatment	Liveweight gains (kg/head/day)		Gastrointestinal parasites (total number/ animal)	
	Control animals	Parasitized animals	Control animals	Parasitized animals
Nonirrigated	0.85	0.47	2,500	95,762
Irrigated	0.70	0.33	1,414	128,333

Source: Calder and Smith, 1970.[16]

As with the plant component of the grassland ecosystem, numerous diseases, parasites, and predators may lessen productive capacities of grazing animals. Every reasonable effort should be made to maintain animal thrift at high levels and ensure that efficient production is not adversely affected. An example of the effects of parasitism on cattle performance is provided by the data of Calder and Smith.[16] Yearling steers were grazed on irrigated and non-irrigated pastures in Canada. Steers were lightly infested with gastrointestinal parasites at the start of the experiment. Some of the steers were treated with an approved anthelmintic to control parasites, while others were not. Average daily liveweight gains and representative parasite burdens of the two groups are shown in Table 5.2. Gains of the treated group were nearly twice those of the parasitized animals, illustrating the great effect of animal health on productivity of animal products from pasture.

❧ INTERRELATIONSHIPS AMONG ANIMALS, PLANTS, AND SOILS

ANIMAL EFFECTS

Grazing has been defined as the partial defoliation of pasture plants by the animal.[2] Degrees of grazing intensity are described in many ways, such as lenient or light grazing; moderate grazing; short, hard, tight or close grazing; top and bottom grazing; and undergrazing and overgrazing. Other terms that describe systems of management are zero, ration, strip, rotational, and continuous grazing.

In consuming grassland herbage, grazing livestock are continually destroying the source of their feed supply. Each green leaf consumed is one less to contribute to the continued life of the plant from which it came. There is much variation among grassland plant species with respect to their ability to tolerate grazing and defoliation. An intensity of grazing suitable for white clover may result in the loss of alfalfa from a pasture. Also, the degree of defoliation that plants of a given species can tolerate depends on the environment in which they are growing and their stage of development. Plants under stress from lack of water or nutrients are more sensitive to defoliation than those more adequately supplied. Much research has been done to determine optimum levels of stocking pastures and ranges, but definitive answers are seldom if ever obtained except for a rather specific set of conditions. Skilled grassland farmers possess the ability to assess pasture and range conditions and to make appropriate adjustments in animal-management practices.

The effect of grazing animals on changes in botanical composition is of great significance in grassland management and utilization. Different species of grassland plants often differ markedly with respect to their acceptability to animals, some being highly palatable and much sought while others are scarcely eaten or left untouched. Different species of animals and even individuals of a species may exhibit different preferences. Cattle, sheep, goats, and horses usually prefer herbaceous plants, but sheep and especially goats readily consume browse vegetation. Camels eat coarse salty plants and, as goats and sheep, utilize the tender portions of thorny plants.[17] In

16. Calder, F. W., and H. J. Smith. 1970. The role of irrigation in the development of gastrointestinal parasitism in cattle on dikeland and upland pastures. Proc. 11th Int. Grassl. Congr., pp. 884–87 (Surfers Paradise, Queensland, Aust.).

17. Larin, I. V. 1956. Pasture economy and meadow cultivation (translated from Russian). Israel Program for Sci. Transl., Jerusalem, 1962.

Africa, giraffes feed largely on trees; rhinoceros eat mostly shrubby brush vegetation; and wildebeests subsist almost exclusively on grass.[18] Such differences in grazing habits may permit fuller exploitation of range resources by mixed animal populations than by single species. For example, acacia-savanna ranges of the Masailand region of Kenya support yearlong 12.26–17.51 t/sq km of mixed wild ungulates but only 1.96–2.8 of domestic cattle, goats, and sheep.[18]

Under the conditions of stress characteristic of dry zones, excessive defoliation of plants is likely to result in their death. A rule-of-thumb which sometimes serves as a guide for grazing management in such areas is to graze half and leave half the vegetative growth of desirable species. An example of the influence of grazing on changing botanical composition is given by data of Canfield.[19] Vegetation inside several enclosures which prevented grazing was compared with that of adjacent areas grazed for 25 years.

Relative amounts of different species present at two different sites is shown in Table 5.3. The more desirable species such as Arizona cottontop, bush muhly, black grama, and sideoats grama decreased under grazing, while curly mesquite, rothrock grama, and slender grama increased. Overgrazing of grassland often leads to dramatic changes in botanical structure, plant and animal productivity, and soil stability. In extreme cases the original conditions may never be restored.

Grazing animals not only gnaw, bite, trample, and lie on the pasture plants; in addition, they soil them with their body wastes, resulting in rejection or lowered acceptability of affected plants. The latter is particularly true for humid grasslands on which stocking rates may be very high. Rejection of 20% of pasture forage due to dung contamination after 200 cow-days of

TABLE 5.3 ❧ Relative amounts of perennial grasses on areas protected from grazing for approximately 25 years and on comparable adjacent areas grazed continuously

Species	High elevations		Intermediate elevations	
	Protected areas (%)	Grazed areas (%)	Protected areas (%)	Grazed areas (%)
Arizona cottontop	31	6	26	2
Bush muhly	0	0	11	*
Curly mesquite	1	13	0	0
Grama				
Black	7	5	26	15
Hairy	3	2	0	0
Rothrock	2	12	7	64
Sideoats	10	6	2	*
Slender	15	49	1	5
Three-awns	9	5	14	10
Tanglehead	5	1	3	3
Other grasses	17	1	10	1
Total	100	100	100	100

Source: Canfield, 1948.[19]
Note: Data refer to basal areas.
* Less than 0.5%.

grazing per ha has been reported,[20] while up to 47% of the herbage in a pasture has been observed to be unpalatable and dung affected by the end of the grazing season.[21] It has been concluded that the dung itself, rather than some feature such as the imbalance of herbage P and K, causes cattle to reject dung-affected pasture grass.[22] About 33% of total fecal output has been found on less than 5% of most grazed pastures.[23] Consequently, in some instances an exhaustive transfer of plant nutrients occurs from each pasture as a whole to smaller areas within it.

Some of the effects of dung and urine on yield and botanical composition of a grazed grass-legume pasture were studied by Sears in New Zealand, and some of his

18. Talbot, L. M., and L. W. Swift. 1965. Production of wildlife in support of human populations in Africa. Proc. 9th Int. Grassl. Congr., pp. 1355–59 (São Paulo, Brazil).

19. Canfield, R. H. 1948. Perennial grass composition as an indicator of condition of southwestern mixed grass ranges. *Ecology* 29:190–204.

20. MacLusky, D. S. 1960. Some estimates of the areas of pasture fouled by the excreta of dairy cows. *J. Brit. Grassl. Soc.* 15:181–88.

21. Tayler, J. C., and R. V. Large. 1955. The comparative output of two seed mixtures. *J. Brit. Grassl. Soc.* 10:341–51.

22. Marten, G. C., and J. D. Donker. 1966. Animal excrement as a factor influencing acceptability of grazing forage. Proc. 10th Int. Grassl. Congr., pp. 359–63 (Helsinki, Finland).

23. Hilder, E. J. 1966. Distribution of excreta by sheep at pasture. Proc. 10th Int. Grassl. Congr., pp. 977–81 (Helsinki, Finland)

TABLE 5.4 ❧ Herbage yields and relative amounts of grasses, legumes, and other species during a four-year period with and without the return of sheep dung and urine to a grazed grass-legume sward in New Zealand

Disposition of dung and urine	Grass t/ha	%	Clovers t/ha	%	Other species t/ha	%	Total yield (t/ha)
Fully returned	27.5	56	20.9	43	0.6	1	49.0
Not returned	13.4	40	20.0	59	0.3	1	33.7

Source: Sears, 1953.[24]
Note: Ground limestone was applied to both sets of plots.

data are shown in Table 5.4.[24] Grazing sheep were fitted with appropriate harnesses to permit complete collection of urine and feces, which were then either returned or withheld from selected plots. Two noticeable effects were observed during the four years immediately following establishment of the pastures. Returning dung and urine resulted in increased herbage production and a shift in botanical composition to a higher proportion of grass and less clover. Incidentally, use of fertilizer N on grass-legume swards usually results in a similar but often more drastic shift toward grass.

PLANT EFFECTS ON ANIMALS

Effective grassland management is directed toward sustained high levels of production of useful animals and animal products. Thus grassland plants are produced and utilized by grazing animals for maintenance; reproduction; and the production of meat, milk, wool, mohair, or hides. The nutritive requirements for these different life processes vary, and a particular type of grassland may or may not be suitable for supporting all of them simultaneously.

Grasslands throughout the world supply feed for many different kinds of agricultural animals, the largest and by far the most important group being ruminants; 73 living genera have been listed.[25] Cattle and sheep are the most important domesticated ruminants. United Nations estimates place the world population of cattle and sheep at 1,123,627,000 and 1,068,839,000 head respectively in 1969–70, with India having the greatest concentration of cattle (176,450,000) and Australia the largest number of sheep (180,079,000).[26]

The suitability of grasslands for producing animals or animal products is determined primarily by the extent to which they supply the nutritive requirements of the animals as cheaply as possible without producing any deleterious side effects. The supply of a nutrient by a particular forage plant depends on the content in the plant, the amount of plant material consumed, and the degree of digestion and utilization of the herbage by the animal.

Herbage plants supply energy, protein, minerals, and vitamins to the animals that consume them. Gross caloric value of herbage plant materials is fairly uniform, averaging approximately 4.4 kcal/g of dry matter.[27] Protein, mineral, and vitamin content are more variable, being markedly affected by stage of plant development, species, soil, fertilization, and management practices. Much control can be exercised to improve the content of these nutrients in the herbage utilized for feeding livestock. For example, liveweight gains of yearling steers grazing either orchardgrass plus N or orchardgrass-clover were compared over a 10-year period in Virginia (Table 5.5).[28] Grass-clover pastures gave fewer steer grazing days per ha per year but higher daily liveweight gains per animal than did grass-nitrogen pastures. However, liveweight gains per ha per grazing season were essentially the same for the two kinds of pasture. (See Chapters 60–65 for animal products per unit of land area.)

Generally, forages are consumed ad libitum; i.e., animals are permitted to eat daily as much as they desire. For this reason the

24. Sears, P. D. 1953. Pasture growth and soil fertility. I. The influence of red and white clovers, superphosphate, lime, and sheep grazing on pasture yields and botanical composition. *N.Z. J. Sci. Tech.* 35:1–29.
25. Moir, R. J. 1965. The comparative physiology of ruminant-like animals. *In* R. W. Dougherty (ed.), Physiology of Digestion in the Ruminant. Butterworths, Washington.
26. United Nations. 1972. Statistical Yearbook, 1971. U.N., New York.
27. Crampton, E. W., and L. E. Harris. 1969. Applied Animal Nutrition, 2nd ed. W. H. Freeman, San Francisco.
28. Blaser, R. E., H. T. Bryant, R. C. Hammes, Jr., R. L. Bowman, J. P. Fontenot, and C. E. Polan. 1969. Managing forages for animal production. Va. Polytech. Inst. Bull. 45, p. 32.

TABLE 5.5 ❧ Liveweight gains of yearling steers grazing orchardgrass and orchardgrass-clover pastures during 10 years

Pasture	Steer-days per ha†	Liveweight gain	
		Daily, per steer (kg)	Per ha (kg)
Orchardgrass–ladino clover	635	0.58	363
Orchardgrass–no clover*	768	0.49	373

Source: Blaser et al., 1969.[28]

* Fertilized each year with 224 kg N/ha from ammonium nitrate.

† Based on 317-kg yearlings, the pasture furnished feed for the steer-days given.

level of voluntary consumption is extremely important and may sometimes be a limiting factor in animal performance. Consumption varies greatly between plant species and sometimes between cultivars of a given species. Intake or consumption of a given kind of forage is closely related to the digestibility of the material, with less being eaten as digestibility decreases.

Forage digestibility depends on the stage of plant development when it is grazed or harvested. As plant parts age and mature, they usually become less digestible. Digestibility of cool-season herbage grasses ordinarily decreases slowly with advancing maturity until near flowering, after which there is a rapid decline in digestibility. Since the youngest part of grassland plants is usually near the top, that portion of the sward is the most highly digestible. Thus animals that have the opportunity to graze first usually perform better than animals following them, as plants are commonly eaten from top to bottom.

Grazing animals choose their diets selectively, and many trials have demonstrated their ability to obtain the most nutritious plants and portions of plants available. Different animal species possess different grazing habits to be considered in planning programs of grassland utilization.

For most efficient utilization of grassland resources, all aspects of the ecosystem must be carefully analyzed and related. Grass-lands of low-quality herbage, either because of inherent low palatability of the plants, inadequate levels of nutrients in the forage, or too advanced plant maturity, do not yield satisfactory performance of young, growing animals or high-producing animals without appropriate feed supplementation. Such pastures and ranges, however, may be perfectly adequate for animals with lower nutritive requirements. By the same token, high-quality grasslands are likely to be most profitably utilized by animals having high nutritive requirements and productive potentials.

In many grassland environments harmful or potentially harmful plants are present along with useful ones. Grazing management should minimize the likelihood of consumption of harmful plants, and appropriate control or eradication measures are normally the preferred means of avoiding losses. A given species may be highly nutritious at most stages of development or under most conditions but may be harmful on occasion. Losses from this group are usually minimized through use of specific plant and animal management practices developed for the particular species involved.

EFFECTS OF PLANTS ON SOIL

The contribution of good grasslands to soil conservation should not be minimized. A plant community that forms a closed canopy is probably the best deterrent to soil erosion that man can devise. Well-nodulated grassland legumes contribute substantial amounts of N to the system, while grasses are thought to contribute much less. However, it has been shown that free-living, N-fixing bacteria accumulate atmospheric N at a considerable rate in a grass community, especially under humid tropical conditions.[29]

A grassland plant community protects the soil from wind and water erosion, adds N to the system, and also improves soil structure and tilth. This improved soil

29. Ruinen, Jakoba. 1971. The grass sheath as a site for nitrogen fixation. *In* T. F. Preece and C. H. Dickinson (eds.), Ecology of Leaf Surface Microorganisms, pp. 567–79. Academic Press, New York.

condition is the result of interactions of living and dead plant roots, microorganisms, and soil.

❧ HARMONIZING PLANT AND ANIMAL PRODUCTION

Harmonizing of plant and animal resources is the crux of successful grassland farming. Livestock producers often restrict utilization of fields, farms, ranches, or even larger areas to a particular kind of animal that can utilize the herbage to best advantage. Examples of such management schemes are the beef cattle fattening pastures of the western Pampa region of Argentina and the eastern lowlands of Aberdeen and Angus counties of Scotland, the winter grazing of ryegrass–small-grain pastures in the southeastern U.S. by young growing calves, the use of deferred tall fescue pasture for winter maintenance of beef brood cows, and the production and utilization of summer annuals such as sudangrass-sorghum hybrids as green chop for high-producing dairy cows.

Provision must be made for the deficit pasture-production periods that occur during drought and low-temperature seasons. In some districts of New Zealand, dairy cows are bred to calve in spring in order to take full advantage of the flush pasture production in spring and early summer. Cows are turned dry during the winter when forage production is low.[30] In the U.S. many beef feeder-calf producers breed their cows for spring calving; and at the end of the grazing season in late autumn or early winter the calves are weaned and sold, while the dams are overwintered on stockpiled

30. Wilson, G. F. 1964. The influence of date of calving on milk production. *N.Z. J. Agr. Res.* 7:80–89.

and/or stored feed. Beef brood cows may gain body weight during the flush grazing period and lose weight during periods of low herbage production without deleterious effects. An example of an adaptation which helps the animal cope with the distribution of feed production is the fat-tailed Karakul sheep of central Asia. The broad fat tail of these animals serves as a nutrient storage organ and has great significance for survival in their native habitat.

In many grassland environments stored feed is essential for efficient animal production. Many methods have been developed for harvesting, storing, and feeding such feeds. The mechanization of plant production, harvesting, storing, and feeding has made it possible and profitable to feed confined lactating cows and fattening animals in certain parts of the world. Nearly perfect harmony between provision of feed and animal production is achieved in some of these operations.

❧ QUESTIONS

1. In your own words define an ecosystem.
2. What are the four main components of a grassland ecosystem?
3. Give two or more examples of how man changes (1) the physical environment, (2) grassland plants, (3) domestic animals, and (4) other biotic factors within the ecosystem.
4. List several effects that grazing animals have on plants.
5. Describe some of the main effects that plants have on animals.
6. List three beneficial effects that a grassland community has on the soil.
7. Give an example of a well-harmonized feed and cattle production program in your home community.

P . J . V A N S O E S T / *Cornell University*

6

COMPOSITION AND NUTRITIVE VALUE OF FORAGES

❧

FORAGES are important in the world's food resources as plant materials containing relatively high amounts of structural carbohydrates. Since many monogastrics including man are very limited in their capacity to handle these fibrous carbohydrates, their usefulness lies in utilization by ruminant animals.[1] However, the ruminant is unique in having the potentiality for cycling forage materials, poor quality protein, and nonprotein N sources into the human food supply as meat and milk.[2]

Forages belong to the class of feeds called roughages, which represent coarser fibrous feeds as opposed to concentrates. The definition that roughages represent feeds over 18% crude fiber is very arbitrary. Roughage examples are forages, browses, seed hulls, and other fibrous by-products of the milling industry. Forages may be considered coarse livestock food that is composed of leaves, stems, and sometimes grain. Substitutes may include cellulosic wastes such as paper, bagasse, cotton linters, and other related products. Concentrates include seed grains and their high-quality by-prod-

ucts. Most forages are inferior to concentrates as energy food sources. Even a kilogram of total digestible nutrients (TDN) or a digestible calorie of forage is generally used less efficiently than the digestible equivalent of concentrate. Hence, there is much emphasis on the improvement of forage quality. This can be accomplished in several ways: by plant improvement, improved management, or processing.

❧ FORAGE COMPOSITION

Constituents of forages can be divided into two classes, those of a concentrate nature and the less digestible fibrous components. The highly digestible fraction termed cellular contents includes protein, sugars, starch, and organic acids. All forages contain some of these constituents, but not as much as concentrates when expressed as a total percentage of the feed. The cellular contents are not inferior in quality to their concentrate counterparts.

The other major fraction is that of the fibrous or cell wall components that are characteristic of forages as a class of feeds. The plant cell wall is the structural part of the plant and represents the total fibrous

❧ PETER J. VAN SOEST is Professor of Animal Nutrition, Cornell University. He received the M.S. degree from Washington State University and the Ph.D. from the University of Wisconsin. His research concerns the role of silicon in forages, the composition of temperate and tropical forages, and the chemical constitution of indigestible forage fractions.

1. Moore, L. A., P. A. Putnam, and N. D. Bayley. 1967. Ruminant livestock: Their role in the world protein deficit. *Agr. Sci. Rev.* 5:1–7.
2. Reid, J. T. 1970. Will meat, milk and egg production be possible in the future? Proc. Cornell Nutr. Conf., pp. 50–63.

TABLE 6.1 ❧ Biochemical components of forages

Component	Availability	Factors limiting animal utilization
Cellular Contents		
Soluble		
carbohydrate	100	intake
Starch	90+	passage and intake
Organic acids	100	intake and toxicity
Protein	90+	fermentation
Pectin	98	fermentation
Plant Cell Wall	variable	lignification, cutinization, and silicification
Cellulose	variable	lignification, cutinization, and silicification
Hemicellulose	variable	lignification, cutinization, and silicification
Lignin, cutin, and silica	indigestible	limit use of cell wall
Tannins and polyphenols	limited (?)	inhibitors of proteases and cellulases

Source: Van Soest, 1970.[4]

fraction. A breakdown of plant dry matter and the nutritive availability of the components is given in Table 6.1.[3,4]

The traditional method by which feeds and foods are analyzed is the proximate system. It was constituted essentially in its present form in 1860 by Henneberg, who used a method that had formed the basis of earlier systems. The essential feature of the proximate system is the partition of the carbohydrate fraction into crude fiber and nitrogen-free extract (NFE). Total carbohydrate is estimated by subtracting the sum of ash, ether extract, and protein (N × 6.25) from 100. Subtraction of crude fiber from total carbohydrate leaves NFE as the remainder unaccounted for by the analyses.

The partition of carbohydrate into fiber and NFE is presumed to represent a separation of less digestible cellulosic carbohydrate from the easily digestible starch and sugars. However, in 20–30% of the feeds listed by Morrison the NFE is less digestible than the crude fiber.[5,6] This comes about for several reasons, the first of which is that the crude fiber method (successive boiling with dilute sulfuric acid and sodium hydroxide) does not recover all the fiber, and large portions of fibrous constituents are extracted into the NFE. The most important of these fractions are lignin and hemicellulose (Table 6.1). Lignin is dissolved by sodium hydroxide, and hemicellulose is dissolved by both acid and alkali.

The basic error of the NFE concept is the assumption that if constituents are soluble they are digestible. Lignin, the rigid component of wood, not only is indigestible but lowers the digestibility of substances with which it is associated.

Another portion of the indigestible part of NFE arises from an artifact in the calculation of fecal NFE, where it is presumed that fecal N is protein (N × 6.25). Actually, 80–90% of fecal N is nonprotein substance and is composed of bacterial residues in which the ratio of organic matter to N is about 14. Thus part of the fecal NFE arises by an underestimation of the organic matter associated with fecal N.

Considerable research has been done to replace the proximate system by a more meaningful division of plant substances according to their availability to rumen bacteria and the animal. Various methods for determining cellulose and lignin have been developed as well as procedures for total cell wall constituents and estimates of hemicellulose. A general system of analysis with use of detergents has been developed that will accomplish this division of plant dry matter (Table 6.2).[3,6,7] The cellular contents represent the completely available proteins, carbohydrates, and other substances, while the plant cell wall is composed of lignin, cellulose, and hemicellulose, all of which contribute 98% of the

3. Goering, H. K., and P. J. Van Soest. 1970. Forage fiber analysis. USDA Agr. Handbook 379.
4. Van Soest, P. J. 1970. The chemical basis for the nutritive evaluation of forages, pp. U1–U19. Proc. Nat. Conf. on Forage Qual. Eval. and Util. (Univ. Nebr.).

5. Morrison, F. B. 1956. Feeds and Feeding, 22nd ed. Morrison, Ithaca, N.Y.
6. Crampton, E. W., and L. A. Maynard. 1938. The relation of cellulose and lignin content to the nutritive value of animal feeds. *J. Nutr.* 15:383–95.
7. Van Soest, P. J. 1971. Newer methods of forage evaluation. *N.Y. Food and Life Sci. Quart.* 4 (Oct.–Dec.): 4–6.

TABLE 6.2 ❧ Basic scheme of forage analysis using detergents

Fraction	Reagent	Treatment	Yield
Neutral-detergent fiber (NDF)	Na lauryl sulfate EDTA† pH 7.0	boil 1 hr	total plant cell wall
Acid-detergent fiber (ADF)	cetyl trimethylammonium bromide in 1 normal H_2SO_4	boil 1 hr	lignocellulose + SiO_2
Lignin*	$KMnO_4$, pH 3.0	treat 1½ hr at 20 C	lignin as loss in weight by oxidation
Cellulose	none	ash residue from lignin step	loss in weight
Silica (SiO_2)	concentrated HBr (48%)	treat ash dropwise, 1 hr at 25 C	residue is SiO_2 and soil silicates
Hemicellulose	none	calculate as NDF-ADF	difference

Source: Van Soest, 1971.[7]
  * Alternately lignin is determined by dissolving cellulose in 72% H_2SO_4 leaving a lignin, cutin, and silica residue. Weight loss upon ashing is crude lignin.
  † Disodium ethylenediaminetetraacetate.

truly indigestible fraction (Table 6.1).[8,9]

The fibrous fraction of forage is of great importance in the diet of ruminants. A minimum level and quality of fiber in the diet are required for proper rumen function and feed efficiency and for normal milk composition. Hay or dehydrated forage that has been finely ground and pelleted will not maintain the normal ratio of volatile fatty acids in the rumen, nor the normal milk fat level. Thus one aspect of fiber quality is destroyed by grinding. However, it is also known that cellulolytic strains of rumen bacteria are responsible for the proper ratios of rumen acids.[10] Therefore, it would seem that digestible cellulose is also an important factor. Digestibility of cellulose is reduced when finely ground forages are fed. The role of hemicellulose in regard to fiber quality is obscure.

PROTEIN

CRUDE PROTEIN. The total N of the plant multiplied by 6.25 is the crude protein content. Thus it includes protein and

8. Jarrige, R. 1965. The composition of sheep feces and its relations to forage digestibility. Proc. 9th Int. Grassl. Congr., pp. 809–14 (São Paulo, Brazil).
  9. Van Soest, P. J. 1967. Development of a comprehensive system of feed analysis and its application to forages. *J. Anim. Sci.* 26:119–28.
  10. Hungate, R. E. 1966. The Rumen and Its Microbes. Academic Press, New York.

nonprotein N (NPN). True protein designates the actual protein in the plant, which is roughly 70% of the total N in fresh forages, 60% in hays, and lower proportions in silages.

NONPROTEIN N. NPN includes a broad class of substances such as glutamine, glutamic acid, asparagine, aspartic acid, and gamma-amino-butyric acid. Small amounts of other substances including nitrate also occur. The NPN fraction of silages differs by containing large amounts of ammonia, amines, and their salts. An insoluble fraction in combination with lignin is indigestible and comprises 5–10% of the total N of most forages. This fraction is usually not determined with the NPN. True protein and soluble NPN usually are completely available, while the quality of the true protein is high, being better than seed proteins.

ORGANIC ACIDS

Collectively, organic acids represent a considerable part of the soluble matter of forages. Principal acids include citric, isocitric, malic, quinic, and aconitic. Many other acids may occur in smaller amounts. These acids are fermentable; in silages and other fermented feeds, lactic, acetic, and butyric acids may predominate. Organic acids are digestible and are associated with high forage quality except in cases of low Mg and high K intakes, where they can be associated with grass tetany, a metabolic disease of grazing animals.[11]

CARBOHYDRATES

Carbohydrates are complex polyhydroxy aliphatic aldehydes and their anhydric polymers in which the proportion of hydrogen and oxygen is generally the same as in water. Soluble carbohydrates are completely digestible and include glucose, fructose, sucrose, fructosan, and amylose starches.

FRUCTOSAN. The main storage carbohydrate in leaves and stems of temperate grasses is fructosan. It consists of a glucose attached to a chain of furanosidic fructose units. It is completely digestible. Fructosan does not occur in legumes or tropical grasses where starch is the main carbohydrate, usually in much smaller amounts.

STARCH. The main storage carbohydrate in many plants is starch, particularly in seed, roots, and tubers. It is composed of the polymers of glucose in alpha 1–4 pyranosidic linkage (amylose) and side chains attached at 1–6 positions (amylopectin). It is highly digestible and available to all animals.

CELLULOSE. The major skeletal carbohydrate in plants is cellulose, which is the chain anhydride of glucose with a beta 1–4 pyranosidic linkage. It is isomeric with starch (amylose) in which the 1–4 linkages are alpha. It is very insoluble and is digested only by microbial action. Rumen cellulolytic bacteria attach themselves to fiber and secrete cellulase enzymes that attack the cellulose. Final products are volatile fatty acids—acetic, propionic, and butyric—that are absorbed by the animal

through the rumen wall. Cellulose has a highly variable nutritive availability depending on its association with lignin, silica, cutin, and other factors.

PECTIN. A polysaccharide from the middle lamella of the plant cell wall, pectin is soluble in hot ammonium oxalate solutions. Main sugar components are galacturonic acid, arabinose, and galactose. True pectin is very highly digestible since it is not in combination with lignin. It should not be confused with the uronide hemicelluloses, which are extracted with pectin under acid hydrolysis.

HEMICELLULOSE. A heterogeneous polysaccharide fraction largely existing in the secondary wall (incrusting layer) of the plant, hemicellulose is more soluble in acids and bases than cellulose but is not more digestible. The mechanism of hemicellulose digestion is very similar to that of cellulose. Some hemicellulose fractions have a very low digestibility and are probably covalently linked to lignin.[12,13] Sugar components include pentoses (pentosan), glucuronic acid, and small amounts of hexoses (mannose and galactose). The term uronide hemicellulose refers to portions containing glucuronic acid. After extraction it resembles pectin. Grasses tend to be higher in hemicellulose than legumes.

NONCARBOHYDRATES

LIGNIN. Generally the noncarbohydrate fraction of the plant cell wall, true lignin is a three-dimensional polymer of substituted phenylpropanes. While adding rigidity to the plant cell wall, it is essentially indigestible and also protects associated portions of the cell wall carbohydrates from biological attack and digestion. Cutin, the outer covering or "skin" of plants, is composed of waxes and waxy polymers that may be integrated with lignin. Like lignin, cutin lowers the avail-

11. Grunes, D. L., P. R. Stout, and J. R. Brownell. 1970. Grass tetany of ruminants. *Advan. Agron.* 22:331–74.

12. Gaillard, B. D. E. 1962. The relationship between cell-wall constituents of roughages and the digestibility of the organic matter. *J. Agr. Sci.* 59:369–73.
13. Sullivan, J. T. 1966. Studies of the hemicellulose of forage plants. *J. Anim. Sci.* 25:83–86.

ability of the cellulose and hemicellulose with which it is associated. Though chemically dissimilar, cutin is included in crude lignin preparations.

MAILLARD PRODUCT. This lignin artifact is an artificial indigestible polymer between proteins or amino acids (particularly lysine) and degradation products of sugars and other carbohydrates. It is generated by the heating of moist feed or forage above 60 C. It is recovered quantitatively in the crude lignin fraction and contains about 11% N in a 1:1 adduct of amino acid and sugar. Its formation results in a marked reduction in digestibility of protein.[14]

TANNIN. Tannin is a broad class of soluble polyphenols with the common property of condensing with proteins (under weakly acidic conditions) to form a leather-like substance that is insoluble and of impaired digestibility. Tannins may impart a bitter taste and influence palatability and may also be inhibitors of cellulolytic digestion. They are usually included in crude lignin preparations unless preextraction is carried out. There are other polyphenol substances in plants that do not have leather-forming properties.

ETHER EXTRACT. A plant lipid or other substance that is soluble in ether from dried plant tissue is termed an ether extract. Components may include galactolipids (leaves), triglycerides (seeds only), waxes, pigments, and some organic acids and essential oils that are steam-volatile lipids occurring in plants. These substances include a wide class of fragrant compounds some of which may be important in palatability.

GLYCOSIDES. Glycosides are low molecular weight organic compounds consisting of a noncarbohydrate portion (aglycone) attached to a sugar. They include

many water and alcohol soluble pigments and occur widely in plants. Some substances in the class are poisonous, for example, those that hydrolyze to yield hydrocyanic acid (prussic acid poisoning). Common sugars linked in glycosides include glucose, galactose, xylose, and ribose.

VITAMINS. Vitamins A and D are required by ruminants. Others including the B complex are synthesized in the rumen or the animal body. Carotene, a yellow pigment occurring in green forage, serves as a source of vitamin A. This pigment is destroyed by light and consequently decreases upon weathering and aging of hay. Its content is highest in fresh herbage and silage.

Vitamin D is much less likely to be limiting than vitamin A in ruminant diets. Its content is increased upon aging and exposure of forage to sunlight.

MISCELLANEOUS. Plants contain small amounts of many substances that may affect grazing animals through drug-like action. These include saponins, which may be important in bloat, and coumestrol in legumes, which possesses female hormone activity. Indolalkylamine bases in some grasses may be toxic or affect palatability.

MINERALS

Mineral composition of plants varies greatly with soil fertilization and plant species. Use of tabular compilations of mineral content of forage is hazardous because of variability in composition of a given material. Chemical analysis is the best way to resolve cases of doubt.

Plants and animals differ in their specific requirements. Some elements like P become limiting to plants at a level below the animal requirement. Consequently, on low-P soils without P fertilization or supplementation, animals may die for lack of this element.

Plants require or use macro amounts of K, Ca, P, Mg, S, and Si and smaller trace

14. Van Soest, P. J. 1965. Use of detergents in analysis of fibrous feeds. III. Study of effects of heating and drying on yield of fiber and lignin in forages. *J. Assoc. Off. Agr. Chem.* 48:785–90.

amounts of Fe, Cu, Mn, Mo, Zn, and B. Animals, on the other hand, do not require B but do require large amounts of Na and Cl and trace amounts of Co (for vitamin B_{12}), Cr, Se, and I in addition to those required by plants. Other trace elements may yet be found to have a role in nutrition.

Because of the differing requirements of plants and animals, supplementation of salt (NaCl), Ca, and P is common to grazing animals. Often trace minerals are included in the mixture. In cases where plant requirements are to be met, fertilization may take care of plant and animal requirements.

Silicon is a unique element in that its oxide (silica) and silicates are major components of soils. In certain north temperate arid regions the high soil availability of Si in combination with cumulator plants can cause a high ingestion of soluble Si through the forage. Renal concentration and shortage of water cause the formation of urinary siliceous calculi. This can be a problem in grazing animals in certain parts of the arid West and Canada. Grazing animals may also ingest large amounts of soil that has little effect other than as a diluent of the diet.

Grasses tend to accumulate more Si than do legumes. Some of the Si that is accumulated is deposited in the plant cell wall with the cellulose carbohydrates. This can be a significant factor lowering organic matter digestibility where soil availability of Si allows a large uptake. The effect of Si upon nutritive value of grass is most important in temperate and northern regions. There is some evidence that Si may play a role as a trace element in nutrition of both plants and animals.

❧ NUTRITIVE VALUE

The feeding value of feedstuffs may be divided into several aspects. No one measure of value adequately accounts for animal response to a feeding regime. The matter of relating measures of feed value to response is still undergoing development and is a difficult and complex subject. Three general categories of feed evaluation are recognized: digestibility, consumption, and the efficiency with which feed that is consumed and digested is used for productive purpose.

DIGESTIBILITY

Digestibility expressed as dry matter, organic matter, energy, or TDN is the most commonly used measure of value. Its common use is related to the relative ease with which it can be applied as well as to its reproducibility as compared with consumption and efficiency, which are usually more important in explaining productivity. Various measures of digestibility are described below.

APPARENT DIGESTIBILITY. This is the balance of feed ingested less the matter lost in the feces, usually expressed as a percentage. The term may be applied to the measured balance of dry matter, energy, or feed components. Organic matter digestibility is often used in a grazing situation where considerable soil ingestion may occur.

DIGESTIBLE ENERGY AND TDN. Digestible nutrients are obtained by multiplying the digestion coefficient by the feed content. Total digestible nutrients represent the sum of digestible fiber, NFE, protein, and ether extract multiplied by 2.25. This constitutes an attempt to equate feeds on an equal energy basis. Direct determination of digestible energy content of feed and feces by analysis with bomb calorimetry has given more accurate estimates of energy availability.

TRUE DIGESTIBILITY. This is the actual digestibility or availability of a feed, forage, or nutrient as represented by the balance between the intake and fecal loss of the same undigested material. True digestibility of whole rations, forage, and protein is always greater than apparent digestibility because part of the feces is of metabolic (nonfeed) origin. Apparent and true digestibility will be identical if there is no metabolic loss as in the case of cellulosic carbohydrates. *In vitro* rumen digestions tend to measure true digestibility because animal metabolic products cannot be generated *in vitro*. However, *in vitro* methods measuring dry matter disappearance may yield lower values because of the generation of bacterial residues that would have considerable digestibility in the lower tract of the animal.

CONSUMPTION

VOLUNTARY INTAKE. The ad libitum intake achieved when an animal is offered an excess of a single feed or forage is termed voluntary intake. Excess usually is specified at 110–115% of that consumed. Because of the problem of selection, voluntary intake is not identical with palatability (see below), although the latter has an influence on intake. Some forages, while they are discriminated against in a situation of choice, may be eaten in high amounts when offered as the sole feed. Rejected feedstuffs left under conditions of ad libitum stall feeding are termed orts. Controlled consumption at lower levels is termed restricted intake.

Feed consumption is a vital factor influencing efficiency with which ingested nutrients are used. Attempts have been made to establish measurements of intake as a feed evaluation characteristic. This has been difficult since the urge to eat varies among animals, depending upon their physiological requirements. Thus lactating animals eat more than pregnant or growing animals, and these in turn eat more than fattening animals. One attempt to provide an evaluation of the intake qualities of forage is that of the nutritive value index (NVI), which is the daily digestible amount of forage eaten per unit of metabolic body size, relative to a standard forage.[15] Metabolic body size is body

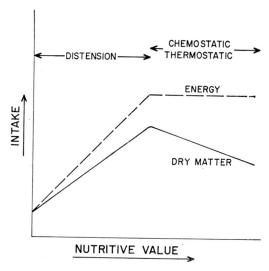

FIG. 6.1. Relationships between nutritive value of rations and feed and dry matter and digestible energy intake. *Graph courtesy B. R. Baumgardt.*

weight to the three-quarter power ($W^{0.75}$). The reason for this is that animal heat production varies with the surface area of the organism. Surface area and heat production are proportional to $W^{0.75}$.

In the NVI, intake and digestibility are assumed to be positively related. This is an oversimplification; later work has shown the relationship between digestibility and intake to be biphasal, as shown in Figure 6.1.[16] The result is that a single value of NVI for a given forage cannot be quoted for all classes of ruminants. Lactating females and growing animals with a greater urge to eat will eat more for metabolic size than other animals and may rank forages differently.

Prediction of NVI and intake is best in the region of positive relationship between intake and digestibility in the left side of Figure 6.1. Under these conditions intake is limited by rumen fill, and intake is predicted from cell wall factors or others related to caloric density. Denser high-quality forage and concentrates are not consumed to the limit of fill since the animal

15. Crampton, E. W., E. Donefer, and L. E. Lloyd. 1960. A nutritive value index for forages. *J. Anim. Sci.* 19:538–44.

16. Baumgardt, B. R. 1970. Regulation of feed intake and energy balance. *In* A. T. Phillipson (ed.), Physiology of Digestion and Metabolism in the Ruminant, pp. 235–53. Proc. 3rd Int. Symp. (Cambridge, England).

is able to satiate itself before that limit is reached. A negative relationship results between intake and quality because the animal does not need to eat as much of the better feed in order to achieve the same state of nutrition.

PALATABILITY. This term refers to plant characteristics eliciting a choice among two or more feeds or forages or different parts of the same forage, conditioned by animal and environmental factors. Palatability connotes the relish with which feed is eaten as stimulated by sensory impulse. Selection is the sorting of forage or feed by the animal for the more desirable (palatable) portions. It occurs only when the animal has a choice and tends to diminish or disappear at high stocking rates, in underfeeding, or under conditions in which the animal is restricted to a single feed. Since the animal cannot tell the observer whether it does or does not eat a forage for a sensory reason, as opposed to a physiological action such as the presence of a metabolically active principle in the forage, the word tends to embrace some ambiguity. Acceptability is a term sometimes used interchangeably to mean either palatability or voluntary intake. These are different aspects of consumption that should not be confused.

ENERGY USE AND EFFICIENCY

METABOLIZABLE ENERGY OR SUBSTANCE. This is the balance of feed ingested less the sum of the feces, urine, and combustible gas (methane). Metabolizable energy is approximately 82% of digestible energy, poorer quality feeds being somewhat less efficient. It is a measure commonly used to evaluate feeds for poultry, but it is less often used for ruminants.

NET ENERGY. The amount of feed energy available for maintenance, work, growth, gain, or milk production is net energy. Values of net energy are expressed in megacalories (Mcal), formerly called therms, obtained by subtracting the

energy lost as heat (heat increment) from metabolizable energy. Net energy values can be determined by placing animals in respiration chambers where the total energy expenditure of the animal can be measured from oxygen consumed and carbon dioxide respired. Respired gas must also be analyzed for methane, a combustible fermentation gas.[17]

Net energy values also can be obtained by slaughter after careful feeding trials. The exact body composition and its caloric content is determined. This latter method is satisfactory for beef animals; however, energy requirement for milk production can only be measured in respiration chambers. Much of this work has been done at the Dairy Cattle Research Branch, USDA, Beltsville, Md.

Net energy should be expressed in reference to animal function, e.g., maintenance, gain, or lactation. Unspecified values such as that of net energy for production (NE_p) are being abandoned because efficiency varies markedly with animal function.

EFFICIENCY. Animal productivity relative to feed use may be expressed in several ways. Daily gain per kilogram of feed or per digestible unit are expressions of gross efficiency. Pasture trials may merely report gains per day since intake estimates are difficult to obtain under these conditions.

In the case of net energy, poor quality feeds are markedly less efficient than better quality ones, as shown in Table 6.3.[18] Poor quality forages are less efficiently used because of the great bulk, low density, and high content of structure carbohydrates and lignin (cell wall). More work of rumination is required for the digestion and passage of these feeds through the digestive tract. Thus there are limitations on the amounts that can be eaten.

17. Blaxter, K. L. 1962. The Energy Metabolism of Ruminants. Hutchinson, London.
18. Van Soest, P. J. 1971. Estimations of nutritive value from laboratory analyses. Proc. Cornell Nutr. Conf., pp. 106–17.

TABLE 6.3 ❧ Composition and nutritive value of feeds (dry basis)

Feed	Crude protein (%)	TDN (%)	Cell wall (%)	Lignin (%)	NE_m (Mcal)	NE_g (Mcal)	Ratio NE_m/g (%)	NE_1 (Mcal)	Lactation* efficiency (%)
Corn grain	11	89	10	1	2.13	1.37	64	2.27	58
Alfalfa hay (early)	22	67	41	6	1.47	0.76	52	1.49	51
Alfalfa (all analyses)	17	57	52	8	1.22	0.51	42	1.17	47
Birdsfoot trefoil	16	61	44	10	1.30	0.60	46	1.29	48
Corn silage	8	70	45	3	1.56	0.99	63	1.70	55
Orchardgrass (very early)	15	71	46	4	1.40	0.71	51	1.47	47
Sorghum silage	8	58	59	8	1.25	0.61	49	1.28	50
Smooth bromegrass before bloom	17	62	62	5	1.22	0.51	42	1.17	43
Tall fescue ('Ky 31')	10	59	64	5	1.25	0.54	43	1.09	42
Timothy (all analyses)	8	54	68	7	1.13	0.42	37	1.05	44
'Coastal' bermuda-grass	8	57	75	9	0.96	0.25	26	0.83	33
Barley straw	5	47	80	8	0.80	0.09	11	0.63	30
Wheat straw	4	46	85	12	0.52	−0.18	−34	0.29	14

Source: Van Soest, 1971, p. 106.[18]
* Net energy as a percent of digestible energy.

MAINTENANCE. Energy is used in the animal body for various purposes, maintenance of the system being the most integral. The body must be maintained before productive function of growth, fattening, or lactation can occur. Consequently, the net energy values of feeds vary, depending on the amount that can be eaten. For example, a very mature forage such as straw cannot be consumed to a high degree because of its bulk and low caloric density. Thus, most of the digestible energy consumed will be used for maintenance. Little will be left over for other functions. Consequently, the net energy for maintenance (NE_m) will be higher than that for gain. In the case of corn grain the net energy for gain (NE_g) is relatively much higher in relation to maintenance, as shown in Table 6.3.

NET ENERGY FOR GAIN. NE_g is the expression of feed value for gain after maintenance requirements have been satisfied. The NE_m and NE_g represent a dual system of feed evaluation known as the California system, which is commonly used in the beef industry for evaluating feeds and estimating gains. This system is one of two net energy systems used in the U.S.[18-20]

NET ENERGY FOR LACTATION (NE_1). This system was developed at Beltsville and is essentially a modification of Morrison's values.[5] It differs from the California system in that the maintenance requirement is expressed in energy equivalents of milk so that the net energy value of a feed is one number. The original Morrison system is similar except that it is based on gain. Combining maintenance with production changes net energy values. Consequently, values by the California system do not correspond to those by the Beltsville system (Table 6.3). Morrison's net energies are 83% of NE_1 since lactation is physiologically a somewhat more efficient process. Values of NE_1 and the efficiency with which digestible energy is used are given in Table 6.3. The efficiency of energy use declines with feed quality.

19. National Research Council. 1970. Nutrient Requirements of Beef Cattle, 4th ed., rev. Natl. Acad. Sci. Washington, D.C.
20. National Research Council. 1971. Nutrient Requirements of Dairy Cattle, 4th ed., rev. Natl. Acad. Sci., Washington, D.C.

FACTORS AFFECTING FORAGE QUALITY

Environmental factors have a profound effect upon forage quality. Knowledge of these is vital for management and proper manipulation of plant maturity, fertilization, and plant species to obtain optimum quality forage.[21]

CLIMATE. The relative importance of temperature, light, and moisture lies in the order listed. Temperature increases metabolic activity of all nonhomeothermic organisms. This means more rapid turnover of energy and pooled metabolites and synthesis of new cells and substances. Since plants accumulate cell wall structures containing lignin and cellulosic carbohydrates that are irretrievable by the organism, it follows that accumulation of lignin and cell wall components is likely to be a temperature-related phenomenon. It has been shown that increasing temperature promotes a lowering of nutritive value at the same physiological age in grasses.[22]

Forages grown in cold climates develop reserves of carbohydrates and proteins in leaves and stems as a requirement of frost-hardiness and are of high nutritive value. Low yield and high nutritive value are characteristics of arctic grazing.

Light, on the other hand, supports photosynthesis, which fosters the synthesis of sugars and organic acids. Independent of temperature, this becomes a vector toward increasing digestibility of the plant.

The effect of moisture is more variable. If moisture is limited, the plant may be prevented from developing toward maturity. However, some adapted perennial plants may go into dormancy in a dry season, pulling reserves into the roots and leaving an aerial part of low value.

MATURITY AND DATE OF CUTTING. Most forages decline in nutritive quality with age. The effect is a complex response and is not guaranteed in all instances. First, it should be recognized that age and physiological maturity are not identical. Thus factors such as cool temperatures and light that retard maturity promote higher quality at a given age. Furthermore, most date-of-cutting studies represent first cuttings taken during the spring and early summer when the effects of warming season and maturity positively interact. Such studies show steep declines in digestibility and protein and increases in fiber, lignin, and other cell wall components. A few exceptions occur, such as in the corn plant where the formation of grain offsets the lignification of the stalk and leaves. Nutritive value of corn silage varies little with date of cutting.

Date-of-cutting information is less useful in evaluating second cuttings or aftermaths grown in July through September. At this time environmental temperature is maximum and no longer increasing, and digestibilities are not as high in immature material as they were in the spring. There is also much less interaction between lignin and cellulose, which are dependent on changing temperature for association. In the fall with declining temperatures, nutritive value may actually increase with the age of the plant.

TROPICAL FORAGES. Many tropical climates are characterized by absence of extreme annual temperature fluctuations. Thus response of tropical grasses is similar to that of summer-grown and aftermath forages in temperate zones. Tropical environment differs in that there is generally a much higher solar intensity, which in combination with adequate moisture and high temperature means extremely rapid plant development and growth toward maturity. Tropical forages on the average are inferior to temperate ones as they are grown.[23,24] However, most of this differ-

21. Raymond, W. F. 1969. The nutritive value of forage crops. *Advan. Agron.* 21:1–108.

22. Deinum, B., A. J. H. van Es, and P. J. Van Soest. 1968. Climate, nitrogen and grass. II. The influence of light intensity, temperature, and nitrogen on *in vivo* digestibility of grass and the prediction of these effects from some chemical procedures. *Neth. J. Agr. Sci.* 16:217–23.

23. McDowell, R. E. 1972. Improvement of Livestock Production in Warm Climates. Freeman, San Francisco.

24. Butterworth, M. H., and J. A. Diaz. 1970. The use of equations to predict the nutritive value of tropical grasses. *J. Range Manage.* 23:55–58.

ence could probably be corrected with management (see Chapter 34).

EFFECT OF FERTILIZATION. Crude protein content as influenced by fertilizer N is the most important effect of fertilization. The effect of other minerals is mainly on yield and content of the mineral in the forage. Digestibility is affected relatively little, although palatability may be.

Nitrogen fertilization of grasses increases crude protein content, depresses soluble carbohydrates in leaves and stems, and promotes more rapid lignification. Such total structural matter as plant cell wall may be depressed if the protein content is greatly increased. These effects are partly compensatory, and digestibility may not be affected even though there is an increase in lignin. However, in some instances digestibility has been decreased by fertilizer N even though it is often considered that this improves forage quality by raising the percent of protein. Caution should be applied in using equations between percent protein and digestibility under these conditions.

True digestibility of well-preserved forage is above 90% in all instances but may decline if the forage has been heat damaged. Apparent digestible protein is about four units lower than total crude protein because of fecal metabolic losses.

GRASSES VERSUS LEGUMES. At the same relative digestibility grasses contain less lignin and much more hemicellulose than do legumes. The lower lignin content is offset by the greater hemicellulose and consequently higher cell wall content, so that digestibility is the same. This promotes lower intake and net energy values for grasses than for alfalfa of the same TDN content. Some comparisons may be seen in Table 6.3.

ESTIMATING NUTRITIVE VALUE. Many equations and tables have been published to aid in estimation of the feeding value of forages and other feeds. In the case of forages many equations reflect age of cutting. In such instances estimation may be reasonably accurate if age is the major difference among samples. Unfortunately, any plant constituent that changes with the age of the plant will be highly correlated with digestibility whether or not it is a primary contributor to quality. When a feed laboratory compares forages from a wide area, factors such as climate, fertilization, and soil may be more important than age in determining forage value. Under these conditions equations based on factors associated with date of cutting or plant maturity are of lesser value. Primary factors in forage influencing nutritive value include available protein, cell wall, cellulose, lignin, and silica. It may not be economical for a farmer to pay for all these analyses in evaluating his forage. However, one alternative is the *in vitro* rumen digestion analysis developed by Tilley and Terry in England.[25] See Chapter 59 for a discussion of forage testing and its opportunities.

25. Tilley, J. M. A., and R. A. Terry. 1963. A two-stage technique for the *in vitro* digestion of forage crops. *J. Brit. Grassl. Soc.* 18:104–11.

❧ QUESTIONS

1. What is the nutritional basis for the role forages play in supplementing world food supply?
2. List some defects of the proximate system of analysis.
3. What factors influence fiber quality?
4. How is fiber important to a ruminant? In particular, to a lactating cow?
5. How are ruminants able to use fibrous carbohydrates such as cellulose as food?
6. What are the characteristics of high-quality forage? List compositional components, the content of which should be high and low respectively.
7. Describe the factors influencing voluntary intake of a forage.
8. Define and distinguish the terms: apparent digestibility, true digestibility, metabolizable energy, and net energy.
9. What happens to forage when it matures? Describe changes in composition and nutritive value.
10. How does climate influence the nutritive value of forages?

DARREL S. METCALFE / *University of Arizona*

7

FORAGE STATISTICS

❧

❧ DARREL S. METCALFE is Associate Dean and Director of Resident Instruction, Assistant Director of the Experiment Station, and Professor of Agronomy at the University of Arizona. He received the M.S. degree from Kansas State University and the Ph.D. from Iowa State University and is active both nationally and internationally in the field of agricultural education.

PERTINENT data not available in other chapters have been assembled here to serve as a convenient reference for the student of forages.

❧ SEED PRODUCTION AREAS

Leading states in the production of the more important legume and grass seed are listed in Table 7.1. Hectarage and ha yields of forage seed crops vary greatly from year to year. However, data for a number of years indicate the areas leading in seed production of any specific crop. Reporting of data for certain seed crops has been discontinued and has been limited for others.

❧ EXPORTS AND IMPORTS

Exports and imports of forage crop seed fluctuate greatly from year to year, depending on the available supply and demand in this country and others. Exports and imports also are restricted by trade barriers, tariffs, staining regulations, and other seed control legislation. Table 7.2 gives the exports and imports for the average of 1968–69 and for 1970. Export

TABLE 7.1 ❧ States leading in production of seed of some more important legumes and grasses, 1962–66, 1969, and 1971; for certain seed, 1969–70 and 1971; U.S. totals

Seed type and area	Hectarage harvested			Kilograms per hectare		
	1962–66 average	1969	1971	1962–66 average	1969	1971
Red Clover						
Illinois	64,476	31,185	38,475	94	73	101
Ohio	48,276	24,300	22,680	82	78	90
Indiana	40,257	25,110	24,300	84	90	90
Missouri	37,098	10,125	13,365	101	90	118
Iowa	22,599	5,265	8,100	73	73	101
Michigan	22,437	22,275	12,150	85	112	90
Wisconsin	14,580	12,150	9,315	82	123	101
Minnesota	14,499	20,250	12,150	110	118	135
Kansas	8,829	3,645	4,050	87	84	129
Oregon	8,708	6,278	7,695	248	342	235
U.S.	321,667	188,973	185,041	101	109	114

TABLE 7.1. ❧ (Continued)

Seed type and area	Hectarage harvested			Kilograms per hectare		
	1962–66 average	1969	1971	1962–66 average	1969	1971
Alfalfa						
California	43,740	38,880	34,830	465	387	549
Kansas	36,369	24,300	24,300	114	106	112
South Dakota	35,883	20,655	36,450	62	62	67
Oklahoma	23,409	24,300	13,365	153	151	123
Nebraska	21,951	11,340	11,745	82	73	73
Idaho	18,873	15,390	15,795	348	420	471
Utah	16,929	9,720	4,860	176	157	258
Montana	16,848	8,505	10,125	105	101	106
Washington	11,340	10,530	14,175	492	589	561
Oregon	8,019	5,265	5,063	520	493	539
U.S.	278,105	201,285	197,195	216	233	269
Lespedeza						
Missouri	23,409	10,125	5,670	232	258	230
Kentucky	19,845	17,415	7,695	278	336	258
North Carolina	14,661	6,075	6,885	180	196	179
Tennessee	14,013	10,125	7,695	234	247	247
Indiana	8,181	5,670	4,860	209	235	168
Arkansas	6,804	4,050	4,253	416	476	235
Illinois	6,075	4,050	4,455	193	191	157
Kansas	5,103	6,075	6,075	244	258	179
Georgia	3,969	2,430	2,025	242	258	280
Maryland	3,888	2,430	1,620	188	202	191
U.S.	116,114	74,115	55,850	239	271	213
Sweetclover						
Minnesota	7,047	7,290	4,455	224	252	308
South Dakota	6,561	2,430	2,025	272	291	308
Kansas	6,237	2,835	2,835	172	157	179
Texas	5,063	2,025	2,430	290	269	336
Nebraska	4,091	2,633	2,025	233	213	219
Ohio	3,767	1,620	2,025	254	213	179
North Dakota	3,078	5,670	4,455	274	314	280
Illinois	1,985	1,823	1,620	156	112	135
Oklahoma	1,831	...	...	148	...	...
Missouri	988	...	...	184	...	...
U.S.	42,047	26,325	21,870	229	244	256
Timothy						
Missouri	26,892	12,555	6,885	158	157	157
Minnesota	20,007	30,780	33,210	193	252	235
Ohio	13,203	8,910	6,075	156	168	157
Iowa	4,941	3,240	2,025	169	140	157
Indiana	3,321	3,645	3,240	135	146	135
Illinois	2,916	2,430	2,633	155	157	157
Wisconsin	2,592	2,430	2,025	130	157	157
Pennsylvania	2,106	2,430	3,038	128	121	123
U.S.	75,978	66,420	59,130	166	200	198

Seed type and area	Hectarage harvested		Kilograms per hectare	
	1969–70 average	1971	1969–70 average	1971
Crimson Clover				
Oregon	7,088	4,253	448	280
Georgia	2,228	2,228	135	112
Alabama	1,094	608	140	135
Mississippi	1,033	972	155	135
Tennessee	587	405	219	224
U.S.	12,029	8,465	327	206

TABLE 7.1 ✤ (Continued)

Seed type	Hectarage harvested		Kilograms per hectare	
and area	1969–70 average	1971	1969–70 average	1971
Hairy Vetch				
Texas	8,708	5,670	191	235
Nebraska	5,063	3,645	163	179
Oklahoma	4,658	3,645	174	135
Oregon	2,430	2,835	454	516
Arkansas	770	567	235	258
U.S.	21,627	16,362	214	250
White Clover				
Idaho-Oregon	2,592	5,913	299	328
Louisiana	1,620	1,418	123	106
U.S.	4,212	7,331	231	286
Ladino Clover				
California	6,581	7,290	342	308
Tall Fescue				
('Alta' and 'Ky 31')				
Missouri	37,260	46,980	278	326
Kentucky	27,945	22,275	272	286
Tennessee	12,555	10,530	233	247
Oregon	6,581	6,885	701	785
South Carolina	6,075	5,265	219	213
Georgia	5,873	4,455	241	247
Alabama	4,455	3,645	247	241
Arkansas	4,354	4,860	222	235
Mississippi	1,418	1,418	174	168
Oklahoma	1,397	1,377	196	179
U.S.	107,709	107,690	286	319
Red Fescue				
Oregon	6,075	6,278	465	583
U.S.	6,116	6,278	464	583
Chewings Fescue				
Oregon	6,683	6,885	499	583
Orchardgrass				
Virginia	6,480	6,075	334	376
Missouri	4,658	4,455	230	235
Kentucky	3,443	3,038	244	263
U.S.	14,580	13,568	279	305
Bentgrass				
Oregon	12,150	12,555	235	336
Washington	71	122	216	280
U.S.	12,221	12,677	235	336
All Ryegrass				
Oregon	63,788	65,205	1,384	1,547
'Merion' Kentucky Bluegrass				
Idaho	2,268	2,430	244	314
Washington	1,438	1,661	297	348
Oregon	1,397	1,782	325	392
U.S.	5,103	5,873	281	348

TABLE 7.1. ❧ *(Continued)*

Seed type and area	Hectarage harvested	
	1969–70 average	1971
	Cured seed (1000 kg)	
	1969–70	1971
Kentucky Bluegrass (other than Merion)		
Northwest	12,756	18,541
North central	6,082	1,736
Kentucky	260	118
U.S.	34,439	20,395

Sources: USDA. 1969. Agricultural statistics.
USDA. 1972. Seed crops annual summary. Crop. Rep. Board, SRS.

data are available for only seven specified kinds of seed, as indicated in the 1970 data.

Tables 7.3 and 7.4 give the number of seed per kilogram, weight per hectoliter, and the usually recommended seeding rates in kilograms per ha of some of the more important grasses and legumes. Since seed vary greatly in size from lot to lot, depending on seasonal and other environmental conditions, actual figures may vary greatly from those shown as average.

❧ CHANGES IN HAY PRODUCTION

The hectarage of tame hay harvested in the U.S. has changed only moderately, but there have been some significant changes in kind and quantity of tame hay pro-duced in different parts of the country. In 1920 nearly 50% of the tame hay hectar-age was clover and timothy, including stands of timothy, clover, and mixtures of the two. The hectarage of clover and timothy now represents only about 19%; while legumes, reported separately, total about 60% of all hay. Wild hay has de-clined from 16 to 7% (Table 7.5). Hectares harvested, yield per ha, and total produc-tion of various kinds of hay are shown in Table 7.6. Table 7.7 lists the leading states in the production of the more im-portant kinds of hay. Data for longtime production averages and certain hay crops no longer are available on a national basis. The percentage of various feeds consumed by different kinds of livestock by periods from 1940 to 1969 is an indication of the forage market as shown in Table 7.8.

TABLE 7.2 ❧ U.S. exports and imports of forage crop seed in thousands of kilograms

Forage	1968–69 Average		1970		Forage	1968–69 Average		1970	
	Exports	Imports	Exports	Imports		Exports	Imports	Exports	Imports
Alfalfa	6,550	192	9,520	25	Bluegrass				
Clover					Merion	*	172	*	30
Red	473	3,923	700	2,317	Other	1,716	527	3,299	38
Sweet	*	6,459	*	4,557	Fescue				
White	*	217	*	248	Chewings	*	7	*	35
Ladino	1,147	†	1,477	†	Red	*	7,006	*	7,574
Crimson	*	†	*	0	Tall (Alta and				
Lespedeza	*	0	*	0	Ky 31)	*	†	*	10
Hairy vetch	*	526	*	2					
Timothy	1,628	112	3,038	118	Bentgrass	2,902	70	3,405	9
Orchardgrass	*	2,977	*	758	All ryegrass	5,811	524	10,585	394

Source: USDA. 1972. Seed crops annual summary. Crop Rep. Board, SRS.
* Data not available.
† Less than 1000 kg.

TABLE 7.3 ❧ Seed per kilogram and seeding rate of some of the more important grasses, arranged alphabetically by scientific name

Scientific and common name	Number of seed per kg	Seeding rate (kg/ha)	Scientific and common name	Number of seed per kg	Seeding rate (kg/ha)
Agropyron cristatum (L.) Gaertn., fairway wheatgrass	385,875	7–13	*Anthoxanthum odoratum* L., sweet vernalgrass	1,600,830	17–28
Agropyron dasystachyum (Hook.) Scribn., thickspike wheatgrass	339,570	7–13	*Arrhenatherum elatius* (L.) Presl., tall oatgrass	330,750	45–56
Agropyron desertorum (Fisch. ex Link) Schult., crested wheatgrass	385,875	7–13	*Astrebla pectinata* (F.) Muell., mitchellgrass	180,810	...
Agropyron elongatum (Host) Beauv., tall wheatgrass	174,195	9–13	*Avena sativa* L., oats	28,665	67–101
Agropyron inerme (Scribn. & Smith) Rydb., beardless wheatgrass	330,750	7–13	*Axonopus affinis* Chase, common carpetgrass	2,694,510	6–13
Agropyron intermedium (Host) Beauv., intermediate wheatgrass	194,040	9–13	*Bouteloua curtipendula* Michx., sideoats grama	421,155	11–17
Agropyron michnoi Rosher	357,210	7–13	*Bouteloua eriopoda* (Torr.) Torr., black grama	2,943,675	11–17
Agropyron repens (L.) Beauv., quackgrass (w)	242,550	7–13	*Bouteloua filiformis* (Fourn.) Griffiths, slender grama	3,148,740	11–17
Agropyron riparium Scribn. & Smith, streambank wheatgrass	343,980	7–13	*Bouteloua gracilis* (H.B.K.) Lag. ex. Steud., blue grama	1,819,125	11–17
Agropyron semicostatum (Steud.) Nees. ex Boiss., drooping wheatgrass	130,095	7–13	*Bouteloua hirsuta* Lag., hairy grama	2,160,900	11–17
Agropyron sibiricum (Willd.) Beauv., Siberian wheatgrass	374,850	7–13	*Bouteloua rothrockii* Vasey, Rothrock grama	9,029,475	11–17
Agropyron smithii Rydb., western wheatgrass	242,550	6–17	*Brachiaria mutica* (Forsk.) Stapf, paragrass	...	vegetative
Agropyron spicatum (Pursh) Scribn. & Smith, bluebunch wheatgrass	209,475	7–13	*Bromus arvensis* L., field bromegrass	617,400	17–34
Agropyron trachycaulum (Link) Malte, slender wheatgrass	350,595	7–13	*Bromus catharticus* Vahl., rescuegrass	126,710	17–28
Agropyron trichophorum (Link) Richt., pubescent (stiffhair) wheatgrass	220,500	9–13	*Bromus bilbersteinii* Roem. & Schult., meadow bromegrass	156,555	11–22
Agrostis alba L., redtop	11,002,950	6–11	*Bromus inermis* Leyss., smooth bromegrass	299,880	11–22
Agrostis canina L., velvet bentgrass	23,814,000	45–67	*Bromus marginatus* Nees., mountain bromegrass	156,555	11–22
Agrostis palustris Huds., creeping bentgrass	17,199,000	45–67	*Bromus secalinus* L., chess (w)	156,555	...
Agrostis tenuis Sibth., colonial bentgrass	19,234,215	45–67	*Bromus tectorum* L., cheatgrass bromegrass (w)	458,480	...
Alopecurus pratensis L., meadow foxtail	1,270,080	17–28	*Buchloe dactyloides* (Nutt.) Engelm., buffalograss	123,480*	4–9*
Ammophila arenaria (L.) Link, European beachgrass	251,370	vegetative	*Calamovilfa gigantea* (Nutt.) Scribn. & Merr., big sandreed	194,040	9–13
Ammophila breviligulata Fernald, American beachgrass	...	vegetative	*Calamovilfa longifolia* (Hook.) Scribn., prairie sandreed	603,509	9–13
Andropogon caucasius Trin. Caucasian bluestem	2,363,760	11–17	*Chloris distichophylla* Lag., weeping chloris	3,902,850	9–17
Andropogon gerardi Vitman, big bluestem	363,825	11–17	*Cynodon dactylon* (L.) Pers., bermudagrass	3,940,335	7–9
Andropogon hallii Hack., sand bluestem	249,165	11–22	*Cynosurus cristatus* L., crested dogtail	1,592,010	17–28
Andropogon ischaemum L., Turkestan bluestem	3,106,845	11–17	*Dactylis glomerata* L., orchardgrass	1,442,070	7–17
Andropogon scoparius Michx., little bluestem	573,300	11–17	*Digitaria decumbens* Stent., 'Pangola' digitgrass	...	vegetative
			Digitaria sanguinalis (L.) Scop., hairy crabgrass (w)	1,819,125	...
			Echinochloa crusgalli var. *frumentacea* (Roxb.) Wight, Japanese millet	341,775	22–28
			Elymus canadensis L., Canada wildrye	253,575	11–17

68

TABLE 7.3 ❧ *(Continued)*

Scientific and common name	Number of seed per kg	Seeding rate (kg/ha)	Scientific and common name	Number of seed per kg	Seeding rate (kg/ha)
Elymus condensatus Presl., giant wildrye	366,030	11–17	*Muhlenbergia porteri* Scribn., bush muhly	4,943,610	...
Elymus giganteus Vahl., Siberian wildrye	220,500	11–17	*Oryzopsis hymenoides* (Roem. & Schult.) Ricker, Indian ricegrass	310,905	9–11
Elymus glaucus Buckl., blue wildrye	302,085	11–17	*Oryzopsis miliacea* (L.) Benth., smilograss	1,949,220	...
Elymus junceus Fisch., Russian wildrye	385,875	9–11	*Panicum antidotale* Retz., blue panic	1,448,685	2–7
Elymus triticoides Buckl., creeping wildrye	112,455	6–17	*Panicum maximum* L., guineagrass	2,438,730	vegetative
Elymus virginicus L., Virginia wildrye	160,965	11–17	*Panicum miliaceum* L., proso	180,810	17–28
Eragrostis chloromelas Steud., Boer lovegrass	6,443,010	1–3	*Panicum obtusum* H.B.K., vine mesquite	315,315	6–11
Eragrostis curvula (Schrad.) Nees., weeping lovegrass	3,225,915	1–3	*Panicum repens* L., torpedograss	1,124,550	vegetative
Eragrostis lehmanniana Nees., Lehmann lovegrass	9,360,225	1–3	*Panicum virgatum* L., switchgrass	857,745	6–9
Eragrostis trichodes (Nutt.) Wood, sand lovegrass	2,866,500	1–3	*Paspalum dilatatum* Poir., dallisgrass	485,100	9–22
Eremochloa ophiuroides (Munro) Hack., centipedegrass	899,640	17–28	*Paspalum laeve* Michx., field paspalum (w)	343,980	...
Euchlaena mexicana Schrad., teosinte	15,281	3–6	*Paspalum malacophyllum* Trin., ribbed paspalum	2,335,095	11–22
Festuca arundinacea Schreb., tall fescue	500,535	11–28	*Paspalum notatum* Flugge, bahiagrass	336,030	11–17
Festuca elatior L., meadow fescue	507,150	11–28	*Paspalum plicatulum* Michx., brownseed paspalum	698,985	11–17
Festuca myuros L., rattail fescue (w)	908,460	...	*Paspalum stamineum* Nash., sand paspalum	568,890	6–11
Festuca octoflora Walt., sixweeks fescue (w)	2,127,825	...	*Paspalum urvillei* Steud., vaseygrass	970,200	11–22
Festuca ovina L., sheep fescue	1,499,400	17–28	*Pennisetum purpureum* Schumach., napiergrass	3,091,410	vegetative
Festuca rubra L., red fescue	1,356,075	17–45	*Pennisetum typhoides* (Burm.) Stapf & C. E. Hubb., pearl-millet	194,040	22–34
Festuca rubra var. *commutata* Gaud., chewings fescue	1,356,075	17–45	*Phalaris aquatica* L., hardinggrass	782,775	28–34
Hilaria belangeri (Steud.) Nash., curly mesquite	593,145	4–9	*Phalaris arundinacea* L., reed canarygrass	1,175,265	6–11
Hilaria jamesii (Torr.) Benth., galletagrass	350,595	4–9	*Phalaris canariensis* L., canarygrass	149,940	28–34
Hilaria mutica (Buckl.) Benth., tobosa	588,735	4–9	*Phalaris caroliniana* Walt., Carolina canarygrass	945,945	11–17
Hilaria rigida (Thurb.) Benth., big galletagrass	72,765	...	*Phleum pratense* L., timothy	2,712,150	7–13
Holcus lanatus L., common velvetgrass	3,360,420	11–28	*Poa ampla* Merr., big bluegrass	1,944,810	7–11
Hordeum bulbosum L., bulbous barley	110,250	9–13	*Poa annua* L., annual bluegrass	2,637,180	17–28
Hordeum vulgare L., barley	30,870	67–101	*Poa arachnifera* Torr., Texas bluegrass	4,132,170	4–7
Hyparrhenia hirta (L.) Stapf	1,353,870	6–11	*Poa bulbosa* L., bulbous bluegrass	1,020,915	22–28
Hyparrhenia rufa (Nees.) Stapf, jaragua	1,558,935	6–11	*Poa compressa* L., Canada bluegrass	5,501,475	17–28
Imperata cylindrica (L.) Beauv., cogongrass	...	vegetative	*Poa nevadensis* Vasey ex. Scribn., Nevada bluegrass	2,385,810	7–11
Koeleria cristata (L.) Pers., junegrass	...	9–13			
Lolium multiflorum Lam., Italian ryegrass	500,535	28–39	*Poa pratensis* L., Kentucky bluegrass	4,800,285	17–28
Lolium perenne L., perennial ryegrass	500,535	28–39			

69

TABLE 7.3 *& (Continued)*

Scientific and common name	Number of seed per kg	Seeding rate (kg/ha)	Scientific and common name	Number of seed per kg	Seeding rate (kg/ha)
Poa secunda Presl., Sandberg bluegrass	2,039,625	7–11	*Sporobolus giganteus* Nash, giant dropseed	3,799,215	2–4
Poa trivialis L., rough bluegrass	5,600,700	17–28	*Sporobolus wrightii* Munro. ex. Scribn., sacaton	4,332,825	2–4
Puccinellia nuttalliana Hitchc., Nuttall alkaligrass	4,648,140	7–11	*Stenotaphrum secundatum* (Walt.) Kuntze, saint augustinegrass	...	vegetative
Redfieldia flexuosa (Thurb.) Vasey, blowoutgrass	579,915	vegetative	*Stipa comata* Trin. & Rupr., needle-and-thread	253,575	9–13
Saccharum officinarum L., sugarcane	...	vegetative	*Stipa viridula* Trin., green needlegrass	399,105	9–13
Secale cereale, L., rye	39,690	101–179			
Setaria italica (L.) Beauv., foxtail millet	485,100	22–34	*Trichcahne californica* (Benth.) Chase, Arizona cottontop	1,583,190	...
Setaria macrostachya H.B.K., plains bristlegrass	672,525	4–7	*Tricholaena rosea* Nees., natalgrass	1,104,705	4–9
Sorghastrum nutans (L.) Nash, indiangrass	385,875	11–17	*Tridens flavus* (L.) Hitchc., purpletop	1,025,325	4–7
Sorghum halepense (L.) Pers., johnsongrass	260,190	11–28	*Tripsacum dactyloides* (L.) L., eastern gamagrass	16,052	vegetative
Sorghum bicolor (L.) Moench, sorghum	61,740	17–84	*Triticum aestivum* L., wheat	33,075	67–168
Sorghum bicolor (L.) Moench, sudangrass	121,275	17–84	*Uniola latifolia* Michx., broadleaf uniola (o)	207,270	...
Sporobolus airoides Torr., alkali sacaton	3,876,390	4–7	*Zea mays* L., corn	2,465	7–11
Sporobolus asper (Michx.) Kunth., tall dropseed	1,109,115	4–7	*Zizania aquatica* L., annual wildrice	25,005	56–112
Sporobolus asper var. *hookeri* (Trin.) Vasey, meadow dropseed	1,814,715	4–7	*Zoysia japonica* Steud., Japanese lawngrass	2,866,500	vegetative
			Zoysia matrella (L.) Merr., manilagrass	1,501,605	vegetative
Sporobolus cryptandrus (Torr.) A. Gray, sand dropseed	11,682,090	2–4	*Zoysia tenuifolia* Willd. ex Trin., mascarenegrass	...	vegetative

Source: Data on the seed and culture of common grasses and legumes—USDA yearbook. 1948. *Grass,* pp. 743–58.

* = in burs or unhulled.

w = weedy in character.

o = ornamentals.

70

Scientific and common name	Number of seed per kg	Weight (kg/hl)	Seeding rate (kg/ha, broad-cast)	Scientific and common name	Number of seed per kg	Weight (kg/hl)	Seeding rate (kg/ha, broad-cast)
Alysicarpus vaginalis (L.) DC., alyceclover	661,500	77	11–13	*Lathyrus hirsutus*, L., roughpea	33,075	71	56–67
Anthyllis vulneraria, L., kidneyvetch	396,900	77	17–22	*Lathyrus sativus*, L., grasspea	11,025	77	78–90
Arachis hypogaea, L., peanut	2,205	28*	45†	*Lathyrus sylvestris*, L., flatpea	17,640	77	67–78
Astragalus cicer, L., cicer milkvetch	286,650	77	22–28	*Lathyrus tingitanus*, L., Tangier-pea	11,025	77	73–90
Astragalus falcatus, Lam., sicklepod milkvetch	286,650	77	22–28	*Lens esculenta*, Moench, lentil	19,845	77	13–17†
Astragalus rubyi, Greene & Morris, ruby milkvetch	529,200	77	11–13	*Lespedeza bicolor*, Turcz., bicolor lespedeza	180,810	77	1–2†
Cajanus cajan (L.) Millsp., pigeonpea	17,640	77	9–11†	*Lespedeza cuneata* (Du-mont) G. Don., sericea lespedeza	771,750	77	11–19
Cassia tora, L., sickle senna	48,510	77	45–50	*Lespedeza cyrtobotrya*, Miq., bush lespedeza	143,325	77	1–2†
Chamaecrista fasciculata, Greene, showy partridge-pea	141,120	73	22–34	*Lespedeza hedysaroides*, (Pall.) Kitagawa, rush lespedeza	661,500	77	11–17
Cicer arietinum, L., garbanzo	2,205	69	22–34†	*Lespedeza latissima*, Nakai, decumbent lespedeza	661,500	77	11–17
Coronilla varia, L., varia crownvetch	242,550	71	17–22	*Lespedeza stipulacea*, Maxim., Korean lespedeza	496,125*	51*	11–17*
Crotalaria incana, L., shak crotalaria	187,425	77	17–20	*Lespedeza striata* (Thumb.) H. & A., common lespedeza	418,850*	32*	11–17*
Crotalaria intermedia, Kotschy, slenderleaf crotalaria	220,500	77	11–19	*Lotus corniculatus*, L., broadleaf birdsfoot trefoil	826,875	77	6–9
Crotalaria juncea, L., sunn crotalaria	33,075	77	39–45	*Lotus pedunculatus*, Cav., big trefoil	2,205,000	77	3–6
Crotalaria lanceolata, E. Mey., lance crotalaria	374,850	77	8–11	*Lotus tenuis*, Waldst. & Kit., narrowleaf birdsfoot trefoil	882,000	77	6–9
Crotalaria mucronata, Desv., striped crotalaria	165,375	77	11–17	*Lupinus albus*, L., white lupine	3,308	77	112–135
Crotalaria spectabilis, Roth, showy crotalaria	66,150	77	28–34	*Lupinus angustifolius*, L., blue lupine	5,513	77	78–112
Cyamopsis tetragonoloba (L.) Taub., guar	44,100	77	34–45	*Lupinus luteus*, Kell., yellow lupine	8,820	77	56–90
Dalea alopecuroides, Willd., foxtail dalea	330,750	77	11–17	*Lupinus subcarnosus*, Hook., bluebonnet	30,870	77	45–50*
Desmodium purpureum, Fawc. & Rend., tall tickclover	441,000	77	9–11	*Medicago arabica*, Huds., spotted burclover	463,050	13*	112*
Dolichos lablab, L., hyacinth bean	3,087	77	22–28†	*Medicago falcata*, L., yellow alfalfa	458,640	77	17–22
Glottidium vesicarium, Harper, bagpod	3,308	72	22–34†	*Medicago lupulina*, L., black medic	661,500	77	11–17
Glycine max (L.) Merr., soybean	11,025	77	50–67	*Medicago minima*, L., little burclover	8,820,000	13*	67*
Hedysarum coronarium, L., sulla	220,500	77	22–28	*Medicago orbicularis*, All., buttonclover	330,750	77	17–22
Indigofera hirsuta, L., hairy indigo	441,000	71	9–11				
Lathyrus cicer, Habl., flatpod peavine	17,640	77	67–78				

TABLE 7.4   (Continued)

Scientific and common name	Number of seed per kg	Weight (kg/hl)	Seeding rate (kg/ha, broadcast)	Scientific and common name	Number of seed per kg	Weight (kg/hl)	Seeding rate (kg/ha, broadcast)
Medicago polymorpha L. = *M. hispida*, Gaertn., California burclover	308,700	77	22–28	*Trifolium fragiferum*, L., strawberry clover	661,500	77	7–11
Medicago sativa, L., purple alfalfa	441,000	77	17–22	*Trifolium glomeratum*, L., cluster clover	2,205,000	77	3–4
Medicago scutellata, Mill., snail medic	94,815	19*	112*	*Trifolium hirtum*, All., rose clover	308,700	77	17–22
Melilotus alba, Desr., white sweetclover	573,340	77	11–17	*Trifolium hybridum*, L., alsike clover	1,543,500	77	7–9
Melilotus indica, All., sourclover	606,375	77	11–17	*Trifolium incarnatum*, L., crimson clover	308,700	77	17–22
Melilotus officinalis, (L.) Lam., yellow sweetclover	573,300	77	11–17	*Trifolium lappaceum*, L., lappa clover	1,499,400	77	4–6
Melilotus suaveolens, Ledeb., Daghestan sweetclover	551,250	77	11–17	*Trifolium nigrescens*, Viv., ball clover	2,205,000	77	2–4
Onobrychis viciifolia, Scop., sainfoin	66,150	71	34–39	*Trifolium pratense*, L., red clover	606,375	77	4–13
Ornithopus sativus, Brot., serradella	352,800	46*	17–22*	*Trifolium repens*, L., white clover	1,764,000	77	1–4
Phaseolus aconitifolius, Jacq., mat bean	44,100	77	39–45	*Trifolium resupinatum*, L., Persian clover	1,488,375	77	4–7
Phaseolus acutifolius, A. Gray, Texas bean	55,125	77	28–34	*Trifolium striatum*, L., knotted clover	509,355	77	9–13
Phaseolus angularis, Wight, adsuki bean	8,820	77	22–28†	*Trifolium subterraneum*, L., subterranean clover	143,325	77	22–28
Phaseolus aureus, Roxb., mung bean	22,050	77	67–78	*Trigonella foenum-graecum*, L., fenugreek	50,715	77	28–39
Phaseolus calcaratus, Roxb., rice bean	22,050	77	78–90	*Vicia articulata*, Hornem., one-flower (monantha) vetch	26,460	77	56–67
Pisum sativum subsp. *arvense* (L.) Poir., field pea	6,615	77	78–101	*Vicia benghalensis*, L., purple vetch	22,050	77	56–67
Pueraria phaseoloides, Benth., tropical kudzu	81,585	69	11–17†	*Vicia cracca*, L., bird vetch	88,200	77	34–39
Pueraria thunbergiana, Benth., Thunberg kudzu	88,200	69	7–11†	*Vicia dasycarpa*, Tenore, woollypod vetch	22,050	77	56–67
Sesbania exaltata (Raf.) Cory, hemp sesbania	88,200	77	22–28	*Vicia faba* var. *equina*, L., horsebean	6,615	77	90–112
Stizolobium deeringianum, Bort., velvetbean	2,205	77	34–45	*Vicia faba* var. *major*, L., broadbean	1,103	77	78–90†
Strophostyles helvola (L.) Ell., trailing wildbean	19,845	64	56–67	*Vicia grandiflora*, Scop., bigflower vetch	70,560	77	39–45
Trifolium agrarium, L., hop clover	2,205,000	77	4–6	*Vicia pannonica*, Crantz, Hungarian vetch	22,050	77	78–90
Trifolium alexandrinum, L., berseem clover	441,000	77	17–22	*Vicia sativa*, L., common vetch	15,435	77	78–90
Trifolium campestre, Schreb., large hop clover	4,410,000	77	3–4	*Vicia sativa*, L., var. *nigra* (L.) Ehrh., narrowleaf vetch	66,150	77	34–45
Trifolium dubium, Sibth., small hop clover	2,205,000	77	4–6	*Vicia villosa*, Roth, hairy vetch	44,100	77	45–50
				Vigna sinensis, (L.) Savi ex. Hassk., cowpea	6,615	77	22–34†

* Unhulled.
† Planted in rows 3 to 4 feet apart.

TABLE 7.5 ✕ U.S. production of all hay in thousands of tons and the leading kinds in percent of the total

Five-year average	All hay (000 t)	Tame hay			Wild hay (%)	Five-year average	All hay (000 t)	Tame hay			Wild hay (%)
		Leg- umes reported sepa- rately* (%)	Clo- ver and tim- othy† (%)	All other tame hay‡ (%)				Leg- umes reported sepa- rately* (%)	Clo- ver and tim- othy† (%)	All other tame hay‡ (%)	
1920–24	82,104	25	46	13	16	1950–54	97,213	53	26	11	10
1925–29	77,182	33	42	11	14	1955–57	103,668	61	20	11	8
1930–34	66,952	40	33	15	12	1958–62	106,638	62	20	10	8
1935–39	76,429	46	28	14	12	1965	113,638	62§	16	14	8
1940–44	87,481	48	28	13	11	1968	113,874	60	19	15	6
1945–49	90,838	45	31	12	12	1970	116,030	60	19	14	7
						1971§	118,801	59	. . .	41	. . .

Source: USDA. 1920–71. Agricultural statistics.

* Alfalfa, lespedeza, sweetclover, soybean, peanut vine, and cowpea exclusive of the clovers reported in "clover and timothy" hay.

†The legume percentage would be increasingly greater in more recent years and the clover and timothy percentage would be considerably smaller if statistics on clover hay grown alone were available and included.

‡ Grains cut green for hay with production reported as miscellaneous tame hay.

§ Beginning in 1965 cowpeas and soybeans are included in "other hay." Beginning in 1971 only two categories are reported.

TABLE 7.6 ❧ Hectarage and production of different kinds of hay in the U.S., 1958-62, 1965, 1970, 1971

Kinds of hay	Hectarage (000 ha)				Yield per hectare (t)				Production (000 t)			
	1958-62	1965	1970	1971	1958-62	1965	1970	1971	1958-62	1965	1970	1971
Alfalfa and mixtures	11,385	12,042	10,983	11,180	5.36	5.94	6.17	6.23	61,019	71,532	68,550	69,587
Clover and timothy and mixtures of clover and grasses	5,905	5,284	5,428	...	3.59	3.45	3.99	...	21,134	18,213	21,665	...
Wild*	4,451	4,085	3,608	...	2	2.13	2.11	...	8,910	8,738	7,591	...
Lespedeza†	1,333	938	573	...	2.74	2.91	3.27	...	3,678	2,727	1,872	...
Peanuts	200	181	122	...	1.52	1.57	1.73	...	307	285	210	...
Grain	1,369	1,128	1,203	...	2.65	3.18	3.18	...	3,597	3,579	3,836	...
Other‡	2,591	3,754	3,638	14,442	2.85	3.32	3.56	3.41	7,350	12,441	13,017	49,215
All§	27,448	27,412	25,479	25,622	3.88	4.15	4.55	4.64	106,632	113,886	115,636	118,802

Sources: USDA. 1967, 1969. Agricultural Statistics.
USDA. 1971. Crop production—annual summary. Crop Rep. Board, SRS.

* Includes prairie, marsh, and salt grasses.
† Additional quantites produced in other states and other years included in "other hay."
‡ In certain states "other" contains small quantities of specific kinds of hay for which separate estimates are not made. Beginning in 1965 cowpeas and soybeans are included in this category.
§ Beginning in 1971 all hay except alfalfa and alfalfa mixtures are included.

74

TABLE 7.7 ❧ States leading in the production of different kinds of hay, 1962–66, later years, and U.S. totals

Kind of hay and state	Hectarage harvested (000 ha)			Metric tons per ha		
	1962–66 average	1969	1970	1962–66 average	1969	1970
Clover and Timothy and Mixtures of Clover and Grasses						
New York	546	472	467	3.45	4.26	4.37
Missouri	526	500	459	2.96	3.81	3.70
Pennsylvania	467	440	449	3.09	3.92	4.04
Iowa	393	243	243	4.30	4.82	4.71
Ohio	379	428	420	3.45	4.15	4.04
Wisconsin	365	343	340	4.35	5.27	5.16
Illinois	265	155	171	3.88	4.26	4.48
Minnesota	241	242	242	3.56	3.81	3.81
Kentucky	222	315	315	3.23	4.26	4.04
Indiana	198	156	162	3.74	4.26	4.26
U.S.	5,534	5,358	5,428	3.43	4.01	3.99
Lespedeza						
Kentucky	205	146	143	2.85	3.59	3.70
Tennessee	189	124	124	2.78	2.80	3.03
Missouri	147	85	77	2.67	3.14	3.03
Arkansas	78	51	53	2.80	3.25	3.81
North Carolina	52	19	17	2.38	3.03	2.91
Mississippi	49	33	30	3.36	3.25	3.14
Virginia	40	23	22	2.24	3.36	3.14
Oklahoma	33	31	28	2.85	3.25	3.14
Alabama	30	23	22	2.71	2.91	2.91
Georgia	21	12	11	2.76	2.91	2.80
U.S.	933	599	573	2.76	3.18	3.27
Wild Hay						
Nebraska	1,068	907	925	1.68	1.68	1.57
South Dakota	842	649	714	1.68	1.79	1.79
North Dakota	642	528	533	2.26	2.13	2.13
Kansas	307	291	300	2.40	2.91	2.35
Montana	240	224	224	2.22	2.35	2.47
Minnesota	160	146	142	2.76	3.03	3.36
Wyoming	156	145	157	1.84	2.02	2.24
Colorado	116	113	128	2.31	2.58	2.69
Oregon	108	119	113	2.58	3.14	3.03
Nevada	86	82	89	2.22	2.69	2.13
U.S.	4,171	3,489	3,608	2.06	2.17	2.11
Kind of hay and state	1962–66 average	1969	1971	1962–66 average	1969	1971
Alfalfa and Alfalfa Mixtures						
Wisconsin	1,168	1,198	1,222	5.63	6.50	6.39
Minnesota	989	925	907	5.76	6.61	6.73
South Dakota	878	907	995	3.39	3.70	3.48
Iowa	857	736	714	6.05	7.17	6.95
Nebraska	736	705	709	5.36	6.05	6.05
Michigan	541	449	446	4.66	5.27	4.71
North Dakota	522	509	566	3.61	3.48	3.81
Kansas	505	456	478	5.45	6.50	6.17
New York	494	435	458	4.91	5.72	5.83
California	465	457	490	12.24	12.33	12.78
U.S.	11,734	10,895	11,180	5.56	6.30	6.23
All Hay						
Nebraska	1,938	1,753	1,698	3.16	3.61	3.77
South Dakota	1,883	1,746	1,892	2.56	2.87	2.74
Wisconsin	1,605	1,629	1,655	5.25	6.10	6.01
Minnesota	1,435	1,351	1,316	5.00	5.65	5.74
North Dakota	1,432	1,335	1,324	2.89	2.76	3.05
Iowa	1,302	1,036	992	5.43	6.43	6.34

TABLE 7.7. *⅍* *(Continued)*

Kind of hay and state	Hectarage harvested (000 ha)			Metric tons per ha		
	1962–66 average	1969	1971	1962–66 average	1969	1971
Missouri	1,215	1,149	1,216	3.59	4.44	3.95
New York	1,181	1,049	1,053	4.01	4.78	4.93
Kansas	989	967	1,003	4.10	4.80	4.75
Montana	949	980	972	3.39	3.59	3.68
U.S.	27,069	25,131	25,622	4.06	4.62	4.64
	1968–69	1970		1968–69	1970	
Grain Hay						
California	173	188		4.15	4.04	
Texas	91	122		2.58	2.58	
Montana	89	113		2.91	2.69	
South Dakota	78	72		2.47	2.47	
North Dakota	71	70		2.87	2.58	
Oregon	51	61		2.98	3.14	
Colorado	50	49		3.03	2.69	
Nebraska	45	41		2.35	2.80	
Tennessee	43	35		3.36	3.25	
Missouri	42	41		3.21	3.36	
U.S.	1,133	1,203		3.25	3.18	
Peanuts						
Texas	36	36		1.12	1.35	
Alabama	22	19		1.52	1.57	
Oklahoma	22	24		1.52	1.68	
Georgia	18	14		1.82	1.73	
North Carolina	15	13		2.35	2.58	
Florida	9	9		1.91	1.91	
Virginia	7	6		2.09	2.58	
U.S.	129	122		1.59	1.73	

Sources: USDA. 1969, 1970, 1971. Agricultural statistics.
USDA. 1972. Crop production annual summary. Crop. Rep. Board, SRS.

TABLE 7.8 ❧ Percentage of specified feeds including pasture consumed by different kinds of U.S. livestock, 1940–69 averages (feeds measured in feed units)

Period	Milk cows	Other dairy cattle	Grain-fattened cattle	Other beef cattle	Sheep and goats	All poultry	Hogs	Horses and mules	Other livestock	Unallocated	Total
All feed, including pastures (%)											
1940–44	21.9	8.0	3.2	19.4	7.4	9.3	18.4	10.5	1.3	0.6	100
1950–54	21.5	8.0	5.2	26.8	4.2	10.6	17.4	4.5	1.8	..	100
1960–64	20.0	5.7	7.3	30.9	4.0	10.1	16.9	2.1	2.8	1.0	100
1965–69	17.4	4.2	10.5	33.5	3.0	10.7	15.4	1.9	2.6	0.8	100
All concentrates (%)											
1940–44	14.4	3.6	5.0	2.6	1.0	22.3	40.7	7.7	2.7	..	100
1950–54	14.6	3.4	8.0	4.6	0.6	24.5	37.8	2.7	3.8	..	100
1960–64	15.2	2.3	12.0	5.7	0.8	22.7	33.7	1.0	4.4	2.2	100
1965–69	14.2	1.6	16.3	6.0	0.6	23.6	29.7	0.8	5.5	1.7	100
All roughage, including pasture (%)*											
1940–44	27.4	11.1	1.9	32.1	12.3	..	2.2	12.7	0.3	..	100
1950–54	26.7	11.4	3.0	44.0	7.0	..	1.7	6.0	0.2	..	100
1960–64	23.7	8.2	3.8	50.0	6.5	..	4.7	2.9	0.2	..	100
1965–69	20.0	6.3	5.8	55.5	4.9	..	4.5	2.7	0.3	..	100
All harvested roughage (%)											
1940–44	43.2	9.4	3.5	18.7	5.4	..	..	19.0	0.8	..	100
1950–54	45.0	10.3	5.8	27.8	3.1	..	..	7.4	0.6	..	100
1960–64	46.3	9.7	9.1	29.4	1.4	..	..	3.5	0.6	..	100
1965–69	39.3	7.9	13.9	33.8	1.1	..	..	3.0	1.0	..	100
Hay (%)											
1940–44	46.2	9.8	3.8	11.7	6.0	..	..	21.3	1.2	..	100
1950–54	46.1	12.1	6.2	25.4	3.5	..	..	5.7	1.0	..	100
1960–64	45.2	11.4	8.8	29.8	1.1	..	..	2.8	0.9	..	100
1965–69	33.9	9.4	13.2	38.4	1.0	..	..	2.6	1.5	..	100
Pasture (%)*											
1940–44	19.4	12.0	1.1	38.9	15.8	..	3.3	9.5	..	..	100
1950–54	16.3	12.1	1.5	53.1	9.1	..	2.8	5.1	..	..	100
1960–64	12.7	7.5	1.2	60.0	9.0	..	7.0	2.6	..	..	100
1965–69	10.0	5.5	1.7	66.7	6.8	..	6.8	2.5	..	..	100

Sources: USDA. 1940–59. Consumption of feed by livestock. Prod. Res. Rept. 79.
Correspondence. 1972.
* Poultry and hogs combined.

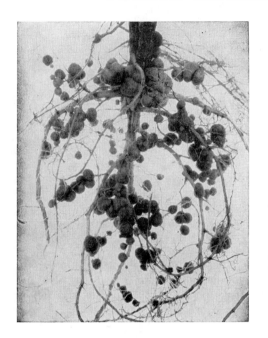

DARREL S. METCALFE / *University of Arizona*

8

THE BOTANY OF GRASSES AND LEGUMES

❧

Our principal forages are largely in the two botanical families, the grasses, Gramineae, and the legumes, Leguminosae.

THE GRASSES

The grasses are grouped into about 600 genera with nearly 5000 species.[1] Of these, about 150 genera and 1500 species are found growing in the U.S.[2] They have a wider range than any other family of flowering plants. The grass family includes about 75% of the cultivated forage crops and all the cereal crops.

❧ DESCRIPTION

Grasses are either annuals or perennials. Almost all are herbaceous (non-woody) plants. The grasses are monocotyledons as distinguished from legumes which are dicotyledons. This distinction between the two groups is based on the structure of the embryo. The major root-stem axis of the embryo carries lateral members known as cotyledons or seed leaves; monocotyledons have only one cotyledon, while dicotyledons have two.

In size the grasses range from a few centimeters to 20 m or more in height. Bamboo attains the greatest size; but corn, sugarcane, and sorghum are also repre-

❧ DARREL S. METCALFE. *See Chapter 7.*

sentative of the larger species of grasses. The organs of the grasses are the stems, roots, and leaves. Modified stems and leaves make up the inflorescences and fruits.[2-4]

❧ MORPHOLOGY

The organs of grasses undergo many modifications from the usual or typical structure. However, they have certain common characteristics.

❧ GROWTH STAGE TERMS

Table 8.1 outlines terms used to identify various growth stages of grasses when harvested.

LEAVES

The leaves are borne on the stem, alternately in two rows, one at each node. The leaf consists of sheath, blade, and ligule (Fig. 8.1, G and J). The sheath surrounds the stem above the node. The margins of the sheath usually are overlapping (open), though they sometimes are

1. Hitchcock, A. S. 1951. Manual of the grasses of the United States. USDA Misc. Publ. 200, rev.
2. Chase, Agnes. 1937. First Book of Grasses, rev. ed. Silveus, San Antonio, Tex.
3. Leithead, Horace L., Lewis L. Yarlett, and Thomas N. Shiflet. 1971. 100 native forage grasses in 11 southern states. USDA Agr. Handbook 389.
4. Gould, Frank W. 1968. Grass Systematics. McGraw-Hill, New York.

TABLE 8.1 ❧ Growth stage terms for grasses and legumes

Terminology	Definition
Grasses	
First Growth	
Vegetative	Leaves only, stems not elongated. (Specify extended leaf length and if seedling or older plants.)
Stem elongation	Stems elongated. (Specify early or late jointing depending on less than or more than one-half the leaves exposed, respectively.)
Boot	Inflorescence enclosed in flag leaf sheath and not showing.
Heading	Inflorescence emerging or emerged from flag leaf sheath but not shedding pollen. (Specify proportion emerged.)
Anthesis	Flowering stage, anthers shedding pollen. (Specify if early or late anthesis.)
Milk stage	Seeds immature, endosperm milky. (Specify if early or late milk.)
Dough stage	Well-developed seeds, endosperm doughy. (Specify if early or late dough.)
Ripe seed	Seeds ripe, leaves green to yellow brown.
Postripe seed	Seeds postripe, some dead leaves and some heads shattered. (Specify amount of dead leaf tissue.)
Stem-cured	Leaves cured on stem, seeds mostly cast. (Specify if frosted.)
Regrowth*	
Vegetative	Leaves only, stems not elongated. (Specify extended leaf length.)
Jointing	Green leaves and elongated stems. (Specify if before or after killing frost.)
Late growth	Leaves and stems weathered. (State age of growth and time of year; specify if before or after killing frost.)
Legumes†	
Spring and Summer Growth	
Vegetative (or prebud)	No buds. (Specify plant height and if seedling or older plants.)
Bud	No flowers. (Specify early or late bud based on the condition of the floral buds.)
First flower	First flowers appear on plants.
Bloom (flower)	Plants flowering. (Specify percent of stems with one or more flowers; determine from 100 randomly selected stems.)
Pod (or green seed) development	Green seedpods developing. (Specify percent of stems with one or more green seedpods formed; estimate amount of leaf loss if any.)
Ripe seed	Mostly mature brown seedpods with lower leaves dead and some leaf loss. (Estimate amount of leaf loss.)
Fall Recovery Growth	Vegetative or with floral development. (Specify plant height and condition of floral development.)

Note: Specify date of observation, cutting number, days of regrowth, and species and cultivar. Dry matter percentage and extended leaf length measurements are recommended at all growth stages.
* If flowering occurs, use nomenclature outlined for first-growth forage.
† These growth stages best describe upright-growing legumes. For stoloniferous legumes like white clover specify if leaves and floral stems only are included or if stolons are also.

united (closed) into a cylinder for a part or all of the distance to the blade.

The blades are parallel veined and typically flat, narrow, and sessile. Some grasses have auricles or earlike appendages projecting from the leaf edges at the junction of the sheath and blade. The ligule is the appendage that clasps the stem where the sheath and blade join (Fig. 8.1 G). The ligule may be a membrane, a fringe of hair, or a hardened ring. The collar is the region at the junction of the sheath and blade.

STEMS

The jointed stem of a grass is distinctly divided into nodes and internodes. The internode may be either hollow, pithy, or solid. The node or joint is always solid. The leaves have their vascular connections with the stem at the node. Lateral buds arise in the axils of the leaves. These lat-

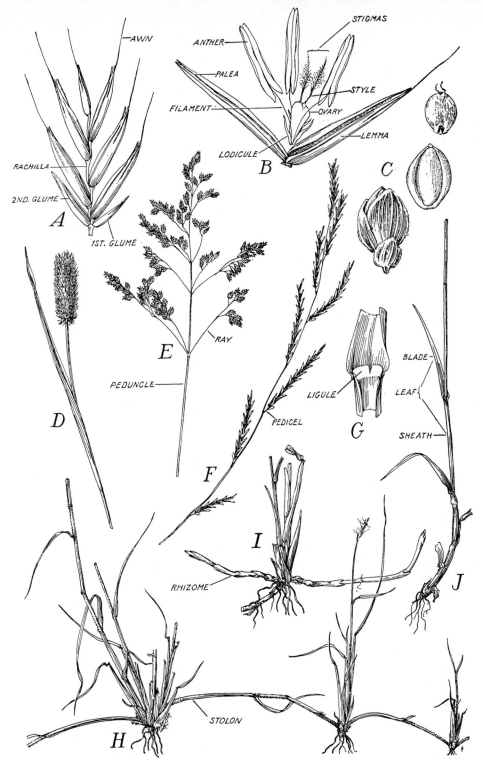

Fig. 8.1. Characteristic growth of grass plant parts: (A) Flowers in a spikelet arranged on a central axis enclosed in two empty glumes or bracts. (B) The different parts of a grass flower. (C) The developed fruit or seed, a caryopsis. The caryopsis is shown successively enclosed in the outer glumes, with the lemma and palea both closely adhering and free. (D) Spikelets arranged in a terminal spike. (E) Spikelets arranged in a panicle. (F) Spikelets in a raceme. (G) A ligule at the junction of the leaf blade and leaf sheath. (H, I, J) Means of propagating or spreading: stolon, rhizome, and bulb respectively. *USDA Yearbook photo, 1948.*

eral buds may become vegetative (sucker) branches of the stem or flower shoots. Brace roots arise from the nodal meristem (keimring), a zone just above the node. The cells of the nodal meristem remain meristematic until the stem has progressed well toward maturity. It is because of the differential growth on the lower side of a lodged stem that such stems are able to turn upward and return to a partially erect position.

In addition to the vertical flowering stems or culms, many grasses have horizontal underground stems called rhizomes, characteristic of quackgrass, johnsongrass, Kentucky bluegrass, and many others (Fig. 8.1I). The rhizome is in most cases the overwintering part of perennial grasses.

Creeping stems above ground are called stolons (Fig. 8.1H). Stolons resemble rhizomes in that they have definite nodes and internodes and nodal meristems from which secondary structures arise. They are more "stemlike" than rhizomes in that they lie above ground and their leaves develop and function normally. Two of the best known stoloniferous grasses are buffalograss and bermudagrass. Certain grasses have thickened lower internodes in which food accumulates and from which new shoots arise, thus serving to perpetuate the plants through the winter or dormant season. These food storage internodes usually are known as corms. The timothy structure differs somewhat and is called the haplocorm.[5] Bulbous bluegrass has true bulbs.

Roots

Grasses have fibrous root systems. The primary grass root may persist for only a short time after germination, as in corn. An extensive system of secondary roots soon arises at the lower nodes of the young stem and comprises the major part of the permanent root system. Secondary roots sometimes form at nodes above the

5. Evans, Morgan W. 1958. Growth and development in certain economic grasses. Ohio Agr. Exp. Sta. Agron. Ser. 147.

ground, as in the case of corn (prop roots) or at the nodes of creeping stems (stolon).

Inflorescence

The unit of the grass inflorescence is the spikelet. The spikelets usually are in groups or clusters, which constitute the inflorescence (Fig. 8.1A). There are several types. The simplest is the raceme, in which case the spikelets are borne along an unbranched axis (Fig. 8.1F). A typical raceme in grasses is rare. The spike differs from the raceme in having sessile spikelets (Fig. 8.1D). Wheat and barley have spikes. The panicle is the most common type of grass inflorescence. Here the spikelets are pedicelled in a branched inflorescence (Fig. 8.1E). The panicle may be either open, diffuse, or contracted. The inflorescences of smooth bromegrass, Kentucky bluegrass, and redtop are panicles.

Specialization usually takes place in the spikelet, which has a variable number of flowers, ranging from one to many depending on the species. The axis of the spikelet is the rachilla. At the base of the spikelet two glumes or bracts are attached on opposite sides of the rachilla. They enclose the flowers of the spikelet.

Flowers

The grasses usually have small perfect flowers arranged in a spikelet (Fig. 8.1B). Below each flower are two bracts. The larger or outer one is the lemma; the smaller or inner one is the palea, which usually is enclosed by the lemma. Stamens vary from one to many, but three is the usual number. The single pistil has a one-celled ovary with one ovule. Two styles are commonly present, each with a feathery (plumose) stigma. The perianth consists of two or sometimes three minute scales called lodicules, located inside the lemma at the base of the flower. These lodicules help force open the lemma and palea at the time of anthesis and thus aid in pollination. The slender filaments bear two-celled anthers. Most grasses flower every year. However, some perennials that spread by rhizomes may cover extensive areas without flowering regularly. Typically, the grasses are adapted to cross pollination by wind, but many species are cleistogamous (self-pollinating in the bud), such as wheat, oats, and barley.

FRUIT OR CARYOPSIS

The fruit of the grasses usually is a caryopsis or kernel (8.1C). The single seed is grown fast to the ovary wall, forming a seedlike grain. The pericarp is the modified ovary wall while the seed is the developed ovule. The caryopsis may be free from the lemma and palea, as in wheat, or it may be permanently enclosed, as in oats. The caryopsis may enlarge during ripening and greatly exceed the glumes, lemma, and palea, as in corn. The pericarp closely adheres to the seed and thus resembles a seed coat. A seed coat (testa), however, is an ovular structure while the pericarp is the modified ovary wall. The pericarp protects the seed against moisture loss, attacks of organisms, and injuries from fungicides and insecticides. The embryo (germ) lies on the side of the caryopsis next to the lemma and can easily be seen as an oval depression. The part of the caryopsis not occupied by the embryo is the endosperm in which food is stored. The embryo consists of a plumule, radicle, and scutellum. Following germination, the plumule develops into the above ground portion of the plant. The radicle develops into the primary root system, which anchors the seedling and absorbs water. During germination the scutellum or cotyledon of the germ secretes from its outer layer of cells certain enzymes that dissolve the stored food in the endosperm. This makes possible the movement of food materials into the plumule and radicle.

THE LEGUMES

There are nearly 500 genera and some 11,000 species of legumes, with almost 4000 species in America.[6]

6. Fernald, Merritt Lyndon. 1950. Gray's Manual of Botany. American Book Co., New York.

❧ DESCRIPTION

The legume family name, Leguminosae, is derived from the term "legume," which is the name of the type of fruit (pod) characteristic of plants of this family. A legume is a monocarpellary fruit that contains only a single row of seed and dehisces along both sutures or ribs.

As the legume plant grows, the symbiotic bacteria responsible for the formation of the nodules on the roots use the N in the air and multiply in the nodules. The N in turn becomes available to the legume plant and aids in its nourishment and growth.

Legumes are dicotyledons. They may be annuals, biennials, or perennials.

❧ MORPHOLOGY

Legume characteristics differ in many ways from those of grasses. Although rather distinct morphological differences exist between genera and between some species, there is much uniformity in the characteristic growth of cultivated legumes.

❧ GROWTH STAGE TERMS

Table 8.1 outlines terms used to identify various growth stages of legumes when harvested.

LEAVES

Leaves of legumes are arranged alternately and have characteristically large stipules. The leaves usually are either pinnately or palmately compound (Fig. 8.2).

STEMS

Stems of legumes vary greatly in the different species in length, size, amount of branching, and woodiness.

ROOTS

Most legumes, especially the herbaceous ones, have taproots. Most important, they nearly all have associated with their roots the N-fixing bacteria that replenish the nitrate supply in soil (Fig. 8.3).

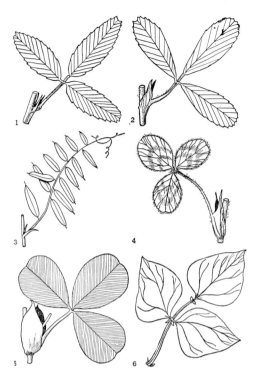

FIG. 8.2. Different types of legume leaves: (1) sweetclover, (2) alfalfa, (3) hairy vetch, (4) red clover, (5) Korean lespedeza, and (6) cowpea. (1 and 2 adapted from Isely, 1951.[7])

FIG. 8.3. The white clovers spread by means of stolons with roots at each node. Leaves and flower heads are borne on long unbranched stalks rising directly from the nodes of the stolons. (Adapted from Isely, 1951.[7])

INFLORESCENCE

Flowers usually are arranged either in racemes as in the pea, in heads as in clover, or in a spikelike raceme as in alfalfa.

FLOWERS

The flowers of the commoner naturally cross-pollinated species of legumes have corollas characteristically papilionaceous, or "butterflylike" (Fig. 8.4). These irregular flowers consist of five petals—a standard, two wings, and a keel consisting of two petals that are more or less united. The calyx normally is four or five toothed. The keel, so named for its boatlike shape, encloses the stigma and the stamens. There

7. Isley, Duane. 1951. The Leguminosae of the north central United States: Loteae and Trifolieae. *Iowa State Coll. J. Sci.* 25(3):439–82.

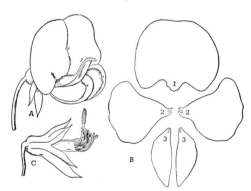

FIG. 8.4. (A) Typical legume flower. (B) The five petals separated (1—standard; 2—two wings; 3—keel, two united petals). (C) Five sepals and ten stamens (one free and nine partially united) and pistil with stigma.

are usually 10 stamens, 9 of which typically have their filaments joined, forming an envelope that encloses the long slender style and ovary. The stigma is not quite capitate or terminal but is somewhat oblique, i.e., extending slightly down the side. The corolla tube formed by the partial joining of the five petals varies in length in the different species. In red clover the corolla tube, sometimes 12 mm or more in length, is relatively long for the size of the flower. In alsike clover, white clover, sweetclover, and alfalfa the tube is much shorter than that of red clover.

Since nectar is secreted at the bottom of the corolla tube, the length of the corolla is a determining factor in the ability of bees and other insects to reach the nectar and thus is also a factor in the pollination of the flower. Some legumes, e.g., many of the beans and peas, are ordinarily autogamous (self-pollinating) and rather completely self-compatible. They pollinate their own stigmas and need no tripping for the pollen to reach the stigma. The pollen contacts the stigma as it rolls out of the opening anthers. In many legumes, the anthers are too far below the stigma for the pollen to contact it when the anthers open. These flowers must be tripped; that is, the keel must be pressed down until the anthers and stigma spring out of the keel and the pollen is flipped into the air and thus given an opportunity to fall back on the stigma. Other legumes, of which red clover is a good example, are self-sterile; therefore, the stigma must be fertilized with pollen from another plant, or no seed will be formed. In such legumes as sweetclover and alfalfa, which are at least in part self-sterile, the flower as a rule must be tripped for the pollen to reach the stigma.

FRUIT

The fruit is a pod containing one to several seed (Fig. 8.5). The seed usually are without an endosperm at maturity. In legume seed the reserve food is stored in the two cotyledons. The hilum is the scar where the seed has been detached from the pod. Near one end and between the edges of the cotyledons is the embryo axis, consisting of the plumule and radicle. Each seed is enclosed in the testa or seed coat. When germination starts, the radicle pushes out and down, developing into the root system. In this case the radicle gives

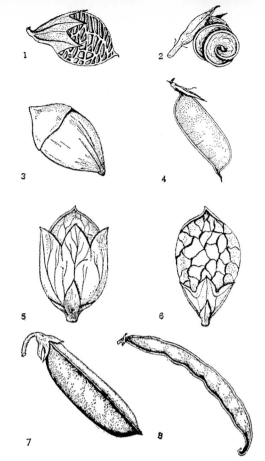

FIG. 8.5. Different types of legume seed and seedpods: (1) yellow sweetclover, (2) alfalfa, (3) red clover, (4) hairy vetch, (5) common lespedeza, (6) Korean lespedeza, (7) fieldpea, and (8) cowpea.

rise to the major part of the permanent root system. The plumule develops into the above ground portion of the plant.

GROWTH STAGE TERMINOLOGY

The feeding value of forages is greatly influenced by the growth stage when harvested. There is a need for uniform terminology to describe growth stages. Table 8.1 is based upon terms to be used in international feed nomenclature.[8,9] Terms for legumes and grasses are slightly different; however, growth stages are divided into three major divisions for both groups: vegetative growth, flowering, and seed

8. Crampton, E. W., and L. E. Harris. 1969. United States–Canadian tables of feed composition, 2nd rev. Natl. Acad. Sci., Natl. Res. Council Publ. 1684.
9. Harris, L. E., J. M. Asplund, and E. W. Crampton. 1968. An international feed nomenclature and methods for summarizing and using feed data to calculate diets. Utah State Univ. Agr. Exp. Sta. Bull. 479.

formation. Postripe and stem-cured stages are included for grasses since they may be harvested beyond the ripe-seed stage under some management systems. Percentages of inflorescences emerging in grasses are recommended rather than specifying early, mid, or late heading. Similarly for legumes, the percentage of stems with one or more flowers should be indicated for bloom or flowering, and a percentage of stems with one or more green seedpods should be indicated for the pod or green-seed development stage.

COMMON AND BOTANICAL NAMES

The accompanying list shows many of the common and scientific names of grasses, legumes, and certain other plants discussed in this book. Many forage crop plants are known by different names in different sections of the U.S.[1,3,6,10-13] The approved common names, listed alphabetically, are written with the first letter of the name capitalized, for example, Alfalfa;

other forms in use but not approved are in italics, *beardgrass* (Bluestem). In this list of scientific names, the genus is in capital letters *(MEDICAGO)*; the species listed under each genus is in lowercase italics *(sativa).* A plant is known by its genus and species. The initial letter of the first or "generic" name is always capitalized; the second or "species" name is written with a lowercase initial letter. The genus corresponds roughly to a last name and the species to a first name, as *Zea mays* would to Brown, John. The scientific name may be followed by the abbreviation of the name of the person who first named the species. Thus, *Zea mays* L. means that this species was named by the great Swedish botanist Linnaeus.

10. Hanson, A. A. 1972. Grass varieties in the United States. USDA Agr. Handbook 170, rev.
11. Kelsey, Harlan P., and William A. Dayton. 1942. Standardized Plant Names. J. Horace McFarland, Harrisburg, Pa.
12. USDA. 1948. Grass. Yearbook Agr.
13. International Code of Nomenclature for Cultivated Plants. 1969. Int. Bur. Plant Taxonomy and Nomenclature of the Int. Assoc. for Plant Taxonomy. Utrecht, Netherlands.

COMMON NAMES	SCIENTIFIC NAMES
Alfalfa	*MEDICAGO sativa* L.
Purple	*sativa* L.
Yellow	*falcata* L.
Variegated	*sativa media*
Alkaligrass, Nuttall	*PUCCINELLIA nuttalliana* Hitchc.
Alyceclover	*ALYSICARPUS vaginalis* (L.) DC.
Bagpod	*GLOTTIDIUM vesicarium* Harper
Bahiagrass	*PASPALUM notatum* Flugge
Balsamroot, Arrowleaf	*BALSAMORHIZA sagittata* Nutt.
Barley	*HORDEUM vulgare* L.
Bulbous	*bulbosum* L.
Foxtail	*jubatum* L.
Meadow	*nodosum* L.
Beachgrass	*AMMOPHILA* Host.
American	*breviligulata* Fernald.
European	*arenaria* (L.) Link
Bean	*PHASEOLUS* L.
Adsuki	*angularis* Wight
Mat *(moth)*	*aconitifolius* Jacq.
Mung	*aureus* Roxb.
Rice	*calcaratus* Roxb.
Siratro	*atropurpureus* DC.
Tepary	*acutifolius* var. *latifolius* Freem.
Texas	*acutifolius* A. Gray
beardgrass (Bluestem)	*ANDROPOGON* L.
beardgrass, prairie (Little bluestem)	*scoparius* Michx.
beardgrass, silver (Silver bluestem)	*saccharoides* Swartz.

COMMON NAMES	SCIENTIFIC NAMES
beardgrass, yellow (Turkestan bluestem)	*ischaemum* L.
Beggarweed; Tickclover	*DESMODIUM* Desv.
beggarweed, Florida (Tall tickclover)	*purpureum* Fawc. & Rend.
Bentgrass	*AGROSTIS* L.
Cloud	*nebulosa* Boiss. & Reut.
Colonial	*tenuis* Sibth.
Creeping	*palustris* Huds.
Velvet	*canina* L.
Winter	*hiemalis* (Walt.) B.S.P.
Bermudagrass	*CYNODON dactylon* (L.) Pers.
big bluejoint (Big bluestem)	*ANDROPOGON gerardi* Vitman
Blowoutgrass	*REDFIELDIA flexuosa* (Thurb.) Vasey
Bluebonnet; Texas lupine	*LUPINUS subcarnosus* Hook.
Bluegrass	*POA* L.
Annual	*annua* L.
Big	*ampla* Merr.
Bulbous	*bulbosa* L.
Canada	*compressa* L.
Kentucky	*pratensis* L.
Mutton	*fendleriana* Vasey
Nevada	*nevadensis* Vasey ex Scribn.
Rough; Roughstalk	*trivialis* L.
Sandberg	*secunda* Presl.
Texas	*arachnifera* Torr.
Upland	*glaucantha* Gaudin
winter (Bulbous)	*bulbosa* L.
bluejoint (Bluejoint reedgrass)	*CALAMAGROSTIS canadensis* (Michx.) Beauv.
bluejoint turkeyfoot (Big bluestem)	*ANDROPOGON gerardi* Vitman
Bluestem	*ANDROPOGON* L.
Big	*gerardi* Vitman
Broomsedge	*virginicus* L.
Cane	*barbinodis** Lag.
Caucasian	*caucasius* Trin.
Little	*scoparius* Michx.
Sand	*hallii* Hack.
Silver	*saccharoides** Swartz.
Slender	*tener* (Nees) Kunth.
Splitbeard	*tenarius* Michx.
Turkestan	*ischaemum* L.
yellowsedge (Broomsedge)	*virginicus* L.
bluetop (Bluejoint reedgrass)	*CALAMAGROSTIS canadensis* (Michx.) Beauv.
Bristlegrass; Millet	*SETARIA* Beauv.
Plains	*macrostachya* H.B.K.
Broadbean	*VICIA faba* var. *major* L.
Bromegrass	*BROMUS* L.
California	*carinatus* Hook. & Arn.
Cheatgrass	*tectorum* L.
Chess	*secalinus* L.
downy (Cheatgrass); Broncograss	*tectorum* L.
Field	*arvensis* L.
Fringed	*ciliatus* L.
Hairy chess	*commutatus* Schrad.
Japanese	*japonicus* Thunb.
Meadow	*bilbersteinii* Roem. & Schult.

* *ANDROPOGON* or *BOTHRIOCHLOA*

88

COMMON NAMES	SCIENTIFIC NAMES
Mountain	*marginatus* Nees.
Nodding	*anomalus* Rupr.
Prairie (Rescuegrass)	*catharticus* Vahl.
Pumpelly	*pumpellianus* Scribn.
Ripgutgrass	*rigidus* Roth
Smooth	*inermis* Leyss.
Soft chess	*mollis* L.
Broomcorn	Sorghum *vulgare* var. *technicum* (Koern.) Jav.
Brunswickgrass	*PASPALUM nicorae* Parodi.
Buffalograss	*BUCHLOE dactyloides* (Nutt.) Engelm.
Buffelgrass	*PENNISETUM ciliare* (L.) Link = CENCHRUS *ciliare* (L.) Link
Burclover; Lucerne; Medic	*MEDICAGO* L.
Burclover	*hispida* Gaertn.
California	*polymorpha* L. = *hispida* Gaertn.
Little; Little medic	*minima* L.
southern (Spotted)	*arabica* All.
Spotted *(spotted medic)*	*arabica* All.
Tifton	*rigidula* Bourg. ex Nym.
Burroweed	*HAPLOPAPPUS tenuisectus* (Greene) Blake ex Benson
Buttonclover; Button medic	*MEDICAGO orbicularis* All.
Cabbage	*BRASSICA oleracea* L.
Caleypea (Roughpea)	*LATHYRUS hirsutus* L.
Canarygrass	*PHALARIS canariensis* L.
Carolina	*caroliniana* Walt.
Hardinggrass	*aquatica* L.
Koleagrass	*tuberosa hirtiglumis* Batt. & Trab.
Littleseed	*minor* Retz.
Reed	*arundinacea* L.
Sunolgrass	*coerulescens* Desf.
Caribgrass	*ERIOCHLOA polystachya* H.B.K.
Carpetgrass	*AXONOPUS* Beauv.
Common	*affinis* Chase
Tropical	*compressus* (Swartz.) Beauv.
catclaw (Acacia)	*ACACIA greggi* A. Gray
Centipedegrass	*EREMOCHLOA ophiuroides* (Munro) Hack.
Centro	*CENTROSEMA pubescens* Benth.
cheat, downy (Cheatgrass bromegrass; Cheatgrass)	*BROMUS tectorum* L.
Cheatgrass; Cheatgrass bromegrass	*tectorum* L.
Chess	*secalinus* L.
Chess, hairy	*commutatus* Schrad.
Chickpea; Garbanzo	*CICER arietinum* L.
Chloris	*CHLORIS* Swartz.
Weeping	*distichophylla* Lag.
Clover	*TRIFOLIUM* L.
Alsike	*hybridum* L.
Arrowleaf	*vesiculosum* Savi
Ball	*nigrescens* Viv.
Berseem *(Egyptian)*	*alexandrinum* L.
Bigflower	*michelianum* Savi
Buffalo	*reflexum* L.
Carolina	*carolinianum* Michx.
Caucasian (Kura)	*ambiguum* Bieb.
Cluster	*glomeratum* L.

COMMON NAMES	SCIENTIFIC NAMES
Crimson	*incarnatum* L.
Egyptian (Berseem)	*alexandrinum* L.
Hollyleaf	*gymnocarpon* Nutt.
Hop (field)	*agrarium* L.
Hungarian	*pannonicum* Jacq.
Kura	*ambiguum* Bieb.
Ladino	*repens* L.
Lappa	*lappaceum* L.
Large hop *(low hop)*	*campestre* Schreb.
least hop (Small hop)	*dubium* Sibth.
Longstalk	*longipes* Nutt. & Gray
Parry	*parryi* Gray
pellett (Kura)	*ambiguum* Bieb.
Persian	*resupinatum* L.
Rabbitfoot	*arvense* L.
red (Zigzag)	*medium* L.
Red—medium; mammoth	*pratense* L.
Rose	*hirtum* All.
seaside (Sierra)	*willdenovii* Spreng.
shaftal (Persian)	*resupinatum* L.
Sierra *(seaside)*	*willdenovii* Spreng. (T. Wormskioldii Lehm.)
Small hop *(least hop)*	*dubium* Sibth.
Strawberry	*fragiferum* L.
Striata *(knotted)*	*striatum* L.
Subterranean	*subterraneum* L.
Whiproot	*dasyphyllum* Torr. & Gray & Parry
White *(white dutch, common)*	*repens* L.
Whitetip	*variegatum* Nutt. ex Torr. & Gray
Zigzag	*medium* L.
cocksfoot (Orchardgrass)	*DACTYLIS glomerata* L.
Cogongrass; Cogon satintail	*IMPERATA cylindrica* (L.) Beauv.
Columbusgrass	*SORGHUM almum* Parodi.
Cordgrass	*SPARTINA* Schreb.
California (Spike)	*leiantha (S. foliosa)* Benth.
Prairie (ripgut)	*pectinata* Link
Spike *(California)*	*leiantha (S. foliosa)* Benth.
Corn; Maize	*ZEA mays* L.
Cottontop, Arizona	*TRICHACHNE californica* (Benth.) Chase
Cowpea	*VIGNA sinensis* (L.) Savi ex Hassk.
Crabgrass, hairy	*DIGITARIA sanguinalis* (L.) Scop.
crabgrass, spreading ('Pangola' digitgrass)	*decumbens* Stent.
Creosotebush	*LARREA tridentata* (DC.) Coville
Crotalaria	*CROTALARIA* L.
Lance	*lanceolata* E. Mey.
Shak	*incana* L.
Showy	*spectabilis* Roth.
Slenderleaf	*intermedia* Kotschy
Striped	*mucronata (C. striata)* Desv.
Sunn	*juncea* L.
Crownvetch	*CORONILLA varia* L.
Curly mesquite	*HILARIA belangeri* (Steud.) Nash.
Dalea; Foxtail	*DALEA alopecuroides* Willd.
Dallisgrass	*PASPALUM dilatatum* Poir.
Danthonia	*DANTHONIA* Lam. & DC.
Oatgrass; California	*californica* Boland

COMMON NAMES	SCIENTIFIC NAMES
Poverty; Povertygrass	*spicata* (L.) Beauv.
Deertongue	*PANICUM clandestinum* L.
Deervetch	*LOTUS* L.
Wetland; Big trefoil	*pedunculatus* Cav.
Desmodium	*DESMODIUM* Desv.
greenleaf	*aparines* (Link) DC. = *intortum* (Mill) Urb.
silverleaf	*uncinatum* (Jack.) DC.
Digitgrass	*DIGITARIA* Stent.
'Kuruman'	*seriata* Stent.
Pangola	*decumbens* Stent.
'Slenderstem'	*pentzii* Stent.
Dogtail, crested	*CYNOSURUS cristatis* L.
Dropseed	*SPOROBOLUS* R. Br.
Blue; Pineywoods	*gracilis* (Trin.) Merr. = *(S. junceus)* (Michx.) Kunth.
Giant	*giganteus* Nash.
Meadow *(meadow tall)*	*asper* var. *hookeri* (Trin.) Vasey
Mesa	*flexuosus* (Thurb.) Rydb.
Pine	*BLEPHARONEURON tricholepis* (Torr.) Nash.
Pineywoods; Blue	*SPOROBOLUS gracilis* (Trin.) Merr. = *S. junceus* (Michx.) Kunth.
Prairie	*heterolepis* (A. Gray) A. Gray
Sand	*cryptandrus* (Torr.) A. Gray
Spike	*contractus* Hitchc.
Tall	*asper* (Michx.) Kunth.
falcon-pea (Flatpod peavine)	*LATHYRUS cicer* Habl.
Fenugreek; Fenugreek trigonella	*TRIGONELLA foenum-graecum* L.
Fescue	*FESTUCA* L.
bluebunch (Idaho)	*idahoensis* Elmer
Chewings	*rubra* var. *commutata* Gaud.
Hard	*ovina* var. *duriuscula* (L.) Koch
Idaho	*idahoensis* Elmer
Meadow	*elatior* L.
Rattail	*myuros* L.
Red	*rubra* L.
Tall	*arundinacea* Schreb.
Sheep	*ovina* L.
Sixweeks	*octoflora* Walt.
Fingergrass	*DIGITARIA* Heister.
spreading (Pangola digitgrass)	*decumbens* Stent.
Flatpea (Wagner pea)	*LATHYRUS sylvestris* L.
foxtail (Millet; Bristlegrass)	*SETARIA* Beauv.
Foxtail	*ALOPECURUS* L.
Creeping (Reed)	*arundinaceus* Poir.
Meadow	*pratensis* L.
Galletagrass	*HILARIA jamesii* (Torr.) Benth.
Big	*rigida* (Thurb.) Benth.
Gamagrass, eastern	*TRIPSACUM dactyloides* (L.) L.
Garbanzo	*CICER arietinum* L.
Gardener's garters	*PHALARIS arundinacea* var. *picta* (L.) Asch. & Graebn.
Grama	*BOUTELOUA* Lag.
Black	*eriopoda* (Torr.) Torr.
Blue	*gracilis* (H.B.K.) Lag. ex Steud.
Hairy	*hirsuta* Lag.
Rothrock	*rothrockii* Vasey
Sideoats	*curtipendula* Michx.

91

COMMON NAMES	SCIENTIFIC NAMES
Slender	*filiformis* (Fourn.) Griffiths
Grasses	*GRAMINEAE* L.
Grasspea	*LATHYRUS sativus* L.
Graythorn	*CONDALIA lycioides* (A. Gray) Suesseng.
Greasewood	*SARCOBATUS* Kees
Guar	*CYAMOPSIS tetragonoloba* (L.) Taub.
Guava	*PSIDIUM guajava* L.
Guineagrass	*PANICUM maximum* L.
Hairgrass	*DESCHAMPSIA* Beauv.
Tufted	*caespitosa* (L.) Beauv.
Hardinggrass	*PHALARIS aquatica* L.
Herdgrass (Timothy)	*PHLEUM pratense* L.
Hilograss	*PASPALUM conjugatum* Bergius.
Hopsage	*GRAYIA* L.
Horsebean	*VICIA faba* var. *equina* L.
Hyacinth bean	*DOLICHOS lablab* L.
Indiangrass	*SORGHASTRUM nutans* (L.) Nash.
Indigo	*INDIGOFERA* L.
Hairy	*hirsuta* L.
Japanese millet	*ECHINOCHLOA crusgalli* var. *frumentacea* (Roxb.) Wight
Jaragua	*HYPARRHENIA rufa* (Nees.) Stapf
Johnsongrass	*SORGHUM halepense* (L.) Pers.
Jointgrass; American jointvetch	*AESCHYNOMENE americana* L.
Junegrass, Prairie junegrass	*KOELERIA cristata* (L.) Pers.
Kaimi clover	*DESMODIUM canum* (Gmel.) Schintz & Thellung
Kale	*BRASSICA oleracea* L.
Kidneyvetch	*ANTHYLLIS vulneraria* L.
Kikuyugrass	*PENNISETUM clandestinum* Hochst. ex Chiov.
Kleingrass	*PANICUM coloratum* Walt.
Koa	*ACACIA koa* A. Gray
Koa haole	*LEUCAENA leucocephala* (Lam.) de Wit.
Kohlrabi	*BRASSICA oleracea* var. *gongylodes* = *B. caulorapa* Pasq.
Kudzu *(kudzubean)*	*PUERARIA* DC.
Thunberg	*thunbergiana* Benth.
Tropical	*phaseoloides* Benth.
Lawngrass, Japanese	*ZOYSIA japonica* Steud.
lawngrass, Korean (Japanese Lawngrass)	*ZOYSIA japonica* Steud.
Legumes	*LEGUMINOSAE* L.
Lentil, common	*LENS culinaris* Medic (*L. esculenta* Moench)
Lespedeza	*LESPEDEZA* Michx.
Bicolor	*bicolor* Turcz.
Bush	*cyrtobotrya* Miq.
Common (striate)	*striata* (Thunb.) H. & A.
Decumbent	*latissima* Nakai
Korean	*stipulacea* Maxim.
Rush	*hedysaroides* (Pall.) Kitagawa
Sericea	*cuneata* (*sericea*) (Dumont) G. Dons.
Shrub (Bicolor)	*bicolor* Turcz.
Thunberg	*thungbergii* (DC.) Nakai
Lovegrass	*ERAGROSTIS* Beauv.
Boer	*chloromelas* Steud.
Lehmann	*lehmanniana* Nees.
Sand	*trichodes* (Nutt.) Wood
Weeping	*curvula* (Schrad.) Nees.
Wilman	*superba* Peyn.

COMMON NAMES	SCIENTIFIC NAMES
Lucerne; Medic; Burclover	*MEDICAGO* L.
Lupine	*LUPINUS* L.
Blue	*angustifolius* L.
Sundial	*perennis* L.
Texas; Bluebonnet	*subcarnosus* Hook.
White	*albus* L.
Yellow	*luteus* Kell.
Maize; Corn	*ZEA mays* L.
Manilagrass	*ZOYSIA matrella* (L.) Merr.
Mannagrass	*GLYCERIA* R. Br.
Mascarenegrass	*ZOYSIA tenuifolia* Willd. ex Trin.
meadow grass, salt (Nuttall alkaligrass)	*PUCCINELLIA nuttaliana* Hitchc.
Medic; Burclover; Lucerne	*MEDICAGO* L.
Black	*lupulina* L.
Button; Buttonclover	*orbicularis* All.
Little; Little burclover	*minima* L.
Snail	*scutellata* Mill.
Spotted; Spotted burclover	*arabica* All.
Mesquite	*PROSOPIS* L.
Velvet	*velutina* Wooton
Algaroba	*pallida* H.B.K. = *juliflora* DC.
Milkvetch	*ASTRAGALUS* L.
Cicer	*cicer* L.
Ruby	*rubyi* (L.) Greene & Morris
Sicklepod *(sickle)*	*falcatus* Lam.
Millet	*SETARIA faberii* Herrm.
Broomcorn	*PANICUM miliaceum* L.
Browntop	*ramosum* L.
Chinese	*SETARIA faberii* Herrm.
Foxtail	*italica* (L.) Beauv.
hog (Broomcorn; Proso)	*PANICUM miliaceum* L.
Mitchellgrass	*ASTREBLA pectinata* F. Muell.
Molassesgrass	*MELINIS minutiflora* Beauv.
Mormon tea	*EPHEDRA trifurca* Torr.
Muhly	*MUHLENBERGIA* Schreb.
Bush	*porteri* Scribn.
Sandhill	*pungens* Thurb.
Napiergrass; Elephantgrass	*PENNISETUM purpureum* Schumach.
Natalgrass	*TRICHOLAENA rosea* Nees.
Needle-and-thread	*STIPA comata* Trin. & Rupr.
Needlegrass	*STIPA* L.
California	*californica* Merr. & Davy
Green	*viridula* Trin.
needlegrass (Needle-and-thread)	*comata* Trin. & Rupr.
Sleepygrass	*robusta* (Vasey) Scribn.
Oatgrass	*ARRHENATHERUM* Beauv.
Bulbous	*bulbosum elatius* var. *bulbosum* (Willd.) Spenner
Tall	*elatius* (L.) Presl.
Oats	*AVENA sativa* L.
Wild oats	*fatua* L., *sterilis* L.
Ohia; Ohia lehua	*METROSIDEROS collina* A. Gray
Orchardgrass	*DACTYLIS glomerata* L.
Pampasgrass	*CORTADERIA selloana* (Schult.) Asch. & Graebn.
Panic, blue	*PANICUM antidotale* Retz.
Panicgrass	*PANICUM* L.

COMMON NAMES	SCIENTIFIC NAMES
blue (Blue panic)	*antidotale* Retz.
giant panicgrass (Blue panic)	*antidotale* Retz.
Green	*maximum* var. *trichoglume* Eyles
Paragrass	*BRACHIARIA mutica* (Forsk.) Stapf
Partridge pea, showy	*CHAMAECRISTA fasciculata* Greene
Paspalum	*PASPALUM* L.
Brownseed	*plicatulum* Michx.
Field	*laeve* Michx.
Ribbed	*malacophyllum* Trin.
Sand	*stramineum* Nash.
pea, Caley (Roughpea)	*LATHYRUS hirsutus* L.
Pea, field	*PISUM sativum* subsp. *arrense* (L.) Poir.
pea, singletary (Roughpea)	*LATHYRUS hirsutus* L.
Pea, Tangier; Tangier peavine	*tingitanus* L.
Peanut	*ARACHIS hypogaea* L.
Pearlmillet	*PENNISETUM typhoides* (Burm.) Stapf & C. E. Hubb.
Peavine	*LATHYRUS* L.
Flatpod	*cicer* Habl.
Tangier; Tangier pea	*tingitanus* L.
Pigeonpea	*CAJANUS cajan* (L.) Millsp.
Pinegrass	*CALAMAGROSTIS rubescens* Buckl.
Porcupinegrass	*STIPA spartea* Trin.
Povertygrass	*DANTHONIA spicata* (L.) Beauv.
Proso	*PANICUM miliaceum* L.
Pumpkin	*CUCURBITA pepo* L.
Purpletop	*TRIDENS flavus* (L.) Hitchc.
Quackgrass	*AGROPYRON repens* (L.) Beauv.
Quakinggrass	*BRIZA* L.
Big	*maxima* L.
Little	*minor* L.
Rape *(winter rape)*	*BRASSICA napus* L.
Rattailgrass; Smutgrass	*SPOROBOLUS africanus* (Poir.) Robyns & Toun. = *S. capensis* Kunth.
rattle-box (Crotalaria)	*CROTALARIA* L.
Redtop	*AGROSTIS alba* L.
Reed, common	*PHRAGMITES communis* Trin.
Reed canarygrass	*PHALARIS arundinacea* L.
Reedgrass	*CALAMAGROSTIS* Adans.
Bluejoint	*canadensis* (Michx.) Beauv.
reedgrass, giant (Big sandreed)	*CALAMOVILFA gigantea* (Nutt.) Scribn. & Merr.
reedgrass, prairie (Prairie sandreed)	*CALAMOVILFA longifolia* (Hook.) Scribn.
Rescuegrass	*BROMUS catharticus* Vahl.
Rhodegrass	*CHLORIS gayana* Kunth.
Ribbongrass	*PHALARIS arundinacea* var. *picta* L.
Ricegrass	*ORYZOPSIS* Michx.
Bloomer	*bloomeri* (Boland) Ricker
Indian	*hymenoides* (Roem. & Schult.) Ricker
Mandan	*STIPORYZOPSIS* (spp.) B. L. Johnson & Rogler
Ripgut grass	*BROMUS rigidus* Roth
Rivergrass (White top)	*SCOLOCHLOA festucacea* Willd.
Ronphagrass	*PHALARIS aquatica* L. = *tuberosa* L. × *arudinacea* L.
Roughpea	*LATHYRUS hirsutus* L.
rushgrass, longleaf (Tall dropseed)	*SPOROBOLUS asper* (Michx.) Kunth.
rushgrass, rough (Tall dropseed)	*asper* (Michx.) Kunth.

COMMON NAMES	SCIENTIFIC NAMES
Rye	*SECALE cereale* L.
Ryegrass	*LOLIUM* L.
Annual	*multiflorum* Lam.
Dalmatian	*subulatum* Vis.
Darnel	*temulentum* L.
Hardy	*remotum* Schrank
Italian	*multiflorum* Lam.
Perennial	*perenne* L.
Persian darnel	*persicum* Boiss. & Honen. ex Boiss.
Swiss	*rigidum* Gaud.
ryegrass (Wildrye)	*ELYMUS* L.
Sacaton	*SPOROBOLUS wrightii* Munro ex Scribn.
Alkali	*airoides* Torr.
Sainfoin	*ONOBRYCHIS* P. Miller
Common	*viciifolia* Scop.
Russian	*transcaucasica* Grossh.
Siberian	*arenaria* (Kit.) DC.
Sagebrush	*ARTEMISIA* L.
Big	*tridentata* Nutt.
Black	*nova* A. Nels.
Sand	*filifolia* Torr.
Threetip	*tripartita* Rydb.
Saint augustinegrass	*STENOTAPHRUM secundatum* Kuntze
Saltbush	*ATRIPLEX* L.
Saltgrass	*DISTICHLIS* Raf.
Inland (Desert)	*stricta* (Torr.) Rydb.
sandgrass, prairie (Prairie sandreed)	*CALAMOVILFA longifolia* (Hook.) Scribn.
Sand reedgrass	*longifolia* (Hook.) Scribn.
Sandreed, big	*gigantea* (Nutt.) Scribn. & Merr.
Sea-oats	*UNIOLA paniculata* L.
Sedge	*CAREX* L.
Threadleaf	*filifolia* Nutt.
Senna; Sickle	*CASSIA tora* L.
Serradella	*ORNITHOPUS sativus* Brot.
Sesbania; Hemp sesbania	*SESBANIA exaltata* (Raf) Cory = *S. macrocarpa* Muhl.
shadscale (Shadscale saltbush)	*ATRIPLEX confertifolia* S. Wats.
Sleepygrass	*STIPA robusta* (Vasey) Scribn.
Sloughgrass, American	*BECKMANNIA syzigachne* (Steud.) Fernald
Smilograss	*ORYZOPSIS miliacea* (L.) Benth.
Sprangletop, green	*LEPTOCHLOA dubia* (H.B.K.) Nees.
Sorghum	*SORGHUM bicolor* (L.) Moench
Sourclover	*MELILOTUS indica* All.
Soybean	*GLYCINE max* (L.) Merr.
Staghorn fern	*NEPHROLEPSIS exaltata* Schott
Stargrass (Star bermuda)	*CYNODON plectostachyum* Pilger
stipa (Needlegrass)	*STIPA* L.
Stylo	*STYLOSANTHES guianensis* (Aubl.) Scv. syn. *gracilis humilis* H.B.K.
Sudangrass	*SORGHUM bicolor* (L.) Moench
Sugarcane	*SACCHARUM officinarum* L.
Suiter's grass (tall fescue)	*FESTUCA elatior* L.
Sulla; Sulla sweetvetch	*HEDYSARUM coronarium* L.
Sweetclover	*MELILOTUS* Mill.
annual yellow (Sourclover)	*indica* All.
Banat	*dentata* (W. & K.) Pers.

COMMON NAMES	SCIENTIFIC NAMES
Daghestan	*suaveolens* Ledeb.
Hubam	*alba* var. *annua* Coe
Israel	*alba* var. *annua* Coe
Sourclover *(sour)*	*indica* All.
White	*alba* Desr.
Yellow	*officinalis* (L.) Lam.
Switchgrass	*PANICUM virgatum* L.
Tanglehead	*HETEROGON contortus* (L.) Beauv. ex Roem. & Schult.
Teosinte	*EUCHLAENA mexicana* Schrad.
Three-awn	*ARISTIDA* L.
Pineland	*stricta* Michx.
Purple	*purpurea* Nutt.
Red	*longiseta* Steud.
Tickclover	*DESMODIUM* Desv.
Tall	*purpureum* Fawc. & Rend.
ticklegrass (Winter bentgrass)	*AGROSTIS hiemalis* (Walt.) B.S.P.
Timothy	*PHLEUM pratense* L.
Alpine	*alpinum* L. (*commutatum* Gaud.)
Turf	*bertolonii* DC. (*nodosum* L.)
Tobosa	*HILARIA mutica* (Buckl.) Benth.
Torpedograss	*PANICUM repens* L.
Townsville stylo	*STYLOSANTHES humilis* H.B.K.
Trefoil	*LOTUS* L.
Big	*pedunculatus* Cav.
Birdsfoot	*corniculatus* L.
marsh birdsfoot (Big)	*pedunculatus* Cav.
Narrowleaf birdsfoot	*tenuis* Waldst. & Kit.
yellow (Black medic)	*MEDICAGO lupulina* L.
Trigonella; Fenugreek	*TRIGONELLA foenum-graecum* L.
Trisetum, yellow	*TRISETUM flavescens* (L.) Beauv.
Tropical kudzu	*PUERARIA phaseoloides*
Tunisgrass	*SORGHUM virgatum* Kuntze
turkeyfoot (Sand bluestem)	*ANDROPOGON hallii* Hack.
Turnip	*BRASSICA rapa* L.
Uniola, broadleaf	*UNIOLA latifolia* Michx.
Vaseygrass	*PASPALUM urvillei* Steud.
Veldtgrass	*EHRHARTA calycina* J. E. Smith
Velvetbean	*STIZOLOBIUM* P. Br.
Florida	*deeringianum* Bort.
Velvetgrass	*HOLCUS* L.
Common	*lanatus* L.
German	*mollis* L.
Vernalgrass, sweet	*ANTHOXANTHUM odoratum* L.
Vetch	*VICIA* L.
Bard	*monantha* Retz.
Bigflower	*grandiflora* Scop.
Bird	*cracca* L.
Bitter	*ervilia* (L.) Willd.
Common	*sativa* L.
Cordateleaf, common	*sativa* (L.) var. *cordata* (Wulfen ex Hoppe) Asch. & Graebn.
Grandiflora (Bigflower)	*grandiflora* Scop.
Hairy	*villosa* Roth
Horsebean	*faba* L.
Hungarian	*pannonica* Crantz
Milk (Single-flowered)	*astragalus rubyi* Greene & Morris

COMMON NAMES	SCIENTIFIC NAMES
Monantha	*articulata* Hornem.
Narrowleaf	*sativa* L. var. *nigra* (L.) Ehrh.
Purple	*benghalensis* L.
Showy	*grandiflora* Scop.
Single-flowered (Monantha)	*articulata* Hornem.
Winter	*villosa* var. *varia* Gunn
Vine mesquite	*PANICUM obtusum* H.B.K.
Wheat	*TRITICUM aestivum* L.
Wheatgrass	*AGROPYRON* Gaertn.
Beardless	*inerme* (Scribn. & Smith) Rydb.
Bluebunch	*spicatum* (Pursh) Scribn. & Smith
Crested	*desertorum* (Fisch. ex Link) Schult.
Drooping	*semicostatum* (Steud.) Nees. ex Boiss.
Fairway	*cristatum* (L.) Gaertn.
Intermediate	*intermedium* (Host) Beauv.
Pubescent	*trichophorum* (Link) Richt.
Quackgrass	*repens* (L.) Beauv.
Siberian	*sibiricum* (Willd.) Beauv.
Slender	*trachycaulum* (Link) Malte
Streambank	*riparium* Scribn. & Smith
Tall	*elongatum* (Host) Beauv.
Thickspike	*dasystachyum* (Hook.) Scribn.
Western	*smithii* Rydb.
Wildbean, trailing	*STROPHOSTYLES helvola* (L.) Ell.
Wildrice, annual	*ZIZANIA aquatica* L.
Wildrye	*ELYMUS* L.
Basin	*cinereus* Scribn. & Merr.
beach (Common, Dune)	*mollis* Trin.
Blue	*glaucus* Buckl.
Canada	*canadensis* L.
Creeping; Beardless	*triticoides* Buckl.
Dune	*mollis* Trin.
Giant	*condensatus* Presl.
Mammoth (Siberian)	*giganteus* Vahl.
Russian	*junceus* Fisch.
Virginia	*virginicus* L.
Yellow	*flavescens* Scribn. & Smith
wiregrass (Bermudagrass)	*CYNODON dactylon* (L.) Pers.
wiregrass (Three-awn)	*ARISTIDA* L.
Woollyfinger	*DIGITARIA stolonifera* Schrad.
Yorkshire fog (Common velvetgrass)	*HOLCUS lanatus* L.

✵ QUESTIONS

1. Discuss the economic value of grasses and of legumes in the U.S.
2. Why are legumes so named? Why are they of special importance?
3. List the more important morphological differences that distinguish grasses from legumes.
4. Draw a grass flower and label its parts. Do the same for a legume flower.
5. Of what value are the cotyledons to the young legume seedling?
6. Why are the activities of bees and other related insects necessary to the production of legume seed?
7. Distinguish between a stolon and a rhizome.
8. Identify: raceme, corm, panicle, lodicule, radicle, and rachilla.
9. Why is it important to be able to identify specific growth stages of grasses and legumes?
10. What is the value of the binomial system for classifying plants? Who is given the credit for this systematic plan?

O. N. ALLEN / *University of Wisconsin*

9

SYMBIOSIS: RHIZOBIA AND LEGUMINOUS PLANTS

⚘

SYMBIOSIS is a "many-splendored thing." It was defined originally to explain the beneficial association of algae within cycad nodules. Over the years latitude of the definition has been broadened to connote various nutritional and morphologic relationships between dissimilar organisms, but none has displayed such a dynamic role as in the association of the root nodule bacteria with leguminous plants (Fig. 9.1).

Culmination of the symbiotic association is the fixation of atmospheric N. This is a mechanism whereby the plant is benefited and in turn the rhizobia profit from having a favorable medium in which they multiply and function. This mutualism often is referred to as one of near perfection. Neither the plant nor the rhizobia fix N individually.

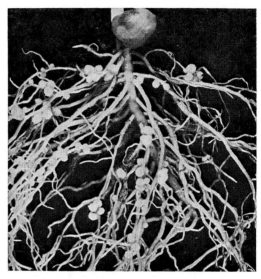

FIG. 9.1. *Dynamic role . . . association . . . with leguminous plants.* Effective nodules on a young pea plant.

⚘ THE LEGUMINOUS PLANT— THE MACROSYMBIONT

The Leguminosae is the second largest family of seed plants. It comprises about 15,000 species distributed in about 600 genera contained in three subfamilies, the

⚘ O. N. ALLEN is Professor of Bacteriology at the University of Wisconsin. He holds the M.A. degree from the University of Texas and the Ph.D. from the University of Wisconsin. His research interests include a global survey of nodulated leguminous and nonleguminous plants with reference to host and symbiont relationships.

Mimosoideae, the Caesalpinioideae, and the Papilionoideae. Plants in each of these subfamilies contribute greatly to the welfare of man. The papilionaceous species are the best known of the leguminous family. The major forage crops of temperate regions are in this group.

The esteemed position of leguminous species as forage and cover crops is attributed to various reasons.

1. They store an abundant amount of

protein in their leaves, stems, and seeds; therefore, they are desirable for livestock as high-quality hay, in feed mixtures, in silage, and as high-protein supplements.

2. They provide adequate quantities of bone-building minerals such as P, K, and Ca; various vitamins; and growth-promoting substances.

3. They are essential in well-balanced crop-rotation programs when they are supplied with the proper nodule-forming bacteria because they utilize air N that is unavailable to nonleguminous plants.

4. They increase the storehouse of soil N when they are turned under properly as green manures.

5. They influence beneficially the numbers, kinds, and activities of various desirable soil microorganisms that are important in the decay of organic matter.

6. Leguminous plants serve as "soil builders," improve soil tilth, and aid in protecting surface soil from erosion.

Nodule occurrence by rhizobia is not universal throughout the leguminous family. It is most common on members of the subfamily Papilionoideae, less common in the Mimosoideae, and least common in the Caesalpinioideae. Explanations of why some leguminous species form nodules and others do not and, still further, why some nodulated plants are benefited and others are not are inadequately defined. Why this unique symbiotic association prevails only between leguminous species and the rhizobia remains to be explained.

Rhizobia may enter the root hairs of various incompatible leguminous species, but they do not penetrate the root cortex, do not incite nodule formation, and do not bring about symbiosis. Presumably, various histological and physiological characteristics of the plant are responsible. The genetic pattern of the plant also is important. Some rhizobial strains that incite nodule formation do not fix N. The explanation is not clear, but it is generally believed that the leguminous plant in such instances does not provide a favorable medium.

Symbiotic effectiveness refers to a beneficially responsive reaction of a plant to nodulation, but it is not uncommon to designate the rhizobial strain as the effective agent. Effectiveness is evidenced by a low to moderate degree of infective ability by the rhizobial strain. Fewer nodules are produced, but these are comparatively large and are formed on the upper primary root system. Effective nodules also contain a red pigment, leghemoglobin, which participates in the N-fixation process. Presence of this pigment permits easy identification of effective nodules since it is discernible by merely slicing the nodule with a pocketknife. Conversely, ineffective plant responses are evidenced by the production of numerous small nodules scattered throughout the secondary and fibrous extremities of the root system. Leghemoglobin is lacking in these nodules.

A strain may cause nodule formation but not bring about N fixation. Also, infectiveness as reflected in high nodule numbers is correlated inversely with ineffectiveness, or low N fixation.

Against the voluminous evidence that a particular rhizobial strain may be highly effective on one host species and yet ineffective on a closely related one, any sweeping conclusion that infectiveness, or effectiveness, is a sole characteristic of the microsymbiont is unsound. The shape and size of beneficial nodules formed on a species of any one genus are markedly similar. Round nodules may be formed on one species by a particular strain, but lobed or coralloid nodules may be incited by the same strain on a compatible plant species in a related genus. Any physiological shock suffered by the plant such as removal of the surface foliage, heavy infestation by insects, or mineral deficiency generally results in nodule shedding. This loss of nodules may be only temporary yet actually beneficial in a sense because countless rhizobia are returned to the rhizosphere where they again invade the root hairs on young roots, form nodules, and reinvigorate growth through N fixation. Because of the mass of nodules on many forage plants in conjunction with the nodules being rich reservoirs of soluble N, nodule shedding often results in the return of considerable N to the soil. The beneficial effect of nodule shedding on grasses grown in mixed stands with legumes is often obvious.

* THE RHIZOBIA—
THE MICROSYMBIONTS

Rhizobia are motile, nonspore-forming, rod-shaped bacteria of the genus *Rhizobium*, family Rhizobiaceae.[1] On special laboratory media and in the nodule these organisms are X, Y, star, and club shaped forms known as bacteroids. Physiologically, the rhizobia are chemoorganotrophs. Their metabolism is respiratory. Molecular O_2 is the terminal receptor. All forms are aerobic and have an optimum temperature for growth between 25 and 30 C. Carbohydrates are used by all strains without the appreciable production of acid, and no gas is produced.

Rhizobia are isolated easily in the laboratory from nodules, but their identity must be confirmed by plant inoculation tests. The host from which the nodule was obtained is the preferred test plant. Isolation and identification of rhizobia directly from soil are fraught with difficulty. Methods for determining the prevalence of root nodule bacteria in soil are not reliable. Thus only by growing a leguminous plant in soil is it possible to ascertain whether rhizobia are present; and only by observing nodule size, location, and effect on plant growth is it possible to assess effectiveness.

Six *Rhizobium* species are defined by their distinctive physiological characteristics and ability to form nodules on certain leguminous species. Plants mutually compatible with the same strains of rhizobia were listed in earlier years in so-called "cross-inoculation groups." Demar-

1. Allen, O. N. 1971. Rhizobiaceae. *In* McGraw-Hill Encyclopedia of Science and Technology, 3rd ed. 11:578.

cations between these plant groups have become less distinct as the scope of experimentation has enlarged, but nonetheless they remain valuable in the differentiation of rhizobia. Commercial inocula are properly labeled relative to plant subgroupings within cross-inoculation categories. These subgroups specify plant species for which the strains of rhizobia in the inocula are appropriate and highly effective.

The number of rhizobia in any soil is diminished greatly by unfavorable environmental conditions. Drought, lack of essential mineral elements (particularly Ca, P, and K), and pH levels below 5 and above 8 are major factors. Numbers of rhizobia also diminish in soils in which compatible leguminous plants are not grown for long periods.

In retrospect to the symbiotic concept, the rhizobia are infective organisms. They enter the root hairs on their own initiative and penetrate the root tissues, where they multiply and incite tissue irritation. Plant response within the root cortex results in rapid host cell proliferation and tissue differentiation that results in a specialized formation, the nodule. Thus the nodule is a pathological structure; but contrary to the literal meaning of the word "pathological," the nodule is beneficial because it contributes to enhanced plant growth.

Behavioral patterns of the rhizobia within effective nodules of the host plant are threefold. In the initial stage of the infection and invasion the rhizobia are aggressors. During the intermediate stage, between nodule maturity and decadence, the rhizobia are true symbionts. During this period their coexistence in the plant tissues is one of equilibrium in which symbiosis is perfected and N is fixed. The plant becomes dominant in the third stage. During this stage the nodules on annuals are shed, and upon decay the rhizobia are returned to the root zone. On short-term annuals, nodules reach their peak of symbiotic association shortly before the flowering stage of the plant, whereupon the N-fixing period is somewhat short-lived. On perennials the N-fixing period extends over many years, as evidenced by nodules that are commonly longitudinally lobed and resemble joined beads on a string.

❧ THE NODULE—THE SITE OF N FIXATION

NODULE ORIGIN

Two types of nodules are recognized in terms of root origin. The *exogenous* type found on alfalfa, clover, peas, beans, and most forage plants arises within the root cortex. With the exception of vascular linkages, tissues within the central stele of the root are not directly involved in nodule formation. The *endogenous* type of nodule typical of those on peanuts consists of tissues differentiated from the pericyclic cell layer of the root. These nodules commonly occur in root axils because rhizobia enter the root through ruptured tissue at the time of root emergence instead of by infection through root hairs. Effective and ineffective nodules are common within each category.

NODULE PATTERN

The mature nodule consists of four areas irrespective of its site of origin and function (Fig. 9.2).

The outermost spongy area consisting of 4–10 layers of noninfected, delicate, thin-walled cells is known as the *cortex*. Attachment of the nodule to the root by this external layer is extremely fragile. This explains why nodules are so easily shed by the plant growing under adverse condi-

tions and why plants removed carelessly from the soil often lack nodules. Only in nodules borne on perennial plants do the cells of this layer contain ligneous tissues or inclusions that contribute to firmness and nodule longevity.

Within the nodule cortex is the all-important *vascular system*. This is the lifeline or "plumbing system" of the nodule. The strands of this system form a network around the inner infection zone through which nitrogenous substances and metabolic by-products of the rhizobia are translocated to the host plant, and in turn the plant supplies the nodule with necessary food materials. Collapse or malfunctioning of this system terminates nodule existence.

The *bacteroid area* is the central part of the nodule where the rhizobia appear as bacteroids in the swollen host plant cells. Some or all of the host cells may be packed with rhizobia, but many of them may not have been invaded. Vacuoles are usually conspicuous where plant nuclei have disappeared. In general, the noninvaded cells in effective nodules are considered beneficial because better aeration is permitted and nodule longevity is enhanced. As N-fixing activity subsides, the leghemoglobin in this area changes in color from red to green and finally to brown.

The *meristem* is the growing area of the nodule. A round nodule is formed if the meristem is hemispherical. A terminal meristem predetermines a long, slender,

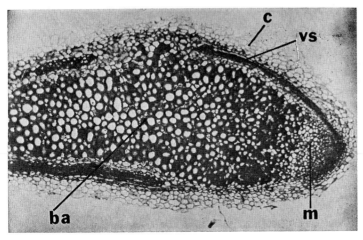

FIG. 9.2. *Mature nodule consists of four areas.* . . . Longitudinal section of an alfalfa nodule showing (c) the cortex, (vs) vascular system, (m) the meristem, and (ba) bacteroid area.

or multilobed nodule. Plant cells of the meristematic area are minute and in a state of active division. Tissue formation continues as long as the nodule is functional.

NITROGEN FIXATION

No part of the nodule is more important than any other, but the bacteroid area is the site of N fixation. The bacteroidal forms of the rhizobia are the loci. The mechanism of N fixation is intricate and has not been fully explained, but it is clear that the enzyme nitrogenase is necessary in the functional system; it is a by-product of the symbiosis. This enzyme, located in the rhizobial bacteroids, catalyzes the absorption and reduction of free N.[2,3] Isotopic studies using ^{15}N show that ammonia is the first stable intermediate. Thereafter, ammonia is catalyzed to form glutamic acid, glutamine, aspartic acid, and alanine. Identity of the intermediates between atmospheric N and ammonia remain unsolved as well as the exact role of leghemoglobin. Presumably, the function of the red pigment is twofold.[4] First, leghemoglobin preserves the low O_2 tension necessary for activity of the N-fixing process; second, it allows O_2, which is necessary for N fixation, to diffuse efficiently and quickly into the bacteroid area.

❧ INOCULATION

Cognizance of the basic need for rhizobia in the culture of leguminous plants gave impetus many years ago to the practice of inoculation. This practice is defined here as the addition of effective rhizobia to leguminous seed prior to planting for the purpose of promoting N fixation. Early practices entailed the transfer of soil from a field where a particular plant had grown satisfactorily to the area where a leguminous crop had failed for need of N, or the transfer of soil to new land being

opened for legume culture. This practice was followed by the bulk culture of the proper rhizobia on agar, in liquids, and in peat-based mixtures. This latter preparation is sold as a separate package and applied by the farmer to the seed immediately before planting.

The innovation of "preinoculation" or "preinoculated seed" appeared in the early 1960s. This practice connotes the treatment of leguminous seed with rhizobia by seed processors, distributors, and dealers months in advance of planting. It embodies two widely different procedures of seed treatment. One process consists of spraying the seed with a broth culture or a reconstituted concentrate of rhizobia followed by subjecting the seed mass to a vacuum treatment. It is claimed that the rhizobia impregnate the interior of the seed, that they are protected against adverse environmental conditions, and that they remain viable for long periods. The other basic process, of which there are variations, entails coating the seed with rhizobia that are usually contained in a peat-based slurry. In the peat-based rhizobial mixture are gums, sugars, and high-molecular polysaccharides that provide adhesive and protective properties.

CRITERIA FOR USE

Justification for the inoculation of leguminous seed rests on the premise that effective rhizobia usually are not present in sufficient numbers in most agricultural soils. Moreover, the appropriate rhizobia for the leguminous species in question may not be present at all. It is imperative to remember that the association between plant species and rhizobial strain is highly specific. Only about 25% of rhizobial strains occurring naturally in most soils are in the most desirable category.

The inoculation process is a selective one. Prior to release of a commercial inoculum or preinoculated seed, highly effective rhizobia for the designated leguminous species are selected. Great numbers of the organisms have been propagated and packaged or affixed to the seed to ensure the most beneficial results. As a result

2. Bergersen, F. J., and G. L. Turner. 1967. Nitrogen fixation by the bacteroid fraction of breis of soybean root nodules. *Biochim. Biophys. Acta* 141:507–15.
3. Evans, H. J. 1969. How legumes fix nitrogen. *In* How Crops Grow—A Century Later, pp. 110–27. Conn. Agr. Exp. Sta. Bull. 708.
4. Fottrell, P. F. 1968. Recent advances in biological nitrogen fixation. *Sci. Progr.*, Oxford, 56:541–55.

of the purposeful addition of these highly beneficial microorganisms to the seed, the rhizobia are readily available in the rhizosphere to initiate invasion and bring about early nodule formation.

Leguminous seed should be inoculated:

1. When the leguminous plant in question has not been grown previously on the land. Maintenance of a satisfactory rhizobial population in the soil depends to a great extent upon successive and successful cropping of leguminous species on which the same rhizobia are mutually effective.
2. If the previously grown leguminous plant followed by the same plant lacked satisfactory nodulation as evidenced by N fixation, or when the legume to be grown follows a nonleguminous species.
3. If the land has been previously fallow or abused or has suffered from unfavorable natural conditions. Uncropped soils usually contain few rhizobia. It is true also that poor soil, in terms of supporting good plant growth, is always lacking in effective rhizobia.
4. When the legume to be planted is a species widely different from the previously grown legume. The host-rhizobial relationship is a highly specific one in terms of infectiveness as well as effectiveness.

Inoculation of legume seed is a simple, economical method of obtaining N (Table 9.1).[5]

BENEFITS

Benefits obtained from legume seed inoculation are fourfold:

1. Early formation of effective nodules is ensured. Rhizobia added to the rhizosphere by means of the seed bring about immediate infection.
2. An adequate supply of N becomes available to the plant soon after the seed protein supply is exhausted. Accordingly, N hunger is short-lived if it occurs at all.

5. Burton, J. C. 1967. *Rhizobium* culture and use. *In* H. J. Peppler (ed.), Microbial Technology, pp. 1–33. Reinhold, New York.

TABLE 9.1 ✣ Cost of inoculating leguminous seed in the U.S.

Species	Rate of seeding (kg/ha)	Cost per ha Inoculant ($)	Cost per ha Labor* ($)	Total cost per ha ($)
Alfalfa	16.80	0.42	0.20	0.62
Birdsfoot trefoil	5.60	0.15	0.07	0.22
Hairy vetch	45.00	1.05	0.55	1.60
Lupine	84.00	1.18	1.01	2.19
Soybeans	56.00	0.30	0.67	0.97
White clover	2.25	0.05	0.03	0.08

Source: Burton, 1965.[5]
* Labor is calculated at $2 per hour; 10 minutes is the time required to inoculate 27 kg of seed by hand. Machine application enables a saving in cost of labor.

3. Crop yield as measured by foliage or seed is increased. Yield increases of 10–15% are usual but may attain 25% on poor land; in addition, the chances of obtaining a good crop stand are greatly improved.
4. Soil N is conserved subsequent to the turn-under of the N-rich, succulent, readily decomposable, leguminous green manure; the soil reservoir of nutrients is augmented; and tilth is improved (Fig. 9.3).

FIG. 9.3. *Benefits from . . . inoculation are fourfold.* Effective inoculation of red clover. Nitrogen was supplied to the inoculated plants by effective rhizobia. All plants received a balanced, N-free, nutrient solution.

TABLE 9.2 ❧ Distribution of N in four leguminous species

Species	Percentage of total N		
	Tops	Roots	Nodules
Alfalfa	50–66	29–43	4.5–12.5
Barrel medic	80–82	13–15	3.4– 7.2
Subterranean clover	69–85	11–21	3.6–12.6
White clover	81–84	11–14	3.5– 4.4

Source: Jensen and Frith, 1944.[6]

The amount of N fixed by properly nodulated legumes averages about 75% of the total N used in the growth of the plant. The amount of N fixed by short-period annual legumes varies between 56 and 112 kg/ha/year. The amount fixed by perennial legumes is higher. Factors making for optimum legume growth influence the quantity of fixed N. This quantity varies greatly from crop to crop and from legume to legume. In general, the N content of leguminous roots is about equal to the amount of N absorbed from the soil. Only about 33% of the N of plants with long taproots is returned to the soil by decay of the root systems. About 16–25% of the N of soybeans and peas is returned in this way. The distribution of N in plant parts of two species each of alfalfa and clover is shown in Table 9.2.[6]

The efficiency resulting from inoculation of soybeans is exemplified in the results of Cartter and Hartwig.[7] On soil to which ground corncobs were added at the rate of 44.82 t/ha to reduce the availability of soil N, nodulated soybeans produced 35.69 hl/ha without added N as compared to a yield of 37.42 hl when 673.57 kg of N were added. A nonnodulated nearly isogenic line of soybeans yielded 13.93 hl/ha of beans without N and 35.69 hl when 673.57 kg of N were added. From the soil not receiving N the increased yield of nodulated over nonnodulated soybeans was 21.76 hl/ha. This increase also contained 107.7 kg of N.

In a Mississippi experiment also cited by these authors, nodulated soybeans yielded 36.56 hl/ha of beans containing 41% protein, as compared with a yield of 12.17 hl and only 28% protein by nonnodulated soybeans.[7] The seed from the nodulated soybeans contained 125.7 kg more N per ha than the seed from the nonnodulated plants. In the same general area, yields as high as 52.21 hl containing 215.55 kg N/ha were obtained, or an increase of about 179.6 kg N/ha over that of the nonnodulated strain.

❧ PERSPECTIVE

Today's world population explosion has generated a massive hunger problem. Legumes are essential for livestock feed, soil conservation, and soil improvement. In many areas inorganic N fertilizers are unavailable. Fertile soil ranks first among any nation's resources. The association of rhizobia and leguminous plants is unique. The symbiotic N-fixation mechanism is a beneficial as well as inexpensive phenomenon. Nitrogen is the most abundant element in our atmosphere and a key element of all living organisms. Thus any dereliction in making this mechanism available in leguminous plant culture is not in keeping with a sound investment.

❧ QUESTIONS

1. Cite the common and scientific names of 10 leguminous species in at least 5 genera cultivated extensively for forage.
2. What is meant by infectiveness? Effectiveness? An exogenous nodule? The nodule as a pathological structure? The rhizosphere? An enzyme? An isotope? Soil tilth? Central stele of the root? Root axils?
3. Postulate several reasons why rhizobial nodules do not occur on nonleguminous plants.
4. Itemize the respective contributions of the rhizobia and the plant to the symbiotic relationship.
5. Discuss the two methods of preinoculating seed. What are the advantages and disadvantages of preinoculated seed as compared with the use of packaged inocula?
6. Itemize various criteria that validate the importance of legume seed inoculation.

6. Jensen, H. L., and D. Frith. 1944. Production of nitrate from roots and root nodules of lucerne and subterranean clover. Proc. Linnean Soc. N.S. Wales 69:210–14.
7. Cartter, J. L., and E. E. Hartwig. 1962. The management of soybeans. Advan. Agron. 14:359–412.

M. W. PEDERSEN AND C. S. GARRISON
Agricultural Research Service, USDA

10

LEGUME AND GRASS SEED PRODUCTION

❦

AVERAGE annual production of 17 small-seeded grasses and legumes for 1969, 1970, and 1971 was 278.6 million kg in the U.S.[1] These figures do not include sudangrass and other large-seeded forages. The leading small-seeded grasses and legumes were annual and perennial ryegrass (32.2%), alfalfa (19.5%), red clover (7.5%), Kentucky bluegrass (6.2%), lespedeza (5.8%), and timothy (4.5%). In addition, a number of native species are used in the Great Plains region.

The species are so varied and produced over such a wide range of conditions that generalizations are likely to be inaccurate. Each species has characteristics that contribute to its adaptability to a certain niche in the ecological position in relation to its use, i.e., climate, soil, and associated species. In addition, it will also have rather specific requirements for seed production.

❧ MARION W. PEDERSEN, Research Agronomist, ARS, USDA, is in charge of alfalfa and seed production at the Crops Research Laboratory, Logan, Utah. He received the M.S. degree from the University of Nebraska and the Ph.D. from the University of Minnesota.

❧ C. S. GARRISON is Staff Scientist, ARS, USDA, Beltsville, Md. He received his agronomic training at the universities of Delaware, Michigan State, and Maryland. From 1949 until 1972 he was in charge of forage seed production investigations for the ARS.

❧ SHIFTS IN AREAS OF SEED PRODUCTION

New technology has made grass and legume seed production a specialized enterprise on many farms and ranches.[2] The increase in efficiency is primarily due to improved cultural and management practices, insect and disease control, use of pollinators, weed control, and harvesting methods. This new technology has been applied most extensively in the irrigated areas of the western states. However, growers elsewhere have developed successful grass or legume seed enterprises such as Kentucky bluegrass and timothy seed production in northern Minnesota, orchardgrass growing in Virginia, or tall fescue seed production in Kentucky.

Application of improved technology has created major shifts in areas producing seed crops. In 1971, 44% of the alfalfa seed was grown in the Pacific Coast states, whereas in 1949 this area was producing less than 15% of the nation's supply of seed.[1] In 1955 most of the orchardgrass seed was grown in Kentucky, Missouri, and Virginia. In 1972, 66% of the crop was being produced in Oregon. Earlier, Kentucky bluegrass seed

1. Crop Reporting Board. 1972. Seed crops annual summary 1971. USDA Stat. Rep. Serv.
2. Garrison, C. S. 1960. Technological advances in grass and legume seed production and testing. *Advan. Agron.* 12:41–125.

was grown mostly in the eastern half of the country. By 1972 the largest part of the seed crop was being produced in the Pacific Northwest. Red clover seed has become an important crop in this area also since most of the certified seed of improved cultivars is grown there.

✤ CULTURE

Seed production of forages has for the most part become a specialized industry, particularly in the West. However, certain species such as lespedeza, timothy, crimson and red clover, and smooth bromegrass are grown for both seed and forage in other parts of the U.S. The aftermath in timothy, orchardgrass, and smooth bromegrass is used for forage after a seed crop is harvested. Crimson and white clovers are grazed first and then allowed to set seed. Red clover is cut for hay before a seed crop is produced.

Row Culture

Where forages are grown for both seed and feed, planting practices appropriate for forage apply. Where seed production is the major objective, special procedures are usually followed.[3] Planting in rows 60–122 cm apart at a seeding rate usually lower than for forage is a common practice. In addition, cross-blocking to remove part of the plants within rows has proved advantageous for alfalfa seed production under certain conditions.[4] Advantages of row stands include easier weed control and irrigation, seed requirement for planting is less than for solid stands, and with certain species a seed crop is obtained the year of planting. Disadvantages include additional labor and equipment requirements and possible reduction in forage yield where the aftermath is grazed.

Irrigation

Water requirements, and hence irriga-tion are in general less for seed than for forage production, although this reduced requirement applies largely to the period of pollination, maturation, and harvest.[4] However, species vary tremendously. White and red clover, for example, cannot survive as long a dry period as alfalfa. Under irrigated conditions the application of water can be controlled. This is a major reason why seed production is concentrated in the West. There is considerable range in acceptable moisture during most of the time a crop is produced. However, during maturity and especially at harvest, dry weather is essential. A seed crop can be heavily damaged by rains and wet weather during harvest.

Fertilization

Most grass seed crops require heavy N fertilization.[5-7] Grasses that initiate floral development in the winter are likely to respond to split applications of N in the early fall and spring. Grasses that develop mostly in the summer are more likely to respond to a single application of N early in the spring. The amount required will depend upon the species, irrigation water, natural soil fertility, and treatment of aftermath. Increasing the rate of N may partially offset the decline in grass seed yields with increasing age. Other elements such as P and K need to be used as local conditions indicate. They are usually not necessary on western soils.

Nitrogen usually is not used on legumes, as they have the capacity to obtain it from the air through N-fixing rhizobia. Requirements for other elements will be determined by local conditions.[3,4] In some areas P, K, S, or B may be needed.

Weed Control

Weed control is a major problem in forage seed production.[3,4,6,7] Control measures vary for different crops, weeds, and areas.

3. Pedersen, M. W., L. G. Jones, and T. H. Rogers. 1961. Producing seeds of the legumes. *In* Seed, pp. 171–81. USDA Yearbook Agr.

4. Pedersen, M. W., G. E. Bohart, V. L. Marble, and E. C. Klostermeyer. 1972. Seed production practices. *In* C. H. Hanson (ed.), Alfalfa Monograph. Am. Soc. Agron., Madison, Wis.

5. Rogler, G. A., H. H. Rampton, and M. D. Atkins. 1961. The production of grass seeds. *In* Seed, pp. 163–71. USDA Yearbook Agr.

6. Cooper, H. W., J. E. Smith, and M. D. Atkins. 1957. Producing and harvesting grass seed in the Great Plains. USDA Farmers' Bull. 2112.

7. Wheeler, W. A., and D. D. Hill. 1957. Seed Production of Grassland Seeds. Van Nostrand, Princeton, N.J.

Small weeds may be easily destroyed by harrowing before the seed is planted. Cultivation is effective in row culture, and hand hoeing can be used for weeds within the rows. Chemicals are useful and generally more effective on grasses than on legumes. Control of dodder is a major problem for alfalfa seed growers in the West. Chemicals such as chlorpropham are fairly effective for controlling dodder if properly applied. Dodder and other weeds not removed in the field will yield seed that must be removed by cleaning. The equipment for removing dodder seed is quite effective, but a certain percentage of alfalfa seed also is removed. Thus the producer takes a loss not only for the expense of cleaning but also for the loss of good seed. The separation of weed seed from the seed crop in the cleaning plant is always a less desirable practice than field weed control.

INSECTS

Legumes grown in the West are especially subject to insect problems. Alfalfa is a good example.[3,4,7,8] Lygus bugs are a problem on the *Trifolium* clovers and are especially serious on alfalfa where control is essential for successful seed production (Fig. 10.1). Aphids, weevils, mites, midges, chalcids, and occasionally other insects must also be controlled. Seed fields must be checked periodically for insect problems. Most insects can be controlled with insecticides; however, their use has caused insects to develop resistance and thus complicates control. The use of persistent insecticides such as DDT has been restricted, and in some cases new insecticide control programs are not completely developed. A problem with insecticides is that they kill not only the harmful insects but also predatory and parasitic insects and pollinators as well.

DISEASES

The crop is vulnerable to attack by diseases for a longer time when grown for seed than for hay. Thus diseases normally

Fig. 10.1. *Control of this insect . . . essential . . . alfalfa seed production in the West.* A lygus nymph feeding on an alfalfa stem tip or bud. *USDA photo.*

of little consequence may be serious problems for seed production. For example, yellow leaf blotch, *Pseudopeziza jonesii* Nannf., is not a serious problem when alfalfa is grown for hay in northern Utah because the disease has not yet developed to a great extent when the crop is cut for hay. However, when alfalfa is grown for seed, this disease can completely defoliate the crop on susceptible cultivars and thus reduce seed yield.

Damage from diseases on legume seed crops is limited mostly to a reduction in health of the plant.[9] However, certain of the grasses have seed and inflorescence diseases. Examples include grass seed nematodes in orchardgrass and 'Astoria' bentgrass seed, blind seed in perennial ryegrass, dwarf bunt in 'Tualatin' oatgrass, and ergot in several grasses.[10]

Control measures are largely limited to the use of resistant cultivars, crop rotation, and field sanitation. However, reports indicate that systemic fungicides will control certain diseases. Excellent control of stripe rust, *Puccinia striiformis* West., and leaf rust, *P. poaenemoralis* Otth., on Kentucky bluegrass was obtained with two to four applications of 1.11–1.68 kg of nickel sulfate hexahydrate plus 1.80–2.69 kg of maneb/

8. Bolton, J. L. 1962. Morphology and Seed Setting: Alfalfa, pp. 97–114. Interscience, New York.

9. Hardison, J. R. 1957. Disease problems in forage seed production and distribution. *In* Grassland Seeds. Van Nostrand, Princeton, N.J.

10. Hardison, John R. 1963. Commercial control of *Puccinia striiformis* and other rusts in seed crops of *Poa pratensis* by nickel fungicides. *Phytopathology* 53:209–16.

ha.[10] Flag smut, *Urocystis agropyri* (Preuss.) Schroet, and stripe smut, *Ustilago striiformis* Niessl., were eliminated and good control of stripe rust on bluegrass was obtained with a thiazole compound (2,4-Dimethyl-5-carboxanilidothiazole).[11,12]

In western Oregon burning of crop residue has proved to be effective in controlling ergot in perennial ryegrass and tall fescue, blind seed disease in perennial ryegrass, and the grass seed nematode on chewings fescue.[9] However, burning of seed fields is restricted because of air pollution. Alternative methods of straw removal and pest control are under investigation. Generally speaking, crop residues and aftermath should be removed for seed production of both legumes and grasses.[3,4,6,7,9] Combining of seed crops presents a residue problem. However, in Utah some growers have modified the combine by adding a straw blower which blows the straw and chaff into a wagon pulled behind the combine. Aftermath production may be effectively removed by grazing or mowing.

❧ POLLINATION

Pollination is the transfer of pollen from the male to the female parts of flowers and is required for all but the apomictic species of which buffelgrass, dallisgrass, and Kentucky bluegrass are examples.[13,14] Some species of both grasses and legumes are self-fertile, others are totally cross-pollinated, and a third group produces seed from both cross- and self-pollination. In the normally self-fertile species (weeping lovegrass, sudangrass, and slender wheatgrass), it is only necessary to move the pollen from the anthers to the stigma within a flower, a fraction of a centimeter. In the normally cross-pollinated grasses, pollen is trans-ferred by the wind. Pollen is moved from the anthers of one plant to the stigma of another by air currents. Dioecious species like buffalograss and saltgrass have male and female flowers on different plants.[13,15] There are no reported monoecious forage plants. However, certain bluestems have both male and perfect flowers on the same plant.[15]

Pollination in forage grasses is not a problem, but the picture is different for legumes. Except for normally self-pollinated forages (Korean and common lespedeza and common and hairy vetch) all legume forages are normally cross-pollinated.[13,16] In contrast to grass pollen, legume pollen is heavy and not transferred easily by wind. Insects, primarily bees, move pollen from plant to plant in the act of collecting pollen and nectar and thus pollinate the flowers. Legume flowers have both male and female parts, but self-incompatability in the normally cross-pollinated species requires that pollen be transferred between plants rather than from flower to flower on the same plant.

The major forage legumes, alfalfa and red clover, have pollination problems and have been studied extensively.[17] Both are normally cross-pollinated by bees. Pollen is dehisced early in flower development and is in close contact with the stigma, but it is not effective until the flower is manipulated. In alfalfa, manipulation of the flower causes tripping, release of the sexual column which forcibly strikes the standard petal and is not reversible. In red clover, manipulation of the flower forces the sexual column out of the keel in a pistonlike action that is reversible. In both cases the stigma touches the bee and picks up pollen from previously visited flowers.

Bees must collect pollen from alfalfa to be efficient pollinators. Bees collecting nectar soon learn to avoid the tripping mechanism and thus pollination is very slow.[4,17]

11. Hardison, John R. 1971. Chemotherapeutic eradication of *Ustilago striiformis* and *Urocystis agropyri* in *Poa pratensis* 'Merion' by root uptake of a(2,4-dichlorophenyl)-a-phenyl-5-pyrimidinemethanol (EL-273). *Crop Sci.* 11: 345–47.

12. Hardison, John R. 1971. Chemotherapy of smut and rust pathogens in *Poa pratensis* by thiazole compounds. *Phytopathology* 61:1396–99.

13. Poehlman, J. M. 1959. Breeding Field Crops. Henry Holt, New York.

14. Bashaw, E. C. 1962. Apomixis and sexuality in buffelgrass. *Crop Sci.* 2:412–15.

15. Frolik, A. L., and F. D. Keim. 1938. Common native grasses of Nebraska. Nebr. Agr. Exp. Sta. Circ. 59.

16. Bohart, G. E. 1960. Insect pollination of forage legumes. *Bee World* 41:64, 85–97.

17. Bohart, G. E. 1957. Pollination of alfalfa and red clover. *Ann. Rev. Entomol.* 2:1–28.

Honeybees collect pollen from alfalfa, but primarily in the southwestern part of the U.S. However, strains of honeybees have been selected and bred for high alfalfa pollen collection and have promise for the future.

Several species of bees are efficient alfalfa pollinators because they primarily collect pollen. Alkali bees and leaf-cutter bees are two species that have been more or less domesticated for alfalfa pollination (Fig. 10.2).[4] The increase of the alkali bee population has resulted from the preparation of ground nesting sites and transfer of soil blocks containing the bee larvae. The nesting sites are primarily excavations lined with plastic sheeting and filled with gravel and soil. Water is added to the bed from pipes to maintain moisture, and salt is added to the surface to maintain the required surface characteristics.

The leaf-cutter bee nests above ground in holes.[4] The holes can be in soda straws, wood, polystyrene, or similar material. The units of nests are placed in shelters throughout a seed field. In contrast to alkali bees, leaf-cutter bee units are portable and can be moved from field to field. Their flight range is limited and requires that shelters be closer together than for other bees. The limited flight range allows the seed grower to control these pollinators better than for other bees, and there is also less contamination from surrounding fields. Bumblebees are sometimes present in legume seed fields such as red clover in sufficient numbers to be effective, but their successful domestication has not been accomplished.

✢ HARVESTING

Harvesting forage crop seed may require specialized equipment. The problem is to collect a large percentage of viable seed with a reasonable cost. The indeterminate growth of the legumes causes new flowers to be forming while seed is maturing on the lower portions of the plant. Trefoils, for example, dehisce the seed as soon as it matures thus making harvest difficult.

FIG. 10.2. *Leaf-cutter bees . . . domesticated for alfalfa pollination.* Ability to manipulate this pollinator has made increased alfalfa seed production in the Northwest possible. *USDA photo.*

In the past, forage crops commonly were harvested with a binder, but this has been largely replaced by the combine with which one of two procedures is followed—direct combining or combining from the windrow.[3,4,5,7,18,19] To facilitate direct combining, a desiccant sometimes is used to speed drying (Fig. 10.3). Combining from a windrow is a popular method but limited to areas where wind will not disturb windrows excessively. In either case seed must

18. Harmond, J. E., J. E. Smith, Jr., and J. K. Park. 1961. Harvesting the seeds of grasses and legumes. *In* Seed, pp. 181–88. USDA Yearbook Agr.
19. Wolff, S. E. 1951. Harvesting and cleaning grass and legume seed in the western Gulf region. USDA Agr. Handbook 24.

FIG. 10.3. *Combining from a windrow . . . limited . . . where wind will not disturb. . . .* Direct combine harvesting of alfalfa in California after applications to dry the foliage. *Arnold-Thomas Seed Serv. photo.*

be dried if there is sufficient moisture to cause heating. Combines usually are modified to reduce seed loss and adjusted to maximize threshing and minimize seed damage. Straw is sometimes collected and rethreshed and a vacuum pickup used on small-seeded legumes such as ladino clover.

A machine known as a stripper is used to harvest Kentucky bluegrass and certain native species in some parts of the country. The comblike action of this machine strips the seed from the stems and deposits it in a collection box.

❦ PROCESSING

Processing includes drying, cleaning, testing, blending, scarification, inoculation, fungicide treatment, pelleting, and packaging.[7,19-22]

Cleaning involves the removal of appendages on the seed as well as the removal of weed seed, other crop seed, and foreign material. Appendages can be removed with a hammer mill or a machine that rubs the seed between rubber belts. The first cleaning is normally done with different sizes of sieves and air. A gravity separator may be used to remove material with a different specific gravity than the seed. Separation is accomplished by running the seed over a slanted, shaking platform covered with a porous cloth through which air is forced. Small-seeded legumes will next go to a dodder mill or roll mill. In the operation of the dodder mill the seed is sprayed with a fine mist of water, followed by addition of iron filings. The seed then flows beneath a magnet which separates the seed to which iron filings have adhered. Dodder seed has a rough coat to which filings adhere more readily than to alfalfa seed, and this results in a fairly efficient separation. The velvet cleaner roll will also separate dodder and other seed with a rough coat. The velvet roll has a series of parallel rollers covered with fuzzy cloth revolving in opposite directions. As the seed flows between the moving rollers, the rough-covered material is removed.

Large seed of legumes may be run through a spiral separator or indented disk or cylinder separators. The spiral separator is used to separate round seed from seed of other shapes. The indented disk or cylinder also separates on the basis of shape. The size of the indents determines the separation. Seed having a size that fits the indent is separated from the others as the cylinder or disk moves through the seed.

After an initial cleaning some plant operators will test for germination and purity. Seed germination may be damaged by threshing, frost, or insects or content of sand or weed seed such as dodder. Additional cleaning may then be used to correct the problem. If a problem such as low germination cannot be corrected by cleaning, a lot of seed of the same cultivar having a higher germination percentage can be mixed or blended with the lot having low germination to raise the overall percentage to meet minimum standards.

Standards are set by the Federal Seed Act of 1939 and state laws.[23] In general, the laws require that the label attached to the container indicate the percentages of pure seed, weed seed, other crop seed, inert matter, germination, hard seed, date of the germination test, and name and address of the shipper or person who labeled the seed. Weed seed recognized as noxious by the state into which the seed is being shipped must also be indicated on the label.

Small-seeded legumes have a high percentage of hard seed and are often scarified. Scarification involves running the seed through a machine that scratches or polishes the seed coat enough so that it will absorb water and germinate without a long delay.

Some legumes need inoculation with the proper symbiotic bacteria and this may be

20. Klein, L. M., J. Henderson, and A. D. Stoesz. 1961. Equipment for cleaning seeds. *In* Seed, pp. 307–21. USDA Yearbook Agr.

21. Purdy, L. H., J. E. Harmond, and G. B. Welch. 1961. Special processing and treatment of seeds. *In* Seed, pp. 322–30. USDA Yearbook Agr.

22. Welch, G. B. 1954. Seed processing equipment. Miss. Agr. Exp. Sta. Bull. 520.

23. Rollin, S. F., and F. A. Johnston. 1961. Our laws that pertain to seeds. *In* Seed, pp. 482–92. USDA Yearbook Agr.

added during processing. Other seed, especially certain grasses, need to be treated with a fungicide to control such diseases as bunt or *Podosporiella*.[9,24]

Seed can be pelleted, a procedure by which a claylike material is added to increase the size.[21] Seed is pelleted when there is need for precision planting or to reduce seeding rates when only a small amount is available. The larger pelleted seed can be planted more accurately but requires additional moisture for germination.

STORAGE AND PACKAGING

Conditions of storage and packaging affect germination. In general, the higher the relative humidity and temperature, the faster seed will deteriorate.[25] Seed produced and stored in the West where relative humidity is low maintains high germination for several years. However, when this seed is marketed in areas with a high relative humidity, storage and packaging are more important. Dry seed kept in moistureproof containers retains viability quite well under various conditions of temperature and humidity.[26]

MARKETING

Seed is marketed as public, proprietary, private, protected, or hybrid cultivars. Some cultivars may fall into more than one category. Public cultivars are those developed by publicly supported agencies such as a state experiment station or the USDA. 'Ranger' alfalfa is an example. In a general sense cultivars are either public or private. Proprietary cultivars are those developed by private breeders or commercial concerns. A proprietary cultivar can also be a public cultivar for which exclusive marketing rights have been given to a firm; 'Regal' white clover and 'Itasca' timothy are exam-

ples. Hybrids are the first generation offspring of a cross between two individuals differing in one or more genes.[13] They must contain at least 95% of crossed seed to be labeled hybrid. A special labeling is required if the crossed seed content is between 75 and 95%. If the crossed seed content is below 75%, the product cannot be labeled hybrid.

❧ SEED CERTIFICATION

Seed certification is the system used to maintain the genetic identity and purity of cultivars during seed production, processing, and distribution. Generally, it ensures reasonable standards of seed quality. Thus certified seed is of known heredity, identified as to variety (cultivar), and traceable through pedigree records to a specific lot of stock seed.

In the U.S., seed is certified by the state seed certifying agencies. The rules and procedure developed by the Association of Official Seed Certifying Agencies are followed to obtain uniformity in certified seed production.[27] They provide for the inspection of fields and seed and the checking on production, harvesting, and cleaning of each seed lot.

Four classes or categories of seed are recognized—breeder, foundation, registered, and certified. In many of the newer cultivars, the registered class is omitted as a means of reducing chances of contamination when a rapid seed increase is possible.

An international seed certification plan was introduced in 1958. It is known as the Organization for Economic Cooperation and Development (OECD) scheme for the varietal (cultivar) certification of herbage seed moving in international trade. The rules and procedures are in principle similar to those of the domestic certification plan. However, it does simplify terminology and provides uniform labels and standards for certified forage seed. Previously, certified seed meant different things in different countries.

24. Kreitlow, K. W., and A. T. Bleak. 1964. *Podosporiella verticillata*, a soil-borne pathogen of some western Gramineae. *Phytopathology* 54:353–57.
25. Barton, L. V. 1961. Seed Preservation and Longevity. Interscience, New York.
26. Bass, L. N., Te May Ching, and F. L. Winter. 1961. Packages that protect seeds. *In* Seed, pp. 330–38. USDA Yearbook Agr.

27. Association of Official Seed Certifying Agencies. 1971. AOSCA Certification Handbook, Publ. 23.

The OECD scheme has two categories or classes of seed: basic seed and certified seed. Basic seed (white label) is available from the breeder of a cultivar and is the stock from which first-generation certified seed is produced. Certified seed includes first-generation (blue label) and advance-generation (red label) seed.

GROWING SEED OUTSIDE THE REGION OF ORIGIN

The seed supply of new forage cultivars developed in the eastern U.S. has been increased rapidly by producing the seed in the West. Weather conditions are favorable for forage seed production, and a large specialized seed industry has developed. For example, over 95% of the certified 'Kenland,' 'Pennscott,' and 'Lakeland' red clover seed and 'Potomac' orchardgrass seed is grown in the West. Seed of new alfalfa cultivars is increased rapidly by utilizing areas in the West favorable for seed production. All the seed of Regal and 'Tillman' white clover is multiplied in the Pacific Coast states as is most of the seed of many new turf grasses.

Much of the forage seed grown outside a cultivar's region of origin is certified. Rules and procedures protect cultivar purity by limiting the number of generations of increase and the number of seed crops that can be harvested from a field. These safeguards preserve the genetic characteristics of a cultivar through the seed multiplication process.[28-34]

28. Smith, Dale. 1955. Influence of area of seed production on the performance of Ranger alfalfa. *Agron. J.* 47:201–6.

29. Bula, R. J., and C. S. Garrison. 1962. Fall regrowth response of Ranger and Vernal alfalfa as related to generations of increase and area of seed production. *Crop Sci.* 2:156–59.

30. Bula, R. J., R. G. May, C. S. Garrison, C. M. Rincker, and J. G. Dean. 1969. Floral response, winter survival, and leaf mark frequency of advanced generation seed increases of 'Dollard' red clover, *Trifolium pratense* L. *Crop Sci.* 9:181–84.

31. Garrison, C. S., and R. J. Bula. 1961. Growing seeds of forages outside their regions of use. *In* Seed, pp. 401–6. USDA Yearbook Agr.

32. Valle, Otto, and C. S. Garrison. 1963. International cooperation in the production of forage crop seed. Amer. Soc. Agron. Spec. Publ. 1, pp. 52–60.

33. Kelly, A. F., and M. M. Boyd. 1966. The stability of cultivars of grasses and clovers when grown for seed in differing environments. Proc. 10th Int. Grassl. Congr., pp. 777–82 (Helsinki, Finland).

34. Parsons, Frank G., Carlton S. Garrison, and Keller E. Beeson. 1961. Seed certification in the United States. *In* Seed, pp. 394–401. USDA Yearbook Agr.

❧ NATIONAL FOUNDATION SEED PROJECT

Adequate supplies of foundation seed are a prerequisite for the successful multiplication of forage seed in the volumes required by farmers and other consumers. To ensure a continuing supply of foundation seed of publicly developed forage cultivars, the USDA in cooperation with the state agricultural experiment stations, seed certifying agencies, and the seed trade organized a national foundation seed program. Its purpose is the rapid build-up and maintenance of foundation seed supplies of superior grass and legume cultivars.

Arrangements for the production of foundation seed are made in areas where a maximum seed increase ratio is possible. Breeder seed of cultivars originating in the central, eastern, and southern states is taken to the western region where the foundation seed is produced under Commodity Credit Corporation contract. After harvest the seed is cleaned in an approved plant, bagged and labeled, and sealed as foundation seed. Arrangements for producing and distributing foundation seed are worked out in cooperation with a representative of a state agricultural experiment station.

❧ VARIETY (CULTIVAR) PROTECTION

A plant variety (cultivar) protection act was passed by the Ninety-first Congress in 1970 and signed into law.[35] Its purpose is to encourage the development of new cultivars of sexually propagated plants and provide protection to those who breed, develop, or discover them. It serves the same purpose as a patent for an inventor. Breeders who develop novel sexually reproduced plants other than fungi, bacteria, or first-generation hybrids are entitled to protection under the act with certain restrictions.[35] The act is administered by the Agricultural Marketing Service of the USDA.

35. Public Law 91–577. 1970. Plant variety protection act. 91st Congress, S. 3070.

❧ QUESTIONS

1. In what respects do cultural practices differ for the production of forage and seed from forage crops?

2. Why is it generally better to grow seed crops in rows?

3. What problems develop as a result of using the chlorinated hydrocarbon type of insecticides for the control of insects on forage crops?

4. Why are diseases more of a problem in seed production than hay production?

5. Why is residue and aftermath control essential for seed production?

6. Is there a difference in the efficiency with which different kinds of bees pollinate legumes? Why?

7. Under certain conditions windrowing a seed crop previous to combining would be advisable. What are they?

8. List the machines that could be used to process a lot of alfalfa seed that contains a certain amount of chaff, fine gravel, and dodder.

9. Explain what is meant by a proprietary, a certified, and a protected cultivar.

SUPPLEMENTAL INFORMATION

❧ REDUCTION IN LEGUMES

A reduction in the use of legumes reflects a changing pattern in American agriculture. Between 1959 and 1974 legume seed production was reduced 14 million pounds per year on the average, or nearly 200 million pounds for the 15-year period. The reduction was mostly in lespedeza, vetch, and crimson clover, but does not include sweetclover because sweetclover seed production was too low to include in the reports.[36]

❧ HYBRID ALFALFA SEED PRODUCTION

One of several problems inhibiting the use of alfalfa hybrids is practical seed production.

The use of cytoplasmic sterility makes possible the production of a 100% hybrid. Nectar production is not reduced and odor production is not believed to be impaired by the pollen sterility. However, pollen production is critical for bee visitation and pollination. A reduction in seed production is associated with an increase in pollen sterility.[37] On the other hand, improvement in seed production results from selection for high seed production among male steriles and male rows, and high pollen production in the males.[38]

36. Pedersen, M. W. 1977. Can legumes make a comeback? *Crops and Soils* 29:7–9.

37. Thomas, J. H., M. W. Pedersen, and P. L. F. Sun. 1973. Some characteristics of the male parent which affect the seed yield of the male sterile in alfalfa hybrids. Agron. Abstr. 65th Ann. Meet., p. 55 (Las Vegas, Nev.).

38. Parker, F. D., P. F. Torchio, W. P. Nye, and M. W. Pedersen. 1976. Utilization of additional species and populations of leafcutter bees for alfalfa pollination. *J. Apic. Res.* 15:89–92.

I. J. JOHNSON / *Cal/West Seeds*

E. H. BEYER / *Farm Seed Research Corporation*

11

FORAGE CROP BREEDING

❧

FROM a genetic point of view improvement programs with forage crops and grain crops are based on the same biological principles. But grain and forage crops differ in many important aspects. An understanding of these differences is necessary to determine the most effective procedures for improvement. (See Fig. 11.1.) Major differences between forage and grain crops that have a bearing on breeding procedures are:

1. The majority of forage crops are naturally cross-pollinated, while many grain crops except corn, rye, and sorghums are naturally self-pollinated.
2. Many forage species exhibit varying degrees of self-sterility which may limit the opportunity for controlled inbreeding.

❧ I. J. JOHNSON was Professor in Charge of Farm Crops at Iowa State University from 1947 until 1959, when he became Director of Research for Cal/West Seeds. He received the Ph.D. degree from the University of Minnesota. Forage crop breeding with emphasis on the fundamental aspects holds his special attention.

❧ EDGAR H. BEYER served on the University of Maryland faculty in the Department of Agronomy from 1963 until 1966, when he assumed the position of Research Director for the Farm Seed Research Corporation. He received the M.S. and Ph.D. degrees from Purdue University.

3. Forage species grown in mixtures add complexity in evaluation and in breeding for mutual compatibility.
4. Perennial forage species require a long period for development and evaluation of new cultivars.
5. The bases for selection and evaluation of breeding material often are not as clear-cut and definite as with grain crops.

Certain of these features may be advantageous in forage breeding programs.

❧ MODE OF POLLINATION IN FORAGE SPECIES

Plants may be cross-pollinated either by wind-blown pollen or by the transfer of pollen by insects. Some plants may be naturally cross-pollinated but may set seed freely when selfed. Other species may have perfect flowers but exhibit varying degrees of self-sterility. Certain crops such as buffalograss may be dioecious, in which case cross-pollination is essential to seed production. In some species such as Kentucky bluegrass, seed may be produced without gametic union in a process called apomixis. Pollination may be necessary in such cases to stimulate seed development even though fertilization does not take place.

FIG. 11.1. *Grain and forage crops differ . . . understanding . . . necessary to determine the most effective procedures for improvement.* A smooth bromegrass spikelet within one minute after anthesis, with the anthers or pollen sacs dangling at the end of the long filaments and the feathery stigmas strikingly in evidence. *Iowa State Univ. photo.*

✷ STERILITY-FERTILITY RELATIONSHIPS

Extensive research has been conducted on the nature and extent of self-sterility in some forage species. The mechanisms involved may be grouped into several general categories.

IRREGULARITIES IN CHROMOSOME BEHAVIOR

Many species of forage crops appear to have had complex evolutionary origins. It is quite possible that interspecific hybridization may have played a major role in the development of existing species. In annual species plants with irregularities in chromosome pairing tend to be eliminated if these plants produce less seed than those with normal pairing. In perennial plants survival is not dependent upon seed production alone, and plants with irregular chromosome behavior could thus persist for a long time. Extensive studies have been made to determine species relationships and to utilize such information in breeding programs. Only a few selected examples are given. Studies in the Bromopsis section of the genus *Bromus* have given important information on chromosome behavior and relationships in this species.[1] In smooth bromegrass, chromosome pairing was found to be very irregular. In an attempt to determine relationships between species in this section, crosses were made between smooth brome-

1. Elliott, F. C. 1949. The cytology and fertility relations of *Bromus inermis* and some of its relatives. *Agron. J.* 41:298–303.

grass and other species having 7, 14, 21, 28, and 35 pairs of chromosomes. Successful crosses were obtained between smooth bromegrass and a 28-chromosome and a 35-chromosome species but not between species with 7, 14, or 21 chromosomes.

Among species in the same genus that have the same chromosome numbers, interspecific crosses usually can be made easily, but in certain species crosses are difficult and the resulting progenies may be sterile or extremely low in fertility. An example of the latter type of relationship has been found in sweetclover species *(Melilotus).*[2]

In some species the original chromosomes apparently have been reduplicated, giving rise to four sets of each instead of two. These species are called autotetraploids. Chromosome pairing as a consequence of doubling may not be normal. Among cultivated forages alfalfa and orchardgrass probably were derived in this manner. Extensive cytological studies have been made on orchardgrass. The percent of seed set by selfing has been shown to be related to the extent of irregularities at reduction division.[3]

To study the effects of chromosome doubling, many experimental autotetraploids have been made to determine their fertility and possible agronomic value. Almost without exception the experimental autotetraploids are low in fertility.[4,5] Selection for higher levels of fertility has been effective in sweetclover, alsike clover, and red clover.

Although abnormal chromosome behavior may have a marked effect on fertility, this factor alone cannot explain the widespread occurrence of low fertility in forage species.

ACTION OF SPECIFIC GENES

An extensive literature review on the mechanisms of self-incompatibility in plants has been presented.[6] Studies with tobacco were the first to show that a multiple series of genes, designated S_1, S_2, S_3 . . . S_n, were responsible for self-sterility through the failure of pollen tube growth in the stylar tissue only when either of the genes in the stylar tissue were the same as the pollen tube of the male gamete.[7]

A similar genetic mechanism has been used to explain self-sterility and cross-fertility in red clover, white clover, and yellow sweetclover.[8,9,10] The number of different self-sterility alleles in these clovers apparently is quite large; therefore intercrossing is not restricted. In addition to the genes for self-sterility found in the above species, a dominant factor for self-fertility also exists. Although this type of self-sterility occurs in at least three legume species, different systems are operative in others.

Variation in seed set by selfing has been found to be quite large among individual plants in alfalfa, smooth bromegrass, orchardgrass, and many other predominantly self-sterile species. In these species it appears that a complex genetic system for self-sterility exists and that its expression may be greatly modified by the level of inbreeding, by the nature of chromosome pairing, and by the environmental conditions under which the plants are grown. In many self-sterile species it is possible to obtain some selfed seed by such means as high-temperature treatments, making possible the evaluation of individual plants by their inbred progenies and the establishment of inbred lines.[11]

2. Webster, G. T. 1950. Fertility relationships and meiosis of interspecific hybrids in *Melilotus. Agron. J.* 42:315–22.

3. Myers, W. M., and H. D. Hill. 1943. Increased meiotic irregularity accompanying inbreeding in *Dactylis glomerata* L. *Genetics* 28:383–97.

4. Johnson, I. J., and J. E. Sass. 1944. Self- and cross-fertility relationships and cytology of autotetraploid sweetclover, *Melilotus alba. J. Amer. Soc. Agron.* 36:214–27.

5. Frandsen, F. K. J. 1948. Lagttajelser over polyploide former of kulturplanter. *Hordisk Jordbrugsforskning* 1–3 Heft:508–27.

6. Stout, A. B. 1938. The genetics of incompatibilities in homomorphic flowering plants. *Bot. Rev.* 4:275–369.

7. East, E. M., and A. J. Mangelsdorf. 1925. A new interpretation of the hereditary behavior of self-sterile plants. *Proc. Natl. Acad. Sci.* 11:166–71.

8. Williams, R. D. 1931. Self- and cross-sterility in red clover, pp. 181–208. Welsh Plant Breeding Sta. Bull. H-12.

9. Atwood, S. S. 1940. Genetics of cross-incompatibility among self-incompatible plants of *Trifolium repens. J. Amer. Soc. Agron.* 32:955–68.

10. Getty, R. E., and I. J. Johnson. 1944. The nature and inheritance of sterility in sweetclover, *Melilotus officinalis* Lam. *J. Amer. Soc. Agron.* 36:228–37.

11. Leffel, R. C. 1963. Pseudo self-compatibility and segregation of gametophytic self-incompatibility alleles in red clover (*Trifolium pratense* L.). *Crop Sci.* 3:377–80.

DEVELOPMENTAL COMPETITION

In the development of the embryo after fertilization, competition for nutrition may occur among the embryo tissue, the endosperm, and the nucellus. Studies have shown this factor to be the major reason for low seed set following selfing of alfalfa. A higher frequency of ovules collapsed following selfing than from crossing, and the rate of growth of the endosperm was much slower in selfed seed than in crossed seed.[12] Apparently the endosperm prevents unfavorable competition between the nucellar tissue and the developing embryo. The large difference in self-fertility among alfalfa plants possibly may be due to genetic systems conditioning the extent of physiologic competition for nutrients in the development of the seed.

The above explanations of types of self-sterility are by no means the sole causes of low seed production from self-pollination. Other factors include unfavorable positional relationships of the stigma and anthers, differential development of the pistillate and staminate portion of the flower, and the presence of stigmatic films that must be ruptured to release stigmatic fluid necessary for pollen germination. The plant breeder should determine the extent of self-sterility in the species under investigation. Often self-sterility may be an important asset rather than a handicap.

CROSS-POLLINATION

The widespread occurrence of cross-pollination is one of the distinguishing features among many forage species. Cross-pollination increases variability within a given population, thus providing the breeder with a wide range of types. Variable populations may have been subjected to sufficiently diverse environments through enough years to permit the establishment of strains of particular adaptive value to best meet the specific conditions under which they were grown. It should be recognized, however, that changes by natural se-lection for any set of genetic factors are relatively slow in perennial species, particularly for those in which individual plant replacements by seedling progenies are not likely to occur. In annual or biennial cross-pollinated species or perennials frequently propagated from seed, population changes under different environments may produce marked differences in adaptation. The classic example of selection to develop 'Grimm' alfalfa is but one of many that could be cited.

Cross-pollination also serves as a mechanism to preserve recessive traits that may have little value under a particular natural environment but may be useful when the species is grown under different conditions or when grown as a cultivated crop. The mode of pollination has been determined for several economic forage species and from results of actual breeding experience and research.[13]

❧ EVALUATION OF BREEDING MATERIALS

The choice of populations from which superior individuals are sought often includes natural ecotypes, older adapted cultivars, germ plasm pools created to produce new gene recombinations, and specific crosses between selected parents. These may originate from foreign or domestic sources.

Selection of superior plants, either for direct utilization as in the case of naturally self-pollinated and apomictic species or for use in some type of recombination with other desirable plants in the cross-pollinated species, is the first step in forage breeding. For crops usually grown alone evaluation is not as difficult as for those commonly grown in two or more component mixtures. Annual species can be evaluated more readily than perennials. In the perennial group, determination of longevity requires a period of years and hence delays the attainment of the ultimate objectives.

For most forage crops, characters desired

12. Brink, R. A., and D. C. Cooper. 1940. Double fertilization and development of seed in angiosperms. *Bot. Gaz.* 102:1–25.

13. Smith, D. C. 1944. Pollination and seed formation in the grass. *J. Agr. Res.* 68:79–95.

in new cultivars (such as winterhardiness, drought tolerance, disease resistance, leafiness, and nutritive value) appear to be inherited in a complex manner. Character expression also may be strongly influenced by the environment under which the breeding materials are grown. The selection of desirable individuals may be based on several types of tests, including:

1. Controlled greenhouse or growth chambers with environments favorable for the expression of disease and insect resistance, response to stresses of moisture and temperature, and the like.
2. Evaluation by growing clonally propagated plants in rows or tiller beds, either alone or in association with other species. This method is applicable largely to perennials that may be propagated by sod pieces or by stem cuttings.
3. Evaluation based on performance of inbred progenies. In naturally self-pollinated species this would be the normal procedure to find desirable pure lines. In self-sterile species it may not be possible to obtain inbred progenies by the conventional method of self-pollination. In this case sib mating may be necessary.
4. Evaluation for general combining ability based on the performance of topcross, polycross, or open-pollinated progenies. The effectiveness of tests for general combining ability depends on the extent of natural cross-pollination.
5. Evaluation for specific combining ability. This is used as a basis for selecting clones (or lines) for recombination into synthetic cultivars. Single-cross seed may be produced by placing the inflorescences of the two parents to be crossed in a single bag, by planting the two in an isolated crossing plot or cage, or by hand crossing.

Several investigations have been reported on comparative methods of evaluation. A highly significant positive correlation has been found between wilt and leafhopper resistance of noninbred alfalfa clones with the same characters in their polycross progenies.[14] Positive associations also were found between polycross performance of noninbred alfalfa clones and single-cross performance for forage yield, wilt resistance, cold resistance, and leafhopper resistance. Significant correlations have been found between the leaf width, panicle number, and winter survival of noninbred clones of orchardgrass and their open-pollinated progenies.[15] Forage yield and leafiness, however, were not significantly associated with these characters in the polycross progenies. Good correlations were found for most plant characters between single crosses and the mean of the two parent clones, but not for forage yield. Correlations between single crosses and open-pollinated progenies of the two parents were generally low and inconsistent in different seasons. Extensive studies also have been reported on methods of evaluating breeding materials and on a proposed plan for orchardgrass breeding.[16]

Comparisons of different methods of evaluating inbred lines in forages also have been investigated. Positive correlations have been found generally between forage and seed yield, growth habit, and disease resistance of inbred lines and their topcross F_1 hybrids.[17,18]

Comparative performance of selected lines or clones grown alone and in associations have been made with only a few forage crops. Differences have been found in competitive ability of Kentucky bluegrass strains when grown with white clover.[19] Similar results were demonstrated when

14. Tysdal, H. M., and B. H. Crandall. 1948. The polycross performance as an index of the combining ability of alfalfa clones. *J. Amer. Soc. Agron.* 40:293–306.
15. Weiss, M. G., L. H. Taylor, and I. J. Johnson. 1951. Correlations of breeding behavior with clonal performance of orchardgrass plants. *Agron. J.* 43:594–602.
16. Kalton, R. R., and R. C. Leffel. 1955. Evaluation of combining ability in *Dactylis glomerata* L. III. General and specific effects. *Agron. J.* 47:370–73.
17. Tysdal, H. M., T. A. Kiesselbach, and H. L. Westover. 1942. Alfalfa breeding. Nebr. Agr. Exp. Sta. Bull. 124.
18. Davis, R. L. 1955. An evaluation of S₁ and polycross progeny testing in alfalfa. *Agron. J.* 47:572–76.
19. Myers, W. M., and R. J. Garber. 1942. The evaluation of individual plants of pasture grasses in association with white clover. *J. Amer. Soc. Agron.* 34:7–15.

different white clover clones were grown in association with Kentucky bluegrass.[20] Differences were also noted in relative performance of orchardgrass cultivars when grown alone with 3-foot row spacing, with 1-foot row spacing, and when grown broadcast with legumes.[21] Studies have been made on the relative performance of different alfalfa cultivars grown with smooth bromegrass and of different smooth bromegrass cultivars grown with alfalfa in comparison with their performance when grown alone. In general these studies show that different cultivars may vary greatly in their response to species associations as well as to planting methods.

It may be concluded that evaluation of such specific characters as winter survival; leafiness; time of flowering; and disease and insect resistance of clones, inbred lines, topcrosses, and single crosses may be made on a progeny row basis. Final evaluation for yielding ability and agronomic utilization preferably should be in accordance with the accepted practice for farm use of the crop.

❧ UTILIZATION OF SELECTED CLONES OR LINES

Emphasis has been placed on the necessity for selecting desirable individual plants or inbred lines. The number of outstanding plants or inbreds is likely to be small if the general results from studies with maize are applicable to forage plants. It also should be emphasized that inbreeding in forage crops is not necessary for the development of superior breeding materials in those species that can be vegetatively propagated. The primary objective of inbreeding is to evaluate the genotype of selected plants or to develop inbred lines homozygous for particular attributes such as disease and insect resistance, winterhardiness, and agronomic type.

DIRECT MULTIPLICATION OF SUPERIOR CLONES

Among species that can be economically propagated vegetatively, the clonal multiplication of desirable individual plants has great value. Extensive use of this method is now being made in bentgrasses for use in golf course greens and for other specialized turf purposes. Development of 'Coastal' and 'Tift' bermudagrasses at the Georgia station illustrates the agricultural use of superior plants by means of their clonal propagation.

DIRECT UTILIZATION OF PROGENIES FROM INDIVIDUAL PLANTS

It is unlikely that the seed progeny from a single plant of a cross-pollinated species would be satisfactory for use as an improved cultivar; this seed would produce inbred progenies. Some first-year selfed lines of smooth bromegrass were equal to the commercial cultivar with which they were compared.[22] The yield performance of a desirable inbred line should not change in successive generations of random sib pollination among plants within the line if the population size is reasonably large.

In self-incompatible species, the first-year selfed progenies usually are sufficiently sib cross-fertile to permit normal seed production. Examples of the direct utilization of the progenies of a single plant in cross-pollinated species are 'Skandia II' and 'Brage' cultivars of orchardgrass developed in Sweden.

USE IN CONTROLLED F_1 CROSSES

In species exhibiting a marked degree of self-sterility, desirable clones or lines may be used as parents of a controlled F_1 cross. This procedure is particularly applicable when the two parental clones can be easily multiplied vegetatively to increase the quantity of parent materials. Seed produced under isolation on both of the parents would be F_1 generation seed. Striking examples of heterosis among F_1 crosses from noninbred clones have been shown in

20. Atwood, S. S., and R. J. Garber. 1942. The evaluation of individual plants of white clover for yielding ability in association with bluegrass. *J. Amer. Soc. Agron.* 34:1–6.
21. Weiss, M. G., and S. K. Mukerji. 1950. Effect of planting method and nitrogen fertilization on relative performance of orchardgrass strains. *Agron. J.* 42:555–59.

22. Murphy, R. P., and S. S. Atwood. 1953. The use of I₁ families in breeding smooth bromegrass. *Agron. J.* 45: 24–28.

breeding programs with many forage species. Extremely high yields of F_1 crosses between inbred lines have been reported in smooth bromegrass and orchardgrass.[23]

In species that exhibit considerable self-fertility, the use of controlled F_1 crosses may be less promising because part of the seed would come from crossing and part from inbreeding. Studies with white clover have shown that clones with a high percentage of self-fertility had a lower percentage of crossing with bees under cages than those that were highly self-sterile.[24] A direct relationship might not exist, however, between the amount of self-pollination and the yield of the F_1 cross. Studies with pearlmillet, in which varying proportions of selfed and crossed seed were blended, showed that as much as 50% selfed seed could be present as a hybrid mixture without a significant reduction in yield.[25] Seedling competition, in which the less vigorous inbred seedlings probably were eliminated, may explain the lack of reduction in yield from mixtures.

In studies with alfalfa as little as 10% admixture of selfed seed caused reduction in forage yields of the hybrids when seeded at lower than normal seeding rates.[26]

The discovery of cytoplasmic sterility in alfalfa and other forage species has opened new possibilities for better control of cross-pollination.[27] For those legume species in which cross-pollination between the male-sterile female (seed) parent and the fertile male parent is accomplished by pollen-gathering bees, hybrid seed yields may be considerably reduced as a result of lesser visitation of bees to the sterile parent. In forage species for which cross-pollination

is accomplished by wind movement, as in sudangrass, the utilization of cytoplasmic male sterility to produce controlled hybrids offers new opportunities to utilize heterosis.

Extensive studies have shown that it also is possible to produce controlled F_1 crosses by using S_1 lines of their respective parents. Several factors impinge upon the success of this procedure, including the reduction in self-fertility as a consequence of inbreeding, the operation of somatic self-incompatibility to enhance the proportion of cross-pollination rather than sib pollination, and the opportunity to produce hybrid seed equally by both parents rather than by only one (the female parent) of the cross.

Potentials for commercial utilization of controlled F_1 crosses in forage crops differ greatly from those in grain crops. Although basic concepts involved in heterosis of forage and grain crops are similar, in forage crops the magnitude of heterosis is likely to be much less. This is due to the selective forces of attrition acting upon seedlings during stand establishment and continuing during maturation.

The use of F_1 crosses as parents in double crosses in alfalfa was first suggested in 1942.[17] In the absence of genetic (or cytoplasmic) controls for crossing, the seed produced consists of a mixture of sib seed from cross-pollination within each of the two parental F_1 crosses and of hybrid seed from reciprocal cross-pollination between the two F_1 parents. The expected yield of a "double cross" would thus not be greatly different from the expected yield of a synthetic cultivar made by recombining the four parental clones. In forage species where the genetics of self-incompatibility has been determined (such as in white clover, red clover, and sweetclover), it is possible to produce a true double cross from four lines when each is homozygous for different self-sterility alleles.

USE IN SYNTHETIC CULTIVARS

The recombination of selected clones or lines into synthetic cultivars probably is the most effective method of utilizing the ad-

23. Hayes, H. K., and A. R. Schmid. 1943. Selection in self-pollinated lines of *Bromus inermis* Leyss., *Festuca elatior* L., and *Dactylis glomerata* L. *J. Amer. Soc. Agron.* 35:934–43.

24. Atwood, S. S. 1943. "Natural crossing" of white clover by bees. *J. Amer. Soc. Agron.* 35:862–70.

25. Burton, Glenn W. 1948. The performance of various mixtures of hybrid and parent inbred pearl millet, *Pennisetum glaucum* (L.) R. BR. *J. Amer. Soc. Agron.* 40:908–15.

26. Carnahan, H. L., and R. N. Paeden. 1967. Effects of vigor of S_1 lines and seeding rates on yield and final stand of an alfalfa two-clone combination admixed with different percentages of S_1 seed. *Crop Sci.* 7:9–12.

27. Davis, W. H., and I. M. Greenblatt. 1967. Cytoplasmic male sterility in alfalfa. *J. Hered.* 58:301–5.

vantages of their superior characters. Several factors may affect the yield potential of synthetic cultivars, including (1) yield of the parent clones or lines, (2) number of parent clones or lines combined, (3) yield of the F_1 crosses among them, and (4) the extent of natural cross-pollination.

Maximum yields of synthetic cultivars will depend to a considerable extent upon the proper balance between each of the above factors. With other factors constant the yield of a synthetic cultivar will be high when the parental clones or S_1 lines are productive. Similarly, the expected yield of a synthetic cultivar will be high if complete cross-pollination is obtained and the number of parents per synthetic cultivar is reasonably large. The actual yield of a synthetic (Syn) cultivar in the Syn-2 and Syn-3 generations usually will be less than the average yield of the F_1 crosses when the number of clones recombined is relatively small.

There may not be a direct relationship between the number of parent plants used to produce a synthetic cultivar and its expected yield unless all parent plants are equal in combining ability. In actual practice it would be expected that the average yield of F_1 crosses from a few highly selected clones or lines might exceed the average performance of F_1 crosses from a larger number.

A high level of cross-pollination is essential to obtain maximum yields of a synthetic cultivar, particularly if the clones themselves are used as parents in the isolated intercrossing plot. Self-pollination usually results in loss of vigor. A synthetic from partially self-pollinated plants consists of a mixture of selfed and crossed seed. The effect of self-pollination on the actual yield of a synthetic cultivar may not be as detrimental as expected because of differential competition for stand survival among the inbred and crossbred seedlings.

A first-generation cultivar (Syn-1) produced by a recombination of self-sterile parent clones is the product of random cross-pollination. The seed consists of all possible F_1 crosses and is not representative of its yield performance in later generations. The next generation from this seed (Syn-2) would consist of the products of random cross-pollination among the F_1 crosses and should produce a yield somewhat lower than in the previous generation.

When a synthetic cultivar is produced from cross-pollination among partially self-fertile clones, the first recombination (Syn-1) consists of intercrosses among clone members (selfs) as well as between different clones. This seed is a mixture of inbred and crossbred seed. It is not equal in performance to the Syn-1 produced with self-sterile clones. In later generations, however, the difference in yields of the two types becomes less but may still differ in Syn-3.

Without natural selection the yield of a synthetic cultivar beyond Syn-2 should remain relatively constant under random complete cross-pollination. Natural selection may become an important factor in changing the genetic composition of a synthetic cultivar in later generations. For this reason it is extremely important that the cultivar be maintained on a limited generation program. If commercial seed is produced under a different climate, it is desirable that foundation stocks be maintained in the area of adaptation.

Because the possible number of experimental recombinations that can be made with a relatively small number of parental clones is very large, it is important to determine possible relationships between the performance of the parental clones or lines and their synthetic cultivars. The association between general combining ability and yield of synthetic cultivars is of great concern to the breeder. Studies with alfalfa, smooth bromegrass, and crested wheatgrass all show significant variation in general combining ability among individual clones.[17,28,29] The relation between general

28. Bolton, J. L. 1948. A study of combining ability of alfalfa in relation to certain methods of selection. *Sci. Agr.* 28:97–126.

29. Knowles, R. P. 1950. Studies of combining ability in bromegrass and crested wheatgrass. *Sci. Agr.* 30:275–302.

combining ability of clones and their performance in synthetic cultivars has been studied by several investigators. Agreement has been found between the actual yield of eight synthetic cultivars of alfalfa and their predicted performance based on the average general combining ability of their parental clones.[14] Similar studies with sweetclover show a good relationship between combining ability of parental plants and the yield of synthetic cultivars from them.[30] These studies suggest that information on general combining ability is an important part of the evaluation program and may replace more costly and difficult work of making F_1 crosses to determine the potential yield of a synthetic cultivar.

In the above discussion major consideration has been given to yield performance as a criterion of superiority. It should be emphasized that many other characteristics may determine the true value of an improved cultivar. Such characters as forage quality, cold resistance, drought tolerance, disease or insect resistance, and growth habit may be the limiting factors for successful use of existing species. In most cases, more than one character must be studied in the improvement program.

Research on the use of *in vitro* techniques to measure forage quality has provided new opportunities for improvement. Use of rumen extracts to determine digestibility and use of detergent techniques have made it possible to study single plants in heterogeneous populations and to obtain meaningful data on their potential feeding values.[31,32] Research has shown that nutritive values in alfalfa are heritable characters and that populations can be modified in these respects by recurrent selection.[33]

Although legumes are recognized as having the highest feeding value of many forage crops, they also may have nonnutritive (negative) compounds that interfere with normal metabolic processes, particularly in monogastric animals. Breeding to reduce these "antimetabolites" may be as important as breeding to improve positive nutritional values. Extensive research has shown that saponins may be injurious and, more important, their content can be altered by breeding.[34,35] Research on protein 18-S (Fraction 1) implicated as a factor in causing bloat in ruminants amply illustrates new potentials in breeding forages to meet animal needs.[36]

❧ MASS SELECTION AND STRAIN BUILDING

Many factors may affect the success of mass selection. For most characters controlled by many genes, each with little effect, the progress that may be expected by mass selection in cross-pollinated species is likely to be slow.

In old stands of perennial forage crops the forces causing natural selection may have included a wide variety of adverse conditions. Individual plants that remain in such old stands may have successfully crowded out the less aggressive and poorly adapted plants, but the surviving individuals may not possess all the desired characteristics. For example, although superior in cold resistance, Grimm alfalfa is extremely susceptible to bacterial wilt and is variable in leafiness, plant height, and other plant characters. Natural selection alone can hardly be expected to produce the kinds of plants desired by the breeder for diverse agricultural uses. Individual plants that survive natural selection may, however, serve as valuable sources of breed-

30. Johnson, I. J., and Max M. Hoover, Jr. 1953. Comparative performance of actual and predicted synthetic varieties in sweetclover. *Agron. J.* 45:495–98.
31. Tilley, J. A., and R. A. Terry. 1963. A two-stage technique for the *in vitro* digestion of forage crops. *J. Brit. Grassl. Soc.* 18:104.
32. Van Soest, P. J. 1967. Development of a comprehensive system of feed analysis and its application to forages. *J. Anim. Sci.* 26:119–28.
33. Shenk, John S., and F. C. Elliott. 1971. Plant compositional changes resulting from two cycles of directional selection for nutritive value of alfalfa. *Crop Sci.* 11:521–24.

34. Jones, J., and F. C. Elliott. 1969. Two rapid assays for saponin in individual alfalfa plants. *Crop Sci.* 9:688–91.
35. Pederson, M. W., and Li-Chun Wang. 1971. Modification of saponin content of alfalfa through selection. *Crop Sci.* 11:833–35.
36. Miltimore, J. E., J. M. McArthur, J. L. Masson, and D. L. Ashley. 1970. Bloat investigations. The threshold Fraction 1 (18S) protein concentration for bloat and relationships between bloat and lipid, tannin, Ca, Mg, Ni, and Zn concentrations in alfalfa. *Can. J. Anim. Sci.* 50:61–68.

ing material for further evaluation. (See Fig. 11.2.) Up to the present time many of the older improved cultivars in forage crops have been developed by some form of mass selection.

In the normal operation of a controlled mass selection program with cross-pollinated forage species, a large population of space-planted individuals should be established and critically examined for desired characters. In cases where seedling reaction to a disease or insect is comparable to adult plant responses, effective selection can be achieved under controlled greenhouse or growth chamber environments. Individual plants that meet specifications required in the objectives of the study may then be handled in a number of different ways.

1. Open-pollinated seed from each plant may be bulked and the selection process repeated in successive generations.
2. Open-pollinated seed may be harvested from each selected individual and grown in separate progeny rows. Further selection may then be practiced both on a maternal-line basis and on a single-plant basis within families.
3. Selected plants may be allowed to intercross only among themselves, either by removing the remaining undesirable individuals before they flower or by vegetatively transferring the selected seedlings or plants to an isolation block for intercrossing. Continued repetition of this process is a form of recurrent selection.

After five years of mass selection in big bluestem marked improvement was obtained in leafiness and other agronomic characters.[37] Seed setting was increased in alfalfa by practicing maternal line selection in the development of the cultivar 'Ferax.'[38] 'Florida 66' alfalfa also is the product of successive cycles of mass selection. The

FIG. 11.2. *Plants that survive natural selection may . . . serve as valuable sources of breeding material.* Indigenous strains of sideoats grama grown under comparable conditions at Ames, Iowa, showing marked differences in earliness of maturity and leafiness: (1) North Dakota, (2) Nebraska, and (3) Oklahoma. *Iowa SCS photo.*

effectiveness of changing populations by selecting plants of different types and allowing each type to intercross has been demonstrated with sideoats grama.[39] Striking progress in breeding for wilt resistance using techniques for infesting seedling alfalfa plants has been reported.[40]

Strain building in forages may include a wide variety of breeding techniques ranging from relatively simple mass selection to more intensive evaluation of the individual plants used in the production of improved cultivars.[41] One of the essential features of strain-building methods, as used by the Welsh plant breeding station at Aberysthwyth, Wales, is the maintenance of the original clones used as members of the improved cultivar. As more desirable

37. Law, Alvin G., and Kling L. Anderson. 1940. The effect of selection and inbreeding on the growth of big bluestem (*Andropon furcatus* Muhl.). *J. Amer. Soc. Agron.* 32:931–43.

38. Fryer, J. R. 1939. The maternal-line selection method of breeding for increased seed setting in alfalfa. *Sci. Agr.* 20:131–39.

39. Harlan, Jack R. 1950. The breeding behavior of sideoats grama in partially isolated populations. *Agron. J.* 42:20–24.

40. Barnes, D. K., C. H. Hanson, F. I. Frosheiser, and L. J. Elling. 1971. Recurrent selection for bacterial wilt resistance in alfalfa. *Crop Sci.* 11:545–46.

41. Jenkins, T. J. 1931. The method and technique of selection, breeding, and strain-building in grasses. *Imp. Bur. Plant Genet. Herbage Plants* 3:5–34.

individuals are found, they either may be incorporated into the cultivar or replace existing clones in a particular cultivar. This procedure requires the maintenance of stocks of the individual components of improved cultivars. The forage breeding program of the Welsh plant breeding station has produced a large number of superior cultivars in several forage crops, including perennial ryegrass, meadow fescue, creeping red fescue, timothy, orchardgrass, red clover, and white clover.

❧ RECURRENT SELECTION

Earlier studies in corn breeding have laid a general background on theory and practice for recurrent selection in forage crop improvement. As the name suggests, recurrent selection is a system of plant breeding in which selected individual plants (or their progeny derived from selfing) are intercrossed to form a new population. The immediate population from intercrossing is designated as the *first cycle* of recurrent selection. Plants are selected for the same characters from the first cycle and again intercrossed to produce progenies designated as the *second cycle* of recurrent selection. Selecting plants as parents for succeeding cycles is continued until further progress does not justify continuation of the program.

There are two general classifications of recurrent selection. When plants are chosen for recombination only on the basis of their characteristics per se, the term *phenotypic* recurrent selection applies. When plants are chosen for recombination on the basis of either their inbred or crossbred progenies, the term *genotypic* recurrent selection is used because such tests aid in revealing the genotype of the selected individuals.

Marked progress has been shown in changing plant type and plant weight by two or three cycles of phenotypic recurrent

selection in sweetclover.[42] These results strongly suggest that this method of forage crop breeding may be a very useful procedure for altering the composition of a strain for plant characters that have a comparatively high transmission to their progenies. In general, the advance per cycle would be expected to be less for characters strongly affected by the environment than for those in which selection could be more accurately made. Further data on recurrent selection as a method in alfalfa breeding have been presented.[43] Marked progress also has been shown in recurrent selection for resistance to southern anthracnose in alfalfa.[44]

❧ SUMMARY

With the extreme diversity in methods of pollination, longevity, method of reproduction, and agricultural utilization it is quite likely that nearly all presently used methods of forage crop breeding will continue to be employed.

Forage breeding is complex. It is made especially difficult by the problems of evaluating breeding materials to fit the many uses for which species may be grown and by the time required for the evaluation of a single generation of breeding. The forage breeder, however, has the opportunity to utilize basic principles of genetics, cytology, and breeding techniques that have become available through research on many forage crops and from analogous studies made with other self- and cross-pollinated crops. In the final analysis these basic principles are the important concepts which may lead to the formulation of the most effective improvement programs.

42. Johnson, I. J., and A. S. El Banna. 1957. Effectiveness of successive cycles of phenotype recurrent selection in sweetclover. *Agron. J.* 49:120–25.

43. Hill, R. R., Jr., C. H. Hanson, and T. H. Busbice. 1969. Effect of four recurrent selection programs on two alfalfa populations. *Crop Sci.* 9:363–65.

44. Devine, T. E., C. H. Hanson, S. A. Ostazeski, and T. A. Campbell. 1971. Selection for resistance to anthracnose (*Colletotrichum trifolii*) in four alfalfa populations. *Crop Sci.* 11:854–55.

❧ QUESTIONS

1. What procedures can be used to determine if a species is primarily cross-pollinated?
2. How could you determine how many different genes were present for self-sterility in a crop such as white clover?
3. If you wished to evaluate foreign plant introductions for possible use in a breeding program, where would you obtain seed?
4. What plant characters important for survival in nature also may be useful under cultivation? Which ones are detrimental?
5. Explain why forage yields of cultivars grown in a space-planted nursery may not agree with their yields when grown in a solid-planted stand.
6. Why is it desirable to maintain production of the *breeder* and *foundation* classes of seed of a cultivar in the area of its adaptation?
7. Why is the rate of gain per generation in recurrent selection procedures dependent upon the complexity of inheritance for the character?

G. O. MOTT / *University of Florida*

12

EVALUATING FORAGE PRODUCTION

⚘

EVALUATING forages requires the measurement of quantity and quality of forages produced per unit of land, labor, and capital. Forages may be harvested as hay, green chop, dehy, silage, or pasture; but each must be converted to animal product to be useful to man. Only hay and dehy are marketed in sufficient quantity in trade channels to establish a market value. As green chop, silage, or pasture, forages are restricted with respect to the time and place they can be used. A direct market value under such restrictions frequently does not exist. Values are best established in terms of the animal product resulting from their utilization. Forages may furnish all or only part of the complete feeding system.

⚘ QUANTITY AND QUALITY

Two basic biological systems are involved in forage production and utilization. They are recognized as the "environment-plant" system and the "plant-animal" system.[1] The economist recognizes these as the "feed production" and "feed utilization and conversion" phases of livestock feeding systems.[2] Yield of ani-

mal product is dependent upon the amount and quality of forage produced and its conversion when consumed by the animal. Forage production per unit area of land in terms of a feed unit may be considered the *quantity* aspect of animal production measurement. Response of the animal to forage is a measure of its *quality in toto,* providing animal potential is a constant and forage is the sole source of feed. Figure 12.1 gives the relationship of some of the important factors associated with estimating output of animal product per ha.

Nutritive value of a forage is characterized by its chemical composition, digestibility, and nature of the digested products. Chemical composition is a factor associated with only the plant and its environment; but digestibility, the nature of the digested products, and their efficiency of utilization are associated with both the plant and animal.[3] Rate of consumption of a forage is related to the readiness with which a forage is selected and eaten.[4] It is also

⚘ G. O. MOTT is Professor of Agronomy, University of Florida, and served on the faculty of Purdue University from 1940–68. He holds the Ph.D. degree from Cornell University. Since 1955 he has been a consultant in pasture research programs.

1. Matches, Arthur G. 1970. Pasture research methods. Proc. Natl. Conf. Forage Qual. Eval. Util., pp. I1–I32. Nebr. Center Continuing Ed., Lincoln.
2. McConnen, R. J., C. M. McCorkle, Jr., and D. D. Caton. 1963. Feed-livestock relationships: A model for analyzing management decisions. *Agr. Econ. Res.* 15:41–48.
3. Raymond, W. R. 1969. The nutritive value of forage crops. *Advan. Agron.* 21:1–108.
4. Marten, Gordon C. 1970. Measurement and significance of forage palatability. Proc. Natl. Conf. Forage Qual. Eval. Util., pp. D1–D55. Nebr. Center Continuing Ed., Lincoln.

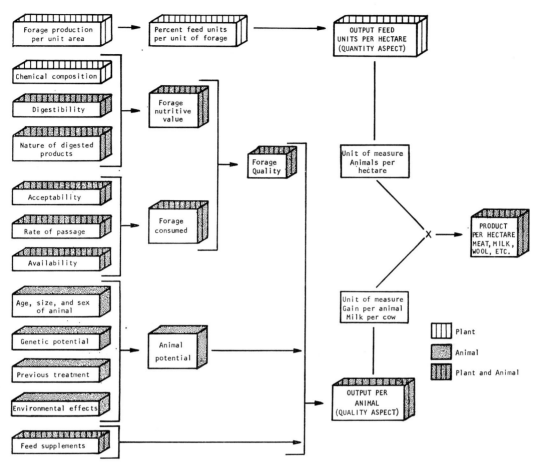

Fig. 12.1. Diagrammatic representation of the relationship of amount and quality of forage to animal response and animal production per unit area of land.

related to the rate of passage in the digestive tract, which is a function of the fiber mass generated during digestion and quantity of forage available to the animal.[5] Forage quality takes into account both nutritive value and rate of consumption. Output per animal in feed-animal production systems is a function of forage quality but is also dependent upon animal potential and feeds other than forages introduced into the system.

Product per ha is dependent upon the output per animal (quality aspect) and the number of animals which a ha of land will support (quantity aspect). These three units of measure are related to each other in that:[6]

Product/animal × animals/ha = product/ha

❦ FORAGE YIELD AND BOTANICAL COMPOSITION

Methods for estimating total yield or yield of component species are based upon the following relationship:

$$\text{Yield/unit area} = f(\text{density, height})$$

5. Waldo, Dale R. 1970. Factors influencing the voluntary intake of forages. Proc. Natl. Conf. Forage Qual. Eval. Util., pp. E1–E22. Nebr. Center Continuing Ed., Lincoln.

6. Joint committee of ASA, ADSA, ASAP, and ASRM. 1962. Pasture and Range Research Techniques. Comstock, Ithaca, N.Y.

In small plot trials or clipped quadrats in the grazed pasture, bulk density or yield is determined by cutting a predetermined area and weighing the harvested forage. Since sampling errors are very large and the sample size represents such a small part of the population, large numbers of samples are required for reliable estimates of yield.[7] Methods have been developed giving estimates of yield based upon density and height measurements.[8,9] Instruments have been constructed that give an integrated estimate of the biomass present in grasslands. By determining the dielectric constant of a fixed volume of a mixture of air and forage, the amount of forage can be estimated.[10,11] Estimation of yield by the attenuation of β-particles has also been proposed.[12,13]

Herbage consumption in the grazed pasture is measured by estimating yield in ungrazed and grazed areas. Under rotational grazing systems in which the grazing period does not exceed four to six days, before and after grazing estimates of yield are made. Under systems of grazing management in which the grazing period exceeds four to six days, cages may be used to protect areas from grazing to estimate yield of ungrazed herbage. Uncaged areas are harvested periodically at the same time as the caged areas to measure consumption by the "difference method."[14]

Hand separation is the most reliable method for estimating yield and percentage composition of component species. Samples for hand separation may be obtained from clipped plots or from cages in the grazed pasture. Separations are best made immediately after harvest, but plant material may be held for short periods at 0 C or for longer periods if frozen. Several other methods have been suggested for measuring population density.[8,9,15,16] The point quadrat, number of tillers per unit area, ground cover, and visual estimates of density methods have been used successfully under specific conditions. Such estimates when multiplied by height usually are closely correlated with yield.

Since the variation between samples for estimating yield, percentage composition, and yield of component species is extremely high, two sampling methods are frequently used in combination to obtain a more reliable estimate of the parameter of interest. A rapid method such as ocular estimation is used in combination with harvested samples to take advantage of the large number of samples that can be acquired by the ocular method and the accuracy of the clipping method. From 10 to 20% of the samples estimated by the ocular method are selected at random, clipped, and the forage weighed. Regression analysis of the two estimates of yield is then used to adjust for systematic error. The number of sample units is dependent upon the magnitude of sample variation and precision desired.[7] If an estimate of sample variation is available and the desired precision known, statistical tables may be consulted to determine the number of samples required.

* MEASURING FORAGE QUALITY

The term "forage quality" takes into account both nutritive value of forages and their rate of consumption (Fig. 12.1). It has been postulated that the level of di-

7. Brown, Dorothy. 1954. Methods of surveying and measuring vegetation. Commonwealth Bur. Past. and Field Crops Bull. 42. Hurley, England.
8. Spedding, C. R. W., and R. V. Large. 1957. A point quadrat method for the description of pasture in terms of height and density. J. Brit. Grassl. Soc. 12:229–34.
9. Evans, R. A., and M. B. Jones. 1958. Plant height times total ground cover versus clipped samples for estimating forage production. Agron. J. 50:504–6.
10. Fletcher, J. E., and H. E. Robinson. 1956. A capacitance meter for estimating forage weight. J. Range Manage. 9:96–97.
11. Campbell, A. G., D. S. M. Philips, and E. D. O'Reilly. 1962. An electronic instrument for pasture yield estimation. J. Brit. Grassl. Soc. 17:89–101.
12. Teare, I. D., G. O. Mott, and J. R. Eaton. 1966. Beta attenuation—A technique for estimating forage yield in situ. Rad. Bot. 6:7–11.
13. Barta, A. L., and I. D. Teare. 1968. Forage density gauging with Sr90 for estimating green forage yield in situ. Crop Sci. 8:53–54.
14. Klingman, D. L., S. R. Miles, and G. O. Mott. 1943. The cage method for determining consumption and yield of pasture herbage. Agron. J. 35:739.

15. Leasure, J. K. 1949. Determining the species composition of swards. J. Amer. Soc. Agron. 41:204–6.
16. Levy, E. B., and E. A. Madden. 1933. The point method of pasture analysis. N.Z. J. Agr. 46:267–79.

TABLE 12.1 ❧ Schematic relationships of digestion measurements

Feed	feed dry matter*	feed organic matter†	feed energy‡
↓ ↘ Feces			
Digestible	digestible dry matter	digestible organic matter	digestible energy
↓ ↘ Urine and Methane			
Metabolizable	. . .	metabolizable organic matter	metabolizable energy
↓ ↘ Heat increment			
Net	. . .	. . .	net energy

* Dry matter—moisture excluded on feed and waste products.
† Organic matter—moisture and ash excluded on feed and waste products.
‡ Energy—energy yield of feed and waste products.

gestible energy intake is the most important factor determining animal performance.[3,17] Ruminant animals are capable of consuming five to six times their maintenance intake on concentrate feeds, but on forages a rate of intake of three times maintenance is in the maximum range.[18] A large number of factors influence both nutritive value and forage consumption, and only the more important ones are indicated in Figure 12.1. Rate of forage intake is limited primarily by the undigested fiber mass generated in the rumenoreticulum and by the limited capacity of the lower digestive tract to handle this residue.[5] If forage is high in digestibility, the residue from digestion is at a minimum and the capacity of the lower tract does not impose any restriction upon rate of passage. Forages that are low in digestibility or have a slow rate of digestion result in accumulation of a fiber mass which passes slowly through the digestive tract. Other factors related to consumption are acceptability of the forage and amount of forage offered to the animal. Deficiencies of protein, minerals, and vitamins also may restrict forage consumption under certain circumstances.

17. Crampton, E. W. 1957. Interrelationship between digestible nutrient and energy content, voluntary dry matter intake, and overall feeding value of forages. *J. Anim. Sci.* 16:546–52.
18. Reid, J. T. 1970. Will meat, milk and egg production be possible in the future? Proc. Cornell Nutr. Conf. for Feed Manufacturers, pp. 50–63.

FORAGE NUTRITIVE VALUE

A clearer understanding of the relationship between various digestion measurements is obtained from the schematic presentation in Table 12.1.

Measurement of digestible energy is a relatively simple procedure and is considered quite satisfactory for estimating nutritive value of forages. Energy yield of feed and feces is determined by standard procedures in a bomb calorimeter. This method of expressing nutritive value is much simpler than total digestible nutrients (TDN). Determination of TDN requires the chemical analysis of feed and feces into component parts: crude protein, crude fiber, nitrogen-free extract, and ether extract. From the analytical information the quantity of each component digested per 100 kg of feed is computed and the sum of these components is TDN.

ESTIMATING DIGESTIBILITY. In conventional digestion trials, feed and feces are measured directly and indigestibility of dry matter (DM) (or some component) is determined according to the following equation:

Indigestibility of DM (%)

$$= 100 \times \frac{\text{fecal DM (kg/day)}}{\text{feed DM (kg/day)}}$$

Under grazing conditions, however, amount

of feed is not known and amount of feces is difficult to determine. Indirect methods known as "indicator ratio" techniques are used to estimate the indigestibility of the DM in grazed pastures according to the following equation:

Indigestibility of DM (%) = 100
$$\times \frac{\text{concentration of indicator, forage DM (\%)}}{\text{concentration of indicator, feces DM (\%)}}$$

In addition to the "conventional digestion trial," and the "indicator ratio" technique, it has been found that certain components of the feces are highly correlated with indigestibility. Chromogen, crude fiber, and fecal N have all been tested as indicators of digestibility; the technique is known as the "fecal index" method. It consists of determining the concentration of one of the indicators in the feces. With the use of previously determined mathematical formulas the digestibility of dry matter can be estimated. Advantages of this method are that no measurements are made on the forage (of which it is difficult to obtain a sample representative of that consumed by the animal) and total fecal collection is not required.

IN VITRO TECHNIQUES. Laboratory procedures for estimating digestibility are proving to be very useful forage evaluation techniques.[19] Extensive reviews have been published of the many procedures that have been studied, and new ones are being proposed.[20] The most widely accepted procedure being used routinely in many laboratories is the Tilley and Terry two-stage *in vitro* rumen fermentation system or some modification of this. This system attempts to simulate the digestive fermentation process in the rumen followed by an acid-pepsin digestion to simulate the process in the lower digestive tract. Each of the two stages requires 48 hours for completion. Since the procedure is empirical, standard conditions must be rigidly followed.

Since *in vivo* digestibility is expressed as digestible DM, digestible organic matter, and digestible energy, results from the *in vitro* system may also be expressed in the same terms by determining appropriate components in the original sample and in the residue after digestion. (See footnote, Table 12.1.) Measurements made of digestibility in the laboratory have been found to be highly correlated with *in vivo* measurements. An advantage of the *in vitro* system is that only a very small sample of 1 g or less of plant material is required to make the test. The method is very useful as a research tool for estimating effects of various factors upon digestibility of forages. It is now possible to study the nutritional value of breeders' lines, effect of physiological stage of growth, effect of fertilizer treatments, and many other factors associated with forage quality.

FORAGE CONSUMPTION

Since rate of forage consumption is generally considered the most important aspect of overall forage quality, several methods have been developed to measure consumption rates under various circumstances. The accepted method for hay, silage, dehydrated, and pelleted forages is to feed weighed quantities daily in excess of the animal's capacity. This ensures that the amount of feed on offer is not limiting rate of consumption.

Under grazing conditions indirect methods have been developed to estimate the consumption rate of the grazing animal.

ESTIMATING RATE OF CONSUMPTION. To measure intake, both digestibility of forage and rate of fecal output must be estimated on animals in the grazed pasture. The relationship is expressed by the following equation:[21]

19. Johnson, Ronald R. 1970. The development and application of *in vitro* rumen fermentation methods for forage evaluation. Proc. Natl. Conf. Forage Qual. Eval. Util., pp. M1–M18. Nebr. Center Continuing Ed., Lincoln.
20. Johnson, Ronald R. 1966. Techniques and procedures for *in vitro* and *in vivo* rumen studies. *J. Anim. Sci.* 25:855.

21. Reid, J. Tom. 1958. Pasture evaluation in relation to feed efficiency. *In* C. R. Hogland et al. (eds.), Feed Utilization of Dairy Cattle. Iowa State Univ. Press, Ames.

Feed DM intake (kg/day)

$$= \frac{\text{fecal DM (kg/day)}}{\text{indigestibility of DM (\%)}}$$

A similar equation may be written for any component of the forage by substituting that component (e.g., crude protein, organic matter, or energy) for "dry matter" in each term of the equation:

Feed energy intake (kcal/day)

$$= \frac{\text{fecal energy (kcal/day)}}{\text{indigestibility of energy (\%)}}$$

Equipment has been designed to make a total collection of feces; however, methods are available for estimating fecal production from a sample. An indigestible indicator is fed to the animal in known amounts and dilution is measured by determining the concentration in a fecal sample. The most widely used indicator is chromic oxide, Cr_2O_3. Fecal production is estimated as follows:[21]

Fecal DM (gm/day)

$$= \frac{Cr_2O_3 \text{ ingested (mg/day)}}{Cr_2O_3 \text{ concentration of feces (mg/gm DM)}}$$

LABORATORY METHODS FOR ESTIMATING CONSUMPTION. Several promising laboratory procedures have been proposed for predicting consumption rate of forages.[22] The initial stage of *in vitro* cellulose fermentation (12-hour digestion) has been found to be closely related to consumption rate within a limited spectrum of forages.[23] Various solubility procedures have been proposed, including dry matter dissolved in distilled water and in 0.075 normal HCl solution of the enzyme pepsin. Correlations of 0.95 have been reported between the latter procedure and intake of digestible energy *in vivo*.[22] The above procedures give results that are related in a positive way to consumption rate. In addition it has been found that cell wall constituents give negative correlations with consumption rate.[24] This suggests that consumption rate of forages is closely related to the ratio of cell content (soluble portion) to fiber (cell wall). This also suggests that within the limits of nutritive value of most forages, physical limitations imposed by rumen fill may be the most important factor regulating consumption rate.[25]

❧ GRAZING TRIAL

Information generated from grazing experiments is useful in developing forage-livestock feeding systems. Output is in terms of animal response and animal product per unit area of land. The grazing trial, if properly conducted, gives reliable estimates of both quality and quantity of feed produced by the pasture. Inputs into the pasture-animal system are associated with climatic factors, grazing intensity, addition of soil amendments, and supplementary feeding.

EXPERIMENTAL PASTURE

In the selection of a site for a pasture experiment, it obviously is impossible to sample a large portion of the population of pastures within a region. Indeed, the investigator may be restricted to land and animals owned by the institution, with little if any opportunity to apply accepted random sampling techniques. The seriousness of this restriction is dependent upon the application of inferences to be made from the experiment and whether treatment $\times$ site interactions exist or are already known. If treatments under study are expected to array themselves in the same order irrespective of site within a region of interest, then restrictions placed upon location may not be very serious. It is assumed the investigator has some prior knowledge of the treatments to be studied

22. Donefer, E. 1970. Forage solubility measurements in relation to nutritive value. Proc. Natl. Conf. Forage Qual. Eval. Util., pp. Q1–Q6. Nebr. Center Continuing Ed., Lincoln.
23. Donefer, E., E. W. Crampton, and L. E. Lloyd. 1960. Prediction of the nutritive value index of a forage from *in vitro* rumen fermentation data. *J. Anim. Sci.* 19:545.

24. Van Soest, P. J. 1965. Symposium of factors influencing the voluntary intake of herbage by ruminants: Voluntary intake in relation to chemical composition and digestibility. *J. Anim. Sci.* 24:834.
25. Baumgardt, B. R. 1970. Voluntary feed intake by ruminants: Models and practical applications. Proc. Cornell Nutr. Conf. for Feed Manufacturers, pp. 85–92.

and of the region with respect to soils, moisture relationships, and previous treatment. The experiment should be located on land representative of the region to which results are to be applied.

Within an experimental site, pastures usually can be grouped in blocks to provide greater uniformity of soils, topography, and previous treatment. On rolling land it usually is preferable to run fences up and down the slope, so that soil variability between pastures is at a minimum.[6] Field designs adapted to agronomic experiments are appropriate for pastures within a grazing trial. The small number of treatments in such trials and the relatively large land area required dictate the use of simple designs. Randomized block designs usually are adequate to control field variability. Use of more complex designs might result in somewhat lower experimental errors, but the accompanying reduction in degrees of freedom for error may offset this advantage.

The complexity of forage measurement by livestock is well illustrated in Figure 12.1. In addition to the factors illustrated, many others are frequently measured directly on the herbage. The number of pastures per treatment (replications) and number of animals per pasture are dependent upon the measurements to be taken.[26] In general, units of measure expressed on a "per ha" basis require more pastures per treatment with fewer animals per pasture than units of measure expressed on a "per animal" basis, which require fewer pastures with more animals per pasture for a given precision.

In "quality" studies the animal variability is the major source of error. Two to three pastures per treatment with 5–11 animals per pasture usually is adequate.[6] In studies requiring measurement of yield per ha, three or more replications are desirable, with as few as two animals per

pasture. Since pasture size is dependent upon number of animals to be grazed and carrying capacity of the pasture, it is only necessary to make the pasture large enough to provide forage for the desired number of animals. It is not necessary that all pastures be the same size, especially if from prior knowledge it is known that carrying capacities of the various treatments will differ. Size of pastures for different treatments may then vary inversely with carrying capacity.

EXPERIMENTAL ANIMALS

In grazing trials, experimenters, should use the class of livestock to which results are to apply.[6] This is particularly true in trials measuring forage quality. If milk production of the dairy cow is the unit of measure of greatest interest, gain of beef cattle or sheep may not be a very good indicator of the milk-producing potential of forage. If yield of feed nutrients is of primary interest, with little or no concern for output of animal product, then class of livestock is not so important if suitable TDN or other feed conversion factors are available for the animals employed.

It frequently is desirable in a grazing trial to study animals that differ in class, milk production level, age, condition, previous treatment, or other factors.[27] Animals differing in one or more characteristics may be grazed in separate pastures, considering the various levels of the factor associated with animals in a factorial set of treatments. Animals that have similar selective habits of grazing may be grazed in the same pasture. Different kinds of animals within the pasture become a split-plot feature of the design. Use of this technique greatly increases information obtained from a grazing trial without an increase in size of experiment. This technique has been used successfully for studies in which grazing steers have been wintered

26. Peterson, R. G., and H. L. Lucas. 1960. Experimental errors in grazing trials. Proc. 8th Int. Grassl. Congr., pp. 747–50 (Reading, England).

27. Mott, G. O. 1959. Animal variation and measurement of forage quality. Symposium on forage evaluation. IV. *Agron. J.* 51:223–26.

at different levels of feeding, for steers of different age groups, and for steers versus heifers.[28-30] The same idea can be applied to dairy cows having different levels of production, provided the investigator accepts the assumption that different animals have the same grazing habits. If this assumption is not tenable, proper interpretation can be obtained only by putting different kinds of animals on separate pastures.

ANIMAL ASPECTS OF GRAZING TRIAL DESIGN

Designs developed for animal feeding experiments also may be applied to animals in a grazing trial.[31] Grouping animals into homogeneous blocks and allotting them at random across all pastures on all treatments or confounding blocks with field replications will reduce the error for treatment contrasts to a minimum. If pretest performance data or data on an initial characteristic are available, covariance may be used to reduce experimental error. This is especially effective for dairy cow milk and fat production.[32]

Change-over designs are frequently used in trials in which output of milk per cow is of primary interest. A comprehensive review of these designs is available.[32] Continuous trials are preferred in experiments measuring increase in liveweight per animal and per unit area of land since weighing errors are usually confounded with time periods in change-over designs. For increase in liveweight, experimental errors associated with animals decrease as the length of experimental period increases.[27]

Since change-over designs require that animals remain on each treatment in a sequence for a relatively short period, day-to-day variation due to fill and other factors accounts for a large proportion of total variation. Differences in treatments are difficult to demonstrate when these designs are used.

TESTER ANIMALS AND THE PUT-AND-TAKE METHOD

Adjusting the number of animals in a pasture to the amount of feed available is a difficult decision facing the pasture investigator. Likewise, the farmer must make similar decisions with respect to the management of his pastures. If there is an excess of forage, then it must be decided whether to reduce the feed supply by harvesting a portion of the pasture, increase number of animals to consume excess feed, or reduce the size of pasture with a temporary fence. In grazing trials in which relatively small pastures are used, many investigators use two types of animals in the pasture. These have been designated as "tester animals" and "put-and-take" animals. The number of tester animals is determined by the predicted minimum carrying capacity of the pasture and usually remains constant throughout the experiment. Put-and-take animals are taken from a group of reserve animals maintained specifically to graze the excess forage beyond that needed for tester animals, and the number varies according to the feed supply during the experiment.[31]

For computing animal performance (*G*) in the put-and-take method, only tester animals are used since these animals remain on pasture during the entire period of the trial and give the best estimate of forage quality. For estimating carrying capacity in terms of animal days per ha (*D*) all animals, including put-and-take animals, are considered. If all animals are essentially alike with respect to their rate of forage consumption, then simply counting the number of animal days per ha will

28. McVey, W. M., R. E. Smith, H. N. Wheaton, and G. O. Mott. 1959. Beef production from alfalfa-grass pastures when grazed by steers wintered at four levels of nutrition. Purdue Univ. Agron. Mimeo. AY 147.

29. Quinn, L. R., G. O. Mott, W. B. Bischoff, and A. C. McClung. 1958. Stilbestrol and its effect on pasture-fed zebu steers. Ibec Res. Inst. Bull. 15.

30. Peterson, R. C., G. O. Mott, M. E. Heath, and W. M. Beeson. 1962. Comparison of tall fescue and orchardgrass for grazing in southern Indiana. Purdue Univ. Res. Prog. Rept. 26.

31. Mott, G. O., and H. L. Lucas. 1952. The design, conduct, and interpretation of grazing trials on cultivated and improved pastures. Proc. 6th Int. Grassl. Congr., pp. 1380–85 (State College, Pa.).

32. Lucas, H. L. 1958. Experimental designs and analyses for feed efficiency trials with dairy cattle. *In* C. R. Hogland et al. (eds.). Feed Utilization of Dairy Cattle, pp. 177–92. Iowa State Univ. Press, Ames.

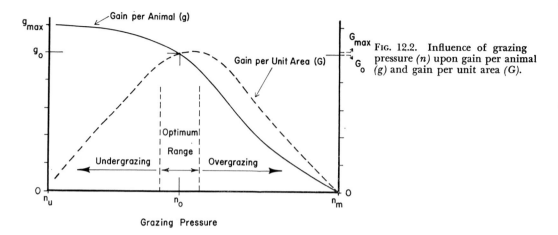

FIG. 12.2. Influence of grazing pressure *(n)* upon gain per animal *(g)* and gain per unit area *(G)*.

suffice. However, if all animals do not have similar requirements, then animal days appropriate for tester animals may be computed as follows: feed units consumed per ha *(F)* are computed from the requirements of all animals for maintenance, changes in body weight, and milk production (dairy cows). Feed unit requirements for a tester animal day *(T)* are then determined in the same manner for tester animals appearing in a particular pasture. Tester animal days per ha *(D')* are then computed as $D' = F/T$ and product per ha *(P)* as $P = D' \times G$.

The put-and-take system of grazing in pasture trials has the advantage of maintaining the number of animals in equilibrium with feed supply without the necessity of harvesting excess forage. It also has the advantage of giving an estimate of changes in carrying capacity of the pasture during the grazing season. At the same time changes in quality of pasture on offer is measured, providing grazing pressure is maintained near the optimum range. Intensity of defoliation may be more easily controlled with the put-and-take system, especially when it is combined with rotational grazing. Decisions to add or remove put-and-take animals are usually determined subjectively. This is no different from deciding how much of a pasture to harvest or to fence out with a temporary fence. However, an error in judgment may be much more serious than

in the put-and-take system where adjustments may be made more frequently if necessary. Since moving animals in and out of a pasture may have a disturbing influence on the performance of tester animals, it is strongly recommended that shifting of animals be held to a minimum.

GRAZING PRESSURE

In a grazing trial it seldom is true that the amount of feed supplied by different treatments is the same. Similarly, replicates of the same treatment may produce different quantities of feed. If all pastures are to be grazed at their optimum stocking rate, provision must be made for equating the number of animals to the forage supply. Adjusting number of animals or area of pasture offered the animals (e.g., strip grazing, harvesting excess forage during flush growth periods, or feeding supplementary feed during periods of low production) are methods used to accomplish equal grazing pressure.[33]

Imperfect knowledge of the optimum for various treatments as well as failure to attain the optima for all pastures may result in biased comparisons. If a pasture is undergrazed, the estimate of animal-days per ha will be too low and the potential production of animal product will not

33. Mott, G. O. 1960. Grazing pressure and the measurement of pasture production. Proc. 8th Int. Grassl. Congr., pp. 606–11 (Reading, England).

be reached. If the pasture is overgrazed, performance per animal will be reduced and potential production of animal product underestimated.

The relationship between grazing pressure (n) and gain per animal (g) and gain per unit area (G) is shown in Figure 12.2. Between n_u and n_o the gain per animal is primarily a function of variation in quality of forage on offer. The greater the variation in forage quality, the greater the degree of selection by the grazing animal. If forage is completely homogeneous so that no selection is possible, gain per animal will be constant at g_o from n_u to n_o.[34,35] In this situation a horizontal line from g_o to the intercept with n_o would then best describe the relationship of gain per animal and grazing pressure. Such conditions occur only rarely in the grazed pasture. Maximum gain per animal (g_{max}) will vary for different species, mixtures, and degree of selective grazing.

From n_o to n_m, rate of forage consumption and gain per animal is determined primarily by the amount of forage on offer. As number of animals is increased and grazing pressure becomes greater than n_o, selective grazing is diminished since the fixed amount of forage available must be shared by more animals. Further increases in stocking rate into the "overgrazing" range result in only enough forage consumption per animal to meet their maintenance requirements, and gain per animal becomes zero. Point n_m is the grazing pressure at which animals are neither losing nor gaining weight.

Gain per unit area is described by the broken line in Figure 12.2. Maximum gain per unit area (G_{max}) is reached in the upper segment of the optimum range $(n > n_o)$ but at some sacrifice in gain per animal. In the lower segment of the optimum range $(n < n_o)$, gain per animal is

increased but at a sacrifice in gain per unit area.

Optimum grazing pressure must then be considered as an optimum range which is a compromise between output per animal and output per unit area. It should be emphasized that this discussion of grazing pressure relates only to animal output and does not take into consideration the optima for plant species in the pasture. For persistence of certain forage species a lower grazing pressure $(n < n_o)$, even into the undergrazing range, may be required.

OTHER FACTORS

Many factors affect animal production and must be considered when evaluating harvested forages and pastures. Variation in age, size, sex, and genetic potential of experimental animals can best be controlled by experimental design. Pretrial information and other factors that can be quantified may be controlled by proper regression procedures. A more comprehensive treatment of these and other techniques is available.[6]

❧ QUESTIONS

1. What are two aspects of pasture measurement?
2. How do forages vary with respect to quality?
3. What is the mathematical relationship between gain per animal, animal-days per ha, and gain per ha?
4. Describe agronomic methods of measuring forage consumed on pasture.
5. How can botanical composition be determined without harvesting the forage?
6. In sampling forage the number of samples to take is dependent upon what factors?
7. Why is it necessary to use an adjusted stocking rate in grazing trials?
8. What is meant by grazing pressure?
9. Why have laboratory *in vitro* methods become an important tool in forage quality evaluation?
10. How is rate of forage consumption related to animal performance, carrying capacity, and the formulation of livestock feeding systems?

34. Owen, J. B., and W. J. Ridgman. 1968. The design and interpretation of experiments to study animal production from grazed pasture. *J. Agr. Sci.* 71:327–35.
35. Peterson, R. G., H. L. Lucas, and G. O. Mott. 1965. Relationship between rate of stocking and per animal and per acre performance on pasture. *Agron. J.* 57:27–30.

C. H. HANSON AND D. K. BARNES

Agricultural Research Service, USDA

13

ALFALFA

ℒ

ALFALFA, *Medicago sativa* L., originated in southwest Asia, although forms of
it and related species are found as wild
plants scattered over central Asia and into
Siberia. It is believed that alfalfa was first
cultivated in Iran. Pliny and Strabo, early
Roman writers, recorded that alfalfa was
introduced into Greece as early as 490 B.C.
by the invading Medes and Persians for the
sustenance of their chariot horses and other
animals. Later, alfalfa was carried into
Italy and other European countries, including Spain. From there it was taken by
the early Spanish explorers to Central and
South America.[1]

The first recorded attempt to grow alfalfa in the U.S. was in Georgia in 1736. It
was grown by both George Washington
and Thomas Jefferson about 1790. However, it was not until about 1850, when it

was introduced on the West Coast, that it
really succeeded. In the gold rush days
gold seekers brought alfalfa seed from
Chile to California where it grew vigorously on the fertile limestone soils. From
California alfalfa spread rapidly to Utah,
Kansas, and other midwestern states and
later to the eastern states.

An introduction in 1857 to Minnesota
from Baden, Germany, by Wendelin
Grimm, paved the way for a great expansion of alfalfa culture in the north central
states. After several generations of natural
selection under severe Minnesota conditions, the 'Grimm' cultivar became sufficiently hardy for that climate.

ℒ DISTRIBUTION AND ADAPTATION

Alfalfa, or lucerne, as it is called in many
European countries, is worldwide in distribution.[2] Figure 13.1 shows alfalfa hay production by regions, with the greatest production in the north central region. In
1970 Wisconsin, Minnesota, and South Dakota each harvested over 800,000 ha of alfalfa for hay. Wisconsin led with 1.62 million ha. The marked increase in hectarage

ℒ C. H. HANSON is Leader of Applied Plant
Genetics Laboratory, Agricultural Research Center,
Beltsville, Md. He received the M.A. degree from
the University of Missouri and the Ph.D. from
North Carolina State University. For twelve years
he was engaged in breeding and genetic research on
alfalfa and lespedeza at Raleigh, N.C.

ℒ D. K. BARNES is Research Geneticist, ARS,
USDA, at the University of Minnesota, St. Paul.
He received the M.S. degree from the University of
Minnesota and the Ph.D. from Pennsylvania State
University. Since 1953 his major area of research
has been alfalfa.

1. Tysdal, H. M., and H. L. Westover. 1937. Alfalfa
improvement, pp. 1122–53. USDA Yearbook Agr.
2. Klinkowski, M. 1933. Lucerne: Its ecological position
and distribution in the world. *Herbage Plants* 12:1–62.

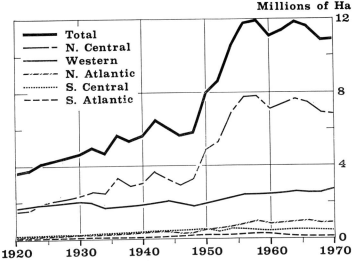

Millions of Ha

Legend:
Total
N. Central
Western
N. Atlantic
S. Central
S. Atlantic

FIG. 13.1. Alfalfa hay produced in different regions of the U.S. In 1970 three states, Wisconsin, Minnesota, and South Dakota, each harvested over 800,000 ha of alfalfa for hay. Wisconsin was in the lead with 1.62 million ha.

during the 1950s in the central and eastern states was the result of improved production practices. Contributing factors were better information; greater use of lime, P, K, and B; recognition of alfalfa as a superior forage and pasture crop; new cultivars; and an adequate supply of high-quality seed.

Alfalfa is well adapted to a wide range of climatic and soil conditions. The yellow-flowered alfalfa, *M. falcata* L., has survived temperatures below —27 C in Alaska, and nonhardy types are grown in Death Valley, Calif., where maximum temperatures may reach 60 C. Alfalfa is best adapted to deep loam soils with porous subsoils. Good drainage is essential. It also requires large amounts of lime and does not do well on acid soils.

Alfalfa grows extremely well in dry climates on irrigated fertile soils. With good fertilization and cultural practices, including inoculation with N-fixing bacteria, alfalfa is being grown successfully under the more humid conditions of the eastern states. Except on a few limestone soils, the addition of lime (calcium) is essential on soils east of the Mississippi River. Alfalfa is relatively tolerant to alkaline soils but does not do well on highly alkaline soils. It is highly drought resistant but goes into dormancy during drought periods and re-

sumes growth only when moisture conditions become favorable.

✤ PLANT DESCRIPTION

Alfalfa is a widely grown herbaceous perennial legume (Fig. 13.2). Its flowers, whose petals are various shades of purples and yellows with some whites, are borne in loose racemes. Pods are twisted with one to five spirals and each contains several small kidney-shaped seed. The leaves, arranged alternately on the stem, are pinnately trifoliolate. The root system has a distinct taproot, which under favorable conditions may penetrate the soil 7–9 m or more. The erect stems usually reach a height of 60–90 cm. There may be 5–25 or more stems per plant, rising from a woody crown from which new stems grow when the older ones mature or are cut.

✤ IMPORTANCE AND USE

Alfalfa, sometimes called the "Queen of the Forages," is one of the most important forage plants in the U.S. It has the highest feeding value of all commonly grown hay crops.[3] Alfalfa produces more protein

3. Barnes, R. F., and C. H. Gordon. 1972. **Feeding value and on-farm feeding.** *In* C. H. Hanson (ed.), **Alfalfa Science and Technology.** Agronomy 15:601–30. Amer. Soc. Agron., Madison, Wis.

FIG. 13.2. The alfalfa plant: (A) Crown and plant, showing several elongating young shoots at the top and an extensive root system. (B) Upper part of a shoot showing flowers. (C) Three views of a single flower—(left) face view, (center) flower before tripping showing the closed keel, and (right) flower after tripping showing the sexual column. (D) Close-up of young seedpods and enlargement of a single seed. Alfalfa is a herbaceous perennial legume whose roots may penetrate the soil 7–9 m. There may be 5–25 or more stems per plant. *USDA drawing.*

per ha than any other crop for livestock. In Wisconsin, high yields of alfalfa compared favorably with corn silage in production of energy and protein when harvested at the proper stage of maturity.[4] In some situations the most efficient use of alfalfa is in combination with corn silage, where the protein of alfalfa complements the energy from corn. Alfalfa is high in mineral content and contains at least 10 different vitamins. It has long been considered an important source of vitamin A. These

characteristics make alfalfa (used as hay, pellets, or low-moisture silage) a desirable ration component for most farm animals. Alfalfa also helps minimize pollution by reducing water runoff and soil erosion.

PASTURE

Alfalfa is excellent pasture for swine, and despite the bloat hazard it also is being used more widely as a pasture for cattle and sheep. In general, mixtures with a grass such as smooth bromegrass, timothy, or orchardgrass are recommended when it is used primarily for pasture or home-grown hay. Bloat is less likely to occur when alfalfa is sown with grasses. Supplemental feeding of grain to dairy cows, sheep, and fattening cattle balances the high protein level of alfalfa pastures with energy and extends the usefulness of pasture.[5]

Alfalfa will tolerate pasturing when rotationally grazed. Stands weaken rapidly if grazed continuously.[6,7] 'Ladak' is superior on rangelands in the northern Great Plains. Creeping-rooted alfalfas are also well adapted for dryland conditions.[8]

ALFALFA MEAL

About 1.54 million t of artificially dehydrated alfalfa, commonly known as "dehy," are produced annually. At one time, all dehy was fed in the form of alfalfa meal, but now over 90% is pelleted. Pelleting nearly eliminates the dust problem. Pellets are also free-flowing and easy to handle mechanically. They are stored in bulk storage tanks under inert gas prior to shipping to prevent deterioration of nutrients. Much of this high-quality product is used in mixed feeds. It serves as a valuable feed supplement to provide carotene (provita-

4. Niedermeier, R. P., N. A. Jorgensen, C. E. Zehner, Dale Smith, and G. P. Barrington. 1972. Evaluation of alfalfa-brome forage harvested two and three times annually, stored as low-moisture silage, and fed to lactating dairy cows. Wis. Agr. Exp. Sta. Res. Rept. 2378.

5. Van Keuren, R. W., and G. C. Marten. 1972. Pasture production and utilization. *In* C. H. Hanson (ed.), Alfalfa Science and Technology. Agronomy 15:641–58. Amer. Soc. Agron., Madison, Wis.
6. Meyer, J. H., G. B. Lofgreen, and N. R. Itner. 1956. Further study on the utilization of alfalfa by beef steers. *J. Anim. Sci.* 15:64–75.
7. Pratt, A. D., and R. R. Davis. 1954. Continuous vs. rotational grazing. *J. Dairy Sci.* 37:665.
8. Heinrichs, D. H. 1963. Creeping alfalfas. *Advan. Agron.* 15:317–37.

min A), tocopherol (vitamin E), vitamin K, xanthophylls (pigmenters for better color of poultry skin and egg yolks), and unidentified growth and reproduction factors.[9,10,11] (See Chapter 50.)

Commercial pilot plants have been constructed to produce specialized alfalfa products for monogastric and ruminant animals by dry fractionation and wet processing. Studies also are under way to test the feasibility of developing a palatable protein product for human consumption.[9]

✴ PRINCIPAL SPECIES AND TYPES

Alfalfa cultivars grown in the U.S. were developed from two species, *M. sativa* and *M. falcata,* and an intermediate form, *M. sativa media,* commonly known as variegated alfalfa. The latter is often classified as a species by itself. Actually, *M. sativa* and *M. falcata* are sufficiently interfertile to be classified as subspecies of the same species. For that reason, these three forms of *Medicago* are frequently referred to as the *M. sativa* complex. Commercial cultivars are tetraploid, with 32 chromosomes.

Medicago sativa, native to southwest Asia, is purple flowered, and tends to be narrow crowned and erect. The Turkestan, Flemish, and common types of alfalfa also are classed as *M. sativa,* but they vary in winterhardiness. As a group they are less hardy than *M. falcata,* which is native to Siberia and is very cold-hardy. It is yellow flowered and decumbent with widely branching roots and a deep-set crown. This species is part of the parentage of numerous U.S. cultivars, but none of them is solely of *M. falcata* origin. The following terms are useful for describing alfalfa cultivars.

Variegated alfalfas are believed to have arisen from natural crossing between *M. sativa* and *M. falcata.* Their flower color ranges from purple through blue and yellow to white. Most cold-resistant cultivars grown successfully in the northern U.S. and in Canada are variegated. 'Vernal' is a strongly variegated cultivar.

Common alfalfas in the U.S. originated principally from the Chilean introduction into California about 1850. They are characterized by purple flowers and are composed of regional strains with different climatic adaptations resulting from natural selection.

Flemish or Flamande-type naturalized alfalfas of northern France are purple flowered, quick to recover after cutting, and only moderately winter-hardy.

Nonhardy alfalfas are rapid growers, even in cool weather and short days. They make rapid recovery after cutting but have little cold resistance. Examples of the extremely nonhardy alfalfas are the cultivars that trace to 'African,' 'Indian,' and 'Peruvian.' They are very productive for hay and seed in the far southwest.

Spreading of two principal types has been observed in alfalfa. One is by rhizomes which are crown bud shoots growing more or less horizontally before emerging from the soil. None of the commercial cultivars have had sufficiently rapid rhizomatous development to win general acclaim as a spreading alfalfa. The second type of spreading is by means of adventitious stem shoots which develop at enlarged points of the root, principally along lateral roots.[12] The latter has become known as the creeping-root habit. It was discovered in a strain of *M. falcata.* The cultivars 'Rambler' and 'Travois' were bred for this character. They are grown mostly in the northern Great Plains of the U.S. and Canada.

✴ CULTIVARS AND BREEDING

The common alfalfas were the first cultivars of the U.S. Regional strains became

9. Kohler, George O., E. M. Bickoff, and W. M. Beeson. 1972. Processed products for feed and food industries. *In* C. H. Hanson (ed.), Alfalfa Science and Technology. Agronomy 15:659–76. Amer. Soc. Agron., Madison, Wis.

10. Schrenk, W. G., H. L. Mitchell, R. E. Silker, E. L. Sorensen, W. H. Honstead, R. G. Taecker, and C. C. Burkhardt. 1959. Dehydrated alfalfa. Kans. Agr. Exp. Sta. Bull. 409.

11. Meyer, J. H., W. C. Weir, J. B. Dobie, and J. L. Hull. 1959. Influence of the method of preparation on the feeding value of alfalfa hay. *J. Anim. Sci.* 18:976–82.

12. Murray, Beatrice E. 1957. The ontogeny of adventitious stems on roots of creeping-rooted alfalfa. *Can. J. Bot.* 35:463–75.

known by the state of origin, such as California Common and Kansas Common. Common alfalfas were usually variable; for this reason they are not recognized as distinct cultivars under the Federal Seed Act.

In 1897 the USDA began sending men to other continents in search of winter-hardy strains and other germplasm useful in breeding.[13] Some of the early introductions were fairly well adapted. They were increased and became cultivars of commerce.

The principal introductions still in production include Grimm from Germany, Ladak from Kashmir, 'Cossack' from Russia, African from Egypt, and Peruvian from Peru. The demand for better adapted and disease-resistant cultivars prompted the initiation of alfalfa breeding programs. Hectarages in the old cultivars have been largely replaced by improved cultivars.

DISEASE RESISTANCE

In 1924 bacterial wilt was found in northern Illinois and southern Wisconsin.[14] In 1942 the first two wilt-resistant cultivars 'Ranger' and 'Buffalo' were released for seed increase; many other wilt-resistant cultivars are available to the grower. The contribution of these cultivars is valued at more than $100 million annually. Breeding for resistance is the most practical and economical means of controlling wilt and most other alfalfa diseases.[15] (See Fig. 13.3.) Cultivars or breeding lines are available with varying degrees of resistance to a number of diseases such as common leafspot, anthracnose, Phytophthora root rot, rust, and downy mildew.

INSECT RESISTANCE

In 1954 the spotted alfalfa aphid was discovered in New Mexico, and within a year it became a serious problem. Due to the pressure of urgency and the fortunate

13. Barnes, D. K., E. T. Bingham, R. P. Murphy, O. J. Hunt, D. F. Beard, W. H. Skrdla, and L. R. Teuber. 1977. Alfalfa germplasm in the United States: Genetic vulnerability, use, improvement, and maintenance. USDA Tech. Bull. 1571.
14. Jones, F. R. 1925. A new bacterial disease of alfalfa. *Phytopathology* 15:243–44.
15. Kehr, W. R., F. I. Frosheiser, R. D. Wilcoxson, and D. K. Barnes. 1972. Breeding for disease resistance. *In* C. H. Hanson (ed.), Alfalfa Science and Technology. Agronomy 15:335–54. Amer. Soc. Agron., Madison, Wis.

FIG. 13.3. *Ranger . . . developed . . . for resistance to bacterial wilt. . . . Vernal . . . bacterial wilt-resistant synthetic cultivar . . . outstanding in the north central states.* An alfalfa cultivar trial 10 years after seeding at the Wisconsin station, demonstrating the contribution of resistance to bacterial wilt: (A) 'Rhizoma'; (B) Ranger; (C) 'Narragansett'; (D) Vernal. *Wis. Agr. Exp. Sta. photo.*

circumstance of finding resistant plants, the pressure of urgency and the fortunate the resistant cultivars 'Moapa' and 'Zia' were developed in only three years. By 1961 Moapa alone saved farmers $1.5 million annually in spray costs. Since 1957 more than 25 resistant cultivars have been developed and made available to farmers.

Plant breeders and entomologists, working in teams, also have developed cultivars with high resistance to the pea aphid. (See Fig. 13.4.) Breeding for resistance to other pests such as the meadow spittlebug, potato leafhopper, and alfalfa weevil also has been successful though less spectacular.[16] Many of the newer cultivars have resist-

16. Sorensen, E. L., M. C. Wilson, and G. R. Manglitz. 1972. Breeding for insect resistance. *In* C. H. Hanson (ed.), Alfalfa Science and Technology. Agronomy 15:371–90. Amer. Soc. Agron., Madison, Wis.

FIG. 13.4. *Plant breeders . . . entomologists . . . developed cultivars with high resistance to the pea aphid.* On the left in a two-cultivar test near Manhattan, Kans., is susceptible 'Cody.' On the right is 'Kanza,' a new cultivar bred for resistance to pea aphid, spotted alfalfa aphid, and bacterial wilt. *USDA photo.*

ance to several disease and insect pests and are described as having multiple pest resistance.[16]

SYNTHETICS

Most of the newer cultivars are synthetics. A synthetic cultivar of alfalfa consists of the advanced-generation progenies from a set of selected clones or seed lines, produced and maintained under conditions specified by the originator. A common practice used to develop an improved synthetic is to vegetatively propagate promising plants to obtain clonal lines, test their polycross progenies to determine the relative general combining ability of each clone, and test clones with high general combining ability in specific combinations.[17,18,19] Yields of synthetics usually decline in generations following the one of synthesis.[20,21,22] It is important to determine the actual performance of advanced generations for a new synthetic.

HYBRID ALFALFA

A hybrid is the product of a cross between individuals of unlike genetic constitution.[23] Unlike corn, which is monoecious, the alfalfa flower is bisexual and cross-pollinated by bees. This makes pollination control difficult in alfalfa. For years it was assumed that alfalfa was 90–95% cross-pollinated, but studies indicate that the percentage of crossing is less.

Some type of pollen control must be used in hybrid seed production. The use of self-incompatibility was proposed nearly 30 years ago for production of commercial alfalfa hybrids.[24] However, this procedure has not proved successful.

Use of cytoplasmic male sterility is a more efficient method of pollen control.[25] A scheme to produce three-way hybrids is:

$$A(ms) \quad X \quad B$$
$$\downarrow$$
$$AB(ms) \quad X \quad C$$
$$\downarrow$$
$$ABC \text{ commercial hybrid}$$

A is a male-sterile parent, B is a male-fertile parent that when crossed to A produces male-sterile progeny, and C is a male-fertile pollen parent. The first commercial hybrids using cytoplasmic sterility were marketed in 1968. Commercial production includes planting four rows of male steriles, omitting one row, and planting four rows of male fertiles. Hybrid seed is harvested only from the male-sterile rows. Because of low seed yields of present male steriles and lack of multiple pest resistance in early experimental hybrids, it has not been possible to determine the potential role of hybrid alfalfa.

INDUSTRY BREEDING PROGRAMS

Historically, the alfalfa seed industry has been concerned with the processing and marketing of alfalfa seed. About 1958 private industry entered the field of alfalfa breeding. Within several years commercial seedsmen were an active force in the development of improved alfalfa cultivars. Cultivars developed by commercial firms as well as by public agencies are now available to farmers.

CHOOSING A CULTIVAR

Certified seed of more than 80 cultivars are produced in the U.S. A listing of the

17. Tysdal, H. M., T. A. Kiesselbach, and H. L. Westover. 1942. Alfalfa breeding. Nebr. Agr. Exp. Sta. Res. Bull. 124.
18. Davis, R. L., and C. Panton. 1962. Combining ability in alfalfa. *Crop Sci.* 2:35–37.
19. Frakes, R. V., R. L. Davis, and F. L. Patterson. 1961. The breeding behavior of yield and related variables in alfalfa. III. General and specific combining ability. *Crop Sci.* 1:210–12.
20. Kehr, W. R., H. O. Graumann, C. C. Lowe, and C. O. Gardner. 1961. The performance of alfalfa synthetics in the first and advanced generations. Nebr. Agr. Exp. Sta. Res. Bull. 200.
21. Dudley, John W. 1964. A genetic evaluation of methods of utilizing heterozygosis and dominance in autotetraploids. *Crop Sci.* 4:410–13.
22. Busbice, T. H., R. R. Hill, Jr., and H. L. Carnahan. 1972. Genetics and breeding procedures. *In* C. H. Hanson (ed.), Alfalfa Science and Technology. Agronomy 15:283–318. Amer. Soc. Agron., Madison, Wis.
23. Knight, R. L. 1948. Dictionary of Genetics, p. 75. Chronica Botanica, Waltham, Mass.
24. Tysdal, H. M., and T. A. Kiesselbach. 1944. Hybrid alfalfa. *J. Amer. Soc. Agron.* 36:649–67.
25. Barnes, D. K., E. T. Bingham, J. D. Axtell, and W. H. Davis. 1972. The flower, sterility mechanisms, and pollination control. *In* C. H. Hanson (ed.), Alfalfa Science and Technology. Agronomy 15:123–41. Amer. Soc. Agron., Madison, Wis.

cultivars developed by public agencies and private firms is available.[13, 26] There are no hard-and-fast rules for the selection of a cultivar. It should produce high yields of high-quality forage, have sufficient winter-hardiness but no more than needed to escape injury, and be resistant to diseases and insect pests that are problems in the area of production. In the upper north central states, for example, a high level of winterhardiness and resistance to bacterial wilt and foliar diseases are especially important. In the Southwest it is important for the cultivar to be nonhardy (nondormant) and resistant to spotted alfalfa aphids and crown and root rots. When a cultivar has all the agronomic and resistance requirements to produce sustained high yields of good quality forage in a given area, it is said to be well adapted.

❦ CULTURE AND MANAGEMENT

Fertile soil is desirable, and the availability of lime and other minerals should be checked. A fine, mellow, firm seedbed should be prepared.

LIME AND FERTILIZER REQUIREMENTS

Alfalfa requires plentiful available calcium (lime). Practically all areas east of the Mississippi River require application of lime. Alfalfa also does best when P and K are readily available. Studies indicate that alfalfa often is underfertilized for most economical returns. With higher yields it is necessary to increase maintenance applications, especially K, if stands are to survive. Fertilization must take into account alfalfa's high removal of nutrients.[27] In the Southeast, applications of B have proved beneficial. In some areas B means the difference between success and failure. A comprehensive report on 25 years of lim-

ing and fertilizing studies on low-fertility acid soils is typical of many other studies throughout the East.[28]

SEEDINGS

In regions south of South Dakota late summer seedings usually are more successful than spring seedings. In the northern part of this area the seedings must become established before fall; therefore, alfalfa should be sown early, preferably in August. Time of seeding may become progressively later as plantings are made southward, so that toward the Gulf alfalfa may be sown as late as October. In the Southwest, plantings are made as late as December and should not be made in the heat of summer. North and east of Nebraska spring sowing is usually best. A companion grain crop, sown at about half the usual rate, is often used. Adequate moisture must be available to support both the companion crop and the alfalfa. Alfalfa seedings that utilize chemical weed controls without companion crops are becoming popular in some areas where growers plan to harvest alfalfa during the year of seeding.

Most experiment stations east of the Appalachians recommend 17–22 kg/ha of seed, although several, particularly those in the Southeast, recommend 22–34 kg/ha.[29] In the Corn Belt 11–13 kg are used.

In general, band-seeding (the placement of a band of alfalfa seed on top of the ground directly over a band of fertilizer placed 2.5–5 cm deep) gives best stands. Under this method seeding rates can be reduced.[29] The use of press wheels to pack the seed and fertilizer area has improved stands.[30] The cultipacker seeder, where the seed is broadcast between two corrugated rollers, has given good results. When seed is drilled, care must be taken not to seed it too deep, preferably 0.6–1.3 cm on silt loam soils.

26. Lowe, C. C., V. L. Marble, and M. D. Rumbaugh. 1972. Adaptation, varieties, and usage. *In* C. H. Hanson (ed.), Alfalfa Science and Technology. Agronomy 15:391–413. Amer. Soc. Agron., Madison, Wis.

27. Rhykerd, C. L., and C. J. Overdahl. 1972. Nutrition and fertilizer use. *In* C. H. Hanson (ed.), Alfalfa Science and Technology. Agronomy 15:437–68. Amer. Soc. Agron., Madison, Wis.

28. Brown, B. A. 1961. Fertilizer experiments with alfalfa, 1915–1960. Conn. Agr. Exp. Sta. Bull. 363.

29. Tesar, M. B., and J. A. Jackobs. 1972. Establishing the stand. *In* C. H. Hanson (ed.), Alfalfa Science and Technology. Agronomy 15:415–35. Amer. Soc. Agron., Madison, Wis.

30. Parsons, J. L. 1958. Improved practices reduce risk in planting alfalfa. *Ohio Farm and Home Res.* 43(311):25–26.

ROTATIONS

Alfalfa has great value as a soil-improving crop.[31] It is used extensively in irrigated regions not only for its feeding value but for its beneficial effect on succeeding crops. In newly irrigated areas it often is the first crop seeded.

Alfalfa may deplete subsoil moisture in the root zone; crop management should take this into account. In drier areas a crop such as sorghum often follows alfalfa. Wheat, oats, and flax are used to some extent. In regions of abundant rainfall corn after alfalfa is a good rotation.

HARVESTING

Continuously cutting alfalfa at an immature stage, such as the prebud or bud stage, will reduce total tonnage and prematurely kill the stand. Death of the plants is due primarily to a continuous reduction of the food reserves in the roots. Alfalfa with low root reserves is especially susceptible to winter-killing. However, alfalfa cut at an immature stage has a higher protein content and higher feeding value than when cut at later stages of growth. Thus it becomes a question of a balance between early cutting and later cutting. The main considerations are production, quality of hay, and longevity of stand. The availability of cultivars with high persistence has made it possible to put more emphasis on cutting at early maturity to obtain high nutrient yield.[32]

The best time to harvest alfalfa is at early flower (first flower to 1/10 bloom). Where bloom is delayed or sparse, the new growth at the crown may indicate time of cutting. If this starts growing vigorously or the stand is lodged, it usually is desirable to cut. One cutting a year may be taken at a prebloom stage without unduly injuring the stand or production. However, this early cutting should not be taken in the fall because this would tend to lower the root reserves.

Most research indicates that fall is the critical period for the alfalfa plant.[33] In Wisconsin, early fall cutting gave a 26% higher yield in the subsequent year than late fall cutting. The latter reduced the food reserves in the roots and weakened the plants.[34] In Kansas an increase of 16% was obtained in a similar test.[35] In general, it seems advisable to make the last cutting in the fall at least four weeks before the average date of the first killing frost. This will permit considerable top growth and abundant food storage in the roots before final freeze-up.

The number of cuttings per year varies from one in the northern drier areas to six to nine under irrigation in the Southwest. In the central latitudes three to four cuttings are normal.

Slightly more than half the alfalfa plant at early bloom consists of leaves, which contain most of the protein and vitamins. It is therefore essential to retain the leaves to make high-quality hay.[3]

EQUIPMENT. The increasing cost of labor has forced significant improvements in the harvesting, storing, and feeding of alfalfa forage. In the 1960s mowing, conditioning, and windrowing were combined into one machine of a pull-type or self-propelled unit. Balers have been functionally improved and bale handling is being mechanized from field to storage. Field and stationary cubing machines have been developed for use in arid, irrigated areas. Where weather permits outside storage, one-man operated machines are available for stacking, moving, and feeding. Equipment is available for complete mechanization from harvesting through feeding for low-moisture silage, loose hay, cubes, and

31. Grandfield, C. O., and R. I. Throckmorton. 1945. Alfalfa in Kansas. Kans. Agr. Exp. Sta. Bull. 328.
32. Smith, Dale. 1972. Cutting schedules and maintaining pure stands. *In* C. H. Hanson (ed.), Alfalfa Science and Technoloy. Agronomy 15:481–96. Amer. Soc. Agron., Madison, Wis.

33. Smith, Dale. 1960. The establishment and management of alfalfa. Wis. Agr. Exp. Sta. Bull. 452.
34. Graber, L. F., and V. G. Sprague. 1938. The productivity of alfalfa as related to management. *J. Amer. Soc. Agron.* 30:38–54.
35. Grandfield, C. O. 1935. The trend of organic food reserves in alfalfa roots as affected by cutting practices. *J. Agr. Res.* 50:697–709.

pellets. Engineers state that completely mechanized systems for harvesting and utilizing all forage are realistic goals for the future.[36,37] (See Chapter 48.)

❧ SEED PRODUCTION

Since 1940 a marked shift to the western states has occurred in the area of alfalfa seed production. As of 1977 California, Idaho, and Washington were the principal seed-producing states. Total U.S. production in 1975 was 42 million kg.

Alfalfa seed production has become a specialized industry in which there is a high degree of precision required for management of the crop, water, pests, and pollinators. This can best be obtained under irrigation. Nevertheless, much seed is produced in nonirrigated areas, and the same principles apply. A successful seed-production program requires keeping abreast of new developments in alfalfa breeding, recognizing the necessity of shifting from old to new cultivars to meet consumer demand, and adjusting cultural and management practices to meet local conditions and the needs of the cultivar.

GROWTH

A normal, moderately vigorous growth appears to produce maximum seed yields.[38,39] Row spacings of 60–110 cm are generally superior to solid plantings. In dryland areas wider spacings are frequently used. Dense stands often result in lower nectar production, less attractiveness to insects, and increased ovule abortion.[40] In California, row spacing is based primarily on soil type and water availability and the effect these factors have on plant growth.[41]

POLLINATION

Practically all alfalfa flowers must be tripped to set seed; moreover, this tripping must be done by insects.[38,42,43,44,45] Tripping is the release of the sexual column from the keel of the flower and can be caused by many insects.[40] *Megachile rotundata* (F.), commonly called the alfalfa leaf-cutter bee, is found over most of the country, while *Nomia melanderi* Ckll., the alkali bee, is found in the western states. Both are important trippers. Bumblebees, *Bombus* spp., also are distributed over the country and are effective trippers. Honeybees, *Apis mellifera* L., are effective trippers when they gather pollen or when the nectar collectors are sufficiently numerous. At present, the honeybee, alkali bee, and leaf-cutter bee are propagated for alfalfa pollination.

Under midwestern conditions it has been observed that nectar-collecting honeybees trip from 0.5 to 2% of the flowers visited. This figure may be higher under certain conditions. Pollen collectors trip essentially 100% of the flowers from which they gather pollen. Unfortunately, alfalfa is not an attractive pollen source for honeybees and rarely, therefore, are pollen collectors in abundance except in some western fields. Placing the colonies throughout the field or moving them frequently has increased pollination. In addition, every care should be taken to preserve and encourage local wild bees and eliminate competing sources of pollen. If leaf-cutter bees are not present in the area, nesting material filled with nests may be purchased. Since the bees forage close to their nests, field shelters for them are placed at regular intervals (usually

36. Zachariah, P. John, K. C. Elliott, and R. A. Phillips. 1958. Performance of forage crushers. W. Va. Agr. Exp. Sta. Bull. 418.

37. Miller, H. F., Jr., and W. F. Wedin. 1972. Equipment for harvesting, storing, and feeding. *In* C. H. Hanson (ed.), Alfalfa Science and Technology. Agronomy 15: 575–99. Amer. Soc. Agron., Madison, Wis.

38. Tysdal, H. M. 1946. Influence of tripping, soil moisture, plant spacing, and lodging on alfalfa seed production. *J. Agr. Res.* 70:123–32.

39. Grandfield, C. O. 1945. Alfalfa seed production as affected by organic reserves, air temperature, humidity and soil moisture. *J. Agr. Res.* 70:123–32.

40. Pedersen, M. W., G. E. Bohart, V. L. Marble, and E. C. Klostermeyer. 1972. Seed production practices. *In* C. H. Hanson (ed.), Alfalfa Science and Technology. Agronomy 15:689–720. Amer. Soc. Agron., Madison, Wis.

41. Marble, V. L. 1970. Producing alfalfa seed in California. Calif. Agr. Ext. Serv. AXT-349.

42. Armstrong, J. M., and W. J. White. 1935. Factors influencing seed setting in alfalfa. *J. Agr. Sci.* 25:161–79.

43. Tysdal, H. M. 1940. Is tripping necessary for seed setting in alfalfa? *J. Amer. Soc. Agron.* 32:570–85.

44. Knowles, R. P. 1943. The role of insects, weather conditions, and plant character in seed setting of alfalfa. *Sci. Agr.* 24:29–50.

45. Vansell, George H., and Frank E. Todd. 1946. Alfalfa tripping by insects. *J. Amer. Soc. Agron.* 38:470–88.

about 90 m apart). Since 1950 many farmers have given increased attention to preserving nesting sites for the alkali bee; some have built "artificial" sites.[40]

HARMFUL INSECTS

Sorenson and Carlson were the first to show that lygus bugs are detrimental to alfalfa seed production.[46,47] Not only *Lygus* spp. but many others such as the seed chalcid, *Bruchophagus roddi* (Guss.), spotted alfalfa aphid, and alfalfa weevil are harmful. However, the lygus bug has been one of the most serious. Harmful insects can be effectively controlled with insecticides.[40,48]

HARVESTING

Technological advances in harvesting practices have greatly reduced seed losses. All the alfalfa seed does not mature at the same time. Harvesting is necessary when most of the pods, usually about two-thirds, have turned a dark brown. When the seed is mature, it is an olive green color. The seed shatters rather easily, so the crop should be handled carefully. Limited amounts are windrowed and then picked up with the combine.[49] Nearly all alfalfa seed is direct combined and use of spray defoliants has increased the success. Proper adjustment of the combine is very important to avoid injury to the seed and thus poor germination.

❧ DISEASES

Bacterial wilt, caused by *Corynebacterium insidiosum* (McCull.) H. L. Jens., is one of the most destructive alfalfa diseases in the U.S., being found in practically every state.[50,51] Affected plants are stunted and finally die. On wilt-infested soil a susceptible cultivar usually lives only one to three years. The disease is controlled by growing wilt-resistant cultivars.

Anthracnose, *Colletotrichum trifolii* Bain, now is considered the principal cause of "summer decline" of alfalfa in the eastern U.S. Typical symptoms are large sunken lesions on stems near the soil level, occasional dead shoots, and crown rot. The general weakening and killing of crown buds either result in death of plants or predispose them to winter damage. Resistant strains have been developed.[52]

Leaf diseases, caused by *Pseudopeziza medicaginis* (Lib.) Sacc., *P. jonesii* Nannf., *Leptosphaerulina briosiana* (Poll.) Graham & Luttrell, *Stemphylium* spp., and other organisms such as rust, *Uromyces striatus* Schroet., and downy mildew, *Peronospora trifoliorum* DBy., lower the quality of alfalfa hay. Foliage diseases also may cause forage to be estrogenic.[53]

Spring black stem and leaf spot, *Phoma medicaginis* Malbr. & Roum, and *Ascochyta imperfecta* Pk.; crown and stem rot, *Sclerotinia trifoliorum* Eriks; Fusarium wilt and root rot, *Fusarium* spp.; Phytophthora root rot, *Phytophthora megasperma* Drechs.; dwarf disease (a virus); and crown wart are other diseases that may cause serious damage.

❧ INSECTS

Alfalfa weevil, *Hypera postica* (Gyll.), occurs in the western and eastern U.S. and under some conditions is very damaging.[54] Progress has been made in developing re-

46. Sorenson, C. J. 1939. *Lygus hesperus* Knight and *Lygus elisus* Van Duzee in relation to alfalfa seed production. Utah Agr. Exp. Sta. Bull. 284.
47. Carlson, J. W. 1940. Lygus bug damage to alfalfa in relation to seed production. *J. Agr. Res.* 61:791–815.
48. App, B. A., and G. R. Manglitz. 1972. Insects and related pests. *In* C. H. Hanson (ed.), Alfalfa Science and Technology. Agronomy 15:527–54. Amer. Soc. Agron., Madison, Wis.
49. Arnold, Lloyd E. 1972. The seed industry. *In* C. H. Hanson (ed.), Alfalfa Science and Technology. Agronomy 15:721–36. Amer. Soc. Agron., Madison, Wis.

50. Jones, F. R. 1928. Development of the bacteria causing wilt in the alfalfa plant as influenced by growth and winter injury. *J. Agr. Res.* 37:545–69.
51. Peltier, G. L. 1933. The relative susceptibility of alfalfas to wilt. Nebr. Agr. Exp. Sta. Res. Bull. 66.
52. Devine, T. E., C. H. Hanson, S. A. Ostazeski, and T. A. Campbell. 1971. Selection for resistance to anthracnose (*Colletotrichum trifolii*) in four alfalfa populations. *Crop Sci.* 11:854–55.
53. Hanson, C. H., G. M. Loper, G. O. Kohler, E. M. Bickoff, K. W. Taylor, W. R. Kehr, E. H. Stanford, J. W. Dudley, M. W. Pedersen, E. L. Sorensen, H. L. Carnahan, and C. P. Wilsie. 1965. Variation in coumestrol content of alfalfa as related to location, variety, cutting, year, stage of growth, and disease. USDA Tech. Bull. 1333.
54. USDA. 1971. The alfalfa weevil: How to control it. Leaflet 368.

sistant cultivars. The spotted alfalfa aphid, *Therioaphis maculata* (Buckton),[55] particularly in the southwestern and south central U.S., and the pea aphid, *Acyrthosiphon pisum* (Harris), are serious pests of alfalfa. Resistant cultivars are available in areas of greatest damage.

Alfalfa yellows, caused by the potato leafhopper, *Empoasca fabae* (Harris), is very serious in the eastern half of the U.S. It causes a yellowing of foliage, loss in carotene, and loss of leaves and feeding value. The meadow spittlebug, *Philaenus spumarius* (L.), may cause damage on the first cutting of alfalfa in some Corn Belt states.

Nematodes—both stem, *Ditylenchus dipsaci* (Kuehn) Filipjev, and root-knot, *Meloidogyne* spp.—cause much damage in alfalfa. Two cultivars, 'Lahontan' and 'Washoe,' are resistant to the stem nematode.

❧ OTHER SPECIES

There are approximately 20 other relatively common species of *Medicago,* but only three are widely distributed in the U.S. They are the annuals, spotted burclover, *M. arabica* Huds.; California burclover, *M. polymorpha* L. (syn. *M. hispida* Gaertn.); and black medic, *M. lupulina* L., which also includes perennial forms.

BURCLOVER

The common name "burclover" is used for most of the annual species of *Medicago,* which occasionally are referred to as "medics." All are native to the Mediterranean region; some are well adapted in western Australia.[56] They are weak-stemmed plants resembling the true clovers. The several species now found in the U.S. came in as escapes. The species found in greatest abundance in the western states is California burclover, while spotted burclover is

most abundant in the southern states. Both have been long established.[57]

California burclover is an important constituent of the range pastures in the California and Arizona foothills. A number of other annual species of *Medicago* introduced from Australia are being grown successfully on California rangelands. In eastern Texas burclover provides considerable grazing. In the deciduous orchards of California volunteer burclover is used as a winter cover crop for decreasing soil erosion and adding organic matter and fertility to the soil. (See Fig. 13.5.)

All burclovers lack winterhardiness and cannot endure summer heat. In the South or where winter temperatures are mild, the seed germinate in the fall, growth is made in the winter, and the plants mature in the spring. California burclover is adapted to drier and sunnier situations than spotted burclover. In the southeastern states spotted burclover is the dominant species. Burclovers require a moderately fertile soil for good growth and do best on neutral or slightly alkaline soils.

In the western states burclover volunteers naturally in range and orchard lands and is seldom seeded. In the southeastern states seeding is required for establishment. Once established, stands can be maintained almost indefinitely if well managed. When burclover is plowed under in late winter or early spring as a green manure crop, it is advisable to allow the crop to fully mature about every fifth year if a good stand is to be maintained without reseeding.

BLACK MEDIC

Black medic is native to Europe and Asia. It was introduced early into the U.S. as an escape. It is an annual with procumbent stems that rise in thick stands. The stems are rather small and leafy and usually attain a length of 30–60 cm. The plant is widely adapted to reasonably fertile soils that are fairly well supplied with moisture

55. USDA. 1957. The spotted alfalfa aphid: How to control it. Leaflet 422.

56. Quinlivan, B. J. 1965. The naturalised and cultivated medics of western Australia. *W. Aust. Dept. Agr. J.* 6(9):532–43.

57. McKee, Roland. 1949. Burclover cultivation and utilization. USDA Farmers' Bull. 1742, rev.

FIG. 13.5. Burclover-producing areas of the U.S.

and not distinctly acid. Most of the hectarage is volunteer in pastures and waste places. Its greatest value is as pasture.

No commercial cultivars are recognized but the species is quite variable, both with reference to appearance and adaptation. Naturalized strains occur in sections where plants have volunteered for a number of years. These usually are superior for local use and should be given preference whenever such seed is available.

1. How do you account for the steady increase in alfalfa hectarage of the U.S. during the 1950s?
2. Why is alfalfa rated a superior forage crop?
3. List the advantages and disadvantages of using alfalfa for pasture.
4. Why is alfalfa–smooth bromegrass a superior combination for pasture?
5. List the kind of alfalfa cultivars you would recommend in your locality and tell why in each case.
6. Why are cultivars of the nonhardy type recommended over the variegated cultivars for the southwestern U.S.?
7. Which cultivars would you recommend for a short rotation on your farm? Why?
8. You are to seed 50 ha of alfalfa on your farm. Discuss choice of field, soil fertilization, time of seeding, choice of companion crop, seed inoculation, rate of seeding, and method of seeding.
9. What are the problems in producing alfalfa seed in your area? How would you best handle these problems?
10. How would you manage an alfalfa field for hay to ensure high-quality forage and to maintain a strong vigorous stand?

SUPPLEMENTAL INFORMATION

Alfalfa breeders have continued to develop cultivars with multiple pest resistance.[58] Three new alfalfa pests have been identified as problems in the United States. They include two insects: the alfalfa blotch leafminer, *Argomyza frontella* (Rondani), in the Northeast and the blue aphid, *Acyrthosiphon kondoi* Shinji, in the Southwest. Verticillium wilt, caused by *Verticillium albo-atrum* Reinke et Berth. was identified in several northwestern states. Resistance to the blue aphid and Verticillium wilt has been isolated.

Concern about use of fossil fuels has increased interest in the nitrogen fixation potential of alfalfa. Alfalfa in combination with *Rhizobium meliloti* can fix from 300 to 600 kg N/ha. It appears that nitrogen fixation potential can be improved through breeding.[59] This should increase the usefulness of alfalfa in many agricultural systems for supplying N to grain and pasture crop production.

58. Barnes, D. K., F. I. Frosheiser, E. L. Sorensen, et al. 1974. Standard tests to characterize pest resistance in alfalfa varieties. ARS-NC-19.

59. Seetin, M. W., and D. K. Barnes. 1977. Variation among alfalfa genotypes for rate of acetylene reduction. *Crop Sci.* 17:783–87.

N. L. TAYLOR / *University of Kentucky*

14

RED CLOVER AND ALSIKE CLOVER

❧

RED CLOVER

RED CLOVER, *Trifolium pratense* L., is the most widely grown of all the true clovers. Grown alone and with grasses, it constitutes the most important legume hay crop in the northeastern U.S. It is used for hay, pasture, and soil improvement and fits well into three- and four-year rotations. Nationwide, red clover and grass mixtures have declined from approximately 6 to 5.5 million ha in the last decade, but total production remains about the same as a consequence of increased yields.[1]

Red clover is thought to have originated in Asia Minor and southeastern Europe. An early flowering type known in Spain by 1500 spread to Holland and Lombardy by 1550 and then to the German Rhineland. Red clover was introduced to England from Germany about 1650 and was carried to America by English colonists.[2,3,4]

❧ DISTRIBUTION AND ADAPTATION

All red clovers may be grouped into three divisions: early flowering, late flow-

ering, and wild red.[5] The wild red clover found in England is unknown in North America. Most American red clovers are of the early flowering type, known collectively as medium red clover. This type is characterized by producing two or three hay crops per year and having a biennial or short-lived perennial growth habit. American mammoth red clover is the principal late flowering type grown in the U.S. The late flowering or single-cut type usually produces one crop plus an aftermath.

In addition to early and late types there are many intermediate forms in Europe. The major difference among early and late flowering types is related to daylength response, the single-cut type requiring a longer photoperiod.[2,6,7,8]

❧ N. L. TAYLOR is Professor in Charge of Legume Breeding at the University of Kentucky. He received the M.S. degree from the University of Kentucky and the Ph.D. from Cornell University. His area of special interest is breeding and genetics of red clover and evolutionary genetics of *Trifolium*.

In previous editions this chapter was written by C. P. Wilsie, deceased.

1. USDA. 1958–70. Crop production. Annual summary by states. Agr. Mkt. Serv., Crop Rept. Board.
2. Whyte, R. O., G. Nelsson-Leissner, and H. C. Trumble. 1953. Legumes in agriculture. Agr. Studies 21. FAO, Rome.
3. Merkenschlager, F. 1934. Migration and distribution of red clover in Europe. *Herb. Rev.* 2:88–92.
4. Fergus, E. N., and E. A. Hollowell. 1960. Red clover. *Advan. Agron.* 12:365–436.
5. Hunter, H., and H. M. Leake. 1933. Recent Advances in Agricultural Plant Breeding. Blakiston's, Philadelphia.
6. Williams, Watkin. 1945. Varieties and strains of red and white clover—British and foreign. Welsh Plant. Breeding Sta. Bull. Ser. H., 16.
7. Ludwig, R. A., H. G. Barrales, and H. Steppler. 1953. Studies on the effect of light on the growth and development of red clover. *Can. J. Agr. Sci.* 33:274–87.
8. Gorman, L. W. 1956. Effect of photoperiod on varieties of red clover, *Trifolium pratense* L. *N.Z. J. Sci. Tech.* (Sect. A) 37:40–54.

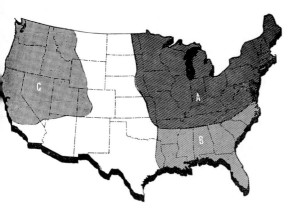

FIG. 14.1. The three major red clover–producing areas of the U.S. are: (A) general region, extensively grown; (B) used as a winter annual except at high elevations; and (C) grown under irrigation except at high elevations.

Red clover is best adapted where summer temperatures are moderately cool to warm and adequate moisture is available throughout the growing season. It is extensively grown in the humid region of the U.S., extending into eastern North and South Dakota, Nebraska, and Kansas. It extends north into Ontario and Quebec and south into Tennessee and North Carolina and is used as a winter annual in the southeastern U.S. It is also grown in much of the Pacific Northwest, primarily under irrigation (Fig. 14.1).

✤ PLANT DESCRIPTION

Red clover is a herbaceous plant made up of numerous leafy stems rising from a crown. The flowers are borne on heads (compact clusters) at the tips of the branches. Heads usually consist of up to 125 flowers.[9]

Most American strains when grown under favorable conditions have corolla tubes 9–10.5 mm in length.[10] Flower color usually is rose purple or magenta. The shape is somewhat similar to pea flowers but more elongated and much smaller. Seed

are short and mitten shaped, 2–3 mm long, and vary in color from pure yellow to purple.

The stems and leaves of American strains are generally hairy, but those of European strains are smooth. Each leaf is divided into three oblong leaflets, usually with a characteristic light-colored marking in the center of each (Fig. 14.2). Red clover has a taproot system with many secondary branches. Plants of the single-cut type form a leafy rosette growth the first year, producing no flowering stems. In the double-cut type many plants flower in the seeding year. In Wisconsin, plants which flowered in the seeding year appear to be more susceptible to winter injury than nonflowering plants.[11]

11. Smith, Dale. 1963. Reliability of flowering as an indicator of winter survival in red clover. *Can. J. Plant Sci.* 43:386–89.

FIG. 14.2. *Stems and leaves are hairy . . . each leaf divided into three oblong leaflets . . . characteristically light-colored marking in the center. Iowa State Univ. photo.*

9. Wilsie, C. P. 1949. Producing alfalfa and red clover seed in Iowa. *Agron. J.* 41:545–50.
10. Starling, T. M., C. P. Wilsie, and N. W. Gilbert. 1950. Corolla tube length studies in red clover. *Agron. J.* 42:1–8.

❧ CULTIVARS AND STRAINS

Red clover is highly self-incompatible and sets seed almost entirely by cross-fertilization.[12] Distinct plant types have evolved through natural selection. In Europe these types are distributed largely according to latitude. Early blooming forms predominate south of 50° N, while late, single-cut types are favored north of 60° N. Between these latitudes a full range is found, with medium-late and late types predominating.[6] Numerous European cultivars have been listed and described.[2,13] European workers have developed tetraploid cultivars which are reported to be more disease resistant and higher yielding than diploid types.[14,15]

In North America many regional and local strains have evolved. Both single-cut and double-cut cultivars are grown in Canada, whereas in the U.S. the double-cut type predominates. Practically all American cultivars are of the diploid type.[16]

Seed from foreign sources often does not perform well throughout the U.S. Red Clover Belt. In Iowa six English cultivars produced only 65% as much forage as standard U.S. cultivars. Although Canadian cultivars have performed well in the northern U.S., most red clover cultivars are not adapted in areas far removed from where the cultivar was developed.

In addition, seed of cultivars increased outside the area of origin may be subject to genetic shifts. Genetic shift in 'Kenland' red clover has been greater at Shafter, Calif., than at Prosser, Wash., and appears to be related to higher seed yield of early plants than of late plants.[17] More flowering and fewer winter-hardy types in 'Dollard' red clover plants have been found from seed increased at Shafter than from seed increased at Prosser.[18] Multiplication of seed of the Finnish 'Tepa' tetraploid red clover cultivar in Israel has resulted in an increase in the number of early flowering plants as compared to the original seed.[19] These examples suggest that studies should be made to indicate practices which will maintain trueness to type in cultivars under seed multiplication outside their areas of origin.

In North America two principal sources of strains are available: old, well-established farm strains produced locally and improved cultivars developed through breeding programs.

Farm strains and older cultivars have been described in detail.[4] The Association of Official Seed Certifying Agencies reports the production of certified seed for the following cultivars:[20]

'Chesapeake' is a naturalized high-yielding cultivar from the eastern shore of Maryland with some resistance to southern anthracnose disease.[21]

Kenland was developed by the Kentucky station and the USDA. It has good persistence and is highly resistant to southern anthracnose. It has been maintained since release in 1947 by continually resowing seed from third-year (second harvest year) stands.[22]

12. Thomas, H. L. 1955. Inbreeding and selection of self-fertilized lines of red clover, *Trifolium pratense*. *Agron. J.* 47:487–89.
13. Nelsson-Leissner, G. 1958. Swedish seed production. Kgl. Lantbrukshogskol. och Statens Lantbruksforsok, Statens Jordbruksforsok, Sartryck och Smaskrifter 109 (First printed as No. 81/1954).
14. Hertzsch, W. 1959. Experiences with polyploid fodder legumes. *Genet. Agraria* 2:116–21.
15. Frandsen, K. J. 1945. Iagttagelser over polyploide Former a nogle Kulturplanter. *Tidsskr. Planteavl* 49:445–96.
16. Thomas, H. L. 1969. Breeding potential for forage yield and seed yield in tetraploid versus diploid strains of red clover (*Trifolium pratense*). *Crop Sci.* 9:365–66.

17. Taylor, N. L., E. Dade, and C. S. Garrison. 1966. Factors involved in seed production of red clover clones and their polycross progenies at two diverse locations. *Crop Sci.* 6:535–38.
18. Bula, R. J., R. G. May, C. S. Garrison, C. M. Rincker, and J. G. Dean. 1969. Floral response, winter survival, and leaf mark frequency of advanced generation seed increases of 'Dollard' red clover, *Trifolium pratense* L. *Crop Sci.* 9:181–84.
19. Dovrat, A., O. Valle, and M. Waldman. 1968. Varietal stability of Finnish red clover (*Trifolium pratense* L.), white clover (*T. repens* L.) and alsike clover (*T. hybridum*) from seed produced in Israel. *Crop Sci.* 8:457–61.
20. Garrison, R. H., and F. S. Morris. 1970. Report of acres approved for certification in 1970 by seed certification agencies. *Prod. Publ.* 22:93–99.
21. Hollowell, E. A. 1958. Registration of varieties and strains of red clover. IV. Chesapeake (Reg. no. 5). *Agron. J.* 50:692.
22. Hollowell, E. A. 1951. Registration of varieties and strains of red clover. II. Kenland (Reg. no. 3). *Agron. J.* 43:242.

FIG. 14.3. *Lakeland . . . high degree of resistance to both powdery mildew and northern anthracnose . . . outyielded all other cultivars . . . persistent.* Lakeland (left) after three years in Wisconsin cultivar trials. *Wis. Agr. Exp. Sta. photo.*

'Lakeland,' developed at the Wisconsin station, is a synthetic cultivar with a high degree of resistance to powdery mildew and northern anthracnose (Fig. 14.3). In Wisconsin, Lakeland has outyielded all other cultivars and has been more persistent. It is adapted to the northern and north central range of states.[23]

'Ottawa' was developed by the experimental farm, Ottawa, Can. It was bred by mass selection for winterhardiness, high yield, and adaptation to conditions of eastern Canada.[4]

'Pennscott' is a naturalized cultivar originating from Lancaster County, Pa. It is characterized by seedling vigor, high yield, and adaptation to conditions of Pennsylvania.[24]

'Tensas' was developed by the Louisiana station for use as a winter annual. It is mildew resistant and adapted to conditions of Louisiana and surrounding states.[4]

Private plant breeding companies also have developed several cultivars of which some seed is being increased. The passage of the U.S. Plant Variety Protection Act is expected to stimulate further development of red clover cultivars.

New cultivars under development for which seed should become available include 'Kenstar,' a cultivar developed by the Kentucky station and the USDA. It was developed by selecting persistent clones from Kenland which were resistant to bean yellow mosaic virus and southern anthracnose. The final selection of ten clones was based on polycross progeny tests. Foundation seed was produced in 1971, and certified seed is expected to be available in 1973.

At the Wisconsin station attention is being directed toward persistence and resistance to powdery mildew, northern anthracnose, and viruses. Several strains and germ plasm lots being tested appear superior to the best-adapted cultivar, Lakeland.

SINGLE-CUT CULTIVARS

Mammoth red clover produces no flowering stems the first year but forms a rosette type of growth instead (Fig. 14.4). During the second year this type comes into bloom 10–14 days later than the double-cut type. Usually only one crop of hay may be harvested, but if moisture is favorable, some aftermath develops.

American mammoth-type cultivars are listed by Fergus and Hollowell.[4] It is doubtful that much seed of these cultivars would be available. 'Altaswede' was developed by the University of Alberta, Edmon-

23. Hanson, E. W., W. K. Smith, and J. H. Torre. 1960. Lakeland red clover performs well in tests. *Crops and Soils* 12:19.

24. Hollowell, E. A. 1953. Registration of varieties and strains of red clover. III. Pennscott (Reg. no. 4). *Agron. J.* 45:574.

Fig. 14.4. *Mammoth red clover . . . no flowering stems the first year.* In the seeding year, even under most favorable conditions, true mammoth red clover produces only basal leaves as (1) at the left. Medium red clover under the same conditions will sometimes bloom freely and even make a good seed crop in the first year (2). *Iowa State Univ. photo.*

ton, Can., from Swedish red clover. It is extremely hardy and well adapted to conditions in Alberta, Canada.

Hybrid Red Clover

The possibility of developing double-cross hybrid medium red clover has been under investigation in the U.S., but no hybrids had been released by 1972. The breeding procedure utilizes inbreds homozygous for S-alleles of the gametophytic self-incompatibility system. Even though red clover is largely self-incompatible, some self-seeds may be produced through a process known as pseudo self-compatibility.[25] Inbreds thus produced are greatly reduced in vigor, but the vigor is regained in single crosses.[26]

The first report of double-cross performance under field conditions was made by Anderson et al.[27] They have shown that crossing was effectively controlled by the self-incompatibility system. In a limited study no hybrids were found that were superior to the best synthetic cultivar. Many technical problems such as methods of maintenance of parental lines remain to be worked out before double-cross hybrids in red clover will become feasible.

Interspecific Hybrids

Because genetic variability for persistence and resistance to certain diseases is

25. Leffel, R. C. 1963. Pseudo self-compatibility and segregation of gametophytic self-incompatibility alleles in red clover, *Trifolium pratense* L. *Crop Sci.* 3:377–80.

26. Taylor, N. L., K. Johnston, M. K. Anderson, and J. C. Williams. 1970. Inbreeding and heterosis in red clover. *Crop Sci.* 10:522–25.

27. Anderson, M. K., N. L. Taylor, and R. Kirithavip. 1972. Development and performance of double-cross hybrid red clover. *Crop Sci.* 12:240–42.

limited in red clover, efforts have been made to hybridize it with other species of the genus. To date, hybridization has been possible with only two annual species, *T. diffusum* Ehrh.[28] and *T. pallidum* Waldst. & Kit.,[29] and greater persistence and disease resistance has not resulted. In spite of many efforts to hybridize red clover with perennial species such as zigzag clover, *T. medium* L., no success had been reported by 1972. However, the use of high temperature and other techniques for overcoming interspecific barriers appears promising.[30]

❧ CULTURE

Fertile, well-drained soils of high moisture-holding capacity are best for red clover. Loams, silt loams, and even fairly heavy-textured soils are preferred to light sandy or gravelly soils. The red clover taproot often is much branched, and a large part of the root system is concentrated in the top 30 cm of soil. Red clover will grow on moderately acid soils, but maximum yields are obtained only when Ca is adequate and the pH is 6 or higher.

Phosphorus is used in large quantities by red clover. This is a limiting factor on most Red Clover Belt soils. Potassium also may be limiting in some areas.

SEEDING

Red clover usually is sown with a small-grain companion crop such as oats, barley, flax, or winter wheat. Small-grain seeding rates are preferably reduced 50–75% from normal.

Red clover is apparently quite tolerant of shading. It has been suggested that photosynthetic saturation for isolated plants of red clover was reached near 16,000 lx of white light, which is a fairly low light intensity.[31]

Early spring seeding is favored for red clover establishment, especially in the northern part of the Red Clover Belt, because of the more favorable moisture conditions. Some clover is seeded still earlier, broadcast on winter wheat or winter rye in February or March.

Farther south, as in Kentucky and Tennessee, seeding between February 15 and March 15 usually is preferred. Red clover may be seeded in the late summer in the southern section of the Red Clover Belt if moisture conditions are favorable, but in the northern section summer seedings are likely to fail. South of Tennessee where clover is used as a winter annual, seedings are usually made from October 15 to December 15. In the western states, seedings may be made in the winter through January.

When seeded alone in the Midwest, the usual rate is 9–11 kg/ha.[4] In the eastern states a little more seed is often used. Red clover usually is seeded in mixtures with a grass, in which case 4.5–7 kg/ha is usual.

PASTURE RENOVATION

Red clover is used extensively in pasture mixtures and for renovating old pastures. It is the easiest legume to establish in closely grazed or renovated sods.[4] Experience in the upper South has shown that it is usually best to disturb the existing sod by disking or other means of mulch tillage in the late fall or winter and to sow the clover in February. Grass should be kept clipped or grazed until the clover is well established. Rotational rather than continuous grazing will result in longer life of the stand.

The inclusion of grass in clover pastures is desirable to control soil erosion, and cattle are less likely to bloat on mixtures than on clover alone. Reproductive disturbances of livestock also have been reported

28. Taylor, N. L., W. H. Stroube, G. B. Collins, and W. A. Kendall. 1963. Interspecific hybridization of red clover (*Trifolium pratense* L.). *Crop Sci.* 3:549–52.
29. Armstrong, K. C., and R. W. Cleveland. 1970. Hybrids of *Trifolium pratense* × *Trifolium pallidum*. *Crop Sci.* 10:354–57.
30. Newton, D. L., W. A. Kendall, and N. L. Taylor. 1970. Hybridization of some *Trifolium* species through stylar temperature treatments. *Theoret. Appl. Genet.* 40:59–62.

31. Bula, R. J. 1960. Vegetative and floral development in red clover as affected by duration and intensity of illumination. *Agron. J.* 52:74–77.

from grazing of predominantly red clover pastures. These are apparently caused by the estrogenic activities of the isoflavones—formononetin, biochanin A, and to a lesser extent daidzein and genistein.[32,33]

❧ MANAGEMENT

Many stands of red clover are lost by improper management in the first year. It is desirable to remove the small-grain companion crop and straw before it can smother the clover. Clover should be clipped in August in the Corn Belt and probably not later than September 15 in the southern section of the Red Clover Belt. If the small grain is harvested for hay or silage, it is usually possible to harvest at least one hay crop or two rotational grazings. After renovation seedings made in February, two crops of hay may be harvested.

In the second year, the first crop of red clover should be harvested at the prebloom to early bloom stage for the best compromise between forage quality and yield. Protein content declined from 28 to 14% and total digestible nutrients from 88 to 65%, whereas dry matter yields increased from 933 to 7105 kg/ha with advance in maturity from the vegetative to full-bloom stages.[34] The second crop is used for additional hay, is grazed, or is left for a seed crop. In many seasons it is difficult to determine the date of first bloom because of lack of flowering as a result of attack by the lesser clover leaf weevil. Usually the first harvest will be made in early May in the southern part of the Red Clover Belt and in early to mid-June in the northern part. Subsequent harvests as hay or pasture may be made at six- to seven-week intervals depending upon moisture availability.

Second-cutting hay also should be made at the early bloom stage for greatest nutritive value. At this stage red clover will produce optimum amounts of protein, carotene, fat, Ca, and P and minimum amounts of undesirable substances such as fiber.[35]

In years when moisture is adequate, regrowth will occur after the second hay or seed crop. This growth may be removed by pasturing or for hay if flowering occurs early. Three hay harvests in the second year usually will result in lower yields in the third year than will two harvests, but quality is higher in the second year for the three-cutting system. A management of one hay harvest and one seed harvest usually is no more detrimental to the stand than are two hay harvests. As in the first year it is best not to cut or graze late in the season. The growth present after a killing frost may be grazed or removed as hay. In the third year, management should be similar to that of the second year.

❧ SEED PRODUCTION

Production of red clover seed in the humid region of the U.S. usually is secondary to forage production. The first crop generally is harvested for hay and the second crop for seed. In the northwestern states where seed production is the primary enterprise, yields have been much higher and more dependable.

Red clover seed production depends upon pollination by insects (Fig. 14.5). Bumblebees, *Bombus* spp., are especially effective in pollinating red clover but are sometimes inadequate to ensure a good seed crop. Honeybees, *Apis mellifera* L., pollinate red clover, particularly when they are collecting pollen.[4] The presence of more attractive nectar-producing plants in the vicinity is a factor. Sweetclover, white clover, and alsike clover plus the flowers of many weed plants growing in the vicinity of the red clover field often result in inadequate red clover pollination.

32. Wong, E. 1962. Detection and estimation of oestrogenic constituents in red clover. *J. Sci. Food Agr.* 13:304–8.
33. Dedio, W., and K. W. Clark. 1968. Biochanin A and formononetin content in red clover varieties at several maturity stages. *Can. J. Plant Sci.* 48:175–81.
34. Smith, D. 1964. Chemical composition of herbage with advance in maturity of alfalfa, medium red clover, ladino clover, and birdsfoot trefoil. *Wis. Agr. Exp. Sta. Res. Rept.* 16:3–10.
35. Van Riper, G. E., and D. Smith. 1959. Changes in the chemical composition of the herbage of alfalfa, medium red clover, ladino clover, and bromegrass with advance in maturity, pp. 1–25. *Wis. Agr. Exp. Sta. Rept.* 4.

Fig. 14.5. *Seed production depends upon pollination by insects.* A good red clover crop on an Indiana farm.

Regardless of whether the second crop is to be used for seed or hay, early harvesting (10–15 days after first bloom) of the first crop for hay is recommended.

Red clover is harvested for seed with combines when the heads have turned brown and the stems are yellow brown. Windrow curing is a common method. Cutting may be with a mower equipped with a curler attachment or with a swather of the type used for windrowing small grain. Direct combining is used by some growers with little attempt being made to obtain clean seed. The "rough" seed is dried to prevent heating, is rethreshed, and then cleaned by use of a stationary combine.

❧ DISEASES

Red clover is subject to a number of diseases.[36,37,38] Crown rot, *Sclerotinia trifoliorum* Eriks., attacks red clover in winter and early spring at relatively low temperatures. It is one of the more destructive diseases in the southern part of the Red Clover Belt. The induction of tetraploidy in red clover has been reported by Norwegian workers to increase resistance to crown rot.[39]

In the northern states, root rot may seriously deplete or even eliminate the stand after the first cutting. Organisms commonly associated with root rot are *Fusarium oxysporum* Schl., *F. solani* (Mart.) Sacc., and *F. roseum* Link. These are weakly pathogenic organisms that may severely injure red clover when it is in a poor state of nutrition or under stress.[40,41] Rots also are associated with an internal breakdown of the root, which appears to be a physiological disorder inasmuch as no causal agent has been found.[42,43]

Northern anthracnose is a major disease in the cooler parts of the Red Clover Belt. It occurs from Massachusetts to Minnesota and south to Delaware and Missouri. The disease is caused by the fungus *Kabatiella caulivora* (Kirch.) Karak. and is most destructive in wet weather at temperatures of 20–25 C. The Wisconsin cultivar Lakeland and the Canadian cultivar Dollard have

36. Kilpatrick, R. A., E. W. Hanson, and J. G. Dickson. 1954. Root and crown rots of red clover in Wisconsin and the relative prevalence of associated fungi. *Phytopathology* 44:252–59.
37. Elliot, Edward S. 1952. Diseases, insects and other factors in relation to red clover failures in West Virginia. W. Va. Agr. Exp. Sta. Bull. 351T.
38. Kreitlow, K. W., J. H. Graham, and R. J. Garber. 1953. Diseases of forage grasses and legumes in the northeastern states. Pa. Agr. Exp. Sta. Bull. 573.
39. Vestad, R. 1960. The effect of induced autotetraploidy on resistance to clover rot (*Sclerotinia trifoliorum* Eriks.) in red clover. *Euphytica* 9:35–38.
40. Chi, C. C., and E. W. Hanson. 1961. Nutrition in relation to the development of wilts and root rots incited by *Fusarium* in red clover. *Phytopathology* 51:704–11.
41. Siddiqui, W. M., P. M. Halisky, and S. Lund. 1968. Relationship of clipping frequency to root and crown deterioration in red clover. *Phytopathology* 58:486–88.
42. Newton, R. C., and J. H. Graham. 1960. Incidence of root-feeding weevils, root rot, internal breakdown, and virus and their effect on longevity in red clover. *J. Econ. Entomol.* 53:865–67.
43. Cressman, R. M. 1967. Internal breakdown and persistence of red clover. *Crop Sci.* 7:357–61.

considerable resistance to northern anthracnose.[23,44]

Southern anthracnose caused by *Colletotrichum trifolii* Bain has been reported as far north as southern Canada but usually is destructive mainly in the southern part of the Red Clover Belt. In some seasons, however, it has been important as far north as central Iowa. Resistant cultivars include Kenland and Kenstar.

Virus diseases have been shown to be destructive to red clover stands.[45] Bean yellow mosaic virus (BYMV) was first and red clover vein mosaic virus was second in prevalence in Minnesota from 1957 to 1960.[46] After the stress of high temperature or cold weather was applied, BYMV reduced stands of clones of red clover as much as 100%. Seed formation was about 10% that of healthy plants.

Stem blackening diseases include spring black stem, *Phoma trifolii* Johnson & Valleau, and summer black stem, *Cercospora zebrina* Pass. Other diseases often causing serious losses include: target spot, *Stemphylium sarcinaeforme* (Cav.) Wiltshire; powdery mildew, *Erysiphe polygoni* DC.; and pepper spot, *Pseudoplea trifolii* (Rostr.) Petr.

Second-cutting red clover hay occasionally has been reported to be unpalatable or to cause slobbering by livestock. This condition apparently is associated with black patch caused by *Rhizoctonia leguminicola* Gough & Elliott. An alkaloid salivation factor, "slaframine," has been isolated from the fungus. Slaframine itself is not the active compound but is converted to the active metabolite by liver enzymes.[47]

The most promising approach toward control of the important red clover diseases would appear to be the development of resistant cultivars. Notable progress has been made in cultivars resistant to northern and southern anthracnose and to powdery mildew.

❧ INSECTS

The clover root borer, *Hylastinus obsurus* (Marsham), often kills many plants by the end of the first crop year. Studies in the Midwest indicate that it is a major factor in reduction of second-year stands.[48]

Another insect which causes considerable damage is the clover root curculio, *Sitona hispidula* (F.), which is closely related to the sweetclover weevil, *S. cylindricollis* Fåhr.[49]

The clover seed chalcid, *Bruchophagus platyptera* (Walker), is one of the most damaging insects to clover and other legume seed. Eggs are laid in the soft green seedpods when the pods are about half grown. The larvae feed on the young developing seed. Several generations may develop in one season. Late developing larvae overwinter in dry seed, either harvested or on plants growing along field borders. The lesser clover leaf weevil, *Hypera nigrirostris* (F.), often attacks the developing clover head.

The potato leafhopper, *Empoasca fabae* (Harris), often causes great damage to strains of European origin which lack the heavy pubescence of stems and petioles characteristic of most plants in strains of American red clover.[50]

Other insects injurious to red clover include: the yellow clover aphid, *Therioaphis trifolii* (Monell); meadow spittlebug, *Philaenus spumarius* (L.); the clover seed midge, *Dasineura leguminicola* (Lintner); the clover leafhopper, *Aceratagallia sanguinolenta* (Prov.); and the pea aphid, *Acyrthosiphon pisum* (Harris).

44. Hanson, E. W. 1959. Relative susceptibility of seven varieties of red clover to diseases common in Wisconsin. *Plant Dis. Reptr.* 43:782–86.
45. Diachun, S., and L. Henson. 1956. Symptom reaction of individual red clover plants to yellow bean mosaic virus. *Phytopathology* 46:150–52.
46. Goth, R. W., and R. D. Wilcoxson. 1962. Effect of bean yellow mosaic virus on survival and flower formation in red clover. *Crop Sci.* 2:426–29.
47. Aust, S. D., H. P. Broquist, and K. L. Rinehart. 1968. Slaframine: A parasympathomimetic from *Rhizoctonia leguminicola. Biotech. Bioeng.* 10:403–12.

48. Pruess, K. P., and C. R. Weaver. 1958. Estimation of red clover yield losses caused by clover root borer. *J. Econ. Entomol.* 51:491–92.
49. Herron, J. C. 1953. Biology of sweet clover weevil and notes on the biology of the clover root curculio. *Ohio J. Sci.* 53:105–12.
50. Hollowell, E. A., J. Montieth, Jr., and W. P. Flint. 1927. Leafhopper injury to clover. *Phytopathology* 17:399–404.

ALSIKE CLOVER

Alsike clover, *Trifolium hybridum* L., is a perennial although it is often treated agriculturally as a biennial. Its history is somewhat obscure, but it is believed to have originated in Sweden. It has been grown commercially in temperate Europe for centuries and is known to have been introduced into England and Scotland about 1832.

❧ DISTRIBUTION AND ADAPTATION

Alsike clover has become an important legume in the clover-timothy area since its introduction into the U.S. about 1839 and into the Midwest by 1854. It is grown widely in the eastern and northern midwestern states, particularly as a complement to red clover in meadow mixtures. It also is important in eastern Canada and in northern Europe. Alsike is especially well adapted to cool climates and wet soils, even tolerating flooded conditions for considerable periods. It will do well on soils that are too acid for red clover and also will tolerate more alkalinity than most other clovers (Fig. 14.6).

❧ PLANT DESCRIPTION

Alsike clover tillers profusely from the crown, with stems at least as long or longer than those of red clover but more slender

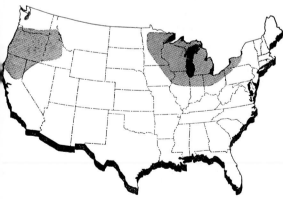

FIG. 14.6. Alsike clover–producing areas of the U.S.

and prostrate. Stems and leaves are smooth, heads are somewhat smaller than red clover, and the flowers are pink or white. The seed are about one-third the size of red clover and are various shades of green mixed with yellow.

The growth habit differs from red clover in that the main axis of the stem does not terminate in a flowering head but keeps growing. Flower-bearing branches arise successively from each leaf axil, so that the youngest flowers are in the terminal heads and the older heads are located farther down on the stem toward the crown.

❧ CULTIVARS AND STRAINS

Variation within this species appears to be less than that found in red clover. The Canada Department of Agriculture has released the cultivar 'Aurora' which is outstanding in hardiness and seed yield. It is a selection of eight indigenous seed lots from areas in western Canada where alsike clover seed has been produced commercially for more than 20 years.[51]

Some evidence exists that tetraploid alsike clover may be more persistent and higher yielding than the diploid form.[52] 'Tetra' is a tetraploid cultivar developed in Sweden.[2]

❧ CULTURE AND MANAGEMENT

Alsike clover grows well on rather heavy soils abundantly supplied with moisture. Although somewhat tolerant of acid soil conditions, the crop responds to lime.

The time and method of seeding is much the same as for red clover. The usual rate of seeding is 4.5–7 kg/ha. On wet, acid soils alsike clover is often sown with redtop, but probably its greatest use is in mixtures with red clover and timothy. Inclusion of timothy with alsike is highly desirable since the clover is likely to lodge badly

51. Elliott, C. R. 1968. Registration of Aurora alsike clover. *Crop Sci.* 8:398.
52. Armstrong, J. M., and R. W. Robertson. 1960. Studies of colchicine-induced tetraploid of *Trifolium hybridum* L. II. Comparison of characters in tetraploids and diploids. *Can. J. Genet. Cytol.* 2:371–78.

and make curing a difficult problem. Alsike clover usually produces only one crop of hay and cannot be expected to produce a hay crop and a seed crop in the same year.

Because of its natural adaptation to wet soils, alsike is a valuable plant to establish on wet natural meadows or those under irrigation. Establishment on poorly drained and overflow land is often possible with alsike clover. Farmers with bottomland fields have found that alsike may succeed where either alfalfa or red clover may be wholly unsuccessful. However, alsike clover generally lacks persistence, living only two years.[53]

❧ DISEASE AND INSECT PESTS

In general, alsike is susceptible to many of the same diseases and insects that damage red clover. It is considered resistant, however, to both northern and southern anthracnose.

ZIGZAG CLOVER

Zigzag clover, *Trifolium medium* L., is a high-polyploid, perennial species which resembles red clover. It is apparently native to central and southern Europe and western Asia but is now naturalized in North America in eastern Canada and New England.[54] Zigzag clover possesses a strong perennial root system and spreads vigorously by rhizomes. Stems and leaves are smooth. Heads are somewhat larger than those of red clover. Florets contain one pale brown seed. Many different forms exist, but no cultivars have been developed. It is highly self-incompatible and is cross-pollinated primarily by bumblebees inasmuch as the corolla tube is too long for pollination by honeybees. Its usage has been limited by low seed yields. Seed failure has been reported to be due to genetic factors, to clover seed chalcid damage, and to preference of pollinators for other plants.[55]

55. Townsend, C. E. 1967. Self- and cross-incompatibility and general seed setting studies with zigzag clover, *Trifolium medium* L. *Crop Sci.* 7:76–78.

❧ QUESTIONS

1. What is the relationship between latitude and adaptation of the principal types of red clover?
2. Suggest reasons why red clover cultivars from one region are not likely to be adapted to another region.
3. How is red clover normally pollinated? Why are honeybees less effective pollinators in Illinois or Iowa than in California?
4. What are two of the newer developments in the breeding of red clover? Why were they undertaken?
5. In the management of red clover, why is it important not to harvest or graze late in the growing season?
6. What is the optimum time for harvesting the first crop of red clover for hay? What are the benefits of harvesting at this time?
7. Name several important diseases of red clover. What is the most promising method of attacking these disease problems?
8. What are the principal factors that influence seed production? Where in the U.S. is seed production best? Why?
9. Why has red clover been such a popular forage crop in short rotations?
10. Is alsike clover superior to red clover in any way or for any purpose? Why has a small amount of alsike been recommended in clover-grass mixtures?

53. Townsend, C. E. 1964. Correlation among characters and general lack of persistence in diverse populations of alsike clover, *Trifolium hybridum* L. *Crop Sci.* 4:575–77.
54. Hermann, F. J. 1953. A botanical synopsis of the cultivated clovers (*Trifolium*). USDA Monogr. 22.

SUPPLEMENTAL INFORMATION

The cultivar 'Arlington' was released in 1973 by the Wisconsin Agricultural Experiment Station in cooperation with the USDA. It is an advanced generation synthetic of six heterogenous populations selected for persistence and resistance to northern anthracnose, powdery mildew, and bean yellow mosaic virus. It is adapted to north central and northeastern U.S. and south central Canada.[56]

56. Smith, R. R., D. P. Maxwell, E. W. Hanson, and W. K. Smith. 1973. Registration of Arlington red clover. *Crop Sci.* 13:771.

HERMAN J. GORZ / *Agricultural Research Service, USDA and University of Nebraska*

W. K. SMITH / *University of Wisconsin*

15

SWEETCLOVER

Sweetclover, *Melilotus,* is native to temperate Europe and Asia as far east as Tibet. It was reported growing in North America as early as 1739, when it was found in Virginia. By 1900 its value as a soil-improving crop was recognized. Its use as a field crop spread gradually through the Corn Belt and Great Plains. This spread was made possible by various improvements in breeding as well as in methods of culture and management. Much of the fundamental information pertaining to sweetclover improvement has been summarized in a comprehensive review published in 1965.[1]

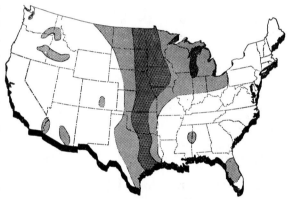

Fig. 15.1. Sweetclover-producing areas of the U.S.

❦ DISTRIBUTION AND ADAPTATION

Sweetclover thrives under a wide range of soil and climatic conditions. It has one

❦ HERMAN J. GORZ, Research Geneticist, ARS, USDA, and Professor of Agronomy at the University of Nebraska, has been in charge of sweetclover improvement work for the northern Great Plains and western Corn Belt regions since 1954. He received the M.S. and Ph.D. degrees at the University of Wisconsin.

❦ W. K. SMITH was on the faculty of the departments of Agronomy and Genetics, University of Wisconsin, and with the Crops Research Division, USDA, until his retirement in 1965. He was widely recognized as an authority on sweetclover.

important restriction, however, in that it does not tolerate acid soils. It is drought resistant and also grows well in parts of the Great Plains with as much as 430 mm of rainfall fairly well distributed through the growing period. It is winter-hardy and productive throughout the Corn Belt and makes a lush growth in areas of adequate rainfall in Texas and on the limestone soils of Alabama and Mississippi. It is one of the first plants to invade and make a successful growth on highway cuts where

1. Smith, W. K., and H. J. Gorz. 1965. Sweetclover improvement. *Advan. Agron.* 17:163–231.

nonacid subsoil is exposed. Use of sweet-clover as a crop plant in eastern North America has been limited, possibly because of the soil tendency toward acidity (Fig. 15.1).

✵ PLANT DESCRIPTION

The cultivated sweetclovers are typically biennial, although certain annual forms are in use. The first season's growth of biennials consists of one central, much branched stem. Like alfalfa, sweetclover has a deeply penetrating taproot. Toward the end of the first year several buds form at the crown, which is usually slightly below the soil surface. During the fall months the root becomes fleshy as storage of food reserves proceeds (Fig. 15.2). In the spring of the second year the crown buds start growth quickly with vigorous, rapidly growing stems that are much coarser than in alfalfa.

Leaves of sweetclover are trifoliolate as in alfalfa, but the leaflets tend to be toothed around the margin and not only at the tip as alfalfa. The stipule of the common sweetclovers is small, narrow, and entire in contrast with the large and broad alfalfa stipule, which is toothed at the base.

Sweetclover flowers are either white or yellow. They are much smaller than those of alfalfa and red clover and are borne in long, loose racemes (Fig. 15.3). The pods are not firmly attached, so that seed shatter readily as they mature. Pods usually contain one seed but sometimes have two. Sweetclover seed can be positively distinguished from those of alfalfa by the fluorescence of germinating alfalfa seed under an ultraviolet light.[2] Sweetclover seed do not fluoresce under these conditions.

✵ IMPORTANCE AND USE

Sweetclover has no equal as a soil-improving crop. Like other legumes, when properly inoculated with the symbiotic

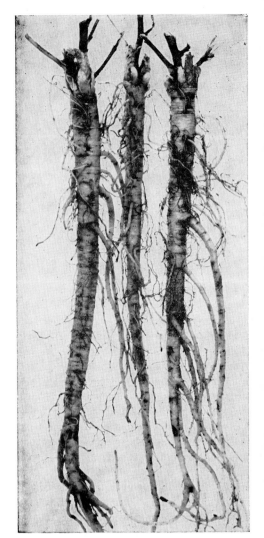

Fig. 15.2. *Sweetclover . . . deeply penetrating taproot . . . in fall stores food reserves . . . spring of the second year crown buds start growth quickly. Univ. Wis. photo.*

nodule-forming bacteria, it utilizes free atmospheric N. Its strong taproot opens up the subsoil, increasing aeration and providing conditions favorable for growth in succeeding crops.[3] Roots break down and decay rapidly at maturity. Plant nutrients become readily available for the succeeding crops, while the organic matter improves

2. Brink, V. C. 1958. Note on a fluorescence test to distinguish seeds of alfalfa and sweetclover in mixtures. *Can. J. Plant Sci.* 38:120–21.

3. Hervey, R. J., L. C. Kapp, J. R. Johnston, and J. C. Smith. 1951. Use of sweetclover for deep placement of phosphorus. *Soil Sci. Soc. Amer. Proc.* 15:258–62.

FIG. 15.3. *Sweetclover flowers . . . much smaller than those of alfalfa and red clover.* (Left) sweetclover, (center) red clover, and (right) alfalfa. Single flowers as shown are of the same magnification. *Univ. Wis. photo.*

the tilth of the soil. Sweetclover gives a high tonnage of organic matter per ha.

In a seven-year test in Ohio, sweetclover sown in the spring with an oat crop has yielded 2450 kg/ha of air-dry roots of 3.5% N content by November.[4] Plots cut for hay on June 15 of the second year averaged over 6700 kg/ha of air-dry hay with N content of 2.35%.

Sweetclover is annually seeded in the Corn Belt and Great Plains for use either as green manure or as a combination pasture and soil-improving crop. In the Dakotas it is often utilized as hay or silage, while to the south pasture is more important. The Texas station has reported that sweetclover is the outstanding legume for general purpose use on the black uplands of the region.[5] Texas also reports that a rotation which includes a crop of sweetclover grown to maturity offers the best means yet known for the control of cotton root rot.[6] In the Palouse region of eastern Washington and adjacent Idaho, soil de-

terioration is halted by using sweetclover-grass mixtures as green manure in rotations with cereals and peas.[7]

Sweetclover from the first has been recognized as one of the most valuable of all our plants for honey production. It yields much nectar; and if early and late flowering cultivars are available, nectar can be gathered over a long period. The honey is of good quality, being of light color and mild flavor.

❧ SPECIES, CULTIVARS, AND STRAINS

Most of the sweetclover seed used in North America is either yellow-flowered, *M. officinalis* (L.) Lam., or white-flowered, *M. alba* Desr. Only biennial forms of *M. officinalis* are grown. Most of the hectarage of this species is "common yellow," although different lots vary in time of maturity and productivity. Both biennial and annual forms of *M. alba* are grown, but by far the larger part of the hectarage is common biennial white. As with the yellow species, individual lots of seed differ markedly. The yellow-flowered species tends to

4. Ohio Agr. Exp. Sta. 1938. Handbook of experiments in agronomy. Spec. Circ. 53.
5. Dunkle, P. B., and I. M. Atkins. 1944. Experiments with small grain and other crops. Tex. Agr. Exp. Sta. Progr. Rept. 892.
6. Lyle, E. W., A. A. Dunlap, H. O. Hill, and B. D. Hargrove. 1948. Control of cotton root rot by sweetclover in rotation. Tex. Agr. Exp. Sta. Bull. 699.

7. Horner, G. M., A. G. McCall, and F. G. Bell. 1944. Investigations in erosion control and the reclamation of eroded land at the Palouse Conservation Experiment Station, Pullman, Wash., 1931–42. USDA Tech. Bull. 860.

be finer stemmed and of better quality but is earlier maturing and somewhat less productive than the white.

CULTIVARS OF *M. officinalis*

'Madrid' originated from seed introduced from Spain.[8] It has good seedling vigor, and the foliage is relatively resistant to fall freezing. It is an excellent seed producer.

'Goldtop' was developed in Wisconsin. It has excellent seedling vigor, is two weeks later in maturity, gives a higher yield of better quality forage, and has slightly larger seed than Madrid.

'Yukon' is a winter-hardy cultivar derived from Madrid by natural selection in northern Saskatchewan. It was released in Canada in 1970. It is equal to or better than Madrid in forage and seed yields in both the U.S. and Canada.

CULTIVARS OF *M. alba*

'Denta' is a low-coumarin, late maturing biennial cultivar developed in Wisconsin.[9] It is vigorous and productive and flowers three to four weeks later than common white.

'Arctic' is an early maturing, winter-hardy cultivar selected in Saskatchewan from common white. 'Polara,' released in Canada in 1970, is similar to Arctic except that it is low in coumarin and produces lower yields of both forage and seed. Arctic and Polara are adapted to western Canada but not to the U.S.

Several annual cultivars of *M. alba* are in use, although the annuals have proved less valuable than the biennial white in the Corn Belt, especially for soil improvement.[10] 'Hubam,' selected at the Iowa station is the best known. 'Floranna,' developed in Florida, is similar to Hubam except that it produces greater forage yields, particularly during the winter months.[11]

'Israel,' a tall, late maturing cultivar, originated as an introduction from Israel and was released as a cultivar in Texas in 1958.[12]

Sourclover, *M. indica* (L.) All., an annual yellow-flowered species, is used as a green manure in the Southwest. It is less productive than Hubam and the forage is less palatable.

❧ COUMARIN

Coumarin is an aromatic compound that occurs in a wide variety of plants. It is used in perfumes and as a flavoring agent and is the substance which gives new-mown sweetclover its characteristic odor.

Most unimproved strains of commonly grown sweetclovers contain large amounts of bound coumarin. When tissues from such plants are chewed by animals, free coumarin is liberated, producing an undesirable taste. This reduces the palatability of the forage to livestock. Coumarin also is objectionable because feeding of spoiled hay or silage from a coumarin-containing cultivar may cause "sweetclover bleeding disease" in livestock.[13] During heating and spoilage in sweetclover hay or silage, coumarin is converted to a toxic substance which reduces the clotting power of the blood of animals eating the forage.[14] Such animals may bleed to death from slight wounds or internal hemorrhages. The toxic substance has been isolated and identified as dicoumarol.[15]

To overcome the undesirable effects, cultivars low in coumarin content have been developed and released. Such cultivars have been made possible by discovery of a low-coumarin gene in an unproductive wild species, banat, *M. dentata* (W. & K.) Pers.[16]

8. Hollowell, E. A. 1943. Registration of varieties and strains of sweetclover. I. *J. Amer. Soc. Agron.* 35:825–29.
9. Smith, W. K. 1964. Denta sweetclover (Reg. no. 5). *Crop Sci.* 4:666-67.
10. Stickler, F. C., and I. J. Johnson. 1959. The comparative value of annual and biennial sweetclover varieties for green manure. *Agron. J.* 51:184.
11. Hollowell, E. A. 1959. Sweetclover. USDA Leaflet 23.
12. Texas Agr. Exp. Sta. 1958. Israel sweetclover. Leaflet. 399.
13. Roderick, L. M., and A. F. Schalk. 1931. Studies on sweetclover disease. N. Dak. Agr. Exp. Sta. Bull. 250.
14. Smith, W. K., and R. A. Brink. 1938. Relation of bitterness to the toxic principle in sweetclover. *J. Agr. Res.* 57:145–54.
15. Campbell, H. A., and K. P. Link. 1941. Studies on the hemorrhagic sweetclover disease. IV. The isolation and crystallization of the hemorrhagic agent. *J. Biol. Chem.* 138:21–33.
16. Brink, R. A., and W. L. Roberts. 1937. The coumarin content of *Melilotus dentata*. *Science* 86:41–42.

The low-coumarin gene was transferred from *M. dentata* to *M. alba* by crossing the two species and grafting the resulting albino seedlings on normal green plants.[17] Later, this same gene was transferred from *M. alba* to *M. officinalis* by excising and culturing the immature hybrid embryos on a nutrient medium.[18]

Low-coumarin cultivars can be contaminated rapidly by volunteer seedlings and by outcrossing to high-coumarin plants during seed increase.[19] Feeding trials with spoiled sweetclover hay in Canada have shown that sheep could safely tolerate 25% contamination and young cattle, 10%.[20,21] Care must therefore be taken to maintain the purity of cultivars during seed increase. Rapid tests for coumarin are available for determining contamination in seed fields and lots.[22]

❧ CULTURE AND MANAGEMENT

Requirements for establishing a good stand of sweetclover are similar to those for alfalfa. However, the seed of sweetclover are "hard" and should be properly scarified before seeding. It usually is recommended that if the pH of the soil is below 6, lime should be applied well in advance of seeding. Scarified seed is sown at the rate of 11–17 kg/ha.

In the Corn Belt, seedings usually are made in the spring with either spring or winter small grain as a companion crop to provide for weed control during establishment.[23]

When the first-year growth is to be used for pasture in the southern half of the Corn Belt and in the Pacific Northwest or where moisture is limited, as in many areas of the Great Plains, the clover usually is seeded without a companion crop.

Sweetclover is unusually susceptible to injury from a number of chemicals used for weed control, particularly 2,4-D. Spraying for weed control in the companion crop will almost always eliminate the seedling stand of sweetclover. In the second season of growth, 2,4-D spray drift results in the shedding of leaves, distortion of leaves and stems, and shedding of flowers.[24] There is also a delay in maturity of the seed crop, smaller yields are obtained, and seed quality is reduced.

THE SEEDLING YEAR

The growth habit of sweetclover in the seedling year differs from that of alfalfa and red clover and calls for careful management. The biennial sweetclover plant in the first year has a single main stem. If the upper portion is cut off, any new growth must come from buds along the stem, not from the crown as in alfalfa. Removal of a substantial amount of the stem in any clipping treatment will result in a marked reduction in root size going into the winter and in plant vigor in the second year.[25] When the companion crop is harvested, the binder or combine should be set as high as possible. Removal of top growth during the first year for use as pasture or hay should be done before mid-August or after mid-October.[26]

PASTURE

Biennial sweetclovers produce a large amount of forage early in the second year.

17. Smith, W. K. 1948. Transfer from *Melilotus dentata* to *M. alba* of the genes for reduction in coumarin content. (Abstr.) *Genetics* 33:124–25.
18. Webster, G. T. 1955. Interspecific hybridization of *Melilotus alba* × *M. officinalis* using embryo culture. *Agron. J.* 47:138–42.
19. Gorz, H. J., and F. A. Haskins. 1969. Contamination of Denta sweetclover during successive generations of seed increase. *Crop Sci.* 9:367–69.
20. Linton, J. H., B. P. Goplen, J. M. Bell, and L. B. Jaques. 1963. Dicoumarol studies. II. The prothrombin time response of sheep to various levels of contamination in low-coumarin sweetclover varieties. *Can. J. Anim. Sci.* 43:353–60.
21. Goplen, B. P., J. H. Linton, and J. M. Bell. 1964. Dicoumarol studies. III. Determining tolerance limits of contamination in low-coumarin sweetclover varieties using a cattle bioassay. *Can. J. Anim. Sci.* 44:76–86.
22. Haskins, F. A., and H. J. Gorz. 1970. Rapid detection of o-hydroxycinnamic acid and beta-glucosidase in *Melilotus alba. Crop Sci.* 10:479–81.

23. Burnside, O. C., and H. J. Gorz. 1965. Oats and amiben for weed control during sweetclover establishment. *Weeds* 13:35–37.
24. Greenshields, J. E. R., and W. J. White. 1954. The effects of 2,4-D spray drift on sweetclover plants in the second year of growth. *Can. J. Agr. Sci.* 34:389–92.
25. Stickler, F. C., and I. J. Johnson. 1959. The influence of clipping on dry matter and nitrogen production of legume green manures. *Agron. J.* 51:137–38.
26. Smith, Dale, and L. F. Graber. 1948. The influence of top growth removal on the root and vegetative development of biennial sweetclover. *J. Amer. Soc. Agron.* 40:818–31.

Growth tapers off rapidly after midsummer as the plants flower and mature. Grazing should begin when the tops are 20–25 cm high, but during the period of rapid growth heavy stocking is desirable to prevent the forage from becoming coarse and unpalatable. First-year growth may provide substantial amounts of pasture in southern areas (Fig. 15.4).

HAY AND SILAGE

A good quality hay, somewhat comparable in palatability and feeding value to alfalfa, can be made from the first-year growth. The second-year growth is less satisfactory for this purpose. The coarse stems have a high percentage of moisture and dry slowly. Leaves tend to become brittle and shatter during handling. If the crop is cut in the bud stage and cured under favorable conditions, it has about the same feeding value as alfalfa.

Because of difficulty in making the second-year growth into high-quality hay, sweetclover forage often is converted to silage. The best quality silage is made when the crop is cut before the plants begin to bloom. Mixtures of grasses or small grains with sweetclover also make high-quality silage.

SOIL IMPROVEMENT

Biennial sweetclover makes a rapid growth both in tops and roots as moisture becomes available after removal of the companion crop. Plowing may be done in late fall of the first year, but best results usually are obtained when this legume is plowed down in the following spring after it has made a top growth of 15 cm. If plowing is deferred beyond this time, some additional N and organic matter will be added to the soil, but depletion of soil moisture reserves in making the additional growth may be a hazard for a corn crop in a dry season.

An Iowa experiment indicates that biennial sweetclover in a two-year corn-oat rotation gave an average annual increase during a 16-year period of 13.8% in the yield of corn.[27] Under irrigation in western Nebraska biennial sweetclover plowed down as green manure increased the yields of the two succeeding corn crops by an average of 13 q/ha on soil of average fertility and by 39 q/ha on soil of lower N content.[28]

Benefits derived from sweetclover as a green manure in humid areas and under irrigation may not be obtained in areas where moisture is limited, as in the Great Plains.[29] Sometimes the large amounts of N released may cause "burning," as the heavy growth of the succeeding crop made early in the season uses up the available moisture.

❧ SEED PRODUCTION

The bulk of sweetclover seed produced in North America is harvested in a relatively narrow north-and-south band, fanning out in the north to include the prairie

FIG. 15.4. *Biennial sweetclovers . . . large amount of forage early in the second year . . . during rapid growth heavy stocking . . . desirable to prevent forage from becoming coarse and unpalatable.* Good sweetclover pasture on an Ingham County, Mich., farm. *USDA photo.*

27. Johnson, I. J., C. P. Wilsie, and A. T. Leffler. 1945. Sweetclover on Iowa farms. *Iowa Farm Sci.* 6:17–20.
28. Pumphrey, F. V., and F. E. Koehler. 1958. Forage and root growth of five sweetclover varieties and their influence on two following corn crops. *Agron. J.* 50:323–26.
29. Army, T. J., and J. C. Hide. 1959. Effects of green manure crops on dryland wheat production in the Great Plains area of Montana. *Agron. J.* 51:196–98.

of western Canada. It narrows in the U.S. to include only the western parts of Minnesota and Iowa and the eastern parts of the Dakotas, Nebraska, Kansas, and Oklahoma and extends into Texas.

POLLINATION

When tripped, flowers of white sweetclover, *M. alba,* set seed readily with their own pollen. However, there is much self-incompatibility in plants of yellow *M. officinalis,* so that cross-pollination is necessary for a full set of seed. This tripping is done readily by various bees and other insects. By far the most important pollinator is the honeybee, *Apis mellifera* L. Increasing the population of bees by placing 3–10 hives of honeybees per ha near the field will ensure adequate pollination.

None of the three species now in cultivation, *M. alba, M. officinalis,* and *M. indica,* will intercross under natural conditions. However, intercrossing can occur between cultivars and strains within *M. alba* or *M. officinalis* unless adequate isolation is maintained. Plants of *M. indica* are self-fertile and the flowers set seed without insect visitation.

CROP MANAGEMENT

Sweetclover sets a heavy crop of seed, but the indeterminate habit of growth and the loose attachment of the mature pods on the rachis result in heavy loss of ripe seed before and at harvest. Yields average about 225 kg/ha of clean seed, but this has been estimated to be only 60% of the seed actually produced on the plants.[30] To minimize this loss, the crop usually is cut when about two-thirds of the pods are brown or black. When methods of harvest in Nebraska were compared, windrowing the crop when damp and threshing after four or five days with a combine equipped with pickup attachment was the most efficient. Combining the standing crop is recommended in some states, particularly following the use of desiccants.[31]

❧ DISEASES

Sweetclover suffers little damage from disease in the Great Plains area in most years. In the more humid Corn Belt the plants usually remain healthy during the seeding year. In the spring of the second year heavy losses have been caused in certain seasons by a root rot caused by *Phytophthora cactorum* (Led. & Cohn) Schroet.; this and other organisms are also associated with root and crown injury in western Canada in the spring of the second year.

Black stem frequently occurs in the Corn Belt. The blackened stems may be stunted, with poor flowering and reduced seed set. *Ascochyta meliloti* Trus. and *Cercospora davisii* El. & Ev. are the organisms most frequently associated with this disease. Stem canker, *Ascochyta caulicola* Laub., sometimes causes serious damage, with the stems stunted and bent at the tip to give a characteristic "goose-neck" effect.[32] Adequate control of these diseases appears to lie in the breeding of resistant cultivars.

❧ INSECTS

The adult sweetclover weevil, *Sitona cylindricollis* Fåhr., is the major insect pest of sweetclover, destroying stands by completely defoliating newly emerged seedlings.[33] The presence of the weevil is indicated by crescent-shaped notches on the leaf margins. Although effective control is provided by various insecticides, the breeding of a weevil-resistant cultivar offers the greatest promise for practical control.[34] No evidence of true resistance has been found within the commonly grown species; but a noneconomic species, *M. infesta*

30. Potts, R. C. 1955. Sweetclover in Texas. Tex. Agr. Exp. Sta. Bull. 791.

31. Garver, S., and T. A. Kiesselbach. 1947. Growing and harvesting the sweetclover seed crop. Nebr. Agr. Exp. Sta. Bull. 387.
32. Gorz, H. J. 1955. Inheritance of reaction to *Ascochyta caulicola* in sweetclover (*Melilotus alba*). Agron. J. 47:379–83.
33. Munro, J. A., M. A. Leraas, and W. D. Nostdahl. 1949. Biology and control of the sweetclover weevil. J. Econ. Entomol. 42:318–21.
34. Haws, B. A., and F. G. Holdaway. 1954. Sweetclover weevil and its control in Minnesota. Minn. Agr. Ext. Folder 180.

Guss., has been found to be virtually immune to weevil feeding.[35] Attempts to transfer the resistance to *M. alba* or *M. officinalis* have been unsuccessful. However, biochemical studies of the mechanism of resistance to weevil feeding have shown that nitrate, found in higher concentrations in *M. infesta* than in the susceptible species, strongly deters weevil feeding.[36] This suggests the possibility of developing a weevil-resistant cultivar by selecting plants with a higher nitrate content.

The sweetclover root borer, *Walshia miscecolorella* (Chambers),[37] and the sweetclover aphid, *Therioaphis riehmi* (Boerner), have caused some damage to sweetclover in the Great Plains. Resistance to the sweetclover aphid is readily available and has been incorporated into breeding lines for use in improved cultivars of sweetclover.[38] Blister beetles, *Epicauta* spp., feed selectively on the leaves of low-coumarin strains of sweetclover and may cause considerable damage when populations are high.[39] Other insects such as grasshoppers, leafhoppers, cutworms, caterpillars, green cloverworms, webworms, and the clover leaf weevil, *Hypera punctata* (F.), have been reported to be pests of sweetclover but rarely cause serious damage.

❧ QUESTIONS

1. Why has the previous large hectarage of sweetclover been reduced?
2. Where are the sweetclover seed-producing areas of the U.S. located? Why?
3. List three ways in which sweetclover can be distinguished from alfalfa.
4. Discuss the relative merits of sweetclover for hay, pasture, and green manure.
5. What factors are responsible for the contamination of low-coumarin cultivars of sweetclover?
6. Under what conditions would you seed Hubam sweetclover on your farm?
7. What is the danger in feeding sweetclover hay or silage made from a high-coumarin cultivar? How can this danger be prevented?
8. When would you plow under biennial sweetclover as a green manure crop? Why?
9. Why are losses high in harvesting sweetclover seed?
10. What method offers the greatest promise for a practical means of controlling the sweetclover weevil? Would this also apply to other insects and to diseases?

35. Manglitz, G. R., and H. J. Gorz. 1964. Host-range studies with the sweetclover weevil and sweetclover aphid. *J. Econ. Entomol.* 57:683–87.

36. Akeson, W. R., F. A. Haskins, G. R. Manglitz, and H. J. Gorz. 1969. Sweetclover weevil feeding deterrent B: Isolation and identification. *Science* 163:293–94.

37. Manglitz, G. R., H. J. Gorz, and H. J. Stevens. 1971. Biology of the sweetclover root borer. *J. Econ. Entomol.* 64:1154–58.

38. Manglitz, G. R., and H. J. Gorz. 1961. Resistance of sweetclover to the sweetclover aphid. *J. Econ. Entomol.* 54:1156–60.

39. Gorz, H. J., F. A. Haskins, and G. R. Manglitz. 1972. Effect of coumarin and related compounds on blister beetle feeding in sweetclover. *J. Econ. Ent.* 65:1632–35.

SUPPLEMENTAL INFORMATION

Seed of common cultivars of sweetclover are quite small and should be planted shallowly to obtain satisfactory stands. A comparison of various seed sizes showed that improved stands were obtained by using strains with larger seed.[40] These types also were able to emerge from greater depths, thus permitting deeper planting to reach moist soil.

In a crop such as sweet clover, the development of cultivars that are resistant to insect attack provides the ideal solution to insect control. Sources of resistance in several species of *Melilotus* to four different insects, including the sweetclover root borer,[41] have been found. Studies to determine why certain plants were resistant to insect attack led to the discovery that the insects responded to specific chemical components in the plant tissues.[42] Knowing which chemical components are responsible for resistance permits more efficient selection of resistant plants in breeding for resistant cultivars.

40. Haskins, F. A., and H. J. Gorz. 1975. Influence of seed size, planting depth, and companion crop on emergence and vigor of seedlings in sweetclover. *Agron. J.* 67:652–54.

41. Manglitz, G. R., H. J. Gorz, and F. A. Haskins. 1974. Resistance in sweetclover to the sweetclover root borer. *ARS-NC-18*, pp. 1–4.

42. Manglitz, G. R., H. J. Gorz, F. A. Haskins, W. R. Akeson, and G. L. Beland. 1976. Interactions between insects and chemical components of sweetclover. *J. Environ. Quality* 5:347–52.

R. C. LEFFEL AND P. B. GIBSON
Agricultural Research Service, USDA

16

WHITE CLOVER

❦

THE NEAR EAST center described by Harlan is generally regarded as the origin of many forage plants and may have included white clover, *Trifolium repens* L.[1] Certainly animal caravans and routes of migratory grazing animals spread white clover throughout Europe and western Asia prior to recorded history. Reports abound of indigenous white clovers in European countries prior to importations of domesticated white clovers. The cultivation of white clover by the use of seed apparently had begun in the Netherlands by the latter half of the sixteenth century.[2,3,4] Cultivated white clover was introduced into England soon after 1700.[4]

The history of white clover in the U.S. is also obscure; white clover was probably introduced into America by colonists from Europe.[5] Reportedly, American Indians

called white clover "white man's foot grass" because it appeared simultaneously with the early European colonists. White clover apparently was well established in North America by 1750 and preceded English settlers to Ohio and Kentucky. The earlier French settlers and missionaries probably introduced white clover to the Ohio Valley.

The first record of the large type of white clover, ladino, in the U.S. was made by the North Carolina station in 1891.[6] The ecotype failed here because of poor seed production. Reintroduction of ladino clover in 1903 and successful seed production in the western U.S. early in the twentieth century have been reported.[7] Adaptation of ladino white clover to the northeastern U.S. was recognized during the 1930s and adaptation to the north central and southeastern U.S. was realized a few years later.[8]

❦ R. C. LEFFEL is Research Agronomist and Laboratory Leader, Plant Nutrition Laboratory, Plant Physiology Institute, ARS, USDA, Beltsville, Md. He received the M.S. and Ph.D. degrees from Iowa State University. He has worked extensively on breeding and culture of soybeans and forage crop breeding.

❦ P. B. GIBSON is Research Agronomist, Southern Region, ARS, USDA. He received the M.S. degree from Auburn University and the Ph.D. from the University of Wisconsin. Since 1955 he has conducted research at Clemson, S.C., on the genetics, breeding, and culture of white clover.

1. Harlan, Jack R. 1971. Agricultural origins: Centers and noncenters. *Science* 174:468–74.
2. Sansone, Antonio. 1905. Il Ladino. Bibl. Agr. Ottavi 51. Casale Monferrato, Italy.
3. Erith, Adela Gwendolyn. 1924. White Clover (*Trifolium repens* L.). (monogr.). Duckworth, London.
4. Ware, W. M. 1925. White clover. Min. Agr. Fish. Misc. Publ. 46, London.
5. Carrier, Lyman, and Katherine S. Bort. 1916. The history of Kentucky bluegrass and white clover in the United States. *J. Amer. Soc. Agron.* 8:256–66.
6. McCarthy, Gerald, and F. E. Emery. 1894. Some leguminous plants. N.C. Agr. Exp. Sta. Bull. 98.
7. Madson, B. A., and J. Earl Coke. 1933. Ladino clover. Calif. Agr. Ext. Serv. Circ. 81.
8. Ahlgren, Gilbert H., and R. F. Fuelleman. 1950. Ladino clover. *Advan. Agron.* 2:207–32.

Popularity of ladino white clover grew rapidly during the 1940s and 1950s. Hectarage of ladino white clover in the U.S. has been about 3 million ha since 1957.

✗ DISTRIBUTION AND ADAPTATION

The general geographical distribution of white clover within and beyond the temperate regions of the world is presented by Daday.[9] White clover is found from the Arctic Circle throughout the temperate regions of the world. The species is found in subtropical regions such as the Gulf Coast of the U.S. and Queensland, Australia. The species has been found near the equator in Colombia at altitudes from 1600 to 3000 m.[10] It appears to be limited geographically only by the cold of the Arctic, the drought of deserts, and the heat and plant competition of lowland tropical jungles. Optimum performance of white clover as a pasture plant is in the mild humid climates of New Zealand and northwest Europe. In the U.S., white clover is found in the humid eastern half of the country, in the Pacific Northwest, and along river valleys and in irrigated pastures of the intermountain region.

White clover is best adapted to well-drained silt loam and clay soils of pH 6–7. It can be grown on sandy soils with adequate soil moisture and fertility. In eastern Canada natural selection has been noted for an acid-tolerant white clover in soils of pH 4.5.[11] White clover is not tolerant of saline or highly alkaline soils (Fig. 16.1).

Natural selection among white clovers of the world for frequencies of two independent genes has been found.[12] The Ac/ac alleles govern the presence or absence of

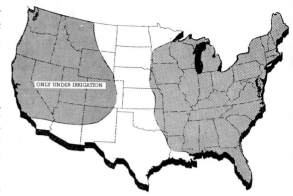

FIG. 16.1. White clover–producing areas of the U.S.

the glucosides producing hydrocyanic acid (HCN) in white clover. The Li/li alleles govern the presence or absence of the enzyme which hydrolyzes the glucosides. The gene frequencies for the genes for glucoside and enzyme were 100% in warm regions and decreased to 0% in cold northern latitudes or at high elevations. Daday found that the enzyme was activated by low temperature, and the HCN produced caused an irreversible inhibition of the respiratory system of the AcLi genotype, causing tissue death. Other workers conclude there is no evidence of discrimination among cyanogenic or acyanogenic white clovers by herbivores, snails, or slugs.[13] How cyanogenesis is associated with greater fitness of white clovers in warm climates is not understood.

✗ PLANT DESCRIPTION

White clover is a glabrous pasture plant with prostrate habit of growth. The species is polymorphic and ranges from a perennial plant in temperate areas to a winter annual in subtropical areas. There is a great range in size of plants and plant parts. Largest plants occupy a square meter or more in area and are 30–45 cm high.

White clover germinates as a typical clover does, producing a pair of cotyledons;

9. Daday, Hunor. 1958. Gene frequencies in wild populations of *Trifolium repens* L. III. World distribution. *Heredity* 12:169–84.
10. Crowder, Loy V. 1960. The response of white clover varieties grown at high elevations in Colombia. *Agron. J.* 52:608–9.
11. McConkey, O. 1935. The origin and ecological adaptation of the agricultural grasses, clovers and alfalfa of eastern Canada. *Herb. Rev.* 3:185–92.
12. Daday, Hunor. 1965. Gene frequencies in wild populations of *Trifolium repens* L. IV. Mechanisms of natural selection. *Heredity* 20:355–65.
13. Bishop, J. A., and M. E. Korn. 1969. Natural selection and cyanogenesis in white clover, *Trifolium repens*. *Heredity* 24:423–30.

a simple leaf bearing a single leaflet; and many compound leaves, each normally composed of three leaflets. The primary stem of the white clover plant is short and contains a number of internodes. The axillary buds of the primary stem give rise to stolons six to eight weeks after germination. Elongation of the primary stem stops or is limited after stolon growth begins. Stolons develop radially from the primary stem. The stolon, contrasted to the primary stem, has elongated internodes and an apical bud that remains vegetative. Leaves arising from the stolons are borne alternately, one per node on long petioles. Leaflets usually are sessile and are elliptical to heart shaped. The presence or absence of a V-shaped white mark in the middle of the leaflet is simply inherited. The life of the leaf from bud to senescence is about 40 days under favorable conditions. In the axil of a leaf is an axillary bud, which may remain dormant or develop into either a flower or a branch stolon. The stolon is solid, varies greatly in size depending on the size type of white clover, and may develop one, or more, adventitious root at each of its nodes (Fig. 16.2).

The white clover plant develops a primary taproot which may grow to a depth of 1 m or more but dies before or during the second year of growth of the plant.[14] Perenniality of white clover eventually depends upon the secondary root system from the nodes of stolons and upon the proportion and rate of axillary buds developing into stolons rather than flowers. Branch stolons achieve independence when the main stolon decays. Nodules are present on the roots of white clover as a result of the symbiosis between host plant and *Rhizobium trifolii* Dangeard.

Flowering depends on many factors among which genotype, age and degree of development of the plant, temperature, and photoperiod are prominent. Flowering is greatly enhanced by long days and optimum temperature for growth following

14. Westbrooks, Fred E., and Milo B. Tesar. 1955. Tap root survival of ladino clover. *Agron. J.* 47:403–10.

FIG. 16.2. *Life of the leaf . . . bud to senescence . . . about 40 days.* The axillary buds of the primary stem (A) give rise to stolons (B) six to eight weeks after germination. The axillary bud may remain dormant or may develop into either a flower or a branch stolon (C). *USDA photo.*

short days and low temperatures. Flowering heads are produced on peduncles somewhat longer than the petioles of leaves. The almost round head is composed of individual perfect flowers or florets, each of which is borne on a short pedicel. Number of florets per head ranges from 20 to 150. The predominantly white flower color, sometimes with a pinkish hue, is responsible for the common name of the species (Fig. 16.3).

FIG. 16.3. *Flowering heads . . . produced on peduncles somewhat longer than the petioles of leaves . . . almost round head . . . composed of individual perfect flowers. USDA photo.*

Seed mature in 22–30 days after cross-fertilization. The seed is small, approximately 1540/g, and is heart shaped or oval. Seed are usually yellow, sometimes reddish, and become brownish in color with age or weathering. The seed coat may be impermeable, causing hard seed. Hard seed of white clover may pass intact through the digestive tract of grazing animals, thus allowing reseeding and spread of the species.

❧ IMPORTANCE AND USE

White clover is the most important pasture legume in many parts of the temperate zones. It is almost always used in association with grasses but may be seeded alone for poultry and swine pastures. The ryegrass–white clover pasture system in northwestern Europe and New Zealand is exemplary of grass-legume pasture combinations. Nevertheless, the system encounters competition from grasses fertilized with N.

In 1969 the Federal Extension Service estimated 5 million ha in the U.S. seeded to cultivars of white clover.[15] Of this hectarage, 70% was in the southeastern U.S. Perhaps at least 20 million ha of humid or irrigated pastureland in the U.S. have varying amounts of white clover.[16] If the pasture is not overgrazed, consumption by grazing animals is limited mostly to leaves and petioles.

Practical experience by grassland farmers suggests that white clover herbage improves the feeding value of a pasture above that of the grass alone. The only conclusive experimental evidence available confirms the hypothesis.[17] Forages containing white clover, compared with pure grass forages, were of superior productive value for growing and fattening lambs. This superiority was a complex of factors, including higher levels of voluntary intake and digestibility and possibly the more efficient utilization of the digested nutrients. Susceptibility of cattle to bloat when fed on white clover often obscured any possible nutritional differences among forages. White clover, compared with grasses, was generally higher in crude protein, which may be important in amino acid metabolism of rapidly growing animals. White clover contains higher crude protein and, generally, a higher percentage of each of 16 amino acids than birdsfoot trefoil, alfalfa, or red clover.[18]

Legumes are generally higher in mineral content than grasses and white clover is outstanding among legumes, with consistently higher contents of Na, P, Cl, and Mo.[17] The difficulty of determining how extensively the nutritional superiority of white clover can be utilized in practical livestock production should be emphasized. Grass pastures fertilized with N produce higher dry matter yields than white clover-grass pastures. Voluntary intake may be influenced by level of forage production. White clover frequently displays estrogenic activity, and its dominant estrogen is coumestrol.[19] Reproductive problems with animals grazing white clover can be explained by its presence. Diseased leaves of white clover are more estrogenic late in the season than nondiseased leaves.[20] The role of estrogens in white clover on the anabolism of the ruminant is not clear.[19,20] Bloat is particularly associated with grazing of lush green legumes such as white clover.[21] The risk of bloat probably reduces the use of white clover, but the danger can be minimized by proper management and methods of control.

15. Paulling, John R. 1970. Trends in forage crop varieties—1969. Fed. Ext. Serv., USDA.
16. Gibson, Pryce B., and E. A. Hollowell. 1966. White clover. USDA Agr. Handbook 314.
17. Thomson, D. J., and W. F. Raymond. 1970. White clover in animal production—Nutritional factors (review). *In* J. Lowe (ed.), White Clover Research. Occasional Symp. 6:277–84. (Brit. Grassl. Soc., Hurley.)

18. Loper, G. M., Dale Smith, and M. A. Stahmann. 1963. Amino acid content of legumes as influenced by species and maturation. *Crop Sci.* 3:522–25.
19. Bickoff, E. M., R. R. Spencer, S. C. Witt, and B. E. Knuckles. 1969. Studies on the chemical and biological properties of coumestrol and related compounds. USDA Tech. Bull. 1408.
20. Newton, J. E., J. E. Betts, Hilary M. Drane, and N. Saba. 1970. The oestrogenic activity of white clover. *In* J. Lowe (ed.), White Clover Research. Occasional Symp. 6:309–14. (Brit. Grassl. Soc., Hurley.)
21. Todd, J. R. 1970. White clover in animal production—Animal health factors (review). *In* J. Lowe (ed.), White Clover Research. Occasional Symp. 6:297–307. (Brit. Grassl. Soc., Hurley.)

In the grass–white clover pasture the white clover supplies N to the grass, increasing production and protein quality of the forage (Fig. 16.4). This transfer of N from white clover to grass is a direct movement of nitrogenous compounds from nodules to grass roots; a transfer of products of decomposition of nodules, roots, and aerial parts of the white clover; and a transfer of N compounds through the grazing animal.[22] Estimates of the N-fixing ability of grass–white clover pastures, obtained by comparing their production with that of grass pastures receiving different levels of N, are as high as 225 kg N/ha in the U.S. and twice this in the 10-month growing season of the North Island, New Zealand.

White clover is widely used in renovation of permanent pastures lacking legumes. White clover–grass mixtures may be used for hay or silage of high nutritive value. The species is used as a cover crop, especially in orchards and in road-bank seedings as an N-fixing legume. White clover is included in some lawn seed mixtures for the northern and western states. White clover–grass mixtures contribute to soil conservation, watershed management programs, and protection of the environment.

✣ CULTIVARS

The indigenous white clovers of an area are often designated as "wild." They evolved under conditions of continuous and heavy grazing and are recognized by small leaf size and dense, spreading habit of growth. They persist well under the environment in which they were produced. 'Kent' and 'Aberystwyth S184' are British cultivars of this type. The closest approach to wild white clovers in the U.S. are those marketed as of Idaho or New York origin. These are small, prostrate white clovers with good winterhardiness.

Most white clovers in the U.S. without a cultivar name, of known origin and often designated as "common," are intermediate

22. Martin, T. W. 1960. The role of white clover in grassland. *Herb. Abstr.* 30:159–64.

FIG. 16.4. *White clover supplies N to the grass, increasing production . . . protein quality.* A white clover–grass pasture in the Columbia River basin of Washington. *USDA photo.*

in size. Approximately 40% of the hectarage in the U.S. is seeded to intermediate white clovers. White clover of Louisiana origin is adapted to and is extensively grown in the lower Mississippi Valley and Gulf Coast. 'Dutch' white clover should designate only a source or strain of the species from Holland.

Other important foreign cultivars of intermediate type include New Zealand's 'Grasslands Huia' and 'Aberystwyth S100' and 'Kersey' from the U.K.

Ladino has been treated as a botanical variety, ecotype, type, or cultivar of white clover and as a kind of clover. In Italy, this large white clover is considered a botanical variety on the basis of the greater number of vascular bundles in the petiole, larger petiole and lamina, smaller seed, and low content of cyanogenetic glucoside. Its origin around Lodi and Cremona is an area with a light podzolized alluvial soil and a warm temperate and maritime climate with mild winters. Here the white clover is irrigated frequently during the summer, is cut five or six times annually, and is grazed a short period in the fall.

'Ladino Gigante Lodigiano' is the local ecotype in the Lodi-Cremona area of Italy.

TABLE 16.1 ❧ Improved white clover cultivars of the U.S.

Cultivar	Type	Year of release	Originator	Adaptation	Characteristics
Louisiana S1	intermediate	1952	Louisiana station	Gulf Coast states	5-clone synthetic; reseeds well
Pilgrim	large	1953	Northeast stations and USDA	Northeast and Canada	21-clone synthetic; trueness to type
Merit	large	1960	Iowa station	central Corn Belt and Northeast	30-clone synthetic; leafhopper damage and drought resistance; winter-hardy
Regal	large	1962	Auburn University station	Southeast	5-clone synthetic; persistence, summer production
Tillman	large	1965	South Carolina station and USDA	Southeast	6-clone synthetic; summer production, persistence, disease resistance, sparse flowering, profuse stolon branching

This is the large type of white clover preserved at its origin.

'Espanso' is a selection from Ladino Gigante Lodigiano for uniformity of type, maximum size and yield, and resistance to low temperatures and drought. This is the largest white clover cultivar available.

In Italy the word "ladino" is not sufficient to define the giant cultivar of white clover of Lodi.[23] There also is the question as to whether the present "ladino" of the U.S., adapted as it is to nonirrigated land, is still the same as the giant cultivar of North Italy. Italian ladino has a relatively longer leaflet than other cultivars of white clover and is in a class by itself, but this does not invariably apply to ladino from the U.S.[24]

Half the white clover hectarage in the U.S. is seeded to large white clovers, most of it as ladino. Ladino is extensively used in temporary pastures with the taller growing grass species such as orchardgrass or tall fescue. Plants and plant parts of ladino are larger than those of intermediate white clovers; stolon diameter is considered by some as the most stable characteristic of ladino in the U.S. Ladino does not flower as profusely as smaller types of white clover, nor does it bloom as early. It lacks winter-hardiness and persistence but is the most productive white clover under conditions of optimum soil moisture and fertility.

During the 1950s and 1960s in the U.S., breeding programs developed the improved cultivars of white clover listed in Table 16.1.

❧ CULTURE AND MANAGEMENT

Small, intermediate, and large white clovers evolved on relatively infertile, medium fertile, and fertile soils respectively and in association with grasses. Correspondingly, the intensity of grazing decreased and forage production increased with the utilization of larger white clovers. Optimum management of a white clover–grass pasture cannot ignore these associations between the genotype and its environment.

The establishment of a grass–white clover pasture requires an adequate ratio of clover to grass in the seeding mixture. In almost all situations, 2–4 kg/ha of white clover are adequate. The white clover seed should be inoculated with the proper *Rhi-*

23. Biasutti, E. 1948. Research and problems overseas—Italy. New species for irrigated meadows in northern Italy and the origin of ladino clover. *J. Brit. Grassl. Soc.* 3:207–10.

24. Hawkins, R. P. 1959. Botanical characters for the classification and identification of varieties of white clover. *J. Nat. Inst. Agr. Bot.* 8:675–82.

zobium. Drilling grass in adequately spaced rows and overseeding the entire area with white clover reduces competition from the grass. Liming to achieve a minimum soil pH of 6 is recommended, and adequate Ca, P, and K should be supplied. Some soils may require minor element fertilization.

The main problem in the management of a grass–white clover pasture is the maintenance of the white clover component. It must be realized that the conditions for growth of white clover are more exacting than those required by grasses and, additionally, that white clover's performance may be adversely affected by drought or disease. Grasses continue to benefit by application of fertilizer N, but white clover is affected adversely. It is generally accepted that the ideal balance of grass to clover for maintaining pasture productivity is about 2:1.[22] Since dry matter yield decreases and crude protein increases with increased percentage of clover in the pasture, this ratio provides maximum production of dry matter and crude protein. The clover content is greatly influenced by the amount of inorganic N in the soil. When mineral N is high, grasses tend to dominate; at lower levels of N with adequate major plant nutrients, white clover becomes dominant.

Species and cultivars of companion grasses vary in the amount of competition they provide white clover. When mineral N is low, however, the great influence on the performance of white clover is by frequency and stage of defoliation. Frequent defoliation during the period of maximum grass growth encourages white clover by minimizing grass competition. Grass–white clover forage should be utilized prior to maximum competition by the grass. One of the great mistakes in management of grass–white clover pastures is allowing overgrowth of the grass. Clipping or harvesting surplus forage in understocked pastures controls the grass and weeds.

The larger white clovers require rotational or controlled continuous grazing. If pastures are grazed continuously, the height of forage should be maintained at 5–15 cm. Management in the fall should allow good regrowth of clover and thus rooting of new stolons. If the white clover component disappears from a permanent pasture, it may be reestablished by proper renovation practices. Reseeding white clover annually in summer perennial grasses in the South requires close grazing, harvesting, or burning of the grass. Soil fertility requirements must be met, the soil surface scarified, and the white clover seed must be accurately placed in contact with the soil within the weakened sod. Compacting the soil about the seed is advisable.

❧ SEED PRODUCTION

Seed production of white clover is of two categories: harvest of a seed crop from an area predominantly utilized as a pasture and growth and management as a highly specialized crop for seed only. The only significant remaining area for white clover seed production from pastures in the U.S. is in Louisiana. Current production there is approximately 1600 ha, with an average yield of about 100 kg seed/ha. Persistency of small white clovers requires harvest of seed from pastures exhibiting this characteristic under grazing.[25] A pasture from which a seed crop is harvested requires special management during the year of seed harvest. Early season pasture production should be fully utilized by heavy grazing or harvest to reduce the grass component. Subsequently, optimum growth and development of the white clover must be allowed to provide adequate flowering heads for the seed crop.

The remaining white clover seed production in the U.S. is a specialty in irrigated areas of the West. High seed yields of excellent quality are obtained under optimum conditions for growth, flower production, insect pollination, and seed harvest. Special procedures such as choice of area

25. Haggar, R. J., and W. Holmes. 1963. Kent wild white clover—the growth and management of wild white clover with special reference to seed production. Dept. Agr. Wye Coll., Ashford, Kent, England.

and limited generations of seed increase ensure maintenance of adaptation of cultivars. Through the 1960s Idaho and Oregon had a total of 2000–10,000 ha annually, with an average annual yield of about 300 kg seed/ha.

Production of ladino white clover seed in the U.S. is mostly in California. Through the 1960s annual production has been 5000–8000 ha, with an average annual yield of about 350 kg seed/ha. Nearly all this production is certified. Seed yields twice those of the average are obtained by best production practices.[26] Time and frequency of irrigations are critical; lush growth of ladino white clover lodges and exposes mature seed heads to moisture. Honeybee hives, 3–10/ha, provide pollinators. The seed crop is accumulated throughout the blooming season; the degree of bloom and seed-head maturity serve as a guide to stop irrigation in preparation for seed harvest. Most of the crop is harvested from the windrow, but spray curing followed by direct combining can be efficient. Straw and chaff from the combine may be rethreshed and the field vacuumed to recover seed. Fields must be irrigated immediately after harvest to revive ladino white clover stands.

❧ DISEASES AND INSECTS

Insect pests and diseases of white clover are discussed by Gibson and Hollowell.[16] Insects threatening the ladino white clover seed crop and their control are discussed by Bacon et al.[27]

DISEASES

Stolon and root rots may seriously deplete stands of white clovers. Species of *Fusarium, Rhizoctonia, Colletotrichum, Leptodiscus,* and *Curvularia* are involved and are part of the stolon and root rot com-

plex that also involves environmental conditions; age of plant tissue; and virus, insect, and nematode attacks upon the plant. *Sclerotium rolfsii* Sacc. may be prevalent in the South during hot humid periods. *Sclerotinia trifoliorum* Eriks. occurs mostly in northern areas under snow cover or in dense stands during winter or early spring. While resistance to stolon and root rots is rare, there is some tolerance among white clovers to most of these diseases. Adapted cultivars and recommended cultural practices reduce the potential of these diseases.

Virus diseases are common in white clovers; most field plants are infected by the third year of the stand. Resistance to viruses in white clover is rarely found, but there is evidence of tolerance. Symptoms include mild to severe mottling of leaves, clearing of the veins of leaves, rugose leaves, and stunting of plants. Viruses that infect white clover, singly or in combination, include the alfalfa mosaic, white clover mosaic, clover yellow mosaic, clover yellow vein mosaic, red clover vein mosaic, and peanut stunt viruses. Viruses are spread by grazing, mowing, and insect vectors. A mycoplasm-induced disease causing phyllody also occurs in white clover.

Foliar pathogens include pepper spot, *Leptosphaerulina trifolii* (Rostr.) Petr., during cool wet weather; Cercospora leaf and stem spot, *Cercospora zebrina* Pass., throughout the season; Curvularia leaf spot, *Curvularia trifolii* (Kauff.) Boed., during warm humid weather; sooty blotch, *Cymadothea trifolii* (Pers. ex Fr.) Wolf, during cool seasons; and rust, *Uromyces trifolii* var. *trifoliirepentis* (Liro) Arth., in late summer and fall. These diseases cause leaf loss and reduce the quality of forages. Good resistance is available for some of the foliar diseases.

Nematode damage to white clover is most widespread in the South, principally by root-knot nematodes, *Meloidogyne* spp. Tolerance in white clovers to *M. incognita* (Kofoid & White) Chitwood is available. Sting, meadow, and clover cyst nematodes also attack white clovers. Root-knot nema-

26. Marble, V. G., L. G. Jones, J. R. Goss, R. B. Jeter, V. E. Burton, and D. H. Hall. 1970. Ladino clover seed production in California. Calif. Agr. Exp. Sta. Ext. Serv. Circ. 554.
27. Bacon, O. G., V. E. Burton, and John E. Swift. 1970. Pest and disease control program for ladino clover seed production. Calif. Agr. Exp. Sta. Ext. Serv. Leaflet.

todes induce galls on roots. Shortened, thickened, or discolored roots are symptoms of meadow and sting nematodes. All nematodes may cause stunting, reduced vigor, and untimely death of plants.

INSECTS

The glabrous leaves of white clover are especially susceptible to the potato leafhopper, *Empoasca fabae* (Harris). Feeding by the insect causes stunting and a reddening-bronzing and browning of the leaves. Spittlebugs, *Philaenus spumarius* (L.), stunt and cause a rosetting of terminal growth and are identified by their spittle masses. Clover leaf and alfalfa weevils, *Hypera punctata* F. and *H. postica* (Gyll.) respectively, are leaf feeders, especially in early spring. The larvae of the clover root curculio, *Sitona hispidula* F., feed upon the roots and introduce soil-borne, root-rotting fungi to the root system.

The seed crop in the South is threatened especially by the lesser clover leaf and clover head weevils, *H. nigrirostris* F. and *H. meles* F. respectively. Larvae of these insects attack parts of the flowering head, stunting or destroying heads and preventing seed formation. Seed production in California and the Pacific Northwest is further threatened by the clover seed weevil, *Miccotrogus picirostris* F., the larvae of which feed on the developing seed; the ladino clover seed midge, *Dasineura gentneri* Pritchard, which feeds on flower parts and prevents seed formation; the lygus bugs, *Lygus hesperus* Knight and *L. elisus* Van D., which suck juices from plant and seed and cause shrivelling or loss of seed; and by several species of spider mites, *Tetranychus* spp., which feed and spin delicate webs on the underside of leaves.

❧ OTHER SPECIES

Taxonomists estimate that the genus *Trifolium* contains 250–300 species. A worldwide taxonomic treatment of the genus is not available to date. Coombe has revised the European species of *Trifolium*

and recognizes six distinct subspecies of *T. repens* within the variation of wild plants of the species.[28] The need for improved white clovers and the lack of genetic diversity within the species for persistence and resistance to root and stolon rots arouse much interest in prospects of improving the species by interspecific hybridization. The first interspecific hybrid with white clover, *T. repens* (a 32-chromosome tetraploid species), was a cross with ball clover, *T. nigrescens* Viv. *Trifolium nigrescens* is an annual diploid species closely related to diploid species *T. petrisavii* Clem. and *T. meneghinianum* Clem. These latter two species have also been crossed with *T. repens,* but the *T. nigrescens* complex involving these three species offers no major characteristic for improvement of *T. repens.*

Stolons of white clover are subjected to trampling by livestock and are exposed to temperature extremes at the soil surface. Hybridization of white clover with a rhizomatous species is desired. *Trifolium ambiguum* Bieb. is very close to *T. repens* taxonomically and possesses rhizomes and many other desirable characteristics including persistence and disease resistance. *Trifolium ambiguum* has been crossed with alsike clover, *T. hybridum* L., but not with *T. repens.* Chen and Gibson have studied the karyotypes of 14 of the 17 species in section *Amoria* Presl. and *T. occidentale* Coombe.[29] Similarity of karyotypes of *T. nigrescens, T. occidentale, T. petrisavii,* and *T. repens* suggests a close phylogenetic relationship among these species.

Trifolium occidentale is a diploid, perennial, stoloniferous species very similar morphologically to the small type of white clover. Gibson and Bienhart have crossed this species with *T. repens* and *T. nigrescens.*[30] *Trifolium uniflorum* L. is a peren-

28. Coombe, D. E. 1968. *Trifolium* L. *In* T. G. Tutin et al. (ed.), Flora Europeae, vol. 2, pp. 157–72. Cambridge Univ. Press.

29. Chen, Chi-Chang, and Pryce B. Gibson. 1971. Karyotypes of fifteen *Trifolium* species in Section *Amoria. Crop Sci.* 11:441–45.

30. Gibson, Pryce B., and George Bienhart. 1969. Hybridization of *Trifolium occidentale* with two other species of clover. *J. Hered.* 60:93–96.

nial tetraploid quite distinct from *T. repens* and was first hybridized with *T. repens* by Pandey.[31] Gibson et al. have crossed *T. uniflorum* with *T. repens* and *T. occidentale* and also have obtained trispecies hybrids.[32] *Trifolium occidentale* tolerates more adverse growing conditions than *T. repens* and is more tolerant to some of the white clover virus diseases. *Trifolium uniflorum* exhibits short internodes, woody taproots, large seed, and tolerance to virus diseases. The barriers to improvement of white clover are being removed by interspecific hybridization.

31. Pandey, Kamla K. 1957. A self-compatible hybrid from a cross between two self-incompatible species in *Trifolium. J. Hered.* 48:278–81.
32. Gibson, Pryce B., Chi-Chang Chen, J. T. Gillingham, and O. W. Barnett. 1971. Interspecific hybridization of *Trifolium uniflorum* L. *Crop Sci.* 11:895–99.

✣ QUESTIONS

1. What characteristics of white clover contribute to its distribution throughout the moist, temperate regions of the world?
2. Why is white clover valuable as a legume component of pastures?
3. Give the management practices which affect the botanical composition of a grass–white clover pasture causing a shift toward (a) more grass, (b) more white clover.
4. What are the apparent relationships among edaphic factors and the evolution and utilization of types of white clover?
5. List the steps which must be taken in producing seed of a white clover cultivar to ensure maintenance of its characteristics.
6. Why are white clovers less persistent than several of the other forage legumes?
7. Compare the life histories of the primary root and stem of white clover with those of alfalfa.

SUPPLEMENTAL INFORMATION

Recently increased interest in forage legumes, including white clover, is the result of diminishing supplies of fossil fuels and the consequential increase in cost of nitrogen fertilizers. Privately developed cultivars 'Arcadia,' 'Sacramento,' and 'Lucky,' developed by the Oregon Agricultural Experiment Station, were recently released. All three cultivars are the large type white clover.

Past research indicates that viruses reduce production of white clover forage and seed and weaken plants, making them more susceptible to competition and to diseases other than viruses. Thus much of the current white clover research in the U.S. is directed toward the control of virus diseases. Developing cultivars resistant to alfalfa mosaic, clover yellow vein, and peanut stunt viruses is in progress. Resistance to each of these viruses exists at a low frequency in white clover, whereas *Trifolium ambiguum* is resistant to all three viruses. The transfer of the virus resistances of *T. ambiguum* to white clover is attempted by species hybridization. Other current research in the U.S. and other countries includes efforts to improve rhizobial relationships and culture and management.

SUPPLEMENTAL LITERATURE CITATIONS

Brockwell, J., W. G. Bryant, and R. R. Gault. 1972. Ecological studies of root nodule bacteria introduced into field environments. III. Persistence of rhizobium trifolii in association with white clover at high elevation. *Aust. J. Exp. Agr. Anim. Husb.* 12:407–13.

Chen, Chi-Chang, and Pryce B. Gibson. 1972. Chromosome relationships of *Trifolium uniflorum* to *T. repens* and *T. occidentale. Can. J. Genet. Cytol.* 14:591–95.

Lucas, L. T., and C. R. Harper. 1972. Mechanically transmissible viruses from ladino clover in North Carolina. *Plant Dis. Reptr.* 56:774–76.

Chen, Chi-Chang, and Pryce B. Gibson. 1974. Seed development following matings of *Trifolium nigrescens* x *T. occidentale* at different ploidy levels. *Crop Sci.* 14:72–77.

Thompson, J. A., R. J. Roughley, and D. F. Herridge. 1974. Criteria and methods for comparing the effectiveness of rhizobium strains for pasture legumes under field conditions. *Plant and Soil* 40:511–24.

Barnett, O. W., and P. B. Gibson. 1975. Identification and prevalence of white clover viruses and the resistance of *Trifolium* species to these viruses. *Crop Sci.* 15:32–37.

Barnett, O. W., P. B. Gibson, and A. Seo. 1975. A comparison of heat treatment, cold treatment, and meristem tip-culture for obtaining virus-free plants of *Trifolium repens. Plant Dis. Reptr.* 59:834–37.

Gibson, P. B., and Chi-Chang Chen. 1975. Registration of SC-2 and SC-3 clover germplasms. *Crop Sci.* 15:605–6.

Miller, J. D., P. B. Gibson, W. A. Cope, and W. E. Knight. 1975. Herbivore feeding on cyanogenic and acyanogenic white clover seedlings. *Crop Sci.* 15:90–91.

Hale, C. N. 1976. Some factors affecting the survival of rhizobium trifolii on white clover. Proc. N.Z. Grassl. Assoc. 38:182–86.

Jutras, M. W., and P. B. Gibson. 1976. White clover (*Trifolium repens* L.) for South Carolina. S.C. Agr. Exp. Sta. Bull. 592.

Williams, E., and D. W. R. White. 1976. Early seed development after crossing of *Trifolium ambiguum* and *T. repens. N.Z. J. Bot.* 14:307–14.

Barnett, O. W., and P. B. Gibson. 1977. Effect of virus infection on flowering and seed production of the parental clones of Tillman white clover (*Trifolium repens*). *Plant Dis. Reptr.* 61:203–7.

Cope, W. A., S. K. Walker, and L. T. Lucas. 1978. Evaluation of selected white clover clones for resistance to viruses in the field. *Plant Dis. Reptr.* 62:267–70.

ROBERT R. SEANEY / *Cornell University*

17

BIRDSFOOT TREFOIL

❧

Birdsfoot trefoil, *Lotus corniculatus* L., is a perennial forage legume used for pasture, hay, and silage. Two distinct types of birdsfoot trefoil are grown in the U.S. and Canada, the New York or Empire type and the European type. Empire types are related to the cultivar 'Empire,' a naturalized ecotype discovered in Albany County, N.Y. The European-type cultivars such as 'Cascade,' 'Granger,' 'Mansfield,' and 'Viking' were developed from introductions from Europe. Compared to the European cultivars, Empire is finer stemmed, is more prostrate in growth habit, is 10–14 days later in flowering, is more indeterminate in growth and flowering habit, is more winter-hardy, and has slower seedling growth and slower recovery growth rate after harvest.

Species of *Lotus* are widely distributed throughout the world. The greatest diversity occurs in the Mediterranean basin, indicating this region was probably the center of origin. *Lotus corniculatus* is native to Europe and parts of Asia. Nineteenth-century reports indicate birdsfoot trefoil grew naturally in many pastures and was a good feed for cattle and horses. However,

it was not until after 1900 that birdsfoot trefoil was cultivated in Europe.[1]

It is not certain when or how birdsfoot trefoil was introduced into the U.S. The crop first received recognition in 1934 when D. B. Johnston-Wallace of Cornell University found a naturalized stand growing in Columbia County, N.Y.[2] During the following 10–15 years, research on management and improvement demonstrated the potential value of birdsfoot trefoil as an important forage legume.

❧ DISTRIBUTION AND ADAPTATION

Birdsfoot trefoil is grown in the British Isles; throughout much of Europe; in several South American countries such as Brazil, Chile, and Uruguay; and in areas of India, Australia, and New Zealand. In the U.S. birdsfoot trefoil first became naturalized in New York, Washington, Oregon, and California. Major hectarage now occurs in the area shown in Figure 17.1. Birdsfoot trefoil does not persist well in most parts of the southeastern U.S. where crown and root diseases cause serious stand losses. The southern limit of adaptation includes higher elevations in North Carolina, Tennessee, and northern Arkansas.

❧ ROBERT R. SEANEY is Professor of Crop Science and Plant Breeding, Cornell University. He completed his professional training at Purdue and Cornell universities. From 1955 to 1967 he conducted research on the breeding and management of birdsfoot trefoil for the ARS, USDA, in cooperation with the New York station at Cornell.

1. MacDonald, H. A. 1946. Birdsfoot trefoil (*Lotus corniculatus* L.): Its characteristics and potentialities as a forage legume. Cornell Univ. Agr. Exp. Sta. Mem. 261.
2. Johnstone-Wallace, D. B. 1938. Pasture improvement and management. N.Y. State Coll. Agr. Ext. Bull. 393.

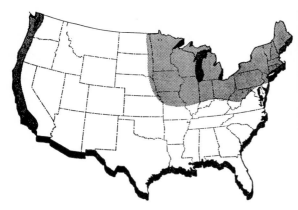

FIG. 17.1. Birdsfoot trefoil–producing areas of the U.S.

FIG. 17.2. *Birdsfoot trefoil . . . many well-branched stems arising from a single crown . . . can be propagated from stem cuttings. N.Y. Agr. Exp. Sta. photo.*

In Canada considerable hectarage of birdsfoot trefoil occurs in the eastern provinces.

Birdsfoot trefoil grows on many different types of soils, from clays to sandy loams. It will grow on poorly drained, droughty, infertile, acid, or mildly alkaline soils. Although it tolerates rather adverse soil conditions, it is most productive on fertile, moderately well-drained to well-drained soils having a pH of 6.2–6.5 or higher. Most cultivars are winter-hardy in the northern U.S. and southern Canada. Under severe winter conditions tests in Minnesota and Canada have shown Empire to be more winter-hardy than Viking and other European-type cultivars.[3]

❧ PLANT DESCRIPTION

Mature plants of birdsfoot trefoil have many well-branched stems arising from a single crown. Under favorable growing conditions the main stems attain a length of 60–90 cm. Stems are generally smaller in diameter and less rigid than those of alfalfa. Plants can be propagated by stem cuttings since roots develop from callous tissue of stem internodes and both roots and shoots develop from axillary buds of the node. (See Fig. 17.2.)

Compound leaves are attached alternately on opposite sides of the stem and consist of five leaflets, three attached to the terminal end of the petiole and two smaller ones at the base. During darkness the leaflets close around the petiole and stem.[1] When birdsfoot trefoil is cut and dried for hay, the leaves also fold around the stem and become inconspicuous, often giving the impression of excessive leaf loss. The inflorescence is a typical umbel having four to eight florets attached at the end of a relatively long peduncle or flower stem. Flower color varies from light to dark yellow and may be tinged with orange or red stripes. (See Fig. 17.3.)

Fertilization and seed set depend on pollination of flowers by insects, primarily species of *Hymenoptera*. Although flowers are perfect, having both stamens and pistils, most seed results from cross-pollination. Even though self-pollination occurs, a self-incompatibility mechanism limits the development of self-seed.[4] Ten to 15 seed are borne in long cylindrical pods which turn brown to almost black at maturity. An average of five or six pods, 2.5–4 cm

3. Rachie, K. O., and A. R. Schmid. 1955. Winter-hardiness of birdsfoot strains and varieties. *Agron. J.* 47: 155–57.

4. Giles, W. L. 1949. The morphological aspects of self-sterility in *Lotus corniculatus* L. Ph.D. thesis, Univ. Mo., Columbia.

long, are attached at right angles to the end of the flower stem giving the appearance of a bird's foot, thus the common name birdsfoot trefoil. Pods ripen 25–30 days after pollination. They split along both sides when mature and twist spirally to scatter the seed. Seed are very small, 825,000–925,000/kg,[1] and vary in color from olive green to brown and almost black. Seed coats are often mottled with black spots varying in size from small dots to large patches.

Birdsfoot trefoil has a well-developed taproot with numerous lateral branches in the upper 30–60 cm of soil. The taproot does not penetrate as deeply as alfalfa and the distribution of branch roots in the upper soil is more extensive. Birdsfoot trefoil roots have the ability to produce new shoots. Root segments taken below the crown will develop shoots and roots from callous tissue and grow into new plants. This ability to develop shoots from roots may aid plant survival when heaving occurs and roots are severed.[5]

Birdsfoot trefoil is a long-day plant requiring approximately a 16-hour day for full flowering. A shorter daylength restricts flowering and results in plants having a more prostrate, rosette growth habit.[6] Flower buds may abort even under optimum photoperiod. Factors causing bud abortion or flower drop include temperature, nutrient level, insects, and diseases.

Most birdsfoot trefoil plants contain a cyanogenetic glucoside which can be hydrolyzed by enzymatic action to produce free hydrocyanic acid (HCN), although some cultivars and selections have plants which do not. For example, about 4% of the plants of Viking are acyanogenetic.[7] The concentration of HCN in some species of *Lotus* is poisonous to animals;[8] however, there have been no authenticated reports of *L. corniculatus* causing HCN poisoning when grazed.

NUTRITIVE VALUE

The chemical composition and nutritive value of birdsfoot trefoil equal that of alfalfa and other legumes.[1] As spring growth of birdsfoot trefoil matures, there is a decrease in protein and an increase in fiber content.[9] The feeding value of early cut hay of Empire and Viking is greater than that of late cut hay. There is little difference in feeding value of Empire and Viking hays harvested on the same date.[10]

With good harvest and storage practices, birdsfoot trefoil makes excellent silage.

FIG. 17.3. *Inflorescence of birdsfoot trefoil . . . four to eight florets attached . . . end of a relatively long flower stem . . . flower varies . . . light to dark yellow . . . tinged with orange or red stripes. Iowa State Univ. photo.*

5. Midgley, A. R., and A. Gershoy. 1946. Birdsfoot trefoil may propagate by root cuttings. *J. Amer. Soc. Agr.* 38:197–99.

6. Joffee, A. 1958. The effect of photoperiod and temperature on the growth and flowering of birdsfoot trefoil. *S. African J. Agr. Sci.* 1:435–50.

7. Seaney, R. R., and P. R. Henson. 1970. Birdsfoot trefoil. *Advan. Agron.* 22:119–57.

8. Gurney, E. H., and C. H. White. 1941. Red-flowered lotus or birdsfoot trefoil (*Lotus coccinius*) a possible danger to stock. *Queensland Agr. J.* 55:297–99.

9. Smith, D. 1964. Chemical composition of herbage with advance in maturity of alfalfa, medium red clover, ladino clover, and birdsfoot trefoil. *Wis. Agr. Exp. Sta. Res. Rept.* 16.

10. Trimberger, G. W., W. K. Kennedy, J. T. Reid, J. K. Loosli, K. L. Turk, and V. N. Krukovsky. 1962. Feeding value and digestibility of birdsfoot trefoil hay harvested at different stages. *N.Y. Agr. Exp. Sta. Bull.* 974.

The forage should be cut, wilted to 60–65% moisture, chopped fine, and ensiled to exclude all air. Feeding studies comparing birdsfoot trefoil silage to other legume silage show similar consumption and milk production results.[11]

❧ IMPORTANCE AND USE

Birdsfoot trefoil is presently grown on an estimated 900,000 ha in the U.S. Because of its wide adaptation, persistence, and relatively high yield potential, it has replaced much of the red and ladino white clovers previously grown in the Northeast. In this area it is also used on the poorly drained shallow soils previously planted to timothy. In the Midwest it has gained importance as a permanent pasture legume, filling the need for a widely adapted legume that is both persistent and productive when grazed by cattle or sheep.

In the Northeast, birdsfoot trefoil is grown extensively in New York, Pennsylvania, and Vermont. The erect European-type cultivars, Viking, Mansfield, and common, account for about 75% of the total ha grown, and Empire accounts for 25%. In the north central region, birdsfoot trefoil is grown in Ohio, Iowa, Illinois, Michigan, Minnesota, Missouri, and Nebraska. In contrast to the Northeast, Empire accounts for about 60% of the total ha grown in the north central region.[12]

PASTURE

Empire or Empire-type cultivars persist better in permanent pastures than the erect European-type cultivars like Viking and Mansfield. European cultivars can be used for pasture but must be rotationally grazed and managed like alfalfa and red clover.[13]

Ohio studies have compared both rota-tional and continuous grazing of Empire and Viking, using sheep and cattle. Both animal product per ha and persistence of Empire and Viking were greater with rotational than with continuous grazing. In the six-year study Empire was more persistent and resulted in greater animal gains than Viking.[14,15]

Birdsfoot trefoil is an excellent legume to use when renovating permanent grass pastures. In comparing birdsfoot trefoil–Kentucky bluegrass pastures with grass or grass fertilized with N, most studies show higher animal production on trefoil-grass pastures and suggest it is more profitable to renovate pastures and establish birdsfoot trefoil than to invest in yearly applications of N on established grasses.[16,17]

Reseeding contributes to the long-term persistence of Empire in pastures. Even when closely grazed, it will often flower and set seed on stems near the ground. Where the perennial habit of birdsfoot trefoil is shortened by environment or diseases, natural reseeding is of definite advantage in maintaining stands.[18, 18a]

Deferred grazing of birdsfoot trefoil can be used to reapportion forage production during the summer months. Pennsylvania studies have shown forage yield and quality of Empire to be relatively high when grazing is delayed until July.[19]

The wide adaptation, relatively high yield, persistence, and nonbloat characteristic make Empire a prominent pasture legume. It has been grazed in pure stands

11. Wittwer, L. S., W. K. Kennedy, G. W. Trimberger, and K. L. Turk. 1958. Effects of storage methods upon nutrient losses and feeding value of ensiled legume and grass forage. N.Y. Agr. Exp. Sta. Bull. 931.
12. Paulling, J. R. 1970. 1969 trends in forage crop varieties. Fed. Ext. Serv., USDA.
13. Davis, R. R., and D. S. Bell. 1957. A comparison of birdsfoot trefoil and ladino clover–bluegrass for pasture. I. Response of lambs. Agron. J. 49:436–40.
14. Van Keuren, R. W., and R. R. Davis. 1968. Persistence of birdsfoot trefoil (Lotus corniculatus L.) as influenced by plant growth habit and grazing management. Agron. J. 60:92–95.
15. Van Keuren, R. W., R. R. Davis, D. S. Bell, and E. W. Klosterman. 1969. Effect of grazing management on the animal production from birdsfoot trefoil pastures. Agron. J. 61:422–25.
16. Mott, G. O., R. E. Smith, W. M. McVey, W. M. Beeson. 1952. Grazing trials with beef cattle. Purdue Agr. Exp. Sta. Bull. 581.
17. Wedin, W. F., R. L. Vetter, J. M. Scholl, and R. W. Woods. 1967. An evaluation of birdsfoot trefoil (Lotus corniculatus) in pasture improvement. Agron. J. 59:525–28.
18. Templeton, W. C., Jr., C. F. Buck, and D. W. Wattenbarger. 1967. Persistence of birdsfoot trefoil under pasture conditions. Agron. J. 59:385–86.
18a. Taylor, T. H., W. C. Templeton, Jr., and J. W. Wyles. 1973. Management effects on persistence and productivity of birdsfoot trefoil (Lotus corniculatus L.). Agron. J. 65:646–48.
19. Mays, D. S., and J. B. Washko. 1960. The possibility of stockpiling legume-grass pasture. Agron. J. 52:190–93.

and also cut and fed green with no apparent bloat problem. (See Fig. 17.4.)

HAY

The faster growing cultivars of European origin can be harvested twice in a year, and three times in areas with a longer growing season.[20,21,22] Hay yields under a two-cut system range from 4.5 to 10 t/ha. Studies in New York report Viking to be more productive than Empire. When tested over a wide range of soil and climatic conditions, yields of Viking were 10–15% greater than Empire. Higher yields of Viking occurred primarily in the second harvest. In these same tests Viking produced about 80% of the yield of Narragansett alfalfa. The appropriate interval between cuttings depends on location and environmental conditions. In most areas of the north central and northeastern U.S., six to eight weeks are required for regrowth and flowering of second or third growths. Late fall harvest of birdsfoot trefoil should be avoided in order to maintain stand.[23]

Cutting heights of 7.6–11.4 cm are necessary to maintain maximum yields and persistence of Empire stands. Lower cutting reduces the number of axillary buds from which regrowth arises and removes leaf area needed to produce carbohydrates for regrowth.[20,24] The carbohydrate root reserve of Empire decreases during spring growth and remains at a relatively low level during the summer until it again increases near the end of the growing season. Thus regrowth after cutting is primarily

FIG. 17.4. *Birdsfoot trefoil . . . excellent . . . renovating permanent grass pastures . . . wide adaptation . . . high yield, persistence and non-bloat characteristics . . . prominent pasture legume. N.Y. Agr. Exp. Sta. photo.*

dependent on carbohydrates synthesized by top growth left after cutting, rather than on reserves stored in the roots as with alfalfa.[25]

If birdsfoot trefoil is cut repeatedly for hay and not allowed to reseed, stands will not persist over long periods. Gradual thinning of stands occurs by loss of individual plants from insects, disease, heaving, and other environmental stresses.[26]

Under most conditions birdsfoot trefoil should be grown in association with a grass. There are several advantages: the associated grass often adds to the total forage production by filling in areas where birdsfoot trefoil does not establish or persist; it prevents encroachment of weeds, reduces lodging, decreases severity of heaving, and aids in hay curing and harvesting. Most northeastern states report highest yields from birdsfoot trefoil–timothy mixtures.[1] Kentucky bluegrass, smooth bromegrass, orchardgrass, tall fescue, reed canarygrass, bentgrass, and perennial ryegrass are

20. Pierre, J. J., and J. A. Jackobs. 1953. The effect of cutting treatments on birdsfoot trefoil. *Agron. J.* 45:463–68.
21. Duell, R. W., and H. W. Gausman. 1957. The effect of differential cutting on the yield, persistence, protein, and mineral content of birdsfoot trefoil. *Agron. J.* 49:318–19.
22. Langille, J. E., L. B. MacLeod, and F. S. Warren. 1968. Influences of harvesting management on yield, carbohydrate reserves, etiolated regrowth and potassium uptake of birdsfoot trefoil. *Can. J. Plant Sci.* 48:575–80.
23. Parsons, J. L., and R. R. Davis. 1964. Establishment and management of birdsfoot trefoil in Ohio. Ohio Agr. Exp. Sta. Res. Bull. 967.
24. Greub, L. J., and W. F. Wedin. 1971. Leaf area, dry matter production, and carbohydrate reserve levels of birdsfoot trefoil as influenced by cutting height. *Crop Sci.* 11:734–38.

25. Smith, D. 1962. Carbohydrate root reserves in alfalfa, red clover, and birdsfoot trefoil under several management schedules. *Crop Sci.* 2:75–78.
26. Chevrette, J. E., L. P. Folkins, F. M. Gauthier, and J. E. R. Greenshields. 1960. Evaluation of birdsfoot trefoil. I. Compatibility of *Lotus corniculatus* L. with other legumes and grasses. *Can. J. Plant Sci.* 40:259–67.

also grown with birdsfoot trefoil; under proper management these mixtures produce well and persist over a number of years.

In New York a mixture of Viking birdsfoot trefoil, alfalfa, and timothy is recommended for planting fields having variable drainage. Birdsfoot trefoil persists in wet areas of the field and the alfalfa grows on the better drained areas. Under such conditions the birdsfoot trefoil–alfalfa mixture is more productive than either species grown alone. Except for such special purposes birdsfoot trefoil should not be grown with aggressive legumes like alfalfa or red clover since competition during establishment is often detrimental to growth and persistence.[26]

❧ CULTIVARS

Empire is a selected ecotype found in Albany County, N.Y.[27] It is semierect, fine stemmed, and flowers 10–14 days later than common European types. Growth and flowering are indeterminate, with new stems developing during the summer from node buds along the main stem. Compared to European-type birdsfoot trefoils the seedling growth rate and spring and recovery growth rates are relatively slow. Empire is very winter-hardy and, because of its ability to reseed and establish new plants, persists well when used for pasture.

'Dawn' was developed in Missouri for its greater resistance to root rots. It is an Empire type although slightly more erect and earlier flowering.

'Leo' was developed in Canada. In Quebec it has excellent early spring vigor and greater winterhardiness than Empire or Viking.[7]

'Carroll,' developed in Iowa, is a winter-hardy pasture type which is less prostrate and slightly earlier in maturity than Empire.

Cascade, Granger, 'Maitland,' Mansfield, 'Tana,' and Viking are all European types having earlier spring growth, semierect to erect growth habit, and more rapid seedling and recovery growth than Empire. Their comparative performance varies in tests at different locations; however, all cultivars are used similarly and respond the same to recommended management practices.[7]

Common or 'European' are names given to commercial seed lots imported from Europe. They have different origins and genetic makeup and are often variable in performance, less winter-hardy, and less productive than adapted domestic cultivars.

❧ CULTURE AND MANAGEMENT

INOCULATION

A special strain of *Rhizobium* bacteria is required for effective inoculation of birdsfoot trefoil. Strains commonly used to inoculate other legumes like alfalfa and red clover are not effective for birdsfoot trefoil. With effective inoculation, small pink nodules are formed on plant roots and symbiotic bacteria fix N from the air. Seed should be mixed with adequate amounts of inoculant immediately before planting. Prolonged exposure to sunlight or drying can result in less effective nodulation.[28]

SEEDING

The seedling growth rate of birdsfoot trefoil is slower than alfalfa or red clover. Empire has less seedling vigor than European cultivars. Because of the relatively slow growth rate and small seed size, good seeding practices must be used to obtain vigorous stands. Preparation of a smooth firm seedbed and proper placement of the seed into the soil is very important since seedling emergence is related to the depth of planting. In Maryland the percent of seedling emergence of Empire and Viking planted in a silt loam soil at depths of 0.6, 1.3, 1.9, and 2.5 cm was 31, 18, 8, and

27. MacDonald, H. A. 1963. The spread and use of birdsfoot trefoil (*Lotus corniculatus* L.) as a farm crop. *The Cornell Plantations* 14:55–57.

28. Alexander, C. W., and D. S. Chamblee. 1965. Effects of sunlight and drying on the inoculation of legumes with *Rhizobium* species. *Agron. J.* 57:550–53.

3% respectively.[7] On most soils birdsfoot trefoil should be planted no more than 1.3 cm deep.

Band-seeding, the placement of seed in the soil surface directly over a fertilizer band, can increase emergence and vigor of seedlings.[29,30] The increased seedling growth rate from band-seeding is often observed the first year and may result in increased forage production the second year. Firming the soil with a press wheel, cultipacker, or roller after seeding will improve the contact of seed with soil moisture and can result in more uniform germination and emergence.

In the central and northern U.S. birdsfoot trefoil is seeded in early spring to ensure optimum soil moisture for germination and to allow development of large plants capable of winter survival. Although midsummer seedings can be successfully established, chances for winter survival are usually less. In areas having moderate winters, fall or winter seeding is recommended.

Recommended seeding rates of birdsfoot trefoil range from 5.5 to 12 kg/ha. Higher rates often increase the number of seedlings that emerge but do not increase forage yields after establishment.[1] At a seeding rate of 1 kg/ha there are approximately 75–85 seed/sq m of soil surface.

Birdsfoot trefoil can be seeded with a small-grain companion crop, which is used to reduce erosion on slopes, suppress weed growth, or produce feed grain and straw during the year of establishment. In the Northeast, seeding birdsfoot trefoil in winter grains in the spring is less successful than seeding with a spring grain such as oats.[31] When seeding with any small grain, early removal of the companion crop as silage or green chop increases the probability of successful establishment.

Studies comparing the establishment of birdsfoot trefoil with and without a companion crop demonstrate that companion crops are often very detrimental to seedling growth and persistence.[32,33] More uniform and productive stands can be obtained by seeding without a companion crop and using herbicides for weed control. Under favorable growing conditions in New York, Viking trefoil seeded without a companion crop has produced up to 5.5–6.5 t/ha of forage the seeding year.

WEED CONTROL

Weeds can be controlled during establishment by clipping or mowing. However, success of control depends upon the particular weed problem and relative growth stage of weeds and trefoil. Under some conditions mowing broad-leaved weed species allows weed grasses such as foxtail, *Setaria* spp., and fall panicum, *Panicum dichotomilflorum* Michx., to grow and become more competitive than the original broad-leaved weeds.[34]

Chemicals are available for control of both broad-leaved weeds and grasses in seedling stands of birdsfoot trefoil. EPTC (S-ethyl dipropylthiocarbamate) or benefin (N-butyl-N-ethyl-a,a,a-trifluoro-2,6,-dinitro-p-toluidine) incorporated into the surface 5–7.5 cm of soil before planting control some annual broad-leaved weeds and nearly all annual grasses. EPTC is also effective in control of yellow nutsedge. When EPTC or benefin are used, companion grasses cannot be seeded with birdsfoot trefoil. Broad-leaved weeds are controlled by using postemergence sprays of 2,4-DB [4-(2,4-dichlorophenoxy) butyric acid] or dinoseb (2-sec-butyl-4,6-dinitrophenol). Under certain conditions, particularly when growth rate is slow, birdsfoot trefoil shows symptoms of injury when 2,4-DB is used. However, seedlings soon recover and under favorable growing conditions continue

29. Tesar, M. B., K. Lawton, and B. Kawin. 1954. Comparison of band-seeding and other methods of seeding legumes. *Agron. J.* 46:189–94.
30. MacDonald, H. A. 1963. Birdsfoot trefoil in New York. N.Y. Agr. Exp. Sta. Bull. 1110.
31. Eakin, J. H. 1954. Birdsfoot trefoil. Pa. Agr. Ext. Serv. Circ. 411.
32. Scholl, J. M., and R. E. Brunk. 1962. Birdsfoot trefoil stand establishment as influenced by control of vegetative competition. *Agron. J.* 54:142–44.
33. Wakefield, R. C., and N. Skaland. 1965. Effects of seeding rate and chemical weed control of establishment and subsequent growth of alfalfa and birdsfoot trefoil. *Agron. J.* 57:547–50.
34. Kerr, H. D., and D. L. Klingman. 1960. Weed control in establishing birdsfoot trefoil. *Weeds* 8:157–67.

rapid growth. Studies have shown that birdsfoot trefoil seedlings are more susceptible to injury from dinoseb than is alfalfa, thus lower rates are recommended for birdsfoot.[35] Since dinoseb can cause severe injury if temperatures are high at the time of application, this herbicide is not recommended in all regions. A postemergence spray of either 2,4-DB or dinoseb can be used in combination with a preplant treatment of EPTC to control both grasses and broad-leaved weeds. The chemicals mentioned here are examples of herbicides that can be used for control of weed competition during establishment. Local recommendations should be reviewed each year to determine available herbicides and to ensure their proper use.

Soil and Soil Fertility

Birdsfoot trefoil has greater tolerance than alfalfa to acid, infertile, or poorly drained soils. Even though it will grow and persist on such soils, forage yields are significantly increased by proper applications of lime and fertilizer.[1]

At a pH lower than 6.2–6.5 birdsfoot seedling growth and establishment may be slow, and nodulation and N fixation may be retarded or completely inhibited.[36] Although birdsfoot trefoil persists on acid soils, the soil pH required for maximum forage production is only slightly lower than for alfalfa. (See Fig. 17.5.)

On many soils, growth and survival of birdsfoot trefoil seedlings can be increased by use of fertilizer at the time of planting. Since seedling growth rate is relatively slow, it is important to use adequate amounts of P to promote early vigorous seedling growth, thereby increasing chances of successful establishment. On medium- to fine-textured soils which have been adequately limed, large applications of P, 45–90 kg P/ha, can be made at time of seeding. The advantage of such large ap-

Fig. 17.5. *Greater tolerance . . . than alfalfa to acid, infertile, . . . soils.* Birdsfoot trefoil and alfalfa grown on poorly drained soil at Aurora, N.Y. After one year very little alfalfa survived (right) but birdsfoot (left) was vigorous and productive.

plications is the saving of yearly topdressing of P for a period of four to five years.[37]

Birdsfoot trefoil responds to applications of K on both clay and sandy loam soils. Potassium applied in early summer to midsummer is essential in maintaining productive trefoil stands.[38] Applications of N to either seedling or established stands is usually detrimental because N stimulates the growth of competing grasses and weeds.[39,40]

Birdsfoot trefoil is tolerant of a wide range of soil moisture conditions but is most productive on moderately well-drained to well-drained soils that retain adequate moisture throughout the growing season. Although more drought resistant than ladino clover, it is more susceptible to drought than alfalfa; and growth is severely checked during long periods of inadequate soil moisture. Birdsfoot trefoil is more persistent and productive than alfalfa on wet shallow soils with impervious fragipans or on wet heavy clays. Its adaptation to poorly drained soils has been of great importance in the Northeast and in the north central states which have large hectarages too wet for growing alfalfa.

35. Linscott, D. L., and R. D. Hagin. 1968. Interaction of EPTC and DNBP on seedlings of alfalfa and birdsfoot trefoil. *Weeds* 16:182–84.
36. McKee, G. W. 1961. Some effects of liming, fertilization, and soil moisture on seedling growth and nodulation in birdsfoot trefoil. *Agron. J.* 53:237–40.

37. Reid, W. S. 1972. Fertilizer recommendations. Cornell Recommendations for Field Crops, pp. 20–25.
38. Varney, K. E. 1958. Birdsfoot trefoil, its establishment and maintenance on light and heavy soils. Vt. Agr. Exp. Sta. Bull. 608.
39. Ward, C. Y., and R. E. Blaser. 1961. Effect of nitrogen fertilizer on emergence and seedling growth of forage plants and subsequent production. *Agron. J.* 53:115–20.
40. Wolf, D. D., and D. Smith. 1964. Yield and persistence of several legume-grass mixtures as affected by cutting frequency and nitrogen fertilization. *Agron. J.* 56:130–33.

PASTURE RENOVATION

The production of perennial grass pastures can often be increased by renovating and establishing birdsfoot trefoil in the grass sod. Animal production per ha is usually increased, and the economic return from birdsfoot trefoil–grass pastures is greater than that from grasses fertilized with N.[17] Several methods can be used to introduce birdsfoot trefoil into unimproved pastures. In Ontario, Canada, good stands were obtained on high-pH soils by broadcasting a mixture of seed, fertilizer, and herbicide on roughland pastures. Pasture yields were increased 4- to 5-fold, and the grazing season extended two to five months.[41,42] This method of establishment often is combined with light grazing later in the season to control broad-leaved weeds. Various types of planters or sod drills are useful in establishing birdsfoot trefoil in grass sods. These machines essentially prepare a small partially tilled strip in the sod and place seed and fertilizer into the soil.[43] Herbicides can be applied by the sod planter or in a separate operation to control competition from the sod.

HARD SEED

Seed coats of mature trefoil seed often are impermeable to water. New York studies have found that hand-harvested seed contained an average of 90% hard seed. After harvest with a combine, the amount of hard seed was reduced to 40%.[44] Hard seed is of little value for carryover and production of new seedlings the year following establishment.[44] Seed lots containing a significant amount of hard seed should be scarified to encourage quick germination.

❧ SEED PRODUCTION

POLLINATION AND GROWTH

Pollination and seed set in birdsfoot trefoil depends on insects, primarily species of *Hymenoptera*. Seed growers usually bring bees into seed-production areas to ensure maximum pollination and seed set. Studies have shown that populations of about one bee per 0.9/sq m are needed to pollinate all flowers.[45]

Pollination takes place when insects force their way toward the base of flowers causing extrusion of the pistil through the keel tip and transfer of pollen from insect to stigma. Fertilization occurs within 24–48 hours after pollination. Ovaries contain an average of 45 ovules, but only about 20 per ovary develop into mature seed.[46] Pods develop rapidly after pollination and reach maximum size within three weeks. As pods mature, they change in color from green to light brown and finally to black. The seed becomes physiologically mature slightly before the pods turn light brown. Pod and seed maturity occur 25–50 days after pollination, depending upon location and weather conditions.[47,48] As the long narrow seedpod matures, the loss of moisture from the tissue results in increased tension between fiber layers and a twisting and splitting of the two valves of the pod. Both the amount and rate of moisture loss influence pod dehiscence.[49] In the Midwest and Northeast, pod shattering and subsequent seed loss can be high when relative humidity drops below 40%.

The major production of birdsfoot trefoil seed in the U.S. is centered in New

41. Winch, J. E., E. M. Watkin, G. W. Anderson, and T. L. Collins. 1969. The use of mixtures of granular dalapon, birdsfoot trefoil seed, and fertilizer for roughland pasture renovation. *J. Brit. Grassl. Soc.* 24:303–7.
42. Watkin, E. M., and J. E. Winch. 1970. Assessment and improvement of roughland pasture in Ontario. Ont. ARDA Proj. 25021 and 6011.
43. Decker, A. M., H. J. Retzer, M. L. Sarna, and H. D. Kerr. 1969. Permanent pastures improved with sod-seeding and fertilization. *Agron. J.* 61:243–47.
44. Brown, C. S. 1955. Hard seed in birdsfoot trefoil. Ph.D. thesis, Cornell Univ., Ithaca. (Libr. Congr. Card No. Mic. 55-723.) Univ. Microfilms, Ann Arbor, Mich.
45. Morse, R. A. 1955. The pollination of birdsfoot trefoil (*Lotus corniculatus* L.) *Diss. Abstr.* 15:946.
46. Giles, W. L. 1949. The morphological aspects of self-sterility in *Lotus corniculatus* L. Ph.D. thesis, Univ. Mo., (Libr. Congr. Card No. Mic. AC–1 No. 1467). Univ. Microfilms, Ann Arbor, Mich.
47. Anderson, S. R. 1955. Development of pods and seeds of birdsfoot trefoil, *Lotus corniculatus* L., as related to maturity and to seed yields. *Agron. J.* 47:483–87.
48. Winch, J. E. 1958. Development, crop management, and harvest of birdsfoot trefoil (*Lotus corniculatus* L.) seed. Ph.D. thesis, Cornell Univ., Ithaca. (Libr. Congr. Card No. Mic. 58-2453.) Univ. Microfilms, Ann Arbor, Mich.
49. Buckovic, R. G. 1952. Some of the morphological and agronomic factors associated with pod dehiscence in *Lotus corniculatus*. M.S. thesis, Oreg. State Coll., Corvallis.

York and Vermont. Canada also produces significant quantities of seed, with Empire being the main cultivar grown for certification. Under optimum conditions in these areas, estimates of potential seed yields range from 500 to 1000 kg/ha. However, because of indeterminant flowering and pod dehiscence, the amount of seed harvested usually represents only a small portion of the seed actually produced by the plants. Although harvested yields can be as high as 200–575 kg/ha, average production ranges from 50 to 175 kg/ha.[48] Year-to-year variations in seed set and success of harvest cause wide differences in average annual seed yields.

HARVEST

Growing birdsfoot trefoil alone gives higher seed yields than growing it in combination with a grass such as timothy, smooth bromegrass, orchardgrass, or tall fescue. However, growing birdsfoot trefoil with a grass often prevents lodging, which can substantially reduce seed yield.[50] In actual practice, grasses are usually present in most seed-production fields of the Northeast. Excessive grass competition is prevented by using herbicides or by rotating crops.

Birdsfoot trefoil flowers and sets seed over an extended period. Plants approaching maturity will have pods in all stages of development from green to fully mature. Because of this, frequent observation and critical timing of harvest are necessary to obtain maximum seed yields. Recommendations for exact timing of harvest vary from when pods are light brown to brown to the time when maximum number of pods are light green to light brown.[47,48] Any delay in cutting after pods are completely mature results in significant seed loss from pod dehiscence and seed shattering. (See Fig. 17.6.)

The commonest method of seed harvest used in the Northeast is to mow, windrow, and then combine directly from the par-

FIG. 17.6. *Sets seed over an extended period . . . pods in all stages of development.* Seedpods are attached to the end of the flower stem, giving the appearance of a bird's foot—thus the common name birdsfoot trefoil. *Iowa SCS photo.*

tially dried windrow. Direct combining has been used to some extent, but the processing of large quantities of green forage through the combine slows harvest and causes increased seed loss by clogging the cleaning mechanism. Chemical defoliants may be used to defoliate and dry plants before harvest, making direct combining faster and reducing seed loss,[51] but this method is not extensively used in seed harvest.

Clipping seed fields in early spring will delay seed harvest. New York studies have found that clipping Empire at bud stage or at early flowering delayed seed maturity from 5 to 10 days. Later clipping treatments also delayed harvest but significantly lowered seed yields.[48] In Iowa, clipping any time during the spring has resulted in decreased seed yields.[52]

50. Anderson, S. R., and D. S. Metcalfe. 1957. Seed yields of birdsfoot trefoil (*Lotus corniculatus* L.) as affected by preharvest clipping and by growing in association with three adapted grasses. *Agron. J.* 49:52–55.

51. Wiggans, S. C., D. S. Metcalfe, and H. E. Thompson. 1956. The use of desiccant sprays in harvesting birdsfoot trefoil for seed. *Agron. J.* 48:281–84.
52. Bader, K. L., and S. R. Anderson. 1962. Seed yields of birdsfoot trefoil, *Lotus corniculatus* L., as affected by preharvest clipping combined with control of injurious insects. *Agron. J.* 54:306–9.

Even though clipping can be used to vary timing of seed harvest, the practice is not generally recommended or used by seed growers.

Control of insects can increase seed yields. In Vermont the use of insecticides has resulted in more flowers, a shorter flowering period, and higher seed yields of both Viking and Empire.[53] Seed yields may also be increased by controlling weeds, particularly the perennial grasses. Although herbicides often do not completely eliminate grass, the reduction in the amount of competition can increase seed yields.

❧ DISEASES

Crown and root rots are the most important diseases of birdsfoot trefoil. Severe loss from these diseases is usually associated with warm weather and high humidity. Thus crown and root rots are of greater importance in the South than in the northeastern or north central region of the U.S.[54]

Root rot is not caused by a single organism but is the result of a parasite-saprophyte complex which may vary in different environments. Organisms which have been found in this complex are species of *Fusarium, Verticillium, Macrophomina, Mycoleptodiscus, Rhizoctonia,* and *Sclerotinia.*[55,56] Plants severely infected with root rot have extensive decay in the central portion of the upper taproot and crown and often fail to regrow after harvest. Entire fields may be decimated after harvest when environmental conditions are optimum for development of the diseases. Differences in susceptibility and tolerance to root rots have been noted, and selection and breeding have been carried on to increase re-

sistance.[57] The variety, Dawn, developed cooperatively by the USDA and the Missouri station shows significant tolerance to root rots in Missouri when compared to Viking and Empire.

Several disease organisms attack stems and leaves of birdsfoot trefoil. *Sclerotinia trifoliorum* Eriks. causes a rot of lower stems and crown, usually under heavy snow cover in late winter or early spring.[58] Under warm humid conditions *Sclerotium rolfsii* Sacc. and *Rhizoctonia solani* Kuehn attack the crown and lower foliage causing blight of the leaves and eventual death of the affected plants. *Rhizoctonia solani* is partially controlled by harvesting when plants first show symptoms of infection.[58] The most widespread foliar disease of birdsfoot trefoil is caused by *Stemphylium loti* Graham. This organism causes reddish brown stem and leaf lesions and results in premature leaf drop or death of individual stems. Immature seedpods may also be attacked, resulting in shriveling and discoloration of seed.[59]

❧ INSECTS

A number of insects cause losses of birdsfoot trefoil forage and seed.[60] The meadow spittlebug, *Philaenus spumarius* (L.), feeds by sucking plant sap and causes stunting of the plant and abortion of flower buds. This insect produces a characteristic white foamy mass on stems and leaves. Other sucking insects such as the alfalfa plant bug, *Adelphocoris lineolatus* (Goeze), and the potato leafhopper, *Empoasca fabae* (Harris), also cause injury. The alfalfa plant bug destroys stem terminals and flowers. The potato leafhopper causes a characteristic yellowing and reddening of leaves and a general

53. MacCollom, G. B. 1958. Control of insects affecting birdsfoot trefoil seed production in Vermont. *J. Econ. Entomol.* 51:492–94.
54. Drake, C. R. 1958. Diseases of birdsfoot trefoil in six southern states in 1956. *Plant Dis. Reptr.* 42:145–46.
55. Kainski, J. M. 1959. A study of fungi involved in root rots and seedling diseases of birdsfoot trefoil. Ph.D. thesis, Cornell Univ., Ithaca. (Libr. Congr. Card No. Mic. 59-2951.) Univ. Microfilms, Ann Arbor, Mich.
56. Ostazeski, S. A. 1967. An undescribed fungus associated with a root and crown rot of birdsfoot trefoil (*Lotus corniculatus* L.). *Mycologia* 59:970–75.

57. Henson, P. R. 1962. Breeding for resistance to crown and root rots in birdsfoot trefoil, *Lotus corniculatus* L. *Crop Sci.* 2:429–32.
58. Kreitlow, K. W. 1962. The trefoils—Adaptation and culture. USDA Agr. Handbook 223.
59. Graham, J. H. 1953. A disease of birdsfoot trefoil caused by a new species of *Stemphylium* (*S. loti*). *Phytopathology* 43:577–79.
60. Neunzig, H. H., and G. G. Gyrisco. 1955. Some insects injurious to birdsfoot trefoil in New York. *J. Econ. Entomol.* 48:447–50.

stunting of the plant. Heavy infestations of potato leafhopper can reduce forage yield and quality.

The trefoil seed chalcid, *Bruchophagus kolobovae* Fed., a small black wasplike insect, can be desructive in seed fields. Eggs are laid in developing seedpods, and the larvae feed inside the maturing ovule, leaving only a hollow inviable seed. Large amounts of seed left on the ground after harvest may increase infestations of this insect the following year.[61] Since insecticides do not control the seed chalcid, proper management of seed harvest is one way to decrease populations.

Studies have shown the use of insecticides to be profitable in preventing loss of forage and seed.[52,62] However, the kinds of insects and control methods vary from region to region; therefore, local recommendations should be consulted to determine the feasibility of economic control.

❧ OTHER SPECIES

In addition to *L. corniculatus*, two other species of *Lotus* are important as pasture legumes in the U.S. Narrowleaf trefoil, *L. tenuis* Waldst. & Kit., is adapted to low wet soil and found in New York, Oregon, and California. California studies have shown it to be very tolerant of saline soils.[63] *Lotus tenuis* has linear-lanceolate leaflets and small flowers which turn orange red with age. Plants are less erect than Empire and have very shallow root systems. Because of its close resemblance and cross-compatibility with *L. cornicu-* *latus,* some investigators suggest that *L. tenuis* may be a progenitor species.[64]

Big trefoil, *L. pedunculatus* Cav., is a perennial having fine stems, relatively large leaves, and vigorous underground stems or rhizomes.[65] It is grown primarily on the wet, poorly drained coastal soils of the Northwest and to some extent in states along the Atlantic and Gulf coasts.

Two cultivars of *L. pedunculatus* have been developed by the Oregon station and the USDA. 'Beaver' has glabrous leaves, while 'Colombia' has pubescent stems and leaves. General growth habits of these cultivars are similar to *L. corniculatus,* and both are well adapted to the wet winter and cool summers of coastal Oregon and Washington. In 1964 several naturalized cold-tolerant ecotypes of big trefoil were discovered in Crawford County, Ind. Selections have shown promise for use with tall fescue on the fragipan soils in the lower Ohio Valley.[66]

❧ QUESTIONS

1. What are the desirable and undesirable characteristics of birdsfoot trefoil?
2. Discuss the optimum soil requirements for birdsfoot trefoil, red clover, and alfalfa.
3. How would you manage European-type cultivars differently than Empire-type cultivars? Why?
4. What factors determine the successful establishment of birdsfoot trefoil?
5. What characteristics of birdsfoot trefoil make seed production difficult?
6. What additional information on culture and use is needed to increase birdsfoot trefoil's value to agriculture?
7. What objectives might plant breeders have for the improvement of birdsfoot trefoil used for hay? For pasture?

61. Neunzig, H. H. 1957. Biological and ecological studies of the seed chalcid with particular reference to populations associated with birdsfoot trefoil. Ph.D. thesis, Cornell Univ., Ithaca.
62. Ridgway, R. L., and G. G. Gyrisco. 1959. Control of insects injurious to birdsfoot trefoil in New York. *J. Econ. Entomol.* 52:836–38.
63. Ayers, A. D. 1948. Salt tolerance of birdsfoot trefoil. *J. Amer. Soc. Agron.* 40:331–34.

64. Dawson, C. D. R. 1941. Tetrasomic inheritance in *Lotus corniculatus. J. Genet.* 42:49–72.
65. Howell, H. B. 1948. Legume for arid soils *(Lotus uliginosus).* Oreg. Agr. Exp. Sta. Bull. 456.
66. Heath, M. E. 1970. Naturalized big trefoil (*Lotus pedunculatus* Cav.) ecotypes discovered in Crawford County, Ind. Proc. Ind. Acad. Sci. 79:193–97.

MARION S. OFFUTT / *University of Arkansas*

JOE D. BALDRIDGE / *Agricultural Research Service, USDA, and University of Missouri*

18

THE LESPEDEZAS

ᨍ

T HE LESPEDEZAS are important legumes for pasture, hay, and soil improvement in the southeastern states. They are warm-season plants and grow well only during the summer months.

Lespedezas are native to eastern Asia and to the eastern part of the U.S. Approximately 140 species have been identified and classified; 125 are of Asiatic origin. All but two are perennials, and they are either herbaceous or shrubby. The two annual species—striate, *Lespedeza striata* (Thunb.) H. & A., and Korean, *L. stipulacea* Maxim. —are introductions from the Orient.[1] The first record of striate lespedeza is in 1846 at Monticello, Ga. Presumably it came in as an adulterant in other seed and eventually became naturalized as far north as 40° N under the names "common" and "wild

ᨍ MARION S. OFFUTT is Professor of Agronomy at the University of Arkansas. He received the M.S. and Ph.D. degrees from the University of Missouri. His major research efforts have been directed toward the improvement and management of the annual lespedezas, alfalfa, and white lupine.

ᨍ JOE D. BALDRIDGE is Professor of Agronomy at the University of Missouri and Research Agronomist, ARS, USDA. He received the Ph.D. degree from the University of Missouri. His research is particularly concerned with breeding the lespedezas and birdsfoot trefoil.

Jap" lespedeza. An introduction of striate from Kobe, Japan, in 1919 and first grown in South Carolina was later designated as the cultivar, 'Kobe.'

Korean lespedeza was introduced in 1919 from Korea. The first seed crop was harvested in 1921 at the USDA experimental farm, Arlington, Va. A small quantity of this seed increase was distributed in 1922 and a larger volume in 1923.[2]

Perennial species of lespedeza considered to be of value are sericea, *L. cuneata* (Dumont) G. Don., and the closely related species, *L. latissima* Nakai, *L. juncea* (L.F.) Pers., and *L. hedysaroides* (Pall.) Kitogawa, all native to eastern Asia. Sericea lespedeza was first tested in North Carolina in 1896. Additional seed was introduced from Japan in 1899 and again in 1924 and tested at the Arlington experimental farm. Seed from the more productive of these sericea lines was distributed to agricultural experiment stations in the South.[3]

Several shrubby species such as *L. bicolor* Turcz., *L. thungbergii* (DC.) Nakai, *L. cyr-*

1. Henson, Paul R. 1957. The lespedezas. I. *Advan. Agron.* 9:113–22.
2. Pieters, A. J. 1939. The annual lespedezas as forage and soil-conserving crops. USDA Circ. 536.
3. Pieters, A. J., P. R. Henson, W. E. Adams, and A. P. Barnett. 1950. Sericea and other perennial lespedezas for forage and soil conservation. USDA Circ. 863.

tobotrya Miq., and *L. japonica* Bailey have
value as ornamentals or for soil conservation and as food and shelter for wildlife.
'Natob,' an early maturing cultivar of *L.
bicolor,* is adapted to the more northern
part of the lespedeza region. None of the
shrubby species have been used for forage
in the U.S.

❦ DISTRIBUTION AND ADAPTATION

Three species of lespedeza (Korean, striate, and sericea) are important in American
agriculture. Collectively, the practical limit of these three species extends in a belt
from eastern Texas, Oklahoma, and Kansas eastward to the Atlantic Coast (Fig.
18.1).

Korean cultivars are well adapted to the
upper two-thirds of the lespedeza region.
Striate cultivars require a longer growing
season and are more important in the
southern part of the region. Sericea cultivars grow well over most of the area.

Daylength and temperature influence
vegetative growth, floral initiation, and
seed maturity in the annual lespedezas.
Plants remain in a vegetative condition
when daylengths are longer than their
critical photoperiod and flower when daylengths are shorter. The critical photoperiod for floral initiation is longer for early
maturing cultivars than it is for those
which mature later. When a cultivar is
grown at a more northern latitude, floral
initiation and seed maturity are delayed
because its critical photoperiod occurs later
in the season. Frost may kill the plants before they mature seed if a cultivar is grown
too far north. When a cultivar is grown at
a more southern latitude, floral initiation
and seed maturity occur earlier because
daylengths are always shorter to the south
between March 21 and September 21. Temperatures are higher in the more southern
latitudes, and this tends to reduce the number of days between flowering and maturity.
Rate of vegetative growth is retarded when
seedlings of a cultivar emerge before the
daylengths in the spring are equal to or

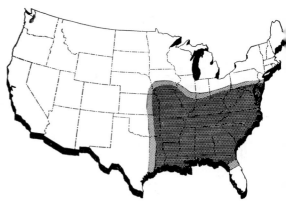

FIG. 18.1. Lespedeza-producing areas of the U.S.

greater than the critical photoperiod for
that cultivar (Fig. 18.2). Careful selection
of annual lespedeza cultivars for any given
area is essential, therefore, if the highest
yields of forage and seed are to be obtained.[4,5]

❦ PLANT DESCRIPTION

Cultivars of striate lespedeza are easily
distinguished from those of Korean (Fig.
18.3). Both have trifoliolate leaves, but
leaflets of striate are not as wide as those of
Korean. The stipules on Korean are larger
and more prominent than on striate. Also,
hairs on the stems of striate are appressed
downward, and those on Korean are appressed upward. Seedlings of the two annual species can be differentiated soon after emergence. Cotyledons of striate are
bluish green and have an indentation on
one edge near the outer end, whereas those
of Korean are dark green, nearly elliptical,
and distinctly veined. In both annual species the first two true leaves are opposite
and unifoliolate. Unifoliolate leaves on
Korean tend to be heart shaped, while
those on striate are more rounded on the
outer end. Flowers of the two annual lespedezas appear in late summer to early
fall and vary from light pink to purple.

4. Smith, G. E. 1941. The effect of photo-period on
the growth of lespedeza. *J. Amer. Soc. Agron.* 33:231–36.
5. Offutt, M. S. 1968. Some effects of photoperiod on
the performance of Korean lespedeza. *Crop Sci.* 8:309–13.

FIG. 18.2. *Careful selection . . . essential . . . if the highest yields . . . obtained.* On July 30, the early maturing cultivar had made more growth from the May 13 planting (C) than from the March 16 planting (A), whereas the opposite was true for the later maturing cultivar, which had made more growth from the March 16 planting (B) than from the May 13 planting (D). The daylengths in March were shorter than the critical photoperiod for the early maturing cultivar and this retarded the vegetative growth. *Univ. Ark. photo.*

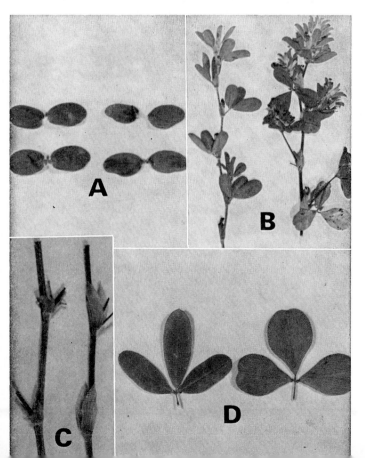

FIG. 18.3. *Striate lespedeza . . . easily distinguished from . . . Korean.* (A) Note distinct indentation in cotyledons of striate on right. (B) Plants of striate set their seed in leaf axils along entire length of stems (left), while seed of Korean are borne in clusters at the tips of all branches developing from leaf axils (right). Also, note the turning forward of the leaves around the flowers and seed of Korean. (C) Stipules of Korean (right) are much larger than those of striate (left), and the hairs on the stems of Korean are appressed upward and those on the stems of striate are appressed downward. (D) Leaflets of striate (left) are not as wide as those of Korean (right). *Univ. Ark. photo.*

Striate lespedeza sets its seed in the leaf axils along the entire length of the stems. In contrast, seed of Korean lespedeza is borne in clusters at the tip end of all branches developing from the leaf axils. After flowering starts, the leaves on Korean turn forward around the developing seed so that the tips of the branches resemble small cones. This gives a measure of protection against shattering when the seed is mature. Leaves of striate do not turn forward after flowering, so this species is more subject to seed shatter than Korean.

The two annual species are small stemmed and leafy. In thin stands plants produce more branches and tend to grow prostrate. Plants in thick stands, resulting from high seeding rates or volunteering from seed shattered the previous season, grow more erectly. Both species of annual lespedeza have a shallow taproot system.

Sericea lespedeza is a long-lived, perennial, erect to semierect, leafy herbaceous plant with relatively coarse stems. If left uncut, it will grow to heights of 60–100 cm. Sericea produces trifoliolate leaves which are well distributed along the stems. Leaflets are long, narrow, and square at the end. Flowers are borne on short pedicels in leaf axils along the stems and vary from cream to purple. Top growth of sericea is killed back to the ground each fall and renews its growth from crown buds the next spring. Sericea develops an extensively branched, deep taproot system.

❧ IMPORTANCE AND USE

Lespedezas have played an important role in the agriculture of the southeastern states since the early 1930s. Production reached its peak about 1950 when the total production of hay and seed in the U.S. exceeded 3 million ha. At that time the quantity of lespedeza seed produced annually was greater than that of any forage crop in the U.S. A substantial portion of the land used for grazing in the Southeast contains lespedeza, either in pure stands or in mixture with one or more pasture species.

The greater part of the lespedeza seed produced in the U.S. is of the Korean cultivars.

Lespedezas are used widely for pasture, hay, and soil conservation. Many fields of lespedeza are also harvested for seed.

❧ CULTIVARS

Korean and its improved cultivars are adapted and most used in the northern part of the lespedeza region. Toward the south Korean progressively declines in favor of striate lespedeza.

'Iowa 6' is an early maturing cultivar of Korean developed by the Iowa station. It is rapid growing, high yielding, and has some resistance to bacterial wilt. Because of its early maturity it is well adapted across the northern part of the lespedeza region.[6]

'Rowan' was developed by the North Carolina station in cooperation with the USDA. It is intermediate in maturity between Iowa 6 and 'Yadkin.' It is moderately resistant to the root-knot nematode and is resistant to powdery mildew. Rowan is more productive than common Korean, decidedly so on root-knot infested soils.

'Summit' was developed by the Arkansas and Missouri stations in cooperation with the USDA. Summit is high in yield, medium in maturity, and adapted to the same area as Rowan except where root-knot nematodes are a problem. It is more resistant to bacterial wilt than other cultivars and is equal to Rowan and Yadkin in resistance to tar spot.[7]

Yadkin was developed by the North Carolina station in cooperation with the USDA. It produces high forage and seed yields and is about 10–14 days later in maturity than Rowan and Summit. Because of its later maturity Yadkin can be grown farther south in the lespedeza region than other Korean cultivars. It is moderately re-

6. Wilsie, C. P., and H. D. Hughes. 1947. Development of early maturing, wilt resistant strains of Korean lespedeza. *J. Amer. Soc. Agron.* 39:615–22.
7. Offutt, M. S. 1963. Registration of Summit lespedeza. *Crop Sci.* 3:368.

sistant to tar spot and two root-knot nematode species. Yadkin is distinguishable from other Korean cultivars by its light pink flowers.[8]

Common striate lespedeza was being grown in the U.S. when Kobe and Korean were introduced. It is a low-growing form, frequently preferred for grazing since it will withstand continuous close grazing and still reseed. Common is smaller and less productive than the improved annual lespedeza cultivars.

Kobe striate lespedeza is a larger, taller growing cultivar than common striate. It is more erect in growth habit and more productive for hay and pasture than common. Kobe is slower growing in the spring than Korean cultivars, but late summer production usually is high. It is several days later in maturity than Yadkin and generally produces higher forage yields than any of the other annual lespedeza cultivars in the southern part of the lespedeza region.

'Arlington' sericea lespedeza was the first improved cultivar of this species in general use. It was developed at the USDA Arlington farm. Arlington is productive and widely adapted in the lespedeza region.

'Serala' was developed by the Alabama station and released in 1962. It is a high-yielding sericea cultivar with relatively fine soft stems and produces numerous stems per plant. It is more palatable than other sericea cultivars because the stems do not become as coarse or woody.[9]

'Interstate' is a multipurpose cultivar developed by the Alabama station. It was developed specifically for use on highway rights-of-way. Interstate is shorter growing, branches more profusely, has finer stems, and grows more uniformly than other sericea cultivars. It also has promise for grazing and hay in many parts of the lespedeza region.[10]

8. Cope, W. A. 1967. Registration of Yadkin Korean lespedeza. *Crop Sci.* 7:401.

9. Donnelly, E. D. 1963. Serala—A new sericea variety. Ala. Agr. Exp. Sta. Leaflet 70.

10. Donnelly, E. D., R. Dickens, D. G. Sturkie, and J. D. Miller. 1970. Interstate sericea lespedeza—A multipurpose legume. Ala. Agr. Exp. Sta. Leaflet 80.

❧ MANAGEMENT OF ANNUAL LESPEDEZA

The annual lespedezas are adapted to a wide range of soil types and fertility levels. Annual lespedezas will, without soil treatment, grow relatively well on eroded, acid soils low in P. They grow best, however, on productive, well-drained land.

Korean is less tolerant of acid soil and more tolerant of alkaline soil than striate. On the high-lime soils in the Coastal states, therefore, it is generally used to replace striate.

Annual lespedezas respond favorably to lime on acid soils and to mixed fertilizers on deficient soils. Data from 34 tests in eight states have been assembled in Table 18.1 to show the generalized response to soil treatment.[11]

Liming to pH 6 or 6.5 and applying 11–20 kg of P/ha annually, or less often in larger amounts, has given successful production. If applied along with lime and P, K often gives a marked response.

High rates of fertilization may lower the forage quality of annual lespedeza because of an increase in the proportion of stems to leaves. Usually, however, the increase in yield from fertilization more than offsets any decrease in forage quality.[12]

11. Baldridge, J. D. 1957. The lespedezas. II. Culture and utilization. *Advan. Agron.* 9:122–42.

12. Offutt, M. S., L. H. Hileman, and O. T. Stallcup. 1966. Effect of lime, phosphorus, and potassium on yield and composition of Korean lespedeza. Ark. Agr. Exp. Sta. Bull. 717.

TABLE 18.1 ❧ Response of annual lespedezas to soil treatments

Soil treatment	Hay yield (kg/ha)	Relative yield
None	1,745	100
Lime	2,899	166
Phosphorus	2,348	135
Potassium	1,976	113
Lime-phosphorus	3,398	195
Lime-phosphorus-potassium	4,048	232

Note: Average response to soil treatments in 34 tests conducted in 8 states of the upper part of the lespedeza region during the period 1930–50.

SEEDING

Annual lespedeza may be sown from midwinter to early spring. Broadcasting without covering normally will give adequate stands in pastures and meadows, on idle land, and in small grains. When seeding is done in late spring, some method of shallow covering should be used such as shallow drilling or cultipacker seeding.

General farming methods usually are not feasible on hilly, rocky, brush-covered land. Where these conditions exist, brush may be controlled with aerial applications of herbicides one spring and seeding of annual lespedeza with an adapted grass such as tall fescue by air that fall or early the following spring without disturbing the soil.

A succession of small grain and annual lespedeza may be maintained for many years if the small grain is not fertilized too heavily with N. Lespedeza normally shatters enough seed to ensure a heavy volunteer stand the next spring. Small grain may be seeded in late fall or early spring before the lespedeza seed germinate. The seedbed for small grain may be prepared by shallow plowing, by disking, or with a field cultivator, to keep the lespedeza seed near the soil surface. Lespedeza will maintain itself indefinitely in open or closely grazed sods by volunteering.

To obtain normal yields of hay, pasture, or seed the first year, 28–33 kg/ha of good quality seed should be sown. This rate is based on unhulled seed of Korean. Seeding rates for striate lespedeza should be increased 4–5 kg/ha. As little as 12–17 kg/ha is sufficient through volunteer reseeding to ensure a full stand in the second and following seasons. Lespedeza seed should be inoculated the first time it is seeded on a new area.

Annual lespedeza seed do not germinate well soon after maturity. The amount of hard seed will range from 40 to 60% during the first two months following harvest but normally will decline to 10% or less by February. This seed characteristic of annual lespedeza is the main reason why stands can be maintained so successfully through volunteer reseeding.

CULTURE

The annual lespedezas seldom make enough growth for good pasture before late spring or early summer. From then until late summer the growth is rapid and vigorous when soil moisture is adequate. By fall the usefulness of the crop is largely past except for the value of the seed to livestock and wildlife and of the crop residue for erosion control.

Annual lespedeza does not compete effectively with many weedy plants because of the shortness of its growing season. Good land-use management, therefore, requires that it be grown in association with other crops. Lespedeza is most effective when grown in small grain or in grass sods for utilization as pasture, hay, or seed after the spring growth of the grain or grass is removed. Higher production will result if competition from the small grain or grass is reduced by its early removal as pasture, silage, or hay. High rates of fertilizer N will increase the competition of the small grain or grass and should be avoided where annual lespedeza is included.

Annual lespedeza makes a large contribution in pastures or meadows without special management. Less competition is encountered when the lespedeza is seeded with bunchgrasses, especially if the seeding rate of the grass is reduced to ensure moderately open stands. In well-sodded vigorous grasses, early moderately close grazing or early cutting in the spring is needed to successfully maintain annual lespedeza for use later in the season.

A combination of winter wheat and annual lespedeza can provide the key to a balanced pasture and forage system. Both crops can be grown on the same land each year, and good returns can be obtained even on soils of marginal fertility. Winter wheat normally provides earlier spring grazing than most permanent pastures. When permanent pastures are ready for grazing, livestock can be removed and the wheat utilized later for silage or grain. Annual lespedeza can be used for summer pasture, hay, or seed as the need arises. If all the wheat or annual lespedeza is not needed for pasture, the area can be divided with an electric fence any time during the season, allowing the surplus to be used for hay, silage, or seed. These two crops are available for grazing when permanent pastures generally are lowest in production, providing a more uniform carrying capacity throughout the grazing season. Full production is obtained from this combination the first year, and no decision on utilization is required until the need is determined.

To obtain both good quality and yield, annual lespedezas should be cut in the early bloom stage for hay. At this stage of growth annual lespedeza is more nutritious, weedy growth is less advanced, the stand is less likely to be killed, and a larger aftermath is obtained for pasture and reseeding. Late cutting, close cutting, and drought following cutting frequently contribute to losses in stand.

Weeds may compete severely with annual lespedeza, especially if pure stands are used year after year. Mowing just above the lespedeza will control some weedy species, but not all. Rotation grazing permits closer mowing and better weed control.

A herbicide that may be used to control weeds in annual lespedeza is 2,4-D (2,4-dichlorophenoxyacetic acid), amine form, at the rate of 1.12 kg/ha. Application of this herbicide in May or June has given good control of broad-leaved weeds without serious injury to the lespedeza.

Dodder, *Cuscuta pentagona* Engelm., is a parasitic plant and a serious weed. Close grazing and mowing of the hay at early stages are practical methods of control. Small patches can be eliminated by killing the lespedeza with herbicides or by flaming.

❧ MANAGEMENT OF SERICEA LESPEDEZA

Sericea is an excellent soil-building legume. It is especially valuable on badly depleted soil on which it is difficult to establish other legumes.[13] Since it is leafier and less woody than other perennials, sericea has a place as a pasture, hay, and seed crop.

Sericea is quite tolerant to low fertility. It generally gives a profitable response to lime and fertilizer on badly depleted, acid soils only.

SEEDING

Sericea lespedeza normally has a high percentage of hard seed. Germination usually will not exceed 25% unless the seed is scarified, which facilitates prompt germination. A firm seedbed and shallow covering of the seed are essential for good seedling establishment.

Usually sericea is planted in early spring at seeding rates of 34 kg/ha or more of scarified seed with no production the first year. The Alabama station has shown, however, that a herbicide like vernolate (S-propyl dipropylthiocarbamate), when incorporated preplant at the rate of 3.4 kg/ha in conjuction with seeding only 11 kg/ha of scarified sericea seed in early spring, produced excellent and nearly weed-free stands. This method of seeding permitted a cutting of hay or grazing in midsummer of the first year with only a small reduction in yield the second year.[14] If a herbicide is not used at seeding time, it usually is necessary to clip new stands to control tall-growing weeds.

CULTURE

Sericea must be cut early to produce good quality hay. Thick stands make for higher quality because of the finer stems produced. Sericea cures rapidly, and unless handled properly, leaf loss is high, resulting in poor-quality, stemmy, low-protein hay.

The crop should not be cut too low because recovery growth develops from the uncut portion of the stems and not from

13. Bailey, R. Y. 1951. Sericea in conservation farming. USDA Farmers' Bull. 2033.
14. Hoveland, C. S., G. A. Buchanan, and E. D. Donnelly. 1971. Establishment of sericea lespedeza. *Weed Sci.* 19:21–24.

FIG. 18.4. *Sericea . . . grazed when plants are tender and grow-ing vigorously . . . best results.* Serala sericea being grazed by beef cows in Alabama's Piedmont area. *Auburn Univ. photo.*

the crowns. To help ensure good stands in succeeding years, no more than two hay cuttings or one hay cutting followed by a seed crop should be harvested annually.

Sericea should be grazed when plants are tender and growing vigorously for best results (Fig. 18.4). If stands reach a height of more than 25 cm, they should be clipped to promote young growth.

Sericea should not be grazed or mowed in late summer because root reserves for growth the next spring are being accumulated at this time.

❧ PRODUCTIVITY AND NUTRITIVE VALUE

PASTURE

Annual lespedeza is an excellent summer pasture for all classes of livestock. Under favorable conditions a good stand should carry cattle at the rate of one mature animal for each 0.6–0.8 ha. Under such conditions with steers as the unit of measure, annual gains should average 112–168 kg/ha. Mixtures of grasses and annual lespedeza should give 224 kg/ha/yr or more of animal gain.[15]

A combination of fall-sown small grain and annual lespedeza may be utilized profitably by pasturing both the small grain and the lespedeza. Carrying capacity, pasturing period, and ha gains for this com-

15. Brown, E. M. 1951. Good pastures pay. Mo. Agr. Exp. Sta. Bull. 547.

bination are indicated by records of the Missouri station (Table 18.2). About half the gain came from small grain and half from lespedeza.

Annual lespedeza is highly valued as a fattening pasture for livestock. Steers pasturing this legume in summer maintain a high rate of gain, often averaging as much as 1 kg/head daily. The high rates of gain from this pasture probably result from the combination of low water content, high palatability, high quality, and freedom from bloat.

Annual lespedeza also furnishes excellent pasture for dairy cows during early summer and midsummer. Milk flow usually declines later in the season as the plants go beyond the full-bloom stage of growth.

In general, sericea is much less palatable than the annual lespedezas. Digestibility of sericea also is relatively low in comparison with the annual species because of the high tannin content in the leaves, the tend-

TABLE 18.2 ❧ Annual steer gains on small-grain and annual lespedeza pasture in Missouri

Year	Pasture period	Cattle-days per ha	Gain (kg/ha)
1937	4/27–9/25	358	321
1938	3/26–10/1	383	228
1939	4/12–9/24	311	371
1940	4/3–10/5	378	432
1941	5/19–10/11	477	315
Five-year average		380	334

ency of the stems to become coarse and woody, and the relatively high lignin content of the plant.[16] Palatability and digestibility of sericea has been improved, however, through the development of cultivars such as Serala which have finer and softer stems and a lower tannin content.[17]

The fine, soft-stemmed sericea cultivars should provide 300 cow-days/ha or more of pasture and 200 kg/ha or more of steer gain annually in the South. Daily gain per steer should average 0.6 kg or more for the season on well-managed stands.[18]

HAY

The hay yield of annual lespedeza is 2240–3360 kg/ha, although higher yields are common under favorable conditions. About 2240 kg/ha of hay can be expected for each 15–20 cm increment of growth above the cutter bar from good stands cut in the bloom stage.

Best quality sericea hay is obtained from thick stands cut in an immature stage when only 25–30 cm high. A good stand on land of medium fertility may be expected to yield 3360–6720 kg/ha of hay from two cuttings each season.

Clean, early cut, properly cured annual lespedeza hay is nearly equal to alfalfa hay in feeding value for all classes of livestock.[19] Sericea lespedeza hay is somewhat lower in feeding value than annual lespedeza hay of comparable grade.[20]

❧ SEED PRODUCTION

POLLINATION

Seed of the annual species and most of the herbaceous perennials develop from two types of flowers. Both flower types, one with normal petals (chasmogamous) and the other without visible petals (cleistogamous), may occur on the same plant. High temperatures at the time of floral initiation favor development of chasmogamous flowers and lower temperatures favor development of cleistogamous flowers. Cleistogamous flowers are self-pollinated, while chasmogamous flowers may be either self- or cross-pollinated.[21]

In sericea lespedeza up to 80% natural crossing has been found in chasmogamous flowers on selected plants. Occurrence of out-crossed and selfed seed on the same plant is an aid in genetic and breeding studies. Mature seed from the two types of flowers on sericea are morphologically different and can be separated readily, thus providing a convenient method of determining the effects of inbreeding and out-crossing in the species.[22]

GROWTH AND MANAGEMENT

The annual lespedezas usually produce between 225 and 335 kg/ha of seed under average farm conditions. Yields of 675 kg/ha or more are not uncommon, especially if they are grown in rows. In general, conditions that favor good forage yields favor good seed yields. Drought or an epiphytotic of tar spot during the blooming and ripening stages may greatly reduce seed yields.

The seed crop is usually harvested directly with a combine as soon as the leaves have become dry and the seedpods have turned brown from maturity or killing frost. With combine harvesting, seed shattering before and during harvest together with seed left on the uncut stubble is normally sufficient to ensure a dense volunteer stand the next season. Harvesting before the plants become completely dry is often

16. Hawkins, G. E. 1955. Composition and digestibility of lespedeza sericea hay and alfalfa hay plus gallotannin. *J. Dairy Sci.* 38:237–43.
17. Donnelly, E. D., and G. E. Hawkins. 1959. The effects of stem type on some feeding qualities of sericea lespedeza, *L. cuneata,* as indicated in a digestion trial with rabbits. *Agron. J.* 51:293–94.
18. Anthony, W. B., R. R. Harris, C. S. Hoveland, E. L. Mayton, and J. K. Boseck. 1967. Serala sericea as a grazing crop for beef cattle. Ala. Agr. Exp. Sta. Highlights of Agr. Res. vol. 14, no. 4.
19. Anderson, K. L. 1956. Lespedeza. Kans. Agr. Exp. Sta. Circ. 251.

20. Holdaway, C. W., W. B. Ellett, J. F. Eheart, and A. D. Pratt. 1936. Korean lespedeza and sericea lespedeza hays for producing milk. Va. Agr. Exp. Sta. Bull. 305.
21. Hanson, C. H. 1953. *L. stipulacea:* Stamen morphology, meiosis, microgametogenesis, and fertilization. *Agron. J.* 45:200–203.
22. Stitt, R. E. 1946. Natural crossing and segregation in sericea lespedeza, *L. cuneata* (Dumont) G. Don. *J. Amer. Soc. Agron.* 38:1–5.

recommended to avoid seed shattering, particularly for cultivars of *L. striata*. Provision will then need to be made for drying the seed.

Sericea seed yields usually range from 335 to 1000 kg/ha. The largest yields are obtained when the total season's growth is allowed to accumulate and mature. Growers often prefer to remove the first cutting for hay, however, and then harvest seed from the second crop because the shorter growth makes for easier combining.

❧ DISEASES AND INSECTS

Diseases often cause losses of economic importance in the lespedezas, with *L. stipulacea* being the most susceptible to damage. Bacterial wilt, *Xanthomonas lespedezae* (Ayers et al.) Starr, is serious in the northern part of the lespedeza region, especially on Korean. The entire plant may wilt and die, but usually only a part of the plant is affected, causing stunting and loss of leaves.[23] Tar spot, *Phyllachora lespedezae* (Schw.) Sacc., causes heavy spotting of the leaves with subsequent defoliation and reduction in yield and quality.[24] Seed yields usually are reduced more from this disease than forage yields.[25] Damage from Rhizoctonia, *Rhizoctonia solani* Kuehn; powdery mildew, *Microsphaera diffusa* C. & P; and southern blight, *Sclerotium rolfsii*

Sacc., is sometimes serious in the Cotton Belt. In the coastal plain area of the southeastern states, nematode, *Meloidogyne incognita* (Kofoid & White) Chitwood, damage to the annual lespedezas is serious. Several of the improved cultivars carry resistance to one or more of these diseases, and their use is usually the most practical means of control.

The lespedezas are remarkably free from serious insect damage. American grasshoppers, *Schistocera americana* (Drury); army worms, *Pseudaletia unipuncta* (Haworth); lespedeza webworms, *Tetralopha scortealis* (Lederer); the three-cornered alfalfa hopper, *Spissistilus festinus* (Say); and other insects feed to some extent on the plants but damage usually is slight.

❧ QUESTIONS

1. Compare the plant and seed characteristics of Korean and striate lespedeza.
2. Explain how daylength affects flowering and seed maturity in the annual lespedezas.
3. Why can lespedeza succeed where alfalfa and red clover fail?
4. Why are the annual lespedezas more palatable and digestible than sericea lespedeza?
5. For what reasons are the lespedezas adapted only to the southeastern part of the U.S.?
6. Name some cultivars of lespedeza and tell where they are adapted and why they are superior.
7. A combination of winter wheat and annual lespedeza can provide the key to a balanced pasture and forage system. Explain how this may be done.
8. How may annual lespedeza be established and utilized on hilly, rocky, brush-covered land?

23. Offutt, M. S., and J. D. Baldridge. 1956. Inoculation studies related to breeding for resistance to bacterial wilt in lespedeza. Mo. Agr. Exp. Sta. Res. Bull. 603.
24. Hanson, C. H., W. A. Cope, and J. L. Allison. 1956. Tar spot of Korean lespedeza caused by *Phyllachora* sp.: Losses in yield and differential susceptibility of strains. *Agron. J.* 48:369–70.
25. Offutt, M. S., and H. J. Walters. 1964. Annual lespedeza variety and strain trials, 1957–1962. Ark. Agr. Exp. Sta. Rept. Ser. 127.

W. E. KNIGHT / *Agricultural Research Service, USDA*

C. S. HOVELAND / *Auburn University*

19

CRIMSON CLOVER AND ARROWLEAF CLOVER

CRIMSON CLOVER

CRIMSON CLOVER, *Trifolium incarnatum L.* (also called scarlet, Italian, or incarnate) is native to southeastern Europe and southwestern Turkey. It was grown in Italy, France, Hungary, and other Balkan countries in the eighteenth century.

Crimson clover was first introduced into the U.S. in 1819 from Italy. It spread rapidly throughout the southeastern states after 1880 and by 1900 was considered a good crop as far north as Kentucky.

DISTRIBUTION AND ADAPTATION

Crimson clover is grown widely as a winter annual from the Gulf Coast region, except peninsular Florida, as far northward as Maryland, southern Ohio, and Illinois. It also is grown in the Pacific Coast states and is an important seed crop in western Oregon. If planted in late May or early June, it can be grown as a summer annual in northern Maine.

The increase in use of crimson clover was rapid after 1942. Before that time the largest hectarages of crimson clover were located in Tennessee, Georgia, Alabama, Kentucky, and Oregon (Fig. 19.1).

The clover is tolerant of medium soil

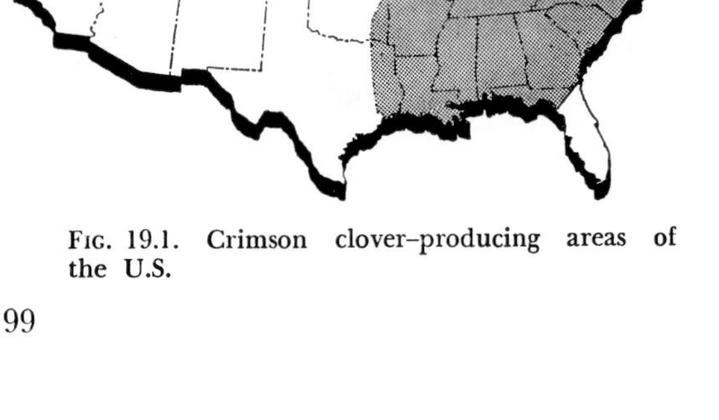

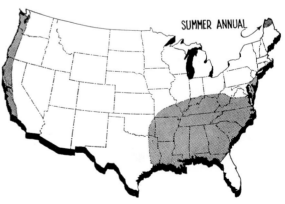

FIG. 19.1. Crimson clover-producing areas of the U.S.

W. E. KNIGHT is Research Agronomist, ARS, USDA, in charge of annual clover research for the southern region at the Mississippi station, Mississippi State University. He received the Ph.D. degree from Pennsylvania State University. For the last twenty years he has studied annual clover improvement with major emphasis on crimson clover.

C. S. HOVELAND is Professor of Agronomy and Soils at Auburn University. He received the M. S. degree from the University of Wisconsin and the Ph.D. from the University of Florida. He has conducted forage research in Texas, Florida, and New Zealand.

acidity and will thrive on both sandy and clay soils. Crimson clover does not tolerate calcareous soils nor those with poor drainage. After seedings become well established, it makes more growth at lower temperatures than most other clover species. This clover was probably the most important legume in the early expansion of winter grazing programs in the South.[1]

❧ PLANT DESCRIPTION

Crimson clover seed are yellow, and they are larger and rounder than seed of red clover. There are approximately 330,000 seed/kg. Under favorable soil moisture conditions seedlings make rapid growth, forming a dense crown or rosette type of leaf development. A central taproot develops, supported by many fibrous roots. Growth continues throughout the winter, the amount influenced by temperature. Leaves are composed of three leaflets, broadly obovate at the tip, narrow at the base, and densely covered with hairs. In the spring, erect hairy flower stems develop with many nodes. Development of flower stems is initiated when daylength is over 12 hours.[2] Growth is terminated by the formation of a pointed, conical flower head composed of 75–125 florets. Florets are usually a bright crimson color, opening in succession from the bottom to the top of the head. (See Fig. 19.2.) Flowers are mostly self-fertile but not self-pollinating. Bees seeking nectar or pollen trip the flowers and bring about pollination. Seed mature in approximately 24–30 days, and the plant dies. Plant height may range from 30 to 90 cm.

❧ IMPORTANCE AND USE

Crimson clover is regarded as one of the most important winter annual legumes for

Fig. 19.2. *Erect hairy flower stems develop . . . with many nodes . . . florets . . . bright crimson.* A crimson clover field in full bloom in southern Indiana.

the South.[3] It will grow under a wide range of climatic and soil conditions, has many uses, produces large yields of easily harvested seed, thrives in association with other crops, and fits well into many crop sequences.

The total hectarage of crimson clover is not known; however, a rapid increase occurred between 1942 and 1952. Since then, domestic use of seed has declined from 16,647,272 kg to 3,097,642 kg in 1969. Several factors contributed to this: (1) there was a sudden increase in seed losses in the mid-1950s from clover seed weevils; (2) over 60% of the crimson clover hectarage planted was in reseeding cultivars and did not require annual seeding, thus reducing demand for seed; and (3) there was a decline in price of seed.

Crimson clover will provide good winter grazing followed by a good yield of seed. This profitable combination fits well into grazing sequences with other crops. During winter, carrying capacity is considerably less than during the spring months when growth is the most rapid. Livestock

1. Stewart, Fred, and J. Boseck. 1947. Feed and forage cropping system for processed milk production in the Alabama-Tennessee Valley. Ala. Agr. Exp. Sta. Ser. 9.
2. Knight, W. E., and E. A. Hollowell. 1958. The influence of temperature and photoperiod on growth and flowering of crimson clover. *Agron. J.* 50:295–98.
3. USDA. 1971. Growing crimson clover. Leaflet 482, pp. 1–10.

FIG. 19.3.   *Crimson clover . . . good winter grazing followed by . . . good yield of seed . . . fits well into grazing sequences.* A good crop of crimson clover in Coastal bermudagrass.

can be shifted from clover to other crops four to six weeks before flowering, permitting the clover to make seed (Fig. 19.3).

High yields of good quality hay may be obtained by harvesting when the majority of the plants are not yet beyond the half-bloom stage. A good stand will yield from 2 to 4 t dry hay/ha, depending upon growth conditions and the intensity of grazing. Crimson clover is high in nutritive value when in the prebloom stage.

Crimson clover is an excellent green manure crop for use in pecan and other orchards. It may be allowed to reseed and does not need to be turned for the N to become available to the trees.[4] Crimson clover also has been used extensively for roadside stabilization and beautification.

❧ CULTIVARS AND STRAINS

Before 1938 most crimson clover was the common type, with more than half the seed imported from France and Hungary.

With the beginning of World War II, foreign seed was unavailable and domestic seed production increased rapidly.

RESEEDING CULTIVARS

The first reseeding crimson clover cultivar, 'Dixie,' was the result of cooperative investigations between several state agricultural experiment stations and the USDA.[5]

Since the development of Dixie, several other cultivars with the reseeding characteristic have been developed. Those of most significance are 'Autauga,' 'Auburn,' and 'Talladega.' Auburn, Autauga, and Dixie cultivars are similar in performance. 'Chief,' 'Kentucky,' and Talladega cultivars are slightly later in maturity.

In 1970 'Tibbee' reseeding crimson clover was released.[6] This cultivar is relatively early maturing and has large seed and excellent seedling vigor. It produces

4. Donnelly, E. D., and J. T. Cope, Jr. 1961. Crimson clover in Alabama. Ala. Agr. Exp. Sta. Bull. 335.

5. Hollowell, E. A. 1946. Dixie crimson clover. Mimeo. BPIA & AE, USDA.
6. Knight, W. E. 1970. Tibbee: A new reseeding variety of crimson clover. Miss. Agr. Forestry Exp. Sta. Inf. Sheet 1131.

greater fall growth than other reseeding cultivars.

The reseeding characteristic in crimson clover is associated with a moderately high percentage of hard seed.[7] These germinate gradually over a considerable period during autumn. This ensures a stand, even though one or more earlier stands of seedlings may have been killed previously due to a period of dry weather after germination. Hard seed content of a cultivar may vary from 30 to 75%. Apparently, this range in hard seed is due to environmental conditions during seed maturation and to genetic factors.[8] A water soaking technique was used successfully to select hard-seeded lines, several of which were composited to develop the cultivar Chief.[9] A nine-year regional test indicates that after a high level of hard-seededness is obtained in a cultivar, the gene frequency is maintained in a population under the climatic environment of the Southeast without reseeding generations.[10]

Seed of reseeding cultivars frequently are scarified during harvesting and processing and may contain as low as 5% hard seed when planted. Seed of reseeding cultivars cannot be distinguished from that of common crimson clover. For this reason, use of certified seed is recommended to ensure cultivar trueness.

* MANAGEMENT

Crimson clover is sown from the middle of July until November, depending upon the location and the use for which it is grown. If fall and winter grazing is desired, clover must be planted sufficiently early for plants to develop before the advent of cold weather.[11] Where temperatures are low and clover is subjected to soil heaving, plants must be well established or they may winter-kill. On the other hand, a rank thick growth throughout the winter months is conducive to the development of crown and stem rot disease which may completely kill the plants. Utilization of growth by grazing or cutting will prevent development and spread of the disease.[12] Seeding crimson clover either immediately preceding or soon after a heavy rain increases the chances of a stand; adequate soil moisture is essential.[13]

The recommended seeding rate is 22–34 kg/ha, the higher rate being desirable. The amount of seed to use depends on the condition of the seedbed, use to be made of clover, price of seed, and companion crops planted with the clover.[14] When clover is planted with small grain or ryegrass, seeding rate may be reduced to 17–22 kg/ha.

Crimson clover can be grown successfully with other crops such as the winter grains, annual ryegrass, and other winter annual legumes. Excellent stands of crimson have been obtained on established bermudagrass, dallisgrass, johnsongrass, and broad-leaved bahiagrass.[15] Removal of excess summer forage is essential for successful establishment of clover in the fall. Crimson clover has been grown successfully in sericea lespedeza and to a lesser degree with kudzu. In the lower South one of the most productive combinations is reseeding crimson clover and 'Coastal' bermudagrass.[16]

On practically all soils it is necessary to apply fertilizers before seeding and to make annual applications after the reseeding cultivars have been established. Phosphate and potash fertilizers are the most important.[17] Where crimson clover is grown with

7. Tennessee Agr. Exp. Sta. 1946. 59th Ann. Rept.
8. James, E. 1949. The effect of inbreeding on crimson clover seed coat permeability. *Agron. J.* 41:261–66.
9. Bennett, H. W. 1939. The effectiveness of selection for the hard-seeded character in crimson clover. *Agron. J.* 51:15–16.
10. Knight, W. E., E. D. Donnelly, J. M. Elrod, and E. A. Hollowell. 1964. Persistence of the reseeding characteristic in crimson clover, *Trifolium incarnatum*. *Crop. Sci.* 4:190–93.
11. Naftel, J. A. 1950. Reseeding crimson clover adds new income for the South. *Better Crops* 34:11–12.

12. Knight, W. E., and E. A. Hollowell. 1959. The effect of stand density on physiological and morphological characteristics of crimson clover. *Agron. J.* 51:73–76.
13. Stitt, R. E. 1944. Effect of moisture, seeding dates and fertilizers on stands and yields of crimson clover. *J. Amer. Soc. Agron.* 36:464–67.
14. Knight, W. E. 1967. Effect of seeding rate, fall disking, and nitrogen level on stand establishment of crimson clover in a grass sod. *Agron. J.* 59:33–36.
15. Kight, T. G., and H. W. Wellhausen. 1968. Cashing in on clover: Crimson the old standby. *Progressive Farmer*, Sept.
16. Knight, W. E. 1970. Productivity of crimson and arrowleaf clovers grown in a Coastal bermudagrass sod. *Agron. J.* 62:773–75.
17. Naftel, J. A. 1942. Soil liming investigations. VI Response of crimson clover to boron with and without lime on coastal plain soils. *J. Amer. Soc. Agron.* 34:975.

heavily nitrated permanent grass sods, attention must be given to soil pH and K level, particularly if hay crops are removed.[18,19] Boron may be needed if a seed crop is to be harvested.[17]

Crimson clover seed should be inoculated when planted on soil where clover was not grown the previous year. When grown in association with a perennial grass and if plants are thoroughly nodulated the first year, it usually is not necessary to inoculate in succeeding years.

❧ SEED PRODUCTION

With good stands and pollination, crimson clover seed set may range from 1000 to 1200 kg/ha. Seed losses during combining decrease the average harvested yield to approximately 250 kg. Tripping of florets is important in setting seed. Placing colonies of honeybees, *Apis mellifera* L., in or adjacent to seed fields is highly recommended.[20] If spring growing conditions are unfavorable, grazing or clipping during late winter or early spring may reduce seed yields. On the other hand, if some growth is not grazed off and spring growing conditions are favorable, growth may be so rank that the plants will lodge and result in low seed yield or failure.[21,22]

Crimson clover seed production has shifted from the Southeast to the West as a result of seed losses from seed weevils and for economic reasons. In 1951 Oregon produced 726,400 kg of seed on 1700 ha, and Alabama produced 2,633,200 kg on 19,035 ha. By 1970 Oregon production had reached 3,869,960 kg of seed on 7695 ha, while Alabama produced only 119,856 kg on 890 ha.

❧ DISEASES AND INSECTS

Although crimson clover is attacked by several diseases, no one consistently causes great damage. The most widespread and serious disease is crown and stem rot, caused by *Sclerotinia trifoliorum* Eriks. This disease attacks during cool wet weather.[23] Grazing during fall and winter destroys most of the initial infection and reduces subsequent spread of the disease. Crimson clover is highly susceptible to sooty blotch, *Cymadothea trifolii* (Pers. ex Fr.) Wolf; leaf and stem spot, *Cercospora zebrina* Pass.; and viruses. Sooty blotch is a leaf spot disease most in evidence at blooming. No great loss will occur if affected areas are mowed or grazed before severe leaf damage occurs.

Two species of insects, the clover head weevil, *Hypera meles* (F.), and the lesser clover leaf weevil, *Hypera nigrirostris* (F.), are responsible for seed losses and reduction in the crimson clover hectarage harvested for seed in the Southeast. The principal damage is caused by the larvae feeding on the flowers, ovules, and growing seed. Adults feed on stems, breaking off the flower heads. Insecticides applied in granular form or in sprays have given satisfactory control of these insects.[24]

ARROWLEAF CLOVER

Arrowleaf clover, *Trifolium vesiculosum* Savi, is a relatively new winter annual legume in the U.S. Early selections were made in the 1930s from plants growing in uncultivated places of central Italy.[25,26] Several introductions of this clover were made to the U.S. in 1956 and grown at the Southern Regional Plant Introduction Station, Griffin, Ga.

18. Adams, W. E., and M. Stelly. 1958. A comparison of Coastal and common bermudagrass, *Cynodon dactylon* (L.) Pers., in the Piedmont region: Yield response to fertilization. *Agron. J.* 50:457–59.
19. Adams, W. E., and R. A. McCreery. 1959. What are the fertility needs of crimson clover when grown with Coastal bermudagrass and Coastal bermudagrass grown alone? *Better Crops* 43 (4): 6–15.
20. Hollowell, E. A. 1947. Crimson clover. USDA Leaflet 160.
21. Knight, W. E., and E. A. Hollowell. 1962. Response of crimson clover to different defoliation intensities. *Crop Sci.* 2:124–27.
22. Rampton, H. H. 1969. Influence of planting rates and mowing on yield and quality of crimson clover seed. *Agron. J.* 61:92–95

23. Wolf, F. A., and R. O. Cromwell. 1919. Clover stem rot. N.C. Agr. Exp. Sta. Bull. 16.
24. Reed, J. K., J. K. Park, S. B. Hays, and B. K. Webb. 1962. Control of clover weevil on crimson clover. S.C. Agr. Exp. Sta. Circ. 134.
25. Petri, L. 1938. Rassegna dei casi fitopatologici osservati nel (Survey of phytopathological records in 1938). *Boll. Staz. Pat. veg. Roma.* 19:115–88. 1939. (*Herb. Abstr.* 10:1045. 1940).
26. Favilli, R. 1952–53. Alcune ricerche ed osservazioni sopra il trifoglio 'Ruffodi Calabria' (*Trifolium vesiculosum* Savi) (Research and observations on Ruffodi Calabria clover, *Trifolium vesiculosum* Savi). Pisa Universita, *Esperienze e Ricerche* 6:33–51.

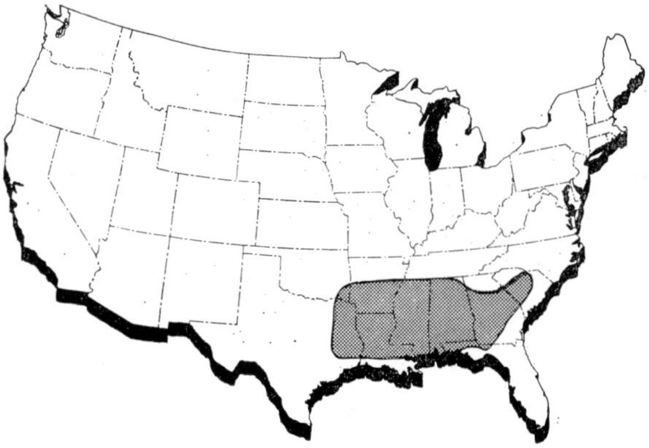

FIG. 19.4. Arrowleaf clover adaptation and growing areas in the U.S.

DISTRIBUTION AND ADAPTATION

Arrowleaf clover is successfully grown from east Texas to South Carolina and southward from Arkansas and Tennessee to the Gulf of Mexico. Hectarage has expanded most rapidly in Alabama, east Texas, and Arkansas (Fig. 19.4). Some arrowleaf clover is grown for seed production in western Oregon. Characteristics contributing to rapid farmer acceptance are: long productive season with high yield and quality, high percentage of hard seed and good reseeding ability, no problems with alfalfa weevil and clover head weevil, and low incidence of bloat.

Arrowleaf clover will thrive on well-drained sandy and clay soils but is less tolerant of acidity and low fertility than crimson clover. Arrowleaf does not tolerate high lime soils or those with poor drainage.[27]

PLANT DESCRIPTION

Arrowleaf clover makes its early growth from a leafy rosette similar to crimson clover, later producing branching stems that curve upward to a length of 60–150 cm. The smooth, thick, hollow stems are often purple, becoming hard near maturity.

27. Hoveland, C. S., E. L. Carden, G. A. Buchanan, E. M. Evans, W. B. Anthony, E. L. Mayton, and H. E. Burgess. 1969. Yuchi arrowleaf clover. Auburn Univ. Agr. Exp. Sta. Bull. 396.

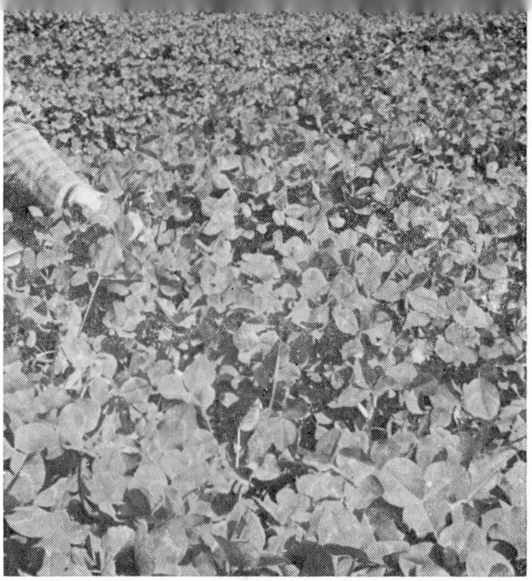

FIG. 19.5. *Leaf marking . . . none, to a large white V-shaped mark.* Large leaflets on vigorously growing arrowleaf clover during late March in central Alabama.

Long, white, pointed stipules are at the base of each leaf petiole. Each arrow-shaped, glabrous leaflet is 3.5–7 cm long and has pronounced veins. Leaf marking ranges from none to a large, white V-shaped mark (Fig. 19.5).

Flower heads are conical, often exceeding 5 cm in length and 3 cm in diameter (Fig. 19.6). From 150 to 170 individual florets make up the head, the corolla being white initially and later turning pink to purple. Flowering occurs over a long period, the later cultivars blooming from late May to July in central Alabama. New blooms continue to develop, while other heads have mature seed. Each floret produces two to three rough brown seed, each about twice the size of white clover seed. There are about 880,000 seed/kg.

FIG. 19.6. *Flower heads . . . conical, often exceeding 5 cm.* Arrowleaf clover in bloom shows the characteristic large flower heads.

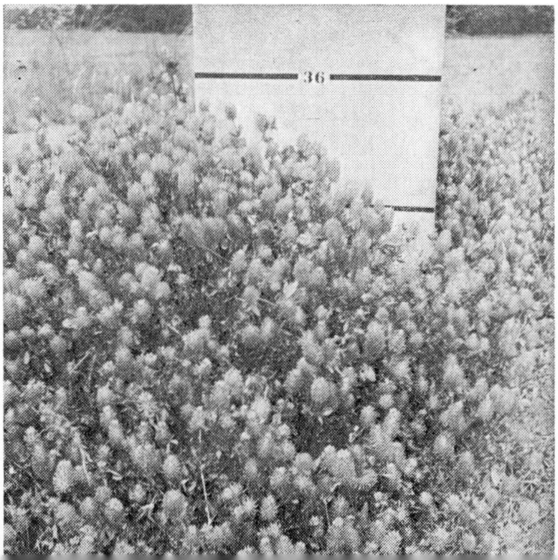

TABLE 19.1 ❧ Dry forage production of winter annual mixtures in central Alabama, two-year average

Mixture	Yield of oven-dry forage (kg/ha)			
	November–December	January–March	April–May	Total
Rye–Yuchi arrowleaf clover	1,870	3,440	3,180	8,390
Rye-ryegrass–Yuchi arrowleaf clover	1,610	3,490	2,810	7,910
Rye-ryegrass–crimson clover	1,790	3,620	2,210	7,620
Rye–crimson clover	2,000	3,710	840	6,550

Source: Hoveland et al., 1969.[27]

❧ IMPORTANCE AND USE

Arrowleaf clover hectarage is expanding rapidly in the southeastern U.S. and in some areas has become the major pasture legume. A survey in 1971 showed over 28,000 ha in the U.S. Hectarage is expected to increase, particularly on droughty upland soils of the lower South where white clover does not persist.

Crimson clover generally produces more early winter growth than arrowleaf clover, but the latter remains productive six to eight weeks later in the spring. Yields of 3500–8000 kg/ha dry forage have been obtained when arrowleaf clover is grown on prepared land.[28,29] (See Table 19.1.)

Forage quality of arrowleaf is high. Cell wall content remains relatively low until bloom stage even though stem percentage may be high.[30] Digestible dry matter remains high until maturity in late May or June.[29,31] Arrowleaf clover is ideally suited for extending the grazing season of small grains. Rye-ryegrass–arrowleaf clover can provide high-quality forage during April and May with little risk of bloat.[29]

In grazing trials arrowleaf clover has helped maintain animal gains over a long season. On hilly Piedmont soil in central Alabama over a four-year period, yearling steers were grazed continuously on ryegrass–'Yuchi' arrowleaf clover from November 24 to June 6 at a stocking rate of 0.4–0.8 steers/ha. Gains were 182 kg/steer, with an average daily gain of 0.91 kg.[32] In the Tennessee Valley of northern Alabama, yearling steers grazed from October to late December and early March to June. Gains were 0.91 kg/steer on small grains with Yuchi arrowleaf clover as compared to only 0.64 kg on small grains alone.[33]

Arrowleaf clover can be overseeded in autumn on perennial warm-season grass sods to furnish grazing in late winter and spring. On clipped plots of bermudagrass sod in Georgia and Mississippi, crimson has been more productive than arrowleaf clover.[15,34] However, in Alabama, arrowleaf yields were higher than crimson on both bermudagrass and bahiagrass sods.[35] Arrowleaf will usually reduce spring growth of the summer grass, and if the clover is not removed, grass stands may be injured. Continuous grazing prevents heavy clover accumulation and shading of grass. Overseeding of Coastal bermudagrass with Yuchi arrowleaf in central Alabama furnished clover grazing from early April to July with no damage to the grass.[36] Beef calf gains on this sward were superior to grass alone.

28. Hoveland, C. S., and H. L. Webster. 1965. Flooding tolerance of annual clovers. *Agron. J.* 56:304.

29. Hoveland, C. S., R. F. McCormick, and W. B. Anthony. 1972. Productivity and forage quality of Yuchi arrowleaf clover. *Agron. J.* 64:552–55.

30. Stanley, R. L., E. R. Beaty, and D. N. Palmer. 1968. Effect of age at harvest on yield and cell wall content of Amclo clover. *Agron. J.* 60:343–44.

31. Hoveland, C. S., E. L. Carden, W. B. Anthony, and J. P. Cunningham. 1970. Management effects on forage production and digestibility of Yuchi arrowleaf clover (*Trifolium vesiculosum* Savi). *Agron. J.* 62:115–16.

32. Anthony, W. B., C. S. Hoveland, E. L. Mayton, and H. E. Burgess. 1971. Rye-ryegrass–Yuchi arrowleaf clover for production of slaughter cattle. Ala. Agr. Exp. Sta. Circ. 182.

33. Harris, R. R., C. S. Hoveland, J. K. Boseck, and W. B. Webster. 1972. Wheat, oats, or rye with ryegrass and Yuchi arrowleaf clover for stocker beef steers. Ala. Agr. Exp. Sta. Circ. 197.

34. Beaty, E. R., and J. D. Powell. 1969. Forage production of Amclo and crimson clover on Pensacola and Coastal bermudagrass sods. *J. Range Manage.* 22:36–39.

35. Hoveland, C. S., E. L. Carden, J. R. Wilson, and P. A. Mott. 1971. Summer grass residue affects growth of winter legumes under sod. Auburn Univ. Highlights Agr. Res., vol. 18, no. 3.

36. Hoveland, C. S., W. B. Anthony, E. L. Mayton, and H. E. Burgess. 1972. Pastures for beef cattle in the Piedmont. Ala. Agr. Exp. Sta. Circ. 196.

Arrowleaf clover makes excellent quality hay. One cutting of hay can be obtained in May if grazing is terminated by early April.

❧ CULTIVARS

Three cultivars of arrowleaf clover are grown in the U.S., all of which are seed increases of plant introductions from Italy to the U.S. in 1956. The major difference between the three cultivars is length of growing season and maturity.

'Amclo,' the earliest maturing cultivar, reaches full bloom in central Georgia by mid-May.[37]

The Yuchi cultivar blooms three to four weeks later than Amclo, while 'Meechee' is about five weeks later.[38,39] When soil moisture is sufficient, the later maturing cultivars are the most productive. Meechee is the most winter-hardy of the three cultivars.[39] Seed of the three cannot be distinguished, so the use of certified seed is recommended to ensure cultivar trueness.

❧ MANAGEMENT

Arrowleaf clover is sown from August until November, depending upon the location. Early planting is essential on prepared land if early grazing is desired. On summer grass sods it is desirable to plant later after the grass is dormant and not competing for water. Arrowleaf clover will germinate at low temperatures.[40] A seeding rate of 6–9 kg/ha of scarified seed is adequate. Since combine-harvesting yields 75–80% hard seed, scarification is essential.[41]

Slow nodulation may be a problem with arrowleaf clover, particularly on fields where it is planted for the first time. Where plants develop nodules early, autumn and winter growth of the clover may exceed crimson clover.[27] A special arrowleaf inoculum is available. Two to three times the recommended inoculum rate has improved nodulation and increased winter growth of arrowleaf clover.[42] Pelleting of seed with inoculum just prior to planting has also given excellent results.

Since seed are small, care should be taken to avoid planting deeper than 0.7 cm. On bahiagrass and bermudagrass sods, broadcasting seed on the surface is satisfactory. Scarification of the sod with a disk is unnecessary.[34] On dense sods such as bahiagrass, old grass residue must be mowed or grazed off to leave a stubble of 2.5–5 cm, or clover stands and forage yield will be reduced.[35]

Lime and P and K fertilizer generally are needed. Arrowleaf clover is more sensitive than crimson clover to low soil P and acidity.[27] Arrowleaf clover is extremely sensitive to Mn. On soils with a pH of 7.5 or higher, plants become chlorotic and make little growth.

Grazing or mowing practices in spring may greatly affect yield and persistence. Arrowleaf clover can be grazed continuously until maturity in June or July and still make a seed crop for reseeding.[36] However, if a hay or seed crop is desired, grazing of Yuchi should be terminated by early April.[29,31,43] Regrowth is reduced by cutting hay in mid-April, and stands are virtually eliminated by cutting in May. Arrowleaf clover, at hay stage in late April and May, has virtually no buds at the base of plants, which accounts for the lack of regrowth after cutting. Bud numbers remain high under grazing. Maximum forage yields of Yuchi have been obtained by frequent cutting or grazing to early April followed by a hay harvest at early bloom in late May.[29] However, reseeding will not be obtained following a cutting for hay.

❧ SEED PRODUCTION

Yuchi and Meechee arrowleaf begin blooming in late May or early June and

37. Beaty, E. R., J. D. Powell, and R. A. McCreery. 1963. Amclo arrowleaf clover. *Crop Sci.* 5:284.
38. Hoveland, C. S. 1967. Yuchi arrowleaf clover. *Crop. Sci.* 7:80.
39. Knight, W. E., V. E. Aldrich, and M. Byrd. 1969. Registration of Meechee arrowleaf clover. *Crop Sci.* 9:393.
40. Hoveland, C. S., and D. M. Elkins. 1965. Germination response of arrowleaf, ball, and crimson clover varieties to temperature. *Crop Sci.* 5:244–46.
41. Andrews, C. H. 1969. Scarify arrowleaf clover seed. Miss. Farm Res., vol. 32, no. 10.

42. Wade, R. H., C. S. Hoveland, and A. E. Hiltbold. 1972. Inoculum rate and pelleting of arrowleaf clover seed. *Agron. J.* 64:481–83.
43. Knight, W. E. 1971. Influence of spring mowing on reseeding and productivity of selected annual clovers in grass sod. *Agron. J.* 63:418–20.

mature seed in late June or July. The Amclo cultivar is two to three weeks earlier. Seed are borne in clustered pods produced at tips of stems that remain erect if plants have not made too much vegetative growth. Shattering is not a major problem. Seed yields of 100–700 kg/ha are obtained in the southeastern U.S.

Several problems account for the wide diversity in seed yields. Weeds such as curly dock, *Rumex crispus* L.; cutleaf evening primrose, *Oenothera laciniata* Hill; and dodder, *Cuscuta* spp., may be serious and require a herbicide. Dodder seed are extremely difficult to separate from arrowleaf clover seed since they are of similar size and have rough seed coats. Several herbicides are effective and cause little or no injury to the clover.[44]

Potential seed fields should be grazed until early April. Failure to graze often will result in extremely heavy growth that mats down, rots, and produces only a small number of seed heads. Thin stands or late planted clover may give little or no grazing but often are the most productive seed fields.

Arrowleaf clover is cross-pollinated, and bees are essential for pollination. Unless enough native bees are present, 2–3 colonies/ha should be placed in the seed field.

Seed harvest is often difficult since maturity of the two later maturing cultivars, Meechee and Yuchi, often coincides with the normally rainy month of July in the Southeast. In addition, the clover continues to flower and stems may remain green even though there is a heavy crop of mature seed heads. Cutting and swathing may be done, but seed losses can occur. Desiccants are more effective and permit direct combining of the dry plants two to four days after application.[27]

❦ DISEASES AND INSECTS

Arrowleaf, like other clovers, is susceptible to crown and stem rot, so stand losses may occur during warm, wet winter periods. The problem is more severe where a heavy accumulation of forage occurs. Grazing the clover to remove surplus growth and permit light to penetrate the sward will reduce disease losses. Arrowleaf is also susceptible to virus diseases. Severely affected plants may be dwarfed or weakened and unable to withstand prolonged drought and heat in late spring and early summer.

Small seedlings of arrowleaf in bahiagrass and bermudagrass sods may be destroyed in autumn by the striped field cricket, *Nemobius fasciatus* Deg.[45] Good control can be obtained with a safe, effective insecticide at planting. Clover head weevil has little effect on arrowleaf clover.[27] Alfalfa weevil, *Hypera postica* (Gyll.), numbers are low and damage minor on arrowleaf clover as compared to alfalfa or bigflower clover, *T. michelianum* Savi.[46]

44. Buchanan, G. A., and C. S. Hoveland. 1971. Tolerance of Yuchi arrowleaf clover to herbicides. *Weed Sci.* 19:354–56.
45. Hoveland, C. S., E. M. Evans, C. C. King, and M. H. Bass. 1966. Annual clover stands reduced by pygmy crickets. Auburn Univ. Highlights Agr. Res., vol. 13, no. 2.
46. Hoveland, C. S., and M. H. Bass. 1963. Susceptibility of mike clover (*Trifolium michelianum* Savi) to alfalfa weevil. *Crop Sci.* 3:452–53.

❦ QUESTIONS

1. How long has crimson clover been used as an agricultural crop in the U.S. and what is its range of adaptation?
2. What are the outstanding characteristics that make crimson clover so important?
3. How important are the "reseeding cultivars" of crimson clover?
4. How important is seed inoculation in the area of adaptation?
5. How does flowering of arrowleaf clover differ from that of crimson clover?
6. Why does the spring grazing or cutting management of arrowleaf clover greatly affect forage or seed production in late spring?
7. What characteristics of arrowleaf clover make it so desirable for pastures in the lower South?
8. What precautions must be taken in getting good stands of annual clovers on warm-season perennial grass sods?

R. C. LEFFEL / *Agricultural Research Service, USDA*

20

OTHER LEGUMES

꙳

T HE DIVERSE CLIMATES and soils of the U.S. have been responsible for the introduction and cultivation of many species of forage legumes. Some of the species are specific in adaptation, and none is capable of profitable forage production throughout the country. Legumes are a source of N for associated grasses or for the succeeding crop in a rotation; however, the development of the commercial N industry provides farmers with an alternative to legume N. Emphasis is on a specialized highly productive agriculture. Many of the species discussed herein were more important a generation ago than they are today. Extensive discussions of forage legumes and their culture in the 1920s are given by Piper.[1] Need for improved forage legumes continues and may be met by known or new species. Many species of plants may be used for hay, pasture, or silage in such emergencies as drought.

꙳ PERENNIALS

CROWNVETCH

Crownvetch, *Coronilla varia* L., is most widely distributed about the Mediterra-

nean Sea and is found in central and southern parts of Europe and in parts of southwestern Asia and northern Africa. It has been used as an ornamental for many years and was commercially available in the U.S. by 1890.[2] The species is best adapted to fertile well-drained soils of pH 6 or above; but once established, crownvetch tolerates some degree of soil infertility and acidity. Crownvetch appears to be well adapted in the U.S. north of 35° N and east of the 97th meridian.

Crownvetch derives its common name from its "vetchlike" leaves and the arrangement of its florets in an umbel resembling a crown. The species has a deeply penetrating taproot and numerous lateral roots. Adventitious buds on the the roots may produce stems or rhizomes.[3]

The author acknowledges the reviews of the chapter or sections thereof as follows: A. E. Carleton and C. S. Cooper, sainfoin and cicer milkvetch; G. W. McKee and M. L. Risius, crownvetch; W. E. Kight, winter annuals; E. D. Donnelly and C. R. Gunn, vetches; and C. E. Townsend and I. Forbes, Jr., the chapter.

1. Piper, Charles V. 1924. Forage plants and their culture, 2nd ed. Macmillan, New York.
2. Henson, P. R. 1963. Crownvetch—A soil conserving legume and a potential pasture and hay plant. USDA Publ. ARS 34-63.
3. Alex, J. F. 1971. Botanical aspects of crownvetch. *In* E. M. Watkin (ed.), The Potential for Crownvetch in Ontario, pp. 35–42. Univ. of Guelph, Ont., Can.

꙳ R. C. LEFFEL. *See Chapter 16.*

Leaves are alternate and stipulate and pinnately compound, bearing 9–25 leaflets per leaf on mature plants. Stems are angular, hollow, decumbent to ascending, and 30–120 cm long. Flowers are a variegated white to purple color. Seed are borne in a long, slim, cylindrically shaped pod of 3–12 segments. When dry, the pod breaks into sections. Each segment of the pod contains a predominantly rod-shaped seed, yellow ochre to mahogany in color, about 3.5 mm long and 1 mm in diameter. There are approximately 245 seed/g.

Crownvetch is used extensively as ground cover for highway embankments, mine spoil areas, and other disturbed environments. Much interest exists in the potential of crownvetch as a forage plant. Major research problem areas with the species include seed production, stand establishment, and forage use; there is no documented evidence that crownvetch forage is either toxic or unpalatable to sheep and cattle.[4] Some species of *Coronilla* contain cardiac glycosides. Such glycosides may be present in the seed and plant of crownvetch.[5] Liveweight gain by sheep was less on early cut crownvetch hay than on alfalfa hay of similar chemical composition, and the difference was attributed to differences in voluntary intake and digestibility.[6] Intake of crownvetches was lower than that of alfalfa at comparable digestibilities; digestibility and intake of three crownvetch cultivars varied greatly from year to year.[7] Beef cattle performance on crownvetch pasture was acceptable.[8] Crownvetch is especially well suited to improvement of permanent bluegrass pastures by sod-seeding.[9]

The three most widely used cultivars of crownvetch, 'Penngift,' 'Emerald,' and 'Chemung,' developed as ecotypes in Pennsylvania, Iowa, and New York respectively. Penngift has relatively fine stems and small leaves, and is somewhat shorter in plant height than the other two cultivars.

Crownvetch is slower in germination and seedling growth when compared to alfalfa and red clover. Lack of a firm seedbed and competition from associated grasses and weeds are the biggest problems in establishment of crownvetch for forage purposes.[4] Competition from other plants may be controlled with herbicides and timely clipping.[10] Dry matter yields of crownvetch appear to be highest when it is harvested at eight-week intervals.[11] Decreasing regrowth intervals progressively decreased yields. Good stands were maintained with frequent harvests that left a 15-cm stubble. Sheep grazing crownvetch consumed mostly leaves and the pattern of leaf and stem removal under grazing was quite different from that under clipping.[12]

The cost of establishing seed fields, the shattering of seed, excessive vegetative growth attributed to its indeterminate growth habit, a slow and nonuniform maturing of seed, and relatively low seed yields are the major problems encountered in seed production.[4] Crownvetch is relatively free of insects and diseases. There are 21 species of *Coronilla;* a 2n chromosome number of 24 has been found for crownvetch and the species is probably an autotetraploid.[13,14]

4. McKee, Guy W. 1971. Crownvetch in the United States—Present status, future developments. *In* E. M. Watkin (ed.), The Potential for Crownvetch in Ontario, pp. 49–62. Univ. of Guelph, Ont., Can.

5. Cassady, John M. 1968. Toxic constituents of *Coronilla* species. *In* Proc. 2nd Crownvetch Symp., pp. 99–100. Pa. State Univ. Agron. Mimeo. 6.

6. Reynolds, Paul J., Charlie Jackson, Jr., and Paul R. Henson. 1969. Comparisons of the effects of crownvetch (*Coronilla varia* L.) and alfalfa hays on the liveweight gain of sheep. *Agron. J.* 61:187–90.

7. Reid, R. L., G. A. Jung, and R. O. Thomas. 1968. Nutritive value of crownvetch using sheep and cattle. *In* Proc. 2nd Crownvetch Symp., pp. 86–98. Pa. State Univ. Agron. Mimeo. 6.

8. Burns, J. C., W. A. Cope, L. Goode, R. W. Harvey, and H. D. Gross. 1969. Evaluation of crownvetch (*Coronilla varia* L.) by performance of beef cattle. *Agron. J.* 61:480–81.

9. Decker, A. M., H. J. Retzer, M. L. Larna, and H. D. Kerr. 1969. Permanent pastures improved with sod-seeding and fertilization. *Agron. J.* 61:243–47.

10. Peters, E. J., and S. A. Lowance. 1971. Establishment of crownvetch with herbicides. *Agron. J.* 63:230–32.

11. Woodruff, John Meredith. 1971. I. Morphological development and physiology of crownvetch (*Coronilla varia* L.) as influenced by defoliation intensity. II. Net carbon exchange of crownvetch leaves as influenced by light and temperature. Ph.D. thesis, Va. Polytech. Inst., Blacksburg.

12. Hart, Richard H. 1970. Frequency and severity of defoliation of crownvetch stems by grazing sheep. *Agron. J.* 62:626–27.

13. Uhrova, A. 1935. Revision der Gallung *Coronilla* L. *Beik Bot. Centralbl.* 53B:1–174.

14. Berchtold, Donald Joseph. 1970. Meiosis in two cultivars of *Coronilla varia* L. M.S. thesis, Pa. State Univ., University Park.

SAINFOIN

Sainfoin, *Onobrychis viciifolia* Scop., is found in most of southern Europe and eastward to Lake Baykal in Siberia.[1] It has been cultivated in Europe for at least 400 years and was evaluated at most agricultural experiment stations in the U.S. during the early part of the twentieth century. It has never achieved status as a major forage crop in the U.S., but interest is renewed with the threat to alfalfa by the alfalfa weevil.[15]

Sainfoin is especially well adapted to the dry calcareous soils of the northern Rocky Mountain region; it is long-lived on dryland but short-lived on irrigated land. Sainfoin grows well on soils low in P; N fixation is sometimes inadequate.[16] It is a deep-rooted species with stout erect stems arising from a crown. Leaves are oddly pinnate with 13–21 leaflets per leaf. Flowers are borne on an erect raceme and are pink, rarely white, in color. A single seed is produced in a bean-shaped, bilaterally compressed pod. Seed are kidney shaped, yellowish green to brown in color, and weigh about 15 g/1000 seed.

As of 1972 sainfoin is recommended in Montana and is being evaluated in adjacent states for irrigated land with limited water and for pasture or hay on dryland areas receiving 330 mm or more of annual rainfall. At similar stages of maturity sainfoin was lower in crude protein and higher in total digestible nutrients than alfalfa, and the hay supplies adequate protein for both young and mature beef animals.[17] The species is recognized as a nonbloating forage legume.

Cultivars 'Eski' and 'Remont' were released in 1964 and 1971 respectively by the Montana station. Remont is earlier than Eski in maturity and recovers more rapidly after harvest. 'Melrose,' licensed in Canada in 1969, is phenotypically similar to Eski but is also earlier in maturity and more rapid in recovery growth after harvest. Cultivars with good regrowth are considered more adaptable for grazing purposes. The grazing management of sainfoin should probably be dependent on the cultivar's pattern of accumulation and utilization of total available carbohydrates.[18]

As seed mature, they are susceptible to shattering from the pod. The seed crop should be windrowed when the seed is at about 40% moisture. Seed is dried in the windrow before threshing and is stored at 12% moisture.[19] The most important diseases in the U.S. are root, crown, and stem rots.[20] Insect pests in the U.S. include lygus bugs, the sainfoin bruchid, and many of the pests that occur on alfalfa.[21] Other cultivated species of *Onobrychis* in the USSR include *O. arenaria* (Kit.) DC. and *O. transcaucasica* Grossh.; many other wild species are known.

CICER MILKVETCH

Cicer milkvetch, *Astragalus cicer* L., introduced from Europe, has potential for irrigated and dryland hay and pasture in the Great Plains and western states.[22,23] (See Fig. 20.1.) It is rhizomatous and decumbent with coarse, succulent hollow stems that attain a length of 3 m under

15. Eslick, R. F. 1968. Sainfoin—Its possible role as a forage legume in the West. *In* C. S. Cooper and A. E. Carleton (eds.), Sainfoin Symp., pp. 1–2. Mont. Agr. Exp. Sta. Bull. 627.
16. Krall, J. L., C. S. Cooper, C. W. Crowell, and A. J. Jarvi. 1971. Evaluations of sainfoin for irrigated pasture. Mont. Agr. Exp. Sta. Bull. 658.
17. Carleton, A. E., C. S. Cooper, R. H. Delaney, A. L. Dubbs, and R. F. Eslick. 1968. Growth and forage quality comparisons of sainfoin *(Onobrychis viciaefolia* Scop.) and alfalfa *(Medicago sativa* L.). *Agron. J.* 60:630–32.
18. Cooper, C. S., and C. A. Watson. 1968. Total available carbohydrates in roots of sainfoin *(Onobrychis viciaefolia* Scop.) and alfalfa *(Medicago sativa* L.) when grown under several management regimes. *Crop Sci.* 8: 83–85.
19. Carleton, A. E., L. E. Wiesner, A. L. Dubbs, and C. W. Roath. 1967. Yield and quality of sainfoin seed as related to stage of maturity. Mont. Agr. Exp. Sta. Bull. 614.
20. Mathre, Don. 1968. Disease in sainfoin. *In* C. S. Cooper and A. E. Carleton (eds.), Sainfoin Symp., pp. 65–66. Mont. Agr. Exp. Sta. Bull. 627.
21. Wallace, L. E. 1968. Current and potential insect problems of sainfoin in America. *In* C. S. Cooper and A. E. Carleton (eds.), Sainfoin Symp., pp. 67–70. Mont. Agr. Exp. Sta. Bull. 627.
22. Townsend, C. E. 1970. Phenotypic diversity for agronomic characters in *Astragalus cicer* L. *Crop Sci.* 10: 691–92.
23. Hafenrichter, A. L., John L. Schwendiman, Harold L. Harris, Robert S. MacLaughlan, and Harold W. Miller. 1968. Grasses and legumes for soil conservation in the Pacific Northwest and Great Basin states. USDA Agr. Handbook 339.

FIG. 20.1. Cicer milkvetch is rhizomatous with coarse, succulent, hollow stems. The leaves are pinnately compound with 10–13 pairs of leaflets plus one terminal leaflet. At maturity the black, bladderlike seedpods contain 3–11 seed. *Mont. State Univ. drawing.*

good growing conditions. Leaves are pinnately compound with 10–13 pairs of leaflets plus one terminal leaflet. Twenty to 60 white to pale yellow flowers are borne on racemes arising from the leaf axils. Pollination is primarily by bumblebees. At maturity the black bladderlike seedpods contain 3–11 seed; there are about 270 seed/g. The seed have an extremely hard, shiny seed coat requiring mechanical scarification. A quick-swell test has been developed to estimate the effectiveness of mechanical scarification.[24]

The species is adapted to a range of growing conditions, preferring cool moist sites and moderately coarse soils. It is adapted to drylands receiving more than 380 mm of precipitation annually and to high-elevation wet areas with a growing season of 50 days or less. Cicer milkvetch is more tolerant to alkaline or acid soils than alfalfa.[24] It is resistant to drought, frost, and pocket gophers; does not cause

24. Carleton, A. E., R. D. Austin, J. R. Stroh, L. E. Wiesner, and J. G. Scheetz. 1971. Cicer milkvetch (*Astragalus cicer* L.) seed germination, scarification and field emergence studies. Mont. Agr. Exp. Sta. Bull. 655.

bloating of animals nor accumulate high levels of selenium; and has no major disease or insect pests. Seedling emergence and growth of cicer milkvetch is slower than that of alfalfa and sainfoin.[24]

The cultivar, 'Lutana,' was released in Montana and Wyoming in 1970; 'Oxley' was licensed in Canada in 1971. Falcatus milkvetch, *A. falcatus* Lam., is another of 2000 species of the genus that is drought resistant and of possible value in drylands.

KUDZU

Kudzu, *Pueraria lobata* (Willd.) Ohwi, is native to Japan and China and was probably first introduced into the U.S. in 1876. It was first used as an ornamental. Interest in kudzu for forage and soil conservation began about 1905 and increased until at least the mid-1940s. The species is best adapted to well-drained loam soils of good fertility in the southeastern U.S.

Kudzu is a rapidly growing, coarse,

FIG. 20.2. *Kudzu . . . rapidly growing, coarse, hairy stoloniferous vine; uncontrolled . . . may be a pest . . . forage is palatable and gives good animal performance.* Ala. Agr. Exp. Sta. photo.

hairy, stoloniferous vine.[25] (See Fig. 20.2.) Stems may attain a length of 20 m in a season, are 1 cm or less in diameter, and are prostrate or climb supports. Uncontrolled, the species may be a pest, invading woodlands or structures and killing trees. Rooting occurs at nodes in contact with moist soil. Leaves are alternate and trifoliolate and resemble those of the grape. The flowers are borne on a raceme, are dark purple in color, and seldom set seed in the U.S. Propagation is by seed, transplanted seedlings, or by rooted nodes called "crowns."[26,27]

Kudzu is used to prevent soil erosion and as a hay and pasture plant. Complete establishment and ground cover require several years. It is susceptible to continual or heavy grazing or frequent cutting. The forage is palatable and gives good animal performance as pasture, hay, or silage. Properly managed, stands persist for many years.[28]

CLOVERS

Strawberry clover, *Trifolium fragiferum* L., originated in the Near East and is a stoloniferous species similar to white clover in morphology and habit of growth. The common name is obtained from the mostly pink to white flower heads that resemble strawberries. It is adapted to wet saline and alkaline soils in the western U.S., tolerates flooding, and is principally a pasture plant.[29] Kura clover, *T. ambiguum* Bieb., is also from the Near East. This species is of interest to forage researchers because of its rhizomatous character, resistance to pests, winterhardiness, and persistence. Kura clover is not effectively

nodulated in field plantings in the U.S.[30] A number of perennial species of clover are native to the western U.S. and contribute considerable high-quality forage to livestock and game animals.[31] These include seaside clover, *T. willdenovii* Spreng., adapted to saline and poorly drained soils; longstalk clover, *T. longipes* Nutt. & Gray, which is similar to alsike clover in morphology and habitat; hollyleaf clover, *T. gymnocarpon* Nutt., adapted to drier sites and sometimes found beneath sagebrush; whiproot, *T. dasyphyllum* Torr. & Gray, and Parry clover, *T. parryi* Gray, both adapted to rocky areas of high altitudes.

OTHER SPECIES

The flatpea, *Lathyrus sylvestris* L., is a rhizomatous species resembling the sweetpea. It has been used for erosion control in Washington, and is established there in rangelands as an escape plant. The seed are toxic to grazing animals, and fatalities have been observed among sheep and other experimental animals fed flatpea forage.[32] 'Lathco' is a cultivar developed by the SCS and released as a soil conservation cover plant for the northeastern U.S. in 1972. Its potential as a forage plant is undetermined. 'Silverleaf,' *Desmodium uncinatum* (Jacq.) DC., from Brazil is a promising perennial summer legume in association with bermudagrass at the Georgia coastal plain station; however, it has not persisted in association with bahiagrass. Commercial seed production of Silverleaf is confined to Australia where the cultivar is widely used in subtropical pastures. Silverleaf will not persist in poorly drained soils and may winter-kill north of central Georgia.

25. Romm, Harry Josef. 1953. The development and structure of the vegetative and reproductive organs of kudzu, *Pueraria thunbergiana* (Sieb. and Zucc.) Benth. *Iowa State Coll. J. Sci.* 27:407–19.

26. Tabor, Paul. 1942. Seed production by kudzu (*Pueraria thunbergiana*) in the southeastern United States during 1941. *J. Amer. Soc. Agron.* 34:389.

27. Tabor, Paul. 1942. Observations of kudzu, *Pueraria thunbergiana* Benth., seedlings. *J. Amer. Soc. Agron.* 39:500–501.

28. McKee, Roland, and J. L. Stephens. 1948. Kudzu as a farm crop. USDA Farmers' Bull. 1923.

29. Hollowell, E. A. 1960. Strawberry clover: A legume for the West. USDA Leaflet 464.

30. Townsend, C. E. 1970. Phenotypic diversity for agronomic characters and frequency of self-compatible plants in *Trifolium ambiguum*. *Can. J. Plant Sci.* 50: 331–38.

31. Hamilton, John W., and Carl S. Gilbert. 1971. Mineral composition of native and introduced clovers. *J. Range Manage.* 24:304–8.

32. Daniel, T. W., F. B. Wolberg, V. L. Miller, J. H. Alswager, M. E. Ensminger, and A. A. Spielman. 1946. Chemical composition and digestibility of flat pea forage in three stages of maturity. *J. Anim. Sci.* 5:80–86.

FIG. 20.3. *With few exceptions cultivated vetches . . . viny annuals with leaves bearing leaflets pinnately . . . terminating in a tendril. USDA photo.*

❧ WINTER ANNUALS

VETCHES

The genus *Vicia* contains about 150 species, including about 15 that are native to the U.S. Cultivated vetches are native to Europe and adjacent parts of Asia and Africa and are widely distributed in temperate areas of the world. With few exceptions cultivated vetches are viny annuals with leaves bearing leaflets pinnately and terminating in a tendril, large flowers, spherical seeds, and elongated, somewhat compressed pods. (See Fig. 20.3.) European species of *Vicia* have been revised by Ball, and his classification is used in this discussion.[33] The Federal Extension Service estimates the 1969 vetch production in the U.S. as 750,000 ha.[34] Of this hectarage 85% was seeded to hairy vetch and 5% each

33. Ball, P. W. 1968. *Vicia* L. *In* T. G. Tutin et al. (eds.), Flora Europaea, vol. 2, pp. 129–36. Cambridge Univ. Press.
34. Paulling, John R. 1970. Trends in forage crops varieties–1969. Fed. Ext. Serv., USDA.

to common and purple vetches. Vetches are used most commonly in the U.S. as winter cover crops in the southern region; 75% of the total hectarage is in Oklahoma, Arkansas, Texas, and Louisiana. Estimates on utilization of vetches as forage are not available, but vetches make hay, silage, and pasture of high quality.

In the southern U.S. and on the Pacific Coast the vetches are seeded in the fall, usually following a cultivated crop. In the northern U.S. only hairy vetch is sufficiently winter-hardy to be a winter annual; the other vetches must be sown early in the spring. Vetches are often seeded with small grains for hay, silage, or pasture. Vetches should be pastured only when the ground is dry to avoid soil compaction and to reduce possibility of bloat in cattle and sheep. Vetches are usually harvested for hay when the first pods are well developed. Most of the seed of hairy vetch is produced in Texas, Nebraska, Oklahoma, and Oregon. Susceptibility to shattering requires harvesting the seed crop as soon as the lower pods are fully ripe as well as minimum handling of the crop prior to threshing.

Diseases of vetches include anthracnose, leaf spot and downy mildew, several stem and root rots, rust, and root-knot nematodes. Many of the insects of forage legumes attack vetches, including the pea aphid, *Acyrthosiphon pisum* (Harris); cutworms, *Euxoa* spp.; corn earworm, *Heliothis zea* (Boddie); fall armyworm, *Spodoptera frugiperda* (J. E. Smith); vetch bruchid, *Bruchus brachialis* Fåhr.; American grasshopper, *Schistocerca Americana* (Drury); lygus bugs, *Lygus* spp.; clover leafhopper, *Aceratagallia sanguinolenta* (Prov.); and potato leafhopper, *Empoasca fabae* (Harris). Resistances to some of the pests exist either in available cultivars or in some species of *Vicia*.

HAIRY VETCH. *Vicia villosa* Roth is the most winter-hardy of the cultivated vetches and can be grown in most crop-producing areas of the U.S. It is adapted to light sandy soils as well as heavier ones.

The plants may be conspicuously hairy or nearly hairless and usually have purple flowers and glabrous pods. A nearly hairless selection, called smooth vetch but sold as hairy vetch, is the most commonly grown vetch in the U.S. It is less winter-hardy than other hairy vetches.

'Madison' is a cultivar of hairy vetch developed in Nebraska. Ball recognized five subspecies of *V. villosa* and one of the subspecies is subsp. *varia,* formerly *V. dasycarpa* Ten.[33] The common name of this subspecies has been changed from woollypod vetch to winter vetch by Gunn.[35] Winter vetch is less cold tolerant and more heat tolerant than hairy vetch. Winter vetch cultivars 'Auburn,' 'Oregon,' and 'Lana' were developed by the agricultural experiment stations of Alabama, Oregon, and California respectively. Lana, the most popular winter vetch, is grown in California and Texas.

COMMON VETCH. *Vicia sativa* L. is also an extremely variable species. It is less winter-hardy than hairy vetch and can be used as a winter annual only in the southern U.S. It is best adapted to well-drained, fertile loam soils.

The cultivar 'Willamette' was developed in Oregon. The cultivar 'Warrior,' released in Alabama in 1958, is resistant to the vetch bruchid and three species of root-knot nematode and produces high forage and seed yields.

Ball cites the variation in basic chromosome number in *V. sativa* as highly correlated with morphology; yet gene exchange between plants of different chromosome numbers can occur with reasonable facility.[33] He classifies narrowleaf vetch (formerly *V. angustifolia* L.) as *V. sativa* L. subspecies *nigra* (L.) Ehrh., with chromosome numbers of 2n = 12, 14. Narrowleaf vetch may be identified by its black pods, which are not constricted between the seeds, and narrow leaflets. Narrowleaf vetch is found throughout the U.S. and is a volunteer legume in southern pastures.

PURPLE VETCH. *Vicia benghalensis* L. is the least winter-hardy of the cultivated vetches. As a winter annual it is adapted only to the mildest climates of the U.S. This species is similar to hairy vetch but can be identified by its wine-colored (reddish purple) flowers and hairy pods.

OTHER SPECIES. Other species of cultivated vetches in Europe and the U.S. include Hungarian vetch, *V. pannonica* Crantz; single-flowered vetch, *V. articulata* Hornem.; bittervetch, *V. ervilia* (L.) Willd.; bard vetch, *V. monantha* Retz.; and horsebean, *V. faba* L. These species are described by Henson and Schoth[36] but make no significant contribution to current forage production in the U.S. Donnelly and Clark[37,38] combined seed coat impermeability and high-temperature dormancy of 10-chromosome common vetch, *V. sativa* L. subsp. *cordata* (Wulfen ex Hoppe) Asch. & Graebn. (formerly *V. cordata*),[33] with desirable characters of 12-chromosome *V. sativa*. These improved vetches have potential as an adapted reseeding winter legume in warm-season perennial grasses in the southeastern U.S. Cultivar 'Nova,' a reseeding vetch developed from the above cross, was released in 1969 by the Alabama station.

CLOVERS

Most of the 250–300 species of *Trifolium* are annuals, and 15 or more of the annual clovers from the Old World contribute to forage production in the U.S. The taxonomy of most of the cultivated clovers in the U.S. is given by Hermann.[39]

ROSE CLOVER. *Trifolium hirtum* All. is the most widely adapted legume for range use in California.[40] Stems, leaves, and

35. Gunn, Charles R. 1971. Seeds of native and naturalized vetches of North America. USDA Agr. Handbook 392.

36. Henson, P. R., and H. A. Schoth. 1968. Vetch culture and uses. USDA Farmers' Bull. 1740.
37. Donnelly, E. D., and E. M. Clark. 1962. Hybridization in the genus *Vicia. Crop Sci.* 2:141–45.
38. Donnelly, E. D. 1971. Breeding hard-seeded vetch using interspecific hybridization. *Crop Sci.* 11:721–24.
39. Hermann, F. J. 1963. A botanical synopsis of the cultivated clovers (*Trifolium*). USDA Monogr. 22.
40. Williams, William A., R. Merton Love, and Lester J. Berry. 1957. Production of range clovers. Calif. Agr. Exp. Sta. Circ. 458.

flower heads are pubescent; the species derives its common name from the rose-colored flower heads. The species is adapted to a wide range of soils and to most of the range area of California. It is not adapted to poorly drained soils nor to areas receiving less than 250 mm annual rainfall or above 1000 m in elevation. With proper grazing management the species reseeds itself and contributes greatly to the grass-legume pasture of the rangeland. Summer grazing of accumulated dry forage shatters the hard seed of rose clover and animals trample it into the soil. The species is highly palatable even when dry. Rose clover is also adapted to the lower southeastern U.S. but does not make a major contribution to pasture production in that area.

SUBTERRANEAN CLOVER. *Trifolium subterraneum* L. is from the Mediterranean and Near East and established a grassland agriculture in Australia.[41] It is established on 10 million ha in Australia, with an estimated potential there of 40 million ha. This species, especially well adapted to relatively warm moist winters and dry summers, is used as a rangeland legume with grasses west of the Cascade Mountains of Oregon and California.[40,42] The inflorescence of subterranean clover is inconspicuous and contains three to seven, usually four, white or pinkish florets. After flowering and fertilization a bur enveloping the seed is formed and the peduncles elongate toward the ground. The stiff forked bristles of the seed bur serve as a mechanism that buries a portion of the burs in the soil, giving rise to the common name and creating a difficult seed harvest. This characteristic, hard seed, and the high temperature dormancy of the seed make the species especially well adapted to reseeding. Most of the seed of the many cultivars, which vary greatly in maturity and other characters, is produced in Australia. In Oregon and California, subterranean clover is adapted to areas with more than 400 mm annual rainfall and below 1000 m elevation. The species is especially tolerant to acid soils. Naturalized ecotypes of subterranean clovers have been identified in the lower southeastern U.S., where they have persisted in permanent pastures for 25 years or longer. Here subterranean clover appears to be an especially promising reseeding legume for permanent pastures if future breeding programs develop adapted and productive cultivars.

BERSEEM CLOVER. *Trifolium alexandrinum* L. has been used for many years in Mediterranean and Near East countries and in India. It was introduced into California in 1896 but has not become a major forage legume because it is the least winter-hardy of cultivated clovers. Adaptation in the U.S. is restricted to the warmest Gulf Coast and southwestern areas, where temperatures seldom fall below freezing. This species exhibits an erect habit of growth, hollow stems, narrow leaflets, and yellowish white flowers borne on a typical clover head. It produces more winter forage than other legumes if it is not damaged by low temperatures. Egyptian cultivars are characterized by the form of stem branching:[43] basal and profuse, basal and along the main stem, and apical along the upper part of the main stem. Once cut, the latter type fails to renew growth.

Kretschmer reports multicut domestic cultivars 'Nile' and 'Hustler' adapted to southern Florida and presents recommended management practices.[44]

BALL CLOVER. *Trifolium nigrescens* Viv. is a diploid nonstoloniferous species closely related and morphologically similar to tetraploid white clover, *T. repens* L. It is adapted to loam and clay soils in the lower southeastern U.S. Ball clover

41. Morley, F. H. W. 1961. Subterranean clover. *Advan. Agron.* 13:57–123.
42. Rampton, H. H. 1952. Growing subclover in Oregon. Oreg. Agr. Exp. Sta. Bull. 432.
43. Kaddah, Malek T. 1962. Tolerance of berseem clover to salt. *Agron. J.* 54:421–25.
44. Kretschmer, Albert E., Jr. 1964. Berseem clover—A new winter annual for Florida. Fla. Agr. Exp. Sta. Circ. S-163.

tolerates grazing, reseeds well even under heavy grazing, and produces most of its growth about one month later in the spring than does crimson clover.[45]

PERSIAN CLOVER. *Trifolium resupinatum* L. is adapted to heavy, moist, low-lying soils in the southeastern U.S. Plants are erect and may grow to a height of 1 m. Flowers are light purple in color; balloon-like capsules containing the seed shatter easily at maturity and distribute seed by wind and water. Persian clover is highly palatable and is used for hay, pasture, silage, and soil improvement.[46]

The improved cultivar 'Abon,' released in 1964 by the Texas station and USDA, is adapted to the Gulf Coast.

HOP CLOVERS. Hop clover, *T. agrarium* L.; large hop clover, *T. campestre* Schreb.; and small hop clover, *T. dubium* Sibth., are similar in appearance. All have small round heads of yellow flowers which turn brown upon ripening of seed, resembling the flower of a hop plant. The middle leaflet of hop clover is not stalked, but in small and large hop clovers it is. All are adapted to infertile and eroded soils of the southern U.S.; hop clover is more prevalent at higher elevations. All three species are highly palatable pasture plants that produce moderate amounts of forage for a relatively short period in the spring.

OTHER SPECIES. Other species of annual clovers include cluster clover, *T. glomeratum* L., adapted to the Gulf Coast and especially to southern Mississippi; bigflower clover, *T. michelianum* Savi, a tall coarse species, with many plant and flower characteristics similar to alsike clover, that is also adapted to the Gulf Coast; lappa clover, *T. lappaceum* L., adapted to the low-lying, dark-colored, heavy, wet calcareous soils of the lower southeastern U.S.; striate clover, *T. stria-*

tum L., adapted to heavy clay soils of the lower Southeast; rabbitfoot clover, *T. arvense* L., adapted to infertile, dry sandy soils of the East; and whitetip clover, *T. variegatum* Nutt. ex Torr. & Gray, a native species adapted to the flood mountain meadows of the West.

LUPINES

Many wild species of *Lupinus* are native to America, but the three cultivated large-seeded lupine species used in the U.S. originated in the Mediterranean basin. Some species of lupines have been cultivated as grain legumes for 3000 years or more. Apparently lupines evolved as plants high in alkaloids, which caused resistance to grazing and repelled insects.[47] Lupines with high alkaloids are termed "bitter." These alkaloids vary with species and include sparteine, lupanine, and hydroxylupanine.[48] Modern lupine improvement began about 1928 with the discovery of alkaloid-free, "sweet" lupines that were nontoxic to livestock. Grazing animals tend to avoid bitter lupines because of the bitterness of the alkaloids in plant and seed; fatalities appear to occur mostly when hungry animals are given access to bitter lupines.[47] Bitter or sweet lupines can be detected by taste, chemical means, or feeding response of an insect such as thrips.[49] Plants of lupines are upright in habit of growth, 1 m or more in height, with coarse stems and digitate (fingerlike) leaves. Lupines are adapted only to the lower South as winter annuals on well-drained soils and are used for soil improvement, late winter and early spring grazing, and for silage. They are under investigation as summer annual feed-grain legumes on sandy soils of the Great Lakes region. A number of genes for improved quality, disease resist-

45. Hoveland, C. S. 1960. Ball clover. Auburn Univ. Agr. Exp. Sta. Leaflet 64.
46. USDA. 1960. Persian clover—A legume for the south. Leaflet 484.

47. Gladstones, J. S. 1970. Lupins as crop plants. *Field Crop Abstr.* 23 (2): 123–48.
48. Nowacki, E. 1963. Inheritance and biosynthesis of alkaloids in lupin. *Genet. Pol.* 4:161–202.
49. Forbes, Ian, Jr., and Homer D. Wells. 1966. Breeding blue lupine forage varieties for the southeastern United States. Proc. 10th Int. Grassl. Congr., pp. 708–11. (Helsinki, Finland).

ance, nonshattering seed, other desirable agronomic characters, and genetic markers are known and utilized in lupine breeding programs.[47,49]

Major diseases of the lupines are gray leaf spot, anthracnose, brown spot, powdery mildew, *Ascochyta* stem canker, viruses, root-knot nematodes, and root rot and seedling blights caused by a number of fungi attacking forage legumes generally. Control of disease can be obtained by use of resistant cultivars, crop rotations, and disease-free seed. Insects include a root weevil which feeds on the nodules, lupine maggot, thrips, white-fringed beetle, and lesser cornstalk borer.

BLUE LUPINE. *Lupinus angustifolius* L. is adapted to neutral or slightly acid soils of at least moderate fertility in the coastal plain of the Southeast. This is the most widely used species in the U.S.; production is centered in northern Florida and southern Georgia. Blue lupines are more winter-hardy than yellow lupines and are moderately susceptible to seed shattering. Blue lupine seed is generally roughly oval and mottled gray to brownish gray in color and contains some hard seed.

Progress in breeding blue lupines in the U.S. has been reviewed.[49] Common bitter blue lupine and bitter cultivar 'Richey' are used for soil improvement only. 'Borre,' 'Blanco,' 'Rancher,' and 'Frost' sweet blue lupines demonstrate especially well the continued improvement of blue lupines as grazing plants. (See Fig. 20.4.) Frost, the most recently released cultivar, has resistance to gray leaf spot and anthracnose diseases, a low alkaloid content, a permeable seed coat, tan-speckled white seeds, blue flowers, and improved winterhardiness. Frost is equal to all previous cultivars in palatability, digestibility, and protein content.

YELLOW LUPINE. *Lupinus luteus* Kell. is adapted to moderately acid, light sandy soils of low fertility. Reduced winterhardiness of this species limits it to Florida. Plants of yellow lupine are quite

FIG. 20.4. *Frost . . . improved winterhardiness . . . equal to all . . . in palatability, digestibility . . . protein content.* Reaction of Rancher (left) and Frost blue lupines to —12 C on January 8, 1970, at the Georgia coastal plain station. *Ga. Agr. Exp. Sta. photo.*

bushy and somewhat shorter than blue or white lupines. The seed is usually white or speckled white and black and is flattened. This species is most susceptible to seed shattering and some seed has an impermeable seed coat. Susceptibility to bean yellow mosaic virus severely limits seed yields of yellow lupine and, consequently, has greatly reduced the use of the crop in Florida. Yellow lupine is the best adapted species in northern Europe where it is grown as a summer annual. 'Weiko III' was developed in Germany for its low alkaloid content, nonshattering, permeable seed coat, white seed, and rapid early growth.[47]

WHITE LUPINE. *Lupinus albus* L. is adapted to neutral fertile soils such as the alluvial soils of the lower Mississippi Delta. It is the most winter-hardy and exhibits the least shattering of seed. Seed are large, flat, and creamy white in color and have a permeable seed coat.

'Hope,' developed especially for use as a winter cover and green manure crop in Arkansas, is high in alkaloid.[50] Short-term weed control is attributed to this alkaloid, which acts as a natural herbicide when the plant material is decomposing in the soil.

50. Offutt, M. S. 1971. Registration of Hope white lupine. *Crop Sci.* 11:602.

FIELD PEA

The field pea, *Pisum sativum* subsp. *arvense* (L.) Poir., differs from the garden pea mostly by the sweeter and more delicate flavor of the latter. The field pea is used as a winter annual in the South and as a summer annual in the North for soil improvement and forage. As a forage it is usually grown with small grain for hay, pasture, or silage.

There were more than 100 cultivars available in 1924.[1] 'Austrian Winter' has been the most widely used cultivar in the South because of its winterhardiness. 'Papago' and 'Romack' were developed in Arizona and Georgia respectively. 'Fenn,' developed by the University of Idaho and released in 1971, is winter-hardy and moderately resistant to *Ascochyta*. This cultivar is expected to replace Austrian Winter in the South. Northern Idaho harvests 20,000 ha of Austrian Winter field peas for seed, most of it for export.

ROUGHPEA

The roughpea, *Lathyrus hirsutus* L., is adapted to heavy soils in areas with mild winters such as the lower South. It is a weak-stemmed decumbent plant similar to the field pea and vetch. The species is used for soil improvement and for early spring pasture. Seed of the roughpea is poisonous to livestock; the active principle, producing the paralytic condition of animals known as lathyrism, is β-aminopropionitrile.[51] Animals should be removed from roughpea pastures when pods begin to form. The species reseeds well, and hard seed persist in the soil for years.

OTHER SPECIES

Winter annuals of limited or past usage in the U.S. include fenugreek, *Trigonella foenum-graecum* L., long used in north Africa and adapted to dry warm areas such

as California, and serradella, *Ornithopus sativus* Brot., adapted to moist sandy soils and used as a summer annual forage in Europe. Serradella has shown some promise as a winter annual in southeastern U.S.

❧ SUMMER ANNUALS

SOYBEAN

The soybean, *Glycine max* (L.) Merr., was first cultivated in the U.S. as a forage crop in 1804 but received little attention until the Perry expedition returned from Japan in 1854 with two cultivars.[1]

The cultivar 'Mammoth,' introduced prior to 1882, made the soybean an important hay crop in the southern states. Between 1900 and 1920 the USDA introduced about 800 cultivars of soybeans from all portions of the Orient.

In 1920 about 20% of the 360,000 ha of soybeans in the U.S. was harvested as seed. Piper, revising his text in 1923, states:[1] "The soybean is the most productive as regards seed of any legume adapted to temperate climates. This fact alone gives the crop a high potential importance and insures its greater agricultural development in America. At the present time the soybean is most largely grown for roughage, but the high value of the seed for human food, as well as animal feed and for oil, will in all probability result in its being more and more grown for the seed and the crop will then become of major importance." By 1970 soybeans in the U.S. exceeded 17 million ha; 98% of this hectarage was harvested for beans. Most of the remaining 350,000 ha was harvested for hay.

Morphology of the soybean varies greatly. In general the plant resembles the field bean. A great range in plant maturity and growth habit exists within the species. Current cultivars are erect and resistant to lodging. Trifoliolate leaves vary greatly in size and shape. The plant is covered with gray or tawny pubescence. Flowers are white or purple in color. Pods contain from one to four seed.

51. Dupuy, Harold P., and Jordan G. Lee. 1956. The toxic component of the singletary pea *(Lathyrus pusillus).* J. Amer. Pharm. Assoc. Sci. Ed. 45:236–39.

Soybeans are a versatile emergency hay crop because they are adapted to a wide range of planting dates.[52] The soybean, like corn, is adapted to most climates and cultivated soils of the eastern U.S. Cultivars have been selected for hay purposes, with somewhat finer stems, a more viny growth, and darker colored seed than cultivars developed for oil and protein. Some hay cultivars possess a delayed abscission of leaves. Either hay or oil cultivars may be planted for hay. Soybean hay is difficult to cure and is subject to loss of leaves and to spoilage. The crop should be cut during good drying conditions and when the seed is about half developed.

COWPEA

The cowpea, *Vigna sinensis* (L.) Savi ex Hassk., is best adapted to the southeastern U.S., where it was one of the most extensively grown legumes. It may be used for hay, pasture, silage, soil improvement, or human food. The hectarage of this species for forage has decreased greatly; the last estimate available is 20,000 ha for hay in 1964. It is especially adapted to a variety of soils under adverse conditions.

The species is viny or semiviny with weak stems, large leaves, and many curved beanlike pods. Seed are kidney shaped and vary in color with the cultivar. Cowpeas should be cut for hay later in maturity than soybeans, when the first pods begin to yellow and prior to leaf drop.

PEANUT

The peanut, *Arachis hypogaea* L., is grown for seed and as a food product in the coastal plain of the southeastern U.S. About 20% of the 600,000-ha harvest also is utilized for peanut-vine hay, a by-product of the seed industry. In the 1950s most of the vines were utilized for hay; the change is a result of the development of the combine method of harvest. About 3% of the peanuts grown in the U.S. are con-

sumed in the field by fattening swine.

OTHER SPECIES

Alyceclover, *Alysicarpus vaginalis* (L.) DC., and hairy indigo, *Indigofera hirsuta* L., were introduced into the U.S. about 1910. Both are adapted to the Gulf Coast. Alyceclover is a low-spreading, rather coarse-stemmed leafy plant that makes good quality hay if cut in early bloom. Hairy indigo plants are coarse and may attain a height of 2 m or more. The leaves are pinnate and resemble those of vetch except they are larger and covered with short pubescence. Hairy indigo must be cut early for hay, as stems become woody with age. Rotational grazing should be practiced to prevent too severe removal of leaves.[53] Small hectarages of hairy indigo and alyceclover are reported in Florida and Texas respectively. Florida velvetbean, *Stizolobium deeringianum* Bort., is used in southern Georgia and northern Florida for late fall and winter pasture. The large-leaved species is planted with corn, since the 3- to 10-m viny stems need support. Pods are 5–15 cm in length with four to eight large kidney-shaped seed. Interest in this species has increased because velvetbean seed is an excellent source of the drug L-dopa used in the treatment of Parkinson's disease.

Guar, *Cyamopsis tetragonoloba* (L.) Taub., is a coarse, upright, branching plant with inconspicuous flowers and long leathery pods. It may be used for soil improvement or forage; and the seed is produced as a source of mannogalactan, an industrial gum used in food, paper, and textile products. Cultivars 'Brooks,' 'Hall,' and 'Mills' are well adapted to Texas and Oklahoma.

Florida beggarweed, *Desmodium purpureum* Fawc. & Rend., behaves as a summer annual in Florida and may be used for pasture or soil improvement. It is an upright branching plant attaining a height of 2 m or more.

52. Johnson, H. W., J. L. Cartter, and E. E. Hartwig. 1967. Growing soybeans. USDA Farmers' Bull. 2129.

53. Wallace, Alvin T. 1957. Hairy indigo—A summer legume for Florida. Fla. Agr. Exp. Sta. Circ. S-98.

Limited hectarages of Townsville stylo, *Stylosanthes humilis* H.B.K., and American jointvetch, *Aeschynomene americana* L., are reported in Florida.

Some tropical legumes are of promise to Florida, especially if they can be improved for cold resistance and an earlier maturity allowing good seed set.[54]

A breeding program is in progress at the Georgia coastal plain station to produce a hyacinth bean, *Dolichos lablab* L., cultivar that sets seed at that latitude.

The *Crotalaria* species are generally no longer recommended for either soil improvement or forage purposes because of their poisonous seed, which are toxic to chickens and livestock when harvested as a contaminant in feed-grain crops such as corn and soybeans. Some species also contain toxic substances in the leaves. The

---

54. Kretschmer, Albert E., Jr. 1970. Production of annual and perennial tropical legumes in mixtures with pangolagrass and other grasses in Florida. Proc. 11th Int. Grassl. Congr., pp. 149–53. (Surfers Paradise, Queensland, Aust.).

'Norman' pigeonpea, *Cajanus cajan* (L.) Millsp., is a suggested replacement for crotalaria for improvement of poorer soils of North Carolina.

℞ QUESTIONS

1. What are the present limiting factors in the use of crownvetch as a forage crop in the U.S.?
2. What are the two most promising dryland pasture legumes? Why?
3. List the characteristics which enable winter annual legumes to persist in perennial warm-season grass pastures.
4. How do blue, yellow, and white lupines differ in adaptation?
5. What special precautions must be taken in the curing and storing of soybean and cowpea hay?
6. What management practice gives good control of kudzu?
7. Name the perennial and annual species of clover which tolerate flooding conditions in the western U.S.

SUPPLEMENTAL LITERATURE CITATIONS

Cooper, Clee S. 1972. Establishment, hay yield and persistence of two sainfoin (*Onobrychis viciaefolia* Scop.) growth types seeded alone with low growing grasses and legumes. *Agron. J.* 64:379–81.

——. 1972. Growth analysis of two sainfoin (*Onobrychis viciaefolia* Scop.) cultivars. *Agron. J.* 64:611–13.

Davis, A. M. 1972. Selenium accumulation in *Astragalus* species. *Agron. J.* 64:751–54.

McKee, G. W., M. L. Resius, and A. R. Langille. 1972. Flowering of crownvetch as affected by thermo-inductive treatment, photoperiod, plant age, and genotype. *Crop Sci.* 12:553–57.

Rahman, M. S., and J. S. Gladstones. 1972. Control of lupine flower initiation by vernalization, photoperiod and temperature under controlled environments. *Aust. J. Exp. Agr. Anim. Husb.* 12:638–45.

Smoliak, S., A. Johnston, and M. R. Hanna. 1972. Germination and seedling growth of alfalfa, sainfoin and cicer milkvetch. *Can. J. Plant Sci.* 52:757–62.

Cooper, Clee S. 1973. Sainfoin-birdsfoot trefoil mixtures for pasture, hay-pasture, and hay-stockpile management regimes. *Agron. J.* 65:752–54.

Davis, A. M. 1973. Protein, crude fiber, tannin, and oxalate concentrations of some introduced *Astragalus* species. *Agron. J.* 65:613–15.

Melton, Bill. 1973. Evaluations of sainfoin and cicer milkvetch in New Mexico. N. Mex. State Univ. Agr. Exp. Sta. Res. Rept. 255.

Townsend, C. E., and W. J. McGinnies. 1973. Factors influencing vegetative growth and flowering in *Astragalus cicer* L. *Crop Sci.* 13:262–64.

Brann, D. E., and G. A. Jung. 1974. Influence of cutting management and environmental variation on the yield, bud activity, and autumn carbohydrate reserve levels of crownvetch. *Agron. J.* 66:767–73.

Burns, J. C., and W. A. Cope. 1974. The nutritive value of crownvetch forages as influenced by structural constituents and phenolic and tannin compounds. *Agron. J.* 66:195–200.

Hollings, E., and C. A. Stace. 1974. Karyotype variation and evolution in the *Vivia sativa* aggregate. *New Phytol.* 73:195–208.

Townsend, C. E. 1974. Productivity of several perennial forage legumes under irrigation and frequent cutting. Colo. State Univ. Exp. Sta. Bull. 562-S.

——. 1974. Selection for seedling vigor in cicer milkvetch. *Agron. J.* 66:241–45.

Forbes, I., J. S. Gladstones, and H. D. Wells. 1975. Gray leaf spot-resistant *Lupinus angustifolius* L. germplasm from plant exploration in the western Mediterranean region. *Crop Sci.* 15:867–68.

Gladstones, J. S. 1975. Lupine breeding in Western Australia. *J. Agr. West. Aust.* 16:44–49.

Johnston, A., S. Smoliak, M. R. Hanna, and R. Hironaka. 1975. Cicer milkvetch for Western Canada. Can. Dept. Agr. Publ. 1536.

Sears, R. G., R. L. Ditterline, and D. E. Mathre. 1975. Crown and root rotting organisms affecting sainfoin (*Onobrychis viciifolia*) in Montana. *Plant Dis. Reptr.* 59:423–26.

Smoliak, S., and M. R. Hanna. 1975. Productivity of alfalfa, sainfoin, and cicer milkvetch on subirrigated land when grazed by sheep. *Can J. Plant Sci.* 55:415–20.

Tolin, Sue A., and John D. Miller. 1975. Peanut stunt virus in crownvetch. *Phytopathology* 65:321–24.

Townsend, C. E., and W. D. Ackerman. 1975. Variability for vigor, height, and flowering in introductions of cicer milkvetch. *Can. J. Plant Sci.* 55:843–45.

Smoliak, S., and A. Johnston. 1976. Variability in forage and seed production and seedling growth in *Astragalus cicer*. *Can. J. Plant Sci.* 56:487–91.

Townsend, C. E. 1976. Combining ability for seedling dry weight and forage yield in cicer milkvetch. *Crop Sci.* 16:480–82.

Hanna, M. R., G. C. Kozub, and S. Smoliak. 1977. Forage production of sainfoin and alfalfa on dryland in mixed- and alternate-row seedings with three grasses. *Can. J. Plant Sci.* 57:61–70.

Townsend, C. E. 1977. Germination of cicer milkvetch seed as affected by year of production. *Crop Sci.* 17:909–12.

——. 1977. Recurrent selection for high seed weight in cicer milkvetch. *Crop Sci.* 17:473–76.

Townsend, C. E., D. K. Christensen, and A. D. Dotzenko. 1978. Yield and quality of cicer milkvetch forage as influenced by cutting frequency. *Agron. J.* 70:109–13.

GEORGE A. ROGLER / *Agricultural Research Service, USDA*

21

THE WHEATGRASSES

THE WHEATGRASSES belong to the genus *Agropyron,* one of the most important genera used as forage in the temperate regions of the world. The *Agropyrons* are of the tribe Hordeae which includes wheat, rye, barley, and forage grasses. Wheatgrasses originally were considered in the same genus with wheat. The first-named species of *Agropyron* were placed under *Triticum,* the generic name of wheat.[1] The common name "wheatgrass" probably was applied because seed heads of many of the species resemble those of wheat. The scientific name *Agropyron* is from the Greek *agrios,* wild, and *puros,* wheat.

The wheatgrasses are in general cross-pollinated but are not completely self-sterile. Slender wheatgrass, *A. trachycaulum* (Link) Malte, is one species which is largely self-pollinated. Numerous intergeneric and interspecific hybrids have been reported, with various wheatgrass species involved.[2-6] Successful crosses have been made between various species and types of wheat—primarily with tall, *A. elongatum* (Host) Beauv.; intermediate, *A. intermedium* (Host) Beauv.; and pubescent, *A. trichophorum* (Link) Richt., wheatgrasses. There also have been crosses with rye. Forage grasses which cross either naturally or artificially with wheatgrasses include species in the *Elymus, Hordeum,* and *Sitanion* genera. With the exception of some natural hybridization that evidently occurs between pubescent and intermediate wheatgrass and within the crested wheatgrass complex, no agronomically important hybrids have been developed as yet from any of the intergeneric or interspecific crosses.

The first native grass to be domesticated and introduced into American agriculture was a wheatgrass. K. McIver of Virden, Man., is said to have first seeded slender

GEORGE A. ROGLER (retired) was Research Leader for the Forage and Range Management and Grass Breeding Research Unit, ARS, USDA, Mandan, N. Dak. He did graduate work at the University of Minnesota and received an honorary D.Sc. degree from North Dakota State University. Nordan crested wheatgrass is one of several grasses developed and released from his breeding program.

1. Dayton, W. A., et al. 1937. Range plant handbook. U.S. Forest Serv.
2. Myers, W. M. 1947. Cytology and genetics of forage grasses. *Bot. Rev.* 13:319–421.
3. Stebbins, G. L., J. I. Valencia, and R. Marie Valencia. 1946. Artificial and natural hybrids in the Gramineae, tribe Hordeae. I. *Elymus, Sitanion,* and *Agropyron. Amer. J. Bot.* 33:338–51.
4. Stebbins, G. L., J. I. Valencia, and R. Marie Valencia. 1946. Artificial and natural hybrids in the Gramineae, tribe Hordeae. II. *Agropyron, Elymus,* and *Hordeum. Amer. J. Bot.* 33:579–86.
5. Nielsen, Etlar L. 1956. Cytology and breeding behavior of a natural Agroelymus hybrid. *Bot. Gaz.* 118:79–88.
6. Dewey, D. R. 1964. Genome analysis of *Agropyron repens* × *Agropyron cristatum* synthetic hybrids. *Amer. J. Bot.* 51:1062–68.

TABLE 21.1 ❧ Common and scientific names and miscellaneous characteristics of important species of wheatgrass, *Agropyron* spp.

Common name	Scientific name	Native (N) or introduced (I)	Bunch (B) or sod (S) type	Number seed per kg	Chromosome number
Fairway	*A. cristatum* (L.) Gaertn.	I	B	551,000	14
Thickspike	*A. dasystachyum* (Hook.) Scribn.	N	S	344,000	28
Crested	*A. desertorum* (Fisch. ex Link) Schult.	I	B	386,000	28
Tall	*A. elongatum* (Host) Beauv.	I	B	187,000	14,56,70
Beardless	*A. inerme* (Scribn. & Smith) Rydb.	N	B	298,000	14,28
Intermediate	*A. intermedium* (Host) Beauv.	I	S	205,000	28,42
Quackgrass	*A. repens* (L.) Beauv.	I	S	242,000	28,42
Streambank	*A. riparium* Scribn. & Smith	N	S	375,000	42
Siberian	*A. sibiricum* (Willd.) Beauv.	I	B	496,000	28
Western	*A. smithii* Rydb.	N	S	242,000	42,56
Bluebunch	*A. spicatum* (Pursh) Scribn. & Smith	N	B	309,000	14,28
Slender	*A. trachycaulum* (Link) Malte	N	B	309,000	28
Pubescent	*A. trichophorum* (Link) Richt.	I	S	298,000	42

wheatgrass in 1885.[7] From this planting its use in seedings spread throughout Canada and the western U.S. Crested wheatgrass, *A. desertorum* (Fisch. ex Link) Schult., an introduced species, came into general use in the 1930s. Many native and introduced wheatgrasses have been tested and released.

❧ DISTRIBUTION AND ADAPTATION

About 150 species of wheatgrasses are widely distributed throughout the temperate regions of the world. Over 30 species are native to North America and about 100 species to Eurasia, most of them in areas of desert or steppe soils under semihumid to arid climatic conditions. A few species occur in southern South America.

Native wheatgrasses predominate in vast areas of the central and northern Great Plains, the intermountain region, and higher altitudes in the Rocky Mountains of the U.S. and Canada. Thirteen species have been reported growing in Alaska, three of which were introduced from Siberia.[8] Quackgrass, *A. repens* (L.) Beauv.,

is the most prominent of the wheatgrasses found in the eastern U.S. Because of its creeping rhizomes and aggressive characteristics, quackgrass has become a troublesome weed throughout many of the eastern and north central states and irrigated areas of the West. Maps showing the producing areas of six of the important wheatgrasses are only general in character.

❧ PLANT DESCRIPTION

The important wheatgrasses are perennial and are classified as cool-season species. Most species are either sod forming from strong creeping rhizomes or have a bunch type of growth which is increased in size by tillering. The division of species by the presence or absence of rhizomes usually is definite, but occasional plants of bunch types may have rhizomes and the usual sod types may not. Since most species are highly cross-pollinated, there is wide variability within species in plant type and in vegetative and floral characteristics. Hitchcock is one of the best sources on identity of species.[9]

Table 21.1 shows the common and scientific names, whether native or introduced, whether sod or bunch type, the number of

7. Waldron, L. R., and W. R. Porter. 1919. Bromegrass, slender wheatgrass and timothy. N. Dak. Agr. Exp. Sta. Circ. 24

8. Aamodt, O. S., and D. A. Savage. 1949. Cereal, forage, and range problems and possibilities in Alaska. Report on exploratory investigations of agricultural problems in Alaska. USDA Misc. Publ. 700, pp. 87–124.

9. Hitchcock, A. S. 1951. Manual of the grasses of the United States. USDA Misc. Publ. 200, rev.

Fig. 21.1. *No other group . . . grasses exceeds . . . the wheatgrasses in the West for the production of highly nutritious, early season forage.* Mixed prairie rangeland near Mandan, N. Dak., of which western wheatgrass is a primary species. *USDA photo.*

seed per kilogram, and the chromosome number of 13 of the most important species.[10] The seed per kilogram are the average of a number of lots. There is wide variation between and within lots depending on strain, growth conditions, and condition and handling at harvest. The germination of seed of most wheatgrasses is rapid, but a few species such as western wheatgrass, *A. smithii* Rydb., and tall wheatgrass may show delayed germination.

❧ IMPORTANCE AND USE

No other group of closely related grasses exceeds the importance of wheatgrasses in the West for the production of highly nutritious early season forage. They also are unexcelled for wind and water erosion control. The vast areas of native wheatgrasses exceed 121 million ha in the western U.S.[11]

10. Hanson, A. A., and H. L. Carnahan. 1956. Breeding perennial forage grasses. USDA Tech. Bull. 1145.
11. Newell, L. C. 1955. Wheatgrasses in the west. *Crops and Soils* 8:7–9.

In addition several million ha of introduced and native species have been seeded on depleted rangelands and on land taken out of crop production (Fig. 21.1).

The most important native wheatgrasses are: the western wheatgrass that grows primarily in the central and northern Great Plains; bluebunch wheatgrass, *A. spicatum* (Pursh) Scribn. & Smith, in the northern intermountain region; and slender wheatgrass which is widespread over the mountains, foothills, and high plains. Crested wheatgrass is the most important introduced species.

❧ SPECIES AND CULTIVARS

NATIVE SPECIES

WESTERN WHEATGRASS. This widely distributed, long-lived, sod-forming grass is of major importance in the central and northern Great Plains. It commonly is associated with blue grama, buffalograss, and the needlegrasses in the plains grassland.

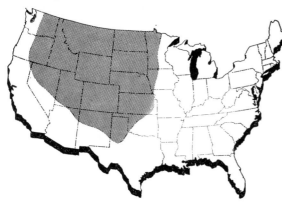

FIG. 21.2. Western wheatgrass–producing areas of the U.S.

In the intermountain areas it often is mixed with bluebunch and thickspike, *A. dasystachyum* (Hook.) Scribn., wheatgrasses on sagebrush rangeland. Pure stands often are found on the heavy and more or less alkaline soils characteristic of the valleys of meandering streams, "gumbo flats," intermittent swales, and shallow lake beds subject to overflow or excess surface drainage from spring runoff. Few other economically important grasses are as tolerant to alkali soils. In the Great Plains it is one of the first grasses to become reestablished on land once cultivated. (See Fig. 21.2.)

Western wheatgrass produces an abundance of forage early in the season before blue grama or buffalograss begin growth. It is readily eaten by livestock until it becomes harsh and fibrous during late summer. The grass cures well on the stem and provides good winter grazing. If grazed too closely over an extended period the plants are soon weakened and will disappear from the stand. Hay yields of 2.3 t/ha were obtained on typical northern plains upland during a favorable year when 100 kg/ha of N were applied.[12]

Western wheatgrass spreads rapidly and forms a dense sod, making it valuable for erosion control. It can be readily transplanted and used for sodding terrace outlets. Plants develop slowly from seed, but

once established are vigorous, hardy, and drought resistant. Most seed harvested is from native stands, but the crop is uncertain and seed is often in short supply.

'Barton' was released in Kansas in 1970 with superior forage production and rust resistance.

'Mandan 456' was selected in North Dakota for vigor, forage quality, and rust resistance.

Other numbered cultivars are being tested at various locations in the western states.

SLENDER WHEATGRASS. This native perennial bunchgrass is distributed from Newfoundland to Alaska; south to the central U.S.; and to California, Arizona, and New Mexico in the Southwest. It was the first native forage grass to be generally used for seeding in western Canada and the U.S. It is a valuable grass on rangeland in the Rocky Mountain states and northern Great Plains. (See Fig. 21.3.)

Slender wheatgrass is more readily established than most grasses because of its high germination and vigorous seedlings. The plants are relatively short lived and should be planted in a mixture with other species. The grass is highly tolerant to alkali soils but is less drought resistant than western or crested wheatgrass.

'Primar' is a superior cultivar of slender wheatgrass, developed in the state of Wash-

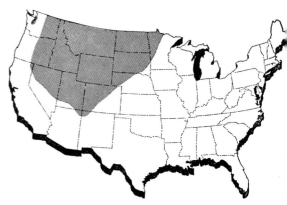

FIG. 21.3. Slender wheatgrass–producing areas of the U.S.

12. Rogler, George A., and Russell J. Lorenz. 1957. Nitrogen fertilization of northern Great Plains rangelands. *J. Range Manage.* 10:156–60.

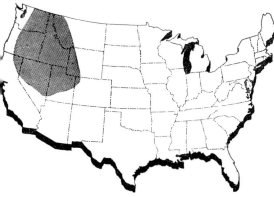

FIG. 21.4. Bluebunch wheatgrass–producing areas of the U.S.

ington.[13] Slender wheatgrass is used extensively in the Pacific Northwest.

'Revenue,' a cultivar developed and released in Canada in 1970, has shown superior establishment ability, salinity tolerance, forage quality, and yield at several western locations in that country.[14]

BLUEBUNCH WHEATGRASS. This long-lived, drought-resistant bunchgrass is widely distributed, ranging from Alaska southward throughout the western U.S. Because of its abundance, high palatability, and nutritive qualities, it is one of the most important native western range plants. Bluebunch wheatgrass withstands proper grazing well but will soon succumb to overstocking and too early grazing. (See Fig. 21.4.)

Seed production is good under favorable conditions. The seed is heavy but because of its awns must be processed to permit satisfactory seeding. Closely related beardless wheatgrass, *A. inerme* (Scribn. & Smith) Rydb., has been more popular for reseeding purposes.

BEARDLESS WHEATGRASS. This grass, sometimes called beardless bluebunch wheatgrass, is similar in growth habit to bluebunch wheatgrass except that it has no awns, or occasionally only short awns. It has the same general area of distribution but is not as abundant as bluebunch wheatgrass.

'Whitmar' is a superior cultivar developed at Pullman, Wash., and released in 1946.[13] It is adapted to the same types of planting as crested wheatgrass in the Northwest but should be grazed later in the season. Seed is readily produced in row plantings and is available commercially.

THICKSPIKE WHEATGRASS. This sod-forming grass has a wider range of distribution than many other wheatgrasses. It occurs from Hudson Bay to Alaska; south throughout the western U.S. to Nevada, Utah, and Colorado; and along the shores of lakes Superior, Michigan, and Huron. It is common in the intermountain region. Thickspike wheatgrass does well on light-textured soils and is found on dry hillsides, exposed ridges, and benchlands up to altitudes of at least 3050 m. It starts growth early in the spring and provides good pasturage until it becomes wiry as the season advances.

'Critana,' developed in Montana, is strongly rhizomatous with good seed production and high seedling vigor. Its main use is for stabilization of roadsides, airports, recreation areas, and construction sites.

STREAMBANK WHEATGRASS, *A. riparium* Scribn. & Smith. This sod-forming grass is found from Montana westward to Washington; north into Alberta and British Columbia; and south to Nevada, Utah, and Colorado. It is drought tolerant and valuable for ground cover, as its dense sod is highly resistant to erosion. Top growth is relatively short and this wheatgrass is lower in forage production than several others. It is well adapted for use on roadsides, airports, and irrigation canal banks.

'Sodar' wheatgrass is a cultivar released in 1954 in Idaho and Washington.[15]

13. Hafenrichter, A. L., J. L. Schwendiman, H. L. Harris, R. S. McLauchlan, and H. W. Miller. 1968. Grasses and legumes for soil conservation in the Pacific Northwest and Great Basin states. USDA SCS Agr. Handbook 339.
14. Crowle, W. L. 1970. Revenue slender wheatgrass. *Can. J. Plant Sci.* 50:748–49.

15. Douglas, Donald S., and Ronald D. Ensign. 1954. Sodar wheatgrass. Idaho Agr. Exp. Sta. Bull. 234.

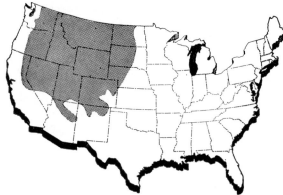

FIG. 21.5. Crested wheatgrass–producing areas of the U.S.

INTRODUCED SPECIES

CRESTED WHEATGRASS. Crested wheatgrass is a hardy, drought-resistant, perennial bunchgrass, native to the cold dry plains of eastern Russia, western Siberia, and central Asia. After an earlier introduction failed,[16] it became widely distributed throughout the West from an introduction from Russian Turkestan in 1906. Crested wheatgrass is especially well adapted to the northern Great Plains and westward to the Sierra Nevada where it has been valuable for regrassing abandoned croplands and depleted rangelands.[17] It has been most successful in areas with 230–380 mm of rainfall, except in more southern locations where from 300 to 380 mm are required. In the more southern areas it has given best results at altitudes of 1500 m or more. The higher elevational limits are from 2600 to 2800 m. (See Fig. 21.5.)

It does well on most productive soils, from light sandy loams to heavy clays. It is low in tolerance to alkali soils and will not persist under prolonged flooding.[18]

Highly cross-pollinated and variable in plant and head type, some plants of crested wheatgrass are leafy and fine stemmed, while others are coarse, with few leaves and stiff stems. Inflorescences may be lax or dense, with seed having pronounced awns, short awns, or none. Seed shatters soon after maturity, and seedlings volunteer readily. A deep, fibrous, extensive root system results in excellent drought resistance. The grass becomes more or less dormant during hot dry periods. Much of the growth of crested wheatgrass is made in early spring; and because of its high production, excellent palatability, and good nutritive qualities it is of special value for early pasture before native grasses are ready for grazing.[19]

Crested wheatgrass is extremely long lived. There have been no reports of established stands being killed by cold and few reports of drought killing except in areas where it is not adapted. The oldest presently identifiable planting in the U.S. was made in 1915 on the Northern Great Plains Research Center, Mandan, N. Dak.

For a period shortly after its introduction until 1950 crested wheatgrass was thought of as one species, *A. cristatum*. Standard crested wheatgrass should be *A. desertorum* (Fisch. ex Link) Schult. and fairway crested wheatgrass, *A. cristatum* (L.) Gaertn.[20] A number of species make up the so-called crested wheatgrass complex and may involve mechanical mixtures from seed or hybrids between closely related species.[21-25]

'Nordan,' a cultivar of crested wheatgrass developed at the Northern Great Plains Research Center, was first released

16. Dillman, A. C. 1946. The beginnings of crested wheatgrass in North America. *J. Amer. Soc. Agron.* 38:237–50.

17. Rogler, George A. 1960. Growing crested wheatgrass in the western states. USDA Leaflet 469.

18. Forsberg, D. E. 1953. The response of various forage crops to saline soils. *Can. J. Sci.* 33:532–49.

19. Rogler, G. A., and R. J. Lorenz. 1969. Pasture productivity of crested wheatgrass as influenced by nitrogen fertilization and alfalfa. USDA Tech. Bull. 1402.

20. Swallen, Jason R., and George A. Rogler. 1950. The status of crested wheatgrass. *Agron. J.* 42:571.

21. Creel, G. C., J. E. Ericson, and J. Schulz-Schaeffer. 1965. Biosystematic investigations in the genus *Agropyron* Gaertn. III. Serological, morphological, and cytological comparison of species within the crested wheatgrass complex (section *Agropyron*). *Crop Sci.* 5:316–20.

22. Dewey, D. R. 1960. Cytogenetics of crested wheatgrass. Rept. 14th Ann. Western Grass Breeders Work Planning Conf., pp. 35–37.

23. Jones, K. 1960. Taxonomic and biosystematic problems in the crested wheatgrasses. Rept. 14th Ann. Western Grass Breeders Work Planning Conf., pp. 29–34.

24. Knowles, R. P. 1955. A study of variability in crested wheatgrass. *Can. J. Bot.* 33:534–46.

25. Sarkar, P. 1956. Crested wheatgrass complex. *Can. J. Bot.* 34:328–45.

FIG. 21.6. *Nordan . . . crested wheatgrass . . . superior . . . in quality of seed and seedling vigor.* An individual plant of Nordan showing its erect growth and dense awnless heads. *USDA photo.*

by the North Dakota station in 1954.[26] It is superior to commercial crested wheatgrass in quality of seed and seedling vigor and is now widely grown throughout the West (Fig. 21.6).

'Summit,' the only other named cultivar for which seed is available, was developed and released in 1953 by the Dominion Forage Crops Laboratory at Saskatoon, Sask.[27] It yields more forage than fairway at most locations in western Canada, grows taller, is somewhat coarser, and seed are considerably larger.

FAIRWAY WHEATGRASS. This drought-resistant bunchgrass is a diploid species distributed in 1927 by the University of Saskatchewan. It was first licensed in Canada as 'Fairway' crested wheatgrass in 1932. The Old World origin of fairway approximates that of other species of the crested wheatgrass complex. One of the original 1906 introductions was the same as or quite similar to fairway wheatgrass.[16] Fairway wheatgrass is grown primarily in Canada but also to some extent in the U.S. The grass is shorter and finer stemmed than crested wheatgrass, seed are smaller with pronounced awns, and seedlings are smaller and less vigorous. Fairway yields somewhat less forage than crested but is more satisfactory for dryland lawns and other turf plantings because of its denser growth and finer appearance. It is generally adapted to higher altitudes and moister sites than crested wheatgrass.

'Parkway,' a cultivar developed and released in Canada, is superior to fairway in forage production and in seed yield and quality.[28] It is not recommended for turf.

SIBERIAN WHEATGRASS. The Old World occurrence of this drought-resistant bunchgrass is about the same as that of crested wheatgrass.[13] A number of introductions have been made but only one— P-27, selected in Washington—has been generally used for seeding purposes. This introduction from the USSR was made by Westover and Enlow in 1934. In some areas it is replacing crested wheatgrass because of its excellent adaptation to poor sites and its ability to do well under adverse conditions. It is closely related to crested wheatgrass and is similar in appearance, but the stems are finer and the heads narrower and more compressed. The seed is slightly smaller and the seedlings less vigorous than those of Nordan crested wheatgrass.

INTERMEDIATE WHEATGRASS. Intermediate wheatgrass is a vigorous sod-forming species native to central Europe, the Balkans, and Asia Minor. It was unsuccessfully introduced in 1907 and the 1920s. The first successful introduction was in 1932 from Maikop in the Caucasus region of Russia. It is well adapted to areas in the eastern Great Plains where the annual rainfall averages 380 mm or more and to many locations at elevations of 1050 m or more in the intermountain region. It is

26. Rogler, G. A. 1954. Nordan crested wheatgrass. N. Dak. Agr. Exp. Sta. Bull. 16, pp. 150–52.
27. Knowles, R. P. 1956. Crested wheatgrass. Can. Dept. Agr. Publ. 986.

28. Elliott, C. R., and J. L. Bolton. 1970. Licensed varieties of cultivated grasses and legumes. Can. Dept. Agr. Publ. 1405.

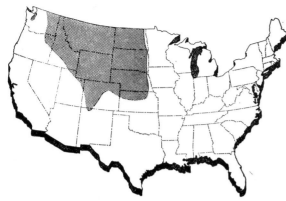

FIG. 21.7. Intermediate and pubescent wheatgrass–producing areas of the U.S.

especially well adapted to parts of the Pacific Northwest. (See Fig. 21.7.)

On well-drained, fertile soils with ample moisture, intermediate wheatgrass grows to a height of as much as 1.2 m or more. Hay yields are higher than for most other adapted grasses, and it makes excellent pasture from early spring to late summer as well. Virtues of the grass are its large seed, ease of establishment, rapid growth, and sod-forming characteristics. It is not as winter-hardy as crested wheatgrass, and if incorrectly managed, stands may deteriorate rapidly. It is not as long lived as crested wheatgrass, and good pasture stands are difficult to maintain for much more than six years.

Cultivars greatly improved in seed production are 'Oahe'[29] and 'Chief,'[28] developed in South Dakota and Saskatchewan respectively. Oahe is a selection from 'Ree,' an older cultivar from the same station.[29,30]

'Greenar' from Washington and 'Amur' from New Mexico are other cultivars.[31]

'Tegmar,' a cultivar released in Idaho in 1968, is a dwarf type developed primarily for erosion control seedings.[32]

29. Ross, J. G., and S. S. Bullis. 1962. Oahe intermediate wheatgrass. S. Dak. Agr. Exp. Sta. Bull. 506.
30. Franske, C. J. 1945. Ree wheatgrass, its culture and use. S. Dak. Agr. Exp. Sta. Circ. 58.
31. Hanson, A. A. 1972. Grass varieties in the United States. USDA Agr. Handbook 170, rev.
32. Harris, H. L., and H. B. Roylance. 1969. Tegmar dwarf intermediate wheatgrass. Idaho Agr. Ext. Serv. Bull. 504.

'Slate' is a Nebraska cultivar released in 1969.[33]

PUBESCENT WHEATGRASS. This sod-forming grass is closely related to intermediate wheatgrass and has the same Old World distribution. The two grasses are quite similar in growth habit, period of growth, and taxonomic characteristics. They differ in that the heads and seed of pubescent wheatgrass are covered with short stiff hairs suggesting the name, "stiff-hair wheatgrass." Plant types intergrade from one species to the other. Commercial seed from the two species usually contain both pubescent and smooth types.

'Topar' is a cultivar released by several cooperating agencies in the Northwest in 1953.[13]

'Mandan 759' was developed in North Dakota and is longer lived and has produced more forage and seed than other cultivars in the northern Great Plains.[31]

'Luna' was developed in New Mexico and released in 1963.[34]

'Trigo,' developed in New Mexico and California and tested under the designation of A-1488 MC, has been superior to other cultivars.[31]

'Greenleaf' is a Canadian cultivar superior in seedling vigor and in forage and seed yields.[28]

TALL WHEATGRASS. Tall wheatgrass is a tall, coarse, late maturing bunchgrass. It is native to saline meadows and seashores of southeastern Europe and Asia Minor. Most plantings in the U.S. are in the West and traceable to seed introduced from the USSR in 1932. (See Fig. 21.8.)

The ability of this grass to establish itself on wet alkaline soils has resulted in its extensive use in reclaiming such areas. Yields are exceptionally high where moisture conditions are favorable. It makes fair hay and can be used successfully for silage. Because of its late maturity, it provides a long graz-

33. Nebraska Crop Improvement Association. 1971. Nebr. Cert. Seed Dir.
34. New Mexico State Univ. 1964. Luna pubescent wheatgrass. N. Mex. Coop. Ext. Serv. Circ. 368.

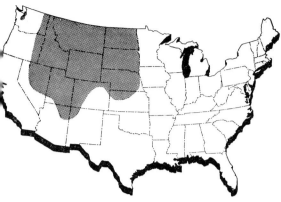

Fig. 21.8. Tall wheatgrass–producing areas of the U.S.

ing period when used for pasture but is not as palatable as most other wheatgrasses.

'Largo,' a New Mexico cultivar, was first released under the designation A-1876 in 1937.[31]

'Jose' is another New Mexico cultivar released in 1965 as a true green type with higher quality forage.[35]

'Alkar' was released in Washington in 1959 and has been used to reclaim large hectarages of saline and alkaline land.[13]

'Orbit' was developed in Canada and first licensed there in 1966.[36] It is a winter-hardy cultivar adapted to wet saline soils in all parts of Canada.

QUACKGRASS. Quackgrass is one of the most widely distributed of all wheatgrasses.

Because of its spread by creeping rootstocks and seed and its aggressive, persistent nature it has become a notorious weed over most of the temperate areas of the world. The history of this grass is somewhat obscure, but it probably is a native of Europe.[37] The first authentic report of the grass in the U.S. was in Connecticut in 1751. It is one of Europe's most troublesome weeds and occurs in every continent of the world. It is most prevalent in the eastern and north central U.S. and in irri-

gated areas of the West. Although quackgrass is so aggressive as to have weedy characteristics, it has good forage qualities and is often used for hay, pasture, or silage in its primary area of adaptation. Its tough sod is useful in holding soil in place on embankments, terraces, and steep slopes. It can be controlled or eradicated with herbicides and power equipment and is no longer the serious weed it was in the past.

❦ CULTURE AND MANAGEMENT

Wheatgrasses are cool-season grasses. In common with most other grasses, the seedlings are tender and require favorable conditions for germination and early growth. Planting of high-quality seed of adapted species at the correct date, a well-prepared seedbed, and proper attention after emergence will ensure the successful establishment of wheatgrasses unless soil moisture conditions are especially unfavorable.

The most favorable time to seed varies with the locality, moisture supply, type of seedbed, and abundance of grasshoppers. In many areas, seedings can be made in early fall if soil moisture is ample so that seedlings will be well started before winter. Other seeding times are late fall (so that germination will be delayed until spring), early spring, and late spring after small weeds have been destroyed by cultivation. Seedings must be made in summer in most mountain areas because of the short season.

A firm seedbed as free of competing plants as possible is of first importance in establishing a stand. Seeding on well-protected summer fallow in early fall or spring is the best method to get seedlings off to a rapid start. Clean grain stubble is another good preparation for early fall seeding. Clean corn ground or lightly worked grain stubble provides a good spring seedbed. Depleted rangelands or rough brush-covered lands will require seedbed preparation. The rangeland can be put in condition with any one of a number of sturdy disk-type machines. In some cases brush can be eliminated by carefully controlled

35. New Mexico State Univ. 1966. Jose tall wheatgrass. N. Mex. Coop. Ext. Serv. Circ. 392.
36. Lawrence, T. 1967. Orbit tall wheatgrass. *Can. J. Plant Sci.* 47:611–12.
37. Kephart, L. W. 1928. Quackgrass. USDA Farmers' Bull. 1307.

burning or by various methods of spraying with chemicals.

Seed must be planted shallow. On heavy soils the depth should not exceed 1.9 cm, on light soils not over 3.8 cm. If possible, seed should be drilled into the soil. Broadcasting is not recommended except for extremely rough terrain. Seeding rates will vary from 4.5 to 11.2 kg/ha depending upon the species, area, site, seed quality, row spacing, and planting method. Most wheatgrasses can be planted successfully in mixtures with other grasses and with alfalfa and sweetclover or other legumes. When seeded with legumes, an alternate-row method is advisable.

❧ SEED PRODUCTION

Most wheatgrasses give good seed yields. Under favorable conditions they can be planted, cultivated, harvested, and the seed cleaned with machinery available on grain farms. Production of seed under dryland conditions is somewhat uncertain, but under irrigation consistent high yields of both seed and forage are obtainable.

Row plantings, both on dryland and under irrigation, produce higher seed yields and better quality seed, and production can be maintained over a longer period. With sod-forming species it is sometimes difficult to keep the grass in rows, but with adequate moisture and fertility good yields can be obtained from solid plantings. Fertilizer N must be applied to maintain high production over the years in both row and solid plantings; P is necessary in some areas.

Seed of wheatgrasses ripen on the head more uniformly than many grasses but shatter easily when mature. Harvest can be with a grain binder, by swathing and pickup combining, or by direct combining. Following direct combining, seed should be dried to avoid heating in storage.

Seed of most species can be prepared for planting by cleaning with a standard farm fanning mill. Seed of species with short awns such as fairway wheatgrass should be processed lightly with a hammer mill or similar machine to facilitate handling and seeding.

❧ QUESTIONS

1. What was the first domesticated native grass introduced into American agriculture? Where is it generally grown and why is it popular?
2. List the major species of the native wheatgrasses grown in the U.S. Give the general area of adaptation for each and how it is best utilized.
3. Why is western wheatgrass one of the first grasses to become reestablished on land once cultivated? How is this grass best utilized?
4. What other sod-forming wheatgrasses besides western wheatgrass are superior for erosion control?
5. Why has crested wheatgrass become the most valuable of the introduced grasses for seeding in the West?
6. Account for the wide variability in crested wheatgrass plants.
7. Why has there been some conflict in the use of the names crested wheatgrass and fairway wheatgrass?
8. What are the main virtues of intermediate wheatgrass?
9. To what extent is quackgrass used as a forage crop? Why?
10. What measures should be taken to ensure the successful seeding and establishment of wheatgrasses?

SUPPLEMENTAL INFORMATION

Several new cultivars of wheatgrasses have been released since the first printing of the third edition of this book. Western wheatgrasses include 'Rosana'[38] from Montana, 'Arriba'[39] from New Mexico, and 'Flintlock'[40] from Nebraska. Other new cultivars from Nebraska are 'Ruff' crested wheatgrass[41] and 'Platte' tall wheatgrass[42].

38. USDA-SCS and Mont. Agr. Exp. Sta. 1972. Notice of release of Rosana western wheatgrass.
39. N. Mex. Coop. Ext. Serv. 1977. Arriba western wheatgrass. Circ. 475.
40. Nebr. Agr. Exp. Sta. and USDA-ARS. 1975. Notice of release of Flintlock western wheatgrass.
41. Nebr. Agr. Exp. Sta. and USDA-ARS. 1974. Notice of release of Ruff crested wheatgrass.
42. Nebr. Agr. Exp. Sta. and USDA-ARS. 1972. Notice of release of Platte tall wheatgrass.

JOHN L. SCHWENDIMAN AND VIRGIL B. HAWK
Soil Conservation Service, USDA

22

OTHER GRASSES FOR THE NORTH AND WEST

❧

SINCE 1930 when slender wheatgrass was the only native American grass of importance under cultivation, many other native grasses have been domesticated. The use of native grasses received its greatest impetus in the droughts of the 1930s during the Dust Bowl years. Concurrent with this was a growing national recognition of soil erosion and its control by use of native grasses in the low-rainfall areas. Large-scale collection of native grass seed by the plant materials centers of the SCS made extensive reseeding possible.

The nine grazing regions of the West, homogeneous as to plant composition or range value, are tall grass, short grass, desert grass, bunchgrass, northern shrub, southern shrub, chaparral, piñon-juniper, and coniferous forest.

Regions based on geography, climate, soils, and vegetation are the Corn Belt, Great Plains, intermountain states, and Pacific Coast. Excellent keys for botanical descriptions may be found in Hitchcock.[1] Descriptions have been prepared by Dayton et al.[2] Colored plates of important native grasses are available.[3]

❧ USES FOR NATIVE GRASSES

Native grasses and closely related introduced species are used chiefly for reseeding abandoned farmlands, severely eroded sites, droughty soils, rangelands, and other areas where common cultivated grasses often fail. As predicted in the nineteenth century, a persistent faith coupled with improvement by plant breeding has led to the development of named improved cultivars of many native grasses.[4-6]

❧ JOHN L. SCHWENDIMAN (retired) was Plant Materials Specialist, SCS, Pullman, Wash. He did graduate work at Washington State University. He has been active in the development of legumes and the 'Alkar,' 'Cougar,' 'Durar,' 'Greenar,' 'Latar,' 'Manchar,' and other "ar" grasses at the Pullman Plant Materials Center.

❧ VIRGIL B. HAWK was Plant Materials Specialist, SCS, Cape May, N.J., before his retirement. He received the M.S. degree from Washington State University and the Ph.D. from Iowa State University. He has worked in many states west of the Mississippi and was among the group that began studies on the development of native grasses for soil conservation in the 1930s.

1. Hitchcock, A. S. 1951. Manual of the grasses of the U.S. USDA Misc. Publ. 200, rev.
2. Dayton, W. A., in charge. 1937. Range plant handbook. U.S. Forest Serv.
3. Phillips Petroleum Co. 1964. Pasture and Range Plants. Bartlesville, Okla.
4. Smith, J. G. 1895. A note on experimental grass gardens. USDA Div. Agrostology, Circ. 1.
5. Hafenrichter, A. L. 1958. New grasses and legumes for soil and water conservation. *Advan. Agron.* 10:349–406.
6. Atkins, M. D., and J. E. Smith, Jr. 1967. Grass seed production and harvest in the Great Plains. USDA Farmers' Bull. 2226.

231

FIG. 22.1. *Native grasses . . . the result of thousands of years of natural selection . . . result . . . very different ecological types.* Sideoats grama grown at Manhattan, Kans., from seed obtained from (A) North Dakota, (B) Nebraska, (C) Kansas, (D) Oklahoma, and (E) Texas.

Cultural and management practices have not been completely developed for many species. Companion crops are not generally used with many of these grasses, but noncompetitive cover crops grown prior to seeding grass are extremely helpful in establishing grass stands in the Great Plains.[7]

The native grasses—bluestems, gramas, some wheatgrasses, and buffalograss—are the result of thousands of years of natural selection. (See Fig. 22.1.) The types best adapted to the environmental conditions of a local area were able to persist and reproduce locally through the years. As the environment varied, many ecological types developed. Seed harvested from indigenous stands toward the northern limit of natural distribution produce a very different growth from seed harvested from indigenous stands to the south. This is especially true of the time of flowering, maturity, and productivity. For this reason it is very important to use locally harvested seed or seed of improved cultivars of known adaptation and performance.

Native grass seed are often low in quality. Some species like little bluestem are difficult to clean, and buffalograss is difficult to germinate. Some species like Can-

ada wildrye have awns or appendages which interfere with seeding. (See Fig. 22.2.) Such undesirable characteristics have prompted establishment by broadcasting hay containing viable seed.[8] Some species may be propagated vegetatively.[9]

Positive-feed fertilizer spreaders have been effectively used for broadcasting trashy seed. Seed dilution with rice hulls, sawdust, and cracked grain can be used to facilitate drilling chaffy seed. Improved processing methods have eliminated some of the need for special drills for handling native grass seed.[10] Low percentages of pure live seed have made the establishment of some native grasses difficult and expensive (Table 22.1).

Seed production of some native grasses has been difficult; therefore, much seed has been collected directly from wild stands. Seed of a few native warm-season grasses is now produced under cultivation.[11-13] Seed can be profitably produced under favorable climatic conditions of the Corn Belt adjacent to the Great Plains, in the West, and under irrigation.[14-16]

Many grasses have been introduced from foreign lands.[17] Improvement of native range depends upon the use of both native and introduced grasses.[18]

The following brief descriptions of several important species are from regional compilations on native grasses. Publica-

8. Wenger, L. E. 1941. Reestablishing native grasses by the hay method. Kans. Agr. Exp. Sta. Circ. 208.
9. Savage, D. A. 1934. Methods of reestablishing buffalograss on cultivated land in the Great Plains. USDA Circ. 328.
10. Schwendiman, J. L., R. F. Sackman, and A. L. Hafenrichter. 1940. Processing seed of grasses and other plants to remove awns and appendages. USDA Circ. 558.
11. Hamilton, L. P., and W. M. Wootan. 1950. Grass seed production. Ariz. Agr. Exp. Sta. Bull. 228.
12. Cooper, H. W., J. E. Smith, Jr., and M. D. Atkins. 1957. Producing and harvesting grass seed in the Great Plains. USDA Farmers' Bull. 2112.
13. Cornelius, D. R. 1950. Seed production of native grasses under cultivation in eastern Kansas. *Ecol. Monogr.* 20:1–29.
14. Hawk, V. B. 1957. Native grass seed. *Crops and Soils* 9:18–19.
15. Oman, H. F., and R. H. Stark. 1951. Grass seed production on irrigated land. USDA SCS Leaflet 300.
16. Windle, L. C., H. C. McKay, and R. B. Foster. 1966. Grass seed production in southern Idaho dryland farms. Idaho Agr. Exp. Sta. Bull. 473.
17. Weintraub, F. C. 1953. Grasses introduced into the United States. USDA Agr. Handbook 58.
18. Schwendiman, J. L. 1956. Improvement of native range through new grass introduction. *J. Range Manage.* 9:91–95.

7. Savage, D. A. 1939. Grass culture and range improvement in the central and southern Great Plains. USDA Circ. 491.

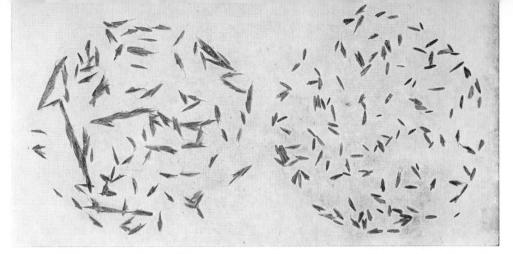

FIG. 22.2. *Some species . . . difficult to clean . . . have appendages which interfere with seeding.* Modern mechanized seeding was made possible with the development of the hammer mill method of seed processing or the use of a debearder to improve seed of big bluestem, little bluestem, Canada wildrye, grama grasses, and indiangrass. Big bluestem seed unprocessed (left); processed seed (right). *Iowa SCS photo.*

tions are available for grasses of the Southwest, Pacific Northwest, Pacific Southwest, southern Great Plains, northern Great Plains, western Canada, and for the western U.S. in general.[19-25]

19. Flory, E. L., and C. G. Marshall. 1942. Regrassing for soil protection in the Southwest. USDA Farmers' Bull. 1913.
20. Hafenrichter, A. L., J. L. Schwendiman, H. L. Harris, R. S. MacLauchlan, and H. W. Miller. 1968. Grasses and legumes for conservation in the Pacific Northwest and Great Basin states. USDA Agr. Handbook 339.
21. Sampson, A. W., A. Chase, and D. W. Hedrick. 1951. California grasslands and range forage grasses. Calif. Agr. Exp. Sta. Bull. 724.
22. Allred, B. W., and W. M. Nixon. 1955. Grass for conservation in the southern Great Plains. USDA Farmers' Bull. 2093.
23. Whitman, Warren. 1941. Grass. N. Dak. Agr. Exp. Sta. Bull. 300.

✣ SPECIES FOR DRYLAND AREAS

BLUESTEMS

There are a large number of bluestems, all warm-season grasses. Only three native and two introduced species are important forage crops in this country.

Big bluestem, *Andropogon gerardi* Vitman, often grows higher than 1.8 m at maturity. Its strong deep roots and short

24. Campbell, J. B., K. F. Best, and A. C. Budd. 1956. Range forage plants of the Canadian provinces. Can. Dept. Agr. Publ. 964.
25. Hoover, M. M., M. A. Hein, W. A. Dayton, and C. O. Erlanson. 1948. The main grasses for farm and home. *In* Grass, pp. 639–700. USDA Yearbook Agr.

TABLE 22.1 ✣ Seed quality standards of some important cool-season and warm-season grasses

Grass	Combine purity (%)	Clean seed			
		Purity (%)	Germination (%)	Pure live seed (%)	Pure seed (seed/kg)
Cool-Season Grasses					
Canada wildrye	65	85	70	59.5	233,700
Green needlegrass	70	90	25	22.5	399,100
Russian wildrye	65	95	90	85.5	385,900
Creeping foxtail	60	75	80	60.0	351,700
Warm-Season Grasses					
Big bluestem	40	60	60	36.0	286,700
Indiangrass	50	70	60	42.0	374,900
Sand bluestem	40	50	60	30.0	249,200
Switchgrass	70	95	70	66.5	857,700
Little bluestem	40	50	60	30.0	562,300
Sideoats grama	40	60	70	42.0	421,200
Sand lovegrass	70	95	80	76.0	2,866,500
Blue grama	30	43	70	30.1	1,567,800
Buffalograss	75	90	65	58.5	92,600
Old World bluestem	35	50	60	30.0	1,896,300
Weeping lovegrass	75	95	80	76.0	3,307,500

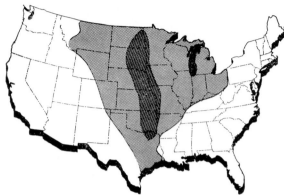

FIG. 22.3. Big bluestem–producing areas of the U.S.

underground stems produce a sod highly resistant to erosion. Growth begins with the warm weather of late spring and continues until fall. Its major distribution is on moist, well-drained loams of relatively high fertility in the central states and on the eastern edge of the Great Plains (Fig. 22.3). The leafy forage is highly palatable to all classes of livestock. It makes good quality hay if mowed before seed heads emerge.

As pasture, big bluestem is palatable and nutritious in its earlier stages of growth. It is vigorous, stands close grazing, and will recover from excessive grazing if protected during the first part of the season. Seed matures in late September and October, and processing is moderately difficult.

Little bluestem, *A. scoparius* Michx., plant height is 0.6–1.2 m. It is more drought resistant than big bluestem. Its major distribution is more westerly and in the drier areas of the Great Plains (Fig. 22.4). It is found on gravelly soils, on ridges, and in other exposed locations. A main area of natural growth is in the flint hills of east central Kansas and Oklahoma. Under some conditions little bluestem is low in palatability. Seed production is difficult.

Sand bluestem, *A. hallii* Hack., resembles big bluestem, but the heads are conspicuously hairy. It is a vigorous perennial grass with creeping underground stems.

A single plant may spread to cover 9 m. It grows to a height of 1.5–2.1 m. It occurs on deep sandy soils with major distribution in western Nebraska, Kansas, Oklahoma, Texas, and eastern Colorado and New Mexico.

Yellow bluestem, *Bothriochloa ischaemum* Keng., is a perennial semiprostrate bunchgrass introduced from India. It appears to be best adapted to the southern Great Plains, is quite leafy and palatable, and is adapted to grazing. Seedlings are vigorous and the grass volunteers readily. Seed production is difficult.

Old world bluestem, *Bothriochloa caucasica* C. E. Hubb., a perennial bunchgrass, is an introduction from Russia that shows promise as a pasture and hay grass in the central and southern Great Plains. It is easily established from seed and makes good growth even if moisture supplies are low. It bears an abundance of small viable seed which shatter readily.

Broomsedge bluestem, *Andropogon virginicus* L., is a weedy grass which grows on low-fertility soils. It often is mistaken for the desirable bluestems. In contrast to the others it has a shallow root system, the heads are partially enclosed in the sheath, and the mature plants have a distinct orange color.[3]

Yellow indiangrass, *Sorghastrum nutans* (L.) Nash., is a perennial grass similar to big bluestem. It differs in its distinctive, plumelike, densely branched panicle of a

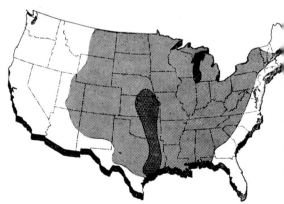

FIG. 22.4. Little bluestem–producing areas of the U.S.

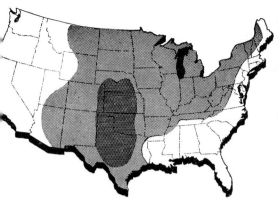

FIG. 22.5. Sidecoats grama–producing areas of the U.S.

golden or coppery color. As a component of the the tall-grass prairie it is a valuable hay species.

GRAMA GRASSES

The gramas are warm-season grasses of major importance in the Great Plains. In general they have received high rank as range forage. Two species are highly important forages of the Great Plains, and four others have shown possibilities in localized areas or in isolated trials.

Sideoats grama, *Bouteloua curtipendula* Michx., a perennial, usually assumes a bunch form and only occasionally forms a sod. Plant height rarely exceeds 1 m. It is easily recognized by its long flower stalks with short, dangling purplish spikes. It is found on favorable sites in the Great Plains (Fig. 22.5). In drier sections it is replaced by blue grama. It rarely forms pure stands but usually grows in association with bluestems. It is palatable to all classes of livestock, having about the same feeding value as big bluestem. Seed mature in late summer and can be combined. Yields of seed are good.[26]

Blue grama, *Bouteloua gracilis* (H. B. K.) Lag. ex Steud., is smaller, finer, and more drought resistant than sideoats grama. It

FIG. 22.6. *Blue grama . . . well adapted . . . lands which . . . should not be plowed.* A good stand of blue grama (top) affords carrying capacity for grazing animals and holds soil in place. Once a verdant and productive range (below) was changed to a desert of drifting sand as a result of the destruction of grass cover. *N. Mex. SCS photo.*

is found in association with buffalograss in the short-grass prairie. Blue grama has no stolons but has a dense mass of fine roots and a low, basal type of growth which forms a sod. The fine, curling basal leaves have a distinctive grayish green color. Plant height at maturity is 15–30 cm. It is found in abundance in the drier sections of the Great Plains (Fig. 22.6). Blue grama will stand more drought and alkali than sideoats grama; thus it is well adapted for use on lands which cannot or should not be plowed. It is highly palatable and retains its feeding value into the winter months. The short growth

26. Smika, D. E., and L. E. Newell. 1965. Irrigation and fertilization practices for seed production from established stands of sideoats grama. Nebr. Agr. Exp. Sta. Res. Bull. 218.

prevents its use for hay. Seed is harvested from native stands, but some improved cultivars are grown commercially.[27] The chaffy material is difficult to process. In seeding, it is important that native strains be used in the vicinity of origin. There is a wide range of types from north to south in the Great Plains. Each is well adapted locally.

BUFFALOGRASS

Buffalograss, *Buchloe dactyloides* (Nutt.) Engelm., is a low-growing perennial which spreads by stolons. The seed is enclosed in a hard bur with one or several caryopses per bur. Plant height is 5–15 cm. The foliage is a grayish green color but at maturity becomes a light straw color. Buffalograss occurs mainly in the central and southern Great Plains. It usually is found on "hard lands" with a high clay content. It is quite drought resistant and if killed by prolonged drought and overgrazing, regenerates from dormant seed in the soil. It is tolerant to alkali but does not succeed on sandy soils. On fertile, deep moist soils it is replaced by tall grasses unless these have been suppressed by overgrazing.[28,29]

Buffalograss has wide renown as a range pasture plant. Not only is it highly palatable and nutritious in the green summer stages but it maintains its feeding value in the dry cured stage during winter months. It is tolerant to heavy grazing.

Buffalograss may be propagated either by sod pieces or seed. Seed is harvested by altering small-grain combines so that the sickle can be run near the ground. When the grass has been closely grazed, suction machines, brooms, or beater equipment must be used to collect the burs.

The one improved cultivar is 'Improved W.'

LOVEGRASSES

The lovegrasses are noted chiefly for their ability to grow on low-fertility or sandy soils. Many produce an abundance of seed which germinate and establish easily. One native and three introduced species are worthy of consideration.[30]

Sand lovegrass, *Eragrostis trichodes* (Nutt.) Wood, is native to the central and southern Great Plains. It is an erect perennial bunchgrass about 1 m tall that was first cultivated about 1937. It is a highly palatable grass that produces good yields from early April to late October and also has some value as a winter feed. It is reported to be much more palatable to livestock than weeping lovegrass.[31] Sand lovegrass has very small seed and usually is seeded at the rate of 0.57 kg/ha in mixtures and about 2.27 kg/ha alone. Seed generally is produced in cultivated rows. The seed is fairly easy to combine, and cleaning presents no problems.

Weeping lovegrass, *E. curvula* (Schrad.) Nees., an introduction from East Africa, has shown considerable promise in the Southwest. It has been used extensively in Oklahoma for erosion control and forage on low-fertility soils.[32] A perennial bunchgrass with an extensive but shallow fibrous root system, it grows to a height of 1.2 m and forms a bunch 30–38 cm in diameter. Like sand lovegrass, seed are very small and heavy with about 4.4 million/kg. Adaptation is south of the Oklahoma-Kansas line. Palatability of weeping lovegrass is not high except during the season of lush spring growth when used as a supplementary pasture.[33] It has become naturalized on rangelands in southern Arizona.[34]

27. Fults, Jess L. 1936. Blue grama grass for erosion control and range reseeding in the Great Plains and a method of obtaining seed in large lots. USDA Circ. 402.
28. Wenger, L. E. 1943. Buffalograss. Kans. Agr. Exp. Sta. Bull. 321.
29. Beetle, A. A. 1950. Buffalograss—Native of the short grass. Wyo. Agr. Exp. Sta. Bull. 293.

30. Crider, F. U. 1945. Three introduced lovegrasses for soil conservation. USDA Circ. 330.
31. Savage, D. A. 1948. Native sand lovegrass: A new seed and pasture crop for the Great Plains. Okla. Agr. Exp. Sta. Bull. B-319.
32. Staten, H. W., and H. M. Elwell. 1944. Weeping lovegrass in Oklahoma. Okla. Agr. Exp. Sta. Bull. 281.
33. Denman, C. E., W. C. Elder, and V. G. Heller. 1953. Performance of weeping lovegrass under different management practices. Okla. Agr. Exp. Sta. Tech. Bull. T-48.
34. Anderson, D., L. P. Hamilton, H. G. Reynolds, and R. R. Humphrey. 1957. Reseeding desert grassland ranges in southern Arizona. Ariz. Agr. Exp. Sta. Bull. 249.

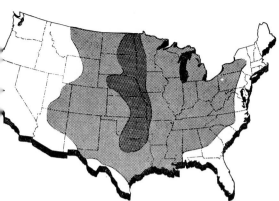

FIG. 22.7. Switchgrass-producing areas of the U.S.

'Morpa' and 'Ermelo' are improved cultivars.[35],[36]

Other lovegrasses of promise include Boer lovegrass, *E. chloromelas* Steud., and Lehmann lovegrass, *E. lehmanniana* Nees. Boer lovegrass is a long-lived perennial bunchgrass, less winter-hardy than weeping lovegrass. Lehmann lovegrass is a perennial grass with prostrate stems which root and produce new plants at the nodes. It is the least winter-hardy of the three introduced lovegrasses.

SWITCHGRASS

Switchgrass, *Panicum virgatum* L., is a tall, perennial sod-forming grass which occurs naturally in most of the U.S. east of the Rocky Mountains (Fig. 22.7). Its chief center of use is in the Great Plains. It is a coarse-stemmed, broad-leaved plant which grows 1–1.5 m high. The grass spreads slowly by short rhizomes. Switchgrass occurs naturally on fertile soils well supplied with moisture. It is a summer grass, and its value for standing winter feed is poor. Excellent yields of seed, vigorous seedling growth, and high forage yields have made it one of the easiest native grasses to bring under cultivation.

Switchgrass is widely used for hay, sum-mer pasture, and erosion control. While best adapted to fertile, moist soil, it will produce better growth and cover on droughty, infertile, eroded soils than most introduced grasses. It is used in combination with sand lovegrass on droughty blowing sands for erosion control. Under certain conditions it is superior to other grasses in permanent waterways.[37]

Selection of the proper switchgrass cultivar is important.

'Blackwell' is a rust-resistant cultivar with a high yield of leafy forage. It is an upland type adapted from Oklahoma north to South Dakota. Seed is readily available.

'Caddo' is a cultivar released by Oklahoma.

'Neb. 28' is an early maturing cultivar from the Nebraska sandhills. It is adapted farther north than Blackwell but is not as vigorous and is susceptible to rust. Newer cultivars are listed in Table 22.2.[38]

Vine mesquite, *P. obtusum* H. B. K., is native to the Southwest where it is used to a limited extent in seeded pastures and for range reseeding.

Blue panicgrass, *P. antidotale* Retz., is an introduction which has shown promise in the Southwest. It is a tall-growing, coarse, vigorous plant like switchgrass but differs in its ability to root at the nodes, its taller growth (1.8–2.4 m), and its definite adaptation to hot summers and mild winters.

DROPSEEDS

The dropseed grasses are characterized by their high yields of small hard seed which shatter at maturity. They are "invader" grasses which grow under unfavorable conditions. Their presence on the range often indicates overgrazing, drought, or unfavorable soil conditions. The forage is of low quality.

Sand dropseed, *Sporobolus cryptandrus* (Torr.) A. Gray, occurs on sandy soils. It

35. Voigt, P. W. 1971. Morpa weeping lovegrass. Okla. Agr. Exp. Sta. Bull. B-690.
36. Dalrymple, R. L. (No date.) Weeping lovegrass management. Noble Foundation, Ardmore, Okla.

37. Atkins, M. D. 1957. Permanent waterways. *Crops and Soils.* 10:2, 14–15.
38. Hanson, A. A. 1972. Grass varieties in the United States. USDA Agr. Handbook 170, rev.

is most common in the Great Plains and the Southwest. It is particularly valuable in mixtures to provide cover until other slow-developing native grasses can become established.

Giant dropseed, *S. giganteus* Nash., is a tall, robust grass resembling in many ways a giant form of sand dropseed.

Tall dropseed, *S. asper* (Michx.) Kunth., is commonly found in the prairies and may occur as a mixture in bluestem seed.

TABLE 22.2 ❧ Available cultivars

Species	Cultivars
Big bluestem	Champ, Kaw, Pawnee
Little bluestem	Pastura, Aldous, Blaze, Imperial
Sand bluestem	Woodward, Elida, Cherry, Garden
Yellow bluestem	El Kan, King Ranch, Formosa, Marash
Old World bluestem	Plains
Indiangrass	Cheyenne, Holt, Llano, Neb. 54, Osage, Oto, Tejas
Sideoats grama	Butte, El Reno, Trailway, Tucson, Uvalde, Vaughn, Premier, Pierre, Killdeer. Block E
Blue grama	Lovington
Black grama	Sonora, Nogal
Buffalograss	Improved W
Weeping lovegrass	Neb. 27, Bend, Mason
Sand lovegrass	A-67, Morpa, Ermelo
Boer lovegrass	A-84, Catalina
Lehmann lovegrass	A-68, Kalahari, Cold Hardy
Switchgrass	Blackwell, Caddo, Neb. 28, Grenville, Kanlow, Summer, Pathfinder, Cave-In-Rock, SD-149, Carthage
Wilman lovegrass	Palar
Blue panicgrass	Algerian, T-15327, A-130
Russian wildrye	Vinall, Sawki, Mayak
Canada wildrye	Mandan
Blue wildrye	P-2662
Basin wildrye	P-5797
Mammoth wildrye	Volga
Indian ricegrass	P-2575
Green needlegrass	Green Stipa, Mandan 2611, Lo Dorm
Creeping foxtail	Garrison, P-14762, Hesa
Tall oatgrass	Tualatin
Koleagrass	Perla
American beachgrass	Cape

Sources: A. A. Hanson, 1972;[38] personal communications from grass breeders in the North and West, 1972.

Alkali sacaton, *S. airoides* (Torr.) Torr., and sacaton, *S. wrightii* Munro ex Scribn., are tall, coarse perennial bunchgrasses found on floodplains and alkali soils of the Southwest. Of the two, alkali sacaton is the more palatable and is more likely to become an important cultivated grass. Both species are unpalatable except when green and tender.

WILDRYES

The wildrye grasses are closely related to the wheatgrasses but are often confused with the unrelated *Lolium* species. Wildrye differs from wheatgrass in having two spikelets at each rachis node.

Russian wildrye, *Elymus junceus* Fisch., is an introduction particularly adapted to the northern Great Plains and adjacent Canadian provinces.[39] It is one of the best cool-season pasture grasses to supplement warm-season grasses. It is a drought-resistant, widely variable, bunch-type grass with erect culms, terminal spikes, and an abundance of basal leaves. Growth starts early in the spring, and the leaves tend to remain green during the summer. Seed production is fair. The best seed yields are obtained in wide-spaced rows with heavy fertilizer N.[40] The seed is easily processed. Russian wildrye has compared favorably with other grasses in digestion trials in Montana.[41]

Canada wildrye, *E. canadensis* L., is a large, coarse, short-lived perennial bunchgrass widely distributed in the U.S. Plant height is 0.92–1.5 m, and the stems are coarse and woody. The seed head is a thick nodding spike 15–25 cm long. The seed is awned, giving the spike a bristle appearance. It is a cool-season grass but begins growth later in the spring and lasts longer into the summer than crested wheatgrass and smooth bromegrass. Palatability

39. Rogler, G. A. 1963. Growing Russian wildrye in the western states. USDA Leaflet 524.
40. McWilliams, J. L. 1955. Effects of some cultural practices on grass production. USDA Tech. Bull. 1097.
41. McCall, R., R. T. Clark, and A. R. Patton. 1943. The apparent digestibility and nutritive value of several native and introduced grasses. Mont. Agr. Exp. Sta. Bull. 418.

is only fair. It produces the best hay when cut at the boot stage.[42] The long awns are readily removed by hammer mill processing. Seedlings are vigorous, establish quickly, and are not highly competitive with other grasses in mixtures.

Virginia wildrye, *E. virginicus* L., appears to be an awnless strain of Canada wildrye, but it is not as productive.

Blue wildrye, *E. glaucus* Buckl., is a short-lived bunchgrass commonly found in cutover or burned-over lands of the Pacific Northwest. It resembles slender wheatgrass in adaptation and use. The plants are 0.92–1.2 m tall. It is shade tolerant. Seed production is good.

Basin wildrye, *E. cinereus* Scribn. & Merr., is a tall, long-lived, coarse perennial grass with short thick rhizomes. It is common on wet alkaline soils of the West.[43] On the range it was an important source of winter feed in pioneer days. The tall growth, 1.7–3 m, was nearly always available even with deep snow cover. A hybrid between basin wildrye and squirreltail has been described.[44]

'Altai' wildrye, *E. angustus* Trin. ex Ledeb., has produced as much forage as Russian wildrye in the arid climate of Saskatchewan.[45]

Beardless wildrye, *E. triticoides* Buckl., is closely related to basin wildrye although not as coarse and tall. It spreads vigorously by rhizomes. It is well adapted to alkaline soils and well regarded as range feed. In many ways beardless wildrye resembles western wheatgrass, and the two are often confused.

Dune wildrye, *E. mollis* Trin.; mammoth wildrye, *E. giganteus* Vahl.; and yellow wildrye, *E. flavescens* Scribn. & Smith, have little forage value but are useful in the control of inland sand dunes. Grasses of value for coastal sand dune control include European beachgrass, *Ammophila arenaria* (L.) Link, and American beachgrass, *A. breviligulata* Fernald. Control of shifting sand dunes is a specialized form of agriculture.[46-48]

NEEDLEGRASSES

Many needlegrasses are found in the arid rangelands of the West. One of the more common is needle-and-thread, *Stipa comata* Trin. & Rupr. It has sharp-pointed seed which may be injurious to livestock.

Sleepygrass, *S. robusta* (Vasey) Scribn., sometimes has a narcotic effect on grazing horses. Porcupinegrass, *S. spartea* Trin., is found from Pennsylvania west to Colorado and Montana. It is readily grazed, but the sharp-pointed seed are sometimes injurious to livestock. California needlegrass, *S. californica* Merr. & Davy, originally constituted an important part of the prairies of California.

Green needlegrass, *S. viridula* Trin., the most important species, is a perennial bunchgrass which grows to a height of 0.45–1.5 m. The seed are awned but not of a type injurious to livestock. Seed quality is good. Green needlegrass is found as a secondary constituent of the native prairie of the northern Great Plains. An improved cultivar known as 'Green Stipagrass' has been developed at Mandan, N. Dak.

An amphidiploid of a natural cross of green needlegrass and Indian ricegrass has been found and increased at Mandan. It is known as 'Mandan' ricegrass, *Stiporyzopsis*.[49]

Many of the grasses listed above are important and the others may become so in grassland agriculture of the arid West.[50,51]

42. Richards, D. E., and V. B. Hawk. 1945. Palatability for sheep and yield of hay and pasture grasses at Union, Oregon. *Oreg. Agr. Exp. Sta. Bull.* 431.
43. Mullen, L. A. 1939. Giant wildrye in the conservation program. *Soil Conserv.* 5:1–3.
44. Dewey, D. R., and A. H. Holgrem. 1962. Natural hybrids of *E. cinereus* × *S. hystrix. Bull. Torrey Bot. Club* 89:217–28.
45. Lawrence, T., D. H. Heinrichs, and R. B. Carson. 1960. An evaluation of Altai wildrye as a forage crop. *Can. J. Plant Sci.* 40:295–305.
46. McLaughlin, W. T., and R. L. Brown. 1942. Controlling coastal sand dunes in the Pacific Northwest. *USDA Circ.* 660.
47. Smith, O. W., H. D. Jacquot, and R. L. Brown. 1947. Stabilization of sand dunes in the Pacific Northwest. *Wash. Agr. Exp. Sta. Bull.* 492.
48. Whitfield, C. J., and J. A. Perin. 1939. Sand dunes reclamation in the southern Great Plains. *USDA Farmers' Bull.* 1825.
49. Neilsen, E. L., and G. A. Rogler. 1952. An amphidiploid of X stiporyzopsis. *Amer. J. Bot.* 39:343–48.
50. Keller, W. R. 1959. Breeding improved forage plants. *AAAS Publ. Grasslands* 53:335–44.
51. Schwendiman, J. L. 1959. Testing new range forage plants. *AAAS Publ. Grasslands* 53:345–57.

TABLE 22.3 ❦ Plant characteristics

Species	Bunch	Sod	Fibrous roots	Rhizomes or stolons	Lowland	Upland	Sand	Silt or clay	Seed Fast	Seed Slow	Rhizomes or stolons Fast	Rhizomes or stolons Slow	Early summer	Late summer	Fall	Height at seed maturity (cm)
Cool-Season Grasses																
Canada wildrye	X		X			X	X	X	X					X		92–123
Green needlegrass	X		X			X		X		X			X			92–123
Slender wheatgrass	X		X			X		X	X				X			92–123
Western wheatgrass		X		X	X	X		X			X			X		61–92
Crested wheatgrass	X		X			X		X		X				X		61–92
Intermediate wheatgrass		X		X		X		X			X				X	123–153
Tall wheatgrass	X		X			X		X		X				X		123–153
Russian wildrye	X		X			X		X		X			X			92–123
Smooth bromegrass		X		X	X	X		X			X			X		92–123
Tall fescue	X		X		X	X		X		X				X		92–123
Creeping foxtail		X		X	X	X		X				X	X			92–123
Warm-Season Grasses																
Big bluestem	X			X	X	X	X	X				X			X	153–184
Indiangrass	X			X	X	X		X			X				X	153–184
Sand bluestem		X		X		X	X				X				X	153–184
Switchgrass		X		X	X	X	X	X			X				X	123–153
Little bluestem	X		X			X	X	X	X						X	92–123
Sideoats grama		X		X		X	X	X				X		X		61–92
Sand lovegrass	X		X			X	X		X					X		92–123
Blue grama	X		X			X		X	X						X	31–61
Buffalograss		X		X		X		X			X				X	15–31
Green sprangletop	X		X			X		X	X					X		92–123
Plains bristlegrass	X		X			X	X	X		X			X			31–61
Old World bluestem	X		X			X	X	X	X				X			92–123
Turkestan bluestem	X		X			X		X	X				X			92–123
Weeping lovegrass	X		X			X	X			X			X			92–123
Kleingrass	X		X			X		X		X			X			92–123

*Early summer, June 1–July 15; late summer, July 16–August 30; fall, September 1–October 30. Species harvested in early summer sometimes produce a second crop.

Recognized cultivars of the species discussed are listed in Table 22.2.

❧ GRASSES FOR COOL MOIST CLIMATES

FOXTAIL

Meadow foxtail, *Alopecurus pratensis* L., is native to temperate Europe and Asia. It has been widely used as a hay grass for wetlands in Europe since 1750. It has been found to be particularly well adapted to the Pacific Northwest and Alaska, making its best growth on fertile soils in a cool moist climate (Fig. 22.8).[52-54] It is not drought hardy or resistant to continuous high temperatures. Under suitable soil and climatic conditions it is a long-lived perennial. At heading, meadow foxtail resembles timothy.

Loosely tufted with narrow leaves and short rhizomes, it produces a dense sod in older stands. It starts growth early in the spring about the earliest of all cultivated moistland grasses. Seed are fluffy and light colored, with an occasional brown or black seed.

Meadow foxtail is primarily a pasture grass. Where adapted, it produces over a long grazing season. Palatability as either pasture or hay is excellent. As pasture it often is seeded with big trefoil or ladino clover. Since 1940 it has increased in importance and use in this country. Because of the light fluffy seed, machine seeding is difficult. Practically all domestic seed is harvested from naturalized stands in mountain meadows of Oregon.

Creeping foxtail, *A. arundinaceus* Poir., is a recent introduction which is broadleaved and strongly rhizomatous and forms a dense sod rapidly. It is sometimes known as reed foxtail.[55] A high percentage of the awnless seed is black.

OATGRASS

Tall oatgrass, *Arrhenatherum elatius* (L.) Presl., is quite generally grown in Europe where it once comprised a part of the grassland climax. It has been cultured in the U.S. since about 1800 and has generally been considered a grass of secondary importance in this country.[56,57] Production is largely limited to Virginia and West Virginia and the Pacific Northwest. It prefers a cool moist climate and is not extremely drought or heat resistant.

Tall oatgrass under favorable conditions is a long-lived perennial; however, in many sections it is used as a rapidly developing, short-lived grass. It is strictly a bunchgrass, growing 1.2–1.8 m tall. Like oats it produces seed in open panicles, but the seed are smaller and much chaffier. The grass comes on early in the spring and remains green during the summer. Its growth period coincides with that of orchardgrass. Studies have shown this grass to be palatable to both sheep and dairy cattle.[41,58]

Tall oatgrass is less valuable for pasture than other grasses because of its tendency to produce heads throughout the season.[59] In Oregon its successful use for pasture depends on rotational grazing, scheduled to keep animals off the grass during the critical heading period.[60] Tall oatgrass cannot stand continuous close grazing. Early maturity is its only disadvantage as a hay plant. The seedlings are not winter-hardy, and spring seedings are best in the Corn Belt. The rate of seeding should be at least triple that for orchardgrass. The test weight per hectoliter and number of seed per kilogram when processed are higher as compared to natural seed. Processing does not injure seed germination if

52. Schoth, H. A. 1947. Meadow foxtail. Oreg. Agr. Exp. Sta. Bull. 433.
53. Irwin, D. L. 1945. Forty-seven years of experimental work with grasses and legumes in Alaska. Alaska Agr. Exp. Sta. Bull. 12.
54. Saxby, S. H. 1945. Pasture production in New Zealand. N.Z. Dept. Agr. Bull. 250.
55. Hawk, V. B. 1954. Reed foxtail—A new plant material. *Iowa Soil and Water* 2:5.

56. Fuelleman, R. F., W. L. Burleson, and W. G. Kammlade. 1949. Pastures for Illinois. Ill. Agr. Exp. Sta. Circ. 647.
57. Keim, F. D., and L. C. Newell. 1955. Introduced forage grasses for Nebraska. Nebr. Agr. Exp. Sta. Circ. 95.
58. Bateman, G. Q., and W. R. Keller. 1956. Improved irrigated pastures. Utah Agr. Exp. Sta. Bull. 382.
59. Stitt, R. E. 1955. Yields of grass species and varieties under irrigation in Montana. Mont. Agr. Exp. Sta. Tech. Bull. 508.
60. Hedrick, D. W. 1956. Grazing tall oatgrass. *Crops and Soils.* 9:3–9.

FIG. 22.8. *Foxtail . . . primarily a pasture grass . . . long grazing season.* Meadow foxtail (right) has narrow leaves with a few short rhizomes. Creeping foxtail (left) has broad leaves and is strongly rhizomatous.

carefully done and the seed planted shortly thereafter.[61] Seed production and cleaning are difficult, although processing facilitates cleaning. Yields are good if seed are not lost by shattering.

'Tualatin,' a selection developed in Oregon, shatters less readily than common tall oatgrass. The caryopses thresh free from the hull, which facilitates processing. In addition, Tualatin is finer, shorter, leafier, and later maturing than common tall oatgrass.

A closely related weedy subspecies known as bulbous oatgrass, *A. elatius* var. *bulbosum* (Willd.) Spenner, develops creeping rhizomes with bulbous swellings about the size of a pea.

MISCELLANEOUS GRASSES

Indian ricegrass, *Oryzopsis hymenoides* (Roem. & Schult.) Ricker, is a densely tufted perennial bunchgrass commonly found on sandy soils subject to wind erosion. It is a highly palatable grass which may be reproduced vegetatively or by seed.

Sand reedgrass, *Calamovilfa longifolia* (Hook.) Scribn., is common on loose sand dunes in the northern Great Plains. It is of low forage value. It spreads rapidly by rhizomes and has been used to stabilize "blowout" areas.

61. Schwendiman, J. L., R. F. Sackman, and A. L. Hafenrichter. 1944. Effects of processing on germinative capacity of seed of tall oatgrass, *Arrhenatherum elatius* (L.) Mert. & Koch. *J. Amer. Soc. Agron.* 36:783–85.

Native grasses which commonly occur on wet soils include eastern gamagrass, *Tripsacum dactyloides* (L.) L.; prairie cordgrass, *Spartina pectinata* Link.; and inland saltgrass, *Distichlis stricta* (Torr.) Rydb.

Eastern gamagrass is related to corn. The seed heads have the female flowers on the lower portion and the male flowers above. It grows in large clumps in low areas, is quite palatable, and often is destroyed by close grazing. It produces a large tonnage of forage and can be used for hay or silage.

Prairie cordgrass grows on deep, heavy, wet lowland soils throughout North America. The leaf blades are coarse and serrated on the margins and will cut the mouths of livestock. Its most prevalent use is as a cover for haystacks.

Inland saltgrass grows in pure stands on alkaline soils with a shallow water table. It is relatively unpalatable except in early stages and withstands close grazing. It must be propagated vegetatively.

See Table 22.3 for characteristics of other grasses not discussed in this chapter.

QUESTIONS

1. What factors favor and what factors limit the adaptation of native grasses to culture in modern grassland farming?
2. Select a particular state, zone, or region and list native grasses best adapted to culture on farmlands. Why did you select them?
3. What methods have been used to overcome the problems of propagation of native grasses?
4. After a review of the literature or key textbooks in plant ecology and range management give a brief discussion of the basic facts underlying the tendency of certain grasses to grow in associations.
5. In the preliminary stages of grassland agriculture what type of grasses are likely to be used? Which are likely to be used in the final or perfected stages? (You will not find the answer in this chapter alone.)
6. What prompted soil conservationists to take such an active interest in the development of native grasses for farm use?

ERNEST N. FERGUS / *University of Kentucky*

ROBERT C. BUCKNER / *Agricultural Research Service, USDA,
and University of Kentucky*

23

THE BLUEGRASSES AND REDTOP

KENTUCKY BLUEGRASS

KENTUCKY BLUEGRASS belongs to the botanical genus *Poa,* a genus of more than 200 species, believed to have originated in central Asia.[1] Hitchcock lists 69 species of *Poa* in the U.S.[2] Perhaps 90% of these are native to North America.

Kentucky bluegrass, *P. pratensis* L., originated many million years ago at a time when barriers to migration differed from the present. Most botanists believe it originated in Eurasia.[3] However, Fernald says it is indigenous to the northwestern U.S. and northern Canada.[4]

❧ ERNEST N. FERGUS was enaged in teaching and in charge of forage research at the University of Kentucky until his retirement in 1962. He holds the M.Sc. from Ohio State University and the Ph.D. from the University of Chicago.

❧ ROBERT C. BUCKNER, Research Agronomist, ARS, USDA, and adjunct Professor of Agronomy, University of Kentucky, is in charge of grass breeding and improvement research at the Kentucky station. He holds the M.Sc. degree from the University of Kentucky and the Ph.D. from the University of Minnesota.

Regardless of where Kentucky bluegrass originated in the northern hemisphere, it had plenty of time to migrate to and become well established in the middle Great Lakes region and the Ohio Valley before the first explorers, traders, hunters, and French missionaries entered the territories.

Doubtless, Kentucky bluegrass was introduced along the Atlantic Coast by early colonists soon after 1600 and for a century or longer thereafter. Eastern Canada introductions are believed to have furnished seed that was carried west and south into the Great Lakes region and the Mississippi and Ohio valleys by French traders and French missionaries before 1700. From introductions into the American colonies the grass was probably carried across the Appalachian Mountains by early settlers after 1770.

There is considerable evidence that the species was abundant in open places and at "licks" (where wild animals came to lick

1. Hartley, W. 1961. Studies on the origin, evolution, and distribution of the Gramineae. IV. The genus *Poa* L. *Aust. J. Bot.* 9:152–61.
2. Hitchcock, A. S. 1951. Manual of grasses of the United States. USDA Misc. Publ. 200, rev.
3. Carrier, Lyman, and Katherine S. Bort. 1916. The history of Kentucky bluegrass and white clover in the United States. *J. Amer. Soc. Agron.* 8:256–66.
4. Fernald, Merritt L. 1950. Gray's Manual of Botany, 8th ed. American Book Co., New York.

the soil for the salt it contained) and "stamping grounds" (normally found near water and on established buffalo trails) around 1775 in central Kentucky. Bluegrass was abundant in these "buffalo pastures," which were valuable land, often having several claimants. The presence of bluegrass sometimes was noted in the testimony presented in court cases and thus became part of the official record.

The name bluegrass seems to be of American origin.[3] It was in use in 1750, but it is not known which *Poa* was first named bluegrass. Possibly it was Canada bluegrass, *P. compressa* L., which has bluish green leaves, whereas Kentucky bluegrass has green leaves. However, the Kentucky species may have been called bluegrass first, since fields of this grass in anthesis usually are dark bluish. Another suggested reason is that some perceptive and enthusiastic colonial farmer appraised Kentucky bluegrass as royalty among the grasses and called it *"blue"* grass.

Poa pratensis became known as "Kentucky" bluegrass between 1833 and 1859. The name doubtless was given to the species because of the excellent bluegrass pastures in Kentucky or to identify the bluegrass seed being sent from Kentucky to other states.

❧ DISTRIBUTION AND ADAPTATION

Kentucky bluegrass is widely distributed in Eurasia and North America. It is present in all states of the U.S. including Alaska but is most important agriculturally only in the northeastern quarter of the country. From the northern boundary of that area it is important north and west in Canada to Alaska. Kentucky bluegrass can also be found in many places in the Southern Hemisphere (Fig. 23.1).

Kentucky bluegrass has wide soil adaptation but does best on well-drained, highly productive soils of limestone origin. It is quite sensitive to slight variations in some soil factors of chemical nature. In general,

FIG. 23.1. Kentucky bluegrass is present in all states of the U.S., including Alaska, but is most important agriculturally in the middle and northeastern sections. It is important as a seed crop in parts of Idaho, Washington, and Oregon.

the grass is dominant in pasture floras only if the soil contains at least 6 ppm of available P (Truog test) and 1500 ppm of N and if its pH is at least 5.[5]

In North America, Kentucky bluegrass is best adapted to the humid areas of Canada and the U.S. north of the average annual isotherm for 15 C, which corresponds closely with the average July isotherm for 25.2 C. Within this region in the U.S. the daily air temperatures vary between 43.5 C and −44 C. Minimum temperatures are somewhat lower in Canada.

Optimum air temperatures for Kentucky bluegrass are between 15.5 C and 32.2 C. Some growth occurs at 4.4 C, and severe injury occurs at continuous soil and air temperatures of 37.8 C. Best root and rhizome growth occurs at 15.5 C. The grass prefers open sunlight, but it grows in lightly shaded situations if soil moisture and nutrients are favorable.

Average annual precipitation varies from 500 mm to 1250 mm within the region of Kentucky bluegrass adaptation in the U.S. Although it essentially goes dormant during dry weather, it survives severe droughts.

5. Watson, James M., G. W. Conrey, and Morgan W. Evans. 1940. The distribution of Canada bluegrass and Kentucky bluegrass as related to some ecological factors. *J. Amer. Soc. Agron.* 32:726–28.

❧ PLANT DESCRIPTION

Kentucky bluegrass is a long-lived perennial. It is rhizomatous and produces dense sod under favorable conditions. Its leaves are glabrous, soft, green to dark green, about 3 mm wide, usually 10–30 cm long, and boat shaped at the tip. In April, May, or early June, depending upon latitude, it produces many erect, unbranched culms, usually 0.3–0.75 m tall. The inflorescence is an open panicle. Seedlings develop into small, leafy stools with two kinds of buds; one produces rhizomes, the other becomes tillers. Some of the tiller buds become culms and bear the panicles; the remainder produce leaves only. New tillers and new rhizomes arise from the lower nodes of aging culms. New rhizomes also arise from the nodes of older rhizomes.[6] (See Fig. 23.2.)

Kentucky bluegrass exhibits a pronounced periodicity in growth and devel-

6. Etter, Alfred Gordon. 1951. How Kentucky bluegrass grows. *Ann. Mo. Bot. Garden* 38:293–375.

FIG. 23.2. Diagram of a mature Kentucky bluegrass plant showing the three types of shoots which develop from the crown. Ordinarily, each plant will develop two to five tillers. (Etter, 1951.[6])

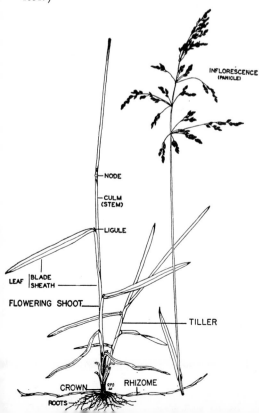

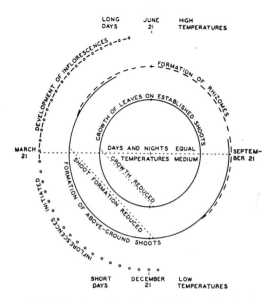

FIG. 23.3. Annual cycles of leaf growth, vegetative reproduction through development of branches, and reproduction through inflorescence in Kentucky bluegrass as it grows in northern Ohio. Since the life processes of the plants are modified by varying environmental conditions, the limits of duration of each phase of growth, development, and reproduction as illustrated here can be only an approximation. (Evans, 1949.[7])

opment, induced by photoperiod and temperature but modified by soil moisture, nutrients, and management.[7] Rhizome buds are initiated mostly during summer and fall; aerial shoots are initiated during fall, winter, and spring when temperatures are favorable. Inflorescences are initiated during the fall in response to combined effects of short days and cool temperatures. Tiller buds that produce only leaves are initiated in the spring and early summer as a rule. (See Fig. 23.3.) Capacity of the individual plant to respond to environmental factors is determined by its genetics.

Kentucky bluegrass is relatively unproductive in midsummer, but yields can be increased by irrigation and fertilizer N. However, these treatments do not prevent the plants from becoming semidormant.

7. Evans, M. W. 1949. Kentucky bluegrass, Ohio Agr. Exp. Sta. Res. Bull. 681.

TABLE 23.1 ❧ Comparative grazing yield indexes of pastures of Kentucky bluegrass and other cool-season grasses

State of test	Number of test years	Test animals	Kentucky bluegrass	Orchard-grass	Smooth bromegrass	'Ky 31' fescue
Pennsylvania*	3	cows and calves	100	105	...	...
Virginia†	10	yearling steers	100	105	...	99
Kentucky*	3	milk cows	100	90	105	80
Missouri†	3	steers	100	98	...	...

Sources: Washko and Wilson, 1971;[9] Blaser et al., 1969;[10] Seath et al., 1956;[11] Brown, 1961.[12]
* Calculated TDN consumption.
† Liveweight gains.

NUTRITIVE VALUE AND PRODUCTIVITY

At similar stages of growth Kentucky bluegrass, smooth bromegrass, and reed canarygrass contained 2399, 1541, and 1819 digestible cal/kg of dry matter respectively in an Illinois experiment.[8] Percentages of calculated maintenance requirements of each grass consumed by the grazing steers were 255, 185, and 139 respectively. Research in Kentucky indicates that fertilized bluegrass which was reserved August 15 for fall to early spring grazing contained the following average percentages of crude protein on the first day of each month, October to April: 19.6, 20.2, 16.2, 13.1, 13.9, 13.9, and 15.5 respectively. The lowest contents are well above that needed by nonlactating brood cows.

The yield of Kentucky bluegrass is similar to other cool-season grasses on good soil when harvested to simulate grazing. In a Kentucky experiment (unpublished), frequently harvested bluegrass produced 2055 kg dry matter/ha/year. Yields of orchardgrass, redtop, timothy, and southern smooth bromegrass were 2195, 2487, 1051, and 1865 kg respectively.

Kentucky bluegrass pastures grazed experimentally in comparison with other cool-season pasture grasses yielded as summarized in Table 23.1.[9-12]

❧ IMPORTANCE AND USE

Kentucky bluegrass has long been one of the most important pasture grasses in North America. It contributes largely to grazing on 20–40 million ha of pasture in the east central and northeastern U.S., and a substantial hectarage in Canada. (See Fig. 23.4.) Nevertheless, bluegrass sometimes is regarded with disfavor as a pasture grass because of its low midseason yield, aggressiveness, and high fertility requirements. By 1952 Kentucky bluegrass was considered the most important lawn grass in the U.S. It is an important seed crop in Kentucky and the north central and northwest U.S.

Usage of Kentucky bluegrass seed in pasture seedings is quite variable. As in the past, most pastures in central Kentucky, central Tennessee, and the Shenandoah Valley of Virginia are sown with Kentucky bluegrass seed or a mixture containing bluegrass seed. Elsewhere in the U.S. the pastures generally are sown with a mixture containing a small amount of Kentucky bluegrass seed; or, more likely, the bluegrass came from seed already in the soil or from pieces of rhizomes and thus was a "volunteer" pasture.

8. Garrigus, W. P., and H. P. Rusk. 1939. Some effects of the species and stage of maturity of plants on the forage consumption of grazing steers of various weights. Ill. Agr. Exp. Sta. Bull. 454.
9. Washko, J. B., and L. I. Wilson. 1971. Progress report: Productivity of pastures utilized by crossbred Angus-Holstein cows and calves, 1968–1970. Pa. Anim. Sci. Res. Sum. 2:20–26.

10. Blaser, Roy E., H. T. Bryant, R. C. Hammes, Jr., R. L. Boman, J. P. Fontenot, and C. E. Polan. 1969. Managing forages for animal production. Va. Polytechnic Inst. Res. Div. Bull. 45.
11. Seath, D. M., C. A. Lassiter, J. W. Rust, M. Cole, and G. M. Bastin. 1956. Comparative value of Kentucky bluegrass, Kentucky 31 fescue, orchardgrass, and bromegrass as pastures for milk cows. I. How kind of grass affected persistency of milk production, TDN yield, and body weight. J. Dairy Sci. 39:574–80.
12. Brown, E. M. 1961. Improving Missouri pastures. Mo. Agr. Exp. Sta. Bull. 768.

FIG. 23.4. *Kentucky bluegrass . . . long . . . one of the most important grasses.* Thoroughbred horses on Kentucky bluegrass in central Kentucky. Many herds of beef cattle also graze these pastures. *Univ. Ky. photo.*

✣ CULTIVARS

Different endemic phenotypes and ecotypes of *P. pratensis* occur in Europe, on the west coast of Canada, in Labrador, and perhaps also on the coast of New England. Individual phenotypes that may differ in productivity have developed through natural selection in old pastures and meadows in America.[13] Selective factors include variations in grazing and harvesting practices and differences in soil productivity. Irrespective of selective factors, the surviving plants are probably individuals of the original population.

Kentucky bluegrass is a pseudogamous, facultative apomict having complex cytological and embryological characteristics.[14] The species is highly but variably apomictic and quite variable in chromosome numbers ($x = 7$; $2n = 28$ to 154). This somewhat unique reproductive habit of the species accounts for the wide range of variability within plant populations and possibly explains its worldwide distribution and adaptation.[15]

Superior cultivars of Kentucky bluegrass have not been developed specifically for pasture or forage purposes, although plants vary greatly in palatability, percent of crude protein, disease and insect resistance, and many morphological characteristics. A number of cultivars have been developed for turf purposes.[16] Most of these trace to a single highly apomictic plant; however, a few are blends from seed of several superior plants.

The most successful method of breeding has been the selection from old sods of highly apomictic individual plants that are superior for some particular character.

Since selections are facultative apomicts, cultivars change morphologically and physiologically from generation to generation. Thus the genetic shift that occurs within the cultivar necessitates rogueing of aberrant plants of each generation to maintain the superior characteristics of the cultivar in seed certification programs.

Intraspecific hybridization and mutagenic agents have been studied as methods of improving the species; however, these methods have not resulted in new cultivars. Recurrent intraspecific hybridization as a breeding method has been proposed.[17] Research indicates that intraspecific hybridization can be used effectively to improve Kentucky bluegrass; however, no improved cultivars have evolved from this method to date.[14]

Before 1950 Kentucky bluegrass seed was harvested from pasture fields in Kentucky and the midwestern states from Missouri northward. The fields of "common" Kentucky bluegrass were a mixture of many plant types. Common Kentucky bluegrass

13. Kentucky Agr. Exp. Sta. 1936. 52nd Ann. Rept., p. 15.
14. Pepin, Gerard W., and C. Reed Funk. 1971. Intraspecific hybridization as a method of breeding Kentucky bluegrass (*Poa pratensis* L.) for turf. *Crop Sci.* 11:445–48.

15. Clausen, Jens. 1961. Introgression facilitated by apomixis in polyploid *Poa* species. *Euphytica* 10:87–94.
16. Hanson, A. A. 1972. Grass varieties in the United States. USDA Agr. Handbook 170, rev.
17. Funk, C. R., and S. J. Han. 1967. Recurrent intraspecific hybridization—A proposed method of breeding Kentucky bluegrass (*Poa pratensis* L.). N.J. Agr. Exp. Sta. Bull. 818, pp. 3–14.

is a general-purpose grass for pasture, lawn, and turf.

The 'Merion' cultivar was released in 1947 cooperatively by the Crops Research Division, ARS, USDA, and the U.S. Golf Association greens section. It is a single-plant selection, is low growing, and where well adapted, it forms a denser sod under short cutting than common bluegrass.

Since the release of Merion, low-growing cultivars have originated as single-plant selections. Among these are 'A-20,' 'Belturf,' 'Campus,' 'Cougar,' 'Flyking,' 'Newport,' 'Midway,' 'Pennstar,' 'Prato,' 'Sodco,' and 'Windsor.' These were selected and increased primarily for lawn and turf purposes. They require higher rates of N, closer mowing, periodic dethatching, and a higher level of management than common Kentucky bluegrass. They are used little if at all for pasture.

'Arboretum,' 'Kenblue,' 'Park,' and 'Troy' cultivars were developed primarily for low-management turf. Their habits of growth are similar to common Kentucky bluegrass and they are useful for pasture. Arboretum, Kenblue, and Park are blends of many selections. They were selected for seedling vigor, disease resistance, sod-forming qualities, and general adaptation to a wide range of conditions.

❧ CULTURE AND MANAGEMENT

Probably 90% of the Kentucky bluegrass pastures in America developed without seeding. Since Kentucky bluegrass has been grown extensively over the northeastern U.S. for more than a century, it is understandable that it should "volunteer" on land taken out of cultivation for a few years.

A new Kentucky bluegrass pasture is usually seeded in the fall with a small-grain companion crop. In the northern part of the U.S., seedings are made in the spring. Except in central Kentucky, timothy is commonly sown to provide cover and forage while the bluegrass is becoming established. A legume is usually used in the mixture. Bluegrass is seeded at rates of 5–10 kg/ha. Lime and fertilizer are used as needed prior to seeding. When a legume is included, little or no N is needed. (See Chapter 36.)

Kentucky bluegrass seed should be selected for high purity and germination. Even more important, the seed should be of a cultivar or ecotype adapted to the area where it is to be sown.

Kentucky bluegrass pasture management goals are a weed-free sod and high production. Both are achieved by adequate liming and fertilization for companion legumes, regulated grazing, and occasional mowing. If legumes disappear from the pasture, liberal applications of fertilizer N will maintain or increase pasture yields. However, legumes can be reestablished in pastures by renovation. Generally this practice increases pasture production more than 100%. (See Chapter 54.)

As a general practice it is important that Kentucky bluegrass pastures be kept to a height of 5–15 cm by grazing or clipping or both; otherwise, the sod becomes weedy and relatively unproductive. When kept extremely short, poor root and rhizome development occurs and the pasture becomes weedy. When undergrazed and not mowed, legumes disappear and weeds and bushes invade the sod. However, overgrazing or undergrazing bluegrass pastures for short periods is not harmful.

❧ SEED PRODUCTION

Commercial Kentucky bluegrass seed is harvested in the Kentucky, north central, and northwest districts of the U.S.[18] The Kentucky district is mainly around Lexington. The north central district is the area between the southern boundaries of east Kansas and Missouri and Canada. The northwest district consists of Idaho, Washington, and Oregon.

All commercial Kentucky bluegrass seed

18. The authors are grateful for personal communications from the following persons in 1971 relative to Kentucky bluegrass seed production in their districts: J. Duane Colburn, S. Dak. Crop Improv. Assoc.; Charles D. Hutchcroft, Iowa Crop Improv. Assoc.; A. G. Law, Wash. State Univ.; Harley J. Otto, Univ. Minn.; Al Slinkard, Univ. Idaho; Harold Youngberg, Oreg. State Univ.

was produced in Kentucky prior to 1897. Iowa then began harvesting seed for the market. Since 1932 more seed has been produced in the north central district than in the Kentucky district. Shortly before 1930 the northwest district began producing commercial bluegrass seed. The enterprise expanded rapidly and in 1967–71 that district produced 86.4% of all Kentucky bluegrass seed harvested in the U.S. Substantial amounts of Kentucky bluegrass seed are produced in Canada, Denmark, and the Netherlands. Variable amounts are exported to the U.S. annually.

There are two main problems in producing good yields of marketable bluegrass seed. The first is removing the cottony filaments at the base of each seed. Unless these are removed, the threshed seed do not flow freely. The second is removing the surplus growth left on a field after seed harvest. This practice greatly improves seed yields the following year.[19]

The standard weight of commercial Kentucky bluegrass seed is about 27 kg/hl, but grades weighing up to 40 kg/hl are offered to a select trade.

Bluegrass seed crops in the Kentucky district are harvested mostly from pasture fields managed for good seed yields. Some fields are grown primarily for seed; these are pastured somewhat, however.

Most bluegrass seed produced in South Dakota and some grown elsewhere in the north central district is harvested from pasture fields managed for good seed yields. The remainder of the bluegrass seed produced in the north central district and essentially all that is produced in the northwest district is harvested from fields grown only for seed. These fields are sown almost wholly in rows of different spacings. As stands become older, the grass fills in between the rows and stands become solid.

In each district, N is the key to high bluegrass seed yields. Therefore, fertilizer N is applied to crops in the fall and/or very early spring. However, adequate soil moisture in fall and spring is more important than fertilizer N for high yields from the pasture fields in South Dakota.

Use of herbicides, insecticides, and fungicides varies from district to district and from place to place within each district depending upon the need. There are few seed crops, however, that are not treated with one or more of these chemicals.

All Kentucky bluegrass seed grown in Kentucky district and some of the crop grown on pasture fields in the north central district are harvested with strippers. Kentucky strippers consist of self-cleaning metal combs. Strippers used in the north central district are essentially revolving studded cylinders that brush the seed into a box that is part of the machine (Fig. 23.5). All other seed crops in the north central district and those in the northwest district are harvested with self-propelled combines modified to effect some rubbing of the seed. Most crops are swathed first, but many are combined standing. (See Fig. 23.6.)

Seed harvested by strippers is dried in curing yards where it is stirred until dry enough to store or thresh. Seed harvested with combines usually is dry enough to be threshed further. If not, the seed is dried in heated drums or on heated floors.

FIG. 23.5. *Strippers . . . revolving cylinders . . . brush seed into . . . machine.* Stripping Kentucky bluegrass seed in central Kentucky with a modern stripper. The revolving reel shears the panicles off a stationary comb along the front edge of the machine; green seed are blown into the wagon. *Ky. Dept. Public Info. photo.*

19. Spencer, J. T., H. H. Jewett, and E. N. Fergus. 1949. Seed production of Kentucky bluegrass as influenced by insects, fertilizers, and sod management. Ky. Agr. Exp. Sta. Bull. 535.

Fig. 23.6. *Most crops swathed first . . . many . . . combined standing.* Direct combining of Kentucky bluegrass seed in Washington. Most of the crop in the Northwest and much in the north central district is combined from the swath. *Wash. State Univ. photo.*

In each district the harvested seed is processed to remove all cottony filaments from each seed that was not defuzzed in combining. In the Kentucky district this is accomplished by rubbing the seed on the inner side of heavy wire screen cylinders. In the other two districts rubbing is done mostly by a series of cylinders and concaves modified for this purpose. Other rubbing devices include rotating drums with beaters inside and double belts moving at different speeds against each other. The defuzzed seed is cleaned with conventional seed cleaning mills and then separated into weight grades by machine.

Surplus growth on fields harvested with strippers is removed by grazing during summer and fall or by mechanical means. Surplus growth on fields harvested with swathers and combines or with combines only is burned in summer or fall. This practice aids in the control of disease and destructive insects.

❧ DISEASES

Kentucky bluegrass is susceptible to several diseases. Among these are powdery mildew, *Erysiphe graminis* DC.; leaf and stem rusts, *Puccinia* spp.; stripe smut, *Ustilago striiformis* (West.) Niessl; leaf eyespot, *Helminthosporium vagans* Drechsl.; and anthracnose, *Colletotrichum graminicola* (Ces.) G. W. Wils.

These and other diseases do not damage bluegrass pastures enough to call for control measures. Neither is any disease important on Kentucky bluegrass seed crops in the Kentucky district or, it seems, in the north central district. However, leaf and stem rusts, powdery mildew, and numerous other fungi and bacteria sometimes affect bluegrass seed crops in the northwest district. They are controlled by stubble burning and occasional use of fungicides.

❧ INSECTS

White grubs cause most of the insect damage to Kentucky bluegrass pastures. Adults, known as May beetles, *Phyllophaga* spp., and the green June beetle, *Cotinis nitida* (L.), are harmless to leaves. The larvae feed on the roots and rhizomes and, when abundant, they kill the grass completely. Destroyed areas should be reseeded. Renovating bluegrass pastures by seeding sweetclover, alfalfa, and red clover in the spring controls these insects effectively.

Sod webworms, *Crambus* spp., sometimes damage Kentucky bluegrass pastures. They feed on leaves, but their damage is noticeable only in dry weather. These insects frequently are destructive in lawns. Leafhoppers frequently injure leaves considerably.

A few insects frequently cause serious damage to Kentucky bluegrass seed crops. In the Kentucky district meadow plant bugs, *Leptopterna dolobrata* (L.) and *Amblytylus nasutus* (Kirsch.), feed on the florets and prevent development of good seed.[19] Experimental control of these insects resulted in 64.5% larger bluegrass seed yields.

In the north central district, whitetop or

silvertop often causes serious losses in seed crops. The disease causes the panicles to wither and turn white or silvery before they are fully expanded. At first, the cause was thought to be an insect. Later, research indictated the cause was a fungus, *Fusarium poae* Pk., and a mite, *Pediculopsis graminum* Reut., the vector of the fungus. In 1971 the Minnesota station found that the capsus bug, *Capsus simulaus* Stal., was the most important cause of silvertop and that use of insecticides and burning of stubble following harvest gave control.[20]

In the northwest district, silvertop or a similar disease sometimes is destructive to Kentucky bluegrass seed crops. The cause appears to be the same as in the north central district. Other insects destructive to bluegrass in the northwest district include billbugs, *Stenophorus* spp. and *Calendra* spp.; wireworms, *Dimonius* spp.; cutworms, *Agrotis* spp.; gelechids, *Gelechia* spp.; mites, *Pediculopsis* spp.; grass thrips, *Anaphothrips obscurus* (Mueller); and grass mealybugs, *Pseudococcus* spp. Control is secured by burning the stubble and using insecticides.

CANADA BLUEGRASS

Canada bluegrass, *P. compressa* L., is believed to be native to Eurasia.[2,4] It was brought to this continent before 1792 and has since spread throughout the areas in which Kentucky bluegrass is found. Although Canada bluegrass is found to some degree in many Kentucky bluegrass pastures, it is dominant only on soils that are too acid, droughty, or deficient in P, N, or other nutrients for Kentucky bluegrass dominance. Optimum temperatures for herbage production are between 27 and 32 C, but roots and rhizomes develop best at 10 C.

Canada bluegrass resembles Kentucky bluegrass somewhat but has a distinct, easily recognized, blue green foliage, flattened stems, and short, semicompact panicles. Culm leaves are short and erect. Its basal

20. Peterson, A. G., and Elymar V. Vea. 1971. Silvertop of bluegrass in Minnesota. *J. Econ. Entomol.* 64: 247–52.

leaves are few, in marked contrast to Kentucky bluegrass, and it matures later. When grazed it makes little recovery growth that year. It is used in pasture mixtures for less productive soils. Canada bluegrass is similar to Kentucky bluegrass in culture and management.

Canada bluegrass seed is produced mostly in Canada. Small amounts are exported to the U.S.

MUTTON BLUEGRASS

Mutton bluegrass, *P. fendleriana* Vasey, is native to North America. It occurs from northern Michigan westward to the Rocky Mountains and southward in the Rockies. It is adapted to cool temperatures and a wide range of soils. Mutton bluegrass is an erect-growing perennial bunchgrass. It is an important palatable and nutritious range grass, especially in early spring. The grass is not cultivated.

TEXAS BLUEGRASS

Texas bluegrass, *P. arachnifera* Torr., is native to North America and occurs from Kansas to Arkansas and Texas and to some extent east to Florida. It grows throughout the winter in its southern range. Texas bluegrass is a vigorous perennial, rhizomatous, dioecious grass that produces much palatable and nutritious herbage. Because of its poor seed habits, it is not cultivated. It has been hybridized with Kentucky bluegrass.

BIG BLUEGRASS

Big bluegrass, *P. ampla* Merr., a native of North America, occurs in all parts of the West. It is a vigorous perennial bunchgrass and an important palatable and nutritious range plant. It has been cultivated to a limited degree.

ROUGHSTALK BLUEGRASS

Roughstalk bluegrass, *P. trivialis* L., is native to Europe. It is adapted to much the same conditions as Kentucky bluegrass but is more tolerant of shade and wet soil. It is much used in pastures in Europe. In the U.S. its use is generally confined to shady lawns. Seed is produced in Europe.

REDTOP

Redtop, *Agrostis alba* L., is believed to be native to Europe, although forms of it are considered native to northern North America.[2,21] It was brought to America by the first colonists, soon became naturalized in New England, and was a valued grass for cultivation.

General distribution of redtop in the U.S. is essentially the same as that of Kentucky bluegrass in the East. However, it succeeds well over most of the U.S. except in drier regions and the extreme South. Reptop grows on very acid soils, on poor clayey soils of low fertility, and on poorly drained land.

Redtop is a perennial grass with both upright and creeping stems. On productive soils it grows to a height of about 1 m. It has flat sharp-pointed leaves. Its ligules are about 0.6 cm long and pointed. Redtop panicles are reddish in color, which explains its common name. The grass matures from mid-June to mid-August, depending upon latitude. Sods of redtop are less compact than Kentucky bluegrass sods.

Redtop is slightly less palatable than Kentucky bluegrass. Its nutritive quality probably is satisfactory if the redtop is grown on good soil. Prior to about 1940 redtop was the second most important pasture grass in the U.S., ranking next to Kentucky bluegrass. It then declined in rank rather rapidly, and by 1971 it was of only minor importance. It is used mainly on poor or wet land for hay and pasture, usually mixed with an annual lespedeza or alsike clover. Other legumes are grown with it on better soils.

Redtop is quite variable in plant type;

21. This discussion of redtop follows closely that of J. A. De France and A. W. Burger in the second edition of *Forages*. Information on the current status of redtop usage was obtained in personal communications from Don W. Graffis, Univ. Ill., and H. N. Wheaton, Univ. Mo., 1971.

therefore, it should be possible to breed superior cultivars. However, no cultivars have been developed in the U.S. nor elsewhere.[16]

Redtop is seldom sown alone. In mixtures it is seeded at rates of 2.5–5.5 kg/ha. Although redtop produces fair yields on unproductive soil, hay yields were greatly increased in southern Illinois experiments by liming and fertilizing with P and K.

Redtop seed production declined sharply after 1945. All seed of this grass harvested in the U.S. is grown in southeastern Illinois and southwestern Missouri. Crops are harvested by combining, which must be done within the short favorable period because seed shatter readily.

Other species of *Agrostis* of some agricultural importance are colonial bentgrass, *A. tenuis* Sibth.; creeping bentgrass, *A. palustris* Huds.; and velvet bentgrass, *A. canina* L. Colonial bentgrass, also known as Rhode Island bent, is grown on unimproved pastures in New England and in places on the Pacific Coast. Creeping bent occupies pastureland in New England and the West. Velvet bent is insignificant agriculturally. Each of these bentgrasses is used for turf. Velvet bent is the preferred grass for putting greens in the northern U.S. Several cultivars of these bents are recognized.[16] (Consult publications on golf course turf culture and management for further information on bentgrasses.)

❧ QUESTIONS

1. Approximately how many species are there in the genus *Poa*? How many are believed to be native to North America?
2. Where do you believe Kentucky bluegrass originated? Give your reasons.
3. Where in the U.S. is Kentucky bluegrass dominant?
4. What are the more important climatic requirements of this grass for optimum growth? Soil requirements?
5. What are the characteristics of Kentucky bluegrass that contribute most to its agricultural value? That limit its usefulness?
6. How would you manage a Kentucky blue-

grass pasture to keep it productive and free of weedy plants?

7. Name the improved cultivars of Kentucky bluegrass that have had general acceptance.

8. Outline and discuss the history of Kentucky bluegrass seed production in the U.S.

9. Under what conditions would you expect Canada bluegrass to replace Kentucky bluegrass?

10. Why the marked decline in usage of redtop in the U.S.?

L. C. NEWELL / *Agricultural Research Service, USDA*

24

SMOOTH BROMEGRASS

&

THE GENUS *Bromus* comprises about 60 species. It is grouped with the small grains in the grass subfamily Festucoideae.[1] As implied by the generic name (from the Greek *Bromus* for oat, hence oatgrass), these grasses resemble oats and are adapted to cool climates or to regions in which cool seasons prevail during parts of the growing season. Such cool-season grasses produce vegetative growth during the early part of the season and mature seed in the long days of early summer.

The bromegrasses vary greatly in adaptation and use and include several important forage and range grasses. Their aggressive reproduction, either through self-seeding or vegetative spread, provides conservation value for establishment of plant cover but also causes them to be classified as weeds in some situations. Hitchcock lists 36 species of this genus in the U.S.[2] These include native and introduced perennials and a large group of introduced annuals. Most of the brome-

grasses are readily grazed and are relatively nutritious during periods of rapid early growth. They differ greatly in the length of time they furnish valuable forage.

Smooth bromegrass, *Bromus inermis* Leyss., is the most widely utilized of the cultivated bromegrasses. It is known as bromegrass, Austrian brome, Hungarian brome, and Russian brome. This grass has been cultivated in the U.S. since the early 1880s. It has gained considerable prominence for pasture, hay, and erosion control, usually with a legume.

The first recorded introduction of smooth bromegrass was by the California station in 1884. The seed may have been obtained from Hungary where this grass had been grown experimentally for about 30 years and was beginning to be utilized as a crop. Trial seed packets were distributed widely by the California station. Smooth bromegrass was grown in the Midwest by the late 1890s. Nebraska recommended it as 'Hungarian bromegrass' as early as 1897–98 on the basis of yield tests.[3]

The Canadian provinces began growing

& L. C. NEWELL, Research Agronomist, ARS, USDA, and Professor of Agronomy, University of Nebraska, is in charge of the cooperative grass improvement program of the Nebraska station and the USDA for central plains latitudes. He received the M.Sc. and Ph.D. degrees from the University of Nebraska. His primary interests include the taxonomy and ecology of introduced and native grasses.

1. Gould, F. Grass Systematics. 1968. McGraw-Hill, New York.
2. Hitchcok, A. S. 1951. Manual of the grasses of the United States. USDA Misc. Publ. 200, rev.
3. Lyon, T. L. 1899. Hungarian bromegrass. Nebr. Agr. Exp. Sta. Bull. 61.

smooth bromegrass from seed initially imported from northern Germany in 1888.[4] A large seed shipment was received in 1898 from the Penza region of Russia (53° N) by N. E. Hanson of the South Dakota station. Large-scale distribution of such importations from northern latitudes in Europe and their successful seed production in Canada and the Dakotas led to early predominance of this northern type in the seed trade.

After the initial recognition of this bromegrass in the early part of the century, interest in grasses as crops lagged. A few fields of smooth bromegrass from the earliest plantings in the Midwest escaped the plow-up programs for wheat production during the war years. Following the drought years of the 1930s, attention was directed to smooth bromegrass as the principal survivor among the introduced grasses. Additional fields were soon established, and local seed supplies were developed. Demand for seed to replace the overstocked and depleted bluegrass and native pastures also promoted the importation of large quantities of smooth bromegrass seed from Canada.

Field plot tests were established in 1939 at the Nebraska station to explain differences among new plantings. Smooth bromegrass seed fields from southern Kansas to Calgary, Canada, were sampled for strain testing. Differences in plant type, establishment, and yield were soon attributed to different seed sources.[5] Adapted strains derived from the old local fields in Nebraska, Kansas, Iowa, and Missouri were shown to be superior in field tests in these states. Subsequent tests indicated that these strains from old fields in the Midwest were adapted throughout the southern part of the Corn Belt. Seed of this southern type soon constituted a considerable part of the amount sold annually in the U.S.

The drought years in the Midwest

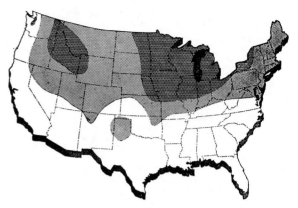

Fig. 24.1. Areas of major use and distribution of smooth bromegrass in the U.S.

brought smooth bromegrass into prominence. Initial problems of seed harvesting and cleaning of the light, chaffy seed were solved. Proper timing and methods of planting were found, and difficulties of stand establishment were overcome. Adapted strains were recognized and utilized and superior cultivars developed.

❧ DISTRIBUTION AND ADAPTATION

Smooth bromegrass, native to Europe and Asia, is adapted to most temperate climates. The region of major adaptation in North America is centered in the Corn Belt and adjacent areas northward and westward into Canada. Its range of distribution and use extends throughout these latitudes on favorable sites or with irrigation (Fig. 24.1).

Smooth bromegrass survives periods of drought and extremes in temperature. In dry summer periods it becomes dormant until the return of cool short days and fall moisture. At an early date it was grown successfully as far north as the Fairbanks station, Alaska.[6]

Smooth bromegrass can be grown on a variety of soil types, including sandy loams. It makes its best growth on deep fertile soils of well-drained silt loam or

4. Knowles, R. P., and W. J. White. 1949. The performance of southern strains of bromegrass in western Canada. *Sci. Agr.* 29:437–50.

5. Newell, L. C., and F. D. Keim. 1943. Field performance of bromegrass strains from different regional seed sources. *J. Amer. Soc. Agron.* 35:420–34.

6. Irwin, D. L. 1945. Forty-seven years of experimental work with grasses and legumes in Alaska. *Alaska Agr. Exp. Sta. Bull.* 12.

FIG. 24.2. *Smooth bromegrass . . . leafy, sod-forming perennial . . . spreads underground by rhizomes . . . readily propagated by seed.*

clay loam. It is deep rooted and fills the surface soil with many roots and rhizomes.

PLANT DESCRIPTION

The smooth bromegrass plant is a leafy sod-forming perennial. It spreads underground by rhizomes and is readily propagated by seed (Fig. 24.2). Inflorescences are initiated in cool short days.[7] Lengthening culms expose large open panicles in late spring or early summer. Numerous spikelets of the inflorescence are made up of many florets which produce the seed. At anthesis visible clouds of pollen are disseminated at intervals over a period of several days.[8] Setting of seed is largely by cross-fertilization.

Forage quality of smooth bromegrass compares well with other cool-season grasses. Under conditions of readily available soil N, the percentage of crude protein is very high during early plant growth. Digestible protein decreases rapidly with maturity. Digestible dry matter

increases until the initiation of seed.[9] The large amount of green forage produced early and late in the season provides grazing through a longer period than many other grasses.

CULTIVARS AND STRAINS

When smooth bromegrass is selected for planting, careful consideration should be given to seed sources and cultivars. The impact of natural selection on plantings from different latitudes in Eurasia disclosed great variation for adaptation and use.[4,5] The north central states and the Canadian prairie provinces are the leading seed-producing areas. Two general types of smooth bromegrass are recognized.

Common seed from the Dakotas and Canada, developed from north European origin, is designated northern commercial. This type produces excellent seed crops but establishes slowly and produces a more open sod than strains which became established farther south. Northern commercial seed is preferred in some of the northern and northeastern states where emphasis on the legume in the mixture is of prime importance.

In the southern Corn Belt the northern commercial seed is unadapted. The more aggressive sod-forming type of central European origin developed in Nebraska and Kansas (Fig. 24.3). Strains of the southern type exhibit superior seedling vigor, establish more readily on critical planting sites, are more drought tolerant, and are better suited for soil conservation purposes than the northern type.

'Parkland' and 'Superior,' developed at the Saskatoon, Canada, station, are the oldest selected cultivars of smooth bromegrass but are no longer produced extensively. Selected for their noncreeping habit, they are low in yield.

'Manchar,' developed from a Man-

7. Newell, L. C. 1951. Controlled life cycles of bromegrass, *Bromus inermis* Leyss., used in improvement. *Agron. J.* 43:417–24.

8. Jones, M. D., and L. C. Newell. 1946. Pollination cycles and pollen dispersal in relation to grass improvement. Nebr. Agr. Exp. Sta. Res. Bull. 148.

9. Wright, M. J., G. A. Jung, C. S. Brown, A. M. Decker, K. E. Varney, and R. C. Wakefield. 1967. Management and productivity of perennial grasses in the Northeast. II. Smooth bromegrass. Northeast Reg. Res. Publ., W. Va. Agr. Exp. Sta. Bull. 554T.

FIG. 24.3. *Strains of the southern type . . . superior.* Of historical interest is this 1941 view of field plots at the Nebraska station, where the first comprehensive research on the development of superior cultivars of the southern type was inaugurated. The Lincoln cultivar (left) was being compared with a strain of northern type (right) which proved inferior. *Nebr. Agr. Exp. Sta. photo.*

churian introduction, is grown in the Pacific Northwest and in Canada.

'Lincoln,' 'Achenbach,' 'Fischer,' and 'Elsberry' are cultivars of the southern type developed and certified respectively by Nebraska, Kansas, Iowa, and Missouri. They were derived from fields originating from the earliest introductions of seed from central Europe. These early cultivars have been planted extensively and also have been used in the development of other cultivars.

A large number of cultivars were compared in the regional uniform tests of the north central, northeastern, and western states.[10,11] 'Lancaster' and 'Lyon' were developed at the Nebraska station, 'Homesteader' by South Dakota, and 'Saratoga' at Cornell University. In the north central interstate trials continued from 1951 through 1956, the cultivars of southern type showed a larger overall production than those of northern type. The differences, greater toward the southern part of the area, appeared to be closely related to latitude.[11]

As the result of continuing development and testing, suitable cultivars are available for most parts of the smooth bromegrass region. Seed is produced under certification programs of several states and Canadian provinces.

'Southland,' selected for Oklahoma conditions, extends the usefulness of smooth

10. Wilsie, C. P. 1949. Evaluation of grass-legume associations, with emphasis on the yields of bromegrass varieties. *Agron. J.* 41:412–20.

11. Thomas, H. L., Earle W. Hanson, and J. A. Jacobs. 1958. Varietal trials of smooth bromegrass. North Central Reg. Publ., Minn. Agr. Exp. Sta. Bull. 93.

bromegrass farther south than the original cultivars of southern type.

'Carlton' is a leading cultivar of northern type particularly adapted in Saskatchewan and Alberta.[12]

'Polar,' a cultivar developed for Alaska, provides adaptation to the far north.[12]

Cultivars of southern type or derivation are used much farther northward and eastward than formerly.[9,12,13] They produce good forage yields but are usually lower in seed yields than the northern smooth bromegrasses. They begin growth earlier in the spring and remain greener in the fall than northern smooth bromegrass and are reasonably winter-hardy in western Canada.[12]

Good yield is combined with disease resistance in the cultivars 'Sac' and 'Fox' from Wisconsin and Michigan respectively.

'Redpatch' is the first cultivar to be derived in Canada from the southern type. It is grown in Ontario and Quebec.

'Magna,' largely of Fischer parentage, combines good forage yield with seed yield in Canadian comparisons.[12]

✿ CULTURE AND MANAGEMENT

Smooth bromegrass is used alone and in mixtures with other grasses and legumes. It was found to be the principal survivor in the early plantings with other introduced grasses and is usually the dominant grass in adapted mixtures.

In much of its region of adaptation suitable cultivars of smooth bromegrass are successfully used for the protection of road shoulders and even steep road cuts. In many areas it is the principal grass to be utilized alone or in mixture with other grasses for constructed waterways and terraces. Fertilizer N is a necessary requirement for the establishment of any grass cover on exposed subsoils or eroded soils

12. Knowles, R. P., D. A. Cooke, and C. R. Elliott. 1969. Producing certified seed of bromegrass. Can. Dept. Agr. Publ. 866.
13. Derscheid, Lyle A., James G. Ross, and Raymond A. Moore. 1970. Tame grasses for pasture or hay. S. Dak. Coop. Ext. Serv. Fact Sheet 299.

FIG. 24.4. *Suitable cultivars of smooth bromegrass . . . used for protection of road shoulders and . . . roadcuts . . . fertilizer N . . . requirement for establishment . . . on exposed subsoils.*

of slopes. Seedling establishment must be at a time to avoid torrential rains. (See Fig. 24.4.)

Smooth bromegrass has been the principal component of grass and legume mixtures for both irrigated and nonirrigated pastures. It is frequently planted with a legume for hay, to be followed by use as pasture. The N supplied by the legume keeps the grass productive for several years. In combination with a legume it makes an excellent sod crop for use in rotation with intertilled crops. Grass roots improve the organic matter content with a resultant improvement of soil structure. Decay of legume roots maintains a balance of available N that aids in decomposition of grass roots and release of N to the subsequent crop.

ESTABLISHMENT

A moist, fertile, firm seedbed is required for the grass and grass-legume mixtures. Time and method of seeding will be influenced by the components of the mixture. In the eastern and northern parts of its region, smooth bromegrass is planted in the spring, often with a legume and companion crop.[14] Conditions for establishment of grass-legume mixtures are usually more favorable in the spring than in

14. Moore, R. A., and Gary B. Harwick. 1969. Establishing pasture and forage crops. S. Dak. Farm and Home Res. 20 (2):6–9.

the fall. In these areas fall-sown mixtures may suffer winter injury, especially to the legume. Farther south and especially in the midcontinent, fall establishment from late summer seedings is greatly preferred. Seedlings that develop in the cool days of autumn grow rapidly the following spring and become fully established before another hot season. There is usually less weed competition with fall establishment.

In the drier parts of the smooth brome-grass belt the companion crop usually is omitted or greatly reduced. Experiments in Pennsylvania show that the companion crop may be detrimental even in areas of ample precipitation.[15]

Smooth bromegrass seed may be either drilled or broadcast. Drilling is much preferred because it permits more accurate control of seeding rate and a uniform shallow depth of planting. Smooth bromegrass and some other grass seeds can be planted with grain drills which have attached seed boxes for legume seed or with special grassland drills with seed boxes for planting both chaffy and free-flowing seed.[14] Most hopper-type fertilizer spreaders can be calibrated to broadcast seed if drills are not available. It is essential to cover the seed.

Rate of planting will vary depending on the planting objective and components of the mixture. In Kansas and Nebraska smooth bromegrass is frequently planted alone at 11.2–16.8 kg/ha or in mixture at 9–11.2 kg with alfalfa at 3.4–5.6 kg/ha. Farther north and east the amount of grass may be decreased and the legume increased. The Michigan station has recommended smooth bromegrass at 5.6 and alfalfa at 9 kg/ha on upland soils, and smooth bromegrass at 16.8 kg/ha when sown alone on muck soil.[16] In Illinois, seeding of alfalfa at 6.7–9 kg and smooth bromegrass at 10.2–13.4 kg/ha has proved

satisfactory.[17] In Indiana smooth bromegrass is seeded at 5.6–7.8 kg/ha in mixture with alfalfa at 9–11 kg/ha, or with alfalfa and red clover at rates of each at 4.5–6.7 kg/ha.[18]

STAND MANAGEMENT

Weeds or companion crops may retard establishment from spring sowing. Competition for moisture and nutrients should be removed by early and repeated mowing at a suitable height without clipping or covering the seedlings. Stands established in the fall may be harvested for seed or cut for hay the following year. Allowing the new planting to stand uncut until seed maturity permits maximum development.

Nitrogen fertilizer should be applied early in the life of the stand if the planting is on infertile soil or subsoil. Old stands may become "sodbound," requiring more N than is readily available in cool seasons to decay the vegetative accumulation and also to maintain a good growth. Stands become yellow in appearance, with greatly reduced seed and forage yields. Numerous experiments have shown that increments of N have increased yields of forage and crude protein as well as seed yields.[9,19-23] Minimum rates for forage production vary from 45 to 112 kg N/ha.

❧ HAYING AND GRAZING

Smooth bromegrass requires careful management. Early spring grazing or mow-

15. Lueck, A. G., V. G. Sprague, and R. J. Garber. 1949. The effects of a companion crop and depth of planting on the establishment of smooth bromegrass, *Bromus inermis* Leyss. *Agron. J.* 41:137–40.
16. Rather, H. C., and C. M. Harrison. 1944. Alfalfa and smooth bromegrass for pasture and hay. Mich. Agr. Exp. Sta. Circ. Bull. 189.
17. Fuelleman, R. F., W. L. Burlison, and W. G. Kammlade. 1943. Bromegrass and bromegrass mixtures. Ill. Agr. Exp. Sta. Bull. 496.
18. Smith, Lester H., and Maurice E. Heath. Forage mixtures for Indiana soils. Purdue Univ. Agron. Guide AY-182.
19. Anderson, Kling L., Ralph E. Krenzin, and J. C. Hide. 1946. The effect of nitrogen fertilizer on bromegrass in Kansas. *J. Amer. Soc. Agron.* 38:1058–67.
20. Fortmann, H. R. 1953. Responses of varieties of bromegrass *(Bromus inermis* Leyss.) to nitrogen fertilization and cutting treatments. Cornell Univ. Agr. Exp. Sta. Memo. 322.
21. Krueger, C. R., and J. M. Scholl. 1970. Performance of bromegrass, orchardgrass and reed canary-grass grown at five nitrogen levels with alfalfa. Wis. Res. Rept. 69.
22. Ukrainetz, H. 1969. Forage crop fertilization—Eastern prairies. Canadian Forage Crop Symposium, pp. 187–221. Can. Dept. Agr. Scott Sask. Exptl. Farm. (Reprint.)
23. Rehm, G. W., W. J. Moline, E. J. Schwartz, and R. S. Moomaw. 1971. Effect of fertilization and management on the production of bromegrass in northern Nebraska. Nebr. Agr. Res. Bull. 247.

ing is detrimental, as is pasturing late in the season. Overstocking too early in the season frequently results if it is the only pasture available. Smooth bromegrass pastures to be grazed continuously are necessarily understocked during the early part of the season to allow growth to accumulate for later use. Forage quality decreases with the advance in maturity. In either case, additional pasture is required for the midsummer period, especially in the midlatitudes.

For full-season use rotational grazing of smooth bromegrass pastures is advantageous over continuous grazing. It provides better timing and utilization of forage for part of the total pasture area in each period of grazing. Primary tillers can be harvested near maximum production, and aftermath tillers extend the period of grazing.[24] Yields of smooth bromegrass, like other tall grasses, decrease with more frequent cutting.[9] Control of regrowth and productivity have been associated with trends in carbohydrate reserves as affected by harvest time and degree of defoliation.[25-27]

Rotational grazing can provide the best use of spring and fall pastures.[28] In midlatitudes cereal grains or wheatgrasses supply very early pasture. Smooth bromegrass pastures may be advantageously stocked heavily in the early part of the season after the growth has been sufficient to restore reserves and before seed formation. Pastures of warm-season grasses provide grazing for midsummer. Fall growth of smooth bromegrass may be grazed judiciously or allowed to accumulate to be utilized after growth ceases. Protection from close grazing during the early fall allows for the accumulation of reserves and ensures vigorous growth the following spring.

Smooth bromegrass in a mixture with alfalfa, either for hay or pasture, appears to be an ideal combination. The mixture is productive and is ideally suited for hay harvests in favorable years with an excess of early pasture. The grass in the mixture is important in decreasing the bloat danger if used as pasture, and it also extends the season for grazing. However, smooth bromegrass tends to make a larger contribution in the early harvests than in aftermath. The legume improves acceptability and feeding value, with resulting better animal performance. The use of a pasture-type alfalfa has been suggested for improved management of a mixture with smooth bromegrass.[29]

❧ SEED PRODUCTION

When sown for seed production, smooth bromegrass is commonly planted solid without a legume. Seed-producing fields seldom continue to give good seed yields after the first two years unless N fertilized.[30]

Responses of tillering and panicle formation to photoperiod, temperature, and N availability have been shown in greenhouse studies.[7] Tillers on which panicles are formed are produced during the short days of fall and very early spring. Soil N must be readily available during short cool days prior to the elongation of the culms for panicles to be formed. Fertilizer N should be applied either in the fall or very early spring. Later applications increase vegetative growth, but their effect on seed production decreases as the season advances.

Early trials showed that applications of fertilizer N were required for maximum seed production.[19] Seed yields increase with

24. Derscheid, Lyle A., Walter N. Parmenter, and Raymond A. Moore. 1969. Grazing management based on . . . how grasses grow. S. Dak. Agr. Ext. Serv. Fact Sheet 302.

25. Eastin, Jerry, M. R. Teel, and Ruble Langston. 1964. Growth and development of six varieties of smooth bromegrass (Bromus inermis Leyss.) with observations on seasonal variations of fructosan and growth regulators. Crop Sci. 4:555–59.

26. Reynolds, J. H., and Dale Smith. 1962. Trend of carbohydrate reserves in alfalfa, smooth bromegrass, and timothy grown under different cutting schedules. Crop Sci. 2:333–36.

27. Smith, Dale, and R. D. Grotelueschen. 1966. Carbohydrates in grasses. I. Sugar and fructosan composition of the stem base of several northern-adapted grasses at seed maturity. Crop Sci. 6:263–66.

28. Moore, R. A. 1970. Symposium on pasture methods for maximum production in beef cattle pasture systems for a cow-calf operation. J. Anim. Sci. 30:133–37.

29. Rumbaugh, M. D., G. Semeniuk, R. Moore, and J. D. Colburn. 1965. Travois—An alfalfa for grazing. S. Dak. Agr. Exp. Sta. Bull. 525.

30. Churchill, B. R. 1944. Smooth bromegrass seed production in Michigan. Mich. Agr. Exp. Sta. Circ. Bull. 192.

increasing rates of N, but severe lodging frequently follows heavy applications. Heads of lodged stems fail to develop caryopses. Rates required for seed production vary with the degree of depletion of available soil N. Old stands usually require more N than new stands. Rates of 45–90 kg N/ha are frequently recommended.[12]

HARVESTING

Seed of smooth bromegrass should be allowed to ripen fully before harvesting with the combine-harvester. To reduce the amount of green material entering the bag with the seed, the crop is harvested when the culms have dried below most of the heads but before shattering occurs. Direct harvesting is seldom satisfactory until this stage is reached. The combine may be set to cut the ripened heads and to leave the green stems and leaves. To avoid loss from early shattering, the crop may be bound and shocked for threshing[30] or mowed and picked up by the combine after the seed has dried in the swath.[12]

WEEDS

Smooth bromegrass for seed production should be planted in fields free of primary noxious weeds. The chief problem weed in northern states is quackgrass, *Agropyron repens* (L.) Beauv.[30] Other wheatgrasses may be troublesome from mixtures at harvest. Weeds on roadsides and field boundaries should be mowed to prevent seed formation. Winter annual bromegrasses are principal invaders.[31] These cool-season grasses mature seed which is harvested with the seed crop and difficult to remove. Another troublesome weed is dock, *Rumex* spp. It may be removed by spraying with 2,4-D, or scattered plants can be rogued.

✲ DISEASES AND INSECTS

In subhumid areas grasshoppers and seedling blight are factors affecting grass establishment. Foliar diseases of smooth bromegrass are more prevalent and serious in humid areas and seasons.[32] Some progress in selection of cultivars with leaf-disease resistance has been made. In some years seed production of smooth bromegrass has been seriously affected by the bromegrass seed midge, *Stenodiplosis bromicola* Marikovsky & Agafonova.[33]

✲ OTHER SPECIES

Relative value of different grasses for forage is well exemplified in the genus *Bromus.* The group includes bromegrasses varying from early maturing winter annuals to the slower maturing, more productive perennials. The annuals for the most part are considered weeds where more valuable perennials are grown. In some areas they provide valuable ground cover or good forage for short periods.

Meadow bromegrass, *B. biebersteinii* Roem & Schult., is a long-lived perennial which offers promise for nonirrigated or irrigated pasture. 'Regar,' is a cultivar selected at the Idaho station from a recent Turkish introduction, PI 172390. It is a relatively early maturing bunchgrass with moderate spread and good regrowth.[34]

Native perennial bromegrasses are important forage plants in the mountain regions of the western U.S. Among these are nodding brome, *B. anomalus* Rupr.; fringed brome, *B. ciliatus* L.; and pumpelly brome, *B. pumpellianus* Scribn. They are abundant up to 3350 m and furnish first-class forage. California brome, *B. carinatus* Hook. & Arn., and the closely related mountain brome, *B. marginatus* Nees., are short-lived perennials. Both produce deep well-branched root systems and make a good leafy growth. They are utilized by grazing animals and are good seed producers.

31. Finnerty, D. W., and D. L. Klingman. 1962. Life cycles and control studies of some weed bromegrasses. *Weeds* 10:40–47.

32. Allison, J. Lewis, and Donald W. Chamberlain. 1946. Distinguishing characteristics of some forage-grass diseases prevalent in the north central states. USDA Circ. 747.

33. Nielsen, E. L., and D. D. Burks. 1958. Insect infestation as a factor affecting seed set in smooth bromegrass. *Agron. J.* 50:403–5.

34. Foster, Ronald B., Hugh C. McKay, and Edward B. Owens. 1966. Regar bromegrass. Idaho Agr. Exp. Sta. Bull. 470.

'Cucumonga' is a cultivar of California bromegrass.

'Bromar' is a mountain bromegrass cultivar released by the Washington station for the intermountain area and the Pacific Northwest. It has been grown with sweetclover in short rotations.

The winter annuals are widespread in their distribution because of prolific seed production. The best known of these is chess, *B. secalinus* L., occurring in waste places and grainfields. Downy bromegrass, *B. tectorum* L.; Japanese chess, *B. japonicus* Thunb.; and hairy chess, *B. commutatus* Schrad., occur widely distributed in pasture and rangelands.[35] These annuals become prominent when they replace perennial grasses depleted by grazing. The former is widespread over the ranges of the West and in some areas constitutes the major source of feed for livestock during the movement of flocks and herds between winter and summer ranges. Such annuals as soft chess, *B. mollis* L., and ripgutgrass, *B. rigidus* Roth, are grazed in their early stages and produce lush pasturage for a short time in the spring. Presence of awns on the matured seed of many of these annuals constitutes a serious hazard to livestock when grazing.

Rescuegrass, *B. catharticus* Vahl., is a native of Argentina introduced into the South before the Civil War. In areas with mild winters this grass makes excellent winter pasture. Several cultivars have been developed.

Field bromegrass, *B. arvensis* L., a winter annual, is adapted to the Corn Belt and eastward. It was introduced into the

U.S. in the late 1920s.[36] Seeded in late summer, this annual grows late in the fall and for a long period the following spring. Its greatest value is as a winter cover and green manure crop. Its superiority to other annual cover crops is in its rapidly developed and very extensive fibrous root growth with great soil-holding capacity. Field bromegrass has not proved troublesome as a weed.

36. Briggs, W. M. 1960. Field bromegrass looks good for the Corn Belt. *Crops and Soils* 12:9.

❧ QUESTIONS

1. What is the general area of distribution and use of smooth bromegrass?
2. What are the growth characteristics of smooth bromegrass that contribute to the recognized values of this grass?
3. Give some characteristics of the original introductions of smooth bromegrass into North America. How did they affect seed production and the development of cultivars?
4. What are the more important recognized cultivars? What is their source or derivation? How do they differ in growth habit and range of adaptation?
5. Indicate the importance of some of the species of *Bromus* other than smooth bromegrass and tell how they are utilized.
6. Explain the cultural practices involved in establishing stands of smooth bromegrass alone or in mixtures.
7. What management practices will provide for the productive use and maintenance of smooth bromegrass over a period of years?
8. How would you manage a field of smooth bromegrass for maximum seed production?
9. How does the time of applying fertilizer N to smooth bromegrass affect the yields of forage and seed?

35. Klemmedson, James O., and Justin G. Smith. 1964. Cheatgrass (*Bromus tectorum* L.). *Bot. Rev.* 30:226–62.

SUPPLEMENTAL INFORMATION

Distribution surveys and life history studies of the bromegrass seed midge, *Stenodiplosis bromicola* Marikovskiy and Agafonova, have shown damage to the smooth bromegrass seed crop.[37] Parasitism by *Tetrastichus* sp. does not

37. Neiman, E. L., and G. R. Manglitz. 1972. The biology and ecology of the bromegrass seed midge in Nebraska. Nebr. Agr. Exp. Sta. Res. Bull. 252.

prevent seed damage but may help control succeeding generations.

Smooth bromegrass pasture returns have been doubled by fertilization.[38] For irrigation responses, see Reference 40, Chapter 44.

38. Rehm, George. 1978. Fertilize; double your beef on bromegrass. *Nebr. Farmer* 120 (7): 88, 89.

G. C. MARTEN / *Agricultural Research Service, USDA, and University of Minnesota*

MAURICE E. HEATH / *Purdue University*

25

REED CANARYGRASS

❧

REED CANARYGRASS, *Phalaris arundinacea* L., was cultivated in Sweden by 1749 and in other parts of northern Europe by 1850.[1,2] Its cultivation in the U.S. probably occurred shortly afterward along the north Atlantic Coast; an Oregon planting was recorded in 1885.[3] Some credit the name "canarygrass" to the fact that seed of the annual species *P. canariensis* L. is used as food for canary birds.[4] Others believed it was named after the Canary Islands where this annual is native.[5]

❧ G. C. MARTEN is Research Agronomist, North Central Region, ARS, USDA, and Professor of Agronomy, University of Minnesota. He received the M.S. and Ph.D. degrees from the University of Minnesota and had postdoctoral study at Purdue University. His research has emphasized pasture management and its influence on forage quality and the development of techniques for forage evaluation.

❧ MAURICE E. HEATH. *See Chapter 1.*

The authors are grateful to the following persons for personal communications in 1970–72 that aided in the preparation of this chapter: I. T. Carlson, Iowa State Univ.; A. W. Hovin, Univ. Minn.; L. Klebesadel, Univ. Alaska; D. P. Knievel, Univ. Wyo.; W. J. Seamands, Univ. Wyo.; A Slinkard, Univ. Idaho; Dale Smith, Univ. Wis.; M. A. Sprague, Rutgers Univ.; D. D. Wolf, Va. Polytech. and State Univ.

❧ DISTRIBUTION AND ADAPTATION

Members of the genus *Phalaris* have been collected on every major land mass except Antarctica and Greenland.[6] Reed canarygrass is indigenous to the temperate portions of all five continents and is well adapted to the northern half of the 48 states and southern Canada. The largest hectarages are found in the Pacific Northwest and the humid north central states (Fig. 25.1).

While its natural habitat is poorly drained and wet areas, it is more drought tolerant than many cool-season grasses grown in the humid and subhumid regions.[7,8] However, it tends to winter-kill

1. Alway, F. J. 1931. Early trials and use of reed canarygrass as a forage plant. *J. Amer. Soc. Agron.* 23: 64–66.
2. Vose, P. B. 1959. The agronomic potentialities and problems of the canarygrasses, *Phalaris arundinacea* L. and *Phalaris tuberosa* L. *Herb. Abstr.* 29:77–83.
3. Schoth, H. A. 1929. Reed canarygrass. USDA Farmers' Bull. 1602.
4. Hoover, M. M., M. A. Hein, W. A. Dayton, and C. O. Erlanson. 1948. The main grasses for farm and home. *In* Grass, pp. 639–700. USDA Yearbook Agr.
5. Lamson-Scribner, F. 1938. Canarygrasses (Phalarideae). *Nature* 31:156.
6. Anderson, D. E. 1961. Taxonomy and distribution of the genus *Phalaris. Iowa State J. Sci.* 36:1–96.
7. Wilkins, F. S., and H. D. Hughes. 1932. Agronomic trials with reed canarygrass. *J. Amer. Soc. Agron.* 24:18–28.
8. Illinois Agr. Exp. Sta. 1938. Yields of reed canarygrass. Ann. Rept., 1937.

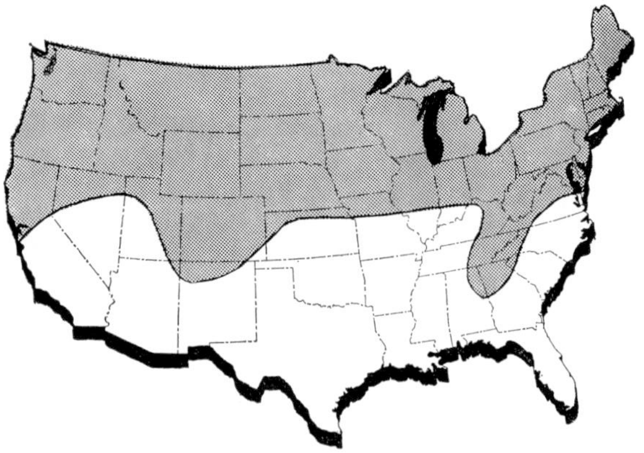

FIG. 25.1. Areas of the U.S. in which reed canarygrass is adapted. In the dry western areas it must be irrigated.

on dry upland soils of the Canadian prairies when snow cover is sparse.[9] Reed canarygrass is very tolerant of flooding and the following range in days for tolerance to spring flooding has been reported: mature plants, 49 or more; seedlings, 35–49; seed, 35–56.[10] No damaging effects were found when this species was grown in pots with 25 mm of water over the soil surface for three months. Reed canarygrass is not adapted to saline soils but tolerates a pH range of 4.9–8.2.[9,11,12]

The leaves of reed canarygrass are killed by temperatures not low enough to kill leaves of timothy or Kentucky bluegrass.[13] The yield of reed canarygrass was reduced more by low temperature than that of smooth bromegrass (soil temperatures ranged from 10 to 21 C).[14] Also, it suffered more winter injury than either intermediate wheatgrass or smooth bromegrass on irrigated land in Saskatchewan.[15] Reed canarygrass is not hardy at Palmer or at College, Alaska.[13] On the other hand, it does not perform well in subtropical or tropical climates. Net photosynthesis of reed canarygrass was maximum at air temperatures of about 20 C and was reduced to 80% of maximum at 38 C.

PLANT DESCRIPTION

Reed canarygrass is a tall, coarse, sod-forming, cool-season perennial. In thin or volunteer stands it often grows in clumps up to 1 m or more in diameter. It spreads underground by short scaly rhizomes which form a heavy sod in well-managed solid seedings. It ranges in height from 60 to 240 cm.[3] Flowers are borne in semidense, spikelike panicles of 5–20 cm.[3] The light gray to gray black waxy seed (about 3 mm long) shatter quickly at ripening; they mature from the top of the panicle downward. The leafy stems are usually sufficiently stout to prevent lodging. Individual plants vary greatly in agronomic characteristics.[13,16]

COMPOSITION AND NUTRITIVE VALUE

CRUDE PROTEIN CONCENTRATION. Crude protein (CP) is the nutrient of reed canarygrass that has been most extensively studied. Early Minnesota research showed a CP range of 7–25% of herbage dry matter, with culms having as low as 3% and panicles as high as 30%. More variation in CP was associated with stage of maturity (lower with increased maturity) and soil N (higher with increased N) than with grass genotype.[17] The vegetative stage of reed canarygrass was found to range in CP from 20 to 27% in British Columbia and to contain up to 30% CP on peat and min-

9. Goplen, B. P., S. G. Bonin, W. E. P. Davis, and R. M. MacVicar. 1963. Reed canarygrass. Can. Dept. Agr. Publ. 805.
10. McKenzie, R. E. 1951. The ability of forage plants to survive early spring flooding. *Sci. Agr.* 31:358–67.
11. Ahlgren, G. H., and C. Eby. 1942. Better pasture and hay crops. N.J. Agr. Exp. Sta. Circ. 448.
12. Decker, A. M., G. A. Jung, J. B. Washko, D. D. Wolf, and M. J. Wright. 1967. Management and productivity of perennial grasses in the Northeast. I. Reed canarygrass. W. Va. Agr. Exp. Sta. Bull. 550T.
13. Evans, M. W., and J. E. Ely. 1941. Growth habits of reed canarygrass. *J. Amer. Soc. Agron.* 33:1018–27.
14. Read, D. W. L., and R. Ashford. 1968. Effect of varying levels of soil and fertilizer phosphorus and soil temperature on the growth and nutrient content of bromegrass and reed canarygrass. *Agron. J.* 60:680–82.
15. Lawrence, T., and R. Ashford. 1969. Effect of stage and height of cutting on the dry matter yield and persistence of intermediate wheatgrass, bromegrass, and reed canarygrass. *Can. J. Plant Sci.* 49:321–32.
16. Baltensperger, A. A., and R. R. Kalton. 1958. Variability in reed canarygrass (*Phalaris arundinacea* L.). I. Agronomic characters. *Agron. J.* 50:659–63.
17. Alway, F. J., and G. H. Nesom. 1930. Protein content of reed canarygrass on peat soils. *J. Agr. Res.* 40:297–320.

eral soils fertilized with about 300 kg N/ha in Minnesota.[9,18] A CP range of 11–18% existed in hay or haylage of reed canarygrass, depending on year and cutting date (150 kg N/ha).[19]

The CP in several cultivars of reed canarygrass at early hay stages increased from 13 to 19% as N rates increased from 75 to 600 kg/ha.[20] In a New Jersey trial unfertilized reed canarygrass contained 13% CP, compared to 20% CP with 224 kg N/ha; CP digestibility also increased with N fertilizer (68% without N and 78% with 224 kg N/ha).[21] Crude protein concentrations of about 11% appeared when second regrowth reed canarygrass was cut after more than three months of growth, compared to about 16% after only two months of growth.[22]

Subherbicidal applications of simazine increased both CP and nitrate N concentrations in reed canarygrass.[23] The CP increased by as much as 5 percentage units (at low levels of fertilizer N) when 0.56 kg simazine/ha was applied. Nitrate N went from less than 75 ppm in control forage to over 100 ppm by applying simazine on low-N plots and from less than 500 ppm to over 750 ppm on high-N plots.

The CP concentration of reed canarygrass has frequently been compared to that of other grasses harvested at similar stages.[24-27] Reed canarygrass has either as much CP or more than smooth bromegrass, orchardgrass, meadow fescue, meadow foxtail, and creeping foxtail. It contains more CP than timothy, tall fescue, tall oatgrass, many wheatgrasses, and quackgrass. Crested wheatgrass and Russian wildrye contain more CP than reed canarygrass. Reed canarygrass liberally fertilized with N contains as much CP as alfalfa cut on the same date.[18,28]

CONCENTRATION OF OTHER NUTRITIONALLY SIGNIFICANT SUBSTANCES. In a trial where eight grasses were harvested at six specific growth stages, reed canarygrass was superior to all except 'Alta' tall fescue in minerals but was desirably lower than all in crude fiber and lignin except Kentucky bluegrass and redtop; other species included smooth bromegrass, orchardgrass, timothy, and tall oatgrass.[27] When hay of several species was harvested on the same dates, first-crop reed canarygrass had lower acid detergent fiber (ADF) and lignin (ADL) than smooth bromegrass, timothy, alfalfa, and birdsfoot trefoil; ADF of several cuttings of reed canarygrass ranged from 27 to 33%, while ADL ranged from 3 to 4%.[29] Reed canarygrass green chop contained lower cellulose and lignin than alfalfa, but reed canarygrass was higher in cell walls; this indicated greater hemicellulose in reed canarygrass.[28] In another study, reed canarygrass hay or haylage had a range of 25–32% crude fiber and 6–8% ash.[19] Early cut reed canarygrass hay contained 25–32% cellulose.[23]

DIGESTIBILITY. Reed canarygrass is as digestible to ruminants as most of the perennial temperate grasses and leg-

18. Marten, G. C. 1971. Unpubl. data, Univ. Minn.
19. Colovos, N. F., R. M. Koes, J. B. Holter, J. R. Mitchell, and H. A. Davis. 1969. Digestibility, nutritive value and intake of reed canarygrass (*Phalaris arundinacea* L.). *Agron. J.* 61:503–5.
20. Niehaus, M. H. 1971. Effect of N fertilizer on yield, crude protein content, and *in vitro* dry matter disappearance in *Phalaris arundinacea* L. *Agron. J.* 63:793–94.
21. Barth, K. M., G. W. VanderNoot, and J. L. Cason. 1959. A comparison of the nutritive value of alfalfa hay with bromegrass and reed canarygrass hays at various levels of nitrogen fertilization. *J. Nutr.* 68:383–91.
22. Asay, K. H., I. T. Carlson, and C. P. Wilsie. 1968. Genetic variability in forage yield, crude protein percentage, and palatability in reed canarygrass, *Phalaris arundinacea* L. *Crop Sci.* 8:568–71.
23. Allinson, D. W., and R. A. Peters. 1970. Influence of simazine on crude protein and cellulose content and yield of forage grasses. *Agron. J.* 62:246–50.
24. Lawrence, T., F. G. Warder, and R. Ashford. 1971. Effect of stage and height of cutting on the crude protein content and crude protein yield of intermediate wheatgrass, bromegrass, and reed canarygrass. *Can. J. Plant Sci.* 51:41–48.
25. Johnson, J. R., and J. T. Nichols. 1969. Production, crude protein, and use of 11 irrigated grasses and alfalfa-grass combinations on clay soils in western South Dakota. S. Dak. Agr. Exp. Sta. Bull. 555.

26. Krueger, C. R., and J. M. Scholl. 1970. Performance of bromegrass, orchardgrass, and reed canarygrass grown at five nitrogen levels and with alfalfa. Wis. Agr. Exp. Sta. Res. Rept. 69.
27. Phillips, T. G., J. T. Sullivan, M. E. Laughlin, and V. G. Sprague. 1954. Chemical composition of some forage grasses. I. Changes with plant maturity. *Agron. J.* 46:361–69.
28. Barnes, R. F., and G. O. Mott. 1970. Evaluation of selected clones of *Phalaris arundinacea* L. I. *In vivo* digestibility and intake. *Agron J.* 62:719–22.
29. Ingalls, J. R., J. W. Thomas, E. J. Benne, and M. Tesar. 1965. Comparative response of wether lambs to several cuttings of alfalfa, birdsfoot trefoil, bromegrass, and reed canarygrass. *J. Anim. Sci.* 24:1159–64.

umes and more digestible than some. Numerous workers have reported that the digestibility of reed canarygrass is equal to or higher than that of alfalfa.[28-33] Reed canarygrass has frequently been found more digestible than other common perennial grasses cut at similar growth stages.[26,31,33-36] Reed canarygrass is often more digestible than timothy, orchardgrass, and tall fescue. However, fall-saved tall fescue pasture (active growth into late fall) was more digestible than fall-saved reed canarygrass (dormant in late fall).[37] Reed canarygrass is as digestible as smooth bromegrass or more so.

A broad-sense heritability of 51–80% of digestibility among fall-saved reed canarygrass clonal means has been noted, indicating the possibility of breeding for improved digestibility in this species.[38] No digestibility differences occurred among available cultivars.[20]

No change in digestibility of reed canarygrass occurred with N rates of 75–600 kg/ha in one study.[20] Subherbicidal applications of simazine increased digestibility.[39]

Silica appears to rival lignin in importance in reducing digestibility of structural carbohydrates in reed canarygrass.[40] An average decline of three units of digestibility has been found per unit of silica in the dry matter, and a correlation of −0.86 has been noted between SiO_2 concentration and digestible dry matter. The grass ranged from 0.6 to 5.4% in SiO_2. On the other hand, another study found no correlation between silica and in vitro digestibility of 33 clones of reed canarygrass when silica comprised from 1.1 to 6.2% of the dry matter.[18]

PALATABILITY, ALKALOIDS, AND INTAKE. Lack of palatability is the most frequently cited reason why this agronomically superior species has not become a leading forage grass in its area of adaptation.[41] However, extremely little sound evidence exists to document the real significance of palatability differences among forage species. The few controlled studies that have attempted to document the significance of unpalatability of reed canarygrass have given contradictory evidence.

Poorer performance of lambs and ewes grazed on reed canarygrass compared to smooth bromegrass has been reported from Michigan.[42] Organic matter intake by sheep of two palatable clones of reed canarygrass was greater than intake of two unpalatable clones in several trials.[32] In contrast, in British Columbia no differences were found in average daily gains of wethers grazing reed canarygrass fertilized with varying levels of N and those grazing a mixture of smooth bromegrass, orchardgrass, and ladino clover.[43] The preference of dairy heifers for smooth bromegrass over reed canarygrass was of no practical significance when the two grasses were grazed

30. Archibald, J. G., H. D. Barnes, H. Fenner, and B. Gersten. 1962. Digestibility of alfalfa hay and reed canarygrass hay measured by two procedures. J. Dairy Sci. 45:858–60.

31. Davis, L. E., G. C. Marten, and R. M. Jordan. 1967. Applicability of chromogen and nitrogen as internal indicators of forage digestibility. Agron. J. 59:544–46.

32. O'Donovan, P. B., R. F. Barnes, M. P. Plumlee, G. O. Mott, and L. V. Packett. 1967. Ad libitum intake and digestibility of selected reed canarygrass (Phalaris arundinacea L.) clones as measured by the fecal index method. J. Anim. Sci. 26:1144–52.

33. Hoveland, C. S., E. M. Evans, and D. A. Mays. 1970. Cool-season perennial grass species for forage in Alabama. Ala. Agr. Exp. Sta. Bull. 397.

34. Hoveland, C. S., and W. B. Anthony. 1971. Winter forage production and in vitro digestibility of some Phalaris aquatica introductions. Crop Sci. 11:461–63.

35. Pritchard, G. I., L. P. Folkins, and W. J. Pigden. 1963. The in vitro digestibility of whole grasses and their parts at progressive stages of maturity. Can. J. Plant Sci. 43:79–87.

36. Pringle, W. L., and J. E. Miltimore. 1966. Digestibility of bog forage. Can. J. Plant Sci. 46:702.

37. Wedin, W. F., I. T. Carlson, and R. L. Vetter. 1966. Studies on nutritive value of fall-saved forage, using rumen fermentation and chemical analyses. Proc. 10th Int. Grassl. Congr., pp. 424–28 (Helsinki, Finland).

38. Carlson, I. T., K. H. Asay, W. F. Wedin, and R. L. Vetter. 1969. Genetic variability in in vitro dry matter digestibility of fall-saved reed canarygrass, Phalaris arundinacea L. Crop Sci. 9:162–64.

39. Allinson, D. W. 1971. Response of reed canarygrass to subherbicidal applications of simazine. Agron. Abstr. p. 53.

40. Van Soest, P. J., and L. H. P. Jones. 1968. Effect of silica in forages upon digestibility. J. Dairy Sci. 51:1644–48.

41. Marten, G. C. 1970. Measurement and significance of forage palatability. In R. F. Barnes et al. (eds.), Proc. Nat. Conf. Forage Qual. Eval. Util., pp. D1–D55. Nebr. Center Continuing Ed., Lincoln.

42. Blakeslee, L. H., C. M. Harrison, and J. F. Davis. 1956. Ewe and lamb gains on brome and reed canarygrass pasture. Mich. Agr. Exp. Sta. Quart. Bull. 39:230–35.

43. Hubbard, W. A., and H. H. Nicholson. 1968. Reed canarygrass vs. grass-legume mixtures under irrigation as pasture for sheep. J. Range Manage. 21:171–74.

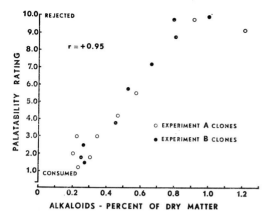

FIG. 25.2. Relationship between palatability rating (high rating = low palatability) and alkaloid concentration of 18 reed canarygrass clones from two experiments at St. Paul, Minn. (Simons and Marten, 1971.[50])

without choice, as heifers gained exactly the same on both.[44]

The discovery of potentially toxic alkaloids in reed canarygrass and the convincing evidence that concentration of total basic alkaloids is negatively correlated with palatability of this species have added a new dimension to the palatability and intake question (Fig. 25.2).[45-50] The lack of palatability may not have adversely affected intake and animal performance in those cases where this has been seemingly so, but the associated alkaloids may have been of sufficient quantity to cause toxicities resulting in poor intake and/or performance.

For example, the assumedly low intake of reed canarygrass by grazing steers (resulting in low daily gains) was accompanied by rough haircoat and profuse watering of the eyes.[51] Also, an alkaloidal type of lesion was found in the livers of dairy cows that were performing poorly and receiving reed canarygrass in the ration.[48]

"Phalaris staggers," a severe neurological and cardiac disease, occurs in livestock grazing hardinggrass, *Phalaris aquatica* L. (formerly named *P. tuberosa* L.), in Australia.[6] This species has three of the same primary alkaloids found in reed canarygrass (gramine, N-N,dimethyltryptamine, and 5-methoxy-N,N-dimethyltryptamine).[46,50,52] A similar nervous disorder and death of sheep grazing ronphagrass (a *Phalaris* hybrid introduced from South Africa) was observed in Florida.[53] However, no case of "phalaris staggers" has ever been reported for animals grazing reed canarygrass in the U.S. Reports of successful use of reed canarygrass as pasture, hay, or silage far exceed the reports of poor performance.

Regardless of the true significance of the existence of alkaloids and low relative palatability in reed canarygrass, sizable genetic differences are known to exist within the species for these factors.[22,49,50,54-56] This points to the possibility of breeding new cultivars low in alkaloids and high in relative palatability (Fig. 25.3). For example, the presence of tryptamine alkaloids in reed canarygrass is controlled by a single dominant gene.[54] No variation in total

44. Marten, G. C., and J. D. Donker. 1968. Determinants of pasture value of *Phalaris arundinacea* L. vs. *Bromus inermis* Leyss. *Agron. J.* 60:703–5.
45. Wilkinson, S. 1958. 5-Methoxy-N-methyltryptamine: A new indole alkaloid from *Phalaris arundinacea* L. *Chem. Soc. J.* 2079–81.
46. Culvenor, C. C. J., R. Dal Bon, and L. W. Smith. 1964. The occurrence of indole alkylamine alkaloids in *Phalaris tuberosa* L. and *P. arundinacea* L. *Aust. J. Chem.* 17:1301–4.
47. Audette, R. C. S., H. M. Vijayanagar, J. Bolan, and K. W. Clark. 1970. Phytochemical investigation of Manitoba plants. I. A new indole alkaloid and associated alkaloids from *Phalaris arundinacea*. *Can. J. Chem.* 48:149–55.
48. Audette, R. C. S., J. Bolan, H. M. Vijayanagar, R. Bilous, and K. Clark. 1969. Phytochemical investigation of Manitoba plants. II. A gas-liquid chromatographic screening technique for the identification of the alkaloids of *Phalaris* species. *J. Chromatog.* 43:295–302.
49. Williams, M., R. F. Barnes, and J. M. Cassady. 1971. Characterization of alkaloids in palatable and unpalatable clones of *Phalaris arundinacea* L. *Crop Sci.* 11:213–17.
50. Simons, A. B., and G. C. Marten. 1971. Relationship of indole alkaloids to palatability of *Phalaris arundinacea* L. *Agron J.* 63:915–19.

51. Van Arsdell, W. J., G. A. Branaman, C. M. Harrison, and J. F. Davis. 1954. Pasture results with steers on reed canarygrass. *Mich. Agr. Exp. Sta. Quart. Bull.* 37:125–31.
52. Oram, R. N., and J. D. Williams. 1967. Variation in concentration and composition of toxic alkaloids among strains of *Phalaris tuberosa* L. *Nature* 213:945–47.
53. Ruelke, O. C., P. E. Loggins, J. T. McCall, C. B. Ammerman, and C. F. Simpson. 1961. Ronphagrass and sheep don't mix. *Fla. Agr. Exp. Sta. Res. Rept.* 6, no. 3, pp. 8–9.
54. Woods, D. L., and K. W. Clark. 1971. Genetic control and seasonal variation of some alkaloids in reed canarygrass. *Can. J. Plant Sci.* 51:323–29.
55. Barnes, R. F., W. E. Nyquist, and R. C. Pickett. 1970. Variation in acceptability and covariation with agronomic characters in *Phalaris arundinacea* L. Proc. 11th Int. Grassl. Congr., pp. 202–6 (Surfers Paradise, Queensland, Aust.).
56. Roe, R., and B. Mottershead. 1962. Palatability of *Phalaris arundinacea* L. *Nature* 193:225–57.

FIG. 25.3. *Reports of successful use . . . exceed reports of poor performance.* Extreme differences in herbage removal of reed canarygrass clones by grazing sheep indicate differences in relative palatability and the possibility of breeding for its improvement. *Minn. Agr. Exp. Sta. photo.*

alkaloid concentration or palatability exists among available cultivars.[18]

Palatability of reed canarygrass may be associated with factors other than alkaloids. Organic solvent extracts of an unpalatable strain if sprayed on a palatable strain caused the latter to become unpalatable; whether alkaloids were present in the extract was not determined.[56] Fertilizer N increased the palatability of reed canarygrass to beef cows in an Alabama study.[57] However, several attempts to repeat this finding gave variable and usually negative results with dairy cattle and sheep in Minnesota.[58] A foul-smelling residue left by the frit fly, *Oscinella frit* L., which was prevalent in Connecticut, may have negatively influenced palatability of reed canarygrass.[59] Reduced palatability with increased maturity is commonly observed for most perennial forages, including reed canarygrass. Insofar as alkaloid concentration is greatly reduced with advancing maturity, another phenomenon (probably buildup of structural components) must be reducing palatability in this case.

Actual intake (measured as units of grass dry matter consumed per animal unit per day) of reed canarygrass has been compared with that of other forages. In one trial, reed canarygrass hay was inferior to birdsfoot trefoil and alfalfa in both total and digestible dry matter intake by sheep, but its intake was usually not significantly different from that of smooth bromegrass or timothy.[29] The following sheep intakes of hay dry matter in grams per kilogram of body weight were reported: alfalfa, 29–33; smooth bromegrass, 28–33; common reed canarygrass, 25–31; and a Siberian source of reed canarygrass, 20.[60] Similarly, other research indicated that sheep intake of alfalfa pasture or green chop was greater than that of four clones of reed canarygrass.[28,32]

Reed canarygrass scored lower in six-hour *in vitro* digestibility (claimed to be a valid measure of nutritive value index, which equals intake $\times$ digestibility) than did alfalfa or birdsfoot trefoil.[61] However, reed canarygrass scored as well as smooth bromegrass and higher than orchardgrass in the test for either two, three, or four seasonal cuttings. Growing rabbits consumed more ground reed canarygrass hay than ground timothy hay cut at the same stage, but they gained more on the timothy.[62] Grazing steers usually consumed more reed canarygrass than tall fescue in an Iowa study.[63] A delay in reed canarygrass harvest of 12–15 days after the first week in June in New Hampshire caused a 20 and 24% loss in dry matter intake by cattle and sheep respectively.[19]

✄ IMPORTANCE AND USE

Reed canarygrass is often successfully used for pasture, hay, and silage. It is a vital part of many soil conservation programs and has become the most popular

57. Andrews, O. N., Jr., and C. S. Hoveland. 1965. Apparent palatability of reed canarygrass and hardinggrass as affected by nitrogen. *Agron. J.* 57:315–16.
58. Marten, G. C., R. M. Jordan, and J. D. Donker. 1971. Unpubl. data, Univ. Minn.
59. Wolf, D. D. 1967. Yield reductions in reed canarygrass caused by frit fly infestation. *Crop Sci.* 7:239–40.

60. Thomas, J. W., A. D. L. Gorrill, G. N. Blank, and M. B. Tesar. 1965. Acceptability of alfalfa, bromegrass, and canarygrass by sheep and their performance. *J. Anim. Sci.* 24:911.
61. Allinson, D. W., M. B. Tesar, and J. W. Thomas. 1969. Influence of cutting frequency, species, and nitrogen fertilization on forage nutritional value. *Crop Sci.* 9:504–8.
62. Crampton, E. W. 1934. Pasture studies. IV. Nutritive value of pasture herbage: Quality of protein. *Emp. J. Exp. Agr.* 2:337–48.
63. Bryan, W. B., W. F. Wedin, and R. L. Vetter. 1970. Evaluation of reed canarygrass and tall fescue as spring-summer and fall-saved pasture. *Agron. J.* 62:75–80.

FIG. 25.4. *Reed canarygrass . . . one of the highest yielding perennial grasses . . . in its area of adaptation.* Here it is successfully used for silage, hay, and pasture on a poorly drained soil in southern Indiana. *Purdue Univ. Agr. Exp. Sta. photo.*

species for irrigation with sewage effluent from municipal and industrial sources as a pollution control measure.

PASTURE

For best quality pasture, reed canarygrass should be grazed when it ranges from 15 to 60 cm tall.[44] Maturer grass will be poorly utilized and will give poor animal intake and performance. Reed canarygrass begins growth early in spring and continues to provide a good distribution of growth until killing frost if moisture and fertility are not severely limiting.

Rotational grazing, with heavy pressure for short periods, provides the best utilization of reed canarygrass. Under continuous light grazing,[2] young growth from unfolding shoots is prominent and selectively grazed, leaving mature growth. With season-long grazing, a stiff short stubble will build up, even under heavy rotational grazing; cattle will not graze below this stubble. A single close (5–7 cm) clipping in midsummer will solve the problem.[44]

Good performance has been obtained with both sheep and cattle on unsupplemented reed canarygrass pasture. Equal daily gains were noted for heifers grazing reed canarygrass or smooth bromegrass.[44] There were no significant differences in daily gains of sheep grazing reed canarygrass alone; reed canarygrass plus ladino clover; or a mixture of smooth bromegrass, orchardgrass, and ladino.[43] Greater steer gains on reed canarygrass than on birdsfoot trefoil pasture were reported.[64] Also, satisfactory milk yields resulted from cows grazing only reed canarygrass.[65]

On the other hand, research also showed poorer performance of lambs and ewes grazing reed canarygrass compared to smooth bromegrass, and steer gains on reed canarygrass–ladino clover pastures were equivalent to those on orchardgrass-ladino only when at least 30–50% clover was present.[42,66]

Reed canarygrass is one of the highest yielding perennial grasses used for grazing in its area of adaptation. (See Fig. 25.4.) It outyielded smooth bromegrass in pasture trials in Iowa, Minnesota, and Nebras-

64. Wedin, W. F., and R. L. Vetter. 1970. Grain feeding on birdsfoot trefoil or reed canarygrass pastures. *Agron. Abstr.*, pp. 77–78.

65. Hodgson, R. E., M. S. Grunder, and J. C. Knott. 1932. Carrying capacity of pure stands of reed canarygrass. Wash. Agr. Exp. Sta. Bull. 275, p. 29.

66. Decker, A. M. 1959. Midland bermudagrass, a new forage grass for Maryland. Md. Agr. Exp. Sta. Bull. 465.

ka.[37,44,67] Reed canarygrass is similar to orchardgrass in that both regrow well throughout the pasture season.[26] It is not as useful as tall fescue for fall-saved winter pasture since tall fescue continues to grow later in the season (after frost) and retains its quality better into the winter.[37]

Reed canarygrass develops a sod sufficiently firm to support grazing animals even on wetland. Farm machinery is supported on sod in areas that were impassable before reed canarygrass was established. It is well adapted to seepy hillside pastures and soils with poor internal drainage.

HAY

The high yield capacity of reed canarygrass hay was recognized as early as 1929 by Schoth in Oregon who reported hay yields of 9–20 t/ha in the U.S.[3] More recent experiments in four northeastern states showed the ease of obtaining over 13 t/ha of dry matter with adequate fertilizer and favorable cutting management.[12] Reports showed nearly 12 t/ha of dry matter with high N fertilization of several cultivars in Ohio and as high as 17 t/ha dry matter in Indiana.[20,68]

An early report from Iowa revealed that reed canarygrass yielded the most hay of seven grasses (including smooth bromegrass, timothy, and orchardgrass) tested on a droughty soil.[7] Reed canarygrass also had higher yields than seven other grasses and five legumes on muck soils in Michigan.[69] In a Pennsylvania study reed canarygrass yielded more hay than smooth bromegrass or tall fescue, but less than orchardgrass.[70] In contrast, it outyielded orchardgrass and smooth bromegrass, but not tall fescue, in Indiana when supplied with adequate N.[68]

Timothy outyields reed canarygrass in eastern Canada on well-drained soils but is outyielded by reed canarygrass on poorly drained soils.[9] Reed canarygrass also yields less hay than intermediate wheatgrass under irrigation in Saskatchewan and Nevada.[24,71] However, reed canarygrass ranked among the highest yielding of 11 irrigated grasses in South Dakota.[25] It outyielded timothy, creeping foxtail, meadow foxtail, and Russian wildrye in irrigated mountain meadows of Wyoming where only tall fescue yielded more.

While early workers recommended cutting the first hay crop of reed canarygrass soon after emergence of the first panicles,[2,3] better quality hay will result if the first crop is taken before heading. If this is done, three excellent quality crops can be obtained (with adequate N and moisture) in all but the northernmost areas of adaptation, where two crops can be harvested.

In low wet areas, which cannot be harvested by machinery early enough in the season to allow good quality hay production, reed canarygrass can be permitted to mature for a high yield of good quality bedding straw.

SILAGE

Reed canarygrass makes a palatable and nutritious silage when harvested at the same stages used for hay.[3,9] Preservation of reed canarygrass silage is excellent, provided it is harvested by early heading time and is chopped fine; it then has a high feeding value for dairy cows. Silage offers the possibility of saving the grass when drying conditions are not suitable for curing hay.

SOIL CONSERVATION

Reed canarygrass is frequently used for gully control and for the maintenance of grassed waterways, stream channel banks,

67. Moline, W. J., E. J. Schwartz, and A. D. Flowerday. 1967. Fertilizers, do they pay? *Nebr. Farm, Ranch, and Home Quart.* Spring.

68. Rhykerd, C. L., C. H. Noller, K. L. Washburn, Jr., S. J. Donohue, K. L. Collins, L. H. Smith, and M. W. Phillips. 1969. Fertilizing grasses with nitrogen. Agron. Guide AY-176. Purdue Univ.

69. Tesar, M. B., and L. N. Shepherd. 1963. Evaluation of forage species on organic soil. *Agron. J.* 55:131–34.

70. Washko, J. B., and R. P. Pennington. 1956. Forage and protein production of nitrogen-fertilized grasses compared with grass-legume associations. Pa. Agr. Exp. Sta. Bull. 611.

71. Jensen, E. H., J. B. Price, F. F. Peterson, H. Harris, N. Ritter, and C. Torell. 1970. Irrigated forages for northern Nevada type climate. Nev. Agr. Ext. Serv. Circ. 105.

and edges of farm ponds because its vigorous, spreading growth prevents soil erosion. It stands in a class by itself for control and healing of gullies.[72] Small pieces of sod are embedded at intervals of 30–60 cm in the bottom of gullies and across them when the soil is moist, either in early spring or late summer. These are not washed away by rain as easily as seed or seedling plants. Great volumes of water will pass over properly embedded sod pieces without removing them. The shoots will penetrate up to 20 cm of sediment if it should be deposited. Small pieces of sod (8 cm or smaller) appear to be as satisfactory as larger ones.[73] Best results occur when the top of the sod piece is placed about 3–5 cm below the soil surface.[74]

Where large gullies are filled and shaped into waterways, sods can be planted with a manure spreader in the center of the waterway at a rate of 35–45 t/ha. They should be disked in, followed by firming with a roller. Grass seed should be distributed over the entire waterway area at the same time that sod pieces are planted.

Reed canarygrass will also produce roots and shoots from the nodes of freshly cut, well-jointed culms that have been covered with 3–5 cm of moist soil (Fig. 25.5).[75] Mature stems produce more vigorous plants. Plants from mature green hay may reach a height of 15 cm in 30 days, with roots up to 20 cm long. Some plants may even head several months after culms are planted. In very wet, muddy conditions this method may be superior to sod planting.[76]

This grass should not be used in drainage ditches or along slow-running, shallow streams because silting may occur. It is considered a serious weed along irrigation banks and ditches. A vigorous program was launched in the 1971 Idaho state legislature to declare reed canarygrass a nox-

FIG. 25.5. *Reed canarygrass will . . . produce roots and shoots . . . nodes of freshly cut, well-jointed culms . . . covered with 3–5 cm of moist soil.* Establishing reed canarygrass for farm pond bank control by pushing fresh culms into moist soil. *Nebr. SCS photo.*

ious weed in that state. Support by university and SCS personnel for retaining it as a forage crop, as well as the fact that the species is widely distributed in Idaho, prevented approval of the action.

❧ CULTIVARS

Relatively few cultivars of reed canarygrass have been developed by plant breeders, and even fewer are available in the U.S. and Canada as commercial seed.

The cultivar 'Superior' was developed in Oregon for use on upland sites.

'Ioreed,' developed at the Iowa station, was released in 1946. It is a recombination of the best selections from a large number of sources grown in Iowa.[77]

'Auburn' is a selection from highly persistent plants released by the Alabama station in 1952.[33]

The cultivar 'Rise,' selected for improved disease resistance and high seed retention, was developed by the Rudy-Patrick Seed Company in Iowa.

72. Hughes, H. D., and V. B. Hawk. 1954. Reed canary stops gullies. *Crops and Soils* 6 (8):14–15, 35.
73. Heimann, H. C. 1949. Vegetative reproduction of reed canarygrass. Unpubl. M.S. thesis, Iowa State Univ.
74. Hughes, H. D. 1949. Gully control with reed canarygrass. *Forage Notes* 4:75–78. (Iowa.)
75. Heath, M. E. 1947. Reed canarygrass propagated from green hay or cuttings. *Forage Notes* 2:90. (Iowa.)
76. Holmberg, G. 1959. Vegetating critical areas. *J. Soil Water Conserv.* 14:165–68.

77. Hanson, A. A. 1972. Grass varieties in the United States. USDA Agr. Handbook 170, rev.

Two leafy cultivars were released by the Ottawa station in Ontario: 'Frontier' is considered somewhat later maturing than most common reed canarygrass, and 'Grove' is 7–10 days later than Frontier.[78] Canadian tests revealed that Rise is even somewhat later in maturity than Frontier and Grove and that it yields slightly more.[79] However, Minnesota tests showed no consistent differences in yield among reed canarygrass cultivars, including Rise.

The cultivar 'Vantage,' developed at Iowa State University, was released in the U.S. in 1972. It has better seed retention and heads two to three days earlier than Rise in Iowa. The most recent Canadian cultivar is 'Castor,' developed by S. G. Bonin in Alberta. It also has high seed retention but otherwise resembles Frontier.[79a]

Considerable plant breeding effort is under way to develop improved cultivars. Much variability in agronomic characteristics and quality components of this species suggests great opportunity for improvement.[16,22,38,50,80] Evaluation of selections in Iowa indicates good prospects for developing synthetic cultivars with improved seed yield and retention, while the development of hybrid cultivars appears to offer promise for improving forage yield.[81]

❧ CULTURE AND MANAGEMENT

SEEDING

Establishing a good stand is the biggest problem in growing reed canarygrass, as the seed germinate slowly and irregularly.[2] Low seed germination may be caused by dormancy; immaturity; overheating during drying; and susceptibility of broken, aged, and dehulled seed to molds after planting.[82–85] Much of the available seed is low in percent of germination; but if germination is 80% or higher, a seeding rate of 6–10 kg/ha is usually adequate on a firm seedbed.

Either spring or late summer seedings are satisfactory if sufficient moisture is available. Reed canarygrass seed and seedlings are not as drought tolerant as Russian wildrye or orchardgrass.[86] Very late fall seeding may be required on poorly drained areas, and it can be successful if the seed do not germinate until spring. Seed and seedlings can withstand 35 or more days of flooding,[10] but reed canarygrass seedlings are more susceptible to freezing than those of most other cool-season grasses.[87]

REED CANARYGRASS–LEGUME MIXTURES

Traditionally, seeding a legume with reed canarygrass has not been advised because of the competition provided by the vigorous grass. However, more frequent cutting of hay and rotational grazing of pasture has increased the success of reed canarygrass–legume mixtures. Management must favor the legume by reducing the competition of the grass for light.

Successful maintenance of reed canarygrass–alfalfa mixtures has been reported in South Dakota, Wisconsin, and Saskatchewan.[25,26,88] Generally, these reports show the N contribution of the alfalfa is substantial. Up to 200 kg N/ha may be required for a pure grass stand to equal the yield of alfalfa or an alfalfa–reed canarygrass mixture.

78. Canada Dept. Agr., Plant Products Div. 1970. License 1268.
79. Canada Dept. Agr., Plant Products Div. 1971. License 1294.
79a. Canadian Seed Growers Assoc. 1972. *The Seed Scoop* 19(5):5.
80. Baltensperger, A. A., and R. R. Kalton. 1959. Variability in reed canarygrass. II. Seed shattering. *Agron. J.* 51:37–38.
81. Carlson, I. T. 1966. Clonal and topcross evaluation of selections of reed canarygrass, *Phalaris arundinacea* L. Proc. 10th Int. Grassl. Congr., pp. 637–41 (Helsinki, Finland).

82. Vose, P. B. 1956. Dormancy of seeds of *Phalaris arundinacea* and *P. tuberosa*. *Nature* 178:1006–7.
83. Morris, G. C. 1938. Germination studies of hull-less seeds of canarygrass. Proc. Assoc. Off. Seed Analysts 39:259.
84. Colbry, V. L. 1953. Factors affecting the germination of reed canarygrass seed. Proc. Assoc. Off. Seed Analysts 45:50–56.
85. Griffith, W. L., and C. M. Harrison. 1954. Maturity and curing temperatures and their influence on germination of reed canarygrass seed. *Agron. J.* 46:163–67.
86. Wood, G. M., and P. A. Kingsbury. 1971. Emergence and survival of cool-season grasses under drouth stress. *Agron. J.* 63:949–51.
87. Arakeri, H. R., and A. R. Schmid. 1949. Cold resistance of various legumes and grasses in early stages of growth. *Agron. J.* 41:182–85.
88. Kilcher, M. R., and D. H. Heinrichs. 1971. Sward assessment of ten irrigated pasture mixtures in southern Saskatchewan. *Can. J. Plant Sci.* 51:391–97.

Ladino clover has also been grown successfully with reed canarygrass.[9,43,66] This mixture is especially adapted to poorly drained soils. However, close control of the height of the grass is often critical for the persistence of the clover; the grass should not be allowed to exceed 40 cm before cutting or grazing. Even then animals may selectively graze the clover, due to its greater palatability, and reduce the clover stand.[43]

Alsike clover mixed with reed canarygrass is recommended for poorly drained burned-over lands in northern Idaho.[89] Red clover and birdsfoot trefoil are recommended legumes for mixtures with reed canarygrass in parts of Canada.[9] Reed canarygrass persists well with crownvetch for hay on fragipan soils in southern Indiana.[90]

FERTILIZATION

On upland soil reed canarygrass becomes "sod-bound" and unproductive within several years unless it is well fertilized, especially with N.[12] While it responds mainly to N, increased yields may occur with added P and K when soils are deficient in these elements.[9,14,91,92] Results in New Jersey indicate that the K requirements of N-fertilized reed canarygrass may be as high as those of alfalfa.[93]

Nitrogen also produced the greatest increase in seed yield of reed canarygrass, even though other elements, including P, were limiting on both peat and upland soils.[94]

Reed canarygrass forage yields continue to increase beyond 200 kg/ha of applied N

per year.[20,68,95] The superior yielding capacity of reed canarygrass compared to other cool-season grasses may not appear until at least this level of N is used.[68] Split applications of N during the growing season result in more uniform production and lengthen the productive period of reed canarygrass.

CUTTING

Reed canarygrass clipped at approximately 10 and 13 cm had faster rates of regrowth and higher yields than grass clipped at 3 and 5 cm.[96] A regional study involving four northeastern states suggested that continual close cutting (at about 4 cm) would result in lower reserve levels and eventually less vigorous plants; however, removing or retaining the growing point when harvesting one aftermath crop (by low versus high clipping) had only a small and inconsistent effect on yield and persistence.[12] In a Wisconsin study frequent cutting (four cuts per season) at close defoliation (4 cm, compared with 10 cm) reduced the stand and yield of reed canarygrass grown between rows of alfalfa. Height of cutting did not affect stand or yield with two or three cuttings per season. In a Pennsylvania study if the spring crop was removed when the growing point was 5, 10, or 20 cm above the soil, slower regrowth resulted at a 4-cm than at a 9-cm cutting height; but if the growing point was 30 cm above the soil or if heads had emerged, cutting height was not critical.[97] A Canadian experiment showed that cutting reed canarygrass at about 4 cm resulted in the highest degree of winter injury and rapid stand deterioration (compared to cutting at about 8 or 15 cm).[15]

In contrast, a more recent study indicated that the dry matter production of

89. Slinkard, A. E., E. O. Nurmi, and J. L. Schwendiman. 1970. Seeding burned-over lands in northern Idaho. Idaho Ext. Serv. Current Info. Ser. 139.
90. Heath, M. E. 1971. Reed canarygrass. Purdue Univ. Agron. Guide AY-60.
91. Mason, J. L., and J. E. Miltimore. 1970. Yield increases from fertilizer on reed canarygrass and sedge meadows. *Can. J. Plant Sci.* 50:257–60.
92. Pringle, W. L., and A. L. van Ryswyk. 1967. Response of reed canarygrass on sedge-organic soil to fertility levels and temperature in the growth room. *Can. J. Plant Sci.* 47:305–10.
93. Ramage, C. H. 1958. Drouth insurance by the bag. *N. J. Agr.* (March–April):14–15.
94. Thompson, J. R. 1964. Yield and seed quality of *Phalaris arundinacea* L. under certain fertilizer and management practices. *Agron. Abstr.*, p. 98.

95. Bonin, S. G., and D. C. Tomlin. 1968. Effects of nitrogen on herbage yields of reed canarygrass harvested at various developmental stages. *Can. J. Plant Sci.* 48:511–17.
96. Davis, W. E. P. 1960. Effect of clipping at various heights on characteristics of regrowth of reed canarygrass. *Can. J. Plant Sci.* 40:452–56.
97. Horrocks, R. D., and J. B. Washko. 1969. Spring growth of reed canarygrass (*Phalaris arundinacea* L.) and Climax timothy (*Phleum pratense* L.) under different harvesting systems. *Crop Sci.* 9:716–19.

reed canarygrass was not affected by the stage of development at which the first harvest was removed, regardless of whether clipping was at 4 or 10 cm.[98] In a northeastern regional study there was no relationship between cutting the first crop at different growth stages and stand persistence, although total yields of dry matter were usually optimum when the first crop was harvested at heading stage.[12]

Studies in British Columbia showed that total dry matter yields declined slightly, while digestible dry matter and crude protein yields declined greatly, if reed canarygrass was harvested after the heading stage.[95]

❧ SEED PRODUCTION

The order of maturity of reed canarygrass seed is from the top of the panicle downward. The first seed to mature shatter before the bulk of the crop is ready for harvest. Only several days elapse between the ripening of the first seed and shattering of a large portion of the crop. Shattering is a two-stage process, the first involving disjointing of the rachilla about 12 days after flowering, and the second allowing release of seed from the glumes. In low-shattering clones the glumes retain the seed within the spikelet.[99] The shattering problem accounts for the continued high price of reed canarygrass seed. Yields of seed vary from under 60 to over 500 kg/ha.[2]

Reed canarygrass may be grown in rows about 90 cm apart for maximum seed production.[100] Wide spacing promotes tillering and allows cultivation for weed control.[9] However, much commercial seed is harvested from solid stands.

Most reed canarygrass seed is harvested with combines. About 40–50% of the seed

should be dark gray or brown before direct combining is begun. The reel may have to be altered to allow raising of the combine table above the green leafy part of the plant when direct combining is used. The seed usually must be dried to prevent heating. This is accomplished by spreading a thin layer (about 8 cm maximum) on the floor of a well-ventilated building, with frequent mixing for several days.[9] Unheated forced air or air heated to a maximum of about 40–45 C may be used in a drying bin for curing large quantities of seed. Swathing is sometimes used to allow drying of the grass before combining; this is essential in humid areas where tall, rank vegetation does not permit direct combining.

Rebuilt grain binders are also commonly used for heading reed canarygrass, especially in low-lying areas. The heads fall into baskets which are later dumped on high land. Several days later the seed crop is combined from partially dried piles.

Heritability estimates were obtained for three primary components of seed yield in reed canarygrass.[101] Estimates were 91% for seed shattering, 74% for seed weight per panicle, and 70% for number of panicles per plant. The heritability for theoretical seed yield was 36%. The researchers concluded that net seed yield could be improved by selection for both low seed shattering and high seed weight per panicle. Seed yield was not correlated with number of panicles per plant.[101]

❧ DISEASES AND INSECTS

Freedom from susceptibility to insects and diseases is a major advantage that reed canarygrass holds over most other forage species adapted to its region. Schoth stated in 1929 that no diseases serious enough to attract any attention attack this grass, and at present it is troubled very little by insects. During occasional years when grass-

98. Horrocks, R. D., and J. B. Washko. 1971. Studies of tiller formation in reed canarygrass (*Phalaris arundinacea* L.) and 'Climax' timothy (*Phleum pratense* L.). *Crop Sci.* 11:41–45.

99. Bonin, S. G., and B. P. Goplen. 1963. A histological study of seed shattering in reed canarygrass. *Can. J. Plant Sci.* 43:200–205.

100. Heath, M. E. 1946. The establishment and testing of grass and legume species with special emphasis on their value for soil conservation. Iowa Agr. Exp. Sta. Ann. Rept., pp. 81–82.

101. Bonin, S. G., and B. P. Goplen. 1966. Heritability of seed yield components and some visually evaluated characters in reed canarygrass. *Can. J. Plant Sci.* 46:51–58.

hoppers and cutworms are numerous, slight damage is done.[3]

The leaf disease *Helminthosporium giganteum* Heald and Wolf sometimes attacks reed canarygrass. A topcross progeny test was effective in discriminating among parent clones for reaction to this disease.[81]

Connecticut researchers recorded the infestation of reed canarygrass with frit fly, *Oscinella frit* (L.).[102] A characteristic symptom of infestation in young shoots was the dying ("flagging") of the central leaf, while other leaves remained green. Reed canarygrass was the only forage grass in the area that was infested. Yields of reed canarygrass were reduced 0.52 t/ha in the second harvest due to frit fly infestation, and fly control increased aftermath yields by 32% in low N plots and 17% in plots fertilized with 200 kg N/ha.[59] However, in a nationwide survey in 1965, frit fly was seldom found on reed canarygrass, even though the insect was present in most states. Frit fly attack of reed canarygrass may be widespread but not recognized.[59]

✲ OTHER SPECIES

According to Anderson 15 species have been identified within the genus *Phalaris*.[6] He gives keys, synonymies, descriptions, illustrations, and distributions of these species.

An interesting taxonomic problem has developed regarding the incorrect naming of the species commonly referred to as *P. tuberosa* var. *stenoptera* (Hack.) Hitchc. in the U.S. and simply *P. tuberosa* L. in Australia. Its common name is hardinggrass in the U.S. and Toowoomba canarygrass in Australia. Other incorrect scientific names for the species have been *P. bulbosa* L. and *P. nodosa* Murr. These names were antedated by *P. aquatica* L., published in 1755, which is the oldest available legitimate name.[6] This name has priority, according to the International Code of Nomenclature, and should therefore be used in all future reference to this species.[34] It is a cool-season perennial, grown in the Southwest and the Southeast for winter pasture and hay.

Koleagrass is an introduction from Morocco classified *P. tuberosa* var. *hirtiglumis* Batt. & Trab. but indistinguishable from introductions labeled *P. aquatica* in an Alabama study.[34] The SCS in California increased another plant introduction from Morocco, received as *P. tuberosa* var. *stenoptera* and later reidentified as *P. tuberosa* var. *hirtiglumis*, which they called 'Perla.'[77] It resembles other cultivars of *P. aquatica* but has better seedling vigor and more winter forage production in Alabama.[33]

Ronphagrass, *P. aquatica* L. (= *P. tuberosa* L.) × *P. arundinacea* L., is a sterile hybrid between hardinggrass and reed canarygrass that was developed in South Africa. It has the high winter production of hardinggrass and the low palatability of reed canarygrass.[33] Hybrids of hardinggrass and reed canarygrass possess the winterhardiness characteristics of reed canarygrass.[103] Hexaploid plants of the first generation backcross to hardinggrass parents were also more winter-hardy than hardinggrass and did not shatter mature seed as readily as reed canarygrass.[104] Embryo abortion following interspecific pollination of these species was attributed to failure of the endosperm to differentiate normally.[105] Ronphagrass may produce "staggers" in sheep similar to that caused by *P. aquatica* in Australia. Supplementation of the diet with cobalt apparently prevents this condition.[53]

Canarygrass, *P. canariensis* L., is an annual grown for bird food. The name should not be confused with reed canarygrass, a perennial.

103. Starling, J. L. 1961. Cytogenetic study of interspecific hybrids between *Phalaris arundinacea* and *P. tuberosa*. *Crop Sci.* 1:107–11.

104. Allison, D. C., and J. L. Starling. 1963. Cytogenetic studies of BC₁ and BC₂ generations from interspecific hybrids between *Phalaris arundinacea* and *P. tuberosa*. *Crop Sci.* 3:154–57.

105. Devine, T. E., and J. L. Starling. 1969. Impediments to hybridization of *Phalaris arundinacea* and *P. tuberosa*. *Crop Sci.* 9:140–43.

102. Wolf, D. D., and M. G. Savos. 1965. Observations of frit fly injuries on reed canarygrass. *FAO Plant Protect. Bull.* 13:14–16.

Littleseed canarygrass, *P. minor* Retz, is a winter annual used for pasture in Brazil, Uruguay, and Argentina.

A distinct variant within reed canarygrass is ribbongrass or gardener's garters, *P. arundinacea* var. *picta* (L.) Asch. & Graebn.[6] The blades have white longitudinal stripes, making it an attractive ornamental.

❧ QUESTIONS

1. Describe the characteristics of reed canarygrass that determine its range of adaptation.

2. Compare the feeding quality of reed canarygrass to that of other forage species.

3. What is the significance of the occurrence of alkaloids in this grass?

4. Why does reed canarygrass have great potential as a forage species?

5. List and discuss the problems associated with the establishment, production, and utilization of reed canarygrass as forage.

6. Why is reed canarygrass so valuable in soil conservation?

7. What are the recommended practices in growing and harvesting reed canarygrass seed?

SUPPLEMENTAL INFORMATION

Alfalfa and reed canarygrass had similar dry matter digestibility when 5-week-old regrowth was fed to lambs either as hay or as fresh forage.[106] However, lambs consumed only 69% as much reed canarygrass as alfalfa and they gained much more weight when fed alfalfa. Lambs lost weight when they received only fresh, immature reed canarygrass but gained 48 g per day when they received reed canarygrass hay. The fresh grass contained nearly twice as much indole alkaloid as did the hay.

Lambs in Minnesota gained significantly more while grazing smooth bromegrass or orchardgrass than reed canarygrass.[107] They suffered recurring diarrhea from reed canarygrass pasture during periods when alkaloid concentration was high. In another Minnesota trial, total alkaloid concentration of this grass was highly negatively associated with gains by both lambs and steers.[108] Poorest gains and greatest diarrhea incidence occurred from grazing plants that had tryptamine-carboline type alkaloids, especially from regrowth following drought.

A ninth indole alkaloid was discovered in reed canarygrass, and the cultivar 'Vantage' was shown to be free of tryptamines-carbolines.[109, 110]

New reed canarygrass pest information has surfaced. Armyworms, *Pseudaletia unipunctata* (Haworth), sometimes preferentially attack reed canarygrass. Within a 72-hour period in 1974, armyworms almost completely devoured a 10-ha field of regrowth reed canarygrass at Rosemount, Minnesota; they avoided adjacent fields of corn and soybeans and left a lone alfalfa plant that had invaded the reed canarygrass meadow. Pennsylvania researchers found that reed canarygrass irrigated with municipal sewage effluent had fewer culms killed by frit fly and fewer cereal leaf beetle, *Oulema melanopus* (L.) larvae than that which was not irrigated.[111] Other Pennsylvania work led to the discovery of tawny blotch, *Stagonospora foliicola* (Bres.) Rubig, on reed canarygrass; sewage effluent application favored tawny blotch infection of mature grass.[112]

106. Donker, J. D., G. C. Marten, R. M. Jordan, and P. K. Bhargava. 1976. Effects of drying on forage quality of alfalfa and reed canarygrass fed to lambs. *J. Anim. Sci.* 42:180–84.

107. Marten, G. C., and R. M. Jordan. 1974. Significance of palatability differences among *Phalaris arundinacea* L., *Bromus inermis* Leyss., and *Dactylis glomerata* L. grazed by sheep. Proc. 12th Int. Grassl. Congr., pp. 305–12 (Moscow, USSR).

108. Marten, G. C., R. M. Jordan, and A. W. Hovin. 1976. Biological significance of reed canarygrass alkaloids and associated palatability variation to grazing sheep and cattle. *Agron. J.* 68:909–14.

109. Gander, J. E., P. Marum, G. C. Marten, and A. W. Hovin. 1976. The occurrence of 2-methyl-1,2,3,4-tetrahydro-β-carboline and variation in alkaloids in *Phalaris arundinacea*. *Phytochemistry* 15:737–38.

110. Hovin, A. W., and G. C. Marten. 1975. Distribution of specific alkaloids in reed canarygrass cultivars. *Crop Sci.* 15:705–7.

111. Byers, R. A., and K. E. Zeiders. 1976. Effect of spray irrigation with municipal sewage effluent on the cereal leaf beetle and the frit fly infesting reed canarygrass. *J. Environ. Qual.* 5:205–6.

112. Zeiders, K. E. 1975. *Stagonospora foliicola*, a pathogen of reed canarygrass spray-irrigated with municipal sewage effluent. *Plant Dis. Reptr.* 59:779–83.

JERREL B. POWELL AND A. A. HANSON
Agricultural Research Service, USDA

26

TIMOTHY

᎓

THE APPEARANCE of timothy, *Phleum pratense* L., in North America has been traced to the early settlements in New England.[1] Early agriculturalists referred to it as Herd grass after John Herd. He reportedly found it about 1711 growing wild along the Piscataqua River near Portsmouth, N.H. Although the record of the early history of timothy cultivation is sometimes equivocal, Timothy Hanson clearly played an important role in promoting the use of this grass in Maryland around 1720 and later in North Carolina and Virginia. By 1747 it was well known as timothy grass in Pennsylvania and as Herd grass in Massachusetts. Benjamin Franklin, in a letter dated July 16, 1747, to Jared Eliot, states that the Herd grass sent to him was "mere timothy." This is the first known recorded use of the name.[1]

Timothy met a critical need in the northeastern U.S. for an adapted, high-quality hay plant. Cultivated timothy was taken to England for forage trials about 1763.[2] Timothy occurred naturally in pastures there and was known as cat's tail or meadow cat's tail. Cultivation of timothy was not practiced in England except in mixtures with other grasses. In Sweden timothy was reportedly cultivated under the name "Angkampe" before seed arrived from America.[2]

Even though early agriculturalists believed timothy was native to North America, evidence clearly indicates that it did not occur in primitive areas of North America. Timothy probably became established from seed carried from Europe by early settlers in hay, litter, manure, and ballast cleaned from ships.[3]

᎓ JERREL B. POWELL is Research Geneticist, ARS, USDA, Beltsville, Md. He received the M.S. degree from Oklahoma State University and the Ph.D. from Washington State University. His research concerns the cytogenetic and mutation breeding of grasses.

᎓ ANGUS A. HANSON is Director, Agricultural Research Center, ARS, USDA, Beltsville, Md. He received the M.S. degree from McGill University and the Ph.D. from Pennsylvania State University. He has done research on the cytogenetics and breeding behavior of grasses.

᎓ DISTRIBUTION AND ADAPTATION

Phleum pratense is native to the Eurasian continent but is distributed through-

1. Piper, Charles V., and Katherine S. Bort. 1915. The early agricultural history of timothy. *J. Amer. Soc. Agron.* 7:1–14.
2. Witte, Hernfrid. 1915. On timothy grass: the history, cultivation, and abundance of varieties developed from experimentation with this forage crop in Svalöf. Sveriges Utsädesförenings Tidskrift. häftena 1. 95 pp. (Swedish) reprint.
3. Edwards, Everett E. 1948. The settlement of grassland. *In* Grass, pp. 16–25. USDA Yearbook Agr.

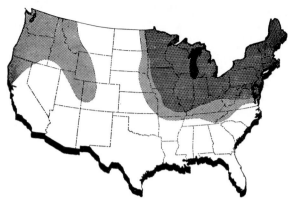

FIG. 26.1. Timothy-producing areas in the contiguous U.S.

out temperate and subarctic climates.[4,5] It occurs from the northern tip of Norway, throughout Scandinavia, and south into Algeria. It grows from England to the Baltic States and into the USSR. Timothy occupies temperate sites in South America and has been introduced into Australia. In North America timothy grows in coastal and central Alaska, the southern portion of the provinces of Canada, and the northern portion of the contiguous U.S. Within the U.S. it is best adapted to the region east of the Great Plains extending south through Missouri, Kentucky, Virginia, and into adjacent states. Also, timothy is found in the Pacific Northwest and northern intermountain regions (Fig. 26.1).[6]

Timothy is adapted to cool humid climates but not to droughty conditions. Considerable differences in daylengths occur between the northern and southern limits of adaptation of timothy. The time required for heading, anthesis, and maturity is affected by daylength (Fig. 26.2).[7,8] Early and late timothy selections re-

sponded differently to latitudes ranging from Washington, D.C., to Guelph, Ontario, Canada. The earliest selection in the South flowered 24 days earlier than the same selection in the North, while the three latest selections flowered 6–16 days earlier in the North than in the South.[9] The optimum temperature for growing timothy under controlled environment ranged from 18.3 to 21.6 C in one test,[10] while in another test day/night temperatures of 15/10 C and 21/15 C were optimum.[11] Cultivars moved too far from their area of adaptation may not produce to their full potential and will not fit with other species grown in mixtures. (See Fig. 26.2.)

✵ PLANT DESCRIPTION

Timothy is a perennial bunchgrass characterized by a dense cylindric, spikelike inflorescence and erect culms. Most cultivated timothy ranges from 80 to 110 cm in height, has flat elongate leaves, and produces many tillers in isolated plants. The spikelets of the inflorescence of timothy are one-flowered. Usually *P. pratense* can be distinguished from other species of *Phleum* by its larger panicle and shorter length of glume awns.[5]

Timothy differs from most grasses in that one and sometimes several basal culm internodes become greatly swollen and produce a haplocorm or corm. New shoots develop from buds at the base of the culm below the haplocorm. From these shoots new culms arise and develop new haplocorms, and the old culm or haplocorm dies.[12] Individual timothy shoots are typically biennial, but the plant maintains itself as perennial through the development

4. Gregor, J. W., and F. W. Sansome. 1930. Experiments on the genetics of wild populations. II. *Phleum pratense* L. and the hybrid *P. pratense* L. × *P. alpinum.* L. *J. Genet.* 22:373–87.
5. Nordenskiöld, H. 1945. Cytogenetic studies in the genus *Phleum. Acta Agr. Suecana* 1:1–137.
6. Evans, Morgan W. 1912. Timothy production on irrigated land in the northwestern states. USDA Farmers' Bull. 502.
7. Allard, H. A., and Morgan W. Evans. 1941. Growth and flowering of some tame and wild grasses in response to different photoperiods. *J. Agr. Res.* 62:193–228.
8. Hanson, A. A., and V. G. Sprague. 1953. Heading of perennial grasses under greenhouse conditions. *Agron. J.* 45:248–51.

9. Evans, Morgan W., H. A. Allard, and O. McConkey. 1935. Time of heading and flowering of early, medium and late timothy plants at different latitudes. *Sci. Agr.* 15: 573–79.
10. Baker, Barton S., and G. A. Jung. 1968. Effect of environmental conditions on the growth of four perennial grasses. II. Response to fertility, water, and temperature. *Agron. J.* 60:158–62.
11. Balasko, J. A., and Dale Smith. 1971. Influence of temperature and nitrogen fertilization on the growth and composition of switchgrass (*Panicum virgatum* L.) and timothy (*Phleum pratense* L.) at anthesis. *Agron. J.* 63:853–56.
12. Sheard, R. W. 1968. Relationship of carbohydrate and nitrogen compounds in the haplocorm to the growth of timothy (*Phleum pratense* L.). *Crop Sci.* 8:658–63.

FIG. 26.2. *Time required . . . heading, anthesis, and maturity . . . affected by daylength.* The effect of the number of hours of daily illumination on the flowering of timothy is strikingly evident. All the plants were propagated vegetatively from a single original timothy plant. The control plant (C) was grown under natural length of day. *Ohio Agr. Exp. Sta. photo.*

and growth of new shoots from bases of older culms.[13] The root system of timothy is relatively shallow and fibrous.[14] It does not spread laterally and form a sod by means of underground rooting stems or rhizomes as do Kentucky bluegrass, smooth bromegrass, or reed canarygrass.

Phleum pratense has a wide range of variation in plant characteristics.[5,15] Much variation is found in growth habit, leaf and stem characteristics, head type, earliness, longevity, winterhardiness, and macrocharacteristics such as glume size and pollen fertility.

✤ IMPORTANCE AND USE

Timothy is grown primarily for hay, but new cultivars are much improved for pasture use. It generally is grown in mixture with clover, alfalfa, or birdsfoot trefoil. The first growth frequently is harvested for hay or silage, and the aftermath pastured.

Where timothy is adapted, its yield compares favorably with that of other grasses. In northern Wisconsin timothy produced more dry matter than smooth bromegrass and orchardgrass when grown in pure stands.[16] It also exceeded the two grasses when grown in association with birdsfoot trefoil and red clover. (See Table 26.1.)[16]

The area of all hays harvested in the U.S. increased from 7.3 million ha in 1866 to 17 million ha by 1900. Timothy was the most important cultivated hay crop of this period. Since 1900 production areas of all hays increased and then decreased slightly. However, the production area of timothy has declined markedly. (See Table 26.2.)[17] In 1919 timothy and clover, mainly red clover, made up 45.6% of all hays harvested, but only 21.5% in 1969. Seed production has declined from approximately 52,200 to 12,000 t.

In the states from Minnesota, Iowa, and Missouri eastward, the production area of clover alone for the 1909, 1919, and 1924 crop years was 5.7, 7.7, and 10.1% respectively of the total timothy and clover production area. This suggests that timothy was included in 90% or more of the total "timothy or clover, alone or mixed" plantings.

In the 12 northeastern states, the amount of timothy seed shipped to retailers and farmers has continued to decline.[18] During the periods 1954–59 and 1960–64 shipments averaged 5412 and 2861 t respective-

13. Langer, R. H. M. 1956. Growth and nutrition of timothy *(Phleum pratense)*. I. The life history of individual tillers. *Ann. Appl. Biol.* 44:166–87.

14. Lambda, P. S., H. L. Ahlgren, and R. J. Muckenhirn. 1949. Root growth of alfalfa, medium red clover, bromegrass and timothy under various soil conditions. *Agron. J.* 41:451–58.

15. Clark, Charles F. 1910. Variation and correlation in timothy. Cornell Univ. Agr. Exp. Sta. Bull. 279, pp. 301–50.

16. Schmidt, D. R., and G. H. Tempas. 1960. Comparison of the performance of bromegrass, orchardgrass, and timothy in northern Wisconsin. *Agron. J.* 52:689–91.

17. USDA. 1936–69. Agricultural statistics.

18. Pardee, W. D., and L. S. Beckham. 1971. Report northeast seed use survey, small-seeded grasses and legumes. Mimeo. Rept. PB 71-8. Dept. Plant Breeding and Biometry, Cornell Univ.

TABLE 26.1 ❧ Three-year average yields of grasses cut at hay (total of two cuttings) and pasture (total of three cuttings) stages when grown in pure stands with and without N fertilization and in two legume associations, Wisconsin

	Hay (kg/ha dry matter)				Pasture (kg/ha dry matter)			
Growing condition	Timothy	Smooth brome- grass	Orchard- grass	Average	Timothy	Smooth brome- grass	Orchard- grass	Average
Pure grass, no-nitrogen	4,560	3,794	3,795	4,050	2,938	2,296	2,938	2,675
Pure grass, 90.8 kg N	10,821	11,053	10,982	10,952	7,175	6,295	8,063	7,178
Grass-alfalfa-ladino- association	8,466	8,485	8,050	8,334	5,759	6,133	5,641	5,844
Grass-trefoil–red clover association	7,182	5,660	5,445	6,095	4,358	3,809	3,783	3,984

Source: Schmidt and Tempas, 1960.[16]

ly, declining steadily to 1454 t in 1971. From 1967 to 1971 timothy seed shipments in the Northeast declined 46%.

The decreasing production of hay and seed of timothy from 1909 to 1971 has been influenced by a number of factors. The number of horses and mules in the U.S. declined during this same period. As their numbers decreased, the demand for timothy hay produced on many farms as a cash crop also decreased. The value of timothy in pasture mixtures is restricted by comparatively poor regrowth under warm dry conditions. The availability of improved cultivars of smooth bromegrass and orchardgrass, with their greater suitability for pasture, has contributed to further reductions in the use of timothy. The

popularity of alfalfa as a high-yielding hay crop and the increased use of corn for silage have resulted in a corresponding reduction in the use of perennial grasses such as timothy for hay.

❧ CULTIVARS AND STRAINS

New improved cultivars of timothy have become available and their use by farmers has been steadily increasing. (See Table 26.3.)[19] Sixty-six cultivars were involved in international trade in 1971. These were certified by the international Organization for Economic Cooperation and Development.[20] Approximately 20 timothy cultivars were in use in the U.S. in 1971.[21]

Regional adaptation is an important consideration in growing timothy. Cultivars developed in northern Europe tend to be later than cultivars developed for the southern timothy-growing region of the U.S.

The cultivar 'Clair' was the only one tested in Tennessee that reached early bloom at the time red clover was at a similar stage for high-quality hay.[22]

TABLE 26.2 ❧ Hectarage harvested of all hay, timothy, and clover, percent timothy and/or clover, and tons of timothy seed produced in the U.S.

Year	All hay (000 ha)	Timothy and clover (000 ha)	Timothy and clover (% of all hay)	Timothy seed (t)
1919	29,600	13,490	45.6	52,180
1929	28,140	12,090	43.0	26,390
1939	28,020	7,560	27.0	26,850
1949	29,470	7,500	25.4	18,180
1959	26,820	5,840	21.8	21,320
1969	25,020*	5,390	21.5	11,970

Source: USDA, 1936–69.[17]
* Preliminary.

19. Fortmann, H. R. 1966. Multiplication and distribution of improved forage varieties. Pa. Agr. Exp. Sta. Bull. 732.
20. Organization for Economic Cooperation and Development. 1971. Scheme for the varietal certification of herbage seed moving in international trade. List of cultivars eligible for certification. OECD, Paris.
21. Hanson, A. A. 1972. Grass varieties in the United States. USDA Agr. Handbook 170, rev.
22. Fribourg, Henry A. 1963. Performance of some forage crop varieties, 1945–1962. Tenn. Agr. Exp. Sta. Bull. 371.

TABLE 26.3 ✤ Use of improved cultivars of timothy seed in the Northeast and the U.S.

Location	1952–54		1961–62	
	Total usage (t)	Improved cultivar (%)	Total usage (t)	Improved cultivar (%)
New York	1,712	1	912	32
Pennsylvania	1,361	0	980	10
Other 10 northeastern states	2,373	trace*	672	3
12 northeastern states	5,491	trace	2,564	16
Total U.S.	20,666	...	14,952	15

Source: Fortmann, 1966.[19]
* Less than 0.5%.

In contrast, 'Essex' timothy is late maturing and therefore matches the late blooming characteristic of 'Empire' birdsfoot trefoil under New York conditions.[23]

The first known attempts to improve timothy by selecting from populations of common timothy were begun in 1889 by Hays at the Minnesota station. Other early investigators were Hopkins at West Virginia and Hunt and Webber at Cornell University. Timothy improvement has been a major objective of several state agricultural experiment stations, the USDA, and other agricultural organizations in Canada and Europe as well as private corporations. Current breeding research in the U.S. has declined, probably in response to reduced use of this grass.

Characteristically, *P. pratense* is self-sterile; however, selection for self-fertility has been practiced and studied for breeding improvement.[24,25] Methods employed to develop new cultivars include mass selection, polycross progeny tests, maternal line selection, and collection of naturalized strains.

A brief description of some improved cultivars is included (Table 26.4);[21] however, for detailed information a description of grass cultivars in the U.S. should be consulted.[21]

✤ CULTURE AND MANAGEMENT

Timothy, when established in mixture with a legume, should be planted at the recommended time for establishment of the legume. If timothy is sown alone, it can be seeded in early spring or late summer. Timothy seed ideally should be sown 1.25 cm deep in moist soil (60% field capacity).[26] Dry conditions or very wet conditions would require seedings somewhat deeper or nearer the surface respectively. Surface seedings are satisfactory if moisture conditions remain ideal throughout the germination period. In mixtures timothy should be sown at the rate of 2–8 kg/ha of good quality seed.

In timothy-legume mixtures, the grass utilizes some of the N fixed by the legume. Higher forage quality is obtained when timothy is grown with an adapted legume. Mixtures of timothy and a legume will sometimes revert to grass after several years. The disappearance of the legume may result from the use of an unadapted cultivar, poor management, winter-killing, diseases, or insects. Application of N to these largely grass hayfields and pastures should extend their profitability and maintain productivity.

PRODUCTION AND QUALITY

Timothy cut for hay will produce maximum dry matter yields when cut at the

23. Chance, C. M., W. L. Griffeth, C. W. Loomis, A. A. Johnson, and C. S. Winkelblech. 1961. Forages: Production, harvesting, utilization. Cornell Univ. Misc. Bull. 39.

24. Clarke, Sidney E. 1927. Self-fertilization in timothy. *Sci. Agr.* 7:409–39.

25. Nath, J., and E. L. Nielsen. 1962. Interrelations of reproductive stages of timothy. *Crop Sci.* 2:49–51.

26. Williams, Stella S. 1954. The effect of depth of sowing and moisture on the germination and seedling development of *Phleum pratense* L. *J. Ecol.* 42:445–59.

TABLE 26.4 ❧ Improved cultivars grown in the U.S.

Cultivar	Releasing authority	Source or breeding methods	Maturity	Other information
Astra	Plant Breeding Inst., Weibullsholm	mass selection of indigenous plants	like climax	resists disease, winter-hardy
Bariton	Barenbrug, Holland, N.V.	from lawns, pastures, uncultivated areas	late	winter-hardy, dark green
Bounty	Canada Dept. Agr. Res., W. R. Childers	from 5 high-yielding progeny Otofte and Wooster, Ohio, materials	late	tall, leaves high on culm, larger culms than Climax
Champ	Canada Dept. Agr. Res., W. R. Childers and L. P. Folkins	from closely grazed farmer field, a 4-clone synthetic	5–7 days earlier than Climax	good aftermath production, fine culms
Clair	Kentucky station, USDA, R. C. Buckner	from naturalized strains from a southern Indiana farm	very early	coarse, good aftermath production and persistence
Climax	Canada Dept. Agr. Res., R. M. Mac-Vicar	selected from wide collection of seed lots, a synthetic from tested clones	7–10 days later than common	rust resistant, leafy, good aftermath production, wide adaptation
Drummond	Macdonald College, J. N. Bird	strains selected from northern Europe, Wales, and U.S.	10–14 days later than common	winter-hardy, rust resistant
Engmo	Agr. Exp. Sta., Tromoso, Norway, K. Flovik	selected from old mountain meadows	early growth	very winter-hardy, leafy
Essex	New York station, R. P. Murphy and S. S. Atwood	synthetic from 4 selected clones	very late	leafy, disease resistant
Itasca	Minnesota station	from 7 inbred lines, a synthetic	like common	desirable growth habit
Verdant	Wisconsin station, USDA, E. L. Nielsen and P. N. Drolsom	a synthetic based on 28 selected clones	late	leaf streak and stem rust resistant

Source: Hanson, 1971.[21]

postbloom stage.[27,28] Only when some other variable such as lodging enters into yield determinations does timothy sometimes produce less at this stage. This was true for tests in Maine conducted in the northeastern states. (See Table 26.5.)[28] Dry matter yield, a valuable attribute of new cultivars, may be underestimated for late maturing cultivars included in tests that are cut on a single date.[29] The total seasonal yield is best estimated for each cultivar when the cultivar is cut at full bloom. A compromise cutting date for early, medium, and late timothy cultivars is the full-bloom stage of the medium maturing cultivars.

Even though the quality of timothy hay can be influenced by location, fertilizer use, and cultivar, stage of harvest is the most important management variable affecting quality. Early cut hay can fur-

27. Evans, Morgan W., and Lloyd E. Thatcher. 1938. A comparative study of an early, a medium, and a late strain of timothy harvested at various stages of development. J. Agr. Res. 56:347–64.
28. Brown, C. S., G. A. Jung, K. A. Varney, R. C. Wakefield, and J. B. Washko. 1968. Management and productivity of perennial grasses in the Northeast. IV. Timothy. W. Va. Agr. Exp. Sta. Bull. 570T.
29. Austenson, H. M. 1964. Chronological versus physiological basis for harvesting grass variety tests. Crop Sci. 4:431–33.

TABLE 26.5 ❧ Dry matter yield and digestibility of first-cut Climax timothy in first harvest year at four stages of growth from different locations

Stage harvested	Total yield (t/ha)					Digestible dry matter (%)		Protein digestibility (%)	
	Maine	Vt.	R.I.	Pa.	W. Va.	Maine	W. Va.	Maine	W. Va.
Prejoint	7.4b*	5.2d	2.5d	7.3b	4.9b	84.9	76.4	22.7	26.6
Early head	7.2b	7.8c	4.8c	6.8b	5.0ab	74.5	62.1	12.4	11.5
Early bloom	8.7a	8.9b	6.7b	8.6a	5.4ab	68.9	58.9	8.5	7.5
Postbloom	7.8ab	10.4a	7.5a	8.8a	5.6a	56.3	55.3	4.5	4.7

Source: Brown et al., 1968.[28]
* Values having the same letter are from the same statistical population at the 5% level of significance. Comparisons may be made within each column.

nish 3.2 times as much digestible protein and 1.25 as much metabolizable energy as late cut timothy hay.[30] Differences in early head and early bloom harvested timothy favored the early head stage in both digestible dry matter and percent protein. (See Table 26.5.)[28] Maximum returns in animal products depend on both forage yield and quality.

PERSISTENCE

Stand persistence and aftermath yields are important in managing timothy for profitable production. Food reserves required to overwinter plants in good condition are influenced by time of harvest and soil fertility. After the first cut the primary haplocorm gives rise to new tillers and secondary haplocorms. After defoliation new sets of buds form, and the timothy plant overwinters as tertiary shoots.[12] Applications of N have been shown to decrease dry weight of primary haplocorms, increase dry weight in secondary haplocorms, and lower dry weight in tertiary shoots. Split applications of N on pure stands of timothy may be advantageous because nitrate, amino, and amide N in tertiary shoots increase as the supply of N is increased. Poor regrowth of tertiary shoots can be expected if they are low in N.[31] The food reserves of timothy corms are mostly

long-chained fructosans.[32] They are lowest in concentration with the initiation of spring growth. Rapid accumulation occurs in culm bases as the plant reaches full bloom. The maximum level of carbohydrate reserves is reached in uncut plants during the interval from flowering to dough stage. If the plants are not cut, reserves decline somewhat and stabilize.[33]

A management system that includes harvesting at the early head stage in combination with high N applications gives a consistent reduction in timothy stands.[28]

❧ DISEASES

More than 31 diseases have been reported as affecting timothy.[34] Most of these are not economically important or can easily be controlled. Stem rust *Puccinia graminis* var. *phlei-pratensis* (Eriks. & E. Henn.) Stakman & Piem. is always a threat to timothy but has been controlled by the breeding and release of rust-resistant cultivars.[35-37] During epidemics damage to susceptible plants of timothy usually peaks

30. Colovos, N. F., H. A. Keener, J. R. Prescott, and A. E. Terri. 1949. The nutritive value of timothy hay at different stages of maturity as compared with second cutting clover hay. *J. Dairy Sci.* 32:659–64.
31. Sheard, R. W. 1970. Characterization of food reserves as a basis for timing nitrogen applications for timothy (*Phleum pratense* L.). Proc. 11th Int. Grassl. Congr., pp. 570–74 (Surfers Paradise, Queensland, Aust.).

32. Smith, Dale, and R. D. Grotelueschen. 1966. Carbohydrates in grasses. I. Sugar and fructosan composition of the stem bases of several northern adapted grasses at seed maturity. *Crop Sci.* 6:263–66.
33. Reynolds, J. H., and Dale Smith. 1962. Trend of carbohydrate reserves in alfalfa, smooth bromegrass and timothy grown under various cutting schedules. *Crop Sci.* 2:333–36.
34. Sprague, Roderick, and George W. Fischer. 1952. Check list of the diseases of grasses and cereals in the western United States and Alaska. Wash. Agr. Exp. Sta. Circ. 194.
35. Johnson, E. C. 1911. Timothy rust in the U.S. USDA Bull. 224.
36. Barker, H. D., and H. K. Hayes. Rust resistance in timothy. *Phytopathology* 14:363–71.
37. Drolsom, P. N., and E. L. Nielsen. 1969. Use of self-fertility in the improvement of *Bromus inermis* and *Phleum pratense*. *Crop Sci.* 9:710–13.

during the spring and early summer and again in the autumn.[38] Plant vigor and the quality of the forage is reduced and winter survival may be affected in rust-susceptible cultivars.[39,40]

OTHER SPECIES

The number of species within *Phleum* has been suggested as 10, although their authenticity and all phylogenetic relationships are not well established. Several have been cytologically studied.[5,41] Turf timothy *P. bertolonii* DC. (*P. nodosum* L.), a diploid with 14 chromosomes, is morphologically very similar to *P. pratense* which is a hexaploid with 42 chromosomes. Closely related to cultivated timothy, *P. nodosum* will intercross to produce unstable hybrids. The cultivar 'Evergreen' is a diploid timothy developed as general-

purpose turf grass and for pasture use. Alpine timothy, *P. alpinum* L. (*P. commutatum* Gaud.), has 28 chromosomes and hybridizes with cultivated timothy with some difficulty.

Since these species may occur as wild or weedy forms throughout the growing area of cultivated timothy, seed-production fields should be isolated. All are inferior to improved cultivars of cultivated timothy in forage productivity.

❧ QUESTIONS

1. What is the general area of adaptation for timothy in North America?
2. Where is timothy believed to be native and where was it first grown as a cultivated grass?
3. Describe the general appearance and habit of growth of timothy.
4. Is there any decided trend in the acreage of timothy in the general area of adaptation? Explain.
5. What are some of the more widely recognized improved cultivars of timothy and where did they originate?
6. What management practices will result in poor persistence of timothy?

38. Nielsen, E. L., and J. G. Dickson. 1958. Evaluation of timothy clones for stem rust reaction. *Agron. J.* 50:749–52.

39. Bird, J. N. 1934. Influence of rust injury on the vigor and yield of timothy. *Sci. Agr.* 14:550–59.

40. Myers, E. M., and S. J. P. Chilton. 1941. Correlated studies of winterhardiness and rust reaction of parents and inbred progenies of orchardgrass and timothy. *J. Amer. Soc. Agron.* 33:215–20.

41. Nath, J. 1967. Cytogenetical and related studies in the genus *Phleum* L. *Euphytica* 16:267–82.

GERALD A. JUNG / *Agricultural Research Service, USDA*

BARTON S. BAKER / *West Virginia University*

27

ORCHARDGRASS

❧

ORCHARDGRASS, *Dactylis glomerata* L., is a native of Europe but has been grown in North America for over 200 years. In 1760 seed from orchardgrass grown in Virginia was sent to England.[1] About 1830, Philip Henshaw collected orchardgrass seed from his father's orchard in Orange County, Va., and planted it on his farm in Oldham County, Ky. From this planting, seed was collected by another farmer and transferred to a farm near Goshen, Ky., where seed was raised commercially.[2]

Since colonial times orchardgrass has spread through a large area of the U.S. and occupies an important place as a cultivated grass for hay and pasture. It is

❧ GERALD A. JUNG is Research Agronomist, ARS, USDA, at the U.S. Regional Pasture Research Laboratory, University Park, Pa., and adjunct Professor of Agronomy at Pennsylvania State University. He holds the Ph.D. degree from the University of Wisconsin. His research includes investigations of the physiology of cold and heat tolerance, plant response to stress, and study of factors that affect forage quality.

❧ BARTON S. BAKER is Agronomist on the West Virginia University Allegheny Highlands Project, Elkins, W. Va. He received the M.S. and Ph.D. degrees from West Virginia University. His research is concerned with forage environmental problems associated with hill pastures.

also found growing along roadsides and in waste areas. Orchardgrass is commonly found growing in shady places such as orchards, which undoubtedly led to its most widely known common name. The characteristic shape of its inflorescence gave rise to the common name "cocksfoot" which is especially used in Europe.

❧ DISTRIBUTION AND ADAPTATION

In the U.S., orchardgrass is found from southeastern Canada to the northern part of the Gulf states and from the Atlantic Ocean to the eastern Great Plains (Fig. 27.1). It is common throughout the Appalachian Mountains and is especially well adapted to Maryland, Pennsylvania, West Virginia, Virginia, Kentucky, and Tennessee. It is also found in the high-rainfall regions of the western mountains and in irrigated areas throughout much of the West. It is common to nearly all of Europe except the most northern regions, the northern half of Asia, and the higher elevations of Africa.[1] It is also found in some

1. Piper, Charles V. 1942. Forage plants and their culture, rev. ed., pp. 202–14. Macmillan, New York.
2. Hein, M. A. 1946. Orchardgrass deserves more friends. *Successful Farming* 44:29, 51.

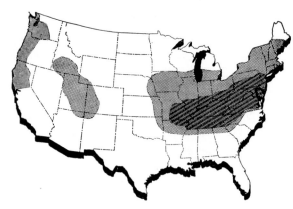

FIG. 27.1. Adaptation and production area of orchardgrass in the U.S.

temperate regions of South America, New Zealand, and Australia.

ENVIRONMENT

TEMPERATURE. The optimum day temperature for the growth of orchardgrass is approximately 21 C.[3-6] However, different optimum day temperatures exist for different night temperatures. When a wide range of day-night temperature combinations were investigated, 22–12 C was found to be the most favorable combination for the production of top growth.[6] It should be remembered, however, that forage growth is a function of many environmental factors and the optimum temperature may vary depending on plant age, carbon dioxide concentration, light intensity, soil fertility, moisture, and the like.

Temperatures above 28 C greatly reduce growth.[3,4,6] Such temperatures also greatly decrease the nucleic acid content of leaves, which appears to occur at temperatures lower than those that suppress growth.[7]

Orchardgrass is more heat tolerant than timothy or Kentucky bluegrass but less so than smooth bromegrass or tall fescue.[6,8,9] Orchardgrass grows rapidly at cool temperatures and is especially productive in early spring. It is reasonably productive in late fall, but less so than tall fescue.

Orchardgrass is only moderately winterhardy and frequently will not survive northern climatic conditions if snow cover is lacking. For this reason timothy and smooth bromegrass are grown farther north and at higher elevations than orchardgrass.

LIGHT. Orchardgrass is shade tolerant and is found growing in many areas where there is reduced light. As much as 33% of the incident light can be intercepted for as long as three years without any detrimental effect on yield or persistence.[10] In contrast, ladino clover stands died when subjected to that much shade for two years. Orchardgrass also withstands high light intensity and is found growing in areas of full sunlight as well as shade. A light intensity of 32,000 lx is sufficient to saturate detached leaves, but 48,000 lx is required to saturate intact leaves that have a leaf-area index (LAI) between 3 and 8. A LAI of 5 is considered optimum and is attained two weeks after clipping if moisture and fertility are favorable for growth.[11]

Under favorable moisture and fertility conditions, plants will develop in 15 days a canopy of leaves that intercept 95% of the sunlight.[11] A high level of photosyn-

3. Brown, E. Marion. 1939. Some effects of temperature on the growth and chemical composition of certain pasture grasses. Mo. Agr. Exp. Sta. Res. Bull. 299.
4. Mitchell, K. J. 1956. Growth of pasture species under controlled environments. I. Growth at various levels of constant temperature. N.Z. J. Sci. Technol. A38:203–16.
5. Davidson, J. L., and F. L. Milthorpe. 1965. The effect of temperature on the growth of cocksfoot (Dactylis glomerata L.). Ann. Bot. 29:407–17.
6. Baker, Barton S., and G. A. Jung. 1968. Effect of environmental conditions on the growth of four perennial grasses. I. Response to controlled temperature. Agron. J. 60:155–58.

7. Baker, Barton S., and G. A. Jung. 1970. Effect of environmental conditions on the growth of four perennial grasses. III. Nucleic acid concentration as influenced by day-night temperature combinations. Crop Sci. 10:376–78.
8. Baker, Barton S., and G. A. Jung. 1968. Effect of environmental conditions on the growth of four perennial grasses. II. Response to fertility, water, and temperature. Agron. J. 60:158–62.
9. Hoveland, C. S., E. M. Evans, and D. A. Mays. 1970. Cool-season perennial grass species for forage in Alabama. Auburn Agr. Exp. Sta. Bull. 397.
10. Blake, Carl T., D. S. Chamblee, and W. W. Woodhouse, Jr. 1966. Influence of some environmental and management factors on the persistence of ladino clover in association with orchardgrass. Agron. J. 58:487–89.
11. Pearce, R. B., R. H. Brown, and R. E. Blaser. 1965. Relationships between leaf area index, light interception and net photosynthesis in orchardgrass. Crop Sci. 5:553–56.

thesis is maintained for 15–20 days after total leaf expansion. Thereafter, the rate of photosynthesis decreases rapidly and is closely associated with a decrease in chlorophyll content.[12]

An increase in light intensity to a point where the leaves are saturated with light can be expected to increase yields, tillering, and carbohydrate reserves.[13] An increase in duration which would increase the photosynthetic period should also increase yields and reserves. Tillering is a function of both intensity and photoperiod, but there is considerable variation among cultivars.[14]

MOISTURE. Orchardgrass is more drought tolerant than either timothy or Kentucky bluegrass. Smooth bromegrass, however, is more drought tolerant than orchardgrass and is better adapted to areas that have a combination of low rainfall and high temperature. The drought tolerance of orchardgrass is probably related to its extensive root system. Orchardgrass does not tolerate flooding and wet soils as well as reed canarygrass. Nevertheless, orchardgrass persists and grows well on soils that have moderately poor drainage.

FERTILITY. Soil requirements of orchardgrass are less exacting than those of either timothy or smooth bromegrass. Orchardgrass will persist on shallow, reasonably infertile soil and be moderately productive. Yet it is responsive to fertilizer applications, especially N, and becomes very competitive when nutrients are available. Tall fescue and Kentucky bluegrass have been found to compete successfully with orchardgrass only when N and K are limiting.[15] In its area of adaptation orchardgrass becomes the dominant species when an abundance of nutrients are available. Under such conditions it may severely reduce the legume content of a mixed sward and prevent weed encroachment even though much of the soil surface is without vegetative cover. Competitiveness of orchardgrass involves light, nutrients, and moisture.[16]

❧ PLANT DESCRIPTION

Orchardgrass is a cool-season grass that grows in clumps, producing an open sod. It starts growth early in spring, develops rapidly, and flowers during late May or early June depending on daylength, temperature, and cultivar.

The inflorescence of orchardgrass differentiates at the base of the plant and moves upward by elongation of internodes. The flowering culms grow from 60 cm to 2 m in height, depending on climatic conditions, but are generally 1–1.3 m high. These culms bear few leaves, but there are many basal leaves associated with the plant. The inflorescence of orchardgrass is 8–15 cm long and is composed of spikelets which bear 2–5 florets.[17] The lowermost branches of the inflorescence are longer and more branching than the ones near the top.

The leaves of orchardgrass are folded in the bud and in cross section appear V-shaped. The sheath is compressed and strongly keeled, and auricles are absent.[18] Leaf blades are 2–12 mm wide and may reach a length of 1 m. Leaves vary in color from light green to dark blue green, with many leaf characteristics varying with environmental conditions and cultivar.

Orchardgrass reproduces sexually by seed formation and asexually by tiller formation. Tillering occurs almost continuously, and within a single tuft, tillers

12. Treharne, K. J., J. P. Cooper, and T. H. Taylor. 1968. Growth response of orchardgrass (*Dactylis glomerata* L.) to different light and temperature environments. II. Leaf age photosynthetic activity. *Crop Sci.* 8:441–45.

13. Auda, H., R. E. Blaser, and R. H. Brown. 1966. Tillering and carbohydrate contents of orchardgrass as influenced by environmental factors. *Crop Sci.* 6:139–43.

14. Nittler. L. W., T. J. Kenny, and Ethel Osborne. 1963. Response of seedlings of orchardgrass, *Dactylis glomerata* L., to photoperiod, light intensity, and temperature. *Crop Sci.* 3:125–28.

15. Henderlong, P. R., R. E. Blaser, and R. E. Worley. 1965. Growth and botanical composition of orchardgrass, tall fescue and bluegrass as affected by potassium and nitrogen fertilization. *Agron. Abstr.*, p. 35.

16. Wilkinson, S. R., and C. F. Gross. 1964. Competition for light, soil moisture, and nutrients during ladino clover establishment in orchardgrass sod. *Agron. J.* 56:389–92.

17. Core, Earl L., Earl E. Berkley, and H. A. Davis. 1944. West Virginia grasses. W. Va. Agr. Exp. Sta. Bull. 313.

18. Philips, C. E. 1962. Some grasses of the Northeast. Del. Agr. Exp. Sta. Field Manual 2.

TABLE 27.1 ❧ Distribution of carbohydrates in orchardgrass tissues

Part of plant	Weight of entire plant (%)	Carbohydrates (% dry wt)		
		Reducing sugars	Sucrose	Fructosan
Upper ⅔ of leaf blades	14.0	1.4	8.4	7.6
Lower ⅓ of leaf blades	12.1	1.2	5.8	22.0
Upper ½ of tiller bases	9.4	1.9	3.6	23.7
Lower ½ of tiller bases	23.6	0.7	2.6	36.2
Roots	40.9	1.2	8.9	8.2

Source: Sprague and Sullivan, 1950.[19]

will be at many stages of development. Under field conditions the production of new tillers gives orchardgrass its perennial character.

Like other grasses, orchardgrass produces a fibrous root system. Carbohydrates are stored in the lower part of the leaf blade, tiller bases, and roots; but the greatest concentration is in the plant base near the soil surface (Table 27.1).[19] Glucose, fructose, sucrose, and starch are stored, but by far the largest fraction is fructosan.[20]

PRODUCTIVITY

If soil fertility is low, a large portion of the total production of orchardgrass occurs in spring, whereas at high fertility levels production is well distributed throughout the growing season. Aftermath production contributes from 33 to 66% of the total production when split applications of fertilizer are applied.[21] By comparison, aftermath of timothy with similar management and fertility contributes only 20% of the total production.[22]

Pure stands of orchardgrass were less productive in Pennsylvania than timothy when 56 kg/ha of N was applied. When 112 kg of N was applied, they were equal in production.[23] At other locations orchardgrass has been more responsive to fertilizer N than timothy.[21,22,24] At high rates of N, orchardgrass is among the most productive of the cool-season grasses. Hay yields of 13.5 t/ha can be expected when orchardgrass is properly fertilized and favorable weather prevails.[21] Yields may be reduced as much as 50% in years of drought.

NUTRITIVE VALUE

Farmers customarily cut first-crop orchardgrass at full bloom or later. In part, this results from the use of early heading cultivars. In addition, heading occurs when field-curing of hay is difficult due to inclement weather, and farmers often delay cutting until more favorable haymaking weather. By this time orchardgrass has frequently declined in feeding value; or if cut earlier, it is often in poor condition when stored. Since this is the usual procedure followed in making orchardgrass hay, its potential feeding value has been underestimated for years. At the vegetative growth stage, orchardgrass approaches the feeding value of alfalfa, whereas at full bloom it has approximately half the value (Fig. 27.2).[25]

As the spring crop advances from the vegetative stage to seed formation, protein concentration and dry matter digestibility decrease, whereas cell wall components increase. These changes are associated with

19. Sprague, V. G., and J. T. Sullivan. 1950. Reserve carbohydrates in orchardgrass clipped periodically. Plant Physiol. 25:92–102.
20. Okajima, H., and Dale Smith. 1964. Available carbohydrate fractions in the stem bases and seed of timothy, smooth bromegrass, and several other northern grasses. Crop Sci. 4:317–20.
21. Washko, J. B., G. A. Jung, A. M. Decker, R. C. Wakefield, D. D. Wolf, and M. J. Wright. 1967. Management and productivity of perennial grasses in the northeast. III. Orchardgrass. W. Va. Agr. Exp. Sta. Bull. 557T.

22. Brown, C. S., G. A. Jung, K. E. Varney, R. C. Wakefield, and J. B. Washko. 1968. Management and productivity of perennial grasses in the northeast. IV. Timothy. W. Va. Agr. Exp. Sta. Bull. 570T.
23. Marriott, L.F. 1961. Nitrogen fertilization of perennial grasses. Pa. Agr. Exp. Sta. Bull. 688.
24. Schmidt, D. R., and G. H. Tenpas. 1960. A comparison of the performance of bromegrass, orchardgrass, and timothy in northern Wisconsin. Agron. J. 52:689–92.
25. Jung, G. A., R. L. Reid, and J. A. Balasko. 1969. Studies on yield, management, persistence, and nutritive value of alfalfa in West Virginia. W. Va. Agr. Exp. Sta. Bull. 581T.

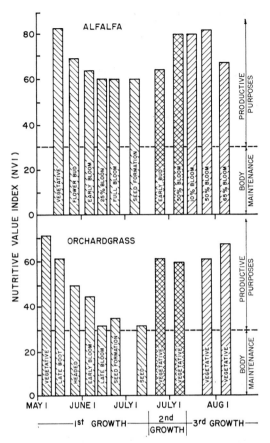

FIG. 27.2. Influence of cutting date on the intake of digestible dry matter (nutritive value index, NVI) from alfalfa and orchardgrass. Horizontal line partitions available forage energy into maintenance and production fractions. (Adapted from Jung et al., 1969.[25])

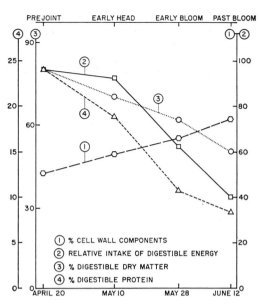

FIG. 27.3. Changes in percent of cell wall components, intake of digestible energy, and dry matter and protein digestibility of orchardgrass associated with several growth stages. (Adapted from Washko et al., 1967.[21])

decreasing levels of consumption, and together they markedly affect the energy available to livestock (Fig. 27.3). Fructosan concentration, which is an indication of available energy, appears to be lower in orchardgrass than in some other grasses such as ryegrass. It is especially low in summer and when fertilized with high rates of N.[26,27]

Aftermath forage is leafy and generally does not decline in feeding value with time. Thus time of harvest is much less important with aftermath than with the first crop. Under field conditions, however, orchardgrass leaves form and senesce at about the same rate after 35 days. Dead leaves will accumulate with infrequent cutting and good growing conditions, so there is little advantage in separating harvests by more than five or six weeks.

Quality, as indicated by mineral composition, has become of concern to many livestock nutritionists. The mineral composition of grass varies with species, stage of growth, soil, season of year, and fertilization.[28,29,30,31] In orchardgrass, percent of K, P, Ca, Mg, Zn, Co, and Mo on a dry

26. Waite, R. 1958. The water-soluble carbohydrates of grasses. IV. The effect of different levels of fertilizer treatments. *J. Sci. Food Agr.* 9:39–43.

27. Waite, R., and J. Boyd. 1953. The water-soluble carbohydrates of grasses. II. Grasses cut at grazing height several times during the growing season. *J. Sci. Food Agr.* 4:257–61.

28. Hemingway, R. G. 1962. Copper, molybdenum, manganese, and iron content of herbage as influenced by fertilizer treatment over a three-year period. *J. Brit. Grassl. Soc.* 17:182–87.

29. Reith, J. W. S., R. H. E. Inkson, W. Holmes, D. S. MacLusky, D. Reid, R. G. Heddle, and J. F. Copeman. 1964. The effect of fertilizer on herbage production. II. The effects of nitrogen, phosphorus and potassium on botanical and chemical composition. *J. Agr. Sci.* 63:209–19.

30. Fleming, G. A., and W. E. Murphy. 1968. The uptake of some major and trace elements by grasses as affected by season and stage of maturity. *J. Brit. Grassl. Soc.* 23:174–84.

31. Reid, R. L., Amy J. Post, and G. A. Jung. 1970. Mineral composition of forages. W. Va. Agr. Exp. Sta. Bull. 589T.

weight basis decreases as stage of growth advances. Copper, however, appears to be uniform at successive stages of growth. First-cut forage is generally higher in K, Cu, Zn, and Fe than aftermath; but P, Ca, and Mg are generally higher in the aftermath.[31]

The influence of fertilization on mineral content is marked but variable, depending on the combination and amount of nutrients applied. In general, fertilizer N increases plant K, Mg, and Ca but depresses P. In some instances fertilizer N has been found to decrease K.[32]

High rates of N may result in excessive uptake of N and K and reduce Mg uptake. This can be of considerable importance in areas where soil and forage Mg levels are too low to meet livestock needs. Magnesium deficiency in cattle causes a condition commonly known as grass tetany, a nutritional disease of common occurrence in many areas. Orchardgrass is a relatively poor accumulator of Mg, especially at cool temperatures.

The rate and type of fertilizer used not only influence forage composition but also palatability.[33] This can influence the amount of forage consumed and contribute significantly to animal performance. Variation may also exist in preference among animal species. Preference of sheep for orchardgrass hay and pasture fertilized with different sources and rates of nitrogen is shown in Table 27.2.

FLOWERING

Temperature and light duration both play an important role in flowering of orchardgrass. Natural induction occurs in fall when days are cool and photoperiods short. Very little induction occurs when daylengths are longer than 12.5 hours. In addition to short days, temperatures of 5 C or less are required for a period of ap-

TABLE 27.2 ❧ Preference of sheep for orchardgrass forage in relation to rate and source of N fertilizer

Fertilizer treatment (kg N/ha)	Hays		Autumn pasture
	1st cutting (%)*	2nd cutting (%)	Dry matter consumption (kg/ha)†
0 Urea	39	27	538
56	27	26	851
112	20	28	1,478
224	...	16	2,262
448	14	3	1,837
	100	100	
112 Sodium nitrate	34	30	1,814
112 Ammonium nitrate	28	28	2,419
112 Ammonium sulfate	20	25	1,590
112 Diammonium phosphate	9	5	2,374
112 Urea	9	12	1,478
	100	100	

Source: Reid et al., 1966.[33]
* Percent of total forage consumed when given a choice.
† Estimates of preference were obtained by clipping before and after grazing.

proximately three weeks. For induction to occur, cool temperatures must accompany or follow short photoperiods.[34]

Floral initiation occurs in spring when days become warmer and photoperiod increases. When days are warm, short photoperiods prevent initiation. Light intensity has very little if any influence on flowering.[35]

❧ IMPORTANCE AND USE

Only in relatively recent years has orchardgrass received much emphasis as a cultivated grass. In Finland, for example, orchardgrass was not used extensively until after 1950.[36] In the U.S., orchardgrass was tested at many experiment stations

32. MacLeod, L. B. 1965. Effect of nitrogen and potassium on the yield and chemical composition of alfalfa, bromegrass, orchardgrass, and timothy grown as pure species. Agron. J. 57:261–66.

33. Reid, R. L., G. A. Jung, and S. J. Murray. 1966. Nitrogen fertilization in relation to the palatability and nutritive value of orchardgrass. J. Anim. Sci. 25:636–45.

34. Gardner, F. P., and W. E. Loomis. 1953. Floral induction and development in orchardgrass. Plant Physiol. 28:201–17.

35. Sprague, V. G. 1948. The relation of supplementary light and soil fertility to heading in the greenhouse of several perennial forage grasses. J. Amer. Soc. Agron. 40:144–54.

36. Huokuna, Erkki. 1964. The effect of frequency and height of cutting on cocksfoot swards. Ann. Acad. Agr. Fennicae 3 (17), suppl. 4.

but was not accepted on a wide scale until about 1940.[37]

Orchardgrass is leafy, productive, and adapted to a wide range of environmental conditions. In its area of adaptation, seedlings are competitive enough to withstand competition from weeds and other plants. Once established, it will survive many years if properly managed. It is suited for pasture, hay, green chop, and silage and can be utilized alone or in combination with legumes.

PASTURE

Growth characteristics of orchardgrass make it well suited to early spring pastures and better suited to rotational grazing than continuous grazing. When it is grazed continuously, animals tend to regraze the same areas until the plants are weakened by frequent, repeated removal of leaf tissue. In some cases, especially with sheep, tillers may be eaten so short that the area of food storage itself is removed. When the erect-growing orchardgrass has become weakened by grazing, it is generally replaced by more prostrate-growing species such as Kentucky bluegrass.

Ladino or white clover is well suited for use in combination with orchardgrass for pasture. Clover provides N for the grass, and if properly managed both species will survive and remain productive for a number of years. When grazing is delayed, excessive competition from the grass may cause elimination of legumes. From clipping trials it appears that grazing when orchardgrass is 20–30 cm tall would give an acceptable balance between yield and persistence of white clover in a stand.[38] If clover needs to be reestablished, it often can be overseeded without conventional seedbed preparation. Legume seed applied in the fall is worked into the soil by freezing, thawing, and trampling of cattle and becomes established the following spring. Orchardgrass may need to be weakened by heavy grazing prior to such seeding. In situations where seedbed preparation is needed, disking is often effective.

The relatively low cost also makes it practical to grow orchardgrass alone and to use commercial fertilizer N. Irrigation also is used in combination with fertilizer N for more intensive forage production.

HAY

Orchardgrass may be grown for hay either in pure stands or with legumes. When pure stands are used for hay production, it is imperative that N be used in combination with other nutrients for high yields. However, with excessive amounts of N, plants tend to lodge, especially in areas of heavy rainfall and winds. Split applications will help prevent lodging and tend to give a better distribution of forage during the growing season. Nitrogen at a rate of 56–84 kg/ha in early spring and after each cutting is generally recommended. The number of applications depends on the length of growing season and need for additional forage.

The open and bunchy orchardgrass sod makes it compatible with alfalfa or other tall-growing legumes. Legumes can become established among bunches of orchardgrass without undue competition when properly managed. Once established, the stand can be managed to favor the legume without being overly concerned about damaging the grass. When a grass-legume mixture is used, N or manure should not be applied because it stimulates growth of orchardgrass, often at the expense of the legume. When orchardgrass is grown with alfalfa, a late maturing cultivar such as 'Pennlate' or 'Masshardy' should be used. These cultivars head about the time alfalfa begins to bloom.

❧ CULTIVARS

Orchardgrass breeders have concentrated on producing cultivars that mature

37. Smith, Dale. 1962. Forage Management in the North. W. C. Brown, Dubuque, Iowa.
38. Wagner, R. E. 1952. Yields and botanical composition of four grass-legume mixtures under differential cutting. USDA Tech. Bull. 1063.

later than common orchardgrass, have improved seasonal distribution of growth, are disease resistant, have improved feeding properties, are high yielding, and are adapted to a wide range of environmental conditions. A large portion of the cultivars exhibiting one or more of these characteristics has been bred from field selections where the desirable trait had been exhibited by the natural population.

Breeding programs are under way at several state experiment stations and by the USDA. New cultivars are released slowly, however, because from 15 to 20 years are required to breed a superior cultivar and release it for commercial production.[39] Some attention has been given to cultivars that do not normally head where they would be grown for forage. They have been found to have a superior chemical composition in some cases, but seed production problems must be overcome before they can be made available to farmers.[40]

The most widely used orchardgrass is the common domestic type, accounting for more ha than all available cultivars combined. 'Potomac' is the most popular cultivar of those being certified. Some of the cultivars used in the U.S. are listed in Table 27.3.

❧ CULTURE AND MANAGEMENT

In its area of adaptation, orchardgrass is usually established with ease. It is frequently recommended that orchardgrass be seeded in early spring or late summer at a rate of 11 kg/ha.[41,42] However, good stands have been obtained at a rate of only 4.5 kg/ha.[43] When orchardgrass is seeded in combination with legumes, the amount of seed is usually decreased by 50% or more. Oats are frequently used as a companion crop with an orchardgrass-legume seeding. The oats are harvested for hay, silage, or grain during the summer and the grass-legume mixture is harvested the following year. The seedbed should be loose on top and firm underneath. The seed should be planted no deeper than 0.6 cm. Press wheels or a cultipacker help to ensure stand survival.[41,42]

Freshly harvested seed will germinate, but germination is enhanced by a period of dormancy. Alternating temperatures from 15 to 30 C or from 10 to 30 C in combination with a 16-hour dark period and 8-hour light period improve germination.[44] A growth inhibitor has been found in dormant seed in the lemma and palea as well as the caryopsis. Germination can be enhanced by removal of the lemma and palea or by storage at temperatures near freezing to decrease the amount of inhibitor.[45] Emergence of germinated seedlings is favored by short days and by moderate temperatures. Temperatures of 30 C or above greatly reduce emergence.[46]

Plants grown at equal radiant energy develop leaves and roots faster when exposed to short photoperiods than when exposed to long ones (Table 27.4).[47] When exposed to equal photoperiods, leaves appear more rapidly with higher light intensity, and they senesce faster.[48] The total leaf area formed, however, is greater when plants are subjected to low light intensity, especially with cool temperatures. Day-night temperatures of 21/13 C and 29/21 C were found to have similar effects on leaf

39. Starling, James. 1964. Orchardgrass. *Pa. Farmer* 170:44–45.

40. Hovin, A. W., C. M. Rincker, and G. M. Wood. 1966. Breeding of nonflowering orchardgrass, *Dactylis glomerata* L. *Crop Sci.* 6:239–41.

41. Pennsylvania State Univ. Coop. Ext. Serv. 1972. Agronomy guide.

42. West Virginia Univ. Coop. Ext. Serv. 1968–69. Field worker's blue book.

43. Sprague, M. A., M. M. Hoover, Jr., M. J. Wright, H. A. MacDonald, B. A. Brown, A. M. Decker, J. B. Washko, V. G. Sprague, and K. E. Varney. 1963. Seedling management of grass-legume associations in the Northeast. N.J. Agr. Exp. Sta. Bull. 804.

44. Sprague, V. G. 1940. Germination of freshly harvested seeds in several *Poa* species and of *Dactylis glomerata*. *J. Amer. Soc. Agron.* 32:715–21.

45. Fendall, R. K., and C. L. Canode. 1971. Dormancy-related growth inhibitors in seeds of orchardgrass (*Dactylis glomerata* L.). *Crop Sci.* 11:727–30.

46. Sprague, V. G. 1944. The effects of temperature and daylength on seedling emergence and early growth of several pasture species. Soil Sci. Soc. Amer. Proc. 8:287–94.

47. Templeton, W. C., Jr., J. L. Menees, and T. H. Taylor. 1969. Growth of young orchardgrass (*Dactylis glomerata* L.) plants in different environments. *Agron. J.* 61:780–83.

48. Taylor, T. H., J. P. Cooper, and K. J. Treharne. 1968. Growth response of orchardgrass (*Dactylis glomerata* L.) to different light and temperature environments. I. Leaf development and senescence. *Crop Sci.* 8:437–40.

TABLE 27.3 ❧ Description of some orchardgrass cultivars adapted to the U.S.

Cultivar	Relative maturity*	Winter-hardiness	Disease resistance	Origin or source	Area of adaptation or use†
Able	late	hardy	resistant to leaf diseases	Farmers Forage Research Cooperative	Indiana
Akaroa	intermediate	intermediate	some resistance to rust	California station and SCS	West Coast, Nevada
Boone	early-intermediate	intermediate	some resistance to rust	Kentucky station and ARS, USDA	Kentucky
Chinook	early	hardy	not available	Canada Dept. Agr. Res. Sta., Lethbridge	northern latitudes
Clatsop	not available	intermediate	resistant to *Mastigosporium rubricosum*	Oregon station and ARS, USDA	Pacific Northwest
Dayton	early-intermediate	hardy	some resistance to rust and leaf blight	Rudy-Patrick Co.	Iowa
Hallmark	early-intermediate	not available	more resistance to leaf diseases than Boone	Farmers Forage Research Cooperative	Indiana
Jackson	intermediate-late	intermediate	some resistance to leaf diseases	Virginia station	Virginia
Kay	not available	hardy	some resistance to rust	Canada Dept. Agr. Res. Sta., Ottawa	northern latitudes
Latar	late	intermediate	not available	Washington and Idaho stations and SCS	Pacific Northwest
Masshardy	late	very hardy	not available	Massachusetts station	Northeast
Napier	early-intermediate	hardy	some rust and leaf blight resistance	Rudy-Patrick Co.	northern latitudes
Nordstern	late	hardy	some resistance to leaf diseases	Northrup, King & Co.	northern latitudes
Palestine	not available	tender (drought resistant)	susceptible to rust	California station	California
Pennlate	late	hardy	moderately resistant to rust	Pennsylvania station and ARS, USDA	Northeast
Pennmead	intermediate	intermediate	some resistance to rust	Pennsylvania station and ARS, USDA	Northeast
Pomar (dwarf type)	late	intermediate	some resistance to leaf disease	Idaho station and SCS	Pacific Northwest
Potomac	early-intermediate	hardy	resistant to rust	ARS, USDA	Northeast, Pacific Northwest
Rideau	late	hardy	not available	Canada Dept. Agr. Res. Sta., Ottawa	northern latitudes
S37	late	intermediate	not available	Welsh Plant Breeding Sta., Aberystwyth	Southeast, Oregon, Washington

TABLE 27.3 ❧ *(Continued)*

Cultivar	Relative maturity*	Winter-hardiness	Disease resistance	Origin or source	Area of adaptation or use†
S143	late	intermediate	not available	Welsh Plant Breeding Sta., Aberystwyth	Southeast, Oregon, Washington
Sterling	early-intermediate	hardy	some resistance to rust and leaf streak	Iowa station	Iowa
Virginia 70	early	intermediate	not available	Virginia station	Southeast
Commercial strain	early	variable	variable	Virginia, Kentucky, Missouri	general

Source: Table based on information from A. A. Hanson, ARS, USDA, with modification by authors.
 * Calendar dates vary with latitude and elevation. Differences between cultivars are generally greater at more southerly latitudes and lower elevations.
 † Area of adaptation not yet well defined in some instances.

appearance and senescence.[48] The influence of photoperiod, light intensity, and temperature on leaf development, however, depends on many factors such as plant age, cultivar, and associated climatic factors.

Insufficient or excessive amounts of water retard seedling growth, especially that of roots. Seedling growth may be retarded when N or P is available in low quantities. Under such conditions growth can be stimulated by an appropriate fertilizer. When both elements are deficient, little response will be obtained with the addition of only one.[47]

FERTILIZATION

In a 14-year study in Virginia in which N, P, and K were used orchardgrass responded to N alone for two years. For the next three years K was required to obtain a yield response from N applications. For the remaining nine years a yield response to any of the nutrients required that the other two nutrients also be applied.[49] Orchardgrass is very responsive to N applications and has been reported to

49. Singh, R. N., D. C. Martens, S. S. Obenshain, and G. D. Jones. 1967. Yield and nutrient uptake by orchardgrass as affected by 14 annual applications of N, P, and K. Agron. J. 59:51–53.

TABLE 27.4 ❧ Leaf development, plant weights, and shoot:root ratios of orchardgrass plants grown under two photoperiods

Age of plants (days)	Photo-period (hours)	Leaves Number/ shoot	Leaves Blade length (cm)	Dry weight of plant or portion (mg) Whole	Dry weight of plant or portion (mg) Shoot	Dry weight of plant or portion (mg) Root	Shoot:root ratio
24	10	2.3*	11.2	13.2	7.5	5.7	1.25
	20	1.9	9.5	9.8	5.8	4.0	1.45
38	10	3.4	22.3	42.7	23.7	19.0	1.24
	20	2.7	21.0	31.2	18.5	12.7	1.38
52	10	4.4	32.2	75.2	43.8	31.3	1.31
	20	3.4	31.5	58.3	37.2	21.3	1.63
66	10	5.2	42.7	124.3	73.3	51.2	1.40
	20	4.3	46.0	115.5	72.3	43.3	1.63
80	10	5.9	48.7	149.0	83.8	65.0	1.29
	20	5.0	54.8	144.2	86.0	58.2	1.48

Source: Adapted from Templeton et al., 1969.[47]
 * Unless italicized, the values of each pair are significantly different at the 0.05 level.

respond to applications as high as 672 kg/ha. In general, the most efficient use of N is made when small split applications are used. When N is used, adequate levels of other nutrients must be maintained if high levels of production are to be sustained.

HARVEST SCHEDULE

GROWTH STAGE. Seasonal yields of dry matter generally increase as maturity advances from the vegetative stage to near full bloom. Intensive studies in six northeastern states have revealed that yields from orchardgrass cut first each year at head emergence were about 14% lower than when cut at early bloom. Delaying first harvest until early bloom decreased aftermath yields 15%. An additional two weeks of delay decreased aftermath yields 26% as compared to yields when the first harvest was taken at early head. Orchardgrass stands become thin and exceedingly clumpy when first growth is cut late, especially when N is readily available, but this usually does not cause severe stand injury.

The proper time to harvest first-growth orchardgrass depends on the use to be made of the forage. Harvesting can be delayed until bloom or later and still provide adequate protein and energy levels for animal maintenance purposes. When high quality is important, orchardgrass should be cut for hay or silage at head emergence. Neither harvest schedule has any detrimental influence on stand longevity. Harvesting may be spread over several weeks by planting early, intermediate, and late maturing cultivars; however, early maturing cultivars are generally more productive.

HARVEST FREQUENCY. Dry matter yields and root weights generally vary inversely with frequency of harvest. The specific effects of harvest frequency depend to a considerable extent on cutting height, which is not important when fewer than five harvests are taken each year.[36] As the frequency of harvest increases, cutting height becomes more important.[50,51]

Regrowth of orchardgrass is a function of energy from photosynthetic activity, carbohydrate reserves, or a combination of the two. With high reserve levels, close cutting does little damage to a stand because new leaves can be produced. Close cutting is a severe management practice when reserves are low because neither sufficient reserves nor photosynthetic tissue is available to provide energy for regrowth. Cutting several times at ground level or continuous close grazing almost always results in a reduction of reserves and serious stand injury. Factors such as soil moisture, temperature, fertility, and disease also have considerable influence on the response of orchardgrass to cutting frequency and height.

❧ SEED PRODUCTION

In 1970 approximately 9 million kg of clean orchardgrass seed worth $4.5 million were harvested in Missouri, Virginia, Kentucky, and Oregon.[52] Oregon produces most of the certified seed. In the northeast region of the U.S. 164,000 kg of orchardgrass seed were sold by wholesale seed companies in 1970 with over 75% of the total being sold in Maryland, Pennsylvania, and West Virginia.[53] This represented a decrease of over 40% in orchardgrass seed sales in the northeast as compared to 1967. This downward trend has been evident for a number of years.

During 1968–70, 23 million kg of orchardgrass seed were produced in the U.S. and 6.7 million kg were imported.[52] U.S. production would seed at least 1.6 million ha. However, probably several times this amount is grown annually since much of this seed is used in mixtures and most orchardgrass stands survive well beyond

50. Reynolds, John H., Charles R. Lewis, and Kenneth F. Laaker. 1971. Chemical composition and yield of orchardgrass forage grown under high rates of nitrogen fertilization and several cutting managements. Tenn. Agr. Exp. Sta. Bull. 479.
51. Davidson, J. L., and F. L. Milthorpe. 1965. Carbohydrate reserves in the regrowth of cocksfoot (*Dactylis glomerata* L.). *J. Brit. Grassl. Soc.* 20:15–18.
52. USDA. 1971. Seed crops annual summary. Stat. Rept. Serv.
53. Pardee, W. D. 1970. Report of 1970 survey of forage seed shipped in the Northeast. Cornell Univ.

three years. Orchardgrass reseeds itself in areas where it is harvested late and fed as a maintenance ration for beef cows.

✣ DISEASES

Many diseases attack orchardgrass. Some are widespread and others are prevalent only in small areas of the U.S. Brown stripe, *Scolecotrichum graminis* Fckl.; scald, *Rhynchosporium orthosporum* Cald.; and rusts and leaf spots are among the most prevalent and destructive diseases.[54] Control by sprays or dusting is generally not economical; control by crop rotation and management has been only partly successful. The best way to control these diseases is with resistant cultivars; however, progress in this area has been slow. Economic losses from orchardgrass diseases are not known, but they are probably greater than most people realize and include loss of yield, decrease in stand longevity, and lower feeding value.

✣ INSECTS

More than 30 insect species have been identified in orchardgrass stands.[55,56] Lar-

vae (grubs) of Japanese beetles, *Popillia japonica* Newman, and green June beetles, *Cotinis nitida* (L.), feed on orchardgrass roots; those of sawflies, *Dolerus* spp., feed on the tops. Although it is generally agreed that insect damage sometimes results in losses of yield, quality, and stand longevity, little is known about the economic losses incurred. Parasites and climate have been important factors in insect control.[57] Crop rotations have been used to reduce insect populations.

54. Kreitlow, Kermit W. 1953. The northern forage grasses. *In* Plant Diseases, p. 264. USDA Yearbook Agr.
55. Newton, R. C. 1959–61. Special reports to entomology research division. USDA.
56. Hardee, D. D., H. Y. Forsythe, Jr., and George G. Gyrisco. 1963. A survey of the Hemiptera and Homoptera infesting grasses (Gramineae) in New York. *J. Econ. Entomol.* 56:555–59.

57. Osborn, Herbert. 1939. Meadow and Pasture Insects. Educators Press, Columbus, Ohio.

✣ QUESTIONS

1. What is the range of climatic adaptation of orchardgrass?
2. What are the factors that affect the nutritive value of orchardgrass? How can these be influenced by the farmer?
3. What are the flowering requirements of orchardgrass?
4. How does orchardgrass compare with other cool-season grasses in terms of area of adaptation, yield, seasonal distribution of forage, feeding value, and persistence?
5. How would you manage an orchardgrass-legume pasture? Hayfield? Seed field? Why?
6. How important are carbohydrate reserves in the regrowth of orchardgrass?
7. Is ground cover a good indication of orchardgrass productivity? Why?

ROBERT C. BUCKNER / *Agricultural Research Service, USDA*

J. RITCHIE COWAN / *Oregon State University*

28

THE FESCUES

୬

THE FESCUES belong to the genus *Festuca* of which there are about 100 species in temperate or cool zones.[1] The species vary greatly in leaf width, height of plants, and longevity. Their growth habit may be creeping or erect and tufted. The annual species are weedy but many of the perennial species are widely used for forage and turf.

The species used for pasture and turf can be classified into fine-leaved and broad-leaved types. Valuable fine-leaved species are sheep fescue, *Festuca ovina* L.; red fescue, *F. rubra* L.; and Idaho fescue, *F. idahoensis* Elmer. The most widely used broad-leaved species are meadow fescue, *F. elatior* L., and tall fescue, *F. arundinacea* Schreb.

୬ ROBERT C. BUCKNER, Research Agronomist, ARS, USDA, and adjunct Professor of Agronomy, University of Kentucky, is in charge of grass improvement research at the Kentucky station. He holds the Ph.D. degree from the University of Minnesota. He has been involved in forage research for many years.

୬ J. RITCHIE COWAN is Head of the Crop Science Department, Oregon State University. He holds the M.S. and Ph.D. degrees from the University of Minnesota. A major area of his research has been the breeding of tall fescue.

Tall fescue is one of the most important grass species in the U.S. Because of its ability to grow over a wide range of soil and climatic conditions, it has been one of the most widely used cultivated grasses for forage, turf, and conservation purposes since the 1940s.

TALL FESCUE

Tall fescue is native to Europe and was introduced into the U.S. by the early settlers about the same time as meadow fescue. Tall fescue and meadow fescue have many similar morphological characteristics. Consequently, confusion existed as to the difference between the two species until the tall fescue cultivars 'Alta' from Oregon and 'Ky 31' from Kentucky became widely used during the 1940s.[2]

Before the release of Ky 31 and Alta cultivars, tall fescue had been listed by botanists as a subspecies, *F. elatior* var. *arundinacea,* of meadow fescue. It was given the scientific name *F. arundinacea* in 1950. The earliest specimen of tall

1. Hoover, Max M., M. A. Hein, William A. Dayton, C. O. Erlanson. 1948. The main grasses for farm and home. *In* Grass, pp. 639–700. USDA Yearbook Agr.
2. Cowan, J. Ritchie. 1956. Tall fescue. *Advan. Agron.* 8:283–319.

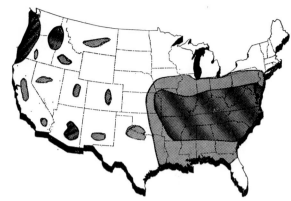

FIG. 28.1. Tall fescue–producing areas of the U.S.

fescue recorded by the U.S. National Herbarium was collected in Oregon in 1886.[3,4] A report in Kentucky Agricultural Experiment Station Bulletin 87 in 1900 on the performance of *F. elatior* (called English bluegrass at that time) strongly suggested that this grass may well have been tall fescue. The report stated that few grasses tested during the period 1892–1900 had performed as well as this species which was thoroughly at home in Kentucky. It made excellent growth, was drought resistant, and remained green through most of the winter.

❧ DISTRIBUTION AND ADAPTATION

The extensive and rapid acceptance of tall fescue since 1950 is due to its wide adaptation and many valuable qualities as a pasture grass.

Tall fescue is adapted to a wide range of climatic conditions and is grown from Florida into Canada (Fig. 28.1). Although tall fescue makes its best growth under relatively cool growing conditions, it is the only cool-season grass that will persist through hot summers and cool winters year after year in many parts of California and the Southwest.[5] At Knoxville, Tenn.,

it is not completely dormant when the mean weekly temperature is 1.1 C and will grow when the mean weekly temperature is about 4.4 C.[6] In the deep South it does not always persist under high summer temperatures and behaves under those conditions more as an annual than as a perennial.

Although tall fescue is widely adapted, it grows best in a transition zone which separates the northern and southern regions of the U.S.; most cool- and warm-season grasses are not well adapted there.[7] Tall fescue is widely used in this zone between the latitudes of Indianapolis, Ind., and Macon, Ga., and the meridian of western Missouri and the eastern edge of the Piedmont area. Within these boundaries it is estimated that 7.2 million ha of tall fescue are grown in pure and mixed stands. Kentucky, Missouri, and Tennessee have large hectarages of tall fescue. It is estimated that Kentucky has about 2.4 million ha.

Tall fescue is tolerant of poor drainage, particularly in the winter. It is found growing in damp pastures and wet places throughout Europe, North Africa, North and South America, New Zealand, and Australia.[1] It is one of the best grasses available for poorly drained soils in irrigated pastures, and it is extensively used as the grass constituent of mixtures in irrigated pastures throughout the western intermountain region from southern California to northern Washington. Its ability to grow on wet soils, to tolerate both alkalinity and salinity, and to produce a heavy turf makes it an excellent grass for such sites.

Tall fescue is one of the more drought-resistant grasses suitable for humid regions. No specific amount of rainfall is known to be the minimum. In Oregon it is grown for forage where the annual rain-

3. Tabor, P. 1951. Tall fescue grown up. *Crops and Soils* 4 (8):9–11.
4. Crowder, L. V. 1953. A survey of meiotic chromosome behavior in tall fescue grass. *Amer. J. Bot.* 40:348–54.
5. Younger, V. B. 1965. A report on tall fescue for turf. *West. Landscaping News* 5 (2):6, 20.

6. Leasure, J. K. 1952. Growth pattern of mixtures of orchardgrass and tall fescue with Ladino clover in relation to temperature. Proc. Assoc. Southern Agr. Workers 49:177–78.
7. Juska, F. V., and A. A. Hanson. 1969. Evaluation of tall fescue, *Festuca arundinacea* Schreb., for turf in the transition zone of the United States. *Agron. J.* 61:625–28.

fall is 370 mm or more and the elevation under 1500 m. However, in the western Gulf states it usually is not recommended for uplands in areas of less than 870 mm of rainfall.

For best growth tall fescue requires good moist soils that are heavy to medium in texture and have considerable humus. It makes fair cover on claypan and other shallow soils and on moist lowlands and sandy loam uplands in the Southeast. Although tall fescue grows well on wet or dry soils, it uses essentially the same amount of moisture during the growing season as alfalfa and bermudagrass.[8]

❧ PLANT DESCRIPTION

Tall fescue is a deep-rooted, long-lived perennial. It is essentially a bunchgrass, though it has short underground stems; and thick stands produce an even sod if kept mowed or grazed. Roots of tall fescue are tough and coarse, contributing to a good sod. In experiments on Class III land at Pullman, Wash., tall fescue produced more than 7.7 t/ha of air-dry roots in the surface 20 cm in six years. Where plots were clipped at three-week intervals, 5.5 t/ha of roots were produced. Tall fescue has numerous shiny, dark green, ribbed leaves. The branched, panicle-type heads are 10–30 cm long and are borne on many to few seed stalks that attain a height of 105–150 cm. The seed are produced five to seven per spikelet. They are similar in size and shape to ryegrass seed but are somewhat darker in general appearance due to a slight purple tinge on the glumes or chaff and a dark purple tinge on the caryopsis. Throughout most of the U.S. it flowers during May and early June. At high elevations in northern areas flowering will sometimes continue into early July.

Tall fescue can be distinguished from meadow fescue by chromosome number, meadow fescue having $2n = 14$, while tall fescue has $2n = 42$. Morphologically, tall

fescue has a number of small hairs on the auricle visible to the naked eye that do not appear on meadow fescue.[9] Numerous investigators have succeeded in producing intergeneric hybrids between tall fescue and *Lolium* spp., suggesting some degree of relationship between these two genera.[10-12]

FORAGE QUALITY

A high-quality forage has been defined as one with the greatest possible concentration of utilizable nutrients in a form highly acceptable to animals.[13] Criteria used to determine forage quality include the contents of crude protein, crude fiber, lignin, soluble carbohydrates, and mineral elements and the digestibility, acceptability, and intake of the forage by livestock.

Contributing factors which govern the quality of tall fescue appear to be age of leaves, fertility of the soil in which it is grown, season of the year, and genetic variation. Usually, quality is improved if the plants are kept grazed rather closely or clipped to prevent accumulation of old leaves if grown with legumes or properly fertilized for good growth. The quality of tall fescue is somewhat poorer in late spring and during summer than most other grasses.[14] The Kentucky station showed the digestibility, total sugar content, and palatability to livestock to be lowest during summer, intermediate in early spring, and highest during the fall.[15] The high quality during the fall months

8. Cowen, O. P., and E. Streckling. 1968. Moisture use by selected forage crops. *Agron. J.* 60:587–91.

9. Crowder, L. V. 1953. A simple method for distinguishing tall and meadow fescue. *Agron. J.* 45:453–54.
10. Buckner, R. C., H. D. Hill, and P. B. Burrus, Jr. 1961. Some characteristics of perennial and annual ryegrass × tall fescue hybrids and of the amphiploid progenies of annual ryegrass × tall fescue. *Crop Sci.* 1:75–80.
11. Carnahan, H. L., and H. D. Hill. 1955. *Lolium perenne* L. × tetraploid *Festuca elatior* L. triploid hybrids and colchicine treatments for inducing autoallohexaploids. *Agron. J.* 47:258–62.
12. Jenkins, T., Jr. 1933. Interspecific and intergeneric hybrids in herbage grasses. Initial crosses. *J. Genet.* 28:205–64.
13. Browning, C. B. 1964. Rept. 21st Southern Pasture and Forage Crop Improvement Conf., Univ. Fla., Gainesville.
14. Van Keuren, R. W. 1970. Summer pasture for beef cows. *Ohio Rept.* 53 (3):43–45.
15. Buckner, R. C., J. R. Todd, P. B. Burrus, II, and R. F. Barnes. 1967. Chemical composition, palatability, and digestibility of ryegrass–tall fescue hybrids, 'Kenwell,' and 'Kentucky 31' tall fescue varieties. *Agron. J.* 59:345–49.

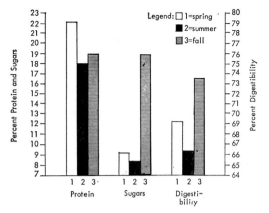

FIG. 28.2. Seasonal changes in percentage crude protein, total sugars, and *in vitro* digestibility of tall fescue and ryegrass–tall fescue hybrid derivatives at Lexington, Ky. Although hybrid derivatives are included in this graph, seasonal trends in forage quality of tall fescue and the hybrid derivatives are similar.

is attributed to an increase in soluble carbohydrates, while crude fiber and lignin remain at about the same level (Fig. 28.2).[16]

The ability of tall fescue to provide the nutrient requirements of an animal is perhaps its best measure of forage quality. Many investigators have studied animal performance on tall fescue pastures in pure seedings and in fescue-legume mixtures in comparison with other grasses, and the results are extremely variable. Average daily gains of cattle grazing fescue was superior in some tests and inferior in others.[17-21] Gains on tall fescue during the three to four months of midsummer were

reported to be nil by workers at the Southern Indiana Forage Farm; however, in a Rowan County, N.C., test, animal performance on tall fescue was superior to that on bermudagrass.[19,20] Poor animal performance on fescue during summer was attributed by the Indiana investigators to a low level of energy intake.[19]

Generally, pure stands of tall fescue supported a longer grazing period, higher stocking rate, and higher gain per ha than pure stands of orchardgrass and grass-legume mixtures.[19-21] Fertilizer N slightly depressed average daily gains, nearly doubled carrying capacities of the tall fescue pastures, and greatly increased liveweight gain per ha.[19-20]

Although tall fescue has many valuable attributes as a pasture grass, cattle grazing pure stands will occasionally have nutritional problems. During 1913 a New Zealand worker reported dry gangrene and lameness of cattle to be associated with consumption of tall fescue.[22] This difficulty was later described and designated as "fescue foot."[23] Usually the first signs are general stiffness and soreness. Affected cattle are slow to move and refuse to graze. They become dull and listless, their rate of breathing increases, and they lose weight rapidly. As the condition progresses, dry gangrene develops, eventually resulting in the sloughing of the extremities of the leg or tail. The syndrome resembles but is not identical to that of ergot or selenium poisoning.[24] However, the alkaloids that cause ergotism have not been detected in tall fescue plant tissue.[25]

Sporadic outbreaks of fescue foot have been reported from most of the southeastern states. The disease is especially prevalent in an area extending from eastern Kansas through Missouri, southern Illinois, and southern Indiana to Kentucky.[24]

16. Brown, R. H., R. E. Blaser, and J. P. Fontenot 1955. Digestibility of fall-grown Kentucky 31 fescue. *Agron. J.* 55:321–24.
17. Jacobson, D. R., S. B. Carr, R. H. Hatton, R. C. Buckner, A. P. Graden, D. R. Dowden, and A. W. Miller. 1969. Growth, physiological responses and evidence of toxicity in yearling dairy cattle grazing different grasses. *J. Dairy Sci.* 53:575–87.
18. Peterson, R. C., G. O. Mott, M. E. Heath, and W. M. Beeson. 1962. Comparison of tall fescue and orchardgrass for grazing in southern Indiana—Four-year summary, 1958–1961. Ind. Agr. Exp. Sta. Res. Rept. 26.
19. Mott, G. O., C. J. Kaiser, R. C. Peterson, Randall Peterson, Jr., and C. L. Rhykerd. 1971. Supplemental feeding of steers on *Festuca arundinacea* Schreb. pastures fertilized at three levels of nitrogen. *Agron. J.* 63:751–54.
20. Gross, H. D., Lemuel Goode, W. B. Gilbert, and G. L. Ellis. 1966. Beef grazing systems in Piedmont, North Carolina. *Agron. J.* 58:307–10.
21. Blaser, R. E., R. C. Hammes, Jr., H. T. Bryant, C. M. Kincaid, W. H. Skrdla, T. H. Taylor, and W. L. Griffeth. 1956. The value of forage species and mixtures for fattening steers. *Agron. J.* 48:508–13.

22. Clifton, E. 1913. Estimation of grasses. *N.Z. J. Agr.* 6:480.
23. Cunningham, T. J. 1948. Tall fescue grass is poison for cattle. *N.Z. J. Agr.* 77 (5):519.
24. Yates, S. G. 1968. Mycotoxins as a possible cause of fescue toxicity. 156th Meet. Div. Agr. Food and Chem., Agr. Chem. Soc. (Atlantic City, N.J.)
25. Riggs, R. K. 1966. The interrelationship of tall fescue and *Claviceps purpurea* upon the development of alkaloids in each. Ph.D. thesis, Univ. Ky.

When the total number of cattle grazing tall fescue is considered, the percentage of cattle affected by this disease is very low; however, severe economic losses may result when it occurs within a herd. Only cattle are susceptible to fescue foot; it has not been reported in other livestock. Most cases of fescue foot occur among cattle that graze poorly managed pure stands of the grass during late fall and winter.

The specific cause of fescue foot is unknown. A vasoconstricter is postulated as the causative agent, which research indicates may be a mycotoxin, an alkaloid of tall fescue or of fungal origin, or a toxin produced in the rumen. The anion fraction of alcohol-soluble material from tall fescue has produced signs of fescue foot. Additional fractionation will be required to identify the specific causative agent.[26]

Fescue foot may be distinct from "fescue poisoning or toxicity." Cattle feeding on tall fescue during late spring and summer may perform poorly at times even though it compares favorably with other cool-season grasses in respect to chemical constituents considered in forage quality. Cattle observed grazing only tall fescue during this period of the year may have rough hair coat, diarrhea, rapid respiration rates, high temperatures, and poor average daily gain.[17]

Tall fescue compares favorably with other cool-season grasses for digestibility; however, it is not consumed as well except during the fall, and intake by cattle is more variable than for other grasses. Although digestibility is a good measure of forage quality in many cool-season grasses, it does not seem so for tall fescue.[27,28] Thus, apparently undesirable constituents are responsible for the erratic nutritional quality of the grass and subsequent poor

performance at times by cattle feeding on it during late spring and summer.

Nine alkaloids have been detected in extracts of tall fescue. Perloline is the major alkaloid, and its content is related to season, genotype, and level of N fertility.[29] Higher perloline levels are found during July and August than during other months of the year. Highest levels occur in grass heavily fertilized with N. Perloline has caused mild toxic effects when injected into animals; therefore, the amount ingested by grazing animals may affect animal health by inhibition of the rumen microflora.[30] It has since been shown to inhibit *in vitro* cellulose digestion by microorganisms of rumen fluid, and growth of certain rumen bacteria has been inhibited at perloline concentrations occasionally found in tall fescue.[31,32] The adverse effect of high perloline levels on rumen microorganisms of cattle may explain the poor relation observed between intake and digestibility and the subsequent erratic performance of cattle when grazing pure stands of tall fescue during late spring and summer.

❧ IMPORTANCE AND USE

The use of tall fescue increased steadily and rapidly during the 1960s. It is widely used for forage, turf, and conservation purposes in the West and Northwest and in the Southeast. The Crop Reporting Board, SRS, USDA, stated that the 1951–60 average annual production of clean seed of tall fescue in the U.S. was 14,490,000 kg and that 32,413,181 kg were produced in 1971. It is the predominant cool-season grass in Kentucky and is widely grown in many other states in the transition zone.

26. Bush, L. P., J. A. Boling, and S. G. Yates. 1978. Animal disorders. *In* Tall Fescue: Amer. Soc. Agron. Monogr., Ch. 13. Amer. Soc. Agron., Madison, Wis.
27. Bryan, W. B., W. F. Wedin, and R. L. Vetter. 1970. Evaluation of reed canarygrass and tall fescue as spring-summer and fall-saved pasture. *Agron. J.* 62 (1): 75–80.
28. Martz, F. A., K. H. Asay, and R. T. Wormington. 1970. Preliminary rept. Plant-animal factors associated with voluntary intake of tall fescue, *Festuca arundinacea* Schreb. Mo. Agr. Exp. Sta. Res Rept., pp. 63–70.

29. Gentry, C. E., R. A. Chapman, L. Henson, and R. C. Buckner. Factors affecting the alkaloid content of tall fescue, *Festuca arundinacea* Schreb. *Agron. J.* 61: 313–16.
30. Butler, G. W. 1961. Genetic differences in the perloline content of ryegrass (*Lolium*) herbage. *N.Z. J. Agr. Res.* 5:158–62.
31. Bush, L. P., R. C. Streeter, and R. C. Buckner. 1970. Perloline inhibition of *in vitro* ruminal cellulose digestion. *Crop Sci.* 10:108–9.
32. Bush, L. P., James Boling, G. Allen, and R. C. Buckner. 1972. Inhibitory effects of perloline to rumen fermentation *in vitro*. *Crop Sci.* 12:277–79.

Tall fescue produces most abundantly under irrigation and high fertility. Where well managed, grazed closely, and with a proper legume balance or high rate of fertilizer N, it provides productive pasture.

Tall fescue is tolerant of continuous close grazing, and a high percentage of the hectarage in the Southeast is used as continuous pasture.[33] The production of tall fescue in terms of carrying capacity and liveweight gain per ha of beef cattle has been superior to other cool-season grasses in this region.[19,20]

It is always advisable to seed a legume with tall fescue when the grass is to be used for pasture. (See Fig. 28.3.) It is used in the Southeast in association with lespedeza; white, red, and alsike clover; alfalfa; and sometimes other legumes. Legumes add greatly to palatability and nutritive value. The choice of legume depends upon adaptation of the legume and the utilization of the forages. Alsike clover has been used successfully on some of the wetter soils. West of the Oregon Cascades, almost 200,000 ha of upland pasture has been improved by seeding subterranean clover with tall fescue.

In the Southeast, tall fescue is a valuable grass for spring, fall, and winter grazing. Forage quality of the grass is equal or superior to most other cool-season grasses during these seasons if properly fertilized and managed. A management system using tall fescue as pasture or as hay and pasture during spring and early summer maximizes the use of tall fescue at its highest quality. Cattle are removed about midsummer, the pasture fertilized, and the growth permitted to accumulate until about the time of frost when the cattle are returned. If stock are removed in midsummer, tall fescue in a mixture with a legume or with an application of fertilizer N should have at least 20–25 cm of leafy growth for winter pasture by the time of first frost. Tall fescue pastures managed in this manner may carry

FIG. 28.3. *Seed a legume with tall fescue . . . for pasture.* Growth on April 25 of tall fescue and ladino clover on rolling, eroded upland Cecil clay near Braselton, Ga. The land received a complete fertilizer at the time of seeding in the fall and 111 kg/ha nitrate of soda the following spring. *SCS photo.*

cattle through the winter with a minimum of supplemental feeding.[34] (See Fig. 28.4.)

Tall fescue makes excellent hay yields when properly fertilized and grown in a grass-legume mixture. For best quality the grass should be harvested when the first seed heads begin to appear and certainly prior to anthesis. The aftermath, even under dry conditions, usually is very productive. Total dry matter yields per year of 7–9 t/ha are consistently reported from hay and aftermath production of well-fertilized pure stands and from tall fescue-legume mixtures.[35,36]

33. Lopez, R. R., A. G. Matches, and J. D. Baldridge. 1967. Vegetative development and organic reserves of tall fescue under conditions of accumulated growth. *Crop Sci.* 7:409–12.

34. Wilson, L. L., R. Peterson, Jr., M. E. Heath, C. J. Callahan, C. J. Kaiser, and K. Hawkins. 1967. Grain supplementation of spring-calving beef cows on tall fescue winter pasture and round bales. Ind. Agr. Exp. Sta., Res. Progr. Rept. 291.

35. Hoveland, C. S., and E. M. Evans. 1970. Cool-season perennial grass and grass-clover management. Ala. Agr. Exp. Sta. Circ. 175.

36. Templeton, W. C., Jr., and T. H. Taylor. 1966. Some effects of nitrogen, phosphorus, and potassium fertilization on botanical composition of a tall fescue-white clover sward. *Agron. J.* 58 (6):569–72.

FIG. 28.4. *Tall fescue pastures . . . carry cattle through the winter.* Formerly abandoned hill land in southern Indiana now producing 450 beef cow days/ha of winter pasture annually from tall fescue round bales and aftermath growth. Spring growth is round baled and left in the field. An application of 111 kg/ha of N is applied annually. *Ind. Agr. Exp. Sta. photo.*

Tall fescue is well recognized for its soil conservation value because of its deep penetrating root system and tolerance to adverse conditions. It provides excellent waterway protection and is ideal for cover in low wetlands. Where waterways can be pastured during certain seasons of the year, it is common practice to seed legumes with the grass. If the waterways cannot be grazed, it is more satisfactory to plant only grass and fertilize with N.

Tall fescue is widely used as a turf grass on play areas, athletic fields, airfields, parks, roadsides, and other areas where tough turf is desired. It is considered wear resistant and compares favorably in shade tolerance with fine-leaved fescues.[7] Tall fescue makes an acceptable lawn where Kentucky bluegrass and other fine-leaved lawn grasses do poorly because of its great tolerance to soil reaction, drainage, sun and shade, disease, insects, and drought.[37] In general, tall fescue has been considered too coarse and bunchy for lawn turf. The formation of tall fescue clumps or bunches may be attributed in part to low seeding rates and inclusion in mixtures with other turf species. A seeding rate of 3.6–4.5 kg of seed per 93 sq m will produce a dense nonbunchy turf with finer leaves.[5] Several stations are attempting to select finer leaved tall fescue for turf purposes.

❧ CULTIVARS

Most tall fescue is either Alta or Ky 31–Alta in the West and Northwest and Ky 31 in the Southeast. It is estimated that approximately 7 million ha in the Southeast is established to Ky 31.

Breeding programs are in progress at a number of agricultural experiment stations with the objective of developing cultivars characterized by improved forage quality and disease resistance. (See Table 28.1.[38])

Tall fescue is a naturally cross-pollinated crop. Approximately 33% of the plants will produce some seed with selfing. A few plants are highly self-fertile.

❧ CULTURE AND MANAGEMENT

Although growth is vigorous, seedling establishment is somewhat slow; therefore, a clean firm seedbed is most desirable. Seed should not be planted more than 6–25 mm in depth, depending upon soil conditions. Recommended seeding rates vary from 2–16 kg/ha. The lighter rates are for seeding well-drained land where a large proportion of legumes is desired. The heavier rates are recommended when seeding is made under adverse conditions, especially if it is to be pastured during the winter. Tall fescue can be seeded either in late summer or

37. Underwood, J. K. 1964. Tennessee lawns. Tenn. Agr. Exp. Sta. Publ. 326.

38. Hanson, A. A. 1972. Grass varieties in the United States. USDA Agr. Handbook 170, rev.

TABLE 28.1 ❧ Tall fescue cultivars, origin, areas of most use, and characteristics

Cultivar	Date of release	Origin or source	Area of most use	Relative maturity	Other characteristics
Alta[2]	1940	Oregon station	West, Northwest	medium, early	adapted to dry summer conditions
Goar[38]	1946	California station	West, Southwest	early	adapted to alkaline soils
Fawn	1964	Oregon station	central U.S., Northwest	early	good seedling vigor, improved palatability
Ky 31[38]	1942	Kentucky station	Southeast, central U.S.	medium	wide adaptation, good winter growth
Kenmont[38]	1963	Kentucky, Montana stations	Southeast, northern Great Plains	medium	good midseason growth
Kenwell[38]	1965	Kentucky station and USDA	Southeast, central U.S.	late	disease resistance, improved palatability
Kenhy[39]	1976	Kentucky station and USDA	Transition zone	medium	improved for quality and yield, wide adaptability

Sources: Cowan, 1956;[2] Hanson, 1965;[38] Buckner et al., 1977.[39]

early spring. However, when legumes are grown in association with tall fescue, better stands are secured from summer than from spring seedings because there is less competition with the grass for light during that time.[40]

Tall fescue is similar to other crops in that it does best on soils of high fertility. However, it is not difficult to establish under rather adverse soil conditions. It will establish on soils of low pH, but production is improved when soils are limed to the neutral range.

Tall fescue responds readily to high rates of N.[35,36] The lack of N may cause an unproductive sod-bound condition. Well-fertilized legumes usually persist in mixtures with tall fescue; weak, starved legumes soon fade out. Usually the liming and fertilizing with P and K necessary to maintain a good vigorous growth of the companion legume will be enough for the fescue, but sometimes applications of N will be necessary to keep the grass green, succulent, and highly productive.

Retaining legumes in a mixture is a major problem, and many pastures become pure stands of tall fescue. When legumes disappear from the stand, they may be reestablished through renovation, which produces increased yields of good-quality forage during summer when the grass is making poor growth and is lowest in nutritive value.[41]

Renovation involves correcting soil fertility deficiencies, making a seedbed by destroying a portion of the grass sod, and distributing the inoculated legume seed evenly over the soil as in an original planting. Fields may be renovated in early fall or spring. Generally spring seedings on a renovated sod are more satisfactory for securing good stands of legumes because severe droughts frequently are encountered in the fall. The grass should be grazed moderately during the spring to prevent undue competition to the legume.

GRAZING MANAGEMENT

Since tall fescue is rather slow to establish and somewhat weak in the seedling

39. Buckner, R. C., P. B. Burrus II, and L. P. Bush. 1977. Registration of Kenhy tall fescue. *Crop Sci.* 17:672–73.
40. Hart, Richard H., G. E. Carlson, and H. J. Retzer. 1968. Establishment of tall fescue and white clover: Effects of seeding method and weather. *Agron. J.* 60 (4): 385–88.

41. Thompson, W. C., and R. F. Cornelius. 1967. Loafing acres go to work. Better crops with plant food. Amer. Potash Inst. (Reprint D-3-67.)

FIG. 28.5. *Annual crop . . . produced in the U.S. . . . increased steadily.* Harvesting tall fescue for seed in Oregon. Field sanitation is being accomplished in the center background by open-field burning.

stage, new stands can be seriously damaged by overgrazing or grazing too soon. A new stand should not be trampled during the first winter while the ground is wet. However, close grazing on well-established stands is a good management practice. Tall fescue will withstand heavy grazing for short periods but may be severely injured by continuous close grazing. Under irrigation where a rotational system of grazing is practiced and forage is grazed quickly and closely, it recovers well. Tall fescue should not be grazed closer than 5–10 cm for best production and longevity.[42]

✣ SEED PRODUCTION

The annual crop of tall fescue seed produced in the U.S. has increased steadily, the average yield rising from 249 kg/ha in 1951–60 to 288 kg/ha in 1969–71. (See Fig. 28.5.) A very high percentage of tall fescue seed grown in the U.S. is produced in the Southeast. Since 1965 tall fescue seed production has made rapid increases in Missouri.[43]

Highest seed yields are obtained from pure stands of tall fescue. Fertilizer N is the most important factor affecting seed production, increasing seed yields up to 100%. In Kentucky, tall fescue sods top-dressed with 73.3 kg/ha of N in December consistently gave the highest seed yields over a five-year period. Nitrogen applied at this rate after March 15 caused lodging and excessive vegetative growth at the expense of seed yields.[44]

Following seed harvest excess herbage should be removed. The regrowth can be grazed during summer and fall or permitted to accumulate and grazed during the winter. Grazing can continue on tall fescue until March without reducing seed yields.

Broadcast seedings produce good seed yields for a year or two, but then yields decline markedly unless definite preventive steps are taken. Thin broadcast stands or row seedings, however, decline less rapidly in seed yields than dense stands. Solid stands can be renovated by skim plowing, with the sod plowed to about 10 cm. The second year after renovation as much as 454.5 kg of seed have been harvested from areas previously yielding less than 45.5 kg.

Tall fescue seed can be harvested with a combine directly from the standing plants or by windrowing. The seed shatter readily as plants ripen. When the seed crop is combined, it has been estimated that 35–40% of the total seed crop is lost through shattering. The loss occurs when the plants are combined directly or picked up from the swath.[45]

The ryegrasses, *Lolium* spp., and orchardgrass, *Dactylis glomerata* L., are among the more serious weedy species in the production of tall fescue seed. Several troublesome annual weedy grasses are cheat and chess, *Bromus* spp., and rattail fescue, *F. myuros* L. Considerable success has been achieved in the control of some weedy grasses by using selective chemicals.

42. Matches, A. G. 1969. Influence of cutting height in darkness on measurement of energy reserves of tall fescue. *Agron. J.* 61:896–98.
43. USDA. 1970. Annual summary. Stat. Rep. Serv. Crop Rep. Board.
44. Buckner, R. C., and P. B. Burrus, Jr. 1959. The effect of certain management and fertilization practices on seed production of tall fescue. Proc. Assoc. Southern Agr. Workers. pp. 67–68.
45. Hill, D. D., and J. E. Harmond. 1955. Survey measures losses during harvest of forage grass and legume seed crops. *Crops and Soils* 8 (1):27.

MEADOW FESCUE

Meadow fescue, *F. elatior* L., is generally a considerably smaller plant than tall fescue. It is a perennial species that flourishes in deep rich soils and can be grown in about the same region as timothy. It is a good grazing grass, has been used to some extent for hay, and is recognized as an excellent pasture grass in western Europe. Meadow fescue has never been used extensively in American agriculture. In areas where adapted it has been used in pasture mixtures on wetland. The chief factor limiting its use in the U.S. is its high susceptibility to leaf rusts, *Puccinia* spp. With the increased use of tall fescue in the late 1940s and the high resistance of tall fescue to crown rust, *Puccinia coronata* Cda., meadow fescue gradually fell into disuse.[2]

FINELEAF FESCUES

Sheep fescue is probably native to North America. It forms dense tufts, with numerous stiff, rather sharp bluish gray leaves. It is adapted to about the same climatic conditions as Kentucky bluegrass. Its greatest use is for making turf in shaded areas.

Red fescue is somewhat similar to sheep fescue, but its leaves are darker green. Commercially, there are two distinct forms, red fescue and chewings fescue. Red fescue is a creeping grass, although this characteristic is variable. Chewings fescue, *F. rubra* var. *commutata* Gaud., is tufted and does not creep. Both forms are used primarily for lawns and turf and are especially adapted to shaded, dry sites.

Idaho fescue is found under range conditions in the Pacific Northwest. Many range investigators recognize it as a grass with considerable potential. Arizona fescue, *F. arizonica* Vasey, is an important forage grass of northern Arizona though it becomes rather tough with age. Greenleaf fescue, *F. viridula* Vasey, locally called mountaingrass, is an outstanding grass in subalpine regions of the northwestern states.[46]

---

46. Hitchcock, A. S. 1951. Manual of the grasses of the United States, 2nd ed., pp. 57–58. USDA Misc. Publ. 200, rev.

❧ QUESTIONS

1. What is the general area of adaptation of tall fescue?
2. Why is tall fescue such a widely adapted species?
3. How can tall fescue be distinguished from meadow fescue?
4. Name the contributing factors which govern the forage quality of tall fescue.
5. During what season of the year is tall fescue of best quality? Why?
6. Describe a system of management to maximize the use of tall fescue when it is of highest quality.
7. Name four tall fescue cultivars, state where they were developed, and give an important characteristic of each.
8. Name two other species of *Festuca*.

ROD V. FRAKES / *Oregon State University*

29

THE RYEGRASSES

A RECENT taxonomic revision of the ryegrass genus, *Lolium,* distinguishes eight species.[1] Perennial ryegrass, *Lolium perenne* L., and annual or Italian ryegrass, *L. multiflorum* Lam., are of economic importance for forage production in cool temperate climates throughout the world. Perennial ryegrass originated in southern Europe, north Africa, and southwest Asia. It is believed to have been first cultivated for forage in England in 1677. The indigenous area for annual ryegrass is questionable, but it was grown in the meadows of northern Italy in the thirteenth century.

Both perennial and annual ryegrasses are considered self-incompatible; however, they cross readily with each other. Natural hybridization between the two species has resulted in great variation in certain plant characteristics earlier believed to be representative of one or the other species. All recognized species of *Lolium* have seven pairs of chromosomes. This has resulted in natural interspecific hybrid variation within the genus.

The ryegrass cultivars being used in forage production are from several sources: (1) perennial ryegrass, $2n = 14$; (2) annual ryegrass, $2n = 14$; (3) autotetraploid ryegrass, $2n = 28$; or (4) perennial $\times$ annual hybrid types, $2n = 14$, referred to as "short-rotation" ryegrasses.

⚜ DISTRIBUTION AND ADAPTATION

The ryegrasses are commonly used for hay and pasture in Australia, New Zealand, the British Isles, and the temperate areas of western Europe and the U.S. for sheep, dairy, and beef production. The worldwide usage of the two species has resulted in many in-depth research programs to study the management, nutritive value, and genetics of these grasses.

Ryegrass is less winter-hardy than certain other forage species, e.g., timothy and orchardgrass. It is grown west of the Sierra Nevada and the Cascade Range and in the southern humid areas of the U.S. Its use also extends northward along the Atlantic Coast (Fig. 29.1).

The ryegrasses can be grown on a wide range of soil types. However, if extended low temperatures, drought, and poor fertility are characteristic of the area to be seeded, ryegrasses may not be the most desirable species. They respond to conditions of high fertility. They are grown in some cases where the area is so wet during certain periods of the year few other forages would survive satisfactorily. Short periods

⚜ ROD V. FRAKES is Professor of Agronomy in charge of forage crop breeding at Oregon State University. He holds the M.S. degree from Oregon State University and the Ph.D. from Purdue University. His special research interests have been the breeding and genetics of cool-season grasses and alfalfa.

1. Terrell, E. E. 1968. A taxonomic revision of the genus *Lolium.* USDA Tech. Bull. 1392.

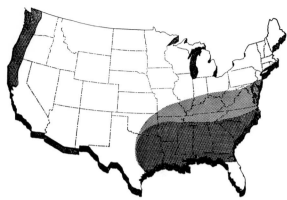

Fig. 29.1. Ryegrass-producing areas of the U.S.

of flooding will not severely reduce the stand of well-established ryegrass.

❧ PLANT DESCRIPTION

The ryegrasses are considered bunch-grasses with no creeping habit of growth. The perennial ryegrasses grow to 90 cm in height with erect culms. The leaf sheaths are glabrous and the leaf blades are folded in the young shoots. The inflorescence is a spike which is usually only slightly curved and up to 30 cm in length. There may be as many as 35 spikelets per spike with 2–10 fertile florets per spikelet. Awns are usually absent from the caryopsis of perennial ryegrass.

The annual ryegrasses sometimes behave as short-lived perennials. They also have erect culms, but usually are taller than perennials when fully grown. The annual ryegrasses may reach 130 cm in height. The annuals also have a glabrous leaf sheath, but the leaf blades are rolled in the young shoots. The inflorescence is a spike, 17–30 cm in length, with up to 38 spikelets and 11–22 fertile florets per spikelet. Awns are typically present on the caryopses of annual ryegrass.

In general, annual ryegrass differs from perennial ryegrass by having attached awns, the annual or biennial habit of growth, leaf blades rolled in the young shoots, a wider leaf blade, more florets per spikelet, and taller mature plant height by about 30 cm.

❧ IMPORTANCE AND USE

Annual, perennial, and short-rotation ryegrasses are widely used in grassland agriculture. Common uses are for pasture, hay, silage, soil conservation, and turf. They can be seeded alone or with other species of grasses, legumes, or cereals. In the milder southern climates it is commonly used for winter pasture.

Annual ryegrass is used for winter pasture in the southeastern U.S. When seeded in September with clover and cereal rye, it provided about 200 days of continuous grazing with beef cattle and about 182 kg of gain at less cost per kg of gain than certain feedlot procedures.[2]

Perennial ryegrass is also used as a common component for pasture mixtures. Seeded alone or with other species, it provides a high-quality forage for the grazing animal. Perennial ryegrass does not persist as long as some other pasture species but is quite satisfactory for three or four years.

Short-rotation ryegrasses have been used more widely in New Zealand and Australia than in the U.S. Where sheep were used as the experimental animal, short-rotation ryegrass usually produced more daily gain than perennial ryegrass. The reasons for the differences among these grasses in animal efficiency of feed utilization are not fully understood, but research in this area is under way.[3] Better liveweight gains are usually obtained if the ryegrass is seeded with a legume.

It is common to graze a ryegrass pasture early in the season, harvest it for hay when about half the heads have shed pollen, and then use the regrowth for either hay or pasture.

2. Anthony, W. B., C. S. Hoveland, E. L. Mayton, and H. E. Burgess. 1971. Rye-ryegrass–Yuchi arrowleaf clover for production of slaughter cattle. Ala. Agr. Exp. Sta. Circ. 182.

3. Wyatt, M. J. 1971. Studies on the causes of the differences in pasture quality between perennial ryegrass, short-rotation ryegrass, and white clover. N.Z. J. Agr. 14:352–67.

Certain areas of the Southeast are using both summer and winter pasture for the production of slaughter steers. In Louisiana, ryegrass was seeded at 45 kg/ha in September.[4] This resulted in 140 days of winter grazing and produced 390 kg/ha of beef. This was in agreement with an earlier study showing steer weight gain of approximately 770 g/day over a 140-day grazing period on ryegrass pastures.[5]

Ryegrass overseeded on bermudagrass pasture will provide 200 days of winter grazing, and studies suggest profits may be greater in a steer fattening program when pasture replaces a portion of the grain.[6]

Three methods of finishing steers for slaughter were compared: (1) feeding in drylot with grass hay and a fattening ration, (2) grazing wheat-ryegrass pasture plus supplemental ration, and (3) grazing wheat-ryegrass pasture without supplemental feed.[7] The results suggest that finishing steers on wheat and ryegrass pasture without supplemental feed offers a good chance for economical returns based on local livestock market prices.

The Alabama station examined the cool-season annual grazing crops, including ryegrass, for a 10-year period.[8] The conclusion was that cool-season annual grazing was a good method of producing a 218-kg feeder steer from a 180-kg stocker calf. Good and choice slaughter steers were produced directly from grazing when calves weighed about 250 kg initially and optimum grazing conditions existed.

Ryegrass forage has been used to make pellets for the feedlot. Pelleting is an accepted method of increasing animal performance on high forage rations. The Louisiana station, using yearling steers, compared ryegrass pellets as comprising 40, 60, and 80% of the ration to ryegrass grazing.[9] Over a 140-day period the daily gain of steers was 994, 1000, and 908 g respectively for the three rations compared to 700 g/day on the ryegrass pasture. The composition of the ryegrass pellets was 89% dry matter, 13.1% crude protein, and 36.7% N-free extract. Carcass grades of slaughtered animals were higher for those fed the pelleted ryegrass.

Ryegrass is used for overseeding turf areas in the southern states. In the fall, established warm-season grasses will go dormant, turn brown, and offer a less desirable appearance. Ryegrass seeded over these areas gives a quick, green cover that will remain during the winter months to be replaced in the spring by the regrowth of the original established species. This permits the homeowner or landowner to have a desirable turf throughout the year. Breeding programs have developed cultivars of perennial ryegrass designed specifically for turf purposes. These are used for play areas as well as for home and industrial turf.

❧ CULTIVARS

Many cultivars of ryegrass have been developed because of its widespread usage in many parts of the world. The most active breeding programs are in the United Kingdom and European countries. In the 1971 list of recognized cultivars for international trade and increase there were 69 cultivars of annual ryegrass and 82 of perennial ryegrass.[10]

The usual methods of grass breeding as well as special techniques have been used to develop ryegrass cultivars. Interspecific hybridization followed by selection has resulted in longer lived annuals or the short-rotation types. The objective is to transfer

4. Carpenter, John C., Jr., R. H. Klett, and Sherman Phillips. 1969. Producing slaughter steers with temporary grazing crops and concentrates. La. Agr. Exp. Sta. Bull. 643.

5. Carpenter, John C., Jr., and Paul B. Brown. 1966. Performance and feed costs for selected methods of feeding beef calves from weaning to market. La. Agr. Exp. Sta. Bull. 612.

6. Carpenter, John C., Jr., R. H. Klett, and F. G. Hembry. 1971. Producing slaughter steers with grain self-fed on pasture. La. Agr. Exp. Sta. Bull. 659.

7. Roark, C. B., H. E. Harris, and J. I. Feazel. 1968. Three methods of finishing steers for slaughter. La. Agr. Exp. Sta. Bull. 630.

8. Harris, R. R., W. B. Anthony, V. L. Brown, J. K. Boseck, H. F. Yates, W. B. Webster, and J. E. Barrett, Jr. 1971. Cool-season annual grazing crops for stocker calves. Ala. Agr. Exp. Sta. Bull. 416.

9. White, T. Wayne. 1969. Dehydrated pellets for fattening steers. La. Agr. Exp. Sta. Bull. 634.

10. Organization for Economic Cooperation and Development. 1971. Scheme for the varietal certification of herbage seed moving in international trade. List of cultivars eligible for certification. OECD, Paris.

the high-yield, high-quality characteristics of annual ryegrass to the longer lived perennials.

Many cultivars of ryegrasses are auto-tetraploid as a result of doubling the chromosome number and selecting for desirable forage types. This has resulted in cultivars with good vigor, large leaves and stems, acceptable regrowth, persistence, and adequate seed production potential.

Ryegrass germplasm is also being examined in plant material produced by crossing ryegrass with tall fescue, *Festuca arundinacea* Schreb. In this procedure special techniques are used to accomplish intergeneric hybridization followed by chromosome doubling and intensive screening for gamete viability and fertility to perpetuate the newly formed hybrids.

❧ CULTURE AND MANAGEMENT

As with many forage crops the time of seeding is a function of severity of winter and cold tolerance of the species. Ryegrasses are fall seeded in areas where the winter months have relatively mild temperatures. If winter pasture is desired, an early fall seeding is in order. Late fall seeding may result in successful stand establishment, but this will not produce an abundance of winter grazing. Late fall-seeded plantings are more susceptible to stand reduction because of winter freezes. Where winters are more severe, an early spring seeding is desirable. Spring and summer rainfall contributes to successful spring seeding of ryegrasses.

Ryegrasses may be seeded alone or with associated forage species. The seed readily emerge from a covering of about 1.25 cm. Seeding may be done in a clean, well-prepared seedbed in existing sod with a sod-seeder or grassland drill. It is a common practice to drill ryegrass in standing stubble. Under favorable conditions the species will germinate and emerge quickly.

Certain cultivars establish more rapidly than others. Mixtures of perennial and short-rotation types are sometimes used for permanent pasture establishment. This is done because the short-rotation type will establish more rapidly, suppress weedy plants, and provide an earlier pasture for grazing than when the perennial is seeded alone. The perennial will ultimately become the dominant species provided the pasture is managed to favor the perennial rather than the shorter lived associated ryegrass.

The seeding rate may vary depending on intended use of the established stand. For forage production in a pure stand, 16–22 kg seed/ha is the common seeding rate. If seeded with a cereal for annual pasture, 9–11 kg/ha is in order. If the ryegrass is grown with an associated legume, 5–6 kg seed/ha is satisfactory. When the seeding is primarily for the control of soil erosion, up to 33 kg/ha are used. Ryegrasses established for turf purposes are observed to be most satisfactory when seeded at the rate of 245–390 kg/ha.

Soon after pollen is shed, the ryegrasses are harvested for hay or silage. The Oregon station has shown that 11,500 kg forage/ha are produced with certain ryegrass cultivars harvested from three to seven times per year.[11] If one crop per year is the common practice, the regrowth after harvest provides considerable late summer and fall grazing.

Harvesting is usually done with a swather, cutting no less than 7.5 cm above the ground, and the forage baled for storage. The grass can also be field chopped and ensiled in the same manner as other forage crops.

The most common use of ryegrass is for pasture. Newly seeded pastures can be grazed within two months after seeding. Because of the rapid growth of these species, rather heavy stocking rates are in order. Pasture is best utilized when grazing pressure does not permit the forage to become coarse and less acceptable because of age. A form of rotational grazing will permit the manager to keep his pasture in a succulent stage of growth. During the early

11. Yungen, J. A. 1969. Ryegrass forage production trial, southern Oregon experiment station. Oreg. Forage and Seed Rept.

TABLE 29.1 ❧ Yield, digestibility, crude protein, total hemicellulose, and water-soluble carbohydrates in a perennial ryegrass (S24) with two rates of fertilizer N

Kg N/ha	Cut	Date	Yield (kg/ha)	Yield of digestible organic matter (kg/ha)	In vitro digestibility of organic matter (%)	Cellulose (g/100 g dry matter)	Crude protein (g/100 g dry matter)	Total water-soluble carbohydrates (g/100 g dry matter)	Total hemicellulose (g/100 g dry matter)
26.9	1	May 11	3,206	2,595	88	19.2	10.7	24.3	17.4
	2	June 18	1,300	1,207	81	23.0	10.1	16.3	19.5
	3	Sept. 15	2,388	1,555	71	27.1	9.1	11.4	22.5
107.6	1	May 5	2,354	1,808	87	20.0	18.7	13.4	14.5
	2	June 4	2,780	2,104	80	22.3	16.9	12.2	16.1
	3	July 15	3,139	2,403	82	22.0	13.2	16.7	16.9
	4	Aug. 27	2,186	1,594	79	22.6	16.8	8.5	18.4

Source: Waite, 1970.[13]

stages, portions of the pasture may need to be harvested as hay or silage for use at a later date when there is not an abundance of grazing forage available.

In South Australia it is an established practice to renovate pastures by sod-seeding perennial ryegrass and subterranean clover.[12] Seeding is done with a disk type of sod-seeder as soon as possible after spraying the undisturbed area with diquat and paraquat. The seed is sown with the fertilizer. Rates of seed and kinds of fertilizer will vary with the situation, but success has been achieved with 13.4 kg perennial ryegrass and 11.2 kg of subterranean clover seed per ha sown with 210 kg/ha of superphosphate.[12] This procedure has resulted in successful establishment of a productive pasture on a weedy site within one year.

The general effect of applying fertilizer N to grass is well known, leading to more rapid growth, a higher percentage of N in the grass, a decrease in the crude-fiber content, and an improvement in digestibility.[13] Table 29.1 shows the effects of period of growth and two rates of N on yield, digestibility of organic matter, crude protein, carbohydrates, cellulose, and hemicellulose in ryegrass.[13] The higher N

rate increased the yield of digestible organic matter and the production of protein. It also reduced the hemicellulose, a fraction less digestible by ruminants than the cellulose, which was also less with the higher N rate.

One study examined the effects of a wide range of N rates on the yields from a perennial ryegrass sward with and without white clover.[14] A near linear response for dry matter yields of perennial ryegrass from 0 to 336 kg N/ha was observed. More N gave additional but smaller increases in dry matter yield. For N rates from 0 to 336 kg/ha, plant response was estimated to be between 11 and 13 kg of dry matter per 454 g of N applied. (See Fig. 29.2.)

In the same study crude protein was observed to be related to N rate in a linear manner from 0 to 336 kg/ha of N applied.[14] The ryegrass produced about 1800 g crude protein for each 454 g of N applied. In a two-year study with a pure stand of ryegrass, anhydrous ammonia appeared to have no advantage over ammonium nitrate as fertilizer N for intensively managed ryegrass pastures.[15]

The response of perennial ryegrass to N

12. Schwerdt, M. A. 1968. From weeds to pasture in one year. *J. Agr. S. Aust.* 72:184–87.
13. Waite, R. 1970. The structural carbohydrates and the *in vitro* digestibility of a ryegrass and a cocksfoot at two levels of nitrogenous fertilizer. *J. Agri. Sci.* 74:457–62.

14. Reid, D. 1970. The effect of a wide range of nitrogen application rates on the yields from a perennial ryegrass sward with and without white clover. *J. Agr. Sci.* 74:227–40.
15. Reid, D., and M. E. Castle. 1970. A comparison of the effects of anhydrous ammonia and a solid ammonium nitrate fertilizer on herbage production from a pure perennial ryegrass sward. *J. Agr. Sci.* 75:347–53.

FIG. 29.2. *Crude protein . . . related to N rate in a linear manner.* Perennial ryegrass and white clover pastures are intensively used in New Zealand. With the use of strip grazing, supplemental irrigation, and a heavy stocking rate, 760 kg/ha of dressed beef was produced annually on this experimental ryegrass-clover pasture at Grasslands DSIR, Palmerston North, N.Z.

in various periods of the growing season has been examined. To produce nearly maximum yields, irrigated grass pastures may require fertilizer N equivalent to 2 kg N/ha/day prior to inflorescence emergence and up to 5 kg N/ha/day for the remainder of the growing season.[16]

ℰ SEED PRODUCTION

Most of the seed for both annual and perennial ryegrass is produced in the Willamette Valley of western Oregon. In 1970 over 92.2 million kg of seed were harvested from 67,230 ha and averaged 1400 kg/ha.

Because of many years of seed production, an ecotype of annual ryegrass has evolved in Oregon. Seed of this ecotype remain dormant in the soil for many years but germinate when they are brought to the surface during seedbed preparation. Because of this situation, special procedures are needed to establish seed fields so the cultivar being produced will not be contaminated with seed from volunteer annual ryegrass plants.[17] This is accomplished by not tilling the soil and by using a contact herbicide to eliminate broadleaf

weeds and weedy grasses prior to seeding with a drill that does not disturb the soil. In some cases, the seed is drilled simultaneously with a band of charcoal. The charcoal will bind the herbicide, rendering it inactive in the drilled row. This allows the drilled seed to germinate and emerge in the row but the herbicide remains functional between drilled rows. This establishment procedure results in production of seed true to type with respect to the cultivar and keeps volunteer annual ryegrass plants to a minimum.

Ryegrass seed growers still follow the practice of open-field burning to (1) remove straw from the field following seed harvest; (2) provide a clean field for the application of herbicides to control weedy species and volunteer seedlings; (3) control certain diseases, particularly blind-seed disease; and (4) stimulate reproductive tiller initiation. Care must be taken to have the residue well distributed over the field, or excessive heat from piles of residue may be lethal to perennial grass stands. Some believe that open-field burning contributes unduly to air pollution. Because of this, research is under way to determine alternate methods of residue removal and uses. Growers have used the open-field burning approach for many years; thus any new method devised must be able to accomplish the items listed above in an inexpensive manner, or ryegrass seed produc-

16. Cowling, D. W., and D. R. Lockyer. 1970. The response of perennial ryegrass to nitrogen in various periods of the growing season. *J. Agr. Sci.* 75:539–46.
17. Warren, Rex, and William O. Lee. 1965. Herbicides as aids in the establishment of grasses for seed production in western Oregon. Oreg. Agr. Coop. Ext. Serv. Fact Sheet 79.

tion may be a marginal enterprise compared to other cropping practices.

Ryegrass seed will shatter from the spike if it reaches full maturity before harvest. Most growers windrow their crop prior to the shattering stage. After several days of air drying in the windrow, a combine with a pickup attachment is used to thresh the seed.

❧ DISEASES

In the more humid areas of ryegrass production, crown rust, *Puccinia coronata* Corda, may severely reduce forage value. It is responsible for considerable defoliation, and the forage is rendered less palatable to livestock.[18] Brown rust, *P. dispersa* Eriks. & Henn., also attacks the ryegrasses.

When rust is present on ryegrass turf, the sod will appear somewhat red instead of green as desired. Certain cultivars of ryegrass offer some resistance to the rust organism and should be used in areas where rust is a problem.

In turf situations red thread, *Corticium fuciforme* (Berk.) Wakef., is often found on ryegrass.[19] This organism is less damaging on sod that is vigorously growing than on turf growing under conditions of low fertility.

The ryegrasses are sometimes attacked by certain *Helminthosporium* species. The common symptom is a spotting of the foliage, but a root rot sometimes develops and causes the sod to decay.

Ergot, *Claviceps purpurea* (Fr.) Tul., and blind-seed disease, *Phialea temulenta* Prill. & Delacr., are organisms that attack

the inflorescence of ryegrass and other grass species. Both cause reduced seed yield and quality. During seed maturation the developing ovary is virtually replaced by the organism. Heat generated by open-field burning of harvested seed fields has proved to be an inexpensive and satisfactory control measure for these two diseases.

❧ OTHER SPECIES

The only two species of the genus *Lolium* used for economic purposes are *L. perenne* and *L. multiflorum*. Swiss ryegrass, *L. rigidum* Gaud., appears to represent one of the weedy types common in southern Europe. Dalmatian ryegrass, *L. subulatum* Vis., is found in Israel. A highly variable species from the Canary Islands is classified as *L. canariense* Steud. Darnel, *L. temulentum* L.; hardy ryegrass, *L. remotum* Schrank; and *L. persicum* Boiss. & Hohen. ex Boiss, are the remaining weedy species listed in Terrell's taxonomic classification of the genus *Lolium*.[1]

❧ QUESTIONS

1. Under what climatic conditions would you expect to find ryegrass being used for pasture?
2. Relate distinguishing differences among perennial, annual, and short-rotation ryegrasses.
3. Discuss methods used to maintain cultivar purity and to produce high-quality ryegrass seed.
4. There are over 150 recognized cultivars of annual and perennial ryegrasses. What reasons can you give for this large number?
5. List and describe five agricultural uses of ryegrass.
6. Discuss different situations where annual ryegrass may be used for pasture.

18. Sampson, K., and J. W. Western. 1954. Diseases of British Grasses and Herbage Legumes, 2nd ed. Cambridge Univ. Press.
19. Smith, J. D., and N. Jackson. 1965. Fungal Diseases of Turf Grasses. Turf Res. Inst., Partridge Printers Ltd., Bradford, Leeds, and London.

COLEMAN Y. WARD AND VANCE H. WATSON
Mississippi State University

30

BAHIAGRASS AND CARPETGRASS

❧

BAHIAGRASS

BAHIAGRASS, *Paspalum notatum* Flugge, is native to South America. It is widely distributed in Argentina, Uruguay, Paraguay, Brazil, and on many islands of the West Indies. It was first introduced into the U.S. in 1913 by the Florida station.[1]

❧ DISTRIBUTION AND ADAPTATION

Bahiagrass is widely grown from east Texas to the Carolinas, and as far northward as northern Arkansas and central Tennessee. It is principally adapted to the coastal area in the southern U.S. (Fig. 30.1).[2] It is adapted to a wide range of coastal plain soils but performs best on sandy soils with a pH of 5.5–6.5.[3] It will

FIG. 30.1. Bahiagrass-producing areas of the U.S.

grow on drier soils with relatively low fertility and on sandier soils than most other pasture grasses in its region of adaptation.

❧ PLANT DESCRIPTION

Bahiagrass is a deep-rooted warm-season perennial. Its short, stout, often exposed rhizomes form dense sods even on sandy soils (Fig. 30.2). The root system is exten-

❧ COLEMAN Y. WARD is Professor of Agronomy, Mississippi State University. He holds the M.S. degree from Texas Tech University and the Ph.D. from Virginia Polytechnic Institute and State University. His major forage research interest is production and management.

❧ VANCE H. WATSON is Associate Professor of Agronomy, Mississippi State University. He holds the M.S. degree from the University of Missouri and the Ph.D. from Mississippi State University. His major forage research interests are forage crops ecology and management.

1. Scott, J. M. 1920. Bahiagrass. *J. Amer. Soc. Agron.* 13:112–14.
2. Burton, Glenn W. 1946. Bahiagrass types. *J. Amer. Soc. Agron.* 28:273–81.
3. Jones, D. W. 1971. Bahiagrass in Florida. Fla. Ext. Serv. Circ. 321A.

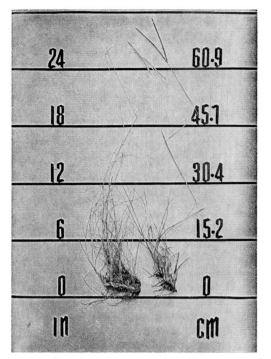

FIG. 30.2. *Short, stout . . . rhizomes form dense sods.* Plant characteristics of a mature plant of bahiagrass.

sive, and once a sod is formed few species are able to encroach. It has many flat or folded basal leaves that are pubescent on the margins, stiffly spreading, and less than 1.25 cm wide. Culms range from 15 to 60 cm in height and occur in dense tufts. The inflorescence is a racemose panicle bearing two or sometimes three racemes. Racemes are curved and ascending with spikelets occurring in two rows. The single-flowered spikelets are smooth and shiny, and the seed are oval in shape, yellowish green in color, glossy in appearance, and about 3 mm in length.[4]

Grazing studies indicate that bahiagrass ranks between carpetgrass and bermudagrass in productivity and in nutritive value. Quality of the forage is highest in early spring, but by midsummer the percentage of cell wall constituents are sufficiently high to suggest that animal intake would be limited.[5]

4. Hitchcock, A. S. 1951. Manual of the grasses of the United States. USDA Misc. Publ. No. 200, rev.
5. Ellzey, H. D. 1967. Annual progress report. Southeast Louisiana Dairy and Pasture Exp. Sta., pp. 30–68.

❧ IMPORTANCE AND USE

Bahiagrass is a popular pasture grass in the South because: (1) it tolerates a wider range of soil conditions than bermudagrass or dallisgrass, (2) it is resistant to encroachment of weeds, (3) it is established by seed, (4) it is relatively free from damaging insects and diseases, (5) it has a unique ability to produce moderate yields on soils of very low fertility, and (6) it withstands close grazing.

Hectarage estimates range from approximately 100 ha in Tennessee to 730,000 ha in Florida. A rapid increase has occurred in most of the southern states since 1945, and bahiagrass is the most important grass in terms of hectarage in the state of Florida.

Primary use of bahiagrass is for permanent pasture for beef cattle, although many farmers use bahiagrass for both grazing and hay production. Conventional hay harvesting equipment may leave as much as 60% of the forage uncut because of its morphology and growth habits.[6,7] Bahiagrass hay is leafy and has few stems and heads.[8]

Beef gains on bahiagrass are intermediate to gains on common and 'Coastal' bermudagrass, and bahiagrass is satisfactory for wintering programs.[9,10] However, bahiagrass pasture or hay is not satisfactory as the sole source of forage for high-producing dairy cows.[11]

Bahiagrass also can be used satisfactorily in rotation with other crops such as corn and sorghum. Recovery of bahiagrass following a crop is usually quite rapid since

6. Stanley, R. L., E. R. Beaty, and J. D. Powell. 1967. Effect of clipping height on forage distribution and regrowth on Pensacola bahiagrass. *Agron. J.* 59:185–87.
7. Beaty, E. R., R. L. Stanley, and J. Powell. 1968. Effect of height of cut on yield of Pensacola bahiagrass. *Agron. J.* 60: 356–59.
8. Hoveland, C. S. 1968. Bahiagrass for forage in Alabama. Ala. Agr. Exp. Sta. Circ. 140.
9. Evans, E. M., L. E. Ensminger, B. D. Doss, and O. L. Bennett. 1961. Nitrogen and moisture requirements of Coastal bermuda and Pensacola bahia. Ala. Agr. Exp. Sta. Bull. 337.
10. McCormick, W. C., W. H. Marchant, and B. L. Southwell. 1967. Coastal bermudagrass and Pensacola bahiagrass hays for wintering beef calves. Ga. Agr. Exp. Sta. Res. Bull. 19.
11. Rollins, G. H., and C. S. Hoveland. 1960. Wanted—Good summer perennial grasses for dairy cows. Auburn Univ. Highlights of Agr. Res., vol. 7, no. 2, Summer.

there are sufficient seed and plants that survive cultivation to quickly reestablish a sod. Extensive use has also been made of bahiagrass for preventing erosion and stabilizing road shoulders. Once a good sod is established, it can be maintained at a relatively low cost. The cultivar 'Pensacola,' is widely used for roadside turf.

❧ CULTIVARS

Bahiagrass introductions and strains have been classified into eight types, of which seven are named cultivars: common, 'Argentine,' 'Paraguay,' 'Paraguay 22,' Pensacola, 'Tifhi-1,' 'Tifhi-2,' and 'Wilmington.'[12]

Until the late 1930s the original common type of bahiagrass was the most widely grown. The plants are small with broad leaves and seed heads that grow 20–45 cm tall. The oval-shaped seed are covered with a tight waxy glume which makes scarification necessary for good germination. Common is lower yielding than later introductions but produces good pasture when well established.

Argentine is a long broad-leaved type that was introduced into Florida in 1945.[13] Seed of this cultivar are very susceptible to ergot, which seriously damages the seed and can cause toxic effects in cattle.

Pensacola, the most popular of the bahiagrass types, was found growing on vacant lots and docks in Pensacola, Fla., in 1935 by E. H. Finlayson.[14] It is characterized by long narrow leaves and large stems and is more winter-hardy than the common, Argentine, or Paraguay types.

Paraguay is a short, coarse, narrow-leaved cultivar that is less productive than Pensacola. It forms a dense sod and provides satisfactory pasture until it becomes tough and unpalatable in midsummer.

Paraguay 22 is quite similar to Argentine in growth habit and cold tolerance and is more productive than Paraguay.

Wilmington is the most cold-hardy of the bahiagrasses. It is a narrow-leaved type of medium size but is less productive than Pensacola and Paraguay.

Tifhi-1 and Tifhi-2 are hybrids developed by Dr. Glenn Burton of the Georgia coastal plain station. They are leafier, have more shatter-resistant seed, and are higher yielding than Pensacola. Tifhi-1 has produced more beef per ha than Pensacola under grazing conditions.[15]

❧ CULTURE AND MANAGEMENT

Bahiagrass generally is sown in early spring after the average date of the last killing frost. Plantings can be made in summer, but weed infestations are usually severe.

Bahiagrass should be planted on a well-prepared seedbed at a depth of 0.64–1.25 cm. Under average farm conditions, 11.2–16.8 kg/ha of seed are required to ensure a good stand. Use of a cultipacker, with a seeding attachment, or a grain drill are good methods of planting. Soil should be firmed around the seed to allow quick germination and rooting.

The small seedlings of bahiagrass are weak competitors with weeds. For quick establishment of a productive bahiagrass sod, weeds must be controlled. Cattle should be restricted from grazing new plantings since trampling will destroy many of the seedlings. To obtain use of the land during the initial year of bahiagrass establishment, sorghum-sudan hybrids may be planted in rows at the time bahiagrass is seeded.

Bahiagrass requires fertilization for satisfactory establishment and production, preferably according to soil test recommendations. During establishment, one or two light topdressings of 18–34 kg/ha of N in mid-June and July will hasten development of young grass plants during their first year.[16]

12. Hanson, A. A. 1972. Grass varieties in the United States. USDA Agr. Handbook 170, rev.
13. Killinger, G. B., G. E. Richey, C. B. Blickensderfer and W. Jackson. 1951. Argentine bahiagrass. Fla. Agr. Exp. Sta. Circ. S-31.
14. Finlayson, E. H. 1941. Pensacola, a new fine-leafed bahia. *Southern Seedsman* 4:9–28.

15. Hodges, E. M., J. E. McCaleb, W. G. Kirk, and F. M. Peacock. 1967. Grazing trials on grass varieties. Ann. Rept. Fla. Agr. Exp. Sta., pp. 50–54.
16. Georgia Agr. Exp. Sta. 1960. Bahiagrass for pastures. Bull. NS 67.

TABLE 30.1 ❧ Forage yield, steer gain, and stocking rate on Pensacola bahiagrass at three N levels in Alabama, four-year average

Nitrogen (kg/ha)	Dry forage yield (kg/ha)	Steer gain (kg/ha)	Stocking rate (number/ ha)
0	3,584	246	3.2
89.6	6,137	325	4.5
179.2	7,246	392	5.0

After establishment, annual applications of 112–224 kg/ha of N, 29 kg/ha of P, and 56 kg/ha of K are required for good production (Table 30.1). Animals prefer fertilized bahiagrass approximately 10 to 1 over unfertilized bahiagrass (Table 30.2). For best results, N should be applied in three to four applications during the growing season.[17-20]

The dense compact sod of bahiagrass is generally not considered good for associated legumes. However, white, crimson, and arrowleaf clovers can be grown in bahiagrass sods provided they are well fertilized and the grass is grazed or mowed short. Where winter legumes are grown in the grass sod, P and K as recommended above should be applied before planting the legume. When legume stands are good, the spring topdressing of N should be omitted. However, for high summer grass production topdressing should be applied in June and early August.[21,22]

Late winter burning of bahiagrass is sometimes practiced to remove litter. When the cover is light, there appears to be little damage from burning. Where a heavy litter is present, such as after seed harvesting or where light grazing has been practiced, burning can cause serious injury to the grass stand.

❧ SEED PRODUCTION

Except for the cultivar Wilmington, most bahiagrasses are rather heavy seed producers. Seed mature progressively, beginning in early June and continuing during the summer. Seed yields vary considerably depending on cultivar, time of harvest, weather conditions, and fertilizer used on the grass. With good fertilization and combining methods, 112–336 kg/ha of cleaned seed can be obtained. When little grazing is done, two or more seed crops can be harvested each year.

Since all seed do not mature at the same time, close examination of fields before harvesting will help prevent shattering loss. Seed color does not always indicate stage of maturity since green-colored seed may be fully ripe. To determine proper time for harvest, the practice of pulling a gathered handful of seed heads through moderately tightly closed fingers is a useful technique. The mature seed readily strip off, while immature seed cling to the seed heads.

Bahiagrass can be easily combined since seed heads extend above the leaves and can be cut without including much forage.

17. Ruelke, O. Charles. 1960. Fertility as a limiting factor for pastures in Florida. Proc. Soil and Crop Sci. Soc. Fla. 20:23–28.
18. Ruelke, O. Charles, and Gordon M. Prine. 1968. Preliminary evaluation of yield and protein content of six hybrid bermudagrasses, Pensacola bahiagrass, and pangolagrass under three fertilization regimes in north central Florida. Proc. Soil and Crop Sci. Soc. Fla. 28:123–29.
19. Wallace, A. T., G. B. Killinger, R. W. Bledsoe, and D. B. Duncan. 1957. Design, analysis and results of an experiment on response of pangolagrass and Pensacola bahiagrass to time, rate, and source of nitrogen. Fla. Agr. Exp. Sta. Tech. Bull. 581.
20. Wallace, A. T., G. B. Killinger, R. W. Bledsoe, and D. B. Duncan. 1955. Effect of nitrogen fertilization on the production of pangolagrass and bahiagrass. Proc. Soil Sci. Soc. Fla. 15:198–207.

TABLE 30.2 ❧ Animal preference for N-fertilized perennial pasture grasses, Mississippi

Nitrogen (kg/ha)	Minutes grazed	
	Common bermudagrass*	Pensacola bahiagrass
0	55	30
36.9	145	75
110.9	190	125
147.8	660	275
295.7	1,320	414

Note: 25 cows grazed for 4 hours.
* All plots received constant rate of P and K.

21. Hoveland, C. W., W. B. Anthony, and E. L. Mayton. 1960. Coastal-vetch-crimson, good for cows and calves. Auburn Univ. Highlights of Agr. Res., vol. 7, no. 3, Fall.
22. Hoveland, C. S., E. L. Carden, J. R. Wilson, and P. A. Mott. 1971. Summer grass residue affects growth of winter legumes under sod. Auburn Univ. Highlights of Agr. Res., vol. 18, no. 3, Fall.

Since combined bahiagrass seed are in various stages of maturity, quick drying is necessary. Seed should be spread a few centimeters deep on a dry floor and stirred thoroughly once or twice a day. Forced-air drying is necessary for large amounts of seed. If heated air is used, the temperature should be kept between 38 and 43 C.

After drying, the seed should be run through a seed cleaner to remove undeveloped seed, empty glumes, and trash. This cleaning process can remove much of the foreign material, and seed should germinate approximately 90%.

❧ DISEASES AND INSECTS

Bahiagrass is relatively free from disease and insect pests. However, ergot, *Claviceps paspali* Stevens & Hall, is serious on the cultivar Argentine. This disease, which attacks the inflorescence and seriously damages the seed, can produce toxic effects in cattle. It is most prevalent in late summer and early fall and can be avoided by mowing the seed heads during that season.[23]

Leaves of most bahiagrass types are susceptible to slight damage by leaf blight, *Helminthosporium micropus* Drechsl. Damage has been widely observed in Alabama and Mississippi, and different types of bahiagrass vary in their reaction to the fungus.[24]

Insect damage to bahiagrass is usually slight.

CARPETGRASS

Carpetgrass, *Axonopus affinis* Chase, is indigenous to Central America and the West Indies. It was introduced into the U.S. during the early colonial period. The first record of domestic use of carpetgrass was in the area of New Orleans. From this and other points of introduction, carpetgrass has spread through the lower

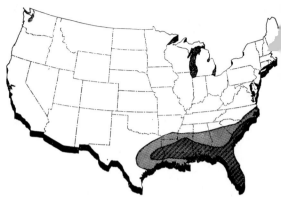

FIG. 30.3. Carpetgrass-producing areas of the U.S.

coastal plain from south central Texas to southern Virginia and inland to Arkansas and northern Alabama and Mississippi.

❧ DISTRIBUTION AND ADAPTATION

Carpetgrass is best adapted to the warmer areas of the Southeast where soils rarely freeze. It is most abundant within 150 km of the Gulf of Mexico on sand and sandy loam soils (Fig. 30.3). Carpetgrass thrives on soils with a high water table, particularly along the many small creeks and rivers in the lower South. Though moisture loving, carpetgrass does not thrive well in swamps or where seepage is continuous most of the year. Because of its adaptation to soils of low fertility, it is a ubiquitous invader of infertile upland sites throughout the entire Gulf Coast. It is often referred to as native pasture grass in the lower South.[25]

❧ PLANT DESCRIPTION

Carpetgrass is a warm-season, low-growing, sod-forming perennial that spreads by stolons and seed. Its prostrate growth habit and abundant rooting of creeping surface runners form a dense sod.

Identification is made from the short, blunt-tipped smooth leaves (6–8 mm wide), which are strongly folded in the bud. In-

23. Dickson, James G. 1956. Diseases of Field Crops. McGraw-Hill, New York.

24. Ivanoff, S. S. 1960. Plant diseases and weed control. Miss. Farm. Res., vol. 23, no. 8., Aug.

25. Stephens, J. L. 1942. Pastures for the coastal plain of Georgia. Ga. Agr. Exp. Sta. Bull. 27.

florescences are borne on delicate seed-stalks which range from 15 to 30 cm in height. Two or three racemes (4–6 cm long) branch from each filiform seedstalk and bear brownish to gray seed about 3 mm in length.[26] A typical carpetgrass pasture has an abundance of basal leaves and nodding seedstalks unless closely grazed.

Nutritional value and dry matter yield of carpetgrass is low, and the forage contains an unusually low concentration of minerals even when well fertilized. The level of crude protein is also low when compared to that of other perennial pasture grasses.

Studies in Georgia show carpetgrass pastures produce about 30% as much beef gain as common bermudagrass. In Florida, unfertilized carpetgrass produced only 178 kg/ha.[27] To produce 1 kg of beef gain, 31 kg of oven-dried forage from the unfertilized carpetgrass were required. When white clover was added to the pasture, only 13 kg of forage were needed per kilogram of gain. Even though carpetgrass produces a close-growing sod, it is easier to maintain white clover in carpetgrass than in 'Pangola' digitgrass or bahiagrass.[28] In spite of its low nutritive value, cattle readily consume carpetgrass. It has smooth and rather tender leaves somewhat like saint augustinegrass.

❧ IMPORTANCE AND USE

Carpetgrass is a chief component in unimproved pasture throughout the Gulf Coast area and in the southern states along the Atlantic Coast. Most of the vast hectarage is the result of low-fertility soils and the prolific seeding characteristic of carpetgrass. Seed spread by birds, livestock, and wind have caused it to become established naturally over extensive areas of cut-over timberland.

Since much of this immense hectarage is never fertilized, a low-yielding forage community of carpetgrass, broomsedge, several wiry three-awns, dropseeds, and native bluestems is perpetuated. Such pastures have a very low carrying capacity; often 5–15 ha are required per animal unit.

The characteristic, low-growing dense sod of carpetgrass makes it useful as turf for lawns and golf courses, especially in flatwoods soil areas. It is easily established as turf from seed, tolerates moderate shade, and requires little care other than mowing. It is also widely used as cut sod from pastures to stabilize waterways and ditches on roadsides. In the past it was frequently a component of seed mixtures for vegetating roadside slopes and fills but has been replaced by bahiagrass. Carpetgrass is ideal for firebreaks in the forests of the Gulf Coast region. Its use for this purpose contributes to widespread dissemination of carpetgrass seed.[29]

❧ CULTIVARS

There are no registered cultivars of the *Axonopus* genus. Hitchcock lists eight species of *Axonopus* as occurring in the West Indies;[26] of these only *A. compressus* (Swartz) Beauv., often called tropical carpetgrass, is of localized importance in the U.S. It has a broader leaf, is less cold-hardy than *A. affinis,* and is restricted to lower Florida and Louisiana.

❧ CULTURE AND MANAGEMENT

Carpetgrass is established from seed, which are available in quantity at moderate prices. Seeding rates range from 5.6 to 16.8 kg/ha. Seed may be broadcast without seedbed preparation or covering. However, good stands are obtained more quickly by seeding on a well-prepared seedbed. The seed require a firm soil for rapid germination and growth. Winter and early spring seedings are preferred.

Carpetgrass is able to withstand more

26. Hitchcock, A. S. 1936. Manual of the grasses of the West Indies. USDA Misc. Publ. 243.
27. Blaser, R. E. 1948. Carpetgrass and legume pastures in Florida. Fla. Agr. Exp. Sta. Bull. 453.
28. Kretschmer, A. E., Jr. 1964. Evaluation of several combinations of grasses and white clover on Immokalee fine sand in southern Florida. Fla. Agr. Exp. Sta. Bull. 676.

29. Hanson, A. A., and Felix Juska. 1969. Turfgrass science. Amer. Soc. Agr. Monogr. 14.

severe grazing or clipping than most of the grasses used for permanent pasture in the deep South.[30-32] Where grown in mixtures, this characteristic often permits carpetgrass to crowd out other forage species in closely grazed pastures. More often, carpetgrass pastures are undergrazed in late spring, resulting in the production of abundant seed heads.

Like most tropical grasses, carpetgrass is continuously forming seed heads throughout the growing season. This lowers acceptability by the grazing animal and results in low daily performance. Since carpetgrass can withstand very close grazing, pastures should be stocked with sufficient animals to prevent the plants from seeding before early fall. In south Florida, carpetgrass grown alone, even when heavily fertilized, did not produce a vigorous permanent pasture compared to other commercial improved grasses.[28] However, during winter and spring a carpetgrass-clover mixture was as good as other grass-clover mixtures when managed properly.

Prior to 1941 carpetgrass was commonly planted for permanent pasture in the lower coastal plain. A typical mixture in kilograms per hectare was lespedeza 16.8, carpetgrass 11.2, white clover 3.3, and hop clover 2.2. Seedings were made on firm well-prepared seedbeds in early spring.[33]

Today, carpetgrass is rarely if ever seeded because other grasses such as dallisgrass, bahiagrass, Pangola digitgrass, and bermudagrass are more nutritious and produce much higher yields. The hectarage presently devoted to carpetgrass may be expected to decrease as more idle land is converted to improved pastures.

❧ SEED PRODUCTION

Carpetgrass produces seed profusely, but the seed crop is harvested with some difficulty. Direct combining recovers about half the seed produced. Cattle should be removed from seed areas a month before harvest for greatest yields. Seedstalks may be mowed, raked immediately, and threshed from the windrow. One kilogram of carpetgrass seed contains approximately 590,000.

33. Watson, C. W. 1931. Pasture mixtures for Mississippi. Miss. Ext. Circ. 70.

❧ QUESTIONS

1. Why is bahiagrass an important forage crop in the deep South?
2. Which cultivars of bahiagrass are most widely used?
3. Give the chief weakness of bahiagrass as a forage.
4. Why is the hectarage devoted to carpetgrass declining?
5. Give the origin and areas of adaptation for carpetgrass.

30. Mayton, E. L. 1935. Permanent pasture studies on upland soils. Ala. Agr. Exp. Sta. Bull. 243.
31. Lovvorn, R. L. 1944. The behavior of dallisgrass and carpetgrass. J. Amer. Soc. Agron. 36:590–600.
32. Levkel, W. A. 1934. Growth behavior and relative composition of pasture grasses. Fla. Agr. Exp. Sta. Tech. Bull. 269.

31

BERMUDAGRASS

ℬ

BERMUDAGRASS, *Cynodon dactylon* (L.) Pers., is found throughout the tropical and subtropical parts of the world. Most early writers expressed the opinion that it probably originated in India. Perhaps the fact that it grows "everywhere" in India and has been used there for centuries led to this conclusion. It should be pointed out, however, that introductions of *Cynodon* from Africa have shown a much greater diversity in type than those coming from India. If these introductions are indicative of the diversity of forms that exist within each country, there is reason to regard Africa rather than India as the primary center of origin of this grass.

One of the earliest written records concerning the introduction of bermudagrass into the U.S. has been found in the diary of Thomas Spalding, owner of Sapeloe Island, Ga., and one of the prominent antebellum agriculturists. In his diary he made the following entries: "Bermudagrass was brought to Savannah in 1751 by

Governor Henry Ellis. If ever this becomes a grazing country it must be through the instrumentality of this grass." Mease, writing in the *Geological Account of the U.S.* published in 1807 referred to bermudagrass as one of the most important grasses in the South at that time.

Howard in 1881 quoted three prominent southerners to lend weight to his opinion that bermudagrass was at that time the most important pasture grass in the South.[1] Many years later Tracy, representing a new generation, said, "Bermudagrass is the most common and most valuable pasture plant in the Southern States, being of the same relative importance in that region that Kentucky bluegrass is in the more Northern States."[2]

Although pioneer agriculturalists in the South were singing the virtues of bermudagrass, most southern farmers, interested in growing only cotton and corn, were trying to destroy the grass that was keeping their fields from washing away. Some states even went so far as to pass laws prohibiting the introduction and planting of bermudagrass.

ℳ GLENN W. BURTON is Research Geneticist, ARS, USDA, and Distinguished Professor of Agronomy, University of Georgia, Tifton. He holds the B.Sc. and honorary D.Sc. degrees from the University of Nebraska and M.Sc., Ph.D. and honorary D.Sc. degrees from Rutgers University. Twenty-five improved grass cultivars have been developed under his direction.

1. Howard, C. W. 1881. Manual of the Cultivation of the Grasses and Forage Plants of the South. James Harrison and Co., Atlanta, Ga.
2. Tracy, Samuel M. 1917. Bermudagrass. USDA Farmers' Bull. 814.

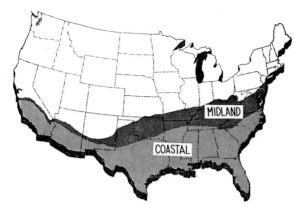

Fig. 31.1. Bermudagrass-producing areas of the U.S.

❧ DISTRIBUTION AND ADAPTATION

In the U.S., bermudagrass is best adapted to the states south of a line connecting the southern boundaries of Virginia and Kansas (Fig. 31.1). It makes its best growth when mean daily temperatures are above 24 C. Very little growth is made when these temperatures drop six to nine degrees. Temperatures of —2 to —3 C usually kill the stems and leaves back to the ground.

Bermudagrass is more drought resistant than dallisgrass, carpetgrass, or bahiagrass. It will grow on any moderately well-drained soil provided it has an adequate supply of moisture and plant nutrients. Although it will tolerate flooding for long periods, it makes little if any growth on waterlogged soils. Better growth generally has been observed on heavy soils than on light sandy soils, probably because heavy soils usually are more fertile and retain soil moisture better. When well fertilized, bermudagrass has made excellent growth on deep sands. It is affected little by soil reaction and has made good growth on both acid and "overlimed" soils. Investigations at the Georgia coastal plain station show that adding lime to soils having a pH below 5.5 favors the growth of this species.

❧ NUTRITIVE VALUE

Nutritive value of any forage plant is greatly influenced by the stage of growth at which it is harvested and the environmental conditions under which it grew. Unfertilized common bermudagrass cut after it has matured seed will analyze 6–7% protein. Grass from the same plots cut frequently, so that most of the sample is leaves, will contain twice as much protein. At Tifton, Ga., it has been possible to double the protein content of bermudagrass in almost any stage of growth by heavy applications of fertilizer N.

Perhaps the best measure of the nutritive value of a grass is the gain that animals make on it. Steers grazing unfertilized common bermudagrass at Tifton, Ga., for an average of 215 days over a three-year period made an average daily gain of 0.39 kg.[3] During the same three years, steers on carpetgrass made an average daily gain of 0.20 kg. During these three years, bermudagrass produced an average of 112 kg/ha of beef. Carpetgrass produced only 74 kg/ha.

Feeding trials designed to evaluate bermudagrass hay in terms of timothy hay were carried out by Lloyd in Mississippi in 1891 and 1892.[4,5] Lloyd concluded that ton for ton, the two hays had practically the same milk and butter-producing values. He also found bermudagrass hay equal to timothy hay when fed to mules.

Genotype also affects the nutritive value of bermudagrass. Cattle grazing 'Coastal' bermudagrass have generally made better average daily gain (ADG) than those grazing common. Dry matter digestibility (DMD), an excellent index of nutritive value, is a heritable character. The *in vitro* DMD of five-week old forage from over 500 genotypes in a bermudagrass

3. Stephens, J. L. 1942. Pastures for the coastal plain of Georgia. Ga. Coastal Plain Exp. Sta. Bull. 27:57.
4. Lloyd, E. R. 1891. Feeding. Miss. Agr. Exp. Sta. Bull. 15.
5. Lloyd, E. R. 1892. Feeding for milk and butter. Miss. Agr. Exp. Sta. Bull. 21.

world collection grown at Tifton, Ga., varied from 40 to 69%.[6]

❧ CULTIVARS

COASTAL BERMUDAGRASS

Coastal bermudagrass, named for the Georgia coastal plain station where it was developed, is an F_1 hybrid between 'Tift' bermudagrass (discovered by J. L. Stephens in an old cotton patch near Tifton, Ga., in 1929) and an introduction from South Africa.[7] This hybrid, selected as the best of 5000 spaced plants set out in 1938, is characterized by larger and longer leaves, stems, and rhizomes than common.

Coastal produces few seed heads, and these rarely contain viable seed. Its much greater resistance to foliage diseases caused by *Helminthosporium cynodontis* Marig. and *H. giganteum* Heald and Wolf enable it to produce more and better quality forage than common bermudagrass.

Coastal tolerates more frost, makes more growth in the fall, and remains green much later than common. It is much more drought resistant than common and other grass species generally grown in the South.[7,8]

Root-knot nematodes lodge their heads in Coastal roots, die before they can lay eggs, and quickly disappear from a soil planted to this grass. As a result, root-knot susceptible legumes grow much better with Coastal than with common.[9]

Repeated tests indicate that Coastal will spread faster and maintain a weed-free sod longer than common. Although its stems and leaves are quite coarse, cattle have consistently grazed Coastal in preference to the finer-stemmed common types. When clipped frequently to simulate close grazing, Coastal has produced over twice as much forage as common. In such tests it has been outstanding in its ability to grow and produce more forage in the late summer and fall than other summer-growing grasses with which it was compared. (See Fig. 31.2.)

Over a five-year period at Tifton, Ga., pastures of common and Coastal fertilized with 40 kg N/ha/yr and 0-35-34 (N-P-K) kg/ha every third year carried 2 and 3.2 steers/ha and produced 181 and 311 kg of LWG (liveweight gain)/ha/yr respectively.[7]

In these grazing studies, Coastal produced more beef in the late summer and fall than common bermudagrass, carpetgrass, or bahiagrass.

Coastal grows tall enough to be cut for hay on almost any soil, whereas common usually is too short to cut. Its fine stems and low moisture content make it easier to cure than any other hay crop adapted to the South. Hay cured in the swath or the windrow usually is dry enough to bale or stack 24 hours after cutting. The four to five cuttings per year afforded by Coastal give the farmer a good chance to save much of his hay, even though one or more cuttings may be damaged by rain. The uniform annual production of hay obtained from Coastal indicates that it is a dependable hay crop. Some 5 million ha of Coastal are grown in the South.

Coastal is becoming increasingly important in rotations. Crops like tobacco, sweet potatoes, and tomatoes that suffer from soil-borne diseases and from nematodes have been remarkably free from such damage when grown in rotation with Coastal. Corn also has done well in Coastal rotations. Turning the sod to a depth of 18–23 cm in the spring facilitates seedbed preparation, planting the crop, and control of the bermudagrass that appears later. A well-fertilized, high-yielding corn crop may shade out and destroy the bermudagrass that regenerates. Frequently, enough

6. Burton, Glenn W., and W. G. Monson. 1972. Inheritance of dry matter digestibility in bermudagrass, *Cynodon dactylon*. *Crop Sci.* 12:375–78.
7. Burton, Glenn W. 1954. Coastal bermudagrass. Ga. Agr. Exp. Sta. Bull. N-52.
8. Burton, Glenn W., Gordon M. Prine, and James E. Jackson. 1957. Studies of drouth tolerance and water use efficiency of several southern grasses. *Agron. J.* 49:498–503.
9. Burton, Glenn W., C. W. McBeth, and J. L. Stephens. 1946. The growth of Kobe lespedeza as influenced by the root-knot nematode resistance of the bermudagrass strain with which it is associated. *J. Amer. Soc. Agron.* 38:651–56.

FIG. 31.2. *When clipped frequently . . . Coastal . . . produced . . . twice as much forage as common.* Grazing Coastal bermudagrass at the Georgia coastal plain station after the removal of a cutting for hay. *USDA photo.*

grass will survive to reestablish itself. In these instances, late summer and fall grazing is available after the cultivated crop is harvested. Such rotations, with the fibrous grass roots reducing soil loss during the cultivation period, provide excellent soil and water conservation.

SUWANNEE BERMUDAGRASS

'Suwanee' bermudagrass is a tall-growing hybrid developed at Tifton.[10] Its dark green color, red seed heads, and more erect leaves distinguish it from Coastal. It outyields Coastal on light sandy infertile soils but is less tolerant of close grazing and is less winter-hardy.

MIDLAND BERMUDAGRASS

'Midland' bermudagrass is an F_1 hybrid between Coastal and a cold-hardy common

from Indiana. Bred in Georgia, Midland was named and released by the Oklahoma station when it greatly surpassed common in Stillwater tests.[11] Although inferior to Coastal in disease resistance and yield, it is more winter-hardy and can be successfully grown where Coastal winter-kills. In Maryland, pastures of Midland overseeded with rye, orchardgrass-ladino, reed canarygrass–ladino, and Kentucky bluegrass–ladino grazed with steers gave respective ADG's of 0.66, 0.59, 0.52, and 0.75 kg and LWG's/ha/yr of 816, 443, 417, and 427 kg.[12]

COASTCROSS-1 BERMUDAGRASS

'Coastcross-1' is a sterile F_1 hybrid between Coastal and bermudagrass PI 255445 from Kenya.[13] It grows taller, has broader

10. Burton, Glenn W. 1962. Registration of Suwannee bermudagrass. *Crop. Sci.* 2:352–53.

11. Harlan, Jack R., Glenn W. Burton, and W. C. Elder. 1954. Midland bermudagrass a new variety for Oklahoma pastures. Okla. Agr. Exp. Sta. Bull. B-416.
12. Decker, A. Morris. 1959. Midland bermudagrass. Md. Agr. Exp. Sta. Bull. 465.
13. Burton, Glenn W. 1972. Registration of Coastcross-1 bermudagrass. *Crop Sci.* 12:125.

softer leaves, and produces more rapidly spreading above-ground stolons than Coastal. Coastcross-1 develops only an occasional very short rhizome. It is highly resistant to foliage diseases and the sting nematode. It makes more growth in the fall but is less winter-hardy than Coastal and is restricted to Florida and the lower third of the Gulf states.

When not injured by cold, Coastcross-1 has yielded about the same as Coastal. Its forage has been about 12% more digestible than forage of comparable age and treatment from Coastal. In a three-year replicated pasture test at Tifton, steers grazing Pensacola bahiagrass, Coastal, and Coastcross-1 made ADG's of 0.49, 0.55, and 0.71 kg respectively.[14] Coastcross-1 has enabled steers to make much better late summer and fall ADG's than other perennial grasses tested at Tifton.

OTHER CULTIVARS

Star bermudagrass is a name given to numerous "giant" introductions from Africa. These are usually tall, coarse, rapidly spreading types that carry high concentrations of prussic acid glucosides. Those tested at Tifton have been less productive and less winter-hardy than Coastcross-1.

Winter-hardy genotypes possessing the desirable traits of Coastal and Coastcross-1 are needed. Breeding programs involving Coastal, winter-hardy bermudagrasses from Europe, and highly digestible types from Kenya should produce such hybrids.

❧ CULTURE

Common bermudagrass may be propagated by planting either seed or vegetative sprigs. Since seed are very small, seeding methods recommended for small-seeded grasses and legumes should be followed. Bermudagrass seed does not germinate well at low temperatures, hence there is little to be gained from planting before mean daily temperatures of 18 C prevail.[15]

Hulled bermudagrass seed germinate more promptly than unhulled and should be used when early establishment is desired. If the best seeding practices are followed, 5–10 kg/ha of seed should give good stands.

More bermudagrass is propagated by planting sprigs than by seeding; farmers generally have had better success by this method. Poor seeding habits of Coastal, Suwanee, Midland, and Coastcross-1 make it mandatory that they be established from vegetative material. This feature of these improved cultivars has led to the development of laborsaving machinery and methods which make it possible to establish them from sprigs at no greater cost than planting common bermudagrass seed.

To have fresh planting material available whenever planting conditions are favorable, farmers are advised to establish bermudagrass nurseries on their farms. Such a nursery can result in a substantial saving in the cost of planting stock. Care should be taken to locate the nursery on land that is free of common bermudagrass, and only pure sprigs of the desired cultivar should be planted. State crop-improvement associations certify vegetatively propagated bermudagrass cultivars to maintain pure sources of planting stock.

A spring-tooth harrow is an excellent tool for digging bermudagrass sprigs (stolons and rhizomes). A side-delivery rake will shake the soil from the sprigs and rake them into windrows from which they can be baled for ease of handling.

Freshly cut green hay makes good low-cost planting stock if baled immediately and properly planted soon after harvesting. Since green hay contains less stored energy and tolerates less drying than rhizomes, it must receive greater care.

Many different methods have been used in the vegetative establishment of bermudagrass. Nurseries have been planted

14. Chapman, Hollis D., W. H. Marchant, G. W. Burton, W. G. Monson, and P. R. Utley. 1971. Performance of steers grazing Pensacola bahia, Coastal and Coastcross-1 bermudagrasses. *J. Anim. Sci.* 32:374. (Abstr.)

15. Nielsen, Etlar L. 1941. Establishment of bermudagrass from seed in nurseries. Ark. Agr. Exp. Sta. Bull. 409.

by pushing the sprigs into freshly prepared moist soil with a broomstick (flattened at one end to 3 mm thickness) so that the tip of the sprig remains above ground. Stepping on the sprig after planting firms the soil around it. Commercial planters designed to plant bermudagrass, trees, vegetable plants, or tobacco plants have been used successfully to plant bermudagrass sprigs. Many good planters have been built in farm shops from discarded farm machinery. Thousands of ha have been planted to bermudagrass by broadcasting sprigs or green hay by hand from trucks, with manure spreaders, or with sprig-scattering machines made from old automobile rear ends. These sprigs have been immediately covered with a tandem disk harrow followed by a cultipacker to firm the soil.

Sprigs should be planted at rates to give one plant every 61–92 cm. Four to six hl/ha of bulk sprigs (one to two bales) will usually give such stands if sprigs are carefully planted in 92-cm rows. Fourteen to eighteen hl of bulk sprigs are usually required to give similar stands with broadcast plantings.

Weed control is essential for quick establishment. Simazine (2.2–3.3 kg/ha) or the amine salt of 2,4-D (2.2 kg/ha) should be applied immediately after the sprigs are planted. If the soil is free of weeds, as it should be, these herbicides will act as preemergents for both grassy and broadleaf weeds. A second application of 2,4-D in three to four weeks following the first may be required if the grass has not covered the ground by that time.

Almost any planting method will succeed if the following rules are observed:

1. Plant only in moist, fertile, weed-free soil.
2. Plant pure live sprigs soon after harvesting.
3. Plant sprigs deep to ensure continued soil moisture, but leave tips above ground.
4. Firm soil around sprigs to keep them moist.
5. Control weeds with herbicides applied *immediately* after planting.
6. Fertilize to hasten coverage as soon as stolons appear.

Coastal has been successfully established from plantings made every month in the year, but spring and summer plantings are usually best.

❧ MANAGEMENT

In the humid southeastern U.S. where most soils are acid, bermudagrass sod should receive dolomitic lime (to supply needed magnesium) as needed to keep the pH above 5.5 for the grass and above 6 if clovers are to be grown with it.

About two weeks before the last average time for killing frost in the spring, bermudagrass sods not containing winter legumes should be burned. This practice will control winter weeds, spittlebug, and other pests; promote early growth; and frequently increase forage yields.

Most soils planted to bermudagrass must be fertilized. If legumes can be grown, P and K plus N from the legume may satisfy the moderate needs of the grass. However, bermudagrass, particularly the named cultivars, can use much more N than the 50–110 kg/ha generally supplied by associated legumes. Annual applications of 448 kg of N/ha/yr plus P and K will usually increase yields manyfold and double the percentage of crude protein (Tables 31.1, 31.2).

LEGUMES IN BERMUDAGRASS

The clovers (white, crimson, and arrowleaf) are the legumes most frequently grown with bermudagrass in the South. These legumes extend the grazing season, improve the quality of the forage, and supply up to 112 kg of N/ha/yr for the bermudagrass. On Mississippi Delta soils near Stoneville, Miss., 459 kg of LWG/ha/yr (three-year average, with 560 kg/ha the best year) have been produced with beef cattle grazing a mixture of Coastal bermudagrass and 'Louisiana S-1' white

TABLE 31.1 ❧ Effect of N yield and chemical composition of bermudagrass hay grown at Tifton, Ga.

Nitrogen (kg/ha)	Total hay yield (t/ha)	Average composition (% dry basis)						
		Crude protein	Ether extract	Crude fiber	N-free extract	Ash	Ca	P
None	1.8	6.9	2.1	29.6	56.3	5.1	0.36	0.31
56	4.7	7.3	2.3	29.3	55.7	5.3	0.46	0.31
112	7.2	8.2	2.3	30.3	53.9	5.2	0.43	0.30
224	10.5	8.8	2.3	30.0	54.2	4.7	0.41	0.28
448	18.8	13.1	2.3	30.9	49.1	4.6	0.46	0.28

Note: Based on yields and chemical composition of hay taken from plots receiving all N from nitrate of soda in March. All plots received 0-49-66 kg/ha.

clover without fertilizer N.[16] Unfortunately, most of the soils planted to bermudagrass are too sandy and droughty to grow legumes dependably.

Most any legume will make an excellent growth in association with bermudagrass provided the soil moisture and plant nutrient requirements of the legume are met and the mixture is managed properly. Lime, P, K, and sometimes some of the secondary and minor elements must be applied in generous amounts to many soils to successfully grow legumes with this grass.

FERTILIZATION

In most years with April 1 to November 1 rainfall ranging from 660 to 760 mm, Coastal bermudagrass yields for any given level of N will be similar (Table 31.2). Applications of 112, 224, and 448 kg N/ha may be expected to produce about 11, 16,

16. Hogg, Peter G., and James C. Collins. 1965. Clover and Coastal bermudagrass. *Miss. Farm. Res.* 28 (5):5.

TABLE 31.2 ❧ Effect of N application rate on t/ha of Coastal bermudagrass hay (16% moisture) produced on Tifton loamy sand in Georgia

Year	Kilogram N per ha, annually			
	112	224	448	Average
1955	11.4	17.0	23.8	17.5
1956	9.2	13.9	20.2	14.2
1957	12.1	16.6	21.3	16.6
1958	12.1	15.5	19.1	15.5
1959	11.0	16.4	22.6	16.6
Average	11.2	15.9	21.3	16.1

Note: Average of six N sources and two frequencies; P and K adequate.

and 21 t/ha of hay (Table 31.2). In such years irrigation has not significantly increased annual forage yields of Coastal fertilized with 448 kg of N/ha/yr.

Drought tolerance of Coastal was well demonstrated in the very dry 1954 season when it produced 13.5 t/ha of hay with 672 kg N/ha (Fig. 31.3). Its ability to respond to N was shown in 1953; when fertilized with 1008 kg N/ha, it produced 30 t/ha of hay (Fig. 31.2).

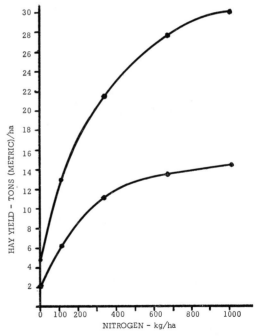

FIG. 31.3. The effect of N rate on the hay production of Coastal bermudagrass cut at five-week intervals during a 25-week period in a wet year (upper) and a dry year (lower). Rainfall from April 1 to November 1 was 1010 mm in 1953 and 350 mm in 1954.

Replicated Coastal pastures fertilized with 56, 112, and 224 kg N/ha/yr (P and K adequate) for a three-year period and grazed with steers produced average LWG's/ha/yr of 339, 539, and 766 kg respectively.[7]

All N sources are not equally effective, kilogram for kilogram of N, when applied as a topdressing to Coastal bermudagrass sod. It was reported in 1954 that N from urea or calcium cyanamid was only about 80% as effective as from ammonium nitrate or nitrate of soda applied broadcast.[17] Results are available from a five-year study in which six sources of N, three rates of application, and two frequencies were compared.[18] In this test, ammonium nitrate, ammonium sulphate, ammonium nitrate solution, anhydrous ammonia, urea–ammonium nitrate solution, and urea gave average relative hay yields of 100, 96, 98, 94, and 82 respectively. The relative N recoveries from these different sources were 100, 99, 95, 96, 86, and 74.

Anhydrous ammonia consistently gave a lag in response (due primarily to placement) that reduced the yield of the first hay cutting 1.1 t or more.[19] Poor response from urea topdressings was due to volitilization of urea to ammonia caused by urease. Since fire destroys urease temporarily, urea N applied soon after the sod is burned in late winter is as effective as other N sources.[19]

Anhydrous ammonia, ammonium nitrate, and ammonium sulphate gave similar responses in percent crude protein of the hay, yields of protein, and N recovery percentages. Urea gave a significantly inferior response in all three of these categories. Percentage recovery in the hay of the applied N decreased significantly as the rate of application increased for all sources except for anhydrous ammonia

which gave a similar recovery regardless of rate.

Splitting the N application for cultivated crops grown on sandy soil usually is considered necessary to prevent leaching losses. In this five-year study splitting the application (with half applied in March and half after the second hay cutting, rather than all in March) increased hay yields by 1.3–2.7 t/ha, except for anhydrous ammonia.[18] Splitting the application reduced the protein content of the hay but had no consistent effect on the yield of protein per ha or the percentage of N recovered. Anhydrous ammonia was equal to the best source of N when the total application was in March but was inferior to most sources when split, because of application injury and lag in response.

Anhydrous ammonia probably will always be the cheapest source of synthetic N, and it can be applied to sod with little loss. However, the high cost of such application has restricted its widespread use.

Coastal established in 1953 and maintained as a hay crop, with annual N applications of from 0 to 1790 kg/ha through 1954 to 1959, continued productive and vigorous through the six-year period. Root weights, including rhizomes which averaged 8500 kg/ha in 1956, were maintained at approximately the same level with all N application rates.[20]

Most sandy soils in the South contain such low reserves of P and K that these elements must be applied annually if much N is used. Maintaining a 9-1-4 fertilizer ratio of N-P-K has generally supplied an adequate minimum of P and K.[21] Although P and K are frequently applied only once a year, splitting the K will reduce luxury consumption and increase the efficiency of this element.[22]

17. Burton, Glenn W., and E. H. DeVane. 1954. Coastal bermudagrass for pasture, hay and silage. Ga. Agr. Exp. Sta. Bull. NS 2.
18. Burton, Glenn W., and James E. Jackson. 1962. Effect of rate and frequency of applying six nitrogen sources on Coastal bermudagrass. *Agron. J.* 54:40–43.
19. Jackson, James E., and Glenn W. Burton. 1962. Influence of sod treatment and nitrogen placement on the utilization of urea nitrogen by Coastal bermudagrass. *Agron. J.* 54:47–49.

20. Holt, Ethan C., and F. L. Fisher. 1960. Root development of Coastal bermudagrass with high nitrogen fertilization. *Agron. J.* 52:593–96.
21. Jackson, James E., Milton E. Walker, and Robert L. Carter. 1959. Nitrogen, phosphorus and potassium requirements of Coastal bermudagrass on a Tifton loamy sand. *Agron. J.* 51:129–31.
22. Burton, Glenn W., and James E. Jackson. 1962. Single vs. split potassium applications for Coastal bermudagrass. *Agron. J.* 54:13–14.

Secondary element (Ca, Mg, S) requirements of bermudagrass will be satisfied if 20% superphosphate is used to supply P and dolomitic limestone is applied as needed. Minor element applications to Coastal have rarely given a measurable response.

Fertilizer rates should be geared to livestock needs. Generally annual applications of 35 kg N/ha are required to maintain good stands of Coastal grown without a legume.

GRAZING

Management greatly influences the results obtained from any pasture. Young growth following close grazing usually is the most nutritious. Such grazing improves the nutritive qualities of the feed but sometimes reduces the total quantity produced to the extent that animals are unable to get enough feed for maximum daily gains. This was demonstrated in a stocking rate experiment conducted at Tifton.

Stocking uniformly fertilized (112-15-56 kg/ha N-P-K) 0.81-ha Coastal pastures at rates of 1.68, 2.24, and 2.8 steers/ha over a five-year period gave ADG's of 0.67, 0.60, and 0.52 kg/steer and annual LWG's of 392, 469, and 508 kg/ha respectively.[23] Thus bermudagrass should be grazed close for maximum carrying capacity and grazed light enough to allow some grass to accumulate for best ADG.

If legumes are growing with bermudagrass, grazing intensity should be adjusted to favor legume requirements. Low-growing legumes like white clover and annual lespedeza can best be maintained in bermudagrass with close grazing. More erect legumes like sweetclover and alfalfa must be given rest periods or be grazed less intensively to keep them in a vigorous condition. Close grazing immediately preceding the planting of a legume greatly facilitates its establishment in bermudagrass sod.

If bermudagrass is to be grazed by lactating cows, it should be well fertilized and mowed frequently to keep an abundance of young succulent grass available at all times.

Research at Clemson, S.C., helps to explain why many dairy farmers obtain only fair milk production from Coastal bermudagrass.[24] When Coastal was fertilized moderately and grazed continuously, as most dairymen have done, cows gave only fair maintenance of milk flow and produced 2800 kg/ha of TDN. With heavier fertilization, rotational grazing, and mowing as needed to keep the grass young and succulent, milk flow was good and production reached 4000–5000 kg/ha TDN. When Coastal was fertilized heavily (448 kg N/ha/yr), green-chopped as short as possible about every 21 days, and fed twice a day, 8200 kg/ha TDN/yr were produced.[24]

Some farmers remove a cutting of hay from a part of their Coastal pastures during the summer. In addition to producing winter feed, this practice helps to control weeds and scatter animal droppings.

Well-fertilized pastures of Coastal, Midland, and Coastcross-1 usually contain very few weeds if burned in late winter or if overseeded with a winter legume or grass. When broadleaf weeds are present, 2,4-D can be safely used to control them. Some perennial weeds can be controlled by turning the sod with a bottom plow, a practice that stimulates the growth of bermudagrass.

HAY, SILAGE, AND PELLETS

Sod of Coastal and similar cultivars should be burned in late winter, sprayed with 2,4-D if additional weed control is needed, and fertilized with about 112 kg/ha of N plus P and K in mid-March. Cuttings for hay or silage should be made when the grass is about 40 cm tall and

23. McCormick, W. C., W. H. Marchant, and B. L. Southwell. 1964. Effects of stocking level on gains of steers grazing Coastal bermudagrass. Ga. Agr. Exp. Sta. Mimeo. NS 183.

24. King, W. A. Coastal bermudagrass as a forage for dairy cows. 1964. Clemson Univ. Dairy Sci. Res. Ser. 34.

TABLE 31.3 ✤ Effect of N rate and clipping frequency upon the yield, leaf percentage and crude protein, and lignin content of Coastal bermudagrass hay at Tifton, Ga.

Clipping intervals (weeks)	Hay yield		Leaf		Crude protein		Lignin	
	112 kg N/ha (t/ha)	672 kg N/ha (t/ha)	112 kg N/ha (%)	672 kg N/ha (%)	112 kg N/ha (%)	672 kg N/ha (%)	112 kg N/ha (%)	672 kg N/ha (%)
1	...	14.0	...	...	...	21.40	...	...
2	6.0	17.4	84.3	87.6	13.60	20.85	10.25	9.45
3	8.9	19.3	81.5	81.3	12.89	18.80	10.20	9.65
4	9.9	21.7	76.9	74.8	11.19	16.98	10.00	10.30
6	12.8	28.1	66.8	57.7	8.44	13.83	9.60	11.20
8	13.7	28.0	59.9	51.4	7.76	12.20	10.25	12.05

Note: P, K, and all other elements adequate. Hay yield adjusted to 16% moisture. Leaf, crude protein, and lignin percentages on dry basis.

every four to six weeks thereafter. Permitting the grass to grow longer than six weeks between cuts in summer lowers quality, increases curing time, and does not increase annual hay yields. Allowing the last cutting to grow about eight weeks until the first killing frost in the fall will enable the grass to build up reserves to give more vigorous growth and better stands the next spring. Often this "last cutting" will supply much needed fall grazing. Hay conditioners will hasten curing so hay can usually be baled or bulk-stacked 24 hours after cutting. Fertilizer (56–112 kg N/ha plus P and K) should be applied after each cutting through August to maintain forage yield and protein content.

Frequency of cutting and fertilization of the tall-growing cultivars like Coastal greatly influence both yield and quality of the hay produced. The effects of these treatments are evident in Table 31.3.[25] A study of these data together with those in Table 31.4 shows that as the age of the plant increases, leafiness, crude protein, and ash content decrease, while yield, lignin, crude fiber, and nitrogen-free extract increase. Digestion trials showed that the digestibility of these constituents de-

creased as the clipping intervals or the age of the grass increased.[26]

The effect of age on hay quality was demonstrated when dairy heifers fed 4-, 8-, and 13-week-old Coastal bermudagrass hays without supplement made daily gains of 0.54, 0.41, and 0.0 kg respectively.[27]

Four years of research at Clemson, S.C., has shown that silage made from heavily fertilized Coastal (properly ensiled before it is 35 days old) can produce as much milk as corn silage (4400 kg/ha of grain) at a saving of $0.21/45 kg of milk.[28]

26. Knox, F. E., Glenn W. Burton, and D. M. Baird. 1958. Effect of nitrogen rate and clipping frequency upon lignin content and digestibility of Coastal bermudagrass. Agr. Food Chem. 6:2, 217–18.
27. McCullough, M. E., and Glenn W. Burton. 1962. Quality in Coastal bermudagrass hay. Ga. Agr. Res. 4 (1):4–5.
28. King, W. A., C. C. Brannon, and H. J. Webb. 1964. Coastal bermudagrass silage for milking cows. S.C. Agr. Sta. Bull. 516.

TABLE 31.4 ✤ Effect of clipping frequency upon chemical composition of Coastal bermudagrass hay

Clipping intervals (weeks)	Average composition (%)					
	Dry matter	Crude protein	Ether extract	Crude fiber	N-free extract	Ash
1 to 2	93.90	20.63	3.11	22.22	42.11	5.83
3	93.90	17.63	2.90	25.00	43.32	5.05
4	93.90	16.25	2.67	25.21	45.62	4.15
6	93.70	11.81	2.30	25.75	50.79	3.05
8	93.70	9.94	1.85	27.00	50.93	3.98

Note: Fertilized with 672 kg N/ha plus adequate P and K during a 24-week period.

25. Prine, Gordon M., and Glenn W. Burton. 1956. The effect of nitrogen rate and clipping frequency upon the yield, protein content and certain morphological characteristics of Coastal bermudagrass, Cynodon dactylon (L.) Pers. Agron. J. 48:296–301.

To make good silage, bermudagrass managed as hay and cut every four to six weeks should be chopped as short as possible and well packed in an airtight silo without wilting. (Coastal usually contains 65–75% moisture when cut at this stage.) Adding 40 kg of ground corn or citrus pulp per ton of chopped grass will improve the quality of the silage.

In repeated feeding trials at Tifton, steers consuming Coastal pellets have averaged 0.82 kg ADG, about 50% more than ADGs usually obtained from Coastal pastures.[29] These pellets have been made from dehydrated chopped forage taken from Coastal fields managed as hay. The potential of Coastal when pelleted and fed was demonstrated in 1960. In that year, F. B. Roebuck, Estill, S.C., won the Progressive Farmers' "Ton of Beef" award when his four steers and four heifers gained 985 kg when fed 7.7 t of pellets and 1.8 t of hay cut from 0.4 ha of heavily fertilized Coastal.

Numerous experiments have shown that dehydrated Coastal bermudagrass may be substituted for alfalfa as a source of vitamin A and xanthophyll for poultry feeds. Processors producing these high-quality pellets manage the grass for hay but apply 672 kg N/ha/yr plus P and K and cut the grass every 21–24 days. Yields of 15.7 t pellets/ha/season are common.

Midland bermudagrass requires fertilization and management practices similar to those described above.[30]

✤ SEED PRODUCTION

Most commercial seed of common bermudagrass is produced in Arizona and southern California. Old cultivated fields abandoned to bermudagrass supply much of the seed, but some is harvested with alfalfa seed from fields that have volunteer bermudagrass growing in association. One to two seed crops are harvested annually, with seed yields ranging from 112 to 224 kg/ha.

✤ CONTROL

The pest potential of every forage plant should be carefully considered before it is planted. Pastures frequently become croplands or urban areas with lawns and golf courses. Homeowners located on or near old Pensacola bahiagrass pastures are denied the beauty and low cost of centipedegrass lawns because the coarse bahiagrass volunteering from hard seed continually produces tall seed stalks that must be mowed twice a week all summer.

Forages that produce hard seed capable of surviving many years in the soil are the most difficult to contain and eradicate. Rhizomatous forages are more difficult to kill than stoloniferous or bunch types without rhizomes. Persistence and ability to crowd out other species, particularly without care, increases pest potential. Rhizomatous seed-producing bermudagrasses, like common, carry a much greater pest potential than the nearly sterile Coastal with its shallow rhizomes. Completely sterile stoloniferous hybrids like Coastcross-1 can be completely eradicated with one shallow cultivation in dry weather.

Growing a high-yielding crop of corn on deeply turned bermudagrass sod followed by disking to kill the few weak survivors after the crop is harvested will usually destroy all but the viable seed left in the soil. Close grazing or mowing followed by disk tilling to a depth of 8–10 cm in dry weather generally kills all plants cut from their roots. One or more additional disk tillings to depths great enough to cut the remaining rhizomes from their roots during dry weather will usually eradicate vegetative bermudagrass.

✤ QUESTIONS

1. What is the range of climatic and soil adaptation of bermudagrass?

29. McCormick, W. C., D. W. Beardsley, and B. L. Southwell. 1965. Coastal bermudagrass pellets for fattening beef steers. Ga. Agr. Exp. Sta. Bull. NS 132.
30. Decker, A. M., R. W. Hemkin, J. R. Miller, N. A. Clark, and A. V. Okorie. 1971. Nitrogen fertilization, harvest management, and utilization of Midland bermudagrass, *Cynodon dactylon* (L.) Pers. Md. Agr. E·). Sta. Bull. 487.

2. Enumerate the differences between Coastal bermudagrass and common bermudagrass; between Coastal and Suwannee; between Coastal, Coastcross-1, and Midland.
3. How is common bermudagrass propagated? Coastal bermudagrass? Suwannee?
4. To what extent can the N needed for large yields be obtained from legumes established in the bermudagrass?
5. How and to what extent is the grazing management changed if legumes are growing in association with the bermudagrass?
6. How and to what extent is the production and quality of hay influenced by height and frequency of cutting?
7. How does bermudagrass rank in importance in comparison with other grasses throughout the South? Why?

SUPPLEMENTAL INFORMATION

✢ OTHER CULTIVARS

'Alicia' bermudagrass is a cultivar selected from an African introduction by Cecil Greer, Harlington, Texas, and distributed through a franchise system. Alicia is similar to Coastal bermudagrass in type, rate of establishment, and dry matter yield; produces more rhizomes; and is less winter hardy. Alicia forage is 3 to 6 percentage points lower in *in vitro* dry matter digestibility (IVDMD) than Coastal and may be expected to give lower livestock gains.

'Callie' bermudagrass, an aberrant plant selected from a plot of PI 290814, has tall, coarse stems; large, broad leaves; spreads rapidly by large stolons; and can be easily propagated from above-ground stems.[31] Its rapid establishment enables it to outyield most other cultivars in the first year. Once established, Callie and Coastal have given similar dry matter yields. Callie has regular meiosis, has fertile pollen, and produces seed. It has a higher IVDMD than most cultivars grown in Mississippi and should give better livestock gains. The severe winter of 1976–1977 killed Callie bermudagrass in the northern half of the Gulf states and reduced stands south to Florida.

'Hardie' bermudagrass is a vegetatively propagated F$_1$ hybrid between bermudagrasses from Elazig, Turkey, and Khanabad, Afghanistan. The cross was made by W. L. Richardson in 1967 and has been evaluated and released by C. M. Taliaferro. Both scientists are staff members at Oklahoma State University. Compared with Midland bermudagrass, Hardie has larger leaves, stems, and rhizomes; yields more dry matter with adequate rainfall or irrigation but less in dry years; makes more early season growth; establishes faster, particularly on heavy soils; gives 6% higher IVDMD values; and should give better daily gains assuming equal intake. Hardie has excellent winter hardiness and is adapted throughout Oklahoma.

'Tifton 44' bermudagrass is the best of several thousand F$_1$ hybrids between Coastal bermuda and a bermudagrass that had survived in Berlin, Germany, for 15 years before it was collected by G. W. Burton in 1966.[32] Compared with Coastal, Tifton 44 is darker green, has finer stems that cure faster when cut for hay, has more rhizomes, makes a denser sod, starts growth earlier in the spring, and yields as much dry matter with a 6% higher IVDMD. It has given 19% better average daily gains than Coastal when grazed or fed as pellets. In a 56-day feeding trial with 250 kg heifers, five-week old Tifton 44 hay with an IVDMD of 65% gave ADGs of 0.54 kg and a hay:gain ratio of 9:1. Reports from cooperators in 14 states indicate that Tifton 44 is as winter hardy as Midland and can be grown as far north as southern Illinois.

31. Watson, Vance H. 1975. 'Callie' bermudagrass. The Agronomist, pp. 18–19.

32. Burton, Glenn W., and Warren G. Monson. 1978. Registration of Tifton 44 bermudagrass. *Crop Sci.* (In Press).

HUGH W. BENNETT / *Agricultural Research Service, USDA*

32

JOHNSONGRASS, DALLISGRASS, AND OTHER GRASSES FOR THE HUMID SOUTH

❧

JOHNSONGRASS, *Sorghum halepense* (L.) Pers., is native to the Mediterranean area of North Africa, South Asia, and southern Europe. It was introduced into the U.S. around 1830. About 1840 Colonel William Johnson carried the grass to the black clay soils of central Alabama, thus the name johnsongrass.[1]

❧ DISTRIBUTION AND ADAPTATION

Originally introduced as a superior forage plant, johnsongrass is best known as a pernicious weed.[2,3] It has spread, by intentional or unintentional means, to all but a dozen northern states. It is most common wherever cotton is grown. (See Fig. 32.1.) The persistence, palatability, and nutritive value of johnsongrass enables its use as a hay and pasture plant to overshadow its disadvantages as a weed in many areas.

Johnsongrass is best adapted to heavy clay soils of relatively high fertility and

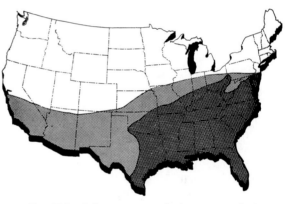

FIG. 32.1. Johnsongrass-producing areas of the U.S.

water-holding capacity. Good yields may be obtained on any soil favorable for cotton or corn.

❧ PLANT DESCRIPTION

Johnsongrass differs from other species of sorghum in that it is a perennial. It produces extensively creeping scaly rhi-

❧ HUGH W. BENNETT is Research Agronomist, Mississippi station, and ARS, USDA. He holds the Ph.D. degree from Iowa State University. Since 1935 he has been involved in research on forage and pasture crop production and improvement.

1. Phares, D. L. 1881. Farmers Book of Grasses. J. C. Hill Printing Co., Starkville, Miss.
2. Hauser, E. W., and A. H. Fred. 1958. Johnsongrass as a weed. USDA Farmers' Bull. 1537.
3. McWhorter, C. G. 1960. Johnsongrass study shows why it is so difficult to control. *Miss. Farm Res.* 23 (12):6.

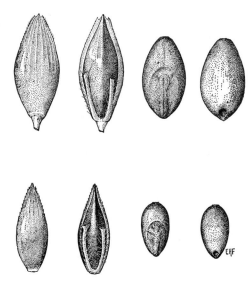

FIG. 32.2. Distinguishing characteristics of johnsongrass seed (below) and sudangrass seed (above). Note differences in the appendages of the seed and the expanded cup-shaped apex in johnsongrass; also note differences in seed size.

zomes from which erect stems grow 90–275 cm in height. The inflorescence is an open panicle resembling sudangrass. Some seed of johnsongrass have short stems because of failure to separate at the articulation of the rachis and spikelet. This distinct suture distinguishes them from seed of sudangrass as shown in Figure 32.2.

A single seed may produce a plant with 1 to more than 170 stems, depending upon

FIG. 32.3. *Mature plants . . . produce rhizomes . . . sprout . . . the following spring.* A johnsongrass rhizome with the soil cover removed to show scales and rootings. *Miss. Agr. Exp. Sta. photo.*

fertility, moisture, space, and inherent differences.[4] A seedling three weeks old is not easily distinguished from plants coming from rhizomes, and both initiate rhizomes at this age. Rhizome growth is relatively slow in relation to top growth until bloom stage. An average plant will produce 19.7 m of rhizomes and 1.7 kg of seed per season.[3] Mature plants continue to produce rhizomes that grow until frost, overwinter, and sprout new plants the following spring. (See Fig. 32.3.)

A rapid change occurs in the plant's metabolism at the bloom stage, influencing its persistence and its resistance to herbicides. Glucose begins to increase when plants are two weeks of age until bloom, then it drops sharply. Carbohydrates stored as sucrose remain at a low level until bloom, then increase as the glucose decreases.[3,5] Total carbohydrates are highest at the bloom stage and constitute 50% of the rhizomes on a dry weight basis.

PRODUCTIVITY

Johnsongrass responds to fertilization on most soils and especially on those that are eroded or depleted.[4,6-9] Dry matter yields are greatly increased by application of fertilizer N up to 1075 kg/ha.[7-10] Economical increases amounting to 8.96 t/ha are obtained with 538 kg/ha of applied N.[8-10] In general, johnsongrass produces higher yields of forage and nutrients when harvested at the boot stage of growth and usually averages three to four harvests per sea-

4. Bennett, H. W. 1949. Plant type, disease resistance, and yield variation in johnsongrass. Proc. Assoc. Southern Agr. Workers 45:56.

5. Rapp, K. E. 1947. Carbohydrate metabolism of johnsongrass. J. Amer. Soc. Agron. 39:869–73.

6. Scarsbrook, C. E. 1963. Nitrogen profitable for johnsongrass. Ala. Agr. Exp. Sta. Highlights of Agr. Res. 10 (4):3.

7. Ward, C. Y., and W. R. Meredith, Jr. 1964. Nitrogen fertilization of johnsongrass will pay big dividends. Miss. Agr. Exp. Sta. Info. Sheet 843.

8. Bennett, H. W., and N. C. Merwine. 1964. Interplanted legumes in johnsongrass. Miss. Agr. Exp. Sta. Bull. 698.

9. Watson, V. H., C. Y. Ward, and Wes Thurman. 1970. Response of johnsongrass swards to various levels of nutrients and management. Proc. Assoc. Southern Agr. Workers 67:51.

10. Miles, J. T., and J. W. Lusk. 1952. Early cut hay produces best results in tests. Miss. Farm Res. 15 (7):1–8.

FIG. 32.4. *Grazed during the summer . . . cut and stacked for reserve feeding.* Baled johnsongrass hay for shipping and feeding. *Miss. Agr. Exp. Sta. photo.*

son.[7-11] Total yield of dry matter cut in the boot stage is 75% of that cut in more mature stages. Feeding value per kilogram of dry matter shows that 1.5 times as much gain is obtained from one ha when the grass is cut in the boot stage as when cut in the milk stage.[10] Crude protein content ranges from 5.9 to 11.9% in hay cut in the boot and milk stages of growth. Fertilized johnsongrass cut at the boot stage averaged 13.5% crude protein with 65.8% digestibility as compared to unfertilized grass containing 7.2% crude protein and 47.5% digestibility cut at the same growth stage.[11] Fertilization increased the percent digestibility of dry matter 61.9–67.6%; cellulose, 73.5–76.6%; and energy, 60.7–66.4%. Maximum yields of dry matter and nutrients are obtained with split applications of at least 270 kg/ha (preferably 540) of N with the majority applied between May 1 and June 15.[7,9-11] If high yields are to continue under heavy fertilizer N, applications of P and K should be made in approximately the ratio of 6 N to 0.5 P to 0.8 K.

✿ IMPORTANCE AND USE

Early feeding tests showed that johnsongrass compared favorably with timothy as

hay.[12,13] Later tests have shown that properly fertilized johnsongrass cut in the boot stage ranked next to alfalfa and ahead of oat and soybean hays for feeding dairy cows.[10,11,14]

Johnsongrass is utilized as a pasture plant throughout the black prairie belt of Alabama, Mississippi, and Texas. A system of grazing johnsongrass seeded with roughpeas has used johnsongrass to good advantage.[8,15] If needed, johnsongrass may be grazed during summer at the low carrying capacity of permanent pastures. If not needed, it may be cut and stacked for reserve feeding. (See Fig. 32.4.) The last growth of johnsongrass is allowed to seed and remain on the field. After frost the cattle are moved from permanent pasture to fields of frosted johnsongrass. Since roughpeas are growing under the grass, adequate green forage is furnished for two months during the winter. When the standing grass has been eaten and severe weather retards the growth of the roughpeas, feed is supplied by the stacked john-

11. Browning, C. B., J. W. Lusk, and J. T. Miles. 1960. Hays for dairy cows. Miss. Agr. Exp. Sta. Info. Sheet 669.

12. Grimes, J. C., and W. C. Taylor. 1930. Johnsongrass hay as a feed for horses and mules. Ala. Agr. Exp. Sta. Circ. 54.
13. Leveck, H. H. 1939. Livestock investigations in Mississippi. *Miss. Farm Res.* 2 (12):1–7.
14. Lusk, J. W., J. R. Owen, W. C. Cowsert, and J. T. Miles. 1956. Three years of hay feeding results. **Miss.** Agr. Exp. Sta. Info. Sheet 539.
15. Baker, K. G. 1950. A system for processed milk production in the Black Belt of Alabama. Ala. Agr. Exp. Sta. Progr. Rept. Ser. 45.

songrass hay. The interplanted legume, although all the top portion is grazed, stimulates the growth of the following johnsongrass.[6,8] Investigations have shown that continuously grazed johnsongrass is equal to sweet sudangrass or pearlmillet for milk production and is preferred over the annual summer forages. More milk was produced from both strip and rotationally grazed johnsongrass in these tests.[16,17]

Heavily fertilized and properly managed johnsongrass meadows produce a high-quality hay with good market value. Higher rates of fertilization and better management coupled with newer types of harvesting machinery are reestablishing the production of johnsongrass hay as a cash crop and for feeding.[7,11,18]

The Black Belt or prairie section of Alabama and Mississippi composes an area of approximately 1.1 million ha. Some 660,-000–825,000 ha are open permanent pasture or hay meadowland. Heavy clay or "gumbo" type of soil, ideally suited to the growth of johnsongrass, is prevalent throughout this area.

❧ CULTIVARS

No established cultivars of johnsongrass exist. Some selections and strains have been made, but they are not in production.[19]

❧ CULTURE AND MANAGEMENT

Johnsongrass should be seeded in early spring on a firm well-prepared seedbed. Excellent results have been obtained by seeding as early as December.[8,12] Under average conditions 11.2–22.4 kg/ha should give a good stand. Sparse stands are thickened

by thorough disking early in the spring.[18,20] The grass should be allowed to become fully established (rhizomes formed) before harvest. Rhizomes make their greatest growth after the plants begin to head.[3,9,18] Any cutting treatment before maturity reduces the production of rhizomes and forage; the more frequent the cuttings, the greater this reduction.[3,6,8,9,15,18,20] This reduction continues the second year, and all cutting treatments show less rhizomes present at the end of the second year than at the end of the first. To produce high-quality forage without stand loss or reduced yield, it is necessary to either permit the plants to develop rhizomes or reseed frequently. This is accomplished by allowing johnsongrass to bloom once during the growing season. Since rhizome production and percent of total carbohydrates are significantly higher in the fall than in the summer,[3,9] allowing the last growth to seed appears the best practice.[8,15,20] Excellent stands and yields have been reported on highly fertilized meadows cut at the boot stage for nine years, whereas stands were sparse on areas receiving no fertilization with the same cutting treatment.[11]

Liberal use of N along with recommended levels of P and K must be practiced to realize the full potential of this grass.[6,7,9,18] This will thicken and maintain stands, eliminate weeds, greatly increase yields, and produce a leafier forage that is higher in nutrients and more digestible.

❧ SEED PRODUCTION

The johnsongrass seed crop is produced in Alabama, Mississippi, and Texas. Seed shatter rather easily. Yields ranged from 188 to 502 kg/ha but 314 kg/ha are considered good. Most of the seed sold is obtained by machine harvest.

Johnsongrass seed are markedly dormant when first mature. They need a number of months for complete after-ripening and then do not germinate completely except

16. Hawkins, G. E., L. A. Smith, R. M. Patterson, and J. A. Little. 1963. Managing johnsongrass for highest possible milk production. Ala. Agr. Exp. Sta. Highlights of Agr. Res. 10 (2):3.

17. Hawkins, G. E., L. A. Smith, H. Grimes, R. M. Patterson, J. A. Little, and C. A. Rollo. 1969. Managing johnsongrass for dairy cows. Ala. Agr. Exp. Sta. Bull. 389.

18. Thurman, C. W., and C. Y. Ward. 1968. Johnsongrass management in Mississippi. Miss. Agr. Exp. Sta. Info. Sheet 1046.

19. Hanson, A. A. 1972. Grass varieties in the United States. USDA Agr. Handbook 170, rev.

20. Sturkie, D. G. 1930. The influence of topcutting treatments on rootstocks of johnsongrass. J. Amer. Soc. Agron. 23:82–93.

with alternating temperatures in a relatively warm temperature range.[21]

The inner integument and various layers of the pericarp of johnsongrass seed contain tannin compounds which decrease seed-coat permeability. These layers and the need for after-ripening explain the excellent stands obtained from fall and winter seeding.[21,22]

✣ DISEASES AND INSECTS

Johnsongrass diseases are not considered serious in the Southeast.[4,23] However, loose smut, *Sphacelotheca holci* Jacks; leaf spot, *Cercospora sorghi* Ell. & Ev.; zonate leaf spot *Gloecercospora sorghi* Bain & Edg.; and anthracnose, *Colletotrichum graminicola* (Ces.) G. W. Wils., do appear in mature johnsongrass. Insects present no problems where johnsongrass is utilized for grazing or hay. The sorghum midge, *Contarinia sorghicola* (Coq.), and sorghum webworm, *Celama sorghiella* (Riley), cause some damage with seed production.

DALLISGRASS

Dallisgrass, *Paspalum dilatatum* Poir., is native to northern Argentina, Uruguay, and southern Brazil. It was introduced into the U.S. by accident about 1842.[24] The value of dallisgrass as a pasture and hay plant for the South was recognized early.[25-27] It was first known simply as paspalum; other common names are watergrass, knotgrass, hairy-flowered paspalum, and Fort Thompson grass.

✣ DISTRIBUTION AND ADAPTATION

Dallisgrass is found from New Jersey south to Tennessee and Florida and west

FIG. 32.5. *More palatable . . . remains nutritious . . . longer period.* Dallisgrass is recognized as one of the most valuable species for the humid South. It has many basal leaves which make rapid recovery following grazing. *Miss. Agr. Exp. Sta. photo.*

to Texas. It is adapted throughout the Cotton Belt where annual rainfall is as much as 760 mm. It has been grown successfully in the far west under irrigation.

Dallisgrass grows well on a wide variety of soils but makes its best growth on moist, fertile clay and loam bottomland. On heavy clay soils dallisgrass will endure extremes of both drought and moisture. It stands extreme drought when there is good rainfall sometime during the year. It is not well suited to extremely sandy soils, but good results have been obtained on such soils with proper fertilization and grazing management.[28,29]

✣ PLANT DESCRIPTION

Dallisgrass is a fast-growing rather stout perennial. It has smooth leaves, a deep root system, and grows in clumps of a few to many stems. Many basal leaves are produced from a knotted base of fleshy and extremely short rhizomes. (See Fig. 32.5.) The leaves, following grazing or drought, make a rapider recovery than any other pasture grass throughout its region of adaptation.[30,31] It is propagated from seed produced on tall (61–122 cm) seedstalks with very few leaves. The stems are slender and usually droop with the weight of the seed. The oval and hairy seed are ar-

21. Taylorson, R. B., and C. G. McWhorter. 1969. Seed dormancy and germination in ecotypes of johnsongrass. *Weed Sci.* 17:359–61.
22. Harrington, G. T., and W. Crocker. 1923. The pericarp and integument of johnsongrass seed in relationship to its physiology. *J. Agr. Res.* 23:193–222.
23. Dean, J. L. 1966. Local injection of sorghum by the johnsongrass loose kernel smut fungus. *Phytopathology* 56:1342–44.
24. Chase, Agnes. 1929. The North American species of *Paspalum. U.S. Nat. Herb.* 28 (1):310.
25. Mississippi Agr. Exp. Sta. 1889. Rept. 2.
26. Louisiana Agr. Exp. Sta. 1892. Grass, clovers, forage crops and small grains. Bull. 19.
27. Tabor, Paul. 1963. Early history of dallisgrass in the United States. *Crop Sci.* 3:449–50.

28. Brown, Otto. 1947. Ala. Agr. Exp. Sta. Progr. Rept. Ser. 36.
29. Holt, E. C. 1956. Dallisgrass. Tex. Agr. Exp. Sta. Bull. 829.
30. Bennett, H. W. 1941. Pastures in Mississippi. Miss. Agr. Exp. Sta. Bull. 356.
31. Lovvorn, R. L. 1945. The effect of defoliation, soil fertility, temperature, and length of day on the growth of some perennial grasses. *J. Amer. Soc. Agron.* 37:570–82.

rayed in two compact rows on the 5–9 racemes of the panicle.[24]

It continues growth later in the fall, is not injured by moderate frosts, and begins growth earlier in the spring than most warm-season grasses.[29,30] Growth continues more nearly through the entire year than any other grass in the Southeast; it is more palatable and remains nutritious over a longer period. Its bunch habit of growth makes it better adapted in association with other grasses and legumes and also prevents it from becoming a pest.[30,32,33]

Depending upon soil moisture and fertility, dry matter yields range from 1230 to 12,000 kg/ha.[29-32] This dry matter is composed of 6.2–19.6% crude protein, 26–33% crude fiber, 1.9–3.2% fat, and 34–42% N-free extract.[30,32,33] Dry matter digestibility ranges from 45 to 60%

❧ IMPORTANCE AND USE

Dallisgrass and adapted legume combinations are primarily utilized for pasture.[30,32,33] They provide grazing over a longer period than many other summer grass-base combinations and produce milk and beef at low feed costs.[30,32-38] The addition of dallisgrass is an effective and economical means of improving native summer permanent pastures.[29,32,33]

Dallisgrass is not extensively used for hay but does produce good yields of fair quality.[29,30] Quality determinations of dallisgrass hay made after seed harvest were equal to that of bermudagrass cut after four weeks of growth.

32. Woodhouse, W. W., and R. L. Lovvorn. 1942. Establishing and improving permanent pastures in North Carolina. N.C. Agr. Exp. Sta. Bull. 338.
33. Brown, J. M., and R. D. Rouse. 1953. Fertilizer effects on botanical and chemical composition of white clover–dallisgrass associations on Sumter clay. J. Amer. Soc. Agron. 45:279–82.
34. Bashaw, E. C., and E. C. Holt. 1958. Megasporogenesis, embryo sac development, and embryogenesis in dallisgrass. Agron. J. 50:753–56.
35. Bennett, H. W. 1959. Artificial pollen germination for selection of improved seed production in Paspalum dilatatum Poir. Agron. J. 50:753–56.
36. Burton, G. W. 1963. Conventional breeding of dallisgrass. Crop Sci. 3:491–94.
37. Roark, D. B., J. W. Lusk, J. T. Miles, W. C. Cowsert, and R. E. Waters. 1953. Pasture for dairy cattle. Miss. Agr. Exp. Sta. Bull. 507.
38. Leveck, H. H. 1949. Wintering bred beef cows. Miss. Agr. Exp. Sta. Ann. Rept.

❧ CULTIVARS

'B230' and 'B430' developed in Louisiana apparently are not sufficiently more fertile than common dallisgrass to warrant commercial seed production.[39] 'Prostrate,' developed at the Georgia coastal plain station, is better adapted to light and poorly drained soils than common.[40] Research shows that desirable characteristics can be combined by hybridization for probable release of more valuable types.[41]

❧ CULTURE AND MANAGEMENT

Late winter or early spring seedings are most dependable.[30,42] Seeding October 1 to November 15 in standing rice or in rice stubble is recommended for the rice areas of Texas and Louisiana.[29] The quantity of seed required to supply 10 live pure seed per square meter or rates adjusted to give 16.8 kg of live pure seed per ha in 50.8-cm rows have resulted in good stands. Soil preparation materially increases establishment in proportion to the amount of preparation.[29,30,32]

Significant increases in yield and density of sward follow applications of N, but heavy applications tend to crowd out legumes. Annual applications of 100–200 kg of N, 67 kg of P, and 34 kg of K are recommended.[30,32,33] Where legumes are grown in the grass sod, the spring application of N can be omitted.

If dallisgrass is not mowed or grazed, it tends to become determinate in growth and the rhizomes decrease in size. For continuous production and for dallisgrass to perennate, some forage must be removed even when harvesting seed. At any stand density if dallisgrass is not grazed or clipped shorter than 5–7.6 cm, it will pro-

39. Owen, C. R. 1966. A hirsute ecotype isolated from common dallisgrass (Paspalum dilatatum Poir.). Crop Sci. 6:374–75.
40. Hart, R. H., and G. W. Burton. 1966. Prostrate vs. common dallisgrass under different clipping frequencies and fertility levels. Agron. J. 58:521–22.
41. Bennett, H. W., B. L. Burson, and E. C. Bashaw. 1969. Intraspecific hybridization in dallisgrass, Paspalum dilatatum Poir. Crop Sci. 9:807–9.
42. Holt, E. C., and H. C. Houston. 1954. The establishment of dallisgrass. Tex. Agr. Exp. Sta. Progr. Rept. 622.

duce up to three times the amount of forage as when grazed or clipped lower. Prevention of extreme defoliation is the principal factor in dallisgrass management.

❧ SEED PRODUCTION

Heavier soil types are best for the production of quality seed. Late winter or early spring applications of 60 kg/ha of N and delayed utilization of forage will increase the yield and quality of the first seed crop. Seed production and seed set are low in the summer. Fields utilized entirely for seed production may be fertilized with N and harvested as many as four times during a growing season. Per ha yields from row and broadcast plantings are similar.[43] Harvesting should begin when 60–80% of the seed heads are a light brown color. Harvesting may be by direct combining or by mowing, windrowing, and threshing from the windrow.[43] Seed containing green material may be dried at 60 C until moisture is reduced to 7–10%.[44] Seed yields range from 90 to 500 kg/ha, depending upon rainfall and growing conditions.[45]

❧ DISEASES AND INSECTS

Ergot, *Claviceps paspali* Stevens & Hall, is the most important disease of dallisgrass. This disease invades the floret and prevents embryo development. Ergotized seed heads are injurious to livestock. Dallisgrass also is attacked by anthracnose, *Colletotrichum graminicola* (Ces.) G. W. Wils., and leaf blight, *Helminthosporium micropus* Drechsl., foliage diseases.

Dallisgrass sometimes is infested with the sugarcane borer, *Diatraea saccharalis* (F.), especially where used largely for seed production.

Insects or diseases are seldom a factor before midsummer. Harvesting the early seed crop avoids most of the ergot, and later grazing or harvesting for hay practically eliminates the insect and foliage disease problems.

PANGOLA DIGITGRASS

'Pangola' digitgrass, *Digitaria decumbens* Stent., is a native of South Africa. It was introduced into the U.S. in 1935, into Puerto Rico and the Virgin Islands in the late 1940s, and subsequently into most of the Caribbean area.[46-48]

❧ DISTRIBUTION AND ADAPTATION

Pangola digitgrass is adapted to Florida, the southern portion of other states bordering the Gulf of Mexico, and into southern California. It rarely withstands the winters 160 km north of the Gulf. Due to winter damage the areas of most extensive use are central and south Florida and the Gulf Coast of Mexico.[47,48]

Pangola digitgrass is best adapted to fertile and moist soils. It does not grow well on flooded soils, but will thrive on well-drained soils. It has been grown successfully in full sun and in partial shade, from near sea level to 300 m, on sandy to heavy clay soils ranging in pH from 4.2 to 8.5, and in rainfall of 2540 mm annually. It is somewhat drought tolerant and is more sensitive to a low N level than carpetgrass or bahiagrass.[46,48-50] It withstands excessive trampling, recovers rapidly from overgrazing, and is among the most palatable of grasses.[46-48]

43. Holt, E. C., and E. C. Bashaw. 1963. Factors affecting seed production of dallisgrass. Tex. Agr. Exp. Sta. MP-662.

44. Bennett, H. W., and W. W. Marclibanks. 1969. Seed drying and viability in dallisgrass. *Agron. J.* 61:175–77.

45. Owen, C. R. 1951. Improvement of native dallisgrass in Louisiana. La. Agr. Exp. Sta. Bull. 449.

46. Oakes, A. J. 1960. Pangolagrass (*Digitaria decumbens*) in the Caribbean. Proc. 8th Int. Grassl. Congr., pp. 386–89 (Reading, England).

47. Nestel, B. L., and M. J. Creek. 1962. Pangolagrass. *Herb. Abstr.* 32:265–71.

48. Hodges, E. M., G. B. Killinger, J. E. McCaleb, O. C. Ruelke, R. J. Allen, Jr., S. C. Shank, and A. E. Kretschmer, Jr. 1967. Pangolagrass. Fla. Agr. Exp. Sta. Bull. 718.

49. Wallace, A. T., G. B. Killinger, R. W. Bledsoe, and D. B. Duncan. 1957. Design analysis and results of an experiment on response of pangolagrass and Pensacola bahiagrass to time, rate, and source of nitrogen. Fla. Agr. Exp. Sta. Tech. Bull. 581.

50. Kretschmer, A. E., Jr., and N. C. Hayslip. 1963. Evaluation of several pasture grasses on Immokalee fine sand in south Florida. Fla. Agr. Exp. Sta. Bull. 658.

❧ PLANT DESCRIPTION

Pangola digitgrass is a creeping perennial that grows to a height of 61–122 cm. It produces many semidecumbent surface runners that form roots at the joints or nodes. Seedstalks produce many branches but few viable seed.[48,51,52]

This grass is established vegetatively by using plants, stems, and runners. Rooted plants spaced 51–91 cm apart in 122-cm rows give good results. Green but rather mature stems and runners spread at the rate of 1 t/ha may be disked into the soil and packed. Planting can be done whenever moisture conditions are adequate and vegetative material is available. A 10-10-10 or similar complete fertilizer mixture should be applied at rates of 336–448 kg/ha before or just after sprigging on land newly prepared from the native condition.[48] Lime should be applied at the rate of 2.2 t/ha.

Composition of Pangola digitgrass compares favorably with other grasses. Dry matter and protein yields show it to be superior to bahiagrass, 'Coastal' bermudagrass, and guineagrass in the utilization of fertilizers. This superiority is demonstrated by significantly larger animal gains, especially under conditions of continuous grazing and during the critical dry seasons.[46,48] Daily gains and gains per ha similar to those of other grasses are produced in the northern area of adaptation.[46]

❧ IMPORTANCE AND USE

Pangola digitgrass has become one of the most important forage grasses in regions where it is adapted. Over 0.25 million ha are in use in central and southern Florida and 0.5 million ha have been planted in the Gulf Coast of Mexico.[47,48] It has been established in pastures in many subtropical and tropical areas throughout the world. Its principal use is as a pasture plant, but it is most suitable in intensive forage systems where some forage is harvested as high-quality hay or silage.

❧ CULTIVARS

Due to sterility and the lack of plant variation within the species no other cultivars of Pangola digitgrass exist. 'Slenderstem' digitgrass, *Digiteria pentzii* Stent., has been released for the poorly drained soils of southern and central Florida.[53] Digitgrass was used as the common name for species of the genus *Digiteria* with the recommendation that the name 'Pangola' be applied only to *D. decumbens*. Adoption of digitgrass as the common name would permit Slenderstem, Pangola, 'Kuruman' digitgrass, *D. seriata* Stent., and other species of *Digiteria* to be treated as cultivars.

❧ CULTURE AND MANAGEMENT

Annual applications of 450 kg/ha of a 12-6-6 or similar fertilizer applied at one or more dates is required to maintain Pangola digitgrass in a productive condition for pastures.[46,48,50] Alternate applications of 10-10-10 or similar fertilizer plus some source of N can be used on pastures fertilized at two or more dates annually. The grass should be 15–30 cm in height at time of treatment.

Harvest of 3 t of grass for hay or 12 t for silage or planting material removes 68 kg of N, 34 kg of P, and 68 kg of K per ha.[48] These nutrients must be replaced following harvest to produce rapid regrowth and high-quality forage. These amounts are contained in 675 kg of a 10–5–10 fertilizer.

Pangola digitgrass should be grazed rotationally, allowing one week between periods in midsummer and two to three weeks during the rest of the growing season. Extremely close grazing is not harm-

51. Sheth A. A., Lillian Yu, and John Edwardson. 1956. Sterility in pangolagrass. *Agron. J.* 58:505–7.
52. Shank, S. C., H. F. Decker, G. B. Killinger, and R. J. Allen, Jr. 1966. Agronomic and cytotoxonomic comparisons between *Digitaria decumbens* and *D. pentzii. Crop Sci.* 6:82–83.

53. McCaleb, J. E., and E. M. Hodges. 1969. Slenderstem digitgrass. Fla. Agr. Exp. Sta. Circ. S-201.

ful if grass is allowed to regrow to a height of 30–45 cm.

Most Pangola digitgrass hay is made in the late fall, October 1 to November 15, but can be made as late as January.[54] Silage made in July and August adds to the feed-producing potential of the grassland areas.[55]

Levels of fertilization above 225 kg N/ha annually should be avoided where winter-killing is an important factor. This grass is sensitive to Cu deficiency and benefits from the application of 0.05 to 0.8 units Cu/ha. This may be obtained from CuO or $CuSO_4$.

❧ INSECTS

The yellow sugarcane aphid, *Sipha flava* (Forbes), is the major pest of Pangola digitgrass, especially in the southern areas of Florida. The nymph and adult forms of the two-lined spittlebug, *Prosapia bicincta* (Say), cause damage from July and August until cold weather.

Controlling or reducing the insect problem is accomplished by the rapid removal of herbage. This can be done by heavy grazing or removal of top growth for hay or silage. No insecticides are recommended. Insect infestations usually start in small isolated areas. Frequent inspections along with spot treatment usually prevent general infestations.[56]

SAINT AUGUSTINEGRASS

Saint augustinegrass, *Stenotaphrum secundatum* (Walt.) Kuntze, is a native of the West Indies, Australia, and southern Mexico. It is also found in South Africa from Cape Town to Natal. It has been introduced into southern France and Italy and probably came to the U.S. from Cuba.

❧ DISTRIBUTION AND ADAPTATION

Saint augustinegrass is found along the southern Atlantic and Gulf Coast regions from South Carolina to Florida and Texas. It is not winter-hardy much over 320 km north of the Gulf. Naturally a seashore plant, it will withstand salt spray. It is adapted to practically all soil types, especially muck soils, provided plenty of moisture is present. This grass thrives in partial shade.

❧ PLANT DESCRIPTION

Saint augustinegrass is broad-leaved and generally light green or yellowish green in color. It is an extensively creeping, rather coarse smooth perennial. It produces stolons with long intervals and branches that are short, leafy, and flat. This grass forms a dense sod and usually crowds out other grasses and weeds.

It will grow to a height of 10–46 cm under conditions of high soil fertility and abundant moisture. A recent summary of 10 years of data showed an average annual animal consumption of 63,222 kg/ha of green forage containing approximately 9408 kg of TDN. Average analyses were 24.4% dry matter of which 15.3% was crude protein, 28.1% crude fiber, 3.1% ether extract, and 8.8% ash.[57]

❧ IMPORTANCE AND USE

Saint augustinegrass is well suited and primarily used for lawns.[58] It is not considered an important pasture plant except in limited areas.[57,59,60] It is especially adapted to moist muck soils and is considered the most dependable pasture grass for

54. Kretschmer, A. E., Jr. 1965. The effect of nitrogen fertilization of mature pangolagrass just prior to utilization in winter on yields, dry matter, and crude protein contents. *Agron. J.* 57:529–34.
55. Semple, J. A. 1966. The preparation and feeding value of pangolagrass silage. *Trop. Agr.* 43:251–55.
56. Strayer, J. R. 1966. Pasture insect control. Fla. Agr. Ext. Serv. Circ. 292.

57. Haines, C. E., H. L. Chapman, Jr., R. J. Allen, Jr., and R. W. Kiddler. 1965. Roselawn saint augustinegrass as a perennial pasture forage for organic soils of south Florida. Fla. Agr. Exp. Sta. Bull. 689.
58. Wise, L. N. 1961. The Lawn Book. Bowen Press, Decatur, Ga.
59. Stansel, R. H., E. B. Reynolds, and J. H. Jones. 1939. Pasture improvement in the Gulf Coast prairie of Texas. Tex. Agr. Exp. Sta. Bull. 570.
60. Jones, D. W., E. M. Hodges, and W. G. Kirk. 1960. Year-round grazing on a combination of native and improved pastures. Fla. Agr. Exp. Sta. Bull. 554A.

the organic soils of southern Florida where growth is practically yearlong.[57,61]

❧ CULTIVARS

The 'Roselawn' cultivar was released in 1943 and 1944 for use as a pasture forage. Much breeding is being conducted at present for the production of improved types for lawns.

❧ CULTURE AND MANAGEMENT

Management practices consist of fertilization, rate of stocking, and pasture supplementation. Saint augustinegrass pastures on muck soil should receive annual applications of 340–560 kg/ha of a 0-8-24, 0-10-20, or 0-12-16 fertilizer containing 1% CuO. The pastures should carry 7 yearlings/ha all year by using the surplus forage for silage.[57,60,62] This plant does not produce seed.

❧ DISEASES AND INSECTS

No serious reduction in forage production has been reported due to diseases and insects. Brown patch, *Pellicularia filamentosa* (Pat.) Rogers, and gray leaf spot, *Piricularia grisea* Cke. & Sacc., are the most common diseases. The chinch bug, *Blissus leucopterus* (Say), is the most serious pest.

OTHER GRASSES OF MINOR IMPORTANCE

❧ RESCUEGRASS

Rescuegrass, *Bromus catharticus* Vahl., is adapted to regions of the South and Southwest where the winters are mild and humid. Its agricultural value is limited to areas southward from North Carolina and Tennessee and in areas of the Pacific Coast. It is a short-lived perennial bunchgrass, acts as an annual under cultivation, and will not make a satisfactory growth on low-fertility soils without fertilization. It grows to a height of 61–122 cm, with drooping open panicles of large flattened spikelets containing seed almost as large as oats. It has a similar nutritive value to oats grown on soil of the same fertility. After the grass has reseeded, the area can be utilized for growing another crop in the summer. 'Lamont,' 'Chapel Hill,' 'Prairie Brome,' 'Naqura,' and 'Texas 46' are cultivars of this grass.

❧ NATALGRASS

Natalgrass, *Tricholaena rosea* Nees., is adapted to Florida, southern Texas, and southern California. It grows only in regions free from freezes and is especially adapted to well-drained, poor, dry sandy soils. A plant may form a tuft 60.9–92 cm in diameter with flowering culms 61–122 cm high. Flowers are produced all season on rosy colored panicles. It is used on areas highly infested with nematodes and produces palatable hay similar to timothy in nutritive value. As a pasture it is nutritious and readily grazed by livestock.

❧ PARAGRASS

Paragrass, *Brachiaria mutica* (Forsk.) Stapf is adapted to Florida and the Texas Gulf Coast. It grows on soils too moist for many other crops, on margins of lakes and streams, on marshes, and on bottomlands subject to prolonged overflow and is a pest in sugarcane fields in the Tropics. It is used as a soiling, hay, and pasture crop.

❧ NAPIERGRASS

Napiergrass, *Pennisetum purpureum* Schumach., is a tall perennial plant growing in clumps of 20–200 stalks, much the same as sugarcane. It grows 243–486 cm tall with stalks up to 2.5 cm in diameter. Its principal use is for soiling and grazing.

61. Chapman, H. L., Jr., R. W. Kidder, C. E. Haines, R. J. Allen, Jr., V. E. Green, Jr., and W. C. Forsee, Jr. 1965. Beef cattle production on organic soils of south Florida. Fla. Agr. Exp. Sta. Bull. 662.

62. Chapman, H. L., Jr., F. M. Peacock, W. G. Kirk, R. L. Shirley, and T. J. Cunha. 1964. Supplemental feeding of beef cattle on pasture in south Florida. Fla. Agr. Exp. Sta. Bull. 665.

New grass introductions and changing fertilizer practices are limiting its use. It is grazed or cut when approximately 180 cm high. With proper fertilization and management it is of considerable importance in the Tropics.[63]

❧ VASEYGRASS

Vaseygrass, *Paspalum urvillei* Steud., is commonly found through the lower South and especially on low wetland. Its general range is from North Carolina to Florida and west to Texas. It is a short erect perennial with many stems 61–183 cm high borne in clumps. It is seldom planted or cultivated but is utilized where found growing. Vaseygrass makes good hay with yields of 2–5 t/ha. This plant loses its palatability and quality with age. It is eliminated by overgrazing but is an excellent plant when properly managed.[64]

❧ CENTIPEDEGRASS

Centipedegrass, *Eremochloa ophiuroides* (Munro) Hack., is a low-growing, creeping perennial with a medium leaf width, light green in color. It spreads by short-jointed, thick leafy stolons. It will grow both on clay soils and sandy soils if enough plant food and moisture are available for establishment. Its yields are less than carpetgrass, bermudagrass, and bahiagrass, and it has a lower protein content. Because of low nutritive value its use is principally for lawns and erosion control.

❧ QUESTIONS

1. Why is johnsongrass considered a noxious weed in some areas, while in others it is considered a valuable forage crop?
2. How does johnsongrass differ from other species of sorghum?
3. How should johnsongrass be managed to obtain high yields and maintain stands?
4. What are the characteristics of dallisgrass that make it one of the leading perennial grasses in the South?
5. How is dallisgrass best utilized?
6. What are the principal factors for establishment and management of dallisgrass for maximum forage production?
7. Compare Pangola digitgrass with other forage grasses grown in its region of adaptation.
8. What is the principal use made of saint augustinegrass? Why is its use for other purposes limited?
9. What is the principal advantage of natalgrass over some of the other grasses grown in the South?
10. Where and why is napiergrass of considerable importance?
11. Where is paragrass best used for pasture? Why?
12. Why is vaseygrass of some importance in the lower South?

---

63. Oakes, A. J. 1967. Effect of nitrogen fertilization and plant spacing on yield and composition of napiergrass in the dry Tropics. *Trop. Agr.* 44:77–82.
64. Bennett, H. W., and C. L. Blount. 1958. Utilization of vaseygrass. Miss. Agr. Exp. Sta. Info. Sheet 594.

HENRY A. FRIBOURG / *University of Tennessee*

33

SUMMER ANNUAL GRASSES AND CEREALS FOR FORAGE

❧

EFFICIENT livestock production is limited by the lack of adequate amounts of high-quality forage in summer. Most perennial cool-season forages become semidormant during the hot summer months, and most perennial warm-season forages do not produce enough high-quality forage. The summer annuals include members of several gramineous genera such as *Sorghum* and *Pennisetum*. The more productive cultivars are characterized by rapid growth of nutritious forage in late spring and summer and are used for pasture, green chop, silage, and hay. Their use depends upon many factors: geographical and environmental conditions, nature and allocation of soil resources, characteristics of the farm enterprise, and economic considerations.

Another limitation to livestock production is low winter temperature which reduces or prevents plant growth in northern climates. Corn silage and small-grain hay or silage are stored for use when other feeds are unavailable. Grazing small grains

❧ HENRY A. FRIBOURG is Professor of Plant and Soil Science, University of Tennessee. He holds the M.S. degree from Cornell University and the Ph.D. from Iowa State University. His special interest is the ecology of forage plants and the prediction of the response of crops to environmental and management factors.

is a common practice in fall, winter, and early spring when climatic factors allow.

Sorghums, millets, and small grains are valuable in the development of year-round forage systems, particularly where quality is important, as with lactating or rapidly growing animals.

❧ DISTRIBUTION AND ADAPTATION

SUMMER ANNUAL GRASSES

Sorghums used for forage in the U.S. include grain sorghums, *Sorghum bicolor* (L.) Moench; sorgos and grass sorghums, *S. bicolor;* and sudangrass, *S. bicolor*[1] [formerly *S. sudanense* (Piper) Stapf]. Sorghums and pearlmillet, *Pennisetum Americanum* (L.) Leeke[1a] [formerly *P. typhoides* (Burm.) Stapf & C. E. Hubb.], can endure considerable moisture stress. They can be grown where annual precipitation is as low as 400–650 mm but grow better with more moisture or when irrigated, especially in the southwestern U.S. They can resume vegetative growth after a dormant period induced by drought.

1. Harlan, J. R., and J. M. J. de Wet. 1972. A simplified classification of cultivated sorghum. *Crop Sci.* 12: 172–76.
1a. Terrell, E. E. 1976. The correct names for pearlmillet and yellow foxtail. *Taxon* 25:297–304.

The most favorable temperatures for growth range between 25 and 30 C; the minimum is about 15 C. Pearlmillet is more sensitive than sorghums to lower temperatures; early plantings of sorghums exposed during germination or the seedling stage to early morning temperatures of 5–10 C may survive when pearlmillet seedlings are killed. Sorghums and pearlmillet are rarely grown above 2000–2700 m in the Southwest, and this elevation limit decreases further north. In the East they are grown from Florida to 42° N. Their range extends from southern Texas to Minnesota and North Dakota in the central grassland regions. Foxtail or Italian millet, *Setaria italica* (L.) Beauv., and other millets sometimes replace them in more northern latitudes.

Census data indicate approximately 7.3 million ha of sorghum are grown in the U.S. About 25% of this hectarage is grown for forage and the other 75% for grain or seed. Pearlmillet is grown on 50% of the 500,000 ha planted in millet. These data do not reflect small fields on farms throughout the U.S. that play an important role in supplying high-quality forage for good animal rations during summer.

The forage sorghums (or cane) are characterized by abundant juice in the culms which are 150–300 cm or more in height. The importance of forage sorghums rapidly increased in the 1960s with the advent of higher yielding hybrids derived from crosses among different groups. Likewise, improved pearlmillets led to an increase in their use. Although pearlmillet is as widely adapted as sorghum, it has been grown primarily in the Southeast because of tolerance to pathogens and high humidity. Most other millets are either not increasing or are decreasing in use.

Some sorghums and pearlmillets are short-day plants. However, many appear to be insensitive to length of dark period.[2] Summer annual grasses are best suited to soils with moderate to high available water supply where erosion is not a problem. They compete with row crops for allocation on highly productive soils; under such conditions their potentially high yields lower the unit cost and may justify their use. Moderately well-drained and imperfectly drained immature soils are well suited to summer annual grasses when excessive surface water is removed. Mature soils that are moderately well drained and imperfectly drained because of layers restrictive to water movement are not as well suited. Planting may be delayed in spring by wet conditions. Green chop or grazing may be difficult or undesirable when the soil is wet. In general, these soils have more available water for summer annual grasses than many well-drained sites. More uniform forage production can be obtained by judicious selection of soils from each of these groups, using appropriate dates of seeding and staggered plantings. Small amounts of alkali in the soil reduce performance considerably, though tolerance to salinity is moderate (4–8 mmhos/cm).[3] Moderately acid soil conditions down to pH 5.7 do not appreciably affect production.

Although seeding can be as early as March in southern Texas, date of planting is determined by the use intended for the crop. Seeding before soil temperature at 10 cm reaches 12–13 C can be hazardous, but later or multiple plantings often are made to equalize forage production throughout the season. In climates approaching subtropical, late summer–early fall plantings may also be made.

CEREALS

The small grains (excluding rice) are cool-season annuals. Fall-seeded small grains, especially in the more humid areas, grow when moisture is seldom a limiting factor. They are suited to a wide range of soils and cropping conditions but vary

2. Begg, J. E., and G. W. Burton. 1971. Comparative study of five genotypes of pearl millet under a range of photoperiods and temperatures. *Crop Sci.* 11:803–5.

3. Bernstein, L. 1964. Salt tolerance of plants. USDA Agr. Info. Bull. 283.

somewhat in their soil suitability and preference. Although rye, *Secale* spp., like wheat, *Triticum* spp., will produce best when grown on fertile well-drained soils of medium or heavier texture, it is more productive than other small grains on soils lower in acidity or fertility, higher in clay or sand content, or more poorly drained.

Warm temperatures during early growth of small grains increase vegetative growth and may delay heading. Winter wheat is generally more winter-hardy than winter barley, *Hordeum* spp., which is hardier than winter oats, *Avena* spp. However, winter rye can survive lower temperatures than other small grains. Some spring barley cultivars mature in about two months, even earlier than spring ryes, wheats, or oats. Winter-hardy barleys mature early enough to escape warm humid conditions. Barley is sensitive to poorly drained soil conditions, grows better in dry than moist hot climates, and can tolerate moderate droughts. Oats grow best in cool moist climates and are more tolerant of wet soil conditions than barley. They require more moisture than other small grains and tolerate a wider soil pH range and finer soil texture than wheat or barley when fertility and drainage are moderate. Wheat is particularly responsive to P fertilization. Generally, small grains tolerate moderate salinity or pH as low as 5–5.5. Barley can tolerate more salinity but less acidity than the other cereals. There is considerable variability for low pH tolerance among barley and wheat cultivars.

Crop improvement has resulted in the development of interspecific plants such as *Agrotricum;* new species such as *Triticale;* as well as many small-grain, corn (*Zea mays* L.) and sorghum cultivars with widely diverse characteristics and broad adaptation and distribution. Although cereal improvement in the past has been geared principally to improve tolerance to environmental factors, pathogens, and pests (and to greater grain yield), better forage production has been a by-product.

Since well-adapted corn cultivars can be harvested either for grain or silage, as feed and market situations and crop prospects dictate, the area devoted to silage production fluctuates with time. Sustained profitable production of corn and summer annual grasses usually is obtained when they are grown on well-drained and moderately well-drained soils which are not droughty and have level to undulating topography (Land Class I and, with adequate erosion control practices, Land Classes II and III). (See Terminology for description of land classes.) Grazing of small grains is practiced in almost every state when livestock is a part of the farm enterprise and environmental conditions permit or demand it. This practice is particularly prevalent south of 40° N. (See Fig. 33.1.)

❧ PLANT DESCRIPTION

SORGHUMS

Sorghum is a coarse erect grass with considerable variability in growth characteristics.[4] Height can range from 45 cm to over 5 m. Some tiller early, while others do not tiller until physiological maturity is reached, or they tiller in response to damage. Culm thickness varies greatly, ranging between 5 mm to over 3 cm. The culms are solid, though spaces may occur in the pith. They may be comparatively dry at maturity or have sweet or insipid juice. Root primordia occur at culm nodes, and prop roots may grow from these. There is a bud at each node from which a tiller may grow. Leaf blades commonly are similar in shape to those of corn but are shorter and may be wider. The blades are glabrous and waxy. The sheaths encircle the culm and have overlapping margins.

The inflorescence of sorghum is a panicle which is compact in most grain sorghums and open in sudangrass and some forage sorghums. Some sorghum cultivars have

4. Artschwager, E. 1948. Anatomy and morphology of the vegetative organs of *Sorghum vulgare.* USDA Tech. Bull. 957.

FIG. 33.1. *Grazing small grains . . . practiced . . . when livestock . . . part of the farm enterprise.* Dairy animals grazing a rye-wheat mixture in April in New Jersey. *Rutgers Univ. photo.*

is a thick cylindrical spike 20–50 cm long and 2–4 cm in diameter. The caryopsis threshes free at maturity. Pearlmillet is largely cross-pollinated since the stigmas appear before the anthers are protruded. The spike flowers from the tip downward over several days.

Pearlmillet seed is usually yellowish and much larger than the hulled seed of other millets. Pearlmillet will average 200,000 seed/kg, and foxtail millet 500,000 seed/kg.

Browntop millet, *Panicum ramosum* L., is a rapidly growing annual, 60–120 cm tall, with a yellow to brown panicle 5–15 cm long. It shatters seed in sufficient amounts to reseed. Foxtail millet is an annual with slender, erect, and leafy culms which grow from 30 to 175 cm. Its inflorescence is a dense, cylindrical, bristly panicle 5–30 cm long. Japanese millet, *Echinochloa crusgalli* var. *frumentacea* (Roxb.) W. F. Wight, is coarser and grows better under cool conditions than foxtail millet.

SMALL GRAINS

The morphology of cereal plants and inflorescences is well known and distinctive for each species. When grown for pasture, it is useful to be able to identify small grains when they are vegetative and small. The wheat ligule encircles the culm and is sharply curved; hairy auricles are present. Rye leaf blades are coarser and more bluish than those of wheat. The ligules are short and rounded; auricles are white, narrow, or absent. In barley the sheath is generally glabrous and ligules are short or truncate. The glabrous auricles partially or entirely clasp the culm and are larger than those of wheat or rye. The ligule of oats is well developed and toothed, whereas it is blunt in other small grains. Oats have no auricles. In all species many differences among cultivars and a wide range of plant characteristics exist. Familiarity with commonly grown cultivars in an area is essential for the identification of small plants.

seed that are completely covered by glumes not removed in threshing; most have seed that thresh free from the glumes. Panicles usually are erect but sometimes recurve. A sorghum panicle may contain as many as 6000 fertile spikelets. Sorghum is generally self-pollinated, but considerable cross-fertilization can occur, depending on environmental conditions.

Sorghum cultivars have grains of different sizes, small in comparison to those of corn. Grain sorghums may have 25,000–60,000 seed/kg, whereas grass sorghums will have 120,000–150,000; seed size of hybrids is intermediate. The seed may be white, yellow, red or brown; and some of the darker colored seed may contain considerable amounts of tannin.

MILLETS

Pearlmillet is an erect annual grass that may grow to a 2–5 m height. The leaf blades are long and pointed and have finely serrated margins. The stems are pithy. Tillering occurs freely from lateral meristems borne at each node. In some cultivars tillering may occur from nodes 20 cm or more from ground level. The inflorescence

❧ IMPORTANCE AND USE

SUMMER ANNUAL GRASSES

Some sorghum cultivars may produce more dry matter per ha than corn; however, these types usually are low in grain content. Cattle, sheep, and horses can use sorghum for maintenance, growth, and fattening, though most consumption is by dairy cattle and some by beef cattle. The use of sorghum silage for lactating dairy cows is increasing. Sorghum and pearlmillet as green chop for dairy cows is an increasingly common practice; grazing of these crops by growing beef cattle is done on a much more limited basis.

Feedlot rations containing 50–65% sorghum forage have been used successfully, and lambs have been fattened on rations of sorghum forage and grain supplemented with protein. Sorghum rations must be supplemented with vitamin A, Ca and other minerals, and protein. If sorghum grain is fed, it should be cracked or rolled for best animal digestibility.

Later maturing sorghum cultivars, which produce more than earlier maturing types, may not reach maturity before a killing frost. However, frosted sorghums and corn can be successfully ensiled with minimal adverse effects on their chemical composition.[5,6]

Sorghum silage has largely replaced corn silage in the high plains region of the Southwest because of high yields.[7] In the higher rainfall areas corn silage is considered superior to sorghum silage because of its higher energy.[8,9] New sorghum hybrid cultivars which produce large quantities of both grain and stover have produced acceptable silage, but the stage of maturity at harvest greatly influences the composition of silage. In general, best animal performance is obtained from feeding silages from plants cut after physiological maturity but before senescence is too marked.[10] The grain, or energy, content is of great importance and should be as high as possible. Highest quality silage is obtained when crop nutrients, as affected by soil fertility, are kept in balance.[11] Differences in yield caused by differences in growing conditions for forage sorghums consist mostly of differences in culm production.[12]

Sorghums are sometimes cut for hay. During a growing season two to five harvests can be attempted, each one having a potential yield of 2 t/ha or more. The plants are difficult to cure because of their thick culms; even grass sorghums, such as sudangrass, which have thinner culms may be difficult to cure due to the large mass of material to be dried. Several days of sunshine are needed, although use of a forage crusher helps reduce this time. Bleaching and discoloration are common side effects. Pearlmillet is seldom made into hay, although sometimes other millets are grown in mixture with soybeans for this purpose.

SMALL GRAINS

The best choice of a small grain for forage depends on the cropping system and the time of seeding. Barley or oats may be preferred for an early fall seeding following corn harvested for silage. Later plantings of wheat or rye may be used because of their greater winterhardiness. Since there is a better market for grain of wheat, oats, or barley than for rye, their use provides greater flexibility. In a multiple

5. Burns, J. C., R. F. Barnes, W. F. Wedin, C. L. Rhykerd, and C. H. Noller. 1970. Nutritional characteristics of forage sorghum and sudangrass after frost. *Agron. J.* 62:348–50.
6. Dotzenko, A. D., W. E. Turner, and K. Takeda. 1968. The effects of frost on the chemical composition of sorghum and corn silages. Colo. Agr. Exp. Sta. Bull. 534S.
7. Quinby, J. R., and P. T. Marion. 1960. Production and feeding of forage sorghum in Texas. Tex. Agr. Exp. Sta. Bull. 965.
8. Moore, J. E., M. E. McCullough, and M. J. Montgomery. 1971. Composition and digestibility of southern forages. Fla. Agr. Exp. Sta. Southern Coop. Ser. Bull. 165.
9. Genter, C. F. 1960. Corn and other crops for silage in Virginia. Va. Agr. Exp. Sta. Bull. 516.
10. Chamberlain, C. C., H. A. Fribourg, K. M. Barth, J. H. Felts, and J. M. Anderson. 1971. Effect of maturity of corn silage at harvest on the performance of feeder heifers. *J. Anim. Sci.* 33:161–66.
11. Keeney, D. R., B. R. Baumgardt, P. J. Stangel, G. B. Beestman, and R. H. Stauffacher. 1967. Effect of soil fertility on the quality of crops grown for silage. Wis. Agr. Exp. Sta. Res. Rept. 29.
12. Thurman, R. L., O. T. Stallcup, and C. E. Reames. 1960. Quality factors of sorgo as a silage crop. Ark. Agr. Exp. Sta. Bull. 632.

cropping system, the earlier maturity of barley over that of wheat will result in less delay in planting of summer annual grasses, corn, or soybeans. Wheat yields as much forage as rye or barley, more than oats, and is higher in quality than rye. Rye grows better at low temperatures but becomes stemmy earlier in spring. Barley is less palatable than wheat but more so than rye. Oats are often preferred because the fine stems lead to easy curing and high palatability. Barley is chosen in the West for its greater drought resistance, and rye in northern areas for its coldhardiness. Smooth-awned or awnless cultivars are preferred since rough awns can seriously irritate livestock mouths.

GENERAL CONSIDERATIONS

Pasturing is the cheapest method of harvesting forage, although efficient utilization of fast-growing summer annuals and cereals demands considerable attention to many details of plant and animal management. Since grazing animals selectively consume certain plant portions, they may produce more milk or meat per animal than if they are hand-fed the whole plant. However, grazing leads to waste by trampling or fouling by excreta. Plant management may be easier under a green chop system, and feed needs are better matched to livestock requirements. Both systems are used with forage sorghums and pearlmillet with equally desirable results.

Summer annuals and small grains are generally more suitable for lactating dairy cows, where a continuous supply of high-quality forage is essential, than when used with steers except for short periods.[13] Small grains are used extensively for both lactating and growing animals in areas where winters are mild, providing high-quality pasture at moderate cost. The seeding of small grains in thin old alfalfa stands or in sods of dormant warm-season perennial grasses may use limited land resources more profitably.

❧ CULTIVARS

Since the mid-1950s, plant breeders have created many sorghum hybrids which are well adapted to specific environments and uses. The term "sorghum-sudangrass hybrids" has been used to describe these, resulting in considerable confusion since the phenotypic expression of genetic characteristics within the genus is a continuum from one extreme to the other.[1] Generally, the male parent used is a fertile sudangrass. The male-sterile female parent can be another sudangrass, a sorghum with either sweet or insipid juice, or a grain sorghum. Crosses involving three or more parents can also be made. Prior to the advent of these hybrids most improved cultivars available in the U.S. were products of breeding programs conducted under the auspices of the USDA and state experiment stations. The hybrids, however, have been developed primarily by industry. Some seed companies have active breeding programs from which have issued unique gene recombinations and cultivars excellent in many characteristics.

There are fewer pearlmillet cultivars than sorghum cultivars. Future breeding goals for summer annuals in addition to high yields will be: lower prussic acid and fiber contents; increased palatability, cold tolerance, and drought tolerance; higher sugar content and leaf-stem ratios; greater resistance to leaf diseases and insect pests; faster regrowth after harvest; and increased intake by ruminants.

In most regions the same corn or small-grain cultivars used for grain production are recommended for forage production, although cultivars within a species can vary widely in their forage production.[14] Small-grain cultivars that are winter-hardy, tiller extensively, and have a high leaf-stem ratio are preferred for forage. Bearded

13. Hoveland, C. S., R. R. Harris, J. K. Boseck, and W. B. Webster. 1971. Supplementation of steers grazing sorghum-sudan pasture. Ala. Agr. Exp. Sta. Circ. 188.

14. Holt, E. C., M. J. Norris, and J. A. Lancaster. 1969. Production and management of small grains for forage. Tex. Agr. Exp. Sta. Bull. B-1082.

wheats and barleys are undesirable for hay.

Since the number of available cultivars is large, reference to the latest cultivar performance reports or descriptions by the USDA, state experiment station, extension service, or state university is advised.[15,16]

❧ CULTURE AND MANAGEMENT

SUMMER ANNUAL GRASSES

ESTABLISHMENT. Adequate germination of sorghums and pearlmillet takes place when the soil temperature is between 20 and 30 C; much poorer germination occurs at lower or higher soil temperatures.[17] Poor stands usually result from very early or very late plantings. Although some late plantings are justified when staggered production is desired, they will result in low yields because growth will be hampered by cool fall temperatures, summer droughts, and long nights.[18] Inadequate surface soil moisture also makes late planting riskier. A well-prepared, firm, moist seedbed is best, though acceptable stands may be established with stubble-planting machinery. Seeding should be at depths of 1.5–5 cm, depending on soil moisture and texture. Compaction of the seedbed is desirable after seeding if it is dry or precipitation is not anticipated before seedling emergence.

SEEDING RATES AND SPACING. Summer annual grasses can be drilled, broadcast, or sown in rows with or without a lister, in double rows on beds, or in rows too narrow to cultivate. The narrower the spacing, the heavier the seeding rate needed. Smaller yields result occasionally from seeding rates of less than 10–20 kg/ha.[19] At low seeding rates, culm diameter may be increased 20–35%, increasing hay drying time. Higher seeding rates, up to 50 kg/ha, give higher first-harvest yields and thinner culms and may decrease drying time.[20] Normal seeding rates are 20–30 kg/ha. The seeding rate should be heavy for large-seeded cultivars and decreased for smaller seeded plants like sudangrass or pearlmillet.

Row spacing has relatively little effect on total forage production, but grazing animals can damage drilled or broadcast seedings. Seeding rate and row spacing therefore will depend upon the intended use. Although broadcast or drilled plantings make more efficient use of solar energy and produce more in the first growth than wide-row stands,[21] total seasonal production is usually the same unless the number of harvests is small.[22] If the number of seed per square meter is kept constant, increasing the width of row may decrease production. As seeding rate increases, intrarow competition reduces the percentage of established plants,[23] because tillering is inversely related to plant spacing and tillering in regrowth compensates for differences in initial plant spacing. Within a row spacing, plant size is inversely related to plant number. Orientation of wide rows may have some effect on yield because of insolation effects. North-south rows may yield 10% more than east-west rows when harvesting is done frequently in an immature stage.

GROWTH HABITS. Species and cultivars within species are widely different in growth habits and performance. Cultivar 'Trudan 2' produced more digestible

15. Hanson, A. A. 1963. Summer annual forage grasses in the United States. USDA Agr. Handbook 238.
16. Hanson, A. A. 1972. Grass varieties in the United States. USDA Agr. Handbook 170, rev.
17. Sumner, D. C., H. S. Etchegaray, J. E. Gregory, and W. Lusk. 1968. Summer pasture and greenchop from sudangrass, hybrid sudangrass, and sorghum × sudangrass crosses. Calif. Agr. Exp. Sta. Circ. 547.
18. Beuerlein, J. E., H. A. Fribourg, and F. F. Bell. 1968. Effects of environment and cutting on the regrowth of a sorghum-sudangrass hybrid. Crop Sci. 8:152–55.
19. Burger, A. W., and W. F. Campbell. 1961. Effect of rates and methods of seeding on the original stand, tillering, stem diameter, leaf-stem ratio, and yield of sudangrass. Agron. J. 53:289–91.

20. Burger, A. W., C. N. Hittle, and D. W. Graffis. 1961. Effect of variety and rate of seeding on the drying rate of sudangrass herbage for hay. Agron. J. 53:198–201.
21. Begg, J. E., J. F. Bierhuizen, E. R. Lemon, D. K. Misra, R. O. Slatyer, and W. R. Stern. 1964. Diurnal energy and water exchanges in bulrush millet in an area of high solar radiation. Agr. Meteorol. 1:294–312.
22. Koller, H. R., and J. M. Scholl. 1968. Effect of row spacing and seeding rate on forage production and chemical composition of two sorghum cultivars harvested at two cutting frequencies. Agron. J. 60:456–59.
23. Holt, E. C. 1970. Relationship of hybrid sudangrass plant populations to plant growth characteristics. Agron. J. 62:494–96.

dry matter than other sorghum hybrids when harvested at a 40-cm height, but 'Sudax SX-11' produced more when harvested at the dough stage, even though the percent digestibility within each stage was about the same for several hybrids.[24] The types of plants are very different among and even within hybrids, ranging from those with long thin stalks to short thick stalks and from very compact heads to open panicles. Just as wide a range probably exists in characteristics of internal morphology, physiology, or chemical components. A gradual increase in digestible dry matter production was observed in 'Gahi-1' pearlmillet when the frequency of harvest was increased from six weeks to four-, three-, and two-week intervals. 'Funk's 77' decreased an abrupt 40% when the cutting frequency was changed from six to four weeks.[25]

MECHANICAL DAMAGE. The wheel pressure of implements on the stubble at the time of cutting can seriously affect regrowth ability and decrease productivity of summer annual grasses. Node tissue can be damaged and bud development prevented.[26] Passage of a tractor wheel over the row at each of five cuttings decreased yield by 20% on a silt loam soil in Tennessee. When the tractor wheel was followed by a loaded wagon wheel, an additional 10% loss was sustained. These treatments increased bulk density about 20% in the top 4 cm of soil, thereby affecting soil aeration and water infiltration. Thus the harvest method contemplated should influence the planting pattern selected, and plants should not be green chopped when the soil is very wet.

HARVESTING MANAGEMENT. A thin-culmed sorghum or pearlmillet recovers more rapidly after cutting and can tolerate closer grazing or cutting than one with thicker culms (Fig. 33.2). Stubble height and height or stage of growth when harvested influence not only total or digestible dry matter yields but leafiness most particularly. Gahi-1 pearlmillet 50-cm growth cut to a 2.5-cm stubble yielded 7 t/ha containing 40% leaf, whereas 75-cm growth cut to a 25-cm stubble yielded 14 t/ha containing 90% leaf.[27] The regrowth of summer annual grasses depends not only on the amount of photosynthetic area left on the stubble but also on the presence and growth of terminal, axillary, and basal meristems. As the height of defoliation is raised, regrowth from terminal meristems increases. Basal and axillary tillering increases as the point of defoliation is lowered.[28] These relationships affect not only total production but also its seasonal distribution, since higher stubbles shift production to later periods in the summer. Low stubbles are more detrimental to some cultivars than to others; pearlmillet is more sensitive to low stubble height than some sorghum cultivars. Since regrowth must come from terminal or axillary meristems, higher stubbles generally lead to more vigorous and leafier regrowth. Stubbles lower than 15–10 cm will result in considerable reduction of regrowth or even death of the plants. However, relationships have not been found between stubble carbohydrate content and yield or further storage after the first cut.[29] (See Fig. 33.3.)

The greatest dry matter yields of pearlmillet and sorghum for forage are realized when the plants are allowed to approach

24. Wedin, W. F. 1970. Digestible dry matter, crude protein, and dry matter yields of grazing-type sorghum cultivars as affected by harvest frequency. *Agron. J.* 62:359–63.

25. Hoveland, C. S., E. L. Carden, W. B. Anthony, and J. P. Cunningham. 1969. Effects of management on yield and digestibility of summer annual grasses. *Ala. Agr. Exp. Sta. Highlights of Agr. Res.* 16 (2):5.

26. Dovrat, A., and N. Ophir. 1965. The effect of number of cuttings, seeding rate and row spacing on the yield and leaf area index of pearl millet (*Pennisetum glaucum* (L.) R. BR.) *Israel J. Agr. Res.* 15:179–86.

27. Fribourg, H. A. 1965. The effect of morphology and defoliation intensity on the tillering, regrowth and leafiness of pearlmillet, *Pennisetum typhoides* (Burm.) Stapf & C. E. Hubb. *Proc. 9th Int. Grassl. Congr.,* pp. 489–91 (São Paulo, Brazil).

28. Clapp, J. G., Jr., and D. S. Chamblee. 1970. Influence of different defoliation systems on the regrowth of pearl millet, hybrid sudangrass, and two sorghum-sudangrass hybrids from terminal, axillary, and basal buds. *Crop Sci.* 10:345–49.

29. Holt, E. C., and G. D. Alston. 1968. Response of sudangrass hybrids to cutting practices. *Agron. J.* 60:303–6.

FIG. 33.2. *Thin culmed . . . recover more rapidly . . . can tolerate closer grazing.* Sorghum cultivars respond differently to management. Both cultivars were planted the same day and when 50 cm tall were cut back to 15 cm. Note the poor regrowth and high culm mortality of the thick-culmed cultivar (left) as compared to the numerous tillers and good regrowth of the thin-culmed cultivar (right).

maturity or at least heights of 80–120 cm. Although such heights may be considered for silage, green chop, or hay, they are not suitable for grazing. Most uniform grazing and least waste are achieved when grazing animals are turned into fields of grass 20–30 cm in height. Best regrowth is obtained if grazing is suspended when at least 15–10 cm of growth and some succulent plant parts containing buds are left. Rotational or strip grazing provide opti-

mum management where two or more areas are grazed successively.

FERTILIZATION. The effects of fertilizer N on summer annual grasses have been studied much more than those resulting from additions of lime and fertilizer P and K. Summer annuals will grow on low-fertility or moderately acid soils but grow best at more favorable soil fertility levels. In the East, lime applications may increase

FIG. 33.3. *Higher stubbles shift production . . . later periods . . . summer.* Summer annual grasses provide high-quality feed in summer when well managed (left), but poor management results in misuse of land resources, little regrowth later in the season, and hungry livestock (right).

production, particularly when the soil pH is less than 5. Sorghum hybrids are more sensitive to low pH and to low soil P and K availability than pearlmillet. Generally, the summer annual grasses are fertilized with 30–60 kg/ha of P and 60–120 kg/ha of K even though yield responses to such applications often have not been demonstrated on soils with medium amounts of available P and K. Since chemical soil testing, coupled in each region with field response studies, is a good method of estimating soil acidity and content of available nutrients, state soil-testing services should be used to pinpoint soil fertility problems and to predict plant response to fertilizer applications.

Approximately 30–50 kg/ha of P and 150–200 kg/ha of K can be removed by a high-yielding summer annual crop. Even higher amounts of K may be removed when K is abundantly available since luxury consumption may lead to more than 6% K in the dry forage. Fertilization affects forage yield and may also influence forage quality and animal performance. High Ca and K fertilizer levels have been associated with more severe milk-fat depression when pearlmillet was fed to lactating cows than when no fertilizer was used. These effects appear related to organic acid constituents of the forage which are themselves influenced by fertilization.[30]

Linear responses of summer annual grasses to N fertilization up to 200 kg/ha have been reported.[17,31] Increased yields are obtained from N fertilization when the N is applied in several increments rather than as a single application. Split applications are essential for uniform growth and balanced nutrition of plants, especially at the higher rates. In warmer and more humid climates with longer growing seasons, up to 15–20 t/ha of dry forage have been produced with 400 kg/ha of N or more. Even though summer annuals are

more drought tolerant than many other plants, the plant response to N applications is greater with adequate moisture; adequate fertilization also increases water-use efficiency if increased yields result from the fertilization.

DIGESTIBILITY AND ANIMAL INTAKE. Since forages are grown to feed animals, the digestibility and composition of the plant material and the voluntary intake by the consumer are of paramount importance. Generally, summer annual grasses are of moderate to high digestibility and are readily consumed by livestock if they are in a vegetative stage of growth. Good quality forage has a high leaf-stem ratio, is high in protein and digestible nutrients, and is low in fiber and lignin. Cutting and grazing management, nature of growth, moisture supply, night length, and sometimes temperature are more important and critical in the production of summer annual forages than of cool-season ones. Positive correlations between leafiness and dry matter digestibility have been established for pearlmillet and for a sorghum.[32,33] Leafiness is related more to stage of growth and height than to time elapsed since a previous harvest. Although the physiologic state and the genotype of the animal as well as soil fertility, moisture availability, and previous management and stage of growth of the plant all have considerable influence on intake and digestibility, cultivars and plant parts are different in animal utilization even when these other factors are held constant.[24] High lignin content has been related to advancing maturity and decreased animal intake and digestibility.[34,35] Young leaf blades may approach

30. Schneider, B. A., N. A. Clark, R. W. Hemken, and J. H. Vandersall. 1970. Relationship of pearl millet to milk fat depression in dairy cows. II. Forage organic acids as influenced by soil nutrients. *J. Dairy Sci.* 53:305–10.

31. Jung, G. A., and R. L. Reid. 1966. Sudangrass—Studies on its yield, management, chemical composition and nutritive value. W. Va. Agr. Exp. Sta. Bull. 524T.

32. Hart, R. H. 1967. Digestibility, morphology, and chemical composition of pearl millet. *Crop Sci.* 7:581–84.

33. Edwards, N. C., Jr., H. A. Fribourg, and M. J. Montgomery. 1971. Cutting management effects on growth rate and dry matter digestibility of the sorghum-sudangrass cultivar Sudax SX-11. *Agron. J.* 63:267–71.

34. Rusoff, L. L., A. S. Achacoso, C. L. Mondart, Jr., and F. L. Bonner. 1961. Relationship of lignin to other chemical constituents in sudan and millet forages. La. Agr. Exp. Sta. Bull. 542.

35. Ademosum, A. A., B. R. Baumgardt, and J. M. Scholl. 1968. Evaluation of a sorghum-sudangrass hybrid at varying stages of maturity on the basis of intake, digestibility and chemical composition. *J. Anim. Sci.* 27:818–23.

75% digestibility, while older leaves may be only 50–60% digestible, and culms may be as low as 30–50%. Well-managed pastures of summer annual grasses result in animal performance levels similar to those obtained from alfalfa.[36] However, consumption varies among cultivars and is related to chemical constituents and their fluctuation with time, environment, and stage of growth.[37,38] The highest protein and digestibility result from the most frequently harvested forage.

MECHANICAL HARVESTING. Harvesting summer annual grasses for green chop or silage is well suited to mechanization because of the bulk and mass involved. Equipment has a low labor requirement and one man can cut, haul, store, and dispense the feed from large areas. Green chop may require daily cutting, but it allows for maximum management control and efficient use of resources by the producer and also limits feed selection by animals. Green-chopped pearlmillet tends to have a laxative effect on cows and has been used only to a limited extent.

Sorghum for silage should be harvested when seed are in the milk to dough stage but before leaf blades reach senescence. Earlier harvest will reduce harvested energy. When grain sorghum for silage was harvested in the milk, dough, and hard-seed stages, dry matter intake increased with maturity, but no differences in milk production were noted.[39] Although harvest in the hard-seed or later stages may lead to some loss of grain passing through the digestive tract, the appearance of some grains in the feces appears to bear little relation to animal performance. Finely chopped material (4–7 cm) will pack more firmly than shredded or coarsely chopped material. The highest quality of silage is obtained from sorghum cultivars of about 2 m mature height that have 20% or more of their dry matter yield as grain, although taller cultivars will produce more tonnage. Sorghum silage is slightly less palatable than corn silage and may require additives if low in grain content. Interplanting corn and sorghum in an attempt to hedge against unfavorable environmental conditions has not been advantageous in the Southeast.

SMALL GRAINS

SEEDING. Forage production in the fall is influenced by species and cultivar, time of seeding, seeding rate, temperature, precipitation, soil fertility, and grazing management.[40] Up to 50–100% heavier seeding rates are recommended in many areas for forage as compared to grain production. The hay is finer stemmed at higher seeding rates, but there is added danger of lodging. Heavier seed rates in early seedings favor early autumn production.[14] Lower seed rates, which encourage tillering, produce just as much spring growth. Early plantings usually result in increased autumn forage production but some early seeded cultivars are susceptible to disease or insects. Oat cultivars resistant to blight and rust in the early growth stages and wheat cultivars resistant to Hessian fly permit earlier planting dates in some regions. (See Fig. 33.4.)

In some areas winter grains are fall seeded into thin alfalfa stands to increase the yield of the first hay crop of the next growing season. In the South small grains and other plants are successfully established in dormant grass sods, using equipment with heavy furrow openers.[41,42] Although this practice may result in slightly

36. Spahr, S. L., E. E. Ormiston, and R. G. Peterson. 1967. Sorghum-sudan hybrid SX-11, Piper sudan grass, and alfalfa-orchardgrass for dairy pastures. *J. Dairy Sci.* 50: 1925–34.

37. Rabas, D. L., A. R. Schmid, and G. C. Marten. 1970. Relationship of chemical composition and morphological characteristics to palatability in sudangrass and sorghum × sudangrass hybrids. *Agron. J.* 62:762–63.

38. Farhoomand, M. B., and W. F. Wedin. 1968. Changes in composition of sudangrass and forage sorghum with maturity. *Agron. J.* 60:459–63.

39. Browning, C. B., and J. W. Lusk. 1967. Effect of stage of maturity at harvest on nutritive value of combine-type grain sorghum silage. *J. Dairy Sci.* 50:81–85.

40. Denman, C. E., and J. Arnold. 1970. Seasonal forage production for small grains species in Oklahoma. Okla. Agr. Exp. Sta. Bull. B-680.

41. Dudley, R. F., and L. N. Wise. 1953. Seeding in permanent pasture for supplementary winter grazing. Miss. Agr. Exp. Sta. Bull. 505.

42. Decker, A. M., H. J. Retzer, F. G. Swain, and R. F. Dudley. 1969. Midland bermudagrass forage production supplemented by sod-seeded cool-season annual forages. Md. Agr. Exp. Sta. Bull. 484.

FIG. 33.4. *Winter grains . . . fall seeded . . . increase the yield . . . first hay crop.* Fall-sown small grains must be winter-hardy. The winter oats cultivar on the left, seeded in the fall, still had an excellent stand the following March. The cultivar on the right did not survive the winter.

less small-grain forage production than could be obtained on prepared seedbeds, it increases returns per ha by using the land in both winter and summer and allows the growing of cereals on slopes normally too steep to plow or disk. Overseeded small grains have furnished 2–3 t/ha more forage in addition to the normal bermudagrass summer production and 33% more beef per ha and have considerably extended the grazing season.

FERTILIZATION. The amount of fertilizer N used on small grains influences yield greatly, although P and K also are important. Since large amounts of N increase the danger of lodging, more N can be used when the stand is to be used for grazing, hay, or silage than when it is to be harvested for grain. In areas of abundant rainfall N, P, and K are applied at planting time, and N is topdressed in winter and/or spring. Yields are increased by 150 kg/ha or more by split applications of N.[43] When grain is to be harvested after graz-

ing, 30–40 kg/ha of N are applied in fall and again in spring. Over 12 t/ha of small-grain silage have been produced with a 50 kg/ha N topdressing in late winter.

GRAZING MANAGEMENT. Grazing management depends on whether the crop is to be used entirely for pasture, or whether hay, silage, or grain is to be harvested also. Heavy fall grazing increases the danger of winter-killing by weakening the plant and decreasing the photosynthetic area needed for vegetative regrowth. Moderate fall and winter grazing has little deleterious effect on subsequent grain yields; sometimes it may prevent lodging and increase tillering and grain yields.[44] Heavy or late spring grazing seriously reduces grain production. Injury from spring grazing is related to the emergence of floral meristems inside the shoots and above ground level. Inflorescence height should be carefully monitored and animals removed from the pasture when the meristems approach 5 cm above the soil surface. Off-flavor milk is sometimes produced by cows pasturing small grains, especially rye, in the spring. The problem can be alleviated by changing the animals from winter feed to pasture gradually and removing them from the pasture a few hours before milking.

HARVESTING FOR HAY OR SILAGE. Small grains, with or without a legume, can be harvested as silage or green chop and used with excellent results. The stage of harvest is critical in determining feeding value. Total dry matter production of oats increases rapidly up through the milk stage but very slowly or not at all from soft dough to maturity.[45] Highest digestibility of oats is attained in boot and early head stages, decreasing thereafter more rapidly than in wheat and barley. Therefore, wheat and barley can be cut some-

43. Morey, D. D., M. E. Walker, W. H. Marchant, and R. S. Lowrey. 1969. Small grain forage production and quality as influenced by rates of nitrogen. Ga. Agr. Exp. Sta. Res. Bull. 70.

44. Day, A. D., R. K. Thompson, and W. F. McCaughev. 1968. Effects of clipping on the performance of spring barley (*Hordeum vulgare* (L.) emend. Lam.) seeded in October. *Agron. J.* 60:11–12.

45. Frey, K. J., P. L. Rodgers, W. F. Wedin, L. Walter, W. J. Moline, and J. C. Burns. 1967. Yield and composition of oats. *Iowa State J. Sci.* 42:9–18.

time between the boot and soft dough stages, but oats should be cut in boot to early head. Rye should be cut at the boot stage or earlier. Generally, rye in the boot stage is ready to cut first, followed by barley, then wheat, and finally oats. This sequence may not hold with newer cultivars selected for early or late maturity. The wilting of small grains cut in the boot stage to 60–70% moisture is desirable to prevent seepage loss from silos and undesirable odors in the silage. Wheat and barley harvested in the soft dough stage contain 65–70% moisture and can be ensiled directly without seepage loss.

Small grains grown alone are easier to cut and will cure more quickly than when grown with a legume. Winter vetch seeded with small grains increases protein level but often not the total dry matter production.[46] In some cases a legume–small-grain–late cut mixture has been inferior to early cut small grains alone as a ration. Since protein content of vegetative small grains is rarely less than 14–16% and often much higher, the presence of legumes adds little to a small-grain pasture and may cause problems in mowing and raking for hay or silage.

❧ SEED PRODUCTION

In growing summer annual grasses for seed, the crop is generally planted in rows about 1 m apart and at low seeding rates (3–6 kg/ha). Most seed production is done in the southern high plains and the Southwest, usually under irrigation. The field should be isolated from others of the same genus to minimize the risk of unwanted hybridization. Although many sorghums are self-pollinated, they will cross freely with other types grown adjacent to them. The seed set on male-sterile heads varies from near 0 to almost 100%, depending on pollen availability and atmospheric conditions. Johnsongrass, *Sorghum hale-*

pense (L.) Pers., is particularly troublesome in sorghum seed production, since it will cross freely with grain or grass sorghums. Crop improvement associations require 200–400 m or more isolation.

Production of the male-sterile parents and of hybrid seed is done by interplanting fertile and male-sterile types in isolated crossing blocks. The maintainer line is used for pollen production. When grown in an isolated and rogued block, the seed produced is either selfed or sibbed. The male-sterile line is wind pollinated by the maintainer line, and the seed produce only male-sterile plants in the next generation. The male parent is produced by selfing or sibbing in another isolated block.

In hybrid seed production the male-sterile line is interplanted with the male (restorer) parent line. The seed harvested from the male-sterile plants is sold as hybrid seed. There is usually a 3:1 ratio of male-sterile to pollinator rows in a production field.

The ease and cost of seed production of the various lines, cultivars, and species can have considerable influence on their use by determining the availability of seed. Some crosses may be difficult to make because the male-sterile line and the pollinator line do not mature at the same time. Staggered or multiple plantings can be used to ensure that sufficient pollen will be available when the male-sterile stigmas are receptive. If the male-sterile parent is tall, this can materially increase the cost of seed production, although combines can be adapted for seed harvest. Some cultivars cannot be produced by the male-sterile method because male-sterile cytoplasm has not been found in the species.

Seed production can be as low as 200 to as high as 6000 kg/ha. Shattering of seed, limited moisture supply, and disease or insect pests help account for low yields. Grain sorghum cultivars produce the intermediate amounts. A seed yield of less than 2000 kg/ha is not considered profitable.

46. Ahlgren, G. H., M. Pool, and H. W. Gausman. 1954. Performance of winter grains alone and with winter vetch for supplemental forage. *Agron. J.* 46:563–65.

❧ QUESTIONS

1. Contrast the ways in which summer annual grasses and small grains fill special needs as forage in different parts of the country.
2. What are the most important features to be considered when selecting a small-grain species and cultivar for pasture? For hay? For silage?
3. What are the most salient characteristics of sorghum and pearlmillet which may lead to their use for green chop? For grazing? For silage? For hay?
4. Discuss the factors that should be considered in making management decisions when considering the use of summer annual grasses and small grains for pasture or green chop.
5. Which cultivars of corn, sorghums, pearl-millet, and small grains would you plant in your locality for forage? Why?
6. In what ways can sorghums, pearlmillet, small grains, and corn for forage fit into different farm enterprises and management strategies in your region?
7. How do climatic and edaphic factors interact with the genetic makeup and the morphology of summer annual grasses and cereals? Discuss how these interactions influence the decisions that must be made by the farm manager for best animal performance or production.
8. What important fertilizer and other soil management practices should be considered in planning for growing summer annual grasses and cereals for forage? Give specific examples applicable to your locality on the most prevalent soil types.

SUPPLEMENTAL LITERATURE CITATIONS

Overton, J. R., and H. A. Fribourg. 1972. Dates of planting summer annual grasses for forage. *Tenn. Farm Home Sci. Progr. Rept.* 83:6–9.

Fribourg, H. A. 1974. Fertilization of summer annual grasses and silage crops. *In* D. A. Mays (ed.), Forage Fertilization, pp. 189–211. Amer. Soc. Agron., Madison, Wis.

Tomeu, A. 1974. Study of forage yield components in sorghum. Proc. 12th Int. Grassl. Congr. 3(2):1004–14.

Bhatia, I. S., R. Singh, K. K. Dogra, and S. Dua. 1975. Changes in cell-wall carbohydrate and lignin of some forage-type millets as affected by growth stage. *J. Sci. Food Agr.* 26:1391–98.

Escalada, R. G., and D. L. Plucknett. 1975. Ratoon cropping of sorghum: I. Origin, time of appearance and fate of tillers. *Agron. J.* 67:473–78.

———. 1975. Ratoon cropping of sorghum: II. Effect of daylength and temperature on tillering and plant development. *Agron. J.* 67:479–84.

Fribourg, H. A., W. E. Bryan, F. F. Bell, and G. J. Buntley. 1975. Performance of selected silage and summer annual grass crops as affected by soil type, planting date, and moisture regime. *Agron. J.* 67:643–47.

Fribourg, H. A., J. R. Overton, and J. A. Mullins. 1975. Wheel traffic on regrowth and production of summer annual grasses. *Agron. J.* 67:423–26.

Fribourg, H. A., B. N. Duck, and E. M. Culvahouse. 1976. Forage sorghum yield components and their *in-vivo* digestibility. *Agron. J.* 68:361–65.

Fribourg, H. A., W. E. Bryan, G. M. Lessman, and D. M. Manning. 1976. Nutrient uptake by corn and grain sorghum silage as affected by soil type, planting date, and moisture regime. *Agron. J.* 68:260–63.

PETER P. ROTAR AND DONALD L. PLUCKNETT
University of Hawaii

34

TROPICAL AND SUBTROPICAL FORAGES

❧

THE world's greatest potential for forage and hence for cattle production lies in the vast areas of the humid Tropics with year-round warm weather, high rainfall, and deep porous soils. Under these conditions yields of dry forage can be increased by intensive management from 500 kg/ha of poor quality forage produced by unimproved volunteer pastures to over 44,800 kg (200 t green) of excellent quality forage with 99 animal units/ha (one animal unit = 454 kg) on green chop and 4.9 animal units/ha on pastures even on steep land. Intensive management practices include planting of high-yielding nutritious grasses, heavy fertilization, liming, weed control, intensive systems of utilization, and careful management so that good

❧ PETER P. ROTAR is Professor of Agronomy, University of Hawaii. He holds the M.S. degree from Washington State University and the Ph.D. from the University of Nebraska. He specializes in tropical forage plant breeding, pasture management, and crop production.

❧ DONALD L. PLUCKETT is Professor of Agronomy, University of Hawaii. He holds the M.S. degree from the University of Nebraska and the Ph.D. from the University of Hawaii. He specializes in tropical crop production, pasture ecology, and tropical farming systems.

quality forage is available all year (see ft.n. 4). These concepts apply to vast humid tropical areas of Latin America, Africa, Southeast Asia, and Australia.

Land areas under U.S. jurisdiction which may be classified as either tropical or subtropical include Hawaii, Puerto Rico, the U.S. Virgin Islands, the trust territory of the Pacific, Guam, American Samoa, southern Florida, and the coastal areas of the Gulf of Mexico. The diversity of climates and forages grown within these areas exceeds that existing between southern Florida and Boston, Mass.

The following discussion deals only with Hawaii and Puerto Rico. These two sets of islands within the Tropics are influenced by the northeast trade winds which are a predominant feature of the climate. In the Tropics, soils play an extremely important role in determining the character of the vegetation that occurs naturally as well as that which may be successfully introduced for forage production. The USDA soil classification system incorporates several soil characteristics that are extremely important in determining potential forage production. These include the diagnostic soil horizons, soil temperature regimes, and soil moisture regimes.[1] By use of this system the best soils for pastures in Hawaii and Puerto Rico may be described as follows: surface horizon, mollic; temperature regime, isothermic to isomesic; and moisture regime, ustic.

❧ HAWAII

The eight major islands forming the state of Hawaii lie at the southeastern end of a chain of islands and shoals more than 2576 km long. Each of the islands was originally built as one or more lava domes, and each owes its shape primarily to volcano building. Parts of the islands have been more or less modified by erosion under strongly localized climatic conditions.

Three factors dominate the climate of Hawaii: the position of the islands, 19°–22° N; their insular position in the largest ocean; and the elevation and topography. Local physiographic features modify the oceanic effects to produce a wide range of microclimates.

The mean annual temperatures at sea level vary from 22 to 28 C depending more on exposure to ocean breeze than on latitude. Mean temperatures decrease at the rate of about 1.6 C/304 m increase in elevation. At the summit of Mauna Kea, 4213 m, temperatures fall below freezing almost every night of the year. At Waimea, 812 m elevation, the average temperature is 17.7 C, with monthly averages ranging from 12 to 24.5 C.

Precipitation is made up of three components: orographic, cyclonic, and conventional rainfall. Annual rainfall varies from less than 300 to over 11,400 mm annually. Large areas of arable land do not regularly receive enough rainfall to support a profitable plant cover. Other large areas have high rainfall but are so steep and inaccessible they cannot be cropped. The arable dry soils, the steep wet soils, and the arable soils with sufficient rainfall occur as relatively small units, often within short distances of each other.

Five general types of vegetation occur: shrub, forest, parkland, bog, and mosslichen. These formations do not exist on all the islands, nor are the altitudinal limits of the formations all the same. These formations tend to occur in regular patterns on the mountain slopes from the very dry leeward side of an island to the wet windward side. On the ascending slopes, the almost tropical conditions at sea level change to a temperate climate in the highlands.

Vegetation zones have been proposed as a means of classifying the potential forage productivity of the islands.[2] These were based on the relationship between vegetation, rainfall, altitude, and soil. Figure 34.1 shows the vegetation zones for the island of Hawaii. Information in Table 34.1 refers to the entire state.

❧ PUERTO RICO

Puerto Rico is the smallest and easternmost island of the Greater Antilles and lies at about 18° N and 66° W longitude. The island is roughly rectangular, about 182 km east to west and about 56 km north to south, and comprises about 8860 sq km. It is surrounded by the Atlantic Ocean to the north and the Caribbean Sea to the south.

In contrast to the volcanic origins of Hawaii, Puerto Rico is the result of massive geological uplifting and erosion. Mountains cover more than 80% of the island. The highest peaks rise to 1338 m in the Cerro de Punta. About 25% of the total land area has slopes of less than 15%, 25% has slopes varying from 16 to 45%, and 50% has slopes over 45%.

Puerto Rico's tropical marine climate is largely conditioned by trade winds and mountainous relief. Trade winds blow from the east-northeast and are forced upward by the terrain. The largest amount of rainfall occurs on the windward slopes and at the highest elevations. According

1. Soil Conservation Service. 1975. Soil Taxonomy: A basic system of soil classification for making and interpreting soil surveys. USDA Agr. Handbook 436.

2. Hosaka, E. Y., and J. C. Ripperton. 1942. Vegetation zones of Hawaii. Hawaii Agr. Exp. Sta. Bull. 89.

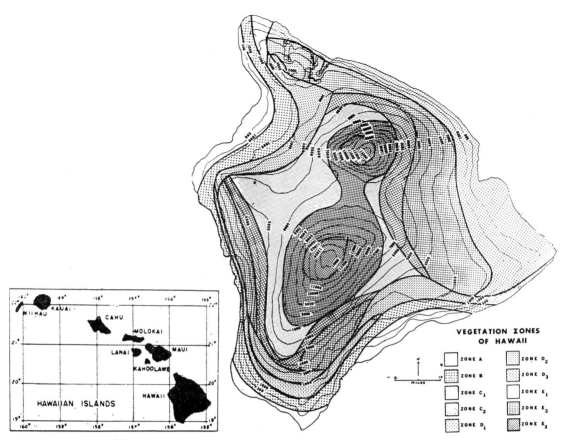

FIG. 34.1. Vegetation zones of the island of Hawaii. Zone E is found only at the higher altitudes on the islands of Hawaii and Maui. Inset shows relative geographic position of the islands.

to Thornthwaite's system of classification the climate of the northern, eastern, and western coasts and the northern foothills is humid tropical.[3] The central mountain ranges are humid mesothermal and wet mesothermal, and the southern coastal areas are semiarid tropical or arid tropical. Annual rainfall varies from 760 mm on the southeast coast to over 6350 mm at the highest elevations. The distribution is uneven, with September and October being the wettest months. Annual temperatures average about 25.6 C along the coastal areas and about 22.2 C in the uplands. Diurnal fluctuation varies from 7 to 10 C throughout the year. Puerto Rico has

high evapotranspiration due to the constant trade winds.

Figure 34.2 and Table 34.2 present vegetational zones. The map follows Thornthwaite's classification and has superimposed upon it the major differences in soils as found on the island. The wide range in elevation, rainfall, and temperatures found in Hawaii are not present in Puerto Rico. Four distinct forage production areas may be recognized.[4]

1. Areas with deficient moisture, including zones B and C found mainly on the south coast. Rainfall is less than 1400

3. Thornthwaite, C. W. 1931. The climates of North America according to a new classification. *Geog. Rev.* 21: 633–55.

4. Vicente-Chandler, J., R. Caro-Costas, R. W. Pearson, F. Abruna, J. Figarella, and S. Silva. 1964. The intensive management of tropical forages in Puerto Rico. P.R. Agr. Exp. Sta. Bull. 187.

Zone	Phase and percent of total land area	Approximate altitude limits (m)	Approximate rainfall limits (mm)*	Natural cover	Diagnostic soil horizons	Key soil characteristics†	
						Temperature regime	Moisture regime
A	11.1	less than 300	500 or less	xerophytic shrub with coastal fringe of trees	umbric ochric	isohyperthermic isothermic	torric or aridic
B	15.1	less than 900	500–1000	xerophytic shrub with some trees in upper part	umbric ochric histic	isohyperthermic isothermic isomesic	torric ustic
C	1-low 8.8	less than 760	1000–1500	mixed open forest and shrubs	umbric mollic histic	isohyperthermic isothermic	torric ustic aquic
	2-high 5.7	760 to 1220	1000–1500	mixed open forest	mollic umbric histic	isothermic isomesic	ustic udic aquic
D	1-low 12.7	less than 450‡	1500 or more	shrub and closed forest	histic ochric umbric	isohyperthermic isothermic	ustic aquic
	2-med. 20.7	variable	1500 or more	closed forest	histic ochric umbric	isohyperthermic isothermic isomesic	ustic aquic
	3-high 5.5 (38.9)	1200 to less than 2130	1500 or more	open forest	histic umbric ochric mollic	isomesic	ustic udic aquic
E	1-low 10.2	1220–2130	1270 or less	open forest and shrub	histic ochric umbric	isomesic	aridic udic
	2-med 8.7	2130–3040	1270 or less	mainly upland open shrub	ochric	isomesic isofrigid	aridic udic
	3-high 1.5 (20.4)	over 3040	1270 or less	no seed-bearing plants present	ochric	isofrigid	aridic

Note: Data presented in the table are approximations and refer to the entire state. Key soil characteristics were provided by H. Ikawa, Associate Soil Scientist, Department of Agronomy and Soil Science, University of Hawaii.

* Minimum rainfall is lower at the higher levels of the C, D, and E vegetation zones.

† The soil characteristics taken from the current USDA Soil Classification Scheme are more precisely defined than the soils as originally described by Hosaka and Ripperton, 1942.³

‡ The boundary between D_1 and D_2 varies with the location and present utilization. In general it represents the highest point of satisfactory utilization for most crops as adjudged by climate, soil type, and present crops grown.

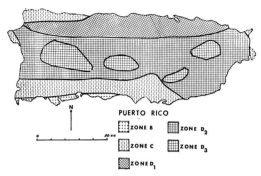

Fig. 34.2. Vegetation zones of the island of Puerto Rico. The vegetation zones as presented here are not completely analogous to those in Hawaii since climate, elevation, and geologic origin are quite different.

mm. There is a marked dry season and no irrigation is practiced.

2. Areas with level topography and abundant moisture (north coast and irrigated south coast), including parts of zone C and zone D_1. These lands are intensively cultivated, and forages are competitive only if they are intensively managed. Highest yields and best utilization are obtained from feeding green chop or silage.

3. Areas of rolling topography and moderate moisture (northwest coast), which includes most of zone D_1 above zone C on that coastline. The natural vegetation was a tropical moist forest with 1600–1900 mm of rainfall.

4. Mountain region with abundant rainfall, which includes the uplands of zone D_1 and all of zone D_2 and D_3. This accounts for more than 75% of Puerto Rico's land area. High yields of forage can be obtained here. There are few alternatives to forage production, as slopes are steep and soils easily eroded.

❧ TYPES OF FORAGES

Relative palatability is of little importance in selecting forages to plant since all those discussed are eaten well by cattle. Well-fertilized and well-managed grasses are relatively similar in composition and digestibility. Legumes, however, generally have much higher protein, Ca, and P content than the grasses.

Methods of harvesting and feeding, however, often determine the species to be used. Napiergrass produces highest yields of cut forage and is therefore best for green-chop feeding or silage. Guineagrass, napiergrass, 'Pangola' digitgrass, and paragrass can be harvested by cutting or grazing. Mollassesgrass does not tolerate repeated cutting and is suited only for grazing.

Topography of the land affects selection. Full use must be made of level or gently sloping land by planting grasses that respond to heavy fertilization and are adapted to cutting or intensive grazing.

Pangola digitgrass, guineagrass, and napiergrass are best for the areas with more favorable topography where it is possible to apply large amounts of fertilizer and lime. Pangola digitgrass is usually preferred to guineagrass and napiergrass since it is easier to establish and manage. Stargrass, *Cynodon* spp., is becoming popular in these areas.

Tropical kudzu and molassesgrass pastures are useful on the steeper, broken, hard-to-reach, or stony lands in the mountain region. Paragrass is usually planted on the poorly drained sites. All the grasses must be maintained separately, as they vary in palatability and management practices.

Value of the land must be considered. On expensive lands the most intensive methods involving green chop or intensive rotational grazing of the highest yielding species can be expected to be profitable; whereas, extensively managed pastures may be best on cheaper land. The farmer's capacity and willingness to make greater investments of time and funds required by intensive management in exchange for higher profits must be considered.

Adaptability of forages to special conditions of the farm within a given region must also be considered. In general it is best to use the highest yielding species unless other factors outweigh this advantage.

TABLE 34.2 ✣ Vegetation zones in Puerto Rico, their altitude and annual rainfall limits, key characteristics of the soil, and the natural vegetation

Zone	Percent of total area	Approximate altitude limits (m)	Approximate rainfall limits (mm)	Natural cover*	Key soil characteristics		
					Diagnostic horizon	Temperature regime	Moisture regime
B†	5	0–150	1240	open thorn bush, semidesert	mollic	isohyperthermic	ustic
C	20	0–150	1240–1400	tropical dry forest	mollic cambic oxic‡	isohyperthermic	ustic udic
D_1	25	low-north coast, 0–150	low-north coast, 1650–1900	tropical moist forest	mollic ustic	isohyperthermic	udic aquic
		150–450	midlands, 1650–2200	tropical and subtropical moist forest	cambic	isohyperthermic	udic
		uplands, 450–900	1900–2400	subtropical moist forest	argillic oxic‡	isothermic	udic
D_2	35	150–900	1900–2400	subtropical moist forest			
D_3	15	900 +	2400–6350	subtropical rain forest	umbic cambic argillic	isothermic	udic

Note: This table was prepared in consultation with F. Beinroth, Soil Scientist, University of Puerto Rico, Rio Pedras.
* The natural vegetation has been nearly completely destroyed, and it is postulated that is the type of cover that would have been present originally.
† Vegetation zones analogous to A, C_2, E_1, E_2, and E_3 in Hawaii are not found in Puerto Rico. The D_3 vegetation zone presented here is not completely analogous to D_3 in Hawaii; the rainfall is higher and temperature and elevation in Puerto Rico are lower.
‡ There are oxisols present on the northwest coast.

TABLE 34.3 ❧ Pasture characteristics of forages commonly grown in Hawaii

Forage	Vegetation zone	Elevation (m) Rainfall (mm)	Companion grass/legume	Growth habit	Propagation, seeding rate
Napiergrass	B, C$_1$	600 m 890–1780 mm	none recommended	erect bunchgrass	stem cuttings, 0.9–1.5-m rows
Guineagrass	B, C, D	0–760 m 500–2000 mm	koa haole, siratro	erect bunchgrass	2.2 kg/ha, sprigs
Green panicgrass	A, B, C$_1$	0–760 m 500–2000 mm	koa haole, alfalfa, greenleaf desmodium	bunchgrass	2.2 kg/ha
Pangola digitgrass	C, D, E$_1$	0–1200 m 1000–5000 mm	big trefoil, greenleaf desmodium, white clover, Kaimi clover	creeping sod to open turf	sprigs or broadcast cuttings
Paragrass	B, C$_1$, C$_2$, D$_1$	0–1200 m 890–5000 mm	greenleaf desmodium	creeping, tuft or clump	sprigs, 1.8 × 1.8 m
Molassesgrass	B, C, D	0–600 m 890–2000 mm	greenleaf desmodium	open sod	4.5–7 kg/ha
Kikuyugrass	B, C, D, E	0–1800 m 890–3000 mm	big trefoil, white clover, greenleaf desmodium, silverleaf desmodium	sod-forming, prostrate, creeping	stem cuttings, 0.9 × 0.9 m or 1.8 × 1.8 m
Buffelgrass	A, B, C$_1$	0–760 m 250–750 mm	none recommended	bunchgrass to sod	1.1–3.4 kg/ha
Bermudagrass	A, B, C, D	0–900 m 375–2000 mm	white clover, Kaimi clover	sod	1.7–5.6 kg/ha
Dallisgrass	B, C, D, E	0–1800 m 750–2500 mm	white clover, big trefoil	open sod	9 kg/ha

364

TABLE 34.3 ❧ (Continued)

Forage	Vegetation zone	Elevation (m) Rainfall (mm)	Companion grass/legume	Growth habit	Propagation, seeding rate
Kazungulu setaria	B, C, D	0–760 m 750–2500 mm	greenleaf desmodium, Clarence glycine	upright, bunchgrass	4.5–5.6 kg/ha
Orchardgrass	C₂, D₃, E₁	900–2100 m 1000–2500 mm	white clover, big trefoil	upright, bunchgrass	4.5 kg/ha
Perennial ryegrass	C₂, D, E	760–2100 m 1000–2500 mm	white clover, big trefoil	open sod	8 kg/ha
Kaimi clover	C, D	0–900 m 1500–3750 mm	bermudagrass, Pangola digitgrass, kikuyugrass	upright to spreading shrub	5.6 kg/ha
Greenleaf desmodium	C, D	0–460 m 1500–3750 mm	Pangola digitgrass, kikuyugrass, paragrass	upright, spreading	2.2 kg/ha, stem cuttings broadcast or 0.9 × 0.9 m or 1.8 × 1.8 m
Silverleaf desmodium	C, D	0–760 m 1125–2500 mm	Pangola digitgrass, kikuyugrass, paragrass	upright, spreading	2.2 kg/ha, stem cuttings broadcast
Clarence glycine	B, C, D	0–900 m > 750 mm	kanzungulu setaria, Pangola digitgrass, kikuyugrass, green panicgrass	twining, spreading	4.5 kg/ha
Koa haole	A, B, C	0–450 m 500–1500 mm	guineagrass, green panicgrass	shrub, small tree	20 kg/ha, stem or crown cuttings
Big trefoil	C, D	150–180 m 150 mm or more	kikuyugrass, Pangola digitgrass, perennial ryegrass, orchardgrass	stoloniferous	2.2 kg/ha, stem cuttings
White clover	C, D, E	300–2100 m 750–3750 mm	kikuyugrass, Pangola digitgrass, dallisgrass, orchardgrass, perennial ryegrass	stoloniferous	2.2 kg/ha

Note: Many of these forages are important in Puerto Rico and other areas of the Tropics and subtropics as well.

365

The following forages are those most commonly used in Hawaii and Puerto Rico. Only a limited number of those adapted are described. A number of these forages are also well adapted to the humid regions of Florida and the deep South, especially the coastal areas along the Gulf of Mexico. Examples of these are dallisgrass, bermudagrass, napiergrass, buffelgrass, and others (see Chapters 30, 31, and 32). A brief summary of the pasture characteristics of forages commonly grown in Hawaii is presented in Table 34.3.

NAPIERGRASS

Napiergrass, *Pennisetum purpureum* Schumach. (introduced from Africa), is a robust, erect, leafy, tufted, branching perennial 2–4 m tall with elongated blades 2–3 cm wide and a dense tawny inflorescence. It grows into clumps and tillers abundantly. It is propagated by stem cuttings since the seed have low viability.

The 'Merker' cultivar generally is used in Hawaii and Puerto Rico because of its resistance to the fungus, *Helminthosporium sacchari* (Breda de Haan) Butl., which seriously affects common napiergrass. It may be grazed but is used most frequently as a green chop for dairy or penned beef animals.

GUINEAGRASS

Guineagrass, *Panicum maximum* L. (introduced from Africa), is an erect, rather robust tufted perennial 1–2.5 m tall with blades 1–3.5 cm in width and open panicles 20–50 cm long. It tillers profusely, producing tufts or clumps up to 30 cm or more in width. Guineagrass is propagated by clump sections or seed. The seed mature gradually, falling to the ground as they ripen. Thus seed harvested at any given time include relatively few mature viable seed, and germination is correspondingly poor. Lack of good seed limits use.

Guineagrass is a highly variable species with many strains. Some cultivars are very tall; 'Coloniao' grows to 3 m while 'Sabi' is about 1 m tall. Leaves are variable in size, 13 mm–5 cm wide and from 30 to 76 cm or more in length. It is used most frequently for pasture but is also used for green chop. In Hawaii, guineagrass is grown extensively with koa haole in B vegetation zone pastures.

GREEN PANICGRASS

Green panicgrass, *P. maximum* var. *trichoglume* Eyles (introduced from Africa), is a leafy perennial bunchgrass, 60–120 cm tall and yellow green in color. The leaves are soft, 7–30 cm long, up to 1.5 cm wide, and well distributed on the stems. The seed heads occur as open panicles 20–35 cm long with the lower branches occurring in a whorl. The branches of the inflorescence are ascending and naked at the base. Seed are very small. Green panicgrass is smaller and lighter green than common guineagrass, and it is usually used as a pasture grass.

PANGOLA DIGITGRASS

Pangola digitgrass, *Digitaria decumbens* Stent. (introduced from Africa), grows to a height of about 50 cm with seed heads to about 1 m. Spreading rapidly by surface runners, it soon produces a dense cover of fine-leaved vegetation. The leaf sheaths are smooth; the seed heads occur as five to seven racemes and are usually 10–15 cm long. Pangola digitgrass is propagated by stem cuttings or tillers, the former being the most widely used. Seed are rarely if ever viable. It is an excellent pasture species.

PARAGRASS

Paragrass, *Brachiaria mutica* (Forsk.) Stapf (introduced from Africa), is a coarse, creeping perennial, sod-forming grass with ascending stems that may grow to about 2 m in height with prostrate to trailing stems over 6 m long. It roots readily at the nodes.

The nodes, leaf sheaths, and leaves are hairy; the leaf blade is flat and 1–2 cm wide. The flower head is 10–20 cm long. It is a sparse seed producer and seed are rarely viable. Paragrass is propagated from stem cuttings or from runners. It is especially useful as a pasture grass or as green chop under irrigation or on poorly drained soils.

MOLASSESGRASS

Molassesgrass, *Melinis minutiflora* Beauv. (introduced from Africa by way of Brazil), grows to a height of about 1 m and roots at the lower nodes. Culms are pubescent and 1 m or more long. The blades are also pubescent, 10–15 cm long, and 5–10 mm wide. The inflorescence is 15–20 cm long and dark purple or reddish, turning brown when mature. Molassesgrass flowers in November. Seed heads should be harvested about two weeks after flowering when they change in color from reddish to dull brown. Molassesgrass is propagated from seed. It has a sweetish, pungent odor, reminiscent of the smell of molasses. Molassesgrass is susceptible to overgrazing.

BUFFELGRASS

Buffelgrass, *Cenchrus ciliarus* L. [syn. *Pennisetum ciliare* (L.) Link] (introduced from South Africa), is a bunch to rhizomatous perennial grass 15–120 cm tall with a tough knotty crown. Roots are dense and long. Leaves are green to bluish green in color, 7.5–30 cm long and 3–6 mm wide. Old plants become stemmy with harsh leaves. Flowering stems are cylindrical, upright to slightly drooping, purplish, and 5–10 cm long. Individual flowers appear singly or clustered and are surrounded by numerous bristles.

Buffelgrass is a highly variable species with many ecotypes. The seed are widely spread by the wind and by sticking to animals. It is an excellent grass for pasture use in dry areas, as it recovers quickly after the first rains of the season.

KIKUYUGRASS

Kikuyugrass, *Pennisetum clandestinum* Hochst. ex Chiov., is a low-growing, very leafy, somewhat hairy, deep-rooted, rhizomatous, sod-forming perennial grass. It spreads by numerous large, fleshy, creeping stolons and rhizomes that sometimes reach 2 m or more in length and depth. The stolons root readily at each node, sending up stout leafy branches up to 60 cm long. The flowering stems are short and leafy, 10–15 cm tall. The inflorescence is often completely enclosed in the terminal leaf shoots. Kikuyugrass has no visible seed head and the seed form inside the leaf sheaths. It is the most important pasture grass in Hawaii, especially in the wetlands. It is often underrated as a pasture species.

KOA HAOLE

Koa haole, *Leucaena leucocephala* (Lam.) de Wit (native to Central America), is a leafy, deep-rooted perennial shrub or small tree. It has bipinnate leaves 12–25 cm long. Each leaf is made up of 10–15 or more paired leaflets. The stipules are triangular, glabrous, and 1.2–1.8 cm long. It has many white flowers clustered in a globular head. The seedpods are flat and occur in palmate groups; each pod is 1.2–1.8 cm wide and 15–20 cm long. The seed are flattened, oblong, and shiny brown. There are about 26,400 seed/kg.

Koa haole is strain-specific for *Rhizobium,* and the proper commercial strain should be used to ensure success in establishment. It is an important browse legume for grazing and can also be used as green chop and for dried high-protein meals. Koa haole combines well with guineagrass for pasture use (Fig. 34.3).

GREENLEAF DESMODIUM

Greenleaf desmodium, *Desmodium aparines* (Link) DC. = *D. intortum* (Mill.) Urb. (native to central and northern South America), is a perennial decumbent plant with long trailing stems that root at

FIG. 34.3. *Koa haole . . . important browse legume . . . also used as green chop.* An excellent stand of guineagrass–koa haole in the B vegetation zone in Hawaii. This combination will carry two or more animal units per ha per year.

the nodes. The main stems are green to reddish brown, 1.3–8 m long, and about 8 mm in diameter. The trifoliate leaves are ovate, 5–7.5 cm wide, and 7.5–12.5 cm long when mature. The inflorescence is a raceme. Flowers are usually pink in color. The hairy seedpods contain 6–10 kidney-shaped seed about 2 mm long and 1.5 mm wide. The plant flowers during the short-day period from November through March. Most of the seed mature within a short time. Greenleaf desmodium may be propagated from seed or stem cuttings. This legume does well in pasture mixtures with Pangola digitgrass and kikuyugrass.

KAIMI CLOVER

Kaimi clover, *D. canum* (Gmel.) Schintz & Thellung (native to Central America), is a small perennial with woody upright stems 25–50 cm high and fibrous to woody trailing and creeping stems 0.5–1 m or more in length. Leaves produced on the upright stems are lanceolate and usually have a white mark along the midrib. Leaflets produced on the trailing stems are oval and/or round and normally have no

markings. The decumbent stems root freely at the nodes. The reddish or lavender flowers are borne on racemes, each bearing up to 12 or more pods. The hairy pods are 2.5–4 cm long, and the seed are light brown and about 3 mm long and 1.5 mm wide.

Kaimi clover is usually propagated from seed. The plant is widespread throughout lowland pastures in the moderate to high rainfall areas of Hawaii. It is an important legume in wet lowland pastures of zone D in Hawaii.

TROPICAL KUDZU

Tropical kudzu, *Pueraria phaseoloides* Benth. (native to the East Indies), is a perennial legume. It is a vigorous twining vine with trifoliate leaves. The numerous above-ground stolons root at both nodes and internodes. It has a deep, widely branching root system. Flowers are borne on long peduncled racemes. Seedpods are 6–10 cm long and 4 mm wide, are black when ripe, and contain 15–20 seed each. Tropical kudzu is propagated easily either from seed, which it produces from January to March, or from stems or crowns. The seedpods mature over a long period, thus the field must be gone over weekly by hand to pick only the black mature pods which open and drop the seed. Tropical kudzu combines well with molassesgrass.

❧ PRODUCTIVITY OF INTENSELY MANAGED FORAGES

Soil fertility is the major factor affecting forage yields in the humid Tropics. Fertilizer requirements are high, primarily due to heavy removal of nutrients in the high yields of forage produced with intensive management and to loss of nutrients by leaching and fixation. To obtain maximum yields of rapidly growing grasses such as napiergrass, guineagrass, and Pangola digitgrass, it is necessary to fertilize regularly with moderate to high rates of N.

Four factors must be considered in rationalizing the fertilizer requirements of forages: (1) quantity of nutrients removed in the forage, (2) quantity of available nutrients in the soil, (3) rate at which soil nutrients become available, and (4) likely losses of applied nutrients.

In Puerto Rico the high pressure for land has dictated a philosophy of intensive forage management involving high rates of fertilization and utilization of the most productive grasses possible, namely napiergrass, guineagrass, and Pangola digitgrass. Yields are highest on the irrigated south coast, followed by unirrigated areas on the north coast, the humid mountain region, and finally the unirrigated south coast.

Napiergrass produces the highest yields of green chop in all regions, followed by guineagrass, Pangola digitgrass, and paragrass (which are similar in productivity) and finally by molassesgrass and tropical kudzu. About 6.4, 8.6, and 10.4 animal units may be fed per ha per year on heavily fertilized cut napiergrass in the humid mountain region, humid north coast, and irrigated south coast respectively. Comparable production of napiergrass,

guineagrass, and paragrass has been obtained in Hawaii.[5-7]

It should be noted that in both areas the highest yields were obtained from green chop for livestock. Whenever animals are allowed to graze these grasses, forage production declines considerably, as measured by forage actually consumed by cattle. This decline is due to waste by trampling and soiling by the grazing animal and to the uneven growth response of the forage after grazing. However, the carrying capacity of these forages is large as measured by animal units per ha or by actual yearly gain in weight per ha.

High fertilization levels are necessary to obtain these high yields since large quantities of nutrients are removed in the forage. At Orocovis in the humid region of Puerto Rico, intensively managed grasses removed an average of 315 kg of N, 51 kg of P, 407 kg of K, 118 kg of Ca, and 78 kg of Mg/ha/year in the harvested crop.

❧ PRODUCTIVITY OF LEGUME-BASED PASTURES

In contrast to Puerto Rico, the general approach to forage production in Hawaii has been to utilize legume-based pastures rather than to rely on fertilizer N for the grasses. Management systems have therefore emphasized the legume and its nutrition and performance in mixtures with desirable grasses.

Legumes which have been used in legume-grass mixtures are listed in Table 34.3. Some problems have occurred in finding suitable legumes for the varied ecological conditions of Hawaii; however, productive legumes are available for each vegetation zone.

Low soil fertility has been a major problem in establishing and maintaining productive legume-grass pastures. The most

5. Takahashi, M., J. C. Moomaw, and J. C. Ripperton. 1966. Studies of napiergrass. III. Grazing management. Hawaii Agr. Exp. Sta. Bull. 28.
6. Younge, O. R., and J. C. Ripperton. 1960. Nitrogen fertilization of pasture and forage grasses in Hawaii. Hawaii Agr. Exp. Sta. Bull. 124.
7. Plucknett, D. L. 1970. Productivity of tropical pastures in Hawaii. Proc. 11th Int. Grassl. Congr., pp. A38–A49 (Surfers Paradise, Queensland, Aust.).

widespread deficiency is P. Liming may be necessary for certain legume species on very acid soils, especially those released to pasture after abandonment from pineapple production.[8] Micronutrient status must also be ascertained to obtain proper functioning of *Rhizobium*.

The most productive legume-grass mixtures in Hawaii have been koa haole–guineagrass, greenleaf desmodium–Pangola digitgrass, kaimi clover–kikuyugrass, and white clover–kikuyugrass. With good management such mixtures can carry from 1.2 to 5 animals/ha/yr, producing from 336 to over 1120 kg liveweight gain/ha/yr, comparable to grasses receiving moderate levels of fertilizer N.[7] As an example of the productivity of legume-based pastures, greenleaf desmodium–Pangola digitgrass pasture produced animal gains of 865 kg/ha with fertilization and lime. Other legumes which show promise for use in legume-grass mixtures are stylo, *Stylosanthes guianensis* (Aubl.) Scv.; glycine, *Glycine wightii* (R. Grah. ex Wight & Arn.) Verdcourt; centro, *Centrosema pubescens* Benth.; and siratro, *Macroptilium atropurpureum* (DC.) Urb.

❧ ESTABLISHING FORAGES

Although forages are sometimes expensive to establish, they should be considered a permanent improvement, thereby enhancing a farm's value. Most of the forages discussed persist indefinitely if properly managed. There are records of productive guineagrass pastures over 100 years old and many fields of napiergrass, molassesgrass, and paragrass are over 30 years old.

HARVESTING AND STORING SEED

Many of the tropical and subtropical forage grasses produce little or no viable seed. Others may produce viable seed, but due to the manner of flowering, indeter-

minate inflorescences, or inclement weather at seed maturity it is difficult to obtain adequate seed.

Seed storage is difficult. Seed cannot be stored for more than one year at normal temperatures and humidity in the humid Tropics. There are no commercial growers of tropical and subtropical forage seed within the U.S., and seed are imported from abroad at considerable cost and effort.

LAND CLEARING AND PREPARATION

Cultivable land covered with low-growing vegetation should be heavily grazed by cattle and then plowed and harrowed to prepare a good seedbed. Lime, if required, and P should be added at the time of plowing. Where complete land preparation is not possible because of broken topography, rocks, or stumps, the area should be heavily grazed, tall weeds cut back, and if possible a heavy rate of herbicides applied before sprigging. Trees and heavy brush may be killed by heavy equipment or, on broken topography or large areas, brush killers may be applied by plane, helicopter, or motorized low-volume spray equipment.[9] After the brush and trees have been killed, the area may be fired at the beginning of the rainy season. The burned areas may then be aerially seeded and fertilized.

SEED AND VEGETATIVE ESTABLISHMENT

In humid regions, forages may be planted at any time, but it is best to plant when the rainy season begins either in the spring (Puerto Rico) or fall (Hawaii). In semiarid regions planting should be during the rainy season.

A generous seeding rate should be used to produce a thick stand quickly. The quantity of seed required depends largely on percent of germination and cost of seed.

8. Plucknett, D. L. 1971. Use of pelleted seed in crop and pasture establishment. Hawaii Coop. Ext. Ser. Circ. 446.

9. Motooka, P. S., D. F. Saiki, D. L. Plucknett, O. R. Younge, and R. E. Daehler. 1967. Aerial herbicide control of Hawaii jungle vegetation. Hawaii Agr. Exp. Sta. Tech. Bull. 141.

Commercial *Rhizobium* inoculum is available and should be used on all legumes listed. Inoculation costs only a few cents per ha, and it is an excellent safeguard for having a useful legume in the pasture.

Many of the forage grasses are established by stem, stolon, or crown cuttings since little or no viable seed is produced. Examples of grasses and legumes which may be established from stem cuttings are napiergrass, paragrass, Pangola digitgrass, greenleaf desmodium, glycine, and tropical kudzu.

Stem cuttings may be broadcast with a manure spreader and disked to cover, laid in furrows 1 m or more apart, or sprigged directly into the soil at regular intervals from 1 m × 1 m to 2 m × 2 m or more. The wider the spacing, the more time required for establishment. Unless the cuttings are distributed onto soil with adequate moisture and fertilizer or during the rainy season, probability of success is low.

Oftentimes unrooted cuttings are scattered with limited success over steep slopes that are impossible to work with machinery or are very difficult to sprig by hand. New plant growth media are now available that allow the rooting of one- or two-node cuttings in self-contained rooting media for field plants.[10] These rooted cuttings are distributed over the surface of the fields at a rate of about 500 packets/ha. This may be achieved from aircraft, jeep, or horseback, or on foot. Such distribution on otherwise erodable lands can lead to good pasture stands and adequate ground cover after 10–15 weeks. When unrooted cuttings are broadcast over the soil surface, several tons per ha of cut vegetation are required to obtain a suitable stand.

This technique of plant propagation is not only advantageous for vegetatively propagated species but also for species setting viable seed. In many areas of the Tropics and sub-Tropics where rainfall and topography increase the danger of soil erosion and generally prevent mechanical drilling of seed, the distribution of both grass and associated legume seed or cuttings in packets has promise.

MANAGEMENT AFTER SEEDING

Establishment of a good grass stand may be helped by good management. A 12-12-12 or similar N-P-K fertilizer at the rate of 200 kg/ha should be applied at planting and 300 kg/ha 2–3 months later. If no legumes have been planted, broadleaf weeds may be controlled with 2,4-D. Tall-growing weeds in low-growing pastures of kikuyugrass and Pangola digitgrass can be controlled by close mowing; low-growing weeds can be shaded out of tall-growing pastures of napiergrass and guineagrass simply by delayed grazing. Methods of establishing pastures must be varied to suit particular conditions.

❦ QUESTIONS

1. What is the range of environments found within tropical Hawaii and Puerto Rico?
2. How does the environment affect the choice of forage to be grown?
3. What are the major differences between the climates of the tropical and temperate regions and how do these differences affect the choice of species?
4. Can grasses be more productive when grown without legumes by substituting fertilizer N for the legume? Under what management circumstances would this be advisable?
5. If napiergrass and guineagrass are as productive as cut forages, why do they drop off considerably when grazed?
6. If we know how to obtain large amounts of good quality forage in the Tropics, why is this information not used to greater advantage?
7. What human factors ultimately limit the overall productivity of a single farm or ranch operation?

---

10. Nicholls, D. F., and D. L. Plucknett. 1971. "Packet" planting techniques for tropical pastures. *Hawaii Farm Sci.* 20:10–11.

DARELL E. McCLOUD / *University of Florida*

R. J. BULA / *Agricultural Research Service, USDA*

35

CLIMATIC FACTORS IN FORAGE PRODUCTION

❧

CLIMATES exert a major influence on plant growth and agricultural production. Agricultural practices often are modified to suit the climate under which a crop is grown. Climate is the principal factor influencing the adaptation of forage plants. Plant geographers for a long time have recognized the relationship between climate and the natural vegetation of the world. Two factors, precipitation and temperature, play the major role in determining climate of any region. These two factors and their influence on natural vegetation have been the basis of most systems for climatic classification.

❧ DARELL E. McCLOUD is Chairman of the Department of Agronomy at the University of Florida. He holds the M.S. and Ph.D. degrees from Purdue University, with advanced study at the Johns Hopkins University Laboratory of Climatology. His research has emphasized the influence of environmental factors on the growth of forages.

❧ R. J. BULA is Research Agronomist, ARS, USDA, and Professor of Agronomy, Purdue University. He holds the M.S. and Ph.D. degrees from the University of Wisconsin. His research has been primarily concerned with the effects of weather factors on the growth and development of forage plants.

❧ CLIMATIC CLASSIFICATION

Thornthwaite, an American geographer, devised a systematic classification of the world's climates, based on precipitation effectiveness and temperature efficiency.[1] Precipitation effectiveness is determined by the ratio of precipitation to evaporation, and climates are divided into five humidity provinces with associated natural vegetation types.

Humidity Type	Characteristic Vegetation
A. Wet	Rain forest
B. Humid	Forest
C. Subhumid	Grassland
D. Semiarid	Steppe
E. Arid	Desert

The two forest types, rain forest and forest, are differentiated by the wetness aspect, as are the two grassland types, which are characterized by tall grasses and short grasses. Sparse vegetation characterizes the desert.

---

1. Thornthwaite, C. W. 1933. The climates of the earth. *Geogr. Rev.* 23:433–40.

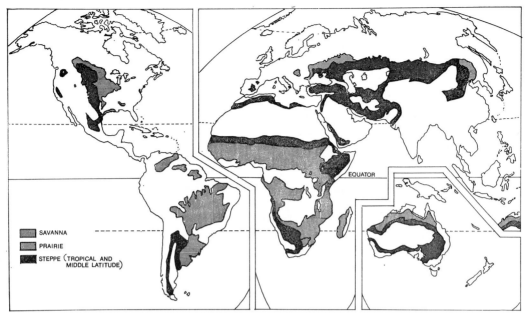

SAVANNA
PRAIRIE
STEPPE (TROPICAL AND MIDDLE LATITUDE)

EQUATOR

FIG. 35.1. World distribution of native grasslands. (Adapted from Trewartha et al., 1967.[2] Used with permission of McGraw-Hill Book Company.)

There are six temperature efficiency provinces:

Temperature Province

A'. Tropical   D'. Taiga
B'. Mesothermal   E'. Tundra
C'. Microthermal   F'. Perpetual frost

When precipitation is not limiting, the first three temperature provinces are easily distinguished. Palms or tall buttressed tropical trees characterize A', deciduous hardwoods B', and spruce and fir are the best indicators of C' provinces. The sparse, stunted, somewhat open forest vegetation characterizes D' taiga, while the treeless feature is indicative of E' tundra province. The F' perpetual frost province has virtually no vegetation.

In addition, the seasonal distribution of effective precipitation provides a basis for subtypes of the humidity provinces. These subtypes are: Precipitation abundant in all seasons (r), sparse in summer (s), sparse in winter (w), and deficient in all seasons (d).

The three factors of humidity, tempera-

ture, and precipitation distribution in all combinations would produce 120 possible climatic types. However, only 32 are recognized as actual climates and, of these, 18 represent the major climatic regions of the world.

The tropical rain forest type (AA') represents the climate most favorable for plant growth, and it produces the densest vegetation on earth. Moisture is abundant and temperatures are never extreme. Reduction in either element will produce a climatic condition less favorable for vegetation growth.

Natural grasslands of the world were developed under restricted precipitation effectiveness (Fig. 35.1).[2] The tall-grass prairies are found in the C humidity type and either B' or C' temperature provinces, as exemplified by the prairies of Iowa and Illinois, eastern South Africa, the lower Danube and the Po Valley of Europe, and the Pampas of Argentina. The drier grasslands, or steppes, are found in the D hu-

2. Trewartha, G. T., A. H. Robinson, and E. H. Hammond. 1967. Elements of Geography, 5th ed. McGraw-Hill, New York.

midity type. The Russian and Australian steppes, the drier portion of the United States Great Plains, and the African veldts are examples of the short-grass vegetation types.

The vast tropical savannas (CA′) of South America, Asia, Australia, and Africa are transitional grasslands with characteristic scattered low-growing, often round-topped trees. The climate is characterized by pronounced wet and dry seasons.

Forage species are found in areas subjected to vigorous temperature and moisture extremes; however, economic forage production is confined to much narrower ranges of temperature and moisture. Winter survival is also an important factor restricting the geographic distribution of perennial forages.

FORAGE ADAPTATION

Forage grasses are especially specific in their temperature adaptation. In the eastern U.S. where moisture is adequate for prairie grasslands or the more humid forests, temperature is the principal factor affecting grass adaptation. Kentucky bluegrass, timothy, smooth bromegrass, orchardgrass, and tall fescue are best adapted to the C′ climate. If they are grown in a B′ climate, it is either in the cooler regions or as a winter grass. Forage legumes such as red clover, birdsfoot trefoil, and alsike clover have similar climatic adaptations. The characteristic grasses of the B′ climates of the humid portions of the U.S. are bermudagrass, dallisgrass, and johnsongrass. In the U.S. only a small A′ area exists. Grasses adapted to this area are 'Pangola' digitgrass, bahiagrass, carpetgrass, and saint augustinegrass. Tropical legumes such as kudzu, stylo, centro, and phasey are adapted to the A′ climates.

In the D climates, blue gramma is found in both the northern (C′) and southern plains (B′) regions. Blue panic and buffalograss have a higher temperature requirement and consequently are mostly restricted to the B′ climates. A few forage species such as alfalfa are well adapted over a wide range of temperatures. Range

grasses particularly well adapted to the drier desert (E′) climates are Boer, Lehmann, and Wilman lovegrasses.

GROWTH INDICES

An alternative approach to climate-plant relationships has been proposed.[3] This involves development of separate models for plant growth response to the three major climatic factors—light, temperature, and water. These are expressed as individual indices which range from 0 when the climatic factor is completely limiting to 1.0 where it is nonlimiting and plant growth is at a maximum for that factor.

From these three climatic indices, a growth index (GI) is developed: $GI = LI \times TI \times MI$, where LI = light index, TI = temperature index, MI = moisture index. These growth indices, computed weekly, provide the bases for determining adaptation and productiveness of forage plants.

❧ MICROCLIMATE

The climate in the lower regions of the atmosphere and at a particular location is called the microclimate. Microclimate is of major importance in the growth and development of forage plants. Light, temperature, moisture, carbon dioxide, and wind are quite variable in the microclimatic zone (Fig. 35.2). Temperature and humidity conditions on a clear day may be more variable across the first 1 m vertical layer above the soil surface at any particular location than measurement of temperature and humidity taken in standard meteorological shelters at 2 m over many locations in a region encompassing several hundred kilometers. Diurnal variations at the same locations are also largest in the microclimatic zone (Fig. 35.3).[4] Near the ground, air is coolest just before sunrise and warmest near midday. At 2 m

3. Fitzpatrick, E. A., and H. A. Nix. 1970. The climate factor in Australian grassland ecology. *In* Australian Grasslands, pp. 3–36. Aust. Natl. Univ. Press, Canberra.
4. Geiger, Rudolph. 1965. The Climate Near the Ground, rev. ed. Harvard Univ. Press, Cambridge.

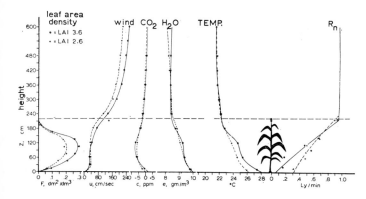

FIG. 35.2. Distribution of leaf area, wind, carbon dioxide, water vapor, air temperature, and net radiation in two stands of corn. (Courtesy E. R. Lemon and Wageningen Centre for Agricultural Publishing and Documentation, PUDOC.)

above the ground, maximum temperature occurs an hour or two later. Since radiation is the primary factor affecting microclimatic temperatures, diurnal variation is much greater on clear days. During clear days incoming radiation from the sun greatly exceeds that reradiated from the earth, with the result that temperatures increase rapidly. At night the reverse is true and surfaces cool rapidly. On cloudy days both the incoming and outgoing radiation are reduced, resulting in a much reduced diurnal temperature variation and much smaller differences between the microclimate and macroclimate. This relationship between incoming and outgoing radiation from plant and soil surfaces largely determines their temperatures.

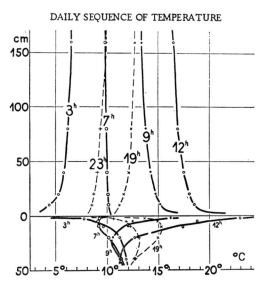

FIG. 35.3. Microclimate temperatures above and below the ground surface. (From Geiger, 1965.[4])

Climatic factors such as air temperature are generally measured by the U.S. National Weather Service at heights 2 m above the ground. This height was selected to avoid the extremes in temperature near the ground.

❧ RADIANT ENERGY

Sunlight provides the energy necessary to sustain plant life. Thus light often is considered the most important environmental factor affecting plants. Sunlight reaching the earth's surface comprises only a minute portion of the total electromagnetic spectrum, which extends from the extremely short wavelength, high-energy cosmic rays to the very long wavelength, low-energy radar, television, and radio waves.

The effects of the various wavelengths of radiant energy on plants are many. Prolonged exposure to cosmic, gamma, and X rays will damage or kill most organisms. Mutations and other chromosomal aberrations are induced by a limited exposure to these high-energy rays. Ultraviolet rays are also deleterious to plants and cause dwarfism.

SOLAR SPECTRUM

In the visible and near visible spectrum, 380–770 nanometers (nm), a division of radiation into eight bands based on effects on plants has been proposed.[5]

5. Van der Veen, R., and G. Meijer. 1959. Light and Plant Growth. Macmillan, New York.

1. Longer than 800 nm, no specific effect on plants except as converted to heat.
2. Between 800 and 700 nm, elongating effects and the farred effect on the phytochrome system.
3. Between 700 and 610 nm, the region of peak chlorophyll absorption and maximum photosynthetic activity, and the red effects of the phytochrome system.
4. Between 610 and 510 nm, the region of minimal phytosynthesis and formative influences.
5. Between 510 and 400 nm, the region of absorption by the yellow pigments and secondary chlorophyll absorption and photosynthetic activity, and phototropism and streaming of chloroplasts.
6. Between 400 and 315 nm, formative effects; plants become shorter and leaves thicker.
7. Between 315 and 280 nm, detrimental to most plants.
8. Shorter than 280 nm, highly deleterious resulting in rapid death of plants.

EFFICIENCY OF ENERGY CONVERSION

Incoming solar energy amounts to about 500 cal/sq cm each day, or 21 million Kcal/ha/day. Of this total about 45% is in the visible spectrum. Albedo (reflection) and inactive absorption in the visible spectrum account for an 18% energy loss. The remaining energy is used in photosynthesis but with an efficiency of about 10%. Of the carbohydrates produced, as much as 33% are used in respiration. Thus, incoming solar radiation could theoretically produce about 770 kg/ha dry matter daily.[6] Under actual conditions with high fertilization and ample water, forage yields of 18 t/ha have been produced during a 200-day growing season. Hence, the energy conversion for high-yielding forage crops is less than 12% of the theoretical maximum. Improvement of this efficiency is the goal of plant breeders and management agronomists.

6. Loomis, R. S., and W. A. Williams. 1963. Maximum crop productivity: An estimate. *Crop Sci.* 3:67–72.

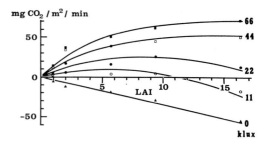

FIG. 35.4. Relation of net photosynthesis of pearlmillet to LAI at various light intensities. (Adapted from D. E. McCloud, 1966.[9])

LEAF AREA AND ENERGY INTERCEPTION

Leaf surfaces are the primary energy interceptors and, since the amount of leaf surface present for forage plants varies widely, it would be expected to be closely related to the rate of growth in forage crops. Leaf area index (LAI) was proposed as an index for relating leaf area to land area.[7] Maintenance of an LAI capable of intercepting a high proportion of the incoming energy is of primary importance in maintaining maximal growth rate. At low LAI values all available energy is not utilized; while at high values of LAI, shading of lower leaves reduces growth rate. A quantity of leaves sufficient to intercept about 95% of the incoming energy results in maximum forage growth.[8] The optimum LAI varies with light intensity (Fig. 35.4). Work with pearlmillet shows an optimum LAI of 2 at 11 k lux light intensity, but at 66 k lux an LAI of 15 is optimum.[9] Maximum growth is reached with 95% light interception. The LAI necessary to intercept 95% of the incident energy varies with species, ranging from 2.1 for ryegrass, 6.5 for timothy, and 3.5 for white clover.[10] Management prac-

7. Watson, D. J. 1947. Comparative physiological studies in the growth rate of field crops. *Ann. Bot.* 11:41–76.
8. Brougham, R. W. 1956. Effect of intensity of defoliation on regrowth of pasture. *Aust. J. Agr. Res.* 7:377–87.
9. McCloud, D. E. 1966. Light relations and photosynthesis within plant communities. Proc. 9th Int. Grassl. Congr., vol. 1, pp. 511–17 (São Paulo, Brazil).
10. Brougham, R. W. 1958. Interception of light by the foliage of pure and mixed stands of pasture plants. *Aust. J. Agr. Res.* 9:39–52.

tices designed to maintain optimal leaf areas to provide maximum interception of the incident energy should result in maximum rates of forage production.

✢ PHOTOPERIOD

In addition to the photosynthetic role of light, the lengths of the daily light and dark periods are of importance to plants. Duration of the photoperiod varies with latitude and season resulting from the tilting of the earth's axis and its orbital path around the sun. Minimum seasonal changes in photoperiod duration occur at the equator and are at a maximum at the earth's poles.

Most forage plants are sensitive to photoperiod, though the responses may be further conditioned by other climatic factors, notably temperature. Temperate grasses and legumes flower during the long photoperiods of summer.[11] Tropical species are less affected by photoperiod than temperate or arctic species.

Photoperiod also affects the vegetative growth habit of many forage species. Under long photoperiods leaf and stem growth is erect, while under short photoperiods growth tends to be prostrate and axillary or adventitious bud activity increases. A knowledge of the photoperiodic response of the various forage species facilitates planning pasture and hay management systems best adapted to the different climatic regions.

✢ TEMPERATURE

The complex interrelated metabolic processes of a plant are catalyzed by enzymes. Temperature is a major factor affecting these enzyme-controlled processes. Respiration rates and the resultant levels of energy available for other metabolic processes thus are related to temperature.

Rates of cell division are closely related to temperature of the meristems because duration of the mitotic cycle is temperature dependent.[12] Temperature also directly affects the rate of respiration which provides the energy needed for cell division. Rates of cell expansion likewise increase with temperature.[13]

Optimal relationships of temperature with cell division and enlargement and the general metabolic process of respiration vary with species. These relationships may represent the major physiological basis for separating forage species into cool- and warm-season and tropical types.

Translocation of photosynthates from the chloroplasts (sources) to growing points (sinks) requires a supply of metabolic energy. Lowering temperatures below threshold levels causes increasing damage to the translocation system, ultimately affecting other metabolic processes including photosynthesis. Reduced growth of tropical forage species like Pangola digitgrass, when grown under cool night temperatures (less than 15 C), has been attributed to decreased rates of translocation.[14] Accumulated starch that had not been translocated from the chloroplasts reduced the rates of photosynthesis the following day even though day temperatures were near 30 C (Fig. 35.5).

Rate of plant development and maturation increases with increasing temperatures (Fig. 35.6). Under hot conditions, plants tend to be shorter and bloom earlier than under cool conditions.[15] Such plant response is part of the reason that forage yields from temperate species decline during hot summer periods. More rapid maturity means that more frequent harvests are needed. Tropical species, on the other hand, are better adapted and more productive under hot humid conditions.

11. Gardner, F. P., and W. E. Loomis. 1953. Floral induction and development in orchardgrass. *Plant Physiol.* 28:201–17.

12. Van't Hof, J., and Huci-Kuen Ying. 1964. Relationship between the duration of the mitotic cycle, the rate of cell production, and the rate of growth of *Pisum* roots at different temperatures. *Cytologia* 29:399–406.

13. Milthorpe, F. L. 1959. Studies on the expansion of the leaf surface. I. The influence of temperature. *J. Exp. Bot.* 10:233–39.

14. Hilliard, J. H., and S. H. West. 1970. Starch accumulation associated with growth reduction at low temperatures in a tropical plant. *Science* 168:494–96.

15. Vough, L. R., and G. C. Marten. 1971. Influence of soil moisture and ambient temperature on yield and quality of alfalfa forage. *Agron. J.* 63:40–43.

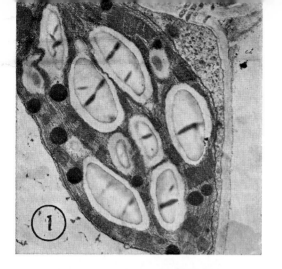

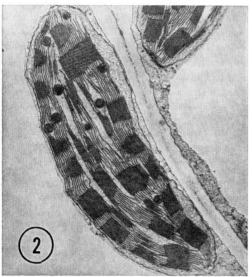

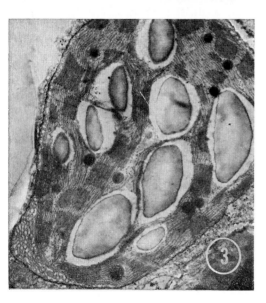

FIG. 35.5. Pangola digitgrass growth stopped by cool temperatures. (1) Starch grains accumulate in chloroplasts during 30 C day; (2) After a 30 C night, starch grains disappear; (3) after a 10 C night, starch grains remain in chloroplasts. (From Hilliard and West, 1970.[14])

TEMPERATURE STRESS

Plants are subjected to continually changing temperature conditions. When temperatures exceed the optimal range, stress is imposed on the plants. Severity of stress depends on the temperature extreme duration and stage of plant development. Stress imposed during an early stage of development may evoke significant physiological responses in later stages.

High-temperature stress frequently occurs concurrently with moisture stress. Thus, it is difficult to separate the two effects. High temperatures lead to a number of metabolic disorders, including enzyme inactivation, imbalance of reaction rates, and reduced metabolic synthesis in plants. Growth depression due to high temperatures has been alleviated by applying essential metabolites such as ribosides to the plant.[16] Excessively high temperatures can induce flower sterility. Plant breeders often use heat to emasculate plants in their breeding programs. High temperatures during seed maturation can reduce subsequent germination as well as vigor of seedlings.[17]

Low-temperature stress can involve either chilling injury at temperatures slightly above freezing or survival during extended periods of subfreezing temperatures. While temperate forage grasses and legumes can withstand considerable overnight frost exposure without appreciable damage to leaf or stem tissue, tropical and subtropical species are damaged by night temperatures in the range of 10–15 C.

Winter injury can be caused by excessively cold temperatures, ice sheets, or heaving. Availability of new cultivars

16. Ketellapper, H. J. 1963. Temperature-induced chemical defects in higher plants. *Plant Physiol.* 38:175–79.
17. Khan, Riaz A., and H. M. Laude. 1969. Influence of heat stress during seed maturation on germinability of barley seed at harvest. *Crop Sci.* 9:55–58.

FIG. 35.6. Temperature affects morphological characteristics of alfalfa plants. *USDA photo.*

capable of withstanding adverse winters has extended forage plant adaptation to more severe winter climates.[18] However, little progress has been made toward increasing heaving or ice sheet tolerance of forage species. Heaving is a serious problem in regions where temperatures fluctuate around the freezing point and on imperfectly drained, fine-textured soils.[19] Prostrate-type plants or those with a branched, creeping rooted habit survive heaving conditions better than plants with a taproot system.

Ice sheets can cause serious damage to overwintering forage plants. When the crown is completely encased in water or ice, plant damage is due to accumulation of respiratory by-products, principally carbon dioxide. Since the hardier species have lower rates of respiration during the winter, differential survival is related to winterhardiness.[20] A high stubble also may reduce ice sheet damage since the protruding stubble provides a passage for gas diffusion from the encased plants.[21]

❧ MOISTURE

Seasonal distribution pattern, total quantity of precipitation, and evapotranspiration demands are important in adaptation of forage species. Also, the quantity of water available to plants depends on the soil reservoir. Fine-textured soils (clays) have a much higher water-holding capacity than coarse-textured soils (sands). Organic soils such as peat and muck also have high water-holding capacities. The depth of rooting also affects the size of the soil reservoir.

Since water loss by plants is a physical evaporative process, net radiation measurements are good indicators of evapotranspiration of a crop canopy, particularly when soil moisture is adequate.[22] Thus the amount of water lost by a forage field through evaporation from the soil surface and transpiration through the plant is de-

18. Klebesadel, L. J. 1971. Selective modification of alfalfa toward acclimatization in a subarctic area of severe winter stress. *Crop Sci.* 11:609–14.

19. Portz, H. L. 1967. Frost heaving of soil and plants. I. Incidence of frost heaving of forage plants and meteorological relationships. *Agron. J.* 59:341–44.

20. Smith, Dale. 1952. Survival of winter-hardened legumes encased in ice. *Agron. J.* 44:469–73.

21. Freyman, S. 1969. Role of stubble in the survival of certain ice-covered forages. *Agron. J.* 61:105–7.

22. Penman, H. L. 1951. The role of vegetation in meteorology, soil mechanics, and hydrology. *Brit. J. Appl. Phys.* 2:145–51.

pendent largely on the amounts of available water and solar radiation. Air temperature, dew point of the air, and wind speed exert a lesser effect on water use.[23]

For any given atmospheric evaporative demand, the water potential in the plant is controlled by the ease with which the water can be restored to the transpiring surface and the rate of water loss from the leaf.[24] The physiological condition of the plant, particularly stomatal activity, also influences the rate of water loss from the plant.

WATER STRESS

When transpiration exceeds water absorption, a stress is imposed upon metabolism, development, growth, and ultimately harvestable yield.[25] The final manifestation of such water stress is permanent wilting and death of the plant. One of the most sensitive plant responses to water stress is cell enlargement. Leaf cell enlargement ceases at very low levels of water stress, when leaf water potentials are less than −3.5 bars. Likewise, cell enlargement in both the shoot and root apex ceases at water potentials of −1 to −2 bars. Even under adequate soil moisture conditions, the atmospheric evaporative demand is high enough during the day to induce a level of stress that results in water potentials of leaf and stem tissue of less than −3.5 bars. Consequently, most leaf and stem cell expansion occurs during the night when transpiration rates are very low.

If the stress has not been too severe or for an extended period, the cessation of cell enlargement and similar plant responses are not permanent, and removal of the stress conditions by reduced transpiration rates or rewatering allows cell enlargement and related development process-es to proceed. As decreasing soil moisture levels and daylight atmospheric demands impose greater water stress on the plant, a longer period for recovery during the dark is required.

Under field conditions drought usually coincides with high temperatures, and both climatic conditions depress plant growth. However, carbohydrate utilization generally is reduced to a greater extent than photosynthesis. Thus drought conditions often result in increased soluble carbohydrate concentration in the plant tissue.[26] This would suggest that forage quality does not decrease during periods of drought stress until death and deterioration of the plant material occurs.

EXCESSIVE MOISTURE CONDITIONS

Poorly drained soils in high-rainfall regions provide an unfavorable environment for growth of many forage species. Some forages such as reed canarygrass or paragrass have an amazing tolerance to waterlogged conditions and often are the only species that can be economically grown in such areas.

Short periods of excessive rainfall that result in temporary waterlogged conditions are more common. Cultivars vary in their tolerance of such excessive moisture conditions. Tolerance may be related to morphology of the root system and stem tissues or an ability to withstand such adverse conditions as low pH or toxicity of aluminum or manganese.

Another important factor is resistance to root diseases. Stand losses of alfalfa growing in poorly drained soils during periods of high precipitation or excessive irrigation often have been attributed to *Phytophthora* root rot.[27] Selection for resistance to this and similar diseases that require very high soil moisture will reduce the deleterious effects of such climatic conditions on forage production. Damping-off

23. Kohler, M. A., T. J. Nordenson, and D. R. Baker. 1959. Evaporation maps for the United States. USDC Tech. Paper 37.
24. Gavande, S. A., and S. A. Taylor. 1967. Influence of soil water potential and atmospheric evaporative demand on transpiration and the energy status of water in plants. *Agron. J.* 59:4–7.
25. Slayter, R. O. 1967. Plant-Water Relationships. Academic Press. New York.

26. Brown, R. H., and R. E. Blaser. 1970. Soil moisture and temperature effects on growth and soluble carbohydrates of orchardgrass (*Dactylis glomerata*). *Crop Sci.* 10:213–16.
27. Frosheiser, F. I. 1967. *Phytophthora* root rot of alfalfa in Minnesota. *Plant Dis. Rept.* 51:679–81.

of seedlings, caused by such soil fungi as *Pythium* spp., *Rhizoctonia* spp., or *Fusarium* spp., can be a serious factor in stand establishment, particularly if periods of high rainfall follow seeding. Other diseases caused by fungi attacking leaf, stem, or floral parts are invariably more serious during periods of excessive rainfall and high humidity. These diseases often cause defoliation with a consequent loss of yield and forage quality. Excessive moisture combined with high temperatures sometimes produces pathological symptoms which cannot be associated with a parasitic organism.[28]

On poorly drained soils excessive rainfall frequently results in serious damage from treading by the grazing animals. Thus excessive rainfall, particularly on poorly drained soils, is a much more important climatic factor in forage production than has been generally recognized.

✦ WEATHER FORECASTS AND FORAGE MANAGEMENT

An understanding of climatic factors and their effects on forage production may allow alteration of production practices to derive maximum yields from the prevailing climate. Forage management decisions involve both short-term (several days to several weeks) and long-term (several months to entire growing seasons) situations. Weather forecasts should play a significant role in making such decisions.

The U.S. Agricultural Weather Service provides meteorological services including forecasts, warnings, and advisories of specific interest to agriculture. The 2- to 5-day weather advisory outlooks provide weather factors useful in forage management. These include air temperatures, humidity, dew intensity and duration, evaporation rates, wind speeds, percent of total possible sunshine, length of rain-free periods, frost warnings, and hay drying rates. An extended 30-day outlook pre-

dicting departures from normal for air temperature and precipitation is issued bimonthly. Considerable effort is being made to attain reliable 14-day outlooks of the weather factors currently forecast in the 2- to 5-day outlooks. Seasonal forecasts of departures from normal temperature and precipitation are being refined. Such long-term forecasts would provide substantially more information on which to base forage management decisions.

SHORT-TERM FORECASTS

Many forage management decisions such as seeding date, insect spraying, and harvesting are based on short-term periods. These management decisions require accurate short-term forecasts. Some operations may have to be performed at times other than the optimum; however, use of weather forecasts will facilitate completion of a major portion of the operations under favorable weather conditions.

Haymaking is one of the more weather-sensitive forage management practices. Loss of feeding value is significant when rains fall on partially cured forage.[29] Ideally, hay should be mowed when at least three rainless days are predicted. In the north central and northeastern portions of the U.S. where field curing of hay can be a problem, such a rain-free period usually begins immediately following the passage of a cold front, which can be recognized by relatively obvious atmospheric conditions (Fig. 35.7).[30]

LONG-TERM FORECASTS

Forage yields differ considerably from one year to the next and also during the season, often as a result of differences in the weather during those years or seasons. Early estimates of anticipated forage yield would be useful in planning management and utilization of the forage.

In areas where moisture is the major

28. Erwin, D. C., B. W. Kennedy, and W. F. Lehman. 1959. Xylem necrosis and root rot of alfalfa associated with excessive irrigation and high temperatures. *Phytopathology* 49:572–78.

29. Hart, R. H., and G. W. Burton. 1967. Curing Coastal bermudagrass hay: Effects of weather, yield, and quality of fresh herbage on drying rate, yield, and quality of cured hay. *Agron. J.* 59:367–71.
30. USDC. 1962. Fronts—Their significance to flying. Aviation Ser. 13.

FIG. 35.7. Hay harvesting is best initiated after passage of a cold front. (Adapted from USDC, 1962.[30])

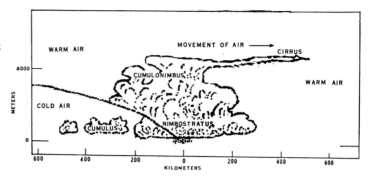

factor limiting plant growth, annual forage yields have been predicted on the basis of normal precipitation.[31] Long-term climatological averages do have limitations because a single season may vary quite widely from the long-term average. In some areas yields of grasslands composed primarily of annual vegetation can be predicted by the amount of precipitation received between September 1 and mid-November of the previous year.[32] Such predictions coupled with long-range weather forecasts could provide considerable information on expected forage yields.

In areas where temperature is the major factor limiting plant growth, the use of heat-unit accumulation provides a basis for predicting yields or harvest dates. Initiation of growth in the spring is related to the accumulated heat units after the midwinter period.[33] Using long-term climatological averages for daily temperatures and combining this with the long-term weather forecasts of departures from normal it should be possible to predict when spring growth will be initiated.

Likewise, the rate of inflorescence development and appearance in grasses is controlled by the weather, primarily temperature.[34] Accumulated daily average temperatures above 5 C during early spring provide a basis for predicting time of head emergence and thus harvest scheduling in grasses.

Refinement of the calculation of the heat units such as weighting of seasonal temperatures to correspond to the sensitivity of the appropriate developmental stage of the plant will increase the usefulness of the heat-unit method. It is entirely within the realm of expectation that within the next quarter-century highly accurate long-range forecasts coupled with predictive methods such as the use of heat units will provide tailored information upon which to base many forage management decisions.

❧ QUESTIONS

1. What climatic factor determines whether the natural vegetation will be forest or grassland?
2. What region of the solar spectrum is most important for plant growth? Why?
3. Why is plant growth maximized when about 95% of increasing solar energy is absorbed?
4. Why is temperature such an important climatic factor in the growth and adaptation of forage plants?
5. Differentiate the climatic factors involved in chilling injury compared with overwinter survival of plants.
6. What climatic factors are involved in the amount of water used to produce a forage crop?
7. How can excessive soil moisture conditions adversely affect forage production?
8. How can climatic factors be used in predicting seasonal forage yields?

31. Sneva, F. A., and D. N. Hyder. 1962. Forecasting range herbage production in eastern Oregon. Oreg. Agr. Exp. Sta. Bull. 588.
32. Murphy, A. H. 1970. Predicted forage yield based on fall precipitation in California annual grasslands. *J. Range Manage.* 23:363–65.
33. Jagtenberg, W. D. 1970. Predicting the best time to apply nitrogen to grassland in spring. *J. Brit. Grassl. Soc.* 25:261–71.
34. Beddows, A. R. 1968. Head emergence in forage grasses in relation to February-May temperatures and the predicting of early or late springs. *J. Brit. Grassl. Soc.* 23:88–97.

PART III

&

FORAGE PRODUCTION PRACTICE

A. MORRIS DECKER / *University of Maryland*

T. H. TAYLOR / *University of Kentucky*

C. J. WILLARD / *Ohio State University*

36

ESTABLISHMENT OF NEW SEEDINGS

THE IMPORTANCE of forage crops to soil conservation and animal feeding is recognized. No erosion was ever stopped and no cow was ever fed by a forage seeding that failed to grow. It takes 2–3 t of forage to pay for establishment; a failure can more than double the cost. Most failures can be prevented with more attention to detail.

Small-seeded forages have establishment problems not common to most crop plants. For example, small variations in planting depth of corn are seldom serious, while similar discrepancies with most forages can be disastrous.

❧ A. MORRIS DECKER is Professor of Agronomy, University of Maryland. He holds the M.S. degree from Utah State University and the Ph.D. from the University of Maryland. His research has been in forage crop management and plant environment.

❧ T. H. TAYLOR. *See Chapter 5.*

❧ C. J. WILLARD was on the faculty of Ohio State University from 1917 until his retirement in 1959. He has been widely recognized for his research on forage management and factors influencing stand establishment.

❧ WHY DO FORAGE SEEDINGS FAIL?

If asked why his seeding failed, the average man may say "poor seed," "dry season," or "winter-kill," but such general reasons seldom tell the whole story. Many more seed are sown than numbers of plants needed (Table 36.1).[1] Why do some plants live but so many die? Stand development may be divided into germination, establishment, and growth stages, each with its own hazards.

Germination of live seed requires:

1. Permeable seed coat. Scarification may be needed.
2. Sufficient air. Seed sown too deeply (especially in wet, heavy soils) may not have enough oxygen to germinate.
3. Favorable temperature. Usually obtained with proper seeding date.
4. Sufficient moisture. Alternating temperature and moisture levels (too low for complete germination) can lower seed viability and result in death.

1. Northeast Regional Publication 42. 1963. Seedling management of grass-legume association in the Northeast. N.J. Agr. Exp. Sta. Bull. 804.

TABLE 36.1 ❧ Number of seedlings 1, 5, and 12 months after seeding plus first harvest forage yields one year after spring seeding

| Companion crop | Number of seedlings per 0.1 sq m | | | | | | Dry matter (t/ha) | |
| | Legume | | | Grass | | | Grass plus legume | Weeds |
	1 mo	5 mo	12 mo	1 mo	5 mo	12 mo		
	Alfalfa at 11.2 kg/ha (54 seed/0.1 sq m) and smooth bromegrass at 6.7 kg/ha (20 seed/0.1 sq m)							
Oats	15	14	8	6	6	5	3.61	0.60
None	17	14	8	9	8	6	3.90	0.49
	Ladino clover at 2.2 kg/ha (43 seed/0.1 sq m) and orchardgrass at 4.4 kg/ha (58 seed/0.1 sq m)							
Oats	13	10	9	9	9	6	3.02	0.38
None	13	9	8	11	11	6	3.27	0.36
	Birdsfoot trefoil at 6.7 kg/ha (56 seed/0.1 sq m) and timothy at 4.4 kg/ha (122 seed/0.1 sq m)							
Oats	13	11	6	30	15	10	3.25	0.67
None	13	11	6	33	17	13	3.56	0.54

Source: Values calculated from tables 2 and 3 of NE Reg. Publ. 42, 1963.[1]
Note: Each value represents the average of four seedling-year management treatments at six northeastern states over a four-year period. All seedings were made with the same cultipacker seeder using one lot of seed at all locations each year.

Establishment after germination may fail because of:

1. Drying. Seed placed in loose surface soil may germinate after a light rain but may dry out and die before developing sufficient roots for establishment.
2. Freezing. Seed are especially sensitive to freezing as the young root breaks the seed coat, and temperatures below —3 C are lethal. Soil coverage reduces the likelihood of injury, and once rooted, seedlings can withstand much lower temperatures.[2]
3. Coverage that is too light. Soil cover or mulch protects against both drying and freezing; without it seed establish only when soil surface remains moist for extended periods.
4. Coverage that is too heavy. More seed probably is wasted in this way than any other.[3]
5. Crusted soil surface. This can prevent emergence, especially when seed are sown deeply on fine-textured soils.

Growth of seedlings after establishment may stop because of:

1. Undesirable pH. Lime should be applied according to soil test to provide desirable pH, plus Ca and Mg as nutrients.[4]
2. Low fertility. A soil test should be used to ensure adequate P, K, or other nutrients.
3. Inadequate legume inoculation. See Chapter 9.
4. Poor drainage. Water accumulation on the surface or in the soil profile can limit growth.
5. Drought. This is the most commonly given reason for stand failures.
6. Competition from companion crops. Cereals compete with forage seedlings for water, light, or nutrients and are not "nurse" crops.[5]
7. Competition from weeds. Weeds are similar to companion crops, but com-

2. Laude, H. M. 1956. The seedling emergence of grasses as affected by low temperature. *Agron. J.* 48:558–63.
3. Beveridge, J. L., and C. P. Wilsie. 1959. Influence of depth of planting, seed size and variety on emergence and seedling vigor in alfalfa. *Agron. J.* 51:731–34.

4. Sullivan, E. F., and L. F. Marriott. 1960. Effect of soil acidity on establishment and growth of orchardgrass seedlings in pot cultures. *Agron. J.* 52:147–48.
5. Klebesadel, L. J., and Dale Smith. 1960. Effects of harvesting an oat companion crop at four stages of maturity on the yield of oats, on light near the soil surface, on soil moisture, and on the establishment of alfalfa. *Agron. J.* 52:627–30.

petition may be more severe and last longer.

8. Insects. Pests like the alfalfa weevil can eliminate new stands.
9. Diseases. Pathogens like anthracnose or pythium can be fatal.
10. Winter-killing. Seeding too late in the fall or seeding poorly adapted cultivars can cause winter-kill.

❧ OBTAINING SUCCESSFUL STANDS FROM NEW SEEDINGS

Hazards associated with seedings have been indicated. Relative importance varies with the crop, its use, and the climate in which it grows. Excellent forage stands are not too difficult to obtain, but success is possible only when rather specific rules are followed.

Selection of species or cultivars should have first priority; one cultivar, species, or combination will best fit the needs for a specific climate, soil condition, and forage use. A single selection may be adequate for one farm, while several may be dictated for another. Research has shown that species respond differently on northern and southern slopes within a single pasture.[6] Thus different managements of these slopes, including seeded mixtures, may mean more efficient production. For example, in warm humid regions species like Kentucky bluegrass or tall fescue would do best on northern slopes, while an adapted warm-season species like bermudagrass would utilize the southern slopes best.

PURE STANDS OR MIXTURES

If one species is exceptionally well adapted to a given location, either naturally or by reason of soil treatment, any mixture is likely to be lower yielding. Few mixtures will outyield well-adapted grasses that are heavily fertilized (especially with N) and given sufficient water; the limitation may lie in forage quality which is usually improved with a legume added. Some reasons for mixtures are:

1. Seeding hazards do not equally affect all crops, and a good mixture is more likely to furnish a uniform supply of quality forage.
2. Legume-grass mixtures are usually more productive than legumes alone, and grasses contain more protein when grown with a legume unless heavily fertilized with N.
3. Grasses reduce soil erosion and winter heaving of legumes.
4. Mixtures resist weed encroachment better and remain productive longer than pure legume stands.
5. Grasses added to legumes will reduce bloat when pastured.
6. Grasses reduce legume lodging, thus saving more leaves.
7. Grass-legume mixtures are more easily cured for hay or preserved as silage than pure legumes.

The best mixture is determined by the interaction of species in the mixture with the climate, soil, seeding method and time, forage use, and expected stand life.[7] General principles for compounding forage mixtures are:

1. Include at least one grass and one legume.
2. Keep the mixture simple; seldom are more than four species justified. Even in the "shot-gun" type of mixture, every species should serve a definite purpose with a reasonable chance of achieving that goal.[8] Too many species can actually decrease yields, as shown by Pennsylvania research (J. B. Washko) where average yields over a five-year period were 7.49, 4.15, and 4.75 t/ha for 2-, 5-,

6. Bennett, O. L., and E. L. Mathias. 1969. Slope direction affects bluegrass yields on hillside pasture. *Crops and Soils* 21:23–24.

7. Blaser, R. E., W. H. Skrdla, and T. H. Taylor. 1952. Ecological and physiological factors in compounding forage seed mixtures. *Advan. Agron.* 4:179–216.

8. Jackobs, J. A. 1963. A measurement of the contributions of ten species to pasture mixtures. *Agron. J.* 55:127–31.

and 14-species mixtures respectively.

3. Plants must be adapted to the use for which the mixture is intended.

4. As nearly as possible, all plants should mature together. It is sometimes said that pasture mixtures should include plants of differing maturity to equalize seasonal yields; but in practice early species outgrow the late ones, which are damaged by untimely grazing. If grazing is delayed to fit requirements of late species, overall quality will be reduced.

5. Grazing mixtures should not include species with widely different palatabilities since unpalatable species will soon dominate.

6. Plants must be good competitors. Bunchgrasses are less competitive than sod grasses if sown at low rates. Sod-forming species ensure more complete soil coverage of seeded crop, leaving less space for weeds. Grasses grown with legumes are most competitive on soils with high native N.

7. Mixtures require more total seed per ha. Enough seed of each species should be included for a stand if others should fail.

8. Species that establish rapidly ensure early production, but too much seed can eliminate others.[9]

LIME AND FERTILITY REQUIREMENTS

Species differ considerably, but persistent, high-yielding stands are always associated with a favorable pH and high fertility. A soil sample prior to seeding, to determine the pH and fertility status of the soil, can be used with the history and intended use of a field to develop a sound fertility program (see Chapters 38 and 39).

In humid regions east of the Missouri River (about the 95th meridian) periodic lime applications are needed, while in more arid climates lime may seldom be required. Where large amounts are needed, liming

6–12 months before seeding and thorough mixing with the plow layer is desirable.

Although high levels of N, P, and K are desirable, P levels are more critical for establishment. Phosphorus carriers in contact or just below the seed are particularly helpful, while large amounts of N and K can be harmful.[10,11] Where the N status of a soil is low, small applications at seeding may be desirable. Virginia research showed that as N rates increased, the numbers of grass and legume seedlings decreased but seedling size increased. However, first harvest year yields were similar.[12]

SEEDBED PREPARATION AND SEED PLACEMENT

A seedbed should be weed-free and firm with just enough loose surface soil for uniform, shallow seed coverage. Any tillage method that accomplishes this is satisfactory. Tillage also provides a means of incorporating slow-moving materials like lime and P into the root zone.

A disk or spring-tooth harrow can be used and may often be preferred to plowing because they leave a protective surface mulch. Nothing will do more to ensure success than a light mulch (Table 36.2).[13] This can be supplied by disking existing vegetation into the surface, or it may be applied immediately after seeding. Straw, manure, or any such material that can be uniformly distributed is satisfactory. About 2 t/ha of straw is ideal; much more may cause "damping off." Mulches conserve surface moisture and reduce summer temperature, crusting, and winter injury (especially heaving) but can be a source of weed seed.

Firming the soil before seeding does two

9. Blaser, R. E., W. L. Griffeth, and T. H. Taylor. 1956. Seedling competition in compounding forage mixtures. *Agron. J.* 48:118–23.

10. Sheard, R. W., G. J. Bradshaw, and D. L. Massey. 1971. Phosphorus placement for the establishment of alfalfa and bromegrass. *Agron. J.* 63:922–27.

11. Brown, B. A. 1959. Band versus broadcast fertilization of alfalfa. *Agron. J.* 51:708–10.

12. Ward, C. Y., and R. E. Blaser. 1961. Effect of nitrogen fertilizer on emergence and seedling growth of forage plants and subsequent production. *Agron. J.* 53:115–20.

13. Moore, R. P. 1943. Seedling emergence of small-seeded legumes and grasses. *J. Amer. Soc. Agron.* 35:370–81.

TABLE 36.2 ❧ Percentage seedling emergence of viable seed after 25 days as affected by seeding depth and mulch

Crop	Depth (not mulched)						Depth (mulched, 2.24 t/ha)					
	0 cm	0.6 cm	1.1 cm	2.5 cm	3.8 cm	5.0 cm	0 cm	0.6 cm	1.2 cm	2.5 cm	3.8 cm	5.0 cm
Alfalfa	42	75	63	48	7	1	76	85	82	73	45	16
Red clover	40	44	39	25	1	1	74	85	86	70	26	3
Orchardgrass	37	58	59	40	9	3	78	95	86	69	39	10
Timothy	30	46	27	3	0	0	49	70	68	23	1	0

Source: Moore, 1943.[13]
Note: Seed sown May 18 on Miami silt loam at Columbus, Ohio. Seed hand placed and hand covered to accurate depths. Several hard showers followed by high evaporation during the germination.

very important things. It prevents placing seed too deep and improves seed-to-soil contact, both very important for germination and early seedling development.[14]

Shallow placement of forage seed is imperative. In most humid areas best results are obtained with seed placed between 0.5 and 1.5 cm deep.[15,16] Deeper than 2.5 cm can be fatal to seed the size of clover or timothy.[17] Even if seedlings emerge from greater depths, they are so weakened that survival is reduced. Emergence and survival of deeply planted seed are greater on sandy soils than on heavier ones. In general, the heavier the texture the shallower the seed must be placed; soil firming is more critical on light soils.

SEEDING RATES

Recommended forage seeding rates vary more than those for grain crops. This is due in part to the fact that forages are sown on such a wide range of soils with widely different climates. It is common for no more than a third of sown seed to produce seedlings, and only half of those survive the first year (Table 36.1). More plants are needed the first year than in subsequent seasons. High seeding rates may appear wasteful, but because of the many hazards they are often justified. Moreover, excessive seeding rates do not reduce forage as much as seed yields. In Ohio, alfalfa yields were similar at 56 and 8.4 kg/ha.[18] Growth of many small plants or a few large ones is dependent upon existing soil and weather conditions if a similar canopy exists in each case. Nevertheless, excessive seed has been shown to reduce vegetative growth.[19] If competition is severe enough, all plants are weakened. Rates are more critical with mixtures. Rates can be lowered by timely sowing and proper seed placement.

SEEDING FORAGES WITH A COMPANION CROP

In humid regions sowing forages with small grains was at one time almost universal. Although the percentage of such seedings has declined, the practice is still used. Cereals grown for grain or forage provide a return from the land while the long-lived forage is establishing. Moreover, experience in humid areas shows that forages sown alone may get a companion crop of weeds, which may do more harm to forage seedlings than cereals that provide erosion-resisting growth more rapidly than forages alone. Winter cereals may protect early sown legumes from frost.

Companion crops may control weeds, but they can also choke out forage seedlings.

14. Triplett, G. B., and M. B. Tesar. 1960. Effects of compaction, depth of planting and soil moisture tension on seedling emergence of alfalfa. Agron. J. 52:681–84.
15. Murphy, R. P., and A. C. Arny. 1939. The emergence of grass and legume seedlings planted at different depths in five soil types. J. Amer. Soc. Agron. 31:17–28.
16. Sund, J. M., G. P. Barrington, and J. M. Scholl. 1966. Methods and depth of sowing forage grasses and legumes. Proc. 10th Int. Grassl. Congr., pp. 319–23 (Helsinki, Finland).
17. Williams, W. A. 1956. Evaluation of the emergence force exerted by seedlings of small-seeded legumes, using probit analysis. Agron. J. 48:273–74.

18. Willard, C. J. 1938. The rate of seeding Grimm and common alfalfa. Ohio Agr. Exp. Sta. Bull. 23.
19. Evans, M. W., F. A. Welton, and R. M. Slater. 1939. Timothy culture. Ohio Agr. Exp. Sta. Bull. 603.

FIG. 36.1. *Companion crop . . . must control . . . weeds but not the forage.* An excellent stand of alfalfa seeded in an oat companion crop.

However, except in the extreme North, cereals mature and are removed early, while most weeds continue to grow throughout the season and thus compete more seriously. Therefore, in humid areas companion crops will continue to be used with spring-seeded forages where it is economically feasible.[20]

Companion crops are seldom used with late summer seedings (often incorrectly called fall seedings) or in areas of limited rainfall. Some cool-season grasses like timothy can be seeded with winter grains, but legumes should not be sown until early the following spring.

The choice of a companion crop depends on many factors. It must control invading weeds but not the seeded forage. It should provide an economic return. Failure in any category makes it unsatisfactory.

Any spring-seeded cereal can be used, but oats are most satisfactory (Fig. 36.1). Fall-sown cereals produce early spring shade, which is particularly detrimental to alfalfa

and birdsfoot trefoil.[21,22] Red clover is less sensitive to early shade, and stands are more likely to be successful from early spring seedings in winter wheat than from late seedings with spring oats, especially in the more southern areas during dry seasons. Winter wheat or barley is more satisfactory than rye.

SEEDING FORAGES WITHOUT A
COMPANION CROP

With the development of effective herbicides the traditional companion crop is no longer needed. Incorporated preemergence herbicides followed by postemergence treatment when necessary will give weed control and excellent legume stands from spring seedings with 6 t/ha or more in the seedling year.[23,24] This is especially important when

20. Schmid, A. R., and R. Behrens. 1972. Herbicides vs. oat companion crops for alfalfa establishment. *Agron. J.* 64:157–59.

21. Gist, G. R., and G. O. Mott. 1958. Growth of alfalfa, red clover and birdsfoot trefoil seedlings under various quantities of light. *Agron. J.* 50:583–86.
22. Peters, R. A. 1961. Legume establishment as related to the presence of an oat companion crop. *Agron. J.* 53:195–98.
23. Peters, E. J., and S. A. Lowance. 1971. Establishment of crownvetch with herbicides. *Agron. J.* 63:230–33.
24. Linscott, D. L., and R. D. Hagin. 1969. Placement of EPTC-fertilizer when seeding birdsfoot trefoil. *Weed Sci.* 17:108–9.

FIG. 36.2. *More reliable than broadcasting . . . on newly prepared seedbed.* Cultipacker seeder operating on a well-prepared seedbed.

the major crops are alfalfa and corn silage and the often lower producing cereal is no longer needed. When herbicides eliminate weed competition, forage seeding rates can be reduced.[25],[26] However, presently available preemergence herbicides cannot be used with grass-legume mixtures.

South of approximately 39° N seeding perennial forages after small-grain harvest is often more practical than sowing them in the spring with a companion crop. Forage seedlings do not have to compete with companion crops or weeds during the hot dry summer, and the cereal does not have to be managed to save the forage. Success of such seedings depends on adequate rain between grain harvest and forage establishment. Ideally, the field is tilled immediately after grain harvest. Surface weed seed germinate and are destroyed at final seedbed preparation. Winter annual weeds like chickweed and henbit can be a problem with late summer seedings, especially during mild winters. When this occurs, herbicides may be needed (see Chapter 37).

METHODS OF SEEDING FORAGES

Forage stands can be obtained by using a variety of techniques. Some are success-

25. Moline, W. J., and L. R. Robinson. 1971. Effects of herbicides and seeding rates on the production of alfalfa. *Agron. J.* 63:614–17.
26. Hoveland, C. S. 1970. Establishing sericea lespedeza at low seeding rate with a herbicide. Ala. Agr. Exp. Sta. Circ. 174.

ful only during short periods when specific soil and climatic conditions exist, while others are reliable over a wider range.

Broadcast seedings without mechanical soil coverage are most successful in late winter or early spring when the soil surface is honeycombed with ice crystals. Freezing and thawing plus rain action usually cover seed to about the right depth. Frost seedings made into fall-seeded cereals produce excellent stands of red clover. However, if sowing is delayed until after freezing and the soil surface has started to dry, drilling is preferred. Frost seeding completes the job early at a slack time with results equal or superior to drilling later.

Cultipacker seeders are more reliable than broadcasting, especially on newly prepared seedbeds. They consist of two corrugated rollers with seed metering boxes. The soil surface is firmed into shallow corrugations by the first roller. Seed is broadcast and the second roller forms new corrugations, with the valleys where the ridges made by the first existed. This firms the soil around the seed which is largely kept within 0.5–2.5 cm of the soil surface (Fig. 36.2).

Band-seeding is the most reliable method of all. Special seeders drill seed 0.5–1.5 cm deep directly over bands of fertilizer placed 3–6 cm deep. Best results are obtained with press wheels to ensure coverage and

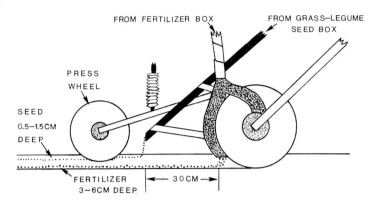

FROM FERTILIZER BOX

FROM GRASS—LEGUME SEED BOX

PRESS WHEEL

SEED 0.5–1.5 CM DEEP

FERTILIZER 3–6 CM DEEP

30 CM

FIG. 36.3. Schematic for converting a grain drill for band-seeding. Flexible tubing from the seed box is attached to a point 30 cm behind openers placing fertilizer.

good seed-soil contact.[27-29] This is especially critical on light soils.

Grain drills equipped with forage seed boxes can be converted for band-seeding by attaching flexible tubing from the seed box to a point 30 cm behind the openers placing fertilizer. This distance is needed to allow soil to flow back into the furrow, with a few centimeters separating fertilizer from seed, and will vary with soil condition and planting speed (Fig. 36.3). Many early band-seeding failures resulted from seed being buried because tubes were too close to fertilizer openers. Tubing should be firmly attached so that seed are placed directly over fertilizer bands; even 3 cm off may be too far.[28]

Soil that is wet does not flow back readily, and deep furrows may result. Seed and young plants at the bottom of these furrows can be silted over by heavy rains. Drilling on a firmer seedbed and using short drag chains in front of the seed tubes will help. Cultipacking after band-seeding is usually not desirable.

Band-seeding correctly done is reliable because:

1. Readily available P promotes more rapid development of large healthier seedlings, which allows for reduced seeding rates.
2. Fewer weeds are fertilized, so forage has a competitive advantage.
3. Less fertilizer is in contact with the soil to be tied up in unavailable forms.
4. Successful seedings can be made later in the fall or spring.
5. Forages can survive adverse soil or climatic conditions better because of rapid early development.

Seeding in row crops has been done in an attempt to go directly from corn to alfalfa without the interim small-grain crop. These seedings have all the hazards of summer seedings plus severe competition from the row crop. They are successful only on fertile soil when adequate moisture is present and where competition is reduced by wide spacing of row crops.[30,31] Since the trend is toward narrower rows, this method is seldom used.

❧ MANAGEMENT OF NEW FORAGE SEEDINGS

The key to success is providing conditions that give a competitive advantage to the seeded forage over the companion crop or invading weeds.

Spring-seeded companion crops should

27. Tesar, M. B., K. Lawton, and B. Kawin. 1954. Comparison of band-seeding and other methods of seeding legumes. *Agron. J.* 46:189–94.
28. Wagner, R. E. 1956. Pasture establishment with special reference to band-seeding. Proc. 7th Int. Grassl. Congr., pp. 104–15 (Palmerston North, N.Z.).
29. Northeast Regional Publication 41. 1960. Band and broadcast seeding of alfalfa-bromegrass in the Northeast. Md. Agr. Exp. Sta. Bull. 804.

30. Pendleton, J. W., J. A. Jackobs, F. W. Slife, and H. P. Bateman. 1957. Establishing legumes in corn. *Agron. J.* 49:44–48.
31. Tesar, M. B. 1957. Establishment of alfalfa in wide row corn. *Agron. J.* 49:63–68.

TABLE 36.3 ❧ Rate of seeding small-grain crops as influencing yield of grain and straw

Rate of seeding (liters)	Oats, grain (27-yr av) (q/ha)	Barley, grain (4-yr av) (q/ha)	Winter wheat (28-yr av)	
			Grain (q/ha)	Straw (kg/ha)
86	32.9	20.3	19.7	3,170
131	36.9	21.2	21.3	3,338
173	38.4	21.8	22.1	3.408
217	39.6	21.1	22.0	3,349

Source: Secrest, 1938.[32]

not be sown heavier than 75% of the usual recommended rate; flax is an exception. This reduces companion crop competition, especially in dry seasons, and decreases the likelihood of lodging in wet seasons. High N topdressing on cereals should be avoided. Early removal of the companion crop as silage or pasture will usually favor forage establishment. When this is removed early, the companion crop seeding rate is less critical.

Fall-seeded companion crops are usually more of a threat to forage establishment than spring cereals. Reduced seeding rates are not practical because of the long period for development, where any reasonable rate produces about the same number of tillers per unit area with similar competition (Table 36.3).[32]

Since winter cereals are usually grown to maturity, spring-sown legumes must be seeded early. When excessive spring growth occurs, pasturing is a good way to reduce competition and is almost essential for vigorous competitors like winter barley and rye. This is also an excellent source of quality feed, but grazing of cereals to be saved for grain must be discontinued before jointing. If grazing is not possible, growth can be clipped. This can save the forage stand and increase grain yields, especially when lodging of the cereal is prevented.

Combined straw should be removed as soon as possible after harvest to avoid plant losses, especially in red clover. This is par-

ticularly true east of the Mississippi.[33] It is often advantageous to clip and remove the stubble with the combined straw. In seasons when forage has made sufficient growth (early bloom), a stubble hay harvest can be made.

Clipping new stands for weed control may be necessary, but should not be done too soon or only the tops of many weeds will be removed. Live buds on the weed stubble produce new branches which can make weeds even more competitive. Weeds should be allowed sufficient growth and then clipped low so that most active buds are removed. Most forages (sweetclover and lespedeza are exceptions) regrow from crown buds and are usually not seriously damaged by low cutting. Clipping during the seedling year can reduce plant development as well as forage yields the following year. In a Maryland study, where an alfalfa–smooth bromegrass mixture was spring-seeded into a field heavily infested with weed seed, alfalfa crown weights were doubled by maintaining weed-free conditions through daily hand weeding. When weeds were allowed to grow, forage yields the following season dropped from 15.9 to 14 t/ha. When weeds were controlled by clipping, yields were 13.3 t/ha. Clipping controlled weeds, but alfalfa seedling development was curtailed. In another phase of the same study, ladino clover stolon growth during the seedling year was increased more than fourfold with a weed-free environment.[1] More productive stands will result in the absence of weeds; clipping for weed control can be detrimental, especially during periods of moisture stress.[34]

Pasturing or harvesting new seedlings can be advantageous, but grazing or cutting should end four to six weeks before a killing frost to allow a buildup of reserves for winter. Less harm will occur with moderate pasturing just before or after frost than by continuous grazing to freeze-up.

32. Secrest, Edmund. 1938. Handbook of experiments in agronomy. Ohio Agr. Exp. Sta. Special Circ. 53.

33. Allen, R. J., Jr., and A. O. Kuhn. 1955. Seedling year management of medium red clover (*Trifolium pratense* L.). Md. Agr. Exp. Sta. Bull. 453.
34. Klebesadel, L. J. and Dale Smith. 1958. The influence of oat stubble management on the establishment of alfalfa and red clover. *Agron. J.* 50:680–83.

Grazing should be avoided during wet periods. Some top growth remaining to serve as a protective mulch for young plants during winter is an advantage. Harvesting or grazing management of seedling stands should be no more severe than for mature stands of the same species.

❧ RENOVATION AND SOD-SEEDING

PASTURE RENOVATION

Pasture renovation is defined by the Crop Science Society of America as "the improvement of a pasture by the partial or complete destruction of the sod, plus liming, fertilizing, seeding, and weed control as may be required to establish desirable forage plants." This technique has been tested and used over a variety of conditions.[35-37] Such seedings are most valuable for hilly rocky areas that cannot or should not be plowed or for areas that are unproductive because of thin weedy stands. Over 1.2 million ha of cool-season grasses were renovated in Kentucky from 1962 to 1971, and the practice is growing.

The objective of renovation is to upgrade the quality and quantity of herbage production. To best accomplish this, fields should be closely grazed to weaken existing sod and to eliminate excess plant material that may interfere with seedbed preparation or seeding operation. The old sod can be renovated with a disk or field cultivator or, if worked on the contour, by shallow plowing. In the spring, plowing may kill more of the existing sod than disking. In late summer the disk is preferred since it leaves root and stubble trash near the surface to protect against erosion and to aid in seedling emergence.

Herbicides can be used alone or in combination with soil tillage.[38,39] This reduces but seldom eliminates all tillage but keeps more of the dead sod mulch near the surface where it does maximum good. When needed, lime and fertilizer can be worked in during seedbed preparation.

SOD-SEEDING

With the development of improved techniques sod-seeding has increased.[40,41,42] It is used primarily to introduce legumes into thin or grass-dominant sods, but the practice of seeding hay crops like alfalfa in regular crop rotations is increasing. The introduction of grasses into low-producing rangelands has also been successful.[43,44] Sod-seeders employ the basic components of the band seeder (Fig. 36.3), with a tillage unit ahead of fertilizer and seed placement. Sod-seeding is successful when competition from the existing sod is reduced and accurate seed placement is achieved. Precision seed placement is the single most consistent factor contributing to successful stands.

Early sod-seeding attempts failed because sod competition was not adequately reduced and precise seed placement was not possible with most available seeders. Sod competition can be controlled by removing a band of sod (10 cm wide, 5 cm deep) with an offset, concave disk placed between the leading straight colter and seeding unit. This modification consistently gave satisfactory stands of birdsfoot trefoil and crownvetch in Maryland.[40] Furrows with sod removed provide a firm seedbed with

38. Sprague, M. A., R. D. Ilnicki, R. J. Aldrich, A. H. Kates, T. O. Evrard, and R. W. Chase. 1962. Pasture improvement and seedbed preparation with herbicides. N.J. Agr. Exp. Sta. Bull. 803.

39. Harrington, J. D., and J. B. Washko. 1962. Sod subjugation with herbicides for pasture renovation. Pa. Agr. Exp. Sta. Bull. 694.

40. Decker, A. M., H. J. Retzer, and F. G. Swain. 1964. Improved soil openers for the establishment of small-seeded legumes in sod. *Agron. J.* 56:211–14.

41. Decker, A. M., H. J. Retzer, M. L. Sarna, and H. D. Kerr. 1969. Permanent pasture improvement with sod seeding and fertilization. *Agron. J.* 61:243–47.

42. Taylor, T. H., E. M. Smith, and W. C. Templeton, Jr. 1969. Use of minimum tillage and herbicide for establishing legumes in Kentucky bluegrass (*Poa pratensis* L.) swards. *Agron. J.* 61:761–66.

43. Dudley, R. F., E. B. Hudspeth, Jr., and G. W. Gant. 1966. Bushland range interseeder. *J. Range Mange.* 19:227–29.

44. Willard, E. W., and J. L. Schuster. 1971. An evaluation of an interseeded sideoats grama stand four years after establishment. *J. Range Mange.* 24:223–26.

35. Burger, A. W., T. S. Ronningen, and A. O. Kuhn. 1954. Pasture renovation. Md. Agr. Exp. Sta. Bull. 449.

36. Gomm, F. B. 1962. Reseeding studies at a small high-altitude park in southwestern Montana. Mont. Agr. Exp. Sta. Bull. 568.

37. Templeton, W. C., C. F. Buck, and N. W. Bradley. 1970. Renovated Kentucky bluegrass and supplementary pastures for steers. Ky. Agr. Exp. Sta. Bull. 709.

FIG. 36.4. *Bermudagrass . . . summer pasture . . . solid footing for grazing animals during wet weather.* The grazing season, especially of warm-season perennials, can be extended with sod-seeded cool-season annuals. *Md. Agr. Exp. Sta. photo.*

just enough loose soil for good seed coverage. Best results are obtained when soil is on the dry side. A band of paraquat sprayed over the row at seeding is equally effective in controlling sod growth and does not leave the field furrowed and rough.[41] In early Kentucky research a powered rotation disk, set at an angle to till the desired width of sod, has also consistently given good stands.[42] Paraquat sprayed over the seeded row reduced sod competition and increased both seedling numbers and size. The John Deere Power Till seeder was developed from the Kentucky research.[45] Other available sod-seeders include the Zip, Bettisen (Melroe), Buffalo, and Tye. No-till corn planters can also be used where the insecticide box is used to deliver seed just in front of the press wheel. A variety of soil tillage and seed placement units were found to give satisfactory stands when sod competition was controlled with herbicides.[46] In old pastures where vegetation is eliminated with broadcast herbicide, annual weeds can be a problem. In such cases, band applica-

tion of the herbicide over the seeded row will often reduce the weeds. The narrow strip of unsprayed sod serves the same function as a companion crop in conventional seedings.[46]

If perennial broad-leaf weeds are present they should be eliminated by herbicides such as 2,4-D and/or Banvel (dicamba). This should be done at least 30 days before sod-seeding.[47] Sod-seeding alfalfa into small grain stubble in late summer works well; best results are obtained with two applications of paraquat 2–4 weeks apart where the last is applied just prior to seeding.

Alternate row sod-seeding of an easily established, short-lived species like red clover with a slower establishing, longer lived species like birdsfoot trefoil provides both early and long-lasting pasture improvement.[48] The frequency of sod-seedings can thus be reduced.

Management of pastures prior to and after sod-seeding is critical. Heavy grazing before will reduce sod competition and

45. Smith, E. M., D. H. Bucher, and J. B. Hackensmith. 1977. A grassland renovator with unique tillage device. Paper 77–1002. Ann. Meet. Amer. Soc. Agr. Engin. (N. C. State Univ., Raleigh).

46. Decker, A. M., and R. F Dudley. 1978. Minimum tillage establishment of forage species. Proc. Int. Hill Land Symp. (W. Va. Univ., Morgantown, 1976) (In Press).

47. Triplett, G. B., Jr., R. W. Van Keuren, and V. H. Watson. 1975. The role of herbicides in pasture renovation. Proc. No-tillage Forage Symp., pp. 29–41. (Ohio State Univ.).

48. Decker, A. M., J. H. Vandersall, and N. A. Clark. 1978. Pasture renovation with alternate row sod-seeding of different legume species. Proc. Int. Hill Land Symp. (W. Va. Univ., Morgantown, 1976) (In Press).

usually facilitate better herbicidal action. After initial establishment, competition from the sod must be controlled to insure satisfactory stands. Controlled grazing is an excellent way to do this, but in some situations clipping may be more desirable.[49] Grazing management is more critical with spring sod-seedings, while drought is more of a problem in late summer.

Sod-seeding of cereals into warm-season perennials for winter grazing was first reported by Dudley and Wise.[50] The practice is widely used in the Southeast. Any heavy-duty drill can be used with good success as long as the seeding is not made too early; wait until after growth of the summer perennial declines as a result of cool nights. This will generally be 3–5 weeks before the first killing frost. When killing frosts are late, paraquat application will make earlier seedings possible.[51] In northern areas most forage produced by sod-seeded, cool-season annuals is in the spring, while fall and winter grazing is more likely farther south. This practice extends grazing, increases yields, reduces winter annual weeds, and provides solid footing for grazing annuals during periods of wet weather (see Fig. 36.4).[52-55] The annual expense of sod-seeding can be eliminated by growing warm- and cool-season perennials in the same pasture. Wilkinson et al.[56] have successfully grown tall fescue and bermudagrass together for a number of years. However, Decker et al.[57] reported that sod-seeded annuals consistently outyielded mixtures of either tall fescue or orchardgrass and Midland bermudagrass, and it was difficult to maintain mixtures of the warm- and cool-season perennials.

Seeding summer annuals into perennial cool-season sods has met with limited success. For such a practice to be successful, irrigation or good rainfall distribution will be necessary, along with chemical sod suppression.[58]

49. Cullen, N. A. 1970. The effect of grazing, time of sowing, fertilizer, and paraquat on the germination and survival of oversown grasses and clovers. Proc. 11th Int. Grassl. Congr., pp. 112–15 (Surfers Paradise, Queensland, Aust.).
50. Dudley, R. F., and L. N. Wise. 1953. Seeding in permanent pasture for supplementary winter grazing. Miss. Agr. Exp. Sta. Bull. 505.
51. Watson, V. H., W. E. Knight, and R. E. Coats. 1975. Pasture renovation and overseeding programs for the lower south. Proc. No-tillage Forage Symp., pp. 97–104 (Ohio State Univ.).
52. Decker, A. M. 1959. Midland bermudagrass—A new forage grass for Maryland. Md. Agr. Exp. Sta. Bull. 465.
53. Decker, A. M., and W. L. Harris. 1971. Can controlled flaming improve bermudagrass yields and forage quality? Proc. Ann. Symp. Thermal Agr. NGPA-NLPGA 8:60–65.
54. Decker, A. M., H. J. Retzer, F. G. Swain, and R. F. Dudley. 1969. Midland bermudagrass forage production supplemented by sod-seeded cool-season annual forages. Md. Agr. Exp. Sta. Bull. 484.
55. Hoveland, C. S., and E. L. Carden. 1971. Overseeding winter annual grasses in sericea lespedeza. Agron. J. 63:333–34.
56. Wilkinson, S. R., L. F. Welch, G. A. Hillsman, and W. A. Jackson. 1968. Compatibility of tall fescue and coastal bermudagrass as affected by nitrogen fertilization and height of clip. Agron. J. 60:359–62.
57. Decker, A. M., H. J. Retzer, and R. F. Dudley. 1974. Cool-season perennials vs. cool-season annuals sod-seeded into a bermudagrass sward. Agron. J. 66:381–83.
58. Hart, R. H., H. J. Retzer, R. F. Dudley, and G. E. Carlson. 1971. Seeding sorghum and sudangrass hybrids into tall fescue sod. Agron. J. 63:478–80.

❧ QUESTIONS

1. What are the main reasons for forage seeding failures?
2. In what way does seeding a grass-legume mixture help ensure successful stands?
3. What makes an ideal seedbed?
4. What determines seeding depth and how can one ensure accurate seed placement?
5. Why do seeding rates vary so much and how can they be lowered?
6. What determines whether forages should be seeded alone or with a companion crop?
7. Why is the term *companion* crop preferred to *nurse crop?*
8. What would be the management of the forage stand after removal of the grain crop? What about the straw after combining?
9. How would you manage a new forage seeding where weeds have invaded the stand?
10. What is meant by the terms pasture renovation, band-seeding, and sod-seeding?

MARVIN M. SCHREIBER / *Agricultural Research Service, USDA, and Purdue University*

37

WEED CONTROL IN FORAGES

⚘

WEEDS are as important in forages as in any crop-production area. The unique aspect of weed control in forages is the close relationship it has with management. To properly discuss weed control in forages the specific problems that can occur must be recognized as well as the relationship of treating the *cause* along with the *symptom,* which is the presence of weeds.

The first principle of weed control in forage crops is prevention. The simplest way to avoid new weeds is not to plant them. Many of the weeds of the U.S. are not native and have been introduced in crop seed. Russian knapweed, *Centaurea repens* L., was introduced in alfalfa seed. Johnsongrass, *Sorghum halepense* (L.) Pers., has been spread in sudangrass seed; and dodders, *Cuscuta* spp., have been spread in clover seed. Since many weed seed are so similar to forages in size, shape, and specific gravity, they have been expensive and difficult to separate. The spread of smooth bedstraw, *Galium mollugo* L., in birdsfoot trefoil seed is a good example. The use of certified seed is one of the best methods of preventing the introduction and spread of weed seed.

Any management system that restricts the optimum production of forage invites weed development within the stand. The key to successful weed prevention in forage crops is to grow the most competitive forage crop possible, utilizing the most advanced technology available. Some weeds are problems even when good management is practiced, however. Since the management aspects will be discussed in other chapters, these will not be covered except as they directly influence control of existing weeds. Although this chapter deals with weed control, the importance of proper management in forage production cannot be overlooked or underestimated. The best control method, whether cultural or chemical, will be ineffective or at best temporary under poor forage management.

⚘ MARVIN M. SCHREIBER is Research Agronomist in Weed Investigations, ARS, USDA. He holds the M.S. degree from the University of Arizona and the Ph.D. from Cornell University. His research is concerned with the botanical, ecological, and physiological characteristics of weeds and their control in forage crops.

⚘ CONTROL PRACTICES

Forage includes animal feed from rangeland, native pastures, rotational pastures, and hay. Although weeds are common to all situations, each of these presents unique weed problems and control practices that warrant individual coverage.

Weeds, whether they are herbaceous or woody (commonly called brush), compete with native or introduced forage plant species for water, nutrients, and light. The extent of this competition most often depends on the growth habit and nature of the weed species as well as their density and distribution. Aspects of their control also differ for the same reasons. Economics is usually a major consideration.

RANGELAND

BRUSH. Under rangeland conditions, brush is the primary weed problem. It has been estimated that of the 130 million ha of grazing lands in the U.S., over 93 million ha are infested with brush and could benefit from weed control. Careful selection from the control methods available is most important in these situations because of the low potential income per ha.[1]

MECHANICAL CONTROL. On large areas mechanical methods are expensive, and for that reason more emphasis has been placed on chemical control. When herbicides are to be used, selection of areas to be improved should have a stand of native grasses present, or the area and climate should provide opportunity for reseeding.[2] If stands of grasses are not available, mechanical methods may be most effective in preparation for reseeding. Where there is not adequate existing grass and without an opportunity for reseeding, brush removal under adverse environmental conditions in arid and semiarid regions is doomed to failure. Where grass is present, good results are apparent in the year following treatment.

The choice of a mechanical method such as cutting, cabling, chaining, bulldozing,

and root plowing depends on the size of the woody plants, soil conditions, terrain, and ability of the plants to send up sprouts. Burning, which has had wide use, is convenient but hazardous and is ineffective on sprouting species.

BIOLOGICAL CONTROL. Interest in the use of biological control methods has been increasing. Successful insect control in St. Johnswort, *Hypericum perforatum* L.; lantana, *Lantana camara* L.; and puncturevine, *Tribulus terrestus* L., in various parts of the world including the U.S., has stimulated the search for other biological control agents.[3,4]

CHEMICAL CONTROL OF BRUSH. This method has increased because of the efficacy of old and new herbicides, ease of application, and economics of application under rangeland conditions. Many species of brush can be controlled by (2,4-dichlorophenoxy)acetic acid (2,4-D), (2,4,5-trichlorophenoxy)acetic acid (2,4,5-T), 2-(2,4,5-trichlorophenoxy)propionic acid (silvex), and 4-amino-3,5,6-trichloropicolinic acid (picloram) alone or in various combinations. In 1973 picloram was not registered for use on grazing lands in most states. As systemic herbicides that translocate within the plant, these chemicals are effective as foliage sprays if applied at the proper stage of growth. In most brush species, this stage coincides with the time of greatest transport of photosynthate to the roots and the time when the root reserves are at their minimum levels. This is usually when new leaf development and terminal growth has stopped.

Climatic conditions always affect the results of herbicide treatments.[5] Moisture stress conditions do not favor good control.[6] Also, it is most unusual for single

1. Hyder, D. N. 1971. Species susceptibilities to 2,4-D on mixed-grass prairie. *Weed Sci.* 19:526–28.
2. Tueller, P. T., and R. A. Evans. 1969. Control of green rabbitbrush and big sagebrush with 2,4-D and picloram. *Weed Sci.* 17:233–35.

3. DeBach, P. (ed.). 1964. Biological Control of Insect Pests and Weeds. Reinhold, New York.
4. Huffaker, C. B. 1959. Biological control of weeds with insects. *Ann. Rev. Entomol.* 4:251–76.
5. Morton, H. L. 1966. Influence of temperature and humidity on foliar absorption, translocation and metabolism of 2,4,5-T by mesquite seedlings. *Weeds* 14:136–41.
6. Badiei, A. A., E. Basler, and P. W. Santelmann. 1966. Aspects of movement of 2,4,5-T in blackjack oak. *Weeds* 14:302–5.

applications to be fully effective on such species as sagebrush, *Artemisia* spp.; mesquite, *Prosopis* spp.; juniper, *Juniperus* spp.; and oak, *Quercus* spp.[7] More often, repeated treatments are necessary in consecutive or alternate years. This is advantageous only in that the second-year treatment kills weeds, thus reducing their competition.

Soil application of granular herbicides is another method for the control of brush.[8] Applications usually are made around the base of large individual plants. Good rainfall is essential for herbicides to move into the soil for plant uptake. Application to the base of the plants or in cuts on the stem are also effective.

CHEMICAL CONTROL OF HERBACEOUS WEEDS. Of great concern on rangeland are grasses such as medusahead, *Taeniatherum asperum* (Sim.) Nevski, which because it is unpalatable is left to accumulate and smother out desirable species. Downy bromegrass, *Bromus tectorum* L., has become quite prevalent but differs from medusahead because it is palatable. However, because it is an annual species, it is not as reliably productive year to year as other more desirable perennial grasses and therefore should be controlled.

Control of these grass weed problems is directly associated with grazing management practices that favor desirable grass species. Good control can often be obtained by preventing seed production for at least two years, since most seed from medusahead or downy bromegrass do not survive longer. Because of the lack of good selective herbicides for weedy grasses, the best control measures are based on reseeding forage grasses such as crested wheatgrass following vegetation kill with the herbicide 1,1'-dimethyl-4,4'-bipyridinium salts (paraquat). Combination of paraquat with 2,4-D is helpful to control broadleaf herbaceous weeds. In 1973 paraquat was not registered for use on grazing lands.

Many broadleaf herbaceous weeds can be problems in rangeland because of their unpalatable characteristics, and some are poisonous. Due to selective grazing, species such as larkspur, *Delphinium* spp.; lupines, *Lupinus* spp.; and mulesear, *Wyethia amplexicaulis* Nutt., have increased. Many perennials such as leafy spurge, *Euphorbia esula* L., and Canada thistle, *Cirsium arvense* (L.) Scop., are even greater problems.

More than half the perennial broadleaf weeds on rangeland are poisonous and most are native.[9,10] These present even greater concern. Toxicity of poisonous plants varies with species and stage of growth and they are not equally poisonous to all classes of livestock. Halogeton, *Halogeton glomeratus* (M. Bieb.) C. A. Mey., causes heavy losses in sheep but little in cattle. Tall larkspur, *Delphinium barbeyi* Huth, and milkvetches, *Astragalus* spp., cause severe poisoning in cattle.

Use of herbicides such as 2,4-D, 2,4,5-T, and picloram are effective for selective control of most of the herbaceous broadleaf weeds.[11] Again, however, grazing management must be used to increase desirable vegetation and to reduce possible reinfestation after weeds are controlled.

The importance of prevention cannot be overemphasized. Early detection of weed species (grasses, broadleaf, or brush) offers the best hope for efficient economical control in rangeland. Many of the weed problems and their control as discussed above are most critical in the western U.S., but the solutions apply to other weed species in other areas of the country as well.

PERMANENT PASTURES

Since it has been estimated that every kilogram of herbaceous weeds grown on

7. Hughes, E. E. 1966. Single and combination mowing and spraying treatments for control of salt cedar (*Tamarix pentandra* Pall.). *Weeds* 14:276–78.

8. McIlvain, E. H., and C. G. Armstrong. 1965. Siberian elm—A tough new invader of grasslands. *Weeds* 13:278–79.

9. Williams, M. C., and L. B. Kreps. 1970. Chemical control of western false hellebore. *Weed Sci.* 18:481–83.

10. Robocker, W. C. 1971. Herbicidal suppression of bracken and effects on forage production. *Weed Sci.* 19:538–41.

11. Klingman, D. L., and W. C. Shaw. 1971. Using phenoxy herbicides effectively. USDA Farmers' Bull. 2183.

a pasture reduces the production of desirable forage by about an equivalent amount, it can be readily appreciated that weed control has direct economic consequences.[12] Because pastures are more intensively managed and have higher carrying capacities than rangelands, more flexibility is available for choices of control methods based on economics. Coupled with this is the increased need for better management practices.

BRUSH AND HERBACEOUS WEEDS. A large part of the land pastured in the eastern U.S. was original forest area. If care is not taken to prevent reestablishment, the land will revert to woody species. Many species are possible, but the sprouting kinds offer the greatest challenge. Wide use of 2,4-D, 2,4,5-T, silvex, picloram, and 3,6-dichloro-o-anisic acid (dicamba) have offered good control of woody species. Also, these same herbicides have been effective against many perennial herbaceous weeds that frequent pastures, namely, Canada thistle; perennial ragweed, *Ambrosia psilostachya* DC.; hoary cress, *Cardaria draba* (L.) Desv.; goldenrod, *Solidago* spp.; ironweed, *Vernonia* spp.; and hoary vervain, *Verbena stricta* Vent.[11]

MECHANICAL CONTROL. Use of the mowing machine as a mechanical means of weed control has been demonstrated as an effective tool in some pastures.[13] In others it is relatively ineffective.[14] Timing and frequency of cutting are extremely important. Some perennial species can be effectively controlled by frequent cutting. Such treatments reduce the root reserves that eventually weaken the plant so the weed cannot compete with the desired forage species. Of equal importance is the prevention of viable seed. Canada thistle

and sowthistle, *Sonchus arvensis* L., often can be mowed three to six days after bloom, which prevents production of significant viable seed.

CHEMICAL CONTROL. Although emphasis on perennial weed control is important in permanent pastures, annual weeds can be a problem. Chemical methods have proven most effective, particularly when forage stands consist of forage grasses. Variable responses to 2,4-D have been found among ecotypes of some weeds such as Canada thistle and perennial ragweed.[15] Nevertheless, 2,4-D and other systemic herbicides have been most effective if applied in the susceptible prebud to early bloom stages of weed growth. Retreatments are required for many perennial species, ironweed for example. Such retreatments also offer control of any annual or biennial species that might develop in the forage stand.[16]

Pastures that have lost their productivity through mismanagement or severe weed encroachment may require complete renovation. Herbicides are especially useful on pastures that are too steep, rocky, or poorly drained to be mechanically tilled.[17]

The first step in renovation is to kill all existing sod prior to reseeding the desired species of grasses and/or legumes. For many years trichloroacetic acid (TCA) and 2,2-dichloropropionic acid (dalapon) have been used to kill existing grasses, and 2,4-D has been used for broadleaf weeds. More recently paraquat has gained wide use because there is no waiting period before seeding since the herbicide is inactivated through soil adsorption.[18] Even though complete kill may not occur, it may be enough to thin the stand of existing grasses to allow forage establishment. If

12. Peters, E. J., and S. A. Lowance. 1969. Gains in timothy forage from goldenrod control with 2,4-D, 2,4-DB, and picloram. *Weed Sci.* 17:473–74.

13. Schreiber, M. M. 1967. Effect of density and control of Canada thistle on production and utilization of alfalfa pasture. *Weeds* 15:138–42.

14. Klingman, D. L., and M. K. McCarty. 1958. Interrelations of methods of weed control and pasture management at Lincoln, Nebr. 1949–55. USDA Tech. Bull. 1180.

15. Hodgson, J. M. 1964. Variations in ecotypes of Canada thistle. *Weeds* 12:167–71.

16. McCarty, M. K., and C. J. Scifres. 1969. Herbicidal control of western ironweed. *Weed Sci.* 17:77–79.

17. Taylor, T. H., E. M. Smith, and W. C. Templeton, Jr. 1969. Use of minimum tillage and herbicide for establishing legumes in Kentucky bluegrass (*Poa pratensis* L.) swards. *Agron. J.* 61:761–66.

18. Linscott, D. L., A. A. Akhavein, and R. D. Hagin. 1969. Paraquat for weed control prior to establishing legumes. *Weed Sci.* 17:428–31.

FIG. 37.1. *Combination of herbicide ... and mowing ... recommended.* Chemically renovated pasture area sown to smooth bromegrass (left), area not renovated (right). Area grazed by dairy cattle. *N.J. Agr. Exp. Sta. photo.*

2,4-D susceptible forage legumes are to be seeded, postemergence application of (2,4-dichlorophenoxy)butyric acid (2,4-DB) may be used to control any broadleaf weeds that might compete with the establishing forage species. (See Fig. 37.1.)

CROPLAND PASTURES AND HAY

CHEMICAL CONTROL. Establishing new stands of forage legumes and grasses with herbicides has received a great deal of attention and has offered the farmer an alternative to using companion grain crops.[19]

With higher fertilizer levels, small grains used as companion grain crops may compete with and injure slow-growing forage species as much as weeds.[20] With the advent of herbicides such as S-ethyl dipropylthiocarbamate (EPTC), N-butyl-N-ethyl-α,α,α-trifluoro-2,6-dinitro-p-toluidine

(benefin), and 4-(methylsulfonyl)-2,6-dinitro-N,N-dipropylaniline (nitralin), forage legume establishment may be made in the spring without a companion grain crop.[21-24] If seedings are made early in the spring, significant yields of 6–10 t/ha of forage may be produced from two to three cuttings and thus may offset the loss from omitting the small grain. If small grain is used, its removal as early as possible (e.g., by grazing) is beneficial to the new seeding.

EPTC, benefin, and nitralin are preplanting incorporated herbicides; that is, they are applied before planting and incorporated within the soil to a depth of 2.5–5 cm. This is done either to reduce vaporization losses or to ensure greater

19. Kust, C. A. 1968. Herbicides or oat companion crops for alfalfa establishment and forage yields. *Agron. J.* 60:151–54.
20. Kust, C. A. 1971. Control of volunteer oats in alfalfa. *Agron. J.* 63:394–96.

21. Elkins, D. M., J. K. Leasure, and J. J. Faix. 1970. Herbicides for spring establishment of crownvetch (*Coronilla varia* L.). *Crop Sci.* 10:95–97.
22. Peters, E. J., and S. A. Lowance. 1971. Establishment of crownvetch with herbicides. *Agron. J.* 63:230–32.
23. Moline, W. J., and L. R. Robinson. 1971. Effects of herbicides and seeding rates on the production of alfalfa. *Agron. J.* 63:614–16.
24. Peters, E. J., and J. F. Stritzke. 1970. Herbicides and nitrogen fertilizer for the establishment of these varieties of spring-sown alfalfa. *Agron. J.* 62:259–62.

soil mixing of insoluble herbicides. If used within proper rates of application, these herbicides will control most of the annual grasses and many of the broadleaf weeds found in new seedings, e.g., pigweed, *Amaranthus retroflexus* L.; lambsquarter, *Chenopodium album* L.; mustards, *Brassica* spp.; crabgrasses, *Digitaria* spp.; barnyardgrass, *Echinochloa crus-galli* (L.) Beauv.; and foxtails, *Setaria* spp. If some broadleaf weeds do escape (such as smartweeds, *Polygonum* spp., and ragweed, *Ambrosia* spp.), they are controlled by postemergence application of 2,4-DB or 2-*sec*-butyl-4,6-dinitrophenol (dinoseb) when the weeds are small and the forage legumes are in the two to three true-leaf stage.

Since EPTC, benefin, and nitralin will severely injure seedling forage grasses, these herbicides cannot be used in mixtures with forage grasses. Where grass-legume mixtures are to be made, postemergence application of 2,4-DB or dinoseb controls the broadleaf weeds but not the weed grasses. However, the stage of growth mentioned above is important. Combination of herbicide treatment and mowing are recommended.

Forage legumes differ in their susceptibility to many of the herbicides mentioned. Alfalfa and birdsfoot trefoil are tolerant to treatments of EPTC, benefin, and 2,4-DB (Fig. 37.2). Sweetclover is susceptible to 2,4-DB. Dalapon has been used in new seedings of alfalfa and birdsfoot trefoil but can kill or severely stunt red and white clover. Isopropyl-m-chlorocarbanilate (chlorpropham) and isopropyl carbanilate (propham) can be used for grass control in alfalfa and clovers when used preemergence or early postemergence. Sericea lespedeza, susceptible to many herbicides, has shown good resistance to *S*-propyl dipropylthiocarbamate (vernolate).[25]

In established cropland pastures and hayfields, forage crops compete very well with summer annual weeds but are susceptible to encroachment by some winter

Fig. 37.2. *Dalapon . . . to kill . . . grasses . . . 2, 4-D for broadleaf weeds.* Birdsfoot trefoil seeding with grasses and broadleaf weeds chemically controlled (above). Same seeding without treatment entirely smothered with grass and weeds (below). *Iowa Agr. Exp. Sta. photo.*

annuals, biennials, and perennial weeds. Some of these can be serious enough to reduce the quality of the forage and often reduce the stand and yield of desirable legumes.

One common problem in the north central and northeast regions of the U.S. is chickweed, *Stellaria media* (L.) Cyrillo, a winter annual that is very competitive with alfalfa in the fall and spring. For many years chlorpropham and dinoseb have been used for chickweed control when alfalfa was dormant. Dinoseb has been used in alfalfa-grass mixtures since chlorpropham injures forage grasses. More recently 2-chloro-4,6-bis(ethylamino)-s-triazine (simazine) and 3-(3,4-dichlorophenyl)-1,1-dimethylurea (diuron) have shown

25. Hoveland, C. S., G. A. Buchanan, and E. D. Donnelly. 1971. Establishment of sericea lespedeza. *Weed Sci.* 19:21–24.

great promise for postemergence control of chickweed and other weeds in dormant alfalfa established for at least a year.[26]

❧ SUMMARY OF CHEMICAL CONTROL

1. Chemical methods of weed control demand careful selection and application of herbicides according to prescribed recommendations.
2. Always follow the recommendations of the local state extension service weed specialist, who is familiar with the problems of the area and the best methods to be used for specific climate and soil conditions.
3. Once selection is made, always read the label. The label on any commercially sold herbicide indicates it is authorized by the federal government and also states that no pesticide used on products consumed directly or indirectly by humans shall leave injurious residues in or on these products if the chemical is used as prescribed. No case of poisoning has ever been shown for any animal when herbicides have been used as

26. Hastings, R. E., and C. A. Kust. 1970. Control of yellow rocket and white cockle in established alfalfa. *Weed Sci.* 18:329–33.
27. Palmer, J. S., and R. D. Radeleff. 1969. The toxicity of some organic herbicides to cattle, sheep, and chickens. ARS, USDA Prod. Res. Rept. 106.

directed.[27] The label also contains information concerning safety precautions for the person applying the herbicide.

❧ QUESTIONS

1. What factors must be considered in the selection of weed control methods on rangelands? Which are of primary concern?
2. On what forage crops in your area can 2,4-D or 2,4,5-T be profitably used? Why?
3. Name five woody and five herbaceous perennial weeds in your state and suggest control methods for each.
4. Discuss the relationship of weeds and management in forage crops.
5. How does palatability influence the competitive aspect of weeds in forage crops?
6. List the steps you would take to establish alfalfa without a companion grain crop, including the handling of any herbicide treatments.
7. Compare the hazard of herbicides to livestock with the hazard of poisonous plants.
8. Why is your state weed specialist your best source of information?
9. Rate cultural, biological, and chemical methods of weed control and explain your rating.
10. Why is the label on a herbicide container important?

W. W. WOODHOUSE, JR. / *North Carolina State University*

W. K. GRIFFITH / *Potash Institute of North America, Inc.*

38

SOIL FERTILITY AND FERTILIZATION OF FORAGES

❧

Soil fertility, the ability of the soil to supply nutrients to plants, is a major factor in forage production. In humid regions the type of forage plant grown is often determined by the fertility level of the soil. High-quality legumes such as alfalfa and ladino clover thrive only on soils well supplied naturally or artificially with P, Ca, Mg, and K. Similarly, grasses such as smooth bromegrass, timothy, and orchardgrass grow well only if there is ample N. In the absence of adequate amounts of these elements, plants having lower requirements must be substituted. This usually means plants of lower nutritive value or reduced yield or both.

Applying fertilizers to maintain and improve soil fertility becomes necessary as soils are depleted of nutrients by crop removal, leaching, and erosion and as attempts are made to push yields higher and higher. This is a practice that becomes more and more vital as the world population increases. Reduced to the simplest terms, the problem becomes one of knowing what the soil can supply and what the crop removes and making up the difference by applying fertilizers. Thus the *soil* and the *crop* are the major factors to consider.

❧ W. W. WOODHOUSE, JR., is Professor of Soils at North Carolina State University. He holds the M.S. degree from North Carolina State College and the Ph.D. from Cornell University. He has been engaged in soil fertility and management research for more than 30 years.

❧ W. K. GRIFFITH is Eastern Director, Potash Institute of North America, Inc. He holds the M.S. degree from the University of Illinois and the Ph.D. from Purdue University. He has worked closely with forage research, extension, and industry personnel in developing and promoting the forage-based agricultural economy in the East.

❧ THE SOIL

Forages are grown on many kinds of soil. Knowledge of the general nature of the soils in a given area enables prediction of the fertilizers likely to be required. Fertilizer application for efficient production must be tailored to the needs of individual farms and specific fields on these farms. For these more specific answers field experiments must be conducted with the forages in question on well-defined soil situations. In this way soil conditions and plant responses are related to the application of kinds and amounts of fertilizers and soil amendments.

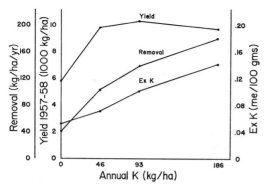

FIG. 38.1. Yield and K removal are both related to the amount of K available; knowledge of all three factors is necessary in the wise use of fertilizer. Exchangeable K (ex K) is in milliequivalents (me) per 100 g.

Figure 38.1 shows the type of information required in predicting the fertilizer needs of one particular forage plant grown on one particular soil. For simplicity this example deals only with K, 'Coastal' bermudagrass, and a Eustis sand with no previous cropping history. Information is presented on crop yield, the removal of the nutrient as related to added K, and the resulting levels of K in the soil.[1]

The results to date indicate that around 0.10 meq of exchangeable (available) K/100 g of soil are adequate for normal growth of this forage plant on this soil. Also, around 50–75 kg/ha of K per year seems to be sufficient to maintain this level. The crop, however, is removing around 90 kg of K/ha/yr, with only 46.5 kg being applied. This sandy soil has an extremely low total K content and cannot be expected to supply much of this element from nonexchangeable sources over any extended period. It may be anticipated that although the soil K level of 0.10 meq is probably about right, the amount of added K required to maintain this level is likely to increase somewhat after the native supply in the soil has been further depleted.

This example illustrates the approach used to evaluate fertilization needs for

other elements such as P, Ca, and Mg. Unfortunately, N soil tests are not satisfactory in predicting N response. Consequently, in the interpretation of N response studies it usually is necessary to fall back on a general knowledge of the soil in question and the behavior of N in it.

❧ THE PLANT

Forage plants require the same 16 elements considered essential for the growth of all other green plants. Differences arise in the amounts required, in the abilities of the various plants to extract elements from the soil, and in the wide range of soils and soil conditions encountered. A knowledge of nutrient removal by a particular crop can be helpful in planning a sound fertilizer program for that crop, as indicated for K in Figure 38.1. Data in Table 38.1 give a general idea of the amounts of nutrients removed by some typical forages.[2-5]

KINDS OF FORAGES

Forage plants constitute a large and diverse group including grasses; legumes; plants of annual, biennial, or perennial nature; and plants adapted to hot and cold climates, wet and dry soils, long days or short, and high or low fertility. Treatment is further complicated by the fact that they often are grown in mixtures. Consequently, in considering fertilization, general principles must be considered rather than details of practice.

It may be helpful to first consider the differences between grasses and legumes from a soil fertility point of view. All forage legumes are quite different from grasses in one respect, that of N fixation—

1. Woodhouse, W. W., Jr. 1959. Fertilizing Coastal bermuda and sericea for optimum production. N.C. State Coll. Soils Info. Ser. 2.

2. Potash Institute of North America. 1972. Plant food content your crops remove. *Better Crops with Plant Food*, Spring.

3. Reid, R. L., Amy J. Post, and G. A. Jung. 1962. Mineral composition of forages. W. Va. Univ. Agr. Exp. Sta. Bull. 589T.

4. Blaser, R. E., and W. E. Stokes. 1943. Effect of fertilizer on growth and composition of carpet and other grasses. Fla. Agr. Exp. Sta. Tech. Bull. 390.

5. Vincente-Chandler, J., R. Caro-Costas, R. W. Pearson, F. Abruna, J. Figarella, and S. Silva. 1964. The intensive management of tropical forages in Puerto Rico. P.R. Agr. Exp. Sta. Bull. 187.

TABLE 38.2 ❧ Effect of placement of 3360 kg/ha of limestone on alfalfa yield, North Carolina

Placement	Yield, kg/ha (3-yr av)
Topdressed	3,788
On plow sole	4,885
Mixed in plow layer	6,064

Source: Woodhouse, 1956.[10]

Lime penetrates the soil slowly so must be applied in the right place to accomplish the most good.[10] Since one of the major objectives in liming is that of reducing acidity, mixing lime with the soil is usually best (Table 38.2).

Mixing lime with an acid soil can greatly enhance alfalfa root growth and nodulation, with the finely branched feeder roots and nodules being confined largely to the limed layers.[11]

Although for many forage plants the mixing of lime into acid soil is most desirable, there are conditions under which very localized applications of this material are to be preferred. For example, where the primary purpose of adding lime is to encourage the growth of nodule bacteria, rather small quantities of limestone, 100–300 kg/ha, either drilled or pelleted with the seed, may be superior to several times that amount broadcast. The widespread growth of subterranean clover on acid soils in Australia following this method is a classic example.[12] Also, there are instances in which the supplying of Ca and Mg as nutrients may be the principal purpose of liming.

❧ NITROGEN AND LIME

The most widely used forms of N fertilizers, those containing ammonia and/or urea, leave acid residues in the soil. Large applications of N without frequent liming may result in excessive soil acidity accompanied by sharp reductions in ex-

changeable bases, reduced P availability, and equally sharp increases in soluble Al and Mn,[13] particularly in the humid Temperate Zone and the Tropics. Under continued N fertilizations these conditions can develop to considerable depths in the soil profile, where they become difficult to correct. The acidity of a soil profile under a Coastal bermudagrass sod increased to a depth of 120 cm by the end of a five-year period as a result of very high applications of N (896 and 1793 kg/ha).[14] Similar findings have been reported under napiergrass in Puerto Rico.[15] Where N was applied over a longer period on a very sandy soil, lower rates of N caused acidification as deep in the profile as 240 cm.[16]

❧ PHOSPHORUS

Phosphorus plays a vital role in both plant and animal growth. It is one of the nutrients most generally deficient in soils and probably the one most universally applied to forage crops. In plants it is required in photosynthesis, transfer of energy within the plant, and the synthesis and breakdown of carbohydrates. It makes up a large part of the nucleus of the plant cell and also is present in the cytoplasm. It is a key nutrient in growth and cell division and tends to be concentrated in young, actively growing tissues. Since these tissues are generally the most palatable and nutritious, high-quality forage requires an adequate supply of P.

FIXATION

Phosphorus is susceptible to "fixation." Most soils are able to rather rapidly tie

11. Pohlman, G. G. 1946. Effect of liming different soil layers on yield of alfalfa and on root development and nodulation. *Soil Sci.* 62:255–66.

12. Brockwell, J. 1963. Seed pelleting as an aid to legume seed inoculation. *World Crops* 15:334–38.

13. Adams, Fred, and R. W. Pearson. 1967. Crop response to lime in the southern United States and Puerto Rico. Soil acidity and liming. *Agron. Monogr.* 12:161–206.

14. Adams, W. C., R. W. Pearson, W. A. Jackson, and R. D. McCreery. 1967. The influence of limestone and nitrogen on soil pH and Coastal bermuda yield. *Agron. J.* 59:450–53.

15. Abruna, F., J. Vicente-Chandler, and R. W. Pearson. 1964. Effects of liming on yields and composition of heavily fertilized grasses and soil properties under humid tropical conditions. Soil Sci. Soc. Amer. Proc. 27:657–61.

16. Woodhouse, W. W., Jr. 1969. Long-term fertility requirements of Coastal bermuda. II. Nitrogen, phosphorus, and lime. *Agron. J.* 61:251–56.

up large amounts of this element in forms not readily available to plants. Several important facts relating to P fertilization are directly concerned with this process.

Usually no more than 10–20% of the P applied is recovered in the first crop. For example, the uptake of P by 'Argentine' bahiagrass was determined at two rates of application using labeled fertilizer. A maximum of 9.9% of the P in the crop for the season came from the fertilizer applied that year.[17]

Annual applications of P almost inevitably result in residual accumulations of this element in the soil. In an extensive study of soils used for potatoes, available P was found to have been increased 25-fold and total P 5-fold by fertilization.[18] The extent to which this residual P is recovered varies widely with soil and cropping conditions. It is an extremely important factor affecting fertilizer practice since a large percentage of the P in a forage crop often comes from fertilizers applied in past years.

The process of "fixation" restricts movement through the soil and minimizes leaching of P. A penetration of P to about 8 cm that had been applied on a pasture surface eight years earlier has been reported.[19] As with lime, rate of application is a factor, and with higher rates on some soils penetration may extend some distance (Table 38.3).[20]

SOIL REACTION

Soil reaction and liming have a very strong bearing on P availability. Iron and aluminum phosphates predominate in very acid soils. These are least soluble at a pH of 4, with their solubility increasing as

TABLE 38.3 ♣ Effects of different rates of surface-applied P on P concentration at different depths in a Cecil sandy loam soil, Georgia

Soil depth (cm)	Rate of P application (kg/ha* and ppm)				
	0	20	39	79	158
0–5	0	6	18	91	143
5–10	0	1	9	23	60
10–20	0	0	10	9	8
20–30	0	0	0	8	21

Source: Sell and Olson, 1946.[20]
* Applied at rates indicated 1936 and 1939. Sampled 1944.

the pH increases to about 8.5. Calcium phosphates begin to form around pH 6, and their solubility decreases with rising pH. Consequently, P is likely to be most available in soils at a pH between 6 and 7. On very acid soils the addition of P without liming may be almost useless.

APPLICATION

AT SEEDING. Phosphorus supply is especially critical for young seedlings. A readily available supply of P within reach of the young roots is essential for normal root development and seedling establishment. Consequently, P applications made at seeding are often beneficial, even on soils with a residual level high enough to sustain normal growth once the plants are established and have roots extending through a large volume of soil. Localized placement in the immediate root zone of the seedlings is usually desirable, both from the standpoint of accessibility to the seedlings and to reduce fixation. So-called band-seeding, drilling the seed in rows with the fertilizer placed in a band just under or to one side of the seed, is designed to accomplish this.[21] Results from this practice have been variable. (See Fig. 38.5.)

FREQUENCY. The question of moderate annual applications of P versus heavy infrequent applications depends large-

17. Neller, J. R., and C. G. Hutton. 1957. Comparison of surface and subsurface placement of superphosphate on growth and uptake of phosphorus by sodded grasses. *Agron. J.* 49:347–51.
18. Cummings, R. W., M. Reech, and A. Hawkins. 1945. Nutrient status of soils in commercial potato-producing areas of the Atlantic and Gulf Coast. *Soil Sci. Amer. Proc.* 10:240–56.
19. Schaller, F. W. 1940. The downward movement of lime and superphosphate in relation to permanent pasture fertilization. *Soil Sci. Soc. Amer. Proc.* 5:162–66.
20. Sell, O. E., and L. E. Olson. 1946. The effect of surface-applied phosphate and limestone on soil nutrients and pH of permanent pasture. *Soil Sci. Soc. Amer. Proc.* 11:238–45.

21. Hunt, O. J., and R. E. Wagner. 1963. Effects of phosphorus and potassium fertilizers on legume composition of seven grass-legume mixtures. *Agron. J.* 55:16–19.

Fɪɢ. 38.5. *Drilling the seed . . . fertilizer in a band . . . under or . . . side of the seed.* Alfalfa seedlings band-seeded (left) and broadcast (right). *Potash Institute of North America, Inc., photo.*

ly on the soil type and perhaps to a lesser degree on the plant. Several workers have reported that an application made once every three years to a pasture sod was more effective than 33% that amount applied annually.[22,23] Others working with legume-dominant sods have found just the opposite, that frequent applications were more efficient.[24] This is probably due to differences in the nature of the fixation process in the respective soils. The plant also may be a factor, since some legumes have been shown to be more directly dependent on fertilizer P than are their companion grasses.[25]

❧ POTASSIUM

The role of K in plant nutrition parallels that of Na in animals. It does not become a part of any particular plant constituent but is vital to many plant functions—the formation of sugars and starch, the translocation of these within the plant, protein synthesis, stomatal action, and the neutralization of organic acids. Potassium is not as universally deficient in soils as P, but it tends to become a limiting factor after soils have been cropped for some time. Eventually, it is often the nutrient that must be added in the largest amount, even on soils not deficient initially. (See Fig. 38.6.)

Potassium is required in fairly large quantities by most forages (Table 38.1), and considerable amounts of it are present in one form or another in most soils. A total K content of 2–3% is common except in sandy-acid or high-organic soils. However, in most cases only a small part of the total K in the soil is available to plants in any one season.[26]

Behavior

Potassium exists in soils in three general forms:

1. Soluble K, which is free to move with the soil water and constitutes only a small portion of the total at any one time.
2. Exchangeable K, held on the soil colloids in position to readily replenish the soluble supply and therefore considered available. It usually makes up a very low percentage of the total.

22. Baker, K. G., and E. L. Mayton. 1944. A year-around grazing program for the alkaline soils of the Black Belt of Alabama. *Agron. J.* 36:740–49.

23. Brown, B. A., and R. I. Munsell. 1943. The effect of fertilizers on grazed permanent pastures. Conn. Agr. Exp. Sta. Bull. 245.

24. Wakefield, R. C., D. A. Shallock, M. Salomon, and C. E. Olney. 1957. Yield and chemical composition of ladino clover as affected by fertilizer treatments. *Agron. J.* 49:374–77.

25. Blaser, R. E., and Clayton McAuliffe. 1949. Utilization of phosphorus from various fertilizer materials. I. Orchardgrass and ladino clover in New York. *Soil Sci.* 68:145–50.

26. Reitemeier, R. F. 1957. Soil potassium and fertility. *In* Soil, pp. 101–86. USDA Yearbook Agr.

Fig. 38.6. *Potassium . . . often the nutrient that must be added in the largest amount.* Growth of alfalfa roots adequately fertilized with K (left) compared with no K fertilization (right). *N.C. Agr. Exp. Sta. photo.*

3. Nonexchangeable K, held within the clay lattice or in primary minerals and not readily available to plants. This form makes up the large proportion of the total K content of most soils. Exceptions are high-organic and acid-sandy soils which are quite low in total K and contain little of the element in this form. The rate of change from nonexchangeable to exchangeable determines the long-term K-supplying power of a soil.

A limited amount of native K is available annually from most soils. This may be adequate to support relatively low-yielding forages without K additions; yet, added K may be required as soon as the yield potential is increased through the introduction of more productive plants or the addition of other fertilizers. Acute K deficiencies may develop on soils containing many tons per ha of total K when annual removal repeatedly exceeds the annual K-supplying power of the soil.

The soluble portion of the soil K supply is subject to loss through leaching. Leaching is an important factor in the use of K fertilizers, particularly on sandy soils. Since this element moves readily with the soil solution, placement usually is unimportant; however, K salts placed too close at seeding time may injure the seed or the young seedlings.

COMPETITION

Competition for K between plants grown in mixture can be serious. Requirements for K of grasses and legumes adapted to the same environment are usually about the same; however, grasses are frequently able to extract K from the soil much more readily than the legumes growing with them. This difference becomes more pronounced as the K supply decreases. An example of this may be seen in Table 38.4 in which the K contents of the grass and legume components of an alfalfa-orchardgrass mixture are compared under varying levels of applied K.[27] Where the supply of K was plentiful, the K content of the legume was essentially equal to that of the grass. However, as the sup-

27. Blaser, R. E., and E. L. Kimbrough. 1968. Potassium nutrition of forage crops with perennials. *In* Role of Potassium in Agriculture, pp. 423–45. ASA, CSSA, SSSA.

TABLE 38.4 ❧ Percentage K in alfalfa and orchardgrass grown together, Virginia

K (kg/ha)	K (% dry weight) Orchard-grass	Alfalfa	Percent K in alfalfa relative to grass
0	2.71	0.70	26
46.5	3.46	1.21	35
93	4.01	1.78	42
372	3.85	3.53	92

Source: Blaser and Kimbrough, 1968.[27]

FIG. 38.7. *Careful adjustment rate ... application ... intervals of one year or less.* Effect of K fertilization on legume-grass ratio with adequate K (left) versus no K (right) after two years. *E. C. Doll, University Ill. photo.*

ply was reduced, legume K dropped rapidly, while the level of this element in the grass fell slowly so that at 0 applied K the alfalfa was acutely deficient (0.7% K), with the grass component of the mixture still containing 2.7% K (probably fully adequate). Thus the problem in fertilizing legume-grass associations is that of applying enough K to maintain the health of the legume without unduly encouraging luxury consumption by the companion grasses.[28] On K-deficient soils, this calls for rather careful adjustment of rate, with applications made at intervals of one year or less. (See Fig. 38.7.)

The demand for K by young seedlings is not large. Thus on soils with fairly good K-supplying powers, a small amount banded or worked into the seedbed at seeding time is usually sufficient. Potassium supply is likely to become much more important once stands are established. Such forages can easily remove 100–200 kg/ha/yr of K (Table 38.1). Some soils can supply this amount or more annually over long periods. Others may be quite adequate for establishment but will require substantial annual additions of K

28. Markus, D. K., and W. R. Battle. 1965. Soil and plant responses to a long-term alfalfa study. *Agron. J.* 57:613–16.

to maintain productivity. Potassium fertilization can be efficient only if it is carefully tailored to the individual situation.

LUXURY CONSUMPTION

"Luxury consumption," the tendency for plants to absorb amounts of certain elements far in excess of actual requirements, can be a problem in K fertilization. For example, a K level in the plant of around 2–3% appears adequate under most circumstances for such forages as alfalfa, ladino clover, orchardgrass, and smooth bromegrass. Yet it is not unusual to find these plants containing 3.5–4.5% K. The extra 1 or 2% K is of no value to the animal consuming the forage and therefore should, except perhaps in cases of very high yields, be considered wasteful absorption by the plant. This is one reason why it is not usually feasible to apply several years supply of this element at one time.

❧ NITROGEN

Nitrogen is extremely vital in both forage quality and yield. It is a major constituent of proteins, and the chlorophyl of green plants is a nitrogenous compound. It is therefore essential for photosynthesis, growth, and reproduction.

Rapid decomposition of organic materials and subsequent leaching has left the N content of most soils of the humid regions relatively low. Some high-organic soils formed under poor drainage and many soils formed under limited rainfall are rather high in this element. But on the vast majority of soils yielding productive forages, much of the required N must come from sources other than the native soil supply. Fertilizers, legumes, and farm manures are major sources.

Most of the N applied in fertilizers is or is soon converted to nitrate or ammonia; both are readily soluble. Ammonia is loosely absorbed by the soil colloids, although in warm, well-aerated soils it is rapidly converted to nitrate. Nitrates remain largely in the soil solution and are quite vulnerable to leaching. Most of the N used by established plants is in nitrate form.

For purposes of N fertilization, most forages have similar requirements during the seedling stage. After establishment, requirements fall into three categories: grasses, legumes, and mixtures of grasses and legumes.

Establishment

Grass or legume seedlings are largely dependent upon the soil for N required during initial growth. Consequently, small additions of this element at seeding usually are desirable on soils low in N.[29]

Maintenance

GRASS. In humid climates, the N available from all sources—soil organic matter, nonsymbiotic fixation, and precipitation—will be much less than the amount necessary for full production. In other words, N supply is usually the first limiting factor. Consequently, for best yields

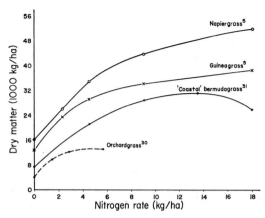

FIG. 38.8. Response of cool-season, warm-season, and tropical grasses to N applications.

and quality these plants must receive fairly large amounts of N from fertilizers or manures.

The amount of N needed depends on several factors such as species, climate, soil, and management. However, where all other plant growth requirements are present, longer growing seasons tend to promote higher dry matter production and the need for more nutrients. This can probably nowhere be better illustrated than with the more productive forage grasses and their response to N, as shown in Figure 38.8.[5,30,31] In production and N utilization the order among the better forage grasses is usually tropical > warm-season > cool-season. Although other factors operate, this is probably more a reflection of length of growing season than anything else.

These data also illustrate the very large capacity of these plants to utilize N. In fact, it is usually safe to assume that productive grasses will always respond to applied N unless the soil supply is exceptionally high or other factors such as moisture, temperature, and other nutrients sharply limit growth. Nitrogen applica-

29. Woodhouse, W. W., Jr., and D. S. Chamblee. 1958. Nitrogen in forage production, rev. N.C. Agr. Exp. Sta. Bull. 383.

30. Rhykerd, C. L., K. L. Washburn, and C. H. Noller. 1970. Nitrogen fertilization increases yields and N-K removal by orchardgrass. *Better Crops with Plant Food* 3:12–13. (Pot. Inst. N. Amer.)

31. Fisher, F. L., and A. G. Caldwell. 1959. The effect of continued use of heavy rates of fertilizers on forage production and quality of Coastal bermudagrass. *Agron. J.* 51:99–102.

tions should be made just before or during periods of active growth if additional forage is desired. Nitrogen will not be very effective on cool-season grasses during their summer dormant period or on warm-season species during the cool season of the year. Heavy applications of N under these conditions may weaken the sod by exhausting food reserves and may make plants more susceptible to drought, cold, or disease injury. Under humid conditions or with irrigation a single application usually is effective over relatively short periods, about 1.5–3 months. This is not true in drier climates where applied N that is not utilized the first season may remain in the soil and become available over several years.[32]

LEGUMES. Legumes are normally expected to obtain most of their N supply from the atmosphere through the symbiotic N-fixing bacteria. Their ability to do this and eventually contribute N to companion grasses or other crops in rotation generally has been considered one of their principal advantages. The amounts of N obtained this way vary widely with the plant and the environment.[33] Estimates run from less than 50 kg/ha/yr from some annuals to around 200 kg for alfalfa and some tropical legumes. In the past, application of fertilizer N to legumes has been confined largely to quick-growing annuals or as an aid in establishing perennials. Attempts to supplement the legume N supply by fertilization have generally been disappointing. The obvious explanation is that N-fixing bacteria tend to cease fixation in the presence of large amounts of available N. Using N as a tracer, it has been shown this can occur and that N applied may then replace rather than supplement the N that would normally be fixed (Table 38.5). Fixation is sharply depressed by the heavier rates of N application.

TABLE 38.5 ❧ Effect of applied N upon N fixed from atmosphere in established ladino clover, North Carolina

N applied, Feb. 24 (kg/ha)	Percent N from atmosphere		
	March 17	April 21	May 16
28	65	91	92
56	42	87	87
112	25	75	87
224	10	43	75

Source: Woodhouse and Chamblee, 1958.[29]

tion, with this effect decreasing as the supply of the element is depleted.

LEGUME-GRASS. The reaction of mixtures of grass and legumes to N applications might be expected to involve complications. A comprehensive review of the literature shows highly variable results and interpretations. There are cases where the applied N appears to act as a supplement to the legume N. It would seem logical to expect this where moisture is adequate and temperatures are high enough to encourage growth but low enough to limit nitrification and related microbiological processes. In practice this seems to be true. Topdressing grass-legume mixtures with N appears to have met with more success in climatic regions having fairly long periods of weather of this description.

It has been demonstrated that where space and light factors were minimized by close and frequent clipping and ample water was applied, application of as much as 390 kg/ha/yr of N had little effect on the clover population. With higher clipping and no irrigation, high N essentially eliminated the clover.[34]

BALANCED FERTILIZATION. Although each nutrient plays a different role, successful forage production requires adequate supplies of all the essential elements. Nitrogen is often the first limiting factor in the growth of forage grasses, but

32. Power, J. R., and J. Alessi. 1971. Nitrogen fertilization of semiarid grassland: Plant growth and soil mineral N levels. *Agron. J.* 63:277–80.

33. Erdman, L. W. 1959. Legume inoculation, rev. USDA Farmers' Bull, 2003.

34. Robinson, R. R., and V. G. Sprague. 1947. Clover populations and the yield of a Kentucky bluegrass sod as affected by nitrogen fertilization clipping treatments and irrigation. *Agron. J.* 39:107–16.

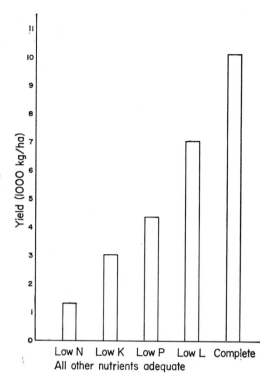

FIG. 38.9. The importance of nutrient balance on the growth of Coastal bermudagrass.

TABLE 38.6 ❧ Effect of fertilization with N or K on uptake of the other nutrient by guineagrass, Puerto Rico

K applied annually (kg/ha)	Fertilizer N in forage (896 kg/ha applied)	N applied annually (kg/ha)	Fertilizer K in forage (672 kg/ha applied)
0	162	0	129
448	549	448	504
896	571	560	672

Source: Vincente-Chandler et al., 1964.[5]

❧ FERTILITY RECYCLING UNDER GRAZING

It is sometimes assumed that since a high proportion of the N, P, and K consumed by the grazing animal passes through (75–90% for mature cattle) and may therefore be subject to recycling,[36] it should be necessary to inject only relatively small amounts of these nutrients into the system from time to time to attain and perpetuate an ample nutrient level over the pasture. Results from studies concerning this phenomenon have been conflicting, with substantial recycling indicated in some cases, considerably less in others.[37-39]

When some factors such as size and distribution of excretal spots and loss rate of individual nutrients within them are examined, it becomes apparent that the effect of nutrient return can be expected to vary widely with stocking rate, climate, soil, and the nutrient involved.[40,41] Re-

the efficiency with which it can be utilized is very much dependent upon the presence of adequate quantities of all the others. This is shown in Figure 38.9 in which N response of Coastal bermudagrass was quite large but was definitely limited by lack of P, K, or lime.[16,35]

There are also interactions between nutrients. One of the easiest of these to demonstrate is between N and K on very productive grasses where the supply of one may greatly affect the uptake of the other, as shown in Table 38.6.

In this trial an application of 448 kg/ha of K increased N uptake by 387 kg, while raising the N fertilization by 112 kg/ha (from 448 to 560) increased K uptake by 168 kg. Obviously, under these conditions one could not afford to consider N fertilization apart from K fertilization, or vice-versa.

35. Woodhouse, W. W., Jr. 1968. Long-term fertility requirements of Coastal bermuda. I. Potassium. *Agron. J.* 60:508–12.

36. Salter, R. M., and C. T. Scholenberger. 1939. Farm manure. Ohio Agr. Exp. Sta. Bull. 605.
37. Sears, P. D., V. C. Goodall, and R. P. Newbold. 1948. Effect of sheep droppings on yield, botanical composition, and chemical composition of pasture. II. Results for the years 1942–1944 and final summary. *N.Z. J. Sci. Tech.* A30:231–49.
38. Sears, P. D., and W. A. Thurston. 1953. Effect of sheep droppings on yield, botanical composition, and chemical composition of pasture. III. Results of field trials at Lincoln, Canterbury, for the years 1944–47. *N.Z. J. Sci. Tech.* A34:445–59.
39. Mott, G. O., L. R. Quinn, and W. V. A. Bisschoff. 1970. The retention of nitrogen in a soil-plant-animal system in guineagrass (*Panicum maximum*) pastures in Brazil. Proc. 11th Int. Grassl. Congr., pp. 414–16 (Surfers Paradise, Queensland, Aust.).
40. Peterson, R. G., H. L. Lucas, and W. W. Woodhouse, Jr. 1956. The distribution of excreta by freely grazing cattle and its effect on pasture fertility. *Agron. J.* 48:440–49.
41. Lotero, J., W. W. Woodhouse, Jr., and R. G. Petersen. 1966. Local effect on fertility of urine voided by grazing cattle. *Agron. J.* 58:262–65.

cycling can have a marked effect where the stocking rate is high and the loss rate of a nutrient such as P is low. On the other hand, under a low stocking rate with a highly mobile nutrient such as N the effect may be insignificant.

❧ OTHER NUTRIENTS

MAGNESIUM. Table 38.1 gives the Mg uptake for some selected legumes and grasses. Magnesium, essential for the formation of chlorophyll, is important to the growth of forage as well as to the health of animals consuming it. (See Chapter 58 for animal health effects.)

SULPHUR. More and more attention must be given to S nutrition as yields increase, the use of high-analysis S-free fertilizer continues, and the demand for cleaner air grows. Legumes remove relatively large amounts of S and require amounts almost equal to that of P. Numerous experiments with legumes have given a response to added S.[42] The S requirement for forage grasses is somewhat less, and thus little work has been done with these species. However, work in North Carolina shows that the addition of S significantly increased the yield of Coastal bermudagrass seven of the eight years.[43] Particularly important in S nutrition is the balance between N and S. An N/S ratio greater than 15:1 is considered detrimental for optimum yield and protein production. A 10:1 N/S ratio is considered optimum for maximum utilization of the forage by ruminants. Thus a balanced N and S fertilization program is essential for both yield and quality forage.

MICRONUTRIENTS. Such micronutrients as B, Cu, Mn, Mo, and Zn are just as essential for plant growth as N, P, K, and Ca. They are required in very small amounts and usually are present in the soil or as impurities in fertilizers in sufficient amounts for the normal growth of forages. The removal of large quantities of plant materials, the use of fertilizers in purer forms, improper liming, and the particular character of some soils will cause deficiencies of one or another of the micronutrients to develop from time to time.[44] Some plants are more likely to require additions of certain of these elements than others. Boron is widely needed on alfalfa in the U.S., and Mo is needed on subterranean clover in Australia. Since excesses of such elements as B, Mo, and Cu can be even more damaging than deficiencies, trace elements should not be added unless the need for them has been established.

44. Sprague, H. B. 1964. Hunger Signs in Crops, 3rd ed. David McKay, New York.

❧ QUESTIONS

1. How and why does climate affect forage fertilization requirements?
2. How do grasses and legumes differ in their response to soil fertility factors?
3. Compare the behavior of K, P, and N applied to soils.
4. What is meant by "luxury consumption," and under what conditions do you expect it to occur?
5. What is meant by nutrient balance? Give some examples, showing its importance in forage production.
6. Is the N requirement for a cool-season, warm-season, and tropical grass likely to differ? Why? What about P and K needs?
7. What is meant by competition for K in a forage mixture? What plants are likely to be at the greatest disadvantage under low levels of K?
8. Do grazed forages have fertilizer requirements different from those harvested in other ways? Explain.
9. Is S as a nutrient receiving more or less attention now than in the past? Why?
10. Is it usually desirable to apply micronutrients in forage fertilizers? Explain.

42. Beaton, J. D. 1966. Sulphur requirements of crops. *Soil Sci.* 101:267–82.
43. Woodhouse, W. W., Jr. 1969. Long-term fertility requirements of Coastal bermudagrass. III. Sulphur. *Agron. J.* 61:705–8.

C. L. RHYKERD AND C. H. NOLLER
Purdue University

39

THE ROLE OF NITROGEN IN FORAGE PRODUCTION

N ITROGEN SUPPLY to grasses is a major limitation in forage production since soils almost universally do not contain sufficient available N for high yields of grasses. The soil may contain a large quantity of combined N which is bound to organic matter and mineral material, but only a few kilograms per ha of available N will be found at any one time. Therefore, fertilizer N, legume N, or both must be relied upon to supply the need. Whether the major source is fertilizer N or legume N depends largely on availability of fertilizer N and climatic conditions.

Where climatic factors such as temperature and moisture are favorable, as in New Zealand, legumes are quite effective in providing N for grasses growing in association with them. However, in other regions of the world such as the Netherlands, fertilizer N has been found to be a much more dependable source for intensive production of grasses for livestock.

The amount of N required for maximum yield of grasses varies with species and climate. Bermudagrass yields have been found to increase with N rates up to 2016 kg/ha/year.[1] Bermudagrass yields of about 25 t/ha/year with N rates of 672 and 896 kg/ha/year have been reported.[2] Studies in the Midwest with cool-season grasses have demonstrated yield increases with increased N up to approximately 560 kg/ha.[3,4] The maximum dry matter yield obtained was 18 t/ha. Rates of N above 560 kg/ha have tended to reduce yields and stands of cool-season grasses (Fig. 39.1).[5]

❧ C. L. RHYKERD is Professor of Agronomy, Purdue University. He holds the M.S. degree from the University of Illinois and the Ph.D. from Purdue University. His research has dealt with the soil-plant-animal environment complex.

❧ C. H. NOLLER is Professor of Animal Nutrition, Purdue University. He holds the M.S. degree from Purdue University and the Ph.D. from Michigan State University. His special interests include silage production and utilization and the soil-plant-animal environment complex as related to forage production and utilization.

1. Woodworth, R. C., R. E. Procter, G. W. Burton, and A. B. Mackie. 1957. Profitable use of fertilizer in the production of Coastal bermuda in the coastal plain area of Georgia. Ga. Agr. Exp. Sta. Tech. Bull. 13.
2. Decker, A. M., R. W. Hemkin, J. R. Miller, N. A. Clark, and A. V. Okorie. 1971. Nitrogen fertilization, harvest management, and utilization of 'Midland' bermudagrass, *Cynodon dactylon* (L.) Pers. Md. Agr. Exp. Sta. Bull. 487.
3. Rhykerd, C. L., C. H. Noller, K. L. Washburn, Jr., S. J. Donohue, K. L. Collins, L. H. Smith, and M. W. Phillips. 1969. Fertilizing grasses with nitrogen. Purdue Univ. Agron. Guide AY-176.
4. Schmidt, D. R., and G. H. Tenpas. 1965. Seasonal response of grasses fertilized with nitrogen compared to a legume-grass mixture. *Agron. J.* 57:428–31.
5. Washburn, K. L., Jr. 1970. Influence of N fertilization on yield and chemical composition of alfalfa, smooth bromegrass, orchardgrass, reed canarygrass, and tal fescue. M.S. thesis, Purdue Univ., Lafayette, Ind.

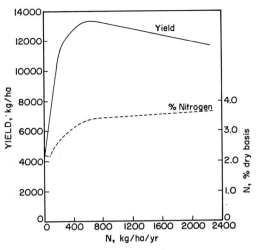

FIG. 39.1. Effect of N fertilization of orchard-grass on average dry matter yields and N concentrations in the plant over a two-year period. (From Washburn, 1970.[5])

In England considerable response to N by grasses can be expected at rates up to 400 kg/ha if the N is uniformly distributed over the growing season.[6]

As the world's need for food protein increases, forage legumes or N-fertilized grass

6. Holmes, W. 1968. The use of nitrogen in the management of the pasture for cattle. *Herb. Abstr.* **38**: 265–77.

may be used as a source of leaf protein. Leaf protein could be used for human food, and the by-products used as livestock feed if a suitable method of processing is developed. Research indicates that alfalfa contains an excellent balance of amino acids. Crude protein yields of approximately 3300 kg/ha have been reported from an alfalfa-grass mixture, while nearly 4500 kg/ha have been obtained from ryegrass and reed canarygrass liberally fertilized with N.[5,7,8]

❧ NITROGEN CYCLE

Nitrogen transformations in a grassland ecosystem are outlined in Figure 39.2. This diagram illustrates the various possible N transformations, rather than a closed system involving the recycling of a given quantity of N. Factors causing shifts in the relative importance of various segments of the N cycle are: application of fertilizer N, presence of a legume, grazing or harvesting the forage as hay or silage, and climatic conditions.

Major inputs into the N cycle come from

7. Rhykerd, C. L., C. H. Noller, J. E. Dillon, J. B. Ragland, B. W. Crowl, G. C. Naderman, and D. L. Hill. 1967. Managing alfalfa-grass mixture for yield and protein. Purdue Univ. Agr. Exp. Sta. Res. Bull. 839.
8. Spedding, C. R. W. 1971. Grassland Ecology. Oxford Univ. Press, London.

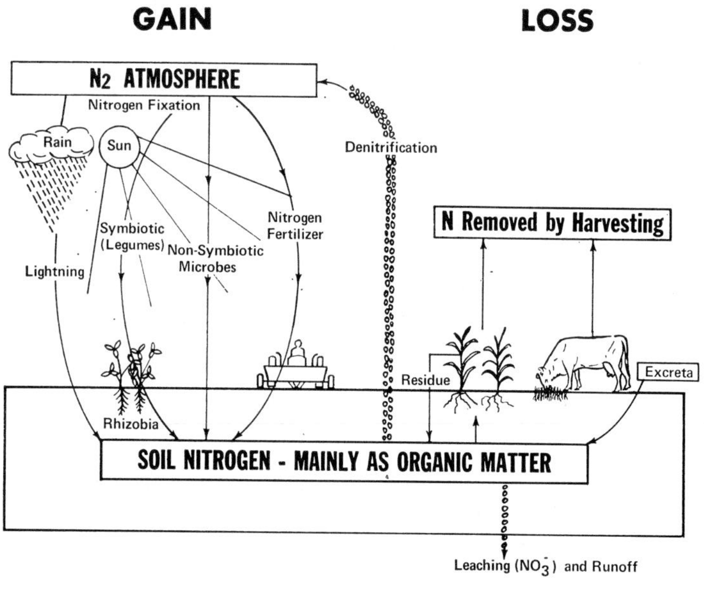

FIG. 39.2. Nitrogen transformations in a grassland ecosystem.

symbiotic N-fixation by nodulated legumes and fertilizer N both of which are provided almost entirely by the atmosphere. Additions of N by rainfall, by absorption of ammonia from the atmosphere, and by nonsymbiotic N-fixation are quite small.

Losses of N from the system vary widely depending upon whether the forage is grazed by livestock or whether it is removed from the field as hay or silage and fed under drylot conditions. The quantity of N removed per ha by hay or silage may amount to several hundred kilograms depending upon the yield and N content. For example, a hay yield of 25 t/ha containing 3% N would remove 750 kg/ha of N.

Under grazing conditions only a small portion of the N consumed by livestock is removed as milk, meat, or wool. Thus most of the N is returned to the soil in excreta. The recycling of N in this manner is an important contribution to total N in some environments and is likely to be more important as stocking rates increase. Other losses of N from the system occur through leaching, denitrification, volatilization of ammonia, and runoff.

❧ BOTANICAL COMPOSITION

Nitrogen fertilization may affect the botanical composition of a mixed grass stand. In general, it appears to promote the growth of the more desirable, more productive grass species. However the effect of N fertilization on botanical composition of mixed grass stands as well as legume-grass mixtures can also be affected by many other factors such as frequency of cutting or grazing and the supply of essential mineral elements in the soil.

Nitrogen fertilization may alter the botanical composition of grass-legume mixtures. Since grasses and legumes differ considerably in chemical composition, any shift in botanical composition may change the chemical composition of the forage produced. As a rule, even small amounts of fertilizer N will tend to depress the growth of legumes in a grass-legume mixture if the forage is harvested as hay or silage. However, under grazing conditions where the grass is continuously being defoliated, legumes are more successful in competing with grasses even at relatively high rates of fertilizer N.[9] The concentration of the various mineral elements in grasses and legumes can be of considerable importance to animal health and performance if forage is the sole feedstuff. For example, low levels of Co and Mg in plants have been reported to cause nutritional deficiencies in grazing animals. These deficiencies are more likely to occur on predominantly grass pastures since legumes tend to be higher in these elements.

Grass tetany is an animal health problem associated with Mg deficiency in grazing animals, especially ruminants under stress. The level of Mg required by plants and animals is quite similar. Legumes tend to have a higher concentration of Mg than grasses. Also, the application of N and K can affect the level of Mg in plants in addition to causing a shift in the proportion of grasses and legumes in a mixture. High levels of K in the soil tend to reduce the Mg level in plants. This effect has been reported to be much greater in grasses than in white clover.[10] Thus the incidence of grass tetany is likely to increase if there is a shift from legume-grass mixtures to pure grass and fertilizer N.

Many factors must be considered when comparing the mineral concentration of grasses and legumes. It has been demonstrated that mineral concentration in plants is affected by stage of maturity, plant part, moisture and temperature conditions, soil pH, and relative ratio of the various elements in the soil.

In general, the Ca, B, and Co concentrations in legumes tend to be considerably higher than in grasses; N, Mg, Zn, Cu, and Fe tend to be somewhat higher in legumes.

9. Robinson, R. R., and V. G. Sprague. 1947. The clover populations and yields of a Kentucky bluegrass sod as affected by nitrogen fertilization, clipping treatments and irrigation. *Agron. J.* 39:107–16.
10. McNaught, K. J. 1970. Diagnosis of mineral deficiencies in grass-legume pastures by plant analysis. Proc. 11th Int. Grassl. Congr., pp. 334–38 (Surfers Paradise, Queensland, Aust.).

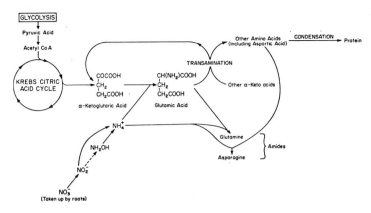

FIG. 39.3. Schematic representation of the incorporation of inorganic N into organic N compounds in plants.

On the other hand, the concentrations of K, Na, and especially Mn usually are higher in grasses.[10]

❧ ABSORPTION OF N BY GRASSES

Nearly all the N absorbed by grasses is as the nitrate ion (NO_3^-) or the ammonium ion (NH_4^+); both are absorbed very rapidly by roots. Soluble organic compounds such as urea and amino acids can be absorbed by plant roots and therefore may contribute to N nutrition of grasses in soils having a large amount of microbiological activity.[11]

The ammonium ion is rapidly oxidized to NO_3^- by nitrifying bacteria in the soil under favorable growing conditions. Therefore, the major portion of the N is probably taken up as NO_3^- even though ammonium fertilizers may have been applied.

❧ UTILIZATION OF N BY PLANTS

The major portion of the N taken up by plants is used in synthesizing protein (Fig. 39.3). About 10–30% of the total N in grasses will be found in nonprotein N (NPN) form. The major constituent of NPN in grasses is amino acids.

For the plant to synthesize protein, NO_3^- taken up by the roots must be reduced to NH_4^+. Some NO_3^- reduction appears to occur in the roots but much of it is translocated to the stems and leaves. Normally the NO_3^- concentration in growing plants under ideal conditions is low. Certain conditions such as drought and mineral deficiencies promote NO_3^- accumulation which may reach levels potentially harmful to the health of livestock. Conditions which allow excessive N absorption in relation to photosynthesis result in NO_3^- accumulation in the plant if the N is absorbed as NO_3^-. Amides such as glutamine and asparagine accumulate if the N is absorbed as NH_4^+ or if there is an excess of this ion in the plant. An accumulation of NO_3^- in the plant does not appear to be harmful.

Plants contain a system of enzymes that reduce NO_3^- to NH_4^+ as outlined in Figure 39.3. Ammoniacal N is converted to amino N and then added to a keto acid to form an amino acid. The major amino acid formed directly from NH_4^+ is glutamic acid.

Amino acids comprise the building blocks of protein. The remaining amino acids may be made from glutamic acid or other organic acids by the process called transamination. Synthesis of protein is carried on by the ribosomes of the cell.

❧ MORPHOLOGICAL EFFECTS OF N ON GRASSES

TILLERS

Application of N usually increases the number of tillers.[12] However, this response

11. Whitehead, D. C. 1970. The role of nitrogen in grassland productivity. Commonwealth Bur. Pastures and Field Crops, Bull. 48.

12. Langer, R. H. M. 1963. Tillering in herbage grasses. *Herb. Abstr.* 33:141–48.

can be modified by factors such as moisture, temperature, light intensity, and plant density. The main effect of N on tillering appears to be on the duration since there is a more pronounced effect on secondary tillers than on primary ones.

LEAVES

The major effect of N on leaves of grasses is thought to be related to leaf size. Nitrogen fertilization appears to have little if any effect on the number of leaves per tiller or leaf senescence.

ROOTS

Increasing the rate of N application increases the top to root ratio of plants. However, the amount of roots may be increased or decreased. The addition of fertilizer N to soil containing low levels of available soil N results in greater acceleration of top growth than root growth. As N rates are increased, smaller and smaller increases in root growth are obtained until a point is reached where a further increase in application of N will cause a retardation.[13]

Number and diameter of roots also are affected by N fertilization. Increasing fertilizer N rates causes an increase in diameter of roots but a decrease in number.[14]

Tropical grasses have been reported to grow better than temperate grasses at low levels of N. The reason may be that temperate grasses have a higher proportion of roots, thereby tying up a higher proportion of the limited supply of N.[15]

❧ NITROGEN RECOVERY

Recovery of N by forage grasses usually is in the range of 50–80%. Occasionally N recovery exceeds 100%, indicating that the application of fertilizer N increased the availability of soil N. A major factor affecting the percentage recovery of N is the rate of application. Other factors are species of grass, temperature, source of N, and time interval between application and harvesting.

In general, percentage recovery is highest at N rates of 200–300 kg/ha/year. At low rates considerable N may remain in the roots and stubble, while at high rates a relatively high proportion of the fertilizer N may not be absorbed.

Differences, although usually relatively small, have been found to exist between grass species relative to recovery of fertilizer N, as illustrated in Table 39.1.[16] Orchardgrass recovered the highest percentage of the N applied. The influence of temperature on N recovery of tropical and temperate grasses has been studied.[17] Day/night temperatures of 35/24 C resulted in greater N recovery by tropical grasses but reduced that of temperate grasses when compared to day/night temperatures of 24/13 C.

What happens to N not recovered by plants? Unrecovered N either is lost from the system or accumulates on or in the soil. If there is a buildup of soil N under permanent grassland, this should be available for recycling after some time with a resultant decrease in amount of fertilizer N required. Data has been obtained from a grazing trial in Brazil suggesting that after application of a high rate of N for several years a much lower annual amount may be needed to maintain near maximum forage production.[18]

13. Troughton, A. 1957. The underground organs of herbage grasses. Commonwealth Bur. Pastures and Field Crops, Bull. 44.
14. Oswalt, D. L., A. R. Bertrand, and M. R. Teel. 1959. Influence of nitrogen fertilization and clipping on grass roots. Soil Sci. Soc. Amer. Proc. 23:228–30.
15. Wilson, J. R., and K. P. Haydock. 1971. The comparative response of tropical and temperate grasses to varying levels of nitrogen and phosphorus nutrition. *Aust. J. Agr. Res.* 22:573–87.

16. Cowling, D. W., and D. R. Lockyer. 1967. A comparison of the reaction of different grass species to fertilizer nitrogen and to growth in association with white clover. II. Yield of nitrogen. *J. Brit. Grassl. Soc.* 22:53–61.
17. Colman, R. L., and A. Lazenby. 1970. Factors affecting the response of some tropical and temperate grasses to fertilizer nitrogen. Proc. 11th Int. Grassl. Congr., pp. 392–97 (Surfers Paradise, Queensland, Aust.).
18. Mott, G. O., L. R. Quinn, and W. V. A. Bisschoff. 1970. The retention of nitrogen in a soil-plant-animal system in guineagrass (*Panicum maximum*) pastures in Brazil. Proc. 11th Int. Grassl. Congr., pp. 414–16 (Surfers Paradise, Queensland, Aust.).

TABLE 39.1 ❧ Percentage recovery of N fertilizer by four grasses

Grass	N, kg/ha/yr		
	90 (%)	180 (%)	360 (%)
Perennial ryegrass, S24	35	48	61
Timothy, S48	48	58	63
Meadow fescue, S215	44	54	64
Orchardgrass, S37	59	63	70

Source: Cowling and Lockyer, 1967.[16]

❧ EFFECT ON CHEMICAL COMPOSITION

DRY MATTER CONTENT

The application of fertilizer N tends to decrease the percent of dry matter of forage crops. The percent dry matter of perennial ryegrass has been found to decrease from approximately 24% to about 17% with the addition of 896 kg/ha of N as shown in Figure 39.4.[19] Other factors affecting percent dry matter are species, stage of growth, time of day, shading, soil moisture, and soil fertility.

INORGANIC FRACTION

A thorough knowledge of the effects of N fertilization on total N and N fractions in forage plants is of considerable importance since it influences forage quality and possibly animal health. Nitrate toxicity, ammonia intoxication, and grass tetany have been associated with N fertilization. (See Chapter 52.)

The application of higher rates of fertilizer N to a grass sward generally causes a progressive increase in N concentration in the forage. However, with legumes there usually is only a very small increase, if any, when N is applied. Although grass yields may be increased with low rates of N there may be little or no change in N concentration (Fig. 39.1). In fact, occasionally a decrease is observed, due possibly to the dis-

19. Lazenby, A., and H. H. Rodgers. 1965. Selection criteria in grass breeding. IV. Effect of nitrogen and spacing on yield and its components. *J. Agr. Sci.* 65:65–78.

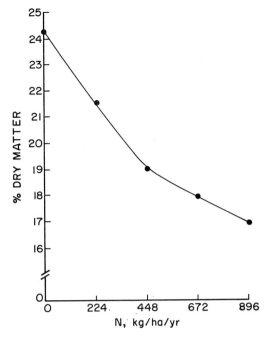

FIG. 39.4. Effect of N fertilization on the percent dry matter in perennial ryegrass. (Adapted from Lazenby and Rodgers, 1965.[19])

appearance of volunteer clover as increased rates of fertilizer N are applied. Nitrogen concentration in grasses will usually continue to increase, even beyond the point where yields cease to increase, with the application of higher rates of N.

Nitrogen content also is influenced by the time interval between application and harvesting by cutting or grazing. The N concentration may be quite high for two to three weeks after application and then declines rather rapidly over the next several weeks.

Inorganic N in the plant may be present in the nitrate or the ammonium form. As a rule, the ammonium form occurs in very minute amounts. Nitrate usually is present in relatively small amounts; however, under unusual growing conditions nearly 50% of the total N in some plant species may be present in the nitrate form.

Many factors affect the nitrate concentration in plants. These include: supply of nitrate to the roots, stage of growth, species, moisture supply, temperature, and light intensity. Deficiencies of S, Mn, Mo, Fe, and Cu may increase nitrate concentration in plants. Sulfur is involved in protein synthesis, while Mn, Mo, Fe, and Cu are components of enzymes involved in nitrate reduction in plants. The N:S ratio has been suggested as a criterion for determining S deficiencies in forages. (See Chapter 38.)

Figure 39.5 shows the effect of N fertilization on the NO_3-N concentration in tall fescue under pasture conditions.[20] The fertilizer N was applied in early spring. It is evident that N had a pronounced effect on the NO_3^- N concentration in tall fescue especially in the earlier part of the growing season. No ill effects on the animals were observed in the experiment. Rhizomatous warm-season grasses like bermudagrass reportedly have less tendency to accumulate nitrate than cool-season grasses.[2]

Reports of the effect of N fertilization on the concentration of the various other mineral elements in plants are often inconsistent. This is not surprising since the form of N as well as level of available elements in the soil affect the uptake of elements.

Nitrogen fertilization appears to increase the concentration of P and K if there is a high level of availability of these elements in the soil. If the soil supply is low, their concentration in the plant may be reduced. Uptake of other elements such as Fe, Mn, and Co is influenced by soil pH. The application of ammonium salts and compounds yielding ammonium salts increases soil acidity, thereby increasing the concentration of Fe, Mn, and Co in plants. Ammonium sulfate also increases the S concentration since it supplies S in addition to N.

The use of anhydrous ammonia results in a decrease in concentration of K, Ca, and Mg. This decrease is believed due to ammonium depressing the uptake of these

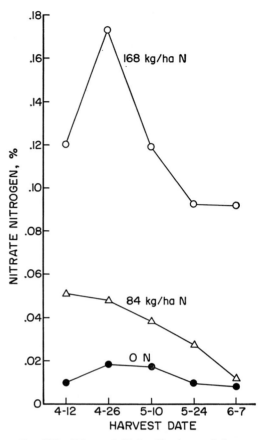

FIG. 39.5. Effect of N fertilization and harvest date on the nitrate N concentration of tall fescue pasture. (From George et al., 1972.[20])

cations. This suggests that the use of anhydrous ammonia might increase the incidence of grass tetany if the level of Mg was already near the deficiency level in the forage.

ORGANIC FRACTION

The percentage of water-soluble carbohydrates in plants generally is decreased by N fertilization. The major change is in the polysaccharides. This decrease appears to have little or no effect on animal nutrition. However, it may affect silage fermentation since adequate readily available carbohydrates are required for making good quality silage.

20. George, J. R., C. L. Rhykerd, G. O. Mott, R. F. Barnes, and C. H. Noller. 1972. Effect of nitrogen fertilization of *Festuca arundinacea* Schreb. on nitrate nitrogen and protein content and the performance of grazing steers. *Agron. J.* 64:24–26.

The percentage of total organic acids and alkaloids in grasses apparently is increased by N fertilization. In addition, carotene is increased considerably.

❧ EFFECT ON SILAGE QUALITY

Readily available carbohydrates are utilized in the ensiling process to form organic acids; consequently, there is a loss of dry matter and an increase in N concentration. Since N fertilization tends to increase the N concentration and decrease the readily available carbohydrates, it may have a detrimental effect on silage quality. This is particularly true with cool-season grasses that tend to be low in readily available carbohydrates. Quality of corn silage is not affected because of a high level of readily available carbohydrates.

High-protein forages are more difficult to ensile because more lactic acid is required to lower the pH. Since the level of readily available carbohydrates in high-protein forages is usually low, there is an insufficient quantity for the lactic acid–forming bacteria to produce the necessary amount of acid. Therefore, the pH of the silage is not lowered sufficiently to ensure good quality.[21] Ensiling forages with less than 70% moisture or adding a preservative will improve the quality of silage made from cool-season grasses fertilized with N.

❧ EFFECT ON THE ANIMAL

Palatability and Intake

Conflicting reports have been published concerning the effect of N fertilization on palatability of forages; it appears that any effect is small. Under pasture conditions bermudagrass has been found to increase in palatability with increased rates of N.[22]

Reports show improved palatability of a number of grasses associated with increased percent of moisture,[23,24] although a marked reduction has been found in dry matter intake by dairy cattle grazing forage oats fertilized with high levels of N.[25] The lower dry matter intake was explained on the basis of a shorter grazing time and higher percentage of moisture associated with N fertilization. Other investigators have suggested that the increase in alkaloid concentration of reed canarygrass and tall fescue may be responsible for the low acceptability of these grasses when they are fertilized with N.[26,27]

Digestibility

Nitrogen fertilization of grasses does not appear to have a very pronounced effect on digestibility. However, differences have been noted where N fertilization affected the presence of legumes and the maturity of the grasses or where soil N was so low that it resulted in reduced digestibility of the forage.[11]

Animal Production

Greater carrying capacity and more livestock products per ha generally result from N fertilization of grasses; however, individual animal performance is usually not improved.[28] In fact, on pastures heavily fertilized with N, performance may not be as good as on comparable grass receiving no N or on grass-legume mixtures.[11] However, lower performance has been obtained

21. Fenner, H., and G. W. Colby. 1969. Effect of nitrogen fertilization and physiological maturity of timothy grass at the time of cutting on silage fermentation. *J. Dairy Sci.* 52:279–80.

22. Burton, G. W., B. L. Southwell, and J. C. Johnson. 1956. The palatability of Coastal bermudagrass, *Cynodon dactylon* (L.) Pers., as influenced by nitrogen level and age. *Agron. J.* 48:360–62.

23. Archibald, J. G., E. Bennett, and W. S. Ritchie. 1943. The composition and palatability of some common grasses. *J. Agr. Res.* 66:341–47.

24. Reid, R. L., G. A. Jung, and S. J. Murray. 1966. Nitrogen fertilization in relation to the palatability and nutrient value of orchardgrass. *J. Anim. Sci.* 25:636–45.

25. Fernando, G. W. E., and O. G. Carter. 1970. The effect of level of nitrogen fertilizer applied to forage oats on the grazing behaviour of dairy cattle. Proc. 11th Int. Grassl. Congr., pp. 853–56 (Surfers Paradise, Queensland, Aust.).

26. Robbins, J. D., S. R. Wilkinson, D. Burdick, and R. B. Russell. 1972. N-acetyl loline in tall fescue seed and forage. *J. Anim. Sci.* 34:352.

27. Barnes, R. F., G. C. Marten, and A. B. Simons. 1969. Indole alkaloid derivatives in *Phalaris arundinacea* L. clones of varying palatability. *Amer. Soc. Agron. Abstr.*, p. 57.

28. Blaser, R. E. 1964. Symposium on forage utilization: Effects of fertility levels and stage of maturity on forage nutritive value. *J. Anim. Sci.* 23:246–53.

from predominantly legume pastures, which tended to produce bloat.

Experiments indicate that high levels of fertilizer N do not appear to have a deleterious effect on animal performance.[11,28] However, health problems in animals have been attributed to the use of high rates of N, especially over a period of years where the ration was largely composed of forage. These problems may not be directly attributed to fertilizer N but rather to an imbalance of nutrients. This may be a deficiency or toxic level of some plant constituent, a reduction in dry matter content, or an unbalanced ration due to an excess of protein in relation to energy where the forage comprises the major portion of the ration. (See Chapter 58 on animal disorders associated with the use of N on grass.)

The ration consumed by grazing animals usually is composed predominantly or entirely of forage. When livestock depend on relatively few feedstuffs, the possibility of animal health being impaired due to a nutritional imbalance increases.[5] Therefore, it is important that grasses contain the necessary nutrients in the proper proportion to meet the nutritional requirements of the grazing animal or that a supplement be supplied to balance the ration. As a rule, the application of N to grass pastures causes an increase in crude protein and possibly a reduction in soluble carbohydrates. Thus the application of N to grass pastures could cause an imbalance between protein and energy, especially in cool-season grasses which tend to be low in energy relative to protein even when fertilized with low levels of N. This imbalance may be in part responsible for the reportedly low animal performance and the health problems frequently associated with the liberal application of fertilizer N.

❧ QUESTIONS

1. The botanical composition of a meadow may be altered by fertilizing with N. What are the major differences in concentration of the various mineral elements in legumes as compared to grasses?

2. Nitrogen is taken up in several different forms by plants. List the forms and indicate which usually serves as the major source of N.

3. What percentage of the N in plants is in the NPN form? List some of the compounds which comprise the NPN fraction.

4. What is the effect of N fertilization on the dry matter content of forage plants?

5. Many compounds found in the organic fraction of grasses are affected by N fertilization. Name at least three of these and indicate whether N fertilization causes an increase or decrease in concentration of these compounds.

6. What is the major effect of N fertilization of forage grasses relative to animal production?

7. Why do legumes disappear from a legume-grass mixture when N is applied and the forage is harvested for hay but may not do so if grazed by livestock?

8. How does the application of fertilizer N affect the top to root ratio of plants?

SUPPLEMENTAL INFORMATION

Prior to World War II, the sources of N required for producing forage crops came primarily from biologically fixed N, the N in rain, and N in animal manure. Technological advancements in the fertilizer industry following World War II along with an abundance of natural gas resulted in low-cost N fertilizers, making it profitable to produce pure grass stands. These high-yielding stands alleviated many of the management problems associated with growing legume-grass mixtures. However, it was generally recognized by livestock producers that animal performance was improved by feeding legume-grass forage rather than pure grass.

The "energy crisis" of 1973 caused a doubling or tripling of the cost of N fertilizers and consequently created a renewed interest in biologically fixed N in forage-animal systems.[29] In the past five years numerous reports have been made of N fixation in tropical grass-bacteria associations.[30] Further research is needed to determine the agronomic practices that will maximize the N fixed from this association.

29. Hoveland, C. S. (ed.). 1976. Biological N fixation in forage-livestock systems. ASA Spec. Publ. 28 (Madison, Wis.).
30. Neyra, Carlos A., and J. Dobereiner. 1977. Nitrogen fixation in grasses. In N. C. Brady (ed.). Advances in Agronomy, vol. 29. Academic Press, New York.

DALE SMITH / *University of Wisconsin*

40

PHYSIOLOGICAL CONSIDERATIONS IN FORAGE MANAGEMENT

❧

T HE GROWTH PATTERN of forage legumes and grasses is influenced by the environmental conditions to which they are exposed. The combination of environmental factors in an area will seldom be the same more than once in any one season. Growth will vary within a season and among seasons, depending on the climatic complex to which the species is exposed. Knowledge of the physiological responses of any particular species to the environment is necessary to determine practical management practices. Management practices should be based on the physiological condition and stage of development of the plant; they seldom can be based on the calendar date.

❧ CARDINAL ENVIRONMENTAL FACTORS

Light, temperature, and moisture are the three cardinal environmental factors influencing the vegetative development and maturation of a forage species.[1-4]

❧ DALE SMITH is Professor of Agronomy, University of Wisconsin. He holds the M.S. and Ph.D. degrees from the University of Wisconsin. His research has dealt with the management, chemical composition, and growth responses of forage plants.

LIGHT

The factors of light that influence growth can be separated into three parts: intensity, quality, and duration.

INTENSITY. Light intensity in the field under full sunlight during the summer reaches levels between 85,000 and 110,000 lx.[1,5] However, the quantity of light energy available rather than the intensity appears to be the important factor.[6] It also has been suggested that the greater the quantity of light energy available up to the highest values in the field, the better the growth.[6] Once the leaf canopy has developed to completely intercept the light, the amount of light energy available sets a limit to production that cannot be

1. Salisbury, F. B., and Cleon Ross. 1969. **Plant Physiology.** Wadsworth, Belmont, Calif.
2. Moss, D. N. 1964. Some aspects of microclimatology important in forage plant physiology. Amer. Soc. Agron. Spec. Publ. 5, pp. 1–14.
3. Alberda, Th. 1966. Responses of grasses to temperature and light. *In* F. L. Milthorpe and J. D. Ivins (eds.), The Growth of Cereals and Grasses, pp. 200–212. Butterworths, London.
4. Cooper, J. P., and N. M. Tainton. 1968. **Light and temperature requirements for the growth of tropical and temperate grasses.** Herb. Abstr. 38:167–76.
5. Larsen, Poul. 1966. Light requirements in plant production and growth regulation. Acta Agr. Scand. (Suppl.) 16:161–72.
6. Black, J. N. 1957. The influence of varying light intensity on the growth of herbage plants. Herb. Abstr. 27:89–98.

exceeded and can be attained only when no other factor is limiting growth. A full canopy of leaves is needed to intercept the available light energy.[7]

Competition for light is an important factor when forages are to be established with a grain companion crop or when forage species are grown in association. Although most forage species are sun plants as opposed to shade plants,[1,5,8] species differ in response to variations in light intensity. Red clover has produced more top growth under low light intensity than alfalfa, and alfalfa more than birdsfoot trefoil.[9,10] It also is well known that orchardgrass will grow under lower light intensities than smooth bromegrass or timothy.

Studies have shown that the individual leaves of most forage legumes and cool-season grasses of temperate origin are light saturated at lower intensities than grasses of tropical origin.[2,4] Light saturation of individual leaves of temperate grasses may occur at 20,000–30,000 lx, while it does not occur in most tropical grasses until 60,000 lx or more. Conversion of light energy at near light saturation may be below 3% in temperate grasses as compared with 5–6% for tropical grasses. Thus tropical grasses have a higher potential photosynthetic rate and very high light saturation values.

The two groups of grasses also differ biochemically.[4] Tropical grasses have no apparent photorespiration and can reduce atmospheric CO_2 to less than 5 ppm in a closed atmosphere. In temperate grasses photorespiration occurs during light exposure, and these grasses can reduce CO_2 to only about 50–60 ppm. Also, tropical grasses have a carbon pathway in photosynthesis where carbon appears to be fixed first into C-4 compounds rather than the C-3 products typical of temperate grasses.

QUALITY. Light quality refers to the wavelength of the light rays. Plant development is better under the full spectrum of sunlight than under any portion. Plants grown only under the long wavelengths of infrared light usually grow continuously, as in darkness, while plants grown only under the short wavelengths of ultraviolet light may be retarded in growth or even injured or killed.

DAYLENGTH. Daylength, or duration of the period of light, influences both vegetative growth and flowering.[1,4,5,11] Early studies emphasized daylength, but later work showed that plant response was controlled by the length of the dark period.[1]

The effect of daylength on flowering has been intensively studied since this influences seed production and geographical distribution. Short-day plants flower only within a range of relatively short daylengths (long nights), while long-day plants flower only within a range of relatively long daylengths (short nights) (Fig. 40.1).[12] Another group of plants, referred to as day-neutral, are capable of flowering under either long or short daylengths. Flowering response has been found to be more complicated than this classification, commonly known as photoperiodism.[1] Many plant species require exposure to specific temperatures in addition to proper photoperiodic conditions.

TEMPERATURE

Temperature influences all physiological processes, and the temperature extremes limit the species or cultivars that can grow at a given location. Growth will vary, depending on the temperature pattern to which a plant is exposed, particularly differences between day and night.[1-4] Opti-

7. Brown, R. H., and R. E. Blaser. 1968. Leaf area index in pasture growth. *Herb. Abstr.* 38:1–9.
8. Böhning, R. H., and C. A. Burnside. 1956. The effect of light intensity on rate of apparent photosynthesis in leaves of sun and shade plants. *Amer. J. Bot.* 43:557–61.
9. Gist, G. R., and G. O. Mott. 1957. Some effects of light intensity, temperature, and soil moisture on the growth of alfalfa, red clover, and birdsfoot trefoil seedlings. *Agron. J.* 49:33–36.
10. Gist, G. R., and G. O. Mott. 1958. Growth of alfalfa, red clover, and birdsfoot trefoil seedlings under various quantities of light. *Agron. J.* 50:583–86.

11. Cooper, J. P. 1960. The use of controlled life cycles in the forage grasses and legumes. *Herb. Abstr.* 30:71–79.
12. Allard, H. A., and M. W. Evans. 1941. Growth and flowering of some tame and wild grasses in response to different photoperiods. *J. Agr. Res.* 62:193–228.

FIG. 40.1. *Daylength . . . influences seed production . . . geographical distribution.* **Response of indiangrass to various constant photoperiods (hours). The control (C) received full length of day. (From Allard and Evans, 1941.[12])**

mum temperature for different species, stages of development, and plant parts can be quite different. Usually, the optimum temperature for vegetative growth is lower than that for either flowering or fruiting and is lower for root than top growth.

Temperate grasses appear to have an optimum temperature for growth of around 20 C but will grow fairly actively at lower temperatures, while tropical grasses have a growth optimum of around 30–35 C and may produce very little below 15 C.[4] Studies have shown that the rates of dry matter accumulation for seven temperate grasses were highest in the range of 10–20 C.[13] However, rates for tropical bermudagrass and bahiagrass were highest at 35 C and decreased rapidly at lower temperatures and more slowly at higher temperatures. The relative growth rates of Panicoideae grass species (warm-season) in another study were highest at 36 C day/ 31 C night temperatures and decreased about 75% as temperatures were decreased to 15/10 C (Table 40.1).[14] In contrast, relative growth rates of Festucoideae grass species (cool-season) were highest between 21/16 and 30/25 C and decreased about 40% as temperatures were increased to 36/

31 C. Warm-season switchgrass has produced the most growth and responded the most to fertilizer N at the highest day/ night temperature used (32/26 C), while this occurred at lower temperatures (15/10 and 21/15 C) for cool-season timothy.[15]

15. Balasko, J. A., and Dale Smith. 1971. Influence of temperature and nitrogen fertilization on the growth and composition of switchgrass (*Panicum virgatum* L.) and timothy (*Phleum pratense* L.) at anthesis. *Agron. J.* 63:853–57.

TABLE 40.1 ❧ Relative growth rates of seedling plants of several warm- and cool-season grass species grown in three day/night temperature regimes

Subfamily and species	Temperature regime (C)		
	15/10	27/22	36/31
Festucoideae			
Agropyron trichophorum (Link) Richt.	70	98	61
Bromus inermis Leyss.	75	98	65
Festuca arundinacea Schreb.	76	99	55
Poa pratensis L.	68	98	62
Trisetum spicatum (L.) Richt.	58	100	64
Phalaris arundinacea L.	66	93	61
Stipa hyalina Nees.	51	95	67
Eragrostoideae			
Chloris gayana Kunth.	22	91	100
Panicoideae			
Setaria sphacelata Stapf & C. E. Hubb.	5	88	100
Cenchrus ciliaris (L.)	11	86	100
Paspalum dilatatum Poir.	23	90	100
Panicum coloratum Walt.	35	82	100
Panicum maximum Jacq.	23	89	100
Digitaria argyrografta (Nees) Stapf	32	86	100
Sorghum almum Parodi.	26	77	100

Source: Kawanabe, 1968.[14]

13. Murata, Y., and J. Iyama. 1963. Studies on the photosynthesis of forage crops. II. Influence of air temperature upon the photosynthesis of some forage and grain crops. Proc. Crop Sci. Soc. Japan 31:315–22.
14. Kawanabe, Sukeo. 1968. Temperature responses and systematics of the Gramineae. Proc. Japan Soc. Plant Taxonomists 2:17–20.

Most studies of grasses and legumes show that increasing temperatures hasten maturity, decrease nonstructural carbohydrate percentages and the digestibility of the herbage, and generally increase protein and mineral percentages. Thus temperature change just prior to harvesting can materially alter the feeding value of forage.[16,17]

SOIL MOISTURE

Adequate soil moisture is essential for normal growth.[18-21] The critical factor, however, is the water status within the plant tissues. This is influenced by the availability of soil moisture and the amount of transpiration from the leaf surfaces. A decrease in internal water will affect certain plant processes more than others. Two of the first to be affected by only a moderate deficiency of water are cell division and cell enlargement, which may be retarded or stopped. A deficiency of internal water may retard growth more at one stage of development than at another. With tall-growing grasses such as timothy, big bluestem, or dallisgrass internal water deficiency during the period of rapid stem elongation can markedly reduce expansion and yield. In general, water deficiencies for any length of time bring a reduction in vegetative growth and promote early maturity (Fig. 40.2).[22]

❧ FOOD RESERVES

Perennial and biennial legumes and grasses store energy as readily available

FIG. 40.2. *Water deficiencies . . . reduction in vegetative growth . . . early maturity.* Growth of sideoats grama in sixty-six days when it was watered at intervals (left to right) of 3, 6, 12, and 20 days. The plants were supplied a total of 21.3, 11.2, 6.1, and 4.1 surface cm of water respectively. (From Olmsted, 1941.[22])

carbohydrates in various plant parts.[23,24] The principal storage organ may be the root as in alfalfa, red clover, and kudzu; the stolons as in ladino clover, bahiagrass, and buffalograss; the rhizomes as in smooth bromegrass, reed canarygrass, and western wheatgrass; or the stem bases as in orchardgrass, dallisgrass, and big and little bluestem. The reserve carbohydrates are used to start growth in the spring and after each cutting. They also are used to develop heat and cold resistance, to support life during periods of dormancy, to promote flower and seed formation, and for many processes that go on within the plant during its life. Reserve carbohydrates are essential to the life of perennial and biennial forage species since regeneration is dependent on an adequate supply of stored reserves.

STARCH AND FRUCTOSAN ACCUMULATORS

Starch is the primary nonstructural polysaccharide accumulated in the Leguminoseae. Grasses of tropical and subtropical origin also accumulate starch, but grasses of temperate origin (species in the

16. Smith, Dale. 1970. Influence of cool and warm temperatures and temperature reversal at inflorescence emergence on yield and chemical composition of timothy and bromegrass at anthesis. Proc. 11th Int. Grassl. Congr., pp. 510–14 (Surfers Paradise, Queensland, Aust.).
17. Marten, G. C. 1970. Temperature as a determinant of quality of alfalfa harvested by bloom stage or age criteria. Proc. 11th Int. Grassl. Congr., pp. 506–9 (Surfers Paradise, Queensland, Aust.).
18. Taylor, S. A. 1964. Water condition and flow in the soil-plant-atmosphere system. Amer. Soc. Agron. Spec. Publ. 5, pp. 81–107.
19. Russell, E. W. 1966. The soil environment and gramineous crops. In F. L. Milthorpe and J. D. Ivins (eds.), The Growth of Cereals and Grasses, pp. 138–52. Butterworths, London.
20. Levitt, J. 1964. Drought. In Forage Plant Physiology and Soil-Range Relationships. Amer. Soc. Agron. Spec. Publ. 5, pp. 57–66.
21. Larson, K. L., and J. D. Eastin (eds.). 1971. Drought injury and resistance in crops. Crop Sci. Soc. Amer. Spec. Publ. 2.

22. Olmsted, C. E. 1941. Growth and development in range grasses. I. Early development of Bouteloua curtipendula in relation to water supply. Bot. Gaz. 102:499–519.
23. McIlroy, R. J. 1967. Carbohydrates of grassland herbage. Herb. Abstr. 37:79–87.
24. Williams, R. D. 1964. Translocation in perennial grasses. Outlook Agr. 4:136–42.

Hordeae, Avenae, and Festuceae tribes) accumulate fructosans in their vegetative tissues.[25-28] Furthermore, species in the Hordeae tribe accumulate only short-chain fructosans (about 26 fructose units in smooth bromegrass), species in the Aveneae tribe accumulate a series of fructosans predominated by those of long-chain length (up to 260 fructose units in timothy), while species in the Festuceae tribe represent both types of fructosan accumulators.[26,28] Species in both the Leguminoseae and Gramineae families accumulate starch in their seed.

SEASONAL CYCLES

Maintenance of a high level of food reserves in the storage organs is necessary to keep a plant vigorous and productive. Plants go through periods when carbohydrate foods are used and when they are stored (Figs. 40.3 and 40.4), and a cyclic pattern occurs between early growth and maturity.[29-33] The general pattern of seasonal carbohydrate trends in the principal storage organs of perennial legumes and grasses is essentially similar but is influenced by the morphology and growth behavior of the species and by climatic conditions. The cyclic pattern in alfalfa is shown in Figure 40.4. With the initiation of growth in the spring (or after cutting), carbohydrates stored in the alfalfa roots were used to initiate new top growth. De-

25. Weinmann, H., and L. Rheinhold. 1946. Reserve carbohydrates in South African grasses. *J. S. African Bot.* 12:57–73.
26. Smith, Dale. 1968. Classification of several native North American grasses as starch or fructosan accumulators in relation to taxonomy. *J. Brit. Grassl. Soc.* 23:306–9.
27. Ojima, K., and T. Isawa. 1968. The variation of carbohydrates in various species of grasses and legumes. *Can. J. Bot.* 46:1507–11.
28. Smith, Dale. 1969. Removing and analyzing total nonstructural carbohydrates from plant tissue. *Wis. Agr. Exp. Sta. Res. Rept.* 41.
29. Graber, L. F., N. T. Nelson, W. A. Luekel, and W. B. Albert. 1927. Organic food reserves in relation to the growth of alfalfa and other perennial herbaceous plants. *Wis. Agr. Exp. Sta. Bull.* 80.
30. Grandfield, C. O. 1935. The trend of organic food reserves in alfalfa roots as affected by cutting practices. *J. Agr. Res.* 50:697–709.
31. Weinmann, H. 1961. Total available carbohydrates in grasses and legumes. *Herb. Abstr.* 31:255–61.
32. Smith, Dale. 1962. Carbohydrate root reserves in alfalfa, red clover, and birdsfoot trefoil under several management schedules. *Crop Sci.* 2:75–78.
33. Sonneveld, A. 1962. Distribution and redistribution of dry matter in perennial forage crops. *Neth. J. Agr. Sci.* 10:427–44.

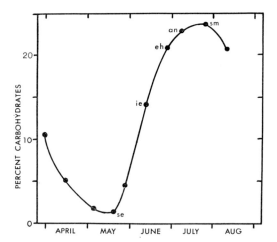

FIG. 40.3. Total nonstructural carbohydrates in the stem bases of timothy at successive stages of development during spring growth at Madison, Wis.: (se) beginning of stem elongation, (ie) inflorescence emergence, (eh) early heading, (an) early anthesis, (sm) seed mature.

pletion continued until about 15–20 cm of top growth were produced. The minimum level of food reserves in other legumes also appears to occur at an early vegetative period (two to three weeks after cutting). It occurs in most temperate grasses at about the beginning of stem elongation (Fig. 40.3). However, few of the

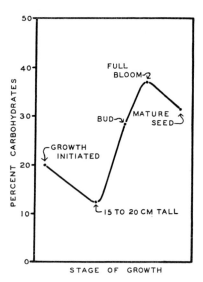

FIG. 40.4. Trend of total nonstructural carbohydrates in roots of alfalfa from the initiation of growth in the spring to the mature seed stage at Madison, Wis. (After Graber et al., 1927.[29])

many legumes and grasses have been studied, and differences no doubt exist among species. For example, it has been found that the minimum carbohydrate level did not occur in mountain brome-grass until after the seed had matured and dropped.[34]

An excess of carbohydrates was produced by photosynthesis in the alfalfa leaves and stems with 15–20 cm of top growth (Fig. 40.4). This excess was translocated to the roots for storage. Storage of carbohydrates in the roots continued as the alfalfa grew. The highest level of storage was reached at near full bloom. There was some removal of carbohydrates from the roots between full bloom and mature seed as new shoots were initiated from the crown. In most forage species the maximum level of food reserves in the storage organs is reached after stem elongation has ceased or at maturity.

The cyclic pattern of use and storage of carbohydrate reserves is influenced by prevailing environmental conditions. The time from start of growth to maturity may proceed rapidly with warm temperatures, limited moisture, and an abundance of sunshine. It may be prolonged with cool temperatures, abundance of moisture, and cloudy weather. For example, a Nevada study found that 'Moapa' alfalfa reached the 10% bloom stage in a hot (33/27 C) temperature regime in half the time (20 days) that it took in a cool (24/4 C) regime (42 days).[35] Other legumes and grasses have shown a similar response. Thus spring weather conditions can make several weeks difference in the time of flowering from one year to the next.[15-17,35]

Seasonal carbohydrate root reserve trends help to explain why birdsfoot trefoil does not survive close cutting as alfalfa and red clover do. Carbohydrate reserves are used to initiate the spring growth but are not restored in the roots of birdsfoot

trefoil at flowering as they are in alfalfa and red clover.[36] They remain at a low level in the roots of birdsfoot trefoil until growth slows down in autumn. Unlike alfalfa or red clover at bloom, a tall stubble needs to be left when birdsfoot trefoil is cut or grazed so that green leaves are available to furnish energy needed for regrowth since little energy is available from the roots. This is another example that the food reserve pattern in one species may not be the same as in another.

RELATION OF CUTTING

Cutting or grazing when food reserves are at a low level may leave very little energy available to start new growth. The greatest damage is done when cutting or grazing occurs during periods of minimum food reserves. Continued cutting at immature stages of growth will eventually exhaust the plant and weaken it to the extent of death. Plants weakened by too early, too heavy, or too frequent cutting usually are more susceptible to drought, heat, winter injury, and invading diseases. Usually, the closer to maturity that cutting or grazing occurs, the higher the stored food reserves will be and the easier it is to maintain vigor and productivity. However, delaying cutting to maturity usually is not compatible with the production of high-protein and low-fiber herbages. Harvesting at somewhat younger growth stages often is necessary to obtain herbage high in feed value, particularly for dairy cattle. It usually is necessary, therefore, to allow the plants to build up their stored food reserves at some period during the growing season. On the other hand, mature grass often is desirable in the western range areas for beef cattle grazing.

PLANT STRUCTURE

Certain forage species are better able to maintain a high level of stored food reserves under frequent and close cutting

34. McCarty, E. C., and Raymond Price. 1938. The relation of growth to the varying carbohydrate content in mountain brome. USDA Tech. Bull. 598.

35. Jensen, E. H., M. A. Massengale, and D. O. Chilcote. 1967. Environmental effects on growth and quality of alfalfa. Nev. Agr. Exp. Sta. Bull. T–9.

36. Smith, Dale. 1966. The unusual growth responses of birdsfoot trefoil. Crops and Soils 18(7): 12.

than others. Tall-growing species with most of the leaf area high on the plant are almost totally dependent on stored foods for recovery, since all or most of the photosynthetic area is removed with close cutting. Short-growing species, the leaf areas of which are near the soil surface, are not totally defoliated with close cutting or grazing. They are not as dependent on stored foods for the initiation of recovery growth. A part of the energy needed to initiate growth comes from the photosynthetic activity of the intact leaves. Various grass species in a Michigan study, rated on the basis of the amount of injury incurred by continuous and close clipping, fell in the following order, beginning with the species least injured: Kentucky bluegrass, quackgrass, and smooth bromegrass, with timothy and orchardgrass about equal.[37] Dallisgrass, a tall bunch-type grass, was injured more in a North Carolina study by close cutting than carpetgrass or bermudagrass, which form sods with most of their leaves near the soil surface.[38]

Forage species dependent on stored food reserves for a long period following the start of spring growth or after cutting, and requiring considerable top growth to replenish their food reserves, usually need careful management to maintain a vigorous condition. Such species cannot be defoliated frequently. This has been found to be the case with kudzu, a vine type of legume grown in the South.[39] This is in contrast to forage species such as Kentucky bluegrass, buffalograss, or bermudagrass that depend on stored food reserves for only a short time following cutting. These forage species begin to replenish food reserves with the initiation of only a few leaves or from basal leaves near the soil surface that were not removed with cutting.

Rate of regrowth and survival of grasses after cutting is influenced greatly by the position of the young shoot apices. The critical stage occurs when internode elongation elevates the shoot apices to a level where they are removed by cutting, and subsequent growth must come from new basal axillary tillers which may or may not be present. In the 1950s this was recognized as a part of the reason why some range grasses survived grazing better than others; little bluestem and sideoats grama resisted heavy grazing better than indiangrass and switchgrass.[40,41] The shoot apices of the former species were not elevated above grazing height until many short basal internodes were mature, while the latter species had only two to four mature basal internodes before the shoot apices were elevated. Grasses having many internodes below or near the soil surface have many sites for the development of new tillers, which in many species are in the form of rhizomes or stolons.[41] Species with a high ratio of flowering shoots to vegetative tillers decreased during grazing in favor of those with many tillers.[40] The critical period when shoot apices are at mowing height differs among grass species, and mowing a mixture of grasses will damage some species more than others.[42,43] This is one of the basic reasons why timothy and smooth bromegrass often fail to persist in an alfalfa association in the Great Lakes states when the spring crop is harvested at the early flower stage of the alfalfa.[44,45]

Decreased production is obtained when timothy and smooth bromegrass are cut

37. Harrison, C. M., and C. W. Hodgson. 1939. Response of certain perennial grasses to cutting treatments. *J. Amer. Soc. Agron.* 31:418–30.
38. Lovvorn, R. L. 1945. The effect of defoliation, soil fertility, temperature, and length of day on the growth of some perennial grasses. *J. Amer. Soc. Agron.* 37:570–82.
39. Pierre, W. H., and F. E. Bertram. 1929. Kudzu production with special reference to influence of frequency of cutting on yields and formation of root reserves. *J. Amer. Soc. Agron.* 21:1079–1101.

40. Branson, F. A. 1953. Two new factors affecting resistance of grasses to grazing. *J. Range Manage.* 6:165–71.
41. Rechenthin, C. A. 1956. Elementary morphology of grass growth and how it affects utilization. *J. Range Manage.* 9:167–70.
42. Scott, J. D. 1956. The study of primordial buds and the reaction of roots to defoliation as the basis of grassland management. Proc. 7th Int. Grassl. Congr., pp. 479–87 (Palmerston North, N. Z.).
43. Booysen, P. De V., N. M. Tainton, and J. D. Scott. 1963. Shoot-apex development in grasses and its importance in grassland management. *Herb. Abstr.* 33:209–13.
44. Rhykerd, C. L., C. H. Noller, J. E. Dillon, J. B. Ragland, B. W. Crowl, G. C. Naderman, and D. L. Hill. 1967. Managing alfalfa-grass mixtures for yield and protein. Purdue Univ. Agr. Exp. Sta. Res. Bull. 839.
45. Smith, Dale, and D. A. Rohweder. 1977. Establishing and managing alfalfa. Wis. Agr. Exp. Sta. Bull. R1741.

during the period from the beginning of internode elongation to inflorescence emergence.[46-48] During this period of growth shoot apices are above cutting height and carbohydrate reserves are at a low level (Fig. 40.3). There are no basal axillary tillers present for regrowth since they are not formed until about the anthesis stage, especially with timothy. Basal tiller development is apparently under control of the apical dominance of the growing shoot until anthesis. Thus regrowth may be delayed two or more weeks, and many cut shoots may die when timothy and smooth bromegrass are harvested during the early stages of stem elongation. Cutting or grazing before the initiation of stem elongation removes only leaf blades, and the intact shoot can elongate to produce a crop. After anthesis, recovery is satisfactory because basal axillary tillers are present to produce the regrowth.

Orchardgrass, in contrast, recovers rapidly when cut at almost any growth stage, even when cut at the early stages of stem elongation. The flowering shoots appear to exert less apical dominance than in timothy or smooth bromegrass. New basal tillers are produced throughout the spring period so that shoots in different stages of development are present at any given time. When orchardgrass is harvested, the cut leaves on the stubble continue to elongate, and new leaves develop rapidly on the axillary tillers so that photosynthesis is only temporarily interrupted.

Care in the management of timothy and smooth bromegrass also is needed in the second crop to maintain stands and yields. Climatic conditions during midsummer are often unfavorable to the growth of cool-season grasses, especially the high temperatures which may be accompanied by low soil moisture levels, and new basal axillary tillers may be slow to develop.[16,48] The best recovery growth occurs when the grasses are cut after new axillary tillers have formed at the base of the second-growth shoots.[46,47]

AUTUMN PERIOD CRITICAL TO OVERWINTERING SPECIES

The period prior to the first killing frost is usually a critical time in the management of forage species, particularly legumes. This is when plants need their top growth to produce carbohydrates through photosynthesis and to store a high level of foods before winter dormancy. Stored foods are needed as energy for the development of cold resistance, for maintenance during the winter dormant period, and for initiation of growth the following spring. The colder and longer the winter, the more imperative it becomes that plants enter it with a high level of food reserves. This can be ensured best by not cutting during the fall (Table 40.2).[49] In the northern areas it is now generally recommended that overwintering legumes should not be cut or grazed during autumn, beginning six to seven weeks before the first killing frost (Fig. 40.5).[45,50-53] Cutting or grazing late in the fall after frost has killed the top growth is less hazardous. However, it removes the winter cover that helps catch snow and hold it for added protection.

COLD AND HEAT TOLERANCE

Forage species differ widely in their ability to withstand cold and heat. Cold

46. Teel, M. R. 1956. The physiological age of bromegrass as it affects recovery rate following defoliation. Ph.D. thesis, Purdue Univ. (Diss. Abstr. 16:844).

47. Sheard, R. W., and J. E. Winch. 1966. The use of light interception, gross morphology and time as criteria for the harvesting of timothy, smooth bromegrass and cocksfoot. J. Brit. Grassl. Soc. 21:231-37.

48. Knievel, D. P., A. V. A. Jacques, and Dale Smith. 1971. Influence of growth stage and stubble height on herbage yields and persistence of smooth bromegrass and timothy. Agron. J. 63:430-34.

49. Fulkerson, R. S. 1970. Location and fall harvest effects in Ontario on food reserve storage in alfalfa (Medicago sativa L.). Proc. 11th Int. Grassl. Congr., pp. 555-59 (Surfers Paradise, Queensland, Aust.).

50. Torrie, J. H., and E. W. Hanson. 1955. Effects of cutting first-year red clover on stand and yield in the second year. Agron. J. 47:224-28.

51. Folkins, L. P., J. E. R. Greenshields, and F. S. Nowosad. 1961. Effect of date and frequency of defoliation on yield and quality of alfalfa. Can. J. Plant Sci. 41:188-94.

52. Jung, G. A., R. L. Reid, and J. A. Balasko. 1969. Studies on yield, management, persistence, and nutritive value of alfalfa in West Virginia. W. Va. Agr. Exp. Sta. Bull. 581T.

53. Smith, Dale, and L. F. Graber. 1948. The influence of top growth removal on the root and vegetative development of biennial sweetclover. J. Amer. Soc. Agron. 40:818-31.

TABLE 40.2 ❧ Plant population, height, and dry matter yield of alfalfa in year following application of postharvest fall cuttings in Ontario, Canada

Fall cutting date*	Plants/0.09 sq m at location:†			Plant height in mid-May at location: (cm)			Hay yield‡ at location: (kg/ha)		
	1	2	3	1	2	3	1	2	3
Uncut	18	27	19	13	13	10	7,329	4,949	6,814
Sept. 3	16	24	20	9	12	6	6,919	4,914	5,764
10	13	19	17	9	11	5	6,584	4,317	5,406
17	15	7	11	9	6	6	6,974	2,533	5,323
24	16	12	14	10	7	7	7,084	2,860	5,677
Oct. 1	20	15	19	10	8	8	6,946	3,523	6,516
LSD, 0.05	4	5	5	1	1	1	§	426	498

Source: Fulkerson, 1970[49]
* Five and 10 days later at location 2 and 3 respectively.
† Locations 1, 2, and 3 were in northern, central, and southern Ontario respectively.
‡ Total yield from two harvests during season after fall cutting.
§ Not significant.

tests have shown biennial sweetclover to be more cold-hardy than 'Ranger' alfalfa and Ranger to be more cold-hardy than northern common red clover.[54-56] Com-

54. Bula, R. J., and Dale Smith. 1954. Cold resistance and chemical composition in overwintering alfalfa, red clover, and sweetclover. *Agron. J.* 46:397–401.
55. Ruelke, O. C., and Dale Smith. 1956. Overwintering trends of cold resistance and carbohydrates in medium red, ladino, and common white clover. *Plant Physiol.* 31:364–68.
56. Jung, G. A., and Dale Smith. 1961. Trends of cold resistance and chemical changes over winter in the roots and crowns of alfalfa and medium red clover. I. Changes in certain nitrogen and carbohydrate fractions. II. Changes in certain mineral constituents. *Agron. J.* 53:359–66.

FIG. 40.5. *High level of food reserves . . . ensured by not cutting during autumn.* Growth of biennial sweetclover in June of the second year at Madison, Wis., showing the effects of cuttings made the previous fall (left to right) on August 16, September 2, September 18, October 18, and not cut. (From Smith and Graber, 1948.[53])

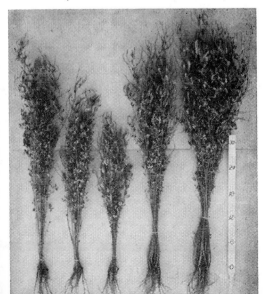

mon white clover was more cold-hardy than ladino clover. Crested wheatgrass seedlings have been found to be more cold-hardy than western wheatgrass and western wheatgrass more than smooth bromegrass.[57]

Buffalograss and bermudagrass were found to be more heat resistant than western and slender wheatgrass.[58] Smooth bromegrass and Kentucky bluegrass had low resistance compared to the other species.

Ability of a forage species to withstand exposure to freezing or to high temperatures is dependent upon ability to make certain metabolic changes.[59-61] Thus some forage species are cold or heat tolerant, while others are not. Many of the metabolic changes occurring during the development of cold or heat resistance are similar. There usually is a decrease in the total water and free water content and an increase in the bound water content of the tissues. Also, there is usually an in-

57. Rogler, G. A. 1943. Response of geographical strains of grasses to low temperatures. *J. Amer. Soc. Agron.* 35:547–59.
58. Julander, Odell. 1945. Drought resistance in range and pasture grasses. *Plant Physiol.* 20:573–99.
59. Smith, Dale. 1964. Winter injury and the survival of forage plants. *Herb. Abstr.* 34:203–9.
60. Smith, Dale. 1968. Varietal chemical differences associated with freezing resistance in forage plants. *Cryobiology* 5:148–59.
61. Laude, H. M. 1964. Plant response to high temperatures. *Amer. Soc. Agron. Spec. Publ. 5,* pp. 15–30.

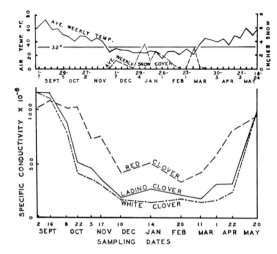

FIG. 40.6. *Development of cold resistance . . . follows a cyclic pattern.* The trend of cold resistance in red clover roots and crowns and in ladino and common white clover stolons at Madison, Wis., as measured by electrical conductance. (After Ruelke and Smith, 1956.[55])

crease in the water-holding colloids, an increase in sugar content, a conversion of starch to sugars, and a slowing down of metabolic activity.

DEVELOPMENT AND MAINTENANCE OF COLDHARDINESS

The development of cold resistance during autumn and its loss during spring roughly follows a cyclic pattern. Studies with several overwintering legumes at Madison, Wis., have shown that plants began to develop cold resistance in early to mid-September, as measured by electrical conductance (Fig. 40.6).[54-56] The development of resistance continued through fall until late November or early December. Prevailing temperatures and a snow cover conditioned the maximum level attained. A near maximum was developed shortly after permanent freezing of the soil surface and after the weekly air temperatures remained below freezing. A high level of cold resistance was maintained from early December to mid-February when substantial snow cover provided protection from low air temperatures. Resistance in some of the legume species began to decrease

in mid-February with the onset of warmer temperatures and reduced snow cover. Resistance began to drop rapidly after the snow had disappeared and the soil surface thawed in late March.

Winter-killing in the northern areas usually occurs in the late winter and early spring when the snow cover has disappeared and the plants are exposed to severe temperature fluctuations above and below freezing. By this time, the plants have lost some cold resistance in response to warmer temperatures. They may be so low in carbohydrate reserves that they are unable to reharden satisfactorily on exposure to a drop in temperature, or the temperature drop is so rapid that they do not have time to reharden.

Overwintering forage species develop cold resistance with the onset of the shorter days and colder temperatures of autumn, within their inherent capacity to do so. The necessity for a plant to develop cold resistance to survive the winter is not limited to the northern areas. Forages of tropical origin are sometimes injured or killed in the southern states by short periods of subfreezing temperatures.[62]

Cold-hardening of alfalfa under artificial conditions was favored by: (1) short daylengths of around seven to eight hours, (2) generally lowering temperatures, (3) an alternation of temperatures between warm (20 C) during the day and cold (0–5 C) at night, and (4) adequate light intensity for good photosynthetic activity.[63] Alfalfa cold-hardened poorly in a warm temperature regime (24/16 C) regardless of daylength.[64] In a cold regime (7/2 C) hardening was better with a short daylength (8 hours) than with a long one (16 hours). Temperature appeared to be of primary importance to coldhardiness, but metabolic processes were influenced by both temperature and photoperiod.

62. Adams, W. E., and Marvin Twersky. 1960. Effect of soil fertility on winter-killing of Coastal bermudagrass. *Agron. J.* 52:325–326.
63. Tysdal, H. M. 1933. Influence of light, temperature, and soil moisture on the hardening process in alfalfa. *J. Agr. Res.* 46:483–515.
64. Shih, S. C., G. A. Jung, and D. C. Shelton. 1967. Effects of temperature and photoperiod on metabolic changes in alfalfa in relation to coldhardiness. *Crop Sci.* 7:385–89.

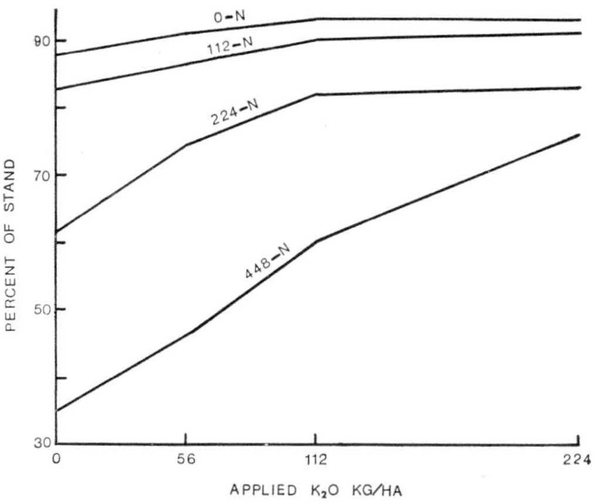

FIG. 40.7. Winter survival of 'Coastal' bermudagrass decreased with increasing levels of applied N at any given level of K, but at high levels of N winter survival increased with increasing levels of applied K. (Adapted from Adams and Twersky, 1960.[62])

Conditions resulting in the initiation of growth during hardening can hinder the development of cold resistance. Resistance may be reduced or development retarded by removal of the top growth (especially with legumes),[45,49-53] the occurrence of warm and rainy weather, and fertilization of grasses with N during the hardening period (Fig. 40.7).[62]

SOIL FERTILITY AND COLDHARDINESS

Soil fertility is as important to the overwintering of plants as it is to their growth during summer. Two nutrients of considerable importance are K and N.[62,65] The role of K is not clear, but a high level of K in the soil solution is essential to the development of maximum coldhardiness. In contrast to K, high levels of N in the soil impede the development of hardiness, particularly in grasses, by forcing the plants to grow when they should be dormant. Coldhardiness in grasses appears to be favored by a high K:N ratio.[62]

MANAGEMENT OF WEAKENED STANDS

Stands that have been weakened or injured following a severe winter, drought, or frequent cutting or grazing usually need careful management to bring them back to a level of high productivity. Plants may appear weak and yellowish, with only a few stems per plant. Weakened stands are sometimes plowed up too hastily. Many will recover with proper cutting management. Delaying the cutting to near full bloom or maturity may allow the plants to heal injured tissue and place a high level of food reserves in the storage organs. The hay harvested may be light and weedy, but with delayed cutting the subsequent crop is often back to normal productivity. Cutting weakened and injured stands at immature stages of growth may kill the plants or keep them in a weakened condition (Fig. 40.8).

65. Jung, G. A., and Dale Smith. 1959. Influence of soil potassium and phosphorus content on the cold resistance of alfalfa. *Agron. J.* 51:585–87.

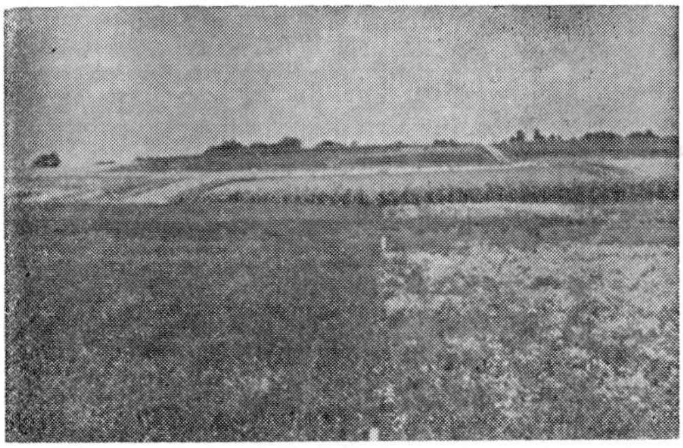

FIG. 40.8. *Stands . . . weakened following a severe winter or frequent cutting . . . need careful management.* Winter-injured alfalfa at Madison, Wis., with the first crop cut at an immature stage (right) was invaded by weeds, in marked contrast to the freedom from weeds (left) where the first crop was not cut until past full bloom.

✤ QUESTIONS

1. What are the most important environmental factors influencing vegetative development and maturation of grasses and legumes?
2. What is the effect of increasing temperatures on maturity? On concentrations of nonstructural carbohydrates, protein, and minerals? On the digestibility of grass and legume herbage?
3. What are some of the biochemical differences between temperate and tropical grasses?

4. Why is a knowledge of the periods of minimum and maximum carbohydrate reserves important to the management of perennial or biennial species?
5. What is the principal vegetative storage organ for readily available (reserve) carbohydrates in alfalfa? In ladino clover? In smooth bromegrass? In orchardgrass?
6. How do alfalfa and birdsfoot trefoil differ in their "cyclic pattern" of use and storage of carbohydrate root reserves? How does this affect their management when cut or grazed?
7. At what stage of growth are grasses vulnerable to cutting damage? Why?
8. What are some of the internal changes that occur during the period that a plant is developing cold or heat resistance?
9. What climatic and soil conditions favor the development of cold resistance?

SUPPLEMENTAL INFORMATION

❧ TRANSLOCATION OF CARBOHYDRATES

This can be considered a transfer from "source" to "sink" down a concentration gradient.[24] Source may be an assimilating organ (green leaf) and sink a metabolizing one (tip of a root or stem, or expanding leaf) or a storage organ (alfalfa root). Later, when stored carbohydrate is used as a substrate for new growth, the former sink becomes a source and new growth a sink to which it exports (as regrowth after cutting).

Expanding young leaves use the carbohydrate they produce; they also import some carbohydrate from older leaves that are exporting, continuing to do so until they are sufficiently expanded to export in turn. First exports of a new expanding leaf usually move upward to the growing point and to younger leaves above it. As the leaf ages, some of its export moves downward; with time, a greater proportion moves downward until finally it all does.

All young expanding leaves have a good chance of receiving carbohydrate from an older leaf, when there are lower leaves. However, distribution of export from an older leaf is restricted by the vascular system, and not every expanding leaf has the same chance of receiving carbohydrate from a lower leaf. Leaves on the stem of many dicotyledonous plants are in a spiral. Many tobacco varieties have the spiral arranged in a phyllotaxy of 3/8.[24] That is, if the spiral is followed upward from leaf to leaf, three complete circuits of stem must be made before arriving at the leaf immediately above the starting one. If a starting leaf is termed leaf 0, the leaf directly above it on the same vascular strand is leaf 8. Thus leaf 8 receives most of its carbohydrate from leaf 0, while the leaf at greatest angular distance from leaf 0 would receive little, if any.

Leaves of grasses have a phyllotaxy of 1/2: two vertical rows, one on each side of the stem. However, vascular strands are scattered throughout the stem, as for monocots generally, rather than being in a discrete ring as in dicots.[24] Since in addition the base of a grass leaf completely surrounds the stem, leaf traces do not connect only with strands on one side of the stem, so that the pattern of assimilate distribution to younger leaves found in dicots does not occur. Sucrose is the normal translocation sugar.

SUPPLEMENTAL LITERATURE CITATIONS

Butler, G. W., and R. W. Bailey (eds.). 1973. Chemistry and Biochemistry of Herbage, vols. 1, 2, 3. Academic Press, London and New York.
Smith, Dale. 1974. Growth and development of timothy tillers as influenced by level of carbohydrate reserves and leaf area. Ann. Bot. 38:595–606.
Sosebee, R. E. (ed.). 1977. Rangeland Plant Physiology. Range Sci. Ser. 4, Soc. Range Manage., Denver, Colo.

CECIL S. BROWN / *University of Maine*

JOHN E. BAYLOR / *The Pennsylvania State University*

41

HAY AND PASTURE SEEDINGS FOR THE NORTHEAST

❧

T HE NORTHEASTERN region extends from New York and New England in the north to West Virginia and Maryland in the south (Fig. 41.1). Most of its people live in concentrated centers of population which serve as ready markets for fluid milk and other livestock products.

Ruminant livestock is the primary source of agricultural income. In some states dairy products alone represent over 50% of the total cash receipts from agriculture.[1] Cattle and sheep number in excess of 6 million head (Table 41.1), with dairy cattle predominating in virtually every state.[2] Beef and sheep are concentrated primarily in the southern part of the region.

Significant changes in livestock numbers have occurred during the past decade. Sheep have declined sharply, while beef

❧ CECIL S. BROWN is Professor of Agronomy, University of Maine. He received the M.S. and Ph.D. degrees from Cornell University. He has carried out research, extension, and teaching responsibilities with perennial forages for over twenty years.

❧ JOHN E. BAYLOR is Professor of Agronomy at Pennsylvania State University. He received the M.S. degree from Rutgers University and the Ph.D. from Pennsylvania State University. His extension work has been in forage production and he has served as a consultant abroad.

cattle have increased. Dairy cattle have decreased in number, but milk production per cow has risen steadily. Total milk production has remained relatively constant in the major dairy states.[3]

❧ CLIMATE AND SOIL

The northeastern region stretches from approximately 47° N in the north to 38° N in the south. The climatic effects of latitude are modified significantly in states bordering the Atlantic Ocean. High elevations occur in several states, with marked effects on temperature and precipitation.

The frost-free season ranges from about 100 days in the northern uplands to 200 days in southern coastal areas.[4] Standard heat units (base 10 C [50 F]) from early March through late September range from about 880 in the cooler areas to 1944 in the warmer zones.[5] Most states exhibit a relatively wide temperature range.

1. New York Crop Rep. Serv. 1971. N.Y. agricultural statistics, 1970.
2. USDA. 1969–71. Livestock and poultry inventory. Stat. Rep. Serv.
3. Cornell Agr. Econ. Ext. Serv. 1970. N.Y. Econ. Handbook 571.
4. Havens, A. V., and J. K. McGuire. 1961. Spring and fall low-temperature probabilities. N.J. Agr. Exp. Sta. Bull. 801.
5. Dethier, B. E., and M. T. Vittum. 1963. Growing degree days. N.Y. (Geneva) Agr. Exp. Sta. Bull. 801.

FIG. 41.1. The northeastern area of the U.S.

Winter temperatures significantly affect the choice of perennial forages. Only the most winter-hardy cultivars of northern species may be safely used in the extreme north. In contrast, improved cultivars of bermudagrass are maintained in the mild winter climate of the southern coast.

Continuity of snow cover is a major variable influencing winter injury. Midwinter thaws along the northern and central coast increase the risk of legume winter-kill. Protective cover is virtually assured in the northern uplands, which in an average winter receive from 2540 to 3810 mm of snow.

PRECIPITATION

The Northeast has a humid climate, with precipitation rather evenly distributed throughout the year. The average annual precipitation ranges from 787 mm in extreme northwestern New York to more

than 1320 mm at some of the higher elevations in West Virginia, New York, Vermont, and New Hampshire. The entire Atlantic seaboard area receives more than 1118 mm/year, as do central West Virginia and northwestern Pennsylvania.[6] Much of the region receives its heaviest rainfall during the spring or early summer, with a secondary maximum usually in late fall.

Moisture conditions throughout the region are generally favorable for forage production. However, short periods of drought occur during midsummer or late summer. Prolonged drought is least likely in New England and the higher elevations of the southern Appalachians. It is commoner in the Hudson River Valley, the Delmarva peninsula, eastern Maryland, northern West Virginia, and extreme southwestern Pennsylvania.[7]

SOIL DRAINAGE

The Northeast exhibits a complex pattern of soil drainage. In some areas gravelly soils seriously limit forage production from drought-sensitive species such as timothy,

6. Dethier, B. E. 1965. The climate of the Northeast: Precipitation probabilities. Cornell Agr. Exp. Sta. Bull. 1005.
7. Dickerson, W. H., and B. E. Dethier. 1970. Drought frequency in the northeastern United States. W. Va. Agr. Exp. Sta. Bull. 595.

TABLE 41.1 ❧ Cattle and sheep on farms of the Northeast, 1970

State	Milk cows* Number (000)	Milk cows* Increase over 1961 (%)	Beef cows* Number (000)	Beef cows* Increase over 1961 (%)	All cattle Number (000)	All cattle Increase over 1961 (%)	Sheep and lambs Number (000)	Sheep and lambs Increase over 1961 (%)
Maine	67	−37	9	0	145	−28	16	−56
New Hampshire	37	−37	2	0	73	−27	5	−38
Vermont	205	−29	6	100	351	−19	6	−45
Massachusetts	64	−38	4	33	116	−26	9	−25
Connecticut	66	−31	4	33	121	−19	5	−29
Rhode Island	8	−47	1	...	13	−35	2	0
New York	1,030	−26	60	50	1,867	−13	100	−35
New Jersey	74	−47	8	100	132	−33	8	−50
Pennsylvania	720	−27	97	3	1,781	− 9	165	−30
West Virginia	62	−56	200	26	475	−11	163	−41
Delaware	15	−48	5	25	32	−40	2	−50
Maryland	167	−28	56	12	426	−15	20	−43
Total	2,515	−30	452	+22	5,532	−14	501	−37

Source: USDA, 1969–71.[a]
* Cows and heifers 2 years and older.

ladino clover, and alsike clover. In others the soils are too poorly drained for successful alfalfa production. These extremes may be found within most any farming community and often within the boundaries of a single farm.

Poorly drained soils are widespread throughout the region.[8,9] Impervious subsoil pans are common in the glaciated soils of northern and central zones. Flat topography and clay subsoils combine to create a serious drainage problem in many alluvial soils.

Drainage improvement practices have been widely adopted. Open-ditch drains have been constructed on many dairy farms, interest in land levelling has increased for the alluvial soils, and subsurface drainage has increased with the availability of improved methods of installation. These practices have contributed to an increasing popularity of alfalfa.

Extensive areas of deep, well-drained soils are also found. These are intensively utilized for corn, alfalfa, and small grains. A concentration of these soils is located in the northern Piedmont area of Maryland and in southeastern Pennsylvania.[8]

SOIL ACIDITY AND FERTILITY

Most unlimed soils of the region are strongly acid. Typical soils have test values of pH 5 or below in the surface horizon.[10] Some areas, however, are favored by natural high-lime soils such as in the agriculturally famous Lancaster County in Pennsylvania.

Soil acidity is a critical factor in the selection of legume species. Alfalfa is preferred for well-drained soils testing pH 6.5 or above. Red clover commonly replaces alfalfa in seedings designed for moderately acid soils. Alsike clover may dominate on strongly acid soils. Continued use of ag-

ricultural limestone has resulted in an increasing number of farm fields suitable for alfalfa production.

Northeastern soils are relatively infertile in their native state. High rates of fertilizer P are recommended for legume establishment. Legume persistence and productivity are closely tied to annual topdressings of fertilizer K. Coarse-textured soils low in K reserves are especially responsive. Nitrogen deficiency is the chief factor limiting the yields of forage grasses.

❧ FEED UTILIZATION BY LIVESTOCK

Pasture and harvested forages are primary sources of feed for cattle and sheep of the region. Dairy cows obtain approximately 20% of their feed energy from pasture, 45% from harvested forages, and 35% from concentrate feeds.[11] Sheep and nonfattening beef cattle obtain most of their feed energy from forages.

The Northeast obtains most of its feed grains from the Midwest. New York, for example, has imported annually over two-thirds of its total concentrate feeds for livestock since the 1930s.[12] No substantial change is predicted through the 1970s.

Feed grain production is of greater significance in the southern part of the region. A longer growing season favors more competitive production of grain corn. Mild winter temperatures permit more consistent yields from barley and other fall-sown small grains.

CORN SILAGE

The production of silage corn has increased rapidly through the 1960s (Table 41.2).[13] Harvested hectarage has risen steadily in almost every state, while yields have increased in response to improved management. The net effect has been a sharp increase in the level of corn silage fed per cow.

8. Brady, N. C. R. A. Struchtemeyer, and R. B. Musgrave. 1957. The Northeast. *In* Soil, pp. 598–619. USDA, Yearbook Agr.

9. Austin, M. E. 1965. Land resource regions and major land resource areas of the United States. USDA Agr. Handbook 296.

10. Prince, A. B., and W. A. Raney. 1961. Some morphological, physical and chemical properties of selected northeastern United States soils. N.H. Agr. Exp. Sta. Misc. Publ. 1.

11. USDC. 1964. U.S. census of agriculture.

12. Casler, G. L. 1970. Toward the year 1985: Field crops. Cornell Spec. Ser. 2.

13. USDA. 1970. Crop production annual summary. Stat. Rep. Serv.

TABLE 41.2 ❧ Silage corn and hay crop production in the Northeast, 1970

State	Corn silage		Hay, all classes	
	1000 ha	1000 t	1000 ha	1000 t
Maine	8	241	117	370
New Hampshire	6	232	50	185
Vermont	32	991	205	820
Massachusetts	13	435	51	217
Connecticut	19	675	41	184
Rhode Island	2	59	5	23
New York	220	6,897	1,074	5,260
New Jersey	13	419	55	300
Pennsylvania	132	4,584	818	3,988
West Virginia	13	421	241	792
Delaware	3	94	14	69
Maryland	30	1,021	133	667
Total	491	16,069	2,804	12,875
Increase over 1960 (%)	+29	+79	−15	−5

Source: USDA, 1970.[12]

Early maturing cultivars have extended the production of silage corn into extreme northern areas. It is predicted that silage corn tonnage will continue to increase during the 1970s in major dairy areas.[12] Increasingly higher yields may permit a gradual levelling off in hectarage during this same period.

HAY AND PASTURE

Nearly half the region's farmland is occupied by hay and pasture crops. Much of this land is poorly suited for intensive cultivation, although part of it is sufficiently tillable for occasional reseeding with improved hayland mixtures. The remainder is utilized as permanent pasture for nonlactating dairy animals, beef cattle, and sheep.

Hayland hectarage has declined substantially during the 1960s (Table 41.2).[13] Dairy production has become concentrated on fewer but larger farms, while marginal farms have gone out of production. Hay yields, however, have generally increased. In states with large numbers of cattle, total hay tonnage has shown little decrease in spite of declining hectarage.

Several types of pasture are important

14. USDC. 1971. 1969 U.S. census of agriculture.

throughout the region (Table 41.3).[14] Cropland pasture is produced commonly in rotation with corn. It may include legume-grass mixtures or annual forage species and is utilized directly by grazing or as green chop.

Nearly half the total pasture hectarage is classified as permanent pasture. About 40% of this land has been improved by liming and fertilization, some of this in conjunction with renovated seedings. (See Fig. 41.2.) This improved pasture is commonly Kentucky bluegrass with varying amounts of wild white clover and other legumes. Unimproved permanent pastures support inferior grasses such as poverty-grass, bentgrasses, and broomsedge along with perennial weeds and brush.

❧ LEGUME SPECIES AND CULTIVARS

The variable nature of northeastern soils requires careful choice of legume species and cultivars. Drainage, acidity, and fertility are major considerations in matching seedings with soil types.

Legume selection is affected also by intended crop use. Alfalfa is commonly utilized in a multiple-harvest system as hay, silage, or green chop. Red clover is useful in short rotations on soils inadequately

FIG. 41.2. *Permanent pasture improved by liming and fertilization . . . with renovated seedings. Beef cows grazing on birdsfoot trefoil–grass. Pa. State Univ. photo.*

limed for alfalfa. Ladino clover is used for rotational pasture, while birdsfoot trefoil is well suited for a delayed hay harvest followed by repeated grazing.

HECTARAGE ESTIMATES

Land use data for forage crops have been compiled by the USDA in repeated surveys

during the 1960s. Extension agronomists in each state were asked to report their estimates of major species and cultivars. The estimates for perennial forages were understandably less precise than for the annuals.

Legume hectarages for the northeastern states, other than West Virginia, are given in Table 41.4.[15,16] In the mid-1960s there were over 900,000 ha of grassland in which alfalfa constituted a major part of the mixture. Red clover was grown on more than 700,000 ha, while considerably smaller hectarages of birdsfoot trefoil and ladino clover were grown. In many cases two or more of these legumes were grown in mixture, even though reported separately.

The data indicate that alfalfa is more important than red clover in major dairy states of the North, while the reverse appears to be true in the South. This subregional difference may have several explanations. Traditionally, red clover has been widely used in the short rotations of southern areas which often include a small-grain companion crop. Its dependable establishment over a wide range of soil conditions is well known. Injury from the

15. Jernigan, J. E. 1965. Trends in forage crop varieties. USDA Fed. Ext. Serv.
16. Paulling, J. R. 1967. Trends in forage crop varieties. USDA Fed. Ext. Serv.

TABLE 41.3 ❧ Pasture production in the Northeast, 1969

State	Cropland pasture* 1000 ha	Increase over 1964 (%)	Improved permanent pasture* 1000 ha	Increase over 1964 (%)	Unimproved permanent pasture* 1000 ha	Increase over 1964 (%)
Maine	35	—17	6	20	10	—52
New Hampshire	. . .	. . .	. . .	. . .	. . .	. . .
Vermont	100	52	26	30	43	—67
Massachusetts	23	—12	6	50	9	—53
Connecticut	21	250	7	17	9	—64
Rhode Island	3	0	1	0	1	—50
New York	492	43	115	37	279	—61
New Jersey	31	3	10	67	9	—59
Pennsylvania	337	76	108	10	121	—66
West Virginia	173	239	120	50	102	—51
Delaware	9	—18	2	100	2	—33
Maryland	94	27	32	—29	23	—63
Total	1,318	+56	433	+24	608	—61

Source: USDC, 1971.[14]

* For farm economic classes 1–5 (farm products exceed $2500).

TABLE 41.4 ❧ Estimated usage of major perennial forages in the Northeast

| State | Legumes (1000 ha) | | | | Grasses (1000 ha) | | |
	Alfalfa	Red clover	Birdsfoot trefoil	Ladino clover	Timothy	Smooth brome-grass	Orchard-grass
Maine	8	15	1	6	55	3	2
New Hampshire	5	5	1	3	67	2	2
Vermont	48	6	23	14	91	18	2
Massachusetts	12	2	tr.	5	45	2	3
Connecticut	15	4	2	2	26	2	4
Rhode Island	2	2	tr.	2	3	tr.	tr.
New York	469	243	288	32	1,035	91	20
New Jersey	34	14	2	16	26	17	32
Pennsylvania	273	326	49	29	567	24	63
Delaware	2	10	1	14	8	tr.	8
Maryland	34	94	tr.	76	113	2	58
Total	902	721	367	199	2,036	161	194

Sources: Jernigan, 1965;[15] Paulling, 1967.[16]
Note: Average of 1965 and 1967 estimates.

alfalfa weevil has been more prolonged and more severe in the southern half of the region. Maryland experienced a 38% reduction in alfalfa hectarage between 1958 and 1967, attributed largely to the increasing severity of weevil damage during that period.[17] Alfalfa, however, is generally more persistent in northern areas because of its superior winterhardiness and tolerance of root rot diseases.

Birdsfoot trefoil is a major species in three states of the region—New York, Pennsylvania, and Vermont. It is used primarily in hayland mixtures on soils of marginal drainage. It is also important, particularly in southern areas, in permanent pastures for beef cattle and young dairy stock. Ladino clover is used for rotational pasture throughout the Northeast. Its use on dairy farms is declining with increasing adoption of year-round stored feeding.

Land use estimates are not available for wild white clover. This prostrate legume is found throughout the region in permanent pastures which have been adequately topdressed with lime and fertilizer. Productivity of at least 40,000 ha of Kentucky bluegrass pasture is increased substantially through N supplied by this legume.

Hectarage data for alsike clover are similarly lacking. For many years, this legume has been a common component of seed mixtures for hay on poorly drained soils. Its use and importance in the Northeast is declining, replaced in part by birdsfoot trefoil.

Crownvetch appears promising as a pasture legume in the Northeast. To 1973, its use for livestock had been confined largely to Pennsylvania and West Virginia. Crownvetch is popular, however, throughout the Northeast as vegetative cover for roadside slopes.

SEED USAGE

Trends in forage crop usage are measured more accurately by seed sales. Data for commercial seed shipments have been compiled annually by Cornell University to monitor changes in species and cultivar usage throughout the Northeast.

Changes in legume seed use are summarized in Table 41.5.[18] Total seed sales have declined coincident with the decrease in hayland. Major shifts in the relative use of legume species have occurred. Red clover has declined to less than 20% of the total legume seed in northern areas and to about 35% in southern areas. Alsike and

17. Barnes, D. K., C. H. Hanson, R. H. Ratcliffe, T. H. Busbice, J. A. Schillinger, G. R. Buss, W. V. Campbell, R. W. Hemken, and C. C. Blickenstaff. 1970. The development and performance of Team alfalfa: A multiple pest resistant alfalfa with moderate resistance to the alfalfa weevil, USDA, ARS 34–115.

18. Pardee, W. D., and L. S. Beckham. 1971. Northeast seed use survey of small-seeded grasses and legumes. Cornell Univ. Dept. Plant Breeding, PB 71–8.

FIG. 41.3. *Alfalfa . . . 50–70% of all the legume seed . . . a dramatic shift to clear seedings of alfalfa without a companion crop.* A productive alfalfa field harvested as high-quality hay. *New Holland Div., Sperry Rand Corp., photo.*

TABLE 41.5 ❧ Seed shipments of major forage legumes in the Northeast

State	Species	Average 1960–64	Average 1965–68	1969	1970	1971
		Regional totals (1000 kg)				
	Alfalfa	2,921	2,160	1,329	1,757	2,099
	Red clover	1,489	1,406	1,122	966	743
	Birdsfoot trefoil	404	276	289	284	225
	Alsike clover	350	263	226	197	168
	Ladino clover	107	76	44	42	37
	Total	5,271	4,181	3,010	3,246	3,272
		Relative usage in selected states (%)				
Vermont	alfalfa	50	57	46	55	64
	red clover	23	22	24	21	16
	birdsfoot trefoil	7	4	7	5	5
	alsike clover	15	13	18	16	12
	ladino clover	5	4	5	3	3
New York	alfalfa	60	64	51	58	70
	red clover	17	18	25	21	14
	birdsfoot trefoil	15	11	17	16	11
	alsike clover	6	5	6	4	4
	ladino clover	2	2	1	1	1
Pennsylvania	alfalfa	55	49	46	54	63
	red clover	35	40	38	34	28
	birdsfoot trefoil	4	5	8	6	4
	alsike clover	5	5	7	5	4
	ladino clover	1	1	1	1	1
Maryland	alfalfa	48	30	25	46	52
	red clover	39	60	69	46	41
	birdsfoot trefoil	1	tr.	tr.	tr.	tr.
	alsike clover	8	7	4	5	5
	ladino clover	4	3	2	3	2

Source: Pardee and Beckham, 1971.[18]

ladino clovers have continued their long-term decline. Seed use of birdsfoot trefoil appears to be levelling off. Alfalfa has shown a strong resurgence since 1969, following a dramatic decline in the alfalfa weevil. (See Fig. 41.3.) Alfalfa constituted 50–70% of all legume seed shipped to major livestock states in 1971. These changes in legume use in the Northeast indicate that the region is moving away from long-lived but low-yielding grasses and legumes toward high-yielding alfalfa and corn. There has been a dramatic shift to clear seedings of alfalfa made without a companion crop, with at least half of New York seedings expected to be made in this way during 1972.[18]

CULTIVAR SELECTION

Significant changes in cultivar usage have also occurred.[18] These reflect the coordinated forage breeding and testing program of the Northeast. Regional testing of promising strains has assured wide adaptation of new cultivars subsequently released from breeding programs concentrated at Cornell University and The Pennsylvania State University (PSU).

Two alfalfa cultivars appear to have particular promise in the Northeast. 'Saranac' (Cornell, 1963) combines the unusual Flamande vigor with improved winter-hardiness and resistance to bacterial wilt. 'Iroquois' (Cornell, 1966) combines wilt resistance with the unique soil adaptability of 'Narragansett.' Iroquois provides long-lived and productive stands over a wide range of soil drainage types. In 1971, these two improved cultivars represented over half the total seed usage of alfalfa.

Breeding efforts have been less intensive with red clover and birdsfoot trefoil; however, 'Pennscott' red clover has shown wide adaptation throughout the region. Two Cornell cultivars dominate most of the seed usage of birdsfoot trefoil. 'Viking' is an erect type with improved winterhardiness. 'Empire' is a semierect type especially adapted for use in permanent pastures.

❦ GRASS SPECIES AND CULTIVARS

Perennial grasses dominate most hay-lands and pastures of the Northeast. In general they are more long-lived than legumes on wet acid soils. The productivity of major grasses in the Northeast has been evaluated in regional research studies.[19-22] With supplemental N, these grasses will produce forage yields nearly equal to that of well-managed alfalfa. However, under intensive management the survival of grass stands may be materially shortened.

PERENNIAL SPECIES

The relative importance of selected hay-land grasses is indicated by the land use and seed shipment data of Tables 41.4 and 41.6.[18] Timothy is clearly the most important species throughout the region. Orchardgrass is considered a major species only in the southern half of the region where milder winter temperatures prevail. Smooth bromegrass is important in some northern areas, but it has never achieved the widespread acceptance accorded it in the north central region.

Use of orchardgrass may increase during the 1970s. It is better adapted than either timothy or smooth bromegrass to multiple-harvest forage systems. It is also more tolerant of grazing than timothy. However, its marginal winterhardiness and rapid decline in forage quality at heading stage may continue to discourage adoption in northern areas.

Two other hay-type grasses have potential value for the Northeast. Reed ca-

19. Decker, A. M., G. A. Jung, J. B. Washko, D. D. Wolf, and M. J. Wright. 1967. Management and productivity of perennial grasses in the Northeast. I. Reed canarygrass. W. Va. Agr. Exp. Sta. Bull. 550T.

20. Wright, M. J., G. A. Jung, C. S. Brown. A. M. Decker, K. E. Varney, and R. C. Wakefield. 1967. Management and productivity of perennial grasses in the Northeast. II. Smooth bromegrass. W. Va. Agr. Exp. Sta. Bull. 554T.

21. Washko, J. B., G. A. Jung, A. M. Decker, R. C. Wakefield, D. D. Wolf, and M. J. Wright. 1967. Management and productivity of perennial grasses in the Northeast. III. Orchardgrass. W. Va. Agr. Exp. Sta. Bull. 557T.

22. Brown, C. S., G. A. Jung, K. E. Varney, R. C. Wakefield, and J. B. Washko. 1968. Management and productivity of perennial grasses in the Northeast. IV. Timothy. W. Va. Agr. Exp. Sta. Bull. 570T.

TABLE 41.6 ✤ Seed shipments of major forage grasses in the Northeast

State	Species	Average 1960–64	Average 1965–68	1969	1970	1971
		Regional totals (1000 kg)				
	Annuals					
	Sudangrass	947	670	307	277	223
	Forage sorghum	782	160	62	75	98
	Sorghum-sudangrass	326	1,114	646	620	843
	Total	2,055	1,944	1,015	972	1,164
	Perennials					
	Timothy	2,857	2,527	1,748	1,633	1,452
	Smooth bromegrass	282	278	178	151	126
	Orchardgrass	318	275	209	164	134
	Total	3,457	3,080	2,135	1,948	1,712
		Relative usage in selected states (%)				
Vermont	timothy	79	84	92	90	90
	smooth bromegrass	17	14	6	8	8
	orchardgrass	4	2	2	2	2
New York	timothy	86	87	88	87	88
	smooth bromegrass	12	12	11	11	10
	orchardgrass	2	1	1	2	2
Pennsylvania	timothy	86	83	84	86	86
	smooth bromegrass	6	9	9	8	7
	orchardgrass	8	8	7	6	7
Maryland	timothy	74	73	64	74	76
	smooth bromegrass	2	3	3	1	2
	orchardgrass	24	24	33	25	22

Source: Pardee and Beckham, 1971.[18]

narygrass is a highly productive species adapted to soils too droughty or too poorly drained for timothy. Tall fescue is used primarily as a soil conservation species but is becoming more widely used for beef pasture in southern areas. The use of these species has been limited by their inferior palatability for dairy cattle.

Kentucky bluegrass is the region's most important grass in improved permanent pastures. It is highly productive when fertilized and associates well with white clover and pasture-type birdsfoot trefoil. Bermudagrass, a relatively new pasture species in the region, is confined to mild winter areas along the southern coast.

Improved cultivars of the perennial grasses are less widely used than those of alfalfa and birdsfoot trefoil. Canadian-bred 'Climax' timothy has become popular in the northern states. 'Saratoga' smooth bromegrass (Cornell, 1955), 'Pennlate' (PSU, 1956) and 'Pennmead' (PSU, 1963) orchard-grass cultivars have become important throughout most of the region.

ANNUAL SPECIES

Cool-season annual grasses are an important source of forage in southern areas. Winter cereals are commonly grazed by beef cattle in late fall or early spring. Along the mild winter southern coast winter rye may be seeded into bermudagrass sod to extend grazing into the cooler months.[23]

Oats, as a companion crop for spring seedings, are often utilized for forage rather than grain. Since the mid-1960s there has been a continuing decline in the use of companion crops in general. New herbicides for alfalfa seedings have accelerated this trend.

Warm-season annual grasses are impor-

23. Decker, A. M., H. J. Retzer, F. G. Swain, and R. F. Dudley. 1969. Midland bermudagrass forage production supplemented by sod-seeded cool-season annual forages. Md. Agr. Exp. Sta. Bull. 484.

tant throughout the region as a source of summer feed. Seed usage has declined during the 1960s (Table 41.6) but at relatively the same rate as the perennial grasses. There has been a marked change in species, with sudangrass replaced to a considerable extent by new hybrids of sorghum-sudangrass. These hybrids are commonly more productive than 'Piper' sudangrass but are less suitable for grazing because of their high levels of hydrocyanic acid at immature growth stages.[24]

Japanese millet is still of some importance in the cooler areas, but its use is generally restricted to the wetter soils. Sudangrass and sorghum-sudangrass hybrids are preferred for most situations throughout the region.

❧ PERENNIAL SEED MIXTURES

Most perennial seedings in the Northeast include both legumes and grasses; however, pure seedings of alfalfa have become popular. Increased rates of alfalfa seed have suppressed the associated timothy and smooth bromegrass so much that some farmers consider their inclusion of little value. All perennial grasses have been excluded from alfalfa seedings treated with preplant herbicides for weedy grass control.

Several mixtures are used on the typical dairy farm. Variability in soil drainage is a major underlying cause. Some farmers program the use of both early and late maturing mixtures to lengthen the harvest period for quality first-crop hay.

TYPICAL SEED MIXTURES

Typical seed mixtures recommended for use in the Northeast are illustrated in Table 41.7. Emphasis on alfalfa for the better hayland soils is readily seen.

Simple mixtures of one legume and one grass are preferred. However, for fields of variable drainage the mixture of Iroquois alfalfa, Viking birdsfoot trefoil, and Climax timothy has become increasingly popular in New York and Pennsylvania. Inclusion of ladino clover in alfalfa-grass mixtures is declining with decreased grazing of dairy cattle. Hayland mixtures rarely contain more than one grass, although two or more may be used for pasture renovation and conservation seedings.

RATES OF SEEDING

Recommended seeding rates vary considerably for the small-seeded perennial forages (see Chapter 36). General levels for the Northeast, expressed in kilograms per ha, are: alfalfa 9–13, birdsfoot trefoil 7–9, red clover 7–9, ladino clover 1–2, timothy 5–7, orchardgrass 5–7, smooth bromegrass 9–11, reed canarygrass 9–11.

Pure seedings require increased seed rates, commonly 50–100% greater than for the same species in mixtures. Alfalfa is commonly sown at 16–22 kg/ha when grown in pure stands.

❧ TRENDS IN FORAGE USE

What changes may be predicted for the 1970s in use of grassland crops in the Northeast? Livestock production will continue to be a very significant factor in the region's economy. New York and Pennsylvania will remain among the five major dairy states of the country.[25] A substantial increase in beef production is expected, particularly in the southern part of the region.

Forage utilization by livestock will continue to change. Corn silage will become increasingly more significant. Pasture will be confined to the less tillable soils. Hay production will become more intensified, with alfalfa the major species. A greater percentage of the spring hay crop will be stored as wilted silage.

More attention will be given to the rapidly expanding use of pleasure horses by the northeastern suburbanite. As of 1969,

24. Harrington, J. D. 1966. Hydrocyanic acid content of Piper, Trudan I, and six sorghum-sundangrass hybrids. Pa. Agr. Exp. Sta. Bull. 735.

25. Groves, Frank. 1971. The dairy enterprise. Proc. 4th Research-Industry Conf., pp. 97–102. Amer. Forage Grassl. Council.

TABLE 41.7 ❦ Typical forage seed mixtures of the Northeast

Soil drainage	Principal use	Legume	Associated grass
Excessively drained to well-drained	silage or green chop	Saranac alfalfa (or other Flamande)	Pennmead orchardgrass
Well-drained to moderately well-drained	short-term hay or silage	Saranac or Iroquois alfalfa	Pennlate orchardgrass
		Iroquois alfalfa	Climax timothy
		Pennscott red clover (or other improved)	Climax timothy
	long-term hay or silage	Saranac or Iroquois alfalfa	Saratoga bromegrass or Climax timothy
		Viking or 'Mansfield' birdsfoot trefoil	Saratoga bromegrass or Climax timothy
	rotational pasture	ladino clover with Iroquois alfalfa or red clover	orchardgrass or smooth bromegrass or timothy
	permanent pasture	Empire birdsfoot trefoil	timothy and Kentucky bluegrass
Variable (spots in field too wet for alfalfa)	long-term hay or pasture	Viking birdsfoot trefoil with Iroquois alfalfa	Climax timothy
Somewhat poorly drained to poorly drained	medium-late cut hay	Viking birdsfoot trefoil or alsike clover	Climax timothy
	late cut hay	Empire birdsfoot trefoil	'Essex' timothy
	rotational pasture	Viking or Empire birdsfoot trefoil or ladino clover	reed canarygrass

Source: Composited from: Maine—Agron. Repts., Fact Sheet D-6, 1970; Maryland—Fact Sheet 94 (rev.); New York—Cornell Recommends for Field Crops, 1971; Pennsylvania—1971 Agron. Guide.

there were about 200,000 horses and ponies in the region.[14] The special needs of horses for pasture and hay will be recognized more fully.[26]

Conservation and recreation uses of grassland species will continue to expand. Improved roadside cover will be achieved through more widespread use of crownvetch and with new cultivars of fescues or other adapted species. The significant and varied role of grassland in urbanized areas is being recognized in the densely populated states of the Northeast.

26. Mitchell, W. H., E. N. Scarborough, and W. T. McAllister. 1962. Horse sense about hay. Del. Agr. Ext. Bull. 78.

❦ QUESTIONS

1. Discuss changes which occurred during the 1960s relative to the production and use of corn silage, hay, and pasture on northeastern farms.

2. Describe natural characteristics of northeastern soils which have retarded adoption of alfalfa. What is being done to minimize these unfavorable conditions?

3. Discuss changes in the relative seed use of the various major legumes of the Northeast during the period 1960–71.

4. Why is red clover of greater significance in the southern part of the region than in the northern part?

5. Contrast ladino clover and birdsfoot trefoil in regard to their use and significance in the Northeast.

6. Why is timothy the most important hayland grass in the Northeast?

7. Predict the future use of orchardgrass in the Northeast. Will it increase or decrease relative to other seeded perennials? Why?

8. Discuss the importance and use of warm-season annual grasses in the Northeast.

9. Illustrate the significance of soil drainage classification in selecting forage seed mixtures for a typical northeastern farm.

MAURICE E. HEATH / *Purdue University*

42

HAY AND PASTURE SEEDINGS FOR THE CENTRAL AND LAKE STATES

⚘

THIRTEEN PERCENT of the total U.S. land area in farms and 28% of the Class I, II, and III land is contained within the boundaries of eight central and Lake states (Fig. 42.1).[1] (See Terminology for land classes.) The area has 61% of the corn hectarage, 19% of the small grain, 61% of the soybeans, 27% of the tame hay, and 8% of the pasture area of the nation, according to the 1969 census (Table 42.1).

⚘ CLIMATE

The annual rainfall is about 510 mm in northwestern Minnesota, increasing to 1150 mm in southeastern Missouri and in the lower Ohio River Valley.[2] Much of the rainfall is torrential in nature.

The average annual snowfall is as little as 250 mm toward the south but exceeds 2500 mm in upper Michigan and Minnesota.[2] Drought periods are more of a forage hazard in the southern part of the area than elsewhere.

The January mean minimum temperature range is from —22 C along the Canadian border of Minnesota to 2 C in southern Missouri. The July mean tem-

⚘ MAURICE E. HEATH. *See Chapter 1.*

Fɪɢ. 42.1. The central and Lake states area of the U.S.

perature range is from 5.5 C in the extreme north to over 32 C in the south. The average freeze-free summer period is from 100 days in the north to 190 in the south.

⚘ SOIL AND NATIVE COVER

The native cover was tall-grass prairie in the western part of the region and forest elsewhere (Fig. 42.2).

1. USDA. 1971. National inventory of soil and water conservation needs, 1967. Stat. Bull. 461.
2. USDC. 1968. Climatic atlas of the United States. Environmental Sci. Admin.

448

TABLE 42.1 ❧ Hectarage in the central and Lake states devoted to forages and field crops, 1969 U.S. census (000 ha)

State	Corn	Sorghum	Small grain	Soybeans	All hay	Crop-land only pastured	Wood-land pastured	Other pasture	Total
Ohio	1,095	5	601	966	560	487	227	352	1,066
Indiana	1,771	6	437	1,244	338	512	289	234	1,035
Illinois	3,841	8	767	2,595	459	788	427	452	1,667
Michigan	482	4	359	191	557	316	179	127	622
Wisconsin	670	3	626	59	1,421	742	735	436	1,913
Minnesota	1,550	8	1,979	1,078	1,104	752	533	515	1,800
Iowa	3,837	19	724	2,094	919	1,526	448	777	2,751
Missouri	1,074	92	408	1,225	1,034	2,371	1,156	1,327	4,854
Regional total	14,320	145	5,901	9,452	6,392	7,494	3,994	4,220	15,708
% of U.S. total	61	2	19	61	27	27	24	3	8

Header note: Pasture lands, 1969* spans the Crop-land only pastured, Wood-land pastured, Other pasture, and Total columns.

* Farms with sales of $2500 and over (economic classes 1–5).

The soils formed under the prairie (mainly the brunizems) lie in a great triangle. The western border of the area is the base, and northwest Indiana is the apex. This large region of dark-colored grassland soils is one of the most fertile areas of its size to be found on the continent. It is well adapted to the production of corn and forages.

FIG. 42.2. The growth and decay of native grasses and legumes produced our great reservoir of deep, rich, granular, dark prairie soils.

On the moister sites, the principal native grasses found by the early explorers and settlers were big bluestem, indiangrass, prairie cordgrass, switchgrass, Canada wildrye, eastern gamagrass, bluejoint, and reed canarygrass. The less favorable upland sites supported a cover of little bluestem, sideoats grama, junegrass, needlegrass, prairie dropseed, and western wheatgrass.[3] About 65% of the tall native grasses extended roots to a depth of 150 cm. The bulk of the prairie growth was below, not above, the soil surface. Growth and decay of native grasses, legumes, and herbs through untold thousands of years produced a reservoir of dark, deep, rich granular soil.[4] (See Fig. 42.2.)

The majority of soils of the area developed under a forest cover. A large belt of soils in northern Minnesota, Wisconsin, and Michigan are low in pH, highly leached, and ashy gray in color. They are known as typical podzol soils (formed largely under mixed conifer-deciduous forest).[5] Their inherent productivity for crop plants is low. The remainder of the forest soils in the area are podzolic in character,

3. Weaver, J. E. 1954. North American Prairie. Johnsen, Lincoln, Nebr.
4. Hughes, H. D., and Maurice E. Heath. 1946. Forage crops that feed the livestock and save the soil. *In* A Century of Farming in Iowa, 1846–1946, pp. 54–65. Iowa State Univ. Press, Ames.
5. USDA and North Central Agr. Exp. Stas. cooperating. 1960. Major soils of the north central region. Wis. Agr. Exp. Sta. Bull. 544, p. 4.

TABLE 42.2 ❧ Livestock on farms in the central and Lake states, 1969 U.S. census

State	All cattle (000)	Milk cows (000)	All hogs (000)	Sheep (000)	Chickens* (000)	Horses and ponies (000)
Ohio	1,910	424	2,479	747	11,878	77
Indiana	1,829	227	4,440	283	14,940	62
Illinois	3,194	292	6,995	377	8,414	73
Michigan	1,442	414	699	272	7,311	54
Wisconsin	3,969	1,723	1,677	150	5,365	48
Minnesota	3,633	894	3,296	521	11,111	51
Iowa	7,021	477	13,439	829	11,155	78
Missouri	4,816	309	4,250	281	7,505	88
Regional total	27,814	4,760	37,275	3,460	77,679	531
% of U.S. total	26	43	67	16	21	24

* Three months old or older.

formed under deciduous forest. Their inherent fertility is intermediate between that of the podzolic and brunizemic soils. Most of these, particularly through the central part of the region, are responsive to soil treatment and produce good yields of forage and grain crops.

❧ FEED UNITS

The 1969 census shows that this area contains 26% of all U.S. cattle, 43% of the dairy cows, 67% of the hogs, 16% of the sheep, and 21% of the chickens three months and older (Table 42.2).

Of the total feed units consumed by livestock, 26% are from pasture, with a total of approximately 43% from all forages, including pasture, hay, silage, and other roughages (Table 42.3).[6]

The total feed units consumed by different classes of livestock of the U.S. and by those of the central and Lake states is shown in Table 42.4.[6] Of the total feed units consumed by the dairy cattle of the U.S., those of this area consumed 45%. For beef cattle the amount is 24%; for sheep and goats, 15%; and for hogs and poultry, 48%.

Of the feed units consumed by the livestock of the U.S., the central and Lake states produced and consumed 33% of the total; of the silage and beet pulp, 22%; of

6. Hodges, Earl F. 1972. Preliminary unpublished data. ERS, USDA.

TABLE 42.3 ❧ Feed units consumed by livestock in the central and Lake states for the 1969–70 feeding year

State	Pasture and grazing (000 t)	Forage sorghum and corn stover (000 t)	Silage and beet pulp (000 t)	Hay (000 t)	Grain (000 t)	Other concentrates (000 t)	Total feed units (000 t)
Illinois	4,177	87	602	2,129	8,372	867	16,234
Indiana	2,882	60	415	1,469	5,776	598	11,200
Iowa	8,580	179	1,238	4,374	17,197	1,781	33,349
Michigan	1,425	30	206	727	2,855	296	5,534
Minnesota	4,242	89	612	2,162	8,501	881	16,487
Missouri	4,501	94	649	2,290	9,020	934	17,488
Ohio	2,493	52	359	1,271	4,997	517	9,689
Wisconsin	4,080	85	589	2,080	8,177	847	15,858
Regional total	32,380	676	4,670	16,502	64,895	6,721	125,844
% of U.S. total	24	26	22	35	49	15	33

Source: Earl F. Hodges, 1972.[6]
Note: A feed unit is a pound of corn or its equivalent in other feed.

TABLE 42.4 ❧ Feed units consumed by different classes of livestock in eight central and Lake states for the 1969–70 feeding year

Feed	Beef cattle (000 t)	Dairy cattle (000 t)	Sheep and goats (000 t)	Hogs and poultry (000 t)	Horses and mules (000 t)
Pasture and grazing	17,394	11,220	1,035	2,063	667
Forage sorghum and corn stover	407	200	41	...	27
Silage and beet pulp	1,546	3,113	12	...	...
Hay	7,675	8,367	190	...	273
Grain	16,148	7,405	153	40,892	296
Other concentrates	776	1,321	...	4,623	...
Regional total	43,946	31,626	1,431	47,578	1,263
% of U.S. total	24	45	15	48	19

Source: Earl F. Hodges, 1972.[6]
Note: A feed unit is a pound of corn or its equivalent in other feed.

the grain, 49%; of the hay, 35%; and of the pasture for grazing, 24%.

GRAIN CROP RESIDUES

In 1969 there were over 28 million ha of grain crop residues in the central and Lake states. Over 13 million ha were from corn (Table 42.1, corn hectarage less silage). Such residues supply excellent maintenance feed for beef cows and stocker cattle. Grain crop residues can be considered free feed since production costs have been charged to the grain crop. Thus the beef cow-calf enterprise is complementary to grain crop production.

❧ LEGUMES FOR HAY AND PASTURE

Alfalfa, either alone or with a grass, is recommended for general use throughout the area over any other legume for hay production and to a considerable extent for pasture. There has been a 26% decline in alfalfa hectarage since 1964, largely caused by the alfalfa weevil, and increased specialization in corn and soybean production (Fig. 42.3). In 1969 there was a ratio of almost 1 ha of alfalfa to each 4.5 ha of corn. The grasses most grown with alfalfa are smooth bromegrass and timothy, although orchardgrass has become increasingly important. A little red or ladino clover often is included in the alfalfa-grass mixtures, depending upon soil conditions and the purpose for which the crop is grown.

Dairy production is particularly important in Wisconsin, Minnesota, and northern Illinois and is relatively so in northeastern Iowa and southern Michigan. Long recognized for its high value as hay in the rations of milk-producing animals, alfalfa for the area increased from 3,330,000 ha, the 1946–55 average, to 4,532,000 ha by 1959, and decreased to 3,229,000 ha by 1969. The greatest concentration is in areas having the larger numbers of dairy animals. On a state basis Wisconsin leads in alfalfa hectarage, but Minnesota and Iowa also produce over 0.5 million ha each. The high-quality protein source of alfalfa-grass complements corn as an energy source in livestock feeding.

Red clover replaces alfalfa in short rotations for hay and pasture and is usually followed by corn (Fig. 42.4). It is valuable as a minor part of the mixture to

FIG. 42.3. The area of major concentration of corn hectarage and production in the central and Lake States.[5]

Fig. 42.4. *Red clover has been the most seeded hay legume . . . exceeded only by alfalfa.* Kenland red clover–timothy aftermath used for pasture in July. *Purdue Univ. Agr. Exp. Sta. photo.*

grow with alfalfa on many soils, where it gives a more adequate stand and quite often a greater yield the first meadow year.

Until recently, red clover has been the most seeded hay legume in the region. Today it is exceeded only by alfalfa. Red clover was not as demanding for its nutrient supply as alfalfa and sweetclover and could be grown on most soils before the advent of general liming and use of commercial fertilizers. Clover failures in Illinois have been more frequently attributed to a lack of lime in the soil than to any other condition.[7]

In 1969, 1,732,000 ha of red clover were grown alone and with grasses for hay, as compared with the 10-year 1946–55 average of 4,556,000 ha. This represents a 62% decrease in the hectarage of red clover, due largely to the increase of alfalfa and the accelerated use of commercial N on corn and grain crops. In 1969 the central and Lake states produced 70% of the red clover seed of the U.S. compared to 77% in 1946–55.

White clover, the common type, occurs naturally in bluegrass pastures over most of the region. The amount and growth varies greatly from year to year. Since the

late 1940s ladino clover has been used rather extensively as a minor part of seeding mixtures.[8] When moisture is available, it makes a valuable contribution, particularly for dairy cattle and swine. The Missouri station, through rotation grazing of bluegrass pastures and soil treatments, has established ladino clover by broadcasting the seed, and maintains the stand without any sod tillage.[9] Ladino clover is susceptible to prolonged drought. Its greatest hazard as a dominant pasture legume is the possibility of bloat in ruminants. This usually can be overcome by increasing the proportion of grass to clover (40–60% or more grass) or by feeding an antibloat agent. It recovers rapidly after grazing and may be grown well where adapted and under intensive management with rapid recovery grasses such as orchardgrass, tall fescue, and reed canarygrass.

Korean lespedeza is grown extensively in Missouri and is found in southern Illinois and Indiana. It is especially suited as pasture on soils of poor to fair productivity.

Lespedeza is best used as a fattening pasture with beef cattle, producing a white fat. When bluegrass pastures are overseeded with Korean lespedeza and grazed rather heavily through April, May, and June, good stands are easily established. In northwest Missouri a fertility level to support a 75% bluegrass stand has allowed lespedeza to volunteer continuously. With normal rain these pastures produced 224–280 kg of beef per ha, with average daily gains of 0.7–0.9 kg.[9] On sloping land subject to erosion it is important that winter cereals or a protective sod of a perennial grass be used with lespedeza. In the past much winter wheat–lespedeza was utilized as pasture, but the increased wheat yields obtained with fertilizer N has discouraged this practice.

Birdsfoot trefoil, used in the renovation of permanent pastures, is gradually in-

7. Heusinkveld, David. 1948. Red clover for Illinois. Ill. Agr. Exp. Sta. Circ. 627.

8. Tesar, Milo B. 1959. The place and contribution of grasslands to the agriculture of the Corn Belt. *In* Grassland, pp. 61–73. Amer. Assoc. Advan. Sci., Washington, D.C.
9. Brown, E. Marion. 1959. Grassland management problems (Mo. Agr. Exp. Sta.). Proc. Amer. Grassl. Council, Norwich, N.Y.

creasing in use, especially in Iowa, Indiana, and Ohio.[10] It is adapted to fields held in pasture for a number of years and makes an excellent legume companion with Kentucky bluegrass. At the Ohio station, lamb gains on birdsfoot-bluegrass over a three-year period ranged from 502 to 533 kg/ha.[11] First recommended as a pasture legume on problem upland soils, birdsfoot trefoil is now also recognized as particularly tolerant of wet, poorly drained soil conditions. It has a wide soil tolerance as to fertility, acidity, and drainage.

Alsike clover has been used in hay and pasture mixtures, especially in the northern part of the region, although total use is small.

Crownvetch is recognized for its slope-control value along roadsides. Its potential use for pasture and possibly for hay has also been reported. As seed supplies become plentiful, more farmers in the central and southerly part of the area will have an opportunity to determine the specific place of this legume in their soil-forage-animal program.[12]

❧ GRASSES FOR HAY AND PASTURE

Kentucky bluegrass grows on more ha in the area than any other grass. It predominates on land in permanent pasture. In 1969 over 8 million ha of permanent pasture were reported. Kentucky bluegrass is very seldom seeded; most stands volunteer from seed scattered by the wind and by livestock when the areas are being grazed. Whatever the species seeded, they are gradually replaced by Kentucky bluegrass if grazed continuously. Canada bluegrass may be found on the less fertile soils. Redtop usually associates with Kentucky bluegrass on the poorly drained soils in the southern part of the region.

The kind and amount of legume species growing with bluegrass largely determine its value as pasture. Pasture improvement research has shown that the carrying capacity of these pastures can be increased two to four times.[13,14] Depending on location, improvement practices may include one or more of the following: lime and fertilizer amendments based on soil tests; introduction of such legumes as lespedeza, ladino clover, red clover, birdsfoot trefoil, and alfalfa; and the conversion of bluegrass pasture to a more productive legume-grass mixture by using such grasses as smooth bromegrass or orchardgrass.

Timothy is probably the second most important grass in the region from the standpoint of hectarage seeded, although its use has decreased. This decline is closely related to the decrease in horse numbers and in more recent years to the competition from other grasses and specialized forage mixtures. Red clover–timothy is one of the mixtures most used for a one-year meadow. Timothy may be seeded with either fall or spring grains. In the southern part of the region, spring seedings are not as reliable as those made in the fall. In 1969 over 98% of the U.S. timothy seed was grown in the area.

Smooth bromegrass not only survived but showed marked drought resistance during the 1934 and 1936 dry years that killed vast areas of Kentucky bluegrass in the western part of the region. In the 1940s the "southern type" bromegrasses were recognized. Cultivar examples are 'Lincoln,' 'Achenbach,' and 'Fischer.' They were found to be not only more productive but also more dependable in stand establishment throughout much of the region, particularly the central and southern parts. Yield differences between northern and southern types have been observed to increase from north to south in this area.[15]

Orchardgrass is not as winter-hardy as timothy and smooth bromegrass but some is used in the north where snow cover is

10. Wedin, W. F., and R. L. Vetter. 1967. Birdsfoot trefoil brings new life to pastures. *Iowa Farm Sci.* 22(6): 3–6.

11. Davis, R. R., and D. S. Bell. 1958. Birdsfoot trefoil. *Ohio Farm Home Res.* 43:90, 95.

12. Van Keuren, R. W. 1968. Crownvetch for forage? *Ohio Rept.* 53:12–14.

13. Scholl, J. M., M. F. Finner, A. E. Peterson, and J. M. Sund. 1970. Pasture renovation in southwestern Wisconsin. Res. Div. Colleges Agr. and Life Sci. Univ. Wis. Res. Rept. 65.

14. Wedin, W. F. 1970. What can Iowa do with 10 million acres of forage? *Iowa Farm Sci.* 24(9):3–8.

15. Thomas, H. L., Earle W. Hanson, and J. A. Jacobs. 1958. Varietal trials of smooth bromegrass in the north central region. Minn. Agr. Exp. Sta. Misc. Rept. 32, North Central Reg. Publ. 93.

dependable. However, it is much more popular in the southern part of the region. Orchardgrass is used as a companion grass with alfalfa on many soils in the central and southern part of the area. Its rapid recovery after harvest makes it an ideal grass for pasture with ladino clover.

Tall fescue is gaining considerable popularity in the southern part of the region, especially on some of the less fertile and less well-drained or tight subsoil areas.[16] The Illinois–Dixon Springs station has reported that a tall fescue–legume mixture used in a rotation is greatly superior to permanent fescue for beef cattle and sheep.[17]

The Indiana station, using yearlings, obtained a three-year average of 433 kg/ha gain from tall fescue topdressed annually with 168 kg N/ha, compared with 278 kg of gain without N. These results were on an unglaciated sandstone-shale soil of low inherent fertility.[18] The Iowa station reports 703 kg/ha of beef from N-fertilized tall fescue pasture using a "three-season" management system. Pasture was grazed in May, June, and July (spring-summer); rested Aug. 1–Oct. 15; and then grazed from mid-October to mid-December (fall).[13] Tall fescue pasture has not generally proved satisfactory for lactating dairy cows.[19]

Tall fescue spring growth harvested as round bales and left in the field, plus aftermath, is becoming popular for winter pasture for beef cow herds. It has been demonstrated that by rationing the bales and aftermath with an electric fence the cleanup is excellent and cow-days per ha may be increased more than 50% compared to a free-choice field.[20,21]

Reed canarygrass stands in a class by itself in its adaptation to very wet lowlands. Iowa recognizes the adaptation of birdsfoot trefoil to low wet areas and even suggests the possibility of the reed canarygrass–birdsfoot trefoil combination under such conditions. This grass has had more extensive use in wet, undrainable bottomland soils in the northern part of the area than farther south.

❧ SEEDING RECOMMENDATIONS

Seedings to be recommended for a given environment need to be related to the specific soil and climatic conditions that prevail and to the use to be made of the forage produced. The recommendations of specialists familiar with the ecological factors that apply in different areas must be the basis for seeding decisions.

There is considerable similarity in the species and combinations recommended for different soils and uses in the eight states of the area. The Wisconsin recommendations especially are applicable to the three northernmost states (where forages for dairy animals are so important), with those of Iowa representative of the more central and southern parts of the area.

COMBINATIONS AND PROPORTIONS

The Wisconsin and Iowa seeding recommendations show that of the many legumes available, only alfalfa, red clover, and ladino clover are generally recommended and extensively used (Tables 42.5 and 42.6).[22,23] Alsike clover, sweetclover, lespedeza, and birdsfoot trefoil are at present seeded on rather limited hectarages,

16. Burger, J. A., J. A. Jacobs, and C. N. Hittle. 1958. The effect of height and frequency of cutting on the yield and botanical composition of tall fescue and smooth bromegrass mixtures. *Agron. J.* 50:629–32.

17. Cate, H. A. 1955. Keeping southern Illinois pastures productive. Ill. Agr. Exp. Sta. Circ. 740.

18. Peterson, R. C., G. O. Mott, M. E. Heath, and William Beeson. 1962. Comparison of tall fescue and orchardgrass for grazing in southern Indiana. Purdue Univ. Agr. Exp. Sta. Res. Progr. Rept. 26, pp. 34–44.

19. Pratt, A. D., and R. R. Davis. 1954. Kentucky 31 fescue is not suited for dairy cattle. *Ohio Farm Home Res.* 39:93–94.

20. Wilson, Lowell, R. C. Peterson, M. E. Heath, and R. E. Erb. 1965. Restricted versus unrestricted winter grazing of round bales and aftermath for the beef cow herd on the forage farm. Purdue Univ. Agr. Exp. Sta. Res. Progr. Rept. 189.

21. Van Keuren, R. W., and E. W. Klosterman. 1967. Winter pasture system for Ohio beef cows. *Ohio Rept.* 52:67–69.

22. Rohweder, D. A., R. F. Johannes, R. L. LaCroix, W. H. Paulson, G. H. Tempas, and G. G. Weis. 1972. Forage crop varieties and seed mixtures for 1972. Wis. Coop. Ext. Serv. Publ. A1525 (C463).

23. Schaller, F. W., and H. E. Thompson. 1968. Forage crop varieties and seeding mixtures. Iowa Coop. Ext. Serv. Pam. 223 (rev.).

TABLE 42.5 ❧ Recommended hay, silage, and pasture seedings for Wisconsin

Mixture	Kg/ha	Use
Well-drained, medium- to fine-textured soils that are limed or nonacid		
1. Alfalfa alone*	11–17	Long rotations for hay only.
2. Alfalfa, smooth bromegrass *or* orchardgrass†	9–13 3–7 2–5	Long rotation for hay, silage, and pasture.
3. Alfalfa, smooth bromegrass, orchardgrass‡	5 11 2	Long rotation for hay, silage, and pasture.
4. Alfalfa, timothy orchardgrass§	9–13 3–5 2–5	Short rotation for hay, silage, and pasture.
5. Red clover, timothy‖	7–9 3–6	Short rotation for hay, silage, and pasture.
Sand soils		
6. Alfalfa, smooth bromegrass	9–11 7–9	For hay and silage.
Poorly drained soils		
7. Red clover, alsike clover, ladino clover, smooth bromegrass *or* timothy	6 3 0.3–0.6 9 5	Especially for pasture.
8. Alsike clover, ladino clover, timothy *or* smooth bromegrass	2 1–2 5 9	Especially for pasture.
9. Alsike clover, timothy *or* smooth bromegrass	6 5 9	Especially for pasture.
Very wet lowlands		
10. Reed canarygrass	7–9	For pasture.
11. Reed canarygrass, timothy	3–6 2–3	For pasture.
Imperfectly drained and rolling soils intended for permanent pasture		
12. Birdsfoot trefoil, Kentucky bluegrass *or* timothy	7 2 3–5	Especially for pasture.
Well-drained soils		
13. Smooth bromegrass	17–22	For waterways or livestock pasture.
14. Reed canarygrass	9–13	For waterways or livestock pasture.
15. Sudangrass	34–39	Supplementary summer pasture.
16. Oats	108	Supplementary summer pasture.
17. Winter rye or winter wheat	135	Supplementary fall or spring pasture sown in August or September.

Source: Rohweder et al., 1972.[22]

* Plant alfalfa alone only on soils with little or no erosion.

† Use heavier rates in southern Wisconsin and lighter rates in eastern Wisconsin. From 0.28 to 0.56 kg ladino clover may be added when used for pasture. One to 2 kg timothy may be substituted for orchardgrass or smooth bromegrass on heavier soils in northern Wisconsin.

‡ Suggested where bloat is a problem, such as in beef pastures. Fertilize with complete fertilizer containing high amounts of N after legume disappears.

§ Timothy is suggested in eastern and northern Wisconsin. Orchardgrass is suggested for green chop and pasture; 0.25–0.5 kg ladino clover may be added when used for pasture.

‖ Especially for hay in eastern and northern Wisconsin on soils not adequately drained and/or limed for alfalfa.

TABLE 42.6 ❧ Recommended hay, pasture, and silage seedings for Iowa

Mixture	Kg/ha	Use
Hay or silage		
1. Alfalfa alone	11–17	Well-drained, limed, or nonacid fertile soils with little or no erosion.
2. Red clover alone	9–11	Well-drained, fertile soils with little or no erosion.
Hay, silage, or pasture		
*(for well-drained, limed, or nonacid and fertile soils)**		
3. Alfalfa,	9	All parts of Iowa.
smooth bromegrass	9	
4. Alfalfa,	9	Especially for pasture.
orchardgrass	6	
5. Alfalfa,	9	Especially for pasture. Mixture should contain at least 50% grass.
smooth bromegrass,	6	
orchardgrass	3	
*(for variable soils, often imperfectly drained and slightly acid)**		
6. Red clover,	8	General.
timothy *or*	4	
orchardgrass	6	
7. Red clover,	8	Poorly drained soils.
alsike,	2	
timothy *or*	3	
smooth bromegrass *or*	9	
orchardgrass	4	
8. Alfalfa,	6	All parts of Iowa.
red clover,	3	
smooth bromegrass *or*	9	Especially for pasture.
orchardgrass	4	
Permanent and semipermanent pasture		
9. Birdsfoot trefoil†	7	General use in pasture renovation, except west of U.S. Highway 71, in sandy soils, and under very acid and low-fertility conditions.
10. Crownvetch†	11	Well-drained sites.
11. Birdsfoot trefoil,	7	General, except west of U.S. Highway 71 and in sandy soils.
orchardgrass	2	
12. Crownvetch,	7	Well-drained areas.
orchardgrass	2	
13. Alfalfa,‡	9	Use Vernal or similar alfalfa. Mixture should contain at least 50% grass.
smooth bromegrass,	6	
orchardgrass	3	
Grass pasture		
14. Smooth bromegrass	17–22	General use.
15. Orchardgrass	9–11	General use except central, north, and west.
16. Reed canarygrass	11–13	Especially low wet areas.
17. Tall fescue	13–17	Southern Iowa.
Green manure		
18. Biennial sweetclover,	6	General use on well-drained, limed, or nonacid fertile soils with little or no erosion.
red clover *or*	6	
alfalfa (southern)	11	
19. Alfalfa (southern)	11–13	Soils adapted to alfalfa.
20. Red clover	9–11	Poorly drained areas.

TABLE 42.6 ❧ *(Continued)*

Mixture	Kg/ha	Use
21. Sweetclover alone	9–11	General use on nonacid soils where weevil control program is used.
Grassed waterways		
22. Smooth bromegrass	17–22	General use.
23. Reed canarygrass	11–13	General use.
24. Tall fescue§	13–17	Pastures, especially low-fertility sites.
Supplemental pasture, hay, or silage		
25. Sudangrass, drilled	22–28	For pasture, hay, green chop, or silage.
26. Sorghum-sudan hybrids, drilled or in 20-inch rows	22–34	Sudan should be 50 cm and hybrids 75 cm tall before grazing to avoid danger of prussic acid poisoning.
27. Forage-sorghum, 40-inch rows	7–9	For silage.
28. Oats	72–108	Seeded as companion crop to forage seeding and grazed or cut for hay or silage.
29. Winter rye	100	Fall-seeded for limited fall grazing and early spring pasture.
30. Soybeans, seeded in rows, drilled	67 135	General use for hay.

Source: Schaller and Thompson, 1968.[23]

Note: Suggested seeding rates are based on uniform distribution and shallow coverage. If seeding rates are changed, the rate for both the grass and the legume should be adjusted proportionately.

 * Ladino clover at 0.6 kg/ha may be added to mixture numbers 3–8 when used mainly for pasture where soil and moisture conditions are suitable.

 † Birdsfoot trefoil and crownvetch are not recommended for seeding in combination with other legumes.

 ‡ When bloat is a problem, alfalfa should be reduced to 4 kg/ha and grass should be increased to 11–13 kg/ha.

 § Tall fescue can be used in mixtures with smooth bromegrass where soil and moisture conditions vary greatly. In the western half of the state 4–7 kg/ha of alfalfa may be added to smooth bromegrass.

and are recommended for use under quite different conditions. Alsike is pretty much limited to the northern part of the area, especially on less well-drained soils. Use of lespedeza is confined to the extreme southern part of the area. Sweetclover was once seeded very generally in small grain as a green manure. The general destruction of sweetclover stands by the sweetclover weevil has resulted in the general discontinuation of its use. Birdsfoot trefoil has been recommended in the area only for pastures which are to remain down through a period of years. The birdsfoot trefoil hectarage is gradually expanding.

Of the many grasses available, timothy, smooth bromegrass, and orchardgrass probably account for well over 90% of those seeded. Orchardgrass is important in the southern part of the area. There is a large hectarage of Kentucky bluegrass, but this grass usually is not seeded. Redtop was once seeded extensively, especially on the more acid, poorly drained areas in the southern part of the region. The more general use of liming and fertilizing programs has resulted in redtop being replaced by more nutritious and palatable grasses.

The legumes and grasses included in a mixture and the proportion of the different species vary greatly, depending upon soil conditions and the use to be made of the forage produced.

The seeding rates suggested by the different states should be regarded only as indicative. They may vary greatly with equally good results.

It will be noted in the forage seeding recommendations of the two states shown that the species included in a given mixture are related to such specific soil conditions as drainage, productivity, and acidity as well as the use to be made of the forage.

SEEDINGS BY ILLINOIS FARMERS

The legume-grass mixtures most seeded by Illinois farmers are of interest and value since Illinois is located almost in the very middle of the central and Lake states, extends over 300 miles from north to south, and includes a relatively wide range of the climatic and soil conditions of the area. An Illinois survey made in 1958 showed that the four most used mixtures for the state as a whole of the 277 reported were, in order of frequency: alfalfa–red clover–timothy; alfalfa–smooth bromegrass; red clover–timothy; and alfalfa–smooth bromegrass–ladino clover.[24] There are great differences in the relative importance of the seedings most used in different parts of the state, however. The variation applies not only to the species included but also to the rates of seeding and the proportion of the different components.

❦ SILAGE CROPS

Corn is the preferred silage crop in the region with 1.25 million ha harvested in 1969.[25] This is 42% of all the corn grown for silage in the U.S. in that year. Wisconsin leads the area with 311,000 ha of corn silage, which was 46% of their total corn hectarage. Minnesota was second and Iowa third with 287,000 and 210,000 ha respectively. Only 24,000 ha of sorghum were grown for silage.

Over 790,000 ha of legumes and grasses were grown for grass silage and green chop in the U.S. in 1969. Of this hectarage 60% was in the central and Lake states.

In this humid and subhumid region spring rains or heavy dews may reduce by half the nutrients from forage made as first-cutting hay. In Missouri it is conservatively estimated that on the average,

35% of the nutrients are lost from all hay harvested.[26] Losses can be as little as 10–15% under favorable preservation when the hay is harvested as silage. In general, however, there is a greater risk of spoilage in making grass silage than corn silage.[27]

❦ FERTILIZATION

Farmers in these states used 54% of all the lime and 34% of all the commercial fertilizer sold in the U.S. in 1969. Less than 5% of this fertilizer was on established hay and pasture. The majority of soils still need additional lime for the best growth of alfalfa and clovers.[28,29] A soil testing service is now available to every farmer in the region.

❦ FORAGE TRENDS

Several trends in forage production are apparent.[30] In the central Corn Belt (Fig. 42.3) continuous row cropping on the more level lands will continue. Forage-animal production will become more intensified on land less adapted to grain production. Commercial use of N on pure grass stands will increase. Fertility programs will become more exacting. Forage plants will be managed more according to growth principles. The hectarage of taller grasses and legumes will increase substantially. Greater emphasis will be placed on pasture renovation. More alfalfa seedings without companion crops will be made to achieve maximum total digestible nutrients and protein per ha. Warm-season grasses will be used to a greater extent in the southern part of the region. More efficient forage handling equipment will be

24. Illinois Crop Reporting Service. 1958. Crop Bull. 58–4.
25. Hildebrand, S. C., L. V. Nelson, H. E. Henderson, Donald Hillman, C. R. Hoglund, R. L. Maddex, and R. C. White. 1969. Corn silage. Mich. Ext. Bull. E-665.

26. Missouri Agr. Exp. Sta. 1958. Silage—Feed of excellence. Bull. 696.
27. Ahlgren, Gilbert H. 1956. Forage Crops, 2nd ed. McGraw-Hill, New York.
28. Peterson, A. E., and Attoe, O. J. 1958. Potash helps alfalfa roots. Wis. Agr. Exp. Sta. Bull. 532.
29. USDA. 1957. Soil Yearbook Agr.
30. The author is grateful for personal communications from the following persons in 1972 relative to forage trends in the central and Lake states: F. W. Schaller, W. F. Wedin, Iowa State Univ.; D. W. Graffis, Univ. of Ill.; L. H. Smith, Purdue Univ.; D. A. Rohweder, Univ. of Wis.; H. N. Wheaton, V. E. Jacobs, Univ. Mo.; D. K. Myers, J. L. Parsons, R. W. Van Keuren, Ohio State Univ.; H. J. Otto, Univ. Minn.; and L. V. Nelson, Mich. State Univ.

available for harvesting, handling, storage, and feeding. Machines and methods will be developed to meet specific needs of pasture renovation, fertilization (especially N), and seedling establishment. Taking inventory of state and regional forage crops by remote sensing for yield and quality may soon become a reality.

Pasture usage will continue to decline in dairying, with continued emphasis on stored and automated feeding systems. Greater use will be made of nonprotein-N with high-energy feeds like corn silage as well as with low-quality crop residues. Beef herd management will emphasize low-cost, year-round forage-animal systems where the cows do most of the harvesting. There will be more emphasis, particularly in the central Corn Belt, on the complementary value of the beef cow for salvaging crop residues, especially corn stover.

❧ QUESTIONS

1. What are the factors responsible for the large number of livestock found in the central and Lake states, which have only 13% of the U.S. farmland area?
2. It is shown that forages furnish approximately 43% of the feed units consumed by livestock in the region. What would happen to the land-use cropping pattern and the population of the different livestock classes if forages furnished 20%? 60%?
3. Discuss why the sharp line of separation exists between the tall-grass prairie and the deciduous forest areas.
4. Explain why there usually are many seeding mixtures recommended for a given state.
5. How do you account for alfalfa being the most seeded legume in the region? Why does alfalfa fit so well into the agricultural pattern of the area?
6. What do you visualize as the future usage and extent of production of red clover, alsike clover, white clover, ladino clover, and crownvetch in the region?
7. Where are lespedeza, birdsfoot trefoil, and sweetclover important? How are they best used in their areas of adaptation in the region?
8. What are the reasons for the large hectarage of Kentucky bluegrass pastures in the region? How can these pastures be improved best?
9. Under what soil and specific use conditions in the region would you recommend timothy? Smooth bromegrass? Orchardgrass? Tall fescue? Reed canarygrass?

SUPPLEMENTAL INFORMATION

When it is economically feasible, there exists a great potential in the north central region to produce relatively higher amounts of forage for ruminants, thereby releasing grain resources for other uses. This can be achieved through increased technology made possible by expanding the existing forage and forage-livestock research programs. Greater emphasis should be placed on research dealing with integrated land-forage-livestock systems.[31]

31. Ewing, S. A., and Gorz, Herman J. (eds.). 1977. Range and forage research needs for red meat production in the north central region. Iowa Agr. Exp. Sta. Bull. 583, or North Central Res. Publ. 247.

DOUGLAS S. CHAMBLEE / *North Carolina State University*

ARTHUR E. SPOONER / *University of Arkansas*

43

HAY AND PASTURE SEEDINGS
FOR THE HUMID SOUTH

⚘

T HE HUMID SOUTH has a relatively high rainfall of 1250 mm or more, with a fairly uniform distribution. The distribution is erratic between years, however, and drought is not uncommon.[1] The growing season in Kentucky ranges from 175 to 200 days, and in Mississippi from 210 to 260. In the lower South mild winters are conducive to year-round grazing. In the upper South little forage is produced in December, January, and February. (See Fig. 43.1.)

The upper South includes all of Kentucky, Virginia, North Carolina, and Tennessee and approximately the northwestern quarter of South Carolina, the northern fourth of Georgia, Alabama, and Mississippi, and the northern third of Arkansas.

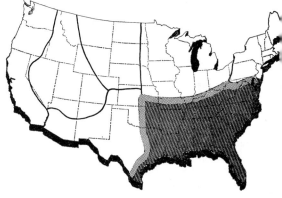

FIG. 43.1. The humid South.

The area below this arbitrary line and a strip along the eastern edge of Oklahoma and Texas will be referred to as the lower South. Six physiographic regions have been described.[2]

The *coastal plain* is a "plainlike" country of sandy soils with an elevation rising from sea level to 180 m. Within the south-

⚘ DOUGLAS S. CHAMBLEE is Professor of Crop Science, North Carolina State University. He holds the M.S. degree from North Carolina State University and the Ph.D. from Iowa State University. His teaching and forage research emphasize adaptation and management problems.

⚘ ARTHUR E. SPOONER is Professor of Crop Science, University of Arkansas. He holds the M.S. degree from Misssssippi State University and the Ph.D. from Purdue University. His area of interest is teaching and research in forage physiology and pasture management.

1. Fribourg, H. A., R. H. Brown, G. M. Prine, and T. H. Taylor. 1967. Aspects of the microclimate at five locations in the southeastern United States. Southern Coop. Ser. Bull. 124.
2. Lovvorn, Roy L. 1948. Grasslands in the south. *In* Grass, pp. 455–58. USDA Yearbook Agr.

ern region it is the low country bordering the Atlantic Ocean and the Gulf of Mexico, extending from the eastern third of Virginia to the mouth of the Rio Grande. The tidewater or flatwoods area of the coastal plain is almost level. Many of these soils have silt loam surface soils and silt loam or silty clay subsoils and contain relatively high amounts of organic matter. If drained, they produce excellent pastures.

The *Piedmont plateau* consists of the area between the Appalachian Mountains and the Atlantic coastal plain. It is a strip through middle Virginia and North Carolina, western South Carolina, and northern Georgia to central Alabama. The elevation ranges from 30 to 455 m. Soils are mostly clays and clay loams.

The *Appalachian province* and the *Cumberland-Allegheny plateau* in the southern area include the western parts of Virginia, North and South Carolina, eastern Kentucky and Tennessee, northwestern Georgia, and northern Alabama.

The *limestone valley* and *uplands* embrace the residual limestone soils north of the Atlantic and Gulf coastal plains and represent the limestone lands of the Appalachian region.

The *Mississippi bluffs* and *loam uplands* are a narrow belt along the east side of the Mississippi River bottoms from western Kentucky to Louisiana. The soils have a brown silt loam surface layer that grades into a yellow brown silt loam subsoil.

The *stream bottom* and *second bottoms* occur throughout the South along the intricate network of the streams. The relatively high rainfall and warm temperatures have contributed to strongly leached soils that are acid in reaction and low in organic matter and mineral plant nutrients.

❧ ADAPTATION AND DISTRIBUTION OF PERENNIAL SPECIES

Perennial forages are the basic pasture plants in the humid South. Cool-season perennial plants adapted in some parts are Kentucky bluegrass, orchardgrass, tall fescue, white clover, red clover, and alfalfa.

Warm-season perennial forages in this area include bermudagrass, dallisgrass, carpetgrass, bahiagrass, johnsongrass, 'Pangola' digitgrass, napiergrass, sericea lespedeza, and kudzu.

Cool-season perennial forages reach their peak production from March 1 to June 1, with a second lesser peak in September and October. Warm-season perennials produce the bulk of their forage between May 1 and September 1. With the onset of freezing weather most of the warm-season perennials turn brown and remain dormant until early spring to midspring.

The adaptation and distribution of forage species in the humid South is considerably influenced by temperature, moisture, diseases and insects, and soil type and fertility.

TEMPERATURE

In the lower South cool-season grasses are seldom grown, with the exception of tall fescue,[3] because of high summer temperatures. In the upper third of the lower South certain warm-season perennials winter-kill, and others are damaged to a lesser extent, particularly in the coastal plain and lower elevations. Sod, even in a dormant condition, has an insulating effect on soil temperature. In the southeastern U.S. freezing temperatures are rarely observed 10.2 cm below the soil surface under sod and only occasionally 2.5 cm below.[1]

In general, temperate species have an optimum temperature for growth around 20 C and will grow in temperatures as low as 5–10 C, while tropical species such as bermudagrass or dallisgrass have growth optimums at 30–35 C and often fail to grow below 15 C.[4] Brown has indicated that orchardgrass and Kentucky bluegrass were severely injured by a continuous air and soil temperature of 38 C.[5] The injury ap-

3. Hoveland, C. S., E. M. Evans, and D. A. Mays. 1970. Cool-season perennial grass species for forage in Alabama. Ala. Agr. Exp. Sta. Bull. 397.

4. Cooper, J. P., and N. M. Tainton. 1968. Light and temperature requirements for the growth of tropical and temperate grasses. *Herb. Abstr.* 38(3):167–76.

5. Brown, E. Marion. 1939. Some effects of temperature on the growth and chemical composition of certain pasture grasses. Mo. Agr. Exp. Sta. Res. Bull. 299

peared to result from high soil temperature rather than high air temperature. When red clover was cultured in the greenhouse at a relatively high temperature (35 C day and 27 C night), approximately 90% of the plants died; whereas the greatest survival occurred at an intermediate temperature, 24 C day and 18 C night.[6]

MOISTURE

The cool-season perennials such as tall fescue and ladino clover will grow in the lower South on the heavier, moister soils, even though growth (particularly of tall fescue) may be checked by the high summer temperatures. In general, irrigation of cool-season perennial grasses in the lower South results in only modest increases in forage yield.[7] Tall fescue, ladino clover, and several other cool-season perennials will not survive on the droughty upland sandy soils of the lower South,[8] nor will they withstand the slightly more limited rainfall conditions of eastern Texas.[9] There, dallisgrass and bermudagrass predominate, along with intermediate white clover. In this area, white clover dies almost every year during the summer but is re-established by volunteering from shattered seed. In eastern Oklahoma, bermudagrass is the principal forage grass.

DISEASES AND INSECTS

In the lower South most of the legumes and cool-season grasses are severely damaged by diseases, nematodes, and other pests. *Rhizoctonia solani* Kuehn is one of the most serious diseases of both cool-season grasses and legumes in this area. In many areas of the upper South, perennial ryegrass and smooth bromegrass are frequently eliminated by *Rhizoctonia,* while tall fescue and orchardgrass are less seriously affected. Rust, *Uromyces dactylidis* Otth., also is a serious problem in the lower South, particularly on orchardgrass.[8]

Increasing difficulty has been experienced in the humid South in maintaining stands of ladino clover for more than three or four years, and intermediate white clovers often behave as reseeding annuals. An entomological-pathological complex has been shown to be the principal causal factor for lack of persistence.[10] Investigators in South Carolina have observed damage to white clover from southern blight and summer dieback, a disease complex incited by soil fungi.[11] Stand losses of white clover may occur in the spring after severe winters.[12] In some areas of the lower South the pygmy cricket, *Nemobius fasciatus* DeGeer, plays an important role in stand loss of new and old seedings of white clover.[13]

SOIL TYPE AND FERTILITY

Soil type and fertility greatly affect the adaptation and distribution of forage species. With the exception of bermudagrass and sericea lespedeza few perennial forages are adapted to upland sandy soils. The tidewater soils with their higher organic content and moisture-holding capacity will often produce more forage than the upland clays or clay loams. The soils are low in fertility and relatively high amounts of fertilizer must be applied for adequate forage production.

❦ PERENNIAL PASTURES AND HAY CROPS—UPPER SOUTH

Cool-season grasses and legumes play a major role in Kentucky, Virginia, Tennessee, North Carolina, and nearby areas. Perennial pasture mixtures of orchardgrass—

6. Kendall, W. A. 1958. The persistence of red clover and carbohydrate concentration in the roots at various temperatures. *Agron. J.* 50:657–59.

7. Hoveland, C. S., and E. M. Evans. 1970. Cool-season perennial grass and grass-clover management. Ala. Agr. Exp. Sta. Circ. 175.

8. Woodle, H. A., and E. C. Turner. 1957. South Carolina pastures. Clemson Agr. Coll. and USDA Ext. Serv. Bull. 115.

9. Holt, E. C., P. R. Johnson, Mark Buckingham. H. C. Hutson, J. K. Crouch, and J. R. Wood. 1958. Pasture, hay, and silage crops for east Texas. Tex. Agr. Exp. Sta. Bull. 893.

10. Blake, Carl T., D. S. Chamblee, and W. W. Woodhouse, Jr. 1966. Influence of some environmental and management factors on the persistence of ladino clover in association with orchardgrass. *Agron. J.* 58:487–89.

11. Halpin, J. E., P. B. Gibson, and G. Beinhart. 1963. Selection and evaluation of white clover clones. II. The role of midsummer diseases. *Crop Sci.* 3:87–89.

12. Gibson, Pryce B., and E. A. Hollowell. 1966. White clover. USDA Agr. Handbook 314.

13. Evans, E. M., Max Bass, L. A. Smith, and H. W. Grimes. 1965. Pygmy crickets—Guilty of damaging white clover. Ala. Agr. Exp. Sta. Highlights of Agr. Res., vol. 12, no. 2.

ladino clover, tall fescue–ladino clover, orchardgrass-alfalfa, Kentucky bluegrass–white clover, or pure sods of these grass species constitute the main perennial species utilized for forage. Mixtures of smooth bromegrass with various legumes are grown on soils with good drainage in northern Arkansas and to a limited extent in Kentucky.[14] Crownvetch is being evaluated and in a two-year trial was found acceptable in beef cattle performance.[15]

In the mountains, upper Piedmont, and other high and cool sections the most prevalent pasture mixture is Kentucky bluegrass–white clover. Many of these pastures are being replaced by more productive, tall-growing mixtures such as orchardgrass-ladino, tall fescue–ladino, or grass-alfalfa.

On the steeper slopes and shallower soils in parts of the mountain area, ladino clover frequently survives for only two or three years. The reason for the loss of stands in this area is not known. In Kentucky under a management program that permitted natural reseeding for a few years, birdsfoot trefoil has shown promise for improving Kentucky bluegrass pasture production.[16]

Kentucky bluegrass–white clover pastures are referred to as permanent pasture since they are seldom renovated. Other mixtures such as orchardgrass-ladino are considered cropland pasture since they generally become less productive in three to five years and are rotated with harvested crops for a year or two before reestablishment.

In the cooler sections of the upper South alfalfa frequently is added to orchardgrass-ladino or tall fescue–ladino mixtures to obtain extra silage or possibly for grazing the first year or two.[17,18] Red clover usually is substituted for alfalfa on moderately to poorly drained soils.

PRODUCTION CAPACITY

ORCHARDGRASS-LADINO AND TALL FESCUE–LADINO. In the upper South orchardgrass-ladino and tall fescue–ladino mixtures give approximately equal amounts of dry forage on soils where adapted.[19,20] Under average conditions they will produce 5.6–6.7 t/ha of dry forage annually.[19] Typically, they produce 60% or more of the total season's production by June 15 (Fig. 43.2). To provide a more uniform supply of feed throughout the season, a silage cut should be made on at least a portion of the ladino-grass pasture. As much as 13.5 t/ha of silage may be harvested in one cut from a ladino-grass pasture in the spring. Tall fescue is usually more competitive with legumes than orchardgrass.[20]

Mixtures of orchardgrass-ladino and tall fescue–ladino produced approximately equal livestock gains in northern Virginia grazing trials (Table 43.1).[21] In another study an average yearly production of about 2912 kg/ha of total digestible nutrients (TDN) were harvested by the animals on each of the ladino-grass mixtures.[22] Lower daily liveweight animal gains have been obtained from grazing tall fescue alone than from orchardgrass.[21,23]

Beef cattle generally graze tall fescue–ladino uniformly. Dairy cows, however, tend to graze ladino clover selectively in preference to tall fescue. In Kentucky, lactating cows averaged in persistency of milk production over a three-year period (for the fourth week as compared with the week prior to the test period) 98.3% on orchardgrass-ladino, 89.3% on tall fescue–ladino, and 81.4% on pure tall fescue which had

14. Wellhausen, Harry W. 1968. Orchardgrass and Southland bromegrass for north Arkansas. Ark. Agr. Exp. Sta. Leaflet 360.
15. Burns, J. C., W. A. Cope, L. Goode, R. W. Harvey, and H. D. Gross. 1969. Evaluation of crownvetch (*Coronilla varia* L.) by performance of beef cattle. *Agron. J.* 61:480–81.
16. Templeton, W. C., Jr., C. F. Buck, and D. W. Wattenbarger. 1967. Persistence of birdsfoot trefoil under pasture conditions. *Agron. J.* 59:385–86.
17. White, Harlan E. 1968. Forages for year-round feeding. Va. Ext. Div. Publ. 156.
18. Seath, D. M., W. C. Templeton, Jr., D. R. Jacobson, Wm. M. Miller, and T. H. Taylor. 1962. Grazing comparisons of two alfalfa-grass–ladino clover mixtures for dairy cows. Ky. Agr. Exp. Sta. Bull. 674.

19. Chamblee, Douglas S. 1960. Adaptation and performance of forage species. N.C. Agr. Exp. Sta. Bull. 411.
20. Templeton, W. C., Jr., T. H. Taylor, and J. R. Todd. 1965. Comparative ecological and agronomic behavior of orchardgrass and tall fescue. Ky. Agr. Exp. Sta. Bull. 699.
21. Virginia Polytech. Inst. 1969. Managing forages for animal production. Res. Div. Bull. 45.
22. Woodhouse, W. W., Jr., J. L. Moore, R. K. Waugh, and H. L. Lucas. 1954. Ladino-orchardgrass and ladino-tall fescue for dairy heifers. N.C. State Coll. Rept. AI-19, DH 10, Agron. 11.
23. Davis, A. M. 1959. Pastures and pasture production in north central Arkansas. Ark. Agr. Exp. Sta. Bull. 607.

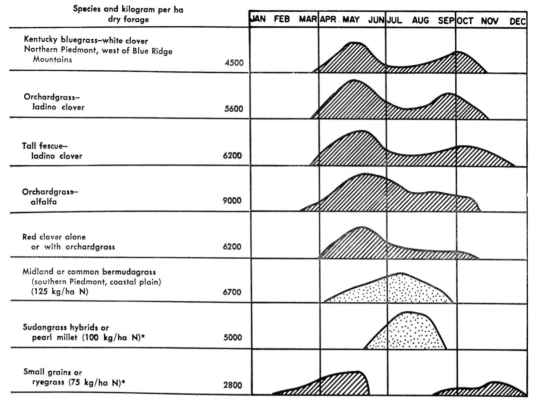

Species and kilogram per ha dry forage		JAN	FEB	MAR	APR	MAY	JUN	JUL	AUG	SEP	OCT	NOV	DEC

Kentucky bluegrass–white clover
Northern Piedmont, west of Blue Ridge
Mountains — 4500

Orchardgrass–
ladino clover — 5600

Tall fescue–
ladino clover — 6200

Orchardgrass–
alfalfa — 9000

Red clover alone
or with orchardgrass — 6200

Midland or common bermudagrass
(southern Piedmont, coastal plain)
(125 kg/ha N) — 6700

Sudangrass hybrids or
pearl millet (100 kg/ha N)* — 5000

Small grains or
ryegrass (75 kg/ha N)* — 2800

Note: Data and estimates for Virginia by R. E. Blaser.
* Higher yields may be obtained when grown for silage or green chop; above assumed grazing management.

FIG. 43.2.   Relative productivity of several forages used in the northern part of the South. All crops are assumed to be limed, fertilized, and topdressed with N as indicated.

been topdressed with 224 kg/ha of N.[24] Excellent stands of ladino clover were maintained with orchardgrass, whereas stands were greatly reduced by the third year in the tall fescue–ladino pastures. In related studies the dry matter intake per 454 kg of body weight by lactating cows grazing orchardgrass and tall fescue was 10.3 and 9.1 kg/day respectively.[25]

Ladino clover–grass mixtures have proved far superior to intermediate white clover–grass mixtures throughout most of the upper South (Fig. 43.3).[19,26] The heavier blooming intermediate white clovers are not as drought resistant as the sparser blooming ladino. Intense two to three week droughts frequently eliminate them.[19] Ladino usually survives the average drought in the upper South. Even when stands occasionally are lost by drought, ladino produces enough seed to volunteer. This is not the case under the shorter day of the lower South where ladino flowers even more sparsely. South Carolina studies have shown that profusely flowering white clover strains tend to be less persistent.[26]

24. Seath, Dwight M., C. A. Lassiter, G. M. Bastin, and R. F. Elliott. 1954. Effect of kind of pasture on the yield of TDN and on persistency of milk production of milk cows. Ky. Agr. Exp. Sta. Bull. 609.

25. Lassiter, C. A., D. M. Seath, J. W. Woodruff, J. A. Taylor, and J. W. Rust. 1956. Comparative value of Kentucky bluegrass, Kentucky 31 fescue, orchardgrass, and bromegrass as pasture for milk cows. J. Dairy Sci. 5:581–88.

26. Gibson, Pryce B. 1957. Effect of flowering on the persistence of white clover. Agron. J. 49:213–15.

TABLE 43.1 ❧ Steer-days and liveweight gains for various grass-legume mixtures compared with pure grass pasture, 1951–60, Middleburg, Va. (northern Piedmont area)

Pasture	Steer-days per ha	Liveweight gains (kg)	
		Per steer/ day	Per ha
Orchardgrass–ladino clover	635	0.58	368
Orchardgrass– no clover*	768	0.49	373
Tall fescue– ladino clover	749	0.46	346
Tall fescue– no clover*	996	0.41	411
Kentucky bluegrass– white clover	638	0.55	349

Source: Virginia Polytech. Inst. Research Division, 1969.[21]
* Pure stands of grass topdressed each year with 224 kg/ha of N split into three or four applications. All pastures received fertilizer and lime at seeding and P and K annually.

ALFALFA-GRASS. The acreage of alfalfa and alfalfa-grass mixtures has declined rapidly in the upper South in recent years because of severe larvae damage of the alfalfa weevil.[27] Alfalfa is primarily harvested for hay, haylage, or silage. Alfalfa-grass mixtures are also used for grazing. A recommended practice is cutting the first growth for silage, then alternating the next three regrowths between grazing and hay.

Yields ranging from 6.7 to 9 t/ha of dry forage are produced from three to four cuts each year. Alfalfa and alfalfa-grass mixtures will yield 9–13.5 t/ha of silage wilted to 70% moisture at the first harvest.[28]

WARM-SEASON PERENNIALS. In the southern half of the upper South, warm-season perennials play an important forage role, particularly bermudagrass and dallisgrass in various legume combinations such as ladino, intermediate white clover, and annual lespedezas and also alone. They are particularly useful for grazing during the hot midsummer.

The use of many warm-season perennial grasses is limited in the upper South by the short growing season and lack of cold tolerance. In the southeastern sandhill area of North Carolina 'Pensacola' and 'Tifhi' bahiagrass and 'Suwannee' bermudagrass suffered 20–40% loss of stand from winter injury each year over a four-year period. In the fifth year they were essentially eliminated when the air temperature reached approximately —12 C;[26] however, 'Coastal' bermudagrass was damaged but quickly recovered and averaged 9 t/ha of dry forage for the five-year period. Coastal and dallisgrass usually survive the winter at the lower elevations in Tennessee, North Carolina, and the coastal plain area of Virginia. In this area dallisgrass has been largely replaced in pastures by tall fescue. Tall fescue is more easily established and grows over a much longer period than dallisgrass. In early spring in the upper South, when clover is making its maximum growth, dallisgrass is essentially dormant.

In the sandhill area of southeastern North Carolina, common and Coastal bermudagrass and sericea lespedeza are practically the only adapted grasses and legume.

27. White, H. E. 1968. Alfalfa production in Virginia. Va. Coop. Ext. Div. Publ. 146.

FIG. 43.3 *Ladino usually survives . . . drought . . . produces enough seed to volunteer.* Ladino clover (left) is probably the most used pasture legume in the upper South. The heavier blooming, volunteering type, intermediate white clover (right), predominates in the lower South.

28. Burns, Joe D. 1969. Silage production in Tennessee. Tenn. Agr. Ext. Serv. EC 548.

CULTURAL PRACTICES

TIME OF SEEDING. In most of Kentucky and parts of Virginia and at higher elevations in other states, best results come from seeding most cool-season perennials in the early spring. However, in most of the humid South they are preferably seeded in the late summer or fall, with less dependable results from late winter or early spring seeding. Late summer or fall seedings of cool-season perennials are often too early or too late for optimum stand establishment.[29] Most cool-season forages are fall seeded in areas of frequent summer droughts.

Certain seedling characteristics may be used for determining the best seeding date and rate. Alfalfa is preferably seeded in late summer or fall since seedlings develop faster in late summer than in the spring. Red clover seedling growth is in reverse and should be seeded in early spring.[30,31] Red clover seedlings seriously suppress those of alfalfa when they are seeded together in the spring.

In Virginia, orchardgrass and tall fescue develop and establish more quickly than Kentucky bluegrass, and alfalfa does so more rapidly than ladino or birdsfoot trefoil. Since birdsfoot develops slowly in the seedling stage, low rates of the companion grass are seeded.

RENOVATION. Keeping legumes in a grass-legume mixture is a major grassland problem in many areas of the upper South. Legumes such as ladino clover can be successfully established in grass-dominant sods without plowing.[32,33] Approximately 50% of the grass should be destroyed or disturbed before seeding with a legume.[33,34] Precision placement of seed below the soil surface (1.2 cm for alfalfa and 0.6 cm for white clover) is the most consistent factor contributing to successful legume establishment in a grass sod.[34]

COMPANION CROPS. Seeding pasture crops with small grain is considered a wise practice on steep land in Kentucky and other nearby areas.[35] The small grain checks development of weeds, protects the soil against erosion, and reduces winter damage to the pasture crops. A companion crop may be beneficial to the seedlings but is strongly competitive later in the season. Consequently, the companion crop is grazed or clipped to reduce competition. In most of the humid South companion crops are not used with pasture seedings due to excessive competition.

❧ PERENNIAL PASTURES AND HAY CROPS—LOWER SOUTH

In the lower South warm-season grasses and legumes are the dominant species. Bermudagrass, dallisgrass, bahiagrass, and johnsongrass are the basic grasses. White clovers and lespedeza are the basic legumes; however, many ha of warm-season grasses are overseeded with one of the annual reseeding clovers. The intermediate white clovers are widely utilized since they produce more seed than ladino and will volunteer readily. This is extremely important since much white clover comes from seed each year rather than from the old rootstock. Pangola digitgrass is an important warm-season forage in Florida.[36] Carpetgrass has limited use for pasture where little or no fertilizer is applied.

Cool-season perennial grasses such as orchardgrass, Kentucky bluegrass and

29. Stephens, R. L., and M. W. Jutras. 1968. The effect of planting date, nitrogen rates, and temperature on seedling vigor of Kentucky 31 fescue. S.C. Agr. Exp. Sta. Circ. 157.

30. Blaser, R. E., W. L. Griffeth, and T. H. Taylor. 1956. Seedling competition in compounding forage seed mixtures. Agron. J. 48:118–23.

31. Blaser, R. E., Timothy Taylor, Walter Griffeth, and Willis Skrdla. 1956. Seedling competition in established forage plants. Agron. J. 48:1–6.

32. Burns, Joe D. 1969. Renovate grass pastures. Tenn. Agr. Ext. Serv. EC 714.

33. Thompson, Warren C., Timothy H. Taylor, and William C. Templeton, Jr. 1970. Renovating grass fields. Ky. Agr. Ext. Serv. Leaflet 277.

34. Taylor, T. H., E. M. Smith, and W. C. Templeton, Jr. 1969. Use of minimum tillage and herbicide for establishing legumes in Kentucky bluegrass (Poa pratensis L.) swards. Agron. J. 61:761–66.

35. University of Kentucky. 1954. Pastures in Kentucky. Circ. 510, rev.

36. Hodges, E. M., G. B. Killinger, J. E. McCaleb, O. C. Ruelke, R. J. Allen, Jr., S. C. Schank, and A. E. Kretschmer, Jr. 1971. Pangolagrass. Fla. Agr. Exp. Sta. Bull. 718.

FIG. 43.4. *Management . . . extremely important in maintaining a stand.* In the lower South, cool-season forages such as tall fescue (foreground) or tall fescue–white clover (background) provide grazing during the cooler periods, while bermudagrass (center) may be used during midsummer. Photo in early November.

smooth bromegrass, are not well adapted to the lower South. Tall fescue is used alone and with legumes, especially on the moister, more fertile soils and on soils having a clay pan or clay layer underneath a sand layer. Management under this condition is extremely important in maintaining a stand.

In general, mixtures of dallisgrass–white clover, tall fescue–white clover, and bahiagrass–white clover are especially well adapted to the moister soils; whereas the bermudagrasses and lespedezas are best adapted to the well-drained, deep, drier soils. (See Fig. 43.4.) Coastal is extremely well adapted to the deep sands where rooting depth is not restricted. Alfalfa is an important hay crop and is best adapted to the deep, well-drained, fertile soils.

Johnsongrass is used primarily as a hay crop in much of the lower South. It is best adapted to the prairie blackland soils of Alabama, Mississippi, Arkansas, and east Texas and to the better drained creek bottom soils. Alfalfa, red clover, white clover, and annual 'Kobe' lespedeza are grown with johnsongrass.

The interseeding of tall fescue into a bermudagrass sod for year-round pasture is receiving much attention. Before this practice can be recommended for general use by the farmer, proper fertilization and grazing management practices must be determined.

PRODUCTION CAPACITY

HYBRID BERMUDAGRASS ALONE AND IN MIXTURES.
The hybrid bermudagrasses, Coastal, 'Coastcross,' and 'Midland,' can be used for both grazing and hay. They are used primarily in pure stands, or with sericea lespedeza for both grazing and hay on the upland sandy soils of the lower South. Yields of 10–16 t/ha of dry forage or 500–700 kg/ha of beef are being produced when stands are fertilized with sufficient N and other nutrients. Yields are largely dependent upon the distribution of rainfall during the growing season. Good fertilization practices tend to overcome many of the deleterious effects of short drought periods.[37,38] Expected seasonal dry matter yields under average conditions of various forages grown in the lower South are presented in Figure 43.5.

Since there are no dependable perennial legumes for many soil conditions, arrowleaf clovers often are seeded in mixtures with annual ryegrass in a hybrid bermudagrass sod in the fall of the year. A major problem in maintaining stands of annual clovers is their inability to reseed annually. Arrowleaf clover normally reseeds better than

37. Hoveland, C. S., C. C. King, E. M. Evans, R. R. Harris, and W. B. Anthony. 1971. Bermudagrass for forage in Alabama. Ala. Agr. Exp. Sta. Bull. 328, rev.
38. Beaty, E. R., J. D. Powell, and J. H. Edwards, Jr. 1969. Forage and animal gains of Coastal bermudagrass and Pensacola bahiagrass. *J. Range Manage.* 22:318-21.

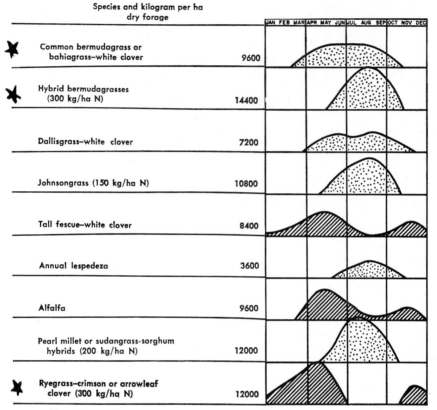

Note: Data and estimates by C. S. Hoveland, Alabama; H. W. Bennett, Mississippi; and A. E. Spooner, Arkansas.

Fig. 43.5. Relative production of several forages utilized in the lower South. Crops are assumed limed, fertilized, and topdressed with N as indicated. (Data and estimates by C. S. Hoveland, Alabama; H. W. Bennett, Mississippi; and A. E. Spooner, Arkansas.)

crimson clover. Beef gains of 400 kg/ha can be expected from annual ryegrass–arrowleaf clover on bermudagrass sod under average to good growing conditions.[39] Extreme damage to hybrid bermudagrass can result when ryegrass and clover are not properly grazed or mowed in the spring. The forage must be removed before the bermudagrass starts growth. Data in Table 43.2 show the beneficial effects that may result from seeding legumes with Coastal.[37,40]

Many grazing and clipping studies have been conducted comparing the bermudagrass hybrids with common bermudagrass, dallisgrass, and bahiagrass. In general, the results have shown the bermudagrass hybrids to be superior in production; however, results have been variable depending on soil type, fertilization practices, and methods of utilization (Table 43.3). Hybrids are normally expected to produce more than common at high N rates. This difference in production diminishes at medium to low rates of N.[37,41]

COMMON BERMUDAGRASS, DALLISGRASS, BA-

39. Anthony, W. B., C. S. Hoveland, E. L. Mayton, and H. E. Burgess. 1971. Rye-ryegrass-Yuchi arrowleaf clover for production of slaughter cattle. Ala. Agr. Exp. Sta. Circ. 182.

40. Hogg, P. G. 1965. Effect of legumes and nitrogen fertilizer on yield of cultivated *Cynodon* (Coastal bermudagrass) pastures in southern U.S.A. Proc. 9th Int. Grassl. Congr., pp. 1099–1101 (São Paulo, Brazil).

41. Spooner, A. E., and Maurice L. Ray. 1969. Pasture fertilization and grazing management studies in southwest Arkansas. Ark. Agr. Exp. Sta. Bull. 741.

TABLE 43.2 ❦ Yields and animal gains from Coastal bermudagrass in pure stand and with legumes at two locations

Species	Alabama[37] (kg/ha oven dry matter)		Mississippi[40]	
	No N	224 kg/ha N	Beef gains (kg/ha)	Daily gain (kg)
Coastal bermudagrass	2,542	9,452	...	...
Coastal + crimson clover	7,425	13,350	...	...
Coastal + woollypod vetch	7,157	13,025	...	...
Coastal + 134 kg/ha N	...	...	316	0.44
Coastal + white clover (no N)	...	...	579	0.64

TABLE 43.3 ❦ Steer gains from various warm-season perennial grasses at different N levels at two locations

Nitrogen treatment* (kg/ha)	Beef gains (kg/ha)		
	Common bermuda-grass	Coastal bermuda-grass	Pensacola bahia-grass
Georgia 1958–60[44]			
112	373	419	412
224	629	827	603
448	836	1,023	783
Arkansas 1963–66[41]			
67	347	332	...
242	535	505	...
672	750	829	...

* Adequate levels of P and K were applied.

HIAGRASS, JOHNSONGRASS, PANGOLA DIGIT-GRASS, AND TALL FESCUE. These grasses, except Pangola digitgrass, are widely used in the lower South. Common bermudagrass and bahiagrass usually are seeded on the sandier soils. Dallisgrass, johnsongrass, and tall fescue are seeded on heavy creek bottom and blackland soils of Alabama, Mississippi, Arkansas, and eastern Texas.[42] Bahiagrass and Pangola digitgrass are the predominant grass species in Florida with about 200,000 ha of each.[36]

Legumes such as white clovers and annual lespedezas are normally seeded with these grasses to provide N and to improve forage quality. The legumes lengthen the grazing season and increase the beef gains or forage production.

Dallisgrass usually is grown with a legume, but legume stands sometimes are lost due to drought and poor grazing management practices. In the Black Belt of Alabama, topdressing dallisgrass pasture with 50–100 kg/ha of N annually is recommended, plus adequate mineral fertilizer and lime, until productive stands of white clover can be reestablished. An annual average production of 180, 290, 325, and 360 kg/ha of beef was obtained over a five-year period when 0, 45, 90, and 112 kg/ha of N respectively were applied annually as a topdressing.[43]

In a four-year Arkansas study, primarily on a Boswell fine sandy loam, Coastal and common bermudagrass were compared at three fertilizer levels on beef produced per ha (Table 43.3).[41,44] Differences in beef gains were slight at the 67 kg/ha of N rate; however, a 79 kg/ha difference in beef production was obtained at the 672 N rate in favor of Coastal. These higher gains of Coastal over common were due to greater forage production rather than to higher forage quality.[41] Daily gains of about 0.5 kg/head were obtained from Coastal and common under the various fertilizer levels. Somewhat different results were obtained in Georgia when common, Coastal, and bahiagrass were compared at different N levels (Table 43.3). The location differences obtained in the lower South are due primarily to soil and climatic conditions. Many soils of the coastal plains have a clay layer near the surface. This layer prevents Coastal from rooting to its normal depths, which limits its production. In deep sandy soil areas where Coastal is grown, unlimited rooting depth is provided. On these soils

42. Hoveland, C. S. 1968. Bahiagrass for forage in Alabama. Ala. Agr. Exp. Sta. Circ. 140.

43. Evans, E. M., L. A. Smith, and H. W. Grimes. 1959. Nitrogen for dallisgrass pastures in the Black Belt. Ala. Agr. Exp. Sta. Circ. 136.
44. Suman, R. F., S. G. Woods, T. C. Peele, and E. G. Godby. 1962. Beef gains from differentially fertilized summer grasses in the coastal plain. *Agron. J.* 54:26–28.

Coastal bermudagrass is superior to common, bahiagrass, and dallisgrass.[42]

Both Pensacola bahiagrass and Pangola digitgrass are widely used for pasture in Florida. When fertilized with 200-22-83 kg/ha of N-P-K, these grasses produced about 8 t/ha of dry matter or 370 kg/ha of beef gains. Pangola outyielded Pensacola bahiagrass at the higher N levels.[45,46]

Yields of 8–14 t/ha or more have been produced by proper management of johnsongrass. Stand maintenance is a major problem; however, this can be accomplished by proper fertilization, especially with N, and cutting management. Johnsongrass produces excellent quality forage which is equivalent to alfalfa in TDN.[47,48]

Tall fescue is used extensively throughout most of the lower South and is usually seeded with white clover on fertile, deep bottomland soils. Yields of 8–14 t/ha of dry matter result from high N rates on tall fescue. It must be allowed to rest during the summer to obtain good production in fall, winter, and spring but withstands heavy grazing pressures when rest periods are provided between defoliations. Tall fescue and white clover, an excellent combination, can be used in conjunction with bermudagrass, dallisgrass, or bahiagrass in a cow-calf program.[3,49]

LEGUME AND LEGUME-GRASS PASTURES. Legume-grass pastures will produce 335–450 kg/ha or more of beef gains in the lower South when properly fertilized and managed. An average of 400 and 520 kg/ha of beef gains were obtained from a bermudagrass–white clover pasture in southern Arkansas.[41,50]

Tall fescue–white clover makes an excellent pasture. Fertilization is extremely important, and proper ratios and amounts of P and K are essential in maintaining stands. Excellent animal gains and growth are obtained from this combination under good management.[29,49]

Sericea lespedeza is used extensively in Alabama. Beef-calf gains over a four-year period were 202, 202, 200, and 150 kg/ha for Coastal with 168 kg/ha of N, Coastal with 112 kg/ha of N, and 'Serala' sericea and 'Goar' tall fescue with 112 kg/ha of N respectively. Sericea grows on a wide range of soils but is most useful on upland sandy soils where few forage legumes are adapted.[51]

Several other legumes are seeded with perennial grasses under specific soil conditions. See the individual legume chapters for their area of adaptation, management, and yield potentials.

CULTURAL PRACTICES

TIME OF ESTABLISHMENT. Except for the extreme lower South, the warm-season perennials must be seeded in late winter or spring. If seeded in the fall, they either fail to germinate because of drought or are killed by the first freeze if in the seedling stage. Bermudagrass hybrids are propagated vegetatively by sprigging during late winter and spring. They can be sprigged in summer if water is available or the soil is moist at planting time. Preferably, most forage legumes except lespedeza and soybeans are fall seeded.

SOD-SEEDING. A large hectarage of warm-season perennial grass sods in much of the lower South is sod-seeded to winter annual grasses and legumes each fall.

45. Wallace, A. T., G. B. Killinger, R. W. Bledsoe, and D. B. Duncan. 1957. Design, analysis and results of an experiment on response of pangolagrass and Pensacola bahiagrass to time, rate, and source of nitrogen. Fla. Agr. Exp. Sta. Bull. 581.

46. Koger, M., W. G. Blue, G. B. Killinger, R. E. L. Green, J. M. Myers, N. Gammon, Jr., A. C. Warnick, and J. R. Crockett. 1970. Production response and economic returns from five pasture programs in north central Florida. Fla. Agr. Exp. Sta. Tech. Bull. 740.

47. Spooner, A. E., Will R. Jeffery, and Herbert J. Huneycutt. 1971. Effects of management practices on johnsongrass for hay production. Ark. Agr. Exp. Sta. Bull. 769.

48. Smith, L. A., H. W. Grimes, J. A. Little, and G. E. Hawkins. 1966. Sorghum-sudan hybrid vs. johnsongrass pasture for dairy cows. Ala. Agr. Exp. Sta. Circ. 151.

49. Ray, Maurice L., and A. E. Spooner. 1969. Cow and calf nutrition and management under different grazing pressures. Ark. Agr. Exp. Sta. Bull. 749.

50. Spooner, A. E., and Maurice L. Ray. 1966. Steer gains on bermudagrass pastures in eastern Arkansas. Ark. Agr. Exp. Sta. Rept. Ser. 150.

51. Hoveland, C. S., W. B. Anthony, R. R. Harris, E. L. Mayton, and H. E. Burgess. 1969. Serala sericea, Coastal bermuda, Goar tall fescue grazing for beef cows and calves in Alabama's Piedmont. Ala. Agr. Exp. Sta. Bull. 388.

A real problem related to sod-seeding is lack of rainfall at seeding time and during germination and growth. Annual ryegrass, small grains, and crimson and arrowleaf clovers are the most widely used forages for over-seeding. The warm-season perennial grass must be grazed or mowed closely immediately before sod-seeding to prevent excessive competition. Sod-seeded grasses and legumes must be grazed or mowed closely in the spring to prevent damage to the warm-season grass. Beef gains of 250–400 kg/ha have resulted from this program. Yields have been low in many trials on sod-seeded small grains primarily because of the lack of fall and early winter grazing caused by insufficient moisture.[52-55] Further research is needed on this practice before it can be recommended.

❧ ANNUAL SUMMER PASTURES

The summer annual plants most frequently used in the humid South are the annual lespedezas, soybeans, sorghum-sudangrass hybrids, and millets. The sorghum-sudangrass hybrids and newer pearlmillet cultivars have gained widespread farmer acceptance for grazing and green chop.[56] Alyceclover and hairy indigo are used to a limited extent in the extreme southern portion. Most summer annuals are seeded from April 15 to July 1 with the exception of the annual lespedezas which generally are seeded between February 1 and April 1.

MILLET, SORGHUM-SUDANGRASS HYBRIDS, AND SOYBEANS

Millet and sorghum-sudangrass hybrids, alone and in mixture with soybeans, are widely used for grazing, silage, and hay. They frequently are grown on the same land following winter annuals. The leading farmers are using more pearlmillet and sorghum-sudangrass in rotation with semi-permanent pastures that are renovated every five to six years. They are excellent forages to utilize the buildup of N in old pasture sods. They also break disease and insect cycles and reduce prevalence of weeds and other undesirable species. When pearlmillet is properly managed, 6.7–9 t/ha of dry forage can be produced annually (Fig. 43.5). In some areas of Alabama, studies have shown that sorghum-sudangrass may not be suited for growing-out steers, due to the large fluctuation in forage growth caused by variable soil moisture.[57]

Pearlmillet has frequently proved superior to most sorghum-sudangrass hybrids on many of the upland sandy soils of the southeast coastal plain.[19,58] However, on clay loams the dry matter yields were practically equal.[19] 'Starr' millet is a leafier cultivar than common pearlmillet; therefore, it is equal or slightly superior for grazing. It usually produces less dry matter.[59] It has been suggested that these species be planted at two-week intervals, until three or four plantings have been made, to permit better distribution of growth.[60]

ANNUAL LESPEDEZA

The annual lespedezas are used throughout the area for hay and grazing. They are often seeded in small grains in late winter and grazed or cut for hay in midsummer to late summer after grain is removed. Typical hay yields range from 2.2 to 5.6 t/ha. Higher N fertilization of small grains has increased stand failures of lespedeza grown with the grains, and the hectarage seeded to annual lespedeza has been drastically re-

52. Elder, W. C. 1967. Winter grazing small grains in Oklahoma. Okla. Agr. Exp. Sta. Bull. B-654.
53. Dudley, R. F., and L. N. Wise. 1953. Seeding in permanent pasture for supplementary winter grazing. Miss. Agr. Exp. Sta. Bull. 505.
54. Brock, W. A., W. W. Kilby, and C. L. Blount. 1968. Wintering beef cows in south Mississippi. Miss. Agr. Exp. Sta. Bull. 758.
55. Harris, R. R., W. B. Anthony, V. L. Brown, J. K. Boseck, H. F. Yates, W. B. Webster, and J. E. Barrett, Jr. 1971. Cool-season annual grazing crops for stocker calves. Ala. Agr. Exp. Sta. Bull. 416.
56. Loden, Harold. 1965. The challenge of sorghum-sudangrass hybrids. *Seedsmen Digest*, vol. 16, no. 2.

57. Hoveland, C. S., R. R. Harris, J. K. Boseck, and W. B. Webster. 1971. Supplementation of steers grazing sorghum-sudan pasture. Ala. Agr. Exp. Sta. Circ. 188.
58. Dunavin, L. S. 1970. Gahi-1 pearl millet and two sorghum × sudangrass hybrids as pasture for yearling beef cattle. *Agron. J.* 62:375–77.
59. Gross, H. Douglass, Beach F. Hollon, R. D. Mochrie, and W. W. Woodhouse, Jr. 1957. Millet for summer grazing. N.C. Agr. Exp. Sta. Rept. FC-5, AI-28, DH-15.
60. Monroe, W. E. 1969. Pastures pay with summer annuals. La. Agr. Ext. Publ. 1571.

duced in some areas. Stands and growth of lespedeza are also reduced when grown with summer grasses well fertilized with N. Nematode damage has caused a reduction in the hectarage of annual lespedeza on sandy soils.

❧ ANNUAL WINTER PASTURES

Annuals for winter grazing, silage, and hay are an important part of the forage program in the humid South (Figs. 43.2, 43.5). The winter small grains, annual ryegrasses, crimson clover, and arrowleaf clover, alone or in mixtures, are used for late fall, winter, and spring grazing. Most of the winter annual forages must be seeded each year in late summer or fall. Reseeding winter annuals like crimson clover, arrowleaf clover, and annual ryegrass produce volunteer stands under favorable management and environmental conditions. In the upper South less growth is produced in the fall and winter than in the lower South where excellent forage production is obtained if rainfall is adequate for germination and growth (Table 43.4).[61]

SMALL GRAINS, RYEGRASS, AND MIXTURES

Generally, winter small grains and crimson clover or arrowleaf clover have been more productive grown in combination than when grown alone. When properly fertilized, 5–8 t/ha of dry forage can be produced from these combinations. Seedings of oats and annual ryegrass have been used to winter beef cows in southern Mississippi. The cows were put on pasture to calve and left there 126 days. The average daily calf gains were 1.02 kg on oats-ryegrass as compared with 0.55 kg on hay and cottonseed meal.[54]

At two locations in southern Alabama stocker beef steers weighing 500–560 kg gained an average of 0.68 kg daily while grazing small grain–crimson clover pastures with supplement as needed. Average gain per animal was 314 kg from October to

TABLE 43.4 ❧ Seasonal forage production of annual winter mixtures, central Alabama, 1965–67

Mixture	Kilograms per ha dry forage			
	Sept.–Dec.	Jan.–Mar.	Apr.–May	Total
Rescuegrass–arrowleaf clover	734	2,648	5,789	9,171
Rescuegrass–crimson clover	631	2,503	5,397	8,531
Rye–arrowleaf clover	1,872	3,436	3,177	8,485
Rye–ryegrass–arrowleaf clover	1,617	3,489	2,815	7,921
Rye–ryegrass–crimson clover	1,789	3,615	2,205	7,609
Rye–crimson clover	2,008	3,705	840	6,553

Source: Hoveland et al., 1967.[61]
Note: 23 to 36 kg/ha N applied in the fall with P and K adequate.

May. Supplemental feed was not required in seven of nine years in one Gulf Coast area test.[55]

Annual ryegrass is used throughout the lower South. It normally is seeded with crimson or arrowleaf clover on a warm-season perennial grass sod. Excellent gains have been obtained from this combination when rainfall has been adequate in late summer and fall. Ryegrass is used extensively in Louisiana to graze beef calves and yearlings in preparation for feeding for slaughter.[62,63] Similar work has been conducted in Alabama using rye-ryegrass–arrowleaf clover for producing slaughter cattle. This combination produced 580 kg/ha of beef gains.[4] Winter annual grasses can be used successfully for wintering beef cattle provided ample fertilizer and management practices are used.

WINTER ANNUAL LEGUMES

The two winter annual legumes used most for forage production in the South are

61. Hoveland, C. S., F. T. Glaze, F. W. Richardson, J. W. Langford, and F. E. Bertram. 1967. Annual grass-clover mixtures for winter grazing. Auburn Univ. Agr. Exp. Sta. Highlights of Agr. Res. 14 (3):12.

62. Roark, C. B., H. E. Harris, and J. I. Feazel. 1966. Winter pastures for fattening feeder calves in the upland area of west Louisiana. La. Agr. Exp. Sta. Bull. 609.
63. Carpenter, J. C., R. H. Klett, and Sherman Phillips. 1969. Producing slaughter steers with temporary grazing crops and concentrates. La. Agr. Exp. Sta. Bull. 643.

crimson and arrowleaf clovers. Arrowleaf clover will normally provide two months longer grazing than crimson in Alabama; it is drought tolerant, has a high percentage of hard seed for reseeding, and has excellent insect and disease resistance.[64]

Hairy vetch and lupines are widely used in the lower South primarily as a green manure crop; however, limited use has been made of these for grazing and hay production.

ESTABLISHMENT PROBLEMS

Early fall or winter growth is an important consideration when winter annuals are used for grazing. For early and maximum growth, winter annuals must be seeded in late summer or early fall and properly fertilized. Double seeding rates of small grain are used compared with grain production usage. Marked advantages also have been demonstrated for relatively heavy seeding rates of certain forage legumes. In these studies dense stands produced earlier fall and winter growth than thin stands.[65]

Erratic rainfall distribution and insect and disease problems make early establishment of winter annuals hazardous in some areas of the Southeast. Weather records of the Georgia Piedmont area show about half the years with less than 6.4 mm of rainfall per week from September through November.[66] Seeding of winter small grains is often delayed until around the first of November to escape the drought hazard.

Small grains frequently are grazed until late February with only a slight decrease in grain yields. Clipping or grazing past this date has resulted in significantly lower grain yields. The lower yield is dependent to some extent on species and cultivars.[67]

Studies have shown that forage yields may be reduced 20–80% by early and frequent pasturing or clipping of small grains. To obtain maximum yields, the plant should be permitted to reach a height of 15–20 cm before grazing.[68]

✢ FERTILIZATION PRACTICES

Soil fertility is the most important factor in the establishment and production of pastures and forages in the humid South. In general, the soils are acid and relatively low in fertility.

LIME, PHOSPHORUS, POTASSIUM, AND MINOR ELEMENTS

Soils vary considerably in their need for lime; however, 2.2–6.7 t/ha at seeding is generally ample for most legume or legume-grass mixtures, with alfalfa requiring 4.5–9 t/ha. Productive pastures are usually re-limed every six years when renovated or rotated with small grain, millet, or corn. In some areas reliming of alfalfa is recommended as a surface application every two years. In most states the annual recommendation for alfalfa is approximately 22 kg/ha of agricultural borax.

The lespedezas can be grown at a lower lime level than the clovers. Frequently, lespedeza may not show a response to liming the first year; however, 3.3 t/ha of lime has doubled lespedeza yields in the third year on the same land.[69]

Production may be doubled on Kentucky bluegrass pastures in the mountain areas by the surface application of approximately 2.2 t/ha of lime each 8–10 years, and 15–25 kg/ha of P annually.[70] Response to K fertilizer is also obtained on many of these soils. The application of lime, P, and K where needed results in more vigorous volunteer stands of white clover and in

64. Hoveland, C. S., E. L. Carden, G. A. Buchanan, E. M. Evans, W. B. Anthony, E. L. Mayton, and H. E. Burgess. 1969. Yuchi arrowleaf clover. Ala. Agr. Exp. Sta. Bull. 396.

65. Knight, W. E. 1967. Effect of seeding rate, fall disking, and nitrogen level on establishment of crimson clover in a grass sod. *Agron. J.* 59:33–36.

66. Crowder, L. V., O. E. Sell, and E. M. Parker. 1955. The effect of clipping, nitrogen application, and weather on the productivity of fall sown oats, ryegrass, and crimson clover. *Agron. J.* 47:51–54.

67. Morris, H. D., and F. P. Gardner. 1958. The effect of nitrogen fertilization and duration of clipping period on forage and grain yield of oats, wheat, and rye. *Agron. J.* 50:454–57.

68. Holt, E. C., M. J. Norris, and J. A. Lancaster. 1969. Production and management of small grains for forage. Tex. Agr. Exp. Sta. Bull. 1082.

69. Woodhouse, W. W., Jr. 1956. Effect of placement and rate of phosphate, potash, and limestone on the growth of alfalfa and lespedeza. Soil Sci. Soc. Amer. Proc. 20:15–18.

70. Woodhouse, W. W., Jr., and R. L. Lovvorn. 1948. Establishment and improving permanent pastures in North Carolina. N.C. Agr. Exp. Sta. Bull. 338.

State and mixture	Establishment (kg/ha)*			Annual maintenance (kg/ha)		
	N	P	K	N	P	K
Arkansas						
White clover-tall fescue	40	80	100	0	60	120 (apply N as needed for desired grass production)
Kentucky†						
Ladino–orchardgrass or Ladino–tall fescue	35	50	95	0	20	75 (use no N if stand is 25% or more clover)
North Carolina†						
Ladino–orchardgrass or Ladino–tall fescue	20	85	165	0	40	130
Virginia†						
Ladino–orchardgrass or Ladino–tall fescue	30	85	100	0	55	100 (apply up to 65 kg N if clover thins or grass yellows)
South Carolina						
Ladino–tall fescue	15	55	110	0	30	110
Alabama†						
White clover-dallisgrass	0	60	110	0	60	110 (apply 65 kg N if legume does not supply sufficient N for desired grass growth)
Mississippi†						
White clover-dallisgrass	0	40	75	0	30	55

* Limestone is usually applied at or prior to establishment on previously unlimed soils at the rate of 2.2–6.7 t/ha. Applications repeated every six years or less.

† Represents average recommendation for soils of low fertility level. Recommendations without symbols are for average fertility conditions.

State	Establishment (kg/ha)*			Annual maintenance (kg/ha)		
	N	P	K	N	P	K
	Alfalfa					
Alabama†	0	60	225	0	60	225
North Georgia†	35	60	110	0	50	185
Tennessee†	10	75	225	0	40	225
	Annual lespedeza					
Mississippi†	0	30	55	...	...	...
South Carolina	0	20	75	...	...	...

* Limestone is applied at or prior to establishment on previously unlimed soils at the rate of 2.2–6.7 t/ha. Boron is also applied at seeding and annually to alfalfa in most of the humid South.

† Represents recommendations for soils of low fertility level. Recommendations for states without symbols are for average fertility conditions.

State	Establishment (kg/ha)*			Topdressing or maintenance (kg/ha)		
	N	P	K	N	P	K
	Coastal bermudagrass					
South Georgia†	55‡	45	85	110–225§	30	110
East Oklahoma†	20‡	20	40	110–225§	20	40
	Tall fescue					
Alabama†	135	40	75	135§	40	75
Kentucky†	35	50	55	225§	20	75
	Small grain					
East Texas	110	50	95	55 kg N Dec., 55 kg Feb.		
Louisiana	110	40	75	80 kg N winter or early spring		
	Pearlmillet or sorghum-sudangrass					
Tennessee†	65	30	85	65 kg N in summer		
South Carolina	45	45	90	45–100§		

* Apply limestone according to soil test.

† Represents recommendations for soils of low fertility level. Recommendations for states without symbols are for average fertility conditions.

‡ Topdress with 67 or more kg N first year.

§ Apply in split application.

some instances of annual lespedezas. Unfertilized Kentucky bluegrass in these studies produced only 1300–1700 kg/ha of forage annually.

The average annual P maintenance requirements for perennial legume-grass or perennial grass pastures range from 15 to 60 kg/ha, with a more typical range of 25–45 kg/ha (Table 43.5). For the same forages, 40–200 kg/ha of K is recommended annually, with a more typical range of 90–130 kg/ha (Table 43.5). In general, the species with high production potential require the higher fertilizer rate. (See Tables 43.5, 43.6, and 43.7.) A soil test will reveal more precisely the amount of each nutrient needed for each soil condition.

NITROGEN

In the upper South a mixture of ladino-orchardgrass (Fig. 43.2) will produce 5600–6700 kg/ha of dry forage without N topdressing,[71] and alfalfa or alfalfa-grass mixtures will produce from 7800 to 9000 kg. To produce 5600 to 9000 kg/ha of dry forage from a pure grass sod (particularly in the upper South), approximately 112–224 kg/ha of N must be applied, plus mineral fertilizer.[72,73] Even so, pure grass stands such as tall fescue, orchardgrass, or bermudagrass may be profitably utilized in many situations. There are many soil and climatic conditions in the humid South where legumes are not well adapted. Grasses must be utilized as the perennial species. Also, pure grass stands that are resistant to trampling are often desired on small hectarages for high seasonal production. For example, tall fescue heavily nitrated will provide extra grazing in late fall and early spring to supplement the legume-grass combinations.

An evener distribution of forage growth has been realized in certain intensified dairy programs of the lower South by use of 112–224 kg/ha of N annually to small hectarages of Pensacola bahiagrass, Coastal bermudagrass, or dallisgrass pastures.[74] Frequently, pure stands of orchardgrass or tall fescue will persist after the associated legume has been killed by competition, drought, or disease. Until these pastures are renovated, they can be heavily fertilized with N for full production. Pure stands of orchardgrass or tall fescue are capable of producing as much or more beef per ha as ladino-grass pastures if 200 kg/ha or more of N are applied.

74. Monroe, W. E. 1959. Pastures pay with dairy cattle. La. Agr. Ext. Serv. Publ. 1240.

❧ QUESTIONS

1. Outline the six major physiographic areas of the humid South and the forages best adapted to each.
2. Discuss the role of the temperature factor in the adaptation of the major forages in the humid South. The moisture factor. Diseases.
3. Develop a suggested pasture program for a farm in the Piedmont area of the upper South. The upper coastal plain area of the lower South. The Mississippi delta. The tidewater area.
4. Why is white clover so valuable as a pasture legume in the South?
5. Compare the range of adaptation of the intermediate white clovers and ladino.
6. Rank the three most prevalent perennial grasses of the upper South as to production capacity. Of the lower South.
7. What is the role of the winter annual and summer annual forages in the pasture production program of the lower South? Of the upper South?
8. Discuss the general fertilizer maintenance requirements for economical production of a pure stand of Coastal bermudagrass. Do the same for an orchardgrass–ladino clover mixture. For pearlmillet. For small grain for grazing.

71. Blake, C. T., J. G. Clapp, S. H. Dobson, W. W. Woodhouse, Jr., D. S. Chamblee, and H. D. Gross. 1967. The place for perennial pure grass and legume-grass pastures in North Carolina. N.C. Ext. Folder 255.

72. Woodhouse, W. W., Jr., and D. S. Chamblee. 1958. Nitrogen in forage production. N.C. Agr. Exp. Sta. Bull. 383, rev.

73. Burns, Joe D. 1969. Bermudagrass for pasture and hay. Tenn. Agr. Ext. Serv. EC 690.

L. C. NEWELL / *Agricultural Research Service, USDA*

RAY A. MOORE / *South Dakota State University*

44

HAY AND PASTURE SEEDINGS FOR THE NORTHERN GREAT PLAINS

❧

Climate and soil factors largely control the choice of small-seeded grasses and legumes used for hay and pasture seedings in the northern Great Plains. The midcontinent area exhibits great extremes in climate, soil, and natural vegetation. This diversity of environment requires special procedures of farming and ranching, including dry farming methods, grazing management, and irrigation practices.

❧ AREA DESCRIPTION

The northern Great Plains area comprises approximately 77.8 million ha. It is bounded on the east by a transition zone, which divides the native short-grass country on the west and the region of tall native and introduced grasses on the east. This line closely corresponds to the ninety-eighth meridian. The intermountain region joins the northern Great Plains on

❧ L. C. NEWELL. *See Chapter 24.*

❧ RAY A. MOORE is Head, Plant Science Department, South Dakota State University. He holds the M.S. degree from South Dakota State University and the Ph.D. from Purdue University. Renovation of grassland, especially by interseeding with pasture-type alfalfas, has been a significant part of his research program.

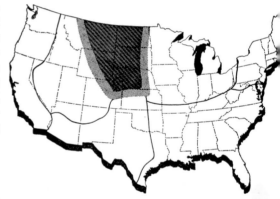

Fig. 44.1. The northern Great Plains area of the U.S.

the west. The latitude of the area of the central and northern Great Plains in the U.S. ranges from central Kansas and central Colorado to the Canadian border. (See Fig. 44.1).

Climate

The climate of the northern Great Plains is semiarid. Precipitation and temperature are the limiting factors in hay and pasture production. The average rainfall gradually decreases from 650 mm along the eastern border to as low as 250 mm in the west. The elevation above sea level averages from 425 m in the east to more than 1500 m in the west. The great difference in elevation and the distance from south to north cause a range in length of growing season from 160 days in the southeast to 110 days in the northwest.

GENERAL CROP CONDITIONS

Conditions for plant growth in the Great Plains region include great extremes, with drier and more adverse conditions increasing from east to west. The types of farming vary with the changes in climate and soil. Along the eastern border of the Great Plains region the hay and pasture crops are a part of general diversified farming systems. Grain crops such as corn, sorghum, wheat, oats, rye, and barley are grown. Most farms have fields of alfalfa and smooth bromegrass or natural grasslands that are used for hay and pasture. The unbroken prairie lands include introduced plants as well as the tall and midtall native grasses. The tall-grass prairie vegetation extends westward into the drier areas along the river valleys and on subirrigated and sandy soils. Farther west on the plains the tall grasses give way to more of the midgrasses and short grasses. Natural grasslands take up more land area than is used for plow crops. General farming and ranching prevail, with greater emphasis on moisture conservation and irrigation.

Hay and pasture seedings have increased rapidly during the past few decades. The drought of the 1930s caused abandonment of some tilled hectarages. Thousands of ha that were marginal for grain production have been returned to rangeland. There is a continuing need for planting such land to grass to bring a return from hay and pasture, making possible a better balanced system of farming. It would be difficult to estimate the value of such plantings for their conservation uses and protection of adjacent good farmland.

❧ TYPES OF VEGETATION

Native grasslands reflect the extremely variable conditions in the northern Great Plains and also show great variation. Range and pasture plants have evolved that have survived low soil fertility and the seasonal extremes of temperature and moisture availability, ranging from subhumid to the most arid conditions. Five general types of vegetation and environments are summarized in Table 44.1.[1] On the basis of area these grasslands provide the outstanding hay and pasture crops of the region, but adapted grasses and legumes also are being planted extensively.

Perennial grasses and legumes constitute most of the useful permanent cover for planting in the Great Plains. New principles of establishment and proper use of planted vegetation are being utilized for the areas of limited rainfall. Not only are adapted cultivars of the introduced grasses being utilized but many of the native grasses are being domesticated.

COOL-SEASON AND WARM-SEASON GRASSES

Grasses fall into two general categories as to season of the year in which they make their growth. Bromegrasses, wheatgrasses, bluegrasses, and needlegrasses make their best growth in the early spring and in the fall; whereas the bluestems, switchgrass, indiangrass, sideoats grama, blue grama, and buffalograss come on slowly in the early part of the season and make best growth during summer.

An understanding of the growth characteristics of the native grasslands and of the adapted grasses and legumes available for planting is essential to their proper management. Such knowledge furnishes the key to proper times of year for seeding or other cultural practices, for grazing of pastures, or for harvesting of meadows.

---

1. Hurtt, Leon E. 1948. The types of plains vegetation. *In* Grass, pp. 484–86. USDA Yearbook Agr.

TABLE 44.1 ❧ Types of northern Great Plains vegetation and related information

Northern Great Plains	Short grasses	Tall and medium-tall grasses	Sandhills	Sagebrush-saltbush	Open forest and foothills
Approximate area in ha	59,097,600	12,960,000	6,572,800	11,550,600	4,665,600
Location	eastern Montana Wyoming Colorado western North Dakota South Dakota Nebraska	eastern North Dakota South Dakota Nebraska	north central Nebraska	dry western Great Plains	Black Hills region, Big Horn and Laramie mountains
Rainfall (mm)	280–430	430–760	380–560	180–300	300–460
Elevation above sea level (m)	610–1830	305–610	457–1067	1525–2287	1525–2287
Soils and topography	chestnut or dark brown soils, flat and rolling plains, some rough broken hills	chernozem or black earth soils, rolling and flat plains, some rough broken hills	rolling dune sand and sand valleys	brown soils, often highly saline or alkaline	brown soils, mostly mountain uplifts
Principal vegetation	greasewood sagebrush saltbush *warm-season* blue grama buffalograss *cool-season* Sandburg bluegrass junegrass needlegrasses western wheatgrass sedges crested wheatgrass	*warm-season* big bluestem little bluestem prairie dropseed blue grama sideoats grama indiangrass switchgrass *cool-season* bluegrass needlegrasses western wheatgrass smooth bromegrass crested wheatgrass	*warm-season* sand bluestem big bluestem little bluestem sand dropseed blue grama indiangrass sandhill muhly sandreed switchgrass *cool-season* bluejoint reedgrass junegrass needlegrasses	greasewood sagebrush saltbush *warm-season* sand dropseed blue grama *cool-season* Sandburg bluegrass needlegrasses ricegrass wheatgrasses wildryes	*warm-season* blue grama *cool-season* bluegrasses mountain bromegrass needlegrasses ricegrass wheatgrasses wildryes
Carrying capacity, ha per animal unit (1 cow or 5 sheep) for a grazing season	2–6	0.4–1.2	1.2–8	1.2–10	1.2–8

Source: Hurtt, 1948.[1]

478

FIG. 44.2. *Larger seed yields . . . obtained with cultivation and fertilization.* Improved cultivars of native prairie grasses grown in cultivated rows provide new sources of adapted seed for planting in pastures and rangelands. *SCS photo.*

❧ ADAPTATION OF HAY AND PASTURE PLANTS

Variation within forage species provides for their wide distribution. Cultivars which do well in one region may not do so in another, or they may be more subject to disease or winter-killing. In the central latitudes strains of smooth bromegrass adapted to the north do not produce a dense sod. In some experiments yields of forage of northern strains are only about half those obtained from southern strains.[2,3] Because of this research suitable cultivars of bromegrass now are grown on most farms bordering the ninety-eighth meridian.[4] Also, cool-season native grasses from the high plains are frequently unadapted at lower elevation and latitude.

The same principles of adaptation hold for the warm-season prairie grasses. It is not good practice to use northern strains farther south where summer days are shorter.[5] Here they mature too early, are subject to disease, and are low in yield.[6] It is not desirable to bring long-season native grasses from southern states too far northward where they may not complete vegetative growth or mature seed before frost. The extra growth of late maturing grasses is valuable for hay or grazing if self-seeding is not important for the perpetuation of stand.[7,8] However, the growth of late maturing strains moved too far northward may be limited by short season or loss of stand by winter-killing.[5,8]

❧ STRAINS AND CULTIVARS

A proper choice of cultivar is the first requirement for success of the planted forage crop. The extensive areas of grassland of the world have provided an array of grasses and legumes for selection. In the Great Plains the different kinds of cool-season grasses are relatively more numerous in the northern latitudes than the warm-season grasses, which increase southward.[9] Following the drought of the 1930s, harvests of the more important of these grasses from meadows and ranges provided seed for plantings. The removal of light chaff, awns, and other appendages by special machinery, such as hammer mills,[10] aided in the planting of many of these grasses. Selected strains of these grasses now are grown in cultivated rows, sometimes with irrigation.[11] (See Fig. 44.2.) Larger seed yields as well as better seed quality for stand establishment are obtained with cultivation and fertilization than from solid stands or mixed stands of wild harvests.[12-14]

Adapted cultivars of grasses and legumes can be readily purchased as the result of

2. Newell, L. C. and F. D. Keim. 1943. Field performance of bromegrass strains from different regional seed sources. *J. Amer. Soc. Agron.* 35:420–34.
3. Thomas, H. L., Earle W. Hanson, and J. A. Jacobs. 1958. Varietal trials of smooth bromegrass. Minn. Agr. Exp. Sta. N. Central Reg. Publ. 93.
4. Derscheid, Lyle A., James G. Ross, and Raymond A. Moore. 1970. Tame grasses for pasture or hay. S. Dak. Coop. Ext. Serv. Fact Sheet 299.
5. Newell, L. C., R. D. Staten, E. B. Jackson, and E. C. Conard. 1962. Sideoats grama in the central Great Plains. Nebr. Agr. Exp. Sta. Res. Bull. 207.
6. Newell, L. C. 1968. Effects of strain source and management practice on forage yields of two warm-season prairie grasses. *Crop. Sci.* 8:205–10.
7. Moore, R. A. 1970. Symposium on pasture methods for maximum production in beef cattle: Pasture systems for a cow-calf operation. *J. Anim. Sci.* 30:133–37.
8. Warnes, D. D., L. C. Newell, and W. J. Moline. 1971. Performance evaluation of some warm-season prairie grasses in Nebraska environments. Nebr. Agr. Exp. Sta. Res. Bull. 241.

9. Gould, F. W. 1968. Grass Systematics. McGraw-Hill, New York.
10. Schwendimann, John L., and Roland F. Sackman. 1940. Processing seed of grasses and other plants to remove awns and appendages. USDA Circ. 558.
11. Atkins, M. D., and James E. Smith, Jr. 1967. Grass seed production and harvest in the Great Plains. USDA Farmers' Bull. 2226.
12. Smika, D. E., and L. C. Newell. 1965. Irrigation and fertilization practices from established stands of sideoats grama. Nebr. Agr. Exp. Sta. Res. Bull. 218.
13. Smika, D. E., and L. C. Newell. 1966. Cultural practices for seed production from established stands of western wheatgrass. Nebr. Agr. Exp. Sta. Res. Bull. 223.
14. Smika, D. E., and L. C. Newell. 1968. Seed yield and caryopsis weight of sideoats grama as influenced by cultural practices. *J. Range Manage.* 21:402–4.

cooperative research of federal agencies and state experiment stations and developments by private companies and seedsmen. The number of cultivars for particular environments and purposes is likely to increase. Information on adaptation and availability of seed can be obtained from agricultural agencies and the seed directories of crop-improvement associations. As a result of improvements in seed production, seed processing, and availability of planting equipment most any kind of grass can be seeded where desired.

❧ ESTABLISHMENT OF GRASSES AND LEGUMES

Since the seeding of grasses in arid and eroded areas is difficult, rejuvenation of the forage plants present is of great importance. Pastures and rangelands can be much improved by deferred grazing, rotational grazing, control of weeds with chemicals, and in some cases interseeding with minimum disturbance of the existing sod.[15,16] Interseeding in rows has been

used extensively on soils that are too steep, thin, or rocky or for other reasons cannot be tilled.[17]

Much progress has been made in the establishment of small-seeded grasses and legumes. Proper equipment is necessary.[17,18] Grain drills are successfully used to plant free-flowing or processed seed; however, it is best to use drills designed for grasses. The essentials of a good grass drill are: (1) separate boxes for free-flowing and nonfree-flowing seed, (2) agitators in the seed boxes to meter the seed uniformly, and (3) depth bands to regulate the depth of planting in the soil. Covering devices and packing wheels may also be used to advantage. (See Fig. 44.3.)

The seedbed is important.[18] Ideally, it should be moist and firm, weed-free, and not an erosion hazard. Firmness is especially important if depth bands or packing devices are not on the drill. Summer fallow is commonly used as a method of seedbed preparation for late summer planting of cool-season grasses where wind movement of the soil is not serious. The

15. Klingman, Dayton L., and M. K. McCarty. 1958. Interrelations of methods of weed control and pasture management at Lincoln, Nebr. USDA Tech. Bull. 1180.
16. Nichols, James T., and Wilfred E. McMurphy. 1969. Range recovery and production as influenced by nitrogen and 2,4-D treatments. *J. Range Manage.* 22: 116–19.

17. Derscheid, Lyle A., Raymond A. Moore, and Melvin D. Rumbaugh. 1970. Interseeding for pasture and range improvement. S. Dak. Coop. Ext. Serv. Fact Sheet 422.
18. Moore, R. A., and Gary B. Harwick. 1969. Establishing pasture and forage crops. S. Dak. Farm Home Res. 20 (2):6–9.

FIG. 44.3. *Best to use drills designed . . . grasses.* (Left) Drill boxes for planting different kinds of seed. (Center) Depth bands on grass drills provide for proper depth of planting in different kinds of seedbeds. (Right) The firmness of the seedbed is important. *S. Dak. Agr. Exp. Sta. photos.*

cool autumn and spring seasons favor seedling growth with a minimum competition from weeds. Planting in undisturbed clean stubble of a preceding small-grain crop has considerable merit, e.g., minimum cost. Attention can be given to weed control in the preceding crop, and if necessary the straw can be scattered or removed. Seeding in stubble is excellent where lands are subject to wind erosion. However, if the soil is too dry for fall establishment, a late seeding of cool-season grasses just before freeze-up may be satisfactory for growth to begin the following spring.

For spring establishment, cover crops are generally used to stabilize the land in the year before the grass and legume crop is planted. Forage sorghum, millet, or sudangrass are planted in late June and mowed high before seed is formed. The cover crop catches snow during the winter, conserves soil moisture for spring growth, and protects the soil from erosion.

Seeding directly into heavy mulch for spring establishment has been the most successful method for planting prairie grasses. Warm-season grasses with light, chaffy, nonfree-flowing seed establish slowly. Mixtures of grasses are planted during late winter or early spring on the firm seedbed beneath the mulch. (See Fig. 44.4.) Grass drills are used with depth controls and different seed boxes for chaffy and free-flowing seed. Mulch delays emergence until the soil is sufficiently warm, holds moisture near the surface for shallow-planted seed that require long periods for germination, protects young seedlings from sun and wind, and reduces weed competition.

Planting warm-season grasses for summer establishment after spring weed control has had some success along the more humid eastern border and in the northern parts of the region. Plowing in early spring is followed by tillage at 10–14-day intervals. A rotary hoe pulled forward effectively kills emerging weeds. Pulled backward at the last operation, the rotary hoe packs the soil. Seed is drilled into the warm moist seedbed in mid-June. Seed with low dormancy must be used; delay in germination for any reason will result in winter-kill of small seedlings. Spring plowing or repeated tillage should not be used if erosion is a problem. The practice is not recommended in the southern and southwestern parts of the region where undisturbed seedbeds under protective crop residues have been the most successful.

FIG. 44.4. *Mixtures of grasses . . . planted . . . late winter or early spring.* The grassland drill plants through heavy mulch or crop residue into an undisturbed firm seedbed. *SCS photo.*

MANAGEMENT OF YOUNG STANDS

Competition from broadleaf weeds in grass mixtures may be checked by light applications of 2,4-D after grass seedling growth is well advanced and protected by a canopy of weed leaves. A companion crop may be planted with the grass-legume mixture, but only where soil moisture is not expected to be limiting. A companion crop of cereal grain competes with the small forage seedlings for soil moisture and plant nutrients but reduces weed competition. It may also protect the seedlings from effects of hot winds and windblown soil. The companion crop has additional value as hay, silage, or cash grain. It must be removed early as a forage crop if soil moisture becomes limiting.

Success of establishment of legumes in mixture or alone often depends on the choice of a planting date that avoids frost damage to seedlings. The legume content of a grass-legume mixture usually decreases with the lateness of planting for fall establishment. Also, late frosts in the spring may damage legume seedlings from plantings made too early in the season.

Initially, good stands of grasses and legumes may be lost by erosion if growth is poor on sloping soils of low fertility. Soil deficiencies should be determined by soil tests and corrected before planting. Nitrogen fertilizer may be applied early in the establishment of cool-season grasses to obtain good grass cover during cool seasons and before weed competition or runoff and erosion can occur. Warm-season grasses also respond to fertilizer N, but these must be well established before its application.[19] Nitrogen should be applied just before their period of warm-season growth. Poorly timed application and excessive amounts of N increase competition from weeds and invasion of cool-season grasses.[8]

PLANNING FOR CONSERVATION AND USE

Feed for livestock is usually the purpose for establishing grasses and legumes. However, at times utilization by livestock is secondary to other objectives including erosion control, soil improvement, wildlife habitat, or weed control as well as longevity of stand. New plantings should be made after considering the total forage needs for livestock. Existing grasslands should also be evaluated in deciding whether new seedings should be for cool-season or warm-season pasture of a single crop or mixture. A wise choice of forage cultivars provides flexibility in managing both livestock and grasslands.[7,20]

Forages make their growth and provide various levels of nutrition in different seasons.[21-23] They also respond differently to cutting or grazing management.[4] Timely grazing or harvesting are essential to ensure quality, optimum regrowth, total

19. Warnes, D. D., and L. C. Newell. 1969. Establishment and yield responses of warm-season grass strains to fertilization. *J. Range Manage.* 22:235–40.
20. Lang, R., and L. Landers. 1960. Beef production and grazing capacity from a combination of seeded pastures versus native range. Wyo. Agr. Exp. Sta. Res. Bull. 370.
21. Streeter, C. L., D. C. Clanton, and O. E. Hoehne. 1968. Influence of advance in season on nutritive value of forage consumed by cattle grazing western Nebraska native range. Nebr. Agr. Exp. Sta. Res. Bull. 227.
22. Valentine, K. A. 1967. Seasonal suitability, a grazing system for ranges of diverse vegetation types and condition classes. *J. Range Manage.* 20:6.
23. Van Riper, G. E., and D. Smith. 1959. Changes in the chemical composition of the herbage of alfalfa, medium red clover, ladino clover, and bromegrass with advances in maturity. Wis. Agr. Exp. Sta. Res. Rept. 4.

yield, and stand survival.[24,25] Thus cool-season and warm-season grasses can be managed best if planted separately.[7,26,27] A maximum of season-long utilization may be developed by carefully planning a pasture and hay program, making use of forages that develop their best quality in different seasons.[7]

KINDS OF PLANTINGS

New grasslands have been established on former cropland. In the southern and eastern parts of the region the warm-season prairie grasses are utilized. Various mixtures now include cultivars of the bluestems, indiangrass, switchgrass, and sideoats grama.[8] These plantings supplement adjoining range or pasturelands for summer grazing. Results of grazing the tall prairie grasses singly or in simple mixtures have shown their value in providing high-quality forage for the midsummer period to complement pastures of cool-season grasses for spring and fall grazing.[7,26,27]

Plantings of cool-season grasses in areas of low rainfall include such grasses as Russian wildrye, green needlegrass, crested wheatgrass, pubescent wheatgrass, slender wheatgrass, and western wheatgrass. Warm-season blue grama is frequently used with western wheatgrass for range seeding. Western wheatgrass occupies extensive areas where it is a principal component of rangelands and hay meadow. Improved production of such rangeland has resulted from practices of pitting, N fertilization with weed control,[28,29] or introduction of biennial sweetclover.[30]

Other cool-season grasses contribute to the forage production for special conditions.[4,31] Creeping foxtail is adapted to wet soils. Tall wheatgrass is especially suitable for planting on low, wet, or saline-alkali soil, periodically subject to spring flooding and summer drought. Timothy, redtop, bluegrass, and reed canarygrass are naturalized components of warm-season prairie haylands of the sandhill meadows.

Also associated with wet meadows are red clover and alsike clover from early introductions for improvement of meadowland.[32] Birdsfoot trefoil is coming into use alone and in grass-legume mixtures in numerous locations in the region.[33] Mixtures of birdsfoot trefoil with sainfoin have given good yields in short rotations at the Montana station.[33] Sainfoin is recommended in Montana for pastures on dryland areas that receive 330 mm or more of annual precipitation.[34]

In the eastern part of the northern Great Plains smooth bromegrass has been the widely grown cool-season grass. Smooth bromegrass and intermediate wheatgrass are principal grasses grown singly or in mixture with alfalfa for pasture or hay in areas with suitable rainfall or with irrigation.[7,35] Where adapted, orchardgrass is sometimes used in irrigated grass-legume mixtures. Pasture types of alfalfa have been developed that are sufficiently similar in growth characteristics to grass com-

24. Newell, L. C. 1968. Chemical composition of two warm-season prairie grasses in three environments. *Crop Sci.* 8:325–29.
25. Derscheid, Lyle A., Walter N. Parmenter, and Raymond A. Moore. 1969. Grazing management based on . . . how grasses grow. S. Dak. Coop. Ext. Serv. Fact Sheet 302.
26. Conard, E. C., and D. C. Clanton. 1963. Cool-season, warm-season pastures needed. Beef Cattle Progr. Rept., Nebr. Agr. Exp. Sta.
27. Conard, E. C., and Vern E. Youngman. 1965. Soil moisture conditions under pastures of cool-season and warm-season grasses. *J. Range Manage.* 18:74–78.
28. Rogler, G. A., and R. J. Lorenz. 1957. Nitrogen fertilization on Great Plains rangeland. *J. Range Manage.* 10:156–60.
29. Nichols, J. T. 1969. Range improvement practices on deteriorated dense clay wheatgrass range in western South Dakota. S. Dak. Agr. Exp. Sta. Bull. 552.

30. Nichols, James T., and James R. Johnson. 1969. Range productivity as influenced by biennial sweetclover in western South Dakota. *J. Range Manage.* 22:342–47.
31. Johnson, James R., and James T. Nichols. 1969. Production, crude protein, and use of 11 irrigated grasses and alfalfa-grass combinations on clay soils in western South Dakota. S. Dak. Agr. Exp. Sta. Bull. 555.
32. Russell, J. S., E. M. Brouse, H. F. Rhoades, and D. F. Burzlaff. 1965. Response of subirrigated meadow vegetation to application of nitrogen and phosphorus fertilizer. *J. Range Manage.* 18:5.
33. Cooper, C. S., H. E. Carleton, and R. F. Eslick. 1971. Birdsfoot trefoil for Montana. Mont. Agr. Exp. Sta. Bull. 652.
34. Carleton, A. E., C. S. Cooper, R. H. Delaney, A. E. Dubbs, and R. F. Eslick. 1968. Growth and forage quality comparisons of sainfoin (*Onobrychis viciaefolia* Scop.) and alfalfa (*Medicago sativa* L.). *Agron. J.* 60:630–63.
35. Moore, R. A. 1970. The efficiency of beef cattle production in South Dakota with various methods of land use and cattle management. Proc. 11th Int. Grassl. Congr., pp. 826–29 (Surfers Paradise, Queensland, Aust.).

ponents to be managed in mixture.[36] Nitrogen fertilization usually is necessary for continued maximum production of large yields of these cool-season grasses.[37]

❧ HARVESTING FOR QUALITY FORAGE

A revolution is in progress in grazing management and harvesting of forages for improved quality and nutritional value. Advances are in proportion to improvements in technology and the greater appreciation of variation among forage crops in their different seasons for grazing or harvest.[7,20-24]

The large hectarages of natural grasslands provide hay crops for winter feeds supplemented by silage from annual crops and pasturing of crop residues. (See Fig. 44.5.) Some areas of rangeland provide good wheatgrass hay. In years favored by good rainfall some areas in the sandhill ranges are mowed. These crops frequently are left in the field in windrows or bales or are stacked for winter use. The prairie hays from the subirrigated meadows provide hay of major importance for wintering feeds. (See Fig. 44.6.) These hays have been improved in quality by introduction of legumes into meadows, fertilization, and timely harvesting before maturity lowers quality.[38] Harvests of pastures not utilized for grazing provide additional forage for emergency uses.

Alfalfa is the principal legume hay of the region. It is usually grown on the best soils, frequently with irrigation, and is the principal high-protein feed for balancing the hay ration. Its production provides the principal forage crop for export to other areas in the form of dehydrated alfalfa used in mixed feeds.

Fig. 44.5. *Hay crops for winter feeds supplemented by silage . . . pasturing crop residues.* Throughout the region forage is conserved as hay or silage.

36. Rumbaugh, M. D., G. Semeniuk, R. Moore, and J. D. Colburn. 1965. Travois—An alfalfa for grazing. S. Dak. Agr. Exp. Sta. Bull. 525.

37. Rehm, G. W., W. J. Moline, E. J. Schwartz, and R. S. Moomaw. 1971. Effect of fertilization and management on the production of bromegrass in northeast Nebraska. Nebr. Agr. Exp. Sta. Res. Bull. 247.

38. Baker, M. L., E. C. Conard, V. H. Arthaud, and L. C. Newell. 1951. Effect of time of cutting on yield and feeding value of prairie hay. Nebr. Agr. Exp. Sta. Bull. 403.

FIG. 44.6. *Crops frequently are left . . . windrows or bales or . . . stacked for winter use.* Forage harvests for winter feed are essential and critical operations. Methods of harvest vary widely.

QUESTIONS

1. List and discuss the limiting factors to the production of hay and pasture in the northern Great Plains.
2. How do you account for the gradual change in the natural vegetation from east to west?
3. What are the distinguishing characteristics of the cool-season and warm-season grasses? Name several grasses in each group.
4. Discuss the importance of planning a program of forage production and the selection of suitable cultivars.
5. What procedure would you follow in the establishment of a hay or pasture crop for a selected purpose and environment in the northern Great Plains?

SUPPLEMENTAL INFORMATION

Analyses of costs and practices in relation to uses and returns showed range reseeding can be a profitable enterprise.[39] Forage production and carrying capacity from reseeding varied with establishment practice but exceeded native range. Livestock benefits from grazing reseeded range were increased weight gains and calf crops. Other benefits included longer seasons of grazing, decreased grazing pressure on native range, and development of special breeding and calving pastures.

At North Platte, Nebr., eight grasses were evaluated under solid-set irrigation.[40] Each grass was fertilized, irrigated, and managed for optimum grazing gains (3 years). Intermediate wheatgrass and smooth bromegrass gave best daily gains, followed by creeping foxtail, orchardgrass, and meadow brome. These five grasses offered choices for irrigated pastures, averaging 1042 kg/ha gain, over Russian wildrye and reed canarygrass (815 kg/ha) and tall fescue (630 kg/ha).

39. Cordingly, R. V., and W. G. Kearl. 1975. Economics of range reseeding in the plains of Wyoming. Wyo. Agr. Exp. Sta. Res. Bull. 98.
40. Nichols, J. T., W. J. Moore, and D. C. Clanton. 1976. Evaluation of eight irrigated pasture grasses. *J. Anim. Sci.* 43(1):268.

WESLEY KELLER AND LESLIE J. KLEBESADEL
Agricultural Research Service, USDA

45

HAY, PASTURE, AND RANGE SEEDINGS
FOR THE INTERMOUNTAIN AREA AND ALASKA

❧

THE INTERMOUNTAIN AREA

THE intermountain area is predominantly mountainous terrain with the intensively cropped land in scattered valleys having access to water for irrigation. The largest concentration of irrigated land occurs in the Snake River Valley of southern Idaho. On higher land where the soil is deep and heavy enough to hold much if not all the winter precipitation, dry farming is practiced.

The climate is Mediterranean with dry summers, although on the eastern and southern borders summer precipitation

❧ WESLEY KELLER was Investigations Leader for Arid Pasture and Range, ARS, USDA, 1956–72, Utah State University. He holds the M.S. degree from Utah State University and the Ph.D. from the University of Wisconsin. His major interests are the improvement of arid rangelands and irrigated pastures.

❧ LESLIE J. KLEBESADEL is Supervisory Research Agronomist, ARS, USDA, University of Alaska. He holds the M.S. and Ph.D. degrees from the University of Wisconsin. His research has dealt with forage crop establishment, management, winter survival, and adaptation as well as evaluation of indigenous Alaskan grasses and legumes.

from adjacent areas may overlap. The average precipitation is about 350 mm/year, but it ranges from less than 120 mm in the drier valleys to over 1250 mm in the higher mountains. Winters are cold and usually have a snow cover of a few to 300 mm or more in the valleys, increasing to 2000 or more mm in the mountains. Deep snow in the larger mountain masses provides water for year-round stream flow, indispensable to life and man's activities in the valleys below.[1]

Idaho, Nevada, and Utah, wholly within the area, occupy 71 million ha. Less than 4% is cultivated cropland.[2] Hay is the most important crop. Land not in farms is used primarily for grazing but has other values including recreation, wildlife, watershed, and timber. The area includes large Indian reservations and land controlled by defense agencies. The predominance of noncropland emphasizes grazing and a livestock-oriented agricultural economy. There are approximately 3 million cattle and more than 4 million sheep in the area as well as nearly 3 million deer, 0.5 million elk, and lesser num-

1. Garnsey, Morris E. 1950. America's New Frontier—The Mountain West. Knopf, New York.
2. USDA. 1970. Agricultural statistics.

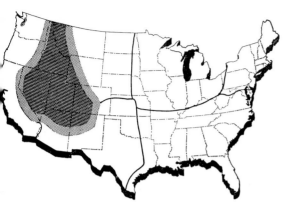

FIG. 45.1. The intermountain area of the U.S.

FIG. 45.1. The intermountain area of the U.S.

bers of other big game animals. Except for antelope, game animals are primarily in the national forests. (See Figs. 45.1, 45.2.)

The mountain rangelands are for the most part accessible only in summer. They constitute the summer range and are used by both sheep and cattle. This resource is declining in importance for domestic livestock and increasing in importance for game, mainly deer, and for recreation.[3]

3. Keller, Wesley. 1960. Importance of irrigated grasslands in animal production. *J. Range Manage.* 13: 22–28.

FIG. 45.2. *Land not in farms . . . primarily for grazing but . . . including recreation, wildlife, watershed, and timber. A summer range in the intermountain area.*

The driest areas, chiefly valley bottoms and adjacent low hills remote from high mountain masses or in the rain shadows of these mountains, are grazed primarily in winter when snow is available to provide water. They are used mostly by sheep. Should snow fail, sheep may be watered at wells where available, or water may be trucked to them. Also an occasional winter snowstorm may cover the range so deeply that hay must be hauled to stock or in extreme emergencies must be flown in.

Cattle usually winter at the home ranch and are fed harvested hay. They also may be pastured in spring and fall on the hay meadows. The spring and fall ranges lie between the desert winter range and the summer range in the mountains. Formerly these ranges were the buffer to absorb livestock when snow had left the desert range, when feed at the home ranch was exhausted or before the animals were permitted on the national forests. The spring and fall ranges were also grazed by the animals when they left the summer ranges en route to the home ranch or the desert. The pattern of use for the spring and fall ranges was clear-cut in the nineteenth century when livestock were trailed, but this pattern is changing because of truck transport of livestock, increased use of spring and fall ranges by game animals, reduction of grazing by domestic livestock on the national forests, and decline in sheep numbers.

The spring and fall ranges have received most of the attention of range researchers, partly because they acutely needed improvement and partly because they were adjacent and amenable to some of the methods and equipment in use on dry farms. They also offered the greatest likelihood of successful rehabilitation. Several million ha have been seeded, primarily to crested wheatgrass. Another large area has been sprayed with 2,4-D to kill sage and release native understory grasses. Much of the remaining spring and fall range is now in private ownership.

In 1906 the Forest Service began administration of the summer ranges in the national forests. These ranges for the most part have been improved considerably. Beginning in 1934 the Bureau of Land Management (BLM), formerly called the Grazing Service, assumed administration of the remaining public domain, chiefly the arid winter range. These drier, inherently less productive lands are more severely depleted, and their improvement will probably be slower.[4]

All the federally owned lands are grazed by permit for which a fee is charged. Although fees have increased over the years, they remain well below the value of the feed; therefore, ranchers with permits have a substantial advantage over those without them. As a result, permits have been known to change hands at a price out of all proportion to their real value.

❧ HAY CROPS

ALFALFA

Alfalfa is the most important seeded hay crop in the intermountain area. Hay is produced primarily on irrigated land but also on dryland. Alfalfa should be sown on well-drained land on a well-prepared seedbed. The seed give best results when drilled at about 1.3 cm depth except on sandy soil which requires deeper drilling up to 2 cm. The usual seeding rate on irrigated land is 11–22 kg/ha and on dryland 7–13 kg/ha.

Alfalfa is most often sown in the spring; but if irrigation water is ample and properly applied, it may be sown in late summer after the harvest of a grain crop, in early summer following a crop of peas harvested for canning, or in early spring with a companion crop of barley harvested for grain or of oats cut for hay. The companion crops are sown at half the usual rate.

NATIVE HAY MEADOWS

Small mountain valleys and lowlands adjacent to streams in many larger valleys are natural hay meadows. In early summer during high streamflow, these meadows flood, and ranchers have constructed diversion ditches to extend the flooding. Wild hay produced on these meadows varies in makeup depending on the degree and extent of flooding in early summer and the intensity of drought in late summer. On the average they yield about 2.5 t/ha.

A Nevada study showed by actual ranch-scale operations that meadow improvement was a good investment.[5] Four ranchers carried out a complete improvement program, involving controlling water, draining, killing the native sod (requiring as much as 3 years; during each year a grain crop is grown), leveling the land, seeding to improved species (productive grasses and legumes), applying fertilizer, and drilling wells for supplemental late season irrigation. They invested $361/ha. Hay yields increased to 10.6 t/ha. These ranchers realized a return of 7.1–56.7% on their investment when hay was valued at $20/t. Seven ranchers applied all the above practices except developing wells for supplemental irrigation. They invested $186/ha. Their hay yields increased to 8.5 t/ha, and they received a return on their investment of 12.8–60.9%. Eleven ranchers did some leveling and limited draining; they controlled water, seeded improved species, and applied fertilizer. They spent $103/ha and obtained a yield of 7.4 t/ha. The return on their investment was 23.2–170.3%. Two ranchers undertook water control only. Their investment was only $5.96/ha. Valuing the native hay produced at $16/t, their investment brought returns of 258.6 and 388.2%. This study shows the great potential for improvement of native hay meadows.

A Wyoming study found alsike clover, red clover, and alfalfa to be legumes adapted to improved meadows. Smooth bromegrass, intermediate wheatgrass, meadow foxtail, orchardgrass, reed canarygrass, and timothy are grasses found to be pro-

4. U.S. Forest Serv. 1936. The western range. U.S. Senate Doc. 199.

5. Fulcher, Glen D. 1960. Economics of meadow improvement in northern Nevada. Nev. Agr. Exp. Sta. Bull. 215.

FIG. 45.3. *Irrigated pastures . . . recent development in the intermountain area.* If harvested by productive animals, pastures are competitive with most cash crops on the best agricultural land, improve the land for crops that follow, and should be part of a farm crop rotation system. *Bert V. Allen photo.*

ductive in these meadows.[6] Other studies in Colorado and Oregon emphasize the value of fertilizer, chiefly N, for maximum yields and of early harvest for high-quality forage.[7,8]

CLOVERS

A modest percentage of hayland is still seeded to red clover. This and alsike clover are well adapted to soils too wet for alfalfa. They are especially valuable in mountain meadows.[6,9] Alsike clover is more tolerant of wet soils than red clover but neither will survive prolonged flooding.

Seedbed preparation for red clover is similar to that for alfalfa. Red and alsike clovers can be established in wet meadows by broadcasting seed near the end of the spring flooding period.

Red clover is highly productive as a hay crop on well-drained irrigated land. Its principle disadvantages when compared to alfalfa are that it is short-lived and does not dry as rapidly after mowing.

SAINFOIN

Ravages of the alfalfa weevil and the withdrawal of insecticides that are effective

in weevil control have increased interest in other possible hay crops. Agronomists in Montana have vigorously sponsored sainfoin, primarily because it is highly resistant if not immune to the weevil and has never been known to cause bloat in ruminants.[10] Sainfoin, however, is short-lived, has rather coarse stems, and strains of rhizobia that work well with it in fixing atmospheric N have not been found in soils in the intermountain area.

Sainfoin seed are nearly 10 times the size of alfalfa seed. Seeding rates range from 9 to 36 kg/ha, but on a firm clean seedbed 18 kg/ha are usually recommended. Sainfoin is best adapted to well-drained, calcareous soils. Because it is non-bloating, sainfoin may find a place in dryland or short-rotation irrigated pastures; however, it is not expected to replace alfalfa as a hay crop.[11]

✣ IRRIGATED PASTURES

Highly productive irrigated pastures on the best farmland are a recent development in the intermountain area (Fig. 45.3). At first the available native forage was used, followed by use of the poorest land that was too wet for cultivation, too shallow or rocky, or uneven and difficult to irrigate. Fertilizer was seldom provided

6. Lewis, Rulon D. 1960. Mountain meadow improvement in Wyoming. Wyo. Agr. Exp. Sta. Bull 350R.
7. Miller, D. E., and M. Amemiya. 1954. Better quality mountain meadow hay through early harvesting and fertilization. Colo. Agr. Exp. Sta. Bull. 434A.
8. Rumburg, C. B. 1961. Fertilization of wet meadows—A progress report. Oreg. Agr. Exp. Sta. Misc. Paper 116.
9. Willhite, Forrest M., Rulon D. Lewis, and Hayden K. Rouse. 1962. Improving mountain meadow production in the West. USDA Agr. Info. Bull. 268.

10. Montana State Univ. 1968. Sainfoin symposium. 31 papers.
11. Krall, J. F., C. S. Cooper, C. W. Crowell, and A. J. Jarvi. 1971. Evaluations of sainfoin for irrigated pasture. Mont. Agr. Exp. Sta. Bull. 658.

TABLE 45.1 ❧ High- and low-yielding species of pasture grasses and legumes, with recommended seeding rates of six palatable, highly productive species

High-yielding species	Kg/ha	Low-yielding species
Red clover	2.7	Kentucky bluegrass
Tall oatgrass	2.7	meadow fescue
Orchardgrass	2.7	meadow foxtail
Alfalfa	2.7	perennial ryegrass
Smooth bromegrass	3.6	Italian ryegrass
Ladino clover	1.8	white clover
Total mixture	16.2	alsike clover
		strawberry clover
Reed canarygrass	…	white sweetclover
Tall fescue	…	yellow sweetclover

Source: Bateman and Keller, 1956.[12]

except by the grazing animal. Kentucky bluegrass and white clover were sown on these lands, and later the Huntley mix which included some other species was used. These early pastures were well adapted to the prevailing management practice, continuous close grazing from early spring until late fall. They were often irrigated to excess without removing the grazing animals. The result was highly compacted soils with a greatly reduced rate of water infiltration.

IMPROVED MIXTURES

A series of comprehensive mixture studies on a field scale with excellent grazing management separated the high- and low-yielding pasture species.[12] The species studied and the separation which resulted, along with recommended seeding rate of the desirable productive species, is presented in Table 45.1.

Tall fescue and reed canarygrass are highly productive and widely adapted. Reed canarygrass is difficult to establish on well-drained land in competition with other more aggressive species. Both species are low in palatability and recommended only for situations where others are not suited. Species low in palatability dominate a pasture under rotation grazing, but they can be held in check by daily ration grazing. None of the high-yielding palatable species that are recommended in Table 45.1 for an irrigated pasture on the best land will tolerate continuous grazing.

In the mixture recommended above, red clover and tall oatgrass are short-lived but develop rapidly. One should never be used without the other since they achieve balance during the early life of a pasture. They give way in the second or third year to alfalfa and orchardgrass. Ladino clover and smooth bromegrass are slightly less productive than alfalfa and orchardgrass, but they thicken the stand where necessary, are extremely palatable, and provide variety in the animal diet.

Researchers in Montana have prepared an excellent pasture guide for the northern intermountain area.[13]

ESTABLISHMENT

Success in establishing an irrigated pasture requires some skill. Seed are small, germinate slowly, and must have close contact with the soil to obtain the moisture necessary to produce seedlings. This requires a firm moist seedbed as free as possible from weeds. The commonest cause of pasture establishment failure is a seedbed that is too loose. A tractor tire should leave tread marks on the surface, not a rut. Planting is preferably by drilling at a depth of 1–1.5 cm, or a little deeper on sandy soil. Pastures are usually sown early in the spring. With ample irrigation water and careful management a pasture can be established following a crop of peas for canning, or later in the summer following harvest of a small-grain crop. In either instance seeding should be directly into the firm soil without cultivation. This requires careful advance preparation of the land for proper irrigation of the pasture.

COMPANION CROPS

In general, a companion crop in pasture establishment is not recommended. The

12. Bateman, George Q., and Wesley Keller. 1956. Grass-legume mixtures for irrigated pastures for dairy cows. Utah Agr. Exp. Sta. Bull. 382.

13. Cooper, C. S., D. E. Baldridge, and C. W. Roath. 1969. Selection and management of irrigated pasture mixtures. Mont. Agr. Exp. Sta. Bull. 622.

determining factors are the skill of the farmer, the adequacy of his water supply, the fertility of his land, and the attention he gives the young pasture seedlings.[14] If a companion crop is not sown, there will be one of weeds. Barley seeded at 55 kg/ha is a good companion crop; the grain should be harvested as soon as it is ripe, and the land promptly irrigated. Such a pasture should provide one good grazing before the close of the season. Oats is a superior companion crop when cut green for hay.

FERTILIZATION

Pasture fertilization assists plants to reach maximum productivity, and helps to maintain the desired balance between grasses and legumes. If the herbage is 50–60% legumes, highest productivity with low risk of bloat will result. Fertilizer N will stimulate the grasses, and P the legumes; the response from N is faster than from P. A pasture containing 50–60% legumes is most economically maintained at high production by fertilizing with barnyard manure and P.

CROP ROTATION

Pastures contribute significantly to the yield of subsequent crops; therefore, they should be part of a crop rotation scheme.[15] Except in special situations, pastures should not remain down longer than about five years, even though they may remain highly productive much longer.

If irrigated pastures are well managed, they will compete successfully with most cash crops under a wide range of conditions. The mixture (Table 45.1) produces excellent hay and yields at least as much as alfalfa. It will require more frequent irrigation, primarily because of shallow-rooted ladino clover, but not necessarily more water per year. Much of the success with irrigated pastures depends on how they are managed and on grazing with a productive dairy herd or good quality animals.

❧ RANGE

SEEDING

Seeding is an important part of range improvement. It is expensive relative to the productive potential of arid land since it takes the land out of productive use one or more years and the likelihood of failure is quite high. Therefore, seeding should never be undertaken unless significant improvement cannot be realized in a reasonable time by simpler methods. Seeding usually is necessary when the desirable native forage species have been lost, when all vegetation must be destroyed to eliminate an undesirable species, or when abandoned cropland is to be returned to productive range. Research has repeatedly shown that success in seeding depends upon destroying all competing vegetation, covering the seed, and providing protection until the seeded species have become established. In some situations rodent control is also necessary.

SELECTING SITES. Sagebrush generally indicates a well-drained soil free of alkali and heavy enough to hold all or most of the precipitation received. All of the good dry farmlands and most of the irrigated lands of the intermountain area were originally a sagebrush-bunchgrass association. The sagebrush-bunchgrass land still in range has changed under heavy use to sage-dominated range with bunchgrasses either killed out or relegated to a weakened understory.[16] The greatest concentration of range seeding has been on this type of land.

If an understory of desirable perennial grasses has survived, seeding is not necessary. The sage can be burned off if it is thick enough to carry a fire, or it can be sprayed with 2,4-D at 1.65–2.42 kg/ha at any time the sage is actively growing.[17]

14. University of Arizona. 1961. Alfalfa for forage production in Arizona. Ariz. Agr. Exp. Sta. Bull. A-16.
15. Gardner, Robert, and D. W. Robertson. 1954. The beneficial effects from alfalfa in a crop rotation. Colo. Agr. Exp. Sta. Tech. Bull. 51.

16. Cook, C. Wayne. 1958. Sagebrush eradication and broadcast seeding. Utah Agr. Exp. Sta. Bull. 404.
17. Hyder, D. N. 1966. Big sagebrush (*Artemisia tridentata* Nutt.). *In* Chemical control of range weeds. USDA and USDI cooperating.

In the intermountain area many million ha of rangeland are dominated by juniper, some of which has invaded sagebrush range. Some juniper-infested land has high potential for forage production if the juniper can be cleared off. Chaining or cabling is the most economical method of destroying mature stands, but the trees must still be disposed of.[18] They may be concentrated and burned, windrowed, or pushed into piles and ignored. On much juniper-infested range after the trees are cleared, the land must still be plowed to destroy understory vegetation and to prepare a suitable seedbed for grass seeding. Because all these operations appear necessary, not much juniper-infested range has been converted to grass.

Range seeding has been successful on highly diverse sites extending from dry sagebrush to high mountain parks. Each site must be analyzed and specifications drawn to meet its particular characteristics.

CHOICE OF SPECIES. On the drier sites where seeding has been successful, crested wheatgrass is used almost to the exclusion of other species. Crested wheatgrass has fairly good seedling vigor, extreme drought and coldhardiness, and tolerance of heavy grazing use; it produces high-quality seed which is widely available. 'Nordan' is the most widely used named cultivar, particularly valuable for its seedling vigor.[19] As conditions improve, usually meaning higher precipitation, other species are competitive. Intermediate wheatgrass is highly productive in the mountain brush zone and at higher elevations. Smooth bromegrass is well adapted to mountain rangelands. Russian wildrye has not been used extensively in intermountain range seeding, chiefly because good stands are difficult to obtain. The species is nutritious, hardy, long-lived, and more salt tolerant than most other range grasses. Many other species are useful in particular situations.[20,21]

RATE AND METHOD. Crested wheatgrass and most other species are seeded at 6 or 7 kg/ha. Drilling at about 2.5-cm depth is preferable to broadcasting. If the site has been plowed, ordinary farm grain drills may be used. If the terrain is rough or rocky, the rangeland drill is better.[22] Drills have been developed for such special conditions as where sagebrush has been killed by herbicides.[23] If drilling is impossible, the seed may be covered by brush drag, or livestock may be driven over the site. In the aspen (*Populus* spp.) zone, leaf fall effectively covers the seed. Higher seeding rates usually are advised if precise distribution and depth of seeding are impossible.

Where a disk type of plow is used to destroy sagebrush, a drill may be trailed to plow and seed in one operation. If the area to be seeded is large, the operation may begin in August and continue until snowed out. If the fall remains dry, the entire seeding may emerge in early spring and be very successful. If there is fall precipitation, fall germination and emergence may occur, depending upon the length of time moisture is available while temperatures are favorable for germination and growth.

The rancher attempting to improve his range by seeding tries to hold cost to a minimum and gambles that it will pay off. The economics of range improvement is always a major factor in the choice of methods used.[24,25]

18. Arnold, Joseph F., Donald A. Jameson, and Elbert H. Reid. 1964. The pinyon-juniper type in Arizona: Effects of grazing, fire, and tree control. U.S. Forest Serv. Prod. Res. Rept. 84.

19. Rogler, George. 1954. Nordan crested wheatgrass. N. Dak. Agr. Exp. Sta. Bimonthly Bull. 16:150–52.

20. Hafenrichter, A. L., John L. Schwendiman, Harold L. Harris, Robert S. Maclauchlan, and Harold W. Miller. 1968. Grasses and legumes for soil conservation in the Pacific Northwest and Great Basin states. SCS Agr. Handbook 339.

21. Plummer, A. Perry, Donald R. Christensen, and Stephen B. Monsen. 1968. Restoring big-game range in Utah. Utah Div. Fish and Game Publ. 68-3.

22. Range Seeding Equipment Committee. 1965. Range seeding equipment handbook. U.S. Forest Serv. Handbook 2244.01.

23. Hyder, D. N., D. E. Booster, F. A. Sneva, W. A. Sawyer, and J. B. Rodgers. 1961. Wheel-track planting on sagebrush-bunchgrass range. *J. Range Manage.* 14:220–24.

24. Caton, D. D., and Christop Beringer. 1960. Costs and benefits of reseeding rangelands in southern Idaho. Idaho Agr. Exp. Sta. Bull. 326.

25. Nielsen, Darwin B. 1967. Economics of range improvements. Utah Agr. Exp. Sta. Bull. 466.

Pellet seeding has been repeatedly tried and has consistently failed[26] because the competing vegetation was not removed nor the seed covered. It is also expensive.

SEED TREATMENT. Nearly all range grasses are susceptible during cold-weather germination to *Podosporiella verticillata* O'Gara, a fungus mildly pathogenic on wheat. It can completely destroy fall-seeded range plantings.[27] Common in soils throughout the range of cheatgrass, this fungus is readily controlled by treating seed with Arasan at 415 g/50 kg seed.

GRAZING MANAGEMENT

Grazing management is the most important tool in range improvement because it deals with all the range. The time and intensity of grazing use are particularly critical. Some range species well adapted to arid conditions are sensitive to any use, particularly when root reserves are low.[28,29] As drought intensifies, plants become increasingly sensitive to defoliation. Range managers may aim at "take half and leave half" as a reasonable guide to forage utilization. But proper use varies with conditions and with the season.[30,31] Range forage species will probably remain vigorous and productive if they can make substantial growth in the spring before grazing begins. Crested wheatgrass withstands early season grazing better than most species and is ideally suited to provide this deferment.

REST-ROTATION GRAZING. A controversial concept in management, rest-rotation grazing, has been advanced.[32] The BLM has adopted the system and is introducing it on grazing allotments throughout the West. The method was developed in northeastern California and was first advocated for bunchgrass range. It has been modified since first announced and is believed to be flexible enough to fit any range situation. The basic idea is heavy range use followed by rest to allow seed of the most important forage species to ripen and be trampled into the soil (covered) by the grazing animal. In a three-pasture system, each year one pasture is rested, one is heavily grazed only after seed has ripened, and one is heavily grazed all season. The three pastures are rotated in the order listed. Proponents claim this system will improve ranges that appear to require artificial seeding.

ALASKA

❧ AGRICULTURAL DEVELOPMENT

Token agricultural activity prevailed in the territory of Alaska until 1935 when a federally sponsored colonization was initiated in the Matanuska Valley with families from the midwestern states. Although only 14.6-ha tracts were made available to the new settlers, this defect gradually has been surmounted with consolidation and enlargement of individual farms. Largely since World War II, land has been cleared in other areas in central and south central Alaska for agricultural development (Fig. 45.4). In general, the progress of Alaskan agriculture has been restrained more by economics than by physical feasibility. Agricultural research in Alaska claims even less history; a significant research program has been in operation only since the 1950s.

❧ CLIMATE

Although Alaska is one of the fifty states, on the basis of great land mass and unique climatic conditions this northwest extension of the continent could well be

26. Hull, A. C., Jr., Ralph C. Holmgren, W. H. Berry, and Joe E. Wagner. 1963. Pellet seeding on western rangelands. USDA Misc. Publ. 922.
27. Kreitlow, K. W., and A. T. Bleak. 1964. *Podosporiella verticillata*, a soil-borne pathogen of some western Gramineae. *Phytopathology* 54:353–57.
28. Jameson, Donald A. 1963. Responses of individual plants to harvesting. Bot. Rev. 29:532–94.
29. Ellison, Lincoln. 1959. Role of plant succession in range improvement. *In* Grasslands. AAAS Publ. 53, pp. 307–21.
30. Cook, C. Wayne. 1971. Effects of season and intensity of use on desert vegetation. Utah Agr. Exp. Sta. Bull. 483.
31. Hyder, D. N., and F. A. Sneva. 1959. Growth and carbohydrate trends in crested wheatgrass. *J. Range Manage.* 12:271–76.

32. Hormay, A. L., and M. W. Talbot. 1961. Rest-rotation grazing . . . a new management system for perennial bunchgrass ranges. U.S. Forest Serv. Prod. Res. Rept. 51.

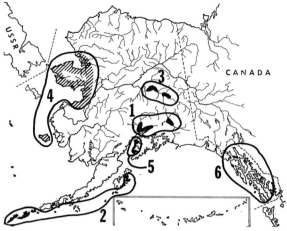

FIG. 45.4. Areas of agricultural development in Alaska in decreasing order of value of agricultural sales: (1) Matanuska-Susitna valleys, (2) southwestern, (3) Tanana Valley, (4) western (reindeer), (5) Kenai Peninsula, and (6) southeastern.

considered a distinct region of the country. In contrast to all other U.S. areas, Alaska occupies northern latitudes similar to those of Norway, Sweden, and Finland. Climatic regions include boreal, subarctic, and arctic, imposing restrictions on which crops can be grown successfully. Very long midsummer photoperiods, cool short growing seasons, and the abrupt advent of relatively long severe winters are common in most of the mainland areas where agriculture has developed.[33] These conditions create an environment for crops quite different from the midtemperate to subtropical climate in the conterminous states and Hawaii.

Alaska is approximately 20% as large as the other 49 states combined, and climatic patterns vary considerably across this large land mass transected by three major mountain ranges. Total annual precipitation along the northernmost arctic coast averages 150 mm, while stations in the southeastern panhandle section record over 5000 mm each year. Temperature extremes recorded in the state are 38 and −62.2 C.

Areas devoted to agricultural activities receive from 250 to 1000 mm of precipitation annually; growing-season temperatures, although somewhat lower than in midtemperate latitudes, are conducive to growth of cool-season crops.

❧ SOILS

Various estimates have been advanced of the total land area in Alaska suitable for agriculture. The area usable as tilled cropland may be near 800,000 ha; however, currently only about 7000 ha are harvested cropland. Land suitable for pasture is believed near 2 million ha; but if reindeer rangelands are considered, this figure becomes significantly greater.

The areas in interior, south central and southwestern Alaska where agriculture has developed are widely separated (Fig. 45.4). Soils of the Tanana Valley in central Alaska are silty to very fine sand, usually deep, near neutral in reaction, and developed from stream alluvium and aeolian deposits. Many of these soil areas are underlain by permafrost. In the Matanuska Valley, soils are slightly to moderately acidic silts and fine sands deposited by winds on outwash gravels. The silt mantle is deep near the loessial origins and becomes shallower with distance from those sources. On the Kenai Peninsula and Kodiak Island, soils are moderately to strongly acidic.[34] Volcanic ash layers are visible in some soils, especially those of Kodiak where a 20- to 40-cm surface layer remains from the massive eruption on the Alaska Peninsula in 1912.

❧ FORAGE CROPS

Major agricultural crops are potatoes, small grains, and forages; the latter two are produced in support of the state's dairy and beef cattle, sheep, and swine operations. Few of the perennial forages cultured in temperate regions perform satis-

33. Watson, C. E., C. I. Branton, and J. E. Newman. 1971. Climatic characteristics of selected Alaskan locations. Alaska Inst. Agr. Sci. Tech. Bull. 2.

34. Rieger, S., and R. E. Wunderlich. 1960. Soil survey and vegetation of northeastern Kodiak Island area, Alaska. SCS Ser. 1956, No. 17.

FIG. 45.5. *Bromegrass . . . dominant perennial forage.* Perennial grasses not adapted to the subarctic environment frequently succumb during severe winters in Alaska. Native Alaskan bromegrass (left) and Polar smooth bromegrass (right) developed in Alaska survived well, while Manchar smooth bromegrass (center) from the Pacific Northwest winter-killed. (The five living plants obvious in the Manchar plot are Kentucky bluegrass present as contaminants.)

factorily in Alaska. Moreover, cultivar differences within species are of marked significance to Alaskan farmers and ranchers. The northernmost adapted cultivars or ecotypes within each species are most winter-hardy and therefore most dependable and useful.[35-37] Warm-season annual forages such as corn, sorghum, and sudangrass, commonly grown in temperate regions, are unadapted and unsuited for use in Alaska's cool summer climate.

PERENNIAL FORAGES

Smooth bromegrass is the dominant perennial forage and timothy is second in importance. 'Manchar' and Canadian commercial bromegrass were widely used before the advent of the more winter-hardy 'Polar' cultivar developed in Alaska (Fig. 45.5).[37] 'Engmo' from northern Norway is the most winter-hardy and most used timothy cultivar.[38]

Quackgrass is a well-adapted, introduced weed that has spread to many cropland fields where it has become a substantial contributor to harvested or grazed forages on many farms. Few other introduced perennial grasses are utilized to any appreciable extent for forage production in Alaska. Meadow foxtail and reed canary-grass are more productive than smooth bromegrass and often surpass timothy where soils tend to be moderately to strongly acidic. Winter-hardy selections and cultivars of Kentucky bluegrass, creeping foxtail, and creeping red fescue show considerable promise for forage production, although they are little used as of 1970.

Perennial and biennial legumes commonly grown in more southern latitudes frequently succumb to winter stress when grown in Alaska.[35] Therefore, grasses are grown principally in monoculture with N supplied in commercial fertilizers.[39] While due in part to the severity of Alaskan winters, survival failures of unadapted legumes and grasses are attributable mostly to inability of those more southern cultivars to achieve maximum coldhardiness under an extremely short conditioning period of appropriate photoperiods and temperatures prior to onset of winter in this subarctic area.[40,41]

Climatic conditions in Alaska are marginal for haymaking; the first cutting of perennial grasses is usually harvested from mid-June to early July. Cooler weather and frequent rains normally preclude field curing of hay at the time of second cuttings during late August and September. This crop and the oat-pea mixtures, cut only once, usually are preserved as silage.

35. Klebesadel, L. J. 1971. Selective modification of alfalfa toward acclimatization in a subarctic area of severe winter stress. *Crop Sci.* 11:609–14.
36. Klebesadel, L. J., A. C. Wilton, R. L. Taylor, and J. J. Koranda. 1964. Fall growth behavior and winter survival of *Festuca rubra* and *Poa pratensis* in Alaska as influenced by latitude of adaptation. *Crop Sci.* 4:340–41.
37. Wilton, A. C., H. J. Hodgson, L. J. Klebesadel, and R. L. Taylor. 1966. Polar bromegrass, a new winter-hardy forage for Alaska. Alaska Agr. Exp. Sta. Circ. 26.
38. Klebesadel, L. J. 1970. Influence of planting date and latitudinal provenance on winter survival, heading, and seed production of bromegrass and timothy in the subarctic. *Crop Sci.* 10:594–98.

39. Laughlin, W. M. 1962. Fertilizer practices for bromegrass. Alaska Agr. Exp. Sta. Bull. 32.
40. Hodgson, H. J. 1964. Effect of photoperiod on development of cold resistance in alfalfa. *Crop Sci.* 4:302–5.
41. Klebesadel, L. J. 1971. Nyctoperiod modification during late summer and autumn affects winter survival and heading of grasses. *Crop Sci.* 11:507–11.

ANNUAL FORAGES

Certain cool-season annual forage crops are important in Alaskan farming. The most used is a mixture of spring-sown oats and Canadian field peas.[42-44] This crop is harvested once in late August or September when oats are in the late milk to early dough stage and peas have filled pods at the base of the vine but may still be flowering at the distal end. Formerly preserved through much hand labor as cocks on wooden stakes in the field, these mixtures now are stored as silage. Mowing, windrowing, and chopping from swaths lowers the moisture content of the crop to desired levels for best preservation.

Because growing seasons are relatively short and the winter feeding periods are longer in Alaska, considerable emphasis must be placed on maximum efficiencies in forage production and fullest use of the entire growing season. Regrowth from spring-seeded annual ryegrass following one harvest near midseason has extended the grazing season in late summer and early autumn.[45] Winter conditions (soil freezing, often accompanied by snowfall) are in effect from October 10 to 20 in south central Alaska and from October 1 to 10 in the interior.[33] During the September and early October span of shortening photoperiods, lowering temperatures, and occasional light frosts, spring-seeded annual ryegrass is more productive than the perennial grasses that prepare for winter during this period. Annual ryegrass is grazed, green chopped for daily feeding, or preserved as silage.

At the other end of the growing season, winter rye shows promise in experimental studies as an earlier spring forage source than the perennial grasses.[46] Winter rye should be planted no later than August 15 for this purpose, and only the most winter-hardy cultivars should be used.

NONCROPLAND FORAGES

A significant amount of native rangeland is utilized in Alaska. Extensive areas are pastured virtually year-round by mixed breeds of beef and sheep on a number of islands from Kodiak to Umnak in the western Gulf of Alaska.[34,47,48] Most of these windswept islands are treeless but with a climate moderated by the warming influence of the Japanese Current that extends the grazing season well beyond that experienced on Alaska's mainland (Fig. 45.6). Except for Kodiak, these islands provide safety from large predators such as the brown bears and wolves common in mainland Alaska. No significant artificial forage seedings have been made on any islands except Kodiak. Native grasses such as dune wildrye, *Elymus mollis* Trin.; bering hairgrass, *Deschampsia beringensis* Hult.; alpine timothy, *Phleum alpinum* L.; *Calamagrostis* spp.; *Festuca* spp.; *Poa* spp.; and numerous forbs and sedges as well as kelp on the beaches provide forage in loosely monitored enterprises where the extent of each island imposes ultimate limits on herd movements. Two native legumes among the forbs are the abundant nootka lupine, *Lupinus nootkatensis* Donn, on uplands and the less common beach pea, *Lathyrus maritimus* L., along many shorelines.

Dairy heifers, dry stock, and dairy steers are transported each summer to subalpine range on mountain slopes adjacent to the Matanuska Valley. There cattle consume mostly grasses and assorted forbs and occasionally browse from woody species.[49,50]

Along Alaska's western coastal region, principally on the Seward Peninsula, the

42. Brundage, A. L., and L. J. Klebesadel. 1970. Nutritive value of oat and pea components of a forage mixture harvested sequentially. *J. Dairy Sci.* 53:793–96.

43. Hodgson, H. J. 1956. Effect of seeding rates and time of harvest on yield and quality of oat-pea forage. *Agron. J.* 48:87–90.

44. Klebesadel, L. J. 1969. Chemical composition and yield of oats and peas separated from a forage mixture at successive stages of growth. *Agron. J.* 61:713–16.

45. Brundage, A. L., and C. I. Branton. 1967. Ryegrass and orchardgrass-alfalfa for annual forage and pasture in south central Alaska. *J. Dairy Sci.* 50:856–62.

46. Klebesadel, L. J. 1969. Winter survival and spring forage yield of winter rye varieties in subarctic Alaska as influenced by date of planting. *Agron. J.* 61:708–12.

47. Boykin, C. C., and T. Q. LeBrun. 1969. Economic aspects of beef cattle production in southwest Alaska. *J. Range Manage.* 22:347–51.

48. Johnson, V. J. 1961. Range and livestock of Kodiak Island. *J. Range Manage.* 14:83–88.

49. Compton, T. L., and A. L. Brundage. 1971. Cattle behavior on subalpine range in south central Alaska. *J. Anim. Sci.* 32:339–42.

50. Mitchell, W. W., and J. Evans. 1966. Composition of two disclimax bluejoint stands in south central Alaska. *J. Range Manage.* 19:65–68.

FIG. 45.6. *Significant amount . . . native rangeland . . . utilized.* Beef cows with calves graze mixed native grasses and forbs on a beach ridge on northern Sitkinak Island in southwestern Alaska.

herding of reindeer is a unique agricultural pursuit.[51] Federal law limits ownership of reindeer to Alaskan natives. Reindeer subsist on a varied range diet of which the very slow-growing foliose lichen is a significant component.[52,53] Lichens have no roots, deriving their nutrients primarily from the air. They are high in starch but low in protein. Forbs are abundant, and sedges are more dominant than grasses on these ranges.

Alaska has a considerable number of native grasses. Some of these represent boreal to arctic ecotypes of species whose ranges extend over much of North America (e.g., Kentucky bluegrass, creeping red fescue, bluejoint, pumpelly bromegrass, slender wheatgrass, bluebunch wheatgrass), while others are uniquely northern latitude species not found in temperate latitudes, e.g., arctic wheatgrass *Agropyron macrourum* (Turcz.) Drobov;

Siberian wildrye, *Elymus sibiricus* L.; salt bluegrass, *Poa eminens* Presl.; and tall arcticgrass, *Arctagrostis arundinacea* (Trin.) Beal. Extensive collections are being continued and agronomic evaluations are measuring the potential of these and other native Alaskan grasses for forage production.

❧ QUESTIONS

1. You are a rancher in the intermountain area with a large native hay meadow naturally flood irrigated. What must you know about your meadow to determine whether an improvement program would be a good investment?

2. What percentage of legumes should a dairy farmer in the intermountain area attempt to have in a highly productive irrigated pasture? If he exceeds this level, to what danger is his stock exposed and how can he best minimize this?

3. As a county agricultural agent how would you advise a farmer as to the use of a companion crop in establishing alfalfa or a pasture on irrigated land?

4. Assume you own a section of rangeland in

51. Brady, J. 1968. The reindeer industry in Alaska. Univ. Alaska Inst. Social, Econ. and Gov. Res. 5(3):1–20.
52. Klein, D. R. 1970. Tundra ranges north of the boreal forest. *J. Range Manage.* 23:8–14.
53. Palmer, L. J., and C. H. Rouse. 1945. Study of the Alaska tundra with reference to its reactions to reindeer and other grazing. USDI Res. Rept. 10.

the arid West that is supporting a very dense stand of sagebrush. What facts must you know to decide whether to burn or plow to improve your range?

5. In converting a deteriorated native range to an improved range by seeding crested wheatgrass, why does not a rancher follow the steps a farmer uses in the preparation of a seedbed for a crop sown on arable land?

6. Why is the arid range a valuable resource even though annual per hectare production is low?

7. What agricultural areas of Alaska depend mostly on seeded forage crops? What areas utilize mostly native rangeland?

8. Why are forage crops used in the mid-temperate U.S. generally unsuited in Alaska?

9. What similarities and differences exist between forage crop production in Alaska and the midwestern states?

CARLTON H. HERBEL / *Agricultural Research Service, USDA*

A. A. BALTENSPERGER / *New Mexico State University*

46

RANGES AND PASTURES OF THE
SOUTHERN GREAT PLAINS
AND THE SOUTHWEST

૪

T HE southern Great Plains and the Southwest often are called "Big Country." This not only refers to the size of individual holdings but the sparseness of urban centers. (See Fig. 46.1.) Annual precipitation averages less than 250 mm in the lower elevations of Arizona, New Mexico, and western Texas. It ranges up to 750 mm in the eastern portions of the southern Great Plains. The precipitation not only varies greatly within and among seasons and years but also among locations separated by only a few kilometers. About 70% of the average annual precipitation occurs during

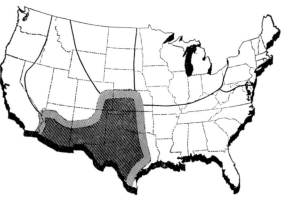

FIG. 46.1. The southern Great Plains and the Southwest.

૪ CARLTON H. HERBEL is Technical Adviser, Range Management, Western Region, and Research Leader, Jornada Experimental Range, ARS, USDA, Las Cruces, N. Mex., and a member of the Graduate Faculty of New Mexico State University. He holds the M.S. and Ph.D. degrees from Kansas State University. His research interests are arid range ecology, grazing management, brush control, seeding, and plant-soil-animal-weather relations.

૪ ARDEN A. BALTENSPERGER is Professor and Head, Department of Agronomy, New Mexico State University. He holds the M.S. degree from the University of Nebraska and the Ph.D. from Iowa State University. He has been engaged in forage research in Texas, Iowa, and Arizona.

the spring-summer period in the Great Plains. In western New Mexico and southern Arizona the growing season precipitation occurs during the summer, and the spring period normally is very dry. (See Fig. 46.2.) The entire region is frequently plagued by drought. During a prolonged drought, the Great Plains may take on a desertlike appearance. The region may also have high winds during some periods; coupled with a reduction in vegetation and

499

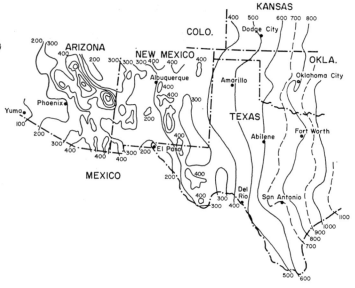

FIG. 46.2. Average annual precipitation in mm. (USDC, 1968.[1])

cover due to drought, this results in considerable wind erosion. The average annual evaporation ranges from 2160 mm at Oklahoma City to 3050 mm at Yuma, Ariz.[1] The frost-free period averages about 180 days in the northeastern part of the region to 340 days in the Yuma area.

Elevations in the southern Great Plains vary from 200 m in southern Texas to 1200 m in northeastern New Mexico. The parts of Arizona and western New Mexico considered in this chapter are desert or desertlike basins interrupted by mountains. The entire region is dissected with rivers and their accompanying floodplains. The soils are highly variable.

Because of the erratic weather conditions dryland farming is high risk in all but the eastern portions of the region. However, because of the favorable temperatures irrigated farming is highly productive where water of good quality is available. A high percentage of the land in the region is used for ranching, a much less intensified operation. Practices common on farmland may not be feasible on rangeland.

1. USDC. 1968. Climate atlas of the United States. Environ. Sci. Serv. Admin.

❧ RANGELANDS

The land used for ranching varies from 50% of the area in the eastern part of the region to more than 95% of the area in Arizona, New Mexico, and the trans-Pecos of Texas. In the latter, farming generally is limited because of low precipitation. Much of the Edwards Plateau in Texas is used for ranching because of shallow and rocky soils and a rolling terrain. Productivity of the rangelands has been greatly reduced by overgrazing, droughts, and an increase in noxious plants. The Edwards Plateau ranches and adjacent areas are stocked with sheep, goats, and cattle. The remaining rangelands of the region are stocked largely with cattle. See Table 46.1.)[2-4]

Much of the rangeland of the region has been invaded by noxious woody plants. An increase of brush is responsible for the loss of grazing lands that formerly made a sig-

2. USDA. 1972. Cattle, sheep, and goat inventory. Crop Rep. Board, Stat. Rep. Serv. LvGn 1 (72).
3. Wooten, H. H., K. Gertel, and W. C. Pendleton. 1962. Major uses of land and water in the United States. USDA Agr. Econ. Rept. 13.
4. USDA. 1972. Crop production, 1971 annual summary. Crop Rep. Board, Stat. Rep. Serv. CrPr 2-1 (72).

TABLE 46.1 ❧ Livestock numbers and selected crops in states of the southern Great Plains and the Southwest

Livestock (000 head) Crops (000 ha)	Arizona	New Mexico	Texas	Oklahoma	Kansas	Colorado
Cattle[2]	1,295	1,441	12,829	5,441	6,757	3,716
Sheep[2]	503	742	3,524	123	337	1,114
Goats[2]	*	*	1,500	*	*	*
Range[3]	23,522	26,488	47,355	9,205	7,675	17,324
Pasture†[3]	83	174	3,319	1,047	585	500
Hay[4]	97	117	898	750	1,002	683
Silage[4]	7	14	78	29	263	116
Fodder[4]	2	28	547	150	179	109
Cereal grains[4]	194	244	3,504	2,003	6,160	1,543

* Small numbers, not estimated.
† Cropland used only for pastures.

nificant contribution to the maintenance of domestic livestock. Stands of brush increase the cost of handling livestock, reduce livestock production, increase parasite damage, and require the use of more breeding males. Mesquite, *Prosopis juliflora* (Swartz) DC., competes with range forage for moisture on about 38 million ha in Arizona, New Mexico, Texas, and southwestern Oklahoma.[5] Shinnery oak, *Quercus havardii* Rydb., occurs on deep sandy soils of western Oklahoma, northern Texas, and eastern New Mexico. Sand sagebrush, *Artemisia filifolia* Torr., is a problem on sandy soils of western Oklahoma and northern Texas. Juniper, *Juniperus* spp., dominates large areas in the Edwards Plateau and rolling plains of Texas[6] and at elevations above the semidesert grasslands and below the ponderosa pine zone in Arizona and New Mexico. Small soapweed, *Yucca glauca* Nutt., is a problem in eastern New Mexico and northern Texas. Tarbush, *Flourensia cernua* DC., occurs on 5.36 million ha in western Texas, southern New Mexico, and southwestern Arizona. Creosotebush, *Larrea tridentata* (DC.) Coville, is a serious problem in Arizona, New Mexico, and western Texas. These are only some of the woody plants of concern to ranchers in the region. Snakeweed, *Gutierrezia sarothrae* (Pursh)

Britt. & Rusby, and burroweed, *Aplopappus tenuisectus* (Greene) Blake, plus poisonous plants such as loco, *Astragalus* spp.; cocklebur, *Xanthium spinosum* L.; and milkweed, *Asclepias* spp., are also a problem. In many instances, as undesirable woody plants increase, there is a corresponding decline in the protective forage grasses and an increase in wind and water erosion. In this region part of the dust during windstorms and the sedimentation in streams and reservoirs comes from rangelands infested with brush. Certain brush species provide browse for wildlife, but heavy stands of those mentioned above have a depressing effect on wildlife, they reduce the recreational value of the land, and in some cases they constitute a serious fire hazard.

Damage of rangeland by rodents and rabbits is often underestimated. On deteriorated mesquite sand dune sites in southern New Mexico there were 81 kg/sq km of rodent biomass.[7] This, plus rabbit populations that may range up to 250/sq km, exerts as much pressure on desirable vegetation as 1 animal unit/sq km. Rodents and rabbits consume vegetation, destroy roots and aboveground plant parts, and collect seed that would otherwise aid in natural revegetation. Even in good grassland areas the banner-tailed kangaroo rats, *Dipodo-*

5. Platt, K. B. 1959. Plant control—Some possibilities and limitations. I. The challenge to management. *J. Range Manage.* 12:64–68.
6. Gould, F. W. 1962. Texas plants—A check list and ecological summary. Tex. Agr. Exp. Sta. MP-585.

7. Wood, J. E. 1969. Rodent populations and their impact on desert rangelands. N. Mex. Agr. Exp. Sta. Bull. 555.

mys spectabilis Merriam, kept 10% of the area from vegetative production by denuding the ground in the vicinity of their mounds.[7] Rangelands in good condition generally have fewer rodents and rabbits than those in poor condition.

Vast range areas in the region are sometimes heavily infested with grasshoppers. Even in a light infestation on a range, with an average of 6 grasshoppers/sq m, those on 4 ha consume grass at about the same rate as a cow.[8] During periods of heavy infestation when there may be 30–60/sq m, all the grass may be destroyed. Like rabbits and rodents, grasshoppers do damage beyond that caused by actual feeding. They cut plant parts and eat only part of them; prevent natural revegetation; eat the grass closer than livestock; and when extremely abundant, sometimes injure the crowns so that growth is reduced for several years. Other insects sometimes causing damage are the New Mexico range caterpillar, *Hemileuca oliviae* Cockerell; armyworms, *Pseudaletia, Laphygma* and *Prodenia* spp.; harvester ants, *Pogonomyrmex* spp.; and thrips, *Frankliniella* and *Thrips* spp.[9]

CONTROL OF NOXIOUS PLANTS

Trends toward dominance by noxious plants can be halted or reduced by judicious use of mechanical and chemical control methods, revegetation of forage species, and control of the numbers of grazing animals and their seasons of use. Sound management principles are essential to the use of any control method on rangeland infested with brush. Once established, woody plants such as mesquite, juniper, oak, and sagebrush cannot be eliminated by good grazing practices alone. On rangelands dominated by brush, control measures are essential before achieving benefits from other improvement practices such as a grazing system, seeding, or water spreading. The most effective control measure may

vary for each particular site, specific vegetation, and degree of infestation. Brush control generally is less costly when invasion is just beginning and the brush plants are small and scattered. In this situation a method should be employed that will not destroy the residual forage plants. On sandy soils heavily infested with brush a broadcast chemical method may provide control of the undesirable plants and result in an increase in forage plants. On medium- to heavy-textured soils with a heavy infestation of brush and a poor stand of desirable plants, a mechanical method accompanied with seeding may be required. Broadcast mechanical methods generally are avoided on sandy soils because of the wind erosion hazard. Fortunately, natural revegetation often is quite rapid on sandy soils following chemical control of the brush. Conversely, natural revegetation following brush control often is very slow on medium- to heavy-textured soils.

CHEMICAL CONTROL. It is often difficult to chemically control stands of mixed brush species with a single application because of different herbicide requirements for various species or a different time of peak readiness among various species. To be effective, foliage applications of herbicides must be applied at the proper stage of growth. Treating mesquite even one week too early drastically reduces the effectiveness of 2,4,5-T treatments.[10] Plants generally are most sensitive to foliage sprays of growth-regulator herbicides when they are actively growing. In dry years herbicide treatments should not be made since plants under moisture stress do not readily translocate phenoxy herbicides.

To achieve adequate initial control of many woody plants, two or more herbicidal applications are necessary. Two aerial spray applications of 0.56 kg of 2,4,5-T/ha from one to three years apart killed 23–64% of the mesquite on sand dunes in southern

8. Parker, J. R. 1954. Grasshoppers, a new look at an ancient enemy. USDA Farmers' Bull. 2064.

9. Randolph, N. M., and C. F. Garner. 1961. Insects attacking forage crops. Tex. Agr. Ext. Serv. Bull. B-975.

10. Valentine, K. A., and J. J. Norris. 1960. Mesquite control with 2,4,5-T by ground spray application. N. Mex. Agr. Exp. Sta. Bull. 451.

FIG. 46.3. *Leveling of sand dunes . . . less wind erosion on sprayed areas.* Aerial spraying of mesquite sand dunes in southern New Mexico. Controlling the mesquite increases forage production.

New Mexico.[11] Perennial grass yields on areas sprayed twice in 1958–61 averaged 234 kg/ha during 1963–68. On an adjacent unsprayed area the perennial grass production averaged 39 kg/ha. There have been a leveling of the sand dunes and less wind erosion on the sprayed areas. (See Fig. 46.3.)

Herbicides such as 2,4-D, 2,4,5-T, silvex, dicamba, and picloram control many species. Applied as broadcast sprays, they may be used on dense stands of weeds or brush. Individual plant treatments of dry herbicides are an effective and economical method of controlling sparse stands of brush. Monuron, fenuron, picloram, and other herbicides are applied as powder, granules, or pellets around the bases of target plants.[12]

MECHANICAL METHODS. Bulldozing and mechanical grubbing, rootplowing, disking, and cabling or chaining are the major mechanical methods of rangeland brush control.

Bulldozing is effective on sparse stands of many species. Bulldozer blades or front-end loaders may be fitted with a stinger blade which is pushed under the crown of the plant to ensure uprooting of the bud

zone. Experienced operators can lift and push over a tree in one smooth operation.[12]

A rootplow is a horizontal blade attached to a track-type tractor. Rootplowing cuts off the brush, generally at depths of 38 cm for mesquite or other resprouting species and at lesser depths for nonsprouting species. Rootplowing kills 90% or more of all of the vegetation growing on the area. The method is best adapted to dense brush areas having little or no residual grass and where seeding of desirable grasses is possible.[13]

Disking is done with a large disk plow or tandem disk which uproots the brush. It is limited to small shallow-rooted plants like sagebrush, creosotebush, and tarbush. It also destroys grasses growing on the area. Thus disking, like rootplowing, should only be done in areas where forages can be established.[12]

Chaining and cabling involve the dragging of a 90–120 m anchor chain or heavy-duty cable in a loop behind two track-type tractors.[14] The method is effective in controlling nonsprouting species like one-seeded juniper, *Juniperus monosperma* (Engelm.) Sarg., and Utah juniper, *J. os-*

11. Herbel, C. H., and W. L. Gould. 1970. Control of mesquite, creosotebush, and tarbush on arid rangelands of the southwestern United States. Proc. 11th Int. Grassl. Congr., pp. 38–44 (Surfers Paradise, Queensland, Aust.).
12. National Research Council Subcommittee on Weeds. 1968. Weed Control. Nat. Acad. Sci. Publ. 1597.

13. Rechenthin, C. A., H. M. Bell, R. J. Pederson, and D. B. Polk. 1964. Grassland restoration. II. Brush control. SCS, Temple, Tex.
14. Fisher, C. E., C. H. Meadors, R. Behrens, E. D. Robison, P. T. Marion, and H. L. Morton. 1959. Control of mesquite on grazing lands. Tex. Agr. Exp. Sta. Bull. 935.

teosperma (Torr.) Little. It also is useful in knocking down mesquite trees previously killed by aerial spraying, thereby reducing the cost of working livestock.

BURNING. Results of burning vary greatly and depend on the susceptibility of a species to fire and the availability of enough fuel. Several range shrubs and weeds are ideally controlled by burning at the proper season if moisture conditions are good and precautions are observed. An example of using fire in range management is the burning of vegetation infested with shinnery oak. Its growth is suppressed for several years and forage production is substantially increased. Summer burning is effective in controlling burroweed in southern Arizona.[15] Burning also is useful in removing old stemmy forage growth from species such as sand bluestem and tobosa.

GRAZING METHODS. Sheep and goats are utilized to control some plants. The animals select the more palatable plants or plant parts and are effective in controlling seedlings and young sprouts. However, continuous heavy utilization of the desirable forage species must be avoided.

SEEDING

In this region the soil surface is infrequently moistened and the evaporation rate is high. Establishing seedlings often is difficult because of an adverse microenvironment (rapid drying, unfavorable temperatures, and crusting of the soil surface). The primary objective in seedling establishment is to place the seed in a favorable environment for germination. Establishment methods vary with site conditions.

Under rangeland conditions most grasses should be seeded 0.7–2 cm deep. In the southern Great Plains sufficient moisture for seedling emergence and establishment cannot be maintained on level bare surface

soil except with very favorable weather.[16] The average annual precipitation in that area ranges from 350 to 600 mm. Establishment is a greater problem in the more arid areas of the Southwest. The use of mulches and land-forming procedures increases the chance of successful seedling establishment under difficult environments.

STUBBLE MULCHES. In forage establishment, plant residue improves soil moisture and protects the soil surface against wind and water erosion.[17] Stubble mulching is being used for seeding grasses in the Great Plains.[18] It consists of planting a residue-producing crop like sorghum a year before the grass is seeded. Sorghum is seeded in mid to late summer to prevent seed formation before frost but in time to make 15–20 cm growth. Grasses are seeded the following spring. Residue from the sorghum improves the microenvironment for the grass seedlings.

RIPPING, PITTING, AND FURROWING. Pitting followed by cultipacker seeding has been the most consistent method of successfully seeding ranges in Arizona.[19] Ripping and contour furrowing have also been good methods of seedbed preparation on fine-textured bottomland soils. Broad shallow pits generally last longer than conventional pits made with a pitter disk. The four-year average annual production of seeded buffelgrass was 773 kg/ha on an area with broad pits and 283 kg/ha on an area with conventional pits.[20]

PLOWING AND SEEDING. Broadcast-seeding native grasses at the time of rootplowing for control of mesquite failed to

15. Tschirley, F. H., and S. C. Martin. 1961. Burroweed on southern Arizona rangelands. Ariz. Agr. Exp. Sta. Tech. Bull. 146.

16. Army, T. J., and E. B. Hudspeth, Jr. 1960. Alteration of the microclimate of the seed zone. *Agron. J.* 52:17–22.

17. Duley, F. L. 1953. Relationship between surface cover and water penetration, runoff, and soil losses. Proc. 6th Int. Grassl. Congr., 2:942–46 (State College, Pa.).

18. Anderson, K. L. 1959. Establishing and reseeding grassland in the Great Plains and western Corn Belt. Proc. Amer. Grassl. Council, pp. 30–36.

19. Anderson, D., L. P. Hamilton, H. G. Reynolds, and R. R. Humphrey. 1957. Reseeding desert grassland ranges in southern Arizona. Ariz. Agr. Exp. Sta. Bull. 249.

20. Slayback, R. D., and D. R. Cable. 1970. Larger pits aid reseeding of semidesert rangeland. *J. Range Manage.* 23:333–35.

provide satisfactory stands at several locations in the high plains of Texas.[21] Loss of seedlings after emergence was attributed to rapid depletion of soil moisture from the loose seedbed after rootplowing and to severe weed competition. Broadcasting is generally a poor method of seeding.

Equipment has been developed for successfully seeding areas infested with brush in the arid Southwest.[22] The brush and other competing vegetation are controlled with a rootplow. The seed are placed in a V-shaped press-wheel groove. Drag chains cover the seed with loose soil to a depth of about 1.3 cm. A conveyor picks up the brush behind the rootplow and deposits it behind the seeder, and a hydraulically operated bulldozer blade in front of the seeder forms basin pits. Thus in a simultaneous operation the competing vegetation is killed; the seed is placed in a firm seedbed; the dead brush is used to partially shade the seeded area, thereby substantially reducing summer soil temperatures; and water is concentrated near the seed.

SPECIES TO SEED. Species for range seedings vary with climatic and site conditions and management of a specific range unit. A species may only be adapted to sandy soils in a fairly small area; other species may have wider adaptation. Considerable use is made of seed harvests of native species. It is important to choose native cultivars or ecotypes of local origin, generally within 300 km north and 450 km south of the area to be seeded. Many native and introduced species are used for seeding in the region.

Big bluestem, little bluestem, switchgrass, and indiangrass are important native species in the eastern part of the southern Great Plains; sand bluestem is adapted to sandy soils. Blue grama and sideoats grama are widely adapted throughout the region except for the most arid

portions of the Southwest. Black grama, Lehmann lovegrass, and Boer lovegrass are some of the major species used in the more arid portions of the Southwest. Blue panicgrass and buffelgrass commonly are used for seeding in Texas. Weeping lovegrass has been seeded in Oklahoma, northern Texas, and the foothills of Arizona.

Seeding rates generally are 100 pure live seed/m of seeded row. Most of the native grass seed is harvested from native stands on rangeland. There is some seed production, particularly of introduced species, under irrigated conditions. Many grass plantings have been ruined by grazing before the seedlings were well established since newly seeded plants must not be grazed until they are well rooted. Severe infestations of rodents, rabbits, and insects are sometimes responsible for seeding failures.

RANGE FERTILIZATION

In some parts of the region low amounts of N in the soil limit plant growth. Fertilizer N is economical only where there is adequate moisture and plant species that give N response.

In Oklahoma, forage yields of weeping lovegrass increased about 50% with 34 kg N/ha.[23] A single application in April increased yearling steer gains 10%; carrying capacity, 25%; beef production per ha, 31%; and profit per ha, 36%. Weeping lovegrass fertilized with N was more palatable, stayed green longer at the beginning of droughts, regrew faster after grazing, and produced more seed. Nitrogen available for plant growth on grazed pastures after a few years of fertilization may amount to 50% of the annual requirement due to recycling through the grazing animal.[24]

In a 380-mm precipitation area in New Mexico, blue grama range fertilized with 45

21. Jaynes, C. C., E. D. Robison, and W. G. McCully. 1968. Root-plowing and revegetation on the rolling and southern high plains. Tex. Agr. Exp. Sta. Rept. 2585.

22. Herbel, C. H. 1972. Environmental modification for seedling establishment. *In* Biology and Utilization of Grasses. Academic Press, New York.

23. McIlvain, E. H., and M. C. Shoop. 1970. Fertilizing weeping lovegrass in western Oklahoma. Proc. 1st Weeping Lovegrass Symp., pp. 61–70 (Noble Foundation, Ardmore, Okla.).

24. Davidson, R. L. 1964. Theoretical aspects of nitrogen economy in grazing experiments. *J. Brit. Grassl. Soc.* 19:273–80.

kg N/ha produced gains of 54 kg/ha, while unfertilized range produced gains of only 26 kg/ha.[25] The increase was due mainly to the greater number of cattle that could be grazed on the fertilized range. Even in more arid areas, some possibilities exist of increasing production on sites that are flooded occasionally.[26]

GRAZING MANAGEMENT

Manipulation of the season of use and intensity of grazing is an important way of increasing range productivity. A decline in grazing capacity has occurred due to overgrazing during droughty periods and a rapid increase in noxious shrubs.

On the Edwards Plateau near Sonora, Tex., average annual net returns for 1959–65 were $1.78, $2.91, and $1.63/ha with light, moderate, and heavy yearlong continuous stocking. The average net return for the same period with a rotation scheme was $4.15/ha.[27] In a four-pasture rotation system each pasture is grazed 12 months then rested 4 months. Thus during a four-year cycle each pasture is deferred once during each of the four-month periods.[28]

Further west on the Edwards Plateau near Barnhart, average annual net returns for 1959–65 were $3.06, $3.90, and $4.17/ha for yearlong continuous use, four-pasture rotation, and two-pasture rotation, all stocked at a moderate rate.[29] At Barnhart a combination of cattle and sheep was more profitable than grazing either alone. At Sonora, combination grazing with cattle, sheep, and goats or cattle and goats was more profitable than using sheep alone or cattle alone. Combination grazing is suc-

cessful because of differential use of species and plant parts.

In the southern rolling plains near Throckmorton, Tex., calf production per animal unit averaged 200, 208, and 221 kg/year for moderate continuous use, two-pasture rotation, and four-pasture rotation for 1960–68.[30]

In studies at Woodward, Okla., continuous yearlong grazing has been equal or superior to several rotation schemes.[31] Major reasons for the success of continuous yearlong grazing in the southern Great Plains are:

1. Forage production is primarily dependent upon summer rainfall, and monthly forage production during the summer can vary from 20 to 670 kg/ha.
2. Most species are grazed by cattle at one time or another.
3. Many "increaser" species are excellent grazing plants, and they are very productive under certain conditions.
4. Cattle compete with natural losses of forages and with other consumers (rodents, rabbits, and insects).
5. Young and regrowth forage is more palatable and more nutritious than mature forage.
6. Grazed plants do not deplete soil moisture as rapidly as ungrazed plants.
7. Favorable seasons combined with proper management allow ranges to recover a desirable species composition.
8. Utilization during the growing season is light.
9. Lighter stocking per unit area means less soil compaction by livestock during wet periods.

Using weather and plant information and considering livestock needs, the "best pasture grazing system" has been developed

25. Dwyer, D. D., and J. G. Schickendanz. 1971. Vegetation and cattle responses to nitrogen-fertilized rangeland in south central New Mexico. N. Mex. Agr. Exp. Sta. Res. Rept. 215.
26. Herbel, C. H. 1963. Fertilizing tobosa on floodplains in the semidesert grassland. *J. Range Manage.* 16:133–38.
27. Merrill, L. B. 1969. Grazing systems in the Edwards Plateau of Texas. Abstr. 22nd Ann. Meet., Amer. Soc. Range Manage., pp. 22–23.
28. Merrill, L. B. 1954. A variation of deferred rotation grazing for use under Southwest range conditions. *J. Range Manage.* 7:152–54.
29. Huss, D. L., and J. V. Allen. 1969. Livestock production and profitability comparisons of various grazing systems, Texas range station. Tex. Agr. Exp. Sta. Bull. B-1089.

30. Kothmann, M. M., G. W. Mathis, P. T. Marion, and W. J. Waldrip. 1970. Livestock production and economic returns from grazing treatments on the Texas experimental ranch. Tex. Agr. Exp. Sta. Bull. B-1100.
31. McIlvain, E. H., and M. C. Shoop. 1969. Grazing systems in the southern Great Plains. Abstr. 22nd Ann. Meet., Amer. Soc. Range Manage., pp. 21–22.

in the Southwest.[32] The system consists of defining an objective relative to the desired species composition for each pasture and then stocking accordingly. The system is opportunistic in that the use of forbs and short-lived grasses is maximized. They are of little value to the permanent range resource but contribute much to livestock nutrition.[33] No set stocking plan is used for a specified time period because great variations in weather affect plant growth. Livestock are moved when vegetation in another pasture can be grazed to the advantage of both plants and animals. In large pastures in the Southwest, periodic opening and closing of watering places is used to rotate grazing pressure to different areas within a pasture.[34]

THE RANCH AS A SYSTEM

Ranches differ in the amount of water development, fencing, and equipment improvements; the proportion of various soil and vegetation types; wildlife values and recreational opportunities; kinds, breeds, and classes of livestock; supplemental feeding practices; and management objectives of the operator. These factors must be collectively considered to maximize production while maintaining the resource. When a variable is introduced, it affects the entire system. For example, in northwestern Oklahoma clearing of brush, seeding, and fertilizing may be used to substantially alter the stocking pattern on a ranch.[35] In that instance only about 10–15% of a ranch should be used for seeded and fertilized weeping lovegrass. Its productivity and season of use dictate this, or a rancher must resort to more intensive management practices than most prefer.

Similarly, a southwestern rancher with a brush problem may want to initiate a program of deferred-rotation grazing. Later, when the brush in a pasture has been controlled, the grazing could be deferred during the growing season for one to three years to allow for a quicker recovery of desirable vegetation. After the brush on a major part of the ranch has been treated, it may be necessary to change to another grazing system to maximize profits.

✤ IRRIGATED PASTURE AND HAY

Alfalfa, sorghums, and a number of grass species are the most important pasture and hay crops produced under irrigation. (See Fig. 46.4.)

ALFALFA

Alfalfa, the most important irrigated forage crop, is adapted to a wide variety of climatic and soil conditions; however, it requires a large amount of water for maximum production. Under irrigation, yields range from approximately 9 to 27 t/ha. On highly productive soils in southern New Mexico light and frequent irrigations using up to 190 cm of water resulted in higher yields and good water-use efficiency.[36]

Irrigation water is usually applied using the border method; however, other methods such as sprinkling, flooding from contour field ditches, and flooding by basins are used. Care should be taken in designing and constructing the system since alfalfa stands are usually maintained for three or more years. Stands are sometimes reduced or lost by excess surface water caused by poor leveling or poor soil drainage.

Alfalfa is moderately tolerant to salts;[37,38] however, special management is required when salts become excessive. Excessive concentrations of either soluble salts or ex-

32. Herbel, C. H., and A. B. Nelson. 1969. Grazing management on semidesert ranges in southern New Mexico. Jornada Exp. Range Rept. 1.
33. Nelson, A. B., C. H. Herbel, and H. M. Jackson. 1970. Chemical composition of forage species grazed by cattle on an arid New Mexico range. N. Mex. Agr. Exp. Sta. Bull. 561.
34. Martin, S. C., and D. E. Ward. 1970. Rotating access to water to improve semidesert cattle range near water. *J. Range Manage.* 23:22–26.
35. McIlvain, E. H., and M. C. Shoop. No date. Grazing weeping lovegrass. Okla. State Univ. Ext. Facts 2558.

36. Hanson, E. G. 1967. Influence of irrigation practices on alfalfa yield and consumptive use. N. Mex. Agr. Exp. Sta. Bull. 514.
37. Bernstein, L. 1958. Salt tolerance of grasses and legumes. USDA Inf. Bull. 194.
38. U.S. Salinity Laboratory Staff. 1954. Diagnosis and improvement of saline and alkali soils. USDA Agr. Handbook 60.

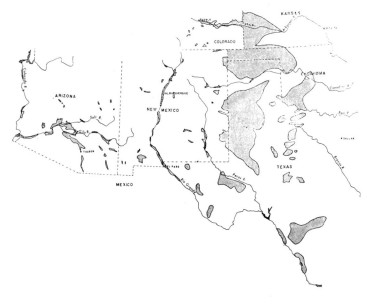

FIG. 46.4. Principal irrigation areas, 1972. Within large blocks shown in Texas, Oklahoma, and Kansas there are significant hectares of nonirrigated land.

changeable sodium or both often cause reduced production. Leaching is the process of dissolving and transporting salts downward through the soil, and is commonly used to help alleviate problems with soluble salts. Productivity of sodium-affected soils has been improved by a combination of leaching and treatment with gypsum and sulfur.[39]

Alfalfa and perennial grasses are well adapted for the improvement of desert and semidesert soils for irrigated agriculture. These forages improve permeability and aeration of soils if managed for high productivity. Alfalfa is especially valuable in crop rotation systems in the irrigated parts of the region.

If a thick stand is maintained, weed control is not as serious with alfalfa as with many other crops. Fall seeding has been popular in much of the region, partially because of fewer weeds compared to spring seedings.

Cultivars have been developed for this region to fit specific insect, disease, and environmental conditions.[40,41] Examples are 'Mesa Sirsa,' 'Sonora,' 'El Unico,' and 'Sonora 70' for Arizona; 'Zia,' 'Mesilla,' 'W.L. 306,' and 'A.S. 13' for New Mexico and western Texas; and 'Kanza' and 'Dawson' for the northern states of the region. Cultivars vary considerably in degree of dormancy. A number have been developed with less dormancy to take advantage of the longer growing season in much of the region.

SORGHUMS

Many different sorghum types and hybrids are used for silage, pasture, and hay under irrigation. Sudangrass and sudangrass hybrids commonly are used for summer pasture and less frequently for hay. Forage sorghum hybrids and hybrids between grain and forage types are used for silage. In parts of the region corn also is important.

Sorghum is a drought-tolerant crop but responds strikingly to irrigation in the arid and semiarid portions of the region. Water requirement ranges from 41 to 61 cm/year.[42] Sorghum is moderately tolerant to salts; however, special management may

39. Chang, C. W., and H. E. Dregne. 1955. Reclamation of salt- and sodium-affected soils in the Mesilla Valley. N. Mex. Agr. Exp. Sta. Bull. 401.

40. Dennis, R. E., et al. 1966. Alfalfa for forage production in Arizona. Ariz. Coop. Ext. Serv. & Agr. Exp. Sta. Bull. A-16.

41. Melton, B. A., N. R. Malm, C. E. Barnes, H. D. Jones, D. H. Williams, P. M. Trujillo, J. E. Gregory, and R. E. Finker. 1971. Performance of alfalfa varieties. N. Mex. Agr. Exp. Sta. Bull. 583.

42. Quinby, J. R., and P. T. Marion. 1960. Production and feeding of forage sorghum in Texas. Tex. Agr. Exp. Sta. Bull. 965.

be needed in the drier portions of the region where salts are excessive. Sorghums do well on a variety of soils but yield best on soils with good tilth and drainage and relatively high fertility. A forage sorghum crop producing 70 t/ha of silage contains about 125 kg of N; therefore, large amounts of N are removed from the soil and must be replaced. The depressing effects sorghum sometimes has on crops that immediately follow may be partially reduced by applying fertilizer N. Choosing forage sorghums resistant to lodging is important for use under irrigated, high-fertility conditions.

OTHER GRASSES

A large number of grasses including bermudagrass, tall fescue, blue panicgrass, tall wheatgrass, and intermediate wheatgrass provide a significant amount of pasture and some hay under irrigation. These grasses require about as much water as alfalfa for maximum production. However, if less water is available, they can be maintained satisfactorily at a lower productivity. Under irrigated conditions these grasses respond to high N levels if other fertilizer elements are adequate.

❧ NONIRRIGATED FORAGES OTHER THAN RANGE GRASSES

In the drier parts of the region, particularly in the lower elevations of the Southwest, tame pastures generally cannot be established or maintained without irrigation. In the eastern part, small-grain pasture is one of the most important forages. Wheat, oats, barley, and rye often are grazed if there is sufficient moisture. It is common practice to harvest grain from these crops, and careful grazing management must be practiced if optimum grain yields are to be realized.

Perennial grasses like bermudagrass, johnsongrass, buffelgrass, several wheatgrasses, and legumes supply considerable forage without irrigation. Generally, their productivity is limited by moisture; however, soil type, fertility, and physical condition may also be limiting.

❧ QUESTIONS

1. How is annual precipitation related to the occurrence of warm- and cool-season forage species on rangeland?
2. What are some of the major brush problems of the region? How does this affect ranch operations? What are the two major methods of controlling noxious brush species? What are three factors governing the selection of control methods?
3. What are the problems associated with seeding rangelands? What seeding procedures are used to help alleviate these problems?
4. List several reasons for the success of continuous yearlong grazing in the southern Great Plains. What classes of livestock have been found to be most profitable in the Edwards Plateau? Why is it important to have flexibility in stocking ranges of the Southwest?
5. What are the major problems associated with irrigated forage production in the region?
6. Contrast the management of sorghums for forage under irrigated versus nonirrigated conditions.
7. List and discuss the most important tame forage species of the region.

A. L. HAFENRICHTER, DONALD S. DOUGLAS,
AND FRANK L. BROOKS, JR.
Soil Conservation Service, USDA

47

HAY AND PASTURE SEEDINGS
FOR THE PACIFIC COAST STATES

❧

Aᴌʟ ʙᴜᴛ ᴀ sᴍᴀʟʟ part of the Pacific Coast states where farms and ranches are found is essentially arid or semiarid. (See Fig. 47.1.) The area west of the Cascade Mountains and high plateaus in eastern Oregon and Washington and adjacent Idaho are classed as subhumid. Even in the humid and subhumid areas the climate is summer-dry, and supplemental irrigation is required to maintain season-long forage production.[1]

Soil conditions such as depth, profile, permeability, pH, wetness, fertility level,

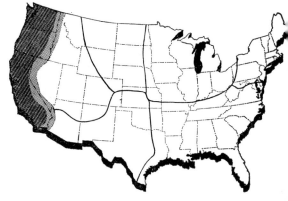

Fɪɢ. 47.1. The Pacific Coast states.

and temperature influence the choice of species for forage production. Temperature is associated with both latitude and elevation. Elevations above sea level vary rapidly in any latitudinal belt because chains of mountains parallel the coast. Farming is carried on from below sea level to more than 2000 m.

Differences in latitude combined with differences in elevation bring about con-

❧ A. L. HAFENRICHTER was Regional Plant Materials Specialist (West), SCS, USDA, Portland, Oreg., until his retirement in 1967. He holds the Ph.D. degree from the University of Illinois. He directed SCS plant materials centers in the western states for over 30 years.

❧ DONALD S. DOUGLAS is Regional Plant Materials Specialist (West), SCS, USDA, Portland, Oreg. He was trained at Washington State University. He has worked as a plant materials specialist and in related areas since 1935.

❧ FRANK L. BROOKS, JR., is Regional Agronomist (West), SCS, USDA, Portland, Oreg. He was trained at Kansas State University. He has worked in agronomy and soil conservation since 1939.

1. Leighly, John. 1941. Settlement and cultivation in the summer-dry climate. *In* Climate and Man, pp. 197–204. USDA Yearbook Agr.

TABLE 47.1 ❧ Hectares and average yield/ha hays in the Pacific Coast states

Kind of hay	Unit	California 1959	California 1969	North Idaho 1959	North Idaho 1969	Oregon 1959	Oregon 1969	Washington 1959	Washington 1969
Alfalfa,	ha (000)	411	400	96	78	124	139	163	179
alfalfa-grass	t/ha	12.20	12.52	5.46	6.40	6.25	7.15	5.51	8.41
Clover and timothy,	ha (000)	55	42	18	18	68	77	32	55
clover and grass	t/ha	3.99	4.25	3.63	3.92	4.08	4.38	4.36	4.79
Grain hay	ha (000)	134	77	7	3	42	36	30	24
	t/ha	3.58	4.14	3.14	4.03	3.05	3.30	3.25	3.25
Wild hay	ha (000)	40	49	4	2	96	91	17	10
	t/ha	2.50	3.00	3.02	4.20	2.44	2.98	2.90	3.43
Other hay	ha (000)	18	60	3	4	23	96	18	16
	t/ha	3.29	3.36	3.36	2.90	3.47	3.04	3.47	3.49

ditions ranging from a long growing season in a hot climate at low elevation to a short growing season in a cold climate at high elevation. Where the growing season is short, provision must be made for supplies of winter feed. The many combinations of climate and soil make it necessary to use several grasses and legumes. Only a few have wide adaptation.

Several changes have occurred in the number and kinds of livestock on farms during the 1960s. The number of stock sheep has decreased 35%; beef cattle, excluding those on feed, increased 13%; dairy cattle decreased about 14%; but the amount of milk per cow increased 27%.[2] These changes have an effect on the kind of forage produced, how it is managed on private lands, and the grazing on public lands.

New species of grasses and legumes have been introduced, and superior cultivars have been developed.[3,4] Alternate-row seedings of mixtures ensure good stands and the desirable proportion of grass and legume in the mixture.[5] The use of fertilizers (based on soil tests) such as lime, manure, P, K, and sometimes S increases production and aids in maintaining the desired components in the mixture.[6-8]

2. USDA. 1970. Agricultural statistics.
3. Hafenrichter, A. L., John L. Schwendiman, Harold L. Harris, Robert S. MacLauchlan, and Harold W. Miller. 1968. Grasses and legumes for soil conservation in the Pacific Northwest and Great Basin states. USDA Agr. Handbook 339.
4. Hanson, A. A. 1972. Grass varieties in the United States. USDA Agr. Handbook 170, rev.
5. MacLauchlan, Robert S., and A. L. Hafenrichter. 1961. Alternate-row grass-legume seedings. *J. Soil Water Conserv.* 16:61–64.
6. Jackson, T. L., and H. B. Howell. 1967. Effect of fertilizers on irrigated grass-legume pastures on an Astoria soil series. Oreg. Agr. Exp. Sta. Tech. Bull. 99.

❧ HAY

KINDS OF HAY

Table 47.1 shows the kind and amount of hay grown in 1959 and 1969 as reported by the U.S. Census of Agriculture and the USDA Statistical Reporting Service. Almost 9 million t of hay were harvested from 1.5 million ha in 1959. In 1969, production was 10.4 million t from 1.45 million ha. The yield increased 1.15 t/ha or 12.5%, and the increase was due to the use of new cultivars and better management of the crop.

ALFALFA. Alfalfa is the principal hay crop in the Pacific Coast states. A total of 794,000 ha was reported in 1969, and this was 55% of the land on which hay was grown. The yield of 8.02 million t was about 75% of all hay produced.

High yields, high quality, market demand, and value in crop rotations are the reasons for the dominant place of alfalfa among hay crops. Intensive plant breeding programs have produced superior cultivars. New cultivars for the continental climatic part of the Pacific Coast states are winter-hardy and resist bacterial wilt, stem nematodes, and spotted alfalfa aphid. Cultivars for the Mediterranean climate are not winter-hardy but resist bacterial wilt, leaf spot, and downy mildew. Preferred and registered cultivars in

7. Turelle, Joseph W., and Wayne W. Austin. 1967. Irrigated pastures for forage and soil conservation in the West. USDA Farmers' Bull. 2230.
8. Turner, Darrell O. 1967. Yield and botanical composition of certain grass-legume mixtures on Puget clay loam. Wash. Agr. Exp. Sta. Bull. 683.

common use are shown in Tables 47.2–47.4 and 47.6–47.8.

Alfalfa is the hay most commonly found in commercial channels. When grown for sale, it is grown alone rather than in mixtures. Much of it is sold baled, but some is dehydrated or pelleted, especially for export. In 1969 an average of 40, 30, 20, and 40% of the alfalfa hay grown in California, Idaho, Oregon, and Washington was sold from the farms where it was produced.[2]

CLOVER, TIMOTHY, GRASS. The second category of hay in Table 47.1 includes clover, timothy, and clover and grass. Only about 9% of the hay is in this category. Much of the clover hay is harvested from seed fields; the first crop is cut for hay and the second for seed. Red clover is seeded with ryegrass for short rotations and on cutover land. Alsike is used with grass on poorly drained land and on acid soils, especially in cool areas. Production of timothy hay is increasing slightly for riding horses.

SMALL GRAIN. About 529,000 t of small-grain hay was harvested in 1969. This was only 5.6% of the hay produced. However, after the rapid decline in use prior to 1950, the amount now remains stable or fluctuates slightly with weather conditions. Grain hay is harvested primarily from semiarid lands, often from plantings originally made for grain but cut for hay when adverse climatic conditions prevent maturity.

WILD HAY. Wild hay harvested from sub-irrigated meadows in the arid interior or from mountain valleys is an important asset to the range livestock industry. The land is not easily tilled, has a high water table, may be flooded in winter or spring, or may be alkaline. The hay consists of native grasses or a mixture of these with sedges, rushes, and forbs. The amount of these meadows is 9.25% of the hayland, but production has increased more than 17% between 1959 and 1969. Yield averages 3.4 t/ha due to better land,

TABLE 47.2 ❧ Legume-grass mixtures for hay in the subhumid part of the continental climatic zone

Mixture	Seeding rate (kg/ha)
Deep, well-drained to moderately well-drained soils	
1. Orchardgrass—Latar *or*	4
timothy—'Climax,'	(5)
alfalfa—Flemish type *or*	13
birdsfoot—'Cascade'*	(6)
Droughty or excessively drained soils	
2. Tall fescue—Fawn, Alta,	5
birdsfoot—Cascade *or*	6
alfalfa—Flemish type	(10)
Moderately well-drained soils with restricted subsoil permeability	
3. Orchardgrass—Latar *or*	5
tall fescue—Fawn, Alta,	(5)
birdsfoot—Cascade* *or*	6
white clover—Grasslands Huia	(5)
Poorly drained soil	
4. Tall fescue—Fawn, Alta *or*	11
reed canarygrass—'Ioreed,'	(11)
big trefoil*	5

Note: Parentheses indicate substitution within the group.
* Birdsfoot and big trefoil should be seeded in alternate rows with grass.

water, and forage management practices.[9,10]

OTHERS. Other tame hays are grown in localized areas where special conditions prevail. Oats and vetch or oats and pea mixtures are grown west of the coast range in Oregon and in western Washington where they can be cured after the rainy season. They also are grown on or along the foothills in parts of California where water is not available for irrigation. In some cases oats are planted and grain harvested the first year, hay is cut from the volunteer oats and vetch in the second year, and the mixture is grazed the third year.

MIXTURES FOR HAY

A large number of legume-grass mixtures are planted for hay on farms in the con-

9. Cooper, C. S., and W. A. Sawyer. 1955. Fertilization of mountain meadows in eastern Oregon. *J. Range Manage.* 8:20–22.
10. Rumburg, C. B. 1969. Yield and concentration of meadow hay fertilized with three nitrogen sources. *Agron. J.* 61:824–25.

TABLE 47.3 ❧ Mixtures for hay on irrigated lands in the semiarid part of the continental climatic zone

Mixture	Seeding rate (kg/ha)
Adequate water, deep well-drained to moderately well-drained soils	
1. Orchardgrass—Latar *or*	5
tall fescue—Alta,	(7)
alfalfa—'Washoe,' 'Ranger'	6
Adequate water, moderately alkaline soils	
2. Tall fescue—Alta,	7
birdsfoot—Cascade* *or*	3
alfalfa—Washoe, Ranger	(5)
Inadequate irrigation water	
3. Intermediate wheatgrass—Greenar,	7
alfalfa—Washoe, Ranger	5
Poorly drained soils	
4. Creeping foxtail—Garrison *or*	6
tall fescue—Alta *or*	(7)
reed canarygrass—Ioreed,	(6)
birdsfoot—Cascade*	3

Note: Parentheses indicate substitution within the group.
* Birdsfoot should be seeded in alternate rows with grass.

tinental climatic part of the Pacific Coast states because there are many combinations of climate, soil, water, drainage, and farm enterprises. State and federal workers have largely standardized mixtures for well-defined but broad categories of factors affecting production. Typical and widely used mixtures are shown in Tables 47.2, 47.3, and 47.4.

Soil conditions divide the four groups of mixtures in the subhumid part of the continental climatic zone west of the Cascade Mountains. Amount of water, degree of drainage, and saline-sodic influences separate the five groups on the irrigated lands of the interior east of the Cascade Mountains and the Sierra Nevada, but on nonirrigated lands the amount of precipitation is the determining factor.

The mixtures in Tables 47.2 and 47.3 contain only one grass and one legume. The practice of seeding the grass and the legume in alternate rows is becoming more common. This ensures establishment of both components because it eliminates competition during the seedling stage, thus allowing control over the percentage of both in the hay.[5,7,11]

'Latar' orchardgrass or 'Fawn' or 'Alta' tall fescue are the most commonly used grasses in the subhumid area. Flemish-type alfalfa or 'Cascade' birdsfoot trefoil are the legumes in the mixtures. Birdsfoot gives better results than alfalfa when soil is restricted in permeability or drainage is poor.[7,11] Reed canarygrass with big trefoil is well adapted to poorly drained soils.

Under irrigation, as shown in Table 47.3, cultivars of alfalfa and Cascade birdsfoot are the major legumes. The grasses used with alfalfa are Latar orchardgrass when there are no soil limitations, 'Greenar' intermediate wheatgrass when the water supply is short, and Alta fescue

11. Turner, Darrell O. 1966. Yield, longevity, and response to lime of certain grass and legume varieties on Nisqually loamy sand. Wash. Agr. Exp. Sta. Circ. 460.

TABLE 47.4 ❧ Hay and pasture species for nonirrigated lands in the semiarid part of the continental climatic zone

Species and cultivars	Annual precipitation (mm)				
	230 (kg/ha)	230–340 (kg/ha)	340–380 (kg/ha)	380–460 (kg/ha)	460–630 (kg/ha)
Siberian wheatgrass	6	7	(7)	...	...
Crested wheatgrass—Nordan	(6)	(7)	(7)	(7)*	...
Beardless wheatgrass—'Whitmar'	...	(10)	(10)	...	...
Big bluegrass—Sherman	...	...	(4)	...	...
Pubescent wheatgrass—Topar	...	...	10	...	...
Intermediate wheatgrass—Greenar	...	...	...	9	(9)
Smooth bromegrass—'Manchar'	...	...	...	...	9
Creeping foxtail—Garrison	...	...	...	...	(7)
Alfalfa for hay—'Ladak,' Ranger, Washoe	...	...	5	5	5
Alfalfa for pasture	...	...	2	2	2

Note: Parentheses indicate substitutions within the group.
* Should be used only on droughty soils.

when moderate alkaline conditions occur. 'Garrison' creeping foxtail or Alta fescue with Cascade birdsfoot produce well on poorly drained soil. 'Alkar' tall wheatgrass, alone or with birdsfoot, is best suited to saline-sodic affected soils with a high water table.[3] This hay is chopped before it is fed.

Table 47.4 shows the species and cultivars used in mixtures under nonirrigated conditions in the interior east of the Cascade Mountains and the Sierra Nevada. Here annual precipitation determines what may be seeded. Hay usually is taken when precipitation exceeds 340 mm, preferably 380 mm. 'Nordan' crested wheatgrass, 'Sherman' big bluegrass, and 'Topar' pubescent wheatgrass with alfalfa make good hay. Greenar intermediate wheatgrass and alfalfa are a preferred mixture when annual precipitation is 390–460 mm. Any of the grass cultivars shown in the table make high-quality hay when precipitation exceeds 460 mm.

❧ PASTURES

A large part of the land in the Pacific Coast states and Idaho is grazed. About 57% of the 31 million ha of land in farms was used for this purpose in 1969, as shown in Table 47.5. Much of this was land that could not be used for crops and included 1.7 million ha of woodland pasture and 14 million ha of rangeland. An average of 22% of the cropland is in seeded pasture, and there are many kinds. Good pasture on irrigated land provides as much as 30 AUM's (animal-unit month)/ha of graz-

ing. Production on some arid rangelands may be so low that 5–10 ha/AUM are required for grazing.

KINDS OF PASTURE. Pastures on farms are either permanent, cropland, or supplemental. Permanent pastures remain on the land for a long time and are usually on the poorer sites. The soil may be shallow, of low fertility, or high in salinity or alkali; drainage may be inadequate, slopes steep, or the land rough or stony. These factors combine to make grazing capacity low as compared with cropland pastures. Areas of native forage plants on farms are grazed and are referred to as rangeland.

Cropland pastures are high in production, are on the better land, and contribute toward maintaining soil structure and fertility. They may or may not be irrigated.

Extensive areas of pasture in the foothills of California are occupied by exotic winter annual grasses and legumes that thrive in the Mediterranean climate. They have a relatively short growing season, but stands are maintained by natural reseeding when the pasture is correctly managed.[12]

Some supplemental pastures are used. Sudangrass or sudangrass hybrids are planted to provide summer feed. Sometimes small grains are grazed during the cool season or early spring. Meadows, seed fields, and grain stubble provide

12. Kay, Burgess L. 1969. Hardinggrass and annual legume production in the Sierra foothills. *J. Range Manage.* 22:174–77.

TABLE 47.5 ❧ Kinds of pasture on private land in the Pacific Coast states and north Idaho

Kind of pasture	California (000 ha)	Idaho (000 ha)	Oregon (000 ha)	Washington (000 ha)
Cropland used only for pasture	747	111	437	338
Woodland pasture	514	183	573	422
Other land pastured	8,146	756	3,367	1,750
Total pasture	9,407	1,050	4,377	2,510
Improved pasture and rangeland	383	54	342	236
Cropland harvested	3,908	497	1,128	1,680
Land in farms	14,468	1,860	7,366	7,120

aftermath grazing. Supplemental pastures contribute only a small part of the pasture feed.[13]

CHOICE OF GRASSES AND LEGUMES. Tables 47.6 and 47.7 list a few typical pasture mixtures. Preferred cultivars are shown and seeding rates are given. These mixtures are the result of many experiments and field trials.

When species and cultivars are chosen, attention is given to yield, season of growth, palatability, and compatibility in mixtures as well as to adaptation to soil conditions, moisture, and climate. Management of the pasture has an important influence on the performance of any cultivar of grass or legume.[14]

New grasses and legumes have been introduced and superior cultivars have been developed by plant breeders. Many studies on performance under use have been made and precise information on cultivars, mixtures, and adaptation is available from local agricultural agencies.[3]

The most important reason for seeding pastures to mixtures in the Pacific Coast states is to obtain a more uniform production of feed during the growing season. Most grasses, even if irrigated, become dormant or make little growth during the hot summer months. Summer-growing perennial grasses are adapted only to irrigated lands in central and southern California. The legumes are the important summer-growing plants in all parts of the region, but even they must be irrigated. (See Fig. 47.2.)

Mixtures, with rare exception, contain only one grass and one legume. This is in contrast to the multiple-species mixtures once in common use. Simple mixtures are easier to manage, and the operator has greater control over the percentage of grass and legume in the pasture.[7,8,11,14] Dairymen prefer mixtures that contain

FIG. 47.2. *Mixtures . . . contain . . . one grass and one legume.* An improved irrigated pasture of Latar orchardgrass and 'Vernal' alfalfa. It is fertilized annually with 170 kg N, 110 kg P, and 34 kg S/ha. Grazing is rotated among 11 units, 2 days on and 28 days off. Grazing capacity is 37 AUM's/ha. *SCS photo.*

half grass and half legume. Those who pasture beef cattle and sheep prefer mixtures that have more grass.

MIXTURES FOR IRRIGATED PASTURES. Irrigated pastures are important sources of feed. They may have a grazing capacity of 28–37 AUM's/ha when they are carefully managed.

Table 47.6 shows the five groups of irrigated pastures for the intermountain part of the continental climatic zone that is east of the Cascade Mountains and the Sierra Nevada. The five groups are divided according to the amount of available water, the degree of drainage, and the presence of saline or saline-sodic soil conditions.

A cultivar of either orchardgrass or tall fescue and one of the alfalfa cultivars make up the mixture when adequate water

13. Van Keuren, R. W., and W. W. Heinemann. 1959. Irrigated sudangrass and millet for forage and seed in central Washington. Wash. Agr. Exp. Sta. Bull. 605.
14. Hafenrichter, A. L. 1957. Management to increase forage production in the West. USDA SCS-TP-128.

TABLE 47.6 *&* Typical pasture mixtures for irrigated land in the continental climatic zone

Mixture	Seeding rate (kg/ha)
Adequate water, good drainage, no soil limitations	
1. Orchardgrass—Latar,	5
alfalfa—Washoe, Ranger	6
Adequate water, moderate alkaline conditions	
2. Tall fescue—Alta, Fawn *or*	7
tall wheatgrass—Alkar,	(11)
alfalfa	6
Inadequate water	
3. Intermediate wheatgrass—Greenar,	7
alfalfa—Ladak, Washoe, Ranger	2
Poorly drained soil	
4. Creeping foxtail—Garrison *or*	6
tall fescue—Alta,	(7)
birdsfoot—Cascade*	6
Saline and saline-sodic affected soil with water table	
5. Tall wheatgrass—Alkar,	11
birdsfoot—Cascade*	4

Note: Parentheses indicate substitutions within the group.
* Should be seeded in alternate rows.

TABLE 47.7 *&* Seedings for irrigated and nonirrigated pastures in the Mediterranean climatic zone

Mixture	Seeding rate (kg/ha)
Pastures for Irrigated Land	
CENTRAL VALLEY OF CALIFORNIA	
Soils with slowly permeable subsoil or shallow over impervious material	
1. Tall fescue—Goar *or*	9
orchardgrass—'Akaroa,'	(6)
ladino clover *or*	2
narrowleaf trefoil	(3)
Saline or saline-sodic affected soil	
2. Tall fescue—Goar,	11
narrowleaf trefoil	6
DESERT VALLEYS OF SOUTHERN CALIFORNIA	
All irrigated pastures	
3. Bermudagrass sprigs—Coastal *or*	29*
giant bermudagrass	(3)
or	
Tall fescue—Goar,	9
narrowleaf trefoil *or*	3
alfalfa—'Mesa Sirsa,' 'El Unico'	(2)
or	
Sudangrass—Piper, Sudax,	22
annual ryegrass (overseeded)	11
Pastures for Nonirrigated Land	
PERENNIAL MIXTURES	
(annual precipitation should exceed 400 mm)	
Soils with no problems	
4. Hardinggrass,	5
alfalfa—'Lahontan,' 'Rambler'	2
Soils fine-textured with slowly permeable subsoils	
5. Hardinggrass,	5
woollypod vetch—Lana *or*	10
subterranean clover—rose clover	(3)
ANNUAL MIXTURES (self-seeding)	
6. Soft chess—Blando bromegrass,	5
woollypod vetch—Lana	11
or	
Subterranean clover—rose clover	
(overseeded)	15

Note: Parentheses indicate substitutions within the group.
* Bermudagrass sprigs at 29 hl/ha.

is available for irrigation. The mixture produces at least 1100 kg/ha of beef in a pasture season of 150–164 days.[15,16] Greenar intermediate wheatgrass and alfalfa are used when water is limited. With poor drainage Garrison creeping foxtail or tall fescue and Cascade birdsfoot are used. Alkar tall wheatgrass with Cascade birdsfoot pastures on saline or saline-sodic affected soils have produced as much beef as orchardgrass and alfalfa on soil with no limitations.[3,17] Birdsfoot is seeded in alternate rows with grass.[5]

Table 47.7 shows typical mixtures used under irrigation in the Mediterranean climatic zone. Those for the central valley of California are of two kinds. The first is for soils with slowly permeable subsoils or for soils that are shallow over impervious material. Birdsfoot-grass pastures have produced 402 kg/ha of beef in the

area.[18] The second is for use on saline or saline-sodic affected soils. 'Goar' tall fescue with narrowleaf trefoil pasture on saline-sodic affected soil produced feed for 32 AUM's/ha for dairy cattle. The cows produced 10,400 kg/ha of milk while they were on the pasture.[19]

15. Heinemann, W. W., and R. W. Van Keuren. 1958. Fattening steers on irrigated pastures. Wash. Agr. Exp. Sta. Bull. 578.
16. Van Keuren, R. W., and W. W. Heinemann. 1958. Forage species in irrigated pastures for market lambs. Wash. Agr. Exp. Sta. Bull. 592.
17. Hafenrichter, A. L. 1956. Improving pastures in difficult environments in the western United States. Proc. 7th Int. Grassl. Congr., pp. 498–508 (Palmerston North, N.Z.).

18. Hull, J. L., and J. H. Meyer. 1967. Irrigated pastures for steers and lambs. Calif. Agr. Exp. Sta. Bull. 835.
19. Miller, H. W., O. K. Hoglund, and A. L. Hafenrichter. 1959. Grasses, legumes, and cultural methods for improving pasture production and aiding conservation on saline-alkali land. Calif. Dept. Nat. Resources Bull. 1.

TABLE 47.8 ❧ Typical pasture mixtures for the sub-humid part of the continental climatic zone

Mixture	Seeding rate (kg/ha)
Deep, well-drained to moderately well-drained soils	
1. Orchardgrass—Latar, 'Pennlate' or	11
tall fescue—Fawn, Alta *or*	(11)
perennial ryegrass,	(17)
white clover—Grasslands Huia	5
Droughty or excessively drained soils	
2. Tall fescue—Fawn, Alta,	11
subterranean clover—'Mt. Barker,'	
'Tallarook'	6
or	
Tall fescue—Fawn, Alta *or*	8
orchardgrass—Latar, Pennlate,	(6)
alfalfa—Flemish type	8
Moderately well-drained to somewhat poorly drained soils with restricted subsoil permeability	
3. Perennial ryegrass *or*	17
tall fescue—Fawn, Alta *or*	(11)
orchardgrass—Latar, Pennlate,	(8)
white clover—Grasslands Huia	5
Poorly drained soils	
4. Meadow foxtail,	7
timothy—Climax,	5
big trefoil,	2
white clover—Grasslands Huia	2

Note: Parentheses indicate substitutions within the group.

Pasture mixtures for the southern desert valleys of California are of two kinds. 'Coastal' bermudagrass is planted with sprigs. Giant bermudagrass and Goar tall fescue are seeded, each with either narrow-leaf trefoil or an adapted cultivar of alfalfa. In one study a bermudagrass seeding yielded 17 t/ha when fertilized with 170 kg/ha of N.[20] 'Piper' or 'Sudax' sudangrass may be used as supplemental summer pasture. Either the bermudagrasses or the sudangrasses may be overseeded with annual ryegrass for winter pasture.

PASTURES FOR THE CONTINENTAL CLIMATE

SUBHUMID CONTINENTAL CLIMATE. The four groups of pastures for the subhumid part of the continental climate west of the Cascade Mountains are shown in Table 47.8. The degree of drainage or relative permeability of the subsoil separate them. Most of the soils in this area have a low pH, and legumes respond to lime. A high increment of production results from applications of N, but response to P and K depends on the ability of the soil to liberate these elements. Soil tests must be made to determine the need.[6,8,11]

Adapted cultivars of orchardgrass and tall fescue and perennial ryegrass with 'Grasslands Huia' white clover dominate the mixtures. On well-drained soils orchardgrass takes precedence over tall fescue and ryegrass. Perennial ryegrass is preferred when drainage is restricted by the subsoil. On poorly drained sites meadow foxtail and timothy with Grasslands Huia clover and big trefoil are used. Latar orchardgrass with a Flemish-type alfalfa on well-drained and fertilized but not irrigated soil produced feed for about 30 AUM's/ha. Latar orchardgrass and Grasslands Huia clover produced feed for about 25 AUM's/ha.[8]

Two mixtures are shown for droughty or excessively drained sites. Tall fescue and one of the subterranean clovers are used on cutover hill soils. Orchardgrass with alfalfa produces good yields on loamy sands if lime, fertilizers, and irrigation can be used.[11]

SEMIARID CONTINENTAL CLIMATE. Pasture mixtures for the semiarid part of the continental climatic zone are shown in Table 47.4. This part of the zone lies east of the Cascade Mountains and the Sierra Nevada. Annual precipitation determines what is planted. Grass is planted alone when annual precipitation is less than 340 mm. These plantings are permanent and are often referred to as range seedings. The grazing season is short in the summer-dry climate, and production varies from 1.25 to 3.6 AUM's/ha.[21]

20. Martin, William E., Victor V. Rendig, Arthur D. Haig, and Lester J. Berry. 1964. Fertilization of irrigated pastures and forage crops in California. Calif. Agr. Exp. Sta. Bull. 815.

21. Douglas, Donald S., A. L. Hafenrichter, and K. H. Klages. 1960. Cultural methods and their relation to establishment of native and exotic grasses in range seedings. *J. Range Manage.* 13:53–57.

When annual precipitation is more than 340 mm, an adapted cultivar of alfalfa is planted with one of the grasses. Such pastures may be relatively long-lived but are usually in a crop rotation. They have produced up to 255 kg/ha of beef.[22] Alfalfa-grass pastures are valuable soil-improving and erosion-preventing crops.

DRYLAND PASTURES FOR THE MEDITERRANEAN CLIMATE

PERENNIAL PASTURES. Table 47.7 lists two kinds of perennial pasture mixtures for the Mediterranean climate. They require at least 400 mm of annual precipitation in this climate. When no limiting factor exists due to soils, hardinggrass and alfalfa are seeded, preferably in alternate rows. On fine-textured soils with slowly permeable subsoils, hardinggrass is used with 'Lana' woollypod vetch or a subterranean clover–rose clover mixture.[12,23]

ANNUAL PASTURES. Annual pasture mixtures combine either 'Blando' bromegrass (soft chess) with Lana woollypod vetch or Blando bromegrass with a mixture of subterranean clover and rose clover. Both Blando bromegrass and Lana vetch were developed for seeding rangelands under limited amounts of precipitation. These seedings can produce feed to provide as much as 15 AUM's/ha of grazing when they are fertilized and properly grazed.[23,24] Sometimes Lana vetch or a mixture of subterranean clovers and rose clover are overseeded into annual range vegetation. Annual pastures of naturalized exotic Mediterranean species when fertilized with N and P and some S give 7.6 AUM's/ha of grazing and 201 kg/ha of beef.[25]

22. Ensminger, M. E., H. G. McDonald, A. G. Law, E. J. Warwick, E. J. Kreizinger, and V. B. Hawk. 1944. Grass and grass-alfalfa mixtures for beef production in eastern Washington. Wash. Agr. Exp. Sta. Bull. 444.
23. Miller, H. W., O. K. Hoglund, and A. L. Hafenrichter. 1964. A range improvement program for Mediterranean climates. Proc. 9th Int. Grassl. Congr., pp. 283–85 (São Paulo, Brazil).
24. Hoglund, O. K., H. W. Miller, and A. L. Hafenrichter. 1952. Application of fertilizer to aid conservation on annual forage range. *J. Range Manage.* 5:55–61.
25. Martin, W. E., and L. J. Berry. 1970. Effects of nitrogenous fertilizers on California range as measured by weight gains of grazing cattle. Calif. Agr. Exp. Sta. Bull. 846.

OTHER PASTURES

Pastures on private land are supplemented by grazing on public lands administered by the USDA Forest Service and the USDI Bureau of Land Management (BLM).[26,27] It is estimated that the lands administered by these agencies provided at least 2.6 million AUM's of grazing in 1969. They were grazed by beef cattle, some horses, and sheep and goats. Lands on the national forests are grazed in the summer, and the public domain lands furnish grazing chiefly in the spring and fall. (See Fig. 47.3.)

Both the Forest Service and the BLM seed some of their lands each year to improved grasses and legumes. More than 300,000 ha have been improved by reseeding in the Pacific Coast states. The grasses or mixtures used for reseeding are those given in Tables 47.4 and 47.7.

🐾 MANAGEMENT

Management is the key for obtaining optimum production of high-quality forage in the Pacific Coast states.

MANAGING THE CROP. Improved cultivars are listed in the tables. Only a few are seeded alone. Simple mixtures of one grass and one legume are easier to manage than complex mixtures. Drilling is commoner than other methods of seeding. The use of the alternate-row seeding method eliminates competition between the grass and the legume, especially in the seedling stage, and gives the operator control over the composition of the mixture.[5] Livestock do not selectively graze one or the other of the components when the pasture is grazed. (See Fig. 47.4.) The deep-furrow press drill, for dryland seedings and seeding on alkali land, and the rangeland drill are examples of new machines for establishing forage crops.[17]

The use of fertilizers is widely accepted.

26. U.S. Forest Service. 1971. Annual grazing statistical report, 1970.
27. Bureau of Land Management. 1969. Public land statistics.

FIG. 47.3. *Public domain lands furnish grazing . . . spring and fall.* Sheep grazing rangeland on the public domain. The Pacific Coast states contain millions of ha of such land. Although grazing capacity is low, it can be maintained with good grazing management. *SCS photo.*

Almost all hay and pasture crops respond to application of N of some form. The increment of increase from N determines the economics of how much is applied. The use of lime, P, K, or S depends on the availability of the nutrient in the soil. There is no indication of deficiencies of minor elements in the Pacific Coast states, except possibly for B in a few places.[6,8,14]

MANAGING IRRIGATION WATER. The amount and frequency of irrigation depend on soil, plant, and climate. The available moisture-holding capacity of loamy sands is about 0.6 cm/dm and on fine-textured silty clays it is 1.3 cm/dm.[28] A general rule is that forage crops should be irrigated when half the available moisture in the root zone has been used. When plants with different root-growth charac-

teristics are used in a mixture, irrigation should satisfy those with the shallowest roots. Ladino clover may extract water to a depth of 1.2 m, birdsfoot to 1.8 m, and alfalfa to 2.5 m on good deep soil.[29] Seasonal use of water by irrigated pastures may vary from 0.63 to 0.85 cm/day depending on temperature.

FORAGE MANAGEMENT PRACTICES. Forage management practices are equally effective on both pasture and range seedings. The aim is high and sustained production of feed.

Rotation grazing practices apply to both cultivated pastures and to the range. On the range the pastures are few in number and large in area, and the grazier must develop a system for rotating three or four pastures among years. Cultivated pastures

28. Myers, V. I., and D. C. Shockley. 1955. Irrigation of hay and pasture crops in Idaho. Idaho Agr. Exp. Sta. Bull. 249.

29. Hagan, R. M., and M. L. Peterson. 1953. Soil moisture extraction by irrigated pastures as influenced by clipping frequency. *Agron. J.* 45:288–92.

FIG. 47.4. *Livestock do not selectively graze one or the other . . . components.* An alternate-row seeding of Latar orchardgrass and alfalfa. Such seedings give the operator good control of the relative percentage of the two components of the mixture. *SCS photo.*

can be as few as three or as many as are needed to provide for daily ration grazing.[7,14,19] The operator must guard against overutilization in both cases.

ENABLING PRACTICES. Enabling practices apply particularly to rangelands and include fencing, herding, salting, and water development. The aim is to obtain more uniform distribution of the livestock and more uniform grazing of the forage.

SPEEDUP PRACTICES. Speedup practices include fertilizing, reseeding, and removal of undesirable plants on rangeland. On cultivated pastures they include occasional mowing to remove weeds or ungrazed grasses and legumes as well as to spread droppings.

❧ QUESTIONS

1. How do differences in climate, soil, and elevation influence the choice of grasses and legumes used for hay and pasture seedings?
2. What changes have occurred in the number and kinds of livestock in the region between 1959 and 1969? How have they affected the level of forage produced?
3. What factors have influenced the increase in hay production between 1959 and 1969?
4. Point out the extent of alfalfa hay production and give reasons for it.
5. List the climatic and soil conditions that determine the mixtures used for hay in the continental and Mediterranean climatic zones.
6. Give the reasons for the importance of cropland pastures and name four other kinds of pasture.
7. Why are simple mixtures used for pasture seedings? What are the advantages of seeding the grass and the legume in alternate rows?
8. Name the important factors that influence the choice of the grass and the legume for pasture in each major part of the continental climatic zone and Mediterranean climatic zone.
9. What publicly owned lands are used to supplement grazing on farmlands? What improvements are made to increase grazing capacity?
10. Name the important practices for managing pastures to obtain optimum production.

PART IV

❧

FORAGE UTILIZATION

K. K. BARNES / *University of Arizona*

48

MECHANIZATION OF FORAGE HARVESTING AND STORAGE

❧

THE MECHANIZATION of forage harvesting and storage is directed toward preserving quality and controlling costs. Forage harvesting has long had a reputation for arduous labor under hot dusty conditions. However, increasing cost and scarcity of labor for this type of field work have stimulated the development of many mechanized systems. With the use of such systems, hay can be harvested and moved into storage with less than one man-hour of labor per ton, and this labor is utilized in controlling machines rather than in supplying energy to lift and place materials.

Many alternatives exist in forage harvesting and storage. They have been developed in response to a variety of needs resulting from climate, topography, scale of operations, and desired product.

❧ MOISTURE LEVELS AND STORAGE CHARACTERISTICS

Forage is stored under a wide range of moisture conditions. Moisture content of

❧ KENNETH K. BARNES is Professor of Agricultural Engineering and Head of the Department of Soils, Water, and Engineering, University of Arizona. He received the M.S. and Ph.D. degrees from Iowa State University. He has been active in many areas of farm machinery research and development since 1952.

crop materials is commonly expressed as percent wet base (WB) but may also be expressed as percent dry base (DB). The two are calculated below; the weight of water and the weight of dry matter (DM) have been determined for a sample of the material to be described:

$$\% \text{ Moisture WB} = 100 \times \frac{\text{weight of } H_2O}{\text{weight of } H_2O + \text{weight of DM}}$$

$$\% \text{ Moisture DB} = 100 \times \frac{\text{weight of } H_2O}{\text{weight of DM}}$$

Three broad terms are applied to indicate the moisture ranges: Silage, 65–75% WB moisture; low-moisture silage, sometimes called haylage, 35–50% WB moisture; and hay, below 25% WB moisture. These boundaries are not well defined, but satisfactory stored forage has been produced within these moisture ranges. Table 48.1 gives the range of bulk volume weights of these forms of forage in storage.[1,2]

1. Iowa State Univ. Staff. 1964. Midwest Farm Handbook, 6th ed., p. 465. Iowa State Univ. Press, Ames.
2. Gustafson, B. W., and H. E. de Buhr. 1965. John Deere "400" hay cuber. Ann. Meet. Amer. Soc. Agr. Engrs. Paper 65-639.

TABLE 48.1 ✄ Volume-weights of various forms of stored forage

Material	Weight (kg/m³)	Volume (m³/t)
Hay		
Loose	54–70	14–19
Chopped	80–110	9–12
Baled	160–320	2.5–6.2
Cubed	420–550	1.8–2.5
Silage, chopped	480–800	1.1–1.8

Sources: Iowa State Univ. staff, 1964;[1] Gustafson and de Buhr, 1965.[2]

SILAGE

In silage the high moisture content makes possible effective compaction of the mass to displace and exclude oxygen. Aerobic processes stop within a few hours to a day after placement in storage.

Silage may be stored in upright cylindrical structures or in horizontal bunkers placed above ground or cut into a knoll or hill. Feeding from either of these types of storage can be mechanized. Upright-silo unloaders that deliver silage to feeding wagons or to mechanized feed bunkers are common. Mechanical unloading of bunker silos is done by tractor-mounted manure loaders or by specially designed, continuous-flow, bunker-silo unloaders.

HAYLAGE

Haylage requires special attention to selection of a structure which will effectively exclude oxygen. If this is not accomplished, the stored forage may char or burst into flame as heat from the aerobic process raises the forage to combustion temperature in the presence of oxygen. Forage that overheats loses feeding value, and the remaining protein decreases in availability.

Compared to silage, haylage involves handling, storing, and feeding of much less water. Compared to hay, it greatly reduces the time involved in field curing and the associated weather risks.

HAY

Hay is stored at a moisture level so low that the biological processes do not proceed rapidly enough to build up heat. However, high-moisture pockets in stored hay may develop enough heat to raise the material to combustion temperature; charring or burning can result in the presence of oxygen, depending upon the supply of air to the hot spot.

It has been common practice to provide hay storage overhead in a barn mow or loft, but this type of storage has become less popular. Reasons favoring the change are: (1) baled and chopped hay are not readily handled in overhead storage, (2) self-feeding or efficient mechanical feeding from storage is desired, and (3) loose housing of animals does not facilitate overhead hay storage to the same degree as stall and stanchion housing.

The heavier, denser forms of hay favor structures where the hay is stored at ground level. Bales are handled most easily in ground-level storage. Self-feeding from ground-level storage can reduce labor requirements in feeding livestock. In low-precipitation areas loose hay, baled hay, and cubed hay are often stored in piles completely exposed to the weather. In other instances, bales and cubes are stacked under roofed structures having no walls or are covered with tarpaulins.

✄ HARVEST-STORAGE SYSTEMS

ALTERNATIVE SYSTEMS

The choice of a harvest-storage system depends upon climatic conditions, ultimate use of the forage, and size of the forage enterprise. A diversified mechanical system is required for on-farm operations. The development of an effective mechanical system depends at least to some extent upon the operator's experience, knowledge, and skill as well as his personal preference for a given system compared to another and the availability of a good, reliable machinery dealer who is capable of providing expert service at reasonable cost during peak work periods.

Silage and haylage must be processed immediately upon removal from oxygen-free storage. The processing usually takes the form of immediate feeding as it is removed from storage on a daily or more frequent basis. Thus these products of high-moisture storage are not readily salable, though they may sometimes be sold to close neighbors on a daily delivery basis.

Long loose hay and chopped hay are also restricted to feeding near the storage area. Because of their bulk, they are uneconomical for long-distance transport. Baled hay is the most common form of forage entering marketing channels. Bales are commonly transported hundreds of miles by truck and may be conveniently stored near the harvest area, near the feeding area, or at intermediate points. The cubing process was developed in response to demand for an improvement in material handling for hay, and cubes are readily shipped long distances. Thus if forage is to enter marketing channels, baled or cubed hay are the practical choices.

Estimates regarding the portions of hay harvested by various methods suggest that in 1972 about 90% of the hay crop was baled, 5% was harvested as long loose hay, 3% was harvested as chopped loose hay, and 2% was field cubed.[3,4] Some forage, usually alfalfa, is field chopped and dehydrated (see Chapter 50) to maximize preservation of nutrients. Dehydrated material is often pelleted to provide a clean, easily handled, specialty feed.

REDUCING WEATHER HAZARDS

HIGH-MOISTURE STORAGE. If climate is such that weather hazards make haymaking risky, the high-moisture storage systems are a good choice for on-farm use. They reduce or eliminate the elapsed time involved in field curing and thus the period of exposure to weather hazards.

ARTIFICIAL DRYING. Exposure to weather risks also may be reduced by artificial drying of hay. Forced circulation of heated or unheated air through hay in storage provides a means of reducing moisture after the crop has been harvested. The barn or storage structure is equipped with air ducts, false floors, or other suitable air passages so that air can be forced through the hay. In this system the hay is partially field cured before being transferred from the field to storage. A moisture of 35–40%, or about half-cured, is best. The hay should not become dry enough in the field (below 30% moisture) for leaves to shatter, or a major advantage of artificial drying will be lost.

All forms of hay (loose, baled, and chopped) have been dried artificially. Feeding value is generally improved because of reduced leaf loss and field exposure. Artificially curing chopped hay is most popular since it may be completely mechanized.

Forced ventilation with an even distribution of unheated air will control heating of hay. The effect of evaporation keeps the hay cool; however, without artificial heat the drying may be prolonged by damp weather, causing mold growth and mustiness. If drying is completed in a week or less, good quality hay results. Hay may be artificially cured in self-feeding structures, barn mows, wagons, or specially designed drying structures.

The depth of hay to be dried must be limited for two reasons: (1) to limit the load on the blower and permit sufficient air to pass through the hay and (2) to insure the relatively early drying of the outer part of the pile. Moisture is moved from the inner part to the outer part of the pile, so that the outer layer dries last. Loose hay may be handled in depths of 2.5–3 m, while chopped and baled hay should be limited to 1.5–2.5 m.[5] Bales must be stacked in a tight and overlapping pattern to prevent channeling of the drying air.

3. Ferguson, W. L., P. E. Strickler, and R. C. Max. 1971. Hay harvesting practices and labor used, 1967, 48 states. Econ. Res. Serv. and Stat. Rep. Serv. USDA Stat. Bull. 460.

4. Miller, H. R. 1971. Trends in equipment for harvesting, storing and feeding alfalfa. Proc. 1st Ann. Alfalfa Symp. Certified Alfalfa Seed Council (Iowa State Univ., Ames).

5. Scarborough, E. N. 1964. Hay drying in the northeastern states. Del. Agr. Exp. Sta. Bull. 349.

FIG. 48.1. *Mowers . . . common to all methods of harvesting.* A semimounted, power take-off driven, cutter bar mower. *International Harvester Co. photo.*

❦ HARVEST PROCESSES AND MACHINES

The selection of the storage moisture condition places the first restraint upon selection of the mechanized harvest system. Though many variations have been tried, silage and haylage are normally field-chopped material. Hay is harvested, handled, and stored long and loose, chopped, baled, or cubed. Many types of machines and processes are available. Only the most important can be discussed here.

Mowing, Conditioning, and Windrowing

Mowers for cutting the standing crop are common to all methods of harvesting. The cutter bar mower (Fig. 48.1) is the most common and is used alone or incorporated into assemblies involving windrowers, conditioners, combinations of these two, or forage choppers.

Conditioners pass freshly cut hay between smooth or corrugated rollers under pressure. This process crushes and opens the stems so that they dry at a rate approaching that of the leaves. Thus leaves

FIG. 48.2. *Windrowing increases field curing time.* A self-propelled windrower. *International Harvester Co. photo.*

are less likely to become overdry and lost in subsequent handling.

Direct windrowing of hay (Fig. 48.2) increases field curing time compared to allowing partial curing in a swath before raking into a windrow. However, combination of a conditioner with a windrower reduces windrow drying time to a level which could have been achieved with unconditioned hay in a swath. Windrowing also protects leaves from the rapid overdrying to which they are exposed in a swath. Hay made by the direct windrowing process has excellent color because of the limited surface exposed to direct bleaching by the sun.

Seventy percent of the 1967 hay crop was cut with a cutter bar mower; windrowers were used to cut 28% of the crop; the remaining 2% was cut with rotary cutters or cut-throw, flail-type cutters.[3] Fourteen percent of the hay harvested with cutter bar mowers was harvested with machines in which the mower was an integral part of a mower-conditioner unit. Nearly 50% of the windrowed hay was cut with windrowers containing an integral conditioner. Of the total hectarage of hay harvested, 28% was conditioned with units integrally constructed with the mowing unit, and an additional 10% was conditioned with separate units. The separate cutter bar mower is most common on farms of less than 40 ha; whereas the windrower, requiring a high investment, is most popular with growers having large hay areas. Tractor mowers are power take-off driven with cut-

TABLE 48.2 ❦ Average labor requirements for mowing, conditioning, and windrowing hay in the U.S., 1967

Operation	Man-hours per ha
Mow, condition, rake	4.1
Windrow, condition, rake	3.5
Mow-condition, rake	2.5
Windrow-condition, rake	2.2
Windrow-condition	1.0

Source: Ferguson et al., 1971.[3]
* Operations separated by commas are separate trips over the field. Operations hyphenated are combined in one trip over the field.

FIG. 48.3. *Handles hay more gently . . . less leaf loss.* A reel-type, side-delivery rake. *International Harvester Co. photo.*

ter bars ranging in length from 1.5 to 3 m. They may be mounted or semimounted. Mower-conditioners are pull-type machines; most windrowers, sometimes referred to as swathers, are self-propelled machines, although pull-type windrowers are available.

FIG. 48.4. *Wheel rakes . . . best suited . . . sparse crops on rough ground.* A wheel-type, side-delivery rake. *International Harvester Co. photo.*

The time required to windrow by various methods is given in Table 48.2.[3]

RAKES. Hay mowed and conditioned without use of a windrower must be raked into a windrow. After partial drying, two or more windrows may be raked together. Rakes are of two types, side-delivery and dump. Side-delivery rakes may be of the reel type (Fig. 48.3), which is most common, or the wheel type (Fig. 48.4). Wheel rakes are best suited to handling sparse crops on rough ground. As compared to dump rakes, side-delivery rakes handle hay more gently and with less leaf loss. They produce uniform windrows that are continuous and well adapted to being picked up with loaders, field balers, and choppers. Raking with the side-delivery rake is a high-capacity operation, and labor requirements may be as low as 0.25 man-hr/t.[6]

Dump rakes work well where hay is stacked outside and sweeps or bucks are used to gather up the hay. They are not satisfactory when balers or choppers are to take up the windrow. The sweep rake or buck rake (Fig. 48.5) is an efficient means of moving hay short distances from the windrow to stack or storage. It is efficient on short hauls from windrow to barn or stack where a fork or stacker is available for lifting the hay into storage. After forage has been placed in the windrow by a windrower or rake, the alternatives of harvest as long loose, chopped, baled, or cubed material are still available.

STORING LONG LOOSE HAY

Forage stored as long loose hay is either loaded onto vehicles for transport to storage or assembled into stacks in the harvest field. Machines are available (Fig. 48.6) for picking up hay from a windrow, forming a stack, transporting that stack to a storage location, and unloading the stack. Capacities of such systems operated by one man

6. Barger, E. L. 1947. Field-to-bale-to-barn. *Iowa Farm Sci.* 1:6–9.

FIG 48.5. *An efficient means . . . moving hay short distances.* An automotive-type buck rake. *Mont. State Univ. photo.*

vary greatly with hay and travel conditions, but capacities of 5–10 t/hr have been reported. This labor requirement of as low as 0.1 man-hr/t compares with labor requirements of 2.5 man-hr/t when hay loaders, wagons, and pole stackers are used. Sweep or buck rake systems of moving long loose hay into stacks have been operated at less than 0.15 man-hr/t.[7]

CHOPPING

Chopping is applicable for storage of forage at any of the moisture ranges. The chief purpose of chopping is to reduce the plant to pieces of a size that can be moved in an airstream. Chopped hay must be stored at lower moisture than other forms of hay. Under most conditions of storing chopped hay, 20–22% moisture has been found safe. For hay cut in 5–6 cm lengths, 25% has been found to be a maximum safe moisture content. Longer lengths of cut hay result in less heating and better keeping qualities, but they increase the storage space required.

Theoretical lengths of 1–3 cm generally are recommended for silage; 5–7 cm are appropriate for chopped hay. The theoretical length of cut is the advance of the feed roller and feeder apron between the cuts of two successive knives.

Direct-cut grass and legume silage pieces will average twice the theoretical setting

7. Larson, W. E. 1971. Capacity measurements on hay harvest systems. Ann. Meet. Amer. Soc. Agr. Engrs. Paper 71-140.

since the stems do not feed in straight at all times. Material cut from a windrow as for wilted silage, haylage, or hay averages much longer than theoretical because few stems move straight into the cutting head.

Forage for silage may be direct cut or chopped after wilting in a swath or windrow. Direct-cut silage is produced by cutting the standing crop and chopping it in one operation. Thus the material is placed into storage at the natural moisture content. This may be too high to produce the best quality of silage. With immature materials, moisture may be as high as 80%. An alternative is to cut and windrow the forage and let it wilt briefly before chopping. Moisture may be reduced by 5–15 percentage points in 0.5–1.5 hours in the windrow. The forage is then picked up and chopped.

Forage to be stored as haylage is also first mowed and then allowed to diminish in moisture in the windrow before chopping. Hay to be artificially dried may be field chopped from the windrow at 35–50% moisture. Field chopping of hay at below 25% moisture results in substantial loss of leaves, the part of the plant containing the most protein.

Field choppers or forage harvesters can be classified under three general types according to the type of cutting mechanism

FIG. 48.6. *Machines . . . for picking up hay . . . forming a stack . . . transporting it to a storage location . . . unloading.* A mechanized hay stacker. *Hesston Corp. photo.*

FIG. 48.7. *Attachments are interchangeable.* A direct-cut, field forage chopper. *International Harvester Co. photo.*

used. Radial-knife or flywheel-type machines have four or six knives attached radially on a wheel which combines cutting and blowing parts. The fan blades or paddles are attached to the outer edge of the wheel. Another common type of chopper utilizes a cutting head similar to that of a reel-type lawn mower. The third category is the flail-type chopper. In this machine, combination knife impellers rotate in planes parallel to the direction of travel. Standing forage is mowed and chopped in a single operation.

Field choppers are made with direct-cut attachments for cutting and chopping standing forage crops, pickup attachments

FIG. 48.8. *Chopped forage . . . adapted to mechanical handling.* A self-unloading wagon feeding a forage blower in silo filling. *Iowa State Univ. photo.*

for taking up and chopping windrows (Fig. 48.7), and row crop attachments for corn and sorghum silage harvest. Usually these attachments are interchangeable. The flail-type harvesters can also be used as beet toppers, stalk shredders, or corn stover harvesters.

CHOPPED FORAGE HANDLING. Chopped forage is blown into a trailer drawn behind the chopper or into a truck or trailer operated alongside. Chopped forage is adapted to mechanical handling (Fig. 48.8).[8] Devices which move the forage to the rear of the wagon or truck box are commonly used. In some cases, the forage is discharged directly from the rear of the box as in Figure 48.8. In others, a cross-conveyor on the wagon replaces the long hopper on the blower. When a cross-conveyor on the wagon is used, discharge may be at either the front or the rear of the box. Cross-conveyor wagons may also be used where green-chopped forage, silage, or other forage feeds are to be delivered from a wagon to feed bunks. Dump boxes and beds for trailers and trucks are also used. The chief disadvantage with dumping is that the unloading rate is not easily related to the blower capacity.

Elevation of chopped material into storage usually is done with a blower designed especially for this purpose. Well-designed blowers will elevate 0.5 t/min of green-chopped forage. Dry material is handled with lesser capacities.

BALING

Balers take up hay from windrows; compress it into rectangular packages; and tie the packages with either two or three bands of wire, hemp, sisal, or plastic (Fig. 48.9). Three wire ties are preferred for commercial hay in the western states, while two ties of hemp, sisal, or plastic are common for farm-fed hay in midwestern and eastern areas.

8. McKibben, J. S. 1971. Mechanized storing and feeding of chopped hay. *Agr. Eng.* 52 (5):274–76.

Fig. 48.9. *Two ties . . . common for farm-fed hay.* A two-tie baler. *International Harvester Co. photo.*

Baled hay is packaged hay. A man's load in handling bales is regulated by the size of the bale, and because of the convenience of measured units the workman is more efficient in handling baled hay than loose hay. A wide range of bale sizes and densities is available. Bale cross-sections, ranging from 25×38 cm (10×15 in.) to 43×56 cm (17 × 22 in.), and lengths from 30 to 130 cm (12 to 52 in.) are available. Most commonly, balers are available with bale cross-sections of 36×46 cm (14×18 in.) or 38×48 cm (15×19 in.) and with bale lengths adjustable from 30 to 124 cm (12 to 49 in.). A common length for a two-wire bale is 90 cm (36 in.), and such a bale would weigh 23–32 kg. Large bales tied with three wires are produced in dimensions up to 41 × 61 × 122 cm (16 × 24 × 48 in.). Bales of this size may weigh 60 kg or more.

Machines have been available which produce cylindrical bales between 36 and 56 cm (14 and 22 in.) in diameter and 90 cm (36 in.) long. Machines have also been developed which produce large round bales ranging in size up to 1800 kg. These machines pick up hay from the windrow, compress it, and roll it into a large cylinder. Common self-tieing balers producing rectangular bales have effective capacities in the range of 5–10 t/hr.

BALE HANDLING. Most commonly bales are dropped onto the ground behind the baler as it travels through the field. In some situations, bale chutes are provided which elevate bales directly from the baler to a pulled trailer where they are stacked by hand (Fig. 48.10).

Bulk bale-handling systems have been developed. A thrower on the baler throws bales into a trailing wagon (Fig. 48.10) where they fall in a random arrangement. The wagonload of bales is then dumped into an elevator, and the bales are dropped in a random manner onto a storage pile.

In another system, bales are accumulated into groups of four to eight as they are discharged behind a baler. These groups of bales are then handled on and off trucks or trailers and in and out of stacks by special tractor-mounted grapples or sweep pickups. These systems can field stack or load onto trucks or trailers at rates of 10 or more t/hr. If bales are placed on a truck or trailer and hauled from the field, removal from the truck and placement in stacks requires additional time equal to the field handling time.[7]

Bales which have been dropped singly onto the ground behind a baler must be picked up and loaded onto vehicles. A three-man crew loading bales by hand has a capacity of 7 t/hr, or 2.33 t/man-hr.

Bale loaders are available that will pick

Fig. 48.10. *Bulk bale-handling systems . . . developed.* Three alternatives in bale handling: (left to right) drop on ground for later pickup, stack on a trailed wagon, throw to a trailed wagon for bulk handling. *International Harvester Co. photo.*

Fig. 48.11. *Mechanized bale-handling equipment . . . for commercial . . . operations.* A pull-type bale handler picks up bales and stacks them on its bed. *New Holland Div., Sperry Rand Corp., photo.*

up bales from the ground and raise them to the bed of a truck or tractor-drawn trailer where they must be stacked by hand. Fully mechanized bale-handling equipment is commonly used for commercial baling operations. The equipment operated by one man consists of a vehicle that picks up bales from the field, arranges them in a stack on its bed (Fig. 48.11), transports them to a storage location, and places them in a stack at the storage area (Fig. 48.12). This equipment is available in both self-propelled and pull-type models. Such equipment can pick up and stack bales at rates up to 10 t/hr when stacking at the harvest field.

The small round bales are sometimes

Fig. 48.12. *Equipment available . . . self-propelled and pull-type models.* A pull-type bale handler placing a stack of bales into storage. *New Holland Div., Sperry Rand Corp., photo.*

Fig. 48.13. *Means to package . . . units small enough . . . handled in bulk.* Hay cubes. *Deere and Co. photo.*

left where they fall from the baler. They are then eaten by cattle turned into the harvest field for wintering when the hay crop is dormant.

CUBING

During the 20-year period 1950–70 much attention was given to the development of means to package hay in units small enough to be readily handled in bulk. The hay cube is the result (Fig. 48.13). The most popular hay "cube" is about 3 cm (1.25 in.) square in cross section and of variable length, ranging from 2.5 to 8 cm. As a cubing machine is used, wear of parts will result in a cube of up to 4 cm (1.5 in.) square in cross section. If cubes beyond this size result, worn machine parts must be replaced.[9]

The cubing process (Fig. 48.14) has become very popular where it is adaptable. Unfortunately, practical field cubing of hay is limited to areas where hay may be field cured to 12% moisture. This has limited field cubing to the arid-land hay areas of New Mexico, Arizona, California, and the Columbia Basin in Washington. With use of the field cuber, the moisture content of the windrowed hay is increased a few percentage points by passing under a water spray. The moistened hay is then chopped

9. Soteropulos, G., and H. E. de Buhr. 1969. Cubing —Past, present, future. *Agr. Eng.* 50 (9):516–18.

FIG. 48.14. *Cubing process . . . popular where . . . adaptable.* A field hay-cubing machine. *Deere and Co. photo.*

to a 3.5-cm (1.38 in.) theoretical cut and forced through the 3-cm square dies. The cubes produced have volume weights of 0.75–0.90 kg/cm (45–55 lb/cu ft), and the bulk volume weight of such cubes is 0.45–0.58 kg/cu cm (28–36 lb/cu ft). Capacities range from 4.5 to 5 t/hr.

In areas where field cubing is adaptable, major portions of the hay crop are being harvested in this manner. In 1968, 17.5% of the Arizona hay, 6.7% of the California hay, 26.1% of the New Mexico hay, and 5.9% of the Washington hay was being cubed.[9] This was early in the history of cubers, and it is predicted that a much greater portion of the hay in these states will be cubed.

The same principle used in field cubing also is applied in stationary machines. For stationary cubing, field-cured hay is stockpiled during hours or seasons of good field conditions and cubed on a continuous operating basis, spreading the operating time of the cuber over a greater period of time than allowed by field conditions. By artificially drying the stockpiled hay, it will be possible to apply cubing to areas where field-curing conditions limit its field application. Drying costs, however, may often limit the application of such a system.

Field cubing has been very successful economically. The savings in handling, transportation, and storage costs together with decreases in feed wastage more than offset the additional costs of cubing. Many cost studies have indicated that as a broad generalization, cubing costs $3/t more than baling, users of cubes will pay $5/t more than they will for baled hay, and the value of cubes to a dairyman is $7/t greater than the value of baled hay.[10]

CUBE HANDLING. Cubes are delivered to a trailing hopper as they are discharged by the cubing machine. At fieldside they are dumped into trucks for hauling to storage locations. Trucks dump cubes into elevators that place them in large storage piles. From there they are easily handled by front-end scoop loaders into hay drags of feed mills or into feed delivery wagons for distribution to feed bunkers. Cubes are hot, 50–60 C, when produced and may need some cooling in storage. They will spoil if stored at over 15% moisture. Where cubes are subject to rainfall, protected storage costing up to $1/t is justified.[11]

10. Barnes, K. K. 1970. More about hay cubing costs. *Implement and Tractor* 85 (23):40.
11. Dobie, J. B., and R. G. Curley. 1970. Storing wafered hay. *Agr. Eng.* 51 (1):22–23.

✧ QUESTIONS

1. What are appropriate moisture levels for storage of alfalfa as silage, haylage, and hay?
2. A metric ton of alfalfa is mowed at 75% moisture. It is field cured to 35% moisture and then chopped and artificially dried to 20% moisture. How much dry hay at 20% results from the original ton? How many kilograms of moisture are removed from the original ton during field curing? How many kilograms of moisture are removed from the original ton during artificial drying?
3. A windrow has been formed by a dump rake. What problems may be expected in attempting to bale from this windrow with a pickup baler?
4. Hay sometimes ignites by spontaneous combustion. What causes this?
5. Why is so much hay baled?
6. What purpose is served by chopping forage?
7. Windrowers have been widely accepted. What advantages do they offer?
8. A farmer from south central Texas has written that his implement dealer will not sell him a hay cuber. He is critical of the dealer and wants an explanation. What should the farmer be told?
9. What is accomplished by cubing hay?

J. T. REID / *Cornell University*

49

QUALITY HAY

˨

Hᴀʏ ɪꜱ ꜰᴇᴇᴅ produced by dehydrating green forage to a moisture content of 15% or less, and it provides a considerable proportion of energy and certain other nutritional essentials of livestock feeds. Its value is especially great when pasturage or silage is not available. The nutrients (energy) provided in field-cured hay undamaged by weather usually cost less to produce than those in any other form of feed except pasturage and corn silage. Figuring the costs of producing various feeds is a complex problem; the final conclusion is influenced by such factors as land productivity, seasonality of growth, methods of harvest and storage, size of the operation, and other conditions.[1,2,3] For example, the annual costs per unit of forage dry matter (DM) are considerably less for hay than for haylage when only 91 t of DM are stored, whereas they are about the same when 272 t of DM are stored.[2]

˨ HAY CONSUMPTION IN THE U.S.

In 1970, forages comprised 54.4% of the energy expressed as total digestible nutri-

Fɪɢ. 49.1. Distribution of all seeded hay crops throughout the U.S.

ents consumed by all farm animals (including fowls and pigs) in the U.S.[4] (See Fig. 49.1.) Of the total energy ingested, hay provided 12.4%; other harvested forage, 5.9%; and pasture, 36.1%. In that year there were 102 million animal units equivalent to lactating cows consuming forage and concentrate and 97 million con-

˨ J. T. REID is Professor and Head, Department of Animal Science, Cornell University. His research has dealt especially with nutritional energetics (i.e., the effects of nutrition upon reproduction, milk and meat production, and longevity of farm animals) as well as with the nutritive value of forages.

1. Hoglund, C. R. 1962. Evaluating the economics of alternative forage crops for the farm business. Mich. Agr. Econ. Mimeo 873.
2. Hoglund, C. R. 1965. Some economic considerations in selecting storage systems for haylage and silage for dairy farms. Mich. Agr. Econ. Rept. 14.
3. Hoglund, C. R. 1967. Economic considerations in selecting silage storage and feeding. Mich. Agr. Econ. Rept. 84.
4. Allen, G. C., E. F. Hodges, and M. Devers. 1972. National and state livestock-feed relationships. ERS, USDA Stat. Bull. Suppl. 446.

532

TABLE 49.1 ❧ Proportions of total energy (TDN) intake provided to certain farm animals by various kinds of feeds

Animal	Proportion of dietary energy supplied by:			
	Concentrates	Hay	Other harvested forage	Pasture
	(%)	(%)	(%)	(%)
Lactating cows	37.9	23.1	19.4	19.6
Other dairy cattle	19.4	29.0	5.9	45.7
Fattening beef cattle	69.8	16.3	8.7	5.2
Other beef cattle	8.7	15.5	4.1	71.7
Sheep and goats	10.4	4.7	3.1	81.8
Horses and mules	20.6	18.3	10.2	50.9
Pigs	85.0	...	...	15.0
Fowls	97.4	...	...	2.6

Source: Adapted from data of Allen et al., 1972.[4]

suming forage. Each forage-consuming animal unit required 1.22 t/year of hay equivalent.

Because of differences in the capacity and morphology of the gastrointestinal tract, in digestive agents available, and in degree of production intensity desired, certain farm animals consume diets containing higher proportions of forages than do others. This is shown in Table 49.1 for various animals, based on 1970 average data for the U.S.[4]

Pasture supplies a greater proportion of the dietary energy than any other feed for nonmilking dairy cattle, nonfattening beef cattle, sheep, goats, and horses. Hay is a more significant energy source for dairy cattle than for any other farm animal. Pigs and fowls consume practically no hay, except as dehydrated alfalfa meal, and only small amounts of pasture. Undoubtedly, hay of higher than average quality could supply considerably more of the energy required by all of the herbivores than it does.

❧ PURPOSE OF HAY IN LIVESTOCK RATIONS

The chief reason for including hay in the rations of ruminant animals (cattle, sheep, and goats) and horses is to provide energy for the support of various productive functions such as those which yield meat, milk, wool, and work. Energy is provided by this kind of feed at a much lower cost than by concentrates (cereal grains and oil meals). For ruminants and horses, hays have much less importance as sources of protein, minerals, and vitamins than they do as energy providers. Hay has greater significance as a source of vitamins, minerals, and protein for animals with simple stomachs (fowls and pigs) than it has as a source of energy. In high-concentrate diets, hay may be an important source of minerals, vitamins, and fiber even for herbivores. The fat content of milk is reduced when cows are fed high-concentrate diets, but when cows eat 3–6 kg/day of hay, the concentration of fat in milk will be maintained.

Differences among animals in the relative value of hay as a source of the various nutrients is briefly explained by the following fundamental facts.

1. Hay contains 40–70% of complex carbohydrates (cellulose and hemicellulose) which require fermentative digestion by bacteria.
2. The gastrointestinal tract of ruminants is large, contains a large population of bacteria, and has its main site (the rumen) of bacterial action near the front of the tract, giving a greater opportunity for the products of digestion to be absorbed into the blood rather than being voided in the feces.
3. Although bacteria inhabit the tract of the pig and fowl, the main sites (namely the large intestines) of fermentation in these species are too near the end of the tract and the extent of digestion is too meager to appreciably benefit the host animal.
4. The symbiotic relationship between the gastrointestinal bacteria and the host is not as well developed in the horse as in the ruminant, but it is considerably better developed than that in the pig or chicken.
5. Animals with simple stomachs have to rely for their energy supply upon

feeds which can be digested by enzymes elaborated by the body.

6. In addition to forming simple substances from complex substances, capable of absorption into the blood, the gastrointestinal bacteria synthesize many substances such as amino acids and certain vitamins which are nutritional essentials.

7. Large quantities of amino acids can be synthesized from simple nitrogenous sources such as ammonia by the ruminants but not by animals with simple stomachs.

8. Animals with simple stomachs require preformed amino acids in their diet.

9. Ruminants require a much smaller percentage of digestible protein in the diet than do animals with simple stomachs.

10. Animals with simple stomachs require the B-complex vitamins and vitamin K in the diet, whereas ruminants, by virtue of their capacity to synthesize them, do not.

❧ HAY QUALITY

Since 96% of the hay produced is consumed by ruminants, it can be concluded that most serves the primary purpose of providing energy. It is axiomatic that the amount of productive energy in a balanced diet determines the size of an animal's response in terms of milk, meat, eggs, and wool produced or in work performed. The total amount of energy is the product of the amount of DM consumed and the concentration of energy in the DM. It follows that the determinants of hay quality are those characteristics which influence the amount of DM animals will consume voluntarily and the energy value derived by the animal per unit weight consumed.

Many conditions and characteristics are either associated with or determine the nutritive quality of hay. It is impossible to predict from one known characteristic of hays the amount of animal response that will be obtained. Among the more important known conditions or charac-

teristics affecting hay quality are: (1) the time during the season and the growth stage at which forage is harvested, (2) whether the forage represents a first growth (not previously harvested or grazed during the same season) or an aftermath growth, (3) leaf content, (4) extent to which the harvested forage is damaged by weather and handling, (5) physical form in which it is fed, and (6) forage species.

HAY INTAKE BY ANIMALS

Properties of hays which influence their acceptability to animals are not well understood. Many qualities such as certain features of the botanical, physical, and chemical composition of hays have been proposed as conditions that might influence the quantity consumed. None has been proved to be a consistently adequate indicator of animal acceptance. During the 1960s, the cell wall content (lignin, cellulose, and hemicellulose) of forage was shown to be inversely related to digestibility and DM intake.[5,6] Because the relationships are species oriented, they do not have a high predictive value when applied generally. However, it seems clear that the cell wall fraction, its digestibility being inhibited by lignin, occupies gastrointestinal space and lowers intake. Cell wall contents become especially limiting as the concentration increases above 50% and the intake decreases at an increasing rate. It has seemed that any condition that would accelerate the digestion of hay and the passage of the undigested residue through the gastrointestinal tract would stimulate the appetite as a consequence. Thus the faster the rate of passage, the larger the quantity voluntarily consumed. If the rate of passage could be increased without seriously depressing digestibility, the net effect on animal production could be increased correspondingly. Practical means

5. Van Soest, P. J. 1965. Symposium on factors influencing the voluntary intake of herbage by ruminants: Voluntary intake in relation to chemical composition and digestibility. *J. Anim. Sci.* 24:834.

6. Van Soest, P. J. 1968. Structural and chemical characteristics which limit the nutritive value of forages. Amer. Soc. Agron. Spec. Publ. 13, pp. 63–76.

TABLE 49.2 & Effect of time of cutting first-growth forage on intake and digestibility of hays by lactating cows

Cutting date	Growth stage*	Number of cows†	Hay intake per day‡ (% of body wt.)	DDM value§ (%)	Relative DDM intake
June 3–4	vegetative	32	2.72	67.2	182
June 9–10	early boot	23	2.64	63.1	166
June 11–12	boot	24	2.36	65.7	154
June 14–15	late boot	94	2.45	62.6	153
June 16–18	early head	24	2.28	58.5	133
July 1	bloom	30	2.30	52.7	121
July 5	bloom	24	2.13	52.2	111
July 7–8	bloom	23	2.05	52.2	107
July 9–10	late bloom	24	1.95	51.5	100

Source: Stone et al., 1959.[8]

* Growth stage of timothy in the grass-legume mixtures fed.

† Number of cows reduced to those consuming forages during periods of five weeks duration; usually in these experiments two to four different forages were compared in a five-week change-over design in which all cows were eventually fed all forages. In some experiments the hays were fed continuously for 20 weeks. The hay crops represented 10 consecutive years.

‡ Concentrates were fed at the average rate of 1 kg/4.1 kg of 4% fat-corrected milk produced. However, considerable variation existed in the level of concentrates fed, which resulted in irregularities in the hay-consumption trend.

§ Digestible dry matter values determined in conventional digestion trials.

of accomplishing this have not been found. The student may gain an appreciation of the complexity of some forage and animal characteristics that influence intake from one worker's attempt to develop a mathematical model to describe forage intake.[7]

TIME OF FIRST-GROWTH HARVEST. Of the known conditions associated with the rate at which hays are consumed by animals, the time when first-growth forage is cut has the most pronounced effect. The data summarized in Table 49.2, obtained in a study of 175 lactating cows and 50 mixed legume-grass forages over a 10-year period, demonstrate this relationship.[8] It is shown that hays made from first-growth forages cut early are consumed in larger amounts than those cut from the same sources later in the season. The cows consumed 35–40% more hay of the crops cut during early June than when cut about a month later. In examining these data, the student should consider that the cows fed

the various hays received concentrates at the average rate of 1 kg/4.1 kg of 4% fat-corrected milk (FCM) produced. Since the cows receiving the early cut hays produced more FCM than those fed the late cut hays (see Table 49.3 for data from one specific experiment),[9] the cows fed the early cut hays were fed more concentrates than those fed the late cut hays. Because of this bias it is reasonable to assume that the effect of time of cutting on acceptability is even more marked than indicated by the Table 49.2 data. Other examples of the effect of harvest time upon the intake of hay by cows and lambs are shown in Tables 49.3 and 49.4 respectively.[10]

An attempt to quantify the relationship between the time of cutting in days after April 30 (X) and the daily DM intake (Y) in kg/100 kg of body weight resulted in the equation, $Y = 3.22 - 0.017X$. Although this equation provides a good estimate of the hay consumption trend in the northeastern states, the estimated and

7. Waldo, D. R. 1970. Factors influencing the voluntary intake of forages, pp. E1–E22. Proc. Conf. Forage Qual. Eval. Util. (Lincoln, Nebr.).

8. Stone, J. B., G. W. Trimberger, C. R. Henderson, J. T. Reid, K. L. Turk, and J. K. Loosli. 1960. Forage intake and efficiency of feed utilization in dairy cattle. *J. Dairy Sci.* 42:1275–81.

9. Slack, S. T., W. K. Kennedy, K. L. Turk, J. T. Reid, and G. W. Trimberger. 1960. Effect of curing methods and stage of maturity upon feeding value of roughages. Cornell Agr. Exp. Sta. Bull. 957.

10. Jones, J. R., D. E. Hogue, and G. L. Hunt. 1959. Effects of date and method of harvesting of mixed hay on the performance of fattening lambs. *J. Anim. Sci.* 18:1539.

TABLE 49.3 ❧ Response of lactating cows to hays prepared from first-growth forage cut at different times from the same source

Item of interest	Early	Late
Cutting date	June 3–12	June 30–July 9
Growth stage*	early to late boot	full to late bloom
Number of cows	20	20
Concentrate intake† (kg/day)	3.9	2.9
Hay intake‡ (kg/day)	15.1	12.5
FCM yield (kg/day)	19.6	14.1
Body weight change (gm/day)	73	—59

Source: Slack et al., 1960.[9]
* Growth stage of timothy in the mixture at the time of harvest.
† Concentrates fed at the rate of 1 kg/5 kg of milk corrected to 4% of fat.
‡ Hay intake expressed on 90% dry basis.

measured intakes frequently are considerably different. This suggests that other or unknown factors not associated with harvest time also influence the consumption rate. It is expected that a different relationship probably exists for forages grown in other geographic regions.

TIME OF CUTTING AFTERMATH FORAGE. No similar trend in the effect of time of cutting on the consumption rate of aftermath forages has been determined. Acceptability of hays from aftermaths approaches that of hays from first-growth forage cut early (Table 49.4). The consumption rate of aftermath hays is not affected as much by the growth stage at the time of harvest as is that of first-growth hays.

LEAF CONTENT. The leaf content of hays is a good index of their palatability. When animals are fed enough hay to allow sorting (known as "selective feeding"), they tend to select the leaves and reject the stems. Hays high in leaf content are usually consumed in larger quantity than those that are low; however, the extent to which leaf content per se influences the amount of hay consumed has not been determined.[11] Since leaf content (like many physical, chemical, and biological characteristics of hays) is related to the stage of growth at harvest time and to several other factors, it is practically impossible to study the effects of this one characteristic unencumbered by the effects of others.

CURING METHODS. Methods commonly used to make hay from green forages are field curing, barn drying with either

11. Moore, L. A. 1958. Influence of forage quality on feed efficiency, pp. 152–66. *In* Feed Utilization of Dairy Cattle. Iowa State Univ. Press, Ames.

TABLE 49.4 ❧ Response of fattening lambs to hays made from an early and a late first cutting and an aftermath of the same source

Item of interest	First growth cut on:		Aftermath* (9-wk regrowth)
	May 31	July 7	
Number of lambs	87	88	88
Concentrate intake (% of body wt.)	1.25	1.25	1.25
Hay intake† (gm/day)	1025	830	953
Digestible DM (%)	67.4‡	53.8	61.5
Weight gain (gm/day)	191	118	168
Live grade§	8.6	5.5	7.3

Source: Jones et al., 1959.[10]
* The second growth was cut from the same area from which the first growth was harvested on May 31.
† All hays were fed ad libitum with sufficient excess to allow considerable selective feeding of the late cut hay; therefore, the differences in the responses were probably considerably less than they would have been with less opportunity to select.
‡ Some rain damage experienced.
§ Relative scale: 1 = lowest and 10 = highest grade.

unheated or heated air, and any of these procedures applied subsequent to the crushing or crimping of the freshly cut crop. A less commonly used procedure involves dehydration at high temperatures for short periods of time. The rate at which animals will consume hay cured by the various methods is about the same if the amount of leaf loss and damage due to leaching and microorganism and enzyme action are not different. In some cases differences in palatability have been attributed to the curing treatment. For example, in experiments in which crushed and uncrushed hays were fed simultaneously to cattle, the crushed hays were preferred.[12] Whether this was the result of the greater mustiness of the uncrushed hays or a preference for crushed stems is not known.

From the sketchy information available it appears that the curing treatment used does not impart any special quality which affects the consumption rate that the forage did not already have at the time of cutting. Based upon the results of numerous experiments, the percentages of the harvested DM conserved by the various curing methods are:[9,11,12] quick drying in an oven, 90%; barn drying with heated air, 87%; barn drying with unheated air, 85%; field curing without rain, 76%; and field curing with rain, 50–76%. The leafy portion of hays suffers from drying and handling more than stems. Thus the leaf content and, as a consequence, the consumption of hay cured under unfavorable weather conditions are affected by the curing method.

PHYSICAL FORM. Leaf content, texture, and brittleness constitute a part of the physical properties of hay. Length of the hay particle and density of the form in which hay is fed are also important. Comparisons have been made of the same hay fed in two or more of the following forms: long, chopped (2.0–10-cm lengths) and fed loose or compressed as wafers,

and finely ground (0.16–0.8-cm particles) fed as meal or pellets. The approximate densities (kilograms per cubic meter) of the various forms of hay are: long, 80 kg; chopped, 144 kg; chopped and wafered, 256–480 kg; finely ground meal, 336 kg; and finely ground and pelleted, 705–961 kg. In the processing of wafers and pellets the amount of pressure applied determines the density and hardness.

It is well established that the voluntary intake of ground, pelleted hay is generally 10–30% greater than that of the same hay fed in the long or chopped form.[13-21] Some typical data demonstrating this difference are summarized in Table 49.5. Although this effect is demonstrated invariably in fattening sheep, beef cattle, and growing cattle, it is not always obtained with lactating dairy cows.[13-24] No essential difference exists in the consumption rate of hay fed in long form or in chopped form fed loose or wafered.[13,22-24]

Much of the increase in the intake of

12. Turk, K. L., S. H. Morrison, C. L. Norton, and R. E. Blaser. 1951. Effect of curing methods upon the feeding value of hay. Cornell Agr. Exp. Sta. Bull. 874.

13. Meyer, J. H., W. C. Weir, J. B. Dobie, and J. L. Hull. 1959. Influence of the method of preparation on the feeding value of alfalfa hay. J. Anim. Sci. 18:976–82.

14. Weir, W. C., J. H. Meyer, W. N. Garrett, G. P. Lofgreen, and N. R. Ittner. 1959. Pelleted rations compared to similar rations fed chopped or ground for steers and lambs. J. Anim. Sci. 18:805–14.

15. Meyer, J. H., R. L. Gaskill, G. S. Stoewsand, and W. C. Weir. 1959. Influence of pelleting on the utilization of alfalfa. J. Anim. Sci. 18:336–46.

16. Paladines, O. L., J. T. Reid, B. D. H. Van Niekerk, and A. Bensadoun. 1964. Energy utilization by sheep as influenced by the physical form, composition and level of intake of diet. J. Nutr. 83:49–59.

17. Heaney, D. P., W. J. Pigden, D. J. Minson, and G. I. Pritchard. 1963. Effect of pelleting on energy intake of sheep from forages cut at three stages of maturity. J. Anim. Sci. 22:752–57.

18. Hogan, J. P., and R. H. Weston. 1967. The digestion of chopped and ground roughages by sheep. 2. The digestion of nitrogen and some carbohydrate fractions in the stomach and intestines. Aust. J. Agr. Res. 18:803.

19. Ronning, M., J. H. Meyer, and G. T. Clark. 1959. Pelleted alfalfa hay for milk production. J. Dairy Sci. 42:1373–76.

20. Ittner, N. R., J. H. Meyer, and G. P. Lofgreen. 1958. Pelleted alfalfa hay: Baled and pelleted alfalfa hay in comparative trial with beef steers. Calif. Agr. 12:8.

21. Webb, R. J., G. F. Cmarik, and H. A. Cate. 1957. Comparison of feeding three forages as baled hay, chopped hay, hay pellets and silage to steer calves. J. Anim. Sci. 16:1057–58.

22. Niedermeier, R. P. 1959. Pelleting forage crops for dairy cows. Proc. Wis. Nutr. School 10:63–65.

23. Blosser, T. H., F. R. Murdock, R. E. Lintott, R. E. Erb, and A. O. Shaw. 1952. The use of dehydrated forages in dairy cattle rations. II. Comparative values of finely ground, chopped and pelleted dehydrated alfalfa as grain replacements for lactating dairy cows. J. Dairy Sci. 35:515–23.

24. Porter, G. H., R. E. Johnson, H. D. Eaton, F. I. Elliott, and L. A. Moore. 1953. Relative value for milk production of field-cured and field-baled, artificially dried-chopped, artificially dried-ground and artificially dried-pelleted alfalfa when fed as the sole source of roughage to dairy cattle. J. Dairy Sci. 36:1140–49.

TABLE 49.5 ✷ Comparison of feeding value of ground, pelleted hay with that of long or chopped hay from the same source

Form of hay	Manner of feeding	Hay DM intake (kg/day)	Body gain (kg/day)	FCM yield (kg/day)	Fat in carcass or milk (%)
		Fattening lambs*			
Chopped†	ad lib.	2.48	0.27	...	30.8
Ground pelleted‡	controlled§	2.54	0.26	...	30.8
Ground pelleted	ad lib.	3.25	0.40	...	28.4
		Fattening steers‖			
Long	ad lib.	14.0	1.80	...	26.4
Ground pelleted#	ad lib.	17.1	2.17	...	25.7
		Lactating cows**			
Chopped††	ad lib.	26.4	−0.11	23.7	4.09
Ground pelleted‡‡	ad lib.	33.3	1.66	28.1	4.01
		Lactating cows§§			
Chopped‖‖	controlled***	29.1†††	0.09	33.7	3.8
Ground##	controlled***	29.8†††	0.63	29.8	2.2

 * Meyer et al., 1959;[15] hay constituted entire ration.
 † Field chopped.
 ‡ Ground through 1.17-mm sieve; made into 9.4-mm pellets.
 § "Controlled" means that intake was restricted to the same amount consumed by the group fed chopped hay ad libitum.
 ‖ Weir et al., 1959;[14] rations provided 0.82 kg of barley and 0.77 kg of oat hay in addition to experimental hays.
 # Ground through 1.17-mm sieve; made into 5.1-mm pellets.
 ** Ronning et al., 1959;[19] hay constituted entire ration.
 †† Chopped into 1.9-cm lengths.
 ‡‡ Ground through 4.7-mm sieve; made into 9.4-mm pellets
 §§ Colenbrander et al., 1967;[16] diets comprised of 50% sorghum grain and 50% alfalfa hay.
 ‖‖ Chopped hay fed with cracked sorghum grain (1:1).
 ## Ground hay fed with expanded sorghum grain (1:1).
 *** "Controlled" means that feed allowance was based on feeding standards.
 ††† Values represent total feed intake of which 50% was alfalfa hay.

pelleted hay is effected by fine grinding (small particle size), but an additional increase is obtained by pelleting or wetting finely ground hay.[13,15] Thus it would appear that the increased intake of hay is caused chiefly by the small particle size which contributes to the increased rate of digestion and passage of the residue through the gastrointestinal tract.[13,15,25] Improvement in intake resulting from pelleting or wetting might be associated with the elimination of dust.[13,15] The effect of density of the hay form fed upon consumption rate has not been completely determined.

25. Blaxter, K. L., N. McC. Graham, and F. W. Wainman. 1955. Interrelations between passage of food through the digestive tract and its digestibility. Proc. Brit. Nutr. Soc. 14:iv–v.

The hypothesis has been proposed that increase in intake attributable to grinding and pelleting is greater for grasses (high cell wall content) than for legumes (low cell wall content).[7] However, this observation is not unequivocal. Within species the degree of improvement in intake effected by grinding and pelleting increases as the stage of maturity progresses.[17] In general, the intake of poor quality hay is increased more by grinding and pelleting than that of good quality hay.

ENERGY CONCENTRATION OF HAYS

The following brief descriptions are intended to remind the students of several criteria of the energy value of hays. A more complete account is found in Chapter 6. In North America the criteria of energy concentration of feedstuffs (including hays) most widely used are total digestible nutrients (TDN), digestible dry matter (DDM), and digestible energy (DE). All these units represent essentially the same thing, disappearance of the feed as it passes through the gastrointestinal tract. Total digestible nutrients are represented by the differences between the feed consumed and feces voided with respect to the weights of protein, carbohydrates, and (fat $\times$ 2.25) contained. Digestible dry matter and DE are the feed-feces differences in DM and calories respectively. When the amount of DM or energy which disappeared during passage of feed through the tract is expressed as a percentage of that consumed, all three units have essentially the same numerical value.

Metabolizable energy (ME) is a more refined nutritive index than DE because it accounts for the energy wasted in urine and methane in addition to feces. Net energy (NE) is that which is put into useful animal products (the heat of combustion value of the body tissue, milk, and fetus). When expressed per unit weight of diet ingested, it becomes the NE value of the diet. The NE value of hay (or the diet) is lower than ME value by the amount of heat lost as the result of the animal transforming ME to NE. As a consequence, the proportion of ME which becomes NE (the net utilization of ME) is a significant index of nutritive value. Since these criteria are expressed as percentages or as calories per unit of weight, they represent indices of energy concentration in hay.

TIME OF FIRST-GROWTH HARVEST. Of all known conditions the time when forage is harvested has the most pronounced effect upon its digestible matter or energy value. In northern states the first growth of grasses and legumes contains 80–85% of DDM during the first two weeks or so of growth. This value declines at the rate of 0.48 percentage units per

TABLE 49.6 ❧ Effect of growth stage and date of cutting on the digestible dry matter value of four different species

Species	Cutting date*	DDM value (%) Measured†	DDM value (%) Estimated‡
Kentucky bluegrass	May 20	72.4	75.4
Orchardgrass	May 26	72.8	72.5
Smooth bromegrass	June 2	70.6	69.2
Timothy	June 15	60.9	62.9

Source: Swift et al., 1950.[27]
* Forages harvested when "head emerged from boot but had not expanded."
† Values determined in conventional digestion trials.
‡ Values estimated from cutting date using the following equation: DDM(%) = 85.0 − 0.48 (days after April 30).

day until another plateau is reached at approximately the 50% level, beginning on about July 10. Some typical values for hays harvested at various times are shown in Tables 49.2, 49.4, and 49.6. In a study of a large number of hays prepared from first cuttings of mixed forages and pure stands of alfalfa, birdsfoot trefoil, red clover, timothy, Kentucky bluegrass, smooth bromegrass, and quackgrass grown in the vicinity of Ithaca, N.Y., it was found that the percentage of DDM (Y) could be predicted quite accurately from the time of cutting (X), expressed as the number of days after April 30, according to the equation, $Y = 85.0 - 0.48X$.[26,27] The student is cautioned that this prediction equation will not necessarily apply to the forages grown in other geographic areas or under climatic conditions different from those at Ithaca. It has been found, however, that first-growth forages from the Pennsylvania, Vermont, New Hampshire, and New Jersey stations, as well as those from England, conform to this equation.[28] Although the rate (0.48 percentage units per day) at which digestible matter declines in forages

26. Reid, J. T., W. K. Kennedy, K. L. Turk, S. T. Slack, G. W. Trimberger, and R. P. Murphy. 1959. Effect of growth stage, chemical composition and physical properties upon the nutritive value of forages. *J. Dairy Sci.* 42:567–71.

27. Swift, R. W., R. L. Cowan, R. H. Ingram, H. K. Maddy, G. P. Barron, E. C. Grose, and J. B. Washko. 1950. The relative nutritive value of Kentucky bluegrass, timothy, bromegrass, orchardgrass, and alfalfa. *J. Anim. Sci.* 9:363–72.

28. Reid, J. T. 1959. Unpubl. data. Cornell Univ.

grown in the northeastern states and in England is the same as that for forages grown in Sweden and Norway, the forage-growing season in the latter two countries is about 19–20 days later than in some of the northeastern states or in England.[26,29,30] Essentially the same equation ($Y = 84.9 - 0.48X$) describes the DDM value of timothy hay harvested in Maine when X is the number of days after May 17.[31]

Thus the forage growing season at Orono, Maine, appears to be about 17 days later than at Ithaca. In the milder climates of Beltsville, Md.; Dover, Del.; Wooster, Ohio; and West Lafayette, Ind., the forage growing season begins earlier and the rate of decline in DM with advancing growth stage is lower (the slopes range from only 0.29 to 0.41).[32-35] The student should understand that starting dates relative to the equations above were arbitrarily selected in order to establish a numerical value for time. Any other day would serve equally as well as the zero time point needed to quantify the relationships.

Although the fundamental reasons for the predictable relationship between time of harvesting and digestible matter content of first-growth forage are not known, it seems possible that it might be a response to light, the extent of root reserves, and/or changes in soil temperature. Whether a dormant period, such as that occurring during the winter in northern states, exerts an effect on this relationship needs to be determined. Research indicates that forages grown in high temperatures contain more stems and cell wall substance and are less digestible than those grown in cooler temperatures.[36,37]

PLANT SPECIES AND CULTIVARS. Although there are several known exceptions, most of the species, cultivars, and strains studied in the northern states follow the general DDM time of cutting relationship discussed above. An excellent example of the greater effect of time than of growth stage upon this nutritional criterion are the data summarized in Table 49.6. In that experiment the timothy had emerged from the boot but had not yet expanded 26 days after this stage was reached in Kentucky bluegrass. However, at this stage timothy contained 19% less DDM than did Kentucky bluegrass. It will be noted in Table 49.6 that the time of cutting DDM equation described above accurately predicted the value of these forages.

Studies made of two cultivars each of birdsfoot trefoil, smooth bromegrass, and timothy (having considerably different flowering dates) revealed no differences in the digestible matter value when forages were harvested at the same time.[26]

Nevertheless, a late maturing timothy cultivar (blooming about 20 days later than common timothy) was found to contain 1.6, 3.4, and 3.8 percentage units more of DDM than did common timothy cut on June 8, June 22, and July 2 respectively.[38] The DDM values of each of four orchardgrass cultivars were 3–7 percentage units lower for various cuttings than the values estimated from the equation discussed above.[38] A first cutting of a late maturing ryegrass cultivar ('S23') was 2–8

29. Jarl, F., and T. Helleday. 1951. Changes in the chemical composition, digestion and nutritive value of growing clover-rich forages (transl. title). *Sartryck och forhansmeddelande* 83:3.

30. Homb, T. 1952. Chemical composition and digestibility of grassland crops (transl. title). Beretning 71, nord. Lantbrukshogskol. Foringsforsok.

31. Mellin, T. N., B. R. Poulton, and J. J. Anderson. 1962. Nutritive value of timothy hay as affected by date of harvest. *J. Anim. Sci.* 21:123–26.

32. Kane, E. A. and L. A. Moore. 1959. Digestibility of Beltsville first-cut forage as affected by date of harvest. *J. Dairy Sci.* 42:936.

33. Haenlein, G. F. W., C. R. Richards, R. L. Salsbury, Y. M. Yoon, and W. H. Mitchell. 1966. Relationship of date of cut to the nutritive value of three varieties of orchardgrass hays. Del. Agr. Exp. Sta. Bull. 359.

34. Conrad, H. R., A. D. Pratt, J. W. Hibbs, and R. R. Davis. 1962. Relationships between forage growth stage, digestibility, nutrient intake, and milk production in dairy cows. Ohio Agr. Exp. Sta. Res. Bull. 914.

35. Martz, F. A., C. H. Noller, and D. L. Hill. 1960. Apparent digestibility of alfalfa-bromegrass using a modified digestion trial. *J. Dairy Sci.* 43:868.

36. Deinum, B., A. J. H. van Es, and P. J. van Soest. 1968. Climate, nitrogen and grass. 2. The influence of light intensity, temperature, and nitrogen on *in vivo* digestibility of grass and the prediction of these effects from some chemical procedures. *Neth. J. Agr. Sci.* 16:217–23.

37. Deinum, B., and J. G. P. Dirven. 1972. Climate, nitrogen and grass. 5. Influence of age, light intensity and temperature on the production and chemical composition of Congo grass. *Neth. J. Agr. Sci.* 20:125–32.

38. Reid, J. T., C. Lowe, and R. Anderson. 1959. Unpubl. data. Cornell Univ.

percentage units higher in digestible organic matter than an early maturing ryegrass cultivar ('S24') harvested at the same time.[39] However, the digestible organic matter value of aftermath forages harvested at the same times was not different for the two cultivars. In the same study an orchardgrass cultivar ('S37') was 4–7 percentage units lower in digestibility than the comparable first-growth or aftermath cuttings of the early maturing ryegrass. It is clear that certain species or cultivars deviate from the general relationship between time of cutting and DDM value of forages discussed above. However, this does not detract from the usefulness of the relationship in the rationing of animals.

More remarkable than the higher digestibility is the greater acceptability of late maturing cultivars. In the comparisons of timothy mentioned above, sheep consumed 6.3, 18.5, and 24.9% more of hay prepared from the late timothy than of that made from common timothy cut on June 8, June 22, and July 2 respectively.[38] The combined advantage of higher digestibility and acceptability made the value of late maturing timothy 38% greater than that of common timothy cut July 2.

AFTERMATH FORAGES. At the stages of growth where aftermath forages are usually harvested in the northern states, the DDM value of aftermath hays generally ranges from about 57–64%, with a majority near 60%.[26] Although the content of DDM in aftermath forage decreases as the stage of growth approaches maturity, changes in the growth stage have much less effect upon aftermaths than upon first-growth forages. For unknown reasons (but possibly because of reduced temperatures), the level of DDM or DE may reach approximately 70% during the fall in the northern states.[36,37] Values this high have been recorded for clippings made at one-

to five-week intervals during the summer in England.

Aftermath forages never contain as high a percentage of DDM as first-growth forages harvested during early spring in the northern states. In this respect, hays (undamaged in curing) made from forage cut before June 10 in the northeastern states are invariably superior to those made from subsequent cuttings at usual hay stages. In practice, the first cutting is often made too late to be superior to the aftermath. A first-growth forage in the head stage or even in early bloom stage contains as much or even slightly more digestible matter than its aftermath in the vegetative stage. Thus in considering the nutritive quality of hays, it is necessary to distinguish between those made from first-growth and aftermath forages.

LEAF CONTENT. Since both concentration of DDM and leaf content decline as forage growth approaches maturity, it is axiomatic that leaf content is associated with DDM content of hay. In one study it was found that the percentage of DDM (Y) was related to the percentage of leaves (X) in the first growth of mixed legume-grass forages by the equation, $Y = 0.4X + 40.8$.[26] The dry weight of the forages involved consisted of 32–87% leaves. In this study the "leaf" of legumes was considered to be the leaf and petiole and that of grasses, the blade and sheath.

Digestibility of the separated leaf and stem fractions, chiefly of alfalfa aftermath, has been studied in a few instances. In certain studies the percentage of DDM was shown to range from 47 to 55% in stems and from 68 to 70% in leaves.[40] For the same population of hays the leaves constituted 45–75% of the hay DM. Thus it would appear that 55–75% of the DDM in hay made from alfalfa aftermath is in the leaves. Since the digestibility of the very immature first growth of both legumes and grasses is as high as 80–85%, it seems probable that either the stems

39. Minson, D. J., W. F. Raymond, and C. E. Harris. 1961. The digestibility of grass species and varieties. Proc. 8th Int. Grassl. Congr., pp. 470–74 (Reading, England).

40. Sotola, J. 1933. The nutritive value of alfalfa leaves and stems. *J. Agr. Res.* 47:919–45.

are highly digestible or a very high proportion of the digestible matter is contained in the leaves or that both these situations exist in early cut, first-growth forage.

CURING METHOD. Like the rate of consumption, DDM content of hay is not affected appreciably by the curing method when harvested forage is not damaged by weather or is not handled in such a way that many leaves are lost. Under conditions of unfavorable curing weather the method of curing used can prevent the depression in the digestibility of hay to varying degrees. In one experiment the DDM value of the portion of a forage cut on June 10 and barn dried with heated air was 67%.[26] That of another portion from the same source cut at the same time but field cured after eight days, during which it was soaked with water or rain on all except the last two days, was only 57%. Heat-dried, unweathered hay prepared from forage of the same source which had been allowed to continue growth until July 8 had only 52% of DDM.

PHYSICAL FORM. The effect upon digestibility of the physical form in which hay is consumed is not entirely settled. The digestibility of hay cut from the same crop at the same time and cured in the same way is not different when fed long or when chopped and fed loose or as a wafer.[22] In some experiments digestibility of finely ground hay (1.6–7.9-mm particles) fed as a meal or pellet has been lower than that of the same hay in long or chopped form.[16,25,41-43] In others it has been the same.[14-16,42,44] The difference in response from experiment to experiment might be related to the sizes of particles compared,

chemical composition of the hay, and intake levels at which the comparisons were made.

With increasing intake levels of chopped or long hay, digestibility of energy is either not affected or is reduced only slightly even at the ad libitum intake level.[45] Nevertheless, a few studies indicate some depression of digestibility with increasing intake.[46] The DE value of pelleted ground hay decreases markedly as the intake level increases.[41,43,45,47-49]

The proportions of energy digestion occurring in various sites of the gastrointestinal tract are quite different for long or chopped hay from those for pelleted ground hay.[43,44,47,48,50] As compared with chopping of hay, grinding and pelleting depress energy digestion in the reticulo-rumen but increase energy digestion in the small intestine. The proportion of the energy digested in the small intestine was 23–51% greater for pelleted ground hay than for the same hay in chopped form, representing three sources.[43,44,47] This means that a higher proportion of the energy of pelleted ground hay is digested by tissue-elaborated enzymes, and a smaller proportion is digested by bacteria. Thus it is expected that the proportions of the products of digestion are quite different for the two forms of hay. Although less of the cellulose and hemicellulose from pelleted ground hay is digested in the rumen, more of these components is digested in the cecum and colon than when hay is fed in chopped form.

Energy retention by sheep fed hays in

41. Blaxter, K. L., and N. McC. Graham. 1956. The effect of the grinding and cubing process on the utilization of the energy of dried grass. J. Agr. Sci. 47:207–17.
42. Swanson, E. W., and H. A. Herman. 1952. The digestibility of coarsely ground and finely ground alfalfa for dairy heifers. J. Anim. Sci. 11:688–92.
43. Thomson, D. J., and D. E. Beever. 1972. The digestion and utilization of grass processed by wafering or by grinding and pelleting. Proc. Nutr. Soc. 31:66A–67A.
44. Thomson, D. J., D. E. Beever, J. F. Coelho da Silva, and D. G. Armstrong. 1972. The effect in sheep of physical form on the sites of digestion of a dried lucerne diet. 1. Sites of organic matter, energy and carbohydrate digestion. Brit. J. Nutr. 28:31–41.

45. Reid, J. T., and H. F. Tyrrell. 1964. Effect of level of intake on energetic efficiency of animals. Proc. Cornell Nutr. Conf., pp. 25–38.
46. Riewe, M. E., and H. Lippke. 1970. Considerations in determining the digestibility of harvested forages, pp. F1–F17. Proc. Natl. Conf. Forage Qual. Eval. Util. (Lincoln, Nebr.).
47. Beever, D. E., J. F. Coelho da Silva, J. H. D. Prescott, and D. G. Armstrong. 1972. The effect in sheep of physical form and stage of growth on the sites of digestion of a dried grass. 1. Sites of digestion of organic matter, energy and carbohydrate. Brit. J. Nutr. 28:347–56.
48. Thomson, D. J., and S. B. Cammell. 1971. The utilization of chopped and pelleted lucerne by growing lambs. Proc. Nutr. Soc. 30:88A–89A.
49. Bull, L. S., J. T. Reid, and D. E. Johnson. 1970. Energetics of sheep concerned with the utilization of acetic acid. J. Nutr. 100:262–76.
50. Hinders, R. G., and F. G. Owens. 1968. Ruminal and postruminal digestion of alfalfa fed as pellets or long hay. J. Dairy Sci. 51:1253–57.

various physical forms has been examined in several experiments. The proportions of ME retained by sheep fed chopped and pelleted finely ground hay of the same source were respectively: dried grass, 36 and 45%; mixed alfalfa-timothy, 31 and 43%; alfalfa, 24 and 45%; and orchardgrass, 14 and 35%.[16,41,43,48,51] It is clear that the ME of pelleted finely ground hay is more efficiently utilized than that of the same hay in chopped form. On the best diets formulated, including those containing concentrates, the approximate maximum efficiency of net utilization of ME for body gain is of the order of 60–65%. In addition to its higher net efficiency for body energy gain, the ME of pelleted ground hay is needed in smaller quantity to maintain body energy equilibrium. For example, the amounts of ME per unit of metabolic size (body weight in kilograms raised to 0.73 power) per day required for maintenance were, for chopped and pelleted ground hay respectively: 96 and 89 kcal and 92 and 87 kcal.[16,51]

The values cited above should not be construed to represent species differences because the growth stage at harvest time is probably a more important determinant of the net utilization of ME. In another experiment NE values of first-growth alfalfa harvested on May 18 and June 15 were 0.88 and 0.67 Mcal/kg respectively.[52] Orchardgrass harvested on May 12 and June 1 had NE values of 0.99 and 0.58 Mcal/kg respectively. All these hays were grown in New Jersey and fed in chopped form.[52] An alfalfa hay harvested on May 25 at Ithaca, N.Y., and fed in pelleted finely ground form had a NE value of 1.24 Mcal/kg.[49] The net efficiency with which the ME of this sample was utilized for body gain was 60%.

At this stage it is not known why pelleted ground hay is utilized more effi-

ciently by growing-fattening ruminants than the same hay in chopped form. It seems possible that the products of digestion of ground hay might be more efficiently utilized than those from chopped hay or that the energy expense of a greater muscular and bacterial activity in the digestion of chopped hay might explain the difference in response associated with particle size.

PROTEIN

Quantitatively, the nutritional significance of protein ranks a distant second to that of energy. For example, only 8.5% as much digestible protein as TDN is needed to maintain a 454-kg cow. A cow of the same size producing 23 kg of milk per day needs 15% as much digestible protein as TDN.[53] While hay can be and often is an important source of protein for ruminants, the protein content should not be considered an important basis on which to select hay. Usually when hay is low in protein, the deficit can be provided by a relatively small quantity of a high-protein concentrate. Unfortunately, hay low in protein is usually low in energy also. Energy-deficient hay requires a considerable quantity of cereal grain or other concentrate to form an adequate diet for animal production.

PROTEIN CONTENT OF HAYS. Crude protein content depends chiefly upon: (1) species, (2) time of cutting or growth stage at harvest, (3) level of N fertilization of grasses, and (4) leaf content.

At the same stage of growth, legumes contain considerably more protein than grasses. In both legumes and nonlegumes the protein content is higher at an early growth stage than at a late stage. Hays may have a wide range in protein content, and a hay from immature grasses may contain more protein than a hay from late cut legumes. In general, hays of first-growth grasses have about the same amount of protein as those from first-growth legumes cut two weeks later in the season. These points are demonstrated by

51. Blaxter, K. L., and N. McC. Graham. 1954. Plane of nutrition and energy utilization by sheep. Proc. Brit. Nutr. Soc. 13:vii–viii.
52. Welch, J. G., M. Clancy, and G. W. Vander Noot. 1969. Net energy of alfalfa and orchardgrass hays at varying stages of maturity. *J. Anim. Sci.* 28:263–67.
53. Reid, J. T., P. W. Moe, and H. F. Tyrrell. 1966. Energy and protein requirements of milk production. *J. Dairy Sci.* 49:215–23.

TABLE 49.7 ❧ Digestible protein content of first cuttings harvested at various times and of aftermaths

Cutting date	Digestible protein (% of DM)	
	Grasses	Legumes
June 1	13.4	19.0
June 15	10.0	14.7
July 1	6.0	10.0
July 15	3.5	6.4
Aftermath	10.5	15.0

Source: Reid, 1966.[54]
Note: Data are averages; variations from these values may be associated with species or fertilization rates.

the data in Table 49.7.[54] Although these figures represent averages of typical data, they are not to be considered as constants. Nevertheless, they are useful guides in feeding practice.

Protein content of aftermath forages, though related to growth stage, is much less variable than that of first-growth forage. The effect of growth stage upon the protein content is considerably less marked in aftermath forage than in first-growth forage. The ratio of protein to TDN is characteristically higher in aftermath hays than in hays made from first-growth forage.

Although N fertilization of soils low in N increases the concentration of crude protein in hay, it does not affect the DDM or energy value. Data demonstrating these effects of N fertilization are summarized in Table 49.8.[55-58]

DIGESTIBILITY OF PROTEIN IN HAYS. Protein is rationed to livestock in terms of "apparently digestible" protein, so

54. Reid, J. T. 1966. Meeting protein needs of milking cows. *Hoard's Dairyman* 111:131, 139.
55. Colovos, N. F., H. A. Keener, H. A. Davis, N. K. Peterson, and P. T. Blood. 1961. The effect of rate of nitrogen fertilization and date of harvest on yield, persistency and nutritive value of bromegrass hay. N.H. Agr. Exp. Sta. Bull. 472.
56. Markley, R. A., J. L. Cason, and B. R. Baumgardt. 1957. Digestibility of bromegrass hays grown under various levels of nitrogen fertilization. *J. Anim. Sci.* 16:1053–54.
57. Poulton, B. R., G. J. Macdonald, and G. W. Vander Noot. 1957. The effect of nitrogen fertilization on the nutritive value of orchardgrass hay. *J. Anim. Sci.* 16:462–66.
58. Barth, K. 1958. Total digestible nutrients expressed in terms of digestible energy. M.S. thesis, Rutgers Univ.
59. Holter, J. A., and J. T. Reid. 1959. Relationship between the concentrations of crude protein and apparently digestible protein in forages. *J. Anim. Sci.* 18:1339–49.

named because it represents the difference between the amount of N $\times$ 6.25 consumed and that voided in the feces and because some of the N in the feces does not originate in the feed (some of the fecal N is contributed by the animal). A very striking relationship of high predictive value exists between the percentage of crude protein (X) and that of apparently digestible protein (Y) in hays: $Y = 0.929X - 3.48$.[59] As crude protein concentration of hays increases, percentage of digestible protein also increases. This equation allows estimation of digestible protein concentration with such a high degree of accuracy that there is no need for a conventional measurement.

❧ ANIMAL PRODUCTION

TIME OF CUTTING. Because of the marked association of time of cutting with rate of voluntary intake by animals, proportion of forage energy digested, and efficiency with which ME is utilized, harvest time of forage is a major determinant of the yields of meat and milk from animals eating it. Data summarized in Table 49.4 show that despite the fact that the hay sample cut on May 31 was rain damaged (after harvesting), lambs consuming it made more rapid gains and had carcasses higher in fat (as indicated by the live grade) than their mates fed either the hay cut 37 days later, or second-cutting forage with nine weeks regrowth (after May 31 cutting).

The amount of energy represented by body tissue gained by sheep ingesting alfalfa hay cut in New Jersey on June 15 was 76% of that by those eating hay from the same source cut on May 18.[52] The body-energy gain of lambs fed orchardgrass hay cut on June 1 was only 58% of those fed hay from the same source cut on May 12.[52]

Cutting time also has been shown to have a marked effect upon milk yield. In an experiment that demonstrates this characteristic effect, advancing the average cutting date from July 4 to June 7 resulted in a 39% increase in milk yield per cow and a difference in weight gain of 0.13 kg/cow/day (Table 49.3).

TABLE 49.8 ✤ Influence of nitrogen fertilization on certain nutritive qualities of grasses

Date of cutting	Fertilizer N (kg/ha)	Concentration in forage		Digestibility	
		Crude protein (% of DM)	Crude fiber (% of DM)	Crude protein (%)	DM or energy (%)
*First growth, smooth bromegrass**					
May 29	56.1	13.1	33.7	68.1	70.8
May 29	224.2	18.0	32.2	75.6	71.6
June 9	56.1	8.9	35.0	59.7	64.6
June 9	224.2	12.1	33.4	69.0	63.1
June 20	56.1	7.2	39.6	54.5	56.9
June 20	224.2	9.8	39.4	61.7	57.3
Second growth, smooth bromegrass†					
. . .	28.0	7.5	30.1	45.8	58.0
. . .	140.1	12.4	29.7	66.6	57.9
. . .	252.2	17.2	27.2	74.3	61.9
Second growth, orchardgrass‡					
. . .	112.1	13.9	35.8	67.4	64.1
. . .	224.2	17.5	35.3	73.8	63.6
. . .	448.4	18.0	35.6	73.8	63.4
Second growth, reed canarygrass§					
. . .	0	14.0	26.1	68.5	63.2
. . .	112.1	16.4	26.6	70.4	58.1
. . .	224.2	22.9	23.3	77.7	62.3

* Colovos et al., 1961.[55]
† Markley et al., 1957;[56] all forages cut at same time.
‡ Poulton et al., 1957;[57] all forages cut at same time.
§ Barth, 1958;[58] all forages cut at same time.

Although DM yield of the first cutting is reduced by advancing the cutting time, the seasonal animal output per ha may be increased. For example, DM yields[60] at Ithaca expressed as a percentage of the maximum first-growth yield (generally obtained by about July 1) are: May 15, 50%; June 1, 73%; June 15, 89%; June 30, 98%; and July 15, 99%. However, from the standpoint of animal productivity per ha the forage yield is a poor index. Although DM yield on June 1 is only 73% of the maximum yield of first-growth forage, the energy yield in terms of DDM on this date is approximately 91% of the expected maximum yield. This apparent sacrifice of 9% of the energy yield is more than compensated for by the larger yields of subsequent cuttings. As much as 25% more energy per ha may be obtained as a result of cutting the first crop early.

60. MacDonald, H. A. 1946. The relationship of stage of growth to the yield and chemical composition of forage grasses and legumes. Cornell Dept. Agron. Mimeo 19.

A high output per animal per unit of time is essential to high profitability. A high output of energy per ha is not necessarily compatible with a large output per animal. This is because animal outputs depend upon the amount of forage ingested above the maintenance requirement and the forage energy value and because the requirements of the animal for maintenance are a relatively high proportion of the total intake. To take advantage of the benefits of early harvesting, special attention must be given to the selection of forage species and cultivars which begin growth early in the spring, are high yielding, tolerate early harvesting, and respond to the liberal use of fertilizer.

PHYSICAL FORM OF HAY. The physical form in which hay is consumed may have a marked effect upon animal production. The extent of response has been more clearly determined for fattening sheep and beef cattle and growing dairy cattle than for lactating cows. In general, response to long hay is similar to that of chopped hay fed loose; however, when enough poor quality long hay is fed to permit selective feeding, animal production may be somewhat greater than that obtained with the same hay in chopped form.

Wafers (7.5–10 cm in diameter by 2.5–5 cm thick) prepared from either long or chopped (2.5–10 cm lengths) hay do not produce animal responses different from those of the same hays fed in loose form.[21,22] The body weight gains effected in sheep, beef cattle, and growing dairy cattle by feeding finely ground (0.16–0.8 cm sieve) and pelleted hay are consistently greater than those produced by long or chopped hay.[13–16,20,21,59,61–63] Some typical comparisons of animal production responses to various forms of hay are shown in Table 49.5.

The increased rate of animal production achieved by the feeding of pelleted ground hay as compared with chopped hay is caused by an increased rate of DM consumption, a change in the proportions of the absorbed products of digestion, and/or a reduction in the energy expense of maintenance as the result of a lower muscular and microbial activity. In one experiment[16] the NE values for body gain of chopped hay and pelleted ground hay were 0.68 and 0.91 Mcal/kg of DM respectively, when each was fed at the two-times-maintenance intake level. In the same study, sheep fed ad libitum ingested 28.4% more DM and 63.4% more NE for body gain as pelleted ground hay than as chopped hay. The greater energy retention by sheep ingesting the pelleted ground hay than by those fed chopped hay was 78.5% attributable to the greater intake of DM and 21.5% attributable to the greater nutritive effect per unit

of DM ingested. That the nutritive value per unit weight is improved by grinding and pelleting has been amply verified.[41,43,48,51]

Nevertheless, in several experiments[15,61] in which equal quantities of pelleted or unpelleted diets of the same composition were fed, no difference was observed in the rate of total gain of body weight or in the gain per unit of DM ingested. Since the amount of gastrointestinal contents is much greater in ruminants ingesting chopped or long hay than in those fed pelleted ground hay, the gains in ingesta-free body weight by the sheep fed pelleted ground hay in equal-intake experiments may have been 20–30% greater than those by sheep fed the chopped hay.[15,16,61]

The response of lactating cows to hays ingested in various physical forms has been variable. Some of the variation seems attributable to the feeding of concentrates with the hay as well as to the particle size of the hay itself. In some experiments the amount of milk produced by cows fed pelleted ground hay or ground hay was the same as that by cows fed chopped or long hay.[23,24,64,65] In other tests pelleted ground hay or ground hay had an advantage in milk yield.[19,66,67] Almost invariably the milk produced by cows ingesting pelleted ground hay has a lower fat percentage than does that of cows fed the same hay in long or chopped form.[22–24,64–69] Associated with the reduction in milk fat is a ruminal

61. Meyer, J. H., R. Kromann, and W. N. Garrett. 1972. Digestion (influence of roughage preparation), pp. 262–71. In Physiology of Digestion in the Ruminant. Butterworths, Washington, D.C.
62. Hazlett, F. S., R. W. Hemken, and R. F. Davis. 1960. Effect of pelleted hays on the growth and development of dairy heifers. J. Dairy Sci. 43:1888.
63. O'Dell, G. D., W. A. King, W. C. Cook, and H. J. Webb. 1963. Feeding value of alfalfa and Coastal bermudagrass when fed as baled or pelleted hays to dairy heifers. J. Dairy Sci. 46:1103–7.

64. O'Dell, G. D., W. A. King, and W. C. Cook. 1968. Effect of grinding, pelleting, and frequency of feeding of forage on fat percentage of milk and milk production of dairy cows. J. Dairy Sci. 51:50–55.
65. Radloff, H. D., and K. D. Allison. 1971. Effect of physical form on alfalfa digestibility and productivity. J. Dairy Sci. 54:773.
66. Colenbrander, V. F., E. E. Bartley, J. L. Morrill, C. W. Deyoe, and H. B. Pfost. 1967. Feed processing. 2. Effect of feeding expanded grain and finely ground hay on milk composition, yield, and rumen metabolism. J. Dairy Sci. 50:1966–72.
67. Keith, J. M., W. A. Hardison, J. T. Huber, and G. C. Graf. 1961. The effect of the physical form on the nutritive value of hay fed to lactating dairy cows. J. Dairy Sci. 44:1174.
68. King, R. L., and R. W. Hemken. 1962. Composition of milk produced on pelleted hay and heated corn. J. Dairy Sci. 45:1336–42.
69. Balch, C. C., W. H. Broster, J. A. F. Rook, and V. J. Tuck. 1965. The effect on growth rate and on milk yield and composition of finely grinding the hay and cooking (flaking) the maize in mixed diets for growing and milking heifers. J. Dairy Res. 32:1–11.

fermentation resulting in a high proportion of propionic acid and a lower proportion of acetic acid. In some of the same experiments, the concentration of protein in milk and the gains in body weight were higher for cows ingesting pelleted ground hay than for those fed long or chopped hay.

Although pelleted ground hay has certain handling, storage, and feeding advantages over long or chopped hay, the degree of ground fineness and the kind of pellet eventually accepted in feeding practice may be a compromise between that which has desirable feeding qualities and that which is possible to process. Its greatest value is for growing and fattening ruminants. Since milk is priced on the basis of its fat concentration, pelleted ground hay is not an economical feed for lactating cows. Economic conditions under which the feeding of highly processed hay, such as that in the form of pellets, is feasible are still to be determined.

FEED INPUT–ANIMAL OUTPUT. Feeding of high-quality hay is an important means of intensifying the energy input when the ruminant production requirement is low (an energy requirement less than three times the requirement of maintenance) and of reducing the effects of diminishing returns. This is because the digestibility of increments of hay does not decrease as much with increasing intake as that of the increments of concentrates. In feeding practice the major limitations of using hay rather than concentrates for this purpose are the stomach capacity of animals, the relatively lower concentration of energy in hay (especially in hay of low to average quality), and the physical and chemical nature of hay that restricts the voluntary consumption rate. These limitations become more restrictive as the productive capacity of animals increases. For ruminants such as lactating cows requiring an energy intake above three times that of maintenance, increments of even high-quality hay provided

above this level of intake will not effectively intensify the energy intake.[53]

❧ SENSORY INDEXES OF HAY QUALITY

Tests or indexes of hay quality based upon sensory analysis are of doubtful value.[26] Though the visual, taste, odor, and feel characteristics of hays appear to be logical criteria of quality, it has not been proven that these characteristics determine animal preference and response.

A hay-grading system based upon standards of odor, color, leafiness, stem texture, and the amount of foreign matter has been formulated and is used in the large hay markets.[70] The adequacy of hay standards as a basis for predicting feeding value has had only limited testing. Studies of the responses of growing cattle and lactating cows to hays of various grades suggest the following conclusions.[11,71-75] For a large population of hays varying over the entire range of grades, the grade reflects the feeding value in a qualitative manner; however, the grade is not a sufficiently precise index of feeding value to predict the quality of hay produced on a given farm. Generally, a difference in animal response is obtained between hays as different as U.S. grades 1 and 3, but even a grade difference of this magnitude is not certain evidence that the higher grade will effect a greater animal response than the lower grade. An important shortcoming of the grading system is that it does not distinguish between first cuttings

70. USDA. 1948. Handbook of official hay and straw standards. Grain Branch, PMA.

71. Gordon, C. H., J. R. Dawson, L. A. Moore, and W. H. Hosterman. 1952. Feeding value of different grades of alfalfa hay for growing dairy heifers. *J. Dairy Sci.* 35:755–63.

72. Gordon, C. H., L. A. Moore, and W. H. Hosterman. 1954. Feeding value of U.S. No. 1 alfalfa hay and U.S. No. 2 alfalfa heavy timothy hay. *J. Dairy Sci.* 37:1116–22.

73. Gordon, C. H., L. A. Moore, and W. H. Hosterman. 1956. The relative feeding value of alfalfa hay and alfalfa light timothy mixed hay at approximately the U.S. No. 1 grade level. *J. Dairy Sci.* 39:1142–48.

74. Horton, O. H., and K. E. Harshbarger. 1951. A comparison of U.S. grades of alfalfa hay for milk production. *J. Dairy Sci.* 34:491.

75. Van Horn, A. G., J. R. Dawson, C. H. Gordon, J. N. Maddux, L. A. Moore, W. H. Hosterman, and R. H. Lush. 1952. Feeding value for milk production of U.S. No. 3 and sample grade Korean lespedeza hay. *J. Dairy Sci.* 35:559–65.

and aftermath. A finer stemmed aftermath of earlier growth stage than a first-cutting hay will not necessarily be a more productive feed for ruminants than the first cutting.

❧ QUESTIONS

1. What is the most important nutritional factor derived from hays by ruminants?
2. Why is the protein content of relatively little importance as an index of the nutritive value of hays fed to ruminants?
3. What conditions or characteristics are associated with the nutritive quality of hay?
4. Is the feeding value of hays made from aftermath forage superior to that of hays made from first cuttings?
5. How much difference exists between the DDM value of hays made from forages cut June 1 and July 10 in the northern states?
6. How many more kilograms would a 500-kg cow eat of hay cut on June 1 than of hay cut on July 1? What conditions could alter these amounts?
7. Under what conditions do nonlegume hays contain more crude protein than legume hays?
8. Why is the animal production response usually greater for pelleted finely ground hay than for the same hay fed in long or chopped form?
9. How is the milk or meat yield per ha affected by the time of cutting forage used as hay?
10. What are the limitations of the federal hay-grading system?
11. How does the method by which forage is cured for hay affect digestibility, rate of intake, and animal productivity?
12. How does the nutritive value of forages grown in the tropics compare with that of forages grown in temperate regions? Why is it different?

JOSEPH CHRISMAN, GEORGE O. KOHLER,
AND E. M. BICKOFF
Agricultural Research Service, USDA

50

DEHYDRATION OF FORAGE CROPS

❧

THE STORY of forage dehydration in the U.S. is primarily the story of alfalfa dehydration. However, since 1960 significant tonnages of dehydrated bermudagrass have been produced in the Southeast. Many alfalfa processors are also dehydrating corn stover, milo stover, or whole plants of these crops. A few dehydrators in northwestern Washington have for many years dehydrated orchardgrass, perennial ryegrass, and mixtures of these with ladino clover.

❧ JOSEPH CHRISMAN is Engineering Technician, Western Regional Research Laboratory, ARS, USDA. He studied at the University of Kansas. He has extensive experience in dehydration of forage crops and related research. He also has worked in operation and quality control in the manufacture of milk by-products.

❧ GEORGE O. KOHLER is Chief, Field Crops Laboratory, Western Regional Research Laboratory, ARS, USDA, where he directs utilization research on cereal feeds, forages, and oilseeds. He holds the Ph.D. degree from the University of Wisconsin.

❧ E. M. BICKOFF is Research Chemist, Western Regional Research Laboratory, ARS, USDA. He has had graduate training at the University of California. His research interest is study of the composition of alfalfa, including antioxidants, carotenoids, phenolics, saponins, plant estrogens, and growth factors.

TABLE 50.1 ❧ Dehydrated alfalfa production, 1944–70

Reporting period	Dehydrated (000 t)	Sun cured (000 t)	Total manufactured (000 t)
1944–45	314	439	753
1949–50	726	269	995
1954–55	965	212	1,178
1959–60	1,063	193	1,256
1964–65	1,429	204	1,633
1969–70	1,577	308	1,884

Source: USDA Consumer and Marketing Service, Grain Division.
Note: Includes pellets, meal, and cubes.

The development of forage dehydration is shown in Table 50.1. A substantial part of this growth has been due to increased exports as shown in Table 50.2. Production of dehydrated bermudagrass is estimated between 90,000 and 136,000 t/year. Most of this product is used by the processor.

Nebraska leads in dehydrated alfalfa production, followed by California and then Kansas. These three states produce about 70% of the U.S. total. The balance is distributed over 25 additional states, with Ohio, Colorado, Iowa, and Pennsylvania leading. Nationwide, there are about 600 individual forage dehydrating units.

TABLE 50.2 ✲ Dehydrated alfalfa exports, 1965–71

Reporting period	Dehydrated (000 t)	Sun cured (000 t)	Total manufactured (000 t)
1965–66	193	149	342
1966–67	184	191	375
1967–68	149	128	277
1968–69	210	167	377
1969–70	210	192	402
1970–71	310	225	535

Source: U.S. Bureau of Census.[2]
Note: Includes pellets, meal, and cubes.

✲ PROCESSING EQUIPMENT

HARVESTERS

Nearly all producers use self-propelled, field-chopping harvesters that discharge the material into self-unloading hoppers which are integral parts of the harvesters. Cutter heads range from 2.4 m to 3.7 m in width, and the hoppers will hold a normal dump-truck load and can be emptied in two to four minutes. Some operators of very large drums use side-dumping trailers with double the load capacity of dump trucks.

DEHYDRATORS

Dehydrators are rotating drums and range in size from 2.4 m in diameter by 7.3 m long to 3.8 m in diameter by 19.8 m long. In evaporative capacity they range from a rated capacity of 2.7–30.8 t/hr of water.

Two general types of dehydrators are in use, triple pass in which the material being dried travels about three times the visible length of drum, and single pass in which the material passes through the rotating drum in one direction only. Figure 50.1 shows construction of the triple pass type. The material is discharged into a cyclone separator or large expansion chamber to separate the product from moisture-laden air.

MILLING EQUIPMENT

A variety of hammer mills is used to grind alfalfa following dehydration. They are customarily connected directly to 3600 rpm motors varying in horsepower from 100 to 250 and are equipped with perforated screens with openings from 1.6 mm upward, depending on customer requirement.

PELLET MILLS

Pellet mills range in size from 25 to 250 hp. Most operators use mills of 50–125 hp, although the trend is toward higher capacities. The most universally used die opening is 6.35 mm. For coarse material going into cattle feeds, die openings range from 9.53 to 31.75 mm. It is essential to supply dry steam to the product-conditioning chamber to obtain suitable pellets.

PELLET COOLER

Immediately following pelleting, both moisture content and pellet temperature are reduced. Two general types of coolers are in use. The vertical type uses gravity

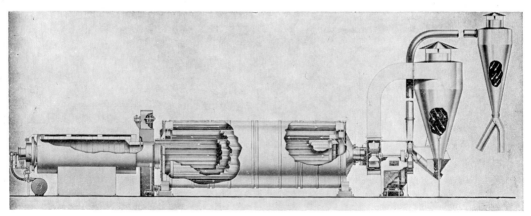

FIG. 50.1.   Cutaway of a triple-pass forage dryer. *Arnold Dryer Co., Division of Heil Co., photo.*

flow and draws air through louvres and through the product; the horizontal type uses a conveyor with air drawn through the perforated screen sections comprising it. Space requirements may dictate which type to use.

INERT GAS STORAGE FACILITIES

Tanks for inert gas storage may be of steel or concrete and must be gastight and equipped with relief valves set for about 5 cm of water pressure. Inert gas machines are regulated to burn nearly all the oxygen from the primary air so the products of combustion are nonoxidizing. Pipelines constantly deliver these gases through condensers to remove water.

DRY SEPARATION

Shaking screens and rotary screens can be used for making two or more fractions

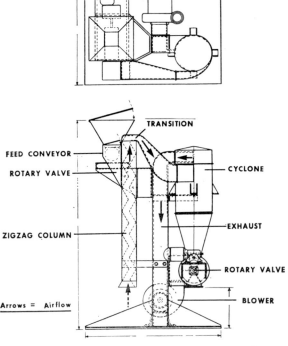

FIG. 50.2. Schematic drawing of air separation and classification machine. *Scientific Separators, Inc., design.*

of forage. Air separation machines readily adjust during operation to produce a wide range of fractions of greater or lesser volume depending on the needs of the animals to which they are to be fed (see Fig. 50.2).

❧ PROCESSING

RAW MATERIAL

In general, alfalfa is produced by independent growers and purchased by the dehydration plant on the basis of dry tons produced. Price will range from $8 to $25/t depending on geographical location and the competitive value of the crop for haymaking or grazing. Harvesting is generally performed by the dehydrating company since plant capacity, stage of growth, and weather conditions must all be considered. Fields are cut in rotation for two reasons: to carry out the agreement with farmers and to ensure forage quality. Under stress of natural gas shortage and cost, most firms are field wilting prior to dehydration.

Harvesting must be coordinated with plant capacity so that there is no plant shutdown and no excessive wait before drying. Delays in drying result in losses of carotene, xanthophyll, and other oxidizable entities. Sharp knives on cutter and chopper blades minimize such losses by reducing maceration. Under practical conditions, the loss of carotene during harvesting and hauling is 5–8%.

DEHYDRATION

Most of the moisture in the alfalfa is removed during dehydration in the "constant rate" drying phase, where moisture diffuses to the surface of the particles as fast as it is evaporated from the surface. Rapid absorption of heat by evaporation keeps the plant substance cool enough (i.e., wet bulb temperature) to avoid burning and permits direct use of combustion gases with temperatures of 871–1093 C. Dryers are designed to permit leaves to pass through as rapidly as possible. The heavier, moist stem particles stay in the hot zone for a longer period.

Chopped alfalfa brought in from the fields is dumped on an automatic feeder which meters it directly into the combustion gases in the dryer. Lifting flights in the cylinders continuously raise the alfalfa and drop it into the gas stream, which moves it through the dryer in a concurrent manner. After remaining in the drum for about 2–10 minutes, the dry alfalfa is separated from the moisture-laden gases at 120–177 C by means of a cyclone or other separator. The alfalfa often passes through another fan and cyclone for cooling before being ground in a hammer mill.

In this process careful control of heat and rate of throughput are essential. Customarily the burners are controlled by the temperature of the discharge gases, while the rate of feed is manually controlled.

Under well-controlled conditions of dehydration and grinding, carotene losses are 5–10%, xanthophyll losses 20–70%, and lysine losses 15–20%.[1,2] Since losses are negatively correlated with moisture content of the final product, the dried product should not contain less water than 8–10%.

GRINDING

Immediately following dehydration the alfalfa is ground in a hammer mill, usually using screen openings of 1.6–3.2 mm. Grinding should be much coarser for feed for ruminants. The screen openings may range from 1.2 to 3.81 cm, which passes many fiber particles 1–2 cm in length.

PELLETING

Ground dehydrated alfalfa is bulky, dusty, and difficult to handle in hoppers and bins. To overcome these adverse qualities, over 90% of the alfalfa is pelleted as it comes from the dehydrator and hammer

mill. Alfalfa pellets normally vary in size from 0.64 to 1.27 cm in diameter, and from 0.64 to 2.54 cm in length. The pellets weigh about 700 kg/cu m compared with 300 kg/cu m for meal. Dustiness is eliminated and the product is free-flowing and easy to handle mechanically. Much tonnage is shipped in bulk pellet form, but pellets destined for feed manufacturers are usually reground prior to shipping.

Development of bulk tank storage under inert gas has effectively solved the problem of storage at the dehydration plant.[3,4] This virtually eliminates oxidative losses in the product up to the time of removal from storage. Collateral benefits are elimination of danger of losses from fire, insects, and rodents. Surveys show inert gas storage capacity of alfalfa pellets in the U.S. at 700,000 t.

When pellets are removed from inert gas storage, oxidative losses of carotene, xanthophyll, and tocopherol begin anew. Losses that occur during blending, shipping, storage at the feed mill, and after mixing in feed should be cut to a minimum. The antioxidant ethoxyquin (6 ethoxy-1,2-dihydro-2,2,4-trimethylquinoline) was subjected to exhaustive pharmacological and physiological tests based on its effectiveness and cost of production.[5] When its safety and practical utility were established, it was generally accepted by the alfalfa processing industry. It is used to treat over 1 million t of dehy annually. Ethoxyquin (0.015%) is added to dehydrated alfalfa at the main hammer mill, pellet mill, or pellet regrind mill. This results in reduction in loss rate of carotene, xanthophyll, and tocopherol to about 35–50% of the losses that would otherwise occur under comparable conditions of time and temperature.[6] Most producers of dehydrated alfalfa use inert gas storage, ethoxyquin, or both to preserve autoxidizable nutrients in their product.

1. Livingston, A. L., R. E. Knowles, J. W. Nelson, and G. O. Kohler. 1968. Xanthophyll and carotene loss during pilot and industrial scale alfalfa processing. *J. Agr. Food Chem.* 16 (1):84–87.
2. Livingston, A. L., M. E. Allis, and G. O. Kohler. 1971. Amino acid stability during alfalfa dehydration. *J. Agr. Food Chem.* 19 (5):947–50.

3. Graham, W. R., Jr. 1944. Method of preserving organic materials. U.S. Patent 2,353,029.
4. Graham, W. R., Jr., and Joseph Chrisman. 1956. Apparatus for charging and storing materials. U.S. Patent 2,592,559.
5. Thompson, C. R. 1958. Antioxidants in feeds. *Feedstuffs* 30 (41):52–53, 56.

OILING

To facilitate handling, the customer may desire a powdered product that is dust-free. This is accomplished by adding 0.5–1% animal fat or vegetable oil to the dehydrated meal.[5-7] The oil is fed by a metering pump to the dehydrated alfalfa as it enters the pellet regrind hammer mill to ensure uniform distribution of oil. In addition to reducing dustiness, oil deepens the desirable green color of the meal.

BLENDING

Usually alfalfa is analyzed at the time of production and stored as pellets in tanks designated for specific quality levels based on protein and/or carotene content. When an order is received for a specific grade, appropriate amounts of pellets are removed from the different tanks and blended for bulk shipment, either as pellets or as reground pellets. Usual market grades of dehydrated alfalfa are: 15% protein, no guarantee on carotene; 17% protein, 13.2 mg carotene/100 gm; 20% protein, 19.8 mg carotene/100 gm; and 22% protein, 26.5 mg carotene/100 gm.

DRY SEPARATION MILLING

Dehydrated forages are fed to two general classes of livestock monogastric or simple-stomached (one) animals and ruminants or multiple-stomached animals. The nutritional needs of these two classes differ markedly. The animals also differ in their ability to use protein, fiber, vitamins, and xanthophyll.

Ruminants such as cattle, sheep, and goats can utilize much higher levels of fiber than monogastric animals such as poultry and swine. Ruminants produce their own water-soluble vitamins; monogastric animals must receive them from an outside

TABLE 50.3 ♣ Distribution of weight, protein, fiber, and xanthophyll resulting from air separation of alfalfa

Factor	Whole	Fine	Coarse
Weight (%)	100.0	48.6	51.4
Protein (%)	20.7	25.4	16.2
Fiber (%)	27.5	20.4	34.2
Xanthophyll (mg/100 g)	29.7	37.2	22.6

Note: 8% bloom 'Ranger' alfalfa at Darr, Neb., July 1968 feed rate, 875 kg/hr; air velocity = 222.5 linear m/min.

source. Xanthophyll is not needed in the ruminant ration; however, it is usually mandatory in poultry rations because of the demand for yellow skin and fat in broilers and for dark yellow egg yolks. The products resulting from fractionating dehydrated alfalfa are better suited to each of the two classes of animals than is whole alfalfa. A product high in protein, vitamins, and xanthophyll and with the least fiber is needed for feeding poultry and swine. A complementary fraction, lower in protein and higher in fiber, is needed for the ruminants.

Dry separation milling is accomplished by passing the dried and leaf-shattered chops into an air-column separator by a distributing conveyor and a rotary valve. Air is drawn up through a zigzag column, as illustrated in Figure 50.2, and carries with it the light or fine particles, allowing the coarse heavier particles to drop free from the bottom of the column. Air carrying the fine particles is passed through a cyclone separator equipped with a rotary valve at the bottom of the cone, and the air is exhausted from the blower as in any negative air system collector. The fine material is lower in fiber and higher in protein, carotene, and xanthophyll than the whole alfalfa. The coarse or heavy fraction is higher in fiber and lower in protein, carotene, and xanthophyll (Table 50.3).[8]

It is advantageous to maintain a higher percent of moisture in the dehydrator output than is customarily done. This allows

6. Livingston, A. L., E. M. Bickoff, and C. R. Thompson. 1955. Effect of added animal fats and antioxidant on stability of xanthophyll concentrates in mixed feeds. *J. Agr. Food Chem.* 3 (5):439–41.

7. Van Atta, G. R., C. R. Thompson, E. M. Bickoff, and W. D. Maclay. 1953. Oiling alfalfa meal for dust control. *Feed Age* 3 (7):30–33, 58, 62, 64.

8. Chrisman, Joseph, G. O. Kohler, A. C. Mottola, and J. W. Nelson. 1971. High and low protein fractions by separation milling of alfalfa. ARS Bull. 74-57.

the coarse fraction to have a higher density and be less subject to breakdown in any milling process. Xanthophyll losses are also greatly reduced.

DEHYDRATION AND SEPARATION COSTS

In a model systems study, costs of dehydration were calculated with and without separation milling.[9] However, capital and operating costs did not include harvesting and hauling costs and the price paid for the raw product. Added costs for separation milling varied from $0.30 to $3.24/t depending on models and alternative separation procedures. A five-year report of semi-commercial scale research on dry separation was published in 1971.[8]

❧ COMPOSITION

In 1965 the American Dehydrators Association promoted a very comprehensive and well-designed research project to analyze the four most commonly used protein grades of dehydrated alfalfa (Table 50.4).

❧ WET PROCESSING

Pressing forages ahead of dehydration or ensiling to reduce their moisture content has been performed experimentally.[10-13] It also has been attempted commercially in an effort to increase the production rate in the dehydrator and reduce fuel costs per ton of finished alfalfa meal. However, processing firms usually have found difficulty in disposing of the expressed liquids. This presents a problem due to emphasis on pollution control; disposition of such liquids is of increasing importance. One

9. Vosloh, C. J., Jr. 1970. Alfalfa, dehydration, separation, and storage costs and capital requirements. USDA Marketing Res. Rept. 881.

10. Goodall, Charles. 1938. Improvements relating to the drying of grasses, crops and other vegetable substances. U.K. Patent 482,312.

11. Ereky, Karoly. 1927. Process for the manufacture and preservation of green fodder pulp or other green plant pulp and of dry products made therefrom. U.K. Patent 270,629.

12. Casselman, T. W., V. E. Green, Jr., R. J. Allen, Jr., and F. H. Thomas. 1965. Mechanical dewatering of forage crops. Univ. Fla. Tech. Bull. 694.

13. Hibbs, J. W., H. R. Conrad, and W. H. Johnson. 1968. Farmers Forage Res. Coop. Mimeo, May-June, Lafayette, Ind.

TABLE 50.4 ❧ Comprehensive analyses of four commercial grades of dehydrated alfalfa

Constituent	Grade of dehy (% protein)			
	15%	17%	20%	22%
Moisture (%)	6.90	6.98	6.88	7.14
Protein (%)	15.22	18.04	20.64	22.47
Fat (ether extract) (%)	2.32	3.00	3.58	3.69
Crude fiber (%)	26.41	24.27	20.15	18.54
Acid detergent fiber (%)	33.9	31.3	27.4	25.6
Ash (%)	8.40	8.96	10.34	10.32
Nitrogen free extract (%)	40.77	38.81	38.42	37.85
Calcium (%)	1.23	1.30	1.47	1.47
Phosphorus (%)	0.22	0.23	0.27	0.28
Potassium (%)	2.30	2.40	2.50	2.50
Sodium (%)	0.07	0.08	0.08	0.10
Chlorine (%)	0.45	0.47	0.57	0.53
Magnesium (%)	0.26	0.26	0.32	0.32
Sulphur (%)	0.17	0.22	0.43	0.30
Manganese (ppm)	27.0	28.0	34.0	39.0
Iodine (ppm)	0.12	0.15	0.14	0.20
Iron (ppm)	230.0	309.0	281.0	306.0
Copper (ppm)	8.6	8.2	8.6	9.0
Zinc (ppm)	19.0	17.0	19.0	21.0
Aluminum (ppm)	226.0	314.0	267.0	295.0
Barium (ppm)	42.0	37.0	32.0	38.0
Strontium (ppm)	75.0	71.0	90.0	95.0
Boron (ppm)	38.0	44.0	47.0	49.0
Chromium (ppm)	2.0	2.3	3.0	3.0
Selenium (ppm)	0.50	0.60	0.50	0.54
Arginine (%)	0.58	0.75	0.98	1.01
Lysine (%)	0.60	0.73	0.87	1.03
Histidine (%)	0.30	0.35	0.42	0.47
Methionine (%)	0.23	0.28	0.33	0.38
Cystine (%)	0.17	0.18	0.23	0.24
Methionine + Cystine (%)	0.40	0.46	0.56	0.62
Tryptophane (%)	0.38	0.45	0.46	0.55
Glycine (%)	0.72	0.88	1.01	1.21
Phenylalanine (%)	0.66	0.91	1.04	1.26
Tyrosine (%)	0.42	0.54	0.64	0.69
Phenylalanine + Tyrosine (%)	1.08	1.45	1.68	1.95
Leucine (%)	1.05	1.31	1.54	1.84
Isoleucine (%)	0.68	0.84	0.98	1.16
Threonine (%)	0.60	0.75	0.88	1.05
Valine (%)	0.84	1.04	1.19	1.42
Aspartic acid (%)	1.63	1.84	2.04	2.40
Glutamic acid (%)	1.40	1.70	2.03	2.43
Proline (%)	0.63	0.79	0.89	1.05
Serine (%)	0.62	0.76	0.88	1.03
Alanine (%)	0.79	0.96	1.23	1.34
Nitrogen recovery (%)	82.4	80.5	81.2	86.0
Xanthophylls (mg/100 g)	17.6	25.77	32.85	40.12
Beta carotene (mg/100 g)	10.2	16.08	21.65	25.26
Thiamine (mg/100 g)	0.30	0.33	0.39	0.42
Riboflavin (mg/100 g)	1.06	1.23	1.55	1.74

TABLE 50.4 ✤ *(Continued)*

Constituent	Grade of dehy (% protein)			
	15%	17%	20%	22%
Pantothenic acid (mg/100 g)	2.09	3.00	3.28	3.30
Niacin (mg/100 g)	4.19	4.58	5.47	5.88
Pyridoxine (mg/100 g)	0.65	0.63	0.79	0.78
Choline (mg/100 g)	155.1	151.9	161.95	185.5
Proline betaine (mg/100 g)	606.5	638	757	853
Folic acid (mg/100 g)	0.15	0.21	0.27	0.30
Vitamin K (mg/100 g)	0.99	0.87	1.47	0.85
Alpha tocopherol (mg/100 g)	9.8	12.81	14.71	15.11
Metabolizable energy (pellets) (kcal/kg)	1,587*	1,653*	1,631†	1,764*

Source: American Dehydrators Assoc.
* Work conducted with chicks by J. D. Summers, Ontario Agr. Coll., University of Guelph, Guelph, Ontario, Canada.
† Results from a joint study with layers by Hobart R. Halloran, Halloran Research Farm, Inc.; H. J. Almquist, Consultant; Pran Vohra, University of California; F. W. Hill, University of California; and George O. Kohler, Western Utilization Research and Development Division, USDA.

approach has been to consider the expressed juices as of primary importance as a source of edible protein and the pressed fibrous fraction or press cake as a by-product or waste product.[14-16]

In contrast to this approach, which focuses on leaf protein for human food, the Pro-xan process has been developed, which involves inserting a "dewatering" or juicing step into the dehydration operation.[17-20]

14. Pirie, N. W. 1969. The production and use of leaf protein. Proc. Nutr. Soc. 28:85–91.
15. Pirie, N. W. 1969. The present position of research on the use of leaf protein as a human food. *Pl. Foods Hum. Nutr.* 1:237–46.
16. Akeson, W. R., and M. A. Stahmann. 1966. Leaf protein concentrates: A comparison of protein production per acre of forage with that from seed and animal crops. *Econ. Bot.* 20:244–50.
17. Bickoff, E. M., A. Bevenue, and K. T. Williams. 1947. Alfalfa has promising chemurgic future—A novel processing method is described. *Chemurgic Digest* 6:213, 216–28.
18. Kohler, G. O., E. M. Bickoff, R. R. Spencer, S. C. Witt, and B. E. Knuckles. 1968. Wet processing of alfalfa for animal feed products. 10th Tech. Alf. Conf. Proc., ARS-74-46, pp. 71–79.
19. Spencer, R. R., E. M. Bickoff, G. O. Kohler, S. C. Witt, B. E. Knuckles, and A. C. Mottola. 1970. Alfalfa products by wet fractionation. Trans. Amer. Soc. Agr. Eng. 13 (2):198–200.
20. Kohler, G. O., and E. M. Bickoff. 1970. Leaf protein. SOS/70 Proc. Inst. Food Tech., pp. 290–95.

The new process, named after the protein-xanthophyll concentrate produced, involves four basic steps: expression of juice, dehydration of dewatered alfalfa, coagulation and separation of protein and xanthophyll in the juice, and drying of the coagulum. Initially, alfalfa is crushed to express some of the liquid from the plant cells to yield a green low-fiber juice and a pressed cake. The green juice containing 8–12% solids is heated to 70 C or higher to coagulate the protein in the form of a green curd. After pressing, the green curd containing about 40% solids is dried and ground to form the Pro-xan product. The brown-colored serum separated from the curd provides another product containing amino acids, sugars, minerals, and vitamins which is usable as a feed supplement or fermentation medium. The pressed cake with a third to half the water removed is dehydrated to produce a dehydrated alfalfa meal which will meet market grades and be salable without penalty. A typical materials balance of the process is shown in Figure 50.3.

Both wet-fractionation and leaf-stem separation could be readily incorporated into the standard dehydration process. Wet fractionation allows more flexibility in marketing than the dry separation procedure. The process allows the dehydrator to tailor-make specialized products for both ruminant and nonruminant animals. At

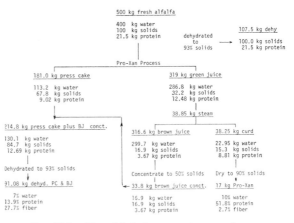

FIG. 50.3. Material balance—wet processing.

the same time it could pave the way for commercial production of an alfalfa protein concentrate suitable for human consumption.

In this operation fresh alfalfa comes out of the field with about 21% protein. The process removes protein and still will meet specifications for a 14% product for ruminants. The protein concentrate contains over 50% protein, no fiber, and about 800 mg/kg of xanthophyll. The content of both carotene and xanthophyll is two to three times greater than that for regular dehydrated alfalfa pellets. By processing in this manner it is possible to increase the dehydrator throughput 40% with a cost reduction.[21]

❧ USE IN FEEDS

POULTRY

Early use of dehydrated alfalfa was primarily in poultry rations. In 1972, half the production was still fed to poultry, in layer rations for yellow egg yolks, to breeding stock for increased fertility and reproduction, and to broilers for skin and fat pigmentation.[22-24]

SWINE

Dehydrated forages making up about 10% of the ration for brood sows have been shown to increase ovulation rate, litter size at birth, and survival rate.[25-29]

Addition of 5% of dehydrated alfalfa to a corn-soybean meal ration significantly depressed the rate of gain of growing-fatten-

ing pigs.[30] Other workers have found similar adverse effects in rations for young swine when levels of over 10% were used.[31,32] A Tennessee study has indicated that increasing dehydrated alfalfa from 3 to 6% in the pelleted diet results in a significant decrease in the number of pigs having ulcers and in the mean ulcer score, with no differences in average daily gain or feed efficiency.[33]

DAIRY

An increased milk yield has been reported when dehydrated alfalfa is fed with other forages.[34] A combination of dehydrated alfalfa meal and urea has been satisfactorily substituted for soybean meal in dairy rations.[35] By furnishing essential nutrients for rumen microorganisms, dehy improves bacterial protein synthesis from urea.

A Maryland study indicates that the vitamin E content of dehydrated forage is effective in controlling oxidized flavor in milk.[36] Increased persistency of lactation has been reported when a high corn silage–timothy hay ration was supplemented with varying levels of dehydrated alfalfa pellets.[37] Low-

21. Harley, Ron. 1970. Is alfalfa our next high-protein source? *Farm Quart.* 25 (4):40, 41, 70, 71.
22. Carlson, C. W., A. W. Halverson, and G. O. Kohler. 1964. Some effects of dietary pigmenters on egg yolks and mayonnaise. *Poultry Sci.* 43:654–62.
23. Kuzmicky, D. D., G. O. Kohler, A. L. Livingston, R. E. Knowles, and J. W. Nelson. 1968. Pigmentation potency of xanthophyll sources. *Poultry Sci.* 47:389–97.
24. Wilkinson, W. S., and Curtis Barbee. 1968. The relative value of xanthophyll from corn gluten meal, alfalfa, Coastal bermudagrass and pearl millet for broiler pigmentation. *Poultry Sci.* 47:1579–87.
25. Teague, H. S. 1955. The influence of alfalfa on ovulation rate and other reproductive phenomena in gilts. *J. Anim. Sci.* 14:621–27.
26. Hogan, A. G., and S. R. Johnson. 1941. Supplementary value of various feedstuffs in brood sow rations. Mo. Agr. Exp. Sta. Res. Bull. 332.

27. Cunha, T. J., O. B. Ross, P. H. Phillips, and G. Bohstedt. 1944. Further observations on the dietary insufficiency of a corn-soybean ration for reproduction of swine. *J. Anim. Sci.* 3:415–21.
28. Seerley, R. W., and R. C. Wahlstrom. 1963A. Dehydrated alfalfa meal for brood sows kept continuously on concrete. S. Dak. State Coll., A.S. Mimeo., Ser. 63–4.
29. Seerley, R. W., and R. C. Wahlstrom. 1963B. The value of dehydrated meal and crude protein for sows kept in confinement. S. Dak. State Coll., A.S. Mimeo, Ser. 63–5.
30. Dinusson, W. E., E. W. Klosterman, E. L. Lasley, and M. L. Buchanan. 1953. Cobalt, alfalfa and meat scraps in drylot rations for growing-fattening pigs. *J. Anim. Sci.* 12 (3):628.
31. DePape, J. G., William H. Burkitt, and A. E. Flower. 1953. Dehydrated alfalfa and antibiotic supplements in gestation-lactation rations for swine. *J. Anim. Sci.* 12 (1):77.
32. Becker, D. E., I. J. Hanson, A. H. Jensen, S. W. Terrill, and H. W. Norton. 1956. Dehydrated alfalfa meal as a dietary ingredient for swine. *J. Anim. Sci.* 15 (3):820.
33. Gamble, C. T., C. C. Chamberlain, G. M. Merriam, and E. R. Lidvall. 1967. Effects of pelleting, pasture and selected diet ingredients on the incidence of esophagogastric ulcers in swine. 1967. *J. Anim. Sci.* 26 (5):1058.
34. Bartley, E. E., D. B. Parrish, F. C. Fountain, and C. H. Whitnah. 1951. Effects of supplementing dairy cow rations with dehydrated alfalfa. *J. Dairy Sci.* 34:309. (Abstr.)
35. Conrad, H. R. 1970. Dehydrated alfalfa, urea in dairy cow nutrition. *Feed Industry,* April, pp. 10–12.
36. King, R. L. 1967. Vitamin A in the dairy ration and oxidized flavor in milk. Proc. 1967 Md. Nutr. Conf. for Feed Mfrs., p. 14.
37. Brown, L. D., C. A. Lassiter, C. F. Huffman, and E. J. Benne. 1960. Supplemental value of dehydrated alfalfa pellets for milking cows fed a high corn silage–timothy hay ration. *J. Dairy Sci.* 43 (6):867.

TABLE 50.5 ❧ Supplement A (32% protein)

Ingredient	Kilograms	% of mix
Soybean meal	290.3	64.0
Cane molasses	63.5	14.0
Dehydrated alfalfa meal (17%)	63.5	14.0
Dicalcium phosphate	23.6	5.2
Iodized salt	8.2	1.8
Premix*	4.5	1.0

* Premix—10 million IU vitamin A, 625 g zinc oxide, 2 g cobalt carbonate, and 3.2 kg soybean meal.

ered percentages of butterfat have been demonstrated when pelleted dehydrated alfalfa was fed as the sole source of forage.[38]

BEEF CATTLE

The amount of dehydrated forages fed to beef cattle is steadily increasing. In 1950 workers found nutritional factors in alfalfa that improved the digestibility of corncobs.[39] Subsequently, others reported that daily addition of 0.23–0.91 kg of dehydrated alfalfa increased gains substantially, and the Purdue Cattle Supplement A was modified to include 14% of dehydrated alfalfa.[40] This successfully used formula is described in Table 50.5. Supplement A has been used to balance all types of beef cattle rations. It has an abundance of essential and unidentified nutrients supplied by dehydrated alfalfa meal.

A high-urea supplement equaling a natural protein supplement was formulated by increasing the dehydrated alfalfa from 14% to 51%.[41-43] It was called Purdue 64 (64% protein). Daily gains and feed efficiency of steers fed Purdue 64 or Supplement A were essentially the same. The

coarse fraction of dehydrated alfalfa derived from air separation produced gains nearly equal to market grade 17% in Purdue 64 ration.[8,44,45]

SHEEP

A 75% faster daily gain with lambs has been observed when dehydrated alfalfa meal was substituted for corncobs and an isonitrogenous comparison was maintained.[46] Lambs receiving alfalfa had more highly finished carcasses, larger loin-eye areas, and higher dressing percentages.

Alfalfa contains factors essential for normal reproduction and lactation in ewes.[47,48] The coarsely ground heavy fraction of air-separated dehydrated alfalfa has been found as suitable nutritionally for ruminants as standard dehydrated alfalfa meal.[49]

42. Beeson, M. W., T. W. Perry, and M. T. Mohler. 1965. The effect of high-urea supplements fed with two levels of tylosin on the performance of steers. Purdue Cattle Feeders Day Rept.

43. Horn, G. W., and M. W. Beeson. 1969. Effects of corn distillers dried grains with solubles and dehydrated alfalfa meal on the utilization of urea nitrogen in beef cattle. *J. Anim. Sci.* 28:412–17.

44. Van Slyke, C. G. 1970. Nitrogen utilization studies with dehydrated alfalfa products and urea ammonium phosphate in beef cattle. Ph.D. thesis, Purdue Univ.

45. Beeson, M. W., T. W. Perry, C. G. Van Slyke, and M. T. Mohler. 1968. The value of dehydrated alfalfa products and distillers dried grains with solubles on the utilization of high-urea supplements for finishing beef cattle. Purdue Cattle Feeders Day Rept.

46. Karr, M. R., U. S. Garrigus, E. E. Hatfield, and H. W. Norton. 1965. Factors affecting the utilization of nitrogen from different sources by lambs. *J. Anim. Sci.* 24:459–68.

47. Shrewsbury, C. L., Claude Harper, F. N. Andrews, and M. R. Zelle. 1942. The limitations of oat straw as a roughage for maintenance, lactation and growth in sheep. *J. Anim. Sci.* 1:126–30.

48. Shrewsbury, C. L., F. N. Andrews, Claude Harper, and M. R. Zelle. 1943. The value of alfalfa and certain of its fractions in the nutrition of breeding ewes. *J. Anim. Sci.* 2:209–20.

49. Tiwari, A. D., and U. S. Garrigus. 1971. Utilization of air-separated stem fraction of dehydrated alfalfa meal of lambs. *J. Anim. Sci.* 33 (4):903–5.

❧ QUESTIONS

1. What are the high-producing states for dehydrated forage?
2. Describe methods and machinery of forage dehydration.
3. Why is dehy included in poultry and livestock rations?
4. How are dehydrated forages protected?
5. What steps can be taken to obtain improved products?

38. Porter, G. H., R. E. Johnson, H. D. Eaton, F. I. Elliot, and L. A. Moore. 1953. Relative value for milk production of . . . alfalfa when fed as the sole source of roughage to dairy cattle. *J. Dairy Sci.* 36 (10):1140.

39. Burroughs, Wise, Paul Gerlaugh, and R. M. Bethke. 1950. The influence of alfalfa hay and fractions of alfalfa hay upon the digestion of ground corncobs. *J. Anim. Sci.* 9:207–13.

40. Beeson, M. W., and T. W. Perry. 1953. Improving the formula of Supplement A with alfalfa meal. Purdue Agr. Exp. Sta. Mimeo. AH-101.

41. Beeson, M. W., M. T. Mohler, and T. W. Perry. 1964. Supplement A (32%) vs. Purdue 64% supplement, and the effect of Co-Ral, selenium and tylosin on the performance of steers. Purdue Cattle Feeders Day Rept.

C. H. NOLLER / *Purdue University*

51

GRASS-LEGUME SILAGE

ॐ

THE FIRST making of silage goes into antiquity. The origin of the process is unknown, but northern Europeans have successfully ensiled grass-legume crops by crude methods for hundreds of years. The process of ensiling became well known in Europe about the middle of the nineteenth century.[1]

The first silo in the U.S. was constructed in Maryland in 1876.[2] However, the practice of making grass-legume silage was slow to gain acceptance until about the middle 1930s. Since then increasing amounts of the nation's potential hay crop have been stored as silage. In 1939, 0.3 million t of grass silage was produced. This amount increased to 1.4 million t in 1946, 6 million t in 1954, 7.3 million t in 1959, and 9.4 million t in 1964 when hay crops cut and fed as green chop were included.[3]

Silage is the product of a controlled anaerobic fermentation of green forage, or in other words fermentation in the absence of air. The process is referred to as ensiling, and the container within which the fermentation occurs is the silo. The objective in ensiling is the storing of the green forage crop to preserve the material with a minimum loss of nutrients.

Silages may be separated into three groups on the basis of moisture level: (1) high-moisture or direct-cut silage, 70% plus moisture; (2) wilted silage, 60–70% moisture; and (3) low-moisture silage, 40–60% moisture. The approximate moisture levels of the forage to be ensiled can be estimated by the "grab test" (Table 51.1). The technique is to take a handful of chopped forage, compress it into a ball, release it, and observe the condition of the forage ball.[4]

ॐ ADVANTAGES OF ENSILING GRASSES AND LEGUMES

The advantages of making grass-legume crops into silage as compared to field-cured hay are:

1. More nutrients are preserved for feeding.
2. Less hindrance results from unfavorable weather conditions.
3. Less need for supplemental feed exists.
4. Silage fits better into mechanized feeding programs.

1. Jenkins, H. M. IV. 1884. Report on the practice of ensilage at home and abroad. *J. Roy. Agr. Soc.*, Ser. 2, 20: 126–45.
2. Plumb, C. S. 1895. Silos and silage. USDA Farmers' Bull. 32.
3. Strickler, P. E., H. V. Smith, and J. R. Kendall. 1968. Silos, silage handling practices and minor feed products. USDA Stat. Bull. 415.
4. Shepherd, J. B., C. H. Gordon, and L. F. Campbell. 1953. Development and problems in making grass silage. USDA Bur. Dairy Ind. Info. Bull. 149.

ॐ C. H. NOLLER. See Chapter 39.

Fig. 51.1. *Objective . . . storing of the green forage crop . . . minimum loss of nutrients.* Conditioning of forage reduces drying time in the field and can reduce field losses. *Deere and Co. photo.*

5. Field losses are reduced with improved harvesting and handling equipment. (See Fig. 51.1.)
6. Costs and storage losses are reduced with use of larger silo structures.
7. A well-made silage can be preserved for long periods with little loss of nutrients.

❧ PRINCIPLES OF PRESERVATION

The principles of the ensiling process are fairly well understood.[5,6] It is governed principally by the interactions of three factors: (1) the composition of the plant material placed in the silo, (2) the amount of air entrapped or allowed to enter the silage mass, and (3) the bacteria on the plant material. These factors are interre-

5. Langston, C. W., H. Irvin, C. H. Gordon, C. Bouma, H. G. Wiseman, C. G. Melin, L. A. Moore, and J. R. McCalmont. 1958. Microbiology and chemistry of grass silage. USDA Tech. Bull. 1187.
6. Barnett, A. J. G. 1954. Silage Fermentation. Academic Press, New York.

lated and govern the outcome of the process.

Direct-Cut Forage

When a forage is harvested, the plant is alive and respiring actively. The plant cells continue to respire for some time after the plant is cut. At the same time, large numbers of aerobic bacteria are present on the surface of the plant material and increase in number as long as oxygen is available. During this initial

TABLE 51.1 ❧ Determining forage moisture content by the grab test

Condition of forage ball	Approximate moisture content (%)
Holds shape, considerable juice	over 75
Holds shape, very little juice	70–75
Falls apart slowly, no free juice	60–70
Falls apart rapidly	below 60

Source: Shepherd et al., 1953.[4]

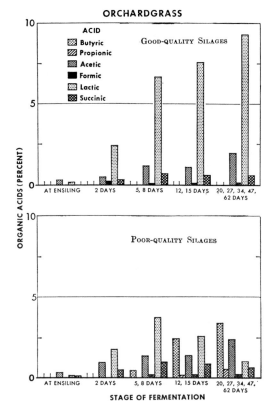

FIG. 51.2. Average amounts of the different organic acids in good and poor quality orchardgrass silages at different stages of the fermentation period. (Langston et al., 1958.[5])

phase plant enzymes and aerobic bacteria use the readily available carbohydrates to produce heat and carbon dioxide, thus decreasing the supply.

After several hours, depending upon the amount of air entrapped, the oxygen is depleted and anaerobic conditions prevail. This permits lactic acid bacteria, found initially in small numbers on the plant, to increase in three or four days to several hundred million per gram of forage.[5]

Lactic acid–producing bacteria act on the readily available carbohydrates in the forage to produce lactic acid and some acetic, propionic, formic, and succinic acids. The sequence of production of the acids and the difference between good and poor quality silages is shown in Figure 51.2. When 1 molecular weight in grams

of glucose is converted by the bacteria to 2 moles of lactic acid, only about 3.1% of the energy is lost as follows:

$$\underset{\text{glucose}}{C_6H_{12}O_6} \longrightarrow \underset{\text{lactic acid}}{2(C_3H_6O_3)}$$
$$673 \text{ kilocalories (kcal)} \rightarrow 652 \text{ kcal}$$
$$\text{loss} = 21 \text{ kcal or } 3.1\%$$

Concentration of lactic acid in the silage may reach 8–9% of the dry matter under favorable conditions. Many times there is not enough readily available carbohydrate in grasses (particularly in legumes), due to low levels in forage or losses during respiration, to produce all the lactic acid needed. When inadequate carbohydrate is a problem under practical conditions, high-carbohydrate feed materials such as cereal grains or molasses may be added to forage at the time of ensiling.

The acid "pickles" the plant material by reducing the pH to 4.2 or below. Low pH inhibits further bacterial growth and enzyme action and preserves the silage. The silage process is complete in about two to three weeks. A high-moisture silage with a pH of 4.2 or less is considered stable and may be kept for years if air is excluded.

Success or failure in making good quality silage may be determined during the first few hours of storage. Long exposure of the chopped forage to air prior to ensiling or large quantities of air entrapped in the silage mass result in the disappearance of much of the readily available carbohydrate. Under these conditions enough readily available carbohydrate may not be left to produce the lactic acid necessary to lower the pH to 4.2 or below.

When a fresh crop is ensiled, approximately 15–25% of the total N will be in the nonprotein nitrogen (NPN) form, with approximately 70–80% of this fraction present as free amino acids.[7,8] During the ensiling process, protein is converted into

7. Whitehead, D. C. 1970. The role of nitrogen in grassland productivity. A review of information from temperate regions. Commonwealth Bur. Pastures and Yield Crops Bull. 48.

8. Synge, R. L. M. 1963. Some nutritional aspects of the nonprotein nitrogen fraction of plants. In D. P. Cuthbertson (ed.), Progress in Nutrition and Allied Sciences. Oliver and Boyd, Edinburgh.

various NPN compounds so that about 65–75% of the total N in a direct-cut silage may be present as NPN.[9] Breakdown of protein by proteolytic organisms is inhibited by a pH below 4.2 or by a dry matter content of at least 33–35%. Increasing the osmotic pressure of the forage liquid phase by removal of water will suppress the development of the undesirable butyric acid–producing bacteria.

When silage has a low dry matter content and a high pH, undesirable bacteria such as the clostridia can grow and produce butyric acid; ammonia; and amines such as cadaverine, histamine, putrescine, tryptamine, and tyramine. Many of these amines and other volatile bases associated with poor quality silage are of interest because of their possible effect upon acceptability of the silages to animals.

The activity of bacteria belonging to the genera *Clostridium,* which are involved in spoilage, can be reduced by two methods.[10] The most direct method is to reduce the moisture in the forage to less than 70%; the other is to increase the acidity of the silage. An indication of clostridial action is the production of butyric acid by the conversion of 2 moles of lactate to 1 mole of butyric acid and carbon dioxide and hydrogen:[10]

$$
\begin{array}{cc}
\text{lactic acid} & \text{butyric acid} \\
2(\text{C}_3\text{H}_6\text{O}_3) \longrightarrow & \text{C}_4\text{H}_8\text{O}_2 + 2\text{CO}_2 + 2\text{H}_2 \\
652 \text{ kcal} \longrightarrow & 524 \text{ kcal} \\
\text{loss} = 128 \text{ kcal or } 19.6\%
\end{array}
$$

Loss of energy in converting the plant glucose to butyric acid is 22.1% of the original energy besides the formation of undesirable butyric acid and other products related to poor silage.

High-protein forages are more difficult to ensile because they require more lactic acid to change the pH. The same is true when the plant or its juices contain min-

eral constituents which interfere with a pH change.

WILTED SILAGE

A wilting procedure was developed by the USDA in the early 1940s and has been used quite extensively.[11] With the advent of the direct-cut forage chopper, the wilting procedure lost favor for a time because of the extra field operation involved. However, problems with seepage from the silo and production of poor quality silage resulted in a return to the wilting procedure.

Many factors associated with making a high-quality direct-cut silage also apply to wilted silage with some modifications. In the wilting method the forage is cut and permitted to wilt in the swath and/or windrow until the moisture reaches approximately 65%. This may require one to four hours on a dry day. No preservative is needed with properly wilted silage, although cereal grains such as corn have been added to increase the energy content.

Silage produced by the wilting method undergoes fermentation and depends upon the lactic acid produced for its preservation; however, there is less fermentation than in direct-cut material. A pH of 4.5 or below is indicative of good quality fermentation in a wilted silage.

LOW-MOISTURE SILAGE

In the early 1960s interest increased in the harvesting and storage of hay crops wilted to between 40 and 60% moisture. These forages generally are stored either in gastight or conventional tower silos. Particular attention must be given to air exclusion, fine chopping, rapid filling, and a good seal.

Low-moisture silages with between 40 and 60% moisture have a limited bacterial growth and fermentation. Extent of fermentation is of little concern since little acid is produced and pH is no criterion of

9. Fatianoff, N., M. Durand, T. L. Tisserand, and S. L. Letter. 1966. Comparative effects of wilting and of sodium metabisulfite on quality and nutritive value of alfalfa silage. Proc. 10th Int. Grassl. Congr., pp. 551–55 (Helsinki, Finland).

10. Whittenbury, R., P. McDonald, and D. G. Bryan-Jones. 1967. A short review of some biochemical and microbial aspects of ensilage. *J. Sci. Food Agr.* 18:441–46.

11. Woodward, T. E. 1944. Making silage by the wilting method. USDA Leaflet 238.

quality. The important factor is the presence and maintenance of air-free conditions. Infiltration of air into the silage mass will cause heating and the growth of molds and yeasts, which are a serious problem. As a rule, low-moisture silages are not stored in bunkers, trenches, or stack silos because of the difficulty of maintaining air-free conditions.

Depending on conditions, low-moisture silages may be subject to spontaneous heating. The condition occurs within a critical range of moisture, availability of oxygen, and heat dissipation.[12] Fires have been reported to occur when at least part of the contents is at 40% or less moisture and oxygen is available. Spontaneous heating that does not result in fires can give rise to the formation of indigestible products with lower protein and energy values. A low-moisture silage with tobacco brown or black color and a caramelized or tobacco odor has undergone some spontaneous heating; protein and energy value should be discounted depending on the degree of heating.

❧ SILAGE QUALITY

No single criterion exists for classifying a silage as good or poor, but a series of factors commonly associated with a given quality of material are known. Although it is difficult to classify silages accurately by subjective evaluations, much useful information can be obtained by carefully noting the color, smell, feel, and taste of the silage and combining this knowledge with information on the nature of the crop ensiled.

Characteristics generally associated with high-quality silages are:

1. A high-quality forage harvested at the proper stage of growth (Table 51.2).
2. A pH of 4.2 or below for high-moisture silages and 4.5 or below for wilted silages. The pH is not an important criterion for low-moisture silages.

12. Koegal, R. G., and H. D. Bruhn. 1969. Inherent causes of spontaneous ignition in silos. Ann. Meet. Amer. Soc. Agr. Eng. Paper 69-164.

TABLE 51.2 ❧ Harvest of crops for silage

Crop	Proper stage for ensiling*
Alfalfa	Late bud, early bloom
Red clover	Late bud, early bloom
Orchardgrass	Boot, early heading
Smooth bromegrass	Boot, early heading
Timothy	Boot, early heading
Bermudagrass	38–46 cm high
Grass mixtures	Boot, early heading
Legume-grass mixture	Grasses—boot, early heading
Cereal grains	Boot, early heading

* Applies to first harvest. Most grasses do not head after the first harvest.

3. Between 5 and 9% lactic acid on a dry basis in high-moisture silages.
4. Freedom from molds and objectionable odors such as ammonia, butyric acid, and mustiness.
5. Absence of caramelized or tobacco odors, particularly in low-moisture silages.
6. A green color, not brown or black.
7. A firm texture with no sliminess.

❧ EFFECTIVENESS OF HARVESTING AND STORAGE METHODS

Many studies have been made on the relative effectiveness of various methods of forage harvesting and efficiency of storage. Relative differences between methods of harvesting and the effect of varying moisture levels on field and harvesting losses and on losses in storage are presented in Figure 51.3.[13]

Harvesting a forage as wilted or low-moisture silage results in the lowest total loss. Wilting a forage to 65% moisture or lower may increase field and harvest losses, but storage losses are reduced. A further reduction in moisture to 40 or 50% will reduce storage losses, but higher field losses may occur due primarily to increased leaf loss. The problem created by water in forage is presented in Table 51.3.[13,14]

13. Hoglund, C. R. 1964. Comparative losses and feeding values of alfalfa and corn silage crops when harvested at different moisture levels and stored in gastight and conventional tower silos: An appraisal of research results. Mich. State Univ. Agr. Econ. Publ. 947.
14. Moore, L. A. 1958. Problems and recent improvements in the preparation and use of grass silage. USDA, ARS 44-23.

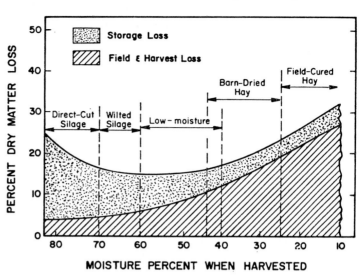

Fig. 51.3. Estimated total field and harvest loss and storage loss when legume-grass forages are harvested at varying moisture levels and by alternative harvesting methods. (Hoglund, 1964.[13])

❧ STORAGE METHODS

In silage making the forage to be ensiled is important, but so is the silo. The type and condition of the silo have considerable influence on the protection it gives the forage, the quality of the product removed, and the losses occurring during storage. Estimates of the effect of moisture level of forage to be ensiled on the dry matter losses in the field and in storage are presented in Figure 51.4.[4,13]

Trenches, Bunkers, Stacks

Farmers often use trench, bunker, or stack silos because of their low initial cost or use them as temporary storage struc-

TABLE 51.3 ❧ The water problem in silage stored in tower silos, and estimated losses

200 tons green forage	80% moisture	Wilted (50% moisture)
Dry matter (t)	40	40
Water (t)	160	40
Dry matter losses	Unwilted	Wilted
Field	2%	8%
Storage	19%	9%
Total	21% or 8.4 t dry matter	17% or 6.8 t dry matter

Sources: Adapted from Hoglund, 1964;[13] Moore, 1958.[14]

tures. Losses tend to be higher with these than tower silos because of the greater surface area exposed and the greater difficulty of excluding air. Thorough packing with a tractor and covering of the silage mass with plastic covers are helpful in reducing losses in the silo. Plastic covers to keep out rain and snow and to exclude air from the surface are most valuable when there is heavy precipitation, a long storage period, and a large surface exposure in relation to silage tonnage.

Vacuum compression has been of some interest in making stack silos. The approach is to make a stack, cover with plastic sealed to a ground sheet and vacuum-compress to 38 cm of mercury. The vacuum technique is laborious and time consuming; however the advantages are that self-feeding is more easily initiated; it is more flexible than a bunker; it allows intermittent filling; and silages are generally superior to those produced in conventional stacks, bunkers, and trenches.[15]

The stack is the simplest method for storing silage, but it is the least efficient of the three types of silos due to the large surface areas exposed. Efficiency of trench and bunker silos is generally superior due to protection from the sides (Fig. 51.4).

15. Lancaster, R. J. 1966. Silage: The research viewpoint. Proc. 28th Conf. N.Z. Grassl. Assoc., pp. 154–62.

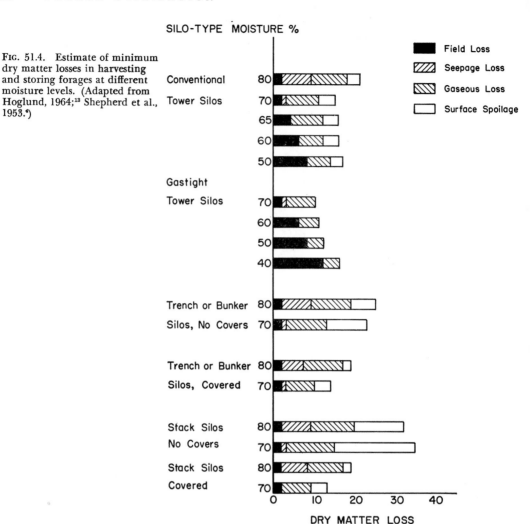

Fig. 51.4. Estimate of minimum dry matter losses in harvesting and storing forages at different moisture levels. (Adapted from Hoglund, 1964;[13] Shepherd et al., 1953.[4])

CONVENTIONAL TOWER SILOS

Conventional tower silos are the most popular means in the U.S. for silage storage. They differ from the gastight silo by not having built-in prevention of the entrance of air. Losses are low with good silage-making procedures and the use of top sealing with plastic or other methods. Silos are used to store materials between 40 and 80% moisture. Losses from seepage increase when moisture levels are over 70%. Due to the necessity for maintaining oxygen-free conditions, a tight silo becomes increasingly important as moisture content of the forage decreases.

SEALED STORAGE

The gastight silo with bottom unloader has found favor among many farmers. The advantages it offers are: (1) no top spoilage occurs, (2) it allows refilling at any time, (3) a low-moisture material between 40 and 60% moisture can be ensiled, (4) it permits automated unloading, and (5) the lowest dry matter losses in the silo are usually associated with sealed storage (Fig. 51.4).

✲ LOSSES

Some losses are incurred in the ensiling process regardless of the procedures used.[16]

Field losses vary with the degree of field drying. Losses in the silo can be grouped under three main headings: (1) surface spoilage, (2) seepage, and (3) gaseous or fermentation losses (Fig. 51.4).

SURFACE SPOILAGE

The amount of surface spoilage is a function of the degree of exposure to air and water. Losses of 20% or more can occur in stack silos (Fig. 51.4). Each 1 cm of surface spoilage represents approximately 3 cm of silage lost. The most effective way to reduce loss from surface spoilage is to reduce the surface area exposed or to provide suitable protection such as a plastic cover.

SEEPAGE

Storage losses tend to be higher with direct-cut materials, due to squeezing out water and movement of feed nutrients out of the silo with the water. In a high-moisture silage 50% or more of the dry matter losses may be due to seepage. These losses usually increase with the percent moisture of the ensiled forage and the height of the silo. A horizontal silo will have less seepage loss because of lower vertical pressures. In general, silages with less than 70% moisture have little or no seepage loss (Fig. 51.4).

GASEOUS LOSS

Gaseous or fermentation loss is due to respiration by the plant in the silo and the subsequent bacterial fermentation. Both of these factors result in loss of dry matter in the silo. Some of this is unavoidable; but unnecessary loss can result because of entry of air into the silo, failure of pH to decline rapidly, and existence of unfavorable fermentations. Adherence to principles of good silage making will keep this loss at a minimum.

16. Gordon, C. H. 1967. Storage losses in silage as affected by moisture content and structures. *J. Dairy Sci.* 50: 397–403.

❧ USE OF ADDITIVES

The use of a preservative should be considered if a grass or legume forage with over 70% moisture is ensiled; additives are not normally needed or used with silages containing less. A preservative is not needed with forages such as corn or sorghum since they normally contain adequate levels of readily available carbohydrates. Use of a preservative does not eliminate the necessity for effective chopping, packing, and sealing of the silo to prevent the entrance of air. Two types of preservatives have been used. One includes grains and feeds such as ground corn, oats, wheat, and molasses. The other includes chemical additives such as sodium metabisulfite, mineral acids, lactic acid, and formic acid.

FEED ADDITIVES

Feed additives furnish a readily available source of carbohydrate for bacterial fermentation of the silage. Some feed additives are used to absorb water, which is a problem with high-moisture silages. Use of a preservative is recommended with high-moisture legume or grass forage to ensure a good quality silage. Approximately 75–85% of feed nutrients added may be recovered as feed.

Some feedstuffs used as additives are:

1. Ground corn, barley, oats, and corn and cob meal in amounts varying from 50 to 100 kg/t, depending upon the moisture content of the crop.
2. Products such as beet pulp, citrus pulp, corn cobs, and chopped hay to reduce seepage losses from the silo.
3. Molasses, either blackstrap or dehydrated, at rates of 20–40 kg/t of green forage.

CHEMICAL ADDITIVES

A large number of chemical additives have been used in silage making with variable results. Mineral acid additives lower the pH immediately, and sodium

FIG. 51.5. Schematic representation of factors affecting silage quality and animal output.

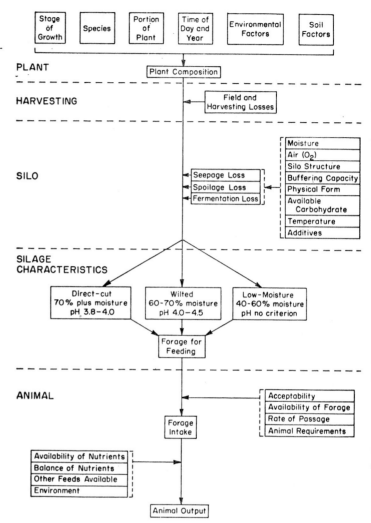

metabisulfite has a bacteriostatic effect. Use of these products has declined markedly.

Some interest has been shown in lactic acid cultures. However, there is no evidence that inoculation of plant material with lactic-acid–producing cultures is necessary or that this will improve the quality of silage.

There is increasing interest in the addition of formic acid to forage being ensiled.[17] Some evidence suggests improved

preservation, animal intake, and production; other data indicate no favorable effects.

❧ SILAGE-MAKING PRACTICES

One of the basic problems in making high-quality silage is the variability of the product even under apparently similar conditions. Generally, the following practices have resulted in making a good grass-legume silage.

1. Use a crop of high quality.

17. Henderson, A. R., and P. McDonald. 1971. Effect of formic acid on the fermentation of grass of low dry matter content. *J. Sci. Food Agr.* 22:157–63.

2. Harvest forage at the proper stage of growth.
3. Fine-chop. Length of cut for unwilted material should be 0.6–2.5 cm in length; for wilted material 0.6–1.2 cm in length.
4. Field-dry to 65% or less to produce either a wilted or low-moisture silage, or use an additive.
5. Use a silo which excludes air and water.
6. Fill the silo rapidly and pack thoroughly.
7. Use a suitable seal to exclude air.
8. Leave silo undisturbed until ready to use the feed.

❧ ACCEPTABILITY AND PRODUCTION

The most important factors influencing crop value are stage of maturity at which forage is harvested, method of harvest, and efficiency of storage. The product available for feeding to the animal represents the result of an interaction of various factors. A schematic representation of those that could have an influence on quality of silage produced, amount consumed, and animal output is presented in Figure 51.5. This illustrates the complexity of the ensiling process and the difficulty of predicting silage quality, intake, and animal output.

When silage is the sole or principal forage fed, the higher the percent of moisture the less dry matter is consumed. Data presented in Table 51.4 show that forage intake and milk production tend to be slightly lower on higher moisture silages than on hay or low-moisture silages. There is some tendency for hay and low-moisture silages to reverse their positions in individual experiments.[18-20] Although dry matter intakes generally are lower with higher moisture silages, a few studies have

TABLE 51.4 ❧ Comparative feeding values of hay, low-moisture silage, and silage for lactating dairy cows

Forage and form of preservation	Dry matter*	Forage dry matter intake	Fat-corrected milk
	(%)	(kg/day)	(kg/day)
Alfalfa			
Hay[18]	88.0	11.9‡	21.4
Low-moisture silage	50.1	11.2	20.9
Wilted silage	37.7	10.7	20.1
		(% body weight)	
Alfalfa–smooth bromegrass			
Hay	86.2†	2.06§	16.0
Low-moisture silage	51.4	2.30	17.2
Wilted silage	29.1	1.92	16.4
Alfalfa			
Hay[20]	89.4	2.46‖	24.3
Low-moisture silage	45.3	2.20	22.4
Direct-cut silage	25.9	2.01	22.1

Sources: Byers, 1965;[18] Roffler et al., 1967;[19] Gordon et al., 1961.[20]

* Dry matter values on as-fed basis.
† Average of three years data.
‡ Forage supplied 64.5% of the total dry matter intake.
§ Forage supplied approximately 70–80% of the total dry matter intake.
‖ Forage supplied 81.5% of the total dry matter intake.

shown that milk production may be equal or superior to that obtained with hay (Table 51.4). Weight gains of dairy heifers fed the lower moisture forages are often higher, due primarily to higher intakes of the drier feed.

The basic reason for the lower dry matter intakes with high-moisture silages is not known. The problem does not appear to be related to the water content per se of forage, but appears to be related to some aspect of fermentation. Intakes of high-moisture silages with a high acid content have been improved with the use of basic materials such as sodium bicarbonate.[21] Other unrecognized materials produced during fermentation may be critical factors influencing acceptability of silage.

Forages stored in conventional tower and gastight silos tend to be of equal value under high levels of management.

18. Byers, J. H. 1965. Comparison of feeding value of alfalfa hay, silage and low-moisture silage. *J. Dairy Sci.* 48:206–8.
19. Roffler, R. E., R. P. Niedermeier, and B. R. Baumgardt. 1967. Evaluation of alfalfa-brome forage stored as wilted silage, low-moisture silage, and hay. *J. Dairy Sci.* 50:1805–13.
20. Gordon, C. H., J. C. Derbyshire, H. G. Wiseman, E. A. Kane, and C. G. Melin. 1961. Preservation and feeding value of alfalfa stored as hay, haylage, and direct-cut silage. *J. Dairy Sci.* 44:1299–1311.
21. McLeod, D. S., R. J. Wilkins, and W. F. Raymond. 1970. The voluntary intake by sheep and cattle of silages differing in free-acid content. *J. Agr. Sci.* 75:311–19.

❧ TOXIC GASES IN GRASS-LEGUME SILAGES

A toxic gas is sometimes produced in grass-legume silage during the first few days of storage.[22,23] Some forages may store fairly large amounts of N in the form of nitrate in the tissues. Normally nitrate entering the silo in the plant will be reduced. The poorer the fermentation the more nitrate is lost.

Sometimes the nitrate is reduced to nitrogen oxide, which on contact with air is oxidized to nitrogen dioxide, a reddish colored gas which may be seen coming from a silo. This gas is highly toxic and dangerous to man and animals. Danger exists only during filling and for about one week after.

A suffocating gas, carbon dioxide, may collect in the silo. This gas is colorless and heavier than air; consequently, it tends to collect in low places. The gas forms shortly after filling begins and continues until fermentation stops. A person entering a silo in which the silage has settled below the open door could suffocate from lack of oxygen.

A simple precaution to follow is: *Never enter recently filled silos without running the blower for a few minutes or using other precautions to provide for adequate ventilation.*

❧ QUESTIONS

1. What are the advantages of making a grass-legume crop into silage as compared to field-cured hay?
2. How do direct-cut, wilted, and low-moisture silages compare relative to degree of fermentation?
3. What are the characteristics associated with a good quality silage?
4. What are some of the advantages and disadvantages of a low-moisture silage as compared to a direct-cut silage?
5. What is the effect of spontaneous heating on the forage?
6. List the losses occurring in the silo and the factors affecting them.
7. Under what conditions should use of additives be considered?
8. List the practices generally associated with the making of good quality grass-legume silages.
9. Discuss the problem of toxic gases in silage making.

22. McCalmont, J. R. 1960. Farm silos. USDA Misc. Publ. 810.
23. Peterson, W. H., R. H. Burris, R. Sant, and H. N. Little. 1958. Production of toxic gas (nitrogen oxides) in silage making. *J. Agr. Food Chem.* 6:121–26.

SUPPLEMENTAL INFORMATION

❧ FORAGE PROTEIN

Numerous experiments have demonstrated that forage protein, including protein from well-made silages, can be substituted for concentrate sources of protein provided the silages have not been heat damaged. Protein is one of the more expensive nutrients in ruminant rations, particularly when oil meals increase in price. Rations with up to 72% of the protein from alfalfa silage have been substituted for soybean meal protein for lactating dairy cows with no significant effect on feed intake and milk production (Table 51.5).

24. Noller, C. H., D. L. Hill, H. M. Saturnino, B. W. Crowl, and C. L. Rhykerd. 1973. Substitution of forage protein for oil meal protein in rations for lactating dairy cattle. Purdue Univ. Res. Progr. Rept. 416.

TABLE 51.5 ❧ Contribution of forage protein to ration protein under three different feeding programs.

	Ration		
	1	2	3
Rations, on dry basis:			
Corn silage, %	50.0	25.0	. . .
Alfalfa silage, %	. . .	25.0	50.0
Grain mixture, %	50.0	50.0	50.0
Protein intake as % of total:			
Corn silage	28	14	. . .
Alfalfa silage	. . .	36	72
Corn grain	18	23	28
Soybean meal	54	27	. . .

Source: Noller, et al., 1973.[24]

R. D. GOODRICH AND J. C. MEISKE
University of Minnesota

52

HIGH-ENERGY SILAGE

❧

THE TERM "high-energy" is applied to those silages that contain considerable grain (corn and sorghum). Thus they contain more digestible energy than the low-energy silages (grass and legume silages). In many instances a high-energy silage is used as the only source of forage in rations for cattle and sheep. (See Fig. 52.1.) Some reasons for the popularity of the high-energy silages are:[1]

1. Maximum yields of nutrients are obtained when a crop is harvested as silage.
2. Crops may be harvested for silage at several moisture contents, thus the silage harvest season may be extended. In addition, silage harvest is earlier

than for grain, which further extends the harvest period for a given crop.
3. Silages allow maximum flexibility in the cropping program. Decisions as to the amount of a crop to harvest as silage can be made late in the season. Also, if drought or early frost occur, much of the value of the crop can be salvaged by harvesting it as silage.
4. Silage harvesting, storing, and feeding are easily mechanized.
5. Silages are highly palatable feeds.
6. Silages may be stored for long periods after they are properly ensiled and protected from spoilage loss.
7. The feeding of rations which contain silage may reduce problems such as off-feed and founder.

The use of silage also has some limitations.[1] These include:

1. Silages do not have a ready market. Thus, once stored, they usually need to be fed on the farm where they were produced.
2. Silage is bulky to store and handle.
3. Storage, handling, transportation, and

❧ RICHARD D. GOODRICH is Professor of Animal Science and Nutrition, University of Minnesota. He holds the M.S. degree from South Dakota State University and the Ph.D. from Oklahoma State University. His research covers nutritional studies, forage quality evaluation, corn silage fermentation, and nitrogen utilization in ruminants.

❧ JAY C. MEISKE is Professor of Animal Science, University of Minnesota. He holds the M.S. degree from Oklahoma State University and the Ph.D. from Michigan State University. His research includes NPN utilization with urea and biuret, energy and forage levels for feedlot cattle, corn silage fermentation, and utilization of by-products by ruminants.

1. Stoneberg, E. G., F. W. Schaller, D. O. Hull, V. M. Meyer, N. J. Wardle, N. Gay, and D. E. Voelker. 1968. Silage production and use. Iowa State Univ. Pam. 417.

569

FIG. 52.1. *In many instances . . . high-energy silage . . . only source of forage . . . cattle and sheep.* In 1971, 12% of all corn and 5% of all sorghum grown in the U.S. was harvested as silage. In New York, 64% of the corn hectarage was harvested for silage. *New Holland Div., Sperry Rand Corp. photo.*

equipment costs are high in relation to its value.

4. Silage must be fed soon after it is removed from storage to prevent spoilage.

5. Losses may be high if it is not stored properly.

6. Rates of gain are reduced and amounts of feed used for maintenance are increased when high levels of silage are fed.

7. With beef cattle the length of feeding time to reach a given grade is increased and dressing percentages are lower than values for cattle fed high-grain rations.

❧ SUPPLEMENTATION OF RATIONS CONTAINING SILAGE

Corn silage contains, on a dry matter basis, an average of 8.9% crude protein, 68.5% total digestible nutrients (TDN), 0.33% Ca, and 0.21% P (Table 52.1). Grain sorghum silage has an average composition similar to that of corn silage. Forage sorghum silage contains less TDN than corn silage but contains similar percentages

TABLE 52.1 ❧ Composition of various silages

Type of silage	Analyses on a dry matter basis (%)			
	Crude protein	TDN	Ca	P
Corn	8.9	68.5	0.33	0.21
Grain sorghum	8.5	65.2	0.28	0.23
Forage sorghum	9.2	57.9	0.30	0.24
Oats	10.5	55	0.26	0.24
Alfalfa	17.1	57	1.64	0.26
Requirement[2]	11.1	69	0.36	0.28

Sources: Stoneberg et al., 1968;[1] NRC, 1970.[3] (Nutrient requirements for a 200-kg steer gaining 0.75 kg daily.)

of protein, Ca and P. In comparison, oats and alfalfa silages contain more protein and less TDN than corn silage. In relation to requirements for growing calves, corn silage and grain and forage sorghum silages are low in crude protein, Ca, and P.[2] The energy (TDN) contents of corn and grain sorghum silages are adequate to support moderate rates of gain even when they constitute a major portion of the ration dry matter. The carotene content of corn silage dry matter is listed by the National Research Council (NRC) as 45.6 mg/kg, with a coefficient of variation of 70%.[3] Thus carotene contents of corn silage are extremely variable.

CRUDE PROTEIN

Corn and sorghum silages are relatively low in protein content. Several studies have shown the value of supplementing rations containing these forages with protein.[4-8]

2. National Research Council. 1970. Nutrient Requirements of Beef Cattle. Nat. Acad. Sci., 4th ed., rev. Washington, D.C.
3. National Research Council. 1964. Joint United States–Canadian Tables of Feed Composition. Nat. Acad. Sci. Publ. 1232, Washington, D.C.
4. Perry, T. W., Donald Webb, C. H. Nickel, and W. M. Beeson. 1962. Levels of supplement A and corn with corn silage for growing and fattening steers. Purdue Univ. Progr. Rept. 11.
5. Klosterman, Earle W., A. L. Moxon, and L. E. Kunkle. 1958. Levels of corn silage and protein in rations for fattening steers. Ohio Agr. Exp. Sta. Beef Cattle Rept.
6. Kolari, O. E., A. L. Harvey, and J. C. Meiske. 1961. Feeding four levels of linseed oil meal and lysine to fattening cattle fed high-corn silage rations. Minn. Beef Cattle–Grassland Field Day Mimeo. B-33.
7. Vetter, R. L., and W. F. Wedin. 1968. Protein and energy level comparisons in a forage sorghum silage ration for finishing steers. Iowa State Univ. A.S. Leaflet R-113.
8. Peterson, L. A., and E. E. Hatfield. 1970. Effect of protein and energy levels for finishing steer calves on corn silage and high-moisture corn diets. Ill. Cattle Feeders Rept. AS-657a.

Feedlot cattle fed rations that contain large amounts of corn or sorghum silage require 0.25–0.30 kg of supplemental crude protein daily. However, to eliminate the possible errors associated with general recommendations that a given weight of supplemental protein be fed or that rations contain a certain percentage of protein, producers should formulate rations to provide the required amount of crude protein. This procedure will allow for ration modifications which result in changes in amounts of feed consumed and hence a change in the percent protein required to provide a given amount of crude protein. The amounts of protein required by cattle of various weights, as established by the NRC, appear to be valid estimates of protein requirements.[2]

Proper amounts of supplemental protein needed by cattle of various weights can be determined by estimating intakes of individual feeds and comparing the supplied protein with requirements. The amount of supplemental protein required is that needed to increase protein intake to the required total amount.

The NRC protein requirements for growing cattle (see Chapters 61 and 62 for NRC requirements) increase as the rate of gain increases. Illinois research suggests that increasing protein levels has little influence on gains or feed efficiencies of cattle fed high-silage rations. However, higher protein levels improve the performance of cattle fed high-grain rations.[8] This suggests that cattle fed high-grain rations require greater amounts of protein than cattle fed high-forage rations. An apparent explanation is that more protein is required by cattle gaining at a rapid rate (high-grain rations) than by cattle gaining at a slower rate (high-forage rations).

USE OF UREA

Urea is widely used as a source of N in ruminant rations. The chief reason for use of a nonprotein nitrogen (NPN) source such as urea in place of oilseed meal is that urea provides N at a lower cost. Practical feeding procedures that have been advanced for the improvement of urea utilization include: (1) full-feeding, (2) frequent feeding of small amounts of urea, (3) thorough mixing of urea-containing supplements, and (4) mixing of urea-containing supplements into the daily feed.[9] These practices are suggested to ensure that a more uniform intake of urea occurs and that conditions in the rumen favor its utilization. Full-feeding (having feed available at all times no matter what type of ration is being fed) will aid in maintaining a low ruminal pH. Also, if urea is mixed with the entire daily ration, the intake of urea at any one time will not be great and the ability of the microbes to synthesize protein will not be as likely to be exceeded.

Most readily available carbohydrates enhance the utilization of urea.[10] The low digestibility of forages results in insufficient available energy to support maximum incorporation of ammonia into microbial protein. Available information has been reviewed concerning the influence of diet energy level on performance of cattle fed urea or preformed protein.[11] Rates of gain of calves and yearlings fed urea with high-energy and medium-energy (high-corn silage) rations averaged 97.2 and 95.5% of the rate of gain of cattle fed preformed protein with rations containing the respective energy levels. Most if not all of this difference could be attributed to adaptation since it has been shown that cattle fed urea gain as well as those fed soybean meal after the initial 28 days of feeding.[12]

Urea can be substituted for all the oilseed meal in high-energy finishing rations with little if any detrimental effect on the performance of cattle, provided the basic nutrition and management practices out-

9. Goodrich, R. D., and J. C. Meiske. 1969. Factors influencing urea utilization by ruminants. Proc. Del IV Simposio Internazionale di Zootecnia, p. 187 (Milan, Italy).

10. Bloomfield, R. A., M. E. Muhrer, and W. H. Pfander. 1958. Relation of composition of energy source to urea utilization by rumen microorganisms. *J. Anim. Sci.* 17:1189.

11. Meiske, J. C., and R. D. Goodrich. 1966. Nonprotein nitrogen utilization with high- and low-energy rations. Proc. Minn. Nutr. Conf. 27:30.

12. Goodrich, R. D., and J. C. Meiske. 1969. Influence of nitrate and Aureomycin on cattle fed urea or soybean meal. Minn. Beef Cattle Feeders Day Rept. B-120.

lined earlier are followed. In nearly all instances use of urea in high-energy rations will lower feed costs.

The use of urea in high-corn silage growing rations has received less research effort than the feeding of urea in high-grain rations. However, it appears that a high percentage of the supplemental crude protein needs of cattle fed rations containing corn silage can be provided by urea.[12-14] Rates of gain may be depressed slightly by feeding large amounts of urea, but feed costs per unit gain should be reduced.

ADDITION OF NONPROTEIN NITROGEN AT ENSILING TIME

Common NPN materials that may be added to silage at ensiling time are urea; biuret; and a mixture of molasses, water, anhydrous ammonia, and minerals. Common rates of addition to 30% dry matter silage are 0.5% urea and 0.6% biuret, and the anhydrous ammonia mixture is added at a rate of 2.5%.[15,16]

A number of considerations influence the decision of whether to add NPN to silage at ensiling time or at feeding time:

1. Mixing NPN with chopped corn plants at ensiling time may be done by farmers themselves, although many may believe that NPN-containing supplements should be purchased for later use. The outlay of capital for supplements may cause some feeders to offer less than required amounts of N in an effort to "save" money.

2. The addition of NPN at ensiling time may increase labor requirements at a time when labor is already stressed.

Dry supplements can usually be mixed or purchased when labor is more available.

3. Most rations fed to feedlot animals require supplementation with nutrients in addition to N (salt, Ca, P, and possibly vitamin A). No matter which method of feeding NPN is used, it is important that the ration be balanced with respect to all required nutrients. The use of NPN-containing corn silage may lead some to think that the ration is complete.

4. The addition of NPN at ensiling time should allow for some diffusion throughout the corn silage. This is important since optimum NPN utilization is partly dependent on its being consumed with the entire ration. Despite the fact that some diffusion will take place in the silo, care must be taken to ensure uniform distribution.

5. Most of the urea added to corn silage may be converted to ammonia and carbon dioxide.[17-19] Since ammonia acts as a weak base, it may retard the normal drop in pH, and fermentation may continue for a longer than normal period. This is reflected in high lactic acid values for NPN-treated silages. Especially with corn silages that contain less than 60% moisture, increased losses of both dry matter and N are possible because of a drop in pH insufficient to cause fermentation to cease in a short period.[18,19]

6. Results of 26 trials have indicated that there is little advantage in daily gain (0.77 versus 0.73 kg/day) but about a 5% advantage in feed efficiency for cattle fed urea-containing silage.[17]

7. Michigan workers have stated that a high percentage of the urea added to corn silage is converted to ammonia and combines with the organic acids

13. Newland, H. W., H. E. Henderson, W. T. Magee, R. J. Deans, L. J. Bratzler, A. L. Pearson, R. W. Luecke, and R. H. Nelson. 1961. Urea and energy levels, lysine supplementation and hormones for fattening steer calves. Mich. Cattle Feeders Day Rept. AH-67.
14. Tolman, W., and W. Woods. 1967. Urea and corn silage. Univ. Nebr. Progr. Rept. Res. Activities.
15. Henderson, Hugh E., David R. Beattie, Mitchell R. Geasler, and W. G. Bergen. 1971. Molasses, minerals, ammonia and Pro-Sil addition to corn silage for feedlot cattle. Mich. State Univ. Rept. Beef Cattle Res. AH-BC-6950.
16. Henderson, Hugh E., D. Barrie Purser, and Mitchell R. Geasler. 1970. Anhydrous ammonia, urea and mineral additives to corn silage. Mich. State Univ. Rept. Beef Cattle Res. AH-BC-684A.

17. Essig, H. W. 1968. Urea-limestone–treated silage for beef cattle. J. Anim. Sci. 27:730.
18. Owens, F. N., J. C. Meiske, and R. D. Goodrich. 1969. Effects of calcium sources and urea on corn silage fermentation. J. Dairy Sci. 52:1817.
19. Owens, F. N., J. C. Meiske, and R. D. Goodrich. 1969. Fate of carbon and nitrogen from ensiled urea and biuret. J. Anim. Sci. 29:168.

produced during fermentation and have suggested that this N is used more effectively than the N in urea-containing supplements.[16] However, others have shown that N retention in lambs is greater for urea in supplements than for urea-treated corn silage.[20]

8. Rate of feeding of urea-treated corn silage may be more critical than for nontreated silage since it has been reported that urea-containing corn silage heated readily upon removal from storage, whereupon the smell of ammonia was noted.[21]

9. Since the amount of corn silage fed is often decreased as cattle reach heavier weights, it may be difficult to use NPN-treated silage effectively for the entire feeding period. Unless the amount of corn-silage feeding is changed abruptly, graded increases in the amount of N supplementation would be needed. However, urea could also be added to high-moisture shelled corn at ensiling time so that it would make no difference how much whole-plant silage was fed.[22]

ADDITION OF LIMESTONE AT ENSILING TIME

Ground limestone has been added to corn and sorghum silages at rates of 0.5–1% to increase the content of organic acids. The pH of limestone-treated silages is higher than nontreated silages because the limestone neutralizes some of the acids as they are produced.[17] Thus fermentation continues for a longer period, and acetic and lactic acid contents are increased. Lactic acid is increased to a greater extent than acetic acid.[23]

It has been concluded that the feeding of limestone-treated silage has little effect on average daily gain.[17] Feed efficiency was slightly improved, but the results were not consistent from station to station. Illinois researchers have also reported that limestone included at feeding time or added at ensiling resulted in similar rates of gain and feed efficiencies.[24] Digestion experiments have shown that the addition of limestone does not improve the digestibility of proximate components.[23]

❧ VITAMIN A VALUE OF CAROTENE IN CORN SILAGE

Vitamin A deficiency symptoms have been observed in cattle full-fed corn silage.[25,26] In one study the silage contained more than 11 mg carotene/kg of fresh silage and the cattle were supplemented with 5000–7000 international units (IU) of vitamin A daily.[25] These observations have led others to question the vitamin A activity of the carotene supplied by corn silage.

Based on the amount of carotene required to prevent elevated cerebrospinal fluid pressures, one study concluded that the carotene in corn silage was as effective as that in dehydrated alfalfa leaf meal in meeting the carotene needs of calves.[27] However, in a later study it was found that liver vitamin A values, adjusted for differences in carotene intake, were higher for steers fed pelleted alfalfa hay than for steers fed corn silage.[28] Other research indicated that 1 mg of corn-silage carotene was equivalent

20. Yamoor, M. Y., J. C. Meiske, and R. D. Goodrich. 1967. Digestibility of corn silage containing urea or biuret and corn silage supplemented with soybean meal, urea or biuret. Minn. Beef Cattle Feeders Day Rept. B-88.

21. Owens, F. N., J. C. Meiske, and R. D. Goodrich. 1967. Supplementation of high-corn silage rations, for wintering calves, with urea, biuret, or soybean meal at ensiling or feeding time. Minn. Beef Cattle Feeders Day Rept. B-87.

22. Hatfield, E. E., and U. S. Garrigus. 1968. Recommended levels of additives for balancing corn silage and high-moisture corn. Ill. Cattle Feeders Day Rept. AS-651g.

23. Klosterman, Earle W., Ronald R. Johnson, A. L. Moxon, and Harold W. Scott. 1963. Feeding value of limestone-treated corn silages for fattening cattle. Ohio Agr. Exp. Sta. Res. Bull. 934.

24. Cmarik, G. F., and G. E. McKibben. 1966. Effect of calcium added to mature corn silage on weight gains of yearling steers. Ill. Cattle Feeders Day Rept. AS-634g.

25. Smith, G. S., A. L. Neumann, W. G. Huber, H. A. Jordan, and O. B. Ross. 1961. Avitaminosis in cattle fed silage rations supplemented with vitamin A. *J. Anim. Sci.* 20:952. (Abstr.)

26. Jordan, H. A., G. S. Smith, A. L. Neumann, J. E. Zimmerman, and G. W. Breniman. 1963. Vitamin A nutrition of beef cattle fed corn silages. *J. Anim. Sci.* 22:738.

27. Miller, R. W., L. A. Moore, D. R. Waldo, and T. R. Wrenn. 1967. Utilization of corn silage carotene by dairy calves. *J. Anim. Sci.* 26:624.

28. Miller, R. W., R. W. Hemken, D. R. Waldo, and L. A. Moore. 1970. Utilization of corn silage carotene as compared to pelleted alfalfa hay carotene by Holstein steers. *J. Anim. Sci.* 30:984.

TABLE 52.2 ❦ Dry matter and TDN yield per ha of corn and sorghum silages

Type of silage	Dry matter yield/ha (kg)	TDN yield/ha (kg)
Corn	13,450	9,220
Grain sorghum	12,330	8,030
Forage sorghum	14,570	8,440
Sorghum-sudangrass hybrids	8,970	4,390

Source: Stoneberg et al., 1968.[1]

to 436 IU of vitamin A.[29] This value is in close agreement with the value used by the NRC (400 IU/mg of carotene).[2] Thus, the conversion of carotene from corn silage to vitamin A probably occurs at a normal efficiency.

❦ COMPARISON OF CORN AND SORGHUM SILAGES

Yields of dry matter and TDN per ha when corn or various types of sorghum are harvested as silage are presented in Table 52.2.[1] Yields are for fertile land with moderate to high management. These data show that yield of TDN from sorghum-sudan hybrids is only 48% of that obtained from 1 ha of corn silage. Since relative yields of corn and sorghum are influenced by climatic conditions, these values probably do not apply to all areas of the U.S.

Assuming approximately equal animal weights, rate of gain is a function of the digestible energy per unit weight of a feed and the amount of that feed consumed. Thus, rates of gain presented in Table 52.3 reflect the animals' ability to consume the silages, as well as the energy value. The TDN values for forage sorghums presented in Table 52.1 are about 85% of the TDN value of corn silage. Rates of gain of cattle fed 'Atlas,' 'Rox Orange,' 'Hidan 39' (cut once), and Hidan 39 (July cutting) are 85% of those for cattle fed corn silage. In many of the studies dry matter values were not reported, thus conclusions relative to the dry matter consumptions of corn and

TABLE 52.3 ❦ Comparison of corn and sorghum silages

Number of comparisons	Sorghum cultivar	Average daily gain of feedlot cattle (kg) Corn silage	Sorghum silage	Sorghum as percent of corn silage
8	Atlas	0.78	0.63	81
10	Rox Orange	1.12	0.98	88
3	sorghum-sudan hybrid	1.11	0.92	83
5	not stated	0.91	0.60	66
1	'Hidan 37'	1.25	0.72	58
1	'Hidan 38'	1.25	0.99	79
2	Hidan 39, cut once	1.12	0.94	84
2	Hidan 39, July cutting	1.12	0.97	87
2	Hidan 39, second cutting	1.12	1.06	95
1	grain sorghum	0.76	0.74	97

Note: A summary of 20 research reports prepared by the authors.

sorghum silages cannot be made. However, it appears that much of the difference in performance of cattle fed corn or forage-sorghum silages is due to the lower energy value of the forage sorghum.

Results of three trials indicate that sorghum-sudan hybrids have a feeding value approximately the same as the forage sorghums (83% of corn silage). In one study cattle fed grain-sorghum silage gained 97% as fast as cattle fed corn silage. It is possible that a portion of the difference between corn and sorghum silages is due to a low digestibility of the intact grain in sorghum silage.[30] Significant improvements in rate of gain and feed efficiency have been obtained by feeding rolled sorghum silage.[31]

When soil and climatic conditions cause moisture stress, yields of dry matter will generally favor the sorghums. Thus, even though the sorghum silages contain less digestible energy than corn silage, yields of digestible energy will favor the sorghums in many areas of the U.S.

29. Martin, F. H., D. E. Ullrey, H. W. Newland, and E. R. Miller. 1968. Vitamin A activity of carotenes in corn silage fed to lambs. J. Nutr. 96:269.

30. Reames, C. E., O. T. Stallcup, and R. L. Thurman. 1961. A comparison of the digestibility of Atlas sorgo silages with corn silage. J. Dairy Sci. 44:693.

31. Pund, William A. 1970. Finishing yearling steers with high-energy grain sorghum silage. Miss. State Univ. Bull. 780.

❧ COMPARISON OF CORN SILAGE AND ALFALFA HAYLAGE

It is difficult to estimate the comparative values of corn silage and alfalfa haylage without feedlot data since these feeds are different in protein, TDN, and Ca contents. Haylage supplies much protein, but corn silage often contains over 45% grain on a dry matter basis. The proper supplement for a ration containing alfalfa or alfalfa-grass haylage will not be adequate for one containing corn silage.

The results of seven trials designed to compare the feeding values of corn silage and alfalfa-grass haylages are presented in Table 52.4.[32-38] In general, rates of gain of cattle fed corn silage or haylage have been similar. It appears that amounts of feed/100 kg gain may favor cattle fed corn silage. In two of these experiments the amount of supplemental crude protein fed (227 g/day) to cattle receiving corn silage may have been inadequate for optimum performance.[33,34]

❧ INFLUENCE OF STAGE OF MATURITY ON NUTRITIVE VALUE

CORN SILAGE

A comprehensive series of experiments concerning the feeding value, composition, and digestibility of corn plants harvested at various stages of maturity have been reported by the Ohio station.[39-42] The greatest yield of corn-silage dry matter oc-curred when corn was harvested between the dent and glaze stages of kernel maturity. When yields were at a maximum, dry matter contents of stalks, leaves, and ears were appproximately 20, 28, and 50% respectively.[40] Maximum dry matter digestibility was obtained for corn plants harvested at the milk–early dough to dough-dent stages of maturity.[42] The influence of maturity on dry matter digestibility was small but significant (Table 52.5). Dry matter digestibility averaged 71.9% for the two years (value for silages without urea or limestone additions) at the dough-dent stage of maturity and decreased to 69% at the postfrost stage (a decrease of 2.9 percentage units).

Crude protein digestibility decreased from 77.5% at the milk–early dough stage to 67% at the flint stage of kernel maturity.[42] Voluntary intake of dry matter increased from the blister to glaze stage of maturity, then decreased at the flint and postfrost stages (Table 52.5). Since maximum dry matter yields were obtained at the dent to glaze stages of kernel maturity[40] and since dry matter digestibility and intake were at or near maximum at these stages,[42] it appears that corn should be harvested for silage at the dent to glaze stages. At this time the forage contained 27.5–33.9% dry matter.[42] Based on the feedlot performance of cattle, others have suggested that corn silage should be made when the corn plants contain about 35% dry matter.[43,44]

Maximum production of beef per ha was

32. Haarer, G., E. Hieber, W. L. Brittain, and R. J. Deans. 1963. Corn silage vs. haylage for feedlot steers. Mich. Cattle Feeders Day Rept. AH-91.

33. Zimmerman, J. E., P. E. Lamb, and A. L. Neumann. 1964. Comparison of corn silage and haylage in steer calf finishing programs. Ill. Cattle Feeders Day Rept. AS-603g.

34. Zimmerman, J. E., A. L. Neumann, F. C. Hinds, B. C. Breidenstein, B. E. Shoemaker, and P. E. Lamb. 1965. Comparisons of haylage and corn silage in steer calf finishing programs. Ill. Cattle Feeders Day Rept., p. 15.

35. Zimmerman, J. E., F. C. Hinds, B. C. Breidenstein, B. E. Shoemaker, and P. E. Lamb. 1966. Comparisons of haylage and corn silage in steer calf finishing programs. Ill. Cattle Feeders Day Rept. As-634h.

36. Henderson, Hugh E., and H. W. Newland. 1965. Corn silage, haylage, vitamins and housing for finishing steer calves. Mich. State Univ. Rept. Beef Cattle Res. AH-BC-642.

37. Henderson, Hugh E., and H. W. Newland. 1967. Alfalfa hay, haylage and corn silage with varying moisture and concentrate levels for finishing yearling steers. Mich. State Univ. Rept. Beef Cattle Res. AH-BC-662.

38. Goodrich, R. D., and J. C. Meiske. 1967. A comparison of haylage and corn silage in finishing rations. Minn. Beef Cattle Feeders Day Rept. B-86.

39. Johnson, R. R., K. E. McClure, E. W. Klosterman, and L. J. Johnson. 1967. Corn plant maturity. III. Distribution of nitrogen in corn silage treated with limestone, urea and diammonium phosphate. *J. Anim. Sci.* 26:394.

40. Johnson, R. R., K. E. McClure, L. J. Johnson, E. W. Klosterman, and G. B. Triplett. 1966. Corn plant maturity. I. Changes in dry matter and protein distribution in corn plants. *Agron. J.* 58:151.

41. Johnson, R. R., T. L. Balwani, L. J. Johnson, K. E. McClure, and B. A. Dehority. 1966. Corn plant maturity. II. Effect on *in vitro* cellulose digestibility and soluble carbohydrate content. *J. Anim. Sci.* 25:617.

42. Johnson, R. R., and K. E. McClure. 1968. Corn plant maturity. IV. Effects on digestibility of corn silage in sheep. *J. Anim. Sci.* 27:535.

43. Henderson, Hugh E., Harlan Ritchie, C. K. Allen, and Erskine Cash. 1971. Effect of housing systems and corn silage maturity on feedlot performance of Holstein steers. Mich. State Univ. Rept. Beef Cattle Res. AH-BC-706.

44. Goodrich, R. D., J. W. Enzmann, H. A. Ronnevik, and J. C. Meiske. 1968. What is the best moisture content of corn silage? Minn. Beef Cattle Feeders Day Rept. B-108.

TABLE 52.4 ❧ Performance of cattle fed corn silage or haylage

| Reference | Footnote | Average daily gain (kg) | | Feed/100 kg gain (kg) | |
		Corn silage	Haylage	Corn silage	Haylage
Haarer et al., 1963[32]	*	1.09	1.11	589	587
Zimmerman et al., 1964[33]	†	0.93, 0.90	1.11, 1.06	922, 899	890, 910
Zimmerman et al., 1965[34]	‡	0.95	1.08	883	862
Zimmerman et al., 1966[35]	§	0.97, 1.02	0.97	852, 814	905
Henderson and Newland, 1965[36]	‖	1.05	1.07	724	732
Henderson and Newland, 1967[37]	#	1.12	1.01, 1.03	897	1,026, 944
Goodrich and Meiske, 1967[38]	**	1.40, 1.40	1.36, 1.37	697, 688	716, 687

* Amount of ear corn for haylage-fed cattle adjusted to give equal rates of gain as for cattle fed corn silage.
† Cattle fed corn silage consumed 6.44 or 5.26 kg of corn (includes that in silage) and those fed haylage consumed 6.44 or 4.90 kg of corn grain.
‡ Approximately equal weights of high-moisture corn were fed to cattle that received corn silage or haylage.
§ See footnote ‡. Cattle fed corn silage received 454 or 567 g of soybean meal (50% crude protein) daily.
‖ Corn grain for haylage-fed cattle adjusted to give equal rates of gain as for cattle fed corn silage.
Approximately equal concentrate to forage ratios (considering grain in the corn silage).
** Cattle fed corn silage consumed 581 and 435 g of crude fiber daily and those fed haylage consumed 662 and 467 g of crude fiber daily.

TABLE 52.5 ❧ Influence of stage of maturity on composition and digestibility of corn silage

| Stage of maturity | Harvest date | | Dry matter (%) | | Crude protein‡ (%) | | Dry matter digestibility (%) | | Crude protein digestibility (%) | | Voluntary intake, g dry matter/ $W^{0.75}$ | |
	1964	1965	1964	1965	1964	1965	1964	1965	1964	1965	1964	1965
Blister	8/17	8/18	20.9	21.3	12.0	11.4	65.3	71.0	74.7	76.7	42.9	51.0
Early milk	8/25	8/25	19.9	22.1	12.1	11.9	66.7	67.9	75.9	75.6	42.6	49.4
Milk–early dough	9/2	9/3	21.9	24.9	10.8	12.3	69.5	72.6	77.6	77.4	54.1	52.7
Dough-dent	9/9	9/10	27.5	27.9	10.4	11.4	71.9	71.9	76.3	75.6	55.6	59.3
Glaze	9/21	9/22	33.5	33.9	9.4	11.0	67.8	68.4	69.1	68.0	58.9	61.9
Flint	10/6	10/5	45.4	38.4	9.0	11.0	71.0	66.6	66.9	67.2	54.1	58.8
Postfrost*	10/15	10/14	49.5†	46.7	8.7	10.5	69.8	68.2	64.8	66.3	54.0	52.4
Mature	...	12/17	...	71.7	...	10.9	...	68.6	...	59.4	...	52.7

Source: Johnson and McClure, 1968.[42]
Note: Data shown here are only for silages that had no urea or limestone additions made at ensiling time. Data are also included in Johnson and McClure for silages with urea and limestone additions.
* Frost dates for 1964 and 1965 were 10/6 and 10/13, respectively.
† Approximately 5% water added at ensiling time.
‡ Dry matter basis.

TABLE 52.6 ❧ Yield, nutrient content, and digestibility of grain sorghum silage at three stages of maturity

| Days after planting | Heads (%)* | Yield (t/ha)* | Dry matter content (%) | Crude protein content of silage (%)* | Digestibility (%) | |
					Crude protein	Energy
First year						
77	39.5	5.83	24.5	10.6	58.0	60.5
84	50.6	6.10	27.3	10.5	55.8	62.3
95	66.4	6.55	32.5	10.2	50.1	62.3
Second year						
77	34.4	4.69	22.4	9.6	51.3	56.6
84	51.0	5.71	26.1	9.3	42.6	56.1
95	69.3	6.05	32.4	9.1	36.4	53.3

Source: Browning and Lusk, 1967.[49]
* Dry matter basis.

obtained when silage was harvested at the late dough stage, followed in decreasing order by early dough, mealy endosperm, and late milk stages of maturity.[45] Animals fed silages which contain low percentages of dry matter apparently consume less dry matter than animals fed higher dry matter silages.[46,47]

SORGHUM SILAGE

The influence of stage of maturity on the nutritive value of bird-resistant grain sorghum, grain sorghum, and forage sorghum silages has been studied.[48-50]

Protein and cellulose contents of bird-resistant sorghum have been shown to decline with advancing maturity, while cell wall constituents and lignin increase.[48] Advancing maturity had little influence on intake or the digestibility of dry matter and organic matter. The digestibilities of protein and cellulose decreased with advancing maturity until after frost, at which time an increase in protein digestibility was observed.

Data presented in Table 52.6 show the influence of maturity on the nutritive value of grain sorghum.[49] Yields of dry matter and the percent of heads it contained increased with advancing maturity. Crude protein contents and crude protein digestion coefficients decreased with advancing maturity. However, stage of maturity had little influence on energy digestibility.

Dry matter contents of Atlas sorghum increased from 23.1 to 28.2% as maturity advanced from the milk to hard dough stage (Table 52.7).[50] Crude protein contents and dry matter and crude protein digestibilities of Atlas sorghum silage decreased as maturity advanced. An increase in dry matter contents was noted for Rox Orange sorghum as maturity advanced. However, crude protein contents and dry matter and crude protein digestibilities of Rox Orange sorghum silage did not decrease as maturity advanced.

❧ MODIFIED CORN SILAGES

Attempts to make corn silage a more versatile feed have resulted in the development of multieared cultivars, dwarf cultivars, high-sugar corn silage, brown midrib mutants, high-cut corn silage, topped corn silage, center-cut corn silage, and high-energy corn silage (corn grain from one row added to chopped plants from another).[51-62]

45. Chamberlain, C. C., H. A. Fribourg, K. M. Barth, J. H. Felts, and J. M. Anderson. 1971. Effect of maturity of corn silage at harvest on the performance of feeder heifers. *J. Anim. Sci.* 33:161.

46. Huber, J. T., G. C. Graff, and R. W. Engel. 1965. Effect of maturity on nutritive value of corn silage for lactating cows. *J. Dairy Sci.* 48:1121.

47. Goering, J. K., R. W. Hemken, N. A. Clark, and J. H. Vandersall. 1969. Intake and digestibility of corn silages of different maturities, varieties and plant populations. *J. Anim. Sci.* 29:512.

48. Johnson, Ronald R., V. P. DeFaria, and K. E. McClure. 1971. Effects of maturity on chemical composition and digestibility of bird resistant sorghum plants when fed to sheep as silages. *J. Anim. Sci.* 33:1102.

49. Browning, C. B., and J. W. Lusk. 1967. Effect of stage of maturity at harvest on nutritive value of combine-type grain sorghum silage *J. Dairy Sci.* 50:81.

50. Owen, F. G., and J. W. Kuhlman. 1967. Effect of maturity on digestibility of forage sorghum silages. *J. Dairy Sci.* 50:527.

51. Neumann, A. L., J. E. Zimmerman, W. W. Albert, and P. E. Lamb. 1963. Regular and multieared corn silage compared with hay as roughage sources in heifer calf wintering rations. Ill. Cattle Feeders Day Rept. AS-593c.

52. Zimmerman, J. E., G. W. Breniman, A. L. Neumann, and G. E. Mitchell, Jr. 1960. Dwarf versus regular corn silage for beef cattle. Ill. Cattle Feeders Day Rept., p. 18.

53. Meiske, J. C., and R. D. Goodrich. 1966. Corn silage, high-sugar corn silage and sorgo-sudan silage rations fed with high-urea supplements. Minn. Beef Cattle Feeders Day Rept. B-69.

54. Barnes, R. F., L. D. Muller, L. F. Bauman, and V. F. Colenbrander. 1971. *In vitro* dry matter disappearance of brown midrib mutants of maize (*Zea mays* L.). *J. Anim. Sci.* 33:881.

55. Muller, L. D., R. F. Barnes, L. F. Bauman, and V. F. Colenbrander. 1971. Variations in lignin and other structural components of brown midrib mutants of maize. *Crop Sci.* 11:413.

56. Muller, L. D., V. L. Lechtenberg, L. F. Bauman, R. F. Barnes, and C. L. Rhykerd. 1972. *In vivo* evaluation of a brown midrib mutant of *Zea mays* L. *J. Anim. Sci.* 35:883–87.

57. Meiske, J. C., A. L. Harvey, and O. E. Kolari. 1961. Wintering steer calves on regular corn silage, high-cut corn silage or forage sorghum silage. Minn. Beef Cattle Feeders Day Rept. B-30.

58. Henderson, Hugh E., H. W. Newland, J. I. Sprague, J. W. Comstock, E. J. Benne, and W. K. Brown. 1961. High-energy corn silage for fattening beef heifer calves. Mich. Cattle Feeders Day Rept. AH-64.

59. Newland, H. W., C. G. Silvernail, and C. M. Hansen. 1962. Effects of adding various levels of shelled corn to topped (butts and ears) corn silage for fattening heifers. Mich. Cattle Feeders Day Rept. AH-76.

60. Newland, H. W., W. K. Brown, R. J. Deans, C. M. Hansen, and J. W. Comstock. 1963. Center-cut corn silage, a complete energy feed. Mich. Cattle Feeders Day Rept. AH-90.

61. Klosterman, Earle W., Ronald R. Johnson, K. E. McClure, and V. R. Cahill. 1964. Feeding value of a complete corn silage for growing-fattening cattle. Ohio Cattle Feeders Day Rept., p. 7.

62. Newland, H. W., and H. E. Henderson. 1966. The effect of melengestrol acetate and stilbestrol on finishing yearling heifers fed regular and high-energy corn silage. Mich. Cattle Feeders Day Rept. AH-BC-654.

TABLE 52.7 ❧ Dry matter and crude protein contents and digestibilities of forage sorghum silages at three stages of maturity

Cultivar and stage of maturity	Dry matter content (%)	Crude protein content (% dry matter)	Digestibility* (%) Dry matter	Digestibility* (%) Crude protein
Atlas				
Milk	23.1	7.75	61.4	11.4
Soft-dough	25.0	9.32	55.8	15.7
Hard-dough	28.2	6.63	52.1	2.2
Rox				
Milk	23.4	9.91	66.6	22.1
Soft-dough	27.7	8.92	67.1	20.8
Hard-dough	29.9	9.26	65.8	33.4

Source: Owen and Kuhlman, 1967.[50]
* Determined by difference.

Useful data are available for predicting the energy value of various portions and combinations of the corn plant.[63] The tops (above the ear), ears, and butts (below the ear) comprised 16, 54, and 30% of the plant dry matter respectively. Data show TDN values (dry matter basis) of 63.2–69.5% for whole-plant silage, 53.5% for dried corn tops, 64.4% for dried butts, 73.4–83.7% for ear corn silage, 73.3% for butts and ears silage, and 58.8–59.1% for cornstalk silage.[63] Corn-grain dry matter contains about 91% TDN.[2] Thus, using these values, the TDN value of various combinations of the corn plant can be calculated. Since corn tops contain less TDN than ears or butts, a higher energy silage would result if this portion of the plant was discarded during harvest.

❧ GROWING-FINISHING RATIONS

The influence of feeding various levels of corn silage and sorghum silage on feedlot performance and carcass characteristics of cattle fed growing or finishing rations has been widely researched.[64-71] Based on these

FIG. 52.2. Corn silage . . . can be fed in a variety of rations . . . several systems. Mechanized feeding of high-energy silage. Purdue Univ. photo.

studies, the following statements appear warranted:

1. Conclusions as to the influence of various levels of silage on costs and returns are greatly dependent on the dry matter content of the silage unless it is priced on a dry matter basis. For example, silage at 30% dry matter and priced at $0.90/100 kg is the same as 40% dry matter silage priced at $1.20/100 kg. Thus both of these silages are priced at $3/100 kg of dry matter. Cattle fed dry silage (40% dry matter) with charges of $0.90/100 kg for the

Judge, and W. M. Beeson. 1964. Calves vs. yearling steers fed on low- and high-corn silage rations. Purdue Cattle Feeders Day Rept.
66. Hammes, R. C., Jr., J. P. Fontenot, H. T. Bryant, R. E. Blaser, and R. W. Engel. 1964. Value of high-silage rations for fattening beef cattle. J. Anim. Sci. 23:795.
67. Newland, H. W., and H. E. Henderson. 1966. The relationship of concentrate level and feeder grade to production factors and carcass characteristics. Mich. Cattle Feeders Day Rept. AH-BC-655.
68. King, H. R., L. B. Embry, R. J. Emerick, and L. J. Nygaard. 1964. Performance of cattle fed various levels of corn silage with and without vitamin A and vitamin D supplements. S. Dak. Cattle Feeders Day Rept., p. 8.
69. Smith, E. F., G. M. Ward, D. Richardson, and H. B. Perry. 1966. The value of grain added to sorghum silage at ensiling. Kans. Cattle Feeders Day Rept., p. 19.
70. Vetter, R. L., and W. F. Wedin. 1967. Feedlot performance of steers fed forage sorghum silage. Iowa State Univ. A.S. Leaflet R-99.
71. Brethour, John R., Donald G. Ely, and W. W. Duitsman. 1969. Modifying forage sorghum silage by adding rolled sorghum grain, rolled wheat and/or cottonseed meal. Kans. State Univ. Bull. 528, p. 6.

63. Newland, H. W. 1963. "Complete energy" corn silage—A new approach for the cattle feeder. Mich. Cattle Feeders Day Rept. AH-89.
64. Miller, K. P., E. C. Frederick, R. D. Goodrich, and J. C. Meiske. 1970. Rations containing various levels of corn silage and corn grain for growing-finishing Holstein steers. Minn. Beef Cattle Feeders Day Rept. B-140.
65. Perry, T. W., Donald Webb, C. H. Nickel, M. D.

silage will be likely to have low feed costs. The method of pricing may explain many of the differences among trials as to the influence of amounts of silage on feed costs and returns.

2. The dry matter content of silage greatly influences the proportion of the total ration dry matter supplied by silage. For example, cattle fed 10, 15, or 20 kg of 30% dry matter silage are fed 2, 4.5, or 6 kg of silage dry matter. Similar levels of 40% dry matter silage supply 4, 6, and 8 kg of silage dry matter. Thus results of trials using 20 kg of 30% dry matter silage may be similar to results when 15 kg of 40% dry matter silage are used. In many studies designed to determine the influence of silage level on performance, dry matter contents of the feeds were not reported. Thus it is impossible to make a valid comparison of the results of such studies.

3. Silage is difficult to price correctly because there are no market quotations for it. The price assigned to silage has a great influence on returns. Obviously, studies comparing silage levels and using underpriced silage (relative to the grain price used) have shown undue advantage for the high-silage rations. Likewise, using overpriced silage (relative to the grain price) unduly penalizes the high-silage rations.

4. Nonfeed costs (labor, interest on cattle and feed, bedding, and electricity) should be included in the economic evaluation of rations. The feeding of rations that result in slow rates of gain causes an increase in the nonfeed costs.

5. Amounts of feed (or TDN) and beef produced per ha are greater when corn or sorghum are harvested as silage than when only the grain is removed from the field. However, beef production per ha is not the only (and possibly not the best) measure of profit. And it may not apply equally well to all levels of silage feeding since it is a land statistic and not one which describes the returns from the cattle feed-

ing operation. A farmer's net farm income will be maximized if he maximizes returns per ha plus returns from the cattle-feeding enterprise. Thus, the level of corn silage feeding that maximizes returns from the land plus the feedlot will be a compromise between the level of feeding that maximizes use of the corn crop as silage and the level that results in maximum profits from the feedlot. The number of cattle fed in relation to the total ha of corn will also influence the percentage of the corn crop that can be profitably harvested as silage. Farmers that feed cattle continuously will often find it desirable to feed less silage than farmers that feed one group per year.

❧ SYSTEMS FOR FEEDING CORN SILAGE TO BEEF CATTLE

Corn silage is versatile and can be fed in a variety of rations and by several systems. (See Fig. 52.2) Programs for use of corn silage can be designed so that amounts of corn silage vary, grain is fed at various rates, or set ratios of grain and corn silage are fed. However, once a cattle feeder decides on the amount of corn to be harvested as silage, the amount of corn silage to be fed is set for a given number of cattle. A farmer's first decision is the amount of corn silage he will feed. He then has several options for systems in which equal amounts of corn silage are offered during the feeding period.

Some feedlot operators feed complete mixed rations. As daily intake increases, animals consume more of each feed making up the ration. When silage is fed by this method, the amount consumed daily increases as the cattle consume more feed, even though the silage remains at a constant percent of the ration.

Research conducted at Minnesota has indicated that differences in gain and efficiency of cattle fed in different programs might exist.[72] However, in those trials equal amounts of corn silage were not fed

72. Meiske, J. C., and R. D. Goodrich. 1967. **Corn silage** for finishing cattle. *Minn. Sci.* 23 (2):5.

TABLE 52.8 ❧ Comparison of four methods of feeding approximately equal total amounts of corn silage

Item	Constant amount	Two-phase	Gradually decreasing	Gradually increasing
Treatment number	1	2	3	4
Number of steers	20	21	20	21
Initial weight (kg)	213	211	214	213
Final weight (kg)	475	474	473	459
Average daily gain (kg)*	1.10	1.11	1.09	1.04
Average daily feed (kg dry matter)				
Corn silage	3.03	2.96	2.97	3.05
Corn grain	4.69	4.24	4.33	4.57
Supplement	0.41	0.41	0.41	0.41
Total†	8.13	7.61	7.71	8.03
Feed/100 kg gain (kg dry matter)				
Corn silage	275	268	274	293
Corn grain	426	383	298	440
Supplement	37	37	38	40
Total‡	738	688	710	773

Source: Dexheimer et al., 1971.[74]
* Significant differences: 1, 2 and 3 > 4 (P < .05).
† Significant differences: 1 > 2 and 3 (P < .01); 4 > 2 (P < .01) and 3 (P < .05).
‡ Significant differences: 4 > 2 (P < .01) and 3 (P < .05); 1 > 2 (P < .05).

in all programs. It has been suggested that following a two-phase program of feeding (an initial high rate of forage feeding followed by a high rate of concentrate feeding) may be beneficial. In addition, feeding corn silage during the first part of the growing-finishing period followed by an ear-corn finishing ration resulted in faster gains than the reverse of this system.[73]

The effects of feeding approximately equal amounts of corn silage in four pro-

73. Embry, L. B. 1967. Varying concentrate to roughage ratio for beef cattle. Proc. Minn. Nutr. Conf. 28:122.

SUPPLEMENTAL INFORMATION

Recent work from the Minnesota station[75] on corn silage levels for steer calves showed that gains declined and amounts of feed per unit of

75. Goodrich, R. D., and J. C. Meiske. 1976. Corn silage: Influence of amounts, feeding systems and drought-damage on feedlot performance. Minn. Cattle Feeders Day Rept. B-219.

grams are presented in Table 52.8.[74] Cattle fed corn silage in the constant amount, two-phase, or gradually decreasing programs gained more rapidly than cattle in the gradually increasing program. Amounts of dry matter required for 100 kg of gain were significantly greater for cattle fed in the gradually increasing program than for cattle fed in the two-phase or gradually decreasing programs. Much of the advantage in feed conversion efficiency for cattle fed in the two-phase or gradually decreasing programs can be explained by the initial slower rates of gain, the resulting smaller average weight during the trial, and the overall high rates of gain. Thus on the average, a smaller amount of feed was used daily for maintenance when the cattle were fed for slower gains early in the feeding program.

74. Dexheimer, C. E., J. C. Meiske, and R. D. Goodrich. 1971. A comparison of four systems for feeding corn silage. Minn. Beef Cattle Feeders Day Rept. B-151.

❧ QUESTIONS

1. Why are corn and sorghum silages popular feeds?
2. Compare the composition of corn and grain sorghum silages with the requirements for growing steer calves.
3. List the nutritional and management factors that should be followed when NPN is included in silage rations.
4. Compare the advantages and disadvantages of adding NPN to silages at ensiling time or at feeding time.
5. Discuss the factors that must be considered when deciding on corn or sorghum as silage crops.
6. Describe how dry matter yields, protein contents, dry matter digestibilities, and feed intakes are influenced by plant maturity.
7. How should the proper level of silage feeding be determined?

gain increased as silage level increased. This work suggested that rations high in corn grain should be fed when corn grain prices are less than $2.13 per bushel ($8.39 per 100 kg), and that rations high in corn silage should be fed when corn grain prices are higher than $2.13 per bushel.

R. E. BLASER, D. D. WOLF, AND H. T. BRYANT
Virginia Polytechnic Institute and State University

53

SYSTEMS OF GRAZING MANAGEMENT

❧

SIMPLE, low-cost, nutritious, and dependable 12-month forage systems of feeding for the various soil and environmental areas are necessary to operate different kinds of profitable livestock operations. To the extent practical, animals must "forage" for themselves to minimize harvesting and refeeding costs and pollution.

Ruminants require large amounts of feed because of inefficient conversion of feedstuffs into meat and milk. For example, steers gaining 0.6 kg daily eat about 7 kg of dry forage, a conversion efficiency of 9% (but only 5% when based on carcass weight per dry matter consumed).[1] Thus feed makes up around 50 and 70% of the cost of producing meat and milk, respectively.

Forage must be consumed and converted to animal products to be of value. Light grazing pressures elevate output per animal but depress animal products per land area because much pasturage is left ungrazed and wasted. Maximum production per animal and per land area cannot be obtained concurrently. (See Chapter 12.) Thus efficient forage utilization for animal products demands wise compromises between production per animal and land unit. Efficient livestock production embodies complex soil-biotic-climatic ecosystems; maximum economic returns should be realized while maintaining environmental quality.[2-4]

❧ UTILIZATION PROBLEMS

SEASONAL DISTRIBUTION

Uneven seasonal growth of perennial grasses and legumes, a universal problem

❧ ROY E. BLASER is Professor of Agronomy, Virginia Polytechnic Institute and State University. He studied at the universities of Nebraska, Rutgers, and North Carolina State. He is involved in research in forage crops ecology and as an agricultural consultant abroad.

❧ DALE D. WOLF is Associate Professor of Agronomy, Virginia Polytechnic Institute and State University. He studied at the universities of Nebraska and Wisconsin. His research emphasizes interrelating microenvironmental factors to plant growth and composition.

❧ HARRY T. BRYANT is Associate Professor of Agronomy, Virginia Polytechnic Institute and State University. He studied at the universities of Maine and Wisconsin. His research specializes in maximizing grass and legume production.

1. Blaser, R. E., H. T. Bryant, R. C. Hammes, Jr., R. Boman, J. P. Fontenot, and C. E. Polan. 1969. Managing forages for animal production. Va. Polytechnic Inst. and State Univ. Res. Bull. 45.
2. Cunningham Laboratory Staff. 1964. Some concepts and methods in subtropical pasture research. CSIRO, Bull. 47, Brisbane, Aust.
3. Donald, C. M. 1963. Competition among crop and pasture plants. *Advan. Agron.* 15:1–114.
4. Blaser, R. E., W. H. Skrdla, and T. H. Taylor. 1952. Ecological and physiological factors in compounding seed mixtures. *Advan. Agron.* 4:179–218.

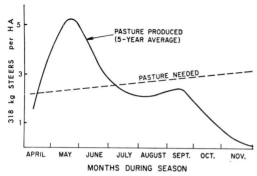

FIG. 53.1. Solid curve is pasture produced for 318-kg steers/ha each month at Middleburg, Va. These are averages for orchardgrass–ladino clover and Kentucky bluegrass–white clover pastures. Dotted line shows seasonal increased feed needs because of weight increases of steers or calves grazing pastures. (Blaser et al., 1969.[1])

TABLE 53.1 ❧ Stages of maturity as related to composition and feeding value of perennial grasses and legumes in Virginia

Item	Pasture	Hay or silage	
		Bud or heading	Full bloom
Leaf/stem ratio	high	medium	low
Water content	high	medium	low
Minerals and vitamins	high	medium	low
Fiber and lignin	low	medium	high
Palatability	high	medium	low
TDN content	65–75%	55–65%	45–55%
Crude protein content	22–34%	10–22%	6–15%
Kind of supplements required	energy or none	energy	energy and protein

Source: Blaser, 1964.[5]

with tropical and temperate plants in all areas of the world, is caused by single or interacting factors that restrict plant growth (temperature, light, moisture, soil fertility, and pests). Variable seasonal animal-carrying capacities of Kentucky bluegrass–clover pastures in the mid-Atlantic region are shown in Figure 53.1. Note that with seasonal advance, feed needs of cow-calf herds or fattening cattle increase as animals grow, but pasture production declines. Lack of winter growth is often a problem, even in warm latitudes.

UTILIZABLE ENERGY

Good performance from animals fed herbaceous annuals and perennials (pasture, hay, or silage) is strongly allied with a leafy morphology best characterized by stage of maturity and usually by age of regrowth (Table 53.1).[5] Well-managed temperate perennials are usually good in nutritive value but low in utilizable energy (intake and/or digestibility), causing suboptimum performance of high-producing animals. Grazing methods and differences in grazing pressures with species, mixtures, and fertilization gave sharp differences in output per animal varying from good to poor. How-

5. Blaser, R. E. 1964. Effects of fertility levels and stage of maturity on forage nutritive value. *J. Anim. Sci.* 23:246–53.

ever, supplementing ground shelled corn for additional energy invariably stimulated gains of growing and fattening cattle or milk per cow. Energy supplements also improved outputs of high-producing animals fed the best quality of perennial hays and silage crops; perennials are of excellent nutritional value for high animal performance when properly supplemented with energy.[1] The nutritional status of well-managed perennial grass-legume mixtures is generally higher than necessary for cow herds and ewes, offering a challenge for improved efficiency in raising calves and lambs with the use of forage systems.

Corn silage (hard dent stage) and certain summer annuals (early leafy stages) are high-energy feeds stimulating near maximum milk or meat production per animal.[1]

❧ FORAGE MANAGEMENT CONCEPTS

Interacting grazing and conservation forage management principles are: (1) maintain the species or mixed plant association and botanical balance; (2) encourage rapid regrowth during and/or after grazing or cutting; (3) make wise compromises between yield and quality; and (4) minimize the need for mowing, weed control, or other costly operations.

Maximum yields and quality of peren-

TABLE 53.2 ❧ Calculated yield of TDN and digestible protein from alfalfa cut at four stages of maturity in California

Item	Prebud	Bud	1/10 bloom	1/2 bloom
Seasonal yield (kg/ha)	13,260	16,430	19,130	19,260
TDN (%)	66.1	60.4	57.2	54.7
TDN yield (kg/ha)	8,765	9,926	10,940	10,533
Protein yield (kg/ha)	3,542	3,908	3,947	3,652
Protein digestion coefficient (%)	78.8	74.6	72.8	70.3
Digestible protein (kg/ha)	2,791	2,916	2,873	2,567

Source: Weir et al., 1960.[6]

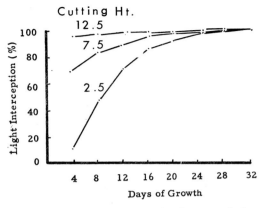

FIG. 53.2. Percentage of light intercepted by perennial ryegrass at 2.5 cm above the soil when cut to leave three sod residue heights (cm). (Brougham, 1956.[7])

nial grasses and legumes cannot be obtained simultaneously (Table 53.2).[6] Cutting alfalfa in a leafy prebud stage gave the highest digestibility and percent of crude protein, but yields of dry matter, protein, and total digestible nutrients (TDN) were low compared with cuttings made at a 0.1 bloom stage. However, with Kentucky bluegrass–white clover pastures highly digestible herbage with heavy grazing can be obtained over prolonged periods, but the principle of depressed yields with maximized quality still applies. Achieving maximum dry matter yields depresses quality. Yield versus quality compromises should be allied with the specific nutritional needs and realistic goals of animal production.

Important concepts that determine management and use of forage plants are the leaf area index (LAI), the amount of total nonstructural carbohydrates (TNC), and their interplay as related to regrowth of old shoots and generation of new ones. Manipulation of these factors is associated with morphological characteristics concurrent with making desirable compromises between yield and quality of herbage, botanical composition, and persistence.

LEAF AREA INDEX

A unit leaf area (one side of leaf) per unit of soil area is an LAI of 1. The rate of regrowth after defoliation is associated with LAI values and light interception.[7] When perennial ryegrass was cut to 2.5-, 7.5-, and 12.5-cm stubble heights, the 12.5-cm stubble intercepted nearly 100% of the light, giving maximum daily regrowth right after cutting. With a 2.5-cm stubble, maximum daily regrowth was reached 24 days later when light interception was also high (Figs. 53.2, 53.3). When regrowth

7. Brougham, R. W. 1956. Effect of intensity of defoliation on regrowth of pasture. *Aust. J. Agr. Res.* 7:377–87.

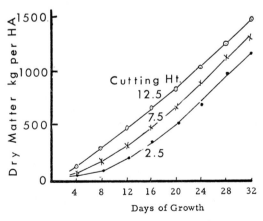

FIG. 53.3. Dry matter accumulation in kilograms per ha after cutting to three stubble heights (cm). (Brougham, 1956.[7])

6. Weir, W. C., L. C. Jones, and J. H. Meyer. 1960. Effect of cutting interval and stage of maturity on the digestibility and yield of alfalfa. *J. Anim. Sci.* 19:5–19.

reached LAI values of about 5, around 95% of the light was intercepted.

Research shows that light interception varies with LAI during seasons within species, and maximum regrowth occurs with less than 95% light interception.[8] Also, there is not an optimum LAI, as maximum regrowth within species plateaus under wide LAI ranges. After reaching nearly complete light interception for dense canopies, the inner leaves photosynthesize progressively less because of shading as the LAI increases. The LAI values for fast regrowth vary within and between species and mixtures, and with season. Leaving a high LAI after grazing is impractical, as yield and new shoot development may be depressed. However, the LAI concept is meaningful since rate of regrowth is associated with high light interception.

Leguminous plants with nearly horizontal leaves require a much lower LAI for high light interception than erectly growing grasses.[8] Erect or semierect leaves allow much light penetration, thus more LAI units in such canopies are photosynthetically active as compared with horizontal leaves.[8,9] Canopy accumulation causes severe leaf losses, depressions in specific leaf weights and photosynthesis of lower leaves, and also reduces forage quality.[1,10-12]

Nonstructural Carbohydrates

Formation of new plant tissue depends on new photosynthates from the present or developing LAI and TNC reserves in basal plant tissues. The TNC is of primary importance for perennial plant survival during dormancy (temperature and moisture stresses) and for reinitiating growth after dormancy or severe defoliation from utili-

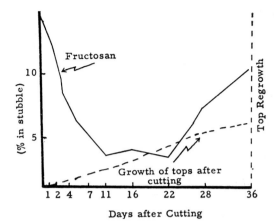

FIG. 53.4. Percent fructosan in ryegrass stubble as related to top growth at different intervals after cutting. (Sullivan and Sprague, 1943.[13])

zation. As the LAI increases, the TNC is usually stored in basal tissues of perennial forages when photosynthesis exceeds respiration. After severe defoliation by cutting or grazing, when respiration for regrowth exceeds photosynthesis, energy for regrowth comes from the TNC. Note the sharp changes in fructosan (similar to starch) utilization and accumulation in ryegrass stubble after cutting and during regrowth (Fig. 53.4).[13] Fructosan made up about 15% of the stubble dry weight at cutting when the LAI was high. During early regrowth (active root and top growth) the fructosan declines to 3% by 11 days after cutting. As the LAI increases, stubble fructosan increases to about 10% of the dry matter 36 days after cutting. Research with other erect perennial forage plants that are easily defoliated show similar cycles of low to high TNC in basal plant tissues resulting from canopy removal and regrowth.[14-17]

8. Brown, R. H., and R. E. Blaser. 1968. Leaf area index in pasture growth. *Herb. Abstr.* 38:1–8.
9. Pierce, R. B., R. H. Brown, and R. E. Blaser. 1967. Photosynthesis in plant communities as influenced by leaf angle. *Crop Sci.* 7:321–24.
10. Wolf, D. D., and R. E. Blaser. 1972. Growth rate and physiology of alfalfa as influenced by canopy and light. *Crop Sci.* 12:23–25.
11. Brown, R. H., R. B. Cooper, and R. E. Blaser. 1966. Effect of leaf age on efficiency. *Crop Sci.* 6:206–9.
12. Fuess, F. W., and M. B. Tesar. 1968. Photosynthesis efficiency, yields and leaf loss in alfalfa. *Crop Sci.* 8:159–63.

13. Sullivan, J. T., and V. G. Sprague. 1943. Composition of roots and stubble of perennial ryegrass following partial defoliation. *Plant Physiol.* 18:656–70.
14. Sprague, V. G., and J. T. Sullivan. 1950. Reserve carbohydrates in orchardgrass clipped periodically. *Plant Physiol.* 25:94–102.
15. Smith, Dale, and L. F. Graber. 1948. The influence of top growth removal on the root and vegetative development of biennial sweet clover. *J. Amer. Soc. Agron.* 40:818–31.
16. Moran, C. H., V. G. Sprague, and J. T. Sullivan. 1953. Changes in the carbohydrate reserves of ladino clover following defoliation. *Plant Physiol.* 28:467–74.
17. Graber, L. F., N. T. Nelson, W. A. Leukel, and W. B. Albert. 1927. Organic food reserves in relation to growth of alfalfa and other perennial herbaceous plants. Wis. Agr. Exp. Sta. Res. Bull. 80.

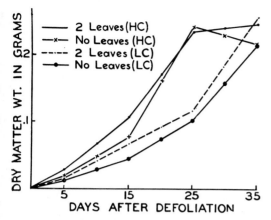

FIG. 53.5. Dry matter increase of apex blades on orchardgrass tillers was influenced by leaf area and low carbohydrate (LC) and high carbohydrate (HC) reserves in the stubble. (Ward and Blaser, 1961.[18])

TILLERING

Fast plant regrowth depends on a dense population of active shoots where light interception is high soon after harvesting or grazing.[3] Accumulating canopies for prolonged periods often deters shoot development and regrowth because of very low light intensity at the stubble base. Conversely, judicious continuous grazing of some species allows light penetration into basal canopies to maintain dense populations of active shoots. For species with determinate growth the regeneration of basal tillers is not as important as for those with indeterminate growth.

THE LAI, TNC, AND TILLERING AS RELATED TO ANIMAL PRODUCTION

During favorable environments the regrowth of orchardgrass is allied with the combined influences of the LAI and TNC (Figs. 53.5, 53.6).[18] Individual orchardgrass tillers had high TNC contents when placed in full light or in darkness for 60 hours. Tillers low and high in TNC with zero and two leaf blades were obtained by cutting blades just above the collar and 5.5

18. Ward, C. Y., and R. E. Blaser. 1961. Carbohydrate food reserves and leaf area in regrowth of orchardgrass. *Crop Sci.* 1:366–70.

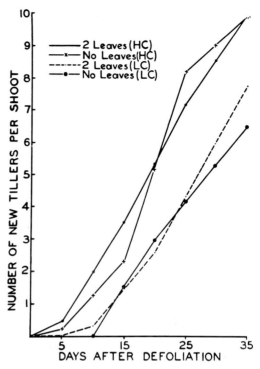

FIG. 53.6. Increase in tillering of orchardgrass was influenced by leaf areas and low carbohydrate (LC) and high carbohydrate (HC) reserves in the stubble. (Ward and Blaser, 1961.[18])

cm above it. Apex blades that had been clipped just above the tiller apex made fastest regrowth from the high TNC tillers, but leaves improved the regrowth of apex blades on low and high TNC tillers. New tillering was most rapid on old original tillers high in TNC; leaf area had little effect (Fig. 53.6). However, regrowth of new tillers was stimulated by leaf areas and TNC in original tillers.[18]

These concepts suggest forage management practices. Grazing and cutting management are related to morphological and physiological interplays as interrelated to regrowth, botanical composition, plant survival, and animal production. Continuous grazing is practical for small semiprostrate species or the taller semiprostrate species where stubble residues have reasonably high LAI's for light interception and insulation against soil temperature increases. Also, species that maintain a strong determinate growth may be grazed continuously by allowing considerable canopy accumulation. Grazing management that allows reseeding is important for annuals. Conversely, tall erect perennial plants that are easily defoliated under continuous grazing require intermittent rest after grazing. When rotation grazing is used, the management of each perennial species or mixture should take into consideration the length of the rest period based on stage of maturity or height of canopy and the quality of forage needed for specific animals, and the height of stubble residue when withdrawing grazing animals or cutting. The LAI and TNC of stubbles should favor fast regrowth. Best regrowths are obtainable when grazing periods are short (three to eight days) since this provides the best control of stubble residues for desirable LAI and TNC.

For example, accumulating tall fescue–ladino clover canopies for prolonged periods advances the growth stage to deter quality, causing wastage when grazing (fouling and lying on the canopy), which also depresses clover and basal tillering due to light competition and disease. Very close grazing of accumulated tall fescue–ladino clover canopies (15–20 cm high) to a low LAI depresses regrowth and animal output (excessive grazing pressure) and nullifies potentially beneficial effects from rotational grazing. For good animal gains tall fescue canopies should be grazed in a young leafy condition (12–16 cm) to improve intake.

Rotational grazing (when considering light competition among species associations in accumulating canopies) is a tool for controlling the botanical components. For example, when accumulating an orchardgrass–ladino clover canopy 18 cm in height, short and tall ungrazed residues will shift the sod to more clover or more grass respectively. A 2-cm stubble residue would depress orchardgrass regrowth because ruminants consumed most of the LAI and much of the TNC in the stubble; the slow grass regrowth would favor clover. Conversely, leaving a tall 6–10 cm ungrazed residue would depress clover since grass with a high LAI would grow rapidly, causing severe light competition for new ladino clover leaves arising from stolon buds at the soil level. In alfalfa mixtures short stubble residues favor alfalfa because of reduced competition due to slow orchardgrass recovery; close grazing would reduce the light competition from grass, thereby favoring the new alfalfa shoots arising from axillary buds near or below the soil surface. Prolonged grazing of alfalfa without allowing rest, where successions of new shoots are grazed, depresses TNC and alfalfa persistence.

The interval allowed for canopy accumulation varies with environmental conditions (growth rates) and with species in mixtures (Table 53.3). Also, with prolonged or massive canopy accumulations the prolonged low light intensity brings about severe leaf losses, often destroys tillering, and causes slow regrowth.

Because rotational grazing management is allied with morphological characteristics and physiological responses of plants coupled with the effects of grazing pressure on animal performance, the scheduling of grazing and regrowth periods on a date basis can seriously harm plants (canopy accumulation and stubble residue uncontrolled). Likewise, ruminants may either starve or have excess pasturage. Rest and grazing periods arranged by dates would be tenable if rate of growth and rate of consumption both remained constant (Fig. 53.1).

Plants are adaptive so that ideal management at all times is unnecessary. During dormancies (low and high temperatures or moisture stresses) accumulated canopies of plants like alfalfa may be grazed continuously in the absence of new shoot development since TNC is not depressed. During late winter or early spring when shoot development is slow, continuous grazing of hay and pasture mixtures is desirable. Enlarged grazing areas reduce grazing pressures for high animal outputs, making it

TABLE 53.3 ❧ Guide for utilizing perennial forages differing in morphology to compromise between leaf area and nonstructural carbohydrates

Species or mixture	Continuous grazing		Rotational grazing or for conservation	
	Season	Residue (cm)	Height (cm)	Stubble residue (cm)
Kentucky bluegrass–white clover	all year	1–8	10–15	2
Orchardgrass–ladino clover	spring	4–10	17–25	5
Tall fescue–ladino clover	spring	2–8	15–20	4
Tall fescue	all year	2–8	15–20	4
Alfalfa	when dormant		*	†
Alfalfa-orchardgrass	when dormant		*	±6
Bermudagrass	all season	1–8	12–20	2–5
Bahiagrass	all season	1–8	. . .	. . .
Dallisgrass–white clover	all season	1–8	12–15	2–4
'Pangola' digitgrass	all season	4–15	17–25	2–4

* Bud to 0.1 bloom.
† Not significant.

possible to start earlier grazing without sacrificing animal gains. Later, as surplus herbage accumulates, the grazing areas should be restricted to supply grazing needs and conserve feed for winter. Placing animals in small paddocks for rotational grazing when there is little pasture depresses animal outputs as compared with the grazing of larger areas continuously.

Continuous grazing with judicious grazing pressures on mixtures like orchardgrass–ladino clover is practical for several spring months. Fast-growing, highly digestible, and palatable pasturage minimizes severe overgrazing and undergrazing. Later, as animal excreta accumulate and growth declines, sod residues and stages of growth can be better controlled with rotational grazing.

❧ FORAGE UTILIZATION METHODS

Methods of utilizing forages for animal feeds are associated with size of canopies, morphology, quality, stand longevity, and botanical composition. Utilization may be flexible combinations of hay, silage, and grazing. Larger, erect, easily defoliated species are best suited for rotational grazing and conservation when yields justify machine harvesting. Short semiprostrate species are ideal for continuous grazing. Additional production obtainable with ro-

tational grazing does not usually justify added expenses for fencing, water, and shade unless grazing pressures are high.

Utilization methods may be classified as follows:

1. Grazing.
   a. Continuous.
   b. Rotational, accumulation, and grazing of canopies.
      1. Ordinary—one group of animals.
      2. Two animal groups—first and last grazers.
      3. Forward creep-grazing.
      4. Strip or ration grazing.
      5. Stockpiling—canopies accumulated for periods of sparse growth or none.
2. Green chop—chopped and fed green.
3. Hay or silage conservation.

PRODUCTION PER ANIMAL

If grazing pressure (forage available per animal) and stage of growth are controlled with utilization methods, output per animal will be similar. Young leafy growth, high in energy and consumed in large amounts, stimulates output per animal. With light grazing pressures (much forage per animal, selective grazing, and wasted pasturage) animals select plant parts high in digestibility and protein and low in fiber and they consume more dry matter.[1,19] Light grazing pressures stimulate daily utilizable energy (amount ingested and digested) and protein intake. The reverse occurs with high grazing pressures. Uncontrolled grazing pressures for many pasture experiments are confusing; pastures with the lightest grazing pressure give the best production per animal but depress animal products per ha.

Effects of changing grazing pressures on output per animal can be characterized and diagnosed during rotational grazing in one pasture. When ruminants consume an accumulated canopy during several days in a pasture, the grazing pressure shifts from very light to high, while grazable herbage per animal decreases as the pasturage is consumed. The change of nutrition from high to low while grazing in one pasture has a sharp influence on daily milk production per cow (Fig. 53.7).[1,19,20] The sharp increase in milk per cow about a day after entering a fresh pasture is attributed to the immediate high utilizable energy available when a fresh pasture is grazed; the delay in milk response is attributed to time needed for the previously consumed low-energy materials to pass through the rumen. Sharp undulations in milk flow from within a rotationally grazed pasture are very closely allied with changing low grazing pressures to high ones and with concurrent changes in digestibility and intake of ingested pasturage.

High selective grazing occurring with low grazing pressures on output per animal was measured with two animal groups in rotational grazing: the first grazers had consumed about half the grazable pasturage when the last group was introduced to consume the rest of the grazable herbage. The first-grazing cows produced much more milk daily than the last grazers and about

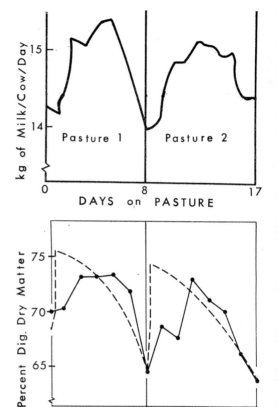

FIG. 53.7. Daily milk fluctuations (kilograms per cow) with rotational grazing (above). The high production soon after cows are turned into a fresh pasture is attributed to selective grazing. Selective grazing is limited toward the end of a grazing period.

Dry matter digestibility of ingested orchardgrass pasturage with rotational grazing (below). High dry matter digestibility is associated with high-energy value. Lag in digestibilities after moving to a fresh pasture occurred because of fecal carryover. Dotted lines are estimations of digestibility changes as pasture was consumed. (Blaser et al., 1969;[1] 1960.[19]) (Data were obtained by the Chromogen technique. Reid et al., 1950.[20])

19. Blaser, R. E., R. C. Hammes, Jr., H. T. Bryant, W. A. Hardison, J. P. Fontenot, and R. W. Engel. 1960. The effect of selective grazing on animal output. Proc. 8th Int. Grassl. Congr., pp. 601–6 (Reading, England).

20. Reid, T. J., P. G. Woolfolk, C. R. Richards, R. W. Kaufman, J. K. Loosli, K. L. Turk, J. I. Miller, and R. E. Blaser. 1950. A new indicator method for determination of digestibility and consumption of forages by ruminants. J. Dairy Sci. 33:60–71.

twice as much milk per cow during the last 14 days (Table 53.4).[1,19] Daily liveweight gains of first-grazing steers were consistently higher than for last grazers for each pasture species or mixture (Table 53.5).[1,19] Mean relative gains per steer for two years for the grazing methods were: 100, ordinary rotational grazing with one animal group; 118, first grazers; and 79, last grazers. High

TABLE 53.4 ❧ Effects of rotational grazing with first and then last grazers for two mixtures on milk production, Virginia

	First grazers		Last grazers	
Feeding period	Grain*	No grain	Grain*	No grain
Standardization period: all cows fed 16% protein feed at the rate of 17% milk weight for a 28-day winter feeding period before experiment started				
4% milk per cow daily during this period (kg)	19.3	18.7	19.5	19.2
Cows then grazed orchardgrass–ladino clover pasture for 49 days				
Milk daily (kg)	20.1	19.5	18.1	13.8
Relative to standardization period (%)	104.0	104.0	93.0	72.0
Cows then grazed alfalfa-orchardgrass mixture for 70 days				
Milk daily (kg)	18.0	14.7	15.3	9.9
Relative to standardization period (%)	93.0	79.0	79.0	52.0
Milk daily for last 14 days (kg)	15.6	12.5	11.4	6.4
Relative to standardization period (%)	81.0	67.0	58.0	36.0

Sources: Blaser et al., 1969;[1] Blaser et al., 1960.[19]
* Ground shelled corn fed at rate of 2.3 kg/day/cow for the season.

gains of first grazers are associated with selection of plant parts high in energy and protein and low in fiber (Table 53.6, Fig. 53.7) and with high utilizable energy.[1,20]

Gains averaged for the first and last grazers were similar to the daily gains for ordinary rotational grazing (Table 53.5). Nearly identical grazing pressures were shown by available forage. Also, liveweight gains per ha were not increased by using two animal groups. In practice two animal groups are used when high output per animal is wanted for first grazers. First grazers could be the high-producing milk cows, steers, or calves where fast gains are desired. Different animal species could be used for first and last grazers. Forward creep-grazing,[21] where calves or lambs graze ahead of the dams or ewes, is an adaptation of selective grazing for high output per animal.

Ungrazed residues and stages of growth with rotational grazing methodology are

21. Whitehouse, A. W. 1956. Rotational forward creep-grazing. *Agriculture* (UK) 56 (8):354.

TABLE 53.5 ❧ Daily liveweight steer gains with two methods of rotational grazing in Virginia

Pasture mixtures	First grazers (kg)	Last grazers (kg)	Average (kg)	Ordinary rotational grazing, one group of steers (kg)
Orchardgrass (N, 91 kg/ha)	0.56	0.36	0.46	0.44
Tall fescue (N, 91 kg/ha)	0.50	0.34	0.42	0.44
Orchardgrass–ladino clover	0.69	0.52	0.61	0.59
Tall fescue–ladino clover	0.60	0.35	0.47	0.54
Kentucky bluegrass–white clover	0.68	0.45	0.57	0.58
Average	0.60	0.40	0.50	0.51
Relative values	118	79	98	100

Available pasturage (kg/ha) (season average for first four mixtures)				
Before first grazers	After first grazers*	After last grazers	Rotational grazing Before	After
971	517	152	941	157

Sources: Blaser et al., 1969.[1] Blaser et al., 1960.[19]
* Same as before last grazers.

TABLE 53.6 ❧ Selection of low-fiber and high-protein pasturage from three mixtures in Virginia, rotational grazing

Rotational grazing methods	Alfalfa-orchardgrass (%)	White clover–Ky bluegrass (%)	Ladino clover–orchardgrass (%)
Two animal groups	*Crude fiber increases in ungrazed residues as pastures are grazed*		
Before first grazers	25	24	25
Before last grazers*	30	25	26
After last grazers	36	25	28
One animal group			
Before grazing	25	23	25
After grazing	34	26	28
Two animal groups	*Protein declines as pastures are grazed*		
Before first grazers	22	20	19
Before last grazers*	16	18	17
After last grazers	13	17	14
One animal group			
Before grazing	21	19	19
After grazing	14	16	14

Source: Blaser et al., 1969.[1]
* Also same as after first grazers.

strongly allied with per animal outputs. Strip or ration grazing where all pasturage is consumed in one day gives even daily nutrition, but animal output would be similar to rotational grazing. Green-chopping may give lower outputs per animal than rotational grazing because there is no selective grazing; however, younger or older plant maturities than for rotational grazing would increase or decrease output per animal. Also, tall stubble residues as compared to short ones would inflate output per animal with green-chopping since upper canopy growths are higher in leafiness and digestibility than basal parts.[1] Grazing to very short stubbles (high grazing pressure) would depress animal outputs for rotational grazing as compared to green chop. In Wisconsin, milk per cow did not differ for green chop, strip grazing, and hay;[22] in California steer gains for green chop and for rotational and strip grazing were similar;[23] and in Virginia cows on rotational pasture gave more milk than those fed hay.[1]

22. Larsens, H. J., and R. F. Johannes. 1965. Summer forage, stored feeding, green feeding, and strip grazing. Wis. Agr. Exp. Sta. Bull. 257.
23. Ittner, N. R., G. P. Lofgreen, and J. H. Myer. 1954. A study of pasturing and soiling alfalfa with beef steers. J. Anim. Sci. 13:37.

ROTATIONAL VERSUS CONTINUOUS GRAZING

When comparing ordinary rotational (one group of animals) with continuous grazing under similar grazing pressures and forage maturities, the output (milk or meat) per animal did not usually differ significantly (Table 53.7).[24-34] By biasing selective

24. Woodward, T. E., J. B. Shepherd, and M. A. Hein. 1932. The Hohenheim system in the management of permanent pastures for dairy cattle. USDA Tech. Bull. 660.
25. Davis, R. R., and A. D. Pratt. 1956. Rotational vs. continuous grazing with dairy cows. Ohio Agr. Exp. Sta. Res. Bull. 778.
26. Hodgson, R. E., M. S. Grunder, J. K. Knott, and E. V. Ellington. 1934. Comparison of rotational and continuous grazing of pastures in western Washington. Wash. Agr. Exp. Sta. Bull. 294.
27. Bryant, H. T., R. E. Blaser, R. C. Hammes, and W. A. Hardison. 1961. Comparison of continuous and rotational grazing of three forage mixtures. J. Dairy Sci. 44:1733–41.
28. McMeekan, C. P., and M. J. Walshe. 1963. The interrelationships of grazing methods and stocking rates in the efficiency of pasture utilization by dairy cattle. J. Agr. Sci. 61:146–66.
29. Comfort, J. E., and E. Marion Brown. 1933. Systems of pasture utilization. Amer. Soc. Anim. Prod. Proc. 26:74–77.
30. Hubbard, William A. 1951. Rotational grazing studies in western Canada. J. Range Manage. 4:25–29.
31. McIlvain, E. H., and D. A. Savage. 1951. Eight-year comparisons of continuous and rotational grazing on the southern plains experimental range. J. Range Manage. 4:42–47.
32. Blaser, R. E., H. T. Bryant, C. Y. Ward, R. C. Hammes, R. C. Carter, and N. H. MacLeod. 1959. Symposium on forage evaluation. VII. Animal performance and yields with methods of utilizing pasturage. Agron. J. 51:238–42.
33. Hein, M. A., and C. A. Cook. 1937. Effect of method and rate of grazing on beef production of pastures at Beltsville, Maryland. USDA Tech. Bull. 538.

TABLE 53.7 ❧ Animal output from rotationally and continuously grazed pastures

Output	Experiment location	Stocking rate	Rotational grazing (kg)	Continuous grazing (kg)
Milk produced (daily/cow or yearly/cow)	Beltsville, Md.[24] Ohio[25]	varied to graze closely varied, excess with rotational for hay	12.9 14.5	12.0 14.3
	Washington[26] Virginia[27]	fixed and same varied, similar moderate grazing pressure	19.2	17.5
		alfalfa-grass	12.9	12.3
		ladino clover–grass	12.4	10.6
		white clover–trefoil-grass	11.6	11.5
	New Zealand[28]	fixed, both light	4,237	4,054
	New Zealand	fixed, both heavy	3,940	3,408
Liveweight gain (daily/head or yearly/head)	Missouri[29] (heifers)	fixed and same	134	156
	Alberta, Canada[30] (calves)	fixed and same	371	396
	Oklahoma[31] (steers)	fixed, both moderate	331	342
		fixed, both heavy	291	293
	Virginia[32] (lambs)	heavier for rotational	0.17	0.23
	Maryland[33] (steers)	fixed and same	0.57	0.57
	Chile[34] (steers)	varied, both moderate	0.83	0.79

grazing and maturity control, either method can give highest production per animal; however, continuous grazing is likely to give best animal outputs because more selective grazing is inadvertently allowed than for rotational grazing. Continuous grazing is very likely to give higher outputs per animal than rotational grazing during flush growth when pressure is apt to be low for continuous grazing; the short sod residues at the end of rotational grazing in each lot with good utilization depress output per animal. After the flush growth it is common to obtain higher output per animal from rotational than continuous grazing because of better growth-stage control; a more uniform leafy canopy is obtained with rotational grazing. With continuous grazing, extreme overgrazing and undergrazing and wide ranges in forage maturity occur as the season advances. This suggests continuous grazing should be used

during the early season followed by rotational grazing (Fig. 53.8).

ANIMAL PRODUCTS PER LAND AREA

With normal medium grazing pressures for species or mixtures adapted to continuous grazing (Kentucky bluegrass, common white clover, perennial ryegrass, bermudagrass, bahiagrass, dallisgrass, 'Pangola' digitgrass, and tall fescue) animal products per land area for continuous and rotational

34. Ruiz, I., and H. Caballero. 1967. Comparacion del remdimento de una pradera de trebol ladino y ballica englesia utilizando sistems de pastereo rotativo y contino. *Memorial Asociacion Latinamericana de Produccion Animal* 2:91–105.

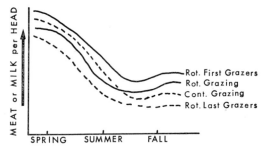

FIG. 53.8. Usual seasonal animal gains with grazing methods associated with changes in selective grazing, grazing pressure, forage quality, and condition of animals.

grazing would be similar. With heavy grazing pressures and judicious canopy management higher outputs per land area may be expected with rotational grazing than for continuous grazing.[28]

With tall species such as alfalfa rotational grazing has given from 42 to 300% more milk and TDN than continuous grazing per land area, especially over periods of years where persistence of alfalfa is allied with high yields.[25,27,35] Under liberal fertilization, green chop, and conservation, utilization of erect plants usually gives more animal products per land area than grazing.[1,22,23]

❧ ANIMAL AND FORAGE MANAGEMENT

Under pasture conditions plants and animals are affected simultaneously. Animal performance usually has first priority, but sometimes pasture factors have temporary priority. However, livestock feed programs usually depend on all phases of forage utilization—grazing, silage, hay, stockpiling, and green chop.

The objective of management is development of a system to produce the best seasonal distribution of good forage and concurrently achieve good utilization so that wise compromises may be made between animal products per animal and land area. Thus, good utilization along with reasonable assurances of adequate forage supplies may be achieved by two interlocked considerations: (1) manage animals to "fit" the nutritional quality and efficiently utilize the seasonal distribution of forage and (2) manipulate factors to produce the quality and quantity of forage needed for the various cycles of animal production. During certain cycles animals, especially ewes and cows, are very tolerant of low nutrition.[1]

Animal Management

With variable seasonal pasture growth, as in mid-Atlantic regions (Fig. 53.1),

TABLE 53.8 ❧ Effects of stocking at twice the rate during spring as for the summer-fall season on animal gains per head and per ha, Virginia (3-year average)

Stocking rates*	Season of year		
	Spring	Summer-fall	Total growing season
Gain in kg/head/day			
Light	0.89	0.44	0.58
Medium	0.68	0.38	0.48
Heavy	0.62	0.32	0.40
Liveweight in kg/ha			
Light	193	105	298
Medium	237	135	373
Heavy	247	122	369
Herbage available in kg/ha			
Light	2,300	1,700	2,000
Medium	1,430	800	1,065
Heavy	900	370	635

Source: Johnson, 1970.[36]
* Field sizes for light, medium, and heavy stocking were 1.22, 0.81, and 0.61 ha respectively; all pastures were stocked with four head during about three spring months and two head for the rest of the season.

stocking at light and constant rates to ensure adequate summer pasture is common. As much as 50% of the flush spring pasturage is often ungrazed and wasted. Later ungrazed stemmy growths will be avoided because of low nutrition and palatability. With severe overgrazing and undergrazing within pastures, weeds accumulate and erect grass growth shades out white clover, causing yield and quality degeneration.

In Virginia a Kentucky bluegrass–white clover pasture was stocked twice as high (at three stocking rates) during the flush spring growth as during the rest of the season. Such high stocking caused a minor sacrifice in gain per animal and improved liveweight gain per land area (Table 53.8).[36] The best quality of spring pasture was utilized, and a good grass–white clover balance without mowing was maintained during the three-year study since weeds were also grazed. With heavy spring stocking, the cattle removed after the flush growth may be sold as feeders or fattened in drylot.

35. Brundage, A. L., and W. E. Petersen. 1952. A comparison between daily rotational grazing and continuous grazing. *J. Dairy Sci.* 35:623–30.

36. Johnson, J. T. 1970. Influence of stocking rates on the production of Kentucky bluegrass, white clover pastures. Ph.D. thesis, Va. Polytechnic Inst. and State Univ.

Pasture utilization may also be improved by heavy stocking during the entire grazing season with energy supplements after flush growth for cattle being fattened, to relieve summer grazing pressures. Stocking rates of cow herds might be increased to utilize the flush spring growth, followed with liberal creep-feeding of calves, beginning in midsummer until fall weaning. Research shows that nursing calves three and one-half to four months old made excellent gains with creep-feeding when feed of the dams was severely restricted.[1,37]

SYNTHESIS OF FORAGE SYSTEMS

Development of a 12-month forage program tailored to the livestock enterprise, soil characteristics, buildings, equipment, and ability of the farmer is a challenge. Such systems can be manipulated for constant or variable animal numbers since they condone flexibility.

A simple Arkansas system (0.91 ha/cow-calf unit per year) has half the land area in each of tall fescue–legumes and bermudagrass-legumes.[38] Pasture furnishes almost all the feed; loose hay stacked from the bermudagrass pasture serves for winter feed. Bermudagrass pastures, of lower nutrition than tall fescue, are used for summer-fall grazing by cows. After fall calving on bermudagrass pastures, accumulated tall fescue is grazed to improve milk flow and pasture quality for calves during winter and spring. Calves before weaning in early summer receive good nutrition from closely grazed tall fescue–clover pastures. Liberal fertilization and good pasture and animal management provide for most of the nutritional needs of cows and calves. Costly buildings, mechanization, and hand feeding are avoided in simple 12-month forage systems (Fig. 53.9).

In Virginia a 12-month forage system

FIG. 53.9. *Buildings, mechanization, and hand feeding . . . avoided.* Tall fescue accumulated during spring or mowed and round baled after seed harvesting and subsequent stockpiled growth is the winter feeding phase of a simple 12-month forage system often used in Missouri and Ohio. *Univ. Mo. photo.*

was compared with continuous grazing. The two pasture systems were:

Continuous grazing. One 1.36-ha field with one mixture (Kentucky bluegrass–white clover–orchardgrass) was grazed continuously. Pastures were stocked about twice as heavily in spring as the rest of the year. This improved the leafiness of pasturage and gave higher gains per ha than farmers received with constant stocking where spring pasturage was wasted.

Twelve-month forage system. A 1.36-ha field was divided into five equal-sized fields and stocked with four yearlings. The first two or three fields (0.14–0.20 ha/head) were grazed rotationally during spring. The other two or three fields were harvested for winter feed in spring. As growth slowed later in the

37. Hammes, R. C., R. E. Blaser, C. M. Kincaid, H. T. Bryant, and R. W. Engel. 1959. Effect of full and restricted winter rations on dams and summer-dropped suckling calves fed different rations. *J. Anim. Sci.* 18: 21–31.

38. Ray, M. L., and A. E. Spooner. 1969. Cow and calf nutrition and management under different grazing pressures. Ark. Agr. Exp. Sta. Bull. 749.

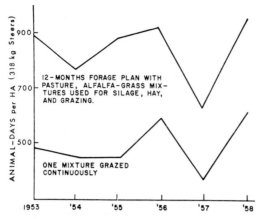

FIG. 53.10. The 12-month forage system averaged 72% more production per ha during six years than grazing one mixture continuously. (Blaser et al., 1969.[1])

season, more or all fields were grazed. Using mixtures flexibly for grazing as needed and harvesting the excess for winter feed increased animal production per ha. Forage was not wasted and growth stage was controlled.

Field 1. Kentucky bluegrass–white clover–orchardgrass for rotational grazing all season.

Field 2. Orchardgrass–ladino clover–red clover for rotational grazing all season.

Field 3. Alfalfa-orchardgrass–ladino clover for silage, then hay, then rotational grazing or hay.

Field 4. Alfalfa-orchardgrass–ladino clover for silage, then hay, then rotational grazing or hay.

Field 5. Alfalfa-orchardgrass for silage, then hay, then aftermath grazing.

The 12-month system with perennials produced enough quality forage per year per ha to feed 2.7 yearlings weighing 318 kg, 72% more than for continuous grazing (Fig. 53.10). During the grazing season the steers gained a little more per head with continuous grazing than with the 12-month plan.[1]

For the 12-month system the pasture area was restricted to grazing needs; excess forage from fields closed off from grazing at any season was saved as hay or silage. During the summer and fall more land (fields or mixtures) was grazed than in spring; thus forage was not wasted nor allowed to grow to a mature low-quality feed. Rotational grazing is most useful as a part of a 12-month forage system. Grazing continuously for brief periods during spring and winter would have simplified the feed plan.

Intensive management with 12-month forage systems increases carrying capacities. To obtain more income, weanling calves could be marketed as yearling feeders or sold even later as fat cattle. Heavier stocking would avoid the wastage of pasture common on many farms.

When adapted, corn silage makes an important contribution to a 12-month system. Over a period of more than ten years, feeder cattle averaged daily liveweight gains of more than 1.14 kg with high-good and choice carcass grades for steers fed corn silage with a protein supplement in Virginia. Early weaned beef calves (four months old) or small dairy calves gained 0.77 kg/day when fed corn silage with a protein supplement. High-producing lactating cows gave as much milk from corn silage supplemented with protein and minerals as from standard rations liberally supplemented with concentrates. Corn silage is a high-energy forage with high yield potentials and is nearly foolproof in the feeding management of any livestock enterprise.[1]

The principle of 12-month feed systems applies to widely different environments and all livestock enterprises. Every livestock farm should tailor a plan to best fit the needs of the animals, environment, and farm facilities. Forage systems support complete economic functioning units of livestock production rather than fragments of it. The challenge is to develop and manage forage-animal systems in various ecosystems to achieve high economic animal production goals (per animal and land area).

✸ QUESTIONS

1. List and explain major feed problems with perennial grasses and legumes.

2. Explain LAI and TNC and their interplay as related to forage management.
3. Is it possible to obtain maximum yields and quality of forages concurrently? Why or why not?
4. Name 4 methods of utilizing forages and explain how each will influence per animal and per ha output and then list a perennial species or grass-legume mixture suitable for each method.
5. Under what conditions is rotational grazing likely to give higher gains per animal than continuous grazing? Higher livestock products per ha? Why?
6. What forage utilization scheme would you use to obtain the highest possible gains per animal? The highest gains per ha? Why?
7. Discuss the effect of overgrazing and undergrazing of pastures on forage longevity, forage yield, and liveweight gains per animal and per ha.
8. Show detailed plans of a practical 12-month forage system for producing animal products efficiently in your region, giving consideration to soils, climate, mechanization, buildings, and animal products.

DWAYNE A. ROHWEDER / *University of Wisconsin*

WARREN C. THOMPSON / *University of Kentucky*

54

PERMANENT PASTURES

❧

P ERMANENT PASTURES are composed of perennial grasses and legumes or self-seeding annuals, frequently both, and are maintained indefinitely for grazing. A permanent pasture may be a natural or indigenous stand, may have been established by seeding, or may have resulted from occupation of abandoned cultivated fields by forage plants that were sufficiently aggressive to spread without man's assistance.

Pasture data are not available on forage yield, quality of cover, seasonal distribution of production, and livestock production per ha. The major source for pasture information is the U.S. census which reports every five years.[1] Pasture hectarage is reported for (1) cropland used as pasture, (2) woodland pasture, (3) other or open permanent pasture on land other than

❧ DWAYNE A. ROHWEDER is Professor of Agronomy, Extension, University of Wisconsin. He holds the M.S. and Ph.D. degrees from Iowa State University. His research is especially concerned with production, management, and utilization of forages.

❧ WARREN C. THOMPSON is Extension Specialist in Forages, University of Kentucky. He holds the M.S. degree from the University of Kentucky. His research has emphasized forage production and utilization.

woodland and cropland used for pasture or grazing, and (4) improved pasture as that portion of open permanent pasture which has received one or more of the following practices: liming, fertilizing, seeding, irrigating, draining, or clearing and control of weed and brush growth. Pastures were inventoried by the USDA Conservation Needs Inventory Committee in 1958, and information was updated in 1967.[2] Pastures were also inventoried as to type. Location with respect to land capability and quality as related to potential for erosion also were reported.

❧ IMPORTANCE OF PASTURE

In the U.S. more than 40% of the 917.8 million ha of land is in forage (Table 54.1).[1,2] Of this area about 389.6 million ha are devoted to various types of pasture. Permanent pasture and rangeland on farms totals 195.2 million ha or 50% of the pasture. In 1964 only 14.5 million ha were reported as improved permanent pasture.

Pastures furnish a large part of the feed

1. Bureau of Census. 1968. U.S. census of agriculture 1964. General report, vol. 2, p. 18.
2. USDA Conservation Needs Inventory Committee. 1971. Basic statistics—National inventory of soil and water conservation needs, 1967. Stat. Bull. 461.

TABLE 54.1 ❧ Hectares of U.S. cropland pasture, other pasture, and woodland pasture, 1949–69

Year	Cropland (mil. ha)	Other (mil. ha)	Woodland (mil. ha)
1949	28.1	168.8	54.7
1954	26.8	186.2	49.1
1959	26.5	188.8	37.5
1964	23.2	198.6	33.3
1967[2]	20.4	195.2*	55.4

Source: Bur. Census, 1968[1]; USDA Stat. Bull. 461.[2]
* Pasture and range with less than 10% canopy of trees and shrubs.

FIG. 54.1. Five major pasture regions of the U.S., with type of forage that provides the majority of pasturage. (USDA, 1946.[5])

consumed by livestock in the U.S. (Table 54.2), contributing 36.3% of the feed consumed.[3] Harvested forages contribute an additional 18.3%, so that all forage crops provide 54.6% of the livestock feed. The balance or 45.4% is obtained from concentrate feed including grain and protein supplements.[4]

As expected, the importance of each kind of feed varies with different classes of livestock. Sheep and goats obtain 82%, beef cattle 73%, horses 51%, other dairy cattle 46%, and milk cows only 20% of their feed from pasture. Cattle on feed, hogs, and poultry use relatively little forage but are heavy consumers of concentrates.

❧ PERMANENT PASTURE REGIONS OF THE U.S.

Natural, varying climatic conditions divide the U.S. into five major pasture re-

gions (Fig. 54.1).[5] Only the permanent pasture of the humid regions (regions 1, 2, and 5) will be considered in this chapter. Permanent pastures generally are not improved over much of the humid region of the U.S.; consequently, yields are low. Many are unproductive fields that have been taken out of row crop production or abandoned. This unaided or undirected establishment of pasture requires many years for full natural development and is a waste of potential resources. Some permanent pasture is on land unsuited to cultivation. It often is covered with thin sods containing broadleaf weeds and annual grass weeds and brush. Permanent pasture may contain remnants of desirable pasture grasses, and these make little growth be-

3. Allen, George C., Earl F. Hodges, and Margaret Devers. 1970. Suppl. 1970, National and state livestock-feed relationships. USDA, ERS Stat. Bull. 446.

4. USDA. 1971. Suppl. 1970, Livestock and meat statistics. ERS Stat. Bull. 333.
5. Semple, A. T., H. N. Vinall, C. R. Enlow, and T. E. Woodward. 1946. A pasture handbook. USDA Misc. Publ. 194.

TABLE 54.2 ❧ Consumption of all feed by kind of livestock, 1969

Kind of livestock	Percent consumed				
	Concentrates*	Hay†	Other harvested forage†	Pasture†	All forage*
Sheep and goats	9.7	4.7	3.7	81.9	90.3
Other beef cattle	7.9	14.6	4.4	73.1	92.1
Horses	20.6	18.4	10.2	50.8	79.4
Other dairy	17.3	30.1	6.6	46.0	82.7
Milk cows	37.1	23.5	19.5	19.9	62.9
Cattle on feed	73.5	13.4	7.7	5.4	26.5
All livestock	45.4	12.2	6.1	36.3	54.6

Source: Allen et al., 1970.[3]
* Concentrates + All forage = 100%.
† Hay + Other harvested forage + Pasture = All forage.

TABLE 54.3 ❧ Dry matter and beef production from unimproved, fertilized, and renovated pastures on selected soils in the humid U.S.

Soil and location	Unimproved (kg/ha)	Fertilized (kg/ha)	Renovated (kg/ha)
Dry Matter			
Shallow soils—Ont.*	610	...	2,060
Gale loam—Wis.			
15–25% slope	1,990	...	3,770
26–35% slope	1,365	...	3,420
wooded†	310	...	...
Fayette-Dubuque—Wis.	2,195	5,875	...
Miami silt loam—Wis.	3,180	...	5,155
Dewey-Humphries—Ala.	...	4,075	3,360
Beef			
Weller-Lindley—Iowa	120	...	375
Nappanee-Brookston—Ind.	160	350	390
Norfolk sandy loam—Ala.	115	330	...

Sources: Ahlgren et al., 1946;[6] Hoveland and Evans, 1970;[7] Mott et al., 1953;[8] Scholl and Llambias, 1966;[9] Sund et al., 1958;[10] Watkins and Winch, 1970;[11] Wedin and Rohweder, 1962;[12] Andrews.[13]
* Twenty-one sites and 78 site years.
† Approximately 50% woods cover.

cause legumes usually are not present in the sward. Consequently, their principal use is for early grazing. It is estimated that 69% of this type of pasture needs treatment through improvement or reestablishment of vegetative cover. Only 28% is adequately treated to control erosion.[2] Production from open permanent pastures where Kentucky bluegrass and white clover are the dominant species generally ranges from 610 to over 3180 kg/ha of dry matter or 115–160 kg/ha of beef (Table 54.3).[6-13]

The soil is an important factor influenc-

ing pasture production. Soil factors causing differences in yield are slope, texture, depth, degree of erosion, soil fertility, and soil acidity. In general, yields increase with increasing soil depth and fineness of texture. In southwestern Wisconsin, yields decreased as slope increased; and production from pastures on comparable soils and slopes, but with some wood cover, was only 310 kg/ha compared to an average of 1625 kg/ha with no wood cover.[6]

Production also varies with the composition of the vegetative cover. Studies in West Virginia have shown that the carrying capacity of an individual pasture was related to the type of vegetation.[14] An Iowa study also has indicated a highly significant association between the percent of ground covered by economic species and yield of forage on four different soils.[15]

In general, the climate in each broad region determines the botanical composition of the permanent pasture there. The important grasses and legumes that occur in permanent pastures depend upon climatic

6. Ahlgren, H. L., M. L. Wall, R. J. Muckenhirn, and J. M. Sund. 1946. Yields of forage from woodland pasture on sloping land in southern Wisconsin. J. Forest. 44:709–11.

7. Hoveland, C. S., and E. M. Evans. 1970. Cool-season perennial grass and grass-clover management. Ala. Univ. Agr. Exp. Sta. Circ. 175.

8. Mott, G. O., R. E. Smith, W. M. McVey, and W. M. Beeson. 1953. Grazing trials with beef cattle on permanent pastures at Miller-Purdue Memorial Farm. Ind. Agr. Exp. Sta. Bull. 581.

9. Scholl, J. M., and C. Llambias. 1966. Response of a permanent grass pasture sward to rate of nitrogen and to nitrogen combined with phosphorus and potassium fertilizer. Proc. 9th Int. Grassl. Congr., pp. 1335–37 (São Paulo, Brazil).

10. Sund, J. M., M. J. Wright, E. H. Zehner, and H. L. Ahlgren. 1958. Comparisons of the productivity of permanent and rotation pastures on plowable cropland. II. Second six-year cycle and summary. Agron. J. 50:637–40.

11. Watkins, E. M., and J. E. Winch. 1970. Assessment and improvement of roughland pasture in Ontario. Project 25021 and 6011. Crop Sci. Dept., Ont. Agr. Coll., Guelph.

12. Wedin, W. F., and D. A. Rohweder. 1962. Pasture trials at Albia, 1940–1960. Iowa Coop. Ext. Serv. Pam. OEF 61-23, pp. 1–5. Mimeo.

13. Andrews, O. N. 1963 Bahiagrass. Ala. Polytech. Inst. Ext. Serv. Circ. 548.

14. Pierre, W. H., J. H. Longwell, R. R. Robinson, G. M. Browning, Ivan McKeever, and R. F. Copple. 1937. West Virginia pastures: Type of vegetation, carrying capacity, and soil properties. W. Va. Agr. Exp. Sta. Bull. 280.

15. Rohweder, D. A. 1963. The nature and productivity of southern Iowa pastures as affected by soil type, slope, erosion, fertility, and botanical composition. Ph.D. thesis, Iowa State Univ., Ames. (Diss. Abstr. 24:3909, 1964.)

and soil characteristics, palatability, fertilizer treatments, cultural practices, and grazing management.

Kentucky bluegrass with varying amounts of white clover is widely distributed on the more fertile soils in northern regions 1-a, 1-b, and 5-a. Smaller percentages of such grasses as orchardgrass, tall fescue, bentgrass, redtop, timothy, Canada bluegrass, and others are also found in permanent pastures. The fine-leaved fescues, Canada bluegrass, redtop, and timothy predominate on drier, less fertile soils along with broadleaf weeds and annual grass weeds having low quality. Bentgrass, timothy, and redtop predominate on the moister soils. In the central belt between the North and South (1-b) white clover and annual lespedezas are also found in many of the permanent pastures. Bermudagrass, bahiagrass, annual lespedezas, and crimson clover are found in upland pastures of the South (regions 2-a and 2-b). In lowland pastures carpetgrass, dallisgrass, and several clover species predominate. Winter annuals predominate in region 5-b.

✦ IMPROVED LEGUMES AND GRASSES

Improved, high-yielding, more palatable legume and grass species are becoming widely distributed in permanent pastures as a result of continuing research and pasture improvement programs. New cultivars having higher yield, improved palatability, increased winterhardiness, and improved disease resistance are being developed and will increase both forage yield and utilization by animals. Other species also are being evaluated.

Alfalfa, red clover, ladino clover, smooth bromegrass, timothy, and reed canarygrass are being used to improve pastures in regions 1-a and 1-b. Alfalfa has been the most productive legume available for pasture renovation on soils having adequate drainage, favorable pH, and adequate fertility. However, alfalfa persists only with rotational grazing. Birdsfoot trefoil is increasing in prominence and offers some advantages over alfalfa in region 1-a. It persists longer under continuous grazing when properly managed and fertilized and does not cause bloat. With increasing beef cattle numbers this latter characteristic gives birdsfoot trefoil more value. Crownvetch is receiving attention, especially in the eastern part of region 1-a.

Tall fescue is a basic winter grass in pastures of regions 2-a and 2-b and for cool season grazing in 1-b. Ladino and white clover are grown in combination with tall fescue, bermudagrass, dallisgrass, and bahiagrass to improve forage quality and production. Coastal bermudagrass, dallisgrass, ryegrass, crimson clover, subterranean clover, and sericea lespedeza are increasing in importance. Red clover, orchardgrass, and timothy are often used in renovating cool-season pastures in region 2-a. 'Pangola' digitgrass has become important in the lower part of region 1-b. Alfalfa, tall fescue, and ladino clover are found on the heavier, more fertile soils of the region.

In general, legumes are seeded with grasses to improve yield, quality, and seasonal distribution of pasturage; however, N-fertilized grasses are best suited for some situations.

✦ POTENTIAL FOR IMPROVEMENT

There is renewed interest in permanent pastures of the humid region for several reasons. Climate and soil characteristics make the region ideally suited for forage production. Rising land prices, higher meat and milk prices, and the pressure placed on level land for grain production are causing farmers to consider ways to make pastures more productive and profitable. (See Fig. 54.3.)

More than 76% of the permanent pasture in the humid regions of the U.S. is located on soils with great potential for improvement (Class I to IV).[2] Of this pasture, over 57% is found on soils suitable for regular cultivation (Class I to III) with hazards to cultivation varying with slope, soil depth, topography, and available moisture. The

FIG. 54.2. *Renewed interest in permanent pastures.* An improved permanent pasture means more profit through more and better cattle. *Univ. Ky. photo.*

FIG. 54.3. *Renovation . . . to restore permanent pasture . . . greater productivity.* An improved and properly managed permanent pasture can be one of the most profitable parts of the farm enterprise. A tall fescue field following renovation, seeded to red and ladino clover—second growth. *Univ. Ky. photo.*

remaining 19% is located on soils suitable for occasional or limited cultivation (Class IV). (See Terminology for definition of soil classes.)

Forage produced on permanent pasture has little or no value unless consumed by livestock, especially cattle. The method of pasture utilization is changing. Since 1950 dairy cow and sheep numbers have declined 42 and 47% respectively in the humid area; however, beef cow numbers increased 50% during the decade 1960 to 1970.[4] About 41% of the beef cows in the U.S. are now found east of the Missouri River. Beef cows can use large amounts of pasturage (Table 54.2). New technology is indicating how the permanent pasture can be improved to better meet the needs of this livestock enterprise.

Considerable evidence indicates that most permanent pastures can be improved. A pasture can be improved by complete seedbed preparation and reseeding, renovation, overseeding or sod-seeding, or fertilization and control of undesirable vegetation. The alternative selected will depend on the soil capability, quality of present vegetative cover, livestock enterprise, use for the pasture, and need for forage.

RENOVATION

Renovation is the improvement of a pasture by partial or complete destruction of a

sod plus liming, fertilizing, weed control, and seeding as may be required to establish desirable forage plants.[16] Renovation can restore permanent pasture to greater productivity with little danger of soil loss because the vegetation remains on or near the soil surface. (See Fig. 54.3.) Research has shown that renovating permanent pasture will improve production twofold to fivefold depending on the soil characteristics and condition of the sod.[17]

Steps to follow for a successful renovation program include:

1. Select the area to be renovated a year ahead of the planned date of seeding.
2. Test the soil to determine soil nutrient deficiencies and apply nutrients needed. Lime should be applied at least six months prior to seeding. Applying P and K during the tillage process so that it can be thoroughly mixed with the soil is preferred.
3. Graze the existing grass sward closely (about 5 cm) before renovating, to permit more effective tillage. Greater suc-

16. Leonard, W. H., R. Merton Love, and M. E. Heath. 1968. Crop terminology today. *Crop Sci.* 8:257–61.
17. Sprague, M. A. 1961. Seedbed preparation and improvement of unplowable pastures using herbicides. **Proc. 8th Int. Grassl. Congr.**, pp. 264–66 (Reading, England).

cess in seeding establishment will be obtained if much of the tillage is done in late summer and fall in the North or fall and winter in the South prior to seeding.

4. Prepare the seedbed by repeated and timely disking, spring-tooth harrowing, field cultivating, chisel plowing, or otherwise destroying the old sod. For best results disturb at least 40–60% of the soil to establish clovers and 80–100% for alfalfa, birdsfoot trefoil, and crownvetch.[18,19] The tillage leaves a surface mulch that reduces soil erosion and reduces the vigor of the existing grasses by killing their vegetative reproductive parts through desiccation and/or freezing. However, tillage alone often has been ineffective because individual diskings or cultivations do not kill the old sward.

Seedling establishment may be improved by combining tillage and herbicide treatments to kill or suppress the existing sod. However, except for broadleaf weed control, only a limited number of herbicides are available for pasture renovation. Considerable work has been conducted with short-lived herbicides, but these are ineffective with some perennial grasses. In these cases, weed infestations can be reduced by seeding a moderate rate of a small-grain companion crop. The small grain should be grazed in early season when it is 15–20 cm tall to reduce competition. Under average to above rainfall conditions, the new seeding will be established by midsummer and can be grazed without injury if properly managed. This will result in essentially no loss in production during the year of renovation.

5. Plant seed of adapted cultivars of high-yielding legumes and grasses at recommended rates in early spring for best results. Place seed at 0.5- to 1.5-cm depth

by band-seeding with a drill having packer wheels or with a cultipacker seeder. A firm seedbed is essential, especially for good seed-soil contact. Seedbeds in renovated sods are often too loose for successful establishment because of trash in the surface. Inoculate legumes with proper N-fixing bacteria.

6. Graze renovated pastures short until the livestock begin to eat the new legume seedings. Then remove livestock to permit forage regrowth. Thereafter, graze the field to best suit the regrowth of the legume. Proper stocking will permit grazing of some species throughout the summer.

COMPLETE SEEDBED PREPARATION WITH RESEEDING

Complete seedbed preparation with reseeding has been superior to renovation in several areas of the North where perennial grass weeds in the sod are difficult to subdue. Legume establishment is markedly improved by plowing compared to tillage with a field cultivator.[20] Studies also indicate that 20–60% less work is required to prepare a seedbed by plowing than may be required with any one of several surface cultivating tools.[21] The steps in reseeding the pasture are identical to renovation except for tillage. Perennial grass weeds should be subdued in late summer by timely and repeated use of a heavy disk or field cultivator, and the seedbed should be prepared in late fall by plowing on the contour to minimize erosion losses. Freezing and thawing over the winter followed by a light disking the following spring provide a firm seedbed. An intervening row crop for one year may or may not be used, depending on soil conditions, to reduce weed population, reduce competition from the sod, and help defray costs.

Renovated and reseeded pastures will soon revert to their former botanical com-

18. Templeton, W. C., Jr., C. F. Buck, and N. W. Bradley. 1970. Renovated Kentucky bluegrass and supplementary pastures for steers. Ky. Agr. Exp. Sta. Res. Bull. 709.

19. Thompson, Warren C., T. H. Taylor, and W. C. Templeton, Jr. 1965. Renovating grass fields. Ky. Coop. Ext. Serv. Leaflet 277.

20. Scholl, J. M., M. F. Finner, A. E. Peterson, and J. M. Sund. 1970. Pasture renovation in southwestern Wisconsin. Wis. Agr. and Life Sci. Res. Rept. 65.

21. Sprague, V. G., R. R. Robinson, and A. W. Clyde. 1947. Pasture renovation. I. Seedbed preparation, seedling establishment, and subsequent yields. *J. Amer. Soc. Agron.* 39:12–25.

position within one to three years unless fertility and proper management are continued on a regular basis.[22] Continuous close grazing and failure to maintain fertility will cause tall-growing legumes to die, resulting in decreased production. A grazing management program should be selected that is consistent with the growth habit of the legume. Topdressing should be applied annually to replace the nutrients removed in meat, milk, and/or forage the previous year.

SOD-SEEDING OR OVERSEEDING

Reseeding of legumes and/or grasses into thin permanent pasture sods by no tillage sod-seeding or overseeding without complete seedbed preparation have given variable results in the humid area. Success depends on the ability of the introduced seedlings to become established in competition with the old pasture sod. Once established, the persistence and vigor of the introduced species will be determined largely by pasture management.

In the North new seedings are made in the spring at a time coinciding with the maximum growth period of grasses in the old sod. Placing lime and fertilizer, especially N, in a band with the seed stimulates the grass in the sod and results in increased competition. Consequently, the introduced seedlings are seldom able to become established.

However, several studies indicate that chemical herbicides, tilled strips of varying widths, and tillage methods have reduced competition from the existing vegetation and improved seedling establishment in the southern part of region 1-a and in region 1-b. Sod-seeding of legumes such as white clover, alfalfa, birdsfoot trefoil, and crownvetch offers an opportunity to economically increase yields from low-producing, cool-season, permanent pastureland on neglected hillsides, steep slopes, and eroded

or stony soils where plowing may be difficult.

Spring seedings generally are most successful,[23-25] and the length of time required for legumes to become successfully established varies with species.[26] The most important factors for successful establishment are proper depth of seeding, good seed-soil contact, and subduing of the existing vegetation to reduce competition. Seeding followed by trampling from livestock often improves on-the-farm results, especially if legumes are seeded prior to the start of competitive growth from the grass in the sod and the soil is not too wet. Chemicals used to kill or suppress the existing vegetation in a band along the row have enhanced legume establishment only when stands of the grass were dense and the growth vigorous. The most satisfactory width for the tilled strip varies and appears to be dependent on soil conditions.

Sod-seeding has been most successful in the South and/or subtropical regions where introduced legumes and grasses are seeded at a time that does not coincide with the maximum growth period of the existing sward.[27] Seedings are made for the most part in late summer or early fall. Winter annuals or perennial grasses and legumes can be incorporated into the sod to provide winter grazing. Fall plantings can be made directly into a thin, dormant, or heavily grazed sod. However, vigorous swards should be closely grazed prior to and following seeding to reduce competition. Overseeding with pelleted seed of legumes, such as white clover and alfalfa, from an

22. Ahlgren, H. L., M. L. Wall, R. J. Muckenhirn, and F. V. Burcalow. 1944. Effectiveness of renovation in increasing yields of permanent pastures in southern Wisconsin. *J. Amer. Soc. Agron.* 36:121–31.

23. Decker, A. M., H. J. Retzer, M. L. Sorna, and H. D. Kerr. 1969. Permanent pastures improved with sod seeding and fertilization. *Agron. J.* 61:243–47.
24. Taylor, T. H., E. M. Smith, and W. C. Templeton, Jr. 1969. Use of minimum tillage and herbicides for establishing legumes in Kentucky bluegrass swards. *Agron. J.* 61:761–66.
25. Taylor, T. H., J. M. England, R. E. Powell, J. F. Freeman, C. K. Kline, and W. C. Templeton, Jr. 1964. Establishment of legumes in old *Poa pratensis* L. sod by use of paraquat and strip tillage for seedbed preparation. 7th Brit. Weed Control Conf. 64-3-65.
26. Van Keuren, R. W., and G. B. Triplett. 1970. Seeding legumes into established grass swards. Proc. 11th Int. Grassl. Congr., pp. 131–34 (Surfers Paradise, Queensland, Aust.).
27. Coats, Robert E. 1957. Sod-seeding—Brown loam tests. Miss. Agr. Exp. Sta. Bull. 554.

airplane has also been successful in parts of the humid region.[28,29]

FERTILIZING AND LIMING

Large areas of permanent pasture have adequate cover but are low in productivity because they lack sufficient fertility. Fertilization can be an economical method of increasing pasture production. When soil fertility is increased and maintained with regular or annual applications of fertilizer, improved, highly productive species can be seeded and maintained.

Legume-grass mixtures give some nutritional, utilization, and possible yield advantages; however it is often easier to manage N-fertilized grasses than legume-grass mixtures. In the absence of legumes, N is the factor most limiting to growth of pasture grasses, especially tall-growing species. However, adequate pH, P, and K soil levels must be maintained to achieve top results from N.

Pasture yields can be increased twofold to fourfold by fertilization with N at 134–269 kg/ha, particularly where the botanical composition is predominantly grass (Table 54.3).

However, considerably higher yields of forage and livestock products have been reported when higher rates of N have been applied to improved tall-growing grasses. Soil and climate characteristics, species, time of fertilizer application, economics, and managerial ability will influence the application rate of N.

Higher N rates may be used when top management is applied to the total forage-livestock enterprise. However, less N is needed for grazing than for hay production because part of the N is recycled through manure, urine, and unconsumed forage.

Nitrogen fertilization not only increases yield per ha but starts growth earlier in the spring, sustains production later in the fall, and increases carrying capacity. The effect of N on the occurrence of high nitrate levels in the forage must also be considered. Studies in Iowa and Indiana have indicated that high nitrates were not a problem in tall grasses fertilized with N at rates to 269 kg/ha, particularly when the N was applied in split applications.[30,31]

From 134 to 269 kg N/ha are needed to equal yields by legume-grass pastures.[32-34] Pasture swards having more than 50% of legume usually do not respond to N fertilization. However, response can be obtained if there is less than 50% of legume in the sward. Nitrogen fertilization of short grasses such as Kentucky bluegrass generally will not equal yields from legume-grass mixtures.

Pastures also may respond to lime, P, and K. Lime and complete fertilizer containing P and K encourage the growth of legumes through which they supply N. In West Virginia, pastures treated with lime and P have increased yields about 75% over untreated pastures. Similar pastures treated with lime, N, P, and K have given increases of almost 125%.[35] Proper liming and fertilization have increased the proportion of desirable pasture plants and the sward density. In North Carolina the total vegetative cover has been increased 33% by the use of fertilizer. Annual lespedezas, white clover, and Kentucky bluegrass have been

28. Robinson, G. S., and M. W. Cross. 1961. Improvement of some New Zealand grassland by oversowing and overdrilling. Proc. 8th Int. Grassl. Congr., pp. 402–5 (Reading, England).

29. White, J. G. H. 1970. Establishment of lucerne (*Medicago sativa* L.) in uncultivated country by sod-seeding and oversowing. Proc. 11th Int. Grassl. Congr., pp. 134–38 (Surfers Paradise, Queensland, Aust.).

30. Krueger, C. R., and J. M. Scholl. 1970. Performance of bromegrass, orchardgrass, and reed canarygrass grown at five nitrogen levels and with alfalfa. Wis. Agr. and Life Sci. Res. Rept. 69.

31. Abbring, F. T., C. L. Rhykerd, C. H. Noller, S. J. Donahue, K. L. Washburn, Jr., and V. L. Lechtenberg. 1969. Nitrogen fertilization of orchardgrass and soil nitrate content. Ind. Agr. Exp. Sta. Res. Progr. Rept. 364.

32. Alexander, C. W., and D. E. McCloud. 1962. Influence of time and rate of nitrogen application on production and botanical composition of forage. *Agron. J.* 54:521–22.

33. Carter, L. P., and J. M. Scholl. 1962. Effectiveness of inorganic nitrogen as a replacement for legumes grown in association with forage grasses. I. Dry matter production and botanical composition. *Agron. J.* 54:161–63.

34. Scholl, J. M., W. H. Paulson, and V. H. Brungardt. 1970. A pasture program for beef cattle in Wisconsin. Wis. Lancaster Cow-Calf Day. Proc.

35. Schaller, F. W., G. G. Pohlman, H. O. Henderson, and R. A. Ackerman. 1945. Pasture fertilization experiments at Reymann Memorial Farm. W. Va. Agr. Exp. Sta. Bull. 324.

increased as much as 65%. Fertilization has resulted in earlier spring grazing and an extended pasture season.[36] Rates of lime, P, and K should be determined by soil test.

❧ GRAZING MANAGEMENT

Lack of proper grazing management probably ruins more pastures than any single cause. Adjusting number of animals to the growth habit of plants is related to varying plant growth rates. Close grazing during the growing season is at the expense of maximum yield and stand persistence. Overgrazing during periods of low rainfall reduces animal performance and photosynthesis, surface soil temperatures may become too high, and the forage plants may lack vigor because of weakened root systems.

Grazing during the growing season of half or more of the foliage of grasses (both cool- and warm-season species) has caused root growth to stop for a time after each removal, with the exception of orchardgrass after the first clipping.[37] Repeated clipping, similar to continuous overgrazing, resulted in complete and permanent cessation of root growth and poor plant development. Annual and perennial weedy species become established under these conditions and compete with forage plants for water and nutrients.

Good pasture is less likely to be ruined by undergrazing than by overgrazing; however, under these conditions tall weeds often increase in number. Excessive wastage of forage occurs because of trampling, fouling, and shading of low-growing species. Insect and rodent infestations also are encouraged, and foliage and root diseases are often more prevalent.

When pastures are grazed too early, productivity of forage plants is lowered by premature leaf removal. Root development is reduced and dry matter production is hampered. With plants at less than optimum height, few leaves remain, sunlight is inefficiently used, and moisture conditions invite growth of weedy annual grasses. Plants are also destroyed by trampling because the ground is soft and loose from freezing and thawing over the winter.

When legume-grass pastures are grazed too late in autumn, the legumes cannot restore food reserves and winter-killing results. A rest period of four to six weeks before growth ceases in autumn is necessary to permit legume plants to store food reserves in the crown and roots as a preparation for winter and for making vigorous growth the following spring.[38] This relationship is not as well determined for grasses. Loss of legumes from a sward eliminates the source of N for the associated grasses. Reduction of ground cover also exposes the crown, tiller buds, and tender growth to frost injury. In the North, stubble and unused vegetation hold snow and provide protection for overwintering plants. In the South, late summer grazing to reduce the competition of the warm-season grasses with the cool-season legumes such as white, hop, and Persian clovers is a desirable practice.

ROTATIONAL VERSUS CONTINUOUS GRAZING

Rotational grazing involves grazing each of a series of pastures in rotation and then moving animals to the next. This system permits the farmer to match grazing more adequately to the growth habit of forage species, condition of pasture, and animal needs than does continuous grazing. Grazing rotationally provides for a comparatively short period of grazing for each field and a recovery period to allow more effective consumption of forage with less waste by trampling, fouling, or selective grazing. Rotational grazing also favors legume persistence and improved yields per ha compared to continuous grazing. Harvesting the mature forage as hay or silage

36. Woodhouse, W. W., Jr., and R. L. Lovvorn. 1942. Establishing and improving permanent pastures in North Carolina. N.C. Agr. Exp. Sta. Bull. 338.

37. Crider, F. J. 1955. Root growth stoppage results from defoliation of grass. USDA Tech. Bull. 1102.

38. Smith, Dale. 1964. Winter injury and the survival of forage plants. *Herb. Abstr.* 34:203–9.

during the maximum growth period when grazing is in surplus supply also will aid in feeding animals through crisis periods such as drought, will increase carrying capacity, and will provide time for regrowth and continued production of high-quality pasturage.

The frequency and intensity of grazing depends on the species used and their vigor. Low-growing species such as birdsfoot trefoil, white clover, Kentucky bluegrass, or ladino clover can be grazed often or continuously. For maximum production, mixtures of Kentucky bluegrass with white or ladino clover should not be grazed closer than 5 cm, and with birdsfoot trefoil not shorter than 7–10 cm. However, tall-growing species such as alfalfa, tall fescue, orchardgrass, smooth bromegrass, and reed canarygrass can be grazed close but not often. Alfalfa and alfalfa-grass mixtures should be permitted to reach 20–45 cm before grazing, and a rest period of five to six weeks should be allowed between grazings. Annuals such as sudangrass and sorghum-sudangrass hybrids also do best under this type of management.

A combined rotational-seasonal grazing program may be necessary to achieve maximum production per hectare and most efficient use of management inputs.[39]

SEASONAL GRAZING

Renovated pastures can be made more effective by growing several species separately in a pasture system and capitalizing on the growth habit of each to obtain full-season grazing. A farmer can select species adapted for the topography and soil conditions on the farm as well as those to hold erosion losses within acceptable limits and to meet the needs of the livestock enterprise in each season of the year. Single species or simple mixtures are easier to manage than complex mixtures.

Grasses start growth earlier in the spring than legumes. Fertilizing grass pastures with a complete fertilizer composed largely of N will encourage earlier growth of the grass. Split applications of fertilizer provide additional increases in production.[40] In the North complete utilization of the forage produced by Kentucky bluegrass and white clover or introduced tall grasses can be obtained during spring and early summer when growth is rapid.

Legume and legume-grass pastures generally provide the most uniform production for the grazing season.[30] Deeper rooted legumes provide higher yields during the critical summer period than do the cool-season grasses; however, production also declines, but at a slower rate than with cool-season grasses. Stockpiling for use in this period has been suggested as one means of obtaining more uniform grazing. Harvesting a portion of the pasture as hay or silage and storing for midsummer use is another form of stockpiling. This also assists the farmer in programming pasture growth so that more of the pasturage can be utilized at stages of highest quality. Legume-grass pastures also may be supplemented with annual pastures such as sudangrass or pearlmillet to provide high carrying capacity in midsummer.

Tall cool-season grasses fertilized with N in late summer can extend forage production and grazing into the fall when legumes should be rested; however, grasses differ in digestibility when grazed during this period.[41]

In the South, winter pastures of small grains and annual ryegrass as well as cool-season legumes and grasses supplement warm-season grasses to provide year-round grazing.

EFFECT OF MIXED GRAZING

The grazing animal influences pasture quantity and quality. Continuous grazing

39. Wedin, W. F., and R. L. Vetter. 1970. Pasture for beef production in the western Corn Belt, USA. Proc. 11th Int. Grassl. Congr., pp. 842–45 (Surfers Paradise, Queensland, Aust.).

40. Matches, A. G. 1968. Performance of four pasture mixtures defoliated by mowing or grazing with cattle or sheep. *Agron. J.* 60:281–85.
41. Wedin, W. F., I. T. Carlson, and R. L. Vetter. 1966. Studies on nutritive value of fall-saved forage, using rumen fermentation and chemical analysis. Proc. 10th Int. Grassl. Congr., pp. 424–28 (Helsinki, Finland).

by sheep alone has a deleterious effect on pasture unless grazing is restricted because sheep are by nature selective, short grazers. Cattle readily select the tender green forage that has been well fertilized, and they prefer forage to be at least 10–12 cm high. Tall-growing palatable grasses are more competitive when grazed by cattle than by sheep.[40]

By selective and close grazing, animals overgraze the palatable species in a pasture and leave unpalatable ones. Continuous overgrazing eventually will eliminate the more palatable species, resulting in a pasture composed principally of those having low palatability.

Little definitive research on mixed grazing has been conducted in the U.S.; however, favorable reports have come from foreign sources. Studies in South Africa and Scotland indicate that sheep grazed in conjunction with cattle increased livestock production and had a beneficial effect on the botanical composition in the pasture. The system favors the spread of more palatable species since sheep and goats eat plants not relished by cattle. In a Canadian study, sheep consumed weeds that cattle did not consume.[42] Sheep also help keep down weeds and brush and may in that way improve the pasture sward.

WEEDS

Weeds are indicative of poor pasture management. Low-quality grass weeds invade pastures largely because of low fertility. These weeds can be easily controlled and eliminated from pastures by liming, fertilizing, and seeding improved species of grasses and legumes on infested areas.

Timely mowing of weeds and brush, ade-quate fertilization, and good grazing management are the best methods of controlling weeds and brush. Herbicides may be included for difficult species. Missouri studies have shown a higher proportion of economic species, fewer weeds, and highest forage consumption from Kentucky bluegrass pastures receiving a combination of high-fertility and 2,4-D herbicide treatments.[43]

43. Peters, Elroy J., and J. F. Stritzke. 1971. Effects of weed control and fertilization on botanical composition and forage yields of Kentucky bluegrass pastures. USDA Tech. Bull. 1430.

❧ QUESTIONS

1. Which legume-grass mixture prevails in permanent pastures on the more fertile soils of the North? Less fertile upland soils? Low or bottomland pasture?
2. Which annual legume is recognized for its pasture value in the central humid region? What perennial legumes are found in permanent pastures? Why are the trends toward using more biennial and perennial legumes?
3. Relate the species found in permanent pastures in the South to soil condition.
4. What changes in the livestock population have occurred during the past two decades? What has sparked the new interest in pastures?
5. Compare the probable value of either reseeding or N fertilization for renovating permanent pastures.
6. How would you proceed to renovate an unproductive upland permanent pasture in your area?
7. Has rotational grazing of permanent pastures usually resulted in increased animal production? Of renovated pastures? Alternate grazing of such pastures? Explain. What is seasonal grazing?
8. Develop a full-season pasture system for your area for beef cows. Include species, system of grazing, and other management practices. How will this vary from a pasture system for dairy cows?

42. Hidiroglou, M., and H. J. Knott. 1963. The effects of green, tall buttercup in roughage on the growth and health of beef cattle and sheep. Can. J. Anim. Sci. 1:68–71.

W. F. WEDIN / *Iowa State University*

ARTHUR G. MATCHES / *Agricultural Research Service, USDA and University of Missouri*

55

CROPLAND PASTURE

❧

Cropland pastures fit well in contemporary American agriculture. Agronomic concepts in the U.S. are shifting the emphasis away from crop rotations (and the "ley" influence) with their definite intervals and proportions of forage crops in the rotation cycle. For row crop production, erosion hazards in monoculture systems are being reduced by land modifications or reduced tillage systems.[1,2] The utility and economic worth of pastures grown on sites which can be planted to intertilled crops must be based more on their role in fitting economically into livestock production systems than on traditional benefits to crops following them in a rotation or system.

Cropland pastures are composed of leg-ume-grass, all-grass, or all-legume swards of improved species grown at varying intervals and duration on land suitable for continuous or intermittent production of agronomic or horticultural crops other than forages. Cropland pastures are grown for their utility in a balanced forage system. The U.S. census considers cropland pasture to include rotation pasture and all other land that is used only for pasture or grazing but could have been used for crops without additional improvement. In 1969 the U.S. census listed 27.9 million ha of cropland pasture.

Permanent pasture (Chapter 54) differs from cropland pasture in that the former is maintained *indefinitely* for grazing.

As previously defined, rotation pasture grown at more or less regular intervals with other crops in a rotation excludes pastures not rotated with other crops.[3] Indeed, crop rotations are still used, but the term "ro-

❧ W. F. WEDIN is Professor of Agronomy, Iowa State University. He holds the M.S. and Ph.D. degrees from the University of Wisconsin. His research and teaching have encompassed pasture and forage production management, with particular emphasis on utilization systems for pastures.

❧ ARTHUR G. MATCHES is Research Agronomist, ARS, USDA, and Professor of Agronomy, University of Missouri. He holds the M.S. degree from Oregon State University and the Ph.D. from Purdue University. His research has emphasized plant-animal interrelationships and development of pasture systems.

1. Meyer, L. L., and J. V. Mannering. 1967. Tillage and land modification for water erosion control. Proc. Tillage for Greater Crop Production Conf., pp. 58–62. Amer. Soc. Agr. Engrs. (Detroit, Mich.).
2. Harrold, Lloyd L. 1972. Soil erosion by water as affected by reduced tillage systems. Proc. No-Tillage Systems Symp., pp. 21–29 (Columbus, Ohio).
3. Hein, Mason A., and R. Wagner. 1962. Rotation pastures. *In* Forages, 2nd ed., pp. 578–88. Iowa State Univ. Press, Ames.

TABLE 55.1 ❧ Types of pasture based on duration of use

Type	Years of use, temperate U.S.
Cropland Pasture	
Short-term	2–4
Long-term	5–8
Permanent	8+
Temporary	<1
Irrigated	variable
Range	

Source: Harlan, 1956.[4]

FIG. 55.1. *Cropland pastures in southern Iowa . . . comprise a great proportion . . . total pasture needed . . . for meeting nutrient needs . . . beef cows and calves. Iowa State Univ. photo.*

tation pasture" is both too restrictive and out of step with changing agriculture.

Pastures have been classified on the basis of elapsed time between establishment and plowing.[4] On this basis, short-term and long-term pastures are defined in Table 55.1.

❧ CONTRIBUTION

The contribution of cropland pastures to farm and ranch enterprises in the U.S. can be firmly supported from several viewpoints, namely, (1) as meeting animal needs, (2) as stretching the bounds which climate imposes on forage species adaptation, and (3) as based on land-use factors.

MEETING ANIMAL NEEDS

Cropland pastures offer several alternatives in the way they may be used because they can produce high yields and are readily accessible to either machine or animal harvest, more so than permanent pastures. Excess forage can thus be readily harvested, conserved, and fed in periods of short supply. For certain classes of livestock it may be necessary to have pastures near farm buildings. Being able to concentrate more animals on cropland pastures can be an advantage in this instance. Permanent pastures may be further away from farm buildings, of lower productivity, and relatively inaccessible to forage-harvesting machinery.

Where the maximization of grazing is an objective in a livestock program, more than one type of pasture is needed to ensure a balance in forage and pasture supply and demand. Cropland pastures in southern Iowa can comprise a great proportion of the total pasture needed (permanent or cropland pasture totaled 75 ha, of which 51 was cropland pasture) for meeting annual nutrient needs of 100 beef cows and calves.[5] (See Fig. 55.1.)

CLIMATE LIMITATIONS

Climate imposes a limit on the adaptability and persistence of species included in cropland pastures. At the same time, cropland pastures are considered favorably for their utility in meeting animal needs, which can be accomplished by more than one species of forage. Therefore, a greater flexibility in use of forage species is envisioned; there is less need to consider a species in terms of its benefit to another crop. The time interval between establishment and plowing is flexible and, therefore, so is the choice of species.

Given the alternative of a short- or long-term pasture, the livestock producer can plan, shift, and adjust the types used as they fit his program. Several alternatives are available in establishing new stands, e.g., alfalfa or pastures and hayfields.[6,7]

4. Harlan, Jack R. 1956. Theory and Dynamics of Grassland Agriculture. Van Nostrand, Princeton, N.J.

5. Wedin, W. F. 1970. What can Iowa do with 10 million acres of forage? *Iowa Farm Sci.* 24 (9):3–8.
6. Moline, W. J., and L. R. Robison. 1971. Effects of herbicides and seeding rates on the production of alfalfa. *Agron. J.* 63:614–16.
7. Tesar, Milo B., and S. C. Hildebrand. 1966. Reestablishment of pastures and hayfields in one year. Mich. Agr. Ext. Serv. Bull. 527.

The producer can use N amendments to bolster production on legume-depleted cropland pasture.[8] He can use management and combinations on the tall, cool-season grasses to extend the grazing season.[9] Given alternatives, the livestock producer may attempt new ideas of high potential.

LAND USE FACTORS

No two farms or ranches are comparable. Pasture and forage needs must fit the operation in question. Of the adapted forages in any area, the species which fit soil conditions and proper land use on an individual farm or ranch must be selected.

In planning forage production, consideration of the USDA land use capability classes is helpful.[10] (See Terminology for description of land classes.)

Cropland pastures fit best in Classes II and III and only sparingly in IV. Class I land will be used primarily for intertilled row crops. Obviously, cropland pastures must be highly productive and well managed if they are to be economic alternatives in I. Factors of wetness and slope may be detrimental to corn production but may be of no consequence or even an advantage in cropland pastures of tall grasses fertilized with N.[11] Cropland pastures thus offer excellent alternatives on sites that are seemingly well suited for row crop production, but because of various factors may restrict corn yields.[12] (See Fig. 55.2.)

Cropland pastures have another favorable aspect with respect to land use, that of curbing environmental pollution. Research has shown that swards of sown leg-

FIG. 55.2. *Cropland pastures fit best in land classes II and III.* Gentle to moderately steep slopes can be maintained in either short-term or long-term stands. *Iowa State Univ. photo.*

umes and grasses are effective "living filter" systems for municipal sewage effluent.[13] The perennial nature of cropland pasture species is an advantage, as effluent of various types may be returned to the land.

✵ TYPES

As indicated in Table 55.1, cropland pastures can be of short-term or long-term duration. Specific species used alone or as mixtures in pasture and hay seedings are discussed for seven U.S. areas in Chapters 41–47. Here considerations will be related to legume-grass, all-grass, or all-legume species or mixtures as they fit for cropland pastures.

LEGUME-GRASS MIXTURES

Properly compounded legume-grass mixtures have provided the basis for economical utilization of pastures on cropland. It has been suggested that legume-grass mixtures were superior to N-fertilized grass

8. Wedin, W. F., J. D. Donker, and G. C. Marten. 1965. An evaluation of nitrogen fertilization in legume-grass and all-grass pasture. *Agron. J.* 57:185–88.
9. Wedin, W. F., R. L. Vetter, and I. T. Carlson. 1971. The potential of tall grasses as autumn-saved forages under heavy nitrogen fertilization and intensive grazing management. Proc. 32nd Conf. N.Z. Grassl. Assoc. (1970), pp. 160–67 (Lincoln).
10. Klingebiel, A. A., and P. H. Montgomery. 1961. Land capability classification. USDA Agr. Handbook 210.
11. Wedin, W. F., and R. L. Vetter. 1970. Pasture for beef production in the western Corn Belt, USA. Proc. 11th Int. Grassl. Congr., pp. 842–45 (Surfers Paradise, Queensland, Aust.).
12. Fenton, T. E., E. R. Duncan, W. D. Shrader, and L. C. Dumenil. 1971. Productivity levels of some Iowa soils. Iowa Agr. Exp. Sta. and Agr. Ext. Serv. Spec. Rept. 66.
13. Kardos, L. T., W. F. Sopper, E. A. Meyers, and J. M. Bollog. 1971. "Living filter" system curbs water pollution by removing effluent. Pa. Agr. Exp. Sta. Sci. in Agr. 18 (3):6–7.

mixtures in total forage production and cost.[14,15]

Frequently, adequate legume stands cannot be maintained in pastures in temperate areas of the U.S. Thus there is need for N fertilization to optimize production of cropland pastures destined for long-term stands. Research has shown this is a practical way to extend the life of a stand.[8,16,17] In research at Purdue, however, it was not beneficial to apply N when alfalfa comprised more than 50% of the mixture.[17]

Efforts to maintain the legume were enhanced by liming and P and K applications in the Purdue research where alfalfa was managed for hay harvest.[17] This suggests that alfalfa stands can be maintained in a grazing management having a large ratio of rest to grazing. However, grazing results in Minnesota and a severe monthly cutting regime used in Alabama showed alfalfa stands to be reduced in the third year.[9,18] In situations typified by these experiments, either N applications to the remaining grass or reestablishment of alfalfa would be necessary.

ALL-GRASS SWARDS

The tall cool-season grasses are excellent in cropland pastures because they offer alternative pasture management schemes when adequate, timely N applications are made.[9] The Alabama station has demonstrated that fall and winter applications of N to grass is necessary for winter grazing.[19] Year-round grazing is not possible in the northern U.S.; however, approximately six months of grazing is possible in southern Iowa, using a three-season grazing program.[5,9] In this system four grasses were grazed (smooth bromegrass, orchardgrass, reed canarygrass, and tall fescue). Pastures were fertilized with N per ha as follows: 45 kg in early spring, 90 kg in June, and 134 kg on August 1. Two grazing periods were possible, spring-summer (late April to August 1) and fall (mid-October to early December). Three-year averages in this continuing grazing study are given in Table 55.2.

ALL-LEGUME SWARDS

Two developments relating to cropland pasture suggest that all-legume pastures are feasible. Bloat prevention is now possible. Work in Utah has shown that irrigated alfalfa pastures, when properly managed with cattle fed a bloat preventive, permit attainment of liveweight gains exceeding 1500 kg/ha for cattle grazing thereon.[20]

The second development is that of nonbloating legumes such as crownvetch and birdsfoot trefoil. While primarily recommended for rolling land in permanent pastures, there are many instances where they may be grown in cropland pasture.

❧ UTILIZATION

Cropland pastures occupy land that has other alternatives. To make these pastures economical in their utilization, good stands of adapted forages are essential. Failure to obtain and maintain good stands is largely due to the selection of forage species, the methods of seeding, and climatic conditions during and following the time of germination. (See Chapter 36 on establishment.)

CROP PRODUCTION

Benefits to other crops grown at intervals in a system including cropland pasture are increased crop production and the preven-

14. Wagner, R. E. 1954. Influence of legume and fertilizer nitrogen on forage production and botanical composition. *Agron. J.* 46:167–71.
15. Wagner, R. E. 1954. Legume nitrogen versus fertilizer nitrogen in protein production of forage. *Agron. J.* 46:233–36.
16. Wedin, W. F. 1966. Legume and inorganic nitrogen for pasture swards in subhumid, microthermal climates of the United States. Proc. 9th Int. Grassl. Congr., pp. 1163–69 (São Paulo, Brazil).
17. Rhykerd, C. L., C. H. Noller, J. E. Dillon, J. B. Ragland, B. W. Crowl, G. C. Naderman, and D. L. Hill. 1967. Managing alfalfa-grass mixtures for yield and protein. Ind. Agr. Exp. Sta. Res. Bull. 839.
18. Hoveland, Carl S., and E. M. Evans. 1970. Cool-season perennial grass and grass-clover management. Ala. Agr. Exp. Sta. Circ. 175.
19. Hoveland, Carl S., E. M. Evans, and D. A. Mays. 1970. Cool-season perennial grass species for forage in Alabama. Ala. Agr. Exp. Sta. Bull. 397.
20. Acord, Clair R. 1969. Beef production on irrigated pastures. *Utah Sci.* (March), pp. 7–9.

TABLE 55.2 ❧ Results using tall cool-season grasses in a continuing grazing study in a three-season pasture system, Iowa, 1967–69

Result	Grazing period*	Tall fescue	Reed canary-grass	Smooth bromegrass	Orchard-grass	Mean of grasses
Average daily gain (kg)	I	0.48	0.55	0.69	0.55	0.57
	II	0.79	0.64	0.92	0.76	0.78
Steer-days/ha	I	788	703	666	751	727
	II	417	349	242	299	327
Total		1,205	1,052	908	1,050	1,054
Liveweight gain/ha (kg)	I	380	388	457	413	410
	II	328	223	222	227	250
Total		708	611	679	640	660

Source: Wedin et al., 1971.[9]

* Grazing period

	Spring-summer (I)	Late fall–early winter (II)
1967	May 4–Aug. 3	Oct. 23–Dec. 18
1968	April 25–Aug. 1	Oct. 21–Dec. 16
1969	May 1–July 31	Oct. 10–Dec. 5

tion or reduction of soil erosion losses. Prior to the use of high fertilizer rates, particularly N, yields of corn following a set rotation with grasses and legumes were greater than yields of continuous corn.[21] In research conducted in a 12-year Wisconsin study, maximum production of dry matter and total digestible nutrients was obtained for a rotation of corn, oats, and four years of alfalfa–smooth bromegrass as compared to continuous Kentucky bluegrass.[22] With higher commercial fertilizer rates and the return of more crop residues to the soil, improvement of soil structure, maintenance of soil organic matter levels, and the fixing of N are important in crop production. Control of certain soil-borne plant diseases and insects by including forages or pastures at varying intervals continues to be very important.

Losses from soil erosion are a serious threat on many sloping croplands. As shown in Table 55.3, forages alleviate soil erosion.[23]

21. Uhland, R. E. 1948. Grass and rotations. *In* Grass, pp. 191–94. USDA Yearbook Agr.

22. Sund, J. M., M. J. Wright, C. E. Zehner, and H. L. Ahlgren. 1958. Comparisons of the productivity of permanent and rotation pastures on plowable cropland. II. Second six-year cycle and summary. *Agron. J.* 50:637–40.

23. Hays, O. E., A. G. McCall, and F. G. Bell. 1949. Investigations in erosion control and the reclamation of eroded land at the Upper Mississippi Valley Conservation Experiment Station near La Crosse, Wis., 1933–1943. USDA Soil Conserv. Serv. Tech. Bull. 973.

FORAGE SYSTEMS

Quantity and quality of forage adequate to meet the nutritional needs of livestock throughout the grazing season can be achieved in many areas through the use of planned forage systems. A single pasture species or mixture of grasses and legumes under one management system cannot provide adequate forage over the entire grazing season, much less an entire year. In the design of forage systems, careful consideration must be given to feed requirements of the livestock throughout the grazing season or year; growth characteristics, especially the seasonal distribution of growth, of forage species adapted to the re-

TABLE 55.3 ❧ Cropping systems for the control of soil losses

Cropping system*	Average soil loss† (t/ha/year)
Corn, annually	119
Corn, barley, sweetclover	74
Corn, barley, hay	49
Corn, barley, hay, hay	29
Corn, barley, hay, hay, hay	18
Corn, barley, hay, hay, hay, hay	16

Source: Hays et al., 1949.[23]

* Hay = clover-timothy.

† 16% slope, plots 22.1 m long, silt loam soil.

gion; and influence of different management and fertilization practices on production of adapted forages. Pasture systems should be planned to ensure reserves of forage for both summer and winter to cover unforeseen hazards.

Cropland pastures are important in forage systems since they may provide either the basic plan around which the rest of the system is developed or they may serve as a stopgap during specific periods when forages are often in short supply.

In many regions midsummer and winter are the deficit periods in forage availability for which pasture systems must be programmed. How these shortage periods are filled will differ not only among regions but also within a region for different classes of livestock. For example, lactating dairy cows require a continuous supply of high-quality feed throughout the year, but forage needs of a steer backgrounding operation may be limited to a grazing period of six months or less (i.e., April to September).

Forage demands for a beef cow-calf enterprise are closely geared to calving dates. Beef cows should be in favorable condition during the breeding season (first three months after calving) to ensure conception. Failure or delay in conception is costly to the producer. The Illinois station reports, "If calving percentage is reduced by 10 percentage points, the producer not only loses 10 calves per 100 cows but also has had to pay the room and board for 10 unproductive cows. If calving is delayed a month, feeder calves will be 40–50 pounds lighter at sale time than calves born on schedule. At a price of $30 a hundredweight, the loss would be between $1200 and $1500 (the equivalent of 10 calves)."[24] Also, heavier calf-weaning weights may be anticipated when cows have access to high-quality forage throughout the suckling period.

Examples of pasture systems that involve cropland pastures in various regions and for various classes of livestock may illustrate how a forage system plan can be used to achieve efficient utilization. Variations in systems include cropland pastures that help to meet feed requirements during critical periods of the grazing season (Table 55.4).

Species mixed, as illustrated, is a grass-legume mixture. Legumes not only provide the grass with N but they enhance the quality of pasture herbage and provide more grazing in the midsummer period. Alfalfa, birdsfoot trefoil, red clover, crownvetch, and lespedeza are especially useful legumes for bridging the summer slump in pasture productivity. Grasses fertilized with N in combinations such as birdsfoot trefoil–grass or alfalfa with smooth bromegrass or orchardgrass (Table 55.5) show the increased forage availability in July and Au-

24. Hinds, F. C. 1971. Forage evaluation–Development, use, value. *Ill. Res.* 14:14–15.

TABLE 55.4 ❧ Cropland pasture in utilization systems

System	Description
Species mixed	Different forage species grown in mixtures for extending the grazing season
Separate pastures of different forages	Different types of forages grown in *separate* pastures for grazing at different times of the year
Overseeding annuals	Annual species overseeded into established stands of perennial forages for extending the grazing season
Separate pastures—vary management and fertility	Separate pastures of the same species under different managements for grazing at different times of the year
Crop residues	Use of crop residues as extenders of the grazing season
Supplement with conserved forage	Supplemental feeding of preserved forage harvested during period of surplus production
Supplement with nonpasture feeds	Supplemental feeding of nonpasture sources of preserved forage or energy concentrates

TABLE 55.5 ❧ Estimated availability of forage for grazing expressed as the percentage available by months

Type of pasture	Percentage available by months							
	May	June	July	Aug.	Sept.	Oct.	Nov.	Dec.
Kentucky bluegrass–white clover, unimproved	25	30	10	5	15	10	5	...
Kentucky bluegrass–white clover + N, P	35	35	8	5	10	4	3	...
Renovated (continuous grazing)								
Birdsfoot trefoil–grass	10	25	25	20	10*	5*	5	...
Birdsfoot trefoil–grass, deferred for midsummer grazing	...	15	35	25	15*	5*	5	...
Tall grasses + N‡	30	30	10	5	10	10	5	...
Tall grasses + N, deferred for fall grazing‡	30	30	...	...	...	25	15	...
Renovated (rotational grazing)								
Alfalfa with smooth bromegrass or orchardgrass	20	25	25	15	5*	5*	5	...
Supplemental								
Sudangrass or sorghum-sudan hybrids	...	...	40	40	15	...†	5	...
Sudangrass or sorghum-sudan hybrids, deferred for fall and winter grazing	...	...	...	...	...	30	45	25
Winter rye	50	20	...	...	5	15	10	...
Miscellaneous								
Meadow aftermath–following one cutting	...	20	30	25	5*	15*	5	...
Meadow aftermath–following one cutting, to be plowed	...	20	30	10	20	20	...	...
Meadow aftermath–following two cuttings	...	...	10	35	25*	25*	5	...
Meadow aftermath–following two cuttings, to be plowed	...	...	10	25	35	30	...	...
Cornstalks	...	...	...	...	...	10	60	...

Source: Schaller, 1967.[25] Compiled originally by W. F. Wedin, Agronomy Department, Iowa State University.
* Allowances have been made for winter hardening of legume from about Sept. 15–Oct. 15.
† Grazing must be avoided between first and definite killing frosts because of prussic acid content in regrowth shoots.
‡ Smooth bromegrass, orchardgrass, tall fescue, reed canarygrass, or combinations.

gust by including legumes in a pasture mixture.[25]

Separate pastures of different forages permit the development of a more detailed system by specifying each pasture for grazing during particular periods of the season. Separate pastures are planted to forages which have different patterns of growth. Perennial and annual types of cool- and warm-season forages are commonly used. For example, from Table 55.5, a pasture of tall grasses fertilized with N may be grazed during May and June, cattle may be shifted to pastures of sudangrass from July to mid-September, and then may be returned to the fall grasses for grazing until the regrowth is exhausted.

In the southern Corn Belt, perennial warm-season grasses such as switchgrass and Caucasian bluestem may provide good midsummer grazing in pasture systems that include tall grasses and N for spring and fall grazing.[26] Temporary pastures of fall-sown grain and pastures of perennial forages like tall fescue are commonly grown in the South for fall, winter, and early spring with a warm-season forage such as bermudagrass for summer grazing.[26,27]

Small grains (oats, barley, wheat, and rye) are especially good sources of winter pasture.[28-30] They produce an abundance of high-quality pasture when forage is generally in short supply. With proper management they may be grazed and then harvested as a cash crop. Average gains above 0.6 kg/day are not uncommon for cattle grazing small grains.[28,29]

Overseeding annuals into stands of pe-

25. Schaller, F. W. 1967. The beef cow herd in Iowa—The forage supply. Iowa Agr. Ext. Serv. Pam. 369.

26. Matches, Arthur G., F. A. Martz, Marion Mitchell, and Stanley Bell. 1971. Research in agronomy: Southwest center grazing trials. Univ. Mo., Dept. Agr. Misc. Publ. 71-3.
27. Baird, D. M., and O. E. Sell. 1956. The performance of beef cattle on winter pastures in the Georgia Piedmont. Ga. Agr. Ext. Bull. NS 36.
28. Gross, H. D., Lemuel Goode, W. B. Gilbert, and G. L. Ellis. 1966. Beef grazing systems in the Piedmont, North Carolina. *Agron. J.* 58:307–10.
29. King, C. C., Jr., W. B. Anthony, S. C. Bell, L. A. Smith, and Harold Grimes. 1971. Beef cow grazing systems compared on Entaw clay. Ala. Agr. Exp. Sta. Bull. 424.
30. Elder, W. C. 1967. Winter grazing small grains in Oklahoma. Okla. Exp. Sta. Bull. B-654.

rennial forage is common in the South and Southwest. Small grains (oats, barley, wheat, and rye) and legumes such as crimson clover, vetch, and winter peas are the annuals often used. When seeded into sods of bermudagrass, they extend the grazing period into the winter months, thus increasing total production per ha.[28,31-33] For example, overseeding 'Coastal' bermudagrass in the fall with crimson clover has increased animal liveweight gain by as much as 300 kg/ha.[32]

Old World bluestems are warm-season perennial grasses which appear to have much potential for late summer pasture, particularly in Oklahoma and parts of Missouri, Kansas, and Texas. Since the Old World bluestems do not initiate vigorous growth until late spring, overseeding with small grain in the fall provides additional early spring grazing.[33]

As may be apparent from the examples cited above, overseeding of annuals works best with forage species that have contrasting periods of production. With the warm-season perennials such as bermudagrass and Old World bluestems, the overseeded cool-season annuals are the pasture extenders for fall, winter, and early spring grazing.

Separate pastures with varied management and fertility can be developed from Table 55.5. For example, the Ohio station has reported steer gains of 0.49–0.60 kg/day during parts of July, August, and September with deferred grazing of Kentucky bluegrass–birdsfoot trefoil.[34]

Another method for providing summer grazing is to round-bale the first growth of the tall grasses and leave the bales in the pasture, utilizing both the regrowth and round bales when summer pasture is

Fig. 55.3. *Round-bale the first growth . . . and leave bales in the pasture, utilizing both the regrowth and round bales. Iowa State Univ. photo.*

needed. This method has been researched in Ohio[34] with orchardgrass, tall fescue, and timothy and in Missouri[26] with tall fescue and an orchardgrass–annual lespedeza mixture. In Missouri the average beef and dairy heifer gains ranged from 0.41 to 0.70 kg/day during July and August. (See Fig. 55.3.)

Using the same species but varied management and fertilization, tall grasses can be used for fall and winter grazing.[5,9,24,35,36] "Late summer-saved forage," "accumulated growth," "stockpiled growth," "forage on the stump," and "fall-saved forage" are some of the terms describing the practice of deferring late summer grazing until fall or winter. This management is best adapted to grasses because unlike legumes they retain most of their leaves after a killing frost. Tall fescue is superior for stockpiling because leaves remain green longer and the forage declines less in digestibility in the fall than orchardgrass, smooth bromegrass, timothy, or reed canary-

31. Holt, E. C., M. J. Norris, and J. A. Lancaster. 1969. Production and management of small grains for forage. Tex. Agr. Exp. Sta. Bull. B-1082.
32. Walker, Odell, Cecil Maynard, and Bill Brant. 1966. Economics of winter pasture. Okla. Agr. Ext. Facts 105.
33. Decker, A. M., H. J. Retzer, F. G. Swain, and R. F. Dudley. 1969. Midland bermudagrass forage production supplemented by sod-seeded cool-season annual forages. Md. Agr. Exp. Sta. Bull. 484.
34. Van Keuren, R. W. 1970. Symposium on pasture methods for maximum production in beef cattle: Pasture methods for maximizing beef cattle production in Ohio. J. Anim. Sci. 30:138–42.

35. Burton, Glenn W. 1970. Symposium on pasture methods for maximum production in beef cattle: Breeding and managing new grasses to maximize beef cattle production in the South. J. Anim. Sci. 30:143–47.
36. McMurphy, W. E., and B. B. Turner. 1971. Pasture research. Okla. Agr. Exp. Sta. Progr. Rept. P-646:10–24.

grass.[5,24,35,36] Spring growth may be grazed or cut as hay. Leaving the hay as round bales in the field for grazing along with the aftermath is practiced in many areas of the Midwest, particularly for beef cows. Such systems have yielded 10 t/ha of dry matter which, when used by the grazing animals, provided over 530 cow-days/ha. Only 0.26–0.29 ha/cow was required for fall and winter grazing from November 15 through April 15 in Ohio experiments.[34]

Harvesting a seed crop from some tall fescue fields and stockpiling the regrowth for winter grazing is practiced in many seed-producing areas.[37] To ensure a good seed crop the following year, the crop residue must be removed; therefore, it is usually clipped, round-baled, and left in the field for winter utilization.

Summer annuals such as sudangrass, sorghum-sudangrass hybrids, and pearlmillet may also be deferred for fall and winter grazing (Table 55.5).[5,34] In Missouri research, heifer daily gains on a stockpiled pearlmillet and sorghum-sudangrass hybrid combination ranged from 0.45 to over 1.30 kg during a two- to six-week grazing period from mid-November to January.[26] Highest gains were obtained when pearlmillet had fully developed seed heads. Generally, one could not expect stockpiled summer annuals to be more than a maintenance ration for cattle.

Crop residues should not be overlooked in grazing systems. They are a very economical source of feed and help fill some of the seasonal voids in pasture availability. Corn, cotton, grain sorghum, small grains, and soybeans are but a few of the crop residues which may be grazed. New growth from shattered small grain may also provide considerable grazing when rains follow soon after combining.

Feed costs for maintaining beef cows can be greatly lowered by grazing cornstalks or by feeding harvested corn-plant residue. For a 6720 kg/ha corn crop with grain representing about 50% of the total plant's dry matter, there is a potential of

Fig. 55.4. *Feed costs for maintaining beef cows . . . lowered . . . grazing cornstalks. Iowa Develop. Comm. Res. Div. photo.*

5600–6720 kg refuse feed per ha. With a stocking rate of 4.9 mature cows/ha, only 10–20% of the potential dry matter will be utilized over a 100- to 200-day grazing period. Composition of cornstalk refuse in Iowa tests ranged from 4.24 to 3.31% crude protein and from 48.2 to 42.3% *in vitro* dry matter digestibility.[38] With proper management a mixture of salt, minerals, and vitamin A is the only supplemental feed required for mature beef cows grazing cornstalks. (See Figs. 55.4, 55.5.)

Supplement with conserved forage and *supplement with non-pasture feeds* offer many possibilities. For conserved forage, preserved forage (hay or silage) is removed from the pasture for feeding back at a later period of need. However, leaving round bales (or loose stacks) of hay within a pasture is considered by the authors as a form of the system of separate pastures.[39]

The producer should consider utilizing

37. Wheaton, Howell N., and K. H. Assay. 1971. Tall fescue. Univ. Mo. Sci. Technol. Guide 4646.

38. Vetter, R. L., Dale Weber, and Nelson Gay. 1970. Grazing cornstalks and feeding corn plant refuse to beef cows. Iowa State Univ. Anim. Sci. Leaflet 137.
39. Matches, Arthur G., F. A. Martz, and T. Wormington. 1968. Pasture grazing trials. Univ. Mo., Southwest Center Res. Rept.

FIG. 55.5. *Feed costs . . . lowered . . . feeding harvested corn-plant residue. Iowa Develop. Comm. Res. Div. photo.*

preserved forage or other feeds in planning his pasture systems. (See Chapters 49 through 52 for methods of preserving and handling forage.) Cropland pastures still form the basis for conserved forage. Crop residues are a by-product of nonpasture feeds when supplemental feeds are grown on the farm.

Output per animal (liveweight increase or milk production), animal output per ha, and carrying capacity of the pasture are all increased by supplemental feeding on pasture.[39-44] With conserved forage, supplemental feeding may be planned only during times when pasture is in short supply, whereas with nonpasture feeds, cattle may receive supplemental feed for the entire grazing season or for only a portion. The type of supplemental program selected is largely dependent on the class of livestock and the economics of feeding on pasture. Lactating dairy cattle may require the feeding of concentrates through the entire season if the producer wishes to maintain high milk production.[41] However, in backgrounding beef cattle on pasture followed by drylot finishing, carry-over effects of supplementation must be considered. Beef cattle gain during a drylot finishing period

40. Bryant, H. T., R. C. Hammes, Jr., R. E. Blaser, and J. P. Fontenot. 1965. Effects of feeding grain to grazing steers to be fattened in drylot. *J. Anim. Sci.* 24: 676–80.
41. Donker, J. D., G. C. Marten, and W. F. Wedin. 1968. Effect of concentrate level on milk production of cattle grazing high-quality pasture. *J. Dairy Sci.* 51:67–73.
42. Hammes, R. C., Jr., R. E. Blaser, J. P. Fontenot, H. T. Bryant, and R. W. Engel. 1968. Relative value of different forages and supplements for nursing and early weaned beef calves. *J. Anim. Sci.* 27:509–15.
43. Hart, Richard H., James Bond, G. E. Carlson, and T. R. Rumsey. 1971. Feeding corn or molasses to cattle on orchardgrass pasture. *Agron. J.* 63:397–401.
44. Mott, G. O., C. J. Kaiser, R. C. Peterson, Randall Peterson, Jr., and C. L. Rhykerd. 1971. Supplemental feeding of steers on *Festuca arundinacea* Schreb. pastures fertilized at three levels of nitrogen. *Agron. J.* 63:751–54.

is negatively correlated with the rate of gain on pasture. For example, Indiana researchers have reported that for each additional kilogram that cattle gained during a 58-day pasture season, they gained 0.2 kg less when cattle from various levels of concentrate feeding were all fed the same daily concentrate ration during the drylot finishing period.[45]

"Good planning well in advance of the need" is the key to successful pasture systems. Each system must be individualized in accordance with the particular farm enterprise. Soil Conservation Service personnel and agricultural college specialists have developed sheets for several planning system methods. A simple, workable guide for planning has been prepared.[46] Utilizing a planning method, the producer can select from the seven basic systems suggested.

45. Perry, T. W., D. A. Huber, G. O. Mott, C. L. Rhykerd; and R. W. Taylor. 1971. Effect of level of pasture supplementation on pasture drylot and total performance of beef cattle. I. Spring pasture. *J. Anim. Sci.* 32:744–48.
46. Schaller, F. W. 1972. Guide for year-around forage supply. Iowa Agr. Ext. Serv. Leaflet AG-81.

✲ QUESTIONS

1. Define cropland pastures in terms of types, species, and use.
2. On what types of land do cropland pastures best fit? Why?
3. What are important criteria in selecting forage cultivars for cropland pasture? Give examples.
4. Could a cropland pasture seeded to alfalfa-grass be both short term and long term? Discuss in relation to longevity of the alfalfa.
5. Would a grass pasture seeded to the tall, cool-season grasses alone be justifiably considered for a short-term cropland pasture?
6. What is the purpose of having pasture systems?
7. How does row crop production fit into a cropland pasture program and a pasture system program?
8. Using the percentage distribution of grazing as given in Table 55.5, outline a tentative six-month grazing sequence for 100 beef cows with calves. State which system or systems are used to provide sufficient pasture and yet avoid excess.

R. MERTON LOVE / *University of California*

C. M. McKELL / *Utah State University*

56

RANGE PASTURES AND THEIR IMPROVEMENT

❧

THERE ARE ABOUT 405 million ha of range and pasture in the continental U.S., as compared with 141 million ha of all crops harvested by machinery and human labor. Over half the nutrients consumed by domestic livestock are from these grazing lands.[1] Their value to the national economy has been estimated from $5 to $10 billion annually as compared with $14 billion for all other crops, including forest products.[1-3]

The term "range" in the pure sense has been applied to grasslands that are a natural climax or which can be developed from climax by natural or induced succession.[4,5] However, we may say that ranges are uncultivated areas that support herbaceous or shrubby vegetation. The range complex (ecosystem) includes not only the vegetation and soil but also the associated atmosphere, water, and animal life. Many ranges are covered with native plants, but extensive areas now include exotics, accidentally introduced or intentionally seeded. Some areas are both range and forest; the tree overstory may be sparse, or the trees may have been harvested or burned, allowing growth of shrubs or herbs. Rangelands have many uses and yield a variety of products. Livestock and game have been the most prominent; but other outputs, especially outdoor recreation, are increasing in importance and are produced even by rangelands that are not grazed.[6]

The 17 western states account for 73% of the nation's pasture and grazing land. Between the deserts and forests of the West are open, arid woodlands and vast expanses

❧ R. MERTON LOVE, Professor Emeritus, is Chairman, Graduate Group in Ecology, University of California, Davis, where he has conducted range research since 1940. He holds the M.Sc. degree from Saskatchewan University and the Ph.D. from McGill University. He has had considerable overseas experience.

❧ C. M. McKELL is Director, Institute for Land Rehabilitation, Utah State University. He holds the M.S. degree from the University of Utah and the Ph.D. from Oregon State University. His research on western rangeland improvement has been extensive. He has been a consultant in Mexico and South America.

1. Sprague, H. B. 1952. Importance of grazing lands in the agricultural economy. *J. Range Manage.* 5:266–70.
2. Owen, O. S. 1971. Natural Resource Conservation. Macmillan, New York.
3. Dana, S. T., and M. Kruger. 1958. California Lands. Livingston, Narberth, Pa.
4. Dyksterhuis, E. J. 1958. Range conservation as based on sites and condition classes. *J. Soil Water Conserv.* 13:151–55.
5. Blaisdell, J. P., D. Vinson, R. W. Harris, R. D. Lloyd, R. J. McConnen, and E. H. Reid. 1970. Range ecosystem research. U.S. Forest Serv. Agr. Info. Bull. 346.
6. Love, R. M. 1971. Rangelands of the western U.S. *In* Man and the Ecosphere, pp. 228–35. W. H. Freeman, San Francisco.

FIG. 56.1. *Between the deserts and forests . . . vast expanses . . . grasslands . . . grasses, broad-leaved herbs . . . the domain of the western livestock industry.* Cattle in Lassen National Forest, California. *U.S. Forest Serv. photo.*

of basins, plateaus, and grasslands with a plant cover of grasses, broad-leaved herbs, shrubs, and noncommercial trees. These, and the mountain meadows constitute the domain of the western livestock industry.[7] (See Fig. 56.1.) The area is characterized by low precipitation, rough topography, and many shallow, rocky, and saline sites. Excellent brief descriptions of the vegetative regions of the West are available.[8]

Much rangeland is federally owned. In the 11 westernmost states this totals almost 54%, ranging from 35% in Washington to a high of 85% in Nevada.[9] Grazing of such land is by permit from the U.S. Forest Service or the Bureau of Reclamation. Permits usually have been granted so that the public land grazed and the home ranch com-

bine to make an economic unit for the operator.

The western range generally is administered on a multiple-use basis: watershed, timber, mining, recreation, and grazing. The ever-increasing population in the West has intensified the problems facing the range operator. This is mainly due to increased recreational use of public and private grazing lands. Since the 1930s annual big-game use of the range has increased from 1 to 5 million animal-unit months (AUM's). During the same period domestic livestock use of the same area has decreased from 15.5 to 5.4 million AUM's annually.[10] Uncontrolled grazing by big game may limit the advantages expected from range improvement practices. Conversely, improvement of game ranges may increase carrying capacity for game and domestic livestock.[11]

Agriculture may be defined as man's attempts to overcome the limitations of nature in order to grow and harvest a desired crop.[12] This and the usage of terms mentioned above indicate that no *intrinsic* difference exists between the range crop and the more intensively cultivated crops. Both involve overcoming difficulties inherent in climate, soil, plants, and harvesting.[13]

Commercial returns from grasslands are almost exclusively in terms of livestock and game production, and it is natural that attention is focused on the animals. However, agriculture is based on *land* and what can be grown on that land with the soil and climatic conditions that prevail. Animals are necessary to convert the forage to the products that man needs. The situation on range is more complicated than that of corn, because of the extremely variable conditions and also because of the

7. USDA. 1958. Agricultural statistics.
8. Stoddart, L. A., and A. D. Smith. 1955. Range Management. McGraw-Hill, New York.
9. Public Land Law Review Commission. 1970. One-third of the nation's land. Rept. of the Commission. USGPO, Washington, D.C.

10. Clawson, M., and B. Held. 1957. The Federal Lands, Their Use and Management. Johns Hopkins, Baltimore.
11. Plummer, A. P., D. R. Christensen, and S. B. Edmonsen. 1968. Restoring big game range in Utah. Utah Div. Fish and Game Publ., pp. 68–73.
12. Love, R. M., and W. A. Williams. 1956. Rangeland development by manipulation of the soil-plant-animal complex. Proc. 7th Int. Grassl. Congr., pp. 509–17 (Palmerston North, N.Z.).
13. Love, R. M. 1961. The range—Natural plant communities or modified ecosystems? *J. Brit. Grassl. Soc.* 16 (2): 89–99.

varied uses and products produced by the range.[6,14] Care must be exercised in the application of improvement practices so that game habitat, yield of clean water, and natural beauty will not be jeopardized. An integrated improvement plan must be prepared and followed that will utilize the most appropriate measures for improving range productivity and retaining or restoring environmental quality. Some of the more important range problems are stated here, with certain suggested principles that apply to their improvement.

❧ THE SOIL FACTOR

Range management and improvement depend to a large extent on a knowledge of the relationship between the soil series and the vegetation, whether it is natural, adventive, or seeded. Data obtained from coordinated soil-vegetation surveys are helpful in planning and applying research. Knowledge of geological formation, topography, drainage, slope aspect, texture, soil horizons, and pH as well as climate and elevation are necessary to develop sound practices.

RANGE FERTILIZATION

In addition to increasing forage yield, range fertilization offers alternatives to management by providing earlier forage growth, increased nutritive quality, greater palatability (to both green and dry feed), and differential species response such as legumes versus grass or annual grass versus perennial grass.[15]

NITROGEN. In the arid West, fertilization has been most useful on mountain meadows, in the northern Great Plains,[14] or in the Pacific Coast region where there is sufficient rainfall.[12,16] A general state-

ment often has been made that moisture is the limiting factor in range production, not lack of fertility. Native or even adventive species may not respond sufficiently to higher fertility levels to make the practice economically sound.[16,17] But there are exceptions. Ammonium sulfate doubled the forage yield of the bluestems in Louisiana and increased range production sixfold in some areas of South Africa.[18] In Wyoming, N fertilization is being used to obtain better utilization of forage away from areas usually grazed by stock. The animals seek out such fertilized areas on the range.[19]

Five conditions must be realized before a range operator can profitably use fertilization: (1) initial soil fertility must be low, (2) climatic conditions must be favorable for increased growth when it is needed, (3) plant species present must respond to higher fertility levels, (4) changes in management are usually necessary to obtain full benefits from fertilization, and (5) fertilization must solve the problem more economically than other means.[20] Micronutrients are important in many regions.[17]

PHOSPHORUS AND SULFUR. Abundant evidence exists that fertilization by P or S to encourage legume growth is one of the best ways to ensure a highly productive and stable grassland agriculture. Until recently this has been practiced primarily in the higher rainfall regions of the world, e.g., New Zealand,[21] the Pacific Northwest region of the U.S.,[22] and the regions of Australia and California[12] with a Mediterranean type of climate. More intensive research on legumes is needed in arid regions.

14. Lorenz, R., and G. A. Rogler. 1972. Forage production and botanical composition of mixed prairie as influenced by N and P fertilization. *Agron. J.* 64 (2):244–49.

15. McKell, C. M., V. W. Brown, R. H. Adolph, and Cameron Duncan. 1970. Fertilization of annual rangeland with chicken manure. *J. Range Manage.* 23:336–40.

16. Kay, B. L., J. E. Street, and C. W. Rimbey. 1957. Nitrogen carryover on range. *Calif. Agr.* 11:5,10.

17. Commonwealth Scientific and Industrial Research Organisation. 1949. The Australian environment. CSIRO, Canberra, Aust.

18. Semple, A. T. 1951. Improving the world's grasslands. Food and Agr. Studies no. 16, FAO, Rome.

19. Smith, D. R., and R. L. Lang. 1958. The effect of nitrogenous fertilizers on cattle distribution on mountain range. *J. Range Manage.* 11:248–49.

20. Martin, W. E., and L. J. Berry. 1970. Effects of nitrogen fertilizers on California range as measured by weight gains of grazing cattle. Calif. Agr. Ext. Bull. 846.

21. Smallfield, P. W. 1956. Techniques of land development in New Zealand. Proc. 18th Conf. N.Z. Grassl. Assoc., pp. 24–32.

22. Williams, W. A., C. M. McKell, and J. Reppert. 1964. Sulfur fertilization of an annual range soil during years of below-normal rainfall. *J. Range Manage.* 17:1–5.

❧ THE PLANT FACTOR

In a given cropland area one species usually is planted and harvested. It is called the "crop." On the range there are many species of plants, usually referred to as the "vegetation." A major problem is to maintain a high proportion of useful, palatable, forage species in the plant population. Often the problem is to replace a relatively undesirable plant population with more desirable types.[23] It is important, therefore, to recognize the types of plants on the range and to know something of their nutrient requirements, growth habits, and responses to management practices.

Weeds are usually easily recognized in a crop. On the range there is often a complete spectrum of weedy species, from slightly undesirable to obnoxious. The latter are the most readily recognized, and brush may be one of them. In addition, a few poisonous species are found on some range pastures. These plants may be controlled by selective herbicides, or they may be avoided by regulating the time or intensity of grazing.

UNDESIRABLE WOODY PLANTS

Shrubs and unwanted trees cover vast hectarages in the Southwest. Estimates in 1937 were 28.3 million ha of mesquite, *Prosopis juliflora* (Swartz) DC., in Arizona, New Mexico, and Texas; at least 22 million ha of burroweed, *Aplopappus tenuisectus* (Greene) Blake, and 1.8 million ha of snakeweed, *Gutierrezia sarothrae* (Pursh) Britt. & Rusby, in Arizona alone; and 24.3 million ha of cholla, *Opuntia* spp., in Texas. Their extent has increased markedly since then.[24] Various forms of sagebrush, *Artemisia* spp., occupy over 46.5 million ha of intermountain country. In California there are 9.7 million ha of brush- and oak-covered land.[25] Brush is a worldwide problem.[18]

It appears that frequent fires formerly restricted shrub invasion in the Southwest. Since fires have been controlled, plant competition, rodents, and the introduction of livestock have been effective agents favoring woody plants at the expense of grasses.[24]

However, not all rangeland shrubs are undesirable. They may provide an important portion of the feed intake of range animals, particularly protein, during the winter months or at other times of the year, depending on the shrub species.[26,27]

CONTROL OF WOODY SPECIES

Six techniques are used to increase forage production on areas with unwanted brush and trees; a combination of methods generally is used. (See Fig. 56.2.)

FIRE. Undoubtedly the oldest brush control tool used by man is fire.[28] It is the least expensive method, though by itself not necessarily the most effective. Extreme care is necessary to prevent escapes. In California neighboring farmers form range improvement associations to help each other. All burns in the fire season are conducted under permit from the state forester. Since the program began in 1945, nearly 1 million ha of brushland have been burned.[25]

Late summer burning is successful in controlling big sage, *Artemisia tridentata* Nutt., and three-tip sage, *A. tripartita* Rydb.[29] In Utah, burning has produced better results than other methods.[30] Burning is probably the most effective method of control for burroweed and snakeweed.[24]

Air pollution must now be considered in planning control burns. Generally,

23. Love, R. M. 1954. Range management standards. *Appraisal J.* 22:409–14.
24. Humphrey, R. R. 1958. The desert grassland. *Bot. Rev.* 24:193–252.
25. California Division of Forestry. 1960. The brush problem on California ranges.

26. Cook, C. W., L. A. Stoddart, and L. E. Harris. 1954. The nutritive value of winter range plants in the Great Basin. Utah Agr. Exp. Sta. Bull. 372.
27. Goodin, J. R., and C. M. McKell. 1971. Shrub productivity—A reappraisal of arid lands. *In* Food, Fiber, and the Arid Lands, pp. 235–46. Univ. Ariz. Press, Tucson.
28. Sauer, C. O. 1956. The agency of man on earth. *In* Man's Role in Changing the Face of the Earth, pp. 49–69. Univ. Chicago Press.
29. Pechanec, J. P. F., and G. Stewart. 1944. Sagebrush burning—Good and bad. USDA Farmers' Bull. 1948.
30. USDA. 1945. Sagebrush to grass, rebuilding western rangelands by eliminating sagebrush and planting grass. U.S. Forest Serv. AIS 27.

FIG. 56.2. *A major problem . . . to replace a relatively undesirable plant population . . . more desirable types.* Cattle grazing on sagebrush-infested range (left) and on brush-controlled range (right) on the Southern Great Plains Field Station, Woodward, Okla. *USDA photo.*

smaller burns produce more satisfactory results than large burns in terms of safety, consumption of brush by fire, and production of a smaller smoke cloud. Although burning as a range improvement tool is not used as extensively by private individuals in the U.S. as it was in the 1940s and 1950s because of local regulations concerning all agricultural burning, federal agencies such as the Forest Service and the Bureau of Land Management and Park Service are conducting control burns (often called prescribed burning) to reduce the amount of fuel on the ground, which in turn reduces the hazards of accidental wildfires.[31]

MECHANICAL EQUIPMENT. Bulldozers and other heavy machines are helpful in preparing brush for burning since crushed brush burns better than standing brush.[32] In Oklahoma heavy-duty mowers or brush beaters eradicated 60% of the sand sagebrush, *A. filifolia* Torr., when treated in June for two successive years.

In Kansas it has been successfully removed by tillage. Care is required to ensure that use of heavy equipment does not open up the soil to erosion.

CHEMICAL TREATMENT. Chemical treatment has been an important avenue of range improvement.[33] Concern about residues and other aspects of the environment has resulted in reduced use of herbicides on public lands. However, careful planning and judicious application of approved chemicals is vital to their continued use.

Probably the most widely used are various formulations of the plant hormone 2,4-D, but diesel oil alone is effective on mesquite. For many brush types best results are obtained from spraying young sprouts and seedlings the first growing season after burning.[34] Much research is being conducted on the relationship between the physiological condition of the plant and the effectiveness of the herbicide. Undoubtedly, costs will decrease as knowledge increases.

BIOLOGICAL CONTROL. The classic example of biological control of undesirable species is the practical elimination of prickly pear, *Opuntia* spp., by *Cactoblastis cactorum* Berg, a moth introduced from Argentina, in the Moonie River Valley, Queensland, Australia, between 1927 and 1932.[35] Utilization of sprouts by big game and domestic animals may be considered a form of biological control. If the burned area is not too extensive in relation to the animal population, this means can be quite effective in killing additional plants.

SEEDING ADAPTED FORAGES. Seeding adapted forages is generally desirable before invasion of the cleared areas by weedy species.[32] Dense brush areas will be unlikely to have enough herbaceous vegetation to

31. Biswell, H. H. 1963. Research in wildland fire ecology in California. Proc. 2nd Tall Timbers Fire Ecol. Conf., pp. 63–97 (Tallahassee, Fla.).
32. Love, R. M., and B. J. Jones. 1952. Improving California brush ranges. Calif. Agr. Exp. Sta. Circ. 371, rev.

33. Valentine, J. F. 1971. Range Development and Improvement. Brigham Young Univ. Press, Provo, Utah.
34. Leonard, O. A., and W. A. Harvey. 1956. Chemical control of woody plants in California. Calif. Agr. Exp. Sta. Bull. 755.
35. Davies, J. Griffiths. 1953. Rural research in CSIRO, no. 3 Canberra, Aust.

provide an adequate cover by natural seeding. Following sagebrush burning, wheatgrasses may be seeded.[33] Monocultures may be easier to manage, but species mixtures have a broader adaptation base and are less susceptible to elimination by insects and diseases. A native species, sand lovegrass, is used successfully in sand sagebrush areas. Where physically possible, drilling is the most effective seeding method. Control of competition in seedling establishment may be approached either by selection of species with a vigorous seedling habit or by modification of the seedling environment with chemicals or tillage equipment.[36,37]

LIVESTOCK CONTROL. Grazing must generally be adjusted for two reasons. Before burning, a good herbaceous cover is needed to carry the fire. After burning, too early grazing results in trampling damage to the young forage plant seedlings, and many of them are pulled up from the loose seedbed by the grazing animal.[32]

❧ THE ANIMAL FACTOR

Important means of range improvement are various arrangements that promote better livestock distribution. Location of water tanks, piping, and troughs in dry areas will draw cattle into remoter parts of a range pasture and increase the utilization of forage there. Construction of drift fences or placement of salt licks will also result in more equal distribution of animals. Diversion of small creeks or intermittent drainage waters to irrigate and spread over dry range sites is another means of improving forage production and better distributing animal grazing use. (See Fig. 56.3.)

The commonest range appraisal method is based on the assumption that the climax

FIG. 56.3. *Location of water tanks . . . increase the utilization of forage.* Water development and cross-fencing are necessary for better distribution of stock and forage utilization. Cattle on five variously treated sagebrush pastures, Great Divide Experimental Range. *Colo. State Univ. photo.*

vegetation is the most stable for the site.[9] Many methods have been developed over the years.[5] In one refinement the steps are as follows:[4]

1. Sites are mapped based on soil differences within a climatic belt.
2. Range condition classes over the site are mapped as excellent, good, fair, or poor. Classification depends upon the percentages of *decreasers, increasers,* and *invaders* as related to climax vegetation for the kind of site.
3. The trend is determined from the current condition. Consider factors permitting either secondary plant succession (upward trend) or causing range degeneration (downward trend).

Other effective methods include an appraisal of soil conditions and the relative abundance of desirable forage species.[23,38]

36. McKell, C. M. 1972. Seedling vigor and seedling establishment. *In* Biology and Utilization of Grasses, pp. 76–89. Academic Press, New York.
37. Cook, C. W., L. A. Stoddart, and P. L. Sims. 1967. Effect of season, spacing, and intensity of seeding on the development of foothill range grass stands. Utah Agr. Exp. Sta. Bull. 467.

38. U.S. Forest Service. 1969. Region IV, Range Environmental Analysis Handbook.

GRAZING MANAGEMENT

GRAZING HABITS. The basic problem in harvesting the range crop is one of overcoming the tendency of animals to graze selectively.[32,39,40] Studies show that given the opportunity an animal will graze one plant, avoid the one adjacent, and move to another, always selecting the most palatable. This results in uneven grazing and leads to a thinning out of the more preferred plants and a predominance of those less desirable. Frequently grazed plants are more preferred by stock than ungrazed plants of the same species. Data reported from Wales with sheep on Italian ryegrass gave plants that had been grazed six times a grazing preference of 100%; those previously grazed twice had a preference of 55%; one previous grazing, 35%; and no previous grazing, a preference of only 14%.[41]

CONTINUOUS STOCKING VERSUS OTHER SYSTEMS. There has been much discussion over the advantages or disadvantages of seasonal stocking compared with some systems of intermittent grazing. Deferred rotation did not show enough advantage over continuous grazing to justify the extra expense involved in fencing and water development in some North American and Australian trials.[42,43] On the other hand, it has been reported from Russia that rest periods are beneficial.[44] Under low rainfall conditions in South Africa continuous grazing has been shown to lead to deterioration, so methods of management allowing for periods of rest during stages of critical growth have been evolved.[45]

The range operator must base his grazing system on a thorough knowledge of all range plants.[39,40,46] It is important for him to realize that proper range use is an ideal toward which he may strive. If the population of desirable plants is gradually increasing year after year, range improvement is being practiced. If the reverse is true, a different management system is necessary.[47]

SPECIES RESPONSE TO GRAZING

Much work has been done in study of the responses of plants to clipping and grazing regimes. This information is valuable if sound grazing management practices are to be established. Three examples are given of excellent work on this problem.

CRESTED WHEATGRASS. This grass was compared under 43 different clipping treatments for five years, with various heights, frequencies, and seasons of harvest. Maximum yields were obtained when grass was harvested in the fall, and minimum yields when plants were clipped frequently in the spring. Late season use resulted in a rapid decrease in yield from year to year. Late season forage was also less nutritious and less palatable.[48]

RED BROMEGRASS AND SOFT CHESS. The differential effects of clipping dates on the production of viable seed of these two adventive annuals were compared.[49] Early clipping increased seed production of soft chess by about 30% because it induced

39. Jones, B. J., and R. M. Love. 1945. Improving California ranges. Calif. Agr. Ext. Circ. 129.
40. Hormay, A. L. 1956. How livestock grazing habits and growth requirements of range plants determine sound grazing management. *J. Range Manage.* 9:161–63.
41. Stapledon, R. G., T. W. Fagan, R. E. Evans, and W. E. J. Milton. 1927. Italian ryegrass for winter and early spring keep. . . . Welsh Plant Breeding Sta. ser. H. no. 5.
42. Hargrave, H. T. 1949. Dominion Range Exp. Sta. Prog. Rept. 1937–47. Manyberries, Alberta, Can.
43. Moore, R. M., N. Barrie, and E. H. Kipps. 1946. Grazing management: Continuous and rotational grazing by Merino sheep. CSIRO Aust. Res. Bull. 291.
44. Larin, I. V. 1956. Rotation of pastures as the system of planned utilization and management of pastures. Proc. 7th Int. Grassl. Congr., pp. 303–12 (Palmerston North, N.Z.).

45. Scott, J. D. 1956. Problems of management of grassland under low rainfall conditions in the Union of South Africa. Proc. 18th Conf. N.Z. Grassl. Assoc., pp. 43–62.
46. Semple, A. T. 1970. Grassland Improvement. Plant Sci. Monogr. Leonard Hill Books, London.
47. Love, R. M. 1956. High country grazing in the western United States. Proc. 18th Conf. N.Z. Grassl. Assoc., pp. 3–15.
48. Cook, C. W., L. A. Stoddart, and F. E. Kinsinger. 1958. Responses of crested wheatgrass to various clipping treatments. *Ecol. Monogr.* 28:237–72.
49. Laude, H. M., A. Kadish, and R. M. Love. 1957. Differential effect of herbage removal on range species. *J. Range Manage.* 10:116–20.

additional tillering. It had no effect on seed production of the weedy red brome-grass, *Bromus rubens* L. Midseason clipping reduced seed production of soft chess about 10% and red bromegrass about 8%, compared with the controls. Animals do not graze red bromegrass after the panicles emerge, while soft chess is taken readily. Therefore, deferred grazing would result in thickening the stands of the weedy red bromegrass in subsequent years.

IDAHO FESCUE. Studies designed to determine response of Idaho fescue to different harvest treatments have shown that under a so-called moderate stocking rate the average stubble height at the end of such season-long use (four months in the summer) is usually 10 cm. The average utilization is 43% of the current season's growth. Detailed measurements of stubble height over many years, however, showed 40% of the plants with a 2.5-cm stubble, 29% with a 5-cm stubble, 13% with a 7.5-cm stubble or higher, and 15% ungrazed. When Idaho fescue plants are cut to a 3.75-cm stubble height, growth is definitely retarded. Therefore, with an average utilization of only 43%, more than 40% of the Idaho fescue plants were weakened under a "moderate" grazing program.[50] (See Fig. 56.4.)

REST-ROTATION GRAZING SYSTEM

Idaho fescue is an important species on the northern desert range. It needs one and one-half seasons of rest to recover from the shock of close grazing, regain vigor, and produce seed. Another season of rest is needed to ensure establishment of seedlings. A minimum of four years is required to complete a cycle of resting and grazing treatments for Idaho fescue. Four range units are necessary to permit grazing of some units and resting of others.

Modifications of the rest-rotation system are being established in many grazing districts of state and federal land management agencies. A key principle of the system is that the physiology of the resident forage species is the basis for decisions as to the time to rest or utilize the range.[51]

FIVE-YEAR CYCLE FOR A SINGLE UNIT. When beginning a rest-rotation system, all animals normally placed on the entire allotment are concentrated on the unit receiving treatment A (Fig. 56.5). This unit is not grazed the second year (treatment B) to improve plant vigor of the key species and to allow buildup of litter. The third year the unit is not grazed until seed are ripe. The fourth year, it is ungrazed to allow for seedling establishment and improvement of vigor and litter. The last year of the cycle the unit is grazed following the time of flowering.

❧ ECONOMICS OF RANGE IMPROVEMENT

Range improvement programs are profitable, depending upon circumstances. The added cost and added return of each level of production should be compared to deter-

FIG. 56.4. *Idaho fescue . . . an important species . . . northern desert range.* Idaho fescue plant at the beginning of a four-month grazing season (upper right) and tuft of squirreltail (middle left). *U.S. Forest Serv. photo.*

50. Hormay, A. L., and A. B. Evanko. 1958. Rest-rotation grazing—A management system for bunchgrass ranges. Calif. Forest and Range Exp. Sta. U.S. Forest Serv. Misc. Paper 27.
51. Hormay, A. L. 1970. Principles of rest-rotation grazing and multiple-use land management. U.S. Forest Serv. Training Text 4 (2200).

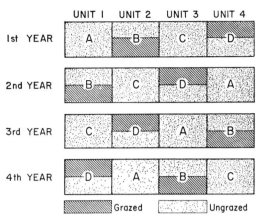

UNIT 1   UNIT 2   UNIT 3   UNIT 4

1st YEAR   A   B   C   D

2nd YEAR   B   C   D   A

3rd YEAR   C   D   A   B

4th YEAR   D   A   B   C

[Grazed]   [Ungrazed]

Fig. 56.5. Schematic schedule of a rest-rotation grazing system.

TABLE 56.1 ❧ Seeding costs, annual basis

Initial Costs ($/ha)	
Plowing, seeding, and drilling	$ 24.28
Fencing	2.48
Water development	5.50
Nonuse	1.58
	$ 33.84
Annual Costs ($/ha)	
Fence maintenance	$ 0.20
Water development maintenance	0.25
	$ 0.45
Summary of Annual Costs of Seeding Maintenance Plus Meadow Fertilization and Increased Operating Costs	
Seeding maintenance (0.45 × 1800 ha)	$ 810.00
Meadow fertilization of 80 ha (70 kg N/ha at $21.50/ha)	1,720.00
Operating (extra costs for 80 cows)	1,846.00
Total	$4,376.00

Source: Nielsen, 1967.[53]

mine what levels of investment are profitable. Investment requirements, the income pattern, and total income will depend on the type of program undertaken and the rate at which it is initiated. One of the main objectives of most reseeding programs is overcoming the lack of balance in seasonal sources of range forage.

The rancher should look beyond the initial investment and examine each system in terms of the average cost per year. This arises from the initial cost spread over the expected life of the vegetation plus any additional costs which may become necessary from time to time. Such considerations have been evaluated.[52,53]

A survey of costs and returns of southern Idaho improvement programs involved nearly 300,000 ha of sagebrush range.[52] The average total cost per ha on seedings under 400 ha was considerably more than on larger seedings, but an overall fourfold increase in returns means that research results had been well applied to range improvement.

There are various options a ranch manager should consider in improving the forage production of his range sufficiently to carry an additional 80 breeding cows: buy more rangeland and hayland, lease range-

land and buy hay, seed some of his own rangeland and improve his meadows, or spray some of his rangeland and fertilize his meadows.[53] Returns on an investment in range improvement might be realized in a number of ways: the range may support more livestock because of additional forage, improved quality and quantity of forage may improve the calf crop, the average weight of salable livestock may be increased, and the value of the land resource may increase.

Annual costs of seeding maintenance and meadow fertilization are summarized in Table 56.1 as well as the existing annual operating costs and extra costs for the 80 additional animals. Using an example of forage production to support an additional 80 breeding cows, returns were calculated to be $11,203/year. Thus over the 20-year period of the expected life of the seeding project the cost-return relationship may show range improvement to be quite profitable (Table 56.2).

The response of rangeland varies in regard to various improvement practices, each of which must be considered in relation to the potential of the range to respond favorably. Matching the site to the

52. Caton, D. D., and C. Beringer. 1960. Costs and benefits of reseeding rangelands in southern Idaho. Idaho Agr. Exp. Sta. Bull. 326.

53. Nielsen, D. B. 1967. Economics of range improvement. Utah Agr. Exp. Sta. Bull. 466.

TABLE 56.2 ✣ Costs and returns from range improvements to support 80 additional breeding cows over a 20-year period

Costs over the Life of the Range Improvement Program	
Original investments in seeding ($33.84/ha × 1800 ha)	$ 60,885
Seeding maintenance, fertilization, and operations ($4376.00 × 20 years)	87,520
Total costs	$148,405
Returns	
Sale of yearling steers, heifers, and cull cows ($11,203/year × 20 years)	$224,060
Profit	$ 75,655

Source: Nielsen, 1967.[53]

appropriate improvement measures can often increase the return on investment far more than conventional interest rates for savings accounts. Proper application of research results to rangelands is the key to success.

PAYMENT FOR NONFORAGE BENEFITS

It is unrealistic to expect a rancher to use livestock production gains to pay for all the many costs involved in improving the vast rangeland areas. This is especially true when the nationwide benefits from these lands—water and recreational areas—are considered. The future may see wider recognition of these public benefits, with other segments of the population sharing the costs of soil and vegetation stabilization.[47,54]

54. Love, R. M. 1970. Better watershed management. Proc. 11th Int. Grassl. Congr., pp. 16–19 (Surfers Paradise, Queensland, Aust.).

✣ QUESTIONS

1. Why are range improvement problems so complex?
2. Discuss the factors that must be considered when undertaking a range improvement program (a) on open grassland and (b) on brushland.
3. Why have brush and other troublesome plants been increasing generally on rangelands?
4. Explain why legumes provide a sound basis for the improvement of grasslands.
5. Compare the rest-rotation system of grazing with deferred rotation and continuous stocking.
6. What is the physiological basis for the success of selective herbicides on brush species?
7. Define range quality in terms of multiple use of rangelands.

SUPPLEMENTAL INFORMATION

Rangelands the world over are receiving greater attention than ever in the past because population pressures require all lands to serve humankind more effectively. Rangelands may well represent the last frontier. Environmental questions regarding grazing use and suitability of improvement practices in the U.S. have challenged existing multiple-use policies. As a result the number of improvement projects have been reduced. As new criteria and priorities are proposed they must still be consistent with the capability of rangelands to produce a combination of goods and services needed by humankind on a sustained yield basis.

SUPPLEMENTAL LITERATURE CITATIONS

Valentine, John F. 1971. Range Developments and Improvements. Brigham Young Univ. Press, Provo.

Interagency Work Group on Range Production. 1974. Opportunities to increase red meat production from ranges of the U.S.A. USDA Ext. Serv., Forest Serv., Soil Conserv. Serv., Agr. Res. Serv., Coop. State Res. Serv., and Econ. Res. Serv.

Gifford, G. F., and F. E. Busby (eds.). 1975. The Pinyon Juniper Ecosystem: a symposium. Utah State Univ., Utah Agr. Exp. Sta.

Heady, Harold F. 1975. Rangeland Management. McGraw-Hill, New York.

Love, R. M. (ed.). 1975. The California Annual Grassland Ecosystem. Inst. Ecol. Publ. 7 (Univ. of Calif., Davis).

McKell, C. M. 1975. Shrubs—A neglected resource of arid lands. Science 187:803–9.

Stoddart, L. A., A. D. Smith, and T. W. Box. 1975. Range Management, 3rd ed. McGraw-Hill, New York.

Box, Thadis W., Don D. Dwyer, and Frederick H. Wagner. 1977. The past, present and future grazing on the public range and its management. U.S. Council on Environ. Quality (Washington, D.C.).

Garrison, George A., Ardel J. Bjugstad, Don A. Duncan, Mont E. Lewis, and Dixie R. Smith. 1977. Vegetation and environmental features of forest and range ecosystems. USDA Agr. Handbook 475.

Heady, Harold F., and James Bartolome. 1977. The Vale Rangeland Rehabilitation program: The desert repaired in southeastern Oregon. USDA Forest Serv. Resour. Bull. PNW-70.

Box, T. W. 1978. The arid lands revisited—100 years after John Wesley Powell. 57th Annual Faculty Honor Lecture (Utah State Univ., Logan).

D. C. CLANTON AND J. T. NICHOLS
University of Nebraska

57

IRRIGATED PASTURES

&

PASTURE IRRIGATION in North America has evolved from the practice used by early settlers of simply diverting water from rivers and streams to adjacent land, commonly referred to as "wild flooding," to sophisticated methods of automated sprinkler irrigation. Center-pivot systems are in common use for numerous crops including irrigated pasture (Fig. 57.1). Permanent-set systems with even greater versatility are being developed and used on a limited basis for irrigated pasture. Surface or gravity-flow irrigation on nearly level land, with refinements for water control such as furrows and borders, has been used extensively. However, the development of automated sprinkler systems and their increased use in the late 1960s have

shown certain advantages for irrigated pasture over surface irrigation:

1. Irrigation on uneven topography and sandy soils not suited to surface irrigation. Some areas of rangeland, especially in the Great Plains region, now have the potential for irrigated pasture.
2. Water and fertilizer applied on a timely basis to more closely approximate plant requirements. Injection of nutrients into the irrigation water permits "spoon feeding" of fertilizer, especially N, throughout the growing season.
3. Livestock management independent of watering and fertilization. Frequent light applications of water do not require livestock to be removed from the pasture being irrigated.
4. Low labor requirements and convenience of operation. This lends itself to intensive grassland agriculture on a large scale.

Because of these considerations irrigated pastures have assumed new importance, especially in ranching areas where large-scale beef cattle production is of primary concern.

Initial investment and annual cost of establishing and maintaining a productive ir-

& D. C. CLANTON is Professor of Animal Science, University of Nebraska, North Platte station, in charge of the beef cattle research program. He holds the M.S. degree from Montana State University and the Ph.D. from Utah State University. He is particularly concerned with beef cattle nutrition and forage evaluation.

& J. T. NICHOLS is Associate Professor of Agronomy, University of Nebraska, North Platte station. He holds the M.S. degree from Fort Hays Kansas State College and the Ph.D. from the University of Wyoming. He is particularly concerned with research and extension in irrigated pasture, range management, and other forage programs.

627

Fig. 57.1. *Center-pivot systems . . . common use . . . numerous crops.* Center-pivot irrigation system on irrigated pasture at the University of Nebraska, North Platte station.

rigated pasture under an automated irrigation system are high. Annual forage production costs under center-pivot irrigation at the Nebraska North Platte station averaged about $275/ha. Fixed costs were approximately 70% of this total. This and the high costs for cattle inventory require intensive management.

⚘ GRASSES AND LEGUMES

Recommendations on suitable grasses and legumes for irrigated pasture may vary widely due to environmental differences among the principal producing areas in the U.S. Grasses and legumes common to most regions include orchardgrass, smooth bromegrass, tall fescue, alfalfa, birdsfoot trefoil, and ladino clover.

Choosing appropriate grasses and/or legumes is important if high production is to be realized from irrigated pasture. High forage production is a prime attribute and must receive primary attention, but not to the exclusion of forage quality.

CLIMATIC AND EDAPHIC ADAPTATION

Irrigated pasture plants must be adapted to climate and soils but in a much less restrictive sense than under dryland conditions where microenvironments are often expressed in relation to soil water and inherent fertility differences. Under proper irrigation and fertilization these soil differences are obscured. Under irrigation, drought tolerance is not an important adaptive characteristic of pasture plants; however, tolerance to temperature extremes, primarily low winter temperatures, must be considered.

Most pervious soils, within limits of erosion hazards and terrain roughness, are suitable for the production of irrigated grasses and legumes. Development of automated sprinkler irrigation has broadened the base of acceptable sites to include rolling terrain and soils of sandy texture. With the exception of areas with a high water table or appreciable salt concentrations, soil textural types do not have any particular influence on the choice of most grasses or legumes for irrigated pasture. For example, a common basic mixture for the Great Plains region is smooth bromegrass, orchardgrass, and alfalfa. This has been used successfully on Pierre clay soils in South Dakota with a clay percentage of 65–70% as well as on Valentine sand in the Nebraska sandhills, which may be 80% sand or more.[1] Soils with alkaline or saline characteristics necessitate the use of species tolerant to these conditions. Sites which include soils with a high water table or

1. Nichols, J. T., J. R. Johnson, F. W. Whetzel, and C. J. Erickson. 1968. Beef production from irrigated pastures. *S. Dak. Farm Home Res.* 19:4–7.

areas subject to prolonged inundation should be seeded to species adapted to these conditions, such as reed canarygrass.

IMPORTANT CHARACTERISTICS

Several characteristics to consider in choosing irrigated pasture plants for seeding either as a mixture or alone are:

1. Adaptation to the climatic and edaphic conditions of the area.
2. Genetic and physiological capability of high forage yields including the ability to respond to high levels of fertilizer and irrigation.
3. Longevity and persistence for reasonably long pasture life.
4. Palatable and readily consumed by the grazing animal.
5. Good forage nutritive value.
6. Regrowth capability after grazing for sustained season-long production.

Grasses and legumes with these morphological and physiological characteristics have the greatest possibility for success when used for irrigated pasture. Cultivar selection can improve these traits; therefore, producers should specify a particular cultivar when buying seed.

SIMPLE VERSUS COMPLEX MIXTURES

Research suggests that simple mixtures of one or two grasses and one legume are the most desirable.[2,3] In the U.S. there is a trend toward simple mixtures where management and utilization practices are based on morphological characteristics of the components.[4] In some cases pure stands have been suggested on the premise that a particular characteristic of agronomic importance can be better exploited

when a species is grown alone. Some research has shown that mixtures do not yield more or less than pure swards.[5]

When mixtures are used, only components that serve an identifiable purpose and are compatible should be included. Adding other components can be detrimental for the following reasons:

1. A management system that is mutually appropriate for numerous components with different morphological and physiological characteristics is impossible to implement.
2. The more palatable components are grazed most heavily, weakened, and eliminated, causing partially depleted and uneven stands consisting mainly of the least preferred plants.
3. Plants differ in their competitive ability for essential factors of the environment during establishment.[4] Relative rankings of rate of seedling development for many grasses and legumes commonly used in irrigated pasture are available and can be used as a guide to formulate compatible mixtures.[6]

Complex mixtures formulated with the objective of combining components with different seasonal growth potential to obtain sustained season-long production have been advocated but have not been successful in practice.[6] Attempts in the Midwest to establish irrigated pastures with both cool- and warm-season grasses in the same stand have had little success. If both cool- and warm-season pastures are desired, they should be established as separate stands and managed according to their respective requirements.

In some areas frequent timely irrigation and fertilization can stimulate certain cool-season grasses to continual regrowth from early spring to late fall. For example, or-

2. Gomm, F. B. 1969. Evaluations of grasses, legumes, and grass-legume mixtures for irrigated pastures grazed by sheep under various fertility and management practices. Mont. Agr. Exp. Sta. Bull. 618.
3. Kopland, D. V., A. H. Post, and R. E. Stitt. 1954. Irrigated pasture investigations, Huntley branch station, Huntley, Mont. Mont. Agr. Exp. Sta. Bull. 496.
4. Blaser, R. E., W. H. Skrdla, and T. H. Taylor. 1953. Advantages and disadvantages of simple and complex mixtures. Proc. 6th Int. Grassl. Congr., pp. 349–55 (State College, Pa.).

5. Cowling, D. W., and D. R. Lockyer. 1968. A comparison of the yield of three grass species at various levels of nitrogenous fertilizer sown alone or in a mixture. *J. Agr. Sci.* 71:127–36.
6. Blaser, R. E., W. H. Skrdla, and T. H. Taylor. 1952. Ecological and physiological factors in compounding forage seed mixtures. *Advan. Agron.* 4:179–216.

chardgrass recovers rapidly after grazing and contributes to sustained seasonal production. Even so, peak growth occurs during the spring, necessitating compensation for this factor in a grazing program.

LEGUME-GRASS MIXTURES

The inclusion of legumes in a simple mixture with grass has been a commonly recommended practice over most of the important irrigated pasture-producing regions of the U.S. Legumes of primary importance seeded with grasses are alfalfa, ladino clover, and birdsfoot trefoil. Alfalfa is the most widely accepted. Others of some importance for localized conditions include the red, alsike, bur, and strawberry clovers.

Several locations have shown grass-legume mixtures to be more productive than pure grass stands.[1,2,7,8] However, the Washington station reports that well-fertilized orchardgrass (364 kg N/ha) and alfalfa are highly productive in pure stands.[9] This compares favorably with production achieved from grass-legume mixtures reported earlier at the same location.[7] In Utah, alfalfa pastures were more profitable than either grass-legume mixtures or grass alone.[10] These two studies are a departure from the concept that grass-legume mixtures are necessary for high production.

Maintaining a desired legume to grass ratio often is difficult because the legume component declines in a mixed stand as a result of winter-kill, differential response to grazing pressure, or fertilization practices. In Washington, alfalfa was maintained at a high percentage of the legume-grass stand over a three-year grazing study, whereas ladino clover disappeared after the second grazing year.[7]

The concept that the botanical composition of legume-grass stands can be manipulated or maintained by application of different kinds and amounts of fertilizer has been proposed.[11,12] The grass component is stimulated by N, P stimulates the legumes, and proper combinations of the two elements help maintain desirable proportions of both grasses and legumes in irrigated pastures.

Bloat is a potential problem with most legumes used for irrigated pasture. Exceptions are birdsfoot trefoil and sainfoin which are nonbloating.[13,14] Their acceptance has been limited because other legumes are generally more productive. In addition, stand establishment is difficult for birdsfoot trefoil, and sainfoin lacks persistence.[13,14] Daily consumption of poloxalene can effectively prevent bloat caused by legumes. It can be fed free choice in blocks or fed with supplements.[9,10]

❧ SITE AND SOIL FACTORS

On new areas being developed for irrigated pasture, suitability of site should be considered before development starts. For land with a cropping history a good potential for irrigated pasture development generally is indicated by high crop production. However, on previously noncultivated land it should be determined that soils and other site factors are capable of supporting pastures with high production capability without causing undue difficulties in the operation of irrigation equipment. Saline or alkaline soil sites severely limit the choice of grasses as well as productivity. Sites may be intermixed with areas that are perennially wet due to poor drainage or natural subirrigation. This can add to the difficulty of maintaining high-

7. Van Keuren, R. W., and W. W. Heinemann. 1958. A comparison of grass-legume mixtures and grass under irrigation as pastures for yearling steers. *Agron. J.* 50:85–88.

8. Bateman, G. Q., and W. Keller. 1956. Grass-legume mixtures for irrigated pastures for dairy cows. Utah Agr. Exp. Sta. Bull. 382.

9. Heinemann, W. W., and L. F. Rogers. 1971. Irrigated pastures and a bloat-preventative supplement for beef production. Wash. Agr. Exp. Sta. Bull. 747.

10. Accord, C. R. 1970. Beef production on irrigated alfalfa pastures. *J. Amer. Vet. Med. Assoc.* 157:1564–67.

11. Wilson, M. L., C. W. Chang, and C. E. Watson. 1959. Effects of fertilization on irrigated pastures. N. Mex. Agr. Exp. Sta. Bull. 439.

12. Martin, W. E., V. E. Rendig, A. D. Haig, and L. J. Berry. 1965. Fertilization of irrigated pasture and forage crops in California. Calif. Agr. Exp. Sta. Bull. 815.

13. Cooper, C. S. 1966. The establishment and production of birdsfoot trefoil–grass compared to alfalfa-grass mixtures under several cultural practices. Mont. Agr. Exp. Sta. Bull. 603.

14. Krall, J. L., C. S. Cooper, C. W. Crowell, and A. S. Jarvi. 1971. Evaluations of sainfoin for irrigated pasture. Mont. Agr. Exp. Sta. Bull. 658.

producing pastures because of differential soil wetness. It also may cause problems in the operation of some types of irrigation equipment.

Sandy soils previously not considered suitable for cultivation or irrigation are successfully producing irrigated pasture in some areas of the Great Plains. However, deviation from normal crop-producing soils can cause pasture establishment difficulty due to wind erosion as well as problems of maintaining pasture productivity because of inherently low soil fertility.

Soil characteristics important for irrigation are:[15] (1) availability of a plentiful supply of good quality water, (2) suitable topography for irrigation or capability of being shaped without exposing undesirable subsoil characteristics, (3) permeable soil profile so that drainage will not be impeded, (4) soil free of salt and adsorbed sodium or readily reclaimable, (5) soil capacity to store sufficient available water yet with satisfactory aeration to permit unrestricted rooting of plants, and (6) structure and other physical soil properties to resist serious erosion with the use of well-planned and well-conducted irrigation.

Automated sprinkler irrigation can supply water frequently and on a timely basis. This reduces the need for soils that can store large quantities of water, which is necessary with flood-type irrigation.

❧ SEEDING

When proper procedures are used, stand establishment should not be difficult, especially under sprinkler irrigation, since frequent light applications of water can ensure seedling emergence. (See Chapter 36 for recommended seeding practices.)

The practice of drilling directly into the existing native vegetation when converting rangeland to irrigated pasture should be discouraged. Tillage to reduce competition is necessary. Growing a small-grain crop the first year followed by fall seeding

into the stubble can be an effective practice.

New stands can be grazed the first year when good plant development is achieved by proper watering and fertilization. Normally, fall seedings are not grazed until the following growing season. Spring seedings can be grazed approximately 90 days after planting. In both situations at least 30 cm of growth should be attained before use. Controlled grazing is extremely important to ensure stand development. A rotation system of grazing is necessary to maintain leaf area, allow recovery after use, and permit continued stand development.

❧ IRRIGATION PRACTICES

Two general means of irrigation are by flood and sprinkler. The most appropriate method will depend on such factors as topography, soil depth, soil texture, permeability of surface soil and subsoil, amount and cost of available water, and surface drainage.

Innovations in sprinkler irrigation equipment (Fig. 57.1) are better adapted to pasture irrigation than flood methods because frequent light applications of water (2.5 cm or less) are possible. Grasses are comparatively shallow rooted and require frequent replenishment of moisture in the top 30 cm of the soil profile to remain growing actively. Irrigation of pasture during establishment is critical. Sprinklers are ideal for this purpose since the soil surface can be kept moist by frequent light application of water.

Soil characteristics determine to a considerable extent the frequency and amount of irrigation necessary. Fine-textured soil stores relatively large quantities of water, allowing heavier, less frequent irrigation. Soil underlain with gravel permits subsurface drainage, thus requiring more frequent irrigation. Coarse-textured soils with low water-holding capacity also need frequent, timely irrigation.

Irrigated pastures require more frequent application and greater total water than most crops. Over a four-year period at the

15. Thorne, D. W., and H. B. Peterson. 1950. Irrigated Soils: Their Fertility and Management. Blakiston, Philadelphia.

Nebraska North Platte station the application of 39–56 cm of irrigation water was necessary each year to maintain adequate soil water in the pasture root zone. Seasonal water applied by irrigation plus precipitation ranged from 88 to 94 cm/year.

✳ FERTILIZATION

Irrigated pastures require adequate soil fertility to be productive; low soil fertility is often a primary limiting factor for pasture. Maximum response may be expected when fertilizer is used with proper grazing management and irrigation.

Results from fertilization of irrigated pasture throughout the world have been well documented.[16] Responses obtained are not always consistent and reflect variability among grasses, amount of legume in the stand, climatic conditions, and soil factors.

Two major considerations dictate the application and amount of fertilizer for irrigated pasture, the level of production desired and the role of legumes in the mixture.[16] Production levels of irrigated pasture have been increased more from fertilizer N than other elements, although responses have been obtained from P and K where soils are deficient in these elements. A more complete fertilization program, including secondary elements, may be important for localized conditions such as sandy soil which is inherently low in fertility. A literature review on fertilizing irrigated grasslands states that many researchers have shown maximum responses of grass-legume mixtures at N rates of 200–250 kg/ha.[16] Yields have increased in response to N up to 896 kg/ha when it was applied to well-irrigated smooth bromegrass, orchardgrass, and alfalfa. The rate and amount of N and P can have an influence on the legume to grass ratio in mixed stands. In general, P stimulates legume growth, N increases the grass component, and a balance of both elements will help maintain a grass-legume mixture.[11,12] A different fertilization program is necessary for mixed stands than for grass alone if legumes are to be maintained as part of the stand.

Nitrogen is needed in greater amounts than other elements for plant growth and can be supplied by either fertilizer N or the legumes. When legumes are a major component of a pasture, economic returns to applied N, measured as animal gain, have not always been obtained.[2,17,18] However, as the legume component declines, fertilizer N is essential to maintain production.[2] When legumes are not part of the mixture, applying N is necessary for high production.

Several applications of N throughout the growing season sustain season-long pasture production. The application of N solutions in irrigation water by means of an injector pump has become a common method of increment feeding of irrigated pastures using sprinkler systems.

✳ USES

Two primary uses are being made of irrigated pasture in beef cattle production. One is by farmers who evaluate it in terms of the competition it may have with other irrigated crops such as corn and sugar beets. The second is by ranchers who use it to complement the forage program in a cow-calf enterprise. In the first use, the kilograms per ha of beef produced as efficiently as possible is of primary concern. In the second, the major objective is increased efficiency of the cow herd through improved reproductive performance and higher calf weaning weights. In many ranching situations green forage is not available during early spring for cows after calving and before the breeding season. Irrigated cool-season pastures pro-

16. Moline, W. J., G. W. Rehm, and J. T. Nichols. 1972. Fertilizer response of irrigated grasslands. In D. Mays (ed.), Proc. Int. Symp. on Forage Fertilization (in press). (TVA Fertilizer Development Center, Muscle Shoals, Ala.).

17. Hull, J. L., J. H. Meyer, and C. A. Raguse. 1967. Rotation and continuous grazing on irrigated pasture using beef steers. J. Anim. Sci. 26:1160–64.

18. Heinemann, W. W., and D. W. Evans. 1966. Effects of fertilizer nitrogen on forage selection by cattle and on in vivo digestibility. Proc. 10th Int. Grassl. Congr., pp. 384–89 (Helsinki, Finland).

vide green forage for several weeks before warm-season grasses are ready for use.

Irrigated pasture also can provide more flexibility in forage production, which can be an asset to good range management. Deferment of native range during early spring can be accomplished by incorporating irrigated pasture into the grazing program, thereby contributing to a range improvement program.

The importance of irrigated pasture in dairy production has been recognized for many years. In Utah a high return per ha has been obtained when such pasture was used with a high-producing dairy herd.[19]

Irrigated pasture is profitable in sheep production.[2] Steers and sheep (ewes and lambs) grazed together have produced more weight gain per ha than steers alone.[20]

The economic worth of the many uses of irrigated pasture will depend greatly on the relationship of the value of animal products versus the value of other crops produced in the area.

BEEF COW-CALF PRODUCTION

Irrigated pasture has been used successfully to improve the breeding efficiency of beef cows nursing calves. Weaning weights of calves raised on such pasture may equal or exceed the weights of comparable calves raised on native rangeland. This improved performance is the result of available green forage early in the growing season. This same improvement may be achieved with nonirrigated, cool-season grass pastures, but not at the high level of production nor as reliably.

At the Nebraska North Platte station weight gains of cows and calves on irrigated pasture beginning in late April excelled those of cows and calves fed grass hay and supplement until native range was

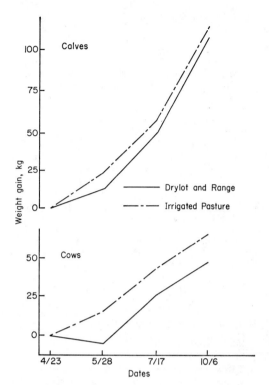

FIG. 57.2. Average weight gains of cows and calves on irrigated pasture compared to cows and calves in drylot and on range at the University of Nebraska, North Platte station. (Clanton et al., 1971.[21])

ready to graze in late May (Fig. 57.2).[21] Cows on irrigated pasture had better reproductive performance, which was the result of having access to green forage approximately a month before their counterparts that were fed hay and supplement during May prior to going on native range forage (Table 57.1).[21] The use of irrigated pasture for meeting requirements of weaned calves in the fall is ideal. Calves from two-year-old heifers gained 225 kg/ha between mid-October and December, averaging 0.54 kg/day.[22] This period of pasture use was from fall regrowth after frost, following a normal summer grazing period.

19. Bateman, G. Q., and J. E. Packer. 1945. Irrigated pastures produce large amounts of milk economically and show a high cash return per acre. *Farm & Home Sci.* 6:10–11.

20. Heinemann, W. W. 1969. Productivity of irrigated pasture under combination and single species grazing. Wash. Agr. Exp. Sta. Bull. 717.

21. Clanton, D. C., J. T. Nichols, and B. R. Somerhalder. 1971. Young cows on irrigated pasture. Univ. Nebr. Beef Cattle Rept. EC 218.

22. Somerhalder, B. R., D. C. Clanton, and J. T. Nichols. 1969. Center-pivot self-propelled irrigated pasture study. Univ. Nebr. Progr. Rept.

TABLE 57.1 ❧ Reproductive performance of cows on irrigated pasture or drylot and range (University of Nebraska, North Platte station)

Factor of reproduction	Drylot and range*			Irrigated pasture†		
	1968	1969	1970	1968	1969	1970
Calving to first heat (days)	71	62	48	54	56	57
First heat by 6/5 (%)	55	44	71	89	76	51
Conception rates (%)	94	84	94	99	88	98

Source: Clanton et al., 1971.[21]
* Remained in drylot receiving grass hay and 0.9 kg of 20% protein supplement until May 28 at which time they were placed on native pasture.
† Cows and calves were placed on irrigated pasture April 23 and were removed July 18 in 1968 and 1969 and taken to native grass pasture. In 1970 they were on irrigated pasture all summer.

Yearling Cattle

Maximum weight gains per ha for yearling cattle are the result of proper relationship of stocking rate and average daily gain (Fig. 57.3).[18] Maximizing either can be at the expense of the other, so the net result may be less weight gain per ha than desirable. An average daily gain of 0.7 kg/head with a carrying capacity of 7–10 head/ha appears optimum. Early in the spring the stocking rate should approach 12 head/ha, decreasing to 7 head by late summer when forage production is lowest. As the animals grow, their nutritive requirements increase, which also necessitates a further reduction in stocking rate.

It is possible to produce 1010 kg/ha of gain during a 140-day grazing season when stocking 10.5 yearlings per ha that gain an average of 0.7 kg/day. This has been accomplished in several locations (Table 57.2).[23-28] Over 1200 kg/ha of gain is pos-

23. Hubbard, W. A., and H. H. Nicholson. 1963. Irrigated grass-legume mixtures as summer pasture for yearling cattle. Can. J. Plant Sci. 44:332–36.
24. Hull, J. L., and J. H. Meyer. 1967. Irrigated pasture for steers and lambs. Calif. Agr. Exp. Sta. Bull. 835.
25. Hull, J. L., C. A. Raguse, and D. W. Henderson. 1971. Further studies on continuous and rotational grazing of irrigated pasture by yearling beef steers and heifers. J. Anim. Sci. 32:984–88.
26. Thomas, O. O., F. S. Willson, and C. B. Baker. 1957. Fattening cattle on irrigated pasture. Mont. Agr. Exp. Sta. Bull. 533.
27. Hildebrand, R. L. 1970. Protein and energy supplementation for yearling steers on native summer range and irrigated pasture. M.S. thesis, Univ. Nebr., Lincoln.
28. Heinemann, W. W. 1970. Continuous and rotation grazing by steers on irrigated pastures. Wash. Agr. Exp. Sta. Bull. 724.

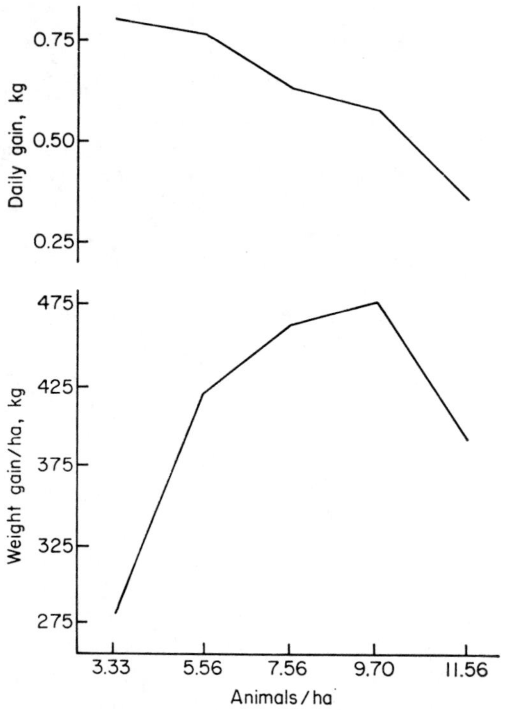

FIG. 57.3. The effect of stocking rate on average daily gain and gains per ha and their relationships as adapted from California data. (Heinemann and Evans, 1966.[18])

sible under ideal conditions. Differences in the genetic potential of cattle and the rate of gain during the preceding winter may contribute more to the variation in gains per ha shown in Table 57.2 than differences in pastures and stocking rates.

In general, animal potential should exceed that of the forage; therefore, reducing the stocking rate may result in improved animal performance but may yield a possible reduction in gains produced per ha. If forage potential exceeds the animal potential, then yields of dry matter produced would be a more reliable measure of forage value. Animal production is generally the most reliable estimate of forage value.[23]

A small amount of high-energy supplement fed to yearling cattle on irrigated pasture is justifiable. This is a reflection of the narrow protein to energy ratio in irrigated pasture forage. Supplemental energy allows for some utilization of excess protein in the forage. One study has

TABLE 57.2 ❧ Relationship of stocking rate and daily gain to gain produced per ha showing great variation from year to year and location to location

Location	Animals per ha (no.)	Gain per head per day (kg)	Gain per ha (kg)	Type of pasture
British Columbia[23]				
1958	7.4	0.77	745	grass-legume
1959	7.4	1.00	1,045	grass-legume
1960	7.4	1.07	1,026	grass-legume
California[24,25]				
3-year average	3.5	0.64	267	grass-legume
1960–62	8.6	0.48	530	grass-legume
	12.6	0.28	439	grass-legume
3-year average	7.2	0.52	546	grass-legume
1963–65	10.9	0.46	668	grass-legume
	7.2	0.53	664	grass-legume
1966	5.2	0.70	407	grass-legume
1967	5.7	0.55	648	grass-legume
1968	6.7	0.75	989	grass-legume
1969	7.9	0.63	1,048	grass-legume
Montana[26]				
1952	5.4	0.66	492	grass-legume
1953	6.2	0.82	552	grass-legume
Nebraska[27]				
1967	6.4	0.68	578	grass-legume
1969	10.1	0.60	745	grass-legume
South Dakota[1]				
1965	4.4	0.64	271	grass mix
1966	4.9	0.55	309	grass mix
1967	4.9	0.66	343	grass mix
1965	5.9	0.72	405	grass-legume
1966	5.7	0.52	337	grass-legume
1967	5.7	0.65	381	grass-legume
Washington[7,22,28]				
1954	7.2	0.85	915	grass
1955	5.4	0.83	641	grass
1956	3.7	0.70	414	grass
1954	7.9	0.98	1,211	grass-legume
1955	5.9	1.01	892	grass-legume
1956	6.2	0.86	884	grass-legume
1965	4.9	0.84	704	grass-legume
1966	4.2	0.83	577	grass-legume
1967	4.4	0.74	603	grass-legume
1968	6.7	0.65	684	grass-legume
1969	6.7	0.67	771	grass-legume

shown an additional 0.13 kg of gain from 0.45 kg of a 12% protein supplement consisting mainly of corn.[27] Experiments using larger amounts of supplemental energy have shown that its efficiency is no higher when fed on pasture than in drylot. A small amount of supplemental energy is desirable to provide readily available carbohydrates which aid in utilization of the nonprotein nitrogen (NPN) in the forage. Levels of supplement above this amount could be used better in drylot following the pasture period.

❧ NUTRITIVE VALUE OF FORAGE

Irrigated pasture forage will range from 75 to 85% moisture, depending upon stage of development, ambient temperature, and humidity or presence of dew. It has been suggested that high moisture content of forage limits dry matter intake; however, limited data show dry matter intake is influenced more by availability of forage.[29]

Protein (N × 6.25) content of irrigated

29. Lake, R. P. 1972. Utilization of irrigated pasture by yearling steers. Ph.D. thesis, Univ. Nebr., Lincoln.

pasture forage is about 20% on a dry matter basis.[29-31] This will vary inversely with the stage of maturity of the forage.[32] In rapidly growing grasses, 20% of the protein equivalence may be present as soluble NPN. As temperatures rise from 18 to 35 C, the percent of soluble N increases, whereas soluble sugars decrease.[33] These changes correspond to the period of rapid plant growth and may be the result of a high percentage of plant N existing in the form of intermediates during protein synthesis. High rates of fertilizer N increase the percentage of forage N that exists as NPN.[34] Nitrogen fertilization also increases the percent of protein but results in a reduction of the highly digestible fructosan fraction of grasses.[35,36] The lower soluble carbohydrate content results from its increased utilization for synthesis of protein and structural materials in increased yields. Cell content of irrigated pasture forage is high in relation to other forages.

Apparent dry matter digestibility of irrigated pasture forage ranges from 55 to 75%, depending upon the stage of forage maturity and the species.[28,30,31,37-39] Thus

30. Heinemann, W. W., and D. W. Evans. 1965. Forage digestibility and animal performance on irrigated grass-legume pastures with variable nitrogen fertilizer. Proc. 9th Int. Grassl. Congr., pp. 887–90 (São Paulo, Brazil).

31. Heinemann, W. W., and T. S. Russell. 1969. Evaluation of rotation-grazed pastures from esophageal and hand-gathered forage samples. *Agron. J.* 61:547–50.

32. Holter, J. A., and J. T. Reid. 1959. The relationship between the concentration of crude protein and apparent digestible protein in forages. *J. Anim. Sci.* 18:1339–49.

33. Bathurst, N. O., and K. J. Mitchell. 1958. The effect of light and temperature on chemical composition of pasture plants. *N.Z. J. Agr. Res.* 1:540–52.

34. Ferguson, W. S., and R. A. Terry. 1954. The fractionation of the nonprotein nitrogen of grassland herbage. *J. Sci. Food Agr.* 5:515–24.

35. Alberda, T. H. 1960. The effect of nitrate nutrition on the carbohydrate content of *Lolium*. Proc. 8th Int. Grassl. Congr., pp. 612–17 (Reading, England).

36. Waite, R. 1958. The water-soluble carbohydrates of grasses. IV. The effect of different levels of fertilizer treatments. *J. Sci. Food Agr.* 9:39–43.

37. Murdock, F. R., A. S. Hodgson, and J. R. Harris. 1958. Observations on the digestibility of orchardgrass pasture as affected by season and grazing management. *J. Dairy Sci.* 41:858–59.

38. Richards, C. R., J. D. Connolly, G. F. W. Haenlein, S. L. Fleeger, and H. G. Weaver. 1961. Comparison of the digestible dry matter harvest from orchardgrass and bromegrass pasture by grazing cows. *J. Dairy Sci.* 44:340–45.

39. Blaser, R. E. 1964. Symposium on forage utilization: Effects of fertility levels and stage of maturity on forage nutritive value. *J. Anim. Sci.* 23:246–53.

digestibility does not appear to be associated as much with intake for irrigated pasture forage as for mature forage. The apparent digestibility of protein will range from 55 to 80% and is influenced greatly by the stage of plant maturity and the amount of fertilizer N.[30,31] High levels of fertilizer N increase forage production; however, they may also lower forage quality by creating too high a percent of protein in relation to the available energy. The highest protein requirement of any class of animals grazed on irrigated pasture would probably not exceed 12–14%. Forage with 20% protein is higher than necessary, requiring the animal to deaminize the protein and eliminate it through the urine. This process uses energy, creating an extra energy expense to the animal.

In a rotation grazing system the dry matter digestibility of the diet may vary as much as 7–8 percentage units from the first to last day of use.[31] This reflects forage availability and selective grazing habits of the animal. During this time the percent of protein in the diet diminishes and the percent of fiber increases.[32] This phenomenon confuses the importance of rotation grazing and emphasizes the need for establishing the proper relationship of forage volume to nutritive value.

❧ GRAZING MANAGEMENT

Grazing management of irrigated pastures is a primary factor determining productiveness. Two types of management are continuous use, where the animals graze the entire pasture season-long, and rotation grazing, where the pasture is divided into several units alternately grazed with relatively long periods of rest and forage regrowth between defoliations. There are many modifications, from the less intensively managed continuous use to more elaborate rotation systems that may involve strip-grazing within a pasture where the fence is moved daily to allow access to fresh forage.

There is no general agreement on the

most appropriate method of grazing irrigated pasture, whether to use continuous or rotation grazing.[40,41] No one system of management is likely to be superior to all others in all situations.[42] However, considerable evidence shows that under intensive but proper use rotation grazing is advantageous to the overall productivity of a pasture.[40] Advantages of rotation grazing are expressed to a greater degree in increased carrying capacity than in animal performance. In California a consistently higher average daily gain of 3–8% was obtained for continuous use as compared to a five-pasture rotation with the same stocking rates.[25] In Washington where stocking rates were adjusted to approximate the optimum for each method of use, pastures grazed in rotation produced 20% more gain per ha than continuous use, with little difference in animal gain.[28]

Regardless of the system used for irrigated pasture it should be designed to optimize the physiological capabilities of the forage being grazed as well as the requirements of the grazing animal. Properly planned rotation grazing permits a higher expression of the plant's forage production potential than continuous use because control can be exercised over the grazing animal as to when the forage is utilized and the degree and intensity of use. This control is not possible under a continuous-use system.

Forages for irrigated pasture are expected to produce a season-long abundance of digestible dry matter, which requires that vital plant processes be active over an extended period. Defoliation by grazing and timely irrigation and fertilization stimulate growth, thereby subjecting the plants to a certain degree of stress. Frequent and severe defoliation of pasture plants is characteristic of any irrigated pasture system that is utilized fully. Limiting

the severity and frequency of defoliation reduces the adverse effects caused by forage removal.

Studies on many forage plants have shown that extensiveness (weight, length, size) of root systems and amount of carbohydrate storage is reduced by defoliation. The degree of root reduction increases with the severity and frequency of defoliation.[43,44] Defoliation also removes leaf tissue necessary for photosynthesis, reducing the growth rate. Maximum rate of growth in a pasture has been shown to take place when the leaf area index is at an optimum value.[45]

Two techniques for managing irrigated pasture under rotation grazing to reduce the negative effects of defoliation on carbohydrate storage, extensiveness of the root system, and reduction of photosynthetic tissue are:

1. Limit the number of times a plant is grazed during a season by using the forage in a particular pasture during a period of a few days and then allowing it to regrow unhampered.
2. Move livestock to the next pasture in the rotation when approximately 25–30% of the forage remains in order to maintain sufficient leaf area to keep the plants productive.

40. Wheeler, J. L. 1962. Experimentation in grazing management. *Herb. Abstr.* 32:1–7.
41. McMeekan, C. P. 1960. Grazing management. Proc. 8th Int. Grassl. Congr., pp. 21–26 (Reading, England).
42. Spedding, C. R. W. 1965. The physiological basis of grazing management. *J. Brit. Grassl. Soc.* 20:7–14.

43. Jamison, D. A. 1964. Effect of defoliation on forage plant physiology. *In* Forage Plant Physiology and Soil-Range Relationships. Amer. Soc. Agron. Spec. Publ. 5, pp. 67–80.
44. Troughton, Arthur. 1957. The underground organs of herbage grasses. Commonwealth Bur. Pastures and Field Crops Bull. 44.
45. Brougham, R. W. 1957. Pasture growth rate studies in relation to grazing management. Proc. N.Z. Soc. Anim. Prod., pp. 46–55.

❧ QUESTIONS

1. Are simple or complex mixtures best for an irrigated pasture? Why?
2. Which is preferred, continuous or rotational grazing? Why?
3. What are the normal ranges of percent dry matter, protein, and dry matter digestibility in irrigated pasture forage?
4. What are the potential gains from irrigated pasture using yearling cattle?

5. What application does irrigated pasture have in a ranching situation?
6. Why is animal production a more reliable estimate of forage value than forage production?
7. Discuss important characteristics of grasses and legumes used for irrigated pasture.
8. What are some of the site and soil factors that are important to consider in determining the suitability for irrigated pasture development?
9. Discuss the effect of stocking rate on average daily gain and gains per ha and their relationship.
10. Discuss fertilization and irrigation practices appropriate for irrigated pasture.

R. L. REID / *West Virginia University*

G. A. JUNG / *Agricultural Research Service, USDA*

58

FORAGE-ANIMAL STRESSES

❦

I<small>T HAS</small> frequently been claimed that the spread of improved methods of pasture establishment and management has been accompanied by the introduction and extension of a miscellany of ailments among grazing stock. Those concerned with animal health and production have often pointed an accusing finger at the plant breeder and agronomist and claimed that by their work they have created many new, or intensified many old problems of animal health."[1]

One of the disturbing features of modern animal husbandry systems is that as the level of intensification of animal production increases, so apparently does the incidence of nutritional disorders. This "production-disease complex" has been most apparent with high-producing ruminant animals where a major part of the natural fiber components of the diet has been replaced by concentrates.[2] Incidence of such problems in grazing animals has been less easy to establish. Development of the use of semipermanent pastures in Europe led earlier workers to conclude that occurrence

of such physiological disorders as bloat and grass tetany in pastured animals was increasing.[3] Reluctance of farmers to use high levels of fertilizer N on their grassland has been attributed not only to the increased level of management required but to a fear that such practices might affect the health and productivity of their livestock.[4,5] It is therefore important to understand the basic causes of these nutritional disorders, how they relate to systems of forage management, and how they may be controlled and treated.

❦ BLOAT

A recent estimate has placed the annual economic loss from bloat in the U.S. in excess of $100 million, with a calculated death loss of more than 0.5% of the cattle population. Similarly, the financial loss to the dairy cattle industry in New Zealand has been put at $NZ 5 million/yr, with a death

❦ R. L. REID is Professor of Animal Nutrition at West Virginia University. He holds the Ph.D. degree from Aberdeen University, Scotland. His major interest is in the chemistry of forage plants and the relationship of plant composition to intake and digestibility by the ruminant animal.

❦ G. A. JUNG. *See Chapter 27.*

1. Worden, A. N., K. C. Sellers, and D. E. Tribe. 1963. Animal Health, Production and Pasture. Longmans, Green, London.
2. Payne, J. M., S. M. Dew, R. Manston, and M. J. Vagg. 1970. Metabolic disorders of the ruminant: Hypocalcaemia and hypomagnesaemia. *In* A. T. Phillipson (ed.), Physiology of Digestion and Metabolism in the Ruminant, pp. 584–98. Oriel Press, Newcastle upon Tyne, England.
3. Muir, W. R. 1948. Pasture herbage as a causal factor in animal disease: A review. *J. Brit. Grassl. Soc.* 3:231–47.
4. Holmes, W. 1968. The use of nitrogen in the management of pasture for cattle. *Herb Abstr.* 38:265–77.
5. Large, R. V. 1968. The effect of nitrogenous fertilizers on animal health. *Nat. Agr. Adv. Serv. Quart. Rev.* 79:110–17.

rate of 1–2% in dairy cows.[6] Factors implicated in these high losses are the increased use of legumes as components of high-quality pasture; more intensive management systems; and, possibly, increased use of fertilizer in pasture production.[7,8]

Bloat in animals may be observed in a variety of feeding circumstances, and the causes of the disease are extremely complex. Feedlot bloat is experienced in the U.S., but the major problem in pastured animals is the subacute or acute condition associated with the feeding of succulent legumes. The condition results in the formation of a stable foam in the rumen of the animal, a retention of gas and an increase of pressure in the chamber, and finally an inhibition of the eructation mechanism (Fig. 58.1). The physiological sequence of events has been clearly described.[7]

FIG. 58.1. *Bloat in pastured animals . . . associated . . . succulent legumes . . . results in formation of a stable foam in the rumen. E. E. Bartley, Kans. State Univ. photo.*

CAUSES

Production of a stable foam in bloating animals is due to a complex interaction of animal, plant, and microbiological factors. There are marked differences among individual animals in their susceptibility to the disease. Within a given herd, some animals are bloaters and some are not. These hereditary differences seem to be due not so much to differences in the rate of intake or total consumption of the herbage as to the state of the animal and the condition of the rumen contents.[9] Studies in New Zealand with cows of high and low susceptibility to bloat showed that susceptibility could be transferred by exchanging the total rumen contents between susceptible and nonsusceptible animals before feeding red clover.[6]

A puzzling feature of bloat research has

been that animals generally are prone to bloat more readily on lush alfalfa pasture than on cured alfalfa hay, although the hay will produce a very stable foam under laboratory conditions. Workers in Kansas therefore concluded that bloat may result from the presence of foam-promoting compounds in the plant *in conjunction with* the absence of an antifoaming agent produced by the animal.[10] They suggest that the antifoaming agent for alfalfa hay is saliva or the mucin compounds in saliva. There is a much higher production of saliva in cows fed hays than in animals fed young herbage, probably due to a reflex stimulation of salivary flow by stemmy food in the rumen. However, New Zealand studies indicate little association between susceptibility to bloat and the supply and composition of saliva in cows fed red clover.[6]

The influence of the animal may be exerted indirectly through the activity and composition of the microflora and microfauna of the rumen. Between bloater and nonbloater animals there seem to be no

6. Clarke, R. T. J., and C. S. W. Reid. 1970. Legume bloat. *In* A. T. Phillipson (ed.), Physiology of Digestion and Metabolism in the Ruminant, pp. 599–606. Oriel Press, Newcastle upon Tyne, England.

7. Dougherty, R. W. 1962. Bloat in ruminants. *In* H. D. Hughes, M. E. Heath, and D. S. Metcalfe (eds.), Forages, 2nd ed., pp. 607–16. Iowa State Univ. Press, Ames.

8. Johns, A. T. 1963. Bloat. *In* Animal Health, Production and Pasture, pp. 384–408. Longmans, Green, London.

9. Johns, A. T. 1956. Bloat. *Vet. Rev. Annot.* 2:107–34.

10. Bartley, E. E. 1967. Progress in bloat prevention. *Agr. Sci. Rev.* 5:5–13.

consistent differences in bacterial species or numbers nor differences in fermentation rates in the rumen. Work in Kansas, however, has shown that both aerobic and anaerobic rumen bacteria have the ability to break down salivary mucins and that there are differences in mucinolytic activity between organisms isolated from bloat susceptible and nonsusceptible cattle.[11,12] If, as suggested, the salivary mucin compounds are effective foam breakers, the destruction of mucin by these bacteria could result in bloat.

Numbers of holotrich ciliate protozoa in the rumen decrease rapidly with the onset of the bloating condition. Polysaccharide cell contents released on the death of these organisms may have a function in foam stabilization. Treatment of animals with dimetridazole to reduce or eliminate the holotrich ciliates markedly reduced the severity and incidence of bloat in both stall-fed and grazing cows, although it was found that bloat could still occur in the holotrich-free animals.[6]

Many plant components have been implicated in the etiology of bloat. Inability of the bloating animal to eliminate ruminal gas indicated a possible role of plant toxins in inhibiting the eructation mechanism or ruminal motility. Such compounds or derivatives produced in the rumen include the cyanogenetic glucosides, flavones, saponins, histamines, and hydrogen sulfide as well as ammonia compounds. For some of these there seems to be little relationship between plant concentration and incidence of bloat. It is also doubtful whether rumen motility is impaired in the affected animal, at least in the earlier stages of the condition.

A variety of adverse physiological effects can, however, be associated with the saponin fraction of alfalfa and it has been claimed that saponins may induce bloat through physiological and surface tension effects.[7] Saponins, which in alfalfa are mainly triterpenoid compounds, have the capacity to stabilize foams. An argument against the saponin theory of bloat is the fact that the optimum pH for maximum foam stability of the saponins is approximately 4.5–5, a considerably more acid pH than required for maximum stability of the rumen contents of bloating cows.[13] Saponin content of alfalfa can be affected significantly by such factors as cultivar, growth stage, and percentage of leaves.[14]

Attention has focused on the role of plant proteins in causing bloat, particularly since the demonstration that the pH for maximum foam stability of rumen liquor is the same as that of foams formed by leaf protein extracts from red clover.[13] Canadian workers claim that a Fraction 1 (18-S) protein is the primary cause of bloat. This is a soluble, high molecular weight protein with a sedimentation constant of 18 Svedberg units. They found marked differences in 18-S protein content between bloating and nonbloating forages and concluded that four conditions are necessary to induce bloat: (1) vigorous gas production to produce the foam gas phase and rumen pressure, (2) sufficient 18-S protein to stabilize the foam, (3) rumen acidity below pH 6, and (4) cations to bind the protein molecules in the surface film. They suggest that when Fraction 1 protein is below 1.8% there will be no significant occurrence of bloat, and when the rumen pH is below 6 severe bloat may result.[15] This definition of a threshold value for a critical component in the bloat-producing complex seems to offer the plant breeder a significant objective in the development of nonbloating legumes.

11. Mishra, B. D., L. R. Fina, E. E. Bartley, and T. J. Claydon. 1967. Bloat in cattle. XI. The role of aerobic (facultative) mucinolytic bacteria. *J. Anim. Sci.* 26:606–12.

12. Mishra, B. D., E. E. Bartley, L. R. Fina, and M. P. Bryant. 1968. Bloat in cattle. XIV. Mucinolytic activity of several anaerobic rumen bacteria. *J. Anim. Sci.* 27:1651–56.

13. Mangan, J. L. 1959. Bloat in cattle. XI. Foaming properties of proteins, saponins and rumen liquor. *N.Z. J. Agr. Res.* 2:47–61.

14. Pedersen, M. W., D. E. Zimmer, D. R. McAllister, J. O. Anderson, M. D. Wilding, G. A. Taylor, and C. F. McGuire. 1967. Comparative studies of saponin of several alfalfa varieties using chemical and biochemical assays. *Crop Sci.* 7:349–52.

15. Miltimore, J. E., J. M. McArthur, J. L. Mason, and D. L. Ashby. 1970. Bloat investigations. The threshold Fraction 1 (18-S) protein concentration for bloat and relationships between bloat and lipid, tannin, Ca, Mg, Ni and Zn concentrations in alfalfa. *Can. J. Anim. Sci.* 50:61–68.

A New Zealand study suggests that the absence of bloat in animals grazing certain temperate and tropical legumes may relate to the presence of protein-precipitating compounds such as tannins in the plant.[16] This also has implications for the agronomist and plant breeder, although whether a selection program designed to increase the tannin levels of plants would have much attraction for the nutritionist interested in improving forage quality is doubtful.

PREVENTION AND TREATMENT

Traditionally, the methods available for the control of bloat have been troublesome, expensive, and generally only partially effective. Pasture management measures may include the use of grass-legume mixtures rather than the legume alone; supplementation of legume pastures with good quality grass hays, e.g., oat hay or sudangrass hay, fed overnight; intensive strip grazing using electric fences; or cutting and feeding the legume herbage in drylot. Treatment with antibiotics such as penicillin has been found to be effective for limited periods (2–3 days) at oral dose levels of 50–100 mg given prior to pasturing. A logical approach has been the use of foam-breaking agents, but here the main problems have been methods of administration and duration of effective control. To be effective, one dose of an antifoaming agent should prevent bloat for at least 12 hours; act within 10 minutes; not be eliminated in milk or cause adverse effects on health, reproduction, feed intake or quality of milk; and not be found in body tissues five days after administration.[10]

Compounds tested have included the vegetable oils, animal fats, paraffin, turpentine, and silicones. Vegetable oils and animal fats are reasonably effective and utilizable by the animal, but their effect is generally short-lived (2–3 hours). Some means of providing continuous intake is therefore necessary. In some countries, the technique of spraying bloat pastures with emulsified vegetable or mineral oils or emulsified tallow has been used successfully.[8]

The most promising advance has been the development of the polyoxypropylene-polyoxyethylene block polymer compounds (Poloxalene in the U.S., Pluronics in New Zealand) as antifoaming agents for the control of bloat. The addition of a Pluronic to the drinking water was highly effective in controlling bloat in cows pastured on red clover.[17] Poloxalene has been tested in feeding studies in Kansas, Iowa, Mississippi, Louisiana, and Utah and has given good control of legume bloat without deleterious side effects.[10] It may be supplied as a topdressing on a grain supplement, compounded into a grain pellet, or incorporated in a salt-molasses block supplied on pasture.

The long-term solution to the problem of bloat would seem to lie in programs of plant breeding designed to select legume species and cultivars of low bloating potential but adequate nutritional quality and of selection of animals with a low hereditary susceptibility to the disease. Some progress in this direction has been made.[6]

❧ MINERAL IMBALANCES

Production of soil-plant-animal mineral imbalances may result from three kinds of situation:[18] (1) where the animal's requirement for a given mineral is much higher than the plant's requirement for normal growth, leading to deficiency states of, e.g., Co, Se, I, Na, Cl, and sometimes Fe and Zn; (2) where the plant is an accumulator of specific minerals to a level toxic to the animal or interfering with the utilization of another mineral, e.g., Se, Mo, Cu; and (3) where both plant and animal have roughly equivalent requirements for normal nutrition, so that a soil deficiency

16. Jones, W. T., and J. W. Lyttleton. 1971. Bloat in cattle. XXXIV. A survey of legume forages that do and do not produce bloat. N.Z. J. Agr. Res. 14:101–7.

17. Phillips, D. S. M. 1968. The use of "Pluronics" administered in the drinking water as a means of bloat control in cattle. N.Z. J. Agr. Res. 11:85–100.

18. Allaway, W. H. 1962. Relation of soil to plant and animal nutrition. Proc. Cornell Nutr. Conf. Feed Manuf., pp. 13–23.

would restrict the growth of both animal and plant, e.g., P and S.

Causes and results of such mineral problems in grazing ruminants have been reviewed in detail.[19,20] Where there is a clearly recognized relationship between a soil mineral deficiency and the incidence of a metabolic problem in animals, e.g., as has been demonstrated for Co and Se in this country, measures may be taken to supply the missing element to the animal.[21,22]

Of equal interest is the increasing incidence of a number of metabolic problems in pastured or forage-fed livestock relating to the intensification of grassland productivity. This may come about through an increasing input of fertilizer to maximize herbage yields or from the selective use of improved grass and legume cultivars as the major component of pasture and hay crops. In many instances the causes of such effects have been hard to define. In reference to trace element problems, it has been stated, "These will not be easily recognizable acute conditions with well-marked stigmata, but mild or marginal deficiencies, difficult to diagnose and expressed mostly as a vague unthriftiness or suboptimal productivity. This has been the recent history of many countries as their animal industries become more intensified and plant productivity from the land is increased."[23] This situation has been noted in the Canterbury district of New Zealand on soils marginally deficient in Se, Cu, and Co. Sheep with no clinical symptoms of Se or Cu deficiency gave significant responses in liveweight gain, wool growth, and fecundity to Se

treatment, and further responses to Se and Cu together.[24]

GRASS TETANY

Grass tetany is a major metabolic and economic problem to farmers in temperate areas of the world (Europe, North America, New Zealand, Australia). Incidence of grass tetany has been placed at 0.5% of all dairy cows in the United Kingdom and at 1–2% of dairy animals in the Netherlands. Similar figures are difficult to come by for the U.S., but reports of serious outbreaks have appeared from California, Pennsylvania, West Virginia, Maryland, Virginia, South Carolina, Georgia, Mississippi, Texas, Oklahoma, Utah, Nevada, and Idaho. In some years death losses in affected herds in California have been as high as 20%.

Classically, grass tetany is most serious on spring pastures, although it may also be observed during the fall. In the Netherlands, outbreaks have been related to weather conditions, the majority of cases occurring with a mean temperature between 8 and 14 C. A higher incidence of spring and fall tetany has been noted in wet years.[25] In the U.S., danger periods for beef animals have been classified as: (1) winter tetany, occurring in cows maintained on grass hay, especially those calving in late fall or winter; (2) transitional tetany, occurring in late winter in cows that are still eating hay but have access to new growth of pasture; (3) spring tetany, the classic condition.[26] The condition of "wheat pasture poisoning," observed in the winter wheat grazing areas of Texas and Oklahoma, occurs in cows near parturition and is apparently similar to grass tetany. Cases of tetany have also been reported in beef cows nursing calves on small-grain pastures in the late winter period in Georgia.

19. Underwood, E. J. 1966. The Mineral Nutrition of Livestock, p. 237. Commonwealth Agr. Bur., Central Press, Aberdeen, Scotland.
20. Underwood, E. J. 1971. Trace Elements in Human and Animal Nutrition, 3rd ed., p. 543. Academic Press, New York.
21. Kubota, J. 1968. Distribution of cobalt deficiency in grazing animals in relation to soils and forage plants of the United States. *Soil Sci.* 106:122–30.
22. Kubota, J., W. H. Allaway, D. L. Carter, E. E. Cary, and V. A. Lazar. 1967. Selenium in crops in the United States in relation to selenium-responsive diseases of animals. *J. Agr. Food Chem.* 15:448–53.
23. Underwood, E. J. 1970. Trace Element Metabolism in Animals. Proc. WAAP/IBP Int. Symp., p. 550 (Aberdeen, Scotland). E. & S. Livingstone, Edinburgh and London.

24. Hill, M. K., S. D. Walker, and A. G. Taylor. 1969. Effects of "marginal" deficiencies of copper and selenium on growth and productivity of sheep. *N.Z. J. Agr. Res.* 12:261–70.
25. Kemp, A., and M. L. t'Hart. 1957. Grass tetany in grazing milking cows. *Neth. J. Agr. Sci.* 5:4–17.
26. Horvath, D. J., and J. R. Todd. 1968. Magnesium supplements for cattle. Proc. 23rd Ann. Tex. Nutr. Conf., pp. 96–104.

FIG. 58.2. *Animal initially shows nervousness, hypersensitivity and muscle twitching . . . staggers while walking . . . acute phase . . . animal will go down . . . show muscular spasms, tetany, and convulsions.* A dairy cow going into hypomagnesemic tetany on grass pasture. *Institute for Biological and Chemical Research on Field Crops and Herbage, Wageningen, The Netherlands.* A. Kemp photo.

Grass tetany generally affects the mature cow, probably due to a relative inability of the older animal to mobilize Mg from its skeleton, and is most common in the 10-week period after calving.[19] The disease can affect any breed of cattle, beef or dairy, although among dairy breeds the Ayrshire seems to be particularly prone to the condition. Sheep also are prone to grass tetany, the most susceptible animal being the ewe with twin lambs in the 1–4-week period after lambing. Clinically, the animal going into tetany initially shows nervousness, hypersensitivity, and muscle twitching, and it staggers while walking; in the acute phase the animal will go down on its side and show muscular spasms, tetany of the fore and hind legs, and convulsions (Fig. 58.2). Consistently there is a depression of serum Mg values to less than 1 mg/100 ml blood, with or without a depression of blood Ca.

CAUSES OF TETANY. The immediate cause of clinical tetany in the animal on spring pasture is the rapid decrease in serum Mg, although the reasons for this decline are not clearly understood. Incidence of grass tetany is not always correlated with the level of Mg in the plant, although workers in the Netherlands concluded that above a critical value of 0.2% Mg in the herbage tetany was unlikely to occur.[27] It also was shown that below this value the risk of tetany increased with increasing herbage levels of N and K.

Magnesium concentration of pasture herbage may be affected by: (1) botanical composition—generally, legumes and herbaceous weeds have higher levels of Mg than grasses;[28] (2) seasonal changes—Mg concentrations are lowest in young spring grass and increase through late summer and fall; and (3) fertilizer treatment—this may be an indirect effect on botanical composition of pasture or a direct effect on Mg concentration of the herbage. Generally, where Mg in the soil is not a limiting element, fertilizer N will increase Mg concentration in the grass. Potassium fertilization, however, will increase herbage K levels but decrease herbage Mg.[29] When high rates of N and K are applied together, the result is frequently a decrease in blood Mg in the animal and an increase in the incidence of grass tetany. Nitrogen fertilization also depresses the level of soluble carbohydrate in the plant, and some workers consider that it is the gross protein-energy imbalance in spring grass that triggers tetany.[30]

In addition to the effect of low dietary intakes of herbage Mg, several factors may affect the availability of the mineral to the

27. Kemp, A. 1960. Hypomagnesaemia in milking cows. The response of serum magnesium to alterations in herbage composition resulting from potash and nitrogen dressings on pasture. *Neth. J. Agr. Sci.* 8:281–304.

28. Todd, J. R. 1961. Magnesium in forage plants. I. Magnesium contents of different species and strains as affected by season and soil treatment. *J. Agr. Sci.* 56:411–15.

29. Wolton, K. M. 1963. Fertilizers and hypomagnesaemia. *Nat. Agr. Adv. Serv. Quart. Rev.* 14:122–30.

30. Metson, A. J., W. M. H. Saunders, T. W. Collie, and V. W. Graham. 1966. Chemical composition of pastures in relation to grass tetany in beef breeding cows. *N.Z. J. Agr. Res.* 9:410–36.

animal.[30,31] Availability in this sense is defined as the percentage of Mg from the feed which is not excreted in the feces. Trials with lactating cows in the Netherlands showed that the availability of Mg increased as the herbage matured (with decreasing crude protein concentrations) and that N and K fertilization depressed Mg availability.[32] This effect of fertilizer N has been related to the release of high levels of ammonia in the rumen of animals eating spring grass and the consequent complexing of Mg as magnesium ammonium phosphate. Dutch workers suggest that the effects of N may result from an increased level of higher fatty acids in the plant and the formation of insoluble Mg soaps in the gastrointestinal tract.[33]

Another factor may be the presence of certain organic acids such as citric and transaconitic in the herbage. The possible significance of transaconitic acid was first demonstrated for California rangeland grasses, many of which were found to contain high levels of the acid in spring.[34] It was suggested that these acids might complex Ca and Mg, making them unavailable to the animal. The oral dosing of potassium chloride with either transaconitic acid or citric acid has been found to cause tetanylike symptoms in cattle.[35] Also, the concentration of organic acids in various grass species responds to fertilization, with increases from the application of both N and K.[31] Reports on the effects of transaconitic and citric acids on Mg metabolism have tended to be inconclusive. There is presently some doubt about a primary function of these plant constituents in the tetany.

PREVENTION AND TREATMENT. Since there is a relationship between the incidence of tetany and the use of high levels of N and K, fertilization practices should be considered first. It is suggested that in tetany-prone areas the risk to animals may be reduced by using no more N than is required for immediate herbage production and by deferring K application until the danger period is past.[29] Steps should also be taken to improve the Mg content of the soil and the herbage. A general experience in various parts of the world has been that Mg fertilization at the rate of roughly 300 kg/ha or more is effective on light or sandy soils but uneconomical on heavy soils.[36] A more effective approach developed under Irish conditions has been to dust the pasture at the rate of 15 kg Mg/ha before grazing. To protect wintering animals, magnesium oxide can be incorporated into forage in the windrow or as it is blown into the silo. A level of 2 kg magnesium oxide per ton of fresh grass has been effective and does not appear to interfere with the silage fermentation.[26]

In tetany-prone areas the farmer may prefer to place more reliance on direct administration of Mg salts to his animals. Daily requirements are high; minimum levels of 50–60 g of magnesium oxide daily for lactating cows have been suggested when given as a drench.[19] Alternative methods would be the use of concentrate mixes; mineral mixes, generally with salt; liquid molasses–magnesium oxide mixtures (this is an effective method of supplementation for cattle on spring pasture); and molasses–magnesium oxide blocks or cubes—here, however, it is difficult to ensure that all cows consume enough to meet their needs. For wintering animals the Mg compounds may also be spread on silage or sprinkled on hay. Use of Mg alloy bullets, which are placed in the rumen and de-

31. Grunes, D. L., P. R. Stout, and J. R. Brownell. 1970. Grass tetany of ruminants. *Advan. Agron.* 22:331–74.
32. Kemp, A., W. B. Deijs, O. J. Hemkes, and A. J. H. van Es. 1961. Hypomagnesaemia in milking cows: Intake and utilization of magnesium from herbage by lactating cows. *Neth. J. Agr. Sci.* 9:134–49.
33. Kemp, A., W. B. Deijs, and E. Kluvers. 1966. Influence of higher fatty acids on the availability of magnesium in milking cows. *Neth. J. Agr. Sci.* 14:290–95.
34. Stout, P. R., J. R. Brownell, and R. G. Burau. 1967. Occurrence of transaconitate in range forage species. *Agron. J.* 59:21–24.
35. Bohman, V. R., A. L. Lesperance, G. D. Harding, and D. L. Grunes. 1969. Induction of experimental tetany in cattle. *J. Anim. Sci.* 29:99–102.

36. Todd, J. R. 1966. Methods of increasing the magnesium contents of herbage, with particular reference to the prevention of hypomagnesaemic tetany in ruminants. Proc. 10th Int. Grassl. Congr., pp. 178–80 (Helsinki, Finland).

signed to release Mg slowly and continuously, has met with mixed success and will require further testing.[31,37]

NITRATE TOXICITY

Nitrate is a normal component of herbage, and indeed the nitrate content of grass has been used as an index of the level of N nutrition of the crop and of the yield obtainable.[38] At abnormally high values in the plant, nitrate can present a serious hazard to livestock consuming the forage. There is also a considerable risk to humans working with high-nitrate silages soon after ensiling. Nitrogen oxide gas released by denitrifying bacteria accumulates at the bottom of the silo and is highly toxic to humans and animals alike.

Early investigations on nitrate toxicity stemmed from the occurrence of "oat hay poisoning" in the western areas of the U.S. Crops such as cereal hays or corn or sorghum fodder were found to accumulate toxic amounts of nitrates when grown under adverse environmental conditions. Consumption of the forage by cattle resulted in the condition of methemoglobinemia resulting from conversion of nitrate into nitrite in the rumen of the animal. In this state, nitrite is absorbed into the blood and converts normal blood hemoglobin into methemoglobin, a form incapable of transporting oxygen to the body tissues. If not treated, the animal dies of anoxia. A more widespread subclinical influence of nitrate ingestion has been recognized with intensification of the practice of heavy fertilization of corn and forage crops, particularly with N. Among these sublethal effects may be effects on growth, reproduction, milk production, and the vitamin A and iodine status of the animal.[39]

Environmental factors controlling nitrate accumulation in the plant are fertilization, light intensity, and drought. Generally, there is a direct response in plant nitrate concentration to increasing levels of fertilizer N,[39,40] and nitrate accumulation is greater from nitrate fertilizers than from ammonium sulfate or urea.[4] Nitrate responses to P and K fertilization have been variable, and the effects of the three fertilizer elements appear to be interdependent.[41] Nitrate accumulation is also greater with delay in application of fertilizer.[42] Low light intensity and drought conditions increase the concentration of nitrate in the plant, and many cases of "cornstalk" poisoning reported from the north central states apparently resulted from the grazing of drought-stricken corn by cattle.

Plant species and cultivars differ markedly in their ability to accumulate nitrate. Earlier classifications tended to rank cereals such as oats, corn, wheat, and certain weeds as "accumulators" and perennial grass and legume species as "nonaccumulators."[42] Under high levels of fertilizer N, however, forage species commonly used for pasture and hay production in the U.S. can develop levels of nitrate potentially dangerous to animal health. A comparison of forage species made in Missouri showed that sudangrass, orchardgrass, and tall fescue under fertilization accumulated nitrate at high levels; that smooth bromegrass, timothy, and ladino clover were intermediate accumulators; and that alfalfa, Kentucky bluegrass, and wheat accumulated only low levels of nitrate.[40] Pearlmillet has been found to build up higher levels of nitrate than sudangrass. It is possible that this property may relate to the marked depression in the milk-fat content of dairy cows grazing pearlmillet that has been observed in such states as Georgia, Maryland, and Illinois. The drop in milk fat has also been related to levels of plant organic acids such

37. Kemp, A., and J. R. Todd. 1970. Prevention of hypomagnesaemia in cows: The use of magnesium alloy bullets. *Vet. Rec.* 86:463–64.

38. Burg, P. F. J. van. 1966. Nitrate as an indicator of the nitrogen nutrition status of grass. Proc. 10th Int. Grassl. Congr., pp. 267–72 (Helsinki, Finland).

39. Wright, M. J., and K. L. Davison. 1964. Nitrate accumulation in crops and nitrate poisoning in animals. *Advan. Agron.* 16:197–247.

40. Murphy, L. S., and G. E. Smith. 1967. Nitrate accumulations in forage crops. *Agron. J.* 59:171–74.

41. Vanderlip, R. L., and J. Pesek. 1970. Nitrate accumulation in smooth bromegrass (*Bromus inermis* Leyss.). I. Effects of applied N, P and K. *Agron. J.* 62:491–94.

42. Crawford, R. F., and W. K. Kennedy. 1960. Nitrates in forage crops and silage: Benefits, hazards, precautions. Cornell Misc. Bull. 37.

as oxalic and succinic acid, with differences in mineral composition and nutrient uptake from the soil and with effects on the relative proportions of volatile fatty acids produced in the rumen.[43] It is therefore not clear whether nitrate is the primary factor in this problem.

Most investigations have shown a pronounced stage of growth effect on the concentration of nitrate in plants. Nitrate levels reach their maximum value at the prebloom stage and then gradually decline with further maturation.[39]

The real problem is the level of nitrate N which will produce symptoms of toxicity or adverse effects on the performance of animals consuming the forage. Unfortunately, there is no simple answer to this question. Cornell University workers point out, rightly, that the total quantity of nitrate consumed is important rather than the concentration in the forage.[39,42] They found no significant increase in methemoglobin values until the level of nitrate ingestion by dairy cattle exceeded 25 g/45 kg of body weight; it was estimated that at an intake of 45 g nitrate/45 kg there was a 50% chance the animal would die. It is, however, difficult to extrapolate from experiments in which graded levels of nitrate are supplied suddenly, as in a drench or solid supplement, to conditions where nitrate is a component of the forage. Composition of the forage, particularly the energy-yielding components, will directly affect the utilization of nitrate. Also, under conditions where food is being ingested over lengthy periods, ruminal microorganisms apparently adapt to rather high levels of nitrate. A study with sheep, for example, showed that while a dose of 50 g of potassium nitrate into the rumen induced methemoglobinemia, adapted animals showed no adverse effects from consuming dried grass containing 0.5% nitrate N over a period of weeks.[44] With these reservations,

levels of 0.34–0.45% nitrate N in the feed may be regarded as potentially toxic.[39] Much lower levels, however, may affect growth performance or metabolism in the animal.

Chronic nitrate toxicity, usually produced by adding nitrate or nitrite to the diet, has been reported to cause abortions, reduced weight gains, and a depression of milk production in beef and dairy cattle, sheep, and swine. Nitrate has also been implicated in a condition of vitamin A deficiency occurring in beef cattle fed fertilized corn silage in the midwestern states. Nitrate may function here as a goitrogenic agent to create a thyroid insufficiency and impair carotene utilization in the animal. Interestingly, a similar depletion of liver vitamin A stores has been found in steers grazing N-fertilized grass.[45] In sheep there is no indication that grazing high-nitrate pastures will adversely affect the vitamin A status of the animal.[46]

The standard treatment for animals suffering from acute nitrate toxicity is an intravenous injection of methylene blue solution; this effects the reconversion of methemoglobin to hemoglobin. Recommendations for treatment or prevention of the chronic or subclinical condition are difficult to give since there is little agreement as to whether nitrate is the sole or major factor in affecting animal performance. Cornell workers suggest that forages with potentially toxic nitrate levels should be mixed with other feeds before use.[39] Provision of an energy supplement is particularly important.

❧ PLANT ESTROGENS

Interest in the estrogenic compounds present in forage plants first developed with the report of severe reproductive disorders in ewes grazing subterranean clover pastures in Australia. It was considered

43. Schneider, B. A., N. A. Clark, R. W. Hemken, and J. H. Vandersall. 1970. Relationship of pearl millet to milk fat depression in dairy cows. II. Forage organic acids as influenced by soil nutrients. *J. Dairy Sci.* 53:305–10.
44. Sinclair, K. B., and D. I. H. Jones. 1964. Nitrate toxicity in sheep. *J. Sci. Food Agr.* 15:717–21.

45. Hinds, F. C., G. F. Cmarik, M. E. Mansfield, and G. E. McKibben. 1969. Vitamin A status of beef cattle grazing orchardgrass. *J. Anim. Sci.* 29:180.
46. Reid, R. L., A. J. Post, and G. A. Jung. 1970. The nutritive evaluation of cocksfoot pasture under different levels of nitrogen fertilization. *Proc. N.Z. Grassl. Assoc.* 32:87–97.

that breeding failures ("clover disease") were due to overstimulation of the reproductive organs of the sheep by phytoestrogens in the pasture. Occurrence of estrogens in pasture plants was then recognized in the U.K., although no adverse effects on reproduction were noted; it was thought that estrogens might be responsible for the increase in the solids-not-fat content of milk observed when cows were turned out to spring pasture. In Australia, it was recognized by the late 1950s that the field problem of clover disease occurred on highly clover-dominant pastures (>80% subterranean clover); that subterranean clover was estrogenic during the entire growing period, but not when dry and mature; and that the risk of clover disease was increased by phosphate deficiency.[47]

Since then the existence of reproductive problems associated with plant estrogen activity has extended throughout the world. Activity is found mainly in legumes, although estrogen compounds have also been identified in grasses. In legumes, the compounds involved are isoflavones such as formononetin and biochanin A; in subterranean clover, genistein is present at high levels. Isoflavones have lower estrogenic activity than the coumestan compounds; coumestrol has been shown to be the main estrogenic component of alfalfa, ladino clover, and the annual medics.[48] Interest in the estrogenic activity of alfalfa in the U.S. arose from apparently conflicting observations of breeding problems in livestock and of favorable effects of synthetic estrogens like diethylstilbestrol on liveweight gains and feed conversion. While earlier observations of favorable growth responses in sheep and cattle from estrogenically active alfalfa have been difficult to confirm, several reports have implicated the heavy feeding of alfalfa with reductions in fertility. In Israel, alfalfa feeding

resulted in irregular estrus, cystic ovaries, and decreased fertility in dairy cows.[49] Similar disturbances of the reproductive cycle have been found in ewes grazing ladino clover.[50]

In Australia where much of the productivity of the southern temperate areas resulted from the introduction of subterranean clover, the major problem is failure of conception in the ewe. Part of this failure has been attributed to embryonic mortality, but a primary cause appears to be a defect of fertilization associated with failure of sperm transport in the genital tract of the ewe.[51] The effect on sperm transport has been related to an increased production of cervical mucus resulting from altered levels of circulating estrogen in the infertile animal.[52] There are marked differences in the estrogenicity of subterranean clover cultivars. Conception rates in ewes grazing different cultivars have been found to relate to the level of the isoflavone formononetin in the leaves.[53] Relative lack of activity of the isoflavones genistein and biochanin A is apparently due to different pathways of degradation in the animal rumen. A main end-product of genistein and biochanin A metabolism is the inactive compound p-ethyl phenol, while formononetin produces the estrogenically active compounds equol and O-desmethyl angolensin.[54] In contrast to previous observations of a relationship between metabolic disease and an increased

47. Rossiter, R. C. 1970. Factors affecting the oestrogen content of subterranean clover pastures. *Aust. Vet. J.* 46: 111–44.
48. Bickoff, E. M., R. R. Spencer, S. C. Witt, and B. E. Knuckles. 1969. Studies on the chemical and biological properties of coumestrol and related compounds. USDA Tech. Bull. 1408, pp. 1–95.
49. Adler, J. H., and D. Trainin. 1961. The apparent effect of alfalfa on the reproductive performance of dairy cattle. Proc. 4th Int. Congr. Animal Reproduction, pp. 451–56 (The Hague).
50. Engle, P. H., D. S. Bell, and R. R. Davis. 1957. The effect of ladino clover, birdsfoot trefoil, and bluegrass pasture on the rate of conception among ewes. *J. Anim. Sci.* 16:703–10.
51. Lightfoot, R. J., K. P. Croker, and H. G. Neil. 1967. Failure of sperm transport in relation to ewe infertility following prolonged grazing on oestrogenic pastures. *Aust. J. Agr. Res.* 18:755–65.
52. Smith, J. F. 1971. Studies on ovine infertility in agricultural regions of western Australia: Cervical mucus production by fertile and infertile ewes. *Aust. J. Agr. Res.* 22:513–19.
53. Davies, H. L., R. C. Rossiter, and R. Maller. 1970. The effects of different cultivars of subterranean clover (*T. subterraneum* L.) on sheep reproduction in the southwest of western Australia. *Aust. J. Agr. Res.* 21:359–69.
54. Braden, A. W. H., and D. A. Shutt. 1970. The metabolism of pasture oestrogens in ruminants. Proc. 11th Int. Grassl. Congr., pp. 770–73 (Surfers Paradise, Queensland, Aust.).

supply of plant nutrients, it has been shown that deficiencies of P, N, and S will substantially increase the concentration of formononetin in subterranean clover.[47] Severity of the disease may also relate to soil levels of Co and Se.

In alfalfa a major factor affecting the amount of coumestrol in the plant is disease and insect attack.[48,55] Disease-free alfalfa contains relatively low levels of coumestan compounds. It is suggested that coumestrol is either synthesized by the plant in response to attack, or by the pathogen itself. A similar relationship seems to hold between disease and estrogenic activity in white clover plants.[56]

The most direct solution to the problem of infertility resulting from plant estrogens lies in a program of selection for cultivars of low estrogen content. This is being practiced for subterranean clover in western Australia. An extensive USDA study has shown significant differences in coumestrol content between alfalfa cultivars.[55] 'Lahontan' had the highest coumestrol concentration, and 'DuPuits' and 'Vernal' the lowest. Selection for this property or for cultivars resistant to disease should be effective in controlling fertility problems resulting from the feeding of high levels of estrogenic alfalfa.

✤ TOXIC COMPOUNDS IN FORAGES

A group of metabolic diseases or problems in ruminant animals has been referred to as "pastoral faux pas."[57] Species or cultivars of a grass or legume which has been developed for a specific agronomic purpose (often to fill a gap in a seasonal grazing program or to increase yield) have been found to contain compounds which in some way depress animal performance. Such problems are often localized in their occurrence but may cause serious economic loss in a given area or at certain times of the year. Some examples associated with different classes of toxic compounds will be considered briefly. A more detailed treatment may be obtained in chapters concerned with individual forage species.

CYANOGENETIC GLUCOSIDES

Hydrocyanic acid (HCN), or prussic acid, is generally not found in healthy plants but is formed by enzymatic action on compounds called the cyanogenetic glucosides when growth is checked by adverse environmental conditions. Hydrolysis of the glucosides also occurs by bacterial action in the rumen, and the resulting cyanide is rapidly absorbed into the blood. Cyanide combines with hemoglobin to form cyanohemoglobin, which does not carry oxygen. The cyanide-poisoned animal shows an increased rate of respiration, increased pulse rate, gasping, muscular twitching, and convulsions; death occurs from respiratory paralysis. Detoxification of the cyanide to thiocyanate is a rapid process; the animal that eats quickly is at greatest risk since the rate of cyanide formation exceeds that of detoxification. Levels of 0–25 mg HCN/100 g dry plant tissue have been considered as safe for pastured animals, levels of 50–75 mg/100 g as doubtful, and concentrations of greater than 100 mg/100 g as highly dangerous.[58]

Of major importance in the U.S. is the problem of HCN poisoning associated with the feeding of forage sorghums and sudangrass. Here the cyanogenetic glucoside is dhurrin. In New Zealand the glucoside lotaustralin in some strains of white clover has caused poisoning of animals. The HCN potential of sudangrass and the sudangrass-sorghum hybrids differs with cultivar, stage of growth, level of N fertilization, and en-

55. Hanson, C. H., G. M. Loper, G. O. Kohler, E. M. Bickoff, K. W. Taylor, W. R. Kehr, E. H. Stanford, J. W. Dudley, M. W. Pedersen, E. L. Sorensen, H. L. Carnahan, and C. P. Wilsie. 1965. Variation in coumestrol content of alfalfa as related to location, variety, cutting, year, stage of growth, and disease, pp. 1–72. USDA Tech. Bull. 1333.

56. Newton, J. E., J. E. Betts, H. M. Drane, and N. Saba. 1970. The oestrogenic activity of white clover, pp. 309–13. Brit. Grassl. Soc. Occas. Symp. 6.

57. Garner, R. J. 1963. Plant toxicology and photosensitivity. *In* Animal Health, Production and Pasture, pp. 737–70. Longmans, Green, London.

58. Boyd, F. T., O. S. Aamodt, G. Bohstedt, and E. Truog. 1938. Sudangrass management for control of cyanide poisoning. *J. Amer. Soc. Agron.* 30:569–82.

vironmental conditions.[59-61] The HCN potential of sudangrass-sorghum hybrids is greater than that of sudangrass cultivars. Generally, higher concentrations of HCN are found in new growth of grass, at high levels of N application, and under environmental stresses such as drought and frost. It is quite possible that under rates of fertilization commonly applied to annual forages animals may be exposed to the dual risk of cyanide poisoning and nitrate toxicity.[61] The two conditions have in fact sometimes been confused.

Prevention of HCN poisoning in livestock may be accomplished most readily by recognition of the environmental factors causing an accumulation of the toxic compound. Sudangrass or the sudangrass-sorghum hybrids should not be grazed at too early a growth stage, and particular precautions should be taken after drought or frost.

ALKALOIDS AND MYCOTOXINS

The alkaloids are nitrogenous bases with a rather complex chemical structure. They occur naturally in a variety of plants or in fungi associated with the plant and cause marked physiological responses in animals. The alkaloids have been implicated in a number of disorders affecting grazing or forage-fed ruminants.

A condition of lameness or "fescue foot" has been observed in cattle on tall fescue pastures in the U.S., Australia, and New Zealand. In the U.S., the problem exists primarily in a belt which stretches from Kansas through Missouri, southern Illinois, and southern Indiana to Kentucky. Fescue foot is a noninfectious disease characterized in cattle by lameness of the hind legs and a dry gangrene of the feet and tail. Outbreaks

are sporadic and seem to occur most frequently in periods of cold weather. Factors influencing the incidence of the disease have been reviewed.[62] (See Chapter 28.) It is interesting to note that one of the alkaloids, perloline, isolated from tall fescue has also been linked to the condition of "ryegrass staggers" in sheep.[63] This is a disease of livestock grazing on perennial ryegrass pastures in Australia and New Zealand and is most frequently observed on new growth of grass in the fall when the alkaloid content is high.

A number of indole alkaloids have been identified in reed canarygrass and hardinggrass. Minnesota studies have shown there is a high correlation between the alkaloid content of reed canarygrass and its palatability to sheep.[64] In Australia the condition of *"Phalaris* staggers" is a serious problem to livestock producers on hardinggrass-dominant pastures. The trouble most commonly occurs in sheep grazing new growth of grass following rain, particularly in cool conditions during the dry season and where levels of soil and pasture N are high.[65,66] Different forms of the disease have been described, a peracute form which results in sudden collapse and death of the grazing animal and a chronic form (staggers) which affects the central nervous system.[67] The chronic form may be prevented by the use of cobalt pellets placed in the rumen, while the acute and peracute forms are not responsive to treatment. A similar subacute or chronic condition has been described in sheep grazing reed canarygrass pastures in New Zealand.[68]

59. Jung, G. A., and R. L. Reid. 1966. Sudangrass. Studies on its yield, management, chemical composition and nutritive value. W. Va. Agr. Exp. Sta. Bull. 524T.
60. Gray, E., J. S. Rice, D. Wattenbarger, J. A. Benson, A. J. Hester, R. C. Loyd, and B. M. Greene. 1968. Hydrocyanic acid potential of sorghum plants grown in Tennessee. Tenn. Agr. Exp. Sta. Bull. 445.
61. Gillingham, J. T., M. M. Shirer, J. J. Starnes, N. R. Page, and E. F. McClain. 1969. Relative occurrences of toxic concentrations of cyanide and nitrate in varieties of sudangrass and sorghum-sudangrass hybrids. Agron. J. 61:727–30.

62. Yates, S. G. 1962. Toxicity of tall fescue forage: A review. Econ. Bot. 16:295–303.
63. Aasen, A. J., C. C. J. Culvenor, E. P. Finnie, A. W. Kellock, and L. W. Smith. 1969. Alkaloids as a possible cause of ryegrass staggers in grazing livestock. Aust. J. Agr. Res. 20:71–86.
64. Simons, A. B., and G. C. Marten. 1971. Relationship of indole alkaloids to palatability of Phalaris arundinacea L. Agron. J. 63:915–19.
65. Gallagher, C. H., J. H. Koch., and H. Hoffman. 1967. Deaths of ruminants grazing Phalaris tuberosa in Australia. Aust. Vet. J. 43:495–500.
66. Moore, R. M., and R. J. Hutchings. 1967. Mortalities among sheep grazing Phalaris tuberosa. Aust. J. Exp. Agr. Anim. Husb. 7:17–21.
67. Gallagher, C. H., J. H. Koch, R. M. Moore, and J. D. Steel. 1964. Toxicity of Phalaris tuberosa for sheep. Nature 204:542–45.
68. Simpson, B. H., R. D. Jolly, and S. H. M. Thomas. 1969. Phalaris arundinacea as a cause of deaths and incoordination in sheep. N.Z. Vet. J. 17:240–44.

The occurrence of cardiac failure in the peracute disease indicated the possibility of a cardiac poison in *Phalaris* spp.; a group of dimethylated tryptamine alkaloids was isolated, with properties related to the pharmacologically active compound serotonin.[69] Under controlled environmental conditions factors that influenced nitrate accumulation in the grass (temperature, light, and nitrate supply) also increased the concentration of tryptamine alkaloids.[70] Characterization of the compounds responsible for *Phalaris* staggers is not complete, however, because study has shown little relationship between toxicity and the tryptamine alkaloid concentration of different strains of *Phalaris*.[71] The possibility of an involvement of other toxins such as hordenine or the interaction of dimethylated tryptamines with compounds such as cyanogenetic glucosides or organic acids has been considered.

A different type of response has been noted in animals consuming the tropical legume, koa haole, *Leucaena leucocephala* (Lam.) deWit. This browse plant, which can produce high levels of protein per ha, has been used in high-rainfall areas of Hawaii and Australia to increase milk and beef production. It contains the alkaloid mimosine, which has been shown to have a goitrogenic effect on cattle. Calves born from cows fed koa haole were found to have enlarged thyroid glands, and thyroid function was also altered in the lamb.[72] Other effects noted have been a loss of hair or wool, infertility, abortion, decreased milk production, and a depression of birth weight in the newborn animal. For these reasons koa haole should be used as a supplement rather than as a sole diet for breeding animals.

Mention should be made of a class of diseases caused by the occurrence of fungi on forage crops. Ergot poisoning is caused by species of the fungus *Claviceps* which infect a number of grasses. Some workers feel that the condition of fescue foot may relate to the presence of mycotoxins produced by common fungi such as *Fusarium*.[73] A condition of excessive salivation, or "slobbers," in cattle associated with the feeding of red clover hay has been reported from Missouri, Illinois, and Wisconsin. It appears to be due to an alkaloid produced by the fungus *Rhizoctonia leguminicola* Gough and Elliott.[74] Moldy hays have been reported to cause respiratory disease in cattle, and a number of photosensitization effects have been reported in animals consuming alfalfa hay or grazing different kinds of pasture.[75]

An important example of mycotoxic diseases is the condition of "facial eczema," found in sheep and cattle on ryegrass pastures in Australia and New Zealand. Facial eczema is a photosensitization disease caused by the toxic compound sporidesmin, produced by the fungus *Pithomyces chartarum* (Berk. & Curt.) M. B. Ellis. The fungus colonizes on dead plant material, and its development is controlled by temperature and the seasonal pattern of pasture growth.[76] The main danger period is in the fall, when warm wet weather and an accumulation of dead herbage on the pasture provide optimal conditions for sporulation of the fungus. When consumed by animals, sporidesmin causes severe liver damage, with photosensitization as a secondary effect. Skin not protected by hair or wool becomes inflamed and scabby

69. Culvenor, C. C. J., R. Dal Bon, and L. W. Smith. 1964. The occurrence of indolealkylamine alkaloids in *Phalaris tuberosa* L. and *P. arundinacea* L. Aust. J. Chem. 17:1301–4.

70. Moore, R. M., J. D. Williams, and J. Chia. 1967. Factors affecting concentrations of dimethylated indolealkylamines in *Phalaris tuberosa* L. Aust. J. Biol. Sci. 20:1131–40.

71. Oram, R. N. 1970. Genetic and environmental control of the amount and composition of toxins in *Phalaris tuberosa* L. Proc. 11th Int. Grassl. Congr., pp. 785–88 (Surfers Paradise, Queensland, Aust.).

72. Donaldson, L. E., R. I. Hamilton, L. J. Lambourne, and D. A. Little. 1970. Assessing *Leucaena leucocephala* for deleterious effects in cattle and sheep. Proc. 11th Int. Grassl. Congr., pp. 780–82 (Surfers Paradise, Queensland, Aust.).

73. Ellis, J. J., and S. G. Yates. 1971. Mycotoxins of fungi from fescue. Econ. Bot. 25:1–5.

74. Rainey, D. P., E. B. Smalley, M. H. Crump, and F. M. Strong. 1965. Isolation of salivation factor from *Rhizoctonia leguminicola* on red clover hay. Nature 205:203–4.

75. Monlux, A. W., and R. J. Panciera. 1963. Bovine hepatogenous photosensitivity associated with the feeding of alfalfa hay. J. Amer. Vet. Med. Assoc. 142:989–94.

76. Brook, P. J. 1969. *Pithomyces chartarum* in pasture, and measures for prevention of facial eczema. J. Stored Prod. Res. 5:203–9.

(hence the name "facial eczema"), and the animal is generally unthrifty.

The disease may be controlled by pasture management or by spraying the herbage with low levels of thiabendazole. Workers in New Zealand have found that heavy sheep stocking rates reduce the amount of dead growth on the pasture, but that lowest incidence of the disease is obtained on a low, set stocking system where animals are not forced to graze too close to the ground.[77] Spraying with thiabendazole, while expensive, provides safe alternative grazing at times when environmental conditions are optimal for occurrence of the disease.

❧ FUTURE PROBLEMS

This discussion has dealt primarily with metabolic problems where there appears to be an established relationship between forage plant composition and the health or performance of the ruminant animal. Under conditions of intensified grassland production it is quite possible that other metabolic "stress" conditions may be recognized in the future. In particular, there are indications that high herbage yields under fertilization may deplete mineral reserves in the soil and create mineral deficiencies and imbalances in the plant. Use of high-analysis phosphate fertilizers and the production of high-yielding alfalfa crops have created S deficiency conditions in forage crops in Wisconsin.[78] A variety of ill-defined effects has been related to the grazing of lush fall pasture, particularly grass which has been fertilized with N and K. Overuse of such pasture has been found to lead not only to hypomagnesemia but to hypocalcemia, hypophosphatemia, and hypoglycemia in cattle.[2] A condition of "ill-thrift" in sheep in New Zealand has been noted, and an increased incidence of milk fever and fertility problems in cattle has been associated with this type of grazing.

The possibility that changes in the mineral balance of forage crops may affect the reproductive performance of ruminant animals has given concern to farmers and advisers in many parts of the world. Infertility in animals may result from a variety of causes. Nutritionally, dietary deficiencies of energy, protein, P, I, Mn, Cu, Co, Se, and vitamin A and an excess supply of plant estrogens have been implicated.[79] The practice of liming soils and the heavy application of fertilizer N changes the pH of the soil and the botanical composition of pastures. This in turn affects the availability of such elements as Co, Cu, Mo, Mn, and Zn. Changes in fertilization practice coupled with the increased use of legumes in seeded pastures may also markedly alter the Ca:P ratio of forage crops. The effect of wide Ca:P ratios on growth and breeding performance has been examined fairly extensively for cattle fed mixed rations, but little is known of the influence of such balances on the health of animals fed forage alone.

Improvement of pasture and hay production often means the selective use of high-yielding forage species and cultivars. On occasion this has resulted in an adverse effect on animal performance due to the presence of toxins or metabolic inhibitors in the forage. It is also recognized that the level of certain plant components, e.g., minerals, is an inherited characteristic and that the availability of minerals may differ between grass species and cultivars. Such differences could well become of practical significance, particularly for growing animals, and for high-producing lactating animals.

There seems to be little justification at present for recommending any major change in the development of forage management systems on the grounds of possible impairment of animal health or productivity. Agronomists and plant breeders should, however, be aware of the plant and

77. Campbell, A. G. 1970. Recent advances in the control of facial eczema. Proc. 11th Int. Grassl. Congr., pp. 774–77 (Surfers Paradise, Queensland, Aust.).

78. Pope, A. L. 1971. A review of recent mineral research with sheep. J. Anim. Sci. 33:1332–43.

79. Bienfet, V., H. Binot, and F. Lomba. 1970. Nutritional infertility in cattle at pasture. In Trace Element Metabolism in Animals. Proc. WAAP/IBP Int. Symp., pp. 474–81 (Aberdeen, Scotland). E. & S. Livingstone. Edinburgh and London.

environmental factors which affect the metabolism and utilization of forage crops by ruminant animals. They should also recognize that current trends toward intensification of both grassland and animal production may lead to an increase in the incidence of metabolic problems in livestock in the future.

❧ QUESTIONS

1. What are the primary plant and animal factors involved in the condition of bloat? If your farm operation involved the pasturing of cows on alfalfa and the labor resource was minimal, what precautionary measures would you take to reduce the risks of this disease?
2. Nitrogen fertilization of grassland has been implicated in aggravating problems of grass tetany and of acute or chronic nitrate toxicity in ruminant animals. Do you consider this charge to be well founded? What sort of pasture fertilization system would you develop to achieve maximum yield of grass with least incidence of metabolic problems?
3. At what times of year and under what en-

vironmental circumstances is grass tetany likely to be a problem? What clinical symptoms characterize a cow suffering from tetany? How would you treat an animal in the initial stages of clinical tetany?
4. What are the main estrogenic substances in (a) alfalfa and (b) subterranean clover? What physiological effects do the estrogens have on the ruminant animal?
5. Under what conditions will potentially toxic levels of (a) nitrate and (b) hydrocyanic acid accumulate in forage plants? How are these substances metabolized at the ruminal level, and what effects do they produce on the animal?
6. Describe some of the effects of alkaloids and mycotoxic substances in forage plants on animal performance and health. Select examples from grazing situations in different areas of the world and comment on techniques that are being used to control the problem.
7. If the present trend toward selection of high-yielding species and cultivars of forage plants is maintained and this is accompanied by the use of increasing levels of high-analysis fertilizers, what metabolic problems do you foresee in ruminant animals consuming the forage?

ROBERT F. BARNES / *Agricultural Research Service, USDA*

59

FORAGE TESTING AND ITS APPLICATIONS

&

F ORAGE TESTING may be described as the evaluation of a given forage or feed in terms of its intended use. The objectives of forage or feedstuff testing include: (1) to provide a basis for estimating the feeding value of available feedstuffs, primarily forages; (2) to allow more efficient use of available feedstuffs, including grains, in formulating rations for year-round feeding programs; (3) to enable specialists to make more accurate diagnoses of nutritional problems associated with overfeeding and underfeeding of various nutrients; and (4) to assist the farmer in making management decisions to maintain the quality of harvested products that is best for his type of livestock operation.

Feeding value of forages is largely dependent upon four interrelated characteristics: (1) chemical composition or nutrient content, (2) nutrient availability or digestibility, (3) intake, and (4) nonnutritive constituents. The general classification of nutrients required for all livestock includes

  ✦ ROBERT F. BARNES is Research Agronomist, ARS, USDA, and Director of the U.S. Regional Pasture Research Laboratory, University Park, Pa. He is also adjunct professor of Agronomy, Pennsylvania State University. He holds the M.S. degree from Rutgers University and the Ph.D. from Purdue University. His research has dealt with development and application of forage evaluation methods.

protein, energy, minerals, vitamins, and water. If a feedstuff does not contain all the essential nutrients for the animal's requirements, it must be supplemented or animal performance will be limited. There may be adequate levels of nutrients in a feedstuff based on its chemical composition; however, they must be digested and absorbed to be of value to the animal. Lastly, sufficient quantities must be consumed if a feedstuff is to attain its potential feeding value based on nutrient content and digestibility.

Since earliest times forage evaluation has been based upon a farmer's experience in assessing forage feeding value. There is still no foolproof method for predicting animal response without actually feeding the forage. However, useful laboratory methods of evaluating forages have been developed. Once the nutrient content of a forage and its digestibility have been estimated, it is then the job of the nutritionist to develop a balanced ration. The nutritional requirements of livestock vary with physiological state and other factors and have been summarized in the respective chapters on various classes of livestock (see Chapters 60–65). As an example, pregnant beef cows require a ration containing 5.9% crude protein on a dry basis, whereas a ration should contain 12.2% crude protein for growing weanling beef calves. Respective requirements for TDN are 50 and 74%. Requirements for other classes of beef cattle are between these two extremes.

Knowledge of the exact biochemical composition of a ration is not necessary, but an understanding of the ration constituents needed by livestock is essential. There is no single ration formulation which may be used as a standard. Circumstances surrounding the source of a given forage dictate how it may be best incorporated into a ration. On-the-farm formulation of rations must take into consideration such factors as the amount of home-grown feedstuffs available, the need for supplementation, and the cost of each ingredient. The specialist attempting to assess the value of a forage sample can be assisted by knowing information on plant species, soil test data, fertilizer treatment of the past and current year, growth stage at harvest, method of harvest and storage, crop yield, animal acceptance and level of consumption, physical texture, and unusual factors such as moldiness which might affect the value of a forage.

❦ RATION CONSTITUENTS

The basis of any forage testing program is its ability to accurately predict the availability and utilization of various ration constituents to a particular class of livestock. An understanding of the nutritive and nonnutritive constituents of rations is essential in developing an effective feeding program.

PROTEIN

Proteins comprise about 80% of the total N in forages. The initial step in protein utilization by ruminants is digestion, followed by synthesis of microbial protein which is assimilated by the animal. Utilization of protein of low biological value may be improved by microbial conversions in the rumen; however, advantages have been shown for bypassing the rumen in improving utilization of high-quality protein.[1] The apparent digestibilities of crude protein vary widely among forages; a typical study showed a range of 35–80% in the apparent digestion coefficients of crude protein of grasses and of 52–80% in alfalfa.[2]

Analysis for crude protein ($N \times 6.25$) includes both soluble and insoluble nonprotein nitrogen (NPN). Soluble NPN may be readily metabolized by rumen microorganisms for synthesis of microbial protein provided the levels are not excessive. Levels of NPN in forages normally are 10–15% of the total N; however, levels up to 40% may occur under certain conditions and may cause digestive disturbances. This is more likely, particularly in grasses, if crude protein exceeds about 25% of the dry weight.[3] Forage protein may be converted to NPN forms during ensiling. Most silages will contain 35–50% of total N as NPN compared to 10–15% for hays. Nitrate nitrogen (NO_3-N) may be reduced during ensiling if nitrogen oxide gas is given off.

Soluble NPN may also accumulate as the result of hay spoilage or reduced plant metabolism associated with severe drought or hail damage. Heavy applications of N fertilizer or manure tend to increase NPN levels in grasses. Feeds with more than 1.5–2% NO_3 may be toxic; thus when high levels of NO_3-N are suspected, it should be measured separately.[4,5]

Where problems with appetite and substandard animal performance occur, the level of NPN in the ration should be checked. Most problems associated with high levels of NPN usually occur from added NPN in the ration, either by design or by accident. Problems may occur as the result of accidental use of fertilizer in the ration; contamination of a water supply;

1. Hungate, R. E. 1966. The Rumen and Its Microbes. Academic Press, New York.
2. Sullivan, J. T. 1964. Chemical composition of forages in relation to digestibility by ruminants. USDA, ARS 34-62.
3. Sullivan, J. T. 1962. Evaluation of forage crops by chemical analysis: A critique. *Agron J*. 54:511–15.
4. Crampton, E. W., and L. E. Harris. 1969. Applied Animal Nutrition, 2nd ed. W. H. Freeman, San Francisco.
5. Hillman, D. 1971. Nitrate in the ration. Mich. Coop. Ext. Serv. Bull. E-728.

feeding hay containing nitrate-accumulating weeds; or inadequate mixing of added NPN sources such as urea, biuret, diammonium phosphate, and anhydrous ammonia.

A decrease in protein digestibility may occur with brown or caramelized hay or haylage resulting from excessive heating in storage.[6] In forages exposed to temperatures above 60 C a nonenzymatic browning reaction may occur which produces an insoluble NPN fraction in combination with lignin. The usual analysis for crude protein (Kjeldahl) overestimates the amount of digestible protein. Determining either acid-detergent insoluble N or pepsin-insoluble N as a concentration in dry matter has been suggested as a means of estimating digestible protein values for hay and haylage samples suspected of heat damage.[7]

ENERGY

Energy is the nutrient most likely to be limiting in forages for optimum animal performance. Energy sources may be expressed in terms of digestible dry matter (DDM), total digestible nutrients (TDN), digestible energy (DE), metabolizable energy (ME), or net energy (NE). A very high correlation exists among DDM, TDN, and DE.[8,9] For most practical situations the terms are interchangeable; however, DE is generally preferred. The TDN may be converted to DE, since pounds of TDN × 2000 = kcal DE.[4] The TDN overestimates the value of low-quality forages in comparison to high-quality forages and concentrates. Losses of energy from heat loss during digestion, expelled gases, feces, and urine are included in measuring NE. Net energy is the amount of energy available to the animal to meet its maintenance requirements (NE_m) and to produce milk, body tissue, and other products.

Techniques for estimating NE are complicated, time consuming, and expensive, which has precluded the routine measurement of NE. Attempts to correct the bias in TDN values include the estimated net energy system (ENE). It has been suggested that the term ENE be reserved for values listed in Morrison's tables or those values based on the equation of Moore et al.[10-12] The term, NE_l, which is the total energy requirement for lactating cows expressed in NE for milk production, is used in some feed programming systems.[10]

Suggested hay and silage standards have been published by the American Forage and Grassland Council (AFGC) based upon the ability of forages to supply protein and energy (Table 59.1).[13] Other standards have been published for use in specific forage testing programs.[14]

MINERALS

Most forages do not contain adequate levels of P, Na, or Cl. In addition to salt and P, the minerals of primary concern are Ca, I, and Mg. Several other minerals are required by livestock, and deficiencies or excesses may occur under local circumstances. Therefore, routine mineral analyses may be desirable to help keep production, health, and reproduction problems at a minimum in animal herds.

The ratio of Ca to P in the ration is important as well as the total amounts and should fall between 1.3:1 and 2.2:1 whenever possible. Supplementation of Ca and

6. Van Soest, P. J. 1965. Use of detergents in analysis of fibrous feeds. III. Study of effects of heating and drying on yield of fiber and lignin in forages. *Assoc. Off. Agr. Chem. J.* 48:785–90.

7. Goering, H. K., C. H. Gordon, R. W. Hemken, D. R. Waldo, P. J. Van Soest, and L. W. Smith. 1972. Analytical estimates of nitrogen digestibility in heat-damaged forages. *J. Dairy Sci.* 55:1275–80.

8. Swift, R. W. 1957. The nutritive evaluation of forages. Pa. Agr. Exp. Sta. Bull. 615.

9. Barth, K. M., G. W. Vander Noot, and J. L. Cason. 1959. The quantitative relationship between total digestible nutrients and digestible energy values of forages. *J. Anim. Sci.* 18:690–93.

10. Moe, P. W., W. P. Flatt, and H. F. Tyrrell. 1972. Net energy value of feeds for lactation. *J. Dairy Sci.* 55: 945–58.

11. Morrison, F. B. 1956. Feeds and Feeding, 22nd ed. Morrison Publ. Co., Ithaca.

12. Moore, L. A., H. M. Irvin, and J. C. Shaw. 1953. Relationships between TDN and energy values of feeds. *J. Dairy Sci.* 36:93–97.

13. American Forage and Grassland Council. 1966. Hay and silage standards. *Forage and Grassl. Progr.* 7:2–3.

14. Bath, D. L., V. L. Marble, and F. F. Smith. 1970. Alfalfa hay testing. Univ. Calif. Agr. Ext. AXT-290.

TABLE 59.1 ❧ AFGC hay and silage standards

Crop	Standard	TDN (%)	Dry matter basis ENE (Mcal/kg)	Crude protein (%)
Legume hay	excellent	65 or above	123 or above	18 or above
(Majority of the plant	good	58–65	101–123	at least 15
material originating	fair	54–58	88–101	at least 12
from legumes)	poor	below 54	below 88	below 10
Grass hay	excellent	65 or above	123 or above	15 or above
(Majority of the plant	good	58–65	101–123	at least 12
material originating	fair	54–58	88–101	at least 10
from grasses)	poor	below 54	below 88	below 10
Corn silage	excellent	65 or above	123 or above	9 or above
	good	60–65	110–123	9–11
	fair	. . .	. . .	. . .
	poor	below 60	below 110	9–11
Hay crop silage	excellent	above 65	123 or above	above 16
	good	60–65	110–123	12–16
	fair	54–59	88–110	below 12
	poor	below 54	below 88	below 12

Source: AFGC, 1966.[13]
Note: To be in a class, a forage must meet both the TDN or ENE and protein requirement of that class.
  Hay crop silage is divided into three classes in terms of dry matter content:
    1. High-moisture silage, contains less than 25% dry matter; pH should be below 4.2.
    2. Medium-moisture silage, contains 25% to 35% dry matter; pH should be below 4.5.
    3. Low-moisture silage, contains more than 35% dry matter; pH is no criterion.

P for dairy cows is best accomplished by force-feeding desired levels in a grain mixture or complete ration. Free-choice supplementation of either dicalcium phosphate or steamed bone meal is generally reserved for other livestock and for insurance purposes with dairy cows.

Magnesium is associated with the problem of grass tetany, particularly during flush periods of pasture growth during cool weather. Magnesium oxide often is used as a supplement when possible problems are anticipated.

VITAMINS

Vitamins are required in very small amounts and most are synthesized by rumen microorganisms. Vitamin A is not produced in the rumen and is generally of most concern, particularly with stored feeds and weathered mature forages. Carotene is a precursor of vitamin A but may be extremely variable in forages. Supplementation often is advised as a precautionary measure.

Vitamin D content of forages is related to sun-curing and thus varies among forages. Also, less vitamin D is obtained from sunlight when cattle are housed year-round. Thus vitamin D also is supplied for insurance purposes. Occasionally problems with vitamin E deficiency may occur in localized situations, particularly in areas associated with deficiencies of Se. Heavy dependence on hays or silages lacking in green color and discontinuance of pasture or green-chopping may also make vitamin E supplementation necessary.

MOISTURE

Moisture content of hay and silage often is an important criterion of its value. The amount of water in silage may limit the total forage utilized in a ration if abnormal fermentation or seepage occurs during ensiling. Approximate levels of moisture in forage to be ensiled may be estimated by the "grab test" (see Chapter 51).[15] A gen-

15. Shepherd, J. B., C. H. Gordon, and L. F. Campbell. 1953. Development and problems in making grass silage. USDA Bur. Dairy Ind. Inf. Bull. 149.

eral rule of thumb used to calculate intake and storage needs is that 3 kg of regular silage or 2 kg of low-moisture silage equals 1 kg of hay.[16] These thumb rules assume that dry matter in hay is 90%, in regular silage 30%, and in low-moisture silage 45%. However, the preferred method of calculating rations is on an actual dry matter basis.

NONNUTRITIVE CONSTITUENTS

Ration constituents not contributing directly to nutrient uptake may influence animal response. For example, there are certain minimum needs for fiber in ruminant rations and sufficient coarse material is required for maintenance of normal rumen function. Other nonnutritive constituents may have deleterious effects on animal response and include toxic compounds produced by some plants under certain conditions.[17] An awareness of the potential problem of poisonous plants or the accumulation of harmful components in plants is desirable, particularly under range conditions.

❧ TECHNIQUES FOR ESTIMATING NUTRIENT AVAILABILITY

Nutrient availability may be measured directly in animal feeding trials or estimated by various indirect methods. To be of value to livestock feeders, a forage testing system should be relatively rapid, economical, and accurate and must fit the nutritional requirements of the animal. The conventional feeding trial is with sheep or cattle fed for a period of 2 to 4 weeks in metabolism cages. The primary disadvantages of such trials are their duration, expense, and the relatively large amount of forage required. Trials to measure animal performance in terms of meat, milk, or

wool are even lengthier and more expensive.

Sensory indices of nutrient availability are of doubtful value. The time of cutting first-growth forage often is closely related to nutrient digestibility, particularly with forages harvested under similar environmental conditions. This factor and the effects of age of plant, growth stage, leaf content, weather damage, physical form, and forage species on hay quality are discussed in Chapter 49. Proposed laboratory methods include chemical analyses, physical methods, *in vitro* rumen fermentation or artificial rumen techniques, and nylon bag techniques.

CHEMICAL ANALYSES

The chemical evaluation of feedstuffs rests largely on methods developed over 150 years ago.[18] The most common scheme has been proximate analysis, which is intended to separate feedstuffs into digestible (nitrogen-free extract) and indigestible (crude fiber) carbohydrates. However, microorganisms in the ruminant digestive system are capable of digesting structural carbohydrates; therefore, crude fiber does not solely represent the indigestible portion of carbohydrates. Likewise, nitrogen-free extract does not solely represent the digestible portion. The significance of crude fiber is that its magnitude is often of the same order as that of the indigestible carbohydrate.

Crude fiber (CF) and crude protein (CP) are used in a number of forage testing programs to predict TDN or ENE. The Axelsson-Reid-Swift equation based on CF and CP was used initially by the Penn State Forage Testing Service which was begun in January 1959.[19,20] A thesis study resulted

16. Crowley, J. W. 1972. Plan your herd's roughage supply. *Hoard's Dairyman* 117 (13): 804–5.
17. Schmutz, E. M., B. N. Freeman, and R. E. Reed. 1968. Livestock-poisoning Plants of Arizona. Univ. Ariz. Press, Tucson.

18. Van Soest, P. J. 1968. Structural and chemical characteristics which limit the nutritive value of forages, pp. 63–76. Amer. Soc. Agron. Spec. Publ. 13.
19. Hershberger, T. V., T. A. Long, E. W. Hartsook, and R. W. Swift. 1959. Use of the artificial rumen technique to estimate the nutritive value of forages. *J. Anim. Sci.* 18:770–79.
20. Adams, R. S. 1961. Symposium: A modern dairy cattle feeding program. Results of feed analysis in feeding dairy cattle. *J. Dairy Sci.* 44:2105–12.

Fig. 59.1. *The Kjeldahl procedure remains . . . standard.* Macro-Kjeldahl system for the determination of total N. *Pa. Agr. Ext. Serv. photo.*

in the adoption by the Penn State Forage Testing Service of separate equations for the prediction of TDN from CF and CP for legumes, grasses, mixed hay-crop and unknown samples, annuals other than corn, and corn silage.[21,22] California workers have adapted a modified CF method for the estimation of TDN and ENE of alfalfa hay.[14] A considerable portion of alfalfa hay has been sold in California on the basis of the modified CF analysis. However, the method is not as satisfactory for the analysis of forage mixtures.

The total N content of feedstuffs includes true protein and nonprotein nitrogen (NPN). Automated analytical systems are being developed for total N; however, the Kjeldahl procedure (Fig. 59.1) remains standard.[23] For most practical situations, percent digestible protein may be satisfactorily estimated from CP.[24] The CP of forages is positively correlated with DDM or TDN; however, the correlation generally is not high and its error of prediction is rather large.[2]

Partitioning of forages into chemical constituents based upon their availability

to ruminants is discussed in Chapter 6. Scientists are increasingly able by chemical means to identify and assess quantitatively the nutrient content of a feed ingredient or a total feed.[18,25] However, they are not able to predict precisely the intake or utilization of feedstuffs.

Summative equations for calculation of dry matter digestibility have been proposed based upon cell wall material and cellular contents of forage samples. A major deterrent to the routine use of such equations is the multiple chemical analyses required.

Solubility indices are chemical methods based upon an estimation of dry matter loss upon acid, solvent, or enzymatic treatment. An example is the dry matter disappearance of forages by an acid-pepsin solution for the estimation of feeding value.[26] Modifications of the pepsin solubility procedure are used as the second stage of the two-stage *in vitro* rumen fermentation technique and for the determination of pepsin-soluble N.[7,27]

For silage samples, the analyses for moisture and pH are of particular importance. Direct-cut grass-legume silage with pH 4.2 or lower and wilted silage with pH 4.5 or lower are indicative of good fermentation (Table 59.1). For low-moisture silage, pH is no criterion of quality, and the forage is subject to spontaneous heating, depending upon conditions.

PHYSICAL METHODS

Physical methods are seldom used for the routine evaluation of forage quality. Examples of such methods include: artificial mastication proposed for estimation of voluntary intake, fibrousness index which relates forage digestibility and intake to the energy expended to grind hay, and histo-

21. Moore, J. H. 1963. The development and educational application of relationships for use in estimating the nutritive content of forages. Unpubl. M.Ed. thesis, Pa. State Univ., University Park.
22. Adams, R. S., J. H. Moore, E. M. Kesler, and G. Z. Stevens. 1964. New relationships for estimating TDN content of forages from chemical composition. *J. Dairy Sci.* 47:1461 (abstr.).
23. Association of Official Analytical Chemists. 1970. Official Methods of Analysis, 11th ed.
24. Holter, J. A., and J. T. Reid. 1959. Relationship between the concentrations of crude protein and apparently digestible protein in forages. *J. Anim. Sci.* 19:1339–49.
25. Goering, H. K., and P. J. Van Soest. 1970. Forage fiber analysis. USDA Agr. Handbook 379.
26. Donefer, E., E. W. Crampton, and L. E. Lloyd. 1966. The prediction of digestible energy intake potential (NVI) of forages using a simple *in vitro* technique. Proc. 10th Int. Grassl. Congr., pp. 442–45 (Helsinki, Finland).
27. Tilley, J. M. A., and R. A. Terry. 1963. A two-stage technique for the *in vitro* digestion of forage crops. *J. Brit. Grassl. Soc.* 18:104–11.

logical methods to study lignification patterns in plants and their relationship to digestibility.[28-30]

In Vitro RUMEN FERMENTATION TECHNIQUES

The most promising laboratory method for estimating digestibility is the two-stage *in vitro* rumen fermentation technique.[27] Stage one simulates the digestion of feedstuffs in the rumen by action of rumen microorganisms. The method involves a small quantity of ground forage (less than 1 g) placed in a test tube to which artificial saliva and rumen fluid inoculum are added. The tube is sealed to exclude oxygen and incubated at body temperature for a specific period, and the dry matter disappearance is measured. Stage two simulates the digestion (primarily of protein) in the lower digestive tract, using acid-pepsin or neutral detergent.[27,31]

In vitro rumen fermentation techniques have been used extensively for evaluating fresh forage and hay samples and to a lesser extent silages and forage-grain mixtures.[32,33] A few forage testing systems have used *in vitro* procedures; however, the many sources of variation inherent with the method make it difficult to standardize and adapt to a routine economic method of testing forages. The method is used primarily as a research tool in assessing the nutritional quality of forages for the animal nutritionist, forage breeder, and forage management specialist.

NYLON BAG TECHNIQUE

The nylon bag technique involves the suspension in the rumen of nylon bags containing forage samples.[34] As an estimate of digestibility, dry matter or nutrient loss is measured after specified periods of incubation. The technique has promise as a tool in evaluating forages. However, it is subject to even more variability than *in vitro* methods and is not readily adapted for use in routine forage testing systems.

⚘ TYPES OF FORAGE TESTING SERVICES

Forage or feedstuff testing has been instituted in over 30 states of the U.S. and in many other countries. It is used as a tool to aid farmers in feed programming for maximum returns and to assist in solving specific metabolic and nutritional problems existing on their farms. Feeding programs involve the development of complete rations including the forage and concentrate components for a given livestock feeding enterprise. As an example, a feeding program for dairy cattle would provide information on grain-to-milk ratios, crude protein content for grain mixtures, formulas for grain mixtures, dry and fresh cow feeding schedules, young stock feeding guides, forage feeding suggestions, and recommendations related to herd health or milk test problems.

The services provided in a given location vary considerably in the types of analyses and the availability of feed programming. Most feedstuff testing services are provided through the cooperative agricultural extension services for the states involved. However, there are many commercial laboratories that provide analytical testing of samples in conjunction with the extension service and other laboratories

28. Troelsen, J. E., J. B. Campbell, and D. H. Heinrichs. 1970. The effect of physical breakdown on the voluntary intake of coarse roughage by sheep. Proc. 11th Int. Grassl. Congr., pp. 747–50 (Surfers Paradise, Queensland, Aust.).

29. Chenost, M. 1966. Fibrousness of forages: Its determination and its relation to feeding value. Proc. 10th Int. Grassl. Congr., pp. 406–11 (Helsinki, Finland).

30. Drapala, W. J., L. C. Raymond, and E. W. Crampton. 1947. Pasture studies. XXVII. The effects of maturity of the plant and its lignification and subsequent digestibility by animals as indicated by methods of plant histology. *Sci. Agr.* 27:36–41.

31. Van Soest, P. J., R. H. Wine, and L. A. Moore. 1966. Estimation of the true digestibility of forages by the *in vitro* digestion of cell walls. Proc. 10th Int. Grassl. Congr., pp. 438–41 (Helsinki, Finland).

32. Barnes, R. F. 1965. Use of *in vitro* rumen fermentation techniques for estimating forage digestiblity and intake. *Agron. J.* 57:213–16.

33. Johnson, R. R. 1970. The development and application of *in vitro* rumen fermentation methods for forage evaluation, pp. M1–M18. Proc. Nat. Conf. Forage Qual. Eval. Util. (Lincoln, Nebr.).

34. Lowrey, R. S. 1970. The nylon bag technique for the estimation of forage quality, pp. 01–012. Proc. Nat. Conf. Forage Qual. Eval. Util. (Lincoln, Nebr.).

that include feed programming services as well. Some grain and feed trade companies provide such services for their customers on a gratis or fee basis.

Considerable variation exists among the available forage testing services as to the methods used to estimate forage quality and to develop feeding programs. Electronic data processing has enabled the researcher to develop least-cost balanced rations. Computerized ration-balancing services are being offered in many areas.[35] The trend toward more intensive cropping and animal practices increases the need for detailed feedstuff testing and feed programming. Routine tests are being made available in some areas for trouble-shooting herd health problems, as well as standard forage tests for estimating digestible protein and TDN or ENE. An example of such tests offered by the Penn State Forage Testing Service is presented in Table 59.2.[36]

❧ ADVANTAGES

Forage testing focuses attention on the critical problems related to forage production and use. Poor animal gains or growth are common where an essential nutrient is limiting. Excessive consumption of a nutrient means poor utilization by the animal. Forage testing may show the need for protein or mineral supplementation or for more or less grain in dairy rations depending on the level of milk production. In other instances a simpler or more complex supplement may be needed.

The savings realized by individuals using forage testing have been sizable in many instances.[37] Forage testing has been cited as responsible for (1) increasing milk production as much as 1952 kg/cow, (2) decreasing grain costs as much as $22/t, (3) increasing returns over feed costs as much as $134/cow, and (4) enabling profitable feed-

TABLE 59.2 ❧ Routine tests available through the Penn State Forage Testing Laboratory, University Park, Pa.

Test	When indicated
Forage	
Standard	routine on all farms
Moisture, protein, fiber, DP, TDN, ENE	
Mineral	routine on good farms
10–14 elements included, Ca, P, K, Mg	problem farms unknown supplements
Sulfur	problem farms unknown supplements
Urea equivalent	problem feeds home-mixed feeds
Nonprotein nitrogen	problem silages urea-silages
Nitrate	problem forages
Water	
Complete chemical test included, pH, most elements, nitrates, and nitrites	problem farms
Nitrate only	problem farms

ing of 454–1226 kg more grain per cow.[38] It was estimated that the value of forage testing in the early 1970s was over $2 million in the state of Pennsylvania alone.

A major contribution of forage testing has been the stimulation of interest in better forage production and feeding practices. Benefits to users from the initial phases of the Penn State Forage Testing Service were attributed to (1) more selective feeding of the available forages, (2) recognizing the value of earlier cutting of perennial forages, (3) making a sounder choice of annuals for silage, and (4) improved methods of making hay-crop silage.[39]

The acceptance of a feedstuff testing program varies from location to location and generally depends on (1) importance of the livestock industry, (2) status of feed programming, and (3) interest of local agri-

35. McGill, S. 1972. Computerized rations: Stage 2. *The Furrow*. July-Aug., pp. 26–27.
36. Veterinary Science Extension. 1970. Feed, water, and blood analyses—Their use in problem solving. Penn State Ext. Vet. News, Special Newsletter 48.
37. Adams, R. S., and J. E. Baylor. 1960. Forage testing is paying off. *Hoard's Dairyman* 105:563.

38. Baylor, J. E., and R. S. Adams. 1961. Forage testing and its value to the livestock farmer, pp. 5–8. Proc. Amer. Grassl. Counc.
39. Washko, J. B., R. S. Adams, and J. E. Baylor. 1964. Forage testing programs to determine forage quality for the farmer or rancher, pp. 17–28. Proc. Amer. Grassl. Counc.

cultural agents or business firms in promoting the program. Acceptance usually is greatest where dairying is the major farm enterprise. Results have been less dramatic with other types of livestock; however, it also is applied to creep-feeding of calves and supplementation of growing steers or heifers. Many commercial feedlot operations maintain a chemical analytical laboratory at their feed mixing facilities to monitor ration composition. In beef cow and calf operations, forage testing is urged as a means of establishing winter feeding programs that use only the amount and quality of forages necessary for profitable cow and calf operations.[40] For example, more efficient utilization of crop residues is possible when the limited nutrients are known and can be economically supplied.

Forage testing provides a means for extension personnel and others to improve their service to farmers. In many instances it has helped to standardize recommendations, which encourages adoption of information by farmers. It also provides a means of keeping feeding programs up to date through quicker on-farm application of recent research.

❧ AREAS OF CONCERN

Limited participation by those who use forage testing only once or twice is a major drawback. Animals must be fed the year-round; their needs change as well as the type and amount of forage available. Feed programming on at least a quarterly basis is recommended, with some producers routinely testing feeds on a monthly or even a more frequent basis. Tests should be made whenever an appreciable ration change is made or contemplated.

SAMPLING

Obtaining a representative sample of forage for testing is a major problem associated with any laboratory estimate of feeding value. It is essential to take whatever steps are necessary to prevent or minimize the time lag between sampling and shipment to the testing laboratory, overheating the sample, and drying the sample. Where fresh forage or silage samples are involved, it may be desirable to refrigerate them prior to shipment.

Hay may be sampled at the time of storage if it is dry enough to keep without further curing, otherwise sampling should be delayed for at least two weeks.[14,41,42] Obtaining at least one core sample per 12 or more bales of hay or a subsample from 12 locations in loose or chopped hay selected at random is recommended. Lots must be adequately identified for reference when feeding, otherwise samples should be taken as fed. Legume hays and mixed hays consisting mainly of legumes should be sampled separately from grass or predominantly grass hays. First-cutting hays should be sampled separately from aftermath cuttings. Samples of aftermath cuttings often are composited since there is usually less variability in quality among aftermath forages than between first and aftermath cuttings.

Sampling of silage usually is recommended as it is fed or at least one month after forage has been ensiled.[14,35,36] Sampling while silage is stored is possible if corn is in the full dent to glaze stage or if the moisture level of haylage is below 60%. Sampling the top portion of the silo or areas adjacent to openings providing moldy or spoiled silage should be avoided. In using a silo unloader or other means of sampling, at least 12 subsample sites are recommended for the test sample. A horizontal silo should be sampled only back of the point where it is of constant depth. Subsamples should be thoroughly mixed and carefully resampled to provide a representative test sample comparable to the forage being fed.

40. Forages and the cow and calf herd. 1971. Va. Poly. Inst. Ext. Div. Publ. 465.

41. Fryman, L. R. 1969. Getting the most from chemical analyses of roughages for dairy cattle. Univ. Ill. Ext. Serv. Circ. 994.
42. Little, H. C., and W. P. Spencer. 1966. Experimental standards and grades for alfalfa hay. Univ. Nev. Bull. B9.

Fig. 59.2. *Type of equipment . . . may influence cost . . . ease of collection.* Sampling baled hay with the Penn State forage sampler. *Purdue Univ. photo.*

SAMPLING EQUIPMENT

The type of equipment for collecting laboratory samples may influence the cost and ease of collection. The "Penn State" forage sampler was developed for use with an electric power drill (Fig. 59.2). However, the weight, bulkiness, expense, and requirement for electric power sometimes make it inconvenient to use. A square-shanked adapter for use with a bit brace also is available for the "Penn State" sampler. Other hand-driven core samplers have been developed and include a section of an old golf club, a heavy-duty core homemade sampler, and a modified hollow ski pole.[14,43]

PROCESSING PERIOD

The length of the processing period required is often a major deterrent to forage testing. Two weeks is normal for most laboratories. This is particularly a problem where rapid turnover time is essential such as with hay marketing.[36,37] Many laboratories have a seasonal sample distribution problem.

43. Little, H. C., and A. J. Baker. 1967. Evaluating experimental standards and grades for alfalfa hay. Univ. Nev. Bull. B12.

Personnel required for servicing feed programming systems is often insufficient or there is inadequate funding to support a large volume. The development of computerized ration-balancing services should help alleviate these problems.

LIMITATIONS

Although a number of laboratory methods have been developed for the estimation of forage digestibility, the primary value of most techniques is as a research tool rather than in a forage testing program. A forage sample submitted for testing is no better than the sampling procedure used to obtain it and the supplemental information provided by the livestock feeder as to its condition and its planned use.

Forage testing programs cannot measure forage intake by livestock; cannot overcome poor plant fertilization, harvesting, or storage programs; and cannot substitute for good livestock management. However, forage testing coupled with feed programming can provide the good forage and livestock manager with a tool to enable improved utilization of forage and other feedstuffs.

❧ QUESTIONS

1. What are the important criteria in the estimation of forage quality?
2. What effect does heat damage of forage have upon nutrient availability?
3. Discuss the relative merits of the TDN system and the ENE system for forage testing.
4. Describe the shortcomings of forage testing for use in a hay marketing situation.
5. Consult an agricultural extension service specialist concerning the forage testing service offered in your state and determine its advantages and disadvantages.
6. Discuss new laboratory methods which may replace the measurements of CP and CF for the estimation of nutrient content and digestibility.

J. T. REID / *Cornell University*

60

FORAGES FOR DAIRY CATTLE

&

Dairying has changed more since 1960 than during any previous 12-year period in history. In the U.S. there were 70% as many lactating cows and about 30% as many dairy farms, but 2.5 times as many cows per farm, in 1972 as in 1960.[1,2] (See Fig. 60.1.) The average cow ingested about 21% more energy and produced about 40% more milk in 1972 than in 1960.[1,3] Accordingly, the 55,842 million kg of milk produced in 1972 was only 2% less than the yield in 1960.

Associated with these changes were radical differences in feeding and management. In addition to consuming more total energy, the lactating cow ate a decidedly different diet. For example, concentrates and silages provided 25 and 44% more of the energy, and hay and pasture provided 24 and 32% less energy in 1970 than in 1960.[3] An average of 880 kg more concentrates, 91 kg less hay, and 1550 kg more silage and haylage were consumed per cow in 1972 than in 1960.[1] This reflects the relatively favorable milk price–grain cost ratio and the high cost of labor that existed during the 1960s. With the trend toward more cows per farm, group handling of cows, more confinement housing, and me-

chanical feeding, the amount of silage and haylage fed was greater and the practice of grazing was less in 1972 than 1960. In many farm situations the feeding of medium-moisture silage has been found to be more compatible with the trends in dairying than has the feeding of hay. Medium-moisture silage is adaptable to mechanized feeding, less prone to the vagaries of weather, and complements corn silage feeding both in handling and nutritionally. When more than 272 t of forage dry matter (DM) are to be stored, the annual costs per unit usually will be less for haylage than for hay.[4]

Despite the great intensification of dairying, pasturage and harvested forages of high quality continue to be the most economical sources of nutrients required by dairy cattle for maintenance, growth, and milk production. Nevertheless, high-producing cows cannot eat enough forage to produce the amount of milk of which they are capable. They need, therefore, a more

& J. T. REID. See Chapter 49.

1. Mathis, A. G., and R. R. Miller. 1972. The dairy situation. ERS, USDA Bull. DS-343.
2. Mathis, A. G., and R. R. Miller. 1972. The dairy situation. ERS, USDA Bull. DS-341.
3. Allen, G. C., E. F. Hodges, and M. Devers. 1972. National and state livestock-feed relationships. ERS, USDA Stat. Bull. 446, suppl.
4. Hoglund, C. R. 1965. Some economic considerations in selecting storage systems for haylage and silage on dairy farms. Mich. Agr. Econ. Rept. 14.

forages do not supply enough Na and Cl, these elements are easily provided as common salt. Cattle must have continual access to this supplement. Forages grown on Co-deficient soils, known to exist in certain regions of the world, will not provide enough of this element. However, it too can be supplied as a supplement mixed in salt or by the provision of "cobalt bullets" which, because of their density, lodge in the rumen of cattle but gradually leach to provide Co.

VITAMINS

Vitamins A and D are needed by cattle throughout life. Dairy animals can obtain adequate vitamin A by consuming feeds that contain it, or they can manufacture vitamin A from carotene in the feed; green plant tissue is the principal source. Good quality forages, especially pasturage and grass silage, are dependable sources of carotene.

The ultraviolet rays of the sun produce vitamin D in the skin of animals and also in plant tissue after the forage has been cut. Thus forage with considerable exposure to the sun provides the extra vitamin D needed when fed to cows in liberal amounts.

❧ PERFORMANCE OF COWS ON FORAGE

It has been amply demonstrated that cows will maintain themselves, reproduce normally, and stay healthy when fed entirely on forages. However, even on high-quality forage, cows cannot maintain a milk output greater than 18–20 kg/day without losing body tissue. Forage is relatively low in energy concentration and lactating cows cannot consume enough to maintain body weight. However, cows fed good quality forage and as little as 1 kg of concentrates per 6 kg of milk produced may yield 1.2–1.4 times as much milk as when fed the forage alone. When fed more concentrates (e.g., 1 kg/4 kg milk), cows may produce as much as 1.5–1.8 times as much

milk as when fed only good quality forage. Response to additional concentrates largely depends upon the cow's capacity to produce milk and the level of feeding at which she tends to deposit body fat.

❧ U.S. DAIRY COWS

The average U.S. dairy cow weighs 520 kg and produces 4480 kg milk/year. Assuming a lactation period of 10 months, her average daily production would be 14.7 kg.[1] During the peak of lactation she would yield about 22 kg/day. To produce these amounts of milk, the average cow would need 16 and 22 kg/day respectively of medium to late cut hay having a TDN content of 50% or its equivalent of other forage. If early cut hay having 70% TDN were fed, she would need only 12 and 16 kg/day respectively.

The major nutrient needs of lactating cows, as reported by the National Research Council, are shown in Table 60.2.[9] The levels of nutrients proposed are adequate to prevent deficiencies, and they provide for acceptable reproduction and milk production when feedstuffs are of at least average quality.

On good pasture or green chop, cows weighing 360–455 kg will consume 11.3–13.6 kg DM/day and cows weighing 590 kg will eat 13.6–18.1 kg.[10,11] Cows will eat almost as much hay or silage (containing 35–60% DM).[12,13,14] However, they usually will not eat as much high-moisture (20–30% DM) silage unless the forage was en-

9. National Research Council. 1971. Nutrient Requirements of Dairy Cattle, 4th ed., rev. Natl. Acad. Sci., Washington, D.C.
10. Reid, J. T., A. M. Smith, and M. J. Anderson. 1958. Difference in the requirements for maintenance of dairy cattle between pasture- and barn-feeding conditions, pp. 88–93. Proc. Cornell Nutr. Conf.
11. Kennedy, W. K., J. T. Reid, and M. J. Anderson. 1959. Evaluation of animal production under different systems of grazing. *J. Dairy Sci.* 42:679–85.
12. Stone, J. B., G. W. Trimberger, C. R. Henderson, J. T. Reid, K. L. Turk, and J. K. Loosli. 1960. Forage intake and efficiency of feed utilization in dairy cattle. *J. Dairy Sci.* 43:1275–81.
13. Merrill, W. G., and S. T. Slack. 1965. Feeding value of perennial forages for dairy cows. A review. Anim. Husb. Mimeo Ser. 3, Cornell Univ.
14. Tyrell, H. F., and J. T. Reid. 1967. Effect of method of forage preservation on the feeding value of perennial forages, pp. 137–45. Proc. Cornell Nutr. Conf.

TABLE 60.2   Daily nutrient requirements of dairy cows

Body weight (kg)	Dry feed (kg)	Protein		Energy		Ca (gm)	P (gm)	Caro- tene (mg)	Vita- min A (1000 I.U.)
		Total (gm)	Digest- ible (gm)	Digest- ible (Mcal)	TDN (kg)				
*Maintenance of mature lactating cows**									
350	5.0	468	220	12.3	2.8	14	11	37	15
400	5.5	521	245	13.6	3.1	17	13	42	17
450	6.0	585	275	15.0	3.4	18	14	48	19
500	6.5	638	300	16.3	3.7	20	15	53	21
550	7.0	691	325	17.6	4.0	21	16	58	23
600	7.5	734	345	18.9	4.2	22	17	64	26
650	8.0	776	365	19.8	4.5	23	18	69	28
700	8.5	830	390	21.1	4.8	25	19	74	30
750	9.0	872	410	22.0	5.0	26	20	79	32
800	9.5	915	430	23.3	5.3	27	21	85	34
Maintenance and pregnancy (last two months of gestation)									
350	6.4	570	315	15.8	3.6	21	16	67	27
400	7.2	650	355	17.2	4.0	23	18	76	30
450	7.9	730	400	19.4	4.4	26	20	86	34
500	8.6	780	430	21.1	4.8	29	22	95	38
550	9.3	850	465	22.9	5.2	31	24	105	42
600	10.0	910	500	24.6	5.6	34	26	114	46
650	10.6	960	530	26.4	6.0	36	28	124	50
700	11.3	1000	555	27.7	6.3	39	30	133	53
750	12.0	1080	595	29.5	6.7	42	32	143	57
800	12.6	1150	630	31.2	7.1	44	34	152	61

Percent fat	Protein		Energy		Ca (gm)	P (gm)
	Total (gm)	Digestible (gm)	Digestible (Mcal)	TDN (kg)		
Milk production (nutrients required per kilogram milk)						
2.5	66	42	1.12	0.255	2.4	1.7
3.0	70	45	1.23	0.280	2.5	1.8
3.5	74	48	1.34	0.305	2.6	1.9
4.0	78	51	1.46	0.330	2.7	2.0
4.5	82	54	1.57	0.355	2.8	2.1
5.0	86	56	1.68	0.380	2.9	2.2
5.5	90	58	1.79	0.405	3.0	2.3
6.0	94	60	1.90	0.430	3.1	2.4

Source: National Research Council, 1971.[9]
* To allow for growth, add 20% to the maintenance allowance during the first lactation and 10% during the second lactation.

siled with an additive such as formic acid.[13,14]

Cows fed 1 kg of concentrates for each 3–4 kg of milk produced will usually eat 12.7–16.0 kg of DM as hay or silage prepared from early cut, first-growth forage or aftermath forage. However, they may consume only 8–11 kg of forage DM if the same crop is harvested at a late stage of growth.

The average lactating cow gets about 62% of her energy from forages and about 38% from concentrates.[3] High-producing cows may get as much as 60% of their feed energy from concentrates. In deciding how much grain to feed the individual cow, the farmer needs to determine whether the saving in forage and the returns from the extra milk obtained by feeding additional concentrates would be worth more than the cost of the added increments of concentrates. Although forages supply the cheapest source of nutrients for dairy cattle, it pays to feed some concentrates to lactating cows under most economic conditions.

IMPORTANCE OF PASTURES

Pasture is a highly nutritious feed for dairy cattle, and under many farming situations it usually is also the lowest cost feed. Therefore, on many dairy farms where the management conditions permit, or at least for dry cows and young stock, the provision of pasturage should be given high priority. This is particularly true in the southern states where pasture can be available during much of the year (Table 60.3). In the northern U.S. the pasture season seldom lasts longer than about five months. Even a part of that may yield poor production unless measures are taken to plan a sequence of crops such as that shown in Table 60.3 to compensate for hot dry weather.

MODERN DAIRYING

In 1970 pastures provided about 20% of the energy consumed by lactating cows and about 46% of that by other dairy cattle.[3] Although these are significant quanti-

ties, the amount of pasture consumed by lactating cows has been decreasing steadily; in 1972 pastures provided less than 60% as much of the total feed as they did in 1960. This downward trend undoubtedly is related to the increasing herd size and the associated movement toward confinement housing, mechanized feeding, group handling of cows, and the increasing use of silage. Also associated with these trends is the steadily increasing milk yield per cow.

At some point in herd size the logistics and time and labor requirements of moving large numbers of cows to and from pasture become overwhelming. The larger the herd, the greater the distance between pasture sites and the milking and feeding center. As herd size increases, additional land must frequently be purchased. In most of the dairy regions land is expensive. As a consequence, in order for the dairyman to

TABLE 60.3 ❧ Sequences of forage crops to maximize pasture production

Kinds of pastures	Grazing periods for central and northern United States											
	Jan.	Feb.	Mar.	Apr.	May	June	July	Aug.	Sept.	Oct.	Nov.	Dec.
Permanent pasture*					▬▬▬▬▬▬				▬▬▬			
Renovated pasture†				▬▬▬▬▬▬▬▬▬▬▬▬▬▬								
Rotation pasture†				▬▬▬▬▬▬▬▬▬▬▬▬▬▬▬								
Hay meadows							▬▬▬					
Small grain–lespedeza‡				▬▬▬▬▬▬▬▬▬						▬▬		
Sweetclover				▬▬▬▬▬▬			▬▬▬					
Sudangrass						▬▬▬▬▬▬▬▬▬▬						

Kinds of pastures	Grazing periods for southern United States											
	Jan.	Feb.	Mar.	Apr.	May	June	July	Aug.	Sept.	Oct.	Nov.	Dec.
Permanent pasture§					▬▬▬▬▬▬▬▬▬▬▬▬▬▬▬▬▬▬							
Oats-vetch‖	▬▬▬▬▬▬										▬▬▬	
Ryegrass–crimson clover‖	▬▬▬▬▬▬▬▬											
Johnsongrass-legumes**	▬▬▬					▬▬▬▬▬▬						
Lespedeza††						▬▬▬▬▬▬▬▬▬▬						
Sudangrass‡‡						▬▬▬▬▬▬▬▬▬▬						
Kudzu						▬▬▬▬▬▬▬▬▬▬▬▬						

  * Kentucky bluegrass–white clover with soil treatment.
  † Seeded to mixture as orchardgrass–ladino clover or smooth bromegrass–alfalfa with soil treatment.
  ‡ If grain crop is taken, grazing season must be shortened at least by six weeks.
  § Dallisgrass or carpetgrass on lowland, bermudagrass on upland with white, hop, and Persian clovers and proper lime-fertilizer treatments.
  ‖ Burclover, crimson clover, or other adapted winter legumes may be used.
  ** Winter oats–rough peas, burclover, and crimson clover can also be seeded where johnsongrass is used.
  †† May be seeded in small grain but not with winter-growing clovers.
  ‡‡ 'Tift' sudangrass should be used in the humid southeastern U.S.

expand his business, he must grow crops more productive than pasture where it is possible to do so.

In addition, pastures are difficult to manage. Although they eliminate some of the labor cost of feeding and manure disposal, pastures entail other costs including fencing, water supply, clipping, reseeding, fertilizing, and other management. Cows have more difficulty maintaining a uniformly high yield on pasture than under the conditions of a more uniform environment and feeding from storage. As the milk yield per cow increases, this problem becomes more critical.

As the result of equipping to harvest and feed silage and haylage, the dairyman then can make dual use of his equipment by feeding from storage or green-chopping during the pasture season. In this way he also can concentrate his labor rather than fragmenting workers' time among more diverse activities.

Use of pasturage for dry cows and young stock is expected to continue. However, whether it is profitable to pasture lactating cows will depend upon the conditions existing on the individual farm. Research is needed to determine economic guidelines which can be applied to various conditions, sizes of operation, and regions of the country.

MILK PRODUCTION

One of the limiting factors in milk production is the inadequate supply of pasturage during the hot, dry, summer months. During this period, the growth of pasture crops falls off greatly and, because farmers do not provide enough other feed, milk production also falls off materially. The condition of the cows deteriorates. As a result, it is difficult to get them back on a higher level of production later in the season when pasturage becomes more plentiful or in the fall when they are maintained under barn-feeding conditions. This contributes greatly to the uneven milk supply and the demoralization of markets.

PASTURE PROGRAMS FOR ABUNDANT GRAZING

Permanent pasture cannot meet the needs of the herd during all the season; it is too irregular in production, except possibly when irrigated. This type of pasture must be supplemented with grazing from rotation pasture, temporary pasture, or meadow aftermath. Grain crops and certain annual or perennial grasses and legumes, with proper fertilization, can be used to provide adequate grazing in the hot, dry, midsummer and also to extend the season earlier in the spring and later in the fall and early winter. This is especially true in the southern states where there is opportunity to approach year-round grazing. To provide such grazing it often is necessary to allow forage crops to grow ungrazed for a period in the late fall and early winter to produce an accumulation of herbage for grazing during periods when the temperature is too low to support growth. Table 60.3 illustrates how different crops and types of pastures can be used to develop an adequate supply of pasturage on farms in northern and southern areas.

EFFECT OF MANAGEMENT METHOD ON PASTURE PRODUCTION

Pasturage gives best results when consumed in an immature stage. For a few weeks in early spring it is highly palatable and contains about 75–80% TDN. These qualities deteriorate rapidly until plant growth is interrupted by grazing or harvesting. If the resulting aftermath is kept in an immature stage and rainfall is adequate, uniformly high nutritive quality is maintained through the remainder of the season. Under these conditions the TDN value usually is between 60 and 70%, but it never again reaches the high early spring value during the same season. The nutritive value of harvested, green forage usually is lower than that of herbage selected from the same sward by cattle grazing conventionally. Also, because of selection by the grazing animal, the nutritive value of grazed forage is higher when the stocking rate is low than when it is high.[10]

In one study with several kinds of pasture, cows grazing the top half of forage produced 42% more milk on the average than their mates grazing the stemmier bottom half of the sward.[15]

Various management practices can be used to maintain high-quality pasturage through the summer. These include dividing a pasture area into small units that can be grazed in rotation or green-chopping at the desired growth stage for bunk feeding. Either plan allows more efficient utilization of herbage than continuous grazing. Animals are confined in both systems so that they can obtain their fill without walking great distances. The intensity of rotational grazing as practiced on dairy farms ranges from the use of two paddocks alternately during the entire season to the use of a fresh strip each day. Several studies have shown that milk yield is about 10% greater from cows grazing under a moderate rotational scheme than from those grazing continuously. The more intensive the method of management, the greater the expense for labor, fencing, and watering. Certain of these expenses and those for additional equipment make the practice of feeding green chop more costly than conventional grazing unless the farm is already equipped for harvesting and feeding mechanically. Also, the intensive methods of utilizing green chop require more management skill.

Variable results have been obtained in comparisons between green chop, rotational grazing, and strip grazing. In general, milk production per cow per day is about the same for all these methods. However, selective grazing at low stocking rates can result in a larger yield per cow per day than the feeding of harvested forage. To obtain an adequate intake, cows grazed rotationally usually require more pasture area than those that are strip grazed. Strip graz-

ing of cows requires a larger area than would be needed when the forage is harvested as green chop. Thus milk yield per ha generally is highest for green chop, intermediate for strip grazing, and lowest for rotational grazing. The degree of superiority of the more intensive grazing system has varied among experiments. This variation seems attributable to differences in the stocking rates imposed upon the pastures grazed rotationally. In at least one experiment comparing green chop, strip grazing, and 3- and 6-paddock rotational grazing, the amount of milk produced per cow per day or per ha was about the same irrespective of method.[11]

Milk yield per ha is the product of the daily production of individual cows and the number of cow-days per ha. It is possible mistakenly to credit a pasture with high productivity by overstocking because cows in good condition can use body tissue to produce considerable amounts of milk. Even though milk yield per ha may be high because of the large number of cows grazing, milk yield per cow may be low and unprofitable. The detriment of body tissue loss may not become manifest until later in lactation when cows are not on pasture.

PASTURE CARE

From the standpoint of efficient utilization of pasturage, it is important to control the amount of ungrazed herbage and weeds and to spread the manure from time to time. This should be done by clipping the pasture as often as seems necessary each season. Clipping should be done right after the cows have finished grazing a paddock and are moved on to the next. Fertilizer should be applied to pastures from time to time as described in Chapters 38 and 39.

A relatively high percentage of legumes in pasture is desirable because they increase the supply of protein and Ca in the forage mixture. But, more important, legumes increase the yield, particularly during the hot part of summer. Nevertheless, it is

15. Bryant, H. T., R. E. Blaser, R. C. Hammes, Jr., and W. A. Hardison. 1961. Method for increased milk production with rotational grazing. *J. Dairy Sci.* 44:1733–41.

also important to have considerable grass present in the herbage mixture to reduce the possibility of bloat in the grazing animals (see Chapter 58).

COMFORT FOR PASTURED COWS

Consideration should be given to the comfort of cows on pasture. They should not be required to travel long distances to and from pasture and during grazing. Energy expended in this way cannot be used for milk production. Grazing cows need 15–30% more feed to produce the same amount of milk as under barn-feeding conditions.[10,16,17] In one experiment the energy expense of continuous grazing was about 11% greater than that of strip grazing.[18] Under conditions which allow cows to graze selectively, the forage consumed usually is more digestible than that cut from the same crop and fed as green chop. However, this difference may be canceled by the greater energy cost of grazing.

Plenty of water, salt, and shade should be provided and the cows should be kept free of flies and other insects. The most ideal environment during summer can be maintained for large herds by feeding green chop under comfortable conditions rather than by grazing.

GRAZING VERSUS DRYLOT FEEDING

Variable results have been obtained in experiments comparing grazing with drylot feeding. In a Louisiana study the response of heifers fed 2.7 kg of concentrates per day and corn silage ad libitum was compared with that of heifers treated the same way but allowed to graze ryegrass or forage sorghum pasture in addition.[19] The rates and costs of body gain were similar. In a Missouri experiment heifers grazing alfalfa (0.57 kg/day) or birdsfoot trefoil (0.62 kg/day) gained decidedly less rapidly than those fed alfalfa haylage in drylot (0.73 kg/day).[20]

No difference in milk production, solids-not-fat, protein, or fat was observed between cows pastured on irrigated ryegrass-clover or orchardgrass-clover and those fed alfalfa hay and grass-legume silages.[21] Concentrates were fed at the same rate to both groups of cows. In another study, cows fed 1 kg of concentrates per 3.5 kg of milk produced yielded significantly more milk while grazing alfalfa than did their mates fed green chop from the same source of an excellent quality, third-cutting alfalfa hay.[22] Sufficient herbage was available to allow selective grazing.

PASTURAGE FOR YOUNG CATTLE AND DRY COWS

When it is abundant and of good quality, pasturage is an excellent and economic feed for dairy calves, heifers, and dry cows. If forage is abundant and actively growing, cattle as young as four months will be able to meet their nutrient requirements.[6] When grazing first-growth forage, growing cattle encounter a deficiency of TDN more frequently and earlier in the season than one of digestible protein. However, these deficiencies exist only when first-growth forage is in the later stages of growth. Even then legumes provide adequate protein. If enough herbage is available to satisfy the appetite for DM, neither deficiency occurs when growing cattle are grazing aftermath of either legumes or nonlegumes.

Dry cows are less sensitive than growing cattle to low-protein forage. When pasturage becomes short, attention must be given

16. Wallace, L. R. 1956. The intake and utilisation of pasture by grazing dairy cattle. Proc. 7th Int. Grassl. Congr., p. 134 (Palmerston North, N.Z.).

17. Holmes, W., J. W. G. Jones, and R. M. Drake-Brockman. 1961. The feed intake of grazing cattle. II. The influence of size of animal on feed intake. *Anim. Prod.* 3:251–60.

18. Holmes, W., and H. el Sayed Osman. 1960. The feed intake of grazing cattle. I. Feed intake of dairy cows on strip and free grazing. *Anim. Prod.* 2:131–39.

19. Hollon, B. F., and D. C. Meyerhoeffer. 1969. Comparison of drylot and pasture feeding for raising replacement dairy heifers. *J. Dairy Sci.* 52:559.

20. Marx, G. D., and F. K. Johnson. 1970. Comparison of birdsfoot trefoil pasture, alfalfa pasture and drylot feeding for dairy heifers. *J. Dairy Sci.* 53:678.

21. Sendagi, A. L., R. H. Kliewer, F. B. Wolberg, M. A. Peters, W. R. Bennett, and K. J. Peterson. 1969. Drylot feeding versus pasturing for milk production in dairy cattle. *J. Dairy Sci.* 52:1404–7.

22. Stiles, D. A., E. E. Bartley, G. L. Kilgore, F. W. Boren, and H. B. Perry. 1971. Comparative value of alfalfa pasture, alfalfa greenchop, or alfalfa hay for lactating dairy cows. *J. Dairy Sci.* 54:65–70.

to providing both growing cattle and dry cows with supplemental feed to maintain satisfactory body condition. Silage, hay, or concentrates will serve this purpose.

❧ HARVESTED FORAGES FOR WINTER FEED

In most dairy regions green chop is the major feed source for at least five months of the year. Harvested forages take the place of green chop during the nonpasture season, and they also are used to supplement deficient pasturage in season.

Since forage crops make their growth in summer but are fed mostly during winter, it is necessary to harvest and store them for later use. This represents one of the most difficult problems with which the farmer has to cope, that of efficiently conserving the high nutritional properties of forages during harvesting and storage.

Hay alone contributes 23% of the total feed energy consumed by dairy cows. Another 19% comes from other harvested forage such as silage (both corn and grass), fodder, and straw. If harvested forages were of higher quality, the amounts included in the average ration could be increased. Generally, silage is of better quality than hay because silage usually is cut earlier in the season and hays cured in the field are often weather damaged. Although alternative methods to field curing will correct this situation, they are expensive to apply. In addition, hay is not as adaptable to mechanical handling and feeding as silage. With increasing herd size and more mechanical feeding, the amount of silage fed relative to that of hay is also increasing. The average cow in the U.S. in 1972, as compared with her counterpart in 1960, ate 91 kg less hay and 1550 kg more silage.

Effect of Stage of Maturity on Value

One of the important factors affecting the feeding value of harvested forages is the stage of maturity at which the crop is cut. As growth proceeds toward maturity, the nutrient value of perennial forages declines steadily. The protein content decreases and the fiber content increases with advancing growth. Associated with these changes is a reduction in digestibility and rate of consumption of forages by cattle.

Many experiments conducted since 1950 have demonstrated the nutritive merit of early cut forage. Notable among these is a Cornell study in which hays prepared from a mixture of alfalfa, red clover, ladino clover, and timothy harvested during the first week of June (when timothy was in the head stage) and between July 5 and 10 (when in postbloom stage) were fed to lactating cows.[23] Milk yield was 19% greater per cow and 27% greater per ha, from cows fed the earlier cut hay. Cows fed forage cut in early June gained 113 gm more body weight per day than those fed late cut hay. In another experiment cows fed first-growth forage harvested on June 11 produced 40% more milk and gained 227 gm more weight per day than those fed forage cut from the same source on July 9.[5] Making the first cutting early has the additional advantage of bringing on aftermath at a time when soil moisture is high. Thus the yield of the second cutting is increased.

Under average conditions most farmers allow forages to become too mature before harvesting. This may result in higher yields of dry matter per ha but, from the standpoint of feeding value and total nutritive effect in terms of animal production, farmers should be more interested in the yield of TDN than in yield of DM.

Preservation Methods

The extent to which harvested forage is damaged by weather has a marked effect upon the amount preserved and its nutritive value. Severe rain damage can reduce the amount of DM stored by as much as 32% and the TDN value per unit weight of DM by as much as 15%. Since first-

---

23. Turk, K. L., S. H. Morrison, C. L. Norton, and R. E. Blaser. 1951. Effect of curing methods upon the feeding value of hay. Cornell Agr. Exp. Sta. Bull. 874.

growth forage of the highest quality can be made only by harvesting early, at which time the climatic conditions generally are unfavorable to field curing, the farmer frequently has to use other means of preserving the crop than field curing. Methods usually employed are ensiling, barn drying with or without heated air, or crushing the green forage to speed up field drying.

The preservation method used does not add any nutritive qualities to the forage that were not present when it was harvested. To varying degrees it may prevent the nutrient loss caused by weathering.

Based upon the results of many experiments, the net percentages of DM in harvested forage that can be preserved for feeding have been found to be:[13,24] barn drying with heat, 88–90%; barn drying without heat, 80–85%; ensiling forage containing 35–45% DM in conventional vertical silos, 85%; ensiling forage containing 20–30% DM in conventional vertical silos, 75–84%; ensiling forage containing 20–60% DM in gastight silos, 85–89%; field curing to a DM content of 75–90%, 68–76%; and field curing with rain damage, as little as 50%.

With increasing dryness of the forage product as removed from the field, the field and harvesting losses increase and the storage losses decrease. For direct-cut silage containing 17–20% DM, the field losses will be only 2–4%. For field-cured hay containing 80–90% DM, the field and harvesting losses will be of the order of 21–28%. On the other hand, the losses in storage are reversed. For the corresponding feeds these are usually 19–23% and 3–5% respectively.

High-moisture silage (less than 30% DM) has the following disadvantages: large DM losses in fermentation and seepage, objectionable odors, low consumption rate by cattle, and handling of a large weight of water per unit of energy.

Although the TDN value of forage does not differ among various preservation methods, DM intake is positively correlated with DM concentration. In one experiment cows were fed rations of alfalfa silage (22–25% DM) alone or with 25, 50, and 75% alfalfa hay containing 87% DM, or they were fed the hay alone.[25] The daily DM intakes were 2.27, 2.49, 2.87, 3.10, and 3.23 kg/100 kg of body weight respectively. Comparisons made of alfalfa stored as hay (89% DM), haylage (39–53% DM), and direct-cut silage (20–27% DM) also show the increasing intake with increasing DM concentration.[26] This study and others also demonstrate that the intake of high-DM (40–60%) silage approaches that of barn-dried hay.

The relative value of preservation methods can be determined by accounting for field and storage losses, DM intake, and milk yield per unit of DM consumed.[13] Thus the relative values of forage for milk yield per ha, when preserved in various ways, become: barn-dried hay, 100; silage (less than 30% DM), 104; silage (30–40% DM), 114; silage (45% DM), 103. These figures are based on silage stored in a conventional upright silo. For gastight silos these values would be 3–8 percentage units higher.

Preservation of forage by ensiling at approximately 40% DM has a number of advantages over other methods. In addition to its high milk-producing potential per ha, it may be mechanically fed and combines in a system with corn silage that is economically and nutritionally advantageous. When both grass and corn silage are utilized on the same farm, greater use can be made of harvesting, storing, and feeding facilities. The combination of corn silage and grass silage simplifies the formulation of the concentrate mixture by making it possible to use a single protein con-

24. Hoglund, C. R. 1964. Comparative storage losses and feeding values of alfalfa and corn silage crops when harvested at different moisture levels and stored in gastight and conventional tower silos: An appraisal of research results. Mich. Agr. Econ. Mimeo 947.

25. Brown, L. D., D. Hillman, C. A. Lassiter, and C. F. Huffman. 1963. Grass silage vs. hay for lactating dairy cows. J. Dairy Sci. 46:407–10.
26. Gordon, C. H., J. C. Derbyshire, H. G. Wiseman, E. A. Kane, and C. G. Melin. 1961. Preservation and feeding value of alfalfa stored as hay, haylage, and direct-cut silage. J. Dairy Sci. 44:1299–1311.

centration in the grain mixture. Silage wilted to a DM of 35–45% does not require gastight storage, which is very expensive. See Chapter 51 for guidelines for making grass silage.

LEGUMES VERSUS GRASSES

The major purpose served by forages in the diet of dairy cattle is the economical provision of energy. When legumes and grasses are cut at the same time, there is little if any difference in their energy value per unit weight.[5] However, the advantage in yield usually obtained emphasizes the importance of growing legumes on farms where possible. Generalizing the relative acceptability to cattle of legumes and grasses is difficult. There probably is as much difference in palatability within grasses or legumes as there is between these two kinds of forage crops.

CORN SILAGE

Corn silage is very palatable and cows consume it in large amounts. It supplements other feeds effectively and appears to have a favorable effect. When good quality corn silage is the only forage fed, it will be consumed in large amounts over long periods. Cows fed corn silage and concentrates have produced as much as 6800 kg of milk annually. For best results, corn should be ensiled when the kernels are in the late dough or early dent stage. When ensiled at this time, corn silage is a good and dependable source of carotene. It is a poor source when ensiled after the grain has matured. Research is needed to determine whether corn silage can be fed as the sole forage for extended periods without the occurrence of metabolic disturbances.

❧ FITTING THE CONCENTRATE MIXTURE TO FORAGE

Harvested perennial forages can make up the major part or all of the ration of dairy cows, depending on the producing ability of the cows or on the level of milk production desired. The extent to which results from forage can be reliable depends upon how much will be eaten per unit of time, its TDN value, and its digestible protein content. However, intake of forage DM will seldom reach 3.3% of body weight even in lactating cows not fed any concentrates. As a consequence, cows producing over 20 kg of milk per day cannot consume enough of even better than usual quality forage to sustain production unless they are fed concentrates in addition.

When harvesting and curing losses are not great, the first cutting of legumes in all growth stages and of grasses up to the flowering stage are dependable for providing enough digestible protein for dairy cattle under almost all conditions.[27] Digestible protein content of aftermath is higher per unit of TDN than that of first-growth forage. At the stages when aftermath usually is harvested, the protein content, even of grasses, generally is adequate. Although nonlegumes in bloom or later growth stages are not always reliable sources of protein, fertilizing the soil on which they are grown with high N levels will markedly increase protein content.

High-protein concentrates are not needed to supplement forages containing considerable first-growth or aftermath legumes, first-growth nonlegumes harvested at prebloom growth stages, or aftermaths of either legumes or nonlegumes cut at the usual stages. Cereal grains or their byproducts containing 8–12% digestible protein in rations with these forages provide sufficient protein for dairy cattle under most conditions.

When corn or sorghum silage is the sole or major forage fed to lactating cows, supplying the appropriate level of protein in the concentrate mixture is a complex problem because of the very low concentration of protein relative to TDN in these forages and the discrepancy between the ratio of protein to energy in the silages and the

27. Reid, J. T. 1966. Meeting the protein needs of milking cows. *Hoard's Dairyman* 111:131, 139.

cow's requirements.[26] To supply sufficient protein to all cows in the herd, representing a wide range of production, a variety of concentrate mixtures of various protein levels would be needed. However, this problem can be alleviated by providing half or more of the forage DM as high-quality perennial hay or silage. This makes it possible to use a concentrate mixture with a single level of protein.

❧ QUESTIONS

1. Develop a cropping program, with major emphasis on grassland farming, for a 150-ha dairy farm that will furnish the necessary pasture, forage, and grain crops to feed a dairy herd. Determine how many lactating cows and young stock the farm will support when average crop yields for your area are used.

2. What factors determine the amount of preserved forages dairy cows will eat?

3. Plan a program for summer feeding based on the utilization of green-chopped forage by a milking herd of 100 cows.

4. What are the relative merits of grazing, green-chopping, and feeding from storage during the usual pasture season?

5. What are the advantages and disadvantages of corn silage as a forage for lactating cows?

6. As the trends in dairying continue, what do you expect in the amounts of various kinds and forms of forages fed to dairy cows?

7. What measures in harvesting and preparation of forage must be taken to make high-quality silage from perennial forages?

8. To what extent can dairymen depend on forages for feeding lactating cows? What factors should be considered in determining the amount and kind of supplemental feed that should be given in addition to the forage?

9. What are the extent and nature of DM losses in forage removed from the field at DM concentrations ranging from 15 to 90%?

L. L. WILSON / *The Pennsylvania State University*

J. C. BURNS / *Agricultural Research Service, USDA, and North Carolina State University*

61

UTILIZATION OF FORAGES
WITH BEEF COWS AND CALVES

❧

ER CAPITA consumption of beef by the U.S. consumer has increased from 29 to 51 kg during 1950–71. Further increases in per capita consumption are anticipated. To supply this amount of beef, the number of beef cattle also has increased (Fig. 61.1). Since 1955 there has been an annual increase of 780,800 beef cows and 1,200,000 other beef animals. Although the retail prices of beef and beef products have increased, the increase has been at a lesser rate than most nonfood consumer items.[1]

❧ LOWELL L. WILSON is Professor of Animal Science, The Pennsylvania State University. He holds the M.S. and Ph.D. degrees from South Dakota State University. His major research is in the area of beef and sheep management and breeding.

❧ JOSEPH C. BURNS is Plant Physiologist, ARS, USDA, and Associate Professor of Crop Science, North Carolina State University. He holds the M.S. degree from Iowa State University and the Ph.D. from Purdue University. His major research is devoted to evaluating organic fractions of forages as related to animal intake and digestibility.

❧ INTERDEPENDENCY OF BEEF CATTLE AND FORAGES

In 1960 and 1969 the tons of concentrates consumed by fed cattle increased by 143% and the amount of forages increased 127% (Table 61.1).[2] The greater increase in consumption of concentrates than of forages is a result of decreased numbers of cattle slaughtered directly off pasture.

In 1960 and 1969, 82.7 and 87.9% respectively of the feed consumed by beef cattle was forages.[2] It is anticipated that the amount of forage consumed by beef will continue to increase.[3]

Traditionally, beef cows have been more important in the western range states. However, cow numbers have increased more rapidly in several Corn Belt states and most states of the mid-South and Southeast. In the former case, increases are associated with large volumes of avail-

1. Hodgson, H. J., and R. E. Hodgson. 1970. Changing patterns in beef cattle production. Agr. Sci. Rev. Agr. Res. Serv. USDA, Fall.
2. USDA. 1970. National and state livestock-feed relationships. Suppl. Stat. Bull. 446.
3. Hodgson, H. J. 1968. Forages: Their present importance and future potentials. Agr. Sci. Rev. Agr. Res. Serv. USDA, Spring.

677

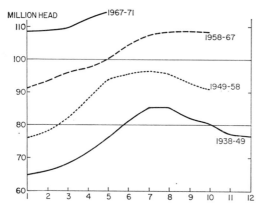

FIG. 61.1. From 1955 through 1971 there has been an annual increase of 780,000 beef cows and 1.2 million other beef animals. *ERS, USDA.*

able grain crop residues like cornstalks. In the Southeast, beef cows have replaced other farm enterprises such as cotton while complementing enterprises like poultry, citrus processing, and tobacco. Increased cow numbers have been accommodated by more efficient production of forages and grains through use of improved plant cultivars, fertilizers, land renovation techniques, and cattle having inherently greater productivity. A major challenge of the beef industry is to maximize the efficiency of each link in the beef production chain.

❧ MEASURES OF PERFORMANCE

The diversity of climate and land types dictates that a wide variety of pasture types and animal and pasture management practices exist in the U.S. In commercial operations the calf is the market-

TABLE 61.1 ❧ Amounts of concentrates and forages consumed by fed cattle and other beef cattle

	Concentrates		Forages	
		All		All
	Fed	other	Fed	other
Year	cattle	beef	cattle	beef
	(000t)	(000t)	(000t)	(000t)
1960	14,407	1,015	20,948	91,639
1969	34,971	992	47,584	124,649
Percent change	+143	−2	+127	+36

Source: USDA, 1970.[2]

able product, while the cow remains on the farm as inventory. Income is realized directly from the cow only when it is sold. Consequently, the following are the main determinants of profitability.

1. Calving percent. The percent of cows exposed to breeding that wean calves is dependent primarily on rebreeding efficiency. This in turn is dependent on adequate energy intake through about 80 days postcalving.[4]
2. Weaning weight. Weight of weaned calves (at 7–8 months) is primarily dependent on the cow's milk production.[5]
3. Building and equipment costs. Elaborate buildings and equipment are not needed in most operations. Wintering areas should consist of adapted grasses that form a dense sod and should be located adjacent to natural windbreaks.
4. Feed costs. Feed costs compose about 70% of all costs. These can be minimized by a forage program that meets the herd's needs without purchased supplements. Closely associated are the economics of different uses of various types of land. (See Chapter 62.)
5. Postweaning performance and markets. The calves' preweaning environment should allow efficient postweaning gains on the chosen ration. Energy intake should never be reduced from weaning to slaughter. Markets for the weight and breed, condition, and quality of calves should be assured before the management program is finally designed.

❧ NUTRITIONAL REQUIREMENTS

The recommended amounts of various nutrients for several types and sizes of cattle for desired rates of gain throughout the

4. Wiltbank, J. N., J. Bond, E. J. Warwick, R. E. Davis, A. C. Cook, W. L. Reynolds, and M. W. Hazen. 1965. Influence of total feed and protein intake on reproductive performance of the beef female through second calving. USDA Tech. Bull. 1314.
5. Wilson, L. L., M. C. Rugh, J. M. Stout, M. J. Simpson, H. Varela-Alvarez, and H. R. Purdy. 1970. Correlations among yield and composition of milk of Angus-Holstein cows and consumption and growth rate of progeny. *J. Dairy Sci.* 54:425–28.

TABLE 61.2 ❧ Nutrient requirements of beef cattle (daily nutrients per animal)

Body weight (kg)	Average daily gain (kg)	Daily dry matter* (kg)	Total protein (kg)	Digestible protein (kg)	Energy ME† (Mcal)	Energy TDN‡ (kg)	Ca (g)	P (g)	Caro-tene (mg)	Vitamin A (000 IU)
				Growing heifers						
150	0.50	3.2	0.39	0.26	8.4	2.3	12	10	17.5	7.0
	0.75	3.2	0.43	0.29	9.0	2.5	17	13	17.5	7.0
300	0.50	7.7	0.77	0.47	15.9	4.4	14	14	43.5	17.4
	0.75	8.0	0.89	0.57	18.2	5.0	17	15	44.5	17.8
400	0.50	9.7	0.86	0.50	20.0	5.5	17	17	54.0	21.6
	0.75	9.9	0.88	0.51	22.6	6.3	18	18	55.0	22.0
				Dry pregnant mature cows						
450	. . .	6.8	0.40	0.19	12.4	3.4	12	12	42.0	16.8
550	. . .	8.0	0.47	0.22	14.4	4.0	12	12	48.8	19.5
				Cows nursing calves, first 3–4 months postpartum						
450	. . .	9.9	0.91	0.53	20.4	5.6	28	22	96.2	38.5
500	. . .	10.5	0.97	0.57	21.6	6.0	28	23	102.5	41.0
				Bulls, growth and maintenance (moderate activity)						
700	0.30	12.7	1.41	0.90	26.2	7.2	23	23	123.5	49.4
900	0.00	10.7	1.07	0.65	22.0	6.1	19	19	104.0	41.6

Source: These values represent a portion of those presented in NRC, 1970.[6]
* Feed intake was calculated from the net energy (NE) requirements and average NE values for the kind of ration being fed.
† ME requirements for growing and finishing cattle were calculated from the NE maintenance and NE gain requirements for weights and rates of gain.
‡ TDN was calculated from ME by assuming 3.6155 kcal of ME per gram of TDN.

year are presented in Table 61.2. Although these allowances are considered adequate under most management situations, they should be increased under conditions of stress, disease, parasitism, or extremely cold temperatures.[6]

The body condition of the cow and her reproductive state are two major factors that must be considered in developing feeding programs. Except for a short "open" period after calving, the brood cow is generally in one of three conditions —lactating with a fall-born calf, pregnant to calve in midwinter (December-January), or pregnant to calve in the spring.

ENERGY AND PROTEIN NEEDS

The notion that low-quality forage should be purposely produced for brood cows simply because they can utilize such forage must be discarded. The determin-

6. Natural Research Council. 1970. Nutrient Requirements of Beef Cattle, 4th ed., rev. Natl. Acad. Sci., Washington, D.C.

ing factors include such items as alternative land use, cost per unit of energy and protein, and managerial ability of the producer. This involves examination of the relationship of energy and protein digestibility with total dry matter yield. It may be cheaper to produce less tonnage of a more digestible forage than a greater tonnage lower in digestibility. Management is more critical in the former case in terms of forage production and limiting energy intake.

In formulating brood cow rations, it is essential to provide approximately 55% more metabolizable energy (ME) for a cow during her first three to four months of lactation than for a dry pregnant cow.[6] Consequently, a midwinter or spring calving program permits efficient utilization of low-quality forages or by-products available during the fall and winter. Also, spring pasture permits the cow to reach the recommended energy intake level for both lactation and for rebreeding. To achieve the latter it is more important for the cow to be in a weight-gaining state than for the absolute amount of postpartum energy intake to be considered. Limitation of prepartum energy intake ensures cows of thin to moderate condition at calving and subsequently permits weight gain more readily than for cows calving in high condition.[4,7,8] If low-energy crop residues are being fed, they should be replaced with lactating rations based on higher quality forage three weeks before calving.

Overfeeding the nonlactating cow and the developing heifer can also be a problem. High-energy rations result in depressed fertility, milk production, calf weaning weight, and longevity and in greater frequency of difficult calvings.[9] Overfeeding of the bull also must be avoided because decreases in sexual urge and breeding ability will occur. However, bulls on range during breeding season travel up to 3–8 km/day and graze less than cows.[10] Therefore, 45 days prior to the breeding season the bulls should be conditioned as recommended in Table 61.2.

Seldom do forage rations for beef cows need protein supplementation. Even during lactation, the ration need only be 9.2% protein. Percent protein of forages seldom falls below this value except perhaps in mature, pure grass stands and when feeding corn silage or grain crop residues. High-quality legume or grass-legume forages have been used frequently to supplement such rations. Protein deficiency is typified by a depressed appetite, leading to decreased energy intake and a decrease in performance.

7. Wiltbank, J. N., W. W. Rowden, J. E. Engalls, and D. R. Zimmerman. 1964. Influence of postpartum energy level on reproductive performance of Hereford cows restricted in energy level prior to calving. *J. Anim. Sci.* 23:1049–53.
8. Wiltbank, J. N., W. W. Rowden, J. E. Engalls, K. E. Gregory, and R. M. Koch. 1962. Effect of energy level on reproductive phenomena of mature Hereford cows. *J. Anim. Sci.* 21:219–25.
9. Arnett, Dudley, and Robert Totusek. 1963. The influence of moderate vs. high levels of nutrition on the performance of twin beef females. *J. Anim. Sci.* 22:239. (Abstr.)
10. Dwyer, Don D. 1961. Activities and grazing preferences of cows with calves in northern Osage County, Oklahoma. Okla. Agr. Exp. Sta. Bull. B-588.

MINERALS AND VITAMINS

Sodium and chlorine should be provided at all times as loose (preferred) or block salt. Since salt toxicity can occur in the absence of sufficient water, extreme care should be taken to provide water near all salting sites.

The proportion of required Ca to P is about 1:1 for dry cows and 1.3:1 for lactating cows (Table 61.2). Most grasses have an ideal ratio, while alfalfa contains approximately 1.35 and 0.22% Ca and P respectively for a ratio of 6.1:1. A supplement for grasses should contain equal amounts of Ca and P, while one for legumes should contain a greater proportion of P than Ca. In addition, low P levels in forages from semiarid areas or P-deficient soils are widespread. Cornstalks are particularly low in P, and concentrates are low in Ca. These inadequacies should be considered in formulating mineral mixes.

Deficiencies of Mg, Cu, Co, Fe, I, S, K, Se, and Zn may occur in certain areas; also, toxic levels of Mo, Se, and F may exist. Specific information within an area should be relied upon to determine the need for ration supplementation. The usual methods of correcting deficiencies are addition to free-choice salt, addition to a mixed ration, or application to the soil.

Only vitamins A, D, and E need to be considered in the beef enterprise. Forages contain beta-carotene which serves as a precursor to A. Since the ruminant stores carotene and A in the liver and body fat during periods of abundant intake, requirements may be met for 4–6 months.[11,12] In cases of prolonged deficiency, vitamin A should be added to mineral or protein supplements or mixed rations or supplied by intramuscular injection. Cattle that are exposed to sunlight or consume sun-cured hay do not require supplemental vitamin D. Most oral or injectable vitamin A products contain vitamins D and E. Vitamin E usually is of little concern. The feeding of 1–1.5 kg/day of grain during the last 60 days of pregnancy or oral administration of alphatocopherol to the calf or to the pregnant cow has reduced the incidence of E deficiencies in problem herds.

SPECIAL WINTERING CONSIDERATIONS

A cow entering the winter in good flesh can lose 10% or more of her weight without adversely affecting either reproduction or calf gains. However, the energy requirement of a fall-calving cow is 55% higher than for a dry pregnant cow. Calf and cow weights from a fall-calving system may be higher in the spring when a high-energy diet is fed, but this is generally not an economical practice.[13] When grain feeding is not profitable for a fall-calving system, it is unlikely to be profitable for spring-calving cows. However, this comparison may not hold in a situation of a scarce forage supply and moderate grain prices.[14]

GRAIN CROP RESIDUES. Grain crop residues play an important role in animal production, but their full potential has not been realized. After corn grain harvest, approximately 40% of the whole-plant energy value remains in the field. In addition, from 180 to 320 kg/ha of corn grain usually remains. Three methods of salvaging corn crop residues are grazing; ensiling stover; and accumulating husks, cobs, and waste kernels behind a picker-sheller. Grazing is best achieved by a spring-calving herd where calves are weaned just before stalk grazing commences in the fall. A stocking rate of 1 cow/ha has maintained nonlactating pregnant cows for 80–130 days. Maximum utilization and more uniform feed intake is achieved by allowing the herd additional ungrazed areas every three to four weeks.[15-17] Stalks have been harvested by flail choppers, row crop forage harvesters, pickup-type harvesters, and specially built stover choppers. This material can be ensiled with the addition of water to ensure at least 50% moisture. Accumulated residues (collected in a wagon behind the combine) can be either dumped for field utilization or ensiled as for cornstalks.

Protein content of corn crop residues averages 4%, which is less than the 7.5% total protein recommended for dry pregnant cows. However, nonprotein nitrogen (NPN) supplements like biuret can supply this difference. Residues which include husks are higher in digestible energy content and more palatable than stalks alone. Two-year-old pregnant heifers have gained weight when fed properly supplemented corn crop residues.[15] Wheat straw is also available in some areas and can replace half the hay or silage in dry-cow rations.[18]

OTHER RESIDUES. Among other by-products that can be fed to cattle are wastes from the processing of apples, oranges, sweet corn, potatoes, and tomatoes. A recent survey conservatively estimated 56,000 head of cattle could be finished from the processing wastes of six Pennsylvania commodities.[19] These wastes are usually low in protein. Concern regarding contamination of these wastes by persistent pesticides is of little importance.[20]

11. Church, D. C., L. S. Pope, and Robert MacVicor. 1956. Effect of plane of nutrition of beef cows on depletion of liver vitamin A during gestation and on carotene requirements during lactation. *J. Anim. Sci.* 15:1078–83.
12. Hayes, B. W., G. E. Mitchell, Jr., C. O. Little, and H. B. Sewell. 1967. Turnover of liver vitamin A in steers. *J. Anim. Sci.* 26:855–57.
13. Nelson, A. B., L. R. Kuhlman, R. D. Farr, W. D. Campbell, and G. R. Waller, Jr. 1963. Creep-feeding fall calves. Okla. Agr. Exp. Sta. Bull. B-610.
14. Jacobsen, N. A., and O. O. Thomas. 1966. Emergency rations for wintering beef cows. Mont. Coop. Ext. Serv. Folder 75.

15. Albert, W. W. 1971. Utilizing cornfield wastes. Ill. Agr. Exp. Sta. Cow-Calf Info. Round-up.
16. Heath, M. E., and M. P. Plumlee. 1971. Using cornstalks for pasture. Purdue Univ. Agron. Field Day Rept.
17. Vetter, R. L., Dale Weber, and Nelson Gay. 1970. Grazing cornstalks and feeding corn plant refuse to beef herds. Iowa Agr. Exp. Sta. Bull. R-137.
18. Dickinson Exp. Sta., N. Dak. State Univ. 1969. Section I. Progress reports on current research. 20th Annual Livestock Research Round-up.
19. Wilson, L. L., D. A. Kurtz, J. H. Ziegler, M. C. Rugh, J. L. Watkins, T. A. Long, M. L. Borger, and J. D. Sink. 1970. Accumulations of certain pesticides in adipose tissues and performance of Angus, Hereford and Holstein steers fed apple-processing wastes. *J. Anim. Sci.* 31:112–17.
20. Wilson, L. L., and M. L. Borger. 1969. An evaluation of the factors affecting the feasibility of recycling solid horticultural wastes through livestock as a horticultural waste disposal method for Pennsylvania. Pa. Dept. Health.

NONPROTEIN NITROGEN SUPPLEMENTS. The beef cow should be fed the recommended level of protein regardless of her reproductive state and body condition. The low cost per unit of N and acceptable utilization of NPN compounds like urea in finishing rations have been established. This relationship has not occurred in beef cow rations since they normally contain lesser amounts of readily available energy than do finishing rations. Misuse of NPN compounds such as poor mixing or feeding in excess can result in adverse physiological conditions that do not generally occur with the use of plant protein. However, providing 10–15% of the total ration protein content from urea or biuret in brood cow and growing-calf rations has not reduced performance.[21-23] This allows approximately 35% of the protein in the supplement to be from NPN sources. The use of biuret instead of urea for low-energy rations has the following advantages: greater palatability, safer because of less free N release in the rumen, and improved handling characteristics when pelleted.[24,25] However, biuret is more expensive per unit of N and may result in slower animal adaptation.[26] Many wintering rations (average quality mixed grass-legume hay or silage) for dry pregnant cows do not require supplemental protein; therefore, producers should decide upon the level of supplementation required based on forage testing results and National Research Council (NRC) requirements.

COW-CALF GRAZING SYSTEMS

Careful consideration must be given a

FIG. 61.2. *Producers must be aware . . . forages are not all the same . . . herd must be capable of consuming and assimilating forages of varying . . . digestibility.*

year-round feed supply. This includes seasonal distribution of dry matter produced as well as total production. Producers must be aware that forages are not all the same, and the herd must be capable of consuming and assimilating forages of varying degrees of digestibility (Fig. 61.2).

MEASURING PASTURE PRODUCTIVITY

Historically, feeder calf producers have given major attention to gain per animal. This occurred because heavier calves generally sell for more total dollars than lighter calves, even though lighter calves may sell at a higher price per kilogram. High investment, operational, land, and labor costs are forcing the producer to balance gain per animal and gain per ha. The major quantitative variables are cow-calf days per ha, calf gain per ha, cow-calf units per ha per day (stocking rate), and estimated total digestible nutrients (ETDN) per ha. (See Chapter 12.) Such per ha responses are greatly altered by the stocking rates used. Generally, light stocking rates result in inefficient pasture utilization, while heavy stocking rates reduce cow weight, reproductive performance, and calf weaning weights.[27,28] Important factors in determining stocking rate are availability and price of emergency feeds, stage

21. Tollett, J. T., R. W. Swart, R. M. Ioset, and J. A. Templeton. 1969. Biuret as a nitrogen source for wintering steers. *J. Anim. Sci.* 28:862. (Abstr.)
22. Turner, H. A., and R. J. Raleigh. 1969. Biuret and urea for growing cattle. *J. Anim. Sci.* 28:869. (Abstr.)
23. Van Horn, J. L., O. O. Thomas, J. Drummond, and R. L. Blackwell. 1969. Biuret and urea in supplements for range ewes. *J. Anim. Sci.* 28:869. (Abstr.)
24. Clark, R., E. L. Barrett, and J. H. Kellerman. 1963. A comparison between nitrogen retention from biuret and urea by sheep on a low-protein roughage diet. *J. South African Vet. Med. Assoc.* 34:419–22.
25. Ioset, R. M. 1969. Handling properties of feed grade biuret in the manufacture of pelleted feed. Proc. Pacific N.W. Anim. Nutr. Conf. 4:32–35.
26. Campbell, T. C. 1962. Biuret and bicarbonate in the rations of ruminants—Their influence on general nitrogen metabolism. Ph.D. thesis, Cornell Univ., Ithaca.

27. Ray, Maurice L., A. E. Spooner, and R. W. Parham. 1969. Cow and calf nutrition and management under different grazing pressures. Ark. Agr. Exp. Sta. Bull. 749.
28. Burzlaff, Donald F., and Lionel Harris. 1969. Yearling steer gains and vegetation changes of western Nebraska rangeland under three rates of stocking. Nebr. Agr. Exp. Sta. Bull. SB-505.

TABLE 61.3 ❧ Cow and calf gains from tall fescue grazed alone or in combination with Coastal bermudagrass

Forage system	Calf gain (kg/head)		Average	Cow gain (kg/head)		Average
	1966	1967		1966	1967	
Tall fescue alone	81	112	97	25	29	27
Tall fescue plus Coastal bermudagrass	96	129	113	42	53	47

Source: Adapted from Goode et al., 1969.[33]

of lactation, reliability of precipitation, and rate of species recovery.

Frequently pasture productivity is expressed as total gain per ha. This value does not contain an estimate of maintenance energy, which for steers approaches 71% of the total energy consumed.[29] Maintenance energy constitutes an even greater percentage of the total energy consumed by a cow-calf unit. Therefore, evaluating pasture productivity only through calf gain per ha appreciably underestimates the total energy utilized. Totaling the ETDN (maintenance and gain) required for all animals on the pasture is a more realistic estimation of pasture productivity. Pastures can then be compared by calculating the ETDN per ha. Obviously, this calculation does not account for forage wasted through improper utilization. The pitfall in using ETDN is the degree of accuracy of the conversion factors. However, no serious error occurs when the same factors are used for similar animals and relative differences are compared.

MAXIMUM GRAZING SYSTEMS

Every region of the U.S. has a number of adapted forage species that grow during different seasons. The best-adapted cultivars of each species can be structured into a forage system that will permit maximum year-round grazing (see Fig. 43.3). Combining cool- and warm-season perennial grasses and legumes with summer and winter annuals can provide dependable grazing from early spring until late fall in most climates and year-round grazing in others.[30-32]

Inclusion of warm-season species provides more reliable midsummer grazing than most cool-season species and such pastures can be stocked to carry more animals per ha. Gains per animal from grazing tall fescue alone were less than gains from tall fescue grazed with 'Coastal' bermudagrass (Table 61.3).[33] Similarly, a three-season grazing system developed in Iowa has appreciably increased calf gain per ha (Table 61.4).[34] In the South and Hawaii, year-round grazing has been achieved through judicious selection of forage species and grazing management.[30-32]

Where forage growth for winter grazing is not dependable or where problems such as poaching, excessive wastage, animal disorders, and periodic restriction of grazing occurs, some stored feed is required.[35] If there is adequate seasonal growth and utilization of winter pasture, the stored feed can be carried over for use the following year. Deferred grazing or stockpiling forage (conservation on the stalk or *in situ*) can extend the grazing season in many

29. Burns, J. C., R. W. Harvey, H. D. Gross, M. B. Wise, W. B. Gilbert, D. F. Tugman, and J. W. Bentley. 1970. Pastures and grazing systems for the mountains of North Carolina. N.C. Agr. Exp. Sta. Bull. 437.

30. Jones, D. W., E. M. Hodges, and W. G. Kirk. 1954. Year-round grazing on a combination of native and improved pasture. Fla. Agr. Exp. Sta. Bull. 554A.
31. Crowder, L. V., O. E. Sell, and E. M. Parker. 1953. Temporary winter grazing practice. Ga. Agr. Sta. Bull. 276.
32. Plucknett, D. L. 1970. Productivity of tropical pastures in Hawaii. Proc. 11th Int. Grassl. Congr., pp. A38–A50 (Surfers Paradise, Queensland, Aust.).
33. Goode, Lemuel, J. C. Burns, H. D. Gross, and H. C. Linnerud. 1969. Grazing systems for the cow-calf enterprise. N.C. State Univ. ANS Rept. 192, AH Ser. 136.
34. Wedin, W. F. 1970. Fortifying good management practices with adequate fertilizer programs. *In* Forage Highlights. Amer. Forage Grassl. Council. Proc. 3rd Res. Industry Conf.
35. Wheeler, J. L. 1968. Major problems in winter grazing. *Herb. Abstr.* 38:11–18.

TABLE 61.4 ❧ Animal performance and production on three-season pastures

Grass	Average daily gain (kg)		Grazing days		Beef per ha(kg)		Total beef per ha (kg)
	Spring-summer	Fall	Spring-summer	Fall	Spring-summer	Fall	
Tall fescue	0.52	0.83	316	167	380	328	708
Reed canarygrass	0.65	0.65	282	140	388	223	611
Smooth bromegrass	0.73	0.92	267	97	457	222	679
Orchardgrass	0.57	0.79	301	120	413	227	641
Average	0.62	0.80	292	131	409	250	...

Source: Wedin, 1970.[34]

regions.[36-38] This principle can be applied to both temperate and tropical regions. In the former case, stored feed is required during the wintering period. Forage can be stored on the stalk and efficiently grazed in winter thereby reducing the stored feed requirement. Such material is the major source of winter feed in western range areas.[36,37] In tropical regions saving forage during the wet season ensures adequate forage for the dry season.

Round bales left in the field for winter grazing have been used successfully from Virginia to Missouri and as far north as central Indiana.[39,40] Tall fescue is the favored grass, although orchardgrass and other species have been used successfully. Percent crude protein of field-stored fescue bales has averaged 14.8%, which was similar to the accompanying fall regrowth.[41] The general practice is to round-bale the first crop, leaving the bales in the field. Regrowth is stored on the stalk, and the bales and regrowth are strip-grazed during the wintering period. An efficient practice is to allow the cattle only sufficient grazing

for three weeks.[39] The same practice is used during late summer droughts.[42]

❧ PASTURE-ANIMAL INTERRELATIONSHIP

The grazing environment is a biological system composed of the soil, plant, and animal. Both management and climate are superimposed upon the system causing interaction within, between, and among the components. Consequently, by altering any factor (e.g., soil pH), it is difficult to anticipate what the ultimate effect will be on the animal in terms of either total gain or net return. Understanding how each component relates to the total grazing environment should lead to wise management decisions.

INFLUENCE OF PASTURE ON THE ANIMAL

A simple grazing environment consists of one soil type, one forage species, and one animal type all in a monoclimate, therefore requiring only one type of management. As each category is expanded, the grazing environment becomes increasingly more involved. Such an example is the cow-calf unit. Not only are many forages used but requirements for two distinct animal types (cow and calf) must be considered, yet the two are closely related. The relationship between the cow

36. Marion, P. T., D. D. McGinty, E. D. Robinson, and J. K. Riggs. 1966. Beef cattle research in Texas. Tex. Agr. Exp. Sta. Consol. Progr. Rept. 2411–26.
37. Nebraska Handbook of Range Management. Nebr. Agr. Exp. Sta. EC 68-131.
38. Wedin, W. F., I. T. Carlson, and R. L. Vetter. 1966. Studies on the nutritive value of fall-saved forage using rumen fermentation and chemical analyses. Proc. 10th Int. Grassl. Congr., pp. 424–28 (Helsinki, Finland).
39. Wilson, L. L., C. J. Kaiser, K. Hawkins, M.E. Heath, and R. C. Peterson. 1966. Performance of beef cows on restricted versus unrestricted winter grazing of tall fescue bales and regrowth. J. Anim. Sci. 25:882. (Abstr.)
40. Van Keuren, R. W., and E. W. Klosterman. 1967. Winter pasture system for Ohio beef cows. Ohio Rept. 52:67–68.
41. Van Keuren, R. W., and C. F. Parker. 1971. Forage systems for sheep. In Sheep Research and Development. Ohio Agr. Res. Sum. 5.
42. Wilson, L. L., M. E. Heath, R. Peterson, and K. J. Drewry. 1967. Comparison of Suchow and field-stored round-baled Kentucky bluegrass for summer and fall pasture for fall-calving beef cows. Purdue Univ. Res. Progr. Rept. 292.

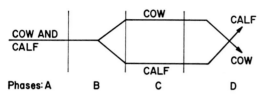

FIG. 61.3. Diagram of the relationship between the cow and calf changes as the lactational period progresses.

and calf as the lactational period progresses is diagrammed in Figure 61.3.

Phase A represents the cow and calf as a unit with the calf obtaining its nourishment from the cow. In phase B, the calf begins to consume either green or dry forage and becomes partially independent. However, adequate milk is still available to be an important source of energy for good calf performance. In phase C the calf becomes less dependent but continues to suckle and obtains some supplemental energy from milk. In phase D the calf competes directly with the cow for its nutrient requirements. If forage is limited during this phase, poor calf gains will occur.

A large percentage of the energy consumed by a beef animal is needed to fulfill its maintenance requirements.[6] This need has precedence over most productive processes. Consequently, if total energy intake is increased, either through increased dry matter intake (quantity) or through more digestible dry matter (quality), an increased amount of energy is available for productive purposes. This assumes the energy expended in assimilation of additional dry matter is not greater than the increased energy consumed. Generally, an increase in forage digestibility is accompanied by an increase in feed intake. Unfortunately, the opposite may also occur. Such relationships are shown in Table 61.5. While the percentage distributions of the energy consumed are only approximations, they are useful in demonstrating how forage quality and intake can greatly alter energy left for productive purposes.

The following points are noted:

1. By increasing digestibility from 50 to 60%, energy left for productive purposes changed from an energy loss to an energy gain situation (columns 1 versus 2).

2. Increasing intake from 2 to 2.5% of body weight and holding digestibility constant at 50% (column 1 versus 3) actually increased energy losses.

3. Increasing dry matter intake from 2 to 2.5% of body weight when dry matter is 60% digestible (column 2 versus 4) increased energy left for productive purposes.

4. Increasing both intake and digestibility (column 1 versus 4) maximizes the energy left for productive purposes.

These factors can and should be applied to grazing management. In pure grass pastures, undergrazing can have the same effect on cattle as moving from column 4 to column 3 and then to column 1 (Table 61.5). This results from a reduction in digestibility generally associated with plant maturity. A 10% unit reduction in digestibility can easily occur if a grass like orchardgrass is undergrazed.[43]

If stocking rates are high, digestibility of forage may actually increase for a time (column 4 versus 3); but if available forage becomes limited, energy intake is reduced and animal response may change as indicated by column 2 versus 4.

In a cow-calf enterprise, the calf is buffered from the above stresses, providing it is still nursing and obtaining a large portion of its energy from milk. However, when its requirements exceed available milk energy, the calf will quickly respond to the situations noted in Table 61.5. This generally occurs at four to five months of age (phase B). It is advantageous at this age to maintain pastures so that forage is always available and of the highest quality possible.

43. Welch, J. G., Martin Clancy, and G. W. Vander Noot. 1969. Net energy of alfalfa and orchardgrass hays at varying stages of maturity. *J. Anim. Sci.* 28:263–67.

TABLE 61.5 ❧ Effects of intake and forage digestibility on the allocation of consumed dry matter (kg) for a 453-kg animal

Feed breakdown categories		Col. 1	Col. 2	Col. 3	Col. 4
	Intake (kg)	9	9	11.3	11.3
	Intake (% body wt.)	2.0	2.0	2.5	2.5
	Digestibility (%)	50	60	50	60
Fecal Losses		4.50	3.60	5.65	4.52
Digestible Quantity*		4.50	5.40	5.65	6.78
Urinary losses (7% of intake)		0.63	0.63	0.79	0.79
Gas losses (8% of intake)		0.72	0.72	0.95	0.95
Metabolizable quantity (left after above losses)		3.15	4.05	3.91	5.04
Heat losses (28.7% of intake)		2.58	2.58	3.24	3.24
Activity of maintenance (10.3% of intake)		0.93	0.93	1.16	1.16
Productive quantity (left after above losses)		−0.36	0.54	−0.49	0.64

* All values are approximations. Constant percentages for urinary, gas, and heat losses and activity of maintenance were used regardless of changes in intake and digestibility.

INFLUENCE OF ANIMAL ON THE PLANT

In a pasture each individual plant is constantly subjected to various frequencies and degrees of defoliation. How this occurs will depend on many factors such as forage availability, forage accessibility, and visual selectivity of the animal as well as simple spatial orientation of the animal to a specific plant. Selective grazing can alter pasture composition and consequently, forage yield and animal productivity. Plants in a pasture are in constant competition for nutrients, moisture, and light. Therefore, repeated defoliation of certain plants in a sward places them at a disadvantage to compete with undefoliated plants. For example, selective grazing of a broad-leaved plant in a grass sward will cause that plant to develop a more upright growth habit if it is to survive. Also, reduction will occur in the root to top ratio. Subsequently, the more erect growth habit forced upon the broad-leaved plant makes it even more susceptible to grazing. Further selective grazing will reduce the root to top ratio and the broad-leaved plant will be in an unfavorable environment to persist in the grass mixture.[44]

The relationship of grazing time and intensity to dry matter production is illustrated in Table 61.6.[45] An intensively grazed pasture (treatment 1) grazed year-round from 7.5 cm to a stubble height of 2.6 cm yielded the least dry matter, while a year-round light grazing intensity (treatment 6) yielded the second highest. Maximum yields were obtained from treatment 2 which was grazed intensively only during the winter. A large change in botanical composition is evident for all treatments. However, intense winter grazing favored yields from perennial ryegrass and red clover. Intensive summer grazing drastically reduced yields of orchardgrass and red clover. A pasture or range can be rendered completely unproductive from improper time and intensity of grazing. Time required to reach an unproductive state depends on the harshness of the environment and degree of management. Other important ways the animal influences the plant, either physiologically or morphologically, are through trampling, poaching, fouling, and selective grazing.

❧ GENERAL MANAGEMENT PRACTICES

Decisions such as season of calving and use of supplemental preweaning grains for calves are important.

44. Norman, M. J. T. 1960. The relationship between competition and defoliation in pasture. J. Brit. Grassl. Soc. 15:145–49.

45. Brougham, R. W. 1960. The effects of frequent hard grazings at different times of the year on the productivity and species yields of a grass-clover pasture. N.Z. J. Agr. Res. 3:125–36.

TABLE 61.6 ❧ Annual yields and species shifts associated with season and intensity of grazing

Treatment*	Total yield (kg/ha)	Species yields (kg/ha)†					
		Perennial ryegrass	Orchard-grass	Other grasses	Red clover	White clover	Other species
1 (7.5–2.6 cm)	10,466	6,151	706	364	280	2,370	605
2 (7.5–2.6 cm, winter)	14,971	7,934	2,398	191	2,409	1,883	157
3 (7.5–2.6 cm, spring)	10,758	5,491†	2,533	286	880	1,322	247
4 (7.5–2.6 cm, summer)	9,805	5,917†	1,109	269	1,009	1,389	112
5 (7.5–2.6 cm, autumn)	12,752	6,477†	3,608	471	1,210	807	179
6 (17.5–7.5 cm)	13,133	6,477	3,227	291	1,770	1,255	112
Signifiant difference at 5% level	1,267	1,184	571	...	971	549	...

Source: Brougham, 1960.[45]

* The designation "7.5–2.6 cm" means grazed continuously yearlong at 7.5–2.6 cm; "7.5–2.6 cm, winter" means grazed from 7.5–2.6 cm during the winter and 17.5 to 7.5 cm for the rest of the year; "17.5–7.5 cm" means grazed continuously at 17.5 to 7.5 cm.

† These do not include a stubble yield of approximately 1,121 kg/ha of dry matter obtained from these treatments when the changeover from the 17.5–7.5 to the 7.5–2.6 system of management occurred.

CALVING SEASON FOR MAXIMUM FORAGE USE

There usually is no better place for calves to be born than on fresh spring pastures. However, the best season for calving depends on such factors as climate, feed supply, labor availability, and equipment. Therefore, the calving season which permits maximum forage use may not be the primary factor when considering the total enterprise.

Some advantages for spring and for fall and winter calving are listed below.[46,47]

Spring calving:
1. Cows are bred on pasture.
2. Dry cows are cheaper to winter.
3. Less labor is required.
4. Calves can be sold directly from cows or can be wintered.
5. Cows milk better on grass.
6. Condition of cows at calving is easier to control.
7. Smaller investment in shelter and equipment.

Fall and winter calving:
1. Calves escape summer heat and flies.
2. Calves utilize spring grass.

3. Spring grass stimulates milk flow.
4. Calves generally bring the highest price per kg.
5. Weight is at least 90 kg heavier in the fall than for a spring calf.
6. Labor is available.

Where herd size is large the producer may diversify and split the herd, producing both spring and fall calves. However, in most situations the herd should calve within 60 days or less.

SUPPLEMENTAL ENERGY FOR SUCKLING OR GRAZING CALVES

Increased preweaning feed consumption results in increased weight gains. However, the economics of such systems depends on age and lactating ability of the cow, season of calving, availability and quality of pastures, kind of supplemental feed, market for the calves, and relative price outlook.

CREEP-FEEDING. Oklahoma results indicate that creep-feeding was not profitable for either spring- or fall-dropped calves.[27,48] Only creep-fed calves from first-calf heifers gained sufficiently more (50.3 kg) than noncreep-fed calves to be profitable.[27]

46. Neumann, A. L., and Roscoe R. Snapp. 1969. Beef Cattle, 6th ed. Wiley, New York.
47. Fowler, Stewart H. 1969. Beef Production in the South. Interstate Printers & Publishers, Danville, Ill.

48. Nelson, A. B., Glen Bratcher, R. D. Humphrey, and R. W. MacVicor. 1955. Creep-feeding spring calves. Okla. Agr. Exp. Sta. Bull. B-462.

In Mississippi, winter ryegrass pastures produced almost as much calf gain but returned more profit than calves fed grain. Suckling calves without supplementation gained poorly and returned little profit.[49]

EARLY WEANING. Calves weaned early (three to five months) and placed on pasture generally require supplemental grains. This practice is advantageous when the cow's lactating ability is impaired by such stress factors as heat and inadequate quality and quantity of feed. North Carolina data indicate it may be desirable under such conditions to wean spring calves in late June or early July. This system permits intensification (doubling animal numbers per ha) of dry cows on pasture during midsummer when forage is frequently lacking. At the same time, gains of calves weaned early were greater than of suckling calves. However, grain and labor costs must be considered. In comparing cost per kg of weaned weight, the least cost occurred for creep-feeding and the greatest for non-creep-feeding. Early weaning costs were intermediate.[50] These comparisons were obtained in a study where a scarce food supply was simulated by feeding the lactating cow 76% of NRC (1970) recommendations.

CONTINUOUS CONFINEMENT OF COWS

Continuous confinement has not depressed weaning weights, cow fertility, herd health, or weaned-calf percentage. At the same time mechanical harvesting of forages results in more forage per ha as compared to grazing. However, poor drylot sanitary conditions can lead to serious losses due to contagious diseases. Conversely, greater calf losses from accidents and wild animals occur on pasture compared to drylot.[36,51-53]

Drylot systems require increased man-hours and capital for forage harvesting and handling. Such systems appear feasible in areas of high grain crop productivity where cows could glean nonmarketable grain crop residues, and where mechanical harvesting has definite advantages compared to grazing.

INTERNAL AND EXTERNAL PARASITES

"Unseen" losses from parasites make it imperative that this problem receive close attention. There is usually some parasite infection in most herds, but only when the degree of infection reaches a certain point does treatment pay. The best method of reducing the economic effect of parasites is to combine proper management with use of medicinals. Rotating and clipping pastures, refraining from overgrazing, avoidance of feeding on the ground, and providing clean fresh water supplies are the best management practices for reducing the incidence of internal parasites. Before any treatment is given, a fresh fecal sample should be collected and observed for parasite indicators. Medicinals can be given as a drench or bolus or added to a mixed ration.

The most frequent external parasites are grubs (warbles), flies, and lice. These are easily controlled by systemic products along with spraying, dusting, or hanging dust bags where cattle walk when going to water, feed, or shade.

❧ QUESTIONS

1. What are the five measures of beef cow performance for profit, and why is each important?
2. Name four factors that may increase an animal's nutritional requirements compared to NRC recommendations.
3. Compare in relative terms the energy re-

49. Crockett, S. P. 1966. Winter grazing for fall-dropped beef calves. Miss. Agr. Exp. Sta. Info. Sheet 947.
50. Wilson, L. L., C. J. Kaiser, and K. Hawkins. 1966. Comparisons of early-weaning, creep-feeding and non-creep-feeding for fall calves. *J. Anim. Sci.* 25:1274. (Abstr.)
51. Albert, W. W., and P. E. Lamb. 1968. Drylot management for beef cows. Ill. Beef Cattle Day Rept. AS-651C.

52. Meiske, J. C., and R. D. Goodrich. 1969. Year-round drylot vs. conventional cow-calf production. *J. Anim. Sci.* 29:115. (Abstr.)
53. McGinty, D. D., H. E. Essig, and Maurice Belew. 1971. Factors affecting performance of beef cattle in confinement. Ariz. Cattle Feeders' Day Rept. P-23.

quirements of dry versus lactating brood cows and collate these needs with fall versus spring calving programs.

4. How is ETDN per ha computed, and why does it provide a better measure of pasture productivity than animal liveweight gain only?

5. Why and under what conditions does a small increase in dry matter appreciably increase energy for productive purposes?

6. The ruminant animal is known for its ability to utilize low-quality forage. Should the cow-calf operator purposely produce forage low in quality? Discuss.

7. Name two NPN supplements and give advantages and disadvantages of these versus plant protein sources for beef cows.

8. Discuss the main advantage and disadvantage of continuous confinement of beef cows.

9. Give five methods of administering internal or external parasite medicinals and four management methods that help control internal parasite infection.

E. R. BARRICK AND S. H. DOBSON
North Carolina State University

62

FORAGE-LAND USE EFFICIENCIES
WITH COMMERCIAL CATTLE

❧

Beef cattle make up approximately 65% of all forage-consuming units in the U.S.[1] This is the result of increasing numbers of beef cattle (Fig. 62.1) and decreasing numbers of dairy cattle and sheep. Beef cattle contribute 23% of the gross agricultural income. A dramatic change in the cattle industry in the 1960–70 decade is the increase in feedlot finishing, with most of the steers and heifers marketed being finished to the choice grade. In 1972, 75% of all cattle marketed were fed cattle. Beef production increased approximately 5% per year during the 1960s. Increased beef cattle numbers accompanied by decreased calf slaughter and an increase in cattle feeding made this possible.

Per capita beef consumption has increased 78% since 1950. Beef accounts for 60% of all red meat consumed in the U.S.—about 52 kg per person in 1971. Continued expansion of beef production will be required for the anticipated population growth and increase in per capita consumption. Thus beef cattle will be expected to consume an ever larger proportion of the total forage produced.

The makeup of the cattle population is shown in Figure 62.1. In this chart, cattle listed as "other beef animals" include calves, steers, and heifers being grown out or finished for market; these make up nearly half the cattle population. The size of the calf crop and ratio of beef to dairy calves is shown in Figure 62.2. Most beef calves and an increasing percentage of male dairy calves are grown out and finished for slaughter.

Marked changes have occurred in handling postweaning cattle, i.e., during the growing or stocker phase and the fattening or finishing phase. Maintenance of cow herds for calf production remains tied to range and farmlands, with many of these herds being in relatively small units. The finishing operations and to a lesser extent

❧ E. R. BARRICK is Professor of Animal Science, North Carolina State University, Raleigh. He holds the M.S. and Ph.D. degrees from Purdue University. He has specialized in beef cattle grazing and forage work and the use of pasture for finishing cattle.

❧ SAMUEL H. DOBSON is Extension Professor of Crop Science, North Carolina State University, Raleigh. He holds the M.S. degree from North Carolina State University. He is primarily concerned with on-farm tests and forage-beef enterprises involving multiple disciplines.

1. Allen, G. C. 1970. National and state livestock-feed relationships. USDA Econ. Res. Serv. Bull. 446.

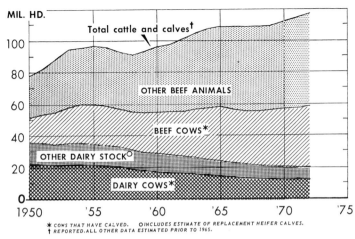

FIG. 62.1. The beef cattle population continues to expand, with a high percentage of the grazing crops being utilized by beef animals. Those being grown out and finished make up approximately half the total cattle population.

the stocker operations tend to be concentrated in large specialized commercial units with grains and high-protein feeds providing most of the nutrients for finishing. For the stocker phase, forages continue to be the primary source of feed. However, with increasing costs cattle are grown out faster with concentrates used to supplement forages when the forage quality is not adequate to maintain satisfactory growth rates. The practice of growing out stockers over a long period with growth spurts related to periods of good grazing is decreasing.

Traditionally, calves are born in the late winter or spring and weaned in the fall; however, some areas produce a significant number of fall calves. Spring-born calves run with their mothers on pasture until weaned in the fall at weights of 150–250 kg, depending on weaning age and feed availability. Spring calves are normally wintered on harvested forage or supplemented range in the cold climates. In the mild climates the cool-season perennials and winter annuals are used in addition to harvested forages. Stockers are also commonly used to glean fields after crops are harvested. They provide a market for available feeds that would otherwise have little market value. Winter wheat–producing areas in the Southwest provide winter grazing for a large volume of stockers in favorable

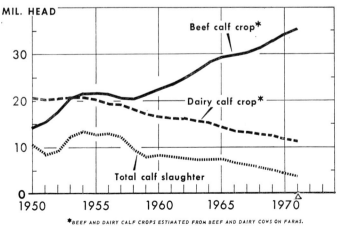

FIG. 62.2. Calf slaughter has declined since the 1950s. Most of the calves are being grown out and finished at heavier weights, and beef calves make up a high percentage of the calf crop.

TABLE 62.1 ❧ Nutrient requirements of growing and finishing cattle (daily nutrients per animal)

Body weight (kg)	Average daily gain (kg)	Daily dry matter/ animal (kg)	Total protein (kg)	Digestible protein (kg)	Energy ME (Mcal)	Energy TDN (kg)	Ca (g)	P (g)	Caro- tene (mg)	Vitamin A (000 IU)
				Finishing steer calves						
200	1.00	5.0	0.61	0.41	13.4	3.7	23	17	27.5	11.0
300	1.10	7.1	0.87	0.58	19.0	5.3	26	19	39.5	15.8
400	1.10	8.8	0.98	0.62	23.5	6.5	25	20	49.0	19.6
450	1.05	9.4	1.04	0.67	25.1	6.9	21	21	52.0	20.8
				Finishing yearling steers						
250	1.30	7.2	0.80	0.51	18.8	5.2	29	20	40.0	16.0
300	1.30	8.3	0.92	0.92	21.7	6.0	29	21	46.0	18.4
400	1.30	10.3	1.14	0.73	26.9	7.4	28	23	56.0	22.8
500	1.20	11.5	1.28	0.82	30.0	8.3	26	26	64.0	25.6
				Finishing heifer calves						
150	0.80	3.5	0.45	0.30	9.9	2.7	18	13	19.5	7.8
200	0.90	5.0	0.61	0.41	13.4	3.7	21	15	27.5	11.0
300	1.00	7.3	0.89	0.59	19.5	5.4	23	18	40.5	16.2
400	0.95	8.7	0.97	0.62	23.2	6.4	23	19	48.5	19.4
				Finishing yearling heifers						
250	1.20	7.6	0.84	0.54	19.8	5.5	27	20	42.0	16.8
300	1.20	8.6	0.95	0.61	22.4	6.2	27	20	48.0	19.2
400	1.20	10.7	1.19	0.76	27.9	7.7	30	24	59.5	23.8
450	1.10	11.0	1.22	0.78	28.7	7.9	24	24	61.0	24.4
				Growing steers						
	0.25	3.1	0.34	0.22	7.1	2.0	8	7	17.0	6.8
150	0.50	3.2	0.39	0.26	8.41	2.3	12	10	17.5	7.0
	0.75	3.2	0.43	0.29	9.0	2.5	17	13	17.5	7.0
	0.25	4.5	0.45	0.27	9.3	2.6	8	8	25.0	10.0
200	0.50	4.9	0.54	0.35	11.2	3.1	13	10	27.0	10.8
	0.75	5.0	0.56	0.36	12.5	3.5	18	14	28.0	11.2
	0.25	6.1	0.54	0.32	12.6	3.5	11	11	34.0	13.6
300	0.50	7.7	0.77	0.47	15.9	4.4	14	14	43.5	17.4
	0.75	8.0	0.89	0.57	18.2	5.0	17	15	44.5	17.8
	0.25	7.7	0.64	0.35	15.9	4.4	14	14	43.0	17.2
400	0.50	9.7	0.86	0.50	20.0	5.5	17	17	54.0	21.6
	0.75	9.9	0.88	0.51	22.6	6.3	18	18	55.0	22.0

Source: NRC, 1970.[2]
Note: See Table 61.2 for growing heifers.

winters. Areas in the Southeast are using increasing hectarages of winter annuals for stocker cattle. Stockers not ready for finishing at the end of the wintering period are commonly grazed on range or perennial pasture during spring and summer for further development. The nutrient requirements for growing and finishing cattle reported by the National Research Council committee on animal nutrition are shown in Table 62.1.[2]

2. National Research Council. 1970. Nutrient Requirements of Beef Cattle, 4th ed., rev. Natl. Acad. Sci., Washington, D.C.

❧ FORAGES AS A SOURCE OF ENERGY

Forages tend to be used in the phase of cattle operations where they have their greatest value. Forages when compared with grains as an energy source have a higher value for animal maintenance in relation to their value for promoting gain. For this reason forages have a higher value where maintenance makes up a large percentage of the total needs of the animal. The beef cow utilizes the highest percentage of her nutrient needs for maintenance; this is followed by the stocker or growing phase and by the finishing phase. Results of research have developed an awareness among cattlemen regarding the energy needs of cattle for maintenance versus their needs for weight gains.[3] Tables have been developed showing the net energy requirements of various weights of cattle for maintenance and for gain and the net energy value of different feeds for maintenance and weight gain. The net energy value of most grains for promoting weight gain is 60–65% of their value for maintenance, while for hay this value is only 45–50%. The corresponding value for high-quality forages (immature grasses and legumes and good corn silage) lies between the values for grain and for hay, with some of the values near those of grain.

For growing cattle the energy requirement for maintenance is a larger part of the total energy needs than it is for fattening cattle. This means that forages have a relatively higher value for stocker than for finishing programs. A 200-kg calf fed to gain 0.70 kg/day has a daily maintenance requirement of approximately 4.10 Mcal and a requirement for growth of 2.14 Mcal for a total of 6.24 Mcal. In this case the maintenance needs constitute about 66% of the total. For a 400-kg fattening steer the maintenance requirement is 6.89 Mcal, and with 1.3 kg/day gain the requirement for gain is 7.17 Mcal, with maintenance less than 50% of total needs.

❧ EFFICIENT USE OF FORAGE BY THE FARM FEEDER

Cattle finishing where forages provide a major source of nutrients is conducted largely on farms. Many operators combine stocker phases with finishing. Some producers with cow-calf operations retain the calves and finish to slaughter weight. Efficient use of forages and crop residues is important in making farm-sized finishing units competitive with large commercial units.

Stocker cattle are used to glean from the fields feed that would otherwise be wasted. Most farms have land not suited for continuous cultivation or land utilized best by sod crops a portion of the time. Forages from this land are often marketed best with stocker cattle or a combination of stocker and finishing cattle, depending on availability of grain. Combining the use of forage crops, field gleanings, and by-products of cultivated crops offers a real opportunity for increased returns on many farms. Use of winter annuals produced on cultivated land or double-cropped with summer annuals is increasing in many areas of the South. This offers a potential for increased production of beef without additional land. Cattle systems can be designed to fit the forage supply under a wide variety of farm conditions.

❧ CONCENTRATE:ROUGHAGE RATIOS AND PHYSICAL FORM OF FORAGE

Investigations have shown that as the ratio of concentrates to roughage in the diet increases, daily gains and feed efficiency improve. This along with the favorable price of grains and their adaptation to mechanical processing and handling has been responsible for the trend toward high-concentrate rations for finishing cattle and predicates their continued use. Work with all-concentrate rations has shown that good gains can be obtained on diets without forage and with better feed efficiency than is normally obtained from diets containing forage.[4] However, the energy intake is no greater than with rations containing forage, and rumen parakeratosis and liver abscesses are more of a problem. The inclusion of 10–15% of a scabrous forage is effective in maintaining a healthy rumen epithelium. A small amount of forage tends to improve feed intake and gain, although feed efficiency may be adversely affected.

An all-concentrate diet has been compared with a pelleted all-forage alfalfa-

3. Lofgreen, G. P., and W. N. Garrett. 1968. A system for expressing net energy requirements and feed values for growing and finishing cattle. *J. Anim. Sci.* 27:793–806.

4. Wise, M. B., R. W. Harvey, B. R. Haskins, and E. R. Barrick. 1968. Finishing beef cattle on all-concentrate rations. *J. Anim. Sci.* 27:1449–60.

based diet.[5] The average daily gain was approximately 21% faster on the all-concentrate diet, and 43% less feed was required per kilogram of gain than on the all-forage diet. When fed to the same slaughter weight the carcasses from the all-forage fed animals had about half as much fat over the rib-eye and slightly less marbling. A taste panel evaluation was slightly higher for the meat from the all-forage than the all-concentrate fed cattle, although the official carcass grade was lower. These results indicate that suitable quality of beef can be produced from all-forage rations when price relationships of grain and forage favor the practice.

Effects of the physical form in which forage is fed have been reviewed.[6,7] Grinding and pelleting influence forage consumption and utilization more than other processing procedures. Ground and pelleted forage when compared to long or chopped forage increased dry matter intake, rate of passage of feed particles from the rumen, and rate of digestion in the rumen and decreased digestibility of crude fiber. There was little or no difference in net energy value compared to long hay. Animal performance is improved markedly as a result of increased intake, and a greater response to processing is obtained on average to low-quality forage than on high-quality forage. An increased incidence of rumen parakeratosis results when finely ground and pelleted forage is fed without any that is coarse or long.

❧ USE OF FORAGES FOR FINISHING CATTLE

Forages used in finishing operations must be of high quality to provide a significant portion of the nutrients required. High-quality pasture, especially grass-legume

mixtures, winter annuals, and good corn silage, provides the forages most adapted for finishing cattle. To meet the market demand for high-good and choice cattle of younger age, supplemental energy is usually provided sometime in the finishing program. Comparatively little finishing is done on pasture alone, as was common when older cattle were marketed.

FINISHING ON PASTURE

Pasture finishing practices in various parts of the country differ markedly. The most effective systems make the most use of pasture when the quality is highest and availability greatest over as long a period as possible. Kansas and Missouri plans for utilizing pasture in finishing cattle have been reviewed.[8] Although the bluestem used in Kansas differs from other areas, the Kansas system works well with any forage that produces its heaviest growth in spring and early summer. Steer calves are wintered well, grazed for approximately 90 days in spring when the grass is most nutritious, and finished in drylot for 100 days. The Missouri plan provides a longer grazing season, utilizing small-grain, bluegrass, and lespedeza pastures in sequence with a shorter grain-feeding period (60–70 days) prior to marketing.

Many grain-on-pasture finishing programs show that it does not pay to feed unlimited grain during pasture periods of high quality. A successful pasture finishing system in North Carolina utilizes steer calves wintered on accumulated pasture or harvested forage and concentrates to gain 0.45–0.6 kg/head daily. Then they are self-fed grain with an intake limiter (10% fat) during the spring and summer finishing period on good pasture.[9] (See Fig. 62.3.) Average daily concentrate intake has been approximately 1 kg/100 kg of body weight for the grazing season. Grain-fat mix fed free-choice reduces labor of daily feeding,

5. Oltjen, R. R., T. S. Rumsey, and P. A. Putnam. 1971. All-forage diets for finishing beef cattle. *J. Anim. Sci.* 32:327–33.

6. Moore, L. A. 1964. Symposium on forage utilization: Nutritive value of forage as affected by physical form. I. General principles involved with ruminants and effect of feeding pelleted or wafered forage to dairy cattle. *J. Anim. Sci.* 23:230–38.

7. Beardsley, D. W. 1964. Symposium on forage utilization: Nutritive value of forage as affected by physical form. II. Beef cattle and sheep studies. *J. Anim. Sci.* 23:239–45.

8. Neumann, A. L., and R. R. Snapp. 1969. Beef Cattle, 6th ed. John Wiley & Sons, New York.

9. Wise, M. B., E. R. Barrick, and T. N. Blumer. 1967. Finishing steers with grain on pasture. N.C. Agr. Exp. Sta. Bull. 425.

FIG. 62.3. *Many . . . programs show . . . does not pay to feed unlimited grain . . . pasture periods of high quality.* Cattle self-fed grain on pasture, with an intake limiter to restrict grain intake to about 1% of the body weight daily, make efficient use of pasture and produce beef economically.

and animals adjust intake as forage quality and weather conditions vary, resulting in more consistent performance. Little or no response has been obtained from added protein when the forage grazed includes clover or a palatable grass like orchardgrass that is properly grazed and clipped to maintain quality. Some response has been obtained to supplemental protein with steers fed grain on 'Coastal' bermudagrass pasture.[10] A 10-year North Carolina study has shown that steers grazing spring and summer pasture from orchardgrass–ladino clover or orchardgrass alone and fed the grain-fat mix have gained 1–1.25 kg/day for grazing periods of 150–170 days. This system requires only 50–60% of the concentrates normally required for drylot finishing and requires no supplemental protein.

Winter annuals have been effectively used in finishing programs in the South. Supplemental grain feeding during or following the grazing period is necessary to obtain a high percentage of good and choice carcasses from young cattle. The cost of gain has been higher when grain was fed. The use of winter annuals has been quite effective in improving performance or in reducing cost of gains compared to drylot finishing.[11-14] Performance data on calves grazing small grain is given in the section on use of forages by stocker cattle.

FINISHING ON SILAGE

The abundance of experiments with corn silage show that more beef can be produced per ha with corn silage grown on productive soil than any other single crop. From 1.5 to 2.5 t of beef per ha can be produced from good corn silage. Choice quality beef can be produced on all-silage rations, but a longer feeding period is required than when additional grain is fed. Cattle performance on sorghum silage has not generally been as good as on corn silage. The wide variety of sorghum types with differing grain and fiber contents is a factor in the results obtained. Steers fed silage from nonbird-resistant grain sorghum have been reported to gain at a significantly faster rate and to produce gains more efficiently than steers fed silage from bird-resistant sorghum.[15] Rolling the silage before feeding was effective in increasing gains. Average daily gains over a three-year period of 1.02 kg with a feed conversion rate of 8.53 kg dry matter/kg of gain on nonbird-re-

10. Wise, M. B., H. D. Gross, R. S. Soikes, E. H. Evans, Jr., and E. R. Barrick. 1967. Supplementation of Coastal bermudagrass for finishing steers. N.C. Agr. Exp. Sta. Bull. 430.

11. Godbey, E. G., R. F. Wheeler, D. H. Kropf, W. C. Godley, and L. V. Starkey. 1959. Winter forage for fattening steers. S.C. Agr. Exp. Sta. Bull. 469.
12. Carpenter, J. C., Jr., and R. H. Klett. 1969. Silage and wheat pasture for wintering and finishing weanling calves. La. Agr. Exp. Sta. Bull. 642.
13. Anthony, W. D., C. S. Hoveland, E. L. Magton, and H. E. Burgess. 1971. Rye-ryegrass–Yuchi arrowleaf clover for production of slaughter cattle. Auburn Univ. Agr. Exp. Sta. Circ. 182.
14. Edwards, R. L., G. C. Skelly, Jr., D. W. Eaddy, W. C. Godley, R. F. Wheeler, J. W. Hubbard, and H. C. Gilliam, Jr. 1968. A comparison of drylot and supplemented pasture systems for finishing beef cattle. S.C. Agr. Exp. Sta. Bull. 537.
15. Pund, W. A. 1970. Finishing yearling steers with high-energy grain sorghum silage. Miss. Agr. Exp. Sta. Bull. 780.

sistant sorghum silage is quite comparable with performance obtained on corn silage. Other harvested forages such as grass or legume silage or hay have not been extensively used as a major source of nutrients for finishing cattle. However, they are valuable as a portion of the diet with grain, and the legumes in particular are effective in meeting the deficiencies of grain in finishing rations. See Chapter 52 for information on high-energy silage.

❧ USE OF FORAGES BY STOCKER CATTLE

Stockers are animals being grown out and developed prior to finishing or entering the breeding herd. The level of energy supplied may be quite variable depending on available feed supplies, intended use of the cattle, and rate of development desired. In general the aim is to provide adequate nutrients to permit maximum development of the skeleton and muscle without appreciable fat deposition. The level of feeding for this purpose will vary with age, type, and stage of maturity of the cattle. Daily gains of 0.45–0.7 kg on cattle of the English breeds are usually considered quite satisfactory for young cattle. In some systems growth and finishing are combined, as when weaned calves are placed on high-energy rations. It is common practice for cattle to be grown out before finishing. There is considerable weight variation in animals put on finishing rations; starting weights for steers of 300–350 kg are common, and heifers usually are 20–45 kg lighter.

Consideration of the use to be made of cattle is important in determining the level of feeding for a given stage of development. For example, calves to be run on pasture following the wintering period are usually wintered at a somewhat lower level than cattle that will go on finishing rations. Fleshy cattle or those wintered at a high level will not make as good gains on pasture as those wintered at a lower level. The operator combining these two phases will be concerned with getting the maxi-

mum output from both phases at the least cost. The increased rate of gain that usually occurs when cattle are put on a good ration following a period of restricted feeding is important in the stocker and finishing operations. The trend is toward a level of feeding that minimizes restriction in rate of development and permits the animals to get to market at an early age.

Most immature grasses and legumes are excellent feed for stocker cattle. Protein is usually higher than actual requirements, and Ca, P, and vitamin A are liberally supplied. Water content and quantity that must be grazed are the principal factors limiting energy intake. For example, a 227-kg stocker steer will consume approximately 6.8 kg of good quality hay. Approximately 4.8 kg of this hay are required for maintenance. The remaining 2.72 kg will permit gain of approximately 0.36 kg. If the potential of immature forage is considered (e.g., wheat pasture on an equal air-dry basis), 3.08 kg would meet the energy needs for maintenance. This leaves 3.72 kg that should support a gain of approximately 1 kg. If the wheat pasture as grazed is 20% dry matter, the steer must consume 30.6 kg to get the equivalent dry matter in 6.8 kg of air-dry feed. The young animal is unable to consume enough wheat pasture for this level of performance.

NATIVE AND IMPROVED SUMMER PASTURES

Native bluestem grasses of the flint hills of Kansas and Osage regions of Oklahoma have long been recognized for their ability to produce cattle gains, as have the grasses of the Nebraska sandhills and Kentucky bluegrass–clover pastures of the Appalachian region. These areas were once noted for production of finished beef. With the advent of plentiful grain and early finishing these areas are being used largely for cow herds and stockers. Performance of stockers on native pastures and ranges may be quite variable. Some of the causes for variability are differences in age, initial condition, kind of cattle, stocking rate, length of grazing season, and weather con-

TABLE 62.2 ❧ Influence of levels of N fertilization on steer gains per ha from Coastal bermudagrass

Nitrogen (kg/ha)	6-year average Georgia (kg/ha)	3-year average South Carolina (kg/ha)
56	292	. . .
112	503	464
224	747	839
448	. . .	1,051

Sources: Stephens and Marchant, 1959;[16] Suman et al., 1964.[17]

TABLE 62.3 ❧ Effect of stocking rate on gains of steers grazing Coastal bermudagrass

Steers per ha	Average daily gain (kg)	Gain per ha (kg)
3.7	0.67	392
5.0	0.60	470
6.2	0.51	509

Source: Hoveland et al., 1971.[18]

ditions. It is well recognized by cattlemen that good native pasture will promote excellent gains during the spring and early summer when forage quality is high. Performance usually declines on tall grasses as they mature; however, short grasses of the Great Plains maintain a relatively high energy value when mature.

In the South, Coastal bermudagrass has provided a tremendous boost to the cattle industry. This warm-season grass responds to high levels of N and provides a very high carrying capacity during the summer months. The Georgia and South Carolina stations report gains per ha on yearling steers with different levels of N as shown in Table 62.2.[16,17] The Georgia station reported the average daily gain to be 0.45 kg and South Carolina reported 0.59 kg.

A five-year Georgia summary on the effects of stocking rates on steer gains when grazing Coastal bermudagrass is shown in Table 62.3.[18] These results are common in studies on stocking rates. Level of stocking that gives the most gain per ha often does not give the best animal performance. The Alabama station has reported an average daily stocking rate of 6.4 yearling steers and gain of 538 kg/ha with an annual average grazing season of 168 days and application of N at the rate of 179 kg/ha.[18] This was somewhat higher production than obtained with either 'Pensacola' bahiagrass or common bermudagrass with the same N level. When the level of N applied to Coastal bermudagrass was doubled, the average daily stocking rate increased to 8.16 and the gain to 695 kg/ha. Average daily gain was 0.34–0.57 kg/head/day.

Achieving the desired individual animal performance is a problem with Coastal. The adverse effect of high summer temperatures on the animals is a factor, as well as the quality of the forage. Alabama workers have investigated the feeding value of a number of bermudagrass hays for dairy cattle. They have reported that the content of total digestible nutrients decreased 1.02% for each percent of increase in crude fiber.[19] The apparent digestible protein content of the hays was linearly related to the crude protein level. It is quite likely that these same relationships hold for the growing forage and are important factors in pasture management for obtaining the best possible animal performance.

The use of a cool-season grass such as tall fescue and a warm-season grass like Coastal bermudagrass at high levels of fertilization and grazed in sequence offers real possibilities for increasing the carrying capacity of an area where both species thrive. In North Carolina nearly twice as many animal grazing days per ha and 23% more beef per ha have been reported from tall fescue and Coastal grazed in sequence than from ladino clover–tall fescue grazed continuously. However, daily gain was superior on the pastures with ladino

16. Stephens, S. L., and W. H. Marchant. 1959. Influence of nitrogen on Coastal bermudagrass. Ga. Agr. Exp. Sta. Circ. NS 13.

17. Suman, R. F., S. G. Woods, T. C. Peele, and E. G. Godbey. 1964. Beef production for summer grasses in the coastal plains. S.C. Agr. Exp. Sta. Bull. 509.

18. Hoveland, C. S., C. C. King, E. M. Evans, R. R. Harris, and W. B. Anthony. 1971. Bermudagrass for forage in Alabama. Auburn Univ. Agr. Exp. Sta. Bull. 328.

19. Hawkins, G. E., and Joe Little. 1970. Some relationships between chemical composition and nutritive qualities of Coastal bermudagrass hays for dairy cows. Auburn Univ. Agr. Exp. Sta. Bull. 405.

clover.[20] Most grazing trials with pure grass and grass-legume mixtures have shown an individual animal performance advantage for the legume-grass pastures. However, on the grass pastures there are indications that careful grazing management and frequent N fertilization can overcome part of the difference in daily gain. On mountain pastures in North Carolina, 32% faster gains have been obtained on Kentucky bluegrass–legume mixtures than on N fertilized Kentucky bluegrass.[21] Workers in Kentucky reported a five-year average gain on steers of 381 kg/ha on Kentucky bluegrass–ladino clover; 500 kg/ha on sequence grazing of rye, sudangrass, or hybrid sorghum–sudangrass and Korean lespedeza; and 600 kg/ha from Kentucky bluegrass–alfalfa.[22] Average daily gains were similar on each of these treatments, i.e., 0.55 kg/day.

WINTER ANNUALS

Depending on the part of the country and type of operation, feeding practices for handling stockers in the winter may include concentrate supplementation on the range, hay or silage feeding, grazing of winter annuals, and gleaning residues from cultivated crops. Most operations will combine two or more of these practices. Hay, silage, and winter annuals are forages produced specifically for winter feeding of stockers, although much of the small-grain grazing in the Southwest is obtained on small grains being grown for grain. Good winter performance can usually be obtained with winter annuals. One problem is to ensure a continuous supply of forage due to variable growing conditions and to supply feeds that will maintain gains when grazing is interrupted. Winter performance of calves grazing winter annuals in different

areas of the South is shown in Table 62.4.[23-29] The gain per ha reported varied from 142 to 460. With the continuous feedlot demand for steers and heifers there is good potential for expanding stocker programs with winter annuals to grow out light calves produced in the South. The vast Southwest winter wheat areas have a marked effect on stocker cattle prices in the fall and winter, causing them to be bullish when wheat pastures are good and bearish when they are poor. (See Chapter 33.)

HARVESTED FEEDS

Stocker cattle have been traditionally wintered on hay or silage in areas where winter range or grazing is not available. Forage quality is the determining factor in rate of gain. In the example given previously, a 227-kg steer calf consuming 6.8 kg of fair to good quality alfalfa hay (28% fiber) would gain about 0.36 kg/day. With high-quality leafy alfalfa hay (24% fiber or less) and the same intake, the potential gain would be 0.58 kg/day. With quality hay the intake and rate of gain would be higher. An increase of 10% in consumption would provide energy for an expected gain of 0.69 kg/day. With poor quality, stemmy alfalfa hay (34% fiber) the expected gain would be about 0.10 kg/day if consumption of 6.8 kg/day could be obtained, which is not likely. In feeding experiments with stocker cattle the performance on hay or

20. Goode, Lemuel, H. D. Gross, G. L. Ellis, and W. B. Gilbert. 1966. Pastures for yearling beef cattle in the Piedmont, North Carolina. N.C. Agr. Exp. Sta. Bull. 428.
21. Burns, J. C., R. W. Harvey, H. D. Gross, M. B. Wise, W. B. Gilbert, D. F. Tugman, and J. W. Bentley. 1970. Pastures and grazing systems for the mountains of North Carolina. N.C. Agr. Exp. Sta. Bull. 437.
22. Templeton, W. C., Jr., C. F. Buck, and N. W. Bradley. 1970. Renovated Kentucky bluegrass and supplementary pastures for steers. Ky. Agr. Exp. Sta. Bull. 709.

23. Baker, F. S. 1957–58. Roughages for wintering calves, 57-11. Wintering stocker cattle, 58-5. N. Fla. Mimeo Repts.
24. Bertrand, J. E., and K. S. Dunavin, Jr. 1969. Small-grain crops grazed by supplemented and unsupplemented growing beef calves. Soil Crop Sci. Fla. Proc. 29: 203.
25. Marron, P. T., C. E. Fisher, and J. H. Jones. 1956. Wintering steer calves at the Spur station. Tex. Agr. Exp. Sta. Bull. 835.
26. Renbarger, R., S. A. Ewing, and D. Stephens. 1968. Effect of supplemented feed and stilbestrol implants on the performance of heifer calves grazing winter wheat pasture. Okla. Agr. Exp. Sta. Misc. Publ. 80.
27. McCrookey, J. E., R. Renbarger, and J. Eason. 1968. A comparison of hormones for heifers grazing wheat pastures. Okla. Agr. Exp. Sta. Publ. 82.
28. Clyburn, T. M., W. C. McCormick, and B. L. Southwell. 1965. Growing and finishing steers on annual pastures. Ga. Agr. Exp. Sta. Mimeo Ser. 240.19.
29. Harris, R. R., W. B. Anthony, V. L. Brown, J. K. Boseck, H. F. Yates, W. B. Webster, and J. E. Barrett, Jr. 1971. Cool-season annual grazing crops for stocker calves. Auburn Univ. Agr. Exp. Sta. Bull. 416.

TABLE 62.4 ✤ Performance of calves grazing winter annuals

Location	Initial weight (kg)	Crops	Average daily gain (kg)
Florida	236	oats and rye	0.63–0.77
Florida	176.6	small grains	0.86
Texas (10-year average)	147–181	wheat	0.75
Oklahoma	218	wheat	0.62
Oklahoma	119–196	wheat	0.48–0.72
Georgia (3-year average)	223	oats	0.87
Louisiana (3-year average)	218	wheat	0.81
Alabama (10-year average)	204–227	small grain–clover	0.63–0.72

Sources: Carpenter et al., 1969;[12] Baker, 1957–58;[23] Bertrand and Dunavin, 1969;[24] Marron et al., 1956;[25] Renbarger et al., 1968;[26] McCrookey et al., 1969;[27] Clyburn et al., 1965;[28] Harris et al., 1971.[29]

silage made from hay crops has been extremely variable. Factors such as forage quality, intake, and nature of cattle fed are involved in this variation. Energy or protein-energy supplements, depending on the protein content of the hay, are usually fed with hay to get the desired performance.

Corn silage, particularly from cultivars yielding a high volume of grain, is usually a more uniform quality of feed in high-rainfall areas than hay or hay crop silage. Corn silage contains 40% or more grain on a dry weight basis and provides a good energy source for stockers. (See Chapter 52 for performance of cattle on silage rations.) Good corn silage fed liberally may increase the condition on stocker cattle more than is desired. This can be controlled by restricted feeding.

✤ ON-FARM EXAMPLES

LARGE FARMS

A Beaufort County, N.C., farm provides a good example of how a forage-cattle program can improve net income on productive corn-soybean land.[30] Land resources on the farm under consideration are primarily Class IIw and Class IIIw soils with 10% organic matter.[31] (See Terminology for definition of land classes.) Open-ditch drainage has made all land suitable for corn and soybean production. In 1966 on this 405-

30. North Carolina State Univ. 1970. Farm Business Records System.
31. USDA. 1966. Land capability classification. SCS Agr. Handbook 210.

ha farm, the 73 ha utilized for forage and cattle returned only $30.89/ha, far below the returns from corn and soybeans. Improvements in forage production and cattle management increased returns to $109.53/ha by 1969. While this was an exceptional year, the enterprise records for five years show that the cattle enterprise makes possible greater net returns than would be realized if all the land were used to produce corn and soybeans. This is on land with average corn yields of over 69 q/ha and soybean yields of over 24 q/ha. A farm enterprise mix analysis has indicated that a cattle operation large enough to utilize most of the grain crop residues and cover crops would optimize returns. At 1972 prices 25–35% of the land on this farm in forages for use with cattle would be desirable.

The cattle program consists of 100 commercial brood cows, with the calves wintered and finished with grain on pasture. The basic forage program on this farm on a per animal unit basis, 454 kg, is 0.12 ha tall fescue, 0.12 ha ladino clover and tall fescue, 0.06 ha pearlmillet, 0.06 ha corn for grain-on-pasture feeding, 0.03 ha corn silage, and 0.03 ha rye for seeding winter cover. This gives 0.43 ha/animal devoted to the cattle enterprise plus grain crop residues, winter cover, and "set aside" acres. The farm is selling over 560 kg/ha of beef for each ha devoted to beef.

To grow palatable nutritious forage in the area, chemical soil amendments are necessary. On land devoted to beef, this

TABLE 62.5. ❧ Land resources, crops, and cattle on Cub Creek Farm

Item	Hectares
Land Resources	
Class I land	0
Class II land	12.58
Class III land	6.52
Class IV land	14.48
Total	33.58
Crops	
Tall fescue	11.36
Ladino clover and tall fescue	16.15
Coastal bermudagrass	2.02
Pearlmillet	1.62
Corn silage	2.43
Total	33.58
Cattle, 1/1/72	
Brood cows	62
Yearling heifers	16
Bulls*	7

Source: N.C. State Univ., 1970.[30]
* Four or five top bull calves are kept each year for sale to neighbors as breeding stock.

farm is using 67 kg/ha of N per year, 29 kg/ha of P per year, 163 kg/ha of K per year, and 0.75 t/ha of dolomitic lime per year. The legume-grass pastures do not receive N fertilization.

Commercial beef herds are replacing cotton on some of the plantations of the old Cotton Belt. An example is a farm near Benton, Miss., where cotton once reigned supreme.[32] Now over 2500 cattle use all the marginal and some of the good cotton land. Coastal and common bermudagrass occupy 650 ha, half of which is over-seeded each fall with wheat and annual ryegrass. In addition, 81 ha are grown as corn and sorghums for silage and as sorghum-sudangrass hybrids and pearlmillet for grazing. The calves are grown to approximately 300 kg. The farm is grossing about as much per ha from commercial cattle as it did from cotton. Labor requirements are quite different because the farm is set up on a limited labor program with a successful adjustment to the decreasing farm labor supply.

While most states in the Southeast now have 1 ha or slightly more of forage for each animal above 225 kg, many feel that the carrying capacity must be at least doubled to two animal units per ha. Research shows this can be done and that some farmers are already doing it. A ranch near Mt. Pleasant, Texas, has a sign which reads, "Pasture Demonstration—500 Cows on 500 Acres."[33] Under this system, fall-dropped calves average 225 kg when weaned in June. They are large enough to make good use of summer forages, and the fall grazing from cool-season annuals prepares them for a short finishing period on grain. This and similar schemes are being followed to utilize summer and fall forages, with cattle going to feedlots for finishing.

SMALL FARMS

Throughout much of the rapidly industrializing Southeast small farms still exist. Many farmers accept work off the farm, yet continue to live there. Pastures and cattle offer the best opportunity on many of these farms. One such farm in Piedmont, N.C., which was entered in the North Carolina State University Farm Business Records Program, has 33.6 ha of cleared land, all devoted to forages and beef cattle.[30]

While the hectarage of cleared land is about average for the state, most farms of this size would have some Class I land. The soils are eroded red clays and clay loams. All the feed for the 85 animals comes from the farm, and with heavier fertilization, indications are that 80–85 brood cows can be supported on this farm yearly with enough feed to carry the calves through the winter to sell in the spring stocker sales. Table 62.5 shows that a little less than half the forage land is in perennial legume-grass mixtures.[30] The remainder of the land is seeded to high-producing grasses that receive heavy N fertilization.

A well-rounded and fairly complete forage program has been developed with

32. Swayze, Harris S. 1971. Southern revolution in forage for beef. Proc. Amer. Forage Grassl. Counc., 4th Res.-Ind. Conf., pp. 39–43.

33. Scruggs, C. G. 1971. A pasture dream realized. Prog. Farmer 86 (6): 23.

TABLE 62.6 ✣ Nutrients used per ha on Cub Creek Farm

Nutrient	Amount	
N	84	kg/year
P	24	kg/year
K	93	kg/year
Dolomitic limestone	0.56	t/year

Source: N.C. State Univ., 1970.[30]

liberal use of fertilizer (Table 62.6).[30] Corn silage and sorghum-sudangrass hybrids are being grown in a rotation program with perennial pasture on Class II and Class III land. (See Chapter 55.) This land grows three annual crops in two years. Corn is planted in the spring in tall fescue sod using zero tillage; rye is planted after corn silage on a prepared seedbed; and corn or sorghum-sudangrass is planted in rye stubble, again using zero tillage. After the corn is cut for silage or the grazing crop grazed off in the late summer of the second year, a seedbed is prepared with lime and phosphate mixed into the soil before seeding for another four years of ladino clover–tall fescue pasture. The system allows for the mixing of lime with the soil every four or five years, a desirable practice on these acid soils. The Kentucky scheme (see Chapter 54) of introducing a legume in a tall fescue sod is being used on the less stony Class IV land.

Utilization is a key word on this farm. Early grazing comes from tall fescue that has received N fertilization. The legume-grass pastures are harvested as grass silage, and fresh aftermath is available for grazing when tall fescue begins to slacken in growth and palatability. From the clover-grass pastures, cattle go to either Coastal bermudagrass or summer annual grasses. Cattle usually have access to the tall fescue pasture while on Coastal or the summer annuals. In this way no tall fescue growth is wasted and the summer grasses keep animal performance at a high level. After calf weaning, brood cows return to tall fescue and the calves utilize the more palatable pastures.

The farmer, his wife, and teen-age son do all the work on the farm. Since man and wife each work 40 hours a week off the farm, no labor charges are made to the farm. Using this system, a return to land, management, and capital investment of $120/ha is obtained. Charging out the investment in machinery and cattle gives a return of $90/ha to land and management.

A cattle system to fit the small to average size of general crop farms is being investigated by the North Carolina station.[34] The system combines high-quality forage during lactation, cows that will supply a liberal amount of milk, and calves with potential to make rapid gains when placed on finishing rations at weaning time. The forage program includes ladino clover–tall fescue, Coastal bermudagrass, and winter and summer annuals grown in the same field when renovated for perennial pastures. The cows are bred to calve in January and early February. After calving they are given access to rye-ryegrass pasture as early as it can be grazed. Following the winter annuals, cattle graze ladino clover–tall fescue, then Coastal and summer annuals (pearl-millet or sorghum-sudangrass). Angus-Holstein F_1 cows mated to Charolais sires are being used. The adjusted 205-day performance test weight on the 1971 calves was 302 kg without creep-feeding. At weaning these calves are put on a self-feeder located on Coastal sod and are finished for market at 13–14 months of age. This system minimizes labor. By moving the feeder occasionally, the problems of mud and hauling manure are avoided. The finishing phase provides a market for farm-raised grain. After the calves are weaned, the dry cows are carried on grain crop residues, pasture, and peanut hay until next calving time. Most of the land used for cattle is not suitable for regular cultivation since it is too wet, sloping, or sandy. These conditions exist on many farms where the proper forage-cattle system can improve productivity and profitability.

34. North Carolina Agr. Exp. Sta. 1971. Progr. Rept. Proj. NCO 5230.

❧ QUESTIONS

1. What is the significance of the beef cattle industry with regard to forage use and agricultural income in the U.S.?
2. What have been the trends in beef cattle finishing from the standpoint of size of operation and kinds of feed used?
3. What contributions can pasture make to a cattle finishing program?
4. Why do forages have a higher value in rations for stockers than finishing cattle?
5. What feed resources help to make the farm operator competitive with large commercial cattle feeders?
6. What influence does fiber content of a forage have on digestibility and animal performance?
7. What type of farm cropping systems are favorable to stocker cattle enterprises?

CLAIR E. TERRILL, IVAN L. LINDAHL
AND DONALD A. PRICE
Agricultural Research Service, USDA

63

SHEEP: EFFICIENT USERS OF FORAGE

❧

RUMINANTS such as sheep convert plant materials to meat, milk, and fiber to provide many essential needs of man for food and protection. These needs very likely led to domestication of sheep, although their convenient size and tractable nature were probably also important.[1] The sheep and goat provided an assured mobile supply of these essentials the year around. Tending sheep made family enterprises desirable. Need for organization and cooperation among families very likely stimulated development of human civilization.

❧ CLAIR E. TERRILL is Animal Scientist, National Program Staff, ARS, USDA, Beltsville, Md. He holds the Ph. D. degree from the University of Missouri. His major interests have been sheep breeding, physiology, and production research.

❧ IVAN L. LINDAHL is Research Chemist, Nutrition Institute, ARS, USDA, Beltsville, Md. His formal training was at William Penn College, George Washington University, and the University of Maryland. He has conducted ruminant nutrition and physiology research since 1943 and has written extensively in this field.

❧ DONALD A. PRICE is Director, U.S. Sheep Experiment Station, ARS, USDA, Dubois, Idaho, and Research Leader for range sheep investigations. He holds the M.S. degree from Colorado State University and the Ph.D. from Oregon Sate University. He has been active in research involving range nutrition and management and sheep breeding.

That the grazing of sheep contributed to the expansion of the human race is amply documented in the Bible. Sheep were intimately related to the domestic, civic, and religious life of the people. Pastures were fought for. Sheep were moved to different areas in different seasons just as in the intermountain West today.

Domestic sheep total about one billion and extend from the Arctic Circle in Iceland and Europe to tips of South America and New Zealand. They are heavily concentrated in warmer temperate zones, especially in the southern hemisphere. Large numbers also are found in tropical areas of South America, Africa, and India. Sheep are adapted to practically every grazing situation known.[2]

Sheep are present in all parts of the U.S. They came with early settlers and aided in development of the country, especially the West. They are most concentrated in west Texas where almost 20% of the nation's sheep are found. Somewhat under half are kept under western range conditions as contrasted with the fenced areas in Texas

1. Zeuner, Frederick E. 1963. A History of Domesticated Animals. Harper and Row, New York.
2. Hafez, E. S. E. (ed.). 1968. Adaptation of Domestic Animals. Lea and Febiger, Philadelphia.

FIG. 63.1. Distribution of sheep throughout the U.S. The state of Texas produces the greatest number of sheep. In 1972 nearly 18 million sheep of all kinds were reported.

and the small flocks prevalent in the Midwest and East. (See Fig. 63.1.)

Sheep have many advantages as grazing animals. Their small size and ease of handling often leads to care by women and children. The sheep's mouth is sufficiently small and narrow with mobility of the lips to permit selective grazing. They eat largely leaves, blossoms, or seed. They prefer finer plants and thus tend to complement cattle grazing. Sheep can graze certain toxic plants such as larkspur in moderate amounts, while cattle cannot.

❧ SHEEP-FORAGE EFFICIENCY

Sheep lead all farm animals in being able to produce marketable products on forage alone. (See Fig. 63.2.) Sheep are more efficient than cattle in utilizing rations high in forage content. With rations of 75% high-quality alfalfa and 25% grain, a ratio of 9 kg feed to 1 kg gain for cattle and 6 or 7 to 1 for lambs was found in Nevada. Grains or other concentrates are generally needed only in late pregnancy and early lactation to supplement low-quality forage or for rapidly growing lambs when forage quality is not sufficiently high.

Sheep have other advantages over cattle in both efficiency and flexibility of production in their short gestation period, high fecundity, and short growing period. A five-month gestation period permits two lamb crops per year, and technology for this is developing. Where climatic conditions permit, sheep may produce more than one lamb crop per year on an irregular schedule. Lambs may now be reared successfully from birth on milk replacers until they consume dry feed and forage. A Finnsheep ewe at Beltsville, Md., recently gave birth to six normal lambs which grew to maturity, demonstrating the tremendous potential of multiple births.[3,4] The short growing period of lambs leads to a marketable product almost in one season and avoids maintenance costs over unfavorable periods. The production of high-quality meat without excess fat on heavier lambs (over 45 kg) also results in increased efficiency.

The development of intensive methods of producing lamb and wool offers potential increased efficiency of production with maximum utilization of forages. Flexibility and adaptability of sheep to highly extensive or intensive methods or combinations thereof permit use of a great variety of forages. Much is experimental, but greater involvement of sheep in rural economy and in production of an abundance of high-quality protein food seems likely.

❧ KINDS OF FORAGES CONSUMED

PASTURES

Sheep pastures may be classified as permanent, cropland, and temporary. Permanent pastures include native pastures and pastures on marginal land unsuited to cropping. In mountainous and semiarid areas, pastures usually consist of native grasses, wild legumes, weeds, and browse plants. Replacement of native grass with crested wheatgrass has increased productivity of some foothill pastures. Native pastures in plains areas include the gramas, buffalograss, and wheatgrasses. Permanent pas-

---

3. *Shepherd Magazine.* 1972. The pack on her back. 17:5.

4. Maijala, K. 1969. Finnish animal husbandry. Rept. Finnish Anim. Breed. Assoc., Helsinki.

FIG. 63.2. *Sheep lead all farm animals . . . able to produce marketable products on forage alone.*

tures in central and eastern states usually are predominantly Kentucky bluegrass, which is very nutritious and palatable when young but soon loses its value when it matures and sets seed. Heavy grazing in early spring and/or frequent clipping not only prolongs feeding value of Kentucky bluegrass but also permits development of summer-growing legumes. Bermudagrass, carpetgrass, and dallisgrass are important in southern areas.

Cropland pastures are usually more productive than permanent pastures. The cropping sequence can vary from one to several years depending on combinations of grasses and legumes used. Clovers are valuable for cropland pastures. Red clover, alsike clover, and sweetclover are mainly used in short-term rotation plans. Ladino clover is important in pasture mixtures in many areas. Other valuable legumes for grass-legume cropland pastures are alfalfa, the lespedezas, and birdsfoot trefoil. Orchardgrass, smooth bromegrass, and timothy are widely used in grass-legume mix-

tures, and good management practices are essential for maximum production. Orchardgrass-ladino mixtures need to be managed to control the abundant early growth of orchardgrass. Alfalfa–smooth bromegrass pastures are most productive when grazing and rest periods are alternated, and smooth bromegrass should neither be grazed closer than 10–12 cm when used in mixtures with clovers nor allowed to get over 45 cm tall. Since many combinations of grasses and legumes can be used to advantage in cropland pastures, recommendations as to the most suitable mixtures should be obtained locally.

Temporary pastures are usually of one species, although mixtures may be used. The cereals (wheat, rye, and winter barley) are valuable late fall, winter, and early spring pastures. Many sheep are pastured on wheat fields in the West. Proper grazing of wheat does not lower subsequent grain production. In other areas cereals are seeded primarily for use as forage. Cereals for forage should be grazed so that they do not joint. Sudangrass grows rapidly for summer pasture; after growth is well started it is drought resistant with high carrying capacity. Rape or rape and oats have been used as temporary pastures in northern states. Combinations such as field peas and oats; field peas, oats, and rape; soybeans and sudangrass; and cowpeas and velvetbeans also have been used.

Other grazed forages include crop residues such as corn, grainfields, and beet tops. Alfalfa regrowth can provide high-quality forage. Sheep also are used to clean up grasses growing along ditches and in other areas. Although these lower quality forages are not suitable for fattening lambs or for ewes in late pregnancy and lactation, they are adequate for dry ewes and maintenance of other sheep. Lambs can be fattened on good pastures adjoining cornfields where they may obtain grain. Lambs also can be fattened in fields planted to a combination of corn and soybeans or cowpeas.

Metabolic disorders and plant poisoning such as bloat and grass tetany may be encountered when sheep are grazed under certain conditions. Proper management procedures and prophylaxis can vary, so it is advisable to consult local experts for advice.

HARVESTED FORAGES

Harvested forages include hay, silage, and green chop. Use of harvested forage may vary from supplementation of pasture and ranges for limited periods to continuous use in confinement rearing.

Legume hays are generally more palatable and nutritious than grass hays; however, there is much variation depending on time of cutting and harvesting conditions. In general, early cut forages (0.10 bloom alfalfa or grasses cut before heading) are preferable to late cut forage for sheep. Grinding and pelleting can increase voluntary intake of forage and feeding value. Pelleted forage may provide cheaper sources of energy than long forage when shipment to feeding areas is required. Under other conditions pelleted forage may be much more expensive than long hay. Either pelleted hay or ground hay is vastly superior to long hay in automated feeding systems.

Silage, either corn or legume-grass, is very satisfactory for sheep. Silage can be used in automated feeding systems but is not adaptable where shipment to feeding areas is required. Value of silage also depends on growth stage at harvest and ensiling procedures. Ensiling part of the early abundant growth of legume-grass pastures can increase total productivity of pastures, especially in areas where it is difficult to harvest high-quality hay.

Sheep generally utilize green chop less effectively than cattle.[5,6,7] Excellent gains

were obtained when lambs were allowed to nurse their dams at night in drylot and were fed high-quality green chop and creep pellets free-choice.[5] However, after weaning at an average age of 120 days, lambs grazing on relatively "parasite clean" pastures gained significantly faster than those fed green chop.

❧ FORAGE CONSUMPTION ON RANGE AND PASTURE

Range and pasture forages are major sources of nutrients for millions of sheep, but relatively little is known about the amount and digestibility of forage consumed. (See Fig. 63.3.) Indirect estimates of feed consumption can be made by using indicators, which include those occurring naturally, such as lignin and plant chromogens. (See Chapter 12 for indicator techniques.) A review of ratio techniques and other methods for determining the consumption and digestibility of herbage by grazing animals has been presented.[8]

The amount of forage consumed by sheep depends primarily on their size, sex, age, stage of reproduction, the palatability and availability of forage, and the environmental factors influencing nutritive requirements for maintenance and reproduction. Using data from many sources, values for voluntary intake of dry matter from range and pasture forage have been calculated. The variation in intake was similar from low- to high-grade dried forages: 55.7 g/kg $W^{0.75}$ (W = body weight) for shadscale, *Atriplex confertifolia* (Torr. & Frem.) Wats., to 82.2 g/kg $W^{0.75}$ for immature orchardgrass. Intake of forage as consumed may vary from 69.6 g/kg $W^{0.75}$ for shadscale to 481.0 g/kg $W^{0.75}$ for lush ladino clover. Forage eaten per day thus could range from 0.8 kg for a 25-kg lamb grazing shadscale to 16.9 kg for a 115-kg ram grazing ladino clover.

Dry matter digestibilities for some representative range forages were 51, 49, 29, 40,

5. Lindahl, I. L., M. L. Colglazier, F. D. Enzie, J. H. Turner, G. E. Whitmore, and R. L. Wilson. 1970. Effect of management systems on the growth of lambs and development of internal parasitism. III. Field trials with lambs on soilage and pasture involving medication with N.F. and purified grades of phenothiazine. *J. Parasitol.* 56:991–99.

6. Hull, J. L., J. H. Meyer, G. P. Lofgreen, and A. Strother. 1957. Studies on forage utilization by steers and sheep. *J. Anim. Sci.* 16:757–65.

7. Meyer, J. H., G. P. Lofgreen, and J. L. Hull. 1957. Selective grazing by sheep and cattle. *J. Anim. Sci.* 16:766–72.

8. Bohman. V. R., L. E. Harris, G. P. Lofgreen, C. J. Kercher, and R. J. Raleigh. 1967. Techniques for range livestock nutrition research. Utah Agr. Exp. Sta. Bull. 471.

Fig. 63.3. *Range and pasture forage . . . major sources of nutrients for millions of sheep.* Ewes and lambs on native grassland range in western Nebraska. *Nebraska SCS photo.*

and 48% for big sagebrush, *Artemisia tridentata* Nutt.; shadscale; winterfat, *Eurotia lanata* (Pursh) Moq.; black sagebrush, *A. nova* Nels.; and squirreltailgrass, *Sitanion hystrix* (Nutt.) J. G. Smith respectively.[9]

Dry matter digestibilities on a tall-forb type of high mountain summer range were 50, 33, and 42 for early, mid, and late summer grazing respectively.[10]

Chemical and botanical composition may also be estimated from the samples collected from esophageally fistulated sheep.[11] Plants on summer ranges usually show a steady decrease in total protein and energy as the season advances. On a tall-forb type of summer range crude protein was 17, 16, and 14% during early, mid, and late summer. Gross energy also decreased from 4297 to 4255 kcal/kg as the season progressed.[10] On a Montana winter range, crude protein intake averaged 7.2%. Crude protein content of forage on Utah desert winter ranges averaged 9% for browse plants and 3.8% for grasses.

Botanical composition of fistula samples may be determined.[12] This method enables estimation of utilization of the different plant species available on a particular range type. On a high-elevation tall-forb range about 75% of the sheep's diet throughout the summer consisted of leaves. The remainder of the diet was 17% stems and 6% flowers.[13]

All senses are related to forage preference for some plant species. Taste is the most important sense and bitter the most unpleasant taste. Smell appears to be supplementary to other senses in determining forage preference. Sight is related to locating plant species preferred by other senses. Touch is of supplementary value for most plants.[14,15]

❧ FORAGE CONSUMPTION IN FEEDLOTS

Voluntary intake of dry forage by sheep varies with a fractional power of body weight approximating 0.73 and is affected by quality, digestibility, and processing as well as by other factors mentioned above. The consumption of poor, medium, and good quality long forage has been found to be 50.5, 77.2, and 94.0 g/kg $W^{0.73}$ respectively.[16] Further studies reveal that the re-

9. Harris, L. E. 1968. Range nutrition in an arid region. Thirty-sixth Faculty Honor Lecture, Utah State Univ., Logan.
10. Price, D. A., I. L. Lindahl, K. R. Fredericksen, P. J. Reynolds, and C. H. Cain. 1964. Nutritive quality of sheep's diet on tall-forb range. Proc. West. Sect. Amer. Soc. Anim. Sci. 15:110–16.
11. Torell, D. T. 1954. An esophageal fistula for animal nutrition studies. *J. Anim. Sci.* 13:878–84.
12. Heady, H. F., and D. T. Torell. 1959. Forage preference exhibited by sheep with esophageal fistulas. *J. Range Manage.* 12:28–34.

13. Buchanan, H., W. A. Laycock, and D. A. Price. 1972. Botanical and nutritive content of the summer diet of sheep on a tall forb range in southwestern Montana. *J. Anim. Sci.* 35:423–30.
14. Krueger, W. C. 1970. Relationships of the special senses to forage selection. Ph.D. thesis, Utah State Univ., Logan.
15. Marten, G. C. 1969. Measurement and significance of forage palatability. Nat. Conf. Forage Qual. Eval. Util. no. D1-D55, Lincoln, Nebr.
16. Blaxter, K. L., F. W. Wainman, and R. S. Wilson. 1961. The regulation of food intake by sheep. *Anim. Prod.* 3:51–61.

lationship between maximal voluntary intake (I) and apparent digestibility of forage (D) by sheep could be expressed by the regression equation, $I = 1.58D - 20.5$.[17] Therefore, digestible energy intake per day and amount of energy available for growth and production is markedly affected by increases in digestibility. Energy digested divided by the maintenance requirement for energy of forages of 40, 50, 60, and 70% energy digestibility is equal to factors of 0.57, 1.40, 2.23, and 3.06 respectively. Thus an increase in apparent energy digestibility from 50 to 60% results in an increase of 59% in energy available for production rather than a mere 10% improvement in feeding value.

Pelleting increases voluntary forage intake, especially of low-quality forages, but digestibility may decrease slightly. For example, voluntary intake of loose and pelleted alfalfa hay was 61.2 and 103.1 g/kg $W^{0.73}$, while apparent digestibility of organic matter was 60% for loose hay and 52% for pelleted hay. Despite the drop in digestibility, the nutritive value index was 44% higher for pelleted hay than for loose hay.[18] The nutritive value index has been defined as that which equals relative dry matter intake per unit of metabolic body size multiplied by percent total digestible nutrients.[19,20] The slight reduction in digestibility of pelleted forage results from a combination of factors, including an increased rate of passage through the intestinal tract and inability to refuse the coarse and less digestible portions.

Voluntary intake of legume-grass silage on a dry matter basis is usually lower than that of hay from the same crop. The high moisture content of silage may limit consumption, but free-acid content also may be important. Perennial ryegrass was treated so that the resulting silage had a range of pH values.[20] Intake of silage with pH values of 3.8, 4.4, 4.8, and 5.4 was 46.9, 53.5, 57.7, and 60.1 g/kg $W^{0.75}$ respectively. Voluntary intake of corn silage harvested at different stages of maturity varied from 52.7 to 60.3 g/kg $W^{0.75}$.[21] Voluntary intake by sheep of perennial ryegrass and corn silage in these trials was comparable to the intakes described above for poor to medium quality loose forages; however, digestibility of dry matter was higher than that of excellent quality hay, averaging 70.1% for corn silage and 75.4% for perennial ryegrass silage.

❧ NUTRIENT REQUIREMENTS FROM FORAGES

Energy is probably the most common nutrient deficiency of ewes. The major factors affecting energy requirement of sheep include ambient temperature, wind velocity, humidity, length of wool, stress, and distance traveled during grazing. The maintenance requirement of mature sheep for energy can be calculated from the following:

DE (digestible energy) $= 119W^{0.75}$
ME (metabolizable energy) $= 98W^{0.75}$
TDN (total digestible nutrients)
$$= 0.027W^{0.75}$$

where W is in kg, DE and ME are in kcal, and TDN are in kg/day.[22,23] These requirements need to be adjusted for activity. Requirements can be reduced by 10–30% for close confinement conditions and may need to be increased by 100% for ewes under sparse grazing conditions such as range in semiarid areas.

Table 63.1 shows that forages can supply energy requirements for maintenance of ewes during the first 15 weeks of gesta-

17. Blaxter, K. L., F. W. Wainman, and J. L. Davidson. 1966. The voluntary intake of food by sheep and cattle in relation to their energy requirements for maintenance. *Anim. Prod.* 8:75–83.
18. Haenlein, G. F. W., R. O. Holdren, and Y. M. Yoon. 1966. Comparative response of horses and sheep to different forms of alfalfa hay. *J. Anim. Sci.* 25:740–43.
19. Crampton, E. W., D. Donefer, and L. E. Lloyd. 1960. A nutritive value index for forages. *J. Anim. Sci.* 19:538–44.
20. McLeod, D. S., R. J. Wilkins, and W. F. Raymond. 1970. The voluntary intake by sheep and cattle of silages differing in free-acid content. *J. Agr. Sci.* 75:311–19.

21. Colovos, N. F., J. B. Holter, R. M. Koes, W. E. Urban, Jr., and H. A. Davis. 1970. Digestibility, nutritive value, and intake of ensiled corn plant in cattle and sheep. *J. Anim. Sci.* 30:819–24.
22. National Research Council. 1975. Nutrient Requirements of Sheep, 5th ed., rev. Natl. Acad. Sci., Washington, D.C.
23. National Research Council. 1968. Nutrient Requirements of Sheep. Natl. Acad. Sci., Washington, D.C.

tion and for yearling ewes and rams. In contrast to simple-stomach animals, quantity of crude protein in the mature sheep's diet is more important than quality. Except for some grass hays, protein requirements can be met by use of forages for these sheep. It also can be seen that energy requirements for lactating ewes, growing lambs, and fattening lambs cannot be met by feeding even the best of the dried forages. High-grade forages approach but do not meet energy requirements for ewes during the last six weeks of gestation. The percentage of the National Research Council requirements that can be met by forage can be calculated by:

$$\frac{\text{nutrient in feed}}{\text{nutrient requirement}} \times 100$$

Thus, midbloom sun-cured alfalfa hay can supply 102, 275, 450, and 79% of digestible energy, digestible protein, Ca, and P requirements respectively for maintenance of ewes weighing 50 kg. With the use of similar calculations it follows that sheep, including lactating ewes, can obtain sufficient protein from legume and high-quality hay, grass or legume silage, and pasture. When pasture becomes mature or sparse and medium or poor quality grass hays are fed, protein must be given as a supplement.

Protein deficiency results in reduced appetite, lowered feed intake, poor feed efficiency, weight loss, and poor reproductive efficiency. The results of energy deficiency are reduced fertility and reproductive failure, lower milk production, and more susceptibility to parasitism.

Calcium supplementation is seldom needed for sheep. However, P deficiencies in pasture and range forages are rather widespread. Almost all forage as it matures is either borderline or deficient in P. Phosphorus supplements can either be added to salt mixtures or mixed with complete feed or concentrates.

Energy and protein intake has a pronounced effect on wool growth. The criti-

cal protein level appears to be near 80% of the recommended requirements (Table 63.1). Below this level, production and quality are adversely affected. Variation in energy intake can result in changes of 400% in the cross-sectional area of wool fibers. Increased energy intake results in greater fiber diameter, longer staple length, and an increase in fiber strength; while limited energy intake reduces fiber diameter, staple length, and fiber strength. Wide fluctuations in energy intake result in wool fibers with varying fiber diameters; severe reductions in feed intake, even of short duration, can result in "wool break."[24]

❧ SUPPLEMENTATION OF FORAGE

Recommendations on range supplementation will vary, depending upon the forage quality, regional climate, and management practices. In the semiarid West plants are of high quality during spring and summer growing seasons; but as forage matures, deficiencies may occur, especially on winter ranges. On pineland ranges of the humid South and the Southeast, soils are relatively infertile and plant quality is lower. Nutritional levels vary by season, but deficiencies prevail most of the year.[25]

Because of difficulty in estimating the nutrient intake of sheep on the range, specific recommendations for supplementation cannot be made. Requirements are shown in Table 63.1. Deficiencies most common on ranges are protein, energy, P, and carotene (vitamin A). These deficiencies may appear singly or in combination and more often when forage is mature. The most pronounced deficiencies occur when sheep are on mature winter ranges or lush washy feeds of low dry matter content for an extended period, under drouth conditions, or when ewes are in the latter stages of gestation. The nutrient requirements of sheep on ranges of the intermountain re-

24. Scott, G. E. 1970. The Sheepman's Production Handbook. Sheep Industry Development Program. Abegg Printing, Denver, Colo.
25. Shepherd, W. O., and R. H. Hughes. 1970. Supplementing range forage. USDA Misc. Publ. 1147, pp. 71–78.

TABLE 63.1 ♋ Nutrient requirements of sheep

Body weight (kg)	Daily dry matter* per animal (kg)	Energy TDN (%)	DE† (Mcal/kg)	Total protein (%)	DP‡ (%)	Ca (%)	P (%)
			Ewes, maintenance§				
50	1.0	55	2.42	8.9	4.8	0.30	0.28
70	1.2	55	2.42	8.9	4.8	0.27	0.25
80	1.3	55	2.42	8.9	4.8	0.25	0.24
			Ewes, nonlactating, first 15 weeks gestation				
50	1.1	55	2.42	9.0	4.9	0.27	0.25
70	1.4	55	2.42	9.0	4.9	0.23	0.21
80	1.5	55	2.42	9.0	4.9	0.22	0.21
			Ewes, last 6 weeks gestation or last 8 weeks lactation suckling singles				
50	1.7	58	2.55	9.3	5.2	0.24	0.23
70	2.1	58	2.55	9.3	5.2	0.21	0.20
90	2.3	58	2.55	9.3	5.2	0.21	0.20
			Ewes, first 8 weeks lactation suckling singles or last 8 weeks lactation suckling twins				
60	2.3	65	2.86	10.4	6.2	0.50	0.36
80	2.6	65	2.86	10.4	6.2	0.48	0.34
			Ewes, first 8 weeks lactation suckling twins				
60	2.6	65	2.86	11.5	7.2	0.50	0.32
80	3.0	65	2.86	11.5	7.2	0.48	0.30
			Ewes, replacement lambs and yearlings‖				
30	1.3	62	2.73	10.0	5.8	0.45	0.25
50	1.5	55	2.42	8.9	4.8	0.42	0.23
70	1.4	55	2.42	8.9	4.8	0.46	0.26
			Rams, replacement lambs and yearlings‖				
60	2.3	60	2.65	9.5	5.3	0.31	0.17
80	2.8	55	2.42	8.9	4.8	0.28	0.16
100	2.8	55	2.42	8.9	4.8	0.30	0.17
			Lambs, fattening#				
30	1.3	64	2.81	11.0	6.7	0.37	0.23
40	1.6	70	3.08	11.0	6.7	0.31	0.19
50	1.8	70	3.08	11.0	6.7	0.28	0.17
			*Lambs, early weaned** *				
10	0.6	73	3.21	16.0	11.5	0.40	0.27
20	1.0	73	3.21	16.0	11.5	0.36	0.24
30	1.4	73	3.21	14.0	9.5	0.36	0.24

Source: National Research Council, 1975.[22]

* To convert dry matter to an as-fed basis, divide dry matter by percentage dry matter.

† 1 kg TDN = 4.4 Mcal DE (digestible energy). DE may be converted to ME (metabolizable energy) by multiplying by 82%.

‡ DP = digestible protein.

§ Values are for ewes in moderate condition, not excessively fat or thin. For fat ewes feed at next lower weight; for thin ewes feed at next highest weight.

‖ Replacement lamb (ewe and ram) requirements start at time they are weaned.

Maximum gains expected: If lambs are held for later market, they should be fed similarly to replacement ewe lambs. Lambs capable of gaining faster than indicated need to be fed at a higher level; self-feeding permits lambs to finish most rapidly.

** 40-kg early weaned lambs fed the same as finishing lambs of equal weight.

gion have been studied. Summer ranges supplied a satisfactory nutrient level, with the possible exception of late summer. Lactating ewes gained during the entire summer, and lambs made substantial gains. On winter ranges, availability of forage is decreased, making intake lower at the same time body maintenance requirements are higher because of severe weather.[26]

Most browse plants on winter ranges meet recommended requirements for protein and carotene, but are low in energy

26. Cook, W. C., and L. E. Harris. 1968. Nutritive value of seasonal ranges. Utah Agr. Exp. Sta. Bull. 472.

and slightly deficient in P. Grasses on the other hand are high in energy, but deficient in protein, P, and carotene. When animals are required to subsist on dry grass ranges for periods longer than six months without intermittent periods of green feed, vitamin A supplements are recommended.[23]

Protein supplements such as concentrate pellets can be used as a source of both energy and protein, and they increase digestibility of range forage. They enhance nutrient intake on the range by increasing digestibility of cellulose and other carbohydrates.

Minerals are very important for sheep, especially the lactating ewe. Salt and most mineral requirements are supplied by making trace-mineralized salt available. Dicalcium phosphate and bone meal are very good sources. Iodine deficiency occurs in some areas of the Northwest, the Dakotas, Montana, Colorado, Utah, Nevada, and Idaho.[25] Iodized salt is recommended to avoid deficiency problems in these areas.

Trace mineral deficiency or excess in soil and plants may cause problems with grazing sheep.[26a] Trace minerals required include iron, copper, cobalt, manganese, zinc, iodine, selenium, and possibly others. Considerable variability exists in amounts required, tolerance levels, and levels in which toxicity symptoms occur. Phalaris staggers may occur with cobalt-deficient soils. Occurrence and extent of deficiency or toxicity involving iodine, cobalt, copper, molybdenum, zinc, and selenium are influenced by complex interrelations between the soil, plant, and animal. Differences in genetics, season and stage of maturity for plants and animals, as well as soil and fertilizer differences complicate trace mineral effects. Interactions among minerals in their metabolism, retention, and excretion may also complicate their effects. Much more information is needed on the interrelationships among minerals in sheep.

Supplementation of range ewes will usually increase production. However, in range livestock production it may not be economical to supplement animals with the intent of achieving maximum production if the increased costs are not commensurate with output of the market animal. Supplementation may be necessary to maintain reasonable condition throughout the year and to support adequate production.

The amount and kind of supplement necessary in feeding of the range flock in the winter drylot is variable and depends on the forage fed. Energy requirements in the drylot are lower than on the range because less energy is expended in obtaining feed and water. When a ration of good quality alfalfa hay is fed, supplementation is not necessary except in those areas where P content is below requirements. With lower quality forage such as grass hay, protein supplements like soybean meal or cottonseed meal increase the digestibility of forages, while grain supplements can reduce the digestibility.

Manipulation of the nutrient intake of animals in the feedlot has reached a high degree of sophistication. Least-cost computer rations which meet all nutrient requirements most economically are readily available. Management of grazing livestock for optimum production is much more difficult because the ration is not available for evaluation. However, advances in evaluating range and pasture forages provide estimates of nutrients supplied by the vegetation.[27] From these studies the range manager can apply supplementation to alter the nutrient intake to meet the requirements of the grazing animal.

✦ PERFORMANCE UNDER VARIOUS GRAZING MANAGEMENT SYSTEMS

Sheep efficiently utilize most types of forage if properly managed. Feed costs are the major expense in sheep production. Therefore, grazing of low-cost range forage, with as little supplementation as possible, is one of the most economical means

26a. Underwood, Eric J. 1977. Trace Elements in Human and Animal Nutrition, 4th ed. Academic Press, New York.

27. Bohman, V. R., L. E. Harris, G. P. Lofgreen, C. J. Kercher, and R. J. Raleigh. 1967. Techniques for range livestock nutrition research. Utah Agr. Exp. Sta. Bull. 471.

of producing lamb and wool. However, grazing must be managed to maintain desirable plants on the range and to provide for sustained yields for an indefinite future.

Large areas of spring, summer, fall, and winter ranges suitable for sheep production exist in the West. In many areas of the Northwest, slaughter lambs of desirable weight and condition can be produced off the range. Lambs that do not reach slaughter weight and condition are sold as feeders. Replacement ewe lambs are also produced in large numbers in these areas and can be grown to breeding age with a minimum of drylot feeding. A successful operation depends on management of available forage and water supply to provide feed for ewe flocks during most of the year. In some instances ewes are maintained on the range the entire year by supplementation of the forage with harvested feeds and protein. On some western ranges, snow covers the range feed supply from 60–90 days, making it necessary to keep ewes in drylot. Because of severe spring storms, shed lambing has proved to be efficient and economical in some areas.

On the arid southwestern ranges production of slaughter lambs off the range may not be possible. The rangelands are much lower in available forage, and production of feeder lambs off the range is most common. The climate is much milder; therefore, ewe flocks in many areas are on the range the year round with some supplementation. Overhead costs for harvested forages and shelter buildings are lower than in the Northwest. In all range operations, where possible, much use is made in the fall of the aftermath from harvested grain, alfalfa, and beet fields.

✣ GRAZING FOR OPTIMUM PRODUCTION

Range Management

Range management skills of a sheep producer are directly related to his success in obtaining optimum production of lamb and wool consistent with maintaining the range in good condition. Range forage should be grazed when of maximum nutritive value, but in a manner to maintain a viable forage cover with plant growth and nutrient storage for the next grazing season.

Formerly, many believed that the range was the exclusive concern of the livestock industry and that forage could be converted into economic uses only by grazing animals. Now ranchers are being subjected to ever-increasing competition from recreation, wildlife, and other uses, especially on public lands.

Multiple Use of Range

There are complementary effects from multiple use by wildlife, timber, recreation, and range livestock uses. After evaluation of studies on grazing habits of cattle and big game, it was concluded that on brush-grass ranges in Nevada the big game strongly preferred browse while cattle consumed mostly grass.[28] There are other indications that deer and cattle do not consume exactly the same browse species; 50% of the browse species consumed by deer have yet to be found in the diets of grazing cattle, and 25% of the deer diet consists of browse species only occasionally taken by cattle. Rangelands should be utilized by both grass- and browse-consuming species in order to maintain a forage habitat that would be beneficial for both deer and livestock. Removal of livestock from Nevada ranges would eventually lead to a reduction in the deer population from excessive use of browse species.

The timber industry also benefits from grazing by range livestock. Grazing may under certain conditions equalize or even exceed the logging damage by aiding tree reproduction and reducing fire hazards. Grazing livestock increased reproduction in the northwest Douglas fir forest by planting seed and decreasing competition from herbaceous plants.

28. Lesperance, A. L., and P. T. Tueller. 1969. Competitive uses of Nevada's range forage by livestock and big game. Renewable Resource Center Rept., Univ. Nevada, Reno.

Water production is complementary to grazing livestock unless grazing is improperly managed. Water production for livestock water and irrigation of livestock forage crops is also of complementary value to the livestock industry.

MANAGEMENT SYSTEMS FOR LAMB PRODUCTION

Several management systems can be used successfully for lamb production on farms in humid areas. Major alternatives are fall, winter, and spring lambing programs. Each program utilizes different types of forage.

Fall lambing is most successful in areas where alfalfa, winter wheat, barley, or rye pastures are available during the fall and winter months. These lush pastures can provide necessary nutritional requirements of ewes during late gestation and lactation. Lambs can reach market weight and condition while nursing, especially if some creep-feed is provided. The ewe flock can be pastured on inexpensive-type forages such as stubble fields and perennial grasses after the lambs are weaned and before breeding.

Winter lambing may be desirable in farm flocks where late fall and winter pasture is not available. Late December, January, and early February lambs can reach slaughter weight and condition during May and June. Relatively inexpensive pasture can satisfy the nutritional needs of ewes during most of the year. Hay, silage, or a combination with grain supplement, however, is required during late fall and winter months. The lambs should be creep-fed a combination of grain and good quality legume hay from a few weeks after birth until slaughter.

Spring lambing may be most profitable under other conditions. Ewes lambing during February, March, and early April usually have the highest lambing percentages. Lambs should reach market weight and condition during July and early August. In areas where snow cover is not prolonged, ewes may receive much of their nutritional needs from pastures and grain or corn stubble. Supplemental feeding of harvested forage and grain may be necessary only during the last four to six weeks of gestation and during lactation and/or during periods of prolonged snow cover. The lambs should be weaned at about 60 days of age and, to reduce parasitism, should not be pastured with their dams. A number of options are available such as weaning before the pasture season, separating ewes and lambs during the day, or either grazing the lambs on separate pastures or feeding them in drylot. Relatively small high-quality pastures are required for lambs under this system and creep-feed should be provided. However, the ewes may be grazed on several types of pastures.

Confinement systems may offer advantages such as effective control of internal parasites, reduction in predator losses, reduced feed requirements, and maximum use of forage from highly productive and valuable land. Confinement is most effective when associated with accelerated lambing programs (three lamb crops every two years) so that maximum utilization of facilities can be obtained. With semiconfinement, lambs are weaned early and finished either in drylot or on slotted floors. The ewes are on pasture during a portion of the year.

With total confinement the flock is kept in drylot or on slotted floors during the entire year. This program is based on automated feeding systems, maximum use of harvested feeds of highly productive crops, and accelerated lambing.

✤ CONTROL OF INTERNAL
PARASITISM ON PASTURE AND RANGE

Control of internal parasitism in sheep requires a combination of good management and strategic treatment with broad-spectrum anthelmintics.[24] Since adult sheep contaminate pastures with fecal eggs which soon become infective larvae, the most effective method of control of internal parasitism of lambs in humid areas or on irrigated pastures is early weaning and grazing of lambs on clean, rested pasture.

It is economically impossible to produce

parasite-free sheep on pasture, but management can be used to hold helminth contamination at a low level. The most successful management and anthelmintic programs will vary among regions. Extension specialists should be consulted regarding effective control procedures.

❧ CO-GRAZING OF SHEEP WITH CATTLE AND/OR GOATS

Several investigators have obtained increased livestock gains per ha by grazing sheep and cattle or sheep, cattle, and goats together. Greater gains and carrying capacity by grazing sheep and cattle together on humid pastures than by grazing the same species separately were obtained in Louisiana.[29] Similar results were obtained in Ohio and Washington.[30,31] Advantages have been demonstrated for grazing cattle, sheep, and goats together on Texas ranges consisting of grass, forbs, and browse.[32,33] Cattle preferred the grass, sheep utilized the forbs or weeds, and goats utilized the browse. Investigators in other parts of the world also obtained increased productivity of pastures by grazing cattle and sheep together.[34,35,36] Results of co-grazing sheep and cattle over a 4-year period on an orchardgrass sward at Beltsville, Md., have been evaluated.[37] When available forage was fixed at fairly high levels by

experimental design and only one species of plant was available for grazing, no effect of co-grazing per se was apparent.

Lambs grazed separately and with steers responded to an increase in pasture height up to 120 mm. Ewes lost weight about six weeks after lambing when weight was below 12 mm but later responded to pasture height. Lambs generally grew faster with mixed than with separate grazing but steer growth was the same.[38]

Maximum use of cereal stubbles may be attained by grazing sheep and cattle either alternatively or together. Sheep will use the short green feed better while cattle will consume more of the remaining cereal residue.[39]

The experimental results obtained by co-grazing mixed pastures in various sections of the U.S. and Australia indicate it may be one means of increasing livestock gains per unit of pasture or range.

38. Hamilton, D., I. D. Ada, and J. J. L. Maden. 1976. Liveweight changes of steers, ewes and lambs in relation to height of green annual pasture. *Aust. J. Exp. Agr. Anim. Husb.* 16:800–807.

39. Mulholland, J. G., J. B. Coombe, and W. R. McManus. 1977. Diet selection and intake by sheep and cattle grazing together on stubbles of wheat, oats or barley. *Aust. J. Exp. Agr. Anim. Husb.* 17:224–29.

❧ QUESTIONS

1. How important are sheep in the utilization of forage resources of the U.S.?
2. What advantages or disadvantages do sheep have relative to cattle in the efficiency of forage utilization?
3. How can forage be best utilized in intensive systems of sheep production?
4. What types of forage are utilized by sheep?
5. Discuss the major factors affecting forage consumption by sheep.
6. What are the advantages and disadvantages of pelleting forages for use by sheep?
7. List the major limitations to the efficient utilization of range forages by sheep.
8. How do sheep perform in a mixed livestock enterprise?
9. What are the critical conditions requiring supplementation of forages for sheep?
10. How does internal parasitism interfere with utilization of sheep pastures and how can this interference be minimized?

29. Snell, M. G. 1935. Pasture gains of cattle, cattle and sheep, and sheep, pp. 142–48. Proc. Amer. Soc. Anim. Prod., 1934.

30. Van Keuren, R. W., and C. F. Parker. 1967. Better pasture utilization—Grazing cattle and sheep together. *Ohio Rept.* 57:12–13.

31. Heinemann, W. W. 1969. Productivity of irrigated pastures under combination and single species grazing. Wash. Agr. Exp. Sta. Bull. 717.

32. Merrill, L. B., and J. E. Miller. 1961. Economic analysis of yearlong grazing rate studies on Substation 14 near Sonora. Tex. Agr. Exp. Sta. MP 484.

33. Merrill, L. B., P. O. Reardon, and C. L. Leinweber. 1966. Cattle, sheep, goats—Mix 'em for higher gains. *Tex. Agr. Progr.* 12:4, 13–14.

34. Campbell, K. O., and W. F. Musgrave. 1958. Economic aspects of the association of beef cattle with sheep production in southeastern Australia. Univ. Sydney Dept. Econ. Bull. 3.

35. Clark, K. W. 1963. Stocking rate and sheep-cattle interactions. *Wool Technol. Sheep Breeding* 10:27–32.

36. Hamilton, D., and J. G. Bath. 1970. Performance of sheep and cattle grazed separately and together. *Australian J. Exp. Agr. Anim. Husb.* 10:19–26.

37. Reynolds, P. J., J. Bond, G. E. Carlson, C. Jackson, R. H. Hart, and I. L. Lindahl. 1971. Co-grazing sheep and cattle on orchardgrass sward. *Agron. J.* 63:533–36.

J A M E S   R .   F O S T E R / *Purdue University*

64

FORAGES FOR SWINE AND POULTRY

SWINE

DRAMATIC CHANGES have taken place in swine production during the 1960s. The total number of producers has declined, while production units have increased substantially in size. As volume has increased, the trend has been to substitute capital for labor. This has resulted in more confinement rearing of hogs with less use of pasture and increased labor efficiency.

Many swine producers report that the move from pasture to confinement has failed to improve performance of their hogs, but this shift has permitted an increase in volume of production with the same or less labor. Pigs in Nebraska farrowed on pasture in the fall and reared in individual lots during the winter had a lower death loss and faster gains than pigs raised in a heated barn.[1]

Prior to about 1950, pasture was considered essential in meeting the nutritional requirements of swine, particularly in regard to reproductive performance. Research before 1950 clearly demonstrated that rations containing 5% or less of alfalfa meal were nutritionally inadequate for gestation and lactation under drylot conditions.[2-6] However, the control rations in most of these experiments consisted of corn, expeller processed soybean meal, salt, limestone, and 5% alfalfa meal.

Following 1950 the use of synthetic vitamins became nearly universal in swine ration formulation. In addition, research identified the need for certain trace minerals and other nutrients, resulting in a better understanding of the complete nutritional needs of the sow.

Most research since 1960 has shown little if any improvement in reproductive performance with levels of up to 10% of dehydrated alfalfa meal or a level of 18% of sun-cured alfalfa in gestation rations.[7,8]

No longer is it a question as to whether pasture or other forages are essential to meet the nutritive needs of swine. Instead, the question is how to meet these requirements most economically. In many swine operations, forages can help to do this.

1. Sumption, L. J. 1959. Pigs should be alone and cool—Pasture vs. confinement, a winter test. Univ. Nebr. Swine Progr. Rept. 371.
2. Ross, O. Burr, Paul H. Phillips, and G. Bohstedt. 1942. The effect of diet on brood sow performance. *J. Anim. Sci.* 1:353.
3. Ross, O. Burr, Paul H. Phillips, G. Bohstedt, and Tony J. Cunha. 1944. Congenital malformations, syndactylism, talipes, and paralysis agitans of nutritional origin in swine. *J. Anim. Sci.* 3:406–14.
4. Cunha, T. J., O. Burr Ross, Paul H. Phillips, and G. Bohstedt. 1944. Further observations on the dietary insufficiency of a corn-soybean ration for reproduction of swine. *J. Anim. Sci.* 3:415–21.
5. Fairbanks, B. W., J. L. Krider, and W. E. Carroll. 1945. Effect of diet on gestation-lactation performance of sows. *J. Anim. Sci.* 4:410–19.
6. Krider, J. L., B. W. Fairbanks, R. F. Van Poucke, D. E. Becker, and W. E. Carroll. 1946. Sardine condensed fish solubles and rye pasture for sows during gestation and lactation. *J. Anim. Sci.* 5:256–63.
7. Seerley, R. W., and R. C. Wahlstrom. 1965. Dehydrated alfalfa meal in rations for confined brood sows. *J. Anim. Sci.* 24:448–53.
8. Teague, H. S., and A. P. Grifo, Jr. 1965. Vitamin intake and the nutritive contribution of alfalfa to successive generation performance of swine. *J. Anim. Sci.* 24:775–81.

⚘ JAMES R. FOSTER is Professor of Animal Sciences, Purdue University. He holds the Ph.D. degree from Iowa State University. He has served as Purdue Extension Swine Specialist since 1960.

❧ KINDS OF FORAGES

The forages most used in swine production are legume pasture and dehydrated alfalfa meal. Additional possibilities include other forms of pasture (rape, winter rye, and certain grasses such as smooth bromegrass) and silages (corn or grass-legume).

❧ PASTURES

The commonest pasture for swine in most parts of the U.S. is alfalfa, ladino clover, or a combination of the two. Analyses of these two pastures indicate slightly higher dry matter, protein, and energy for alfalfa. Both are good sources of calcium and most of the required vitamins except vitamin D (which generally is not a problem when swine are exposed to sunlight) and vitamin B_{12}. Ladino clover generally contains less fiber than alfalfa. Alfalfa and ladino clover pastures have been compared in Indiana and Kentucky experiments.[9-12] These trials failed to show a consistent advantage of either alfalfa or ladino clover over the other, and the average rate of gain and feed efficiency over all trials was about the same for these legume pastures.

Legume pastures used to a lesser extent than alfalfa and ladino clover include red clover, lespedeza, birdsfoot trefoil, and sweetclover.

RAPE

Rape is neither a legume nor a grass; it is an annual, usually seeded in the spring in the Corn Belt and in the fall in the southern states. Frequently it is seeded alone; however, a mixture of oats and rape allows somewhat earlier grazing than rape alone. As the oat pasture passes its peak, the rape continues to grow and furnish high-quality pasture even into the cool fall months. Rape can be seeded in an emergency and within about 8–10 weeks will provide a pasture for hogs which compares favorably with alfalfa. Its nutritional value is nearly equal to the legumes. 'Dwarf Essex' rape is the most commonly used cultivar. (See Fig. 64.1.)

RYE

'Balbo' is the cultivar of winter rye most used for swine pasture. It has very rapid growth in fall and early spring and is adapted to many regions. Experiments in Kentucky evaluated Balbo rye as a winter pasture for bred sows.[13-16] In these trials sows on rye pasture during gestation were fed levels of 0.91, 1.36, or 1.81 kg of supplemental feed daily compared to those fed in drylot receiving 2.7 kg feed/sow/day. Reproductive performance of sows fed on winter rye pasture was essentially equal to those fed in drylot. The advantage of the rye pasture was in lower feed requirements of the sows. The rye pasture had a carrying capacity of approximately 12 sows/ha. In one year Kentucky workers found that 0.91 kg of supplemental feed per sow daily was adequate, whereas in another year it appeared that more than 1.33 kg of feed were needed for sows on rye pasture. Feed costs per live pig farrowed were reduced about 30% when sows were on rye pasture. These costs did not include a charge for the pasture.

The size of the sow, her condition, the ambient temperatures, and the quality of the rye pasture will determine the amount

9. Vestal, C. M., and G. O. Mott. 1948. Alfalfa and ladino clover pasture for swine production. Purdue Univ. AH Mimeo. 35.

10. Vestal, C. M., and G. O. Mott. 1949. A comparison of alfalfa and ladino clover as pasture for hogs. Purdue Univ. AH Mimeo. 43.

11. Vestal, C. M., and G. O. Mott. 1951. Alfalfa and ladino clover as pasture for growing and fattening hogs. Purdue Univ. AH Mimeo. 66.

12. Barnhart, C. E. 1952. Protein and vitamin supplements for growing-fattening pigs on ladino clover and on alfalfa. *J. Anim. Sci.* 11:233–37.

13. Barnhart, C. E., and T. W. Cathey. 1956. Winter pasture versus a drylot for bred sows. Ky. Agr. Exp. Sta. Livestock Field Day Rept.

14. Barnhart, C. E., and T. W. Cathey. 1957. Winter pasture versus a drylot for bred sows. Ky. Agr. Exp. Sta. Livestock Field Day Rept.

15. Barnhart, C. E., M. D. Whiteker, and C. W. Nichols. 1958. Winter pasture versus a drylot for bred gilts. Ky. Agr. Exp. Sta. Livestock Field Day Rept.

16. Selke, Marvin, C. E. Barnhart, R. Ayer, and C. H. Nichols. 1960. Balbo rye pasture and legume silage versus a drylot for bred sows. Ky. Agr. Exp. Sta. Livestock Field Day Rept.

Fig. 64.1. *Rape continues to . . . furnish high-quality pasture . . . into the . . . fall.* Rape is a good annual pasture for hogs. It may be seeded alone or in a mixture with oats. The oats will provide early pasture and the rape will furnish high-quality pasture after the oats are gone.

of concentrate needed for gestating sows to ensure good reproductive performance. This amount may vary from slightly less than 1 to nearly 2 kg/sow/day of a 15% protein ration. Gilts will require slightly more feed than older sows because they are still growing. Cold weather will increase the total feed requirements slightly.

OTHER GRASSES

Smooth bromegrass, alfalfa, and a mixture have been compared.[17] Growing-finishing pigs self-fed to 90 kg required 5.5% more concentrate feed per unit of gain on smooth bromegrass than on alfalfa. Pigs on smooth bromegrass consumed 33% more protein supplement and 13% more minerals per unit of gain compared to those on alfalfa. Pigs gained slightly faster on alfalfa. A pasture mixture of smooth bromegrass and alfalfa was fully equal to the alfalfa pasture for self-fed pigs.

17. Krider, J. L., and S. W. Terrill. 1950. Comparisons of pastures and supplements for growing-fattening pigs. *J. Anim. Sci.* 9:289–99.

ALFALFA MEAL

Probably the most widely used form of forage for swine is alfalfa meal. This product is considered to be a good source of most vitamins and possible unidentified factors. However, due to the relatively high fiber and low energy content of alfalfa meal, rate of gain and feed efficiency generally decline as the level of alfalfa meal in growing-finishing swine rations increases. The commonest form used in swine rations is dehydrated alfalfa meal. Also, in some instances alfalfa hay has been ground and fed as alfalfa meal. Research in Nevada has demonstrated that high levels of alfalfa meal could be used in growing-finishing swine rations.[18,19] Levels of 0, 10, 20, 30, 50, and 60% of the ration were used. Data indicate that hogs utilize up to 50% alfalfa in their ration, although gain and feed efficiency are depressed somewhat as the percent of alfalfa in the ration is increased. Pelleting of the 50% alfalfa ration improved daily gain by 13% and feed efficiency by 25% compared to the ground mixture.

Dehydrated alfalfa meal at levels of 10 and 20% in protein-deficient rations has a very limited ability to provide supplementary protein and improve performance.[20] Most research indicates that levels of dehydrated alfalfa meal above 15% of the ration reduce rate of gain and feed efficiency. Most of this growth depression is due to a lowered energy content in the ration and reduced feed intake by the pig.[21]

California researchers have determined the value of alfalfa meal as a source of energy for swine at three levels of meal (5, 20, and 40%), three stages of maturity

18. Bohman, V. R., J. F. Kidwell, and J. A. McCormick. 1953. High levels of alfalfa in the rations of growing-fattening swine. *J. Anim. Sci.* 12:876–88.
19. Bohman, Verle R., James E. Hunter, and John McCormick. 1955. The effect of graded levels of alfalfa and Aureomycin upon growing-fattening swine. *J. Anim. Sci.* 14:499–506.
20. Becker, D. E., L. J. Hanson, A. H. Jensen, S. W. Terrill, and H. W. Norton. 1956. Dehydrated alfalfa meal as a dietary ingredient for swine. *J. Anim. Sci.* 15:820–29.
21. Hanson, L. J., D. E. Becker, S. W. Terrill, A. H. Jensen, and H. W. Norton. 1956. The inhibitory effect of dehydrated alfalfa meal in the diet of swine. *J. Anim. Sci.* 15:830–39.

(16% bud, 3% bloom, and 34% bloom), and three methods of preparation (sun-cured, dehydrated, and dehydrated reground).[22] Rate of gain was lower on rations containing sun-cured meal compared to others even though feed consumption was not affected by method of preparation. Stage of maturity had no effect. Poor utilization of alfalfa as a source of energy is indicated by the total digestible nutrient (TDN) content of the hays averaging only about 55% of the TDN content of barley. The average replacement value of 1 kg of alfalfa meal was calculated to be 0.28 kg of concentrate.

SILAGE

Indiana, Iowa, Illinois, and Minnesota stations have conducted research demonstrating that good corn or grass-legume silage, properly supplemented, may constitute the major part of the ration for pregnant sows and gilts.[23-27] Advantages of feeding silage to sows include: (1) the cost of pigs at farrowing may be reduced, (2) sows may be prevented from getting too fat, (3) silage is often available on farms where beef and dairy cattle are kept, and (4) silage is nutritionally the next best feed to summer pasture.

The kinds of silages that have been used successfully in swine operations include corn, legume (alfalfa), or grass-legume (alfalfa–smooth bromegrass).

CORN SILAGE. Corn silage is an excellent source of many of the vitamins needed by swine; but it is deficient in protein, energy, and certain minerals. Generally, corn silage is full-fed once or twice daily and supplemented with 1–1.5 kg of concentrate. A wide variation in silage intake has been reported. In many trials sows have consumed 4.5–6.5 kg daily of a good quality silage. However, in an Illinois experiment the sows consumed only 1.5 kg of silage per day.[26] In this case additional concentrate was needed. Purdue studies have shown that feed costs during gestation on a per pig weaned basis were reduced 28% by feeding corn silage. For best results corn silage should be made when the ears are formed but when the plant is still green and not frosted. Silage made from corn nearing maturity is less palatable. Fine-chopped silage is best for sow feed to avoid excesssive waste.

GRASS-LEGUME SILAGE. The most common grass-legume silage is made with either alfalfa or a combination of alfalfa and smooth bromegrass. Nutritionally, grass-legume silage differs from corn silage in that it has more protein and Ca but less energy. Shelled corn is sometimes added at the time of ensiling, which will increase the energy value of the silage. Grass-legume silage has been fed to feeder pigs, but consumption of the silage was very low when a concentrate was self-fed.[27] Reducing the concentrate intake by 25% resulted in a 200% increase in silage consumption, but it was insufficient to overcome the reduction in weight gain from the concentrate restriction. In a Kentucky experiment pregnant sows self-fed alfalfa silage consumed 6.33 kg/day with 1.33 kg of a concentrate.[16] Reproductive performance was about equal to that of sows fed on winter rye pasture and somewhat better than for sows fed 2.67 kg of feed daily in drylot.

LOW-MOISTURE SILAGE. Low-moisture silage may be defined as a legume, grass, or cereal cut near its peak nutritive stage of maturity, wilted to 40–60% moisture, finely chopped, and ensiled. It is sometimes referred to as haylage. Nutritionally, energy is the limiting factor in the use of low-moisture silage for swine.

22. Heitman, Hubert, Jr., and J. H. Meyer. 1959. Alfalfa meal as a source of energy by swine. *J. Anim. Sci.* 18:796–804.

23. Conrad, J. H., and W. M. Beeson. 1954. Grass silage and corn silage as a feed for brood sows. Purdue Univ. AH Mimeo. 133.

24. Catron, Damon, Gordon Ashton, Vaughn Speer, C. C. Culbertson, and E. L. Quaife. 1955. Silage for sows. Iowa State Coll. AH Mimeo. 680.

25. Johnson, C. W., V. C. Speer, G. C. Ashton, C. C. Culbertson, and D. V. Catron. 1957. Supplementary plane of nutrition for sows fed corn silage. *J. Anim. Sci.* 16:600–606.

26. Becker, D. E., S. W. Terrill, and A. H. Jensen. 1959. Silage for sows during gestation. Univ. Ill. Mimeo. AS 507.

27. Bowden, D. M., and M. F. Clarke. 1963. Grass-legume forage fed fresh and as silage for market hogs. *J. Anim. Sci.* 22:934–39.

TABLE 64.1 ❧ Daily nutrient requirements of breeding swine

Nutrient	Bred		Lactating	
	Gilts	Sows	Gilts	Sows
Crude protein (g)	280	280	750	825
Digestible energy (kcal)	6,600	6,600	16,500	18,150
Calcium (g)	15	15	30	33
Phosphorus (g)	10	10	20	22
NaCl (salt) (g)	10	10	25	27.5
Vitamin A (IU)	8,200	8,200	16,500	18,150
Vitamin D (IU)	550	550	1,100	1,210
Riboflavin (mg)	8.2	8.2	16.5	18.2
Niacin (mg)	44	44	88	96.8
Pantothenic acid (mg)	33	33	66	72.6
Vitamin B_{12} (μg)	27.6	27.6	55	60.5

Source: NRC, 1968.[29]

Good reproductive performance has been reported using alfalfa haylage mixed with ground corn at the rate of 4 parts of haylage to 1 part of corn and stored in an airtight silo.[28] The haylage-corn mixture analyzed 45.5% moisture, 19.5% crude protein, and 20.25% fiber. This mixture was full-fed to both gilts and sows beginning about two weeks prior to the start of breeding and continuing through gestation. Average daily consumption of the haylage-corn mixture was 3.8 kg for gilts and 5.3 kg for sows. Sows made satisfactory gains during the middle third of gestation when fed only the haylage-corn mixture. Gilts required some supplemental feed throughout gestation to produce satisfactory gains. Digestion trials with sows indicated the crude protein of the haylage-corn mixture to be 55–60% digestible.

❧ MANAGEMENT SYSTEMS UTILIZING PASTURE

The nutrient requirements for breeding swine have been summarized by the National Research Council. These requirements are presented in Table 64.1.[29]

Fairly reliable information is available regarding the nutrient content of ingredients, and most of the needed vitamins are available in synthetic form. Thus it is possible today to formulate a nutritionally adequate ration without depending on forages as a source of nutrients. Table 64.2 shows the nutritive content of forages commonly used for swine.[30,31] However, these values vary considerably among samples, and the values listed represent averages from a number of analyses.

GROWING-FINISHING PERIOD

The digestive system of the growing-finishing pig is not well adapted for utilization of forages. Research to evaluate the use of pasture for growing-finishing hogs is summarized in Table 64.3.[32-36] Although the difference in feed required per unit of gain between drylot and pasture varies widely among experiments, these results suggest a slight feed saving by legume pasture. Assuming an average difference of 0.1 kg of feed per kilogram of gain in favor

28. Hoagland, J. M., H. W. Jones, and R. A. Pickett. 1963. Haylage as a gestation ration for sows and gilts. Purdue Univ. Res. Progr. Rept. 75.

29. National Research Council. 1968. Nutrient Requirements of Swine. Publ. 1599, Natl. Acad. Sci., Washington, D.C.

30. Crampton, E. W., and L. E. Harris. 1969. Applied Animal Nutrition, 2nd ed. W. H. Freeman, San Francisco.

31. Morrison, F. B. 1956. Feeds and Feeding, 22nd ed. Morrison, Ithaca, N.Y.

32. Hudman, D. B., and E. R. Peo, Jr. 1957. Protein levels for growing-finishing swine on pasture and in drylot. Nebr. Swine Progr. Rept. 348.

33. Terrill, S. W., A. H. Jensen, and D. E. Becker. 1958. Pasture versus drylot for growing-finishing swine. Ill. Coop. Ext. Serv. AS 477.

34. Wallace, H. D., and G. E. Combs. 1958. Pasture vs. concrete for growing-finishing swine. Fla. Agr. Exp. Sta. Mimeo. Ser. 59-3.

35. Christmas, R. B., G. E. McCabe, H. D. Wallace, G. E. Combs, and A. Z. Palmer. 1959. Millet pasture vs. concrete for growing-finishing swine. Fla. Agr. Exp. Sta. Mimeo. Ser. 59-6.

36. Wallace, H. D., G. E. McCabe, A. Z. Palmer, M. Koger, J. W. Carpenter, and G. E. Combs. 1960. Pasture vs. concrete for growing-finishing swine with special emphasis on the carcasses produced. Fla. Agr. Exp. Sta. Mimeo. Ser. 60-11.

TABLE 64.2 ✤ Nutrient composition of forages

| Nutrient | Pasture | | | | Silage | | | Alfalfa meal (dehy) |
	Alfalfa	Ladino clover	Rape	Rye	Corn	Grass-legume	Low moisture	
Dry matter (%)	24	20	16	17	26	28	55	93
Digestible energy (kcal/kg)	660	525	525	575	880	750	975	1,400
Crude protein (%)	6.0	5.1	3.0	5.0	2.1	5.0	6.3	17.0
Ether extract (%)	0.9	1.0	0.6	0.8	0.8	1.1	1.4	3.0
Crude fiber (%)	5.4	2.9	2.8	2.9	6.4	8.2	11.4	25.0
Nitrogen-free extract (%)	10.0	8.9	8.2	5.6	14.7	11.2	13.9	38.9
Calcium (%)	0.5	0.3	0.2	0.1	0.05	0.04	0.5	1.3
Phosphorus (%)	0.1	0.07	0.06	0.1	0.05	0.09	0.12	0.23
Sodium (%)	0.04	0.02	0.01	*	0.01	0.04	0.05	0.09
Chlorine (%)	0.11	*	*	*	0.05	0.11	0.15	0.46
Copper (mg/kg)	*	*	0.6	1.1	0.6	2.9	3.4	9.9
Iron (mg/kg)	0.01	0.01	0.003	*	0.003	0.01	0.01	0.05
Zinc (mg/kg)	3.6	*	*	*	2.5	*	*	16
Vitamin A equivalent (IU/g)	104	118	*	155	7	45	31	268
Vitamin D (IU/g)	0	0	0	0	0.1	0	0.2	*
Riboflavin (mg/kg)	5.0	4.0	*	*	*	*	*	12.3
Niacin (mg/kg)	8.2	*	*	*	5.7	5.7	6.0	46
Pantothenic acid (mg/kg)	4.0	*	*	*	*	*	*	30

Sources: Based on averages of several references. Adapted mainly from tables in Crampton and Harris, 1969;[30] Morrison, 1956.[31]
* Data not available.

of pasture, the feed saving value of 1 ha of good legume pasture can be calculated as follows: 50 pigs per ha gaining 80 kg = 4000 kg of pork, 4000 kg of pork × 0.10 = 400 kg feed saved per ha, and 400 kg feed × 6.2¢ per kg = $24.80 per ha. There appears to be no advantage in rate of gain for pigs fed on pasture.

GESTATION

The digestive system of swine eight months of age or older is sufficiently developed to permit utilization of relatively large amounts of forage. In addition, the swine producer is not striving for maximum gains during gestation, hence the en-

TABLE 64.3 ✤ Effect of pasture on performance of growing-finishing swine

Experiment station	Comparison	Number of pigs	Daily gain (kg)	Daily feed (kg)	Kg feed per kg gain
Nebraska[32]	drylot	80	0.73	2.38	3.28
	alfalfa	80	0.65	1.97	3.02
Illinois[33]	drylot	224	0.64	1.79	3.04
	alfalfa–ladino clover	224	0.63	1.66	2.99
Florida[34]	concrete	17	0.76	2.71	3.56
	legume (full-fed)	16	0.79	2.74	3.45
	legume (limit-fed)	17	0.63	2.13	3.38
Florida[35]	concrete	12	0.73	2.47	3.39
	millet (full-fed)	15	0.70	2.34	3.36
	millet (limit-fed)	15	0.54	1.83	3.42
Florida[36]	concrete	40	0.64	2.13	3.33
	oats-wheat (winter)	40	0.68	2.27	3.34

ergy requirements are somewhat less for the pregnant sow than for the growing-finishing hog. Research has demonstrated that considerable feed can be saved during the gestation period by the use of good pasture.[37,38] The amount of feed saved will depend primarily on the quality of pasture used. For example, Table 64.4 illustrates that sows on good quality legume pasture can meet more than half their nutrient requirements from pasture alone (Fig. 64.2).

The nutrients slightly deficient when good pasture is used include energy, P, salt, and vitamin B_{12}; protein may be borderline. The requirements for these nutrients can be met by feeding about 1 kg of corn and 150 g of a protein supplement per sow per day. Most commercial protein supplements fed at this level will contain adequate amounts of minerals and vitamin B_{12} to meet these needs.

Figuring 24 sows for each ha and a daily rental charge for pasture of 60¢/ha, the daily feed costs for each sow would be about 2.5¢ for pasture and 6.5¢ for supplemental feed. This total daily feed cost of 9¢/sow compares with a daily feed cost of 12–15¢ for a sow in drylot.

LACTATION

The trend toward confinement of swine began mainly with central farrowing facilities. This change has lessened the use of pasture for the lactation period. South Carolina workers have reported a recent four-year study where different forages were compared to a confinement system on gestation-lactation performance of swine from breeding to weaning.[39] The pastures studied included oats, red clover–orchardgrass, ladino clover–orchardgrass, rape, and millet. The litter and individual pig weights at birth were similar for all treat-

37. Barnhart, C. E., and T. W. Cathey. 1957. Legume pasture for bred sows. Ky. Agr. Exp. Sta. Livestock Field Day Rept.
38. Eyles, Dudley E. 1959. Feeding and management of pregnant sows on pasture. Anim. Prod. 1:41–50.
39. Handlin, D. L., J. W. Nickles, G. R. Craddock, and W. E. Johnson. 1972. Forages for gestation and lactation periods. J. Anim. Sci. 34:348–49. (Abstr.)

FIG. 64.2. *Amount of feed saved will depend . . . quality of pasture used.* High-quality legume pasture can be used to meet more than half the nutrient requirements for gestating sows. Good pasture can accommodate up to 24 sows/ha. *Purdue University photo.*

ments. However, pigs produced in the confinement system consumed significantly less creep-feed and were lighter in weight at weaning time. More forage was produced for grazing in the red clover–orchardgrass treatment than for the other forages in this experiment.

✷ GUIDELINES FOR SUPPLEMENTATION OF PASTURE

The general recommendations for supplementing swine on pasture are outlined in Table 64.5. The amount of supplemental feed will depend on the quality of

TABLE 64.4 ✷ Percent of sow nutritional requirement obtained from high-quality alfalfa–ladino clover pasture

Nutrient	Daily requirement[20]	Daily intake*	Percent of requirement
Protein (g)	280	385	138
Digestible energy (kcal)	6,600	4,200	64
Calcium (g)	15	28	187
Phosphorus (g)	10	5.6	56
NaCl (salt) (g)	10	4.2	42
Vitamin A (IU)	8,200	777,000	9,475
Vitamin D (IU)	550	†	†
Riboflavin (mg)	8.2	31.5	384
Niacin (mg)	44	57.4	130
Pantothenic acid (mg)	33	28	85
Vitamin B_{12} (μg)	27.6	0	0

* Based on daily pasture consumption of 7 kg.
† Sows exposed to sunlight will have enough Vitamin D produced by irradiation of the sun on the skin to meet this requirement.

TABLE 64.5 ❧ Suggested feeding program for swine on pasture

Life cycle stage	Number per ha	Feed per day (kg)	Protein level in concentrate (%)
Gestation	24	1	13
Lactation (litters)	12	4–5	13
Growing	75	full feed	15
Finishing	50	full feed	12

the pasture as well as the stage of the life cycle of the hog. The values given in Table 64.5 are for high-quality legume pasture.

POULTRY

❧ CHICKENS

In the past most broilers and layers were maintained on green pasture. With that production system chickens consumed a large supply of xanthophylls, the yellow and red pigments found in grasses and clovers. The xanthophylls imparted a bright yellow color to the skin, shanks, and beaks of broilers and to the yolks of eggs.

Production of broilers and eggs has become a highly intensified industry. As a result it is no longer practical for chickens to roam the range. They are largely confined in houses under controlled environmental conditions and fed an all-mash diet. Many consumers still associate the yellow color of broilers with healthy chickens. Also, there is a demand for orange-pigmented yolks for use in egg noodles, yellow cake mixes, and other products produced by food processors.

The chief forage fed to poultry is alfalfa in the form of dehydrated alfalfa meal, used mainly as a source of pigment for producing yellow color in the skin and shanks of broilers and in egg yolks.[40] Since alfalfa meal (the most plentiful source of xanthophylls among the common poultry feedstuffs) is relatively low in energy, poultrymen have limited the amount in poul-

40. Scott, Milton L., Malden C. Nesheim, and Robert J. Young. 1969. Nutrition of the Chicken, pp. 361–62. M. L. Scott & Assoc., Ithaca.

try feeds to about 2.5–5%, which is sufficient to increase pigmentation. However, levels above 5% significantly increased the feed required per unit of gain in broilers or per dozen eggs produced by laying hens. The most common alfalfa meal used in poultry rations is the 17% dehydrated alfalfa meal containing at least 17% crude protein and not more than 27% crude fiber. Other products include alfalfa leaf meal, containing at least 20% crude protein and not more than 18% crude fiber, and sun-cured alfalfa meal with an average analysis of 14% crude protein and 28% crude fiber.

❧ GEESE

Geese are the best of all domestic poultry foragers. Although geese can go on pasture as early as the first week, a good share of their feed can be forage after they are five to six weeks old. Geese are very selective and tend to pick out the palatable forages. They will reject alfalfa and tough grasses and select the more succulent clovers and grasses. A ha of pasture will support 50–100 birds, depending on the size of the geese and the quality of the pasture.[41]

41. USDA. 1972. Raising geese. Farmers' Bull. 2251.

❧ QUESTIONS

1. Compare alfalfa and ladino clover pasture for use in swine production.
2. What factors should be considered in supplementing pasture with grain for gestating sows?
3. What are the advantages of feeding silage to sows?
4. Compare the nutritional value of corn silage with grass-legume silage.
5. Outline a year-round pasture program for brood sows.
6. Explain why sows apparently benefit from pasture more than growing-finishing swine.
7. Explain how the feed-saving value of a ha of pasture can be calculated for growing-finishing swine.
8. Discuss the reasons for using alfalfa meal in poultry rations.

JOE L. EVANS / *Rutgers University*

65

FORAGES FOR HORSES

❧

Dᴿᴬꜰᴛ ʜᴏʀꜱᴇꜱ, mules, and donkeys make up only a few percentage units of the U.S. horse population, which is mostly light horses.[1] Many of these light horses are serving as family pets and for family recreational activity while others are "work" horses on cattle ranches, in horse shows, and in horse racing. Many books on horses have been written and several are referenced. [1-3] (See Fig. 65.1.)

Over the years these herbivorous mammals have consumed large quantities of lower quality roughages and, when available, higher quality forages. About 60% of the space in the digestive tract of the horse is in the cecum and large intestine; however, this area is smaller in total capacity but equal in relative size to the ruminant's stomach. Unlike the rumen in ruminants, the cecum and large intestine in horses are located at the posterior end of the digestive tract, and many of the products of fermentation may be voided in

the feces and not absorbed to benefit the animal. Many questions are unanswered concerning the contribution of the lower tract to the nutrition of the horse. With these and other limitations in mind, this chapter deals with voluntary intake, digestibility, nutrient requirements, and maximum forage diets in horses.

❧ VOLUNTARY INTAKE

Limited data from controlled experiments with horses are available concerning the voluntary intake of dry matter in feedstuffs and of water. Morrison suggested that horses and mules would consume 60–108 $g/W^{0.75}$ (W = body weight, kg) of dry diet per day composed of varying proportions of forage and grain.[4] Standardbred geldings consumed 70–110 $g/W^{0.75}$ of forage and forage plus grain diets.[5] The voluntary intake ranged from 65 to 95 $g/W^{0.75}$

❧ JOE L. EVANS is Professor of Nutrition, Rutgers University. He holds the M.S. degree from the University of Kentucky and the Ph.D. from the University of Florida. His research has dealt with nutritive evaluation of forages, mineral utilization and metabolism, digestibility and utilization of different N sources or protein, and influence of diet composition on intestinal environment and nutritional state.

1. Simpson, George G. 1961. Horses: The Story of the Horse Family in the Modern World and through Sixty Million Years of History. American Museum of Natural History and Doubleday, New York.
2. Crowell, Pers. 1951. Cavalcade of American Horses. Bonanza Books, New York.
3. Hughes, H. D., and Maurice E. Heath. 1962. Hays and pastures for horses. *In* Forages, 2nd ed., pp. 671–83. Iowa State Univ. Press, Ames.
4. Morrison, F. B. 1959. Feeds and Feeding, 22nd ed. Morrison, Ithaca, N.Y.
5. Fonnesbeck, P. V. 1968. Consumption and excretion of water by horses receiving all hay and hay-grain diets. *J. Anim. Sci.* 27:1350–56.

FIG. 65.1. *U.S. horse population . . . mostly light horses.* In spite of the steady reduction in draft horses, interest in light horses and ponies has never been greater. A 10-kg Shetland foal and a 1000-kg Clydesdale stallion eye each other with evident curiosity. This picture has been reproduced countless times throughout much of the world. *Iowa State University photo.*

in smaller ponies that consumed forage.[6] Other ponies consumed 75 g/$W^{0.75}$ of 17% protein alfalfa in long form, 17% more in wafers, and 24% more in pellets.[7] Lower intakes can be maintained by hand-feeding and by diluting the diet with fiber from straw or strawlike advanced maturity forage.

Water intake ranged from 13 to 34 kg/day for 427-kg standardbred geldings at rest and maintenance.[5] Even though humidity increased water intake, temperature was more influential.[8] Both sweating and lactation increase the water requirement. In addition to environmental conditions, physical activity, and physiological state of the horse, diet composition contributed

to differences in water intake. Water intake for forage diets averaged 3.55 kg/kg dry hay. A forage diluted with corn, barley, or oats (54% forage:46% grain) reduced the water intake to 2.90 kg per kilogram of diet.[5] An increase of fiber or cell wall content in the diet resulted in a reduced digestibility or increased fecal residue and required more water for excretion.

CHEMICAL COMPOSITION AND DIGESTIBILITY OF FEEDSTUFFS

Limitations of the proximate system and the nonuniformity of the crude fiber fraction among forage species are discussed in Chapter 6, and composition of detergent (Van Soest) fiber fractions have been analyzed.[9] Lignin is not digested by the horse, and the remaining cell wall fiber is composed of cellulose and hemicellulose, which

6. Darlington, J. M., and T. V. Hershberger. 1968. Effect of forage maturity on digestibility, intake and nutritive value of alfalfa, timothy and orchardgrass by equines. *J. Anim. Sci.* 27:1572–76.

7. Haenlein, G. F. W., R. D. Holdren, and Y. M. Yoon. 1966. Comparative response of horses and sheep to different physical forms of alfalfa hay. *J. Anim. Sci.* 25:740–43.

8. Yoshida, S., H. Sudo, K. Noro, and C. Nokava. 1967. Measurement of drinking water volume in horses. Exp. Rept. Equine Health Lab. 4:29–36.

9. Colburn, M. W., and J. L. Evans. 1967. Chemical composition of the cell wall constituent and acid detergent fiber fractions of forages. *J. Dairy Sci.* 50:1130–35.

is partly digestible.[10] Digestibility of hemicellulose is slightly but not significantly greater than that of cellulose in the horse, indicating that the total fiber fraction dilutes the amount of digestible energy (DE) provided in the diet.[10] Crude fiber as determined by the proximate system is both nonuniform in composition and noninclusive of the total diet fiber. Procedures used in the determination of digestibility and specific examples using these procedures in the determination of the digestibility of nutrients of forages in horses have been published.[11-13]

❧ DIGESTIBLE DRY MATTER AND ENERGY

Table 65.1 gives the daily diet requirements for protein, energy, Ca, P, and vitamin A for growing horses and for mature horses at maintenance, work, pregnancy, and lactation.[14] The amounts of daily diet given in Table 65.1 contain 62.5% total digestible nutrient (TDN) and 2.75 Mcal/kg on a dry basis. Most forages and other feedstuffs on an as-fed basis average about 90% dry matter.

Digestibility of most forages declines with advancing maturity. An exception is the silage made from cereal-grain crops. As only limited data are available on the influence of advancing forage maturity on its digestibility in the horse,[6] changes in digestible dry matter (DDM) for alfalfa, orchardgrass, and corn silage with advancing maturities were estimated (Table 65.2).[15-19]

10. Fonnesbeck, P. V. 1969. Partitioning the nutrients of forage for horses. *J. Anim. Sci.* 28:624–33.
11. Maynard, L. A., and J. K. Loosli. 1969. Animal Nutrition, 6th ed. McGraw-Hill, New York.
12. Fonnesbeck, P. V., R. K. Lydman, G. W. Vander Noot, and L. D. Seymons. 1967. Digestibility of the proximate nutrients of forages by horses. *J. Anim. Sci.* 26:1039–45.
13. Fonnesbeck, P. V. 1968. Digestion of soluble and fibrous carbohydrate of forage by horses. *J. Anim. Sci.* 27:1336–44.
14. National Research Council. 1966 and 1973. Nutrient Requirements of the Horse. Publ. 1401 and 2045. Natl. Acad. Sci., Washington, D.C.
15. Vander Noot, G. W., and J. R. Trout. 1971. Prediction of digestible components of forages by equines. *J. Anim. Sci.* 33:38–41.
16. Weir, W. C., L. G. Jones, and J. H. Meyer. 1960. Effect of cutting interval and stage of maturity on the digestibility and yield of alfalfa. *J. Anim. Sci.* 19:5–19.
17. Colburn, M. W., J. L. Evans, and C. H. Ramage. 1968. Apparent and true digestibility of forage nutrients by ruminant animals. *J. Anim. Sci.* 51:1450–57.

Equations where crude fiber was used to represent the total cell wall or fiber in the diet were not considered.[15,19,20]

Many horses performing different types of activity do not require a diet that provides 2.75 Mcal DE/kg. This level of energy may be provided by all-forage diets if an early harvesting schedule is followed for both grasses and legumes. Data in Table 65.2 suggest that early head emergence and 42-day regrowth orchardgrass and 11% bloom alfalfa will allow an adequate intake of DE for growth and lactation in the horse. Data for DDM in corn silage are lower than expected, but DDM of low-quality reed canarygrass diluted with 46% corn, barley, or oats averages only 56% in horses.[5] The influence of total diet fiber is apparent as DDM increases to 66% when alfalfa replaces reed canarygrass. The ratio of hemicellulose to cellulose varies in grasses and legumes.[17] Expressing hemicellulose as a percent of cellulose, values for alfalfa, orchardgrass, and corn silage were 43, 76, and more than 80%. These composition data indicate that cellulose does not constitute a uniform percent of all forage fibers and total diet digestibility should not be estimated from cellulose only but from the total diet fiber.

Coefficients of digestibility for both hemicellulose and cellulose are about 25% lower in mature horses than in growing cattle.[5,17] True coefficients of digestibility in horses for hemicellulose and cellulose are 49 and 41% respectively when the diet contains 25% of each.[5] Coefficients of true digestibility for cellular content and nonfibrous carbohydrate are 90% or greater.[5] In the same digestion trials, the coefficient of true digestibility for forage ether extract (fat) is 75%.[5] Of the total fat in forage, true fat constitutes about 42% and is highly digestible.[4,5]

18. Johnson, R. R., and K. E. McClure. 1968. Corn plant maturity. IV. Effects on digestibility of corn silage in sheep. *J. Anim. Sci.* 27:535–40.
19. Vander Noot, G. W., and E. B. Gilbreath. 1970. Comparative digestibility of components of forages by geldings and steers. *J. Anim. Sci.* 31:351–55.
20. Blaxter, K. L. 1961. Efficiency of feed conversion by different classes of livestock in relation to food production. *Fed. Proc.* 20 (part 3, suppl. 7):268–74.

TABLE 65.1 ❦ Nutrient requirements of horses

Body weight (kg)	Age (month)	Daily gain (kg)	Daily diet* (kg)	Daily diet* (g/W^{0.75})	DP† (g)	DE* (Mcal)	Ca (g)	P (g)	Carotene‡ (mg)
Growing horses (200 kg mature weight)									
50	3	0.70	2.9	156	383	7.4	17	11	5
90	6	0.50	3.1	106	315	8.5	17	10	9
135	12	0.20	2.9	73	206	8.0	12	8	14
165	18	0.10	2.9	64	181	8.1	10	7	17
200	42	0	3.0	56	160	8.2	8	6	13
Growing horses (400 kg mature weight)									
85	3	1.00	3.8	136	553	10.4	26	16	9
170	6	0.65	4.5	96	430	12.3	35	22	17
260	12	0.40	5.0	77	370	13.6	22	15	26
330	18	0.25	5.1	66	339	14.1	19	14	36
400	42	0	5.0	56	268	13.9	16	12	25
Growing horses (600 kg mature weight)									
140	3	1.25	5.2	127	705	14.2	52	32	14
265	6	0.85	6.3	95	582	17.2	51	32	27
385	12	0.60	6.9	79	524	18.9	33	21	39
480	18	0.35	7.0	68	458	19.2	31	20	48
600	42	0	6.8	56	364	18.8	24	18	38
Mature horses at light work									
200	...	...	4.0	75§	202	10.4	8	6	13
400	...	...	6.7	75	355	18.4	16	12	25
500	...	...	8.0	75	424	21.9	20	15	31
600	...	...	9.1	75	491	25.4	24	18	38
Mature horses at medium work									
200	...	...	5.3	100§	255	13.2	9	7	13
400	...	...	8.9	100	460	23.8	17	13	25
500	...	...	10.6	100	553	28.7	21	16	31
600	...	...	12.1	100	649	33.6	25	19	38
Mares (last 90 days of pregnancy)									
200	...	...	3.2	60	216	8.7	10	8	25
400	...	...	5.4	60	375	14.9	20	15	50
500	...	...	6.3	60	434	17.4	24	18	63
600	...	...	7.3	60	502	20.0	28	21	75
Mares (peak of lactation)									
		Milk (kg)							
200	...	15	5.5	104	480	15.2	34	23	25
400	...	19	8.9	100	748	24.4	42	36	50
500	...	21	10.0	95	829	27.6	47	39	63
600	...	23	10.9	90	876	30.0	64	43	75

Source: NRC, 1966 and 1972.[14]
* Based upon 2.75 Mcal DE and 62.5% TDN/kg 100% dry feed.
† Total daily protein is calculated by dividing DP by the coefficient of digestibility from Table 65.3.
‡ 1 mg B-carotene equals 400 IU of vitamin A.
§ Adjusted to 75 and 100 g/W^{0.75} for horses at light and medium work respectively.

Limited data on the influence of diet intake on digestibility in the horse are available. A summary statement of research completed in 1929 states that diet intake has no definite effect on digestibility until it exceeds 2% of body weight.[21] This

21. Olson, N. O. 1969. The nutrition of the horse. *In* Nutrition of Animals of Agricultural Importance 17 (2): 921–60. Pergamon Press, New York.

does not seem to be an area of great importance in the horse. An exception might be in younger growing horses and lactating mares. These animals have greater diet ingestion capacity and higher nutrient requirements to meet their physiological conditions. Horses can sleep while standing, and this phenomenon has resulted in

TABLE 65.2 ❧ Advancing maturity of forage and digestible dry matter, horses

Maturity of forage (stage)	DDM* (%)	Dry matter basis				
		Crude protein (%)	Cellulose (%)	Ca (%)	P (%)	Mg (%)
		Alfalfa†				
Prebud	83‡	30.9	15.2§	...§	...	...
Bud (1%)	76	26.9	20.9	2.2	0.33	...
Bud (62%)	72	25.2	21.7	1.6	0.24	0.23
Bloom (11%)	66	21.3	27.3	1.3	0.24	...
Bloom (46%)	62	19.1	28.5	1.2	0.22	0.29
Bloom (96%)	59	16.9	31.4	1.1	0.20	...
		Orchardgrass‖				
First Growth						
Boot	71	22.8	25.9	0.9	0.43	0.14
Head emergence	63	17.9	28.8	0.8	0.42	0.14
Preanthesis	59	15.3	30.3	0.8	0.31	0.14
Postanthesis	55	13.4	31.3	1.1	0.24	0.14
First aftermath (42 days)	67	20.4	26.5	0.7	0.24	0.18
First aftermath (56 days)	61	17.1	28.1	0.6	0.19	0.26
Second aftermath (42 days)	67	21.2	26.2	0.7	0.28	0.28
Second aftermath (56 days)	63	18.9	27.1	0.6	0.26	0.31
		Corn silage#				
Blister	54	11.7	30.8	0.38	0.28	0.28
Early milk	54	12.0	28.8	0.31	0.27	0.26
Milk–early dough	54	11.6	25.1	0.26	0.25	0.22
Dough-dent	53	10.9	22.9	...	0.23	0.22
Glaze	51	10.2	20.0	0.28	0.31	0.22
Flint	51	10.0	18.8	0.23	0.31	0.24
Postfrost	51	9.6	19.3	0.14	0.30	0.19
Mature	52	10.9	16.9	0.09	0.33	0.16

* DDM estimated from ruminant data using the following equation, Equine % DDM = 19.92 + 1.48% crude protein + 0.24% ruminant DDM. Vander Noot and Trout, 1971.[15]
† California data—Weir et al., 1960.[16]
‡ Ruminant DDM estimated from TDN using the equation DDM = (TDN − 16.0) ÷ 0.69. Unpublished data, alfalfa—Evans, Rutgers.
§ For alfalfa, fiber reported as crude fiber. Mineral values—Morrison, 1959, pp. 1001, 1096.[4]
‖ New Jersey data—Colburn et al., 1968.[17] Unpubl. mineral data—Evans, Rutgers.
Ohio data—Johnson and McClure, 1968.[18]

much discussion about the comfort and metabolism or energy requirement in the standing and lying positions. Metabolism in horses while standing and lying has been reported to be the same.[22]

❧ PROTEIN

Digestible protein (DP) requirements of horses decline from birth to maturity both as a percent of diet intake and in total grams per day (Table 65.1).[14] Rate of

22. Brody, Samuel. 1945. *Bioenergetics and Growth.* Hafner, New York.

growth, pregnancy, and lactation increase the DP requirement, but work does not. In the horse, digestibility of protein changes in proportion to diet protein (Fig. 65.2), and the protein requirement for the horse should be expressed as DP. The slope of the regression line in Figure 65.2 indicates that the coefficient of true digestibility is 85% for forage protein, and the constant indicates that obligatory fecal loss or metabolic fecal protein is 2.8% of the ingested diet dry matter. With 6 and 16% diet protein, the respective total fecal losses are 3.7 and 5.2%. Coefficients

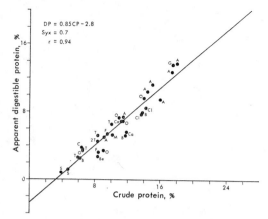

FIG. 65.2. Regression of the percent apparent DP on the percent crude protein content in all-forage diets fed to horses. The number of data points in parentheses follows the reference number: 6 (9), 12 (12), 18 (4), 25 (8). Means were plotted for alfalfa (A), bermudagrass (Be), smooth bromegrass (B), cereal hay (C), reed canarygrass (Ca), tall fescue (F), green chop (G), meadow hay (M), orchardgrass (O), straw (S), and timothy (T).

of true digestibility for forage and grain proteins were 85 and 95% respectively. The respective values for the percent DP and the coefficients of (apparent) digestibility, when protein in all-forage and all-grain diets is increased from 6 to 20%, are given in Table 65.3.

Forages and other feedstuffs are analyzed for protein, and this value can be equated with the DP requirement (Tables 65.1 and 65.3). The DP requirement for the

TABLE 65.3 ❧ Digestibility of dietary protein, horses

Dietary crude protein (%)	Forage*		Grain†	
	DP (%)	Coefficient of digestibility (% × 100)	DP (%)	Coefficient of digestibility (% × 100)
6	2.3	38	3.5	58
8	4.0	50	5.4	67
10	5.7	57	7.3	73
12	7.4	62	9.2	77
14	9.1	65	11.1	79
16	10.8	67	13.0	81
18	12.5	69	14.9	83
20	14.2	71	16.8	84

* DP calculated from equation presented in Figure 65.1.

† Equation, DP = 0.95% crude protein −2.2, based upon data from Olson, 1969, p. 955.[21]

260-kg growing horse with a mature weight of 400 kg is 370 g. The 370 g divided by 5000 g of ingested diet results in 7.5% DP. When regression is used (Fig. 65.2 and Table 65.3), the diet protein should be 12.1% with forage and about 2% lower with an all-grain diet.

If a lower energy diet at a higher intake is fed to the mature horse at medium work, the DP requirements given in Table 65.1 may be too low to meet both the obligatory and endogenous losses in forage diets. It appears that the work of digestion in higher fiber, forage diets results in an increased requirement, not physical work per se.

Protein quality or balance of amino acids in the diet may be deficient in the presence of adequate DP in nonruminant animals such as the horse. The more critical times in the life cycle of the horse are during rapid growth when the foal has a decreasing supply of milk and must depend on other available feedstuffs, during pregnancy when improper diets are fed to prevent fattening, and during lactation when milk production is high. Based upon recent amino acid data for different feedstuffs and the amino acid requirements for growing swine published by the National Research Council (NRC), lower protein forages and several cereal grains may be borderline in some amino acids for the rapidly growing foal.[23,24] Barley, corn, oats, sorghum grains, and more mature alfalfa with less than 15% protein may be borderline in both lysine and methionine. Threonine, isoleucine, and tryptophan are suspect also for several of these feedstuffs. Inclusion of soybean meal or high-protein forage to provide 10–30% of the total diet protein should correct most amino acid deficiencies.

Forages contain varying amounts of nonprotein N (NPN) (see Chapter 6) and 2.5–4% urea in the diet did not appear to be

23. National Research Council. 1968. Nutrient Requirements of Swine. Publ. 1599. Natl. Acad. Sci., Washington, D.C.

24. National Research Council. 1971. Nutrient Requirements of Poultry. Publ. 1861. Natl. Acad. Sci., Washington, D.C.

detrimental to the horse in eight weeks.[25,26] Many questions remain concerning the utilization of NPN and the contribution of the protein digested in the cecum and large intestine to the nutrition of the horse.[27,28]

✄ MINERALS

Large variations in the composition of minerals within and among forage species exist. These variations in most of the minerals considered essential for animals have been recorded for alfalfa,[29] and other mineral composition data for many feedstuffs have been reported by the NRC.[24] Limited experimental data on the mineral requirements for the horse are available.[4,11,14,21,30,31] The complications of mineral interrelationships have been discussed for other animals, and some of these may apply to the horse.[32] A chemical analysis for minerals in a diet gives the amount present, but it does not give the amount biologically available to the horse.

SALT

Most forages supply a deficient amount of Na to the horse. The mature horse at medium work may lose 60 g of sodium chloride daily in the sweat and 35 g in the urine.[14] Self-feeding salt to horses on pasture or on a variable work schedule provides an adequate supply.

PHOSPHORUS AND POTASSIUM

Forage contents of P and K decline with advancing maturity of the forage (Table 65.2) and with lower soil concentrations. Grains usually have higher amounts of P than forages and are deficient in K for the horse. A large amount of P in forage and grain is present as phytate P, and the availability of this form is expected to be lower than inorganic orthophosphate in the horse.

CALCIUM AND MAGNESIUM

Legumes contain more Ca than grasses, and grasses are higher in Ca than most grains. Mixtures of legumes and grains tend to provide a good balance of P, Ca, and Mg in the diet. Cattle have adapted or changed their rate of absorption of Ca with time when diet Ca exceeded the requirement.[33] It may be that the excessive Ca in legumes undergoes the same treatment in the horse when P and Mg are adequate in the diet. Most reports suggest that a proper ratio be maintained between Ca and P and that diet Ca should exceed diet P. The Ca:P ratio in horse milk is 1.7:1.0 and appears to be adequate for the horse.[11] The Mg content of forage is closely related to soil temperature, and for this reason it increases with advancing maturity in spring and summer forages but not in forages harvested in the fall (Table 65.2).[34]

SULFUR

The NRC has concluded that inorganic S is not a diet essential for the horse. However, in addition to adequate S amino acids

25. Slade, L. M., D. W. Robinson, and K. E. Casey. 1970. Nitrogen metabolism in nonruminant herbivores. I. The influence of nonprotein nitrogen and protein quality on the nitrogen retention of adult mares. *J. Anim. Sci.* 30:753–60.
26. Nelson, D. D., and W. J. Tyznik. 1971. Protein and nonprotein nitrogen utilization in the horse. *J. Anim. Sci.* 32:68–73.
27. Reitnour, C. M., J. P. Baker, G. E. Mitchell, Jr., C. O. Little, and D. D. Kratzer. 1970. Amino acids in equine cecal contents, cecal bacteria and serum. *J. Nutr.* 100:349–54.
28. Hintz, H. F., D. E. Hogue, E. F. Walker, Jr., J. E. Lowe, and H. F. Schryver. 1971. Apparent digestion in various segments of the digestive tract of ponies fed diets with varying roughage-grain ratios. *J. Anim. Sci.* 32:245–48.
29. Bear, F. E., and A. Wallace. 1950. Alfalfa, its mineral requirements and chemical composition. N.J. Agr. Exp. Sta. Bull. 748.
30. Squibb, R. L. 1958. Fifty years of research in America on the nutrition of the horse. *J. Anim. Sci.* 17:1007–14.
31. Cunha, T. J. 1971. The mineral needs of the horse. *Feedstuffs* 43 (46):34, 36, 38, 51.
32. Tillman, A. D. 1966. Recent developments in beef cattle feeding. Proc. Pfizer Res. Conf. 14:7–18.

33. Garces, M. A., and J. L. Evans. 1971. Calcium and magnesium absorption in growing cattle as influenced by age of animal and source of dietary nitrogen. *J. Anim. Sci.* 32:789–93.
34. Rook, J. A. F., and J. E. Storry. 1962. Magnesium in the nutrition of farm animals. *Nutr. Abstr. Rev.* 32:1055–77.

TABLE 65.4 ❧ Mineral composition and variation in alfalfa

Mineral	Number of observations	Range	Mean
Sodium (%)	43	0.01–0.33	0.16
Chlorine (%)	110	0.06–0.54	0.28
Phosphorus (%)	882	0.01–0.97	0.26
Potassium (%)	442	0.22–3.37	1.77
Calcium (%)	879	0.15–2.99	1.64
Magnesium (%)	389	0.03–0.84	0.32
Sulfur (%)	76	0.20–0.73	0.36
Iodine (ppm)	56	0.06–0.29	0.12
Cobalt (ppm)	113	0.02–0.31	0.13
Copper (ppm)	58	4–38	14
Iron (ppm)	265	40–1640	240
Zinc (ppm)	67	10–29	17
Manganese (ppm)	231	8–100	52

Source: NRC, 1958.[36]

it has increased both weight gain and femur ash in the rat.[35]

TRACE ELEMENTS

Large variations in trace mineral concentrations in feedstuffs have been related to plant species, soil type, area and mineral content, and growing season (Table 65.4).[29,36] The NRC has recommended 0.1 mg I, less than 0.05 ppm Co, 5–8 ppm Cu, and less than 40 ppm Fe for the horse.[14] It has been suggested that most forages contain adequate Zn and Mn, but this is not always true (Table 65.4). In addition, Fe, Mo, and Se should be considered.[11,21,31]

❧ VITAMINS

Green leafy forage harvested at an early stage of maturity will usually provide adequate diet carotene and B vitamins for the horse. Forages vary in vitamin composition.[14,21,36] In both first-growth and regrowth orchardgrass at all levels of N fertilization studied, carotene has varied with percent protein:[37] Carotene, mg/454 g =

0.79% protein — 3.12. It may be that carotene in lower protein versus higher protein forage has a lower availability in the horse.[38] Limited data on ascorbic acid for horses are available, and the choline content of forages for horses should be evaluated.[36,39] It has been indicated that mature horses do not have a diet vitamin B_{12} requirement; however, this does not mean that the growing horse does not require diet B_{12}.[40] It may be that when a forage supplies the minimum adequate DP to the horse, more consideration should be given to fat-soluble than to water-soluble vitamins.

❧ MAXIMUM FORAGE DIETS

In addition to the feeding value of forage, quality horse pastures should form a high-quality turf and withstand close grazing (Fig. 65.3). Orchardgrass stores its energy reserves above the soil surface and does not withstand as close grazing as timothy, which stores its reserves below the soil surface. Intermediate grasses are Kentucky bluegrass, smooth bromegrass, and reed canarygrass. Horse pastures should include both legumes and grasses that are adapted to a given location. In most cases horse pastures should be clipped, and at times the droppings should be spread to aid in maintaining uniform fertility and in reducing parasite populations.

MAINTENANCE AT MATURE WEIGHT

In most cases, a poor quality mature forage containing 35–40% cellulose and 8–10% protein on a dry basis should provide the maintenance nutrient requirements for the mature horse. Usually, salt and water are provided free-choice. In areas known to have problems related to nutrition, diet

35. Evans, J. L., and G. K. Davis. 1964. Mineral interrelationships (copper, molybdenum, sulfur and phosphorus) in the nutrition of the rat. Proc. 6th Int. Congr. Nutr., p. 520 (Edinburgh, Scotland). (Abstr.)
36. National Research Council. 1958. Composition of Cereal Grains and Forages. Natl. Acad. Sci. Publ. 585, Washington, D.C.
37. Evans, J. L., J. Arroyo-Aguilu, M. W. Taylor, and C. H. Ramage. 1965. Date of harvest of New Jersey forages as related to the nutrition of ruminant animals. N.J. Agr. Exp. Sta. Bull. 814.

38. Fonnesbeck, P. V., and L. D. Symons. 1967. Utilization of the carotene of hay by horses. J. Anim. Sci. 26: 1030–38.
39. Stillions, M. C., S. M. Teeter, and W. E. Nelson. 1971. Ascorbic acid requirement of mature horses. J. Anim. Sci. 32:249–51.
40. Stillions, M. C., S. M. Teeter, and W. E. Nelson. 1971. Utilization of dietary vitamin B12 and cobalt by mature horses. J. Anim. Sci. 32:252–55.

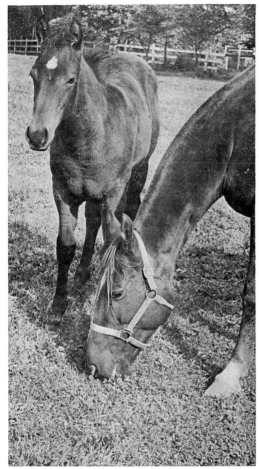

FIG. 65.3. *Quality horse pasture should . . . withstand close grazing.* Foal and mare grazing grass-legume pasture. Horses are close grazers, and pasture mixtures of Kentucky bluegrass and white clover are adapted to this treatment.

However, a supply of nutrients lost in sweat should be provided (e.g., water and Na). The working horse has a reduced eating time and a higher energy requirement. After work the horse should not be allowed to eat too fast or to overeat. Voluntary intake of energy from forage decreases with advancing maturity or increasing fiber (Table 65.2). An amount of work can be supported by a low-quality forage in the mature horse. Condition of the horse should indicate the relationship between diet energy and work intensity. If the horse is losing body condition, a lower fiber forage and/or an 8–10% protein-grain mixture should be fed in an amount that maintains the desired condition.

PREGNANCY

Nutrient requirements for the last quarter of pregnancy are the inverse of work requirements (i.e., energy is similar to the maintenance requirement), and requirements for all other nutrients are greater than maintenance. A large area of poor pasture is desirable for the mature pregnant mare. This provides exercise, and higher fiber forage would reduce energy intake. However, depending on the size of the mare, in addition to this high-fiber forage up to 1 kg/day of protein supplement fortified with minerals and vitamins should be calculated, as discussed in the protein section.

LACTATION

Most forages fed as the average quality of hay presently produced in the U.S. do not provide adequate nutrition without some grain mixture added to the diet. By harvesting forage at an earlier stage of maturity so that fiber will not restrict energy intake, all-forage diets can be consumed in amounts that will meet the nutrient requirements of most mares (Table 65.2). The small mare (pony) and the mare in poor condition are exceptions. In most cases a 14% protein forage would provide

supplements may be required. Should the distended intestinal tract associated with a low-quality forage diet be undesirable, one of two actions could be taken. The horse could be fed the low-quality forage several times per day, or the total diet fiber could be reduced by feeding a limited amount of grain mixture to reach the desired body condition.

WORK

Of all the required nutrients, only that for energy varies with the intensity of work.

adequate protein, but energy intake as limited by forage fiber would not be adequate. Stages of maturity for alfalfa and orchardgrass to provide different levels of DDM are given in Table 65.2.

GROWTH

Like the lactating mare, the growing foal needs a high-quality, low-fiber diet that does not restrict voluntary intake. The diet should supply adequate protein containing a proper balance of amino acids and adequate minerals and vitamins that are biologically available from plant sources. Initially the foal consumes milk, and mare's milk contains 25% protein, 15% fat, 55% lactose, 5% mineral, 0.9% Ca, 0.54% P, 0.9% K, and 4.5 kcal/g.[11]

At a few weeks of age the foal starts to nibble feedstuffs that are available (i.e., forage as hay or pasture and/or grain that is provided for the mare). As the foal grows, the high-energy, 25% protein milk diet is replaced by other feedstuffs. Diet for the growing foal (from before weaning to past one year of age) should be decreased from 17% to about 10% DP. Level of protein depends on the mature weight of the horse and its stage of growth (Table 65.1). The growing horse even past one year should have good quality forage to provide adequate energy at the expense of some overfeeding of protein. When forages are borderline in quality, the protein supplement with minerals and vitamins for the pregnant mare or the grain mixture for the lactating mare may be used to pro-

vide a balanced diet. In areas where the recurrence of anemia is frequent, the supply and availability of diet Co, Fe, and Cu should be evaluated.[32,41,42] The faster gaining horse of larger mature weight requires a large voluntary intake of forage, indicating a requirement for a low-fiber, immature forage (Table 65.1). Teething is another stress, and the diet should be provided in a physical form that does not result in inadequate voluntary intake.

41. Evans, J. L., and P. A. Abraham. 1973. Anemia, iron storage and ceruloplasmin in copper nutrition in the growing rat. *J. Nutr.* 103:196–201.
42. Abraham, P. A., and J. L. Evans. 1971. Cytochrome oxidase activity and cardiac hypertrophy during copper depletion and repletion. Proc. Conf. Trace Substances in Environmental Health 5:335–47 (Univ. Mo.).

❧ QUESTIONS

1. Using the same fibrous diet, will the mature bovine or the mature horse digest more fiber? Why?
2. What is digestible protein? Metabolic fecal protein? Nonprotein N?
3. Distinguish between apparent and true digestibility of protein.
4. What is the percent Ca in calcium carbonate and dicalcium phosphate?
5. A 385-kg horse consumed 6.9 kg of forage. Express body weight in kilograms to the 0.75 power of body weight and calculate the diet intake of $g/W^{0.75}$.
6. How do diet lignin, cellulose, and hemicellulose influence the digestibility of energy in the horse?
7. Using the information in this chapter and your local forage data, balance diets for a mare at maintenance, work, pregnancy, lactation, and growth.

TERMINOLOGY

❧

Aberrant—Differing from the normal type of a species, genus, or higher group in one or more characters, but not readily assignable to another group.

Abiotic substances—Nonliving components of the environment, such as water, sun, oxygen, organic compounds, and soil nutrients.

Acceptability, animal—Readiness with which animals select and eat a forage; sometimes used interchangeably to mean either palatability or voluntary intake. See also Palatability.

Acid soil—Soil with a reaction somewhat below pH 7 (usually less than pH 6.6); more technically, a soil having a preponderance of hydrogen ions over hydroxyl ions in solution.

Ad libitum feeding—Where animals are permitted to eat daily as much as they desire. See also Orts; Voluntary intake.

Aerobic—Pertaining to life in free oxygen or conditions requiring the same. See also Anaerobic.

Aftermath—Recovery growth of forage plants after harvesting by either animal or machine.

Agrostology—Study of grasses; their classification, management, and utilization.

Albedo—Ratio of light reflected by a planet or satellite to that received by it.

Alkaline soil—Soil with pH above 7.

Alkali soil—Soil containing excessive amounts of alkaline salts, usually sodium carbonate (pH 8.5 or higher).

Allele—Any of a group of possible mutational forms of a gene.

Ambient temperature—Air temperature at a given time; not radiant temperature.

Amino acid—Organic acid containing one or more amino groups ($-NH_2$) and at least one carboxyl groups ($-COOH$). Some amino acids such as cystine and methionine contain sulfur. Many amino acids linked together in a definite pattern form a molecule of protein.

Anabolism—Metabolic process by which simple substances are synthesized into complex materials of living tissue.

Anaerobic—Living in the absence of free oxygen; the opposite of aerobic.

Animal day—One day's tenure upon range or pasture by one animal.

Animal unit—One mature cow (454 kg) or the equivalent based upon average daily forage consumption of 12 kg dry matter per day.

Animal-unit conversion factor—A numerical figure expressing the forage requirement of a particular kind or class of animal relative to the requirement for an animal unit. A conversion factor is satisfactory with respect to the amount of forage required to maintain an animal, but may not be applicable in determining stocking rates for range and pasture use for particular kinds of classes of animals because of different grazing preferences.

Animal-unit month (AUM)—The amount of feed or forage required by an animal unit for one month.

Annual—Plant that completes its life cycle from seed in one (year) growing season.

Annual, winter—Plant species that initiates growth in the fall, lives over winter, and dies after producing seed the following season.

Anthesis—Stage in floral development when pollen is shed.

Antimetabolite—Prevents the formation or utilization of organic compounds in particular metabolic processes in living tissue.

Apical dominance—Inhibiting effect of a terminal bud upon the development of lateral buds.

Apomixis—Formation of viable embryos without actual union of male and female gametes, as in Kentucky bluegrass.

Arable—Pertaining to land suitable for the production of crops that require tillage.

Auricle—Earlike lobe at the base of leaf blades of certain grass species.

Autotetraploid—Organism with more than two sets of chromosomes in its body cells; both sets derived from the same species.

Available water—Soil water available to plants;

between the field capacity and the permanent wilting point.

Axillary tiller or bud—New shoot or bud growth arising from the junction of leaf and stem.

Backgrounding—Growing of replacement cattle, usually on high-forage systems. Backgrounding may take place anytime during the postweaning period until the animal goes into the feedlot or the breeding herd.

Bacteriostatic—Preventing or hindering the growth and multiplication of bacteria.

Band-seeding—Placing forage crop seed in rows directly above but not in contact with a band of fertilizer.

Biennial—Plant that normally requires two years to reach maturity, producing leaves in the first year, blooming and producing seed in the second year, and then dying.

Biomass—The part of a given habitat consisting of living matter, expressed either as weight of organisms per unit area or as volume of organisms per unit volume of habitat.

Biota—Animal and plant life of a particular region considered as a total ecological entity.

Biotype—A population in which all individuals have an identical genotype.

Bloat—Excessive accumulation of gases in the rumen of animals.

Boot stage—Growth stage of grasses at the time the head is enclosed by the sheath of the uppermost leaf.

Bound water—Water that is hydrogen-bonded to cell colloidal solutes such as protein and that is not free to act as a solvent for an added crystallite.

Browse—That part of leaf and twig growth of shrubs, woody vines, and trees available for animal consumption; to consume browse.

Calorie (gram calorie)—Unit for measuring chemical energy, defined as the heat necessary to raise the temperature of 1 g of water from 14.5 to 15.5 C at standard pressure; 1 kilocalorie (kcal) raises the temperature of 1 k of water 1 C. Thus 1 kcal = 1000 cal, and 1000 kcal = 1 megacalorie (Mcal).

Canopy interception—Plant cover that protects the soil surface by dissipating raindrop energy.

Carbohydrate—Compound of carbon, hydrogen, and oxygen in the ratio of one atom each of carbon and oxygen to two of hydrogen, as in sugar, starch, and cellulose.

Carbohydrates, nonstructural—Photosynthetic products existing in plant tissue as a solute or as stored insoluble material; function as readily metabolizable compounds, not as structural components of the tissue. Examples are fructose, glucose, sucrose, starch, fructosans, and hemicellulose.

Carotene—Yellow compound of carbon and hydrogen that occurs in plants; a precursor of vitamin A. Alpha, beta, and gamma carotenes may be converted into vitamin A in the animal body.

Caryopsis—Small, one-seeded, dry fruit with a thin pericarp surrounding and adhering to the seed; the seed (grain) or fruit of grasses.

Cellulase—Enzymes that attack cellulose.

Cellulose—Major skeletal material in the cell wall of plants; chemically, an anhydride of beta-D glucose units. A cellulose molecule may contain between 1600 and 2700 beta-D glucose units.

Cereal forage—Cereal crop harvested when immature for either hay, silage, or green chop or as pasturage.

Chlorosis—Yellowing or blanching of leaves and other parts of chlorophyll-bearing plants; usually caused by a mineral deficiency.

Chops—Mixture of dehydrated leaves and stems as they come from the dehydrator.

Chromosome—Dark-staining, rodlike, or threadlike body in the nucleus of the plant cell at the time of cell division that carries the genes controlling the development of the different plant characters.

Climax—Fully developed plant community with plant cover and its environment in equilibrium.

Clone—Individual plant propagated vegetatively by rooting portions from a single original plant.

Combining ability—Average performance of a strain in hybrid combinations.

Companion crop—Crop sown with another crop, usually a small grain with which a forage crop is seeded. Preferred to the term "nurse crop."

Concentrate—All feed, low in fiber and high in total digestible nutrients, that supplies primary nutrients (protein, carbohydrate, and fat), e.g., grains, cottonseed meal, and wheat bran.

Convergent improvement—System of crossing, back-pollinating, and selfing with accompanying selection in an effort to improve inbred lines of cross-pollinated plants without interfering with their behavior in hybrid combinations.

Cool-season grass—Grass species adapted to rapid growth during the cool moist periods of the year; usually dormant during hot weather or injured by it.

Corm—bulblike, short, fleshy, solid stem, e.g., timothy.

Coumarin—White, crystalline compound (C_9H_6 O_2) with a vanillalike odor; gives sweet-clover its characteristic odor.

Coumestrol—Estrogenic factor occurring naturally in forage crops, especially in ladino clover, strawberry clover, and alfalfa.

Crop residue—Portion of plants remaining after seed harvest; said mainly of grain crops such as corn stover or of small-grain straw and stubble.

Cross inoculation—Inoculation of one legume species by the symbiotic bacteria from another.

Crown—Base of stems where roots arise.

Crude fiber—Coarse fibrous portions of plants, such as cellulose, partially digestible and relatively low in nutritional value. In chemical analysis it is the residue obtained after boiling plant material with dilute acid and then with dilute alkali.

Cubing—Process of forming hay into high-density cubes to facilitate transportation, storage, and feeding.

Culm—Jointed stem of a grass.

Cultivar (derived from "cultivated variety")—International term denoting an assemblage of cultivated plants that is clearly distinguishable by any characters (morphological, physiological, cytological, chemical, or others) and that when reproduced (sexually or asexually) retains its distinguishing characters. In the U.S. "variety" is synonomous with "cultivar."

Cutin—Outer covering of plants composed of waxes and waxy polymers.

Daylength—Number of hours of light for each 24-hour cycle.

Day-neutral plant—Capable of flowering under either long or short daylengths.

Decreaser—Forage (range) plant that gradually is replaced by other species in a stand.

Dehiscence (dehisce, verb)—Opening of an organ on an existing line of weakness, such as the opening of anthers to shed pollen and the splitting of a seedpod along a definite line to release seed.

Dehulled seed—Seed from which pods, glumes, or other outer covering have been removed, as sometimes with lespedeza and timothy; also often ambiguously referred to as "hulled" seed.

Denitrification—Biological reduction of nitrate or nitrite to gaseous N (molecular N or the oxides of N).

Desiccant—Compound that promotes dehydration or removal of moisture from plant tissue.

Determinate (growth)—The flowering of plant species uniformly within certain time limits. See also Indeterminate.

Dicotyledon—Plant that produces two seed leaves in each seed.

Dicoumarol—Chemical compound produced microbiologically from coumarin; found in spoiled sweetclover hay.

Digestibility, apparent—Refers to the balance of feed ingested less that matter lost in the feces, usually expressed as a percentage; obtained by multiplying the digestion coefficient for a nutrient by its content in the feed.

Digestibility, true—Actual digestibility or availability of a feed, forage, or nutrient as represented by the balance between intake and fecal loss of the same ingested material.

Digestible dry matter (DDM)—Feed-feces difference expressed in dry matter (DM).

Digestible energy (DE)—Feed-feces difference expressed in calories.

Digestible nutrients—Portion of nutrients consumed that are digested and taken into the animal body. This may be either apparent or true digestibility; generally applied to energy and protein.

Dioecious—Having male and female flowers borne on separate plants.

Diploid—Having two sets of chromosomes; body tissues of higher plants and animals ordinarily are diploid.

Dry matter (DM)—Total amount of matter in a feed less the moisture it contains.

Dry matter percent—Plant substance less water; found by oven-drying a weighed sample, weighing, and determining percent lost. See also Moisture, dry basis; Moisture, wet basis.

Ecosystem—Open system including plants, animals, organic residues, atmospheric gases, water, and minerals that are involved in the flow of energy and circulation of matter.

Ecotype—Plant type or strain within a species, resulting from exposure to a particular environment.

Edaphic—Pertaining to the influence of the soil upon plant growth.

Efficiency, animal—Animal productivity relative to feed use.

Endemic—Species native to a particular environment or locality; not introduced.

Ensile—To store forage as silage.

Enzyme—Specialized protein compound occurring in both plant and animal bodies that is capable of producing chemical transformations without itself being changed or destroyed; functions as a biochemical catalyst.

Epiphytotic—Characterizes a sudden or abnormally destructive outbreak of a plant disease, usually over an extended geographical area.

Eructation—Act of belching or giving off gas from the stomach.

Estrogenic—Pertaining to any hormonal substance capable of producing estrus in a female animal.

Ether extract—Fats, oils, waxes, and similar plant components that are extracted with dry ethyl ether in chemical analysis.

Etiolated—Refers to plants grown in reduced light.

Etiology—Science that deals with the origins or causes of disease.

Evapotranspiration—Total soil moisture lost to the air by plant transpiration and evaporation from the soil surface.

Exchange capacity (soil)—Measure of the total amount of exchangeable cations that can be held by the soil, expressed in terms of milliequivalents per 100 g of soil at neutrality (pH 7) or at some other stated pH value.

Exotic plant—Introduced plant; not native.

Fecal index—Indirect method of estimating indigestibility of dry matter by determining concentration of an indicator in feces.

Feeding value—See Forage quality.

Feedstuff—Material(s) consumed by animals that contributes nutrients to the diet.

Field capacity (water)—Amount of moisture remaining in soil after free water (gravitational) has drained away.

Fistula—Surgically established opening between a hollow organ and the skin for experimental purposes (such as an esophageal fistula).

Flagging—Dying of the central leaf in grasses while other leaves stay green.

Floret—In grasses, the lemma and palea with included flower (stamens and pistil). In legumes, the individual flower, usually belonging to a cluster.

Fodder—Coarse grasses such as corn and sorghum harvested with the seed and leaves and cured for animal feeding.

Foggage—English term meaning forage for winter pasture.

Forage—Herbaceous plants or plant parts fed to domestic animals (generally, the term refers to such material as pasturage, hay, silage, dehy, and green chop in contrast to less digestible plant material known as "roughage"); to graze.

Forage quality—Characteristics that make forage valuable to animals as a source of nutrients; the combination of chemical, biochemical, physical, and organoleptic characteristics of forage that determines its potential to produce animal meat, milk, wool, or work. Considered by some as synonymous with feeding value and nutritive value.

Forage testing—Laboratory evaluation of a given forage or feed in terms of intended use.

Forb—Any herbaceous nongrasslike plant on which animals feed.

Fouled—Pasture spots or areas made unacceptable to the grazing animal by presence of urine or dung.

Fructosan—Polysaccharide yielding primarily fructose on hydrolysis; the primary form of carbohydrate storage in certain forage crops.

Gene—Specific region of a chromosome that is capable of determining development of a specific trait, composed wholly or in part of deoxyribonucleic acid (DNA).

Genotype—Group of organisms with the same genetic makeup. See also Phenotype.

Glabrous—Smooth; not hairy.

Glucoside—Low molecular weight organic compound consisting of a noncarbohydrate portion (aglycone) attached to a sugar.

Glycoside—Any of a group of organic compounds, occurring abundantly in plants, that produce sugars and related substances on hydrolysis.

Grass—Botanically, any plant of the family Gramineae. Generally, in grassland agriculture the term does not include cereals when grown for grain but does include forage species of legumes often grown in association with grasses.

Grassland—Land on which grasses and/or legumes constitute the dominant vegetation.

Grassland agriculture—Farming system that emphasizes the importance of grasses and legumes in livestock and land management.

Grassland farmer—One who plans his row crop and livestock production around his grassland hectarage.

Grass silage—Designating silage from grasses, legumes, or mixtures. Terms such as "alfalfa silage," "clover silage," and "alfalfa-timothy silage" are definite expressions that should be used where applicable.

Grass tetany (hypomagnesemia)—Condition of cattle and sheep marked by tetanic staggers, convulsions, coma, and frequently death; characterized by a low level of blood magnesium.

Grass waterway—Surface drainageway, usually broad and relatively flat, protected from erosion by a natural or seeded grass cover.

Graze—Partial defoliation of forage plants by the animal; to feed animals on growing grass or herbage; to forage. See also Pasture.

Grazer—Animal that grazes growing grass or herbage.

Grazier—One who pastures (grazes) livestock, usually for commercial purposes.

Grazing, alternate—Grazing of two or more pastures in succession.

Grazing, continuous—The grazing of a specific range or pasture by livestock throughout a year or grazing season. The term is not necessarily synonymous with yearlong grazing.

Grazing, deferred—Delay or discontinuance of livestock grazing on an area for an adequate period of time to provide for plant reproduction, establishment of new plants, or restoration of vigor.

Grazing, mixed—Grazing two or more classes of livestock such as sheep and cattle on the same pasture.

Grazing pressure—Number of animals per unit area of available forage.

Grazing, ration—See Grazing, strip.

Grazing, rest-rotation—Intensive system of management whereby grazing is deferred on various parts of the range during succeeding years, allowing the deferred part complete rest for one year; two or more units are required.

Grazing, rotational—System of pasture utilization embracing periods of heavy stocking followed by periods of rest for herbage growth recovery during the same season.

Grazing, strip (ration grazing)—Confining animals to an area of forage to be consumed in a short period of time, usually a day.

Green chop—Mechanically harvested forage fed to animals while it is fresh and succulent. Preferred to "soiling," "zero grazing," or "green feed."

Green manure—Crop grown and plowed under to improve the soil.

Hay—Entire herbage of forage plants, sometimes including seed of grasses and legumes, that is harvested and dried for animal feed.

Haylage—Product resulting from ensiling forage with about 45% moisture, in the absence of oxygen.

Hemicellulose—Heterogeneous polysaccharide fraction existing largely in the secondary cell wall of the plant.

Herbaceous—Plant growth that is relatively free of woody tissue.

Herbage—Leaves, stems, and other succulent parts of forage plants upon which animals feed. See also Forage.

Herbicide—Phytotoxic chemical used to kill or inhibit plant growth.

Herbivore—Animal that subsists principally or entirely on plants or plant products.

Heritability—Portion of observed variability in a progeny that is due to heredity, the remainder being due to environmental causes.

Heterosis—Increased vigor or capacity of growth often resulting from crossing organisms genetically unlike. Negative heterosis also is recognized by some geneticists when decreased vigor results.

Homeostatic—Maintenance of constancy or a high degree of uniformity in functions of an organism or interactions of individuals in a population or community under changing conditions of the environment because of the capabilities of organisms to make adjustments.

Humus—The organic fraction of soil in which decomposition is so far advanced that its original form is not distinguishable.

Hybrid—Product of a cross between individuals of unlike genetic constitution or makeup.

Hydrocyanic acid (HCN)—Poison (also called prussic acid) produced as a glucoside by several plant species, especially sorghums.

Inbred—Pertaining to offspring or progeny produced by self-pollination in normally cross-pollinated plants.

Increaser—Forage plant on the range that spreads under existing management.

Indeterminate—Pertaining to growth of plants, the flowers of which are borne on lateral branches, the central stem continuing vegetative growth, with blooming continued for a long period. Examples are alsike clover, alfalfa, and birdsfoot trefoil.

Indigenous—Produced or living naturally in a specific environment.

Inflorescence—Flowering part of a plant.

Inoculation—Addition of effective rhizobia to legume seed prior to planting for the purpose of promoting N fixation.

Insolation—Solar radiation received by the earth.

International unit (IU)—Unit of measure for vitamin potency.

Internode—The part of a plant stem between joints or nodes.

Interspecific hybrid—Plant or animal progeny resulting from crossing of two species.

In vitro—In glass; in test tubes; outside the organism, as digestion *in vitro*.

In vivo—In a living organism such as in the animal or in the plant.

Karyotype—Chromosomal complement of an individual or a species.

Keto acid—Formed in the liver of the animal from incomplete combustion of fat.

Lactating—Designating an animal that is actively producing and secreting milk. Preferred to "milking."

Land class (land-capability class)[1]—Term used in the USDA land-capability classification system as an interpretive grouping of soils made primarily for agricultural purposes. Hazards and limitations increase from Class I through Class VIII. Only the first four classes are considered usable for cultivated crops under normal conditions. The system also contains subclasses within each land class except for Class I. These four subclasses indicate the dominant limitations for agricultural use: e, erosion hazard; w, excess water or wetness of soil; s, unfavorable soil in root zone; and c, adverse climate.

Land suitable for cultivation

Class I—Few limitations that restrict use.

Class II—Some limitations that reduce choice of plants or require moderate conservation practices.

Class III—Severe limitations that reduce choice of plants, require special conservation practices, or both.

Land suitable for limited cultivation

Class IV—Very severe limitations that restrict choice of plants, require very careful management, or both.

Land not suitable for cultivation

Class V—Little or no erosion hazard but other limitations that are impractical to remove, limiting use largely to pasture, range, woodland, or wildlife food and cover.

Class VI—Severe limitations causing general unsuitability for cultivation and limiting use largely to pasture or range, woodland, or wildlife food and cover.

Class VII—Very severe limitations causing

unsuitability for cultivation and restricting use largely to grazing, woodland, or wildlife.

Class VIII—Limitations that preclude use for commercial plant production and restrict use to recreation, wildlife, water supply, or esthetic purposes.

Lathyrism—Paralytic condition of animals caused by consumption of seed of certain plants of the genus *Lathyrus*.

Leaf area index (LAI)—Ratio of leaf area (one side of leaf) to ground surface.

Leghemoglobin—From "leg" (leguminous) and "hemoglobin," a complex respiratory pigment of red corpuscles; a hemoprotein similar to blood hemoglobin.

Legume—Plant member of the family Leguminosae, with the characteristic of forming nitrogen-fixing nodules on its roots, in this way making use of atmospheric N possible.

Ley—An English term designating the biennial or perennial hay or pasture portion of a rotation that includes cultivated crops.

Lignin—Complex noncarbohydrate strengthening material in the thickened cell walls of plants; practically indigestible.

Line—Group of individuals from a common ancestry; more narrowly defined group than a strain or cultivar.

Maillard product—Lignin artifact that is an artificial indigestible polymer between proteins and amino acids and degradation products of sugar and other carbohydrates.

Maturation—Plant process of coming into full development, as to mature or ripen.

Meadow—Area covered with grasses and/or legumes grown primarily for hay.

Meristem—Growing point or area of rapidly dividing cells at the tip of a stem, root, or branch.

Metabolic body size ($W^{0.75}$)—Weight of the animal raised to the three-fourths power.

Metabolism—Complex of physical and chemical processes involved in the maintenance of life.

Metabolizable energy (ME)—Food intake gross energy minus fecal energy, minus energy in the gaseous products of digestion, minus urinary energy.

Microclimate—Atmospheric environmental conditions in the immediate vicinity of the plant, including interchanges of energy, gases, and water between atmosphere and soil.

Microorganism—Minute living organism such as bacteria, fungi, or protozoa.

Microsymbiont—One of the organisms (bacteria) in a symbiotic relationship.

[1] Klingebiel, A. A., and P. H. Montgomery. 1966 reprint. Land-capability classification. USDA SCS Agr. Handbook 210.

Mitotic cycle—Entire sequence of processes of cell division in which the diploid number of chomosomes is retained in both daughter cells.

Moisture, dry basis—A basis for representing moisture content of a product, as parts of water per part of dry matter (DM), that is equal to the weight of the DM and the answer multiplied by $100 = \%$. It may be more than 100%.

Moisture, wet basis—Used for commercial designation. Obtained by dividing the weight of water present in the material by the total weight of material, including water and dry matter.

Mole (mol)—Amount of a substance that has a weight in grams numerically equal to the molecular weight of the substance; also called gram-molecular weight.

Monocotyledon—Plant having one cotyledon, as in grasses.

Monoculture—Cultivation of a single crop to the exclusion of other potential crops.

Monoecious—Having male and female reproductive organs in separate flowers on the same plant.

Mucin compound—Any of a group of mucoproteins found in various secretions and tissues of man and animals, such as saliva, lining of the stomach, and skin.

Mulch—Any nonliving material that forms a covering on the soil surface.

Mutation—Sudden heritable variation in a gene or in chromosome structure.

Native grass—Grass species indigenous to an area; not introduced from another environment or area.

Naturalized plant—Plant introduced from another environment; has become established in and more or less adapted to a given region by being grown for many generations.

Net energy (NE)—Difference between metabolizable energy and heat increment; includes the amount of energy used either for maintenance only or for maintenance plus production.

Neutral soil—Neither acid nor alkaline, with a pH of 7 or (practically) between 6.6 and 7.3.

Nitrate poisoning—Condition sometimes resulting when ruminants ingest nitrates (NO_3) that rumen bacteria convert to nitrite (NO_2); the nitrites compete with oxygen, tying up the oxygen-carrying mechanism in the blood and causing the animal to suffocate.

Nitrification—Formation of nitrates and nitrites from ammonia (or ammonium compounds), as in soil by microorganisms.

Nitrogen-free extract (NFE)—Obtained by subtraction of the crude fiber from the total carbohydrate analysis in the proximate system of feed analysis.

Node—Joint of a culm or stem.

Nodule—Tubercle, particularly such as formed on legume roots by the symbiotic nitrogen-fixing bacteria of the genus *Rhizobium*. See also Inoculate.

Nonprotein nitrogen (NPN)—Broad class of nitrogenous substances not comprising protein such as glutamine, glutamic acid, asparagine, aspartic acid, and gamma-amino butyric acid.

Nurse crop—See Companion crop.

Nutrient, animal—Food constituent or group of food constituents of the same general chemical composition required for support of animal life.

Nutrient, plant—Element essential to plant growth used in the elaboration of food and tissue.

Nutritive value—Characterizes a forage or feed as to its chemical composition, digestibility, and nature of digested products.

Nutritive value index (NVI)—Daily digestible amount of forage eaten per unit of metabolic body size relative to a standard forage.

Organic matter—Chemical compounds of carbon combined with other chemical elements and generally manufactured in the life processes of plants and animals. Most organic compounds are a source of food for bacteria and are usually combustible.

Organoleptic—Affecting one or more of the organs of special sense (sight, touch, hearing, smell, and taste).

Orts—Rejected feedstuffs left under conditions of ad libitum stall feeding.

Paddock—Small fenced field used for grazing purposes.

Palatability—Plant characteristics eliciting a choice between two or more forages or parts of the same forage, conditioned by the animal and environmental factors that stimulate a selective intake response. See also Acceptability.

Panicle—Inflorescence with a main stem (axis) and subdivided branches. In grasses the panicle may be compact and spikelike (timothy) or open (smooth bromegrass).

Pasturage—Vegetation on which animals graze, including grasses or grasslike plants, legumes, forbs, and shrubs.

Pasture—Fenced area of domesticated forages, usually improved, on which animals are grazed; to graze. See also Range.

Pasture carrying capacity—Number of animals a given pasture will support at a given time or for a given period of time.

Pasture, cropland—Includes rotation pasture and other land used only for pasture but that could be used for crops without additional improvements. Preferred to "rotation pasture."

Pasture, permanent—Pasture of perennial or self-seeding annual plants maintained through several years for grazing.

Pasture renovation—Improvement of a pasture by the partial or complete destruction of the sod, plus liming, fertilizing, seeding, and weed control as may be required to establish desirable forage plants.

Pasture, rotation—See Cropland pasture.

Pectin—Polysaccharide from the middle lamella of the plant cell wall; jelly-forming substance found in fruit.

Peduncle—Primary flower stalk supporting either a cluster or a solitary flower; in grasses, the stalk of an inflorescence.

Perfect flower—Having both stamens and pistils.

Petiole—Stalk by which a leaf blade is attached to the stem; a leafstalk.

pH—The pH scale is the chemist's measure of acidity and alkalinity: pH 7 is neutral; pH above 7 represents alkalinity and below, acidity. The scale is logarithmic; a solution with a pH of 4 is 100 times as acid as one with a pH of 6 and 10 times as acid as one with a pH of 5.

Phenotype—Group of organisms identifiable by their appearance regardless of genetic or hereditary makeup. See also Genotype.

Photoperiod—Period of a plant's daily exposure to light.

Photoperiodism—Response of a plant to the relative lengths of day and night (light and dark), particularly in respect to floral initiation.

Photosynthesis—Process by which carbohydrates are produced from CO_2 and water, chloroplasts or chlorophyll-bearing cell granules, and the energy of sunlight.

Polymorphic—Having many forms.

Polyploid—Plant having more than two basic sets of chromosomes.

Prairie—Level or rolling area of treeless land, naturally covered with grass, under which fertile soils usually have developed.

Preservative, silage—Material added to the forage crop at ensiling to quickly develop the acidity essential for preservation.

Primordia—Earliest stage at which differentiation of organs in a plant can be perceived.

Protein—Complex combination of amino acids, always containing carbon, hydrogen, oxygen, and nitrogen and sometimes phosphorus and sulfur; essential part of all living matter and the feed rations of animals.

Protein, crude—All nitrogenous substances contained in feedstuffs (% crude protein = % N $\times$ 6.25).

Proximate analysis—Analytical system that includes the determination of ash, crude fiber, crude protein, ether extract, moisture (dry matter), and nitrogen-free extract.

Prussic acid—See Hydrocyanic acid.

Pure live seed (PLS)—Percentage of the content of a seed lot that is pure and viable; determined by multiplying the percentage of pure seed by the percentage of viable seed and dividing by 100.

Put-and-take animals—Used in a grazing experiment to graze excess forage beyond that needed for tester animals and to accumulate animal days. See also Tester animals.

Raceme—Inflorescence in which the spikelets are arranged singly along a common main axis.

Rachilla—Small rachis; axis of a spikelet in grasses.

Rachis—Axis of a spikelet or a raceme.

Range—Land and native vegetation (climax or natural potential) that is predominantly grasses, grasslike plants, forbs, or shrubs suitable for grazing or browsing and present in sufficient quantity to justify grazing or browsing use. Includes lands revegetated naturally or artificially to provide a forage cover managed like native vegetation.

Range management—Producing maximum sustained use of range forage without jeopardy to other resources or uses of land.

Ration—A 24-hour allowance of a feed or a mixture of feedstuffs making up the animal diet.

Regional strain—Strain developed under a given environmental condition as a result of the survival of the best adapted individuals through many seed generations; botanically an ecotype.

Rejuvenation, rangeland—Accomplished by soil-plant-animal management practices favorable to forage plants.

Reseeding cultivar—Perpetuates itself by volunteering from shattered seed; usually made possible because of a high percentage of hard seed or seed with high dormancy.

Rhizobia—Species of bacteria that live in symbiotic relationship with leguminous plants within nodules on their roots; carry on the fixation of atmospheric N in forms used as nutrients by the host legumes.

Rhizome—Underground stem, usually horizontal and capable of producing new shoots and roots at the nodes.

Rhizosphere—Interfacial layer of soil between the root and soil bulk that is under the influence of the plant root.

Roughage—Plant materials that are relatively high in crude fiber and low in digestible nutrients, such as straw and stover. See also Forage.

Rumen—First compartment of the stomach of a ruminant or cud-chewing animal.

Saline soil—Soil containing an excess of soluble salts, but not excessively alkaline; pH less than 8.5.

Saponin—Any of various plant glucosides that form soapy colloidal solutions when mixed and agitated with water.

Savanna—Grassland with scattered trees, either as individuals or clumps; often a transitional type between true grassland and forest.

Scarification—Procedure of mechanically scarring the seed coat of "hard" or impermeable seed to permit the rapid imbibition of water to make germination possible.

Seed, breeder—Seed or vegetative propagating material directly controlled by the originator (or in certain cases the sponsoring plant breeder or institution) that provides the source for the initial and recurring increases of foundation seed.

Seed, certified—Progeny of foundation, registered, or certified seed that is so handled as to maintain satisfactory genetic identity and/or purity and that has been approved and certified by the certifying agency.

Seed, foundation—Seed stocks so handled as to most nearly maintain specific genetic identity and purity, such as may be designated or distributed by an agricultural experiment station. Foundation seed is the source of certified seed, either directly or through registered seed.

Seed, hard—With a seed coat impervious to the water or oxygen necessary for germination; common in legume seed and made germinable by scarification.

Seed, registered—Progeny of foundation or registered seed so handled as to maintain satisfactory genetic identity and purity; has been approved and certified by the certifying agency.

Seed, unhulled (in the hull)—Mature seed with the pods, glumes, or other outer covering retained.

Selection, mass—System of breeding in which seed from individuals selected on the basis of phenotype is composited and used to grow the next generation.

Selection, recurrent—Breeding system involving repeated cycles of selection and recombination with the objective of increasing the frequency of favorable genes for yield or other characteristics.

Self-fertilization—Fertilization of the egg cells of a plant by the sperm cells of the same plant.

Self-incompatible—Inability of a plant to set seed as a result of fertilization by its own pollen; also referred to as self-sterility.

Semiarid—Climate in which evaporation exceeds precipitation, a transition zone between true desert and humid climate; usually an annual precipitation between 254 and 508 mm.

Senesce—To age.

Short-grass plains—Area of the Great Plains or other similar areas covered with relatively low-growing native grasses.

Sib—Brother-sister relationship.

Silage—Forage preserved in a succulent condition by partial fermentation.

Silage additive—Material added to forage at the time of ensiling to enhance either its preservation or feeding value.

Silage preservative—Material added to silage at the time of ensiling to enhance the favorable fermentation process.

Sod—Top few centimeters of soil permeated by and held together with grass roots or grass-legume roots.

Sod-bound—Used to describe the unproductiveness of grass sod due to lack of nitrogen.

Sod-seeding—Mechanically placing seed, usually legumes or small grains, directly into a grass sod.

Soil tilth—Physical condition of a soil in respect to its fitness for good plant growth.

Soluble carbohydrate—Completely digestible; includes glucose, fructose, sucrose, fructosan, and amylose starch.

Spikelet—Unit of the inflorescence in grasses, consisting of two glumes and one or more florets.

Spontaneous combustion—Self-ignition of material by the chemical action of its constituents; most often results from high-moisture hay storage.

Sprigging—Vegetative propagation by planting stolons or rhizomes (sprigs) in furrows or holes in the soil.

Starch—Main storage carbohydrate $(C_6H_{10}O_5)_x$ in many plants, particularly seed, roots, and tubers.

Steppe—Vast semiarid grass-covered plain, usually lightly wooded.

Stipule—One of the usually small, paired leaf-like appendages at the base of a leaf or leafstalk in certain plants.

Stocker—Beef animal being backgrounded prior to finishing or entering the breeding herd.

Stocking, continuous—See Grazing, continuous.

Stocking rate—Number of animal units per unit of land area at a specific time.

Stockpiled—Accumulated growth of forage for later use.

Stolon—Trailing or creeping stem at or below the soil surface capable of rooting and sending up new shoots at the nodes.

Stover—Mature, cured stalks of such crops as corn or sorghum from which grain has been removed; a type of roughage.

Strain—Group of organisms of common origin having one or more definite heritable morphological or physiological characteristics.

Stubble mulch—Crop residue left on the surface of land that is being cropped.

Subhumid climate—Climate with sufficient precipitation to support a moderate to dense growth of tall and/or short grasses; usually 508–762 mm of rainfall.

Sward—Sward, turf, and sod may seem nearly synonymous. Sward usually refers to the grassy surface of a pasture, lawn, or playing field; vegetation may be of pure or mixed species; turf and sod refer to the stratum of earth filled with grass roots as well as to the surface.

Symbiosis—The living together of dissimilar organisms in a mutually advantageous partnership.

Symbiotic nitrogen fixation—Fixation of atmospheric N by rhizobia growing in nodules on roots of legumes.

Synthetic cultivar—Advanced generation progeny of a number of clones or lines, or of hybrids among them, obtained by open pollination.

Tall-grass prairie—Area in the western Corn Belt originally covered with tall native grasses, or other similar areas.

Tannin—Broad class of soluble polyphenols with a common property of condensing with protein to form a leatherlike substance that is insoluble and of impaired digestibility.

Tester animals—Used in grazing experiments to measure animal performance or pasture quality. See also Put-and-take animals.

Tiller—Branch or shoot originating at a basal node in grasses.

Tilth—Physical condition of a soil in respect to its fitness for plant growth.

Tocopherol—Any of a group of four chemically related compounds differing slightly in structure that constitute vitamin E.

Top-cross progeny—From out-crossed seed of selections, clones, or lines crossed with a single variety or line that serves as a common pollen parent.

Top-dressing—Application of fertilizer anytime after establishment of a crop.

Total digestible nutrients (TDN)—Sum total of all digestible organic nutrients, i.e., proteins, nitrogen-free extract, fiber, and fat. Fat is multiplied by 2.25 to put its energy value on the same basis as the other nutrients. On the average for all feeds 1 g of TDN = 4.4 kcal.

Tripping—Release of the staminate and pistillate portions from the keel of the leguminous flower in the process of pollination.

Ungulates—Mammals having hoofs.

Variety—See Cultivar.

Vegetative—Term used to designate stem and leaf development in contrast to flower and seed development.

Vegetative cover—Soil cover of plants irrespective of species.

Vitamins—Organic compounds that function as parts of enzyme systems essential for transmitting energy and regulating metabolism.

Voluntary intake—Ad libitum intake achieved when an animal is offered an excess of a single feed or forage.

Warm-season grass—A grass species that makes its major growth during the warmer part of the year. Preferred to "hot weather."

Xanthophyll—Yellow carotenoid pigment ($C_{40}H_{56}O_2$) found with chlorophyll in green plants and egg yolk.

INDEX

❧

Boldface entries denote areas of special importance

743